GENERAL MOTORS S10/SONOMA PICK-UPS 1994-97 REPAIR MANUAL

CHILTON'S™

President Dean F. Morgantini, S.A.E.
Vice President–Finance Barry L. Beck
Vice President–Sales Glenn D. Potere
Executive Editor Kevin M. G. Maher
Production Manager Ben Greisler, S.A.E.
Project Managers Michael Abraham, George B. Heinrich III, S.A.E., Will Kessler, A.S.E., S.A.E., Richard Schwartz
Schematics Editor Christopher G. Ritchie
Editor Thomas A. Mellon

CHILTON™ Automotive Books
PUBLISHED BY **W. G. NICHOLS, INC.**

Manufactured in USA

1020 Andrew Drive
West Chester, PA 19380
ISBN 0-8019-8845-4
Library of Congress Catalog Card No. 96-85110
2345678901 7654321098

Contents

Contents

SAFETY NOTICE

Proper service and repair procedures are vital to the safe, reliable operation of all motor vehicles, as well as the personal safety of those performing repairs. This manual outlines procedures for servicing and repairing vehicles using safe, effective methods. The procedures contain many NOTES, CAUTIONS and WARNINGS which should be followed, along with standard procedures to eliminate the possibility of personal injury or improper service which could damage the vehicle or compromise its safety.

It is important to note that repair procedures and techniques, tools and parts for servicing motor vehicles, as well as the skill and experience of the individual performing the work vary widely. It is not possible to anticipate all of the conceivable ways or conditions under which vehicles may be serviced, or to provide cautions as to all possible hazards that may result. Standard and accepted safety precautions and equipment should be used when handling toxic or flammable fluids, and safety goggles or other protection should be used during cutting, grinding, chiseling, prying, or any other process that can cause material removal or projectiles.

Some procedures require the use of tools specially designed for a specific purpose. Before substituting another tool or procedure, you must be completely satisfied that neither your personal safety, nor the performance of the vehicle will be endangered.

Although information in this manual is based on industry sources and is complete as possible at the time of publication, the possibility exists that some car manufacturers made later changes which could not be included here. While striving for total accuracy, NP/Chilton cannot assume responsibility for any errors, changes or omissions that may occur in the compilation of this data.

PART NUMBERS

Part numbers listed in this reference are not recommendations by Chilton for any product brand name. They are references that can be used with interchange manuals and aftermarket supplier catalogs to locate each brand supplier's discrete part number.

SPECIAL TOOLS

Special tools are recommended by the vehicle manufacturer to perform their specific job. Use has been kept to a minimum, but where absolutely necessary, they are referred to in the text by the part number of the tool manufacturer. These tools can be purchased, under the appropriate part number, from your local dealer or regional distributor, or an equivalent tool can be purchased locally from a tool supplier or parts outlet. Before substituting any tool for the one recommended, read the SAFETY NOTICE at the top of this page.

ACKNOWLEDGMENTS

Portions of materials contained herein have been reprinted with the permission of General Motors Corporation, Service Technology Group.

1

GENERAL INFORMATION AND MAINTENANCE

HOW TO USE THIS BOOK

Chilton's Total Car Care manual for the 1994-97 Chevrolet and GMC Pick-ups is intended to help you learn more about the inner workings of your vehicle while saving you money on its upkeep and operation.

The beginning of the book will likely be referred to the most, since that is where you will find information for maintenance and tune-up. The other sections deal with the more complex systems of your vehicle. Operating systems from engine through brakes are covered to the extent that the average do-it-yourselfer becomes mechanically involved. This book will not explain such things as rebuilding a differential for the simple reason that the expertise required and the investment in special tools make this task uneconomical. It will, however, give you detailed instructions to help you change your own brake pads and shoes, replace spark plugs, and perform many more jobs that can save you money, give you personal satisfaction and help you avoid expensive problems.

A secondary purpose of this book is a reference for owners who want to understand their vehicle and/or their mechanics better. In this case, no tools at all are required.

Where to Begin

Before removing any bolts, read through the entire procedure. This will give you the overall view of what tools and supplies will be required. There is nothing more frustrating than having to walk to the bus stop on Monday morning because you were short one bolt on Sunday afternoon. So read ahead and plan ahead. Each operation should be approached logically and all procedures thoroughly understood before attempting any work.

All sections contain adjustments, maintenance, removal and installation procedures, and in some cases, repair or overhaul procedures. When repair is not considered practical, we tell you how to remove the part and then how to install the new or rebuilt replacement. In this way, you at least save the labor costs. Backyard repair of some components is just not practical.

Avoiding Trouble

Many procedures in this book require you to "label and disconnect . . . " a group of lines, hoses or wires. Don't be lulled into thinking you can remember where everything goes — you won't. If you hook up vacuum or fuel lines incorrectly, the vehicle will run poorly, if at all. If you hook up electrical wiring incorrectly, you may instantly learn a very expensive lesson.

You don't need to know the official or engineering name for each hose or line. A piece of masking tape on the hose and a piece on its fitting will allow you to assign your own label such as the letter A or a short name. As long as you remember your own code, the lines can be reconnected by matching similar letters or names. Do remember that tape will dissolve in gasoline or other fluids; if a component is to be washed or cleaned, use another method of identification. A permanent felt-tipped marker can be very handy for marking metal parts. Remove any tape or paper labels after assembly.

Maintenance or Repair?

It's necessary to mention the difference between maintenance and repair. Maintenance includes routine inspections, adjustments, and replacement of parts which show signs of normal wear. Maintenance compensates for wear or deterioration. Repair implies that something has broken or is not working. A need for repair is often caused by lack of maintenance. Example: draining and refilling the automatic transmission fluid is maintenance recommended by the manufacturer at specific mileage intervals. Failure to do this can ruin the transmission/transaxle, requiring very expensive repairs. While no maintenance program can prevent items from breaking or wearing out, a general rule can be stated: MAINTENANCE IS CHEAPER THAN REPAIR.

Two basic mechanic's rules should be mentioned here. First, whenever the left side of the vehicle or engine is referred to, it is meant to specify the driver's side. Conversely, the right side of the vehicle means the passenger's side. Second, most screws and bolts are removed by turning counterclockwise, and tightened by turning clockwise.

Safety is always the most important rule. Constantly be aware of the dangers involved in working on an automobile and take the proper precautions. See the information in this section regarding SERVICING YOUR VEHICLE SAFELY and the SAFETY NOTICE on the acknowledgment page.

Avoiding the Most Common Mistakes

Pay attention to the instructions provided. There are 3 common mistakes in mechanical work:

1. Incorrect order of assembly, disassembly or adjustment. When taking something apart or putting it together, performing steps in the wrong order usually just costs you extra time; however, it CAN break something. Read the entire procedure before beginning disassembly. Perform everything in the order in which the instructions say you should, even if you can't immediately see a reason for it. When you're taking apart something that is very intricate, you might want to draw a picture of how it looks when assembled at one point in order to make sure you get everything back in its proper position. We will supply exploded views whenever possible. When making adjustments, perform them in the proper order; often, one adjustment affects another, and you cannot expect even satisfactory results unless each adjustment is made only when it cannot be changed by any other.

2. Overtorquing (or undertorquing). While it is more common for overtorquing to cause damage, undertorquing may allow a fastener to vibrate loose causing serious damage. Especially when dealing with aluminum parts, pay attention to torque specifications and utilize a torque wrench in assembly. If a torque figure is not available, remember that if you are using the right tool to perform the job, you will probably not have to strain yourself to get a fastener tight enough. The pitch of most threads is so slight that the tension you put on the wrench will be multiplied many times in actual force on what you are tightening. A good example of how critical torque is can be seen in the case of spark plug installation, especially

where you are putting the plug into an aluminum cylinder head. Too little torque can fail to crush the gasket, causing leakage of combustion gases and consequent overheating of the plug and engine parts. Too much torque can damage the threads or distort the plug, changing the spark gap.

There are many commercial products available for ensuring that fasteners won't come loose, even if they are not torqued just right (a very common brand is Loctite®). If you're worried about getting something together tight enough to hold, but loose enough to avoid mechanical damage during assembly, one of these products might offer substantial insurance. Before choosing a threadlocking compound, read the label on the package and make sure the product is compatible with the materials, fluids, etc. involved.

3. Crossthreading. This occurs when a part such as a bolt is screwed into a nut or casting at the wrong angle and forced. Crossthreading is more likely to occur if access is difficult. It helps to clean and lubricate fasteners, then to start threading with the part to be installed positioned straight in. Then, start the bolt, spark plug, etc. with your fingers. If you encounter resistance, unscrew the part and start over again at a different angle until it can be inserted and turned several times without much effort. Keep in mind that many parts, especially spark plugs, have tapered threads, so that gentle turning will automatically bring the part you're threading to the proper angle, but only if you don't force it or resist a change in angle. Don't put a wrench on the part until it's been tightened a couple of turns by hand. If you suddenly encounter resistance, and the part has not seated fully, don't force it. Pull it back out to make sure it's clean and threading properly.

Always take your time and be patient; once you have some experience, working on your vehicle may well become an enjoyable hobby.

TOOLS AND EQUIPMENT

See Figures 1, 2, 3, 4, 5, 6, 7, 8, 9, 10, 11, 12, 13 and 14

Naturally, without the proper tools and equipment it is impossible to properly service your vehicle. It would also be virtually impossible to catalog every tool that you would need to perform all of the operations in this book. Of course, It would be unwise for the amateur to rush out and buy an expensive set of tools on the theory that he/she may need one or more of them at some time.

The best approach is to proceed slowly, gathering a good quality set of those tools that are used most frequently. Don't be misled by the low cost of bargain tools. It is far better to spend a little more for better quality. Forged wrenches, 6 or 12-point sockets and fine tooth ratchets are by far preferable to their less expensive counterparts. As any good mechanic can tell you, there are few worse experiences than trying to work on a vehicle with bad tools. Your monetary savings will be far outweighed by frustration and mangled knuckles.

Begin accumulating those tools that are used most frequently: those associated with routine maintenance and tune-up. In addition to the normal assortment of screwdrivers and pliers, you should have the following tools:

- Wrenches/sockets and combination open end/box end wrenches in sizes from 1/8-3/4 in. or 3mm-19mm (depending on whether your vehicle uses standard or metric fasteners) and a 13/16 in. or 5/8 in. spark plug socket (depending on plug type).

➡If possible, buy various length socket drive extensions. Universal-joint and wobble extensions can be extremely useful, but be careful when using them, as they can change the amount of torque applied to the socket.

- Jackstands for support.
- Oil filter wrench.
- Spout or funnel for pouring fluids.
- Grease gun for chassis lubrication (unless your vehicle is not equipped with any grease fittings — for details, please refer to information on Fluids and Lubricants found later in this section).
- Hydrometer for checking the battery (unless equipped with a sealed, maintenance-free battery).
- A container for draining oil and other fluids.
- Rags for wiping up the inevitable mess.

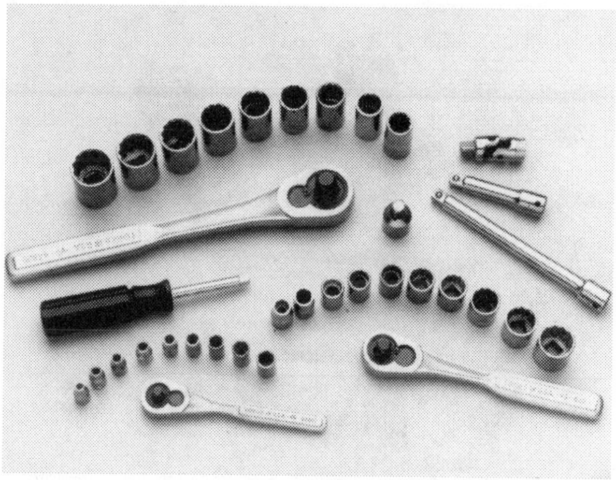
tccs1200

Fig. 1 All but the most basic procedures will require an assortment of ratchets and sockets

In addition to the above items there are several others that are not absolutely necessary, but handy to have around. These include Oil Dry® (or an equivalent oil absorbent gravel — such as cat litter) and the usual supply of lubricants, antifreeze and fluids, although these can be purchased as needed. This is a basic list for routine maintenance, but only your personal needs and desire can accurately determine your list of tools.

After performing a few projects on the vehicle, you'll be amazed at the other tools and non-tools on your workbench. Some useful household items are: a large turkey baster or siphon, empty coffee cans and ice trays (to store parts), ball of twine, electrical tape for wiring, small rolls of colored tape for tagging lines or hoses, markers and pens, a note pad, golf tees (for plugging vacuum lines), metal coat hangers or a roll of mechanics's wire (to hold things out of the way), dental pick or similar long, pointed probe, a strong magnet, and a small mirror (to see into recesses and under manifolds).

A more advanced set of tools, suitable for tune-up work, can be drawn up easily. While the tools are slightly more sophisticated, they need not be outrageously expensive. There are

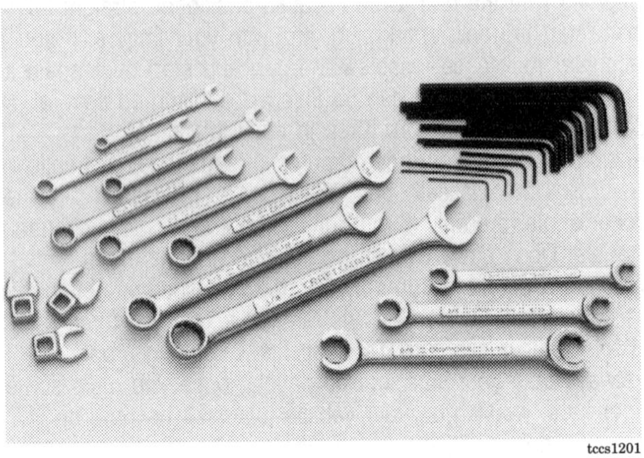

tccs1201

Fig. 2 In addition to ratchets, a good set of wrenches and hex keys will be necessary

tccs1202

Fig. 3 A hydraulic floor jack and a set of jackstands are essential for lifting and supporting the vehicle

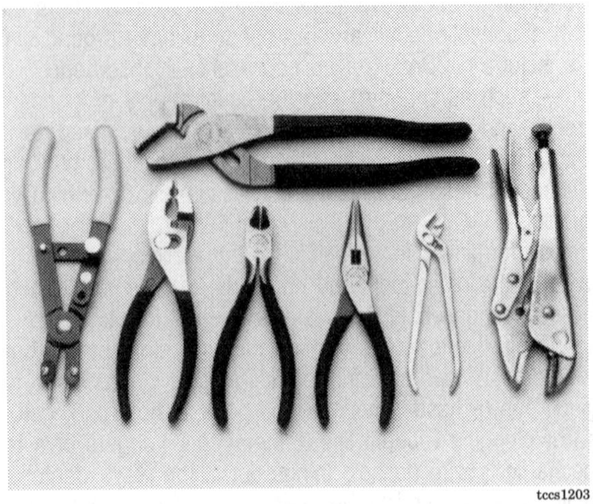

tccs1203

Fig. 4 An assortment of pliers, grippers and cutters will be handy for old rusted parts and stripped bolt heads

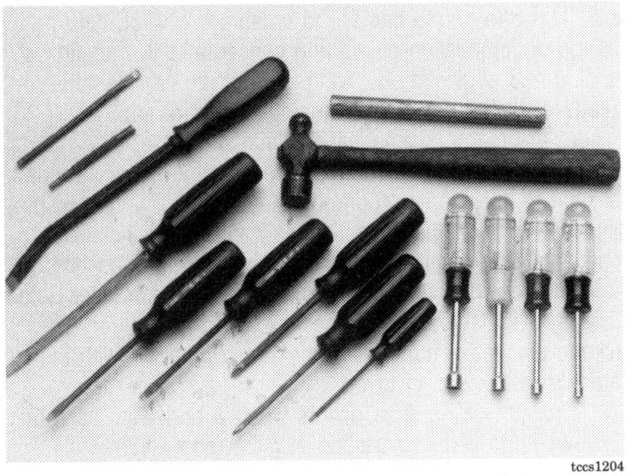

tccs1204

Fig. 5 Various drivers, chisels and prybars are great tools to have in your toolbox

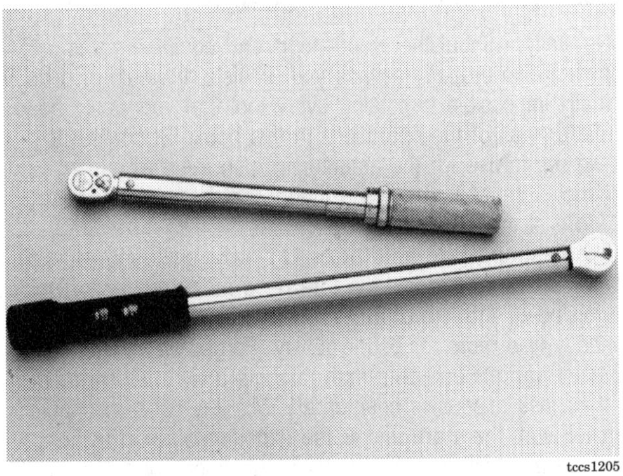

tccs1205

Fig. 6 Many repairs will require the use of a torque wrench to assure the components are properly fastened

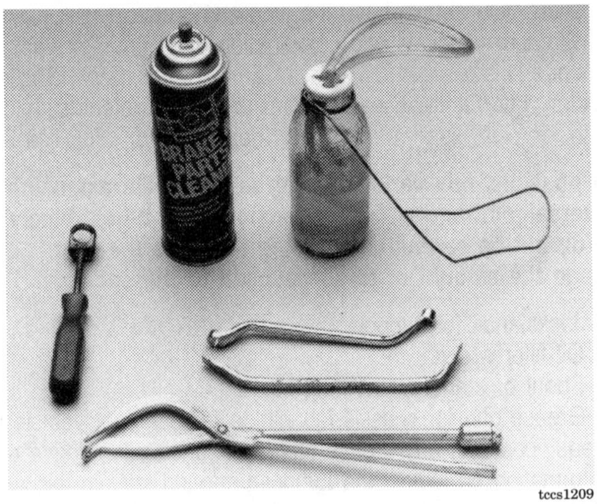

tccs1209

Fig. 7 Although not always necessary, using specialized brake tools will save time

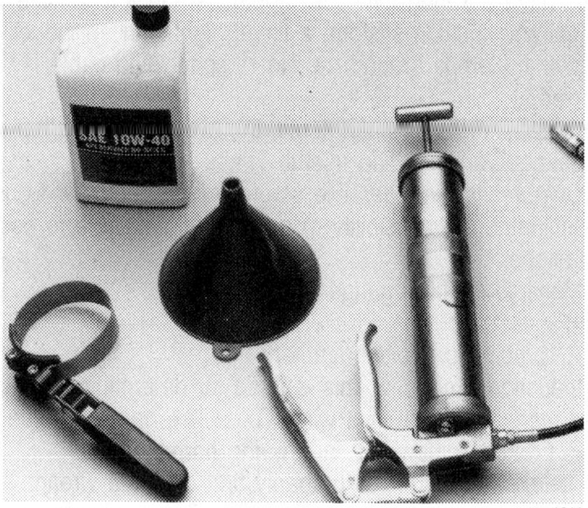

tccs1210

Fig. 8 A few inexpensive lubrication tools will make maintenance easier

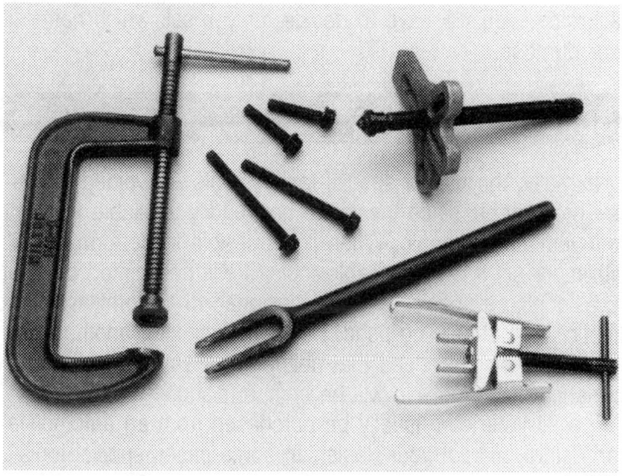

tccs1211

Fig. 9 Various pullers, clamps and separator tools are needed for many larger, more complicated repairs

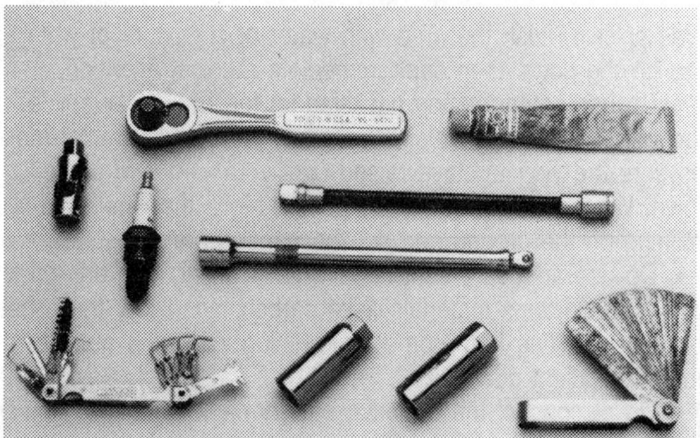

tccs1212

Fig. 10 A variety of tools and gauges should be used for spark plug gapping and installation

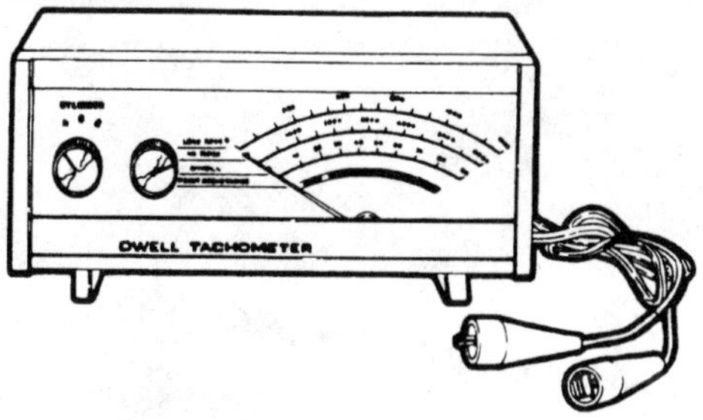

tccs1001

Fig. 11 Dwell/tachometer unit (typical)

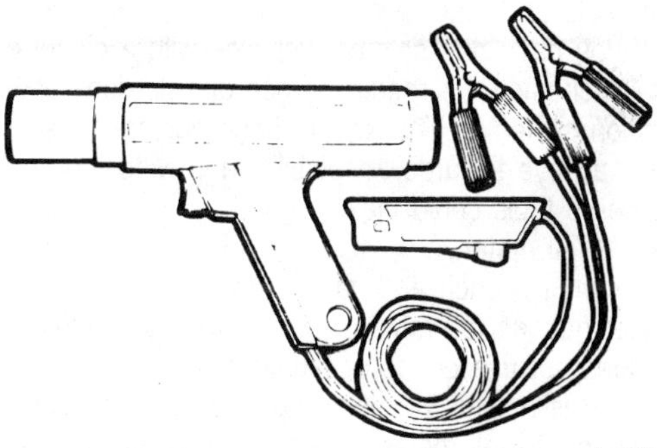

tccs1002

Fig. 12 Inductive type timing light

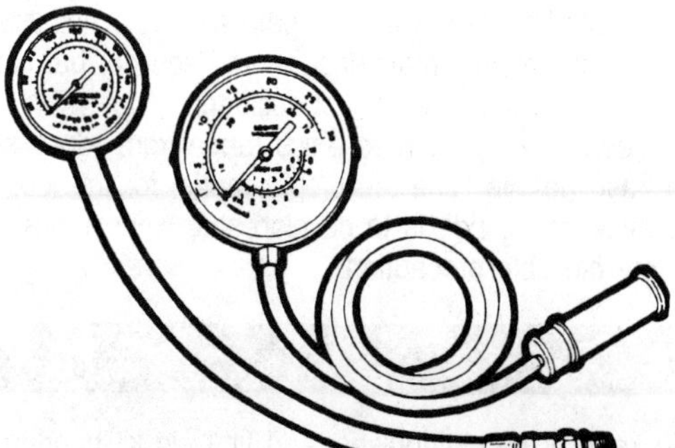

tccs1003

Fig. 13 Compression gauge and a combination vacuum/fuel pressure test gauge

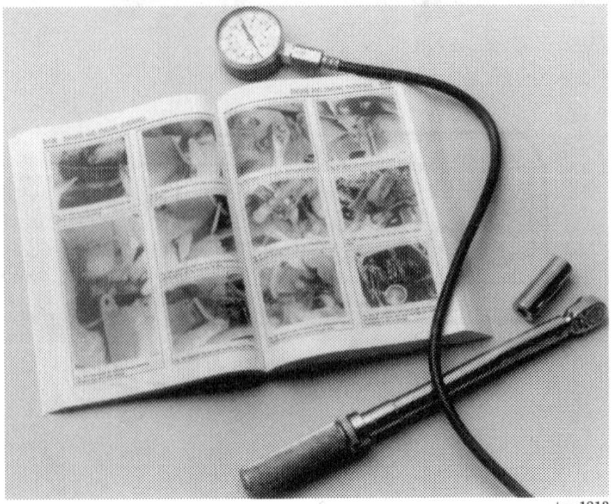

Fig. 14 Proper information is vital, so always have a Chilton Total Car Care manual handy

several inexpensive tach/dwell meters on the market that are every bit as good for the average mechanic as a professional model. Just be sure that it goes to a least 1200-1500 rpm on the tach scale and that it works on 4, 6 and 8-cylinder engines. (If you have one or more vehicles with a diesel engine, a special tachometer is required since diesels don't use spark plug ignition systems). The key to these purchases is to make them with an eye towards adaptability and wide range. A basic list of tune-up tools could include:

- Tach/dwell meter.
- Spark plug wrench and gapping tool.
- Feeler gauges for valve or point adjustment. (Even if your vehicle does not use points or require valve adjustments, a feeler gauge is helpful for many repair/overhaul procedures).

A tachometer/dwell meter will ensure accurate tune-up work on vehicles without electronic ignition. The choice of a timing light should be made carefully. A light which works on the DC current supplied by the vehicle's battery is the best choice; it should have a xenon tube for brightness. On any vehicle with an electronic ignition system, a timing light with an inductive pickup that clamps around the No. 1 spark plug cable is preferred.

In addition to these basic tools, there are several other tools and gauges you may find useful. These include:

- Compression gauge. The screw-in type is slower to use, but eliminates the possibility of a faulty reading due to escaping pressure.
- Manifold vacuum gauge.
- 12V test light.
- A combination volt/ohmmeter
- Induction Ammeter. This is used for determining whether or not there is current in a wire. These are handy for use if a wire is broken somewhere in a wiring harness.

As a final note, you will probably find a torque wrench necessary for all but the most basic work. The beam type models are perfectly adequate, although the newer click types (breakaway) are easier to use. The click type torque wrenches tend to be more expensive. Also keep in mind that all types of torque wrenches should be periodically checked and/or recalibrated. You will have to decide for yourself which better fits your purpose.

Special Tools

Normally, the use of special factory tools is avoided for repair procedures, since these are not readily available for the do-it-yourself mechanic. When it is possible to perform the job with more commonly available tools, it will be pointed out, but occasionally, a special tool was designed to perform a specific function and should be used. Before substituting another tool, you should be convinced that neither your safety nor the performance of the vehicle will be compromised.

Special tools can usually be purchased from an automotive parts store or from your dealer. In some cases special tools may be available directly from the tool manufacturer.

SERVICING YOUR VEHICLE SAFELY

See Figures 15, 16, 17 and 18

It is virtually impossible to anticipate all of the hazards involved with automotive maintenance and service, but care and common sense will prevent most accidents.

The rules of safety for mechanics range from "don't smoke around gasoline," to "use the proper tool(s) for the job." The trick to avoiding injuries is to develop safe work habits and to take every possible precaution.

Do's

- Do keep a fire extinguisher and first aid kit handy.
- Do wear safety glasses or goggles when cutting, drilling, grinding or prying, even if you have 20-20 vision. If you wear glasses for the sake of vision, wear safety goggles over your regular glasses.
- Do shield your eyes whenever you work around the battery. Batteries contain sulfuric acid. In case of contact with the eyes or skin, flush the area with water or a mixture of water and baking soda, then seek immediate medical attention.
- Do use safety stands (jackstands) for any undervehicle service. Jacks are for raising vehicles; jackstands are for making sure the vehicle stays raised until you want it to come down. Whenever the vehicle is raised, block the wheels remaining on the ground and set the parking brake.
- Do use adequate ventilation when working with any chemicals or hazardous materials. Like carbon monoxide, the asbestos dust resulting from some brake lining wear can be hazardous in sufficient quantities.
- Do disconnect the negative battery cable when working on the electrical system. The secondary ignition system contains EXTREMELY HIGH VOLTAGE. In some cases it can even exceed 50,000 volts.
- Do follow manufacturer's directions whenever working with potentially hazardous materials. Most chemicals and fluids are poisonous if taken internally.
- Do properly maintain your tools. Loose hammerheads, mushroomed punches and chisels, frayed or poorly grounded

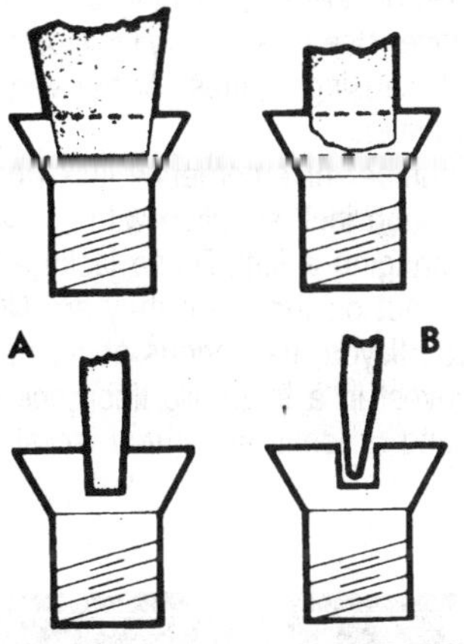

Fig. 15 Screwdrivers should be kept in good condition to prevent injury or damage which could result if the blade slips from the screw

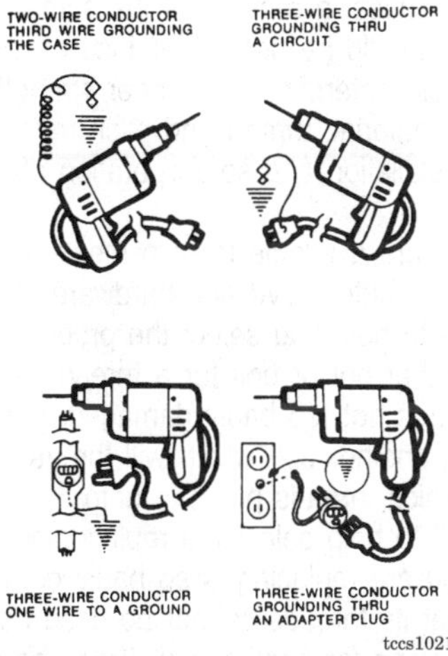

Fig. 16 Power tools should always be properly grounded

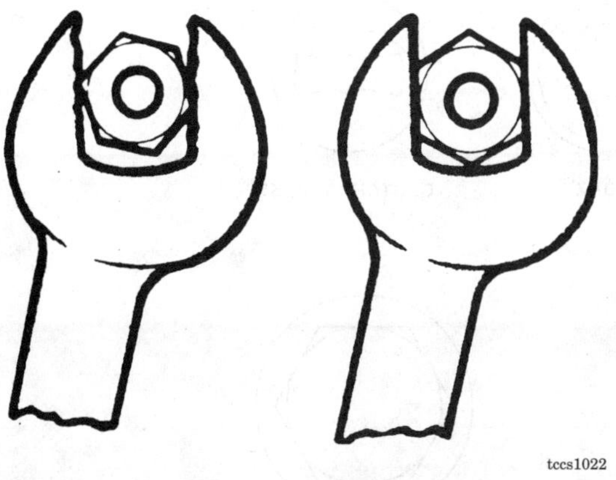

Fig. 17 Using the correct size wrench will help prevent the possibility of rounding off a nut

Fig. 18 NEVER work under a vehicle unless it is supported using safety stands (jackstands)

electrical cords, excessively worn screwdrivers, spread wrenches (open end), cracked sockets, slipping ratchets, or faulty droplight sockets can cause accidents.

- Likewise, keep your tools clean; a greasy wrench can slip off a bolt head, ruining the bolt and often harming your knuckles in the process.
- Do use the proper size and type of tool for the job at hand. Do select a wrench or socket that fits the nut or bolt. The wrench or socket should sit straight, not cocked.
- Do, when possible, pull on a wrench handle rather than push on it, and adjust your stance to prevent a fall.
- Do be sure that adjustable wrenches are tightly closed on the nut or bolt and pulled so that the force is on the side of the fixed jaw.
- Do strike squarely with a hammer; avoid glancing blows.
- Do set the parking brake and block the drive wheels if the work requires a running engine.

Don'ts

- Don't run the engine in a garage or anywhere else without proper ventilation — EVER! Carbon monoxide is poisonous; it takes a long time to leave the human body and you can build up a deadly supply of it in your system by simply breathing in a little every day. You may not realize you are slowly poisoning yourself. Always use power vents, windows, fans and/or open the garage door.
- Don't work around moving parts while wearing loose clothing. Short sleeves are much safer than long, loose sleeves. Hard-toed shoes with neoprene soles protect your toes and give a better grip on slippery surfaces. Jewelry such as watches, fancy belt buckles, beads or body adornment of any kind is not safe working around a vehicle. Long hair should be tied back under a hat or cap.
- Don't use pockets for toolboxes. A fall or bump can drive a screwdriver deep into your body. Even a rag hanging from your back pocket can wrap around a spinning shaft or fan.
- Don't smoke when working around gasoline, cleaning solvent or other flammable material.
- Don't smoke when working around the battery. When the battery is being charged, it gives off explosive hydrogen gas.

• Don't use gasoline to wash your hands; there are excellent soaps available. Gasoline contains dangerous additives which can enter the body through a cut or through your pores. Gasoline also removes all the natural oils from the skin so that bone dry hands will suck up oil and grease.

• Don't service the air conditioning system unless you are equipped with the necessary tools and training. When liquid or compressed gas refrigerant is released to atmospheric pressure it will absorb heat from whatever it contacts. This will chill or freeze anything it touches. Although refrigerant is normally non-toxic, R-12 becomes a deadly poisonous gas in the presence of an open flame. One good whiff of the vapors from burning refrigerant can be fatal.

• Don't use screwdrivers for anything other than driving screws! A screwdriver used as an prying tool can snap when you least expect it, causing injuries. At the very least, you'll ruin a good screwdriver.

• Don't use a bumper or emergency jack (that little ratchet, scissors, or pantograph jack supplied with the vehicle) for anything other than changing a flat! These jacks are only intended for emergency use out on the road; they are NOT designed as a maintenance tool. If you are serious about maintaining your vehicle yourself, invest in a hydraulic floor jack of at least a $1\frac{1}{2}$ ton capacity, and at least two sturdy jackstands.

FASTENERS, MEASUREMENTS AND CONVERSIONS

Bolts, Nuts and Other Threaded Retainers

See Figures 19, 20, 21 and 22

Although there are a great variety of fasteners found in the modern car or truck, the most commonly used retainer is the threaded fastener (nuts, bolts, screws, studs, etc). Most threaded retainers may be reused, provided that they are not damaged in use or during the repair. Some retainers (such as stretch bolts or torque prevailing nuts) are designed to deform when tightened or in use and should not be reinstalled.

Whenever possible, we will note any special retainers which should be replaced during a procedure. But you should always inspect the condition of a retainer when it is removed and replace any that show signs of damage. Check all threads for rust or corrosion which can increase the torque necessary to achieve the desired clamp load for which that fastener was originally selected. Additionally, be sure that the driver surface of the fastener has not been compromised by rounding or other damage. In some cases a driver surface may become only partially rounded, allowing the driver to catch in only one direction. In many of these occurrences, a fastener may be installed and tightened, but the driver would not be able to grip and loosen the fastener again. (This could lead to frustration down the line should that component ever need to be disassembled again).

If you must replace a fastener, whether due to design or damage, you must ALWAYS be sure to use the proper replacement. In all cases, a retainer of the same design, material and strength should be used. Markings on the heads of most bolts will help determine the proper strength of the fastener. The same material, thread and pitch must be selected to assure proper installation and safe operation of the vehicle afterwards.

Thread gauges are available to help measure a bolt or stud's thread. Most automotive and hardware stores keep gauges available to help you select the proper size. In a pinch, you can use another nut or bolt for a thread gauge. If the bolt you are replacing is not too badly damaged, you can select a match by finding another bolt which will thread in its place. If you find a nut which threads properly onto the damaged bolt, then use that nut to help select the replacement bolt. If however, the bolt you are replacing is so badly damaged (broken or drilled out) that its threads cannot be used as a gauge, you might start by looking for another bolt (from the same assembly or a similar location on your vehicle) which will thread into the damaged bolt's mounting. If so, the other bolt can be used to select a nut; the nut can then be used to select the replacement bolt.

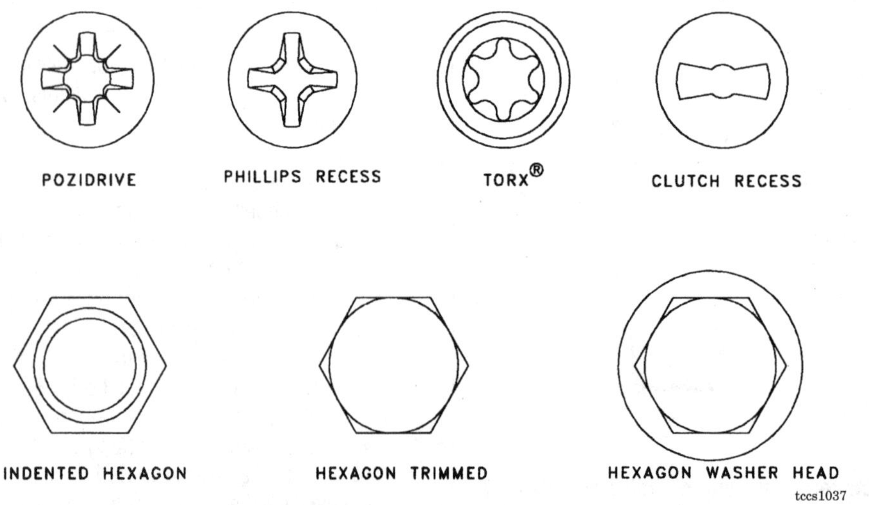

Fig. 19 Here are a few of the most common screw/bolt driver styles

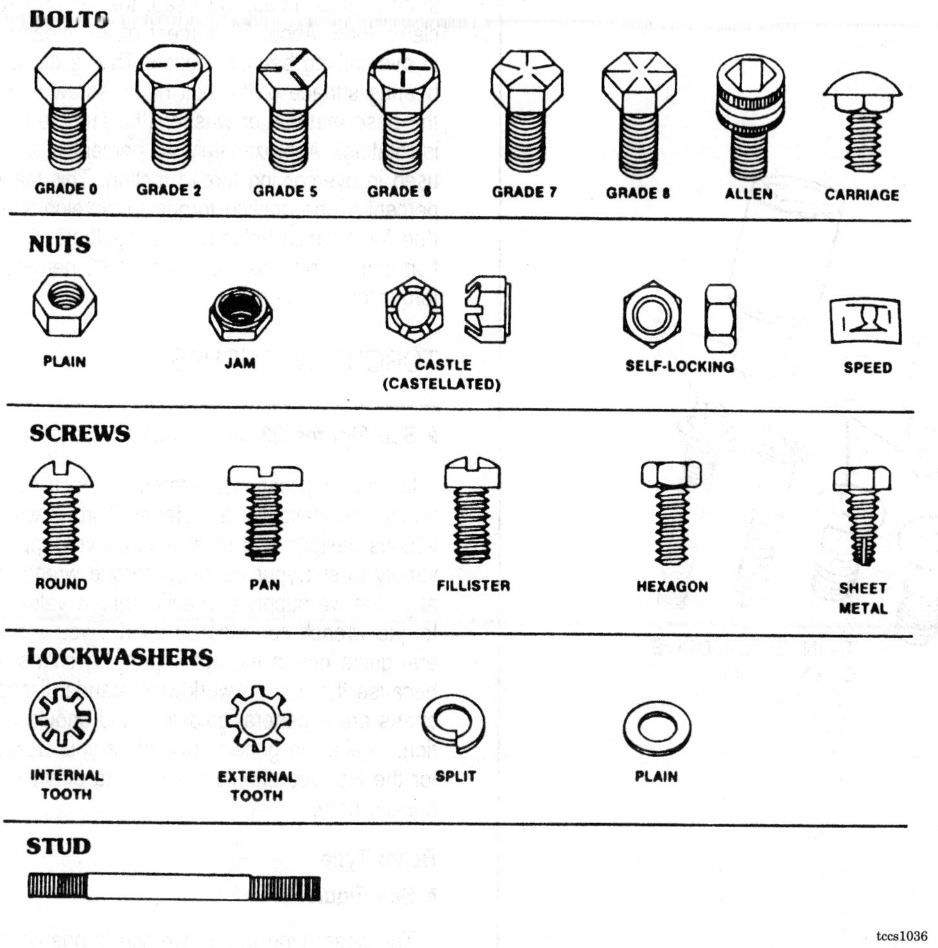

Fig. 20 There are many different types of threaded retainers found on vehicles

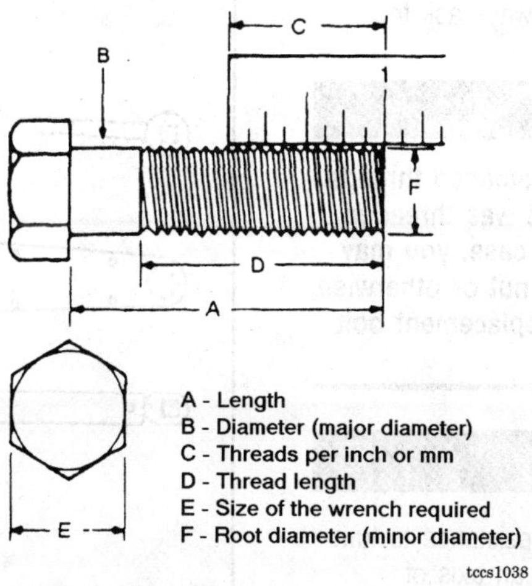

Fig. 21 Threaded retainer sizes are determined using these measurements

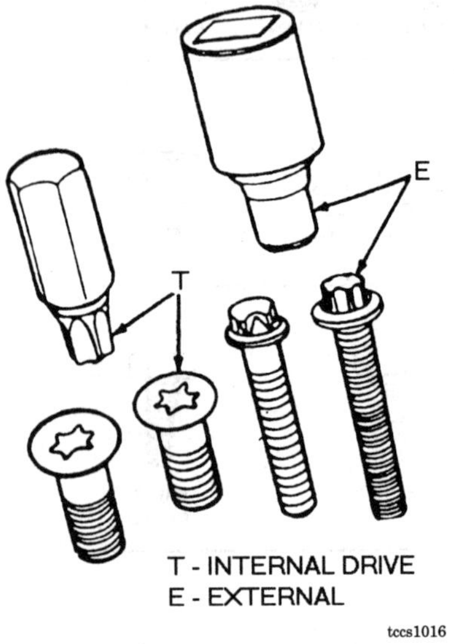

Fig. 22 Special fasteners such as these Torx® head bolts are used by manufacturers to discourage people from working on vehicles without the proper tools

In all cases, be absolutely sure you have selected the proper replacement. Don't be shy, you can always ask the store clerk for help.

WARNING

Be aware that when you find a bolt with damaged threads, you may also find the nut or drilled hole it was threaded into has also been damaged. If this is the case, you may have to drill and tap the hole, replace the nut or otherwise repair the threads. NEVER try to force a replacement bolt to fit into the damaged threads.

Torque

Torque is defined as the measurement of resistance to turning or rotating. It tends to twist a body about an axis of rotation. A common example of this would be tightening a threaded retainer such as a nut, bolt or screw. Measuring torque is one of the most common ways to help assure that a threaded retainer has been properly fastened.

When tightening a threaded fastener, torque is applied in three distinct areas, the head, the bearing surface and the clamp load. About 50 percent of the measured torque is used in overcoming bearing friction. This is the friction between the bearing surface of the bolt head, screw head or nut face and the base material or washer (the surface on which the fastener is rotating). Approximately 40 percent of the applied torque is used in overcoming thread friction. This leaves only about 10 percent of the applied torque to develop a useful clamp load (the force which holds a joint together). This means that friction can account for as much as 90 percent of the applied torque on a fastener.

TORQUE WRENCHES

See Figures 23, 24 and 25

In most applications, a torque wrench can be used to assure proper installation of a fastener. Torque wrenches come in various designs and most automotive supply stores will carry a variety to suit your needs. A torque wrench should be used any time we supply a specific torque value for a fastener. A torque wrench can also be used if you are following the general guidelines in the accompanying charts. Keep in mind that because there is no worldwide standardization of fasteners, the charts are a general guideline and should be used with caution. Again, the general rule of "if you are using the right tool for the job, you should not have to strain to tighten a fastener" applies here.

Beam Type

See Figure 26

The beam type torque wrench is one of the most popular types. It consists of a pointer attached to the head that runs the length of the flexible beam (shaft) to a scale located near the handle. As the wrench is pulled, the beam bends and the pointer indicates the torque using the scale.

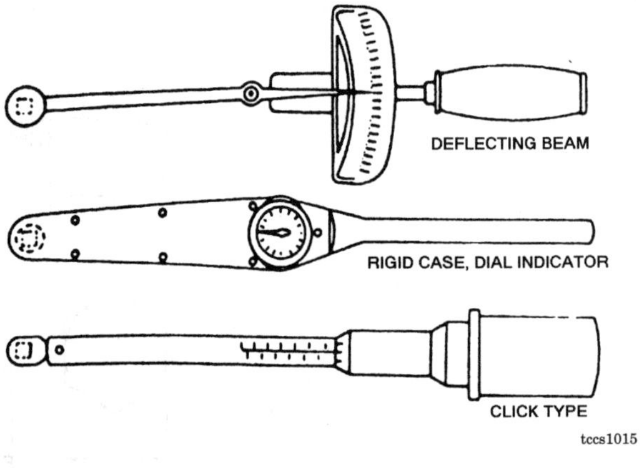

Fig. 23 Various styles of torque wrenches are usually available at your local automotive supply store

	Mark	Class
Hexagon head bolt	 Bolt head No. 4— 5— 6— 7— 8— 9— 10— 11—	4T 5T 6T 7T 8T 9T 10T 11T
	 No mark	4T
Hexagon flange bolt w/ washer hexagon bolt	 No mark	4T
Hexagon head bolt	 Two protruding lines	5T
Hexagon flange bolt w/ washer hexagon bolt	 Two protruding lines	6T
Hexagon head bolt	 Three protruding lines	7T
Hexagon head bolt	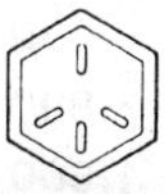 Four protruding lines	8T

	Mark	Class
Stud bolt	 No mark	4T
	 Grooved	6T
Welded bolt	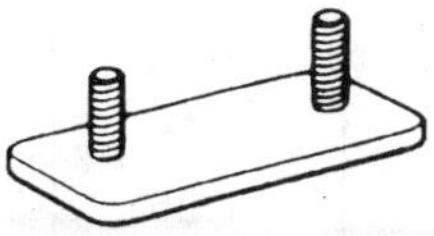	4T

tccs1240

Fig. 24 Determining bolt strength of metric fasteners — NOTE: this is a typical bolt marking system, but there is not a worldwide standard

Class	Diameter mm	Pitch mm	Specified torque					
			Hexagon head bolt			Hexagon flange bolt		
			N·m	kgf·cm	ft·lbf	N·m	kgf·cm	ft·lbf
4T	6	1	5	55	48 in.·lbf	6	60	52 in.·lbf
	8	1.25	12.5	130	9	14	145	10
	10	1.25	26	260	19	29	290	21
	12	1.25	47	480	35	53	540	39
	14	1.5	74	760	55	84	850	61
	16	1.5	115	1,150	83	—	—	—
5T	6	1	6.5	65	56 in.·lbf	7.5	75	65 in.·lbf
	8	1.25	15.5	160	12	17.5	175	13
	10	1.25	32	330	24	36	360	26
	12	1.25	59	600	43	65	670	48
	14	1.5	91	930	67	100	1,050	76
	16	1.5	140	1,400	101	—	—	—
6T	6	1	8	80	69 in.·lbf	9	90	78 in.·lbf
	8	1.25	19	195	14	21	210	15
	10	1.25	39	400	29	44	440	32
	12	1.25	71	730	53	80	810	59
	14	1.5	110	1,100	80	125	1,250	90
	16	1.5	170	1,750	127	—	—	—
7T	6	1	10.5	110	8	12	120	9
	8	1.25	25	260	19	28	290	21
	10	1.25	52	530	38	58	590	43
	12	1.25	95	970	70	105	1,050	76
	14	1.5	145	1,500	108	165	1,700	123
	16	1.5	230	2,300	166	—	—	—
8T	8	1.25	29	300	22	33	330	24
	10	1.25	61	620	45	68	690	50
	12	1.25	110	1,100	80	120	1,250	90
9T	8	1.25	34	340	25	37	380	27
	10	1.25	70	710	51	78	790	57
	12	1.25	125	1,300	94	140	1,450	105
10T	8	1.25	38	390	28	42	430	31
	10	1.25	78	800	58	88	890	64
	12	1.25	140	1,450	105	155	1,600	116
11T	8	1.25	42	430	31	47	480	35
	10	1.25	87	890	64	97	990	72
	12	1.25	155	1,600	116	175	1,800	130

tccs1241

Fig. 25 Standard bolt torque for metric fasteners — WARNING: use only as a guide

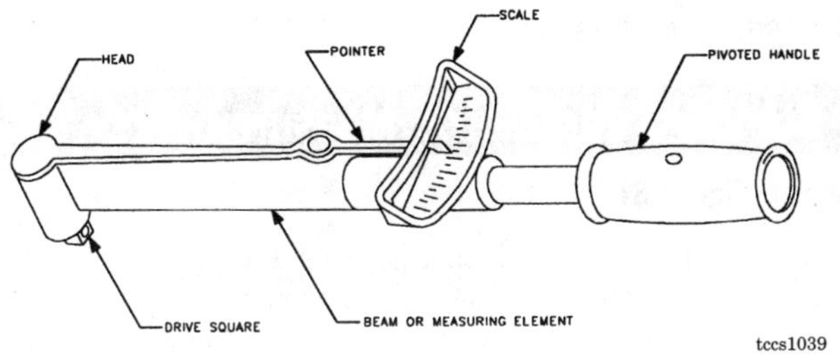

Fig. 26 Example of a beam type torque wrench

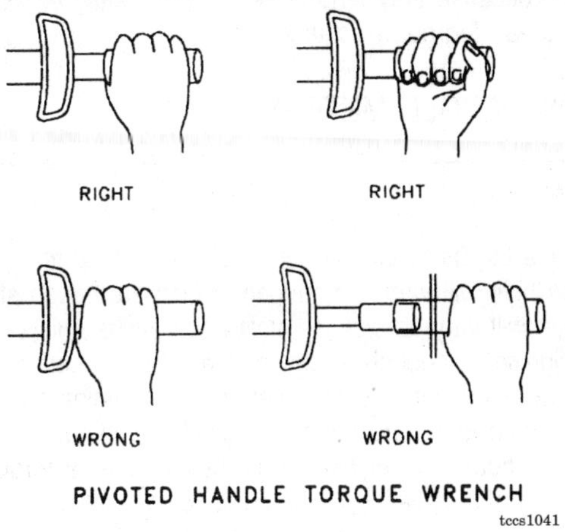

Fig. 28 Torque wrenches with pivoting heads must be grasped and used properly to prevent an incorrect reading

Click (Breakaway) Type

➧ See Figure 27

Another popular design of torque wrench is the click type. To use the click type wrench you pre-adjust it to a torque setting. Once the torque is reached, the wrench has a reflex signalling feature that causes a momentary breakaway of the torque wrench body, sending an impulse to the operator's hand.

Pivot Head Type

➧ See Figures 27 and 28

Some torque wrenches (usually of the click type) may be equipped with a pivot head which can allow it to be used in areas of limited access. BUT, it must be used properly. To hold a pivot head wrench, grasp the handle lightly, and as you pull on the handle, it should be floated on the pivot point. If the handle comes in contact with the yoke extension during the process of pulling, there is a very good chance the torque readings will be inaccurate because this could alter the wrench loading point. The design of the handle is usually such as to make it inconvenient to deliberately misuse the wrench.

➡It should be mentioned that the use of any U-joint, wobble or extension will have an effect on the torque readings, no matter what type of wrench you are using. For the most accurate readings, install the socket directly on the wrench driver. If necessary, straight extensions (which hold a socket directly under the wrench driver) will have the least effect on the torque reading. Avoid any extension that alters the length of the wrench from the handle to the head/driving point (such as a crow's foot). U-joint or Wobble extensions can greatly affect the readings; avoid their use at all times.

Rigid Case (Direct Reading)

➧ See Figure 29

A rigid case or direct reading torque wrench is equipped with a dial indicator to show torque values. One advantage of these wrenches is that they can be held at any position on the wrench without affecting accuracy. These wrenches are often

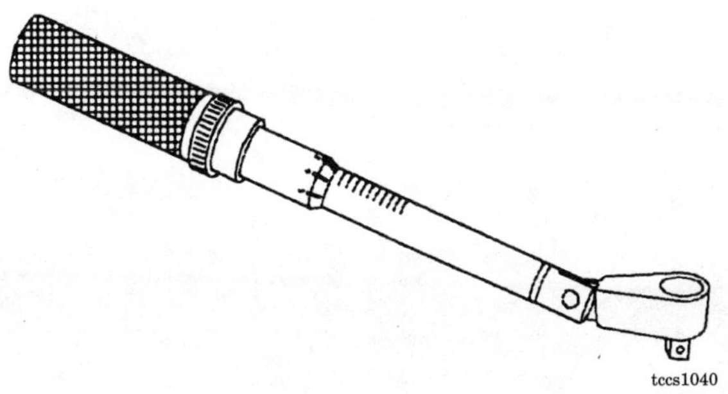

Fig. 27 A click type or breakaway torque wrench — note this one has a pivoting head

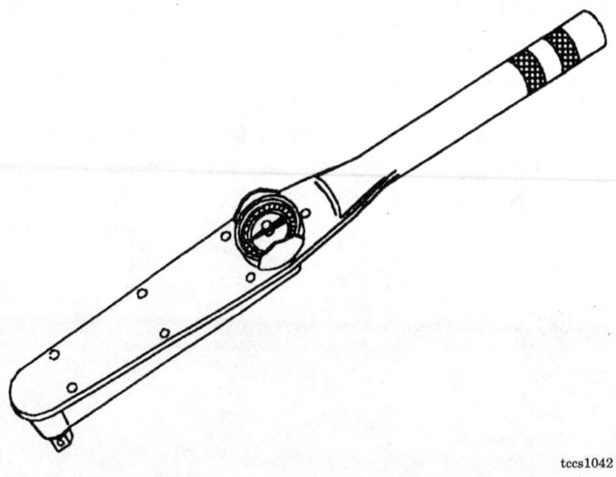

Fig. 29 The rigid case (direct reading) torque wrench uses a dial indicator to show torque

preferred because they tend to be compact, easy to read and have a great degree of accuracy.

TORQUE ANGLE METERS

See Figure 30

Because the frictional characteristics of each fastener or threaded hole will vary, clamp loads which are based strictly on torque will vary as well. In most applications, this variance is not significant enough to cause worry. But, in certain applications, a manufacturer's engineers may determine that more precise clamp loads are necessary (such is the case with many aluminum cylinder heads). In these cases, a torque angle method of installation would be specified. When installing fasteners which are torque angle tightened, a predetermined seating torque and standard torque wrench are usually used first to remove any compliance from the joint. The fastener is then tightened the specified additional portion of a turn measured in degrees. A torque angle gauge (mechanical protractor) is used for these applications.

Fig. 30 Some specifications require the use of a torque angle meter (mechanical protractor)

Standard and Metric Measurements

See Figure 31

Throughout this manual, specifications are given to help you determine the condition of various components on your vehicle, or to assist you in their installation. Some of the most common measurements include length (in. or cm/mm), torque (ft. lbs., inch lbs. or Nm) and pressure (psi, in. Hg, kPa or mm Hg). In most cases, we strive to provide the proper measurement as determined by the manufacturer's engineers.

Though, in some cases, that value may not be conveniently measured with what is available in your toolbox. Luckily, many of the measuring devices which are available today will have two scales so the Standard or Metric measurements may easily be taken. If any of the various measuring tools which are available to you do not contain the same scale as listed in the specifications, use the accompanying conversion factors to determine the proper value.

The conversion factor chart is used by taking the given specification and multiplying it by the necessary conversion factor. For instance, looking at the first line, if you have a measurement in inches such as "free-play should be 2 in." but your ruler reads only in millimeters, multiply 2 in. by the conversion factor of 25.4 to get the metric equivalent of 50.8mm. Likewise, if the specification was given only in a Metric measurement, for example in Newton Meters (Nm), then look at the center column first. If the measurement is 100 Nm, multiply it by the conversion factor of 0.738 to get 73.8 ft. lbs.

CONVERSION FACTORS

LENGTH–DISTANCE

Inches (in.)	x 25.4	= Millimeters (mm)	x .0394	= Inches
Feet (ft.)	x .305	= Meters (m)	x 3.281	= Feet
Miles	x 1.609	= Kilometers (km)	x .0621	= Miles

VOLUME

Cubic Inches (in3)	x 16.387	= Cubic Centimeters	x .061	= in3
IMP Pints (IMP pt.)	x .568	= Liters (L)	x 1.76	= IMP pt.
IMP Quarts (IMP qt.)	x 1.137	= Liters (L)	x .88	= IMP qt.
IMP Gallons (IMP gal.)	x 4.546	= Liters (L)	x .22	= IMP gal.
IMP Quarts (IMP qt.)	x 1.201	= US Quarts (US qt.)	x .833	= IMP qt.
IMP Gallons (IMP gal.)	x 1.201	= US Gallons (US gal.)	x .833	= IMP gal.
Fl. Ounces	x 29.573	= Milliliters	x .034	= Ounces
US Pints (US pt.)	x .473	= Liters (L)	x 2.113	= Pints
US Quarts (US qt.)	x .946	= Liters (L)	x 1.057	= Quarts
US Gallons (US gal.)	x 3.785	= Liters (L)	x .264	= Gallons

MASS–WEIGHT

Ounces (oz.)	x 28.35	= Grams (g)	x .035	= Ounces
Pounds (lb.)	x .454	= Kilograms (kg)	x 2.205	= Pounds

PRESSURE

Pounds Per Sq. In. (psi)	x 6.895	= Kilopascals (kPa)	x .145	= psi
Inches of Mercury (Hg)	x .4912	= psi	x 2.036	= Hg
Inches of Mercury (Hg)	x 3.377	= Kilopascals (kPa)	x .2961	= Hg
Inches of Water (H_2O)	x .07355	= Inches of Mercury	x 13.783	= H_2O
Inches of Water (H_2O)	x .03613	= psi	x 27.684	= H_2O
Inches of Water (H_2O)	x .248	= Kilopascals (kPa)	x 4.026	= H_2O

TORQUE

Pounds–Force Inches (in–lb)	x .113	= Newton Meters (N·m)	x 8.85	= in–lb
Pounds–Force Feet (ft–lb)	x 1.356	= Newton Meters (N·m)	x .738	= ft–lb

VELOCITY

Miles Per Hour (MPH)	x 1.609	= Kilometers Per Hour (KPH)	x .621	= MPH

POWER

Horsepower (Hp)	x .745	= Kilowatts	x 1.34	= Horsepower

FUEL CONSUMPTION*

Miles Per Gallon IMP (MPG)	x .354	= Kilometers Per Liter (Km/L)
Kilometers Per Liter (Km/L)	x 2.352	= IMP MPG
Miles Per Gallon US (MPG)	x .425	= Kilometers Per Liter (Km/L)
Kilometers Per Liter (Km/L)	x 2.352	= US MPG

*It is common to covert from miles per gallon (mpg) to liters/100 kilometers (1/100 km), where mpg (IMP) x 1/100 km = 282 and mpg (US) x 1/100 km = 235.

TEMPERATURE

Degree Fahrenheit (°F)	= (°C x 1.8) + 32
Degree Celsius (°C)	= (°F – 32) x .56

tccs1044

Fig. 31 Standard and metric conversion factors chart

SERIAL NUMBER IDENTIFICATION

Vehicle

VEHICLE IDENTIFICATION PLATE

See Figures 32 and 33

The Vehicle Identification Number (VIN) is stamped on a plate located on the top left hand side of the instrument panel, so it can be seen by looking through the windshield. It is also found on various other anti-theft labels found throughout the vehicle. The VIN is a seventeen digit sequence of numbers and letters which can be important for ordering parts and for servicing. The VIN plate is part of the Federal Vehicle Theft Prevention Standard and cannot be removed or altered in anyway. The 8th digit of the VIN identifies the factory equipped engine while the 10th digit will give the vehicle model year.

SERVICE PARTS IDENTIFICATION LABEL

See Figure 34

The service parts identification label has been developed and placed on the vehicle to aid in identifying parts and options which were originally installed on the vehicle. The service parts identification label is located on the inside of the glove box door. In most cases, the label lists the VIN, wheelbase, paint information and all production options or special equipment on the truck when it was shipped from the factory. Always refer to this information when ordering parts.

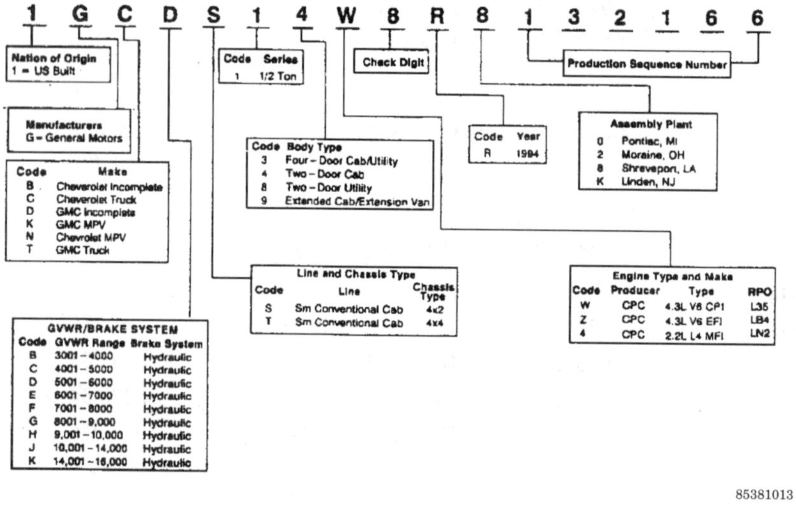

Fig. 32 Example of VIN interpretation

VEHICLE CERTIFICATION LABEL

See Figure 35

The certification label shows the Gross Vehicle Weight Rating (GVWR), the front and rear Gross Axle Weight Rating (GAWR) and the Payload Rating.

Gross Vehicle Weight (GVW) is the weight of the originally equipped truck and all items added to it after leaving the factory. The GVW must not exceed the Gross Vehicle Weight Rating (GVWR) of your truck.

The Payload Rating shown on the label is the maximum allowable cargo load (including the weight of the occupants) that the truck can carry. The payload rating is decreased if any accessories or other equipment is added to the truck after delivery from the factory. Deduct the weight of any added accessories from the original payload rating to determine the new payload rating.

Engine

Engine identification can take place using various methods. The VIN, described earlier in this section, contains a code identifying the engine which was originally installed in the vehicle. In most cases, this should be sufficient for determining the engine with which your truck is currently equipped. But, some older vehicles may have had the engine replaced or changed by a previous owner. If this is the case, the first step in identification is to locate an engine serial number and code which is laser etched, stamped on the block or located on adhesive labels that may be present on valve covers or other engine components.

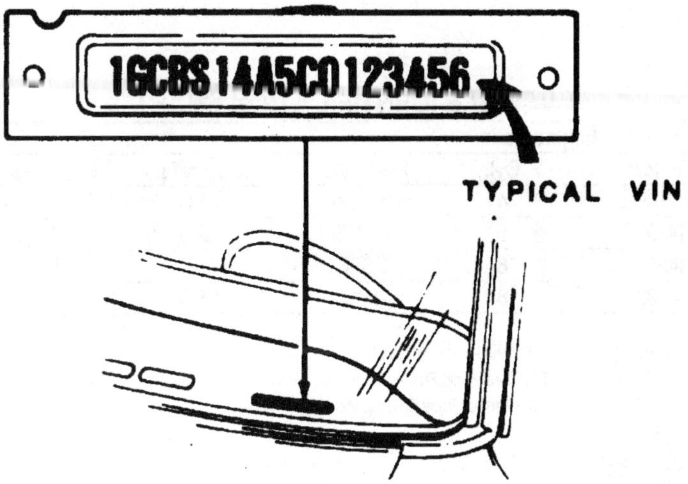

85381015

Fig. 33 VIN location

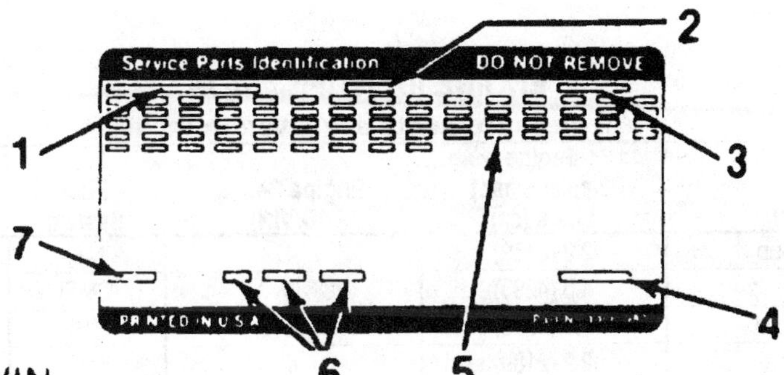

1. VIN
2. Wheel Base
3. Model Number
4. Order Number
5. RPO/SEO Codes
6. Exterior Color WA Number
7. Paint System

85381016

Fig. 34 Service parts identification label

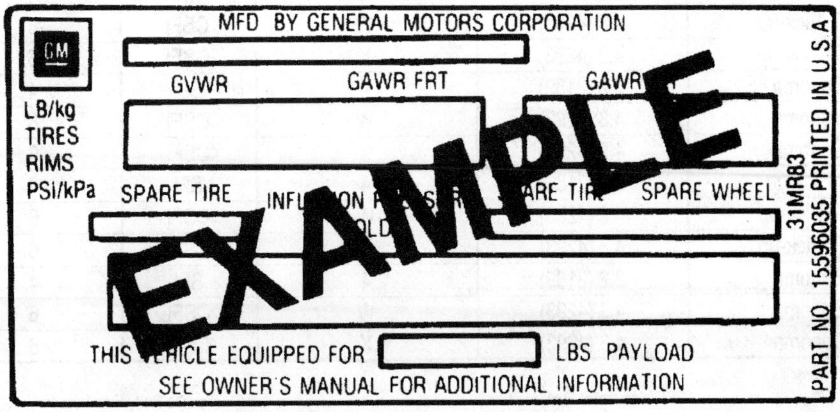

Certification label

85381017

Fig. 35 Vehicle certification label

VEHICLE IDENTIFICATION CHART

Engine Code					
Code	Liters	Cu. In. (cc)	Cyl.	Fuel Sys.	Eng. Mfg.
4	2.2	133 (2189)	4	MFI/SFI	CPC
W	4.3	262 (4293)	6	CMFI/CSFI	CPC
X	4.3	262 (4293)	6	CSFI	CPC
Z	4.3	262 (4293)	6	TBI	CPC

Model Year	
Code	Year
R	1994
S	1995
T	1996
V	1997

CMFI - Central Multi-port Fuel Injection
CPC - Chevrolet/Pontiac/Canada
CSFI - Central Sequential Fuel Injection
MFI - Multi-port Fuel Injection
SFI - Sequential Fuel Injection
TBI - Throttle Body Fuel Injection

88451c01

ENGINE IDENTIFICATION

All measurements are given in inches.

Year	Model	Engine Displacement Liters (cc)	Engine Series (ID/VIN)	Fuel System	No. of Cylinders	Engine Type
1994	S Pick-up	2.2 (2189)	4	MFI	4	OHV
	S/T Pick-up	4.3 (4293)	W	CMFI	6	OHV
	S/T Pick-up	4.3 (4293)	Z	TBI	6	OHV
	Sonoma	2.2 (2189)	4	MFI	4	OHV
	Sonoma	4.3 (4293)	W	CMFI	6	OHV
	Sonoma	4.3 (4293)	Z	TBI	6	OHV
1995	S Pick-up	2.2 (2189)	4	MFI	4	OHV
	S/T Pick-up	4.3 (4293)	W	CMFI	6	OHV
	S/T Pick-up	4.3 (4293)	Z	TBI	6	OHV
	Sonoma	2.2 (2189)	4	MFI	4	OHV
	Sonoma	4.3 (4293)	W	CMFI	6	OHV
	Sonoma	4.3 (4293)	Z	TBI	6	OHV
1996	S Pick-up	2.2 (2189)	4	SFI	4	OHV
	S/T Pick-up	4.3 (4293)	W	CSFI	6	OHV
	S/T Pick-up	4.3 (4293)	X	CSFI	6	OHV
	Sonoma	2.2 (2189)	4	SFI	4	OHV
	Sonoma	4.3 (4293)	W	CSFI	6	OHV
	Sonoma	4.3 (4293)	X	CSFI	6	OHV
1997	S Pick-up	2.2 (2189)	4	SFI	4	OHV
	S/T Pick-up	4.3 (4293)	W	CSFI	6	OHV
	S/T Pick-up	4.3 (4293)	X	CSFI	6	OHV
	Sonoma	2.2 (2189)	4	SFI	4	OHV
	Sonoma	4.3 (4293)	W	CSFI	6	OHV
	Sonoma	4.3 (4293)	X	CSFI	6	OHV

MFI - Multi-port Fuel Injection
CMFI - Central Multi-port Fuel Injection
SFI - Sequential Fuel Injection
CSFI - Central Sequential Fuel Injection
TBI - Throttle Body Fuel Injection

88451C02

2.2L ENGINE

➧ See Figure 30

The engine identification number is stamped on a flat, machined surface, on the left rear of the engine block, near the flywheel.

4.3L ENGINE

➧ See Figure 37

The engine identification number is stamped either on a flat, machined surface, on the right-front of the engine block, just above the water pump (on some earlier model engines), or on the left-rear side of the engine block, where the transmission is joined to the engine.

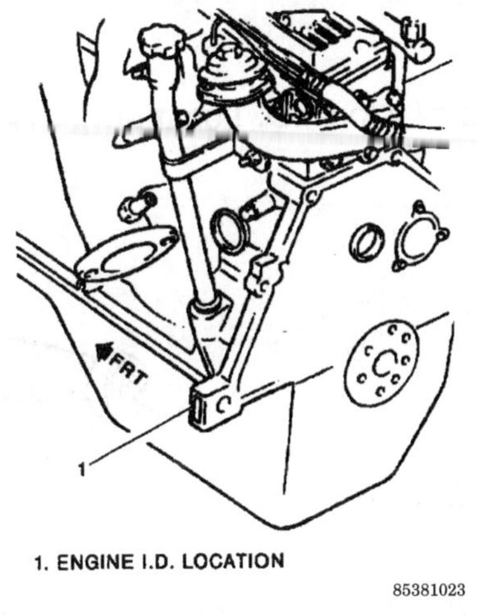

Fig. 36 Location of the engine identification number — 2.2L engine

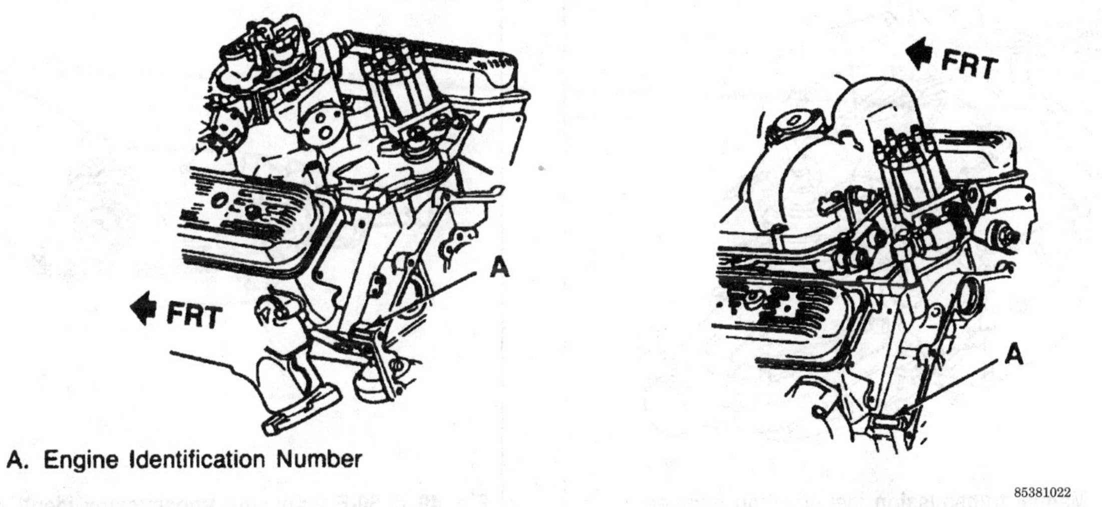

Fig. 37 Location of the engine identification number — 4.3L engine

Transmission

MANUAL

➧ See Figures 38 and 39

A transmission serial number is stamped on each transmission case or to a plate which is welded to the case. Location of the ID number will vary with the transmission manufacturer. With the Borg Warner T-5 transmission or New Venture Gear 1500/3500, locate the transmission ID number on the front right of the housing.

AUTOMATIC

➧ See Figure 40

The identification number for the 4L60-E is stamped on the right rear of the housing just above the pan rail.

Drive Axle

➧ See Figure 41

On most rear axles, the identification number is stamped on the right-front side of the axle tube, next to the differential. On front axles, the ID number is either stamped on a tag, attached to the differential cover by a cover bolt or is stamped, on the top of the carrier case along the edge of the machined face of the left half.

Transfer Case

The New Process 231, New Venture Gear NV231, New Process 233, New Venture Gear NV233 and the Borg-Warner 4472 transfer cases are equipped with an identification tag which is attached to the rear half of the case; the tag gives the model number, the low range reduction ratio and the assembly part number. If for some reason it becomes dislodged or removed, reattach it with an adhesive sealant.

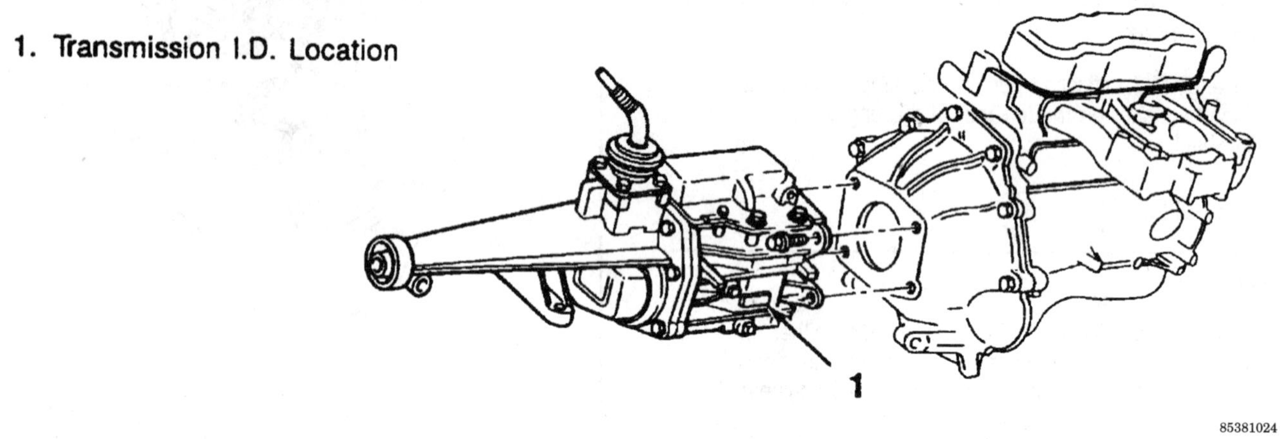

Fig. 38 Manual transmission identification number location — Borg Warner T-5

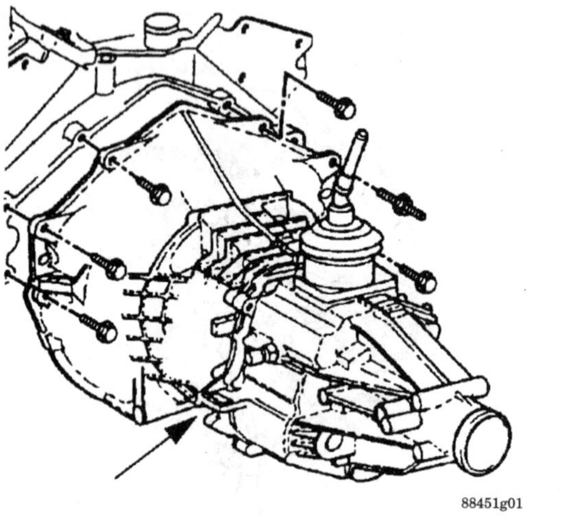

Fig. 39 Manual transmission identification number location — New Venture Gear 1500 and 3500

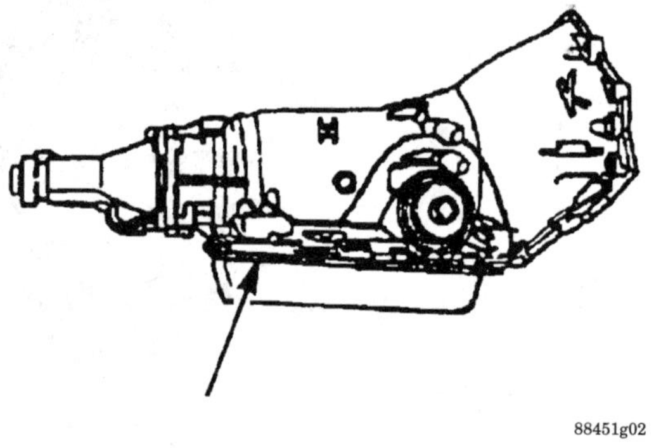

Fig. 40 4L60-E automatic transmission identification number location

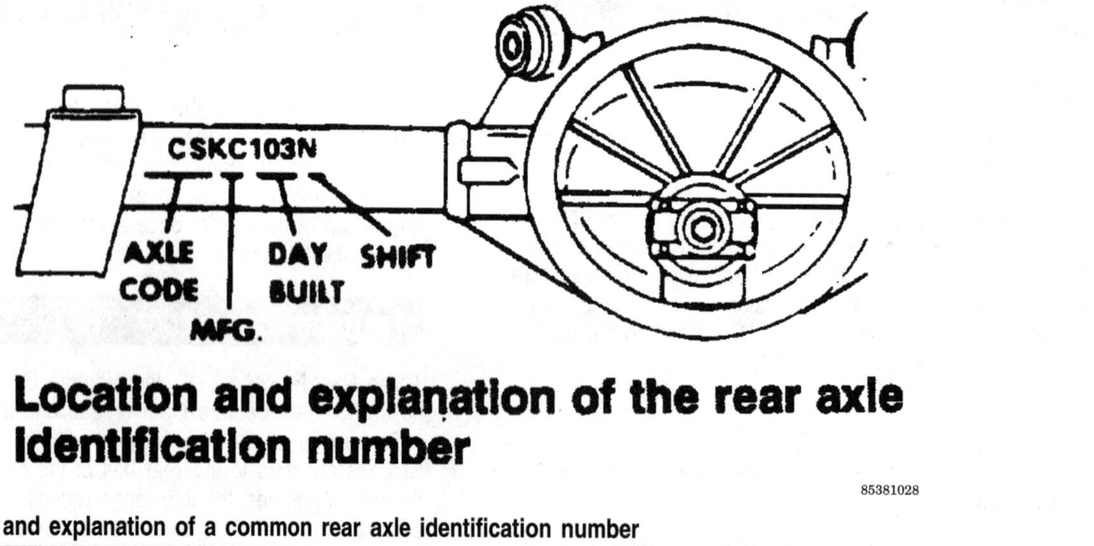

Fig. 41 Location and explanation of a common rear axle identification number

MANUAL TRANSMISSION APPLICATION

Year	Models	Transmission Type
1994	2.2L	Borg-Warner T-5
	4.3L	NVG 3500
1995	2.2L	Borg-Warner T-5
	4.3L	NVG 3500
1996	2.2L	NVG 1500
	4.3L	NVG 3500
1997	2.2L	NVG 1500
	4.3L	NVG 3500

88451C04

AUTOMATIC TRANSMISSION APPLICATION

Year	Models	Transmission Type
1994	All	4L60-E
1995	All	4L60-E
1996	All	4L60-E
1997	All	4L60-E

88451C03

REAR AXLE APPLICATION

Year	Models	Axle Type
1994	All	7½ Ring Gear Semi-Floating 7⅝ Ring Gear Semi-Floating
1995	All	7⅝ Ring Gear Semi-Floating GM 8½ Ring Gear Semi-Floating
1996	All	7⅝ Ring Gear Semi-Floating 8⅝ Ring Gear Semi-Floating
1997	All	7⅝ Ring Gear Semi-Floating 8⅝ Ring Gear Semi-Floating

88451C05

ROUTINE MAINTENANCE AND TUNE-UP

Proper maintenance and tune-up is the key to long and trouble-free vehicle life, and the work can yield its own rewards. Studies have shown that a properly tuned and maintained vehicle can achieve better gas mileage than an out-of-tune vehicle. As a conscientious owner and driver, set aside a Saturday morning, say once a month, to check or replace items which could cause major problems later. Keep your own personal log to jot down which services you performed, how much the parts cost you, the date, and the exact odometer reading at the time. Keep all receipts for such items as engine oil and filters, so that they may be referred to in case of related problems or to determine operating expenses. As a do-it-yourselfer, these receipts are the only proof you have that the required maintenance was performed. In the event of a warranty problem, these receipts will be invaluable.

The literature provided with your vehicle when it was originally delivered includes the factory recommended maintenance schedule. If you no longer have this literature, replacement copies are usually available from the dealer. A maintenance schedule is provided later in this section, in case you do not have the factory literature.

Air Cleaner

The air cleaner has a dual purpose. It not only filters the air, but also acts as a flame arrester if the engine should backfire. The engine should never be run without the air cleaner installed unless an engine maintenance procedure specifically requires the temporary removal of the air cleaner. Operating a vehicle without its air cleaner results in some throaty sounds from the engine giving the impression of increased power but will only cause trouble.

Your truck is equipped with an air cleaner element of the paper cartridge type. The element should be replaced every year or 30,000 miles (48,000 km), whichever comes first. If the truck is operated in heavy traffic or under dusty conditions, replace the element at more frequent intervals.

REMOVAL & INSTALLATION

TBI Models

➧ See Figures 42, 43 and 44

1. If so equipped, unlatch the clamp fasteners around the perimeter of the air cleaner housing.
2. Loosen the wingnut(s) at the center of the air cleaner cover.
3. Remove the cover from the air cleaner assembly, then remove the air cleaner element from the housing.

To install:

4. Using a clean rag, wipe the inside of the air cleaner housing assembly to remove any dirt or debris.
5. Install the air cleaner element to the housing, then position the cover onto the assembly.
6. Secure the cover using the clamp fasteners and/or wingnut(s).

MFI/CMFI Models

➧ See Figures 45, 46 and 47

1. Loosen the housing cover retaining clips and separate the housing cover.
2. Remove the air filter assembly.

To install:

3. Using a clean rag, wipe the inside of the air cleaner housing assembly to remove any dirt or debris.
4. Install the air filter assembly.
5. Engage the housing cover and fasten the retaining clips.

Fuel Filter

The fuel filter should be serviced every 30,000 miles (48,000 km). If the truck is operated under severe conditions, change it more often.

REMOVAL & INSTALLATION

In-line Filter

➧ See Figure 48

✻✻CAUTION

Before removing any fuel system component, always relieve pressure from the system. Refer to Section 5 for this procedure

To locate the inline filter, follow the fuel line back from the throttle body unit or fuel rail. In-line filters are often mounted to the frame rail underneath the vehicle. It may be necessary to raise and safely support the vehicle using jackstands in order to access the filter.

✻✻CAUTION

Before disconnecting any component of the fuel system, refer to the fuel pressure release procedures found earlier in this section.

1. Properly relieve the fuel system pressure.
2. Using a backup wrench (where applicable) to prevent overtorquing the lines or fittings, loosen and disconnect the fuel lines from the filter. Be sure to position a rag in order to catch any remaining fuel which may escape when the fittings are loosened.
3. Remove the fuel filter from the retainer or mounting bolt. For most filters which are retained by band clamps, loosen the fastener(s) and remove the filter. For some filters it may be necessary to completely remove the clamp and filter assembly.

MAINTENANCE COMPONENT LOCATIONS
4.3L TBI (1994 SHOWN)

1. Brake master cylinder reservoir
2. Brake booster
3. Air filter housing
4. Alternator
5. Upper radiator hose
6. Serpentine belt routing label
7. Emission hose routing label
8. Serpentine belt
9. Radiator cap
10. Battery
11. Coolant recovery tank
12. Engine oil dipstick
13. Engine oil filler cap
14. Manual transmission filler cap
15. Windshield washer fluid reservoir
16. Vehicle emission label

88451p46

MAINTENANCE COMPONENT LOCATIONS
4.3L CSFI (1996 SHOWN)

1. Engine oil fill cap
2. Automatic transmission fluid dipstick
3. Brake booster
4. Brake master cylinder
5. Windshield washer fluid reservoir
6. Air filter housing
7. Upper radiator hose
8. Air conditioning line
9. Power steering pump cap
10. Air conditioning compressor
11. Serpentine belt
12. Emission hose routing label
13. Vehicle information label
14. Alternator
15. Engine oil dipstick
16. Radiator cap
17. Air bag warning label
18. Battery
19. Coolant recovery tank

88451p66

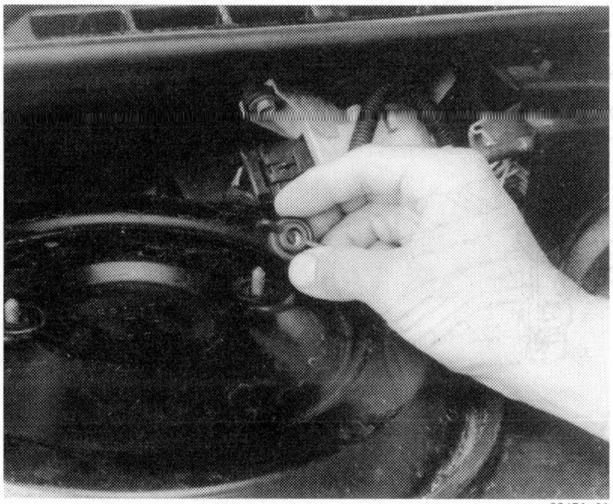
88451p01

Fig. 42 Remove the wingnuts from the air cleaner cover

88451p02

Fig. 43 Remove the air cleaner cover

88451p03

Fig. 44 Remove the old air filter from the housing

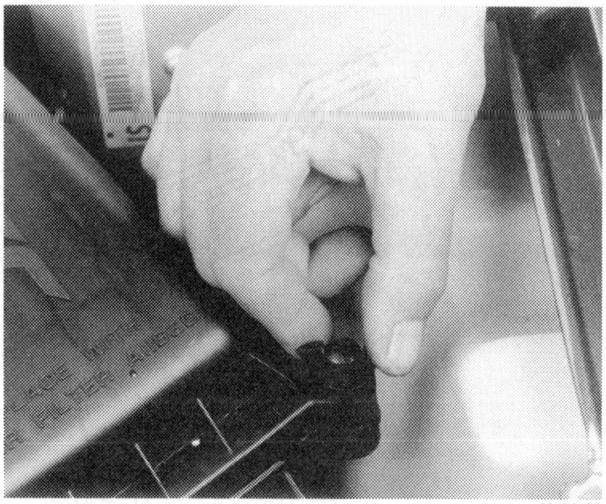
88451p50

Fig. 45 Unfasten the air cleaner housing retainers — 1996 model shown

88451p51

Fig. 46 Remove the air filter from the housing — 1996 model shown

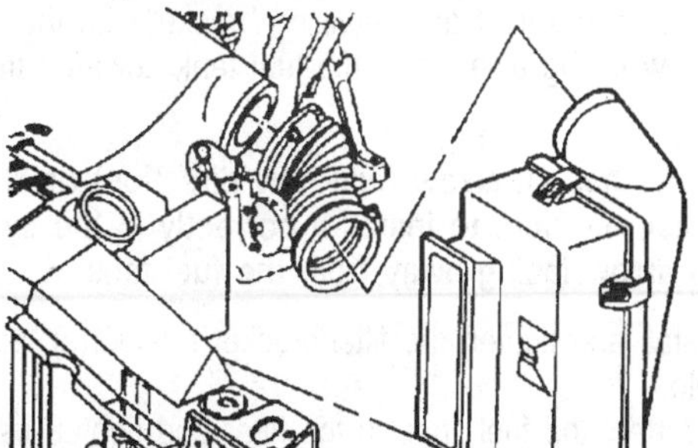
88451g04

Fig. 47 View of the air filter housing and related components — 1996 model shown

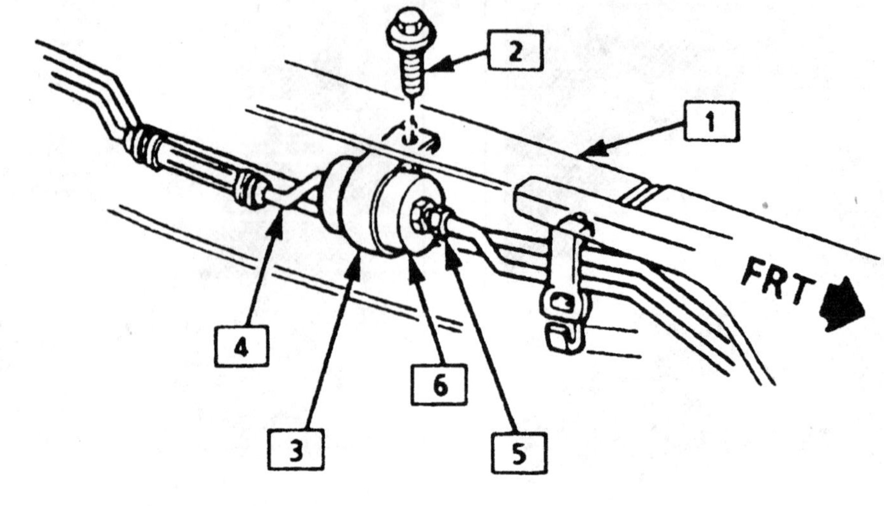

1 LEFT FRAME SIDE MEMBER

2 BOLT - TIGHTEN 16 N·m (24 lb. ft.)

3 CLAMP

4 REAR FUEL FEED PIPE
TIGHTEN 26 N·m (20 lb. ft.)

5 INTERMEDIATE FUEL FEED PIPE
TIGHTEN 26 N·m (20 lb. ft.)

6 IN - LINE FUEL FILTER

85381035

Fig. 48 In-line fuel filter — 4.3L engine

To install:

4. Position the filter and retaining bracket with the directional arrow facing away from the fuel tank, towards the throttle body.

➡The filter has an arrow (fuel flow direction) on the side of the case, be sure to install it correctly in the system, the with arrow facing away from the fuel tank.

5. Install and tighten the filter/bracket retainer(s), as applicable.
6. Connect the fuel lines to the filter and tighten using a backup wrench to prevent damage.
7. Connect the negative battery cable and tighten the fuel filler cap, then start the engine and check for leaks.

In-Tank Filter

➧ See Figure 49

This filter is not part of the vehicles routine maintenance and does not normally require service. To service the in-tank fuel filter, please refer to the electric fuel pump procedures found in Section 5 of this manual.

Positive Crankcase Ventilation (PCV) Valve

➧ See Figures 50 and 51

The PCV system must be operating properly in order to allow evaporation of fuel vapors and water from the crankcase. This system should be serviced and both the PCV valve and filter (located in the air cleaner) replaced every 30,000 miles (48,000 km). Normal service entails cleaning the passages of the system hoses with solvent, inspecting them for cracks and breaks, and replacing them as necessary. The PCV valve contains a check valve and, when working properly, this valve will make a rattling sound when the outside case is tapped. If it fails to rattle, then it is probably stuck in a closed position and needs to be replaced.

The PCV system is designed to prevent the emission of gases from the crankcase into the atmosphere. It does this by

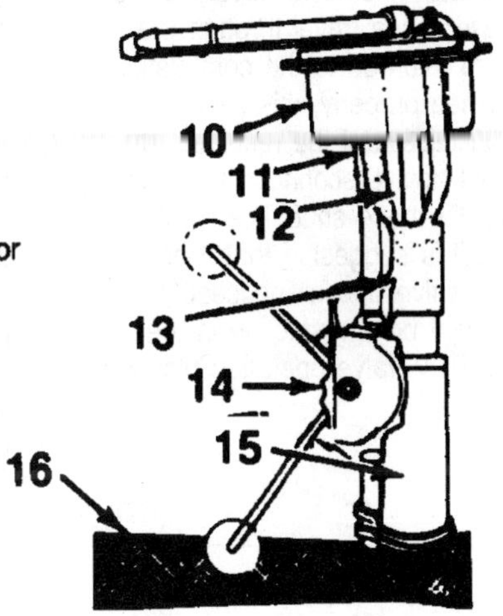

Fig. 49 Common in-tank electric fuel pump and filter assembly

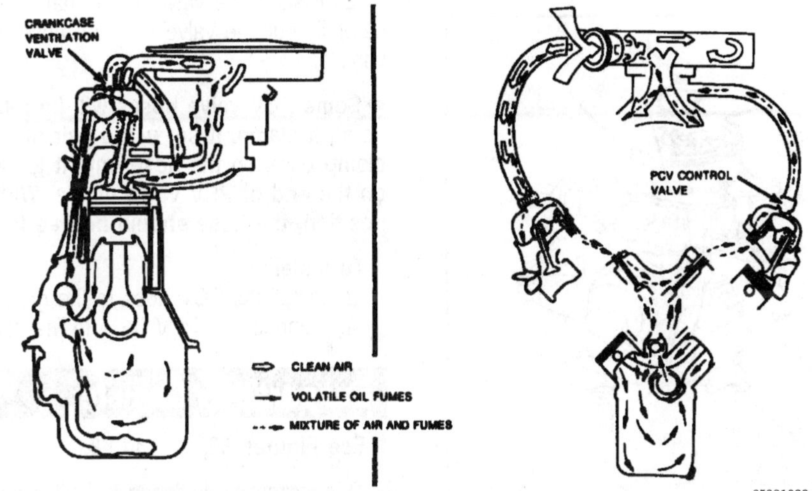

Fig. 50 PCV flow through the engine

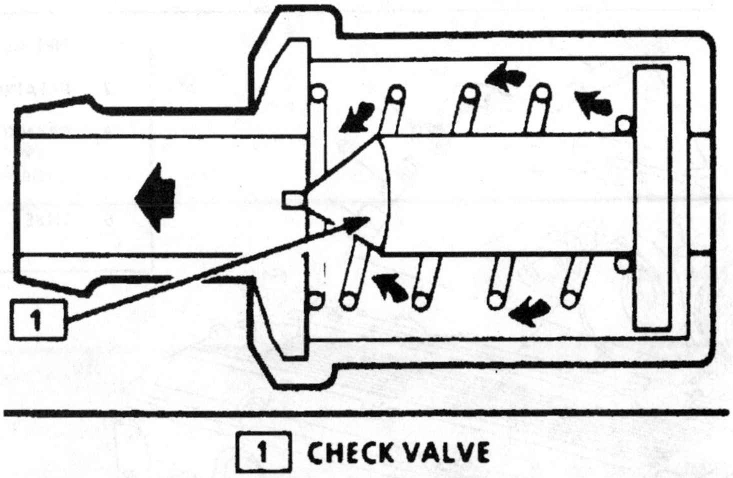

Fig. 51 Cross-section of a PCV valve

connecting a crankcase outlet (usually the valve cover) to the intake with a hose. The crankcase gases travel through the hose to the intake where they are returned to the combustion chamber to be burned. If maintained properly, this system reduces condensation in the crankcase and the resultant formation of harmful acids and oil dilution. Disconnect the valve from the engine or merely clamp the hose shut. The PCV valve is an inexpensive item and it is suggested that it be replaced, if suspected. If the new valve doesn't noticeably improve engine idle, the problem might be a restriction in the PCV hose. For further details on PCV valve operation please refer to Section 4 of this manual.

FUNCTIONAL CHECK

See Figures 52, 53 and 54

If the engine is idling rough, check for a clogged PCV valve, dirty vent filter or air cleaner element, or plugged hose. Test the system using the following procedure and replace components as necessary.

1. Remove the PCV valve from the rocker cover.
2. Run the engine at idle and place your thumb over the end of the valve to check for vacuum. If the engine speed decreases less than 50 rpm, the valve is clogged and should be replaced. If the engine speed decreases much more than 50 rpm, then the valve is good.
3. If no vacuum exists, check for plugged hoses, manifold port.
4. To check the PCV valve, remove the valve from the hose and shake it. If a rattling noise is heard, the valve is good. If no noise is heard, the valve is plugged and replacement is necessary.

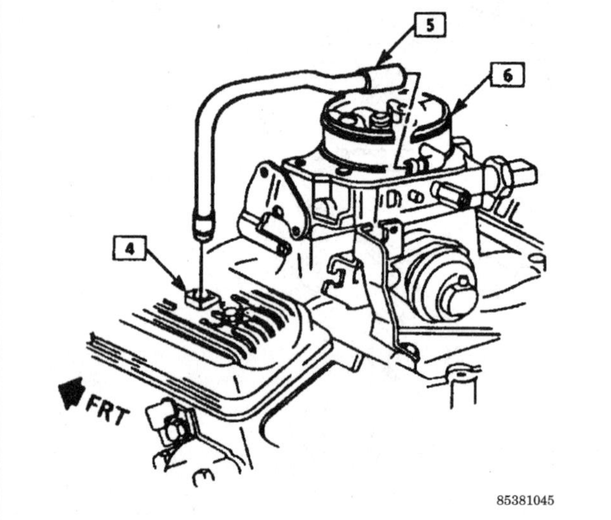

Fig. 52 PCV system — 4.3L TBI engine

REMOVAL & INSTALLATION

See Figure 55

1. Grasp the valve and withdraw it from the valve cover.
2. Holding the valve in one hand and the hose in the other, carefully pull the valve from the hose and remove from the vehicle.

➡Some PCV valve hoses will be retained to the valve using a clamp. If so, use a pair of pliers to slide the clamp back on the hose until it is clear of the bulged area on the end of PCV valve nipple. With the clamp in this position, the hose should be free to slip from the valve.

To install:

3. Install the PCV hose to the grommet in the valve cover.
4. Connect the PCV hose to the valve.

Evaporative Canister

See Figures 56, 57 and 58

This system is designed to limit gasoline vapor, which normally escapes from the fuel tank and the intake manifold, from discharging into the atmosphere. Vapor absorption is accomplished through the use of the charcoal canister. The canister

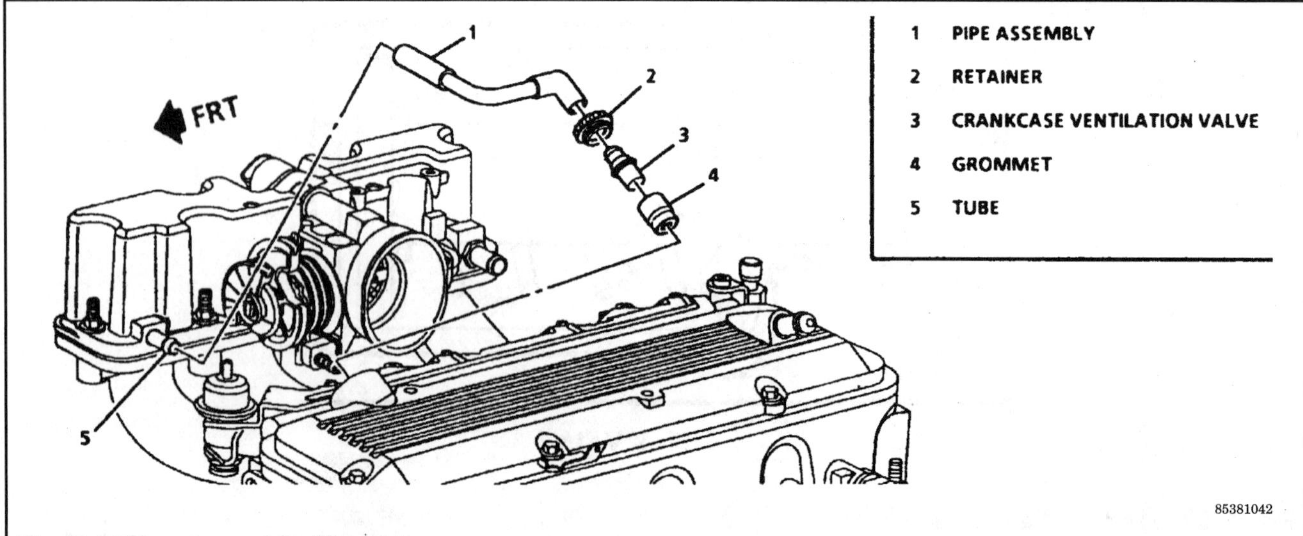

Fig. 53 PCV system — 2.2L MFI engine

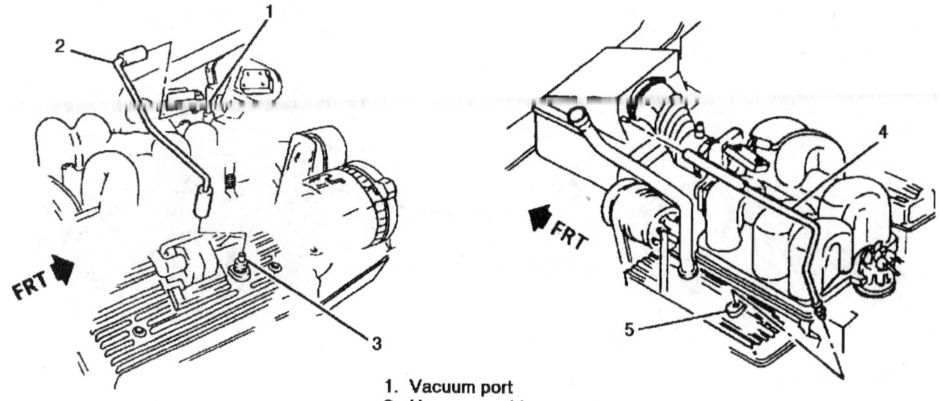

Fig. 54 PCV system — 4.3L CMFI engine

Fig. 55 Remove the PCV valve from the valve cover

absorbs fuel vapors and stores them until they can be removed and burned in the combustion process. Removal of the vapors from the canister to the engine is accomplished through a computer controlled canister purge solenoid.

In addition to the canister, the fuel tank requires a non-vented gas cap. This cap does not allow fuel vapor to discharge into the atmosphere. All fuel vapor travels through a vent line (inserted high into the domed fuel tank) directly to the canister.

SERVICING

Every 30,000 miles (48,000 km) or 24 months, check all fuel, vapor lines and hoses for proper hook-up, routing and condition. If equipped, check that the bowl vent and purge valves work properly. Remove the canister and check for cracks or damage and replace, if necessary.

Battery

GENERAL MAINTENANCE

All batteries, regardless of type, should be carefully secured by a battery hold-down device. If this is not done, the battery terminals or casing may crack from stress applied to the battery during vehicle operation. A battery which is not secured may allow acid to leak out, making it discharge faster; such leaking corrosive acid can also eat away components under the hood. A battery that is not sealed must be checked periodically for electrolyte level. You cannot add water to a sealed maintenance-free battery (though not all maintenance-free batteries are sealed), but a sealed battery must also be checked for proper electrolyte level as indicated by the color of the built-in hydrometer "eye."

Keep the top of the battery clean, as a film of dirt can help completely discharge a battery that is not used for long periods. A solution of baking soda and water may be used for cleaning, but be careful to flush this off with clear water. DO NOT let any of the solution into the filler holes. Baking soda neutralizes battery acid and will de-activate a battery cell.

CAUTION

Always use caution when working on or near the battery. Never allow a tool to bridge the gap between the negative and positive battery terminals. Also, be careful not to allow a tool to provide a ground between the positive cable/terminal and any metal component on the vehicle. Either of these conditions will cause a short circuit leading to sparks and possible personal injury.

Batteries in vehicles which are not operated on a regular basis can fall victim to parasitic loads (small current drains which are constantly drawing current from the battery). Normal parasitic loads may drain a battery on a vehicle that is in storage and not used for 6-8 weeks. Vehicles that have additional accessories such as a cellular phone, an alarm system

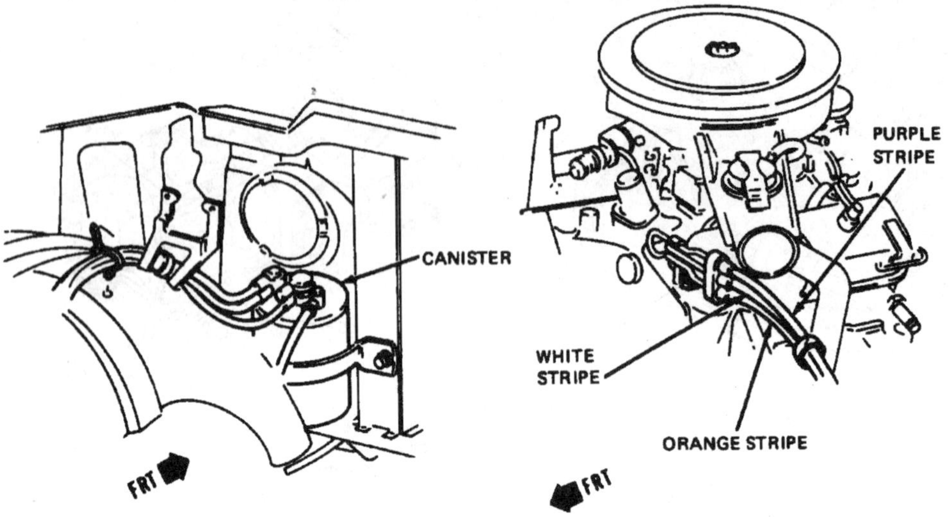

4-cylinder engine evaporative canister and hoses

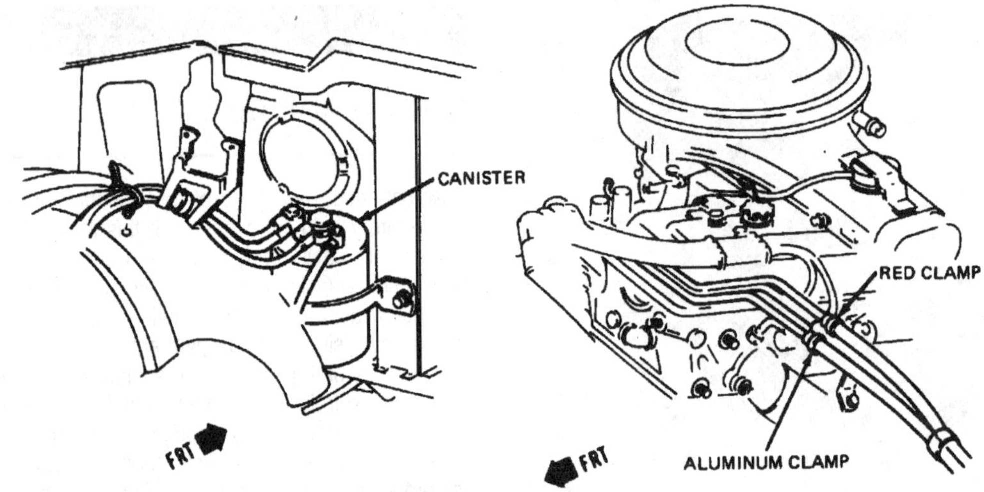

85381048

Fig. 56 Example of a common evaporative canister and hose assembly — 6-cylinder engine

or other devices that increase parasitic load may discharge a battery sooner. If the vehicle is to be stored for 6-8 weeks in a secure area and the alarm system, if present, is not necessary, the negative battery cable should be disconnected at the onset of storage to protect the battery charge.

Remember that constantly discharging and recharging will shorten battery life. Take care not to allow a battery to be needlessly discharged.

BATTERY FLUID

➧ **See Figures 59, 60 and 61**

✻✻CAUTION

Battery electrolyte contains sulfuric acid. If you should splash any on your skin or in your eyes, flush the affected area with plenty of clear water. If it lands in your eyes, get medical help immediately.

The fluid (sulfuric acid solution) contained in the battery cells will tell you many things about the condition of the battery. Because the cell plates must be kept submerged below the fluid level in order to operate, maintaining the fluid level is extremely important. And, because the specific gravity of the acid is an indication of electrical charge, testing the fluid can be an aid in determining if the battery must be replaced. A battery in a vehicle with a properly operating charging system should require little maintenance, but careful, periodic inspection should reveal problems before they leave you stranded.

Fluid Level

Check the battery electrolyte level at least once a month, or more often in hot weather or during periods of extended vehicle operation. On non-sealed batteries, the level can be checked either through the case on translucent batteries or by removing the cell caps on opaque-cased types. The electrolyte level in each cell should be kept filled to the split ring inside each cell, or the line marked on the outside of the case.

If the level is low, add only distilled water through the opening until the level is correct. Each cell is separate from the

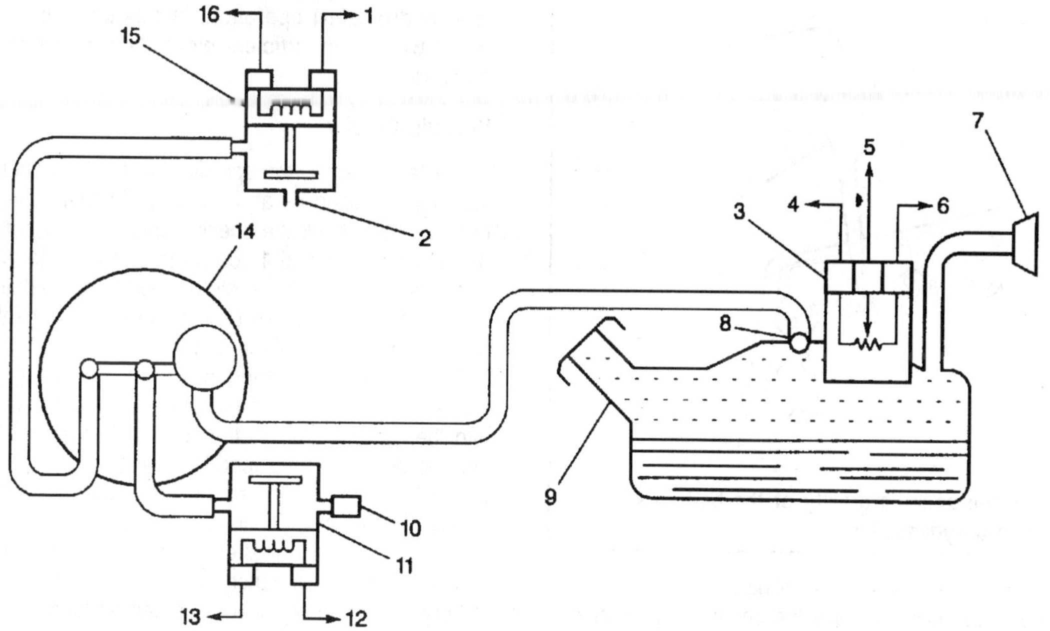

(1) EVAP Purge Solenoid Ignition Feed
(2) Intake Manifold
(3) Fuel Tank Pressure Sensor
(4) Fuel Tank Pressure Sensor Ground Circuit
(5) Fuel Tank Pressure Sensor Signal Circuit
(6) Fuel Tank Pressure Sensor 5 Volt Reference Circuit
(7) Fuel Filler Neck
(8) Rollover Valve
(9) Fuel Tank
(10) EVAP Vent Valve Filter
(11) EVAP Vent Valve
(12) EVAP Vent Valve Control Circuit
(13) EVAP Valve Ignition Feed
(14) EVAP Canister
(15) EVAP Purge Solenoid
(16) EVAP Purge Solenoid Control Circuit

88451g07

Fig. 57 Common evaporative emission system — 1996 model shown

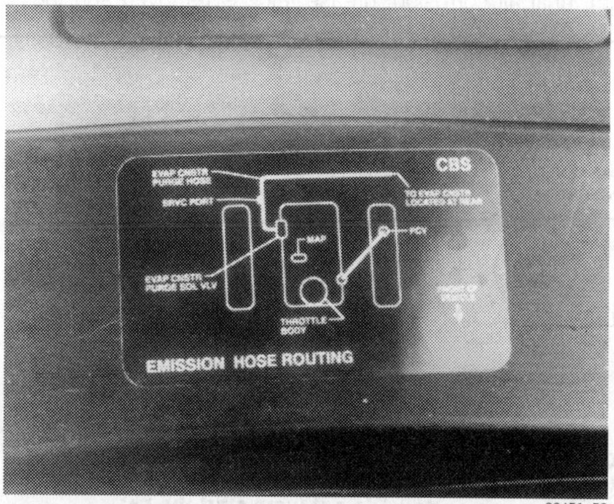

88451p52

Fig. 58 Common emission hose routing label — 1996 model shown

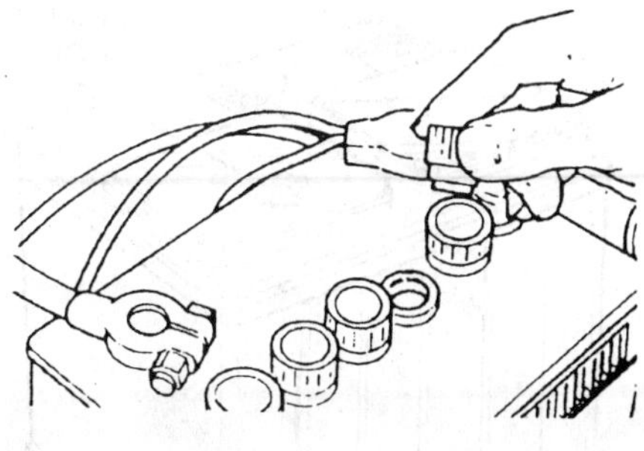

tccs1251

Fig. 59 On non-maintenance free batteries, the level can be checked through the case on translucent batteries; the cell caps must be removed on other models

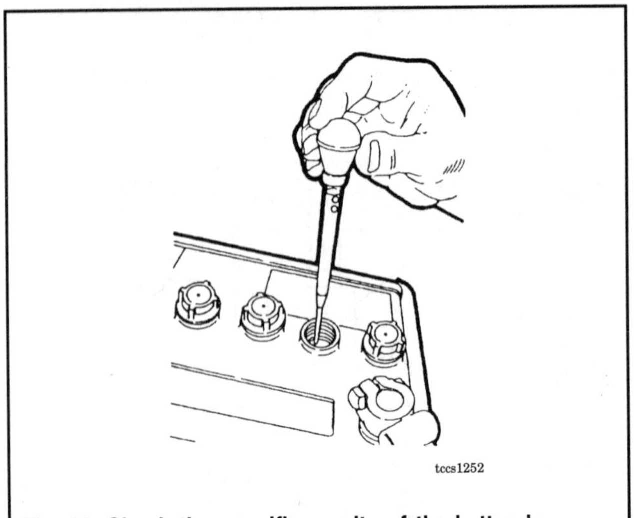

Fig. 60 Check the specific gravity of the battery's electrolyte with a hydrometer

others, so each must be checked and filled individually. Distilled water should be used, because the chemicals and minerals found in most drinking water are harmful to the battery and could significantly shorten its life.

If water is added in freezing weather, the vehicle should be driven several miles to allow the water to mix with the electrolyte. Otherwise, the battery could freeze.

Although some maintenance-free batteries have removable cell caps for access to the electrolyte, the electrolyte condition and level on all sealed maintenance-free batteries must be checked using the built-in hydrometer "eye." The exact type of eye varies between battery manufacturers, but most apply a sticker to the battery itself explaining the possible readings. When in doubt, refer to the battery manufacturer's instructions to interpret battery condition using the built-in hydrometer.

➡Although the readings from built-in hydrometers found in sealed batteries may vary, a green eye usually indicates a properly charged battery with sufficient fluid level. A dark eye is normally an indicator of a battery with sufficient fluid, but one which may be low in charge. And a light or yellow eye is usually an indication that electrolyte supply has dropped below the necessary level for battery (and hydrometer) operation. In this last case, sealed batteries with an insufficient electrolyte level must usually be discarded.

Specific Gravity

As stated earlier, the specific gravity of a battery's electrolyte level can be used as an indication of battery charge. At least once a year, check the specific gravity of the battery. It should be between 1.20 and 1.26 on the gravity scale. Most auto supply stores carry a variety of inexpensive battery testing hydrometers. These can be used on any non-sealed battery to test the specific gravity in each cell.

The battery testing hydrometer has a squeeze bulb at one end and a nozzle at the other. Battery electrolyte is sucked into the hydrometer until the float is lifted from its seat. The specific gravity is then read by noting the position of the float. If gravity is low in one or more cells, the battery should be slowly charged and checked again to see if the gravity has come up. Generally, if after charging, the specific gravity between any two cells varies more than 50 points (0.50), the battery should be replaced as it can no longer produce sufficient voltage to guarantee proper operation.

On sealed batteries, the built-in hydrometer is the only way of checking specific gravity. Again, check with your battery's manufacturer for proper interpretation of its built-in hydrometer readings.

CABLES

➧ See Figures 62, 63, 64, 65, 66 and 67

Once a year (or as necessary), the battery terminals and the cable clamps should be cleaned. Loosen the clamps and remove the cables, negative cable first. On batteries with posts on top, the use of a puller specially made for this purpose is recommended. These are inexpensive and available in most auto parts stores. Side terminal battery cables are secured with a small bolt.

Clean the cable clamps and the battery terminal with a wire brush, until all corrosion, grease, etc., is removed and the

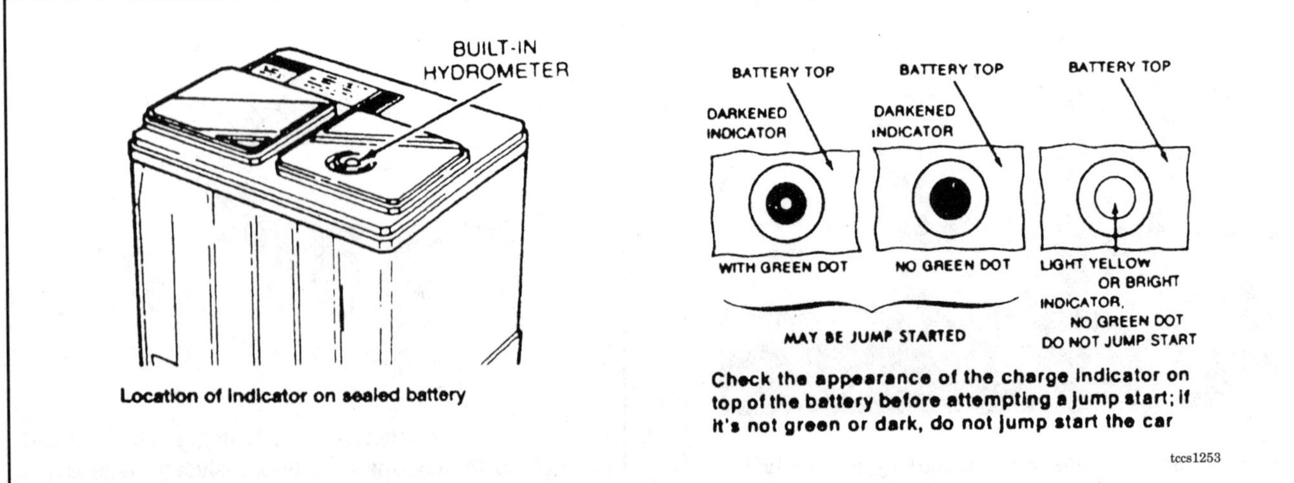

Fig. 61 A typical sealed (maintenance-free) battery with a built-in hydrometer — NOTE that the hydrometer eye may vary between battery manufacturers; always refer to the battery's label

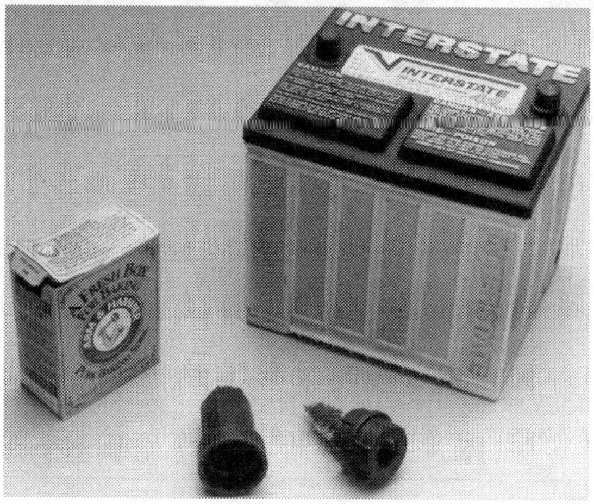

tccs1206

Fig. 62 Maintenance is performed with household items and with special tools like this post cleaner

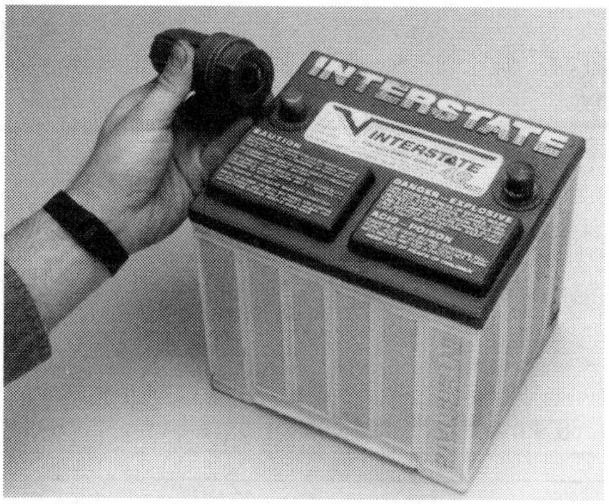

tccs1207

Fig. 63 The underside of this special battery tool has a wire brush to clean post terminals

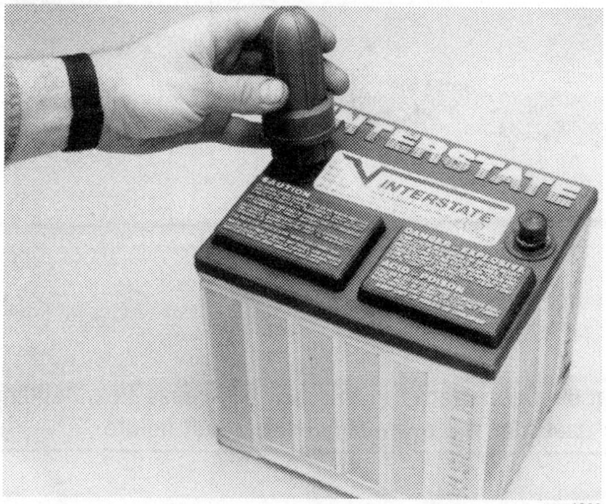

tccs1208

Fig. 64 Place the tool over the terminals and twist to clean the post

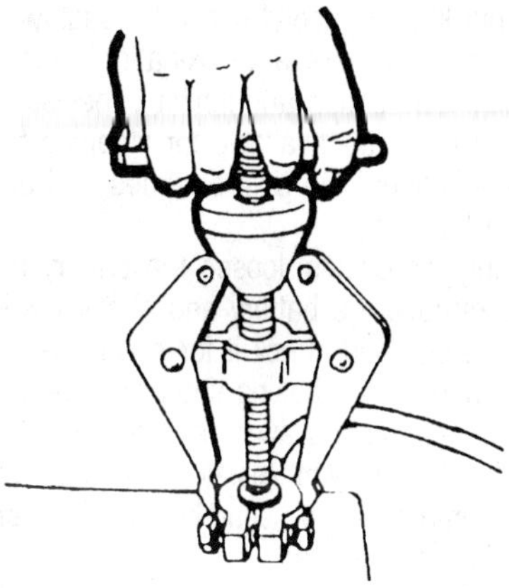

tccs1254

Fig. 65 A special tool is available to pull the clamp from the post

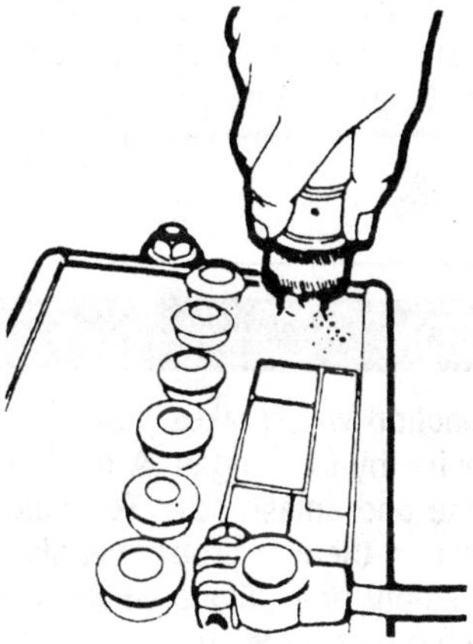

tccs1255

Fig. 66 Clean the battery terminals until the metal is shiny

tccs1256

Fig. 67 The cable ends should be cleaned as well

metal is shiny. It is especially important to clean the inside of the clamp (an old knife is useful here) thoroughly, since a small deposit of foreign material or oxidation there will prevent a sound electrical connection and inhibit either starting or charging. Special tools are available for cleaning these parts, one type for conventional top post batteries and another type for side terminal batteries.

Before installing the cables, loosen the battery hold-down clamp or strap, remove the battery and check the battery tray. Clear it of any debris, and check it for soundness (the battery tray can be cleaned with a baking soda and water solution). Rust should be wire brushed away, and the metal given a couple coats of anti-rust paint. Install the battery and tighten the hold-down clamp or strap securely. Do not overtighten, as this can crack the battery case.

After the clamps and terminals are clean, reinstall the cables, negative cable last; DO NOT hammer the clamps onto post batteries. Tighten the clamps securely, but do not distort them. Give the clamps and terminals a thin external coating of grease after installation, to retard corrosion.

Check the cables at the same time that the terminals are cleaned. If the cable insulation is cracked or broken, or if the ends are frayed, the cable should be replaced with a new cable of the same length and gauge.

CHARGING

****CAUTION**

The chemical reaction which takes place in all batteries generates explosive hydrogen gas. A spark can cause the battery to explode and splash acid. To avoid serious personal injury, be sure there is proper ventilation and take appropriate fire safety precautions when connecting, disconnecting, or charging a battery and when using jumper cables.

A battery should be charged at a slow rate to keep the plates inside from getting too hot. However, if some maintenance-free batteries are allowed to discharge until they are almost "dead," they may have to be charged at a high rate to bring them back to "life." Always follow the charger manufacturer's instructions on charging the battery.

REPLACEMENT

When it becomes necessary to replace the battery, select one with a rating equal to or greater than the battery originally installed. Deterioration and just plain aging of the battery cables, starter motor, and associated wires makes the battery's job harder in successive years. The slow increase in electrical resistance over time makes it prudent to install a new battery with a greater capacity than the old.

Drive Belts

INSPECTION

See Figures 68, 69, 70 and 71

Inspect the belts for signs of glazing or cracking. A glazed belt will be perfectly smooth from slippage, while a good belt will have a slight texture of fabric visible. Cracks will usually start at the inner edge of the belt and run outward. All worn or damaged drive belts should be replaced immediately. It is best to replace all drive belts at one time, as a preventive maintenance measure, during this service operation.

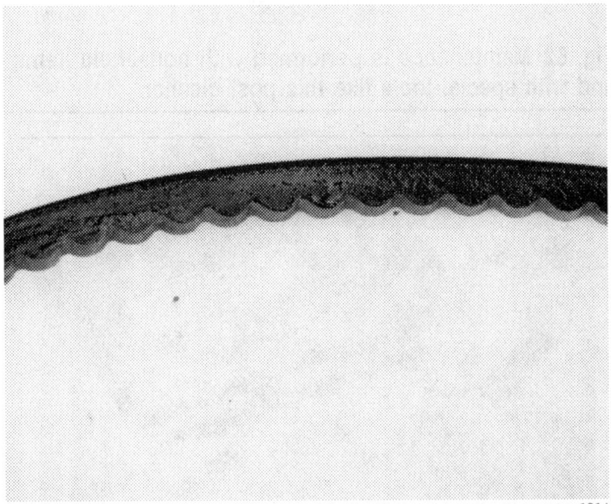

tccs1214

Fig. 68 An example of a healthy drive belt

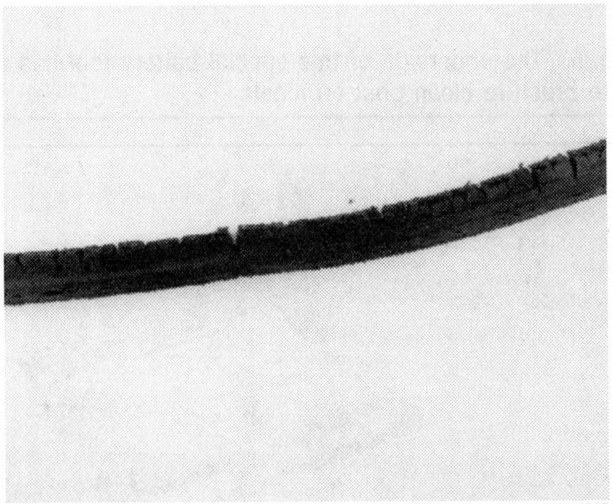

tccs1215

Fig. 69 Deep cracks in this belt will cause flex, building up heat that will eventually lead to belt failure

tccs1216

Fig. 70 The cover of this belt is worn, exposing the critical reinforcing cords to excessive wear

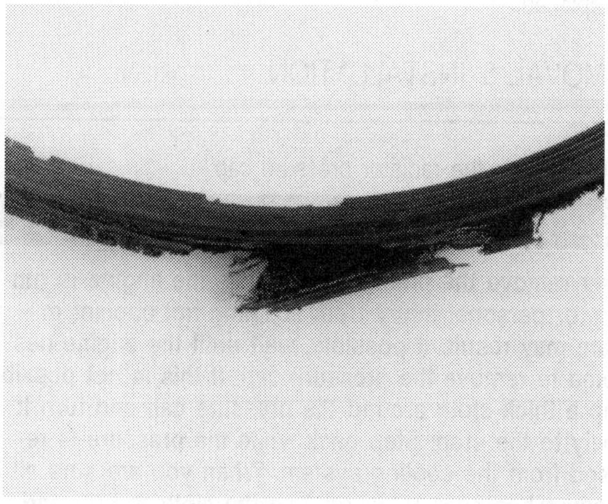

tccs1217

Fig. 71 Installing too wide a belt can result in serious belt wear and/or breakage

ADJUSTMENT

➧ See Figure 72

Serpentine belts are automatically tensioned by a system of idler and tensioner pulleys, thus require no adjustment. The serpentine belt tension can be checked by simply observing the belt acceptable belt wear range indicator located on the tensioner spindle. If the belt does not meet the specified range, it must be replaced.

➡A belt is considered "used" after 15 minutes of operation.

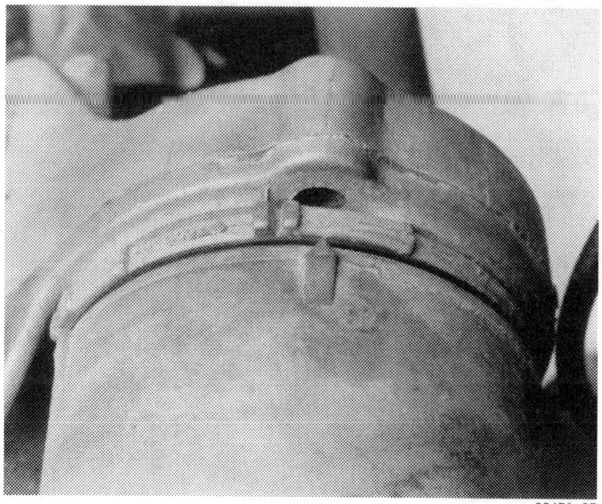

88451p05

Fig. 72 Check the belt tension by simply observing the range indicator located on the tensioner spindle

REMOVAL & INSTALLATION

➧ See Figures 73, 74, 75, 76 and 77

1. Using a ½ in. breaker bar with a socket placed on the tensioner pulley bolt, rotate the tensioner to relieve the belt tension.
2. Remove the serpentine belt.

To install:

3. Route the belt over all the pulleys except the tensioner.
4. Place the breaker bar and socket on the tensioner pulley bolt and rotate the tensioner to the released position.
5. Install the belt and return the pulley to its original position.
6. Check that the belt is properly seated in each pulley.

88451p06

Fig. 73 A decal showing the belt routing may sometimes be found under the hood

88451p07

Fig. 74 Relieve the belt tension and remove the belt — 1994 model shown

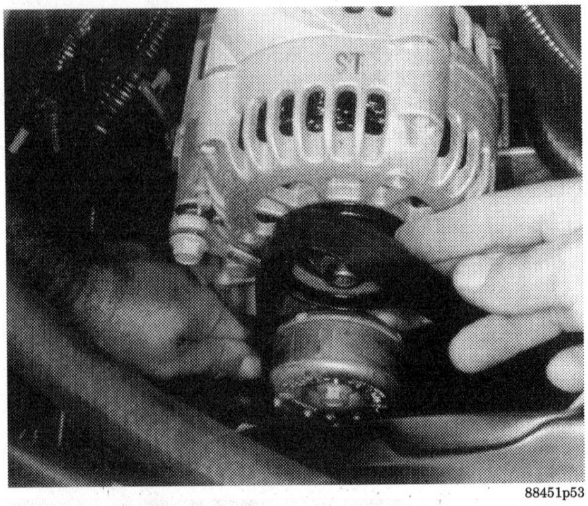

88451p53

Fig. 75 Relieve the belt tension and remove the belt — 1996 model shown

Hoses

INSPECTION

➧ **See Figures 78, 79, 80 and 81**

Upper and lower radiator hoses along with the heater hoses should be checked for deterioration, leaks and loose hose clamps at least every 15,000 miles (24,000 km). It is also wise to check the hoses periodically in early spring and at the beginning of the fall or winter when you are performing other maintenance. A quick visual inspection could discover a weakened hose which might have left you stranded if it had remained unrepaired.

Whenever you are checking the hoses, make sure the engine and cooling system are cold. Visually inspect for cracking, rotting or collapsed hoses, and replace as necessary. Run your hand along the length of the hose. If a weak or swollen spot is noted when squeezing the hose wall, the hose should be replaced.

REMOVAL & INSTALLATION

1. Remove the radiator pressure cap.

⁂CAUTION

Never remove the pressure cap while the engine is running, or personal injury from scalding hot coolant or steam may result. If possible, wait until the engine has cooled to remove the pressure cap. If this is not possible, wrap a thick cloth around the pressure cap and turn it slowly to the stop. Step back while the pressure is released from the cooling system. When you are sure all the pressure has been released, use the cloth to turn and remove the cap.

2. Position a clean container under the radiator and/or engine draincock or plug, then open the drain and allow the

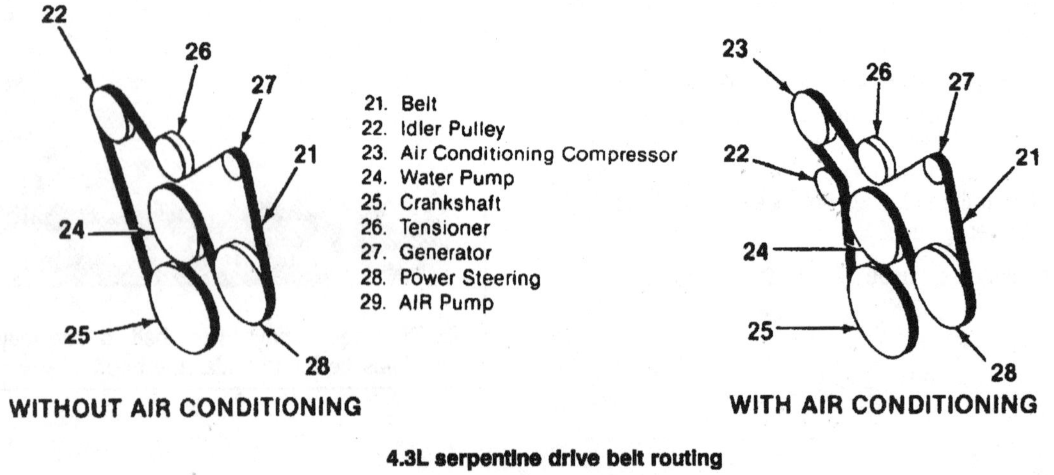

Fig. 76 Serpentine belt routing — 4.3L engine

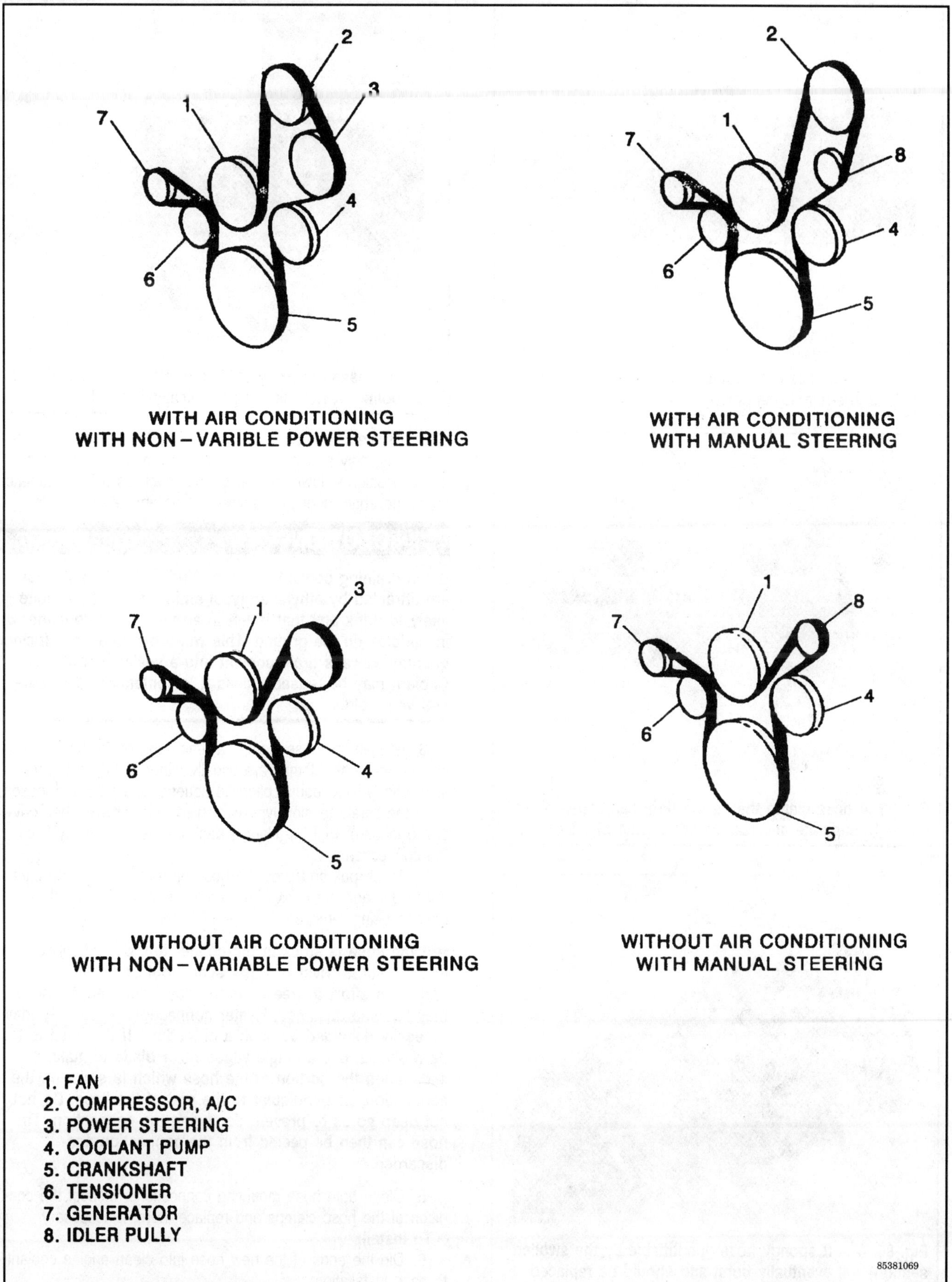

Fig. 77 Serpentine belt routing — 2.2L engine

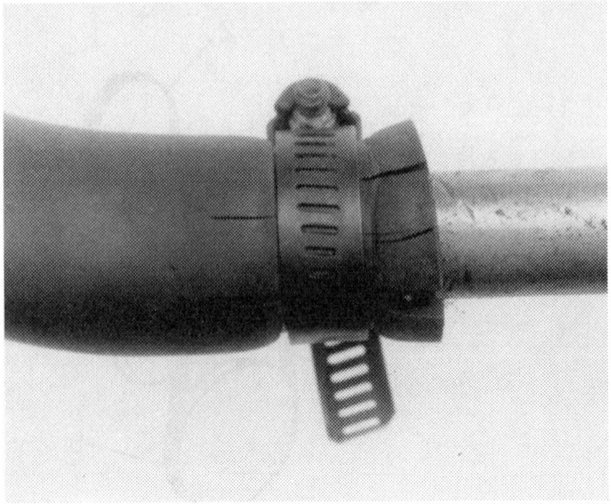

tccs1219

Fig. 78 The cracks developing along this hose are a result of age-related hardening

tccs1220

Fig. 79 A hose clamp that is too tight can cause older hoses to separate and tear on either side of the clamp

tccs1221

Fig. 80 A soft spongy hose (identifiable by the swollen section) will eventually burst and should be replaced

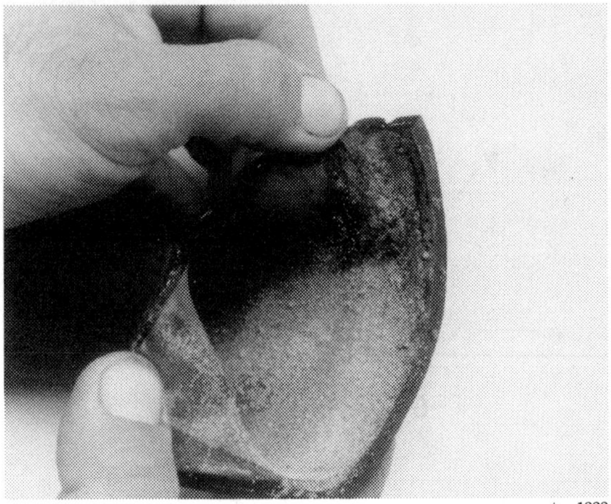

tccs1222

Fig. 81 Hoses are likely to deteriorate from the inside if the cooling system is not periodically flushed

cooling system to drain to an appropriate level. For some upper hoses, only a little coolant must be drained. To remove hoses positioned lower on the engine, such as a lower radiator hose, the entire cooling system must be emptied.

****CAUTION**

When draining coolant, keep in mind that cats and dogs are attracted by ethylene glycol antifreeze, and are quite likely to drink any that is left in an uncovered container or in puddles on the ground. This will prove fatal in sufficient quantity. Always drain coolant into a sealable container. Coolant may be reused unless it is contaminated or several years old.

3. Loosen the hose clamps at each end of the hose requiring replacement. Clamps are usually either of the spring tension type (which require pliers to squeeze the tabs and loosen) or of the screw tension type (which require screw or hex drivers to loosen). Pull the clamps back on the hose away from the connection.
4. Twist, pull and slide the hose off the fitting, taking care not to damage the neck of the component from which the hose is being removed.

➡If the hose is stuck at the connection, do not try to insert a screwdriver or other sharp tool under the hose end in an effort to free it, as the connection and/or hose may become damaged. Heater connections especially may be easily damaged by such a procedure. If the hose is to be replaced, use a single-edged razor blade to make a slice along the portion of the hose which is stuck on the connection, perpendicular to the end of the hose. Do not cut deep so as to prevent damaging the connection. The hose can then be peeled from the connection and discarded.

5. Clean both hose mounting connections. Inspect the condition of the hose clamps and replace them, if necessary.

To install:

6. Dip the ends of the new hose into clean engine coolant to ease installation.

7. Slide the clamps over the replacement hose, then slide the hose ends over the connections into position.
8. Position and secure the clamps at least 1/4 in. (6mm) from the ends of the hose. Make sure they are located beyond the raised bead of the connector.
9. Close the radiator or engine drains and properly refill the cooling system with the clean drained engine coolant or a suitable mixture of ethylene glycol coolant and water.
10. If available, install a pressure tester and check for leaks. If a pressure tester is not available, run the engine until normal operating temperature is reached (allowing the system to naturally pressurize), then check for leaks.

****CAUTION**

If you are checking for leaks with the system at normal operating temperature, BE EXTREMELY CAREFUL not to touch any moving or hot engine parts. Once temperature has been reached, shut the engine OFF, and check for leaks around the hose fittings and connections which were removed earlier.

CV-Boots

INSPECTION

See Figures 82 and 83

The CV (Constant Velocity) boots should be checked for damage each time the oil is changed and any other time the vehicle is raised for service. These boots keep water, grime, dirt and other damaging matter from entering the CV-joints. Any of these could cause early CV-joint failure which can be expensive to repair. Heavy grease thrown around the inside of the front wheel(s) and on the brake caliper/drum can be an indication of a torn boot. Thoroughly check the boots for missing clamps and tears. If the boot is damaged, it should be replaced immediately. Please refer to Section 7 for procedures.

Fig. 82 CV-boots must be inspected periodically for damage

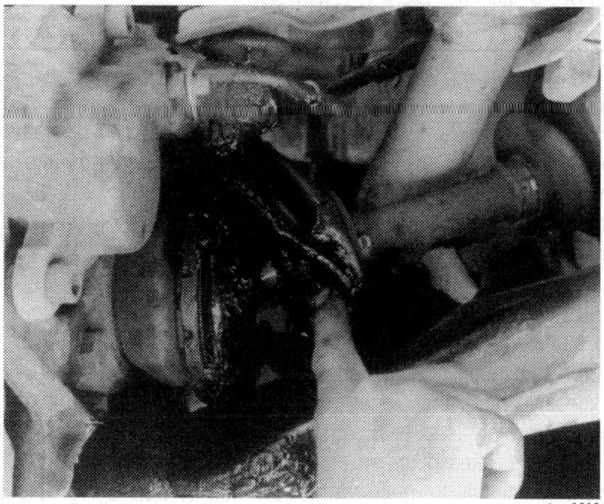

Fig. 83 A torn boot should be replaced immediately

Spark Plugs

See Figure 84

A typical spark plug consists of a metal shell surrounding a ceramic insulator. A metal electrode extends downward through the center of the insulator and protrudes a small distance. Located at the end of the plug and attached to the side of the outer metal shell is the side electrode. The side electrode bends in at a 90° angle so that its tip is just past and parallel to the tip of the center electrode. The distance between these two electrodes (measured in thousandths of an inch or hundredths of a millimeter) is called the spark plug gap.

The spark plug does not produce a spark but instead provides a gap across which the current can arc. The coil produces anywhere from 20,000 to 50,000 volts (depending on the type and application) which travels through the wires to the spark plugs. The current passes along the center electrode and jumps the gap to the side electrode, and in doing so, ignites the air/fuel mixture in the combustion chamber.

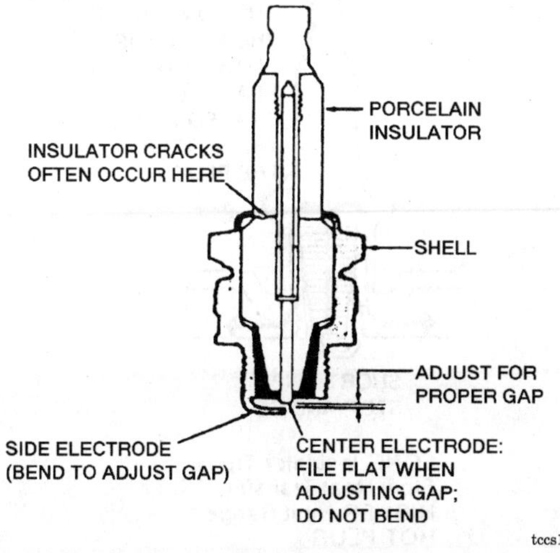

Fig. 84 Cross-section of a spark plug

SPARK PLUG HEAT RANGE

See Figure 85

Spark plug heat range is the ability of the plug to dissipate heat. The longer the insulator (or the farther it extends into the engine), the hotter the plug will operate; the shorter the insulator (the closer the electrode is to the block's cooling passages) the cooler it will operate. A plug that absorbs little heat and remains too cool will quickly accumulate deposits of oil and carbon since it is not hot enough to burn them off. This leads to plug fouling and consequently to misfiring. A plug that absorbs too much heat will have no deposits but, due to the excessive heat, the electrodes will burn away quickly and might possibly lead to preignition or other ignition problems. Preignition takes place when plug tips get so hot that they glow sufficiently to ignite the air/fuel mixture before the actual spark occurs. This early ignition will usually cause a pinging during low speeds and heavy loads.

The general rule of thumb for choosing the correct heat range when picking a spark plug is: if most of your driving is long distance, high speed travel, use a colder plug; if most of your driving is stop and go, use a hotter plug. Original equipment plugs are generally a good compromise between the 2 styles and most people never have the need to change their plugs from the factory-recommended heat range.

REMOVAL & INSTALLATION

See Figures 86, 87 and 88

A set of spark plugs usually requires replacement after about 20,000-30,000 miles (32,000-48,000 km), depending on your style of driving. In normal operation plug gap increases about 0.001 in (0.025 mm) for every 2500 miles (4000 km). As the gap increases, the plug's voltage requirement also increases. It requires a greater voltage to jump the wider gap and about two to three times as much voltage to fire the plug at high speeds than at idle. The improved air/fuel ratio control of modern fuel injection combined with the higher voltage output of modern ignition systems will often allow an engine to run sig-

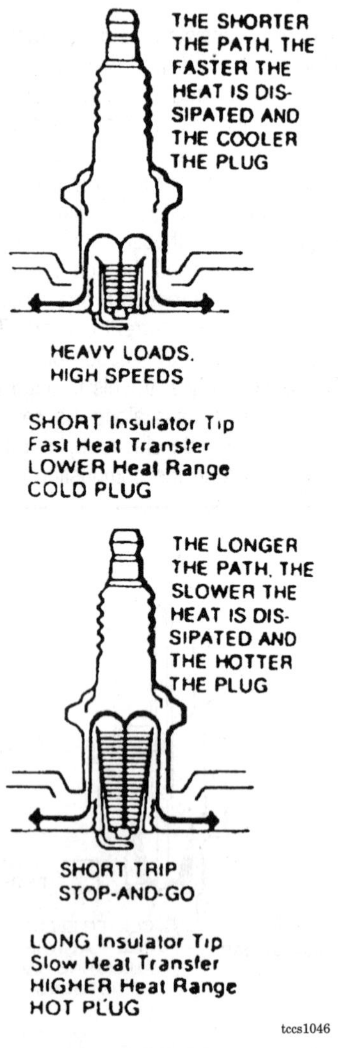

Fig. 85 Spark plug heat range

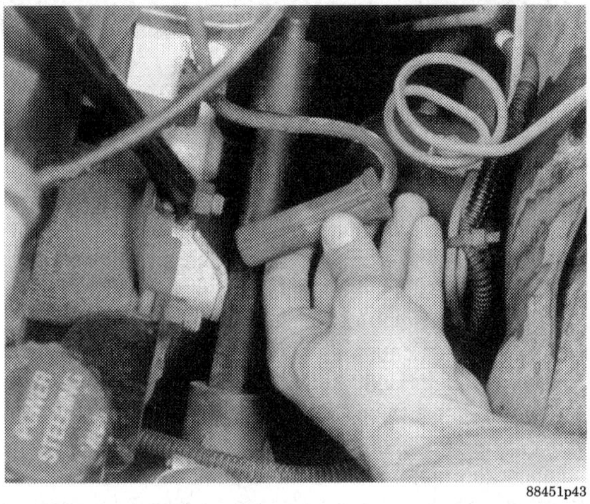

Fig. 86 Remove the spark plug wire by pulling on the boot

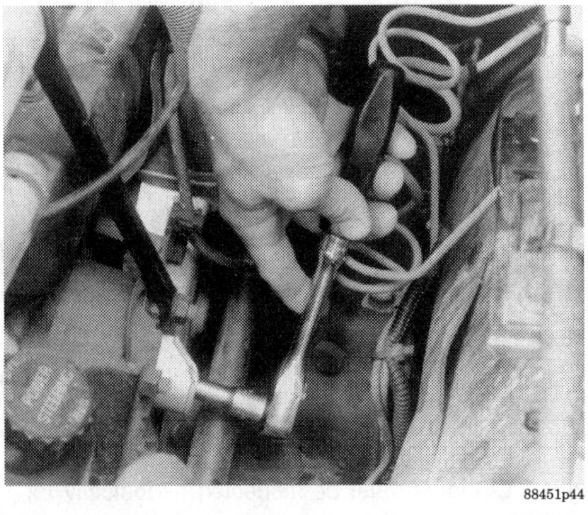

Fig. 87 Using a spark plug socket with a rubber insert, turn the plug counterclockwise to loosen it

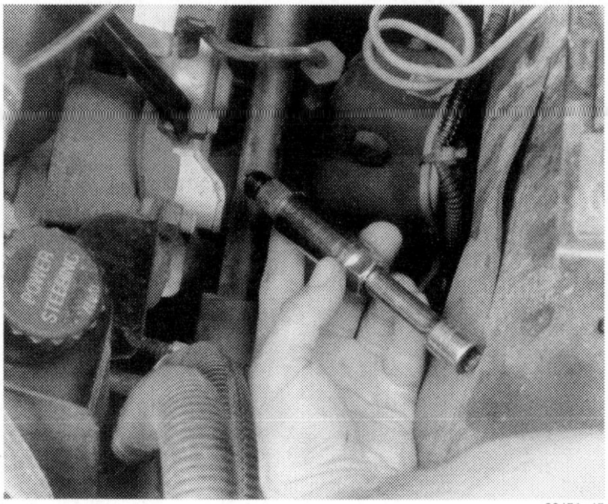

Fig. 88 Remove the spark plug from the bore

nificantly longer on a set of standard spark plugs, but keep in mind that efficiency will drop as the gap widen's (along with fuel economy and power).

When you're removing spark plugs, work on one at a time. Don't start by removing the plug wires all at once, because, unless you number them, they may become mixed up. Take a minute before you begin and number the wires with tape.

1. Disconnect the negative battery cable, and if the vehicle has been run recently, allow the engine to thoroughly cool.
2. Carefully twist the spark plug wire boot to loosen it, then pull upward and remove the boot from the plug. Be sure to pull on the boot and not on the wire, otherwise the connector located inside the boot may become separated.
3. Using compressed air, blow any water or debris from the spark plug well to assure that no harmful contaminants are allowed to enter the combustion chamber when the spark plug is removed. If compressed air is not available, use a rag or a brush to clean the area.

➡Remove the spark plugs when the engine is cold, if possible, to prevent damage to the threads. If removal of the plugs is difficult, apply a few drops of penetrating oil or silicone spray to the area around the base of the plug, and allow it a few minutes to work.

4. Using a spark plug socket that is equipped with a rubber insert to properly hold the plug, turn the spark plug counterclockwise to loosen and remove the spark plug from the bore.

✲✲✲WARNING

Be sure not to use a flexible extension on the socket. Use of a flexible extension may allow a shear force to be applied to the plug. A shear force could break the plug off in the cylinder head, leading to costly and frustrating repairs.

To install:

5. Inspect the spark plug boot for tears or damage. If a damaged boot is found, the spark plug wire must be replaced.
6. Using a wire feeler gauge, check and adjust the spark plug gap. When using a gauge, the proper size should pass between the electrodes with a slight drag. The next larger size should not be able to pass while the next smaller size should pass freely.
7. Carefully thread the plug into the bore by hand. If resistance is felt before the plug is almost completely threaded, back the plug out and begin threading again. In small, hard to reach areas, an old spark plug wire and boot could be used as a threading tool. The boot will hold the plug while you twist the end of the wire and the wire is supple enough to twist before it would allow the plug to crossthread.

✲✲✲WARNING

Do not use the spark plug socket to thread the plugs. Always carefully thread the plug by hand or using an old plug wire to prevent the possibility of crossthreading and damaging the cylinder head bore.

8. Carefully tighten the spark plug. If the plug you are installing is equipped with a crush washer, seat the plug, then tighten about 1/4 turn to crush the washer. If you are installing a tapered seat plug, tighten the plug to specifications provided by the vehicle or plug manufacturer.
9. Apply a small amount of silicone dielectric compound to the end of the spark plug lead or inside the spark plug boot to prevent sticking, then install the boot to the spark plug and push until it clicks into place. The click may be felt or heard, then gently pull back on the boot to assure proper contact.

INSPECTION & GAPPING

➧ See Figures 89, 90, 91, 92, 93, 94, 95, 96, 97, 98, 99 and 100

Check the plugs for deposits and wear. If they are not going to be replaced, clean the plugs thoroughly. Remember that any kind of deposit will decrease the efficiency of the plug. Plugs can be cleaned on a spark plug cleaning machine, which can sometimes be found in service stations, or you can do an acceptable job of cleaning with a stiff brush. If the plugs are cleaned, the electrodes must be filed flat. Use an ignition points file, not an emery board or the like, which will leave deposits. The electrodes must be filed perfectly flat with sharp edges; rounded edges reduce the spark plug voltage by as much as 50%.

Check spark plug gap before installation. The ground electrode (the L-shaped one connected to the body of the plug) must be parallel to the center electrode and the specified size wire gauge (please refer to the Tune-Up Specifications chart for details) must pass between the electrodes with a slight drag.

➡NEVER adjust the gap on a used platinum type spark plug.

Always check the gap on new plugs as they are not always set correctly at the factory. Do not use a flat feeler gauge when measuring the gap on a used plug, because the reading may be inaccurate. A round-wire type gapping tool is the best way to check the gap. The correct gauge should pass through the electrode gap with a slight drag. If you're in doubt, try one size smaller and one larger. The smaller gauge should go through easily, while the larger one shouldn't go through at all. Wire gapping tools usually have a bending tool attached. Use

Tracking Arc
High voltage arcs between a fouling deposit on the insulator tip and spark plug shell. This ignites the fuel/air mixture at some point along the insulator tip, retarding the ignition timing which causes a power and fuel loss.

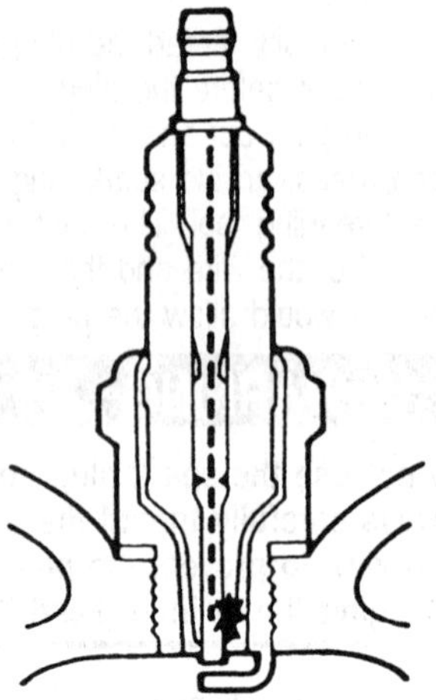

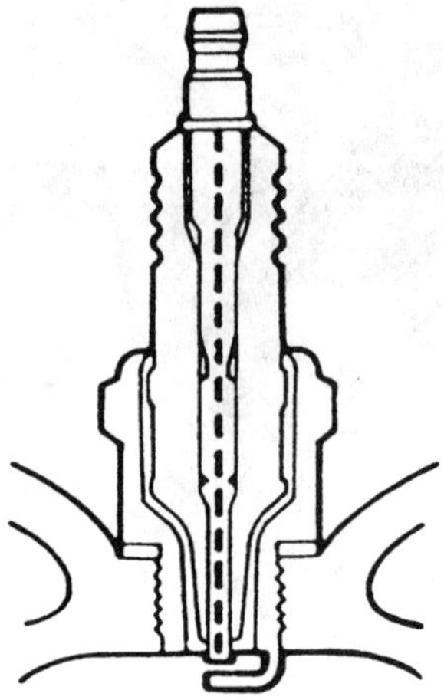

Wide Gap
Spark plug electrodes are worn so that the high voltage charge cannot arc across the electrodes. Improper gapping of electrodes on new or "cleaned" spark plugs could cause a similar condition. Fuel remains unburned and a power loss results.

Flashover
A damaged spark plug boot, along with dirt and moisture, could permit the high voltage charge to short over the insulator to the spark plug shell or the engine. AC's buttress insulator design helps prevent high voltage flashover.

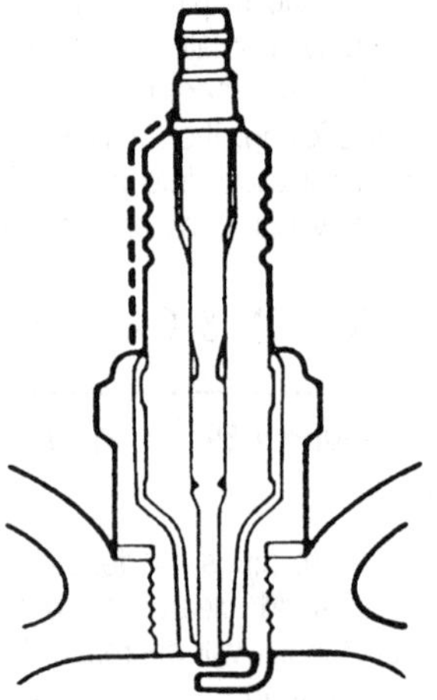

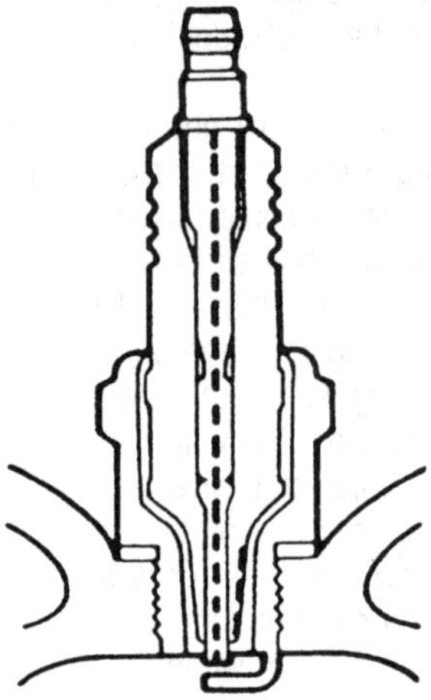

Fouled Spark Plug
Deposits that have formed on the insulator tip may become conductive and provide a "shunt" path to the shell. This prevents the high voltage from arcing between the electrodes. A power and fuel loss is the result.

Bridged Electrodes
Fouling deposits between the electrodes "ground out" the high voltage needed to fire the spark plug. The arc between the electrodes does not occur and the fuel air mixture is not ignited. This causes a power loss and exhausting of raw fuel.

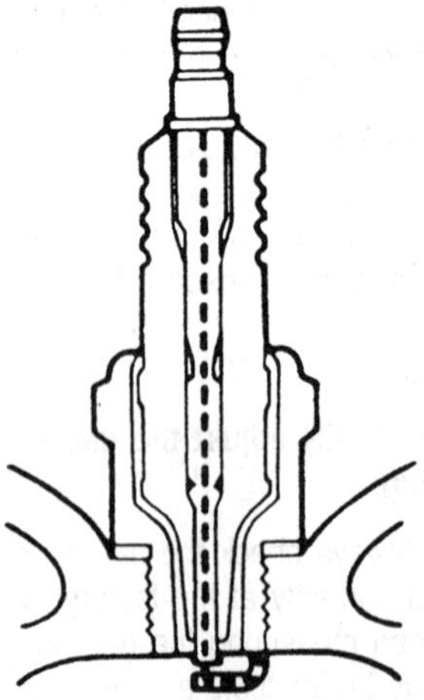

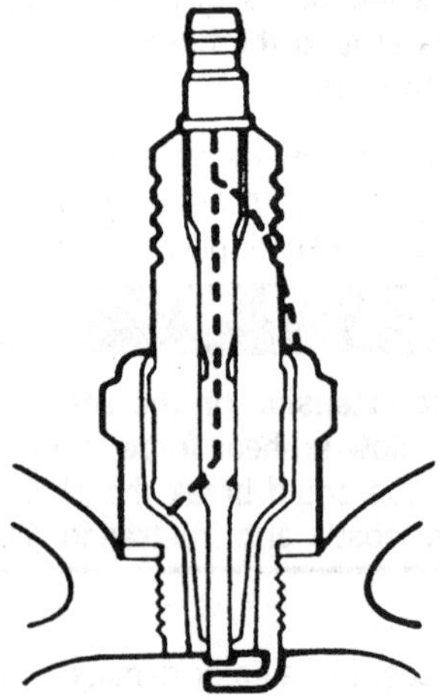

Cracked Insulator
A crack in the spark plug insulator could cause the high voltage charge to "ground out." Here, the spark does not jump the electrode gap and the fuel air mixture is not ignited. This causes a power loss and raw fuel is exhausted.

tccs2001

Fig. 89 Used spark plugs which show damage may indicate engine problems

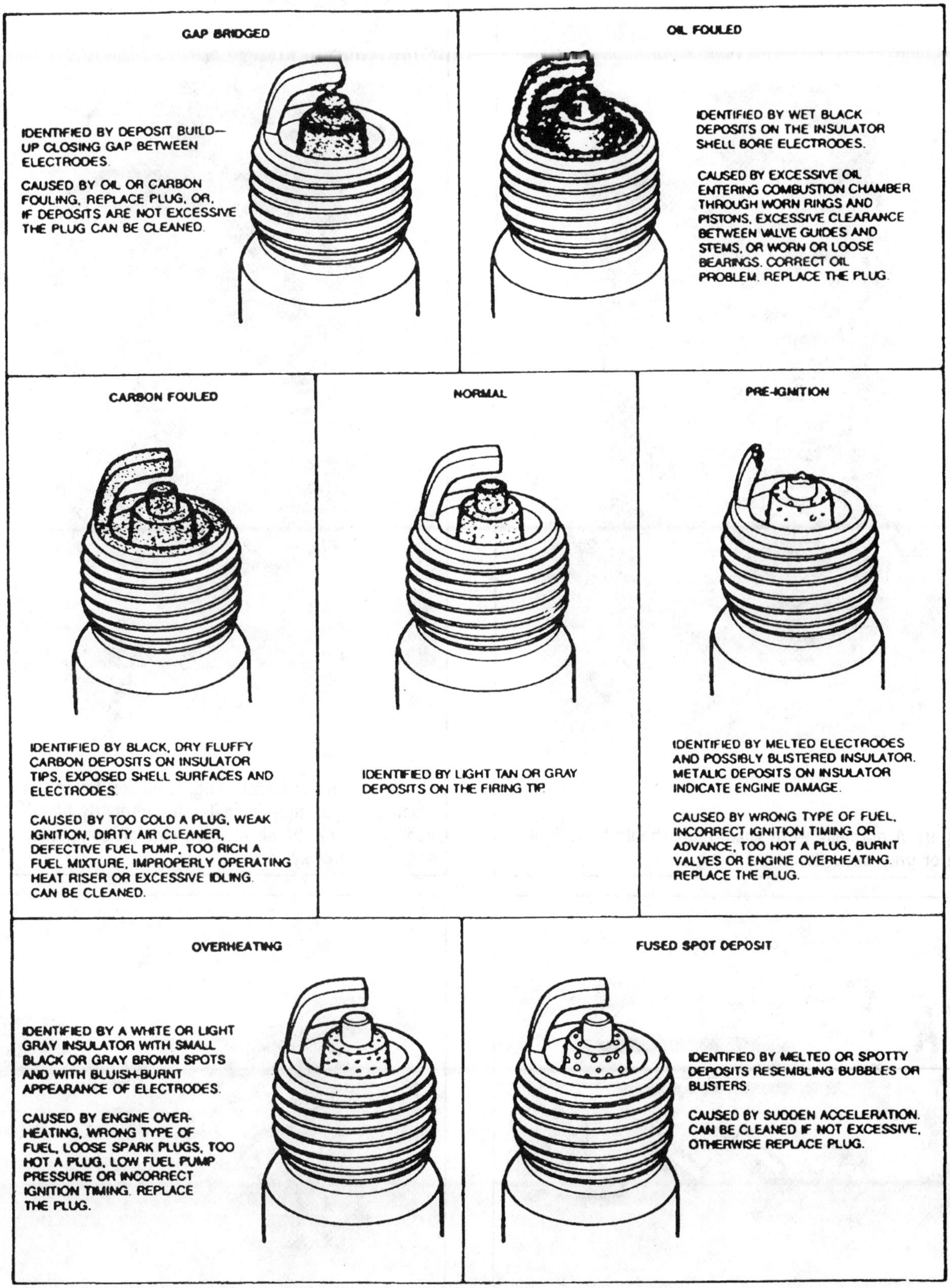

tccs2002

Fig. 90 Inspect the spark plug to determine engine running conditions

tccs2135

Fig. 91 A normally worn spark plug should have light tan or gray deposits on the firing tip

tccs2136

Fig. 92 A carbon fouled plug, identified by soft, sooty, black deposits, may indicate an improperly tuned vehicle. Check the air cleaner, ignition components and engine control system

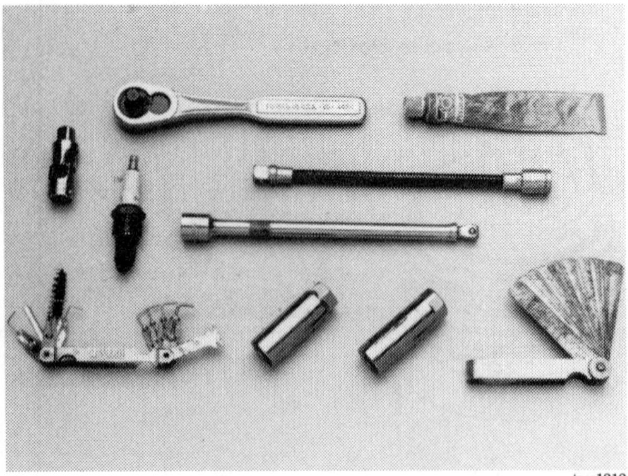

tccs1212

Fig. 93 A variety of tools and gauges are needed for spark plug service

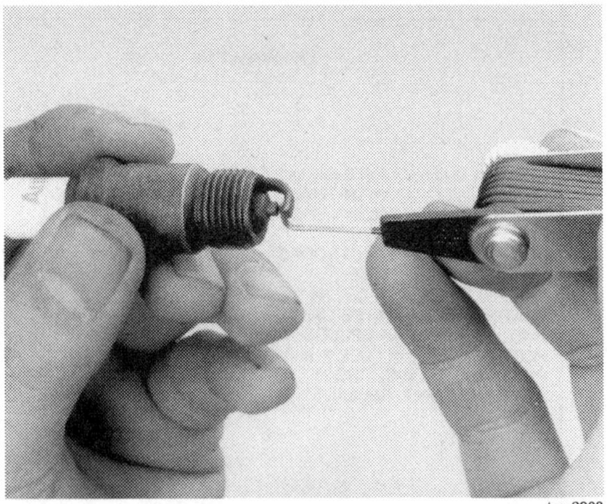

tccs2903

Fig. 94 Checking the spark plug gap with a feeler gauge

Fig. 95 A physically damaged spark plug may be evidence of severe detonation in that cylinder. Watch that cylinder carefully between services, as a continued detonation will not only damage the plug, but could also damage the engine

Fig. 96 An oil fouled spark plug indicates an engine with worn piston rings and/or bad valve seals allowing excessive oil to enter the chamber

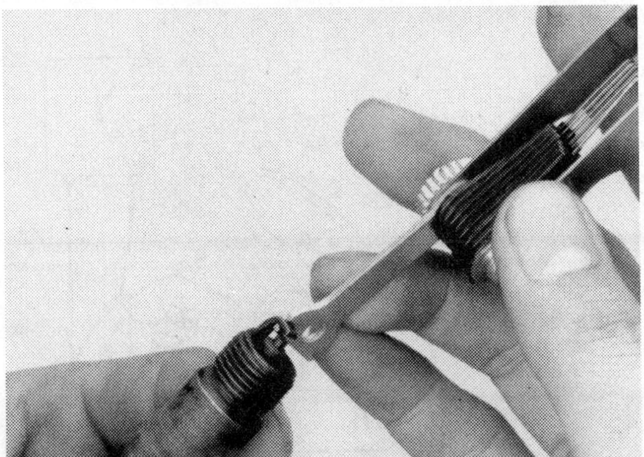
Fig. 97 Adjusting the spark plug gap

that to adjust the side electrode until the proper distance is obtained. Absolutely never attempt to bend the center electrode. Also, be careful not to bend the side electrode too far or too often as it may weaken and break off within the engine, requiring removal of the cylinder head to retrieve it.

Spark Plug Wires

TESTING

See Figures 101 and 102

At every tune-up/inspection, visually check the spark plug cables for burns cuts, or breaks in the insulation. Check the boots and the nipples on the distributor cap and/or coil. Replace any damaged wiring.

Every 50,000 miles (80,000 Km) or 60 months, the resistance of the wires should be checked with an ohmmeter. Wires with excessive resistance will cause misfiring, and may make the engine difficult to start in damp weather.

tccs2139

Fig. 98 This spark plug has been left in the engine too long, as evidenced by the extreme gap. Plugs with such an extreme gap can cause misfiring and stumbling accompanied by a noticeable lack of power

tccs2140

Fig. 99 A bridged or almost bridged spark plug, identified by a build-up between the electrodes caused by excessive carbon or oil build-up on the plug

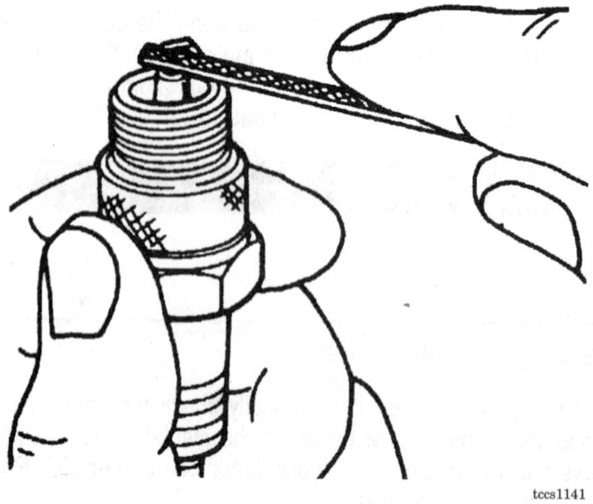

tccs1141

Fig. 100 If the plug is in good condition, the electrode may be filed flat and reused

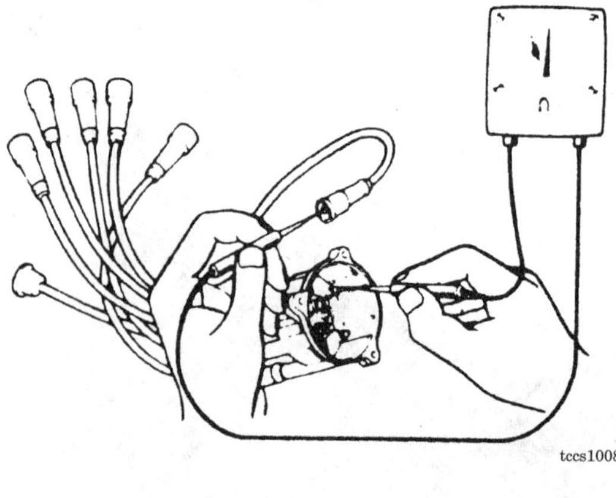

tccs1008

Fig. 101 Checking plug wire resistance through the distributor cap with an ohmmeter

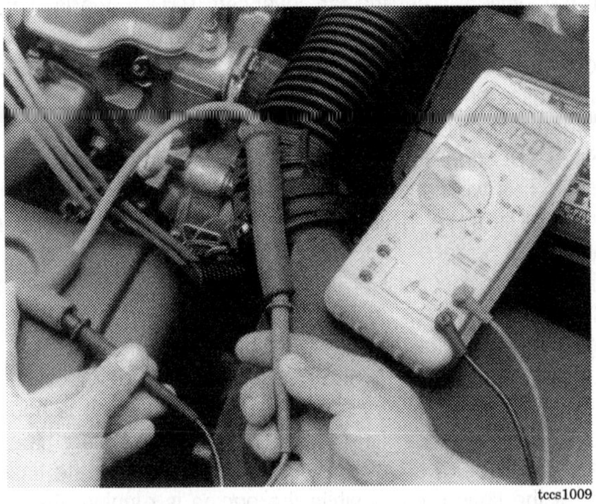

tccs1009

Fig. 102 Checking individual plug wire resistance with a digital ohmmeter

To check resistance:

1. Remove the distributor cap, leaving the wires in place.
2. Connect one lead of an ohmmeter to an electrode within the cap.
3. Connect the other lead to the corresponding spark plug terminal (remove it from the spark plug for this test).
4. Replace any wire which shows a resistance over 30,000 ohms. Generally speaking, however, resistance should not be over 25,000 ohms, and 30,000 ohms must be considered the outer limit of acceptability.

It should be remembered that resistance is also a function of length. The longer the wire, the greater the resistance. Thus, if the wires on your truck are longer than the factory originals, the resistance will be higher, possibly outside these limits.

REMOVAL & INSTALLATION

➧ See Figure 103

When installing new wires, replace them one at a time to avoid mix-ups. Start by replacing the longest one first.

1. Remove the spark plug wire by gripping the boot firmly and disengaging the wire from the spark plug and the distributor.
2. Install the boot of the new wire firmly over the spark plug. Route the wire over the same path as the original.

Distributor Cap and Rotor

REMOVAL & INSTALLATION

➧ See Figures 104, 105 and 106

1. Tag and remove the spark plug wires.
2. Loosen the cap retaining fasteners and remove the cap.
3. Remove the rotor from the distributor shaft.
4. Installation is the reverse of removal.

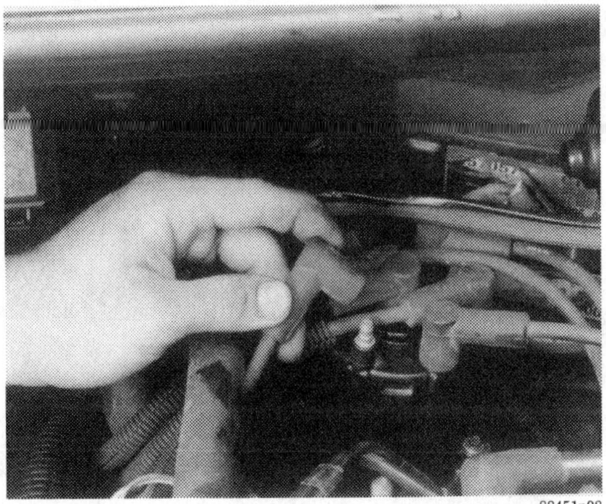

88451p08

Fig. 103 Removing the spark plug boot from the distributor cap

88451p09

Fig. 104 Loosen the distributor cap retaining fasteners

88451p10

Fig. 105 Remove the distributor cap

Fig. 106 Remove the rotor from the distributor shaft

INSPECTION

1. Remove the distributor cap and rotor as described in this section.
2. Check the cap for wear, electrode cracks or damage. Replace if defective.
3. Check the rotor for cracks and wear. Replace if defective.

Ignition Timing

GENERAL INFORMATION

Ignition timing is the measurement, in degrees of crankshaft rotation, of the point at which the spark plugs fire in each of the cylinders. It is measured in degrees before or after Top Dead Center (TDC) of the compression stroke.

Because it takes a fraction of a second for the spark plug to ignite the mixture in the cylinder, the spark plug must fire a little before the piston reaches TDC. Otherwise, the mixture will not be completely ignited as the piston passes TDC and the full power of the explosion will not be used by the engine.

The timing measurement is given in degrees of crankshaft rotation before the piston reaches TDC (BTDC). If the setting for the ignition timing is 5° BTDC, the spark plug must fire 5° before each piston reaches TDC. This only holds true, however, when the engine is at idle speed.

As the engine speed increases, the pistons go faster. The spark plugs have to ignite the fuel even sooner if it is to be completely ignited when the piston reaches TDC. The Electronic Spark Timing (EST) system makes all timing changes electronically based on signals from various sensors. The 1994-97 2.2L engine and 1996-97 4.3L engine uses a distributorless Electronic Ignition (EI) system. Operation of the EI system allows for fully electronic control of the timing.

If the ignition is set too far advanced (BTDC), the ignition and expansion of the fuel in the cylinder will occur too soon and tend to force the piston down while it is still traveling up. This causes engine ping. If the ignition spark is set too far retarded, after TDC (ATDC), the piston will have already passed TDC and started on its way down when the fuel is ignited. This will cause the piston to be forced down for only a portion of its travel. This will result in poor engine performance and lack of power.

Timing marks consist of a notch on the rim of the crankshaft pulley and a scale of degrees attached to the front of the engine (often on the engine front cover). The notch corresponds to the position of the piston in the number 1 cylinder. A stroboscopic (dynamic) timing light is used, which is hooked into the circuit of the No. 1 cylinder spark plug. Every time the spark plug fires, the timing light flashes. By aiming the timing light at the timing marks while the engine is running, the exact position of the piston within the cylinder can be easily read since the stroboscopic flash makes the mark on the pulley appear to be standing still. Proper timing is indicated when the notch is aligned with the correct number on the scale.

➡Never pierce a spark plug wire in order to attach a timing light or perform tests. The pierced insulation will eventually lead to an electrical arc and related ignition troubles.

INSPECTION & ADJUSTMENT

Electronic Ignition (EI) Systems

2.2L ENGINES

On vehicles equipped with this system,the ignition timing is controlled by the Powertrain Control Module (PCM). No adjustment is possible or necessary.

Distributor Ignition (DI) Systems

4.3L ENGINES — 1995 MODELS

➡Refer to the underhood label for the proper timing setting.

1. Engage the parking brake, block the wheels and set the transmission in P.
2. Disconnect the Ignition Control (IC) system by disengaging the "set timing connector". This is a single wire sealed connector that has a tan with black stripe lead. This wire comes out of the wiring harness below the heater case.
3. With the ignition switch **OFF**, connect the timing light pickup lead to the No. 1 spark plug wire.
4. Start the engine and point the timing light at the timing mark on the balancer or pulley and check the timing.
5. If the timing is not within specifications (refer to the underhood emission sticker), loosen the distributor hold-down bolt. Slowly rotate the distributor until the proper timing setting is achieved.
6. Tighten the hold-down bolt and recheck the timing.
7. Turn the ignition **OFF**, remove the timing light and engage the "set timing" connector.

4.3L ENGINES — 1996-97 MODELS

The ignition timing is preset and cannot be adjusted. If the distributor position is moved crossfiring may be induced. To check distributor position, perform tho following:

➡An OBD II compliant scan tool is required for this procedure

1. With the ignition **OFF** install the scan tool to the Data Link Connector (DLC).
2. Start the engine and bring the vehicle to operating temperature.
3. Monitor the cam retard on the scan tool.
4. If cam retard is between -2° and +2° the distributor is properly adjusted.
5. If cam retard is not between -2° and +2° the distributor must adjusted.
6. With the engine **OFF**, loosen the distributor hold-down bolt.
7. Start the engine and check the cam retard reading. Rotate the distributor counterclockwise to compensate for a negative reading and clockwise to compensate for a positive reading.
8. Momentarily raise the engine speed to ovor 1000 RPM and check the cam retard reading.
9. If the proper reading is not achieved, repeat Steps 7 and 8.
10. When the proper reading has been achieved tighten the distributor hold-down bolt and disconnect the scan tool.

Idle Speed and Mixture Adjustments

These vehicles are controlled by a computer which supplies the correct amount of fuel during all engine operating conditions and controls idle speed; no adjustment is necessary or possible.

GASOLINE ENGINE TUNE-UP SPECIFICATIONS

Year	Engine ID/VIN	Engine Displacement Liters (cc)	Spark Plugs Gap (in.)	Ignition Timing (deg.) MT	Ignition Timing (deg.) AT	Fuel Pump (psi)	Idle Speed (rpm) MT	Idle Speed (rpm) AT	Valve Clearance In.	Valve Clearance Ex.
1994	4	2.2 (2189)	①	③	③	41-47 ②	⑥	⑥	HYD	HYD
	W	4.3 (4293)	0.035	⑤	⑤	55-61 ②	⑥	⑥	HYD	HYD
	Z	4.3 (4293)	0.035	⑤	⑤	9-13 ②	⑥	⑥	HYD	HYD
1995	4	2.2 (2189)	0.060	③	③	41-47 ②	⑥	⑥	HYD	HYD
	W	4.3 (4293)	0.035	④	④	58-64 ②	⑥	⑥	HYD	HYD
	Z	4.3 (4293)	0.035	①	①	9-13 ②	⑥	⑥	HYD	HYD
1996	4	2.2 (2189)	0.060	③	③	41-47 ②	⑥	⑥	HYD	HYD
	W	4.3 (4293)	0.045	④	④	60-66 ②	⑥	⑥	HYD	HYD
	X	4.3 (4293)	0.045	④	④	60-66 ②	⑥	⑥	HYD	HYD
1997	4	2.2 (2189)	0.060	③	③	41-47 ②	⑥	⑥	HYD	HYD
	W	4.3 (4293)	0.045	④	④	60-66 ②	⑥	⑥	HYD	HYD
	X	4.3 (4293)	0.045	④	④	60-66 ②	⑥	⑥	HYD	HYD

NOTE: The Vehicle Emission Control Information label often reflects specification changes made during production. The label figures must be used if they differ from those in this chart.

HYD - Hydraulic

① Refer to underhood label for exact setting

② With key on and engine off

③ Distributorless ignition, no adjustment possible

④ Ignition timing is preset and cannot be adjusted

⑤ 0°, disconnect set timing connector (tan with black striped wire taped to engine harness near distributor)

⑥ Idle speed is computer controlled. No periodic adjustments are necessary or possible

88451C06

Air Conditioning System

➡Be sure to consult the laws in your area before servicing the air conditioning system. In most areas, it is illegal to perform repairs involving refrigerant unless the work is done by a certified technician. Also, it is quite likely that you will not be able to purchase refrigerant without proof of certification.

SAFETY PRECAUTIONS

The refrigerant gas R-134a is an extremely cold substance. When exposed to air, it will instantly freeze any surface it comes in contact with, including your eyes. Because of the inherent dangers involved with working on air conditioning systems, these safety precautions must be strictly followed.

- Avoid contact with a charged refrigeration system, even when working on another part of the air conditioning system or vehicle. If a heavy tool comes into contact with a section of tubing or a heat exchanger, it can easily cause the relatively soft material to rupture.
- When it is necessary to apply force to a fitting which contains refrigerant, as when checking that all system couplings are securely tightened, use a wrench on both parts of the fitting involved, if possible. This will avoid putting torque on refrigerant tubing. (It is also advisable to use tube or line wrenches when tightening these flare nut fittings.)
- Do not attempt to discharge the system without the proper tools. Precise control is possible only when using the service gauges and a proper A/C refrigerant recovery station. Wear protective gloves when connecting or disconnecting service gauge hoses.
- Discharge the system only in a well ventilated area, as high concentrations of the gas which might accidentally escape can exclude oxygen and act as an anesthetic.
- Never start a system without first verifying that both service valves are properly installed, and that all fittings throughout the system are snugly connected.
- Avoid applying heat to any refrigerant line or storage vessel. Charging may be aided by using water heated to less than 125°F (50°C) to warm the refrigerant container. Never allow a refrigerant storage container to sit out in the sun, or near any other source of heat, such as a radiator or heater.
- Always wear goggles to protect your eyes when working on a system. If refrigerant contacts the eyes, it is advisable in all cases to consult a physician immediately.
- Frostbite from liquid refrigerant should be treated by first gradually warming the area with cool water, and then gently applying petroleum jelly. A physician should be consulted.
- Always keep refrigerant drum fittings capped when not in use. If the container is equipped with a safety cap to protect the valve, make sure the cap is in place when the can is not being used. Avoid sudden shock to the drum, which might occur from dropping it, or from banging a heavy tool against it. Never carry a drum in the passenger compartment of a vehicle.
- Always completely discharge the system into a suitable recovery unit before painting the vehicle (if the paint is to be baked on), or before welding anywhere near refrigerant lines.
- When servicing the system, minimize the time that any refrigerant line or fitting is open to the air in order to prevent moisture or dirt from entering the system. Contaminants such as moisture or dirt can damage internal system components. Always replace O-rings on lines or fittings which are disconnected. Prior to installation coat, but do not soak, replacement O-rings with suitable compressor oil.

GENERAL SERVICING PROCEDURES

➡It is recommended, and possibly required by law, that a qualified technician perform the following services.

The most important aspect of air conditioning service is the maintenance of a pure and adequate charge of refrigerant in the system. A refrigeration system cannot function properly if a significant percentage of the charge is lost. Leaks are common because the severe vibration encountered underhood in an automobile can easily cause a sufficient cracking or loosening of the air conditioning fittings; allowing, the extreme operating pressures of the system to force refrigerant out.

The problem can be understood by considering what happens to the system as it is operated with a continuous leak. Because the expansion valve regulates the flow of refrigerant to the evaporator, the level of refrigerant there is fairly constant. The receiver/drier stores any excess refrigerant, and so a loss will first appear there as a reduction in the level of liquid. As this level nears the bottom of the vessel, some refrigerant vapor bubbles will begin to appear in the stream of liquid supplied to the expansion valve. This vapor decreases the capacity of the expansion valve very little as the valve opens to compensate for its presence. As the quantity of liquid in the condenser decreases, the operating pressure will drop there and throughout the high side of the system. As the refrigerant continues to be expelled, the pressure available to force the liquid through the expansion valve will continue to decrease, and, eventually, the valve's orifice will prove to be too much of a restriction for adequate flow even with the needle fully withdrawn.

At this point, low side pressure will start to drop, and a severe reduction in cooling capacity, marked by freeze-up of the evaporator coil, will result. Eventually, the operating pressure of the evaporator will be lower than the pressure of the atmosphere surrounding it, and air will be drawn into the system wherever there are leaks in the low side.

Because all atmospheric air contains at least some moisture, water will enter the system mixing with the refrigerant and oil. Trace amounts of moisture will cause sludging of the oil, and corrosion of the system. Saturation and clogging of the filter/drier, and freezing of the expansion valve orifice will eventually result. As air fills the system to a greater and greater extent, it will interfere more and more with the normal flows of refrigerant and heat.

From this description, it should be obvious that much of the repairman's focus in on detecting leaks, repairing them, and then restoring the purity and quantity of the refrigerant charge.

A list of general rules should be followed in addition to all safety precautions:

- Keep all tools as clean and dry as possible.
- Thoroughly purge the service gauges/hoses of air and moisture before connecting them to the system. Keep them capped when not in use.
- Thoroughly clean any refrigerant fitting before disconnecting it, in order to minimize the entrance of dirt into the system.
- Plan any operation that requires opening the system beforehand, in order to minimize the length of time it will be exposed to open air. Cap or seal the open ends to minimize the entrance of foreign material.
- When adding oil, pour it through an extremely clean and dry tube or funnel. Keep the oil capped whenever possible. Do not use oil that has not been kept tightly sealed.
- Purchase refrigerant intended for use only in automatic air conditioning systems.
- Completely evacuate any system that has been opened for service, or that has leaked sufficiently to draw in moisture and air. This requires evacuating air and moisture with a good vacuum pump for at least one hour. If a system has been open for a considerable length of time it may be advisable to evacuate the system for up to 12 hours (overnight).
- Use a wrench on both halves of a fitting that is to be disconnected, so as to avoid placing torque on any of the refrigerant lines.
- When overhauling a compressor, pour some of the oil into a clean glass and inspect it. If there is evidence of dirt, metal particles, or both, flush all refrigerant components with clean refrigerant before evacuating and recharging the system. In addition, if metal particles are present, the compressor should be replaced.
- Schrader valves may leak only when under full operating pressure. Therefore, if leakage is suspected but cannot be located, operate the system with a full charge of refrigerant and look for leaks from all Schrader valves. Replace any faulty valves.

Additional Preventive Maintenance

USING THE SYSTEM

The easiest and most important preventive maintenance for your A/C system is to be sure that it is used on a regular basis. Running the system for five minutes each month (no matter what the season) will help assure that the seals and all internal components remain lubricated.

ANTIFREEZE

See Figure 107

➡Antifreeze should not be used longer than the manufacturer specifies.

In order to prevent heater core freeze-up during A/C operation, it is necessary to maintain a proper antifreeze protection. Use a hand-held antifreeze tester (hydrometer) to periodically check the condition of the antifreeze in your engine's cooling system.

tccs1233

Fig. 107 An antifreeze tester can be used to determine the freezing and boiling level of the coolant

RADIATOR CAP

For efficient operation of an air conditioned vehicle's cooling system, the radiator cap should have a holding pressure which meets manufacturer's specifications. A cap which fails to hold these pressures should be replaced.

CONDENSER

Any obstruction of or damage to the condenser configuration will restrict the air flow which is essential to its efficient operation. It is therefore a good rule to keep this unit clean and in proper physical shape.

➡Bug screens which are mounted in front of the condenser (unless they are original equipment) are regarded as obstructions.

CONDENSATION DRAIN TUBE

This single molded drain tube expels the condensation, which accumulates on the bottom of the evaporator housing, into the engine compartment. If this tube is obstructed, the air conditioning performance can be restricted and condensation buildup can spill over onto the vehicle's floor.

SYSTEM INSPECTION

The easiest and often most important check for the air conditioning system consists of a visual inspection of the system components. Visually inspect the air conditioning system for refrigerant leaks, damaged compressor clutch, compressor drive belt tension and condition, plugged evaporator drain tube, blocked condenser fins, disconnected or broken wires, blown fuses, corroded connections and poor insulation.

A refrigerant leak will usually appear as an oily residue at the leakage point in the system. The oily residue soon picks up dust or dirt particles from the surrounding air and appears greasy. Through time, this will build up and appear to be a heavy dirt impregnated grease. Most leaks are caused by damaged or missing O-ring seals at the component connections, damaged charging valve cores or missing service gauge port caps.

For a thorough visual and operational inspection, check the following:

1. Check the surface of the radiator and condenser for dirt, leaves or other material which might block air flow.
2. Check for kinks in hoses and lines. Check the system for leaks.
3. Make sure the drive belt is under the proper tension. When the air conditioning is operating, make sure the drive belt is free of noise or slippage.
4. Make sure the blower motor operates at all appropriate positions, then check for distribution of the air from all outlets with the blower on **HIGH**.

➡Keep in mind that under conditions of high humidity, air discharged from the A/C vents may not feel as cold as expected, even if the system is working properly. This is because the vaporized moisture in humid air retains heat more effectively than does dry air, making the humid air more difficult to cool.

5. Make sure the air passage selection lever is operating correctly. Start the engine and warm it to normal operating temperature, then make sure the hot/cold selection lever is operating correctly.

DISCHARGING, EVACUATING AND CHARGING

Discharging, evacuating and charging the air conditioning system must be performed by a properly trained and certified mechanic in a facility equipped with refrigerant recovery/recycling equipment that meets SAE standards for the type of system to be serviced.

If you don't have access to the necessary equipment, we recommend that you take your vehicle to a reputable service station to have the work done. If you still wish to perform repairs on the vehicle, have them discharge the system, then take your vehicle home and perform the necessary work. When you are finished, return the vehicle to the station for evacuation and charging. Just be sure to cap ALL A/C system fittings immediately after opening them and keep them protected until the system is recharged.

Windshield Wipers

ELEMENT (REFILL) CARE AND REPLACEMENT

➧ See Figures 108, 109, 110, 111, 112, 113, 114, 115, 116, 117, 118 and 119

For maximum effectiveness and longest element life, the windshield and wiper blades should be kept clean. Dirt, tree sap, road tar and so on will cause streaking, smearing and blade deterioration if left on the glass. It is advisable to wash the windshield carefully with a commercial glass cleaner at least once a month. Wipe off the rubber blades with the wet rag afterwards. Do not attempt to move wipers across the windshield by hand; damage to the motor and drive mechanism will result.

To inspect and/or replace the wiper blade elements, place the wiper switch in the **LOW** speed position and the ignition

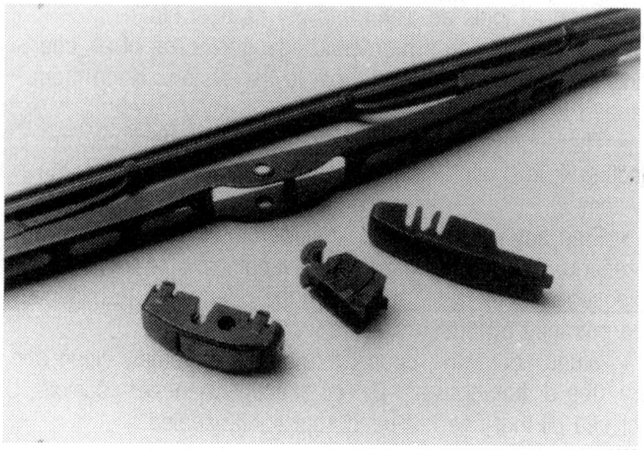

tccs1223

Fig. 108 Bosch® wiper blade and fit kit

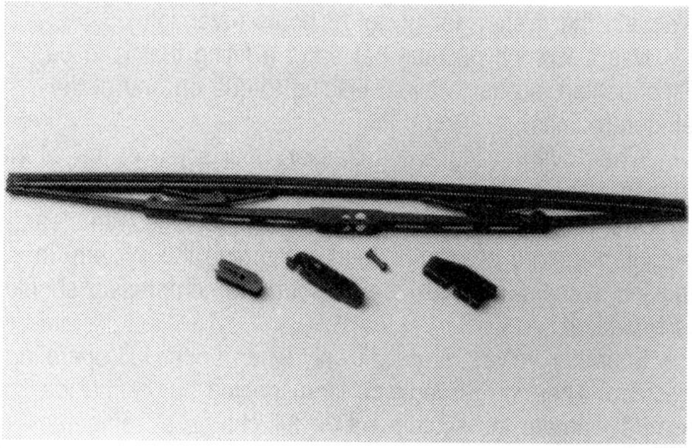

tccs1224

Fig. 109 Lexor® wiper blade and fit kit

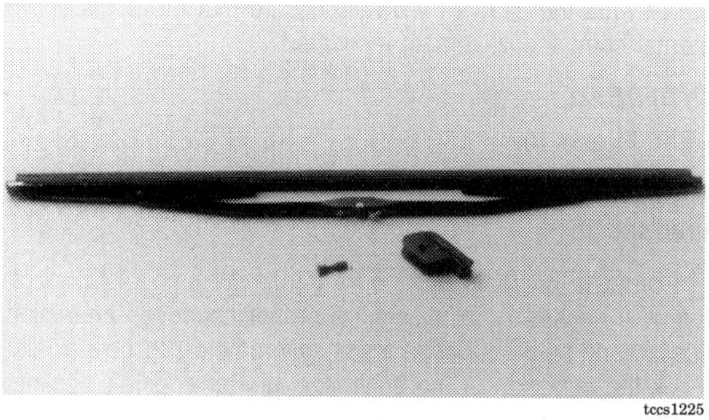

tccs1225

Fig. 110 Pylon® wiper blade and adaptor

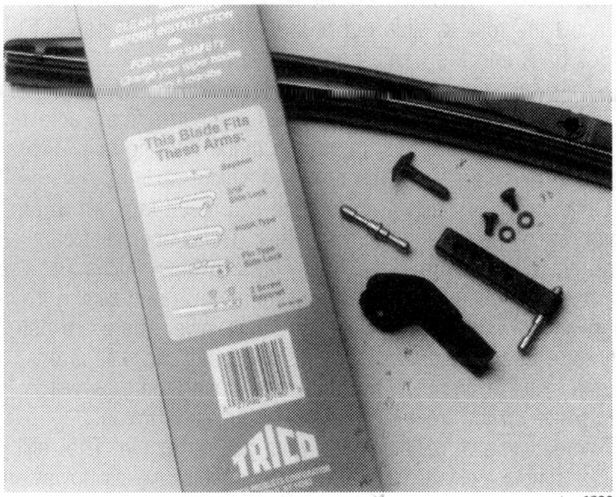

tccs1226

Fig. 111 Trico® wiper blade and fit kit

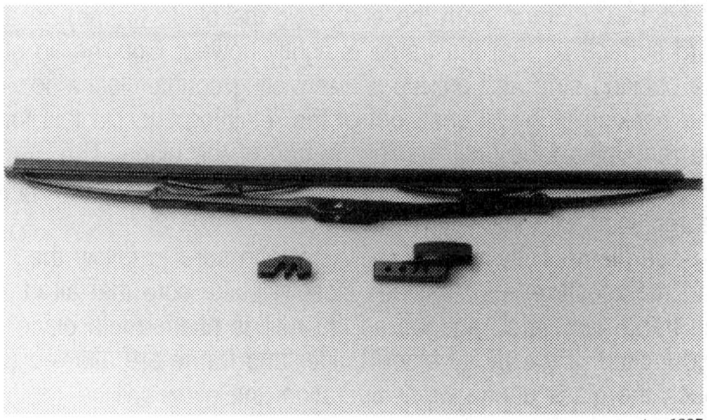
tccs1227

Fig. 112 Tripledge® wiper blade and fit kit

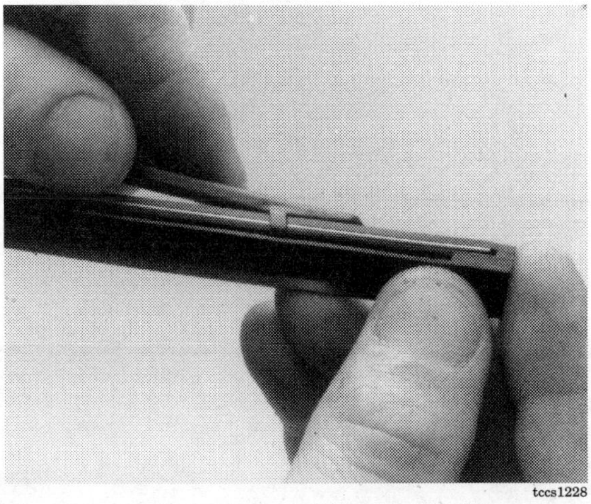
tccs1228

Fig. 113 To remove and install a Lexor® wiper blade refill, slip out the old insert and slide in a new one

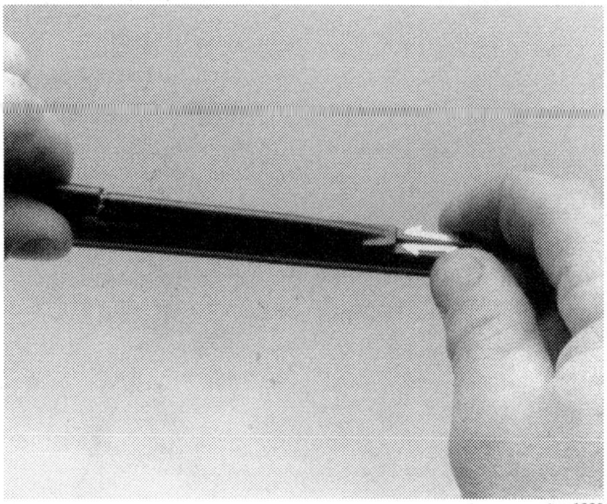
tccs1229

Fig. 114 On Pylon® inserts, the clip at the end has to be removed prior to sliding the insert off

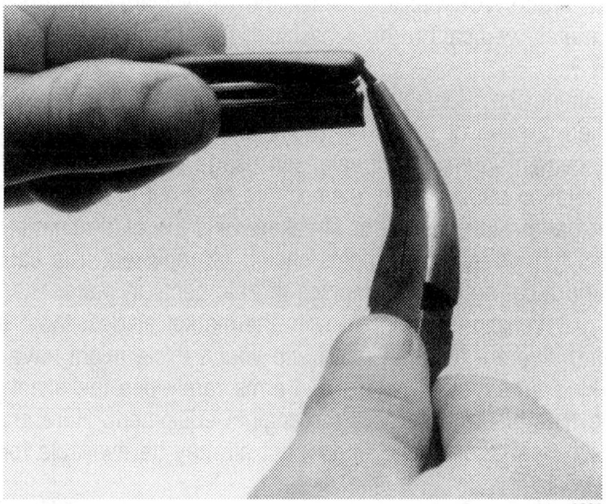
tccs1230

Fig. 115 On Trico® wiper blades, the tab at the end of the blade must be turned up . . .

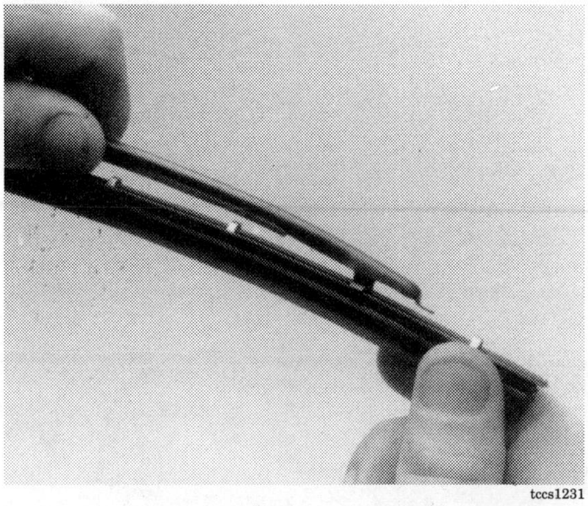
tccs1231

Fig. 116 . . . then the insert can be removed. After installing the replacement insert, bend the tab back

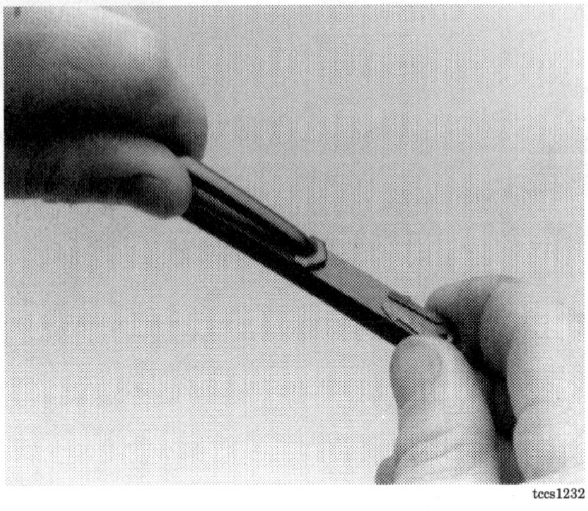

Fig. 117 The Tripledge® wiper blade insert is removed and installed using a securing clip

switch in the **ACC** position. When the wiper blades are approximately vertical on the windshield, turn the ignition switch to **OFF**.

Examine the wiper blade elements. If they are found to be cracked, broken or torn, they should be replaced immediately. Replacement intervals will vary with usage, although ozone deterioration usually limits element life to about one year. If the wiper pattern is smeared or streaked, or if the blade chatters across the glass, the elements should be replaced. It is easiest and most sensible to replace the elements in pairs.

If your vehicle is equipped with aftermarket blades, there are several different types of refills and your vehicle might have any kind. Aftermarket blades and arms rarely use the exact same type blade or refill as the original equipment. Here are some typical aftermarket blades; not all may be available for your vehicle:

The Anco® type uses a release button that is pushed down to allow the refill to slide out of the yoke jaws. The new refill slides back into the frame and locks in place.

Some Trico® refills are removed by locating where the metal backing strip or the refill is wider. Insert a small screwdriver blade between the frame and metal backing strip. Press down to release the refill from the retaining tab.

Other types of Trico® refills have two metal tabs which are unlocked by squeezing them together. The rubber filler can then be withdrawn from the frame jaws. A new refill is installed by inserting the refill into the front frame jaws and sliding it rearward to engage the remaining frame jaws. There are usually four jaws; be certain when installing that the refill is engaged in all of them. At the end of its travel, the tabs will lock into place on the front jaws of the wiper blade frame.

Another type of refill is made from polycarbonate. The refill has a simple locking device at one end which flexes downward out of the groove into which the jaws of the holder fit, allowing easy release. By sliding the new refill through all the jaws and pushing through the slight resistance when it reaches the end of its travel, the refill will lock into position.

To replace the Tridon® refill, it is necessary to remove the wiper blade. This refill has a plastic backing strip with a notch about 1 in. (25mm) from the end. Hold the blade (frame) on a hard surface so that the frame is tightly bowed. Grip the tip of the backing strip and pull up while twisting counterclockwise. The backing strip will snap out of the retaining tab. Do this for the remaining tabs until the refill is free of the blade. The length of these refills is molded into the end and they should be replaced with identical types.

Regardless of the type of refill used, be sure to follow the part manufacturer's instructions closely. Make sure that all of the frame jaws are engaged as the refill is pushed into place and locked. If the metal blade holder and frame are allowed to touch the glass during wiper operation, the glass will be scratched.

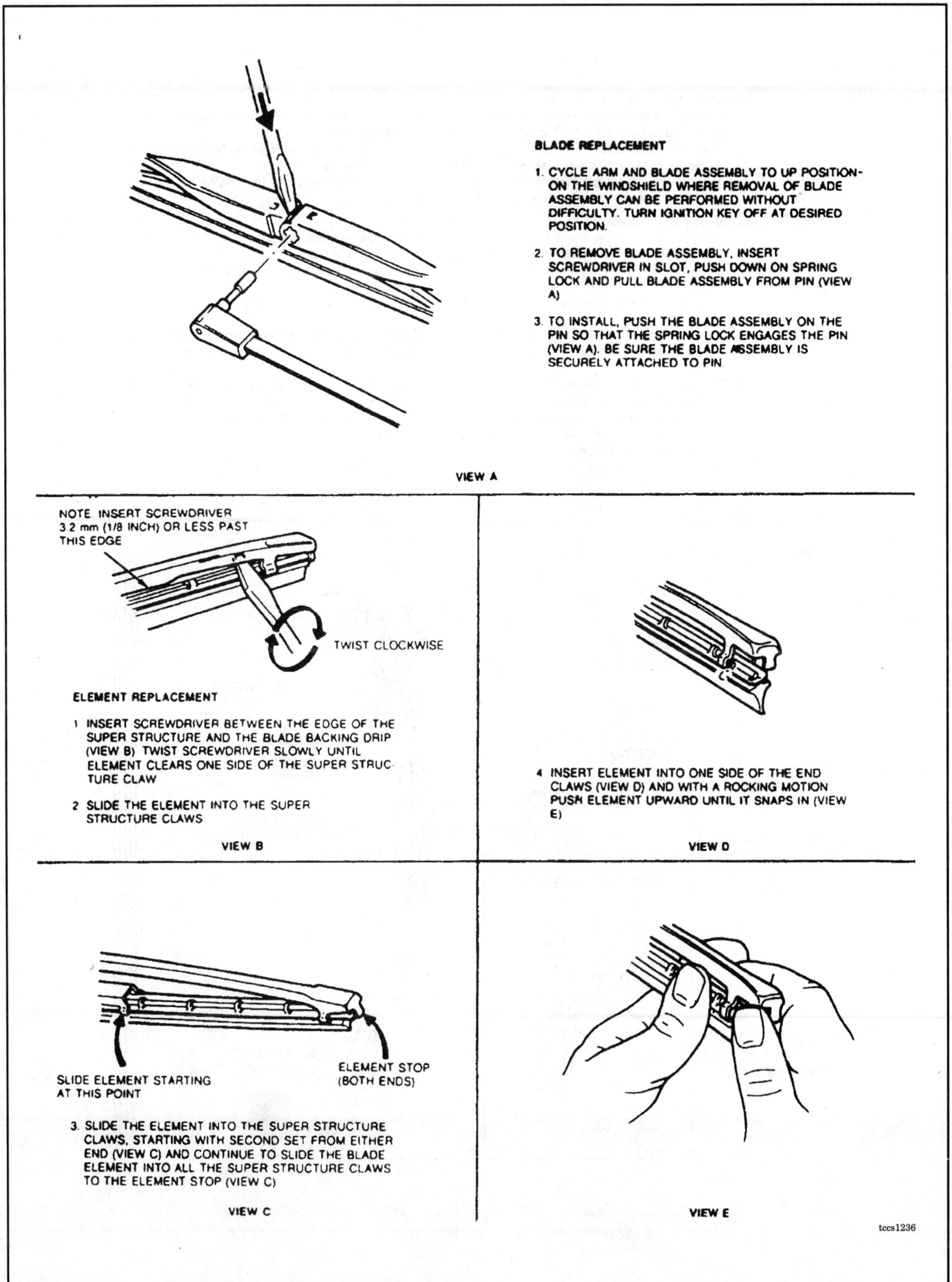

Fig. 118 Trico® wiper blade insert (element) replacement

BLADE REPLACEMENT

1. Cycle arm and blade assembly to a position on the windshield where removal of blade assembly can be performed without difficulty. Turn ignition key off at desired position.
2. To remove blade assembly from wiper arm, pull up on spring lock and pull blade assembly from pin (View A). Be sure spring lock is not pulled excessively or it will become distorted.
3. To install, push the blade assembly onto the pin so that the spring lock engages the pin (View A). Be sure the blade assembly is securely attached to pin.

ELEMENT REPLACEMENT

1. In the plastic backing strip which is part of the rubber blade assembly, there is an 11.11mm (7/16 inch) long notch located approximately one inch from either end. Locate either notch.
2. Place the frame of the wiper blade assembly on a firm surface with either notched end of the backing strip visible.
3. Grasp the frame portion of the wiper blade assembly and push down until the blade assembly is tightly bowed.
4. With the blade assembly in the bowed position, grasp the tip of the backing strip firmly, pulling up and twisting C.C.W. at the same time. The backing strip will then snap out of the retaining tab on the end of the frame.
5. Lift the wiper blade assembly from the surface and slide the backing strip down the frame until the notch lines up with the next retaining tab, twist slightly, and the backing strip will snap out. Continue this operation with the remaining tabs until the blade element is completely detached from the frame.
6. To install blade element, reverse the above procedure, making sure all six (6) tabs are locked to the backing strip before installing blade to wiper arm.

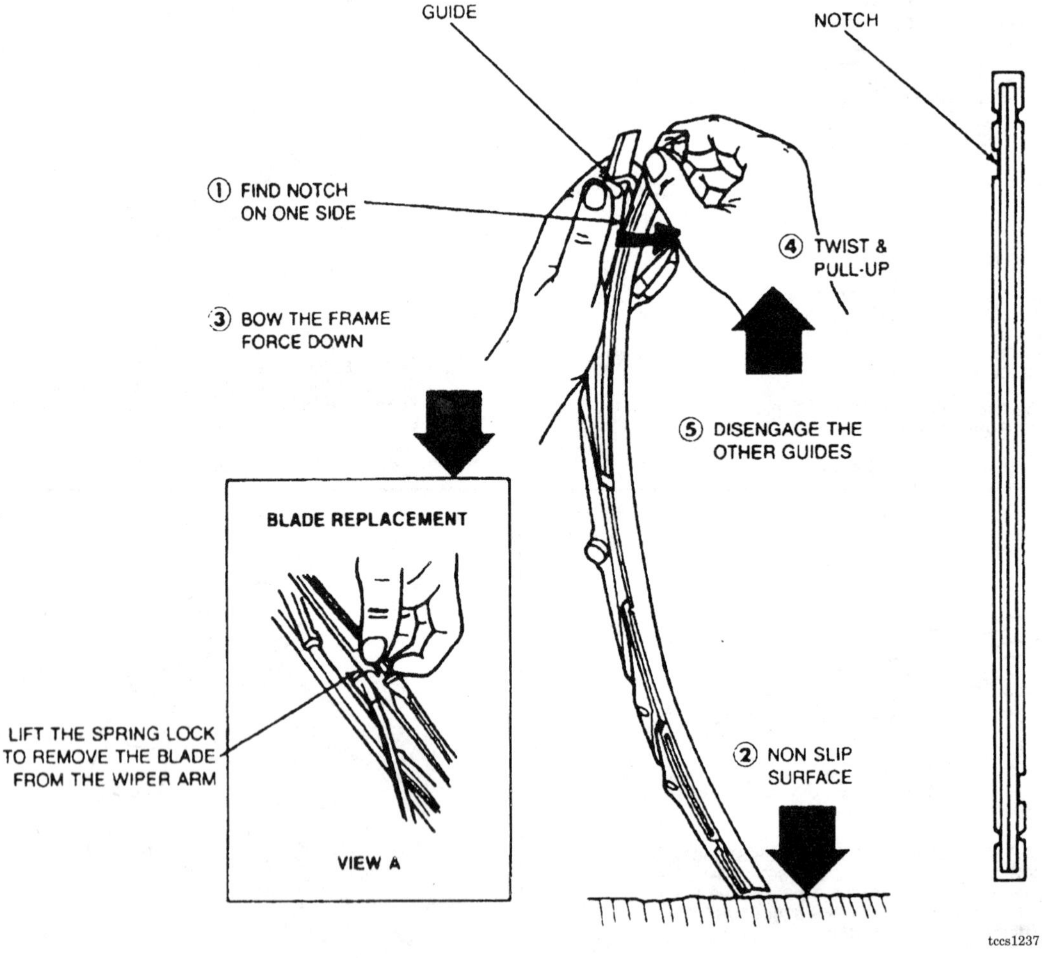

Fig. 119 Tridon® wiper blade insert (element) replacement

Tires and Wheels

Common sense and good driving habits will afford maximum tire life. Fast starts, sudden stops and hard cornering are hard on tires and will shorten their useful life span. Make sure that you don't overload the vehicle or run with incorrect pressure in the tires. Both of these practices will increase tread wear.

➡For optimum tire life, keep the tires properly inflated, rotate them often and have the wheel alignment checked periodically.

Inspect your tires frequently. Be especially careful to watch for bubbles in the tread or sidewall, deep cuts or underinflation. Replace any tires with bubbles in the sidewall. If cuts are so deep that they penetrate to the cords, discard the tire. Any cut in the sidewall of a radial tire renders it unsafe. Also look for uneven tread wear patterns that may indicate the front end is out of alignment or that the tires are out of balance.

TIRE ROTATION

▶ See Figures 120 and 121

Tires must be rotated periodically to equalize wear patterns that vary with a tire's position on the vehicle. Tires will also wear in an uneven way as the front steering/suspension system wears to the point where the alignment should be reset.

Rotating the tires will ensure maximum life for the tires as a set, so you will not have to discard a tire early due to wear on only part of the tread. Regular rotation is required to equalize wear.

When rotating "unidirectional tires," make sure that they always roll in the same direction. This means that a tire used on the left side of the vehicle must not be switched to the right side and vice-versa. Such tires should only be rotated front-to-rear or rear-to-front, while always remaining on the same side of the vehicle. These tires are marked on the sidewall as to the direction of rotation; observe the marks when reinstalling the tire(s).

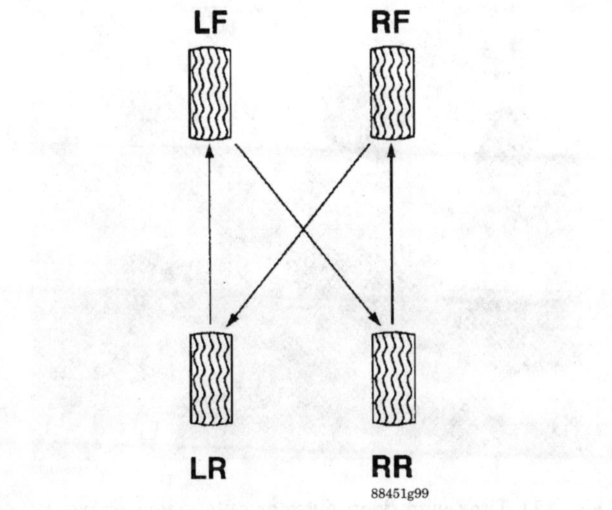

Fig. 120 Common Pick-up tire rotation patterns

Fig. 121 Unidirectional tires are identifiable by sidewall arrows and/or the word "rotation"

Some styled or "mag" wheels may have different offsets front to rear. In these cases, the rear wheels must not be used up front and vice-versa. Furthermore, if these wheels are equipped with unidirectional tires, they cannot be rotated unless the tire is remounted for the proper direction of rotation.

➡The compact or space-saver spare is strictly for emergency use. It must never be included in the tire rotation or placed on the vehicle for everyday use.

TIRE DESIGN

▶ See Figure 122

For maximum satisfaction, tires should be used in sets of four. Mixing of different types (radial, bias-belted, fiberglass belted) must be avoided. In most cases, the vehicle manufacturer has designated a type of tire on which the vehicle will perform best. Your first choice when replacing tires should be to use the same type of tire that the manufacturer recommends.

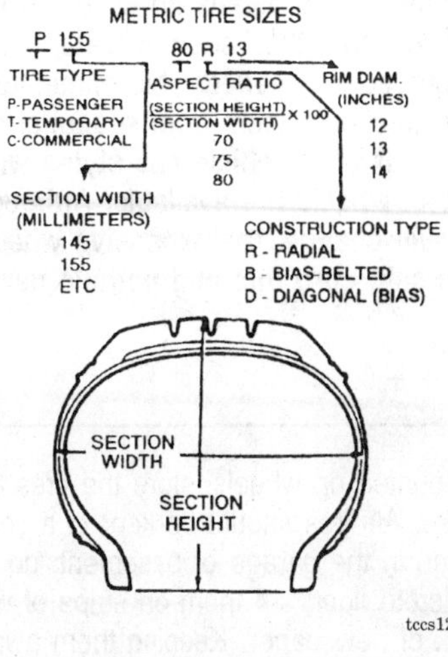

Fig. 122 P-Metric tire coding

When radial tires are used, tire sizes and wheel diameters should be selected to maintain ground clearance and tire load capacity equivalent to the original specified tire. Radial tires should always be used in sets of four.

****CAUTION**

Radial tires should never be used on only the front axle.

When selecting tires, pay attention to the original size as marked on the tire. Most tires are described using an industry size code sometimes referred to as P-Metric. This allows the exact identification of the tire specifications, regardless of the manufacturer. If selecting a different tire size or brand, remember to check the installed tire for any sign of interference with the body or suspension while the vehicle is stopping, turning sharply or heavily loaded.

Snow Tires

Good radial tires can produce a big advantage in slippery weather, but in snow, a street radial tire does not have sufficient tread to provide traction and control. The small grooves of a street tire quickly pack with snow and the tire behaves like a billiard ball on a marble floor. The more open, chunky tread of a snow tire will self-clean as the tire turns, providing much better grip on snowy surfaces.

To satisfy municipalities requiring snow tires during weather emergencies, most snow tires carry either an M + S designation after the tire size stamped on the sidewall, or the designation "all-season." In general, no change in tire size is necessary when buying snow tires.

Most manufacturers strongly recommend the use of 4 snow tires on their vehicles for reasons of stability. If snow tires are fitted only to the drive wheels, the opposite end of the vehicle may become very unstable when braking or turning on slippery surfaces. This instability can lead to unpleasant endings if the driver can't counteract the slide in time.

Note that snow tires, whether 2 or 4, will affect vehicle handling in all non-snow situations. The stiffer, heavier snow tires will noticeably change the turning and braking characteristics of the vehicle. Once the snow tires are installed, you must re-learn the behavior of the vehicle and drive accordingly.

➡Consider buying extra wheels on which to mount the snow tires. Once done, the "snow wheels" can be installed and removed as needed. This eliminates the potential damage to tires or wheels from seasonal removal and installation. Even if your vehicle has styled wheels, see if inexpensive steel wheels are available. Although the look of the vehicle will change, the expensive wheels will be protected from salt, curb hits and pothole damage.

TIRE STORAGE

If they are mounted on wheels, store the tires at proper inflation pressure. All tires should be kept in a cool, dry place. If they are stored in the garage or basement, do not let them stand on a concrete floor; set them on strips of wood, a mat or a large stack of newspaper. Keeping them away from direct moisture is of paramount importance. Tires should not be stored upright, but in a flat position.

INFLATION & INSPECTION

See Figures 123, 124, 125, 126, 127, 128, 129 and 130

The importance of proper tire inflation cannot be overemphasized. A tire employs air as part of its structure. It is designed around the supporting strength of the air at a specified pressure. For this reason, improper inflation drastically reduces the tires's ability to perform as intended. A tire will lose some air in day-to-day use; having to add a few pounds of air periodically is not necessarily a sign of a leaking tire.

Two items should be a permanent fixture in every glove compartment: an accurate tire pressure gauge and a tread depth gauge. Check the tire pressure (including the spare) regularly with a pocket type gauge. Too often, the gauge on the end of the air hose at your corner garage is not accurate because it suffers too much abuse. Always check tire pressure when the tires are cold, as pressure increases with temperature. If you must move the vehicle to check the tire inflation, do not drive more than a mile before checking. A cold tire is

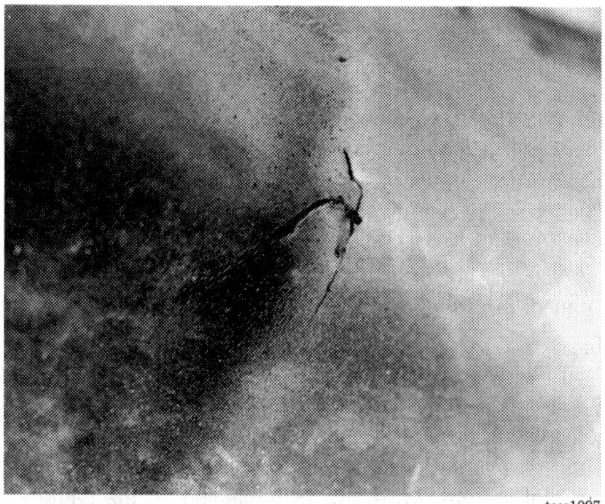

tccs1097

Fig. 123 Tires should be checked frequently for any sign of puncture or damage

tccs1095

Fig. 124 Tires with deep cuts, or cuts which show bulging, should be replaced immediately

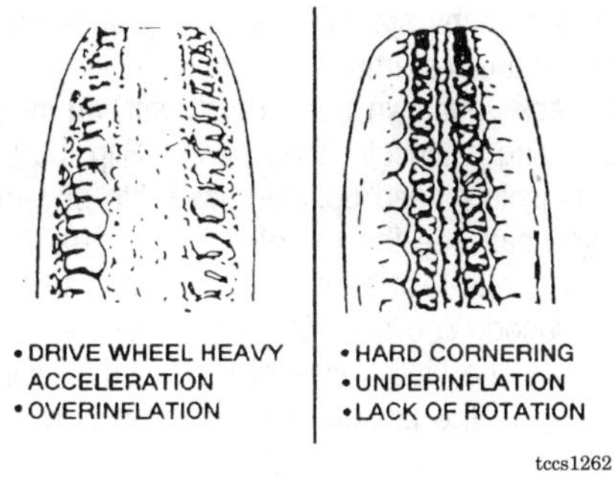

Fig. 125 Examples of inflation-related tire wear patterns

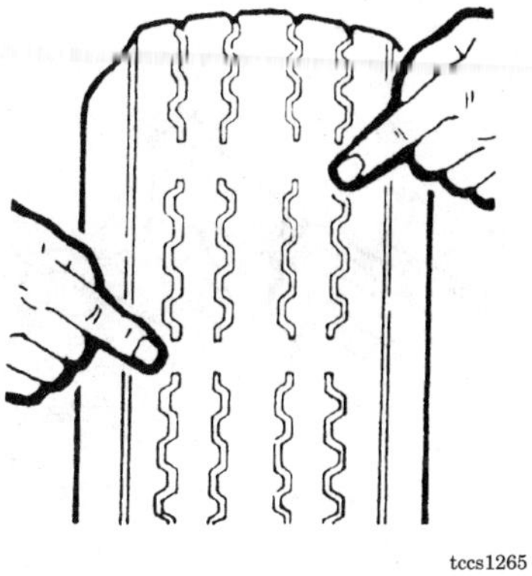

Fig. 128 Tread wear indicators will appear when the tire is worn

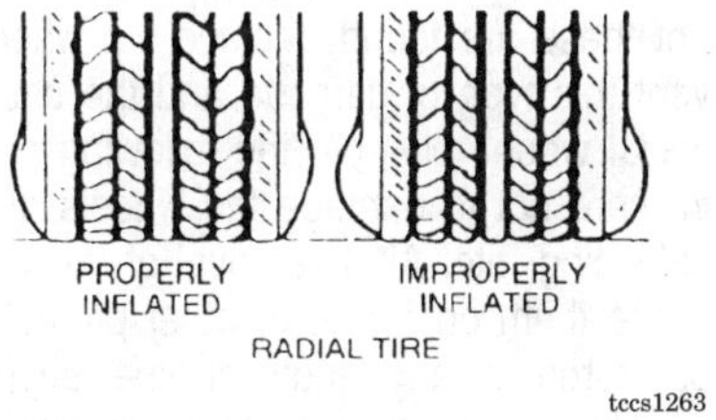

Fig. 126 Radial tires have a characteristic sidewall bulge; don't try to measure pressure by looking at the tire. Use a quality air pressure gauge

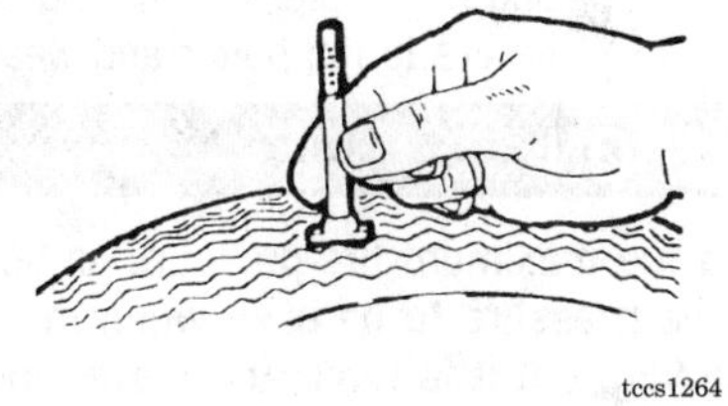

Fig. 129 Accurate tread depth indicators are inexpensive and handy

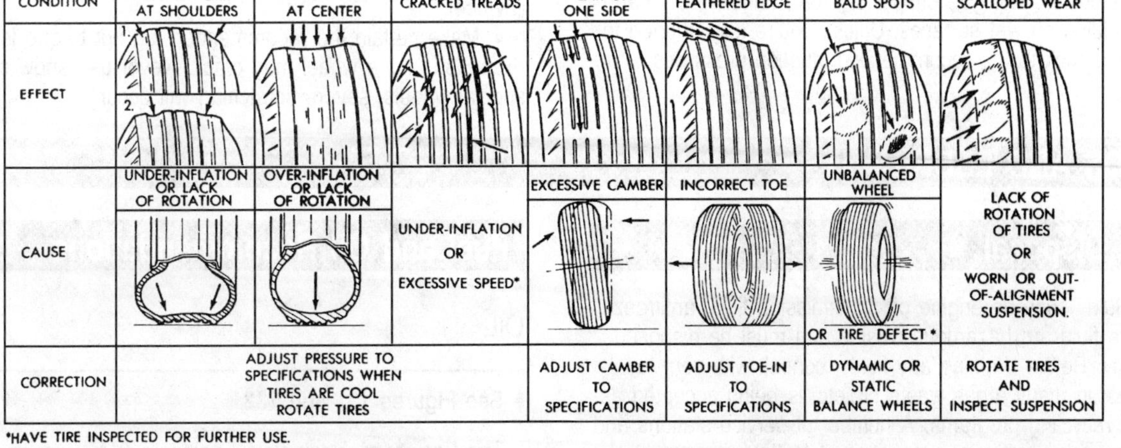

Fig. 127 Common tire wear patterns and causes

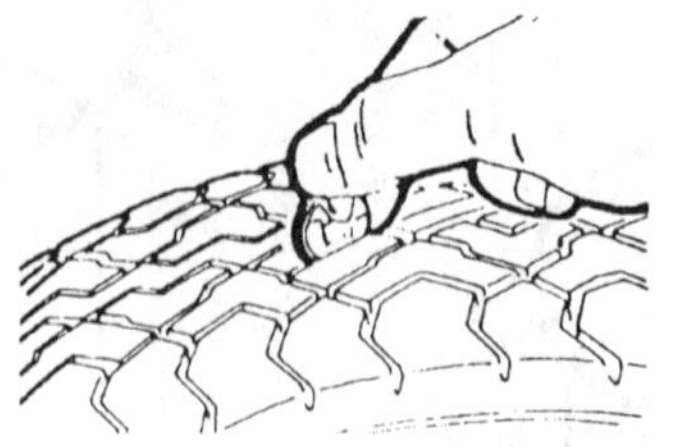

Fig. 130 A penny works well for a quick check of tread depth

generally one that has not been driven for more than three hours.

A plate or sticker is normally provided somewhere in the vehicle (door post, hood, tailgate or trunk lid) which shows the proper pressure for the tires. Never counteract excessive pressure build-up by bleeding off air pressure (letting some air out). This will cause the tire to run hotter and wear quicker.

****CAUTION**

Never exceed the maximum tire pressure embossed on the tire! This is the pressure to be used when the tire is at maximum loading, but it is rarely the correct pressure for everyday driving. Consult the owner's manual or the tire pressure sticker for the correct tire pressure.

Once you've maintained the correct tire pressures for several weeks, you'll be familiar with the vehicle's braking and handling personality. Slight adjustments in tire pressures can fine-tune these characteristics, but never change the cold pressure specification by more than 2 psi. A slightly softer tire pressure will give a softer ride but also yield lower fuel mileage. A slightly harder tire will give crisper dry road handling but can cause skidding on wet surfaces. Unless you're fully attuned to the vehicle, stick to the recommended inflation pressures.

All tires made since 1968 have built-in tread wear indicator bars that show up as 1/2 in. (13mm) wide smooth bands across the tire when 1/16 in. (1.5mm) of tread remains. The appearance of tread wear indicators means that the tires should be replaced. In fact, many states have laws prohibiting the use of tires with less than this amount of tread.

You can check your own tread depth with an inexpensive gauge or by using a Lincoln head penny. Slip the Lincoln penny (with Lincoln's head upside-down) into several tread grooves. If you can see the top of Lincoln's head in 2 adjacent grooves, the tire has less than 1/16 in. (1.5mm) tread left and should be replaced. You can measure snow tires in the same manner by using the "tails" side of the Lincoln penny. If you can see the top of the Lincoln memorial, it's time to replace the snow tire(s).

CARE OF SPECIAL WHEELS

If you have invested money in magnesium, aluminum alloy or sport wheels, special precautions should be taken to make sure your investment is not wasted and that your special wheels look good for the life of the vehicle.

Special wheels are easily damaged and/or scratched. Occasionally check the rims for cracking, impact damage or air leaks. If any of these are found, replace the wheel. But in order to prevent this type of damage and the costly replacement of a special wheel, observe the following precautions:

- Use extra care not to damage the wheels during removal, installation, balancing, etc. After removal of the wheels from the vehicle, place them on a mat or other protective surface. If they are to be stored for any length of time, support them on strips of wood. Never store tires and wheels upright; the tread may develop flat spots.
- When driving, watch for hazards; it doesn't take much to crack a wheel.
- When washing, use a mild soap or non-abrasive dish detergent (keeping in mind that detergent tends to remove wax). Avoid cleansers with abrasives or the use of hard brushes. There are many cleaners and polishes for special wheels.
- If possible, remove the wheels during the winter. Salt and sand used for snow removal can severely damage the finish of a wheel.
- Make certain the recommended lug nut torque is never exceeded or the wheel may crack. Never use snow chains on special wheels; severe scratching will occur.

FLUIDS AND LUBRICANTS

Fluid Disposal

Used fluids such as engine oil, transmission fluid, antifreeze and brake fluid are hazardous wastes and must be disposed of properly. Before draining any fluids, consult with your local authorities; in many areas waste oil, etc. is being accepted as a part of recycling programs. A number of service stations and auto parts stores are also accepting waste fluids for recycling.

Be sure of the recycling center's policies before draining any fluids, as many will not accept different fluids that have been mixed together.

Fuel and Oil Recommendations

OIL

See Figures 131 and 132

The Society of Automotive Engineers (SAE) grade number indicates the viscosity of the engine oil; its resistance to flow at a given temperature. The lower the SAE grade number, the lighter the oil. For example, the mono-grade oils begin with

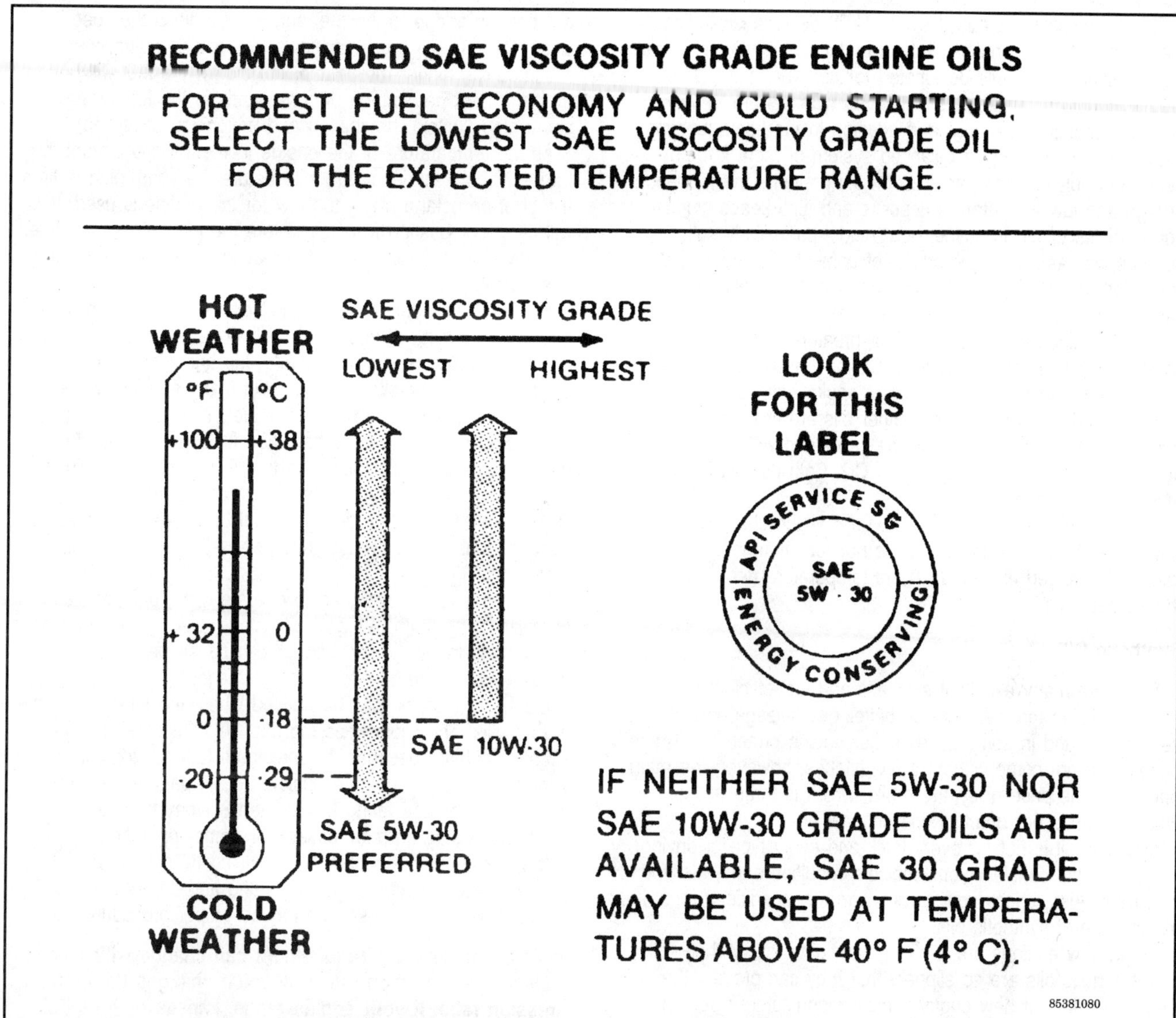

Fig. 131 Recommended SAE engine oil viscosity grades

Fig. 132 Look for the API oil identification label when choosing your engine oil

SAE 5 weight, which is a thin light oil, and continue in viscosity up to SAE 80 or 90 weight, which are heavy gear lubricants. These oils are also known as 'straight weight', meaning they are of a single viscosity, and do not vary with engine temperature.

Multi-viscosity oils offer the important advantage of being adaptable to temperature extremes. These oils have designations such as 10W-40, 20W-50, etc. The 10W-40 means that in winter (the "W" in the designation) the oil acts like a thin 10 weight oil, allowing the engine to spin easily when cold and offering rapid lubrication. Once the engine has warmed up, however, the oil acts like a straight 40 weight, maintaining good lubrication and protection for the engine's internal components. A 20W-50 oil would therefore be slightly heavier than and not as ideal in cold weather as the 10W-40, but would offer better protection at higher rpm and temperatures because when warm it acts like a 50 weight oil. Whichever oil viscosity you choose when changing the oil, make sure you are anticipating the temperatures your engine will be operating in until the oil is changed again. Refer to the oil viscosity chart for oil recommendations according to temperature.

The American Petroleum Institute (API) designation indicates the classification of engine oil used under certain given operating conditions. Only oils designated for use "Service SG" or greater should be used. Oils of the SG type perform a variety of functions inside the engine in addition to the basic function as a lubricant. Through a balanced system of metallic detergents and polymeric dispersants, the oil prevents the formation of high and low temperature deposits and also keeps sludge and particles of dirt in suspension. Acids, particularly sulfuric acid, as well as other by-products of combustion, are neutralized. Both the SAE grade number and the APE designation can be found on top of the oil can.

Diesel engines also require SG or greater engine oil. In addition, the oil must qualify for a CC or greater rating. The API has a number of different diesel engine ratings, including CB, CC, and CD. Any of these other oils are fine as long as the designation CC appears on the can along with them. Do not use oil labeled only SG or only CC. Both designations must always appear together.

For recommended oil viscosities, refer to the chart. Note that 10W-30 and 10W-40 grade oils are not recommended for sustained high speed driving when the temperature rises above the indicated limit.

Synthetic Oil

There are many excellent synthetic and fuel-efficient oils currently available that can provide better gas mileage, longer service life, and in some cases better engine protection. These benefits do not come without a few hitches, however; the main one being the price of synthetic oils, which is three or four times the price per quart of conventional oil.

Synthetic oil is not for every truck and every type of driving, so you should consider your engine's condition and your type of driving. Also, check your truck's warranty conditions regarding the use of synthetic oils.

Brand new engines are a wrong candidate for synthetic oil. The synthetic oils are so slippery that they can prevent the proper break-in of new engines; most manufacturers recommend that you wait until the engine is properly broken in; 3000 miles (4800 km), before using synthetic oil. Also, if your truck is leaking oil past old seals you'll have a much greater leak problem with synthetics.

Consider your type of driving. If most of your accumulated mileage is high speed, highway type driving, the more expensive synthetic oils may be a benefit. Extended highway driving gives the engine a chance to warm up, accumulating less acids in the oil and putting less stress on the engine over the long run. Under these conditions, the oil change interval can be extended (as long as your oil filter can last the extended life of the oil) up to the advertised mileage claims of the synthetics. Trucks with synthetic oils may show increased fuel economy in highway driving, due to less internal friction. However, many automotive experts agree that 50,000 miles (80,000 km) is too long to keep any oil in your engine.

FUEL

It is important to use fuel of the proper octane rating in your vehicle. Octane rating is based on the quantity of anti-knock compounds added to the fuel and it determines the speed at which the gas will burn. The lower the octane rating, the faster it burns. The higher the octane, the slower the fuel will burn and a greater percentage of compounds in the fuel prevent spark ping (knock), detonation and preignition (dieseling).

As the temperature of the engine increases, the air/fuel mixture exhibits a tendency to ignite before the spark plug is fired. If fuel of an octane rating too low for the engine is used, this will allow combustion to occur before the piston has completed its compression stroke, thereby creating a very high pressure very rapidly.

Fuel of the proper octane rating, for the compression ratio and ignition timing of your truck, will slow the combustion process sufficiently to allow the spark plug enough time to ignite the mixture completely and smoothly. Many non-catalyst models are designed to run on regular fuel. The use of some super-premium fuel is no substitution for a properly tuned and maintained engine. Chances are that if your engine exhibits any signs of spark ping, detonation or pre-ignition when using regular fuel, the ignition timing should be checked against specifications or the cylinder head should be removed for decarbonizing.

Most models are designed to operate using unleaded gasoline with a minimum rating of 87 octane. Use of unleaded gas with octane ratings lower than 87 can cause persistent spark knock which could lead to engine damage.

Light spark knock may be noticed when accelerating or driving up hills. The slight knocking may be considered normal (with 87 octane) because the maximum fuel economy is obtained under condition of occasional light spark knock. Gasoline with an octane rating higher than 87 may be used, but it is not necessary (in most cases) for proper operation.

If spark knock is constant, when using 87 octane, at cruising speeds on level ground, ignition timing adjustment may be required. Refer to this section for the proper procedure

➡Your engine's fuel requirement can change with time, mainly due to carbon buildup, which changes the compression ratio. If your engine pings, knocks or runs on, switch to a higher grade of fuel. Sometimes just changing brands will cure the problem. If it becomes necessary to retard the timing from specifications, don't change it more than a few degrees. Retarded timing will reduce power output and fuel mileage and will increase the engine temperature.

Engine

OIL LEVEL CHECK

See Figures 133, 134, 135 and 136

Every time you stop for fuel, check the engine oil making sure the engine has fully warmed and the vehicle is parked on a level surface. If the truck is used for trailer towing or for heavy-duty use, it is recommended to check the oil more frequently. Because it takes a few minutes for all the oil to drain back to the oil pan, you should wait a few minutes before checking your oil. If you are doing this at a fuel stop, first fill the fuel tank, then open the hood and check the oil, but don't

88451p12

Fig. 133 Remove the dipstick from the tube, wipe it clean, then reinsert it

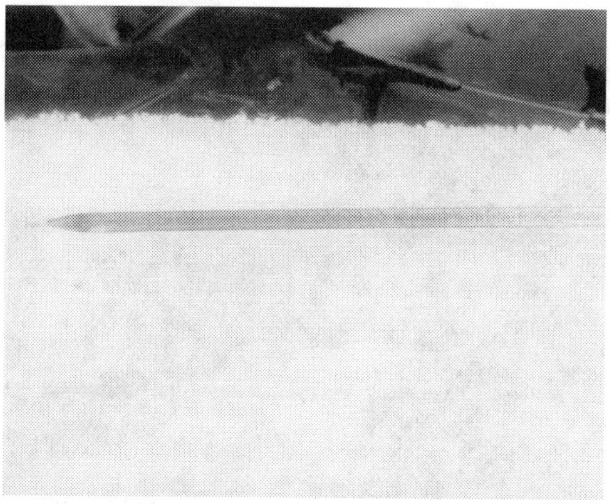

88451p13

Fig. 134 Remove the dipstick again and, while holding it horizontally, read the oil level

88451p14

Fig. 135 If oil needs to be added, remove the oil filler cap . . .

88451p15

Fig. 136 . . . then add the correct amount and grade of oil

get so carried away as to forget to pay for the fuel. Most station attendants won't believe that you forgot.

1. Make sure the truck is parked on level ground.
2. When checking the oil level it is best for the engine to be a normal operating temperature, although checking the oil immediately after stopping will lead to a false reading. Wait a few minutes after turning off the engine to allow the oil to drain back into the crankcase.
3. Open the hood and locate the dipstick which will be in a guide tube mounted in the upper engine block, just below the cylinder head mating surface. The dipstick may be located on the right or left side of the vehicle depending upon your particular engine, but on most of these pick-ups, it will be toward the driver's side of the engine. Pull the dipstick from its tube, wipe it clean (using a clean, lint free rag) and then reinsert it.
4. Pull the dipstick out again and, holding it horizontally, read the oil level. The oil should be between the FULL and ADD marks on the dipstick. If the oil is below the ADD mark, add oil of the proper viscosity through the capped opening in the top of the cylinder head cover or filler tube, as applicable. See the oil and fuel recommendations listed earlier in this section for the proper viscosity and rating of oil to use.
5. Replace the dipstick and check the oil level again after adding any oil. Approximately one quart of oil will raise the level from the ADD mark to the FULL mark. Be sure not to overfill the crankcase and waste the oil. Excess oil will generally be consumed at an accelerated rate.

OIL AND FILTER CHANGE

➧ See Figures 137, 138, 139, 140, 141, 142 and 143

If the vehicle is operated on a daily or semi-daily basis and most trips are for several miles (allowing the engine to properly warm-up), the oil should be changed a minimum of every 12 months or 7500 miles (12,000 Km), whichever comes first.

If however, the vehicle is used to tow a trailer, is made to idle for extended periods of time such as in heavy daily traffic or if used as a service vehicle (delivery) or the vehicle is used for only short trips in below freezing temperature, the oil change interval should be shortened. Likewise, if your vehicle

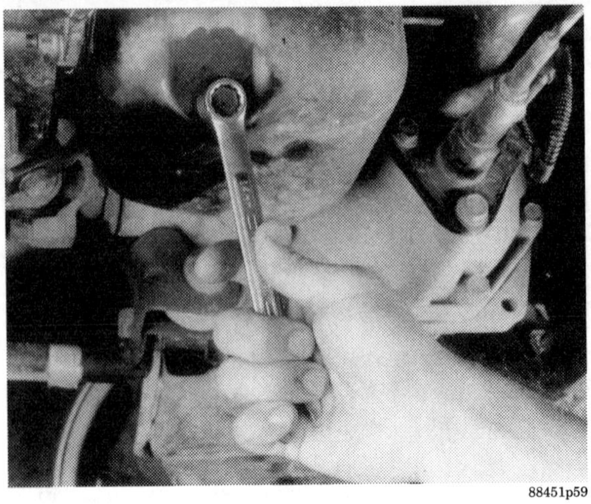
88451p59

Fig. 137 Remove the oil pan drain plug and drain all the oil from the crankcase

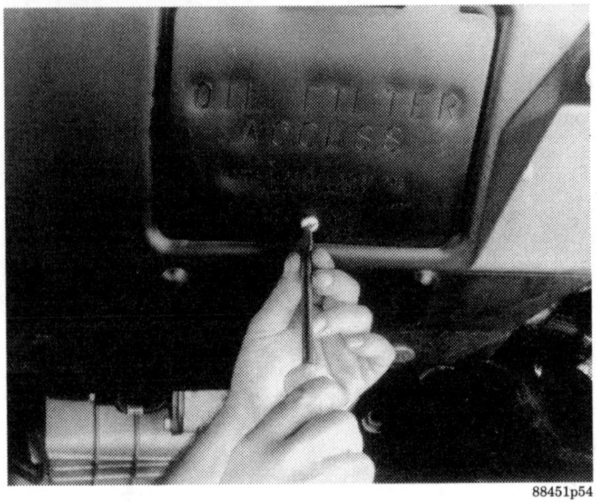

88451p54

Fig. 138 Open the oil filter access panel located at the front of the vehicle

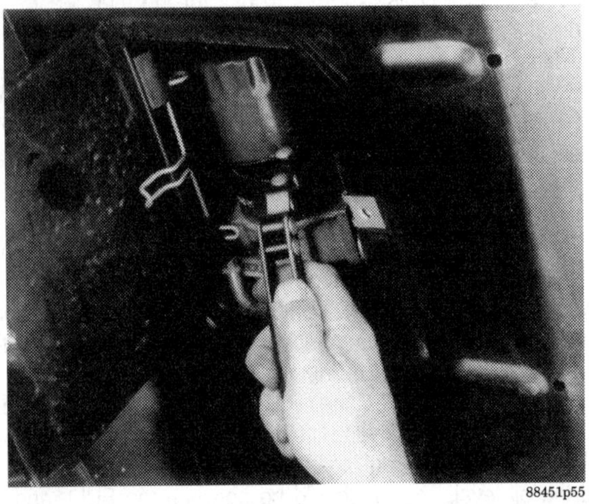
88451p55

Fig. 139 Using the proper size oil filter wrench, remove the old oil filter

88451p56

Fig. 141 Add the proper amount and grade of engine oil to the engine

tccs1901

Fig. 140 Before installing a new oil filter, lightly coat the rubber gasket with clean oil

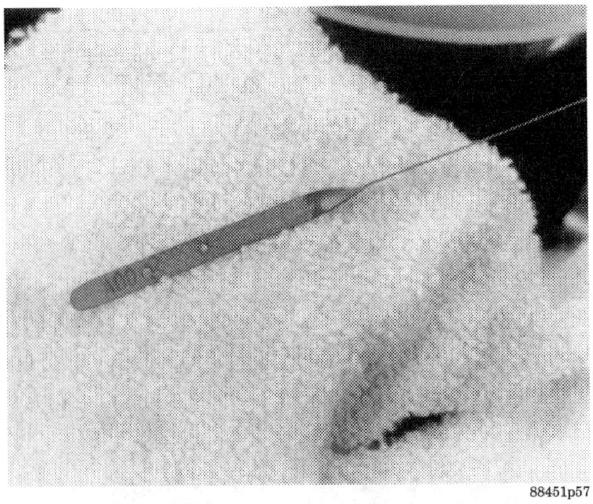
88451p57

Fig. 142 After adding the oil, check the dipstick to ensure that the crankcase is filled to the proper level

Fig. 143 Remember to always replace the engine oil filler cap after adding oil

is used under dusty, polluted or off-road conditions, the oil should be changed more frequently. Under these circumstances oil has a greater chance of building up sludge and contaminants which could damage your engine. If your vehicle use fits into these circumstance, as most do, it is suggested that the oil and filter be changed every 3000 miles (4800 Km) or 3 months, whichever comes first.

Under certain circumstances, Chevrolet and GMC recommend changing both the oil and filter during the first oil change and then only replacing the filter every other oil change thereafter. For the small price of an oil filter, it's cheap insurance to replace the filter at every oil change. One of the larger filter manufacturers points out in its advertisements that not changing the filter leaves one quart of dirty oil in the engine. This claim is true and should be kept in mind when changing your oil.

Oil should always be changed after the engine has been running long enough to bring it up to normal operating temperature. Hot oil will flow easier and more contaminants will be removed along with the oil than if it were drained cold. The oil drain plug is located on the bottom of the oil pan (bottom of the engine, underneath the vehicle). The oil filter is usually located on the left side of the engine and in some cases may be easier to reach through the plastic access flap in the wheel well.

You should have available a container that will hold a minimum of 6 quarts (5.6L) of liquid (to help prevent spilling the oil even after it is drained), a wrench to fit the drain plug, a spout for pouring in new oil and a rag or two, which you will always need. If the filter is being replaced, you will also need a band wrench or a filter wrench that fits the end of the filter.

➡If the engine is equipped with an oil cooler, this will also have to be drained, using the drain plug. Be sure to add enough oil to fill the cooler in addition to the engine.

1. Run the engine until it reaches normal operating temperature, then shut the engine **OFF**, make sure the parking brake is firmly set and block the drive wheels.
2. Clearance may be sufficient to access the drain plug without raising the vehicle. If the truck must be lifted, be sure to support it safely with jackstands and be sure to position the drain plug at a low point under the vehicle.
3. Slide a drain pan of a least 6 quarts (5.6L) capacity under the oil pan. Wipe the drain plug and surrounding area clean using an old rag.

✱✱CAUTION

The EPA warns that prolonged contact with used engine oil may cause a number of skin disorders, including cancer! You should make every effort to minimize your exposure to used engine oil. Protective gloves should be worn when changing the oil. Wash your hands and any other exposed skin areas as soon as possible after exposure to used engine oil. Soap and water, or waterless hand cleaner should be used.

4. Loosen the drain plug using a ratchet, short extension and socket or a box-wrench. Turn the plug out by hand, using a rag to shield your fingers from the hot oil. By keeping an inward pressure on the plug as you unscrew it, oil won't escape past the threads and you can remove it without being burned by hot oil.
5. Quickly withdraw the plug and move your hands out of the way, but be careful not to drop the plug into the drain pan as fishing it out can be an unpleasant mess. Allow the oil to drain completely in the pan, then install and carefully tighten the drain plug. Be careful not to overtighten the drain plug, otherwise you'll be buying a new pan or a trick replacement plug for stripped threads.

➡Although some manufacturers have at times recommended changing the oil filter every other oil change, we recommend the filter be changed each time you change your oil. The added benefit of clean oil is quickly lost if the old filter is clogged and the added protection to the heart of your engine far outweighs the few dollars saved by using a old filter.

6. Move the drain pan under the oil filter. Use a strap-type or cap-type filter wrench to loosen the oil filter. Cover your hand with a rag and spin the filter off by hand; turn it slowly. Keep in mind that it's holding about one quart of dirty, hot oil.

✱✱CAUTION

On most Chevrolet engines, especially the V6s, the oil filter is next to the exhaust pipes. Stay clear of these, since even a passing contact can result in a painful burn. ALSO, on trucks equipped with catalytic converters, stay clear of the converter. The outside temperature of a hot catalytic converter can approach 1200°F.

7. Empty the old filter into the drain pan and properly dispose of the filter.
8. Using a clean rag, wipe off the filter adapter on the engine block. Be sure that the rag doesn't leave any lint which could clog an oil passage.
9. Coat the rubber gasket on the filter with fresh oil, then spin it onto the engine by hand; when the gasket touches the adapter surface, give it another 1/2-1 turn. No more, or you'll squash the gasket and it will leak.

10. Refill the engine with the correct amount of fresh oil. Please refer to the Capacities chart at the end of this section.

11. Check the oil level on the dipstick. It is normal for the level to be a bit above the full mark until the engine is run and the new filter is filled with oil. Start the engine and allow it to idle for a few minutes.

✱✱CAUTION

Do not run the engine above idle speed until it has built up oil pressure, as indicated when the oil light goes out.

12. Shut off the engine and allow the oil to flow back to the crankcase for a minute, then recheck the oil level. Check around the filter and drain plug for any leaks, and correct as necessary.

When you have finished this job, you will notice that you now possess four or five quarts of dirty oil. The best thing to do with it is to pour it into plastic jugs, such as milk or antifreeze containers. Then, locate a service station or automotive parts store where you can pour it into their used oil tank for recycling.

✱✱CAUTION

Pouring used motor oil into a storm drain not only pollutes the environment, it violates Federal law. Dispose of waste oil properly.

Manual Transmission

FLUID RECOMMENDATIONS

On 1994 vehicles equipped with a Borg Warner 5 speed manual transmission, use Dexron® II automatic transmission fluid. On 1995 vehicles equipped with a Borg Warner 5 speed manual transmission, use Dexron® III automatic transmission fluid.

On 1994-97 vehicles equipped with a New Venture Gear 3500/1500 and 1996-97 Borg Warner 5 speed manual transmission, use Synchromesh transmission fluid GM part No. 12345349 or its equivalent.

➡Using the incorrect lubricant in your transmission can lead to significant transmission damage and a costly overhaul.

LEVEL CHECK

Remove the filler plug from the side of the transmission (usually located on the passenger's-side of the housing). If the transmission housing contains 2 plugs, the lower is a drain plug, while the upper plug is the filler. The oil should be level with the bottom edge of the filler hole. This should be checked at least once every 6000 miles (9600 km) on leakage or seepage is observed.

➡When checking the fluid, the vehicle must be level. If it was necessary to raise and support the vehicle to access the filler plug, the vehicle must be supported at sufficient points (all wheels or 4 points on the frame) so it is sitting level and is not tilted forward/backward or to one side.

DRAIN AND REFILL

Under normal conditions, the manual transmission fluid should not need to be changed. However, if the truck is driven in deep water (as high as the transmission casing) it is a good idea to replace the fluid. Little harm can come from a fluid change when you have just purchased a used vehicle, especially since the condition of the transmission fluid is usually not known.

If the fluid is to be drained, it is a good idea to warm the fluid first so it will flow better. This can be accomplished by 15-20 miles (24-32 km) of highway driving. Fluid which is warmed to normal operating temperature will flow faster, drain more completely and remove more contaminants from the housing.

1. Raise and support the vehicle safely using jackstands.
2. Place a fluid catch pan under the transmission.
3. Remove the bottom transmission housing plug and allow the fluid to drain.
4. Install the bottom plug and refill the transmission housing.

Automatic Transmission

FLUID RECOMMENDATIONS

When adding fluid or refilling the transmission, always use Dexron® III automatic transmission fluid.

LEVEL CHECK

▶ See Figures 144, 145 and 146

Check the automatic transmission fluid level at least every 7500 miles (12,000 km). The dipstick can be found in the rear of the engine compartment. The fluid level should be checked only when the transmission is hot (normal operating temperature). The transmission is considered hot after about 15-20 miles (24-32 km) of highway driving.

➡Although the transmission should be checked while the fluid is at normal operating temperature, do not check it if it is at the extreme high end of the operating temperature range. Wait at least 30 minutes if you have just be driving the vehicle in ambient temperatures in excess of 90°F (32°C), at highway speeds for a long time, in heavy traffic (especially in hot weather) or have been pulling a trailer.

Fig. 144 Remove the automatic transmission dipstick from the tube

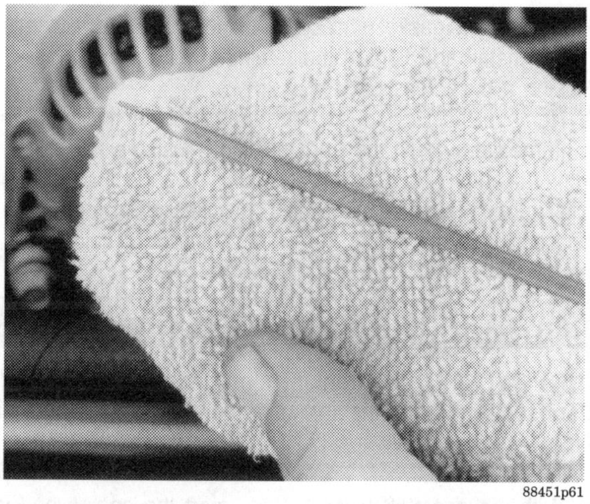

Fig. 145 Check the transmission fluid level on the dipstick

1. Park the truck on a level surface with the engine idling, then shift the transmission into Park and firmly set the parking brake.
2. With your foot on the brake pedal, move the selector through each gear range (pausing for about 3 seconds in each gear), then place it in Park. Allow the engine to run at idle about 3 more minutes.

➡When moving the selector through each range, DO NOT race the engine.

3. With the engine running at a low idle, remove the dipstick, wipe it clean and then reinsert it firmly. Be sure that it has been pushed all the way in, then pause 3 seconds. Remove the dipstick again and check the fluid level while holding it horizontally. The fluid level should be between the upper notch and the FULL HOT line. If the fluid must be checked when it is cool, the level should be between the lower 2 notches.

➡Most of the transmissions for the 4.3L engine are equipped with a flip-top handle on the dipstick. To withdraw these, flip the handle upward, then pull the dipstick from the guide.

4. If the fluid level is low add DEXRON®III automatic transmission fluid. The fluid must be added through the transmission dipstick tube, which is easily accomplished using a funnel. Add fluid gradually, checking the level often as you are filling the transmission. Be extremely careful not to overfill the transmission, as this will cause slippage, seal damage and overheating. Approximately one pint of ATF will raise the fluid level from one notch/line to the other.

✱✱WARNING

Always use DEXRON®III ATF. The use of ATF Type F or any other fluid will cause severe damage to the transmission.

The fluid on the dipstick should always be a bright red color. If it is discolored (brown or black), or smells burnt, serious transmission troubles, probably due to overheating, should be

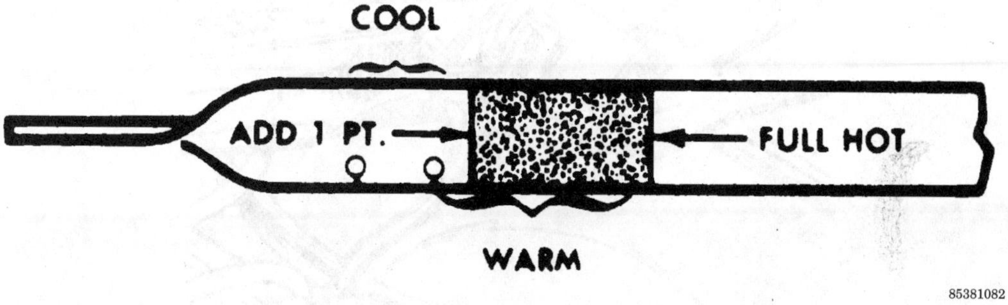

Fig. 146 Automatic transmission dipstick marks; the proper level for a hot transmission is within the shaded area

suspected. The transmission should be inspected by a qualified technician to locate the cause of the burnt fluid.

DRAIN AND REFILL

See Figures 147 and 148

The truck should be driven 15-20 miles (24-32 km) to warm the transmission fluid before the pan is removed.

1. Raise and support the front of vehicle safely using jackstands.
2. Place a drain pan under the transmission housing and fluid pan.
3. Remove the pan bolts from the front and the sides, then loosen the rear bolts 4 turns.

On some vehicles, it may be necessary to support the transmission tailshaft and remove the crossmember just behind the transmission for pan clearance or access to the pan bolts.

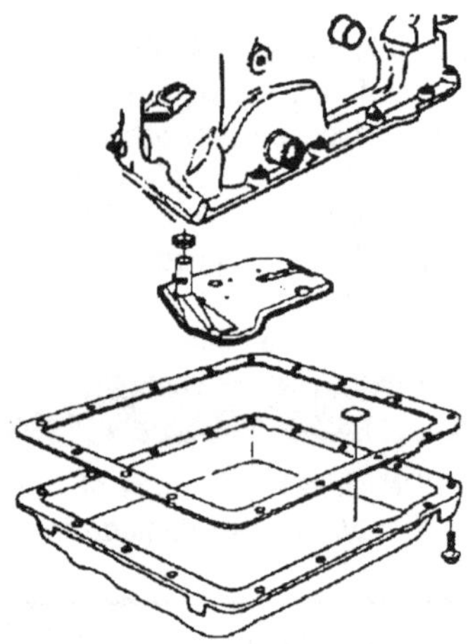

Fig. 148 Exploded view of the automatic transmission oil pan and filter — 4L60-E transmission shown

4. Using a small prybar, carefully pry the pan downward at the front of the transmission. This will allow the pan to partially drain. Remove the remaining pan bolts and lower the pan from the transmission.

If the transmission fluid is dark or has a burnt smell, transmission damage is indicated. Have the transmission checked professionally.

5. Empty the transmission pan of the remaining fluid, then remove the gasket material and clean with a solvent.
6. Using a putty knife, carefully clean the gasket mounting surfaces.
7. Remove the screen and the filter from the valve body. Most screens are retained using a bolt fastener, though some may use an interference fit between the screen tube and valve body.

To install:

8. Install a new filter using a new gasket or O-ring.

If the transmission uses a filter equipped with a fully exposed screen, it may be cleaned and reused.

9. Use a new gasket and sealant and install the transmission pan. Install and tighten the retaining bolts to 8 ft. lbs. (11 Nm) using a crisscross pattern.
10. Remove the jackstands and carefully lower the vehicle.
11. Immediately refill the transmission housing using Dexron® II automatic transmission fluid. Add the fluid through the filler tube. Please refer to the Capacities chart found later in this section to determine the proper amount of fluid to be added.

****WARNING**

DO NOT OVERFILL the transmission. Foaming of the fluid and subsequent transmission damage due to slippage will result.

12. With the gearshift lever in Park, start the engine and let it idle. DO NOT race the engine.
13. Apply the parking brake and move the gearshift lever through each position. Return the lever to Park and check the fluid level with the engine idling. The level should be between

Fig. 147 Fluid may be added to the transmission through the dipstick using a funnel and flexible hose

the two dimples on the dipstick, about 1/4 in. (6mm) below the ADD mark. Add fluid, if necessary.

14. Check the fluid level after the truck has been driven enough to thoroughly warm the transmission.

Transfer Case

FLUID RECOMMENDATIONS

When adding fluid or refilling the transfer case, use Dexron® III automatic transmission fluid for vehicles covered by this manual.

LEVEL CHECK

See Figure 149

➡When checking the fluid, the vehicle must be level. If it was necessary to raise and support the vehicle to access the filler plug, the vehicle must be supported at sufficient points (all wheels or 4 points on the frame) so it is sitting level and is not tilted forward/backward or to one side.

1. If necessary for access to the filler plug, raise and support the vehicle safely using jackstands, but make sure the vehicle is level.
2. Remove the filler plug (upper one of the 2 plugs) from the rear-side of the transfer case.
3. Using your finger, check the fluid level, it should be level with the bottom of the filler hole.
4. If the fluid level is low, use Dexron® III automatic transmission fluid to bring the fluid up to the proper level. Most parts stores will carry a small, hand operated pump which will greatly ease the task of adding fluid to the transfer case.
5. Install and tighten the filler plug.

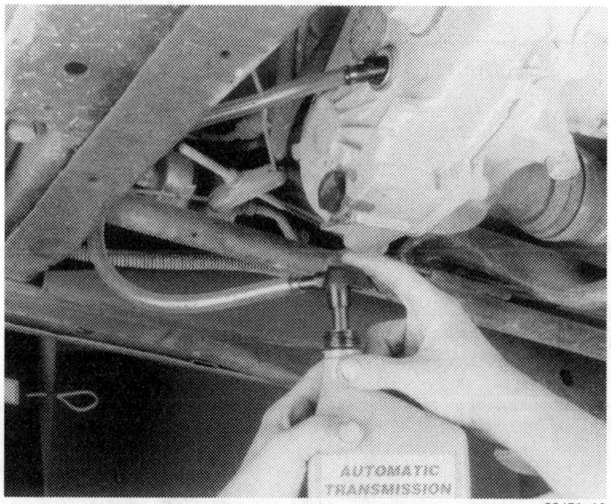

88451p18

Fig. 149 If it is necessary to add fluid, use a small hand operated pump to add the fluid

DRAIN AND REFILL

See Figures 150 and 151

1. Operate the vehicle in four wheel drive in order to warm the fluid to normal operating temperature.
2. If necessary for access to the drain and filler plugs, raise and support the vehicle safely using jackstands. Support the truck so it is level; this is necessary to assure the proper fluid level is maintained when the case is refilled.
3. Position drain pan under transfer case.
4. Remove drain and fill plugs, then drain the lubricant into the drain pan.
5. Install and tighten the drain plug.
6. Remove the drain pan and dump the fluid into a used transmission fluid storage tank, for recycling purposes.
7. Using Dexron® III automatic transmission fluid, fill transfer case to edge of fill plug opening.
8. Install and tighten the fill plug.

88451p16

Fig. 150 Use a wrench to loosen the drain plug

88451p17

Fig. 151 Remove the drain plug and let the fluid drain

9. Remove the jackstands and carefully lower the vehicle, then check for proper operation of the transfer case.

Drive Axles

The fluid in both the rear axle and, if equipped, the front drive axle should be checked at each oil change. The fluid in the rear axle should be changed at the truck's first engine oil change and thereafter at intervals of 15,000 miles (24,000 km). Changing the front drive axle fluid on these vehicles usually requires it's removal and partial disassembly. The fluid in the front drive axle should not need to be changed unless the axle is removed for repair.

The fluid is checked by removing the filler plug, but keep in mind the truck must be sitting level or an incorrect fluid level will be indicated. Maintain the fluid at a level 3/8 in. (9.5mm) below the filler plug hole.

FLUID RECOMMENDATIONS

Always use SAE 80W-90 GL5 gear lubricant, part number 1052271, or equivalent.

LEVEL CHECK

See Figures 152, 153, 154 and 155

When checking the fluid, the vehicle must be level. If it was necessary to raise and support the vehicle to access the filler plug, the vehicle must be supported at sufficient points (all wheels or 4 points on the frame) so it is sitting level and is not tilted forward/backward or to one side.

1. If necessary for access to the filler plug, raise and support the vehicle safely using jackstands, but make sure the vehicle is level.
2. Remove the filler plug, located at the side of the differential carrier.
3. Check the fluid level, it should be 3/8 in. (9.5 mm) below the filler plug hole.

88451p20

Fig. 152 Remove the filler plug from the front drive axle

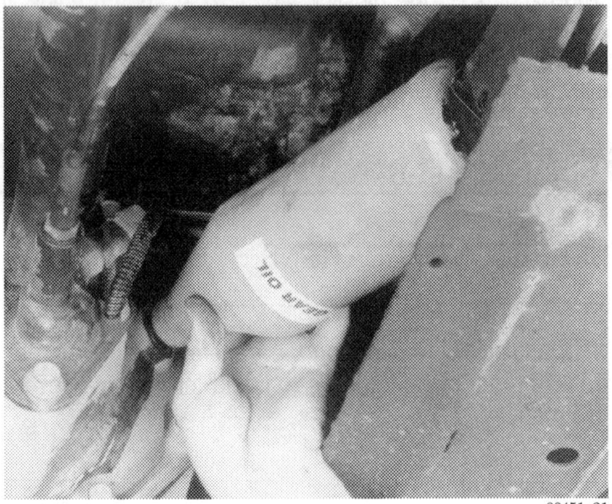

88451p21

Fig. 153 If necessary, add fluid through the filler plug opening

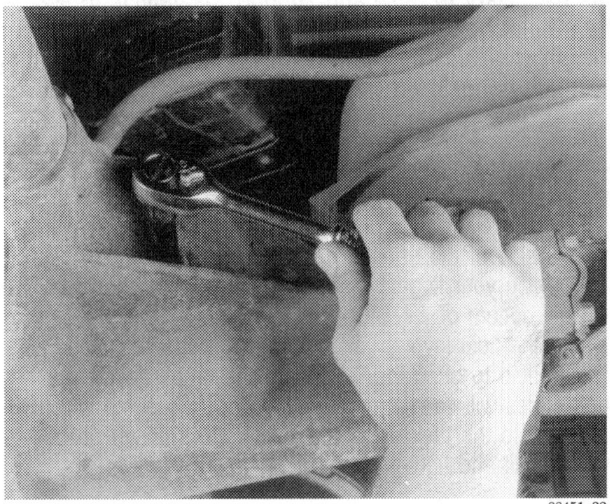

88451p22

Fig. 154 Remove the filler plug from the rear drive axle

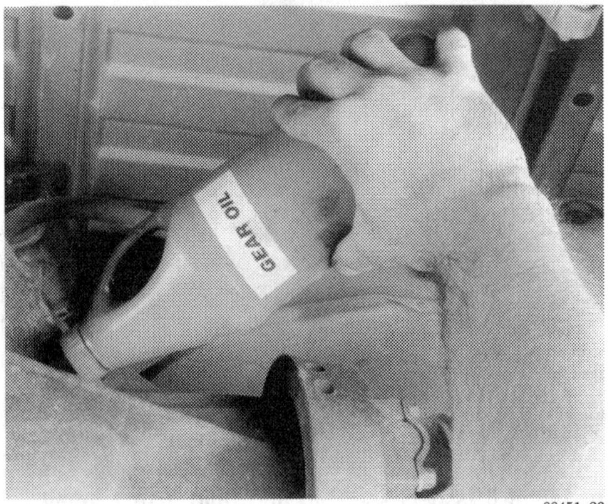

88451p23

Fig. 155 If necessary, add fluid through the filler plug opening

4. If necessary add fluid through the filler plug opening. A suction gun or a squeeze bulb may be used to add fluid. Most parts stores will carry a small, hand operated pump which will greatly ease the task of adding fluid.
5. Install and tighten the filler plug.
6. Remove the jackstands and carefully lower the vehicle.

DRAIN AND REFILL

Rear Axle

See Figures 156, 157, 158, 159 and 160

1. Run the vehicle until the lubricant reaches operating temperature.
2. If necessary for access, raise and support the vehicle safely using jackstands; but make sure that the vehicle is level.
3. Use a wire brush to clean the area around the differential. This will help prevent dirt from contaminating the differential housing while the cover is removed.
4. Position a drain pan under the rear axle.
5. Unscrew the retaining bolts and remove the rear cover. When removing the cover, a small prytool may be used at the base of the cover to gently pry it back from the axle housing, breaking the gasket seal and allowing the lubricant to drain out into the container. Be careful not to use excessive force and damage the cover or housing.

To install:

6. Carefully clean the gasket mating surfaces of the cover and axle housing of any remaining gasket or sealer. A putty knife is a good tool to use for this.
7. Install the rear cover using a new gasket and sealant. Tighten the retaining bolts using a crosswise pattern to 20 ft. lbs. (27 Nm).

Make sure the vehicle is level before attempting to add fluid to the rear axle or an incorrect fluid level will result.

8. Refill the rear axle housing using the proper grade and quantity of lubricant as detailed earlier in this section. Install the filler plug, operate the vehicle and check for any leaks.

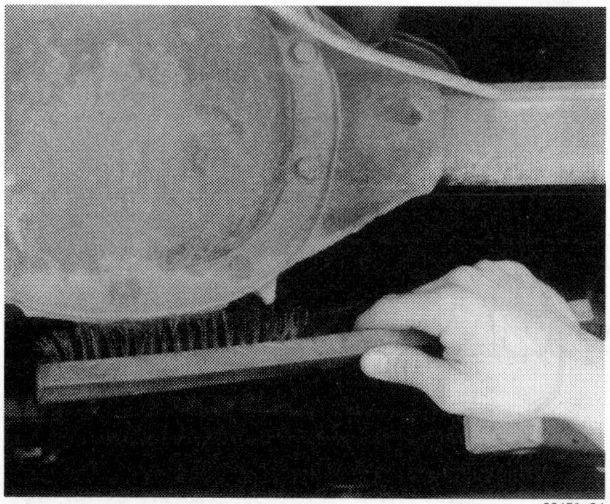
88451p24

Fig. 156 Clean the area around the rear differential using a wire brush

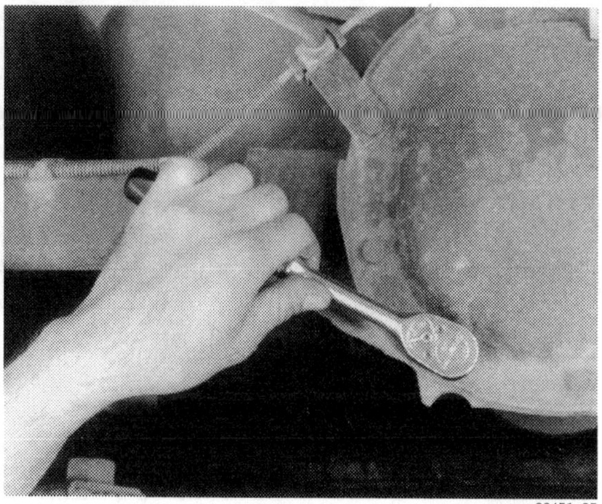
88451p25

Fig. 157 Remove the rear differential cover retaining bolts

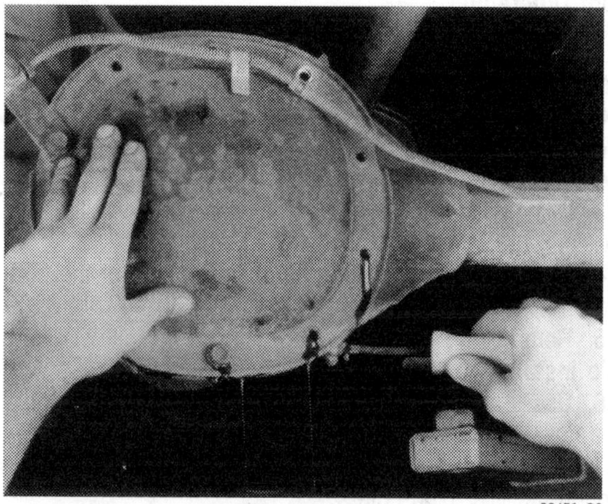
88451p26

Fig. 158 Use a small prytool to pry the cover away from the axle housing

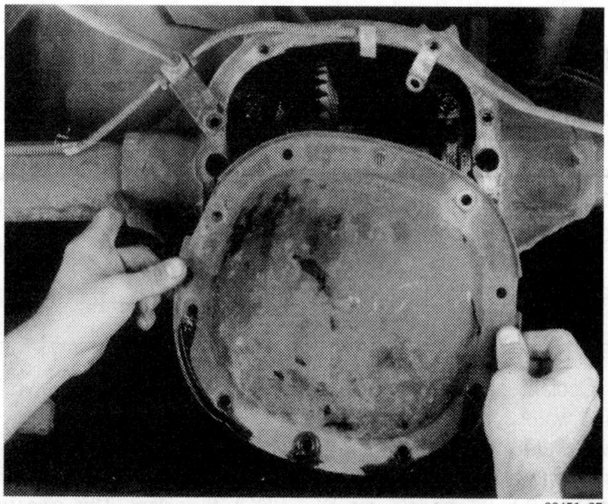
88451p27

Fig. 159 Remove the rear differential cover

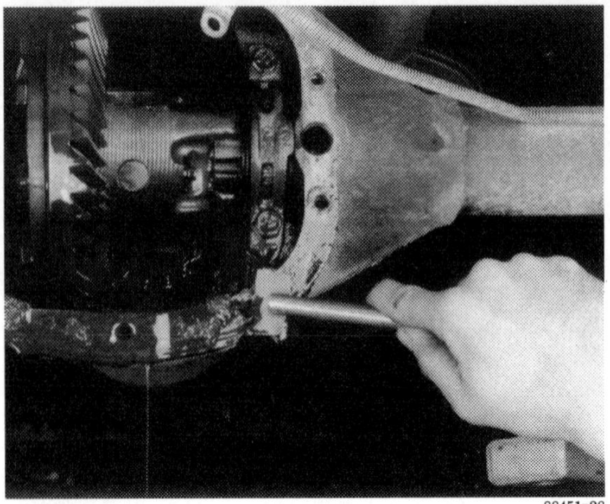

Fig. 160 Clean the old gasket from the surfaces of the cover and axle housing

Front Differential

1. Run the vehicle until the lubricant reaches operating temperature.
2. If necessary for access, raise and support the vehicle safely using jackstands; but make sure that the vehicle is level.
3. Using a floor jack, support the front axle. Position a drain pan under the front axle.
4. Remove the drain plug from the right side of the front axle, then drain the lubricant.
5. Remove the filler plug.

To install:

6. Use a sealant on the drain plug, then torque the plug to 24 ft. lbs. (33 Nm).
7. Using a suction gun or a squeeze bulb, install the fluid through the filler plug hole.
8. Using sealant, coat the filler plug threads, then torque the plug to 24 ft. lbs. (33 Nm).

Cooling System

The cooling system was filled at the factory with a high quality coolant solution that is good for year around operation and protects the system from freezing down to -20°F (-29°C) (-32°F/36°C in Canada).

The hot coolant level should be at the FULL HOT mark on the expansion tank and the cold coolant level should be at the FULL COLD mark on the tank. Do not remove the radiator cap to check the coolant level.

FLUID RECOMMENDATIONS

Coolant mixture in 1994-95 pick-ups is 50/50 ethylene glycol and water for year round use. Use a good quality anti-freeze with water pump lubricants, rust inhibitors and other corrosion inhibitors along with acid neutralizers.

The 1996-97 models use DEX-COOL™ coolant. This silicate free coolant is orange in color and does not require maintenance for 5 years or 100,000 miles (166,000 km). If additonal coolant needs to be added to the system, use only DEX-COOL™ or a silicate free orange coolant meeting GM spec 6277M. If another coolant type is added, the advantage of the prolonged maintence period is lost.

FLUID LEVEL CHECK

See Figures 161, 162, 163 and 164

1. Check the level on the see-through expansion tank.

CAUTION

The radiator coolant is under pressure when hot. To avoid the danger of physical harm, coolant level should be checked or replenished only when the engine is cold. To remove the radiator cap when the engine is hot, first cover the cap with a thick rag, or wear a heavy glove for protection. Press down on the cap slightly and slowly turn it counterclockwise until it reaches the first stop. Allow all the pressure to vent (indicated when the hissing sound stops). When the pressure is released, press down on the cap and continue to rotate it counterclockwise. Some radiator caps have a lever for venting the pressure, but you should still exercise extreme caution when removing the cap.

2. Check the level and, if necessary, add the proper type of coolant (see fluid recommendations) through the expansion tank to the proper level. Anti-freeze solutions should be used, even in summer, to prevent rust and to take advantage of the solution's higher boiling point compared to plain water. This is imperative on air conditioned vehicles; the heater core can freeze if it isn't protected. Coolant should be added through the coolant recovery tank, not the radiator filler neck.

WARNING

Never add large quantities of cold coolant to a hot engine! A cracked engine block may result!

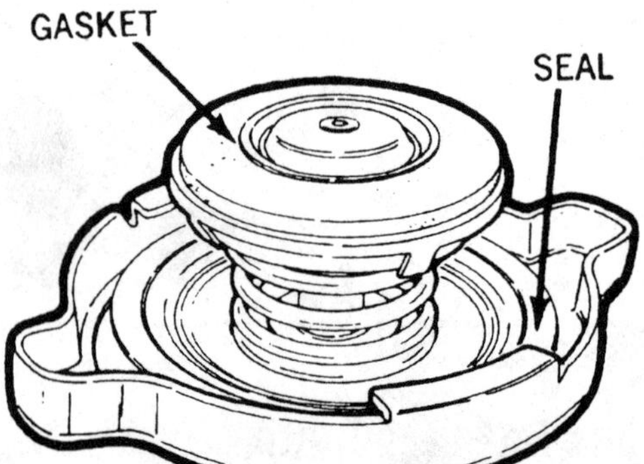

Fig. 161 Be sure the rubber gasket on the radiator cap has a tight seal

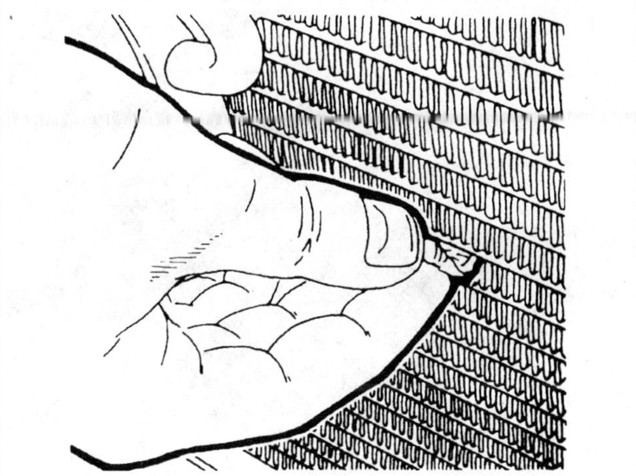

Fig. 162 Periodically remove all debris from the radiator fins

Fig. 164 Cooling systems should be pressure tested for leaks periodically

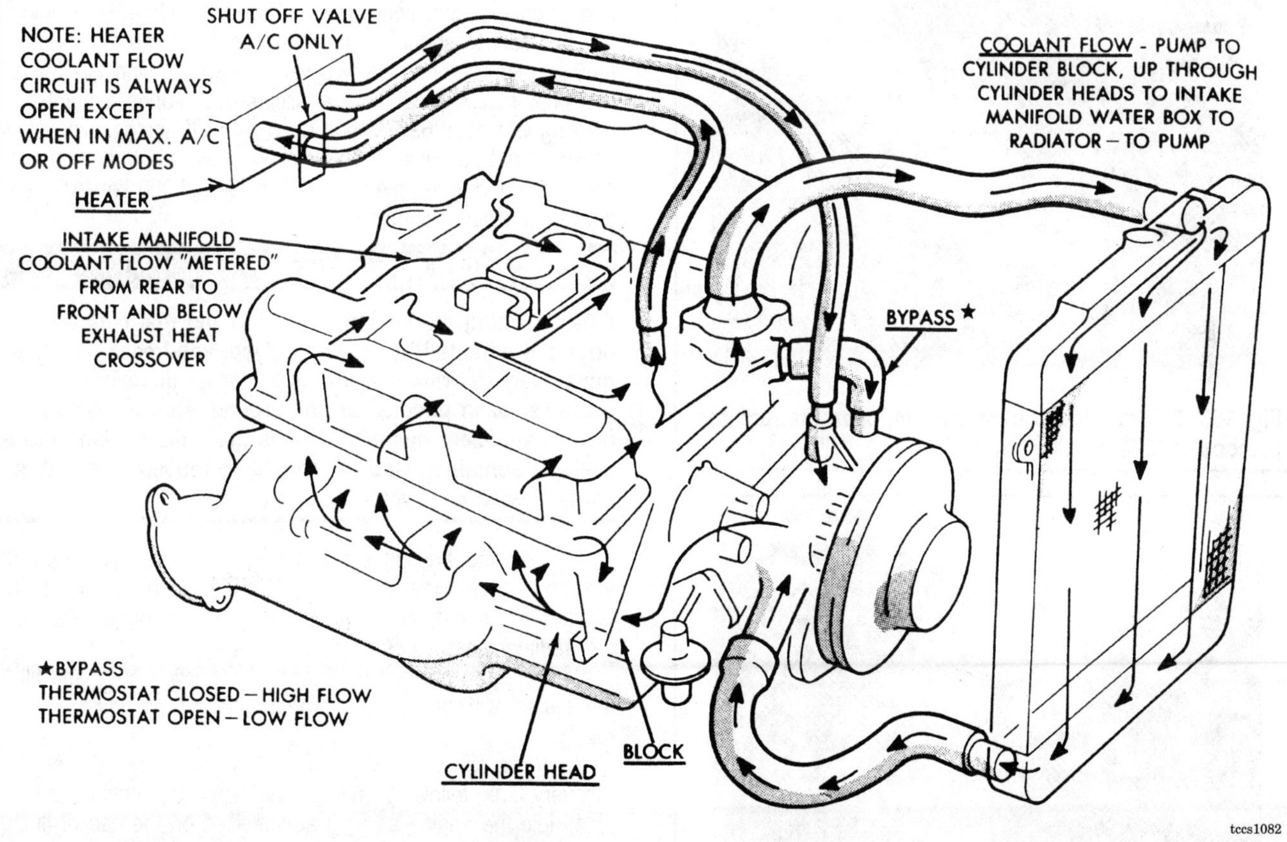

Fig. 163 Cutaway view of a typical cooling system flow

Each year the cooling system should be serviced as follows:

- Wash the radiator cap and filler neck with clean water.
- Check the coolant for proper level and freeze protection.
- Have the system pressure tested at psi. (103 kPa), If a replacement cap is installed, be sure that it conforms to the original specifications.
- Tighten the hose clamps and inspect all hoses. Replace hoses that are swollen, cracked or otherwise deteriorated.
- Clean the frontal area of the radiator core and the air conditioning condenser, if so equipped.

DRAINING AND FLUSHING

See Figures 165, 166, 167, 168, 169, 170 and 171

The cooling system in your vehicle accumulates some internal rust and corrosion in its normal operation. A simple method of keeping the system clean is known as flushing the system. It is performed by circulating a can of radiator flush through the system, and then draining and refilling the system with the normal coolant. Radiator flush is marketed by several different manufacturers, and is available in cans at auto departments, parts stores, and many hardware stores. On 1994-95 models, this operation should be performed every 30,000 miles (48,000 km) or once a year (whichever comes first). On 1996-97 models, this service should be performed every 100,000 miles (166,000 km) or once every 5 years. Keep in mind this holds true only if DEX-COOL™ or a silicate free orange coolant meeting GM spec 6277M has been used. If another type of coolant has been used in this system, then this operation should be performed every 30,000 miles (48,000 km) or once a year (whichever comes first).

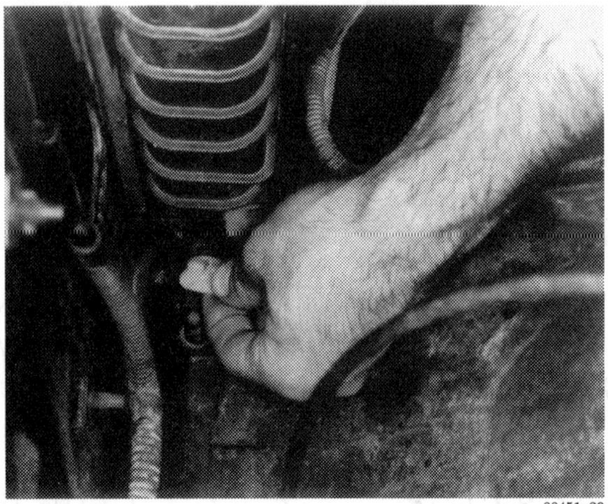

88451p29

Fig. 165 To drain the cooling system, open the radiator petcock — 1994 model shown

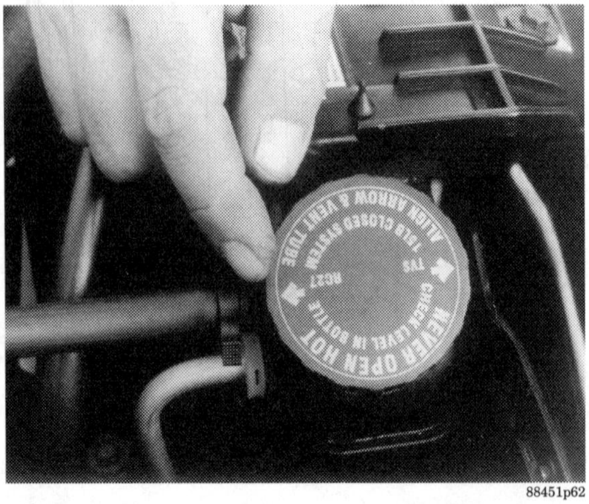

88451p62

Fig. 166 Read the instructions on the radiator cap before removing it — 1996 model shown

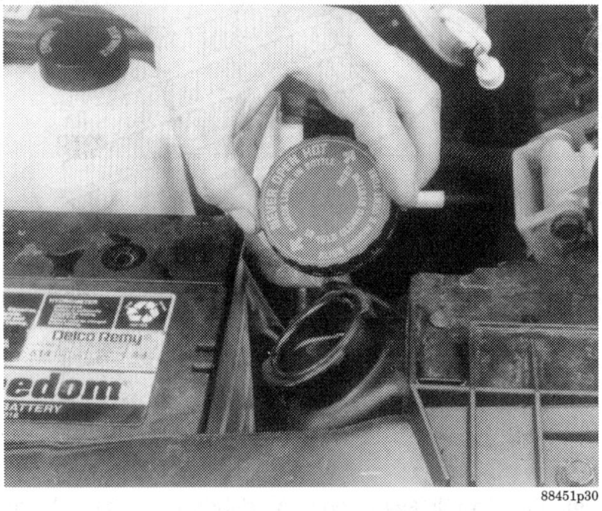

88451p30

Fig. 167 Remove the radiator cap — 1994 model shown

****CAUTION**

When draining the coolant, keep in mind that cats and dogs are attracted by ethylene glycol anti-freeze, and are quite likely to drink any that is left in an uncovered container or in puddles on the ground. This will prove fatal in sufficient quantity. Always drain the coolant into a sealable container. Coolant should be reused unless it is contaminated or several years old.

1. Drain the existing anti-freeze and coolant. Open the radiator and engine drain petcocks (located near the bottom of the radiator and engine block, respectively), or disconnect the bottom radiator hose at the radiator outlet.
2. Close the petcock or reconnect the lower hose and fill the system with water — hot water if the system has just been run.
3. Add a can of quality radiator flush to the radiator or recovery tank, following any special instructions on the can.
4. Idle the engine as long as specified on the can of flush, or until the upper radiator hose gets hot.
5. Drain the system again. There should be quite a bit of scale and rust in the drained water.
6. Repeat this process until the drained water is mostly clear.
7. Close all petcocks and connect all hoses.
8. Flush the coolant recovery reservoir with water and leave empty.

88451p31

Fig. 168 Add a 50/50 mix of ethylene glycol, or other suitable antifreeze, and water — 1994 model shown

88451p63

Fig. 169 Removing the cap from the coolant recovery tank — 1996 model shown

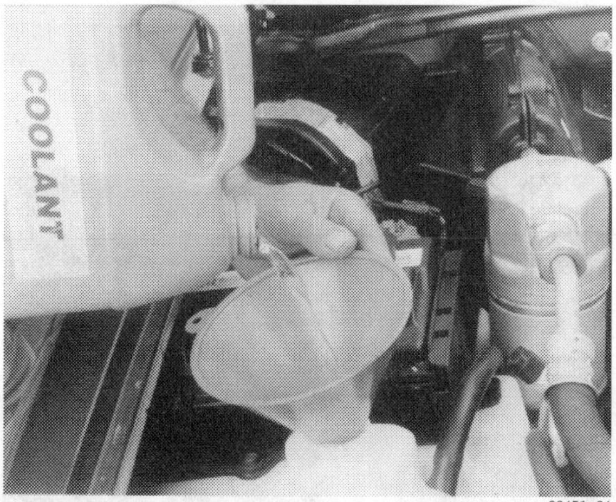

88451p64

Fig. 170 Adding coolant to the recovery tank — 1996 model shown

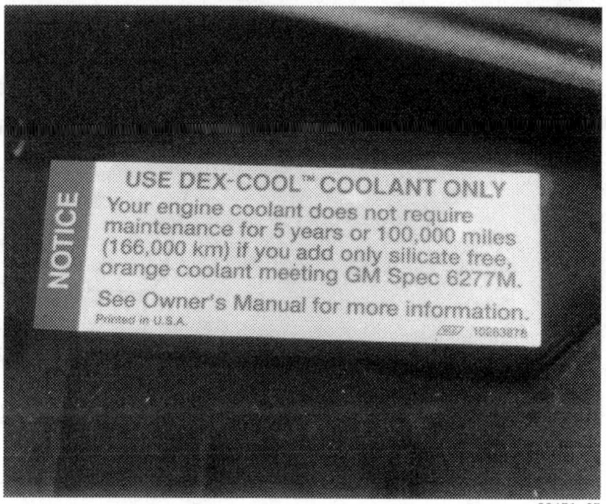

88451p65

Fig. 171 As this label indicates, 1996 and newer models use DEX-COOL coolant

9. Determine the capacity of your truck's cooling system (see the Capacities chart in this guide). Fill the cooling system with the proper type of coolant (refer to fluid recommendations).

10. Run the engine to operating temperature, then stop the engine and check for leaks. Check the coolant level and top up if necessary.

11. Check the protection level of your anti-freeze mix with an anti-freeze tester (a small, inexpensive syringe type device available at any auto parts store). The tester has five or six small colored balls inside, each of which signify a certain temperature rating. Insert the tester in the recovery tank and suck just enough coolant into the syringe to float as many individual balls as you can (without sucking in too much coolant and floating all the balls at once). A table supplied with the tester will explain how many floating balls equal protection down to a certain temperature (three floating balls might mean the coolant will protect your engine down to +5°F (-15°C), for example.

Brake Master Cylinder

FLUID RECOMMENDATIONS

➧ See Figure 172

Use only heavy-duty Delco Supreme 11 or DOT-3 brake fluid.

✱✱WARNING

Brake fluid damages paint. It also absorbs moisture from the air; never leave a container or the master cylinder uncovered any longer than necessary. All parts in contact with the brake fluid (master cylinder, hoses, plunger assemblies and etc.) must be kept clean, since any contamination of the brake fluid will adversely affect braking performance.

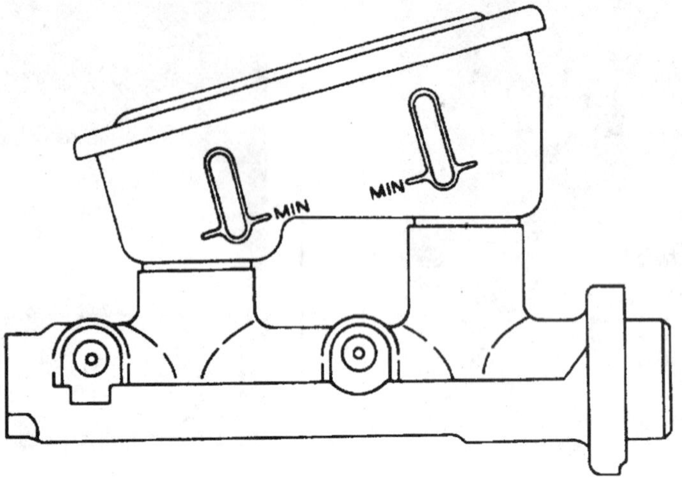

Fig. 172 Most master cylinder reservoirs are marked with MIN level fill lines

FLUID LEVEL CHECK

See Figures 173, 174 and 175

It should be obvious how important the brake system is to safe operation of your vehicle. The brake fluid is key to the proper operation of the brake system. Low levels of fluid indicate a need for service (there may be a leak in the system or the brake pads may just be worn and in need of replacement). In any case, the brake fluid level should be inspected at least during every oil change, but more often is desirable. Every time you open the hood is a good time to glance at the master cylinder reservoir.

The master cylinder is mounted to the left side of the firewall.

The brake fluid level can be checked by observing the MIN and MAX marks on the side of the reservoir.

1. Clean all of the dirt from around the cover of the master cylinder.
2. Be sure that the vehicle is resting on a level surface.

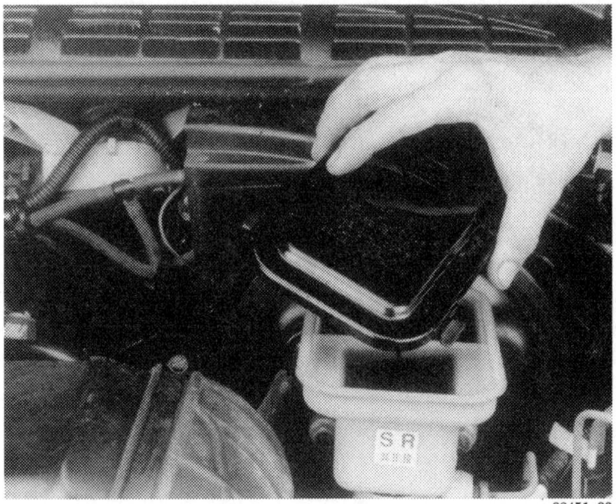

Fig. 174 Remove the master cylinder cover

Fig. 173 The fluid level can be checked by looking at the level marks on the reservoir

Fig. 175 If necessary, add brake fluid until the level is correct

3. Pull up on the tabs on the top of the master cylinder to release the cover.
4. The fluid level should be approximately 1/4 in. (6mm) from the top of the master cylinder or at least above the **MIN** mark. If not, add fluid until the level is correct. Replacement fluid should be Delco Supreme No. 11, DOT 3, or its equivalent. It is normal for the fluid level to fall as the disc brake pads wear.

*****WARNING**

Brake fluid dissolves paint! It also absorbs moisture from the air. Never leave a container or the master cylinder uncovered any longer than necessary!

5. Install the cover of the master cylinder. On most models there is a rubber gasket under the cover, which fits into 2 slots on the cover. Be sure that this is seated properly.
6. Push the cover back into place and be sure that it seats correctly.

Clutch Master Cylinder

FLUID RECOMMENDATIONS

Use only heavy duty Delco Supreme 11 or DOT-3 brake fluid.

FLUID LEVEL CHECK

See Figures 176 and 177

The clutch master cylinder is located on the firewall in the engine compartment.

1. Clean all of the dirt from around the cover of the master cylinder.
2. Be sure that the vehicle is resting on a level surface.
3. Carefully remove the cover from the master cylinder.

88451p35

Fig. 176 Remove the clutch master cylinder cover

88451p36

Fig. 177 If necessary, add DOT-3 brake fluid to achieve the proper fluid level

4. The fluid level should be approximately 1/4 in. (6mm) from the top of the master cylinder or at least above the **MIN** mark. If not, add fluid until the level is correct. Replacement fluid should be Delco Supreme No. 11, DOT 3, or its equivalent.
5. Install the cover of the master cylinder.

Power Steering Pump

FLUID RECOMMENDATION

Use GM Power Steering fluid, or its equivalent.

FLUID LEVEL CHECK

See Figures 178, 179, 180 and 181

➡On models equipped with a remote reservoir, the fluid level should be 1/2-1 in. (13-25.4mm) from the top when the wheels are turned to the extreme left position.

The power steering pump reservoir is located at the front left-side of the engine.

Check the dipstick in the pump reservoir when the fluid is at operating temperature. The fluid should be between the **HOT** and **COLD** marks. If the fluid is at room temperature, the fluid should be between the **ADD** and **COLD** marks. The fluid does not require periodic changing.

On systems with a remote reservoir, the level should be maintained approximately 1/2-1 in. (13-25mm) from the top with the wheels in the full left turn position.

Steering Gear

FLUID RECOMMENDATIONS

Use GM Lubricant (part No. 1051052) or equivalent.

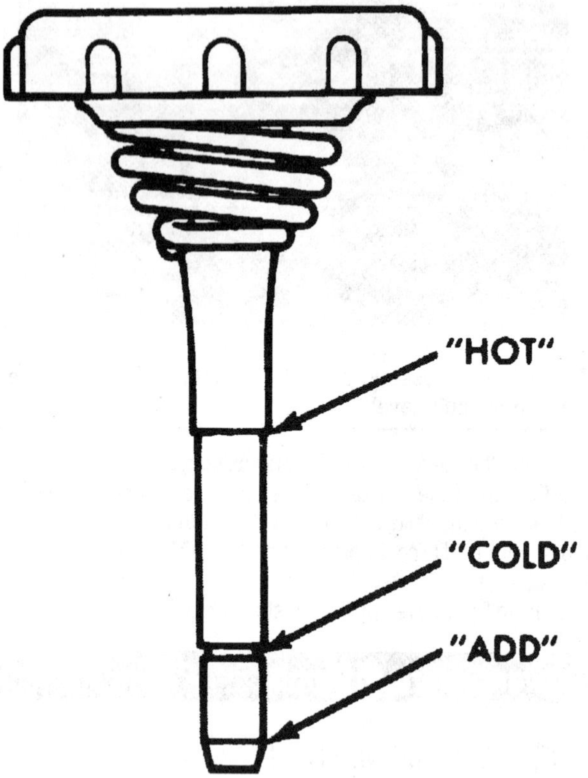

85381087

Fig. 178 The power steering reservoir cap/dipstick is marked for proper fluid levels

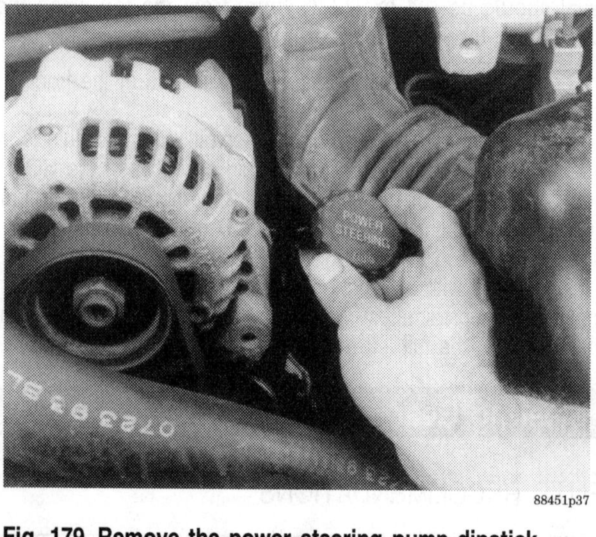

88451p37

Fig. 179 Remove the power steering pump dipstick

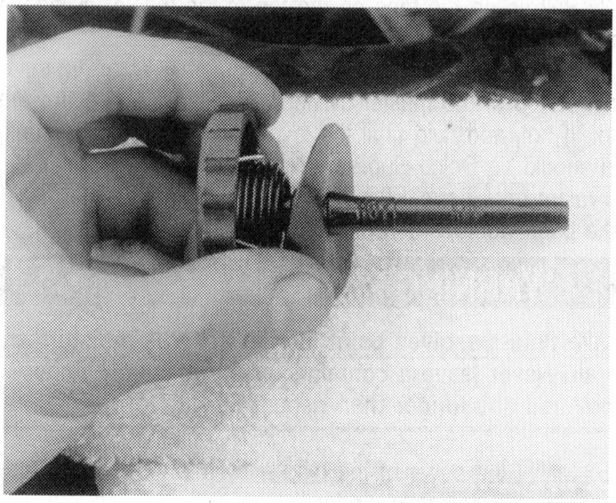

88451p38

Fig. 180 Check the level of the power steering fluid on the dipstick

88451p39

Fig. 181 If necessary, add the proper amount of power steering fluid

FLUID LEVEL CHECK

No lubrication is needed for the life of the gear, except in the event of seal replacement or overhaul, when the gear should be refilled with a 13 oz. container of Steering Gear Lubricant (Part No. 1051052) which meets GM Specification GM 4673M, or its equivalent.

Windshield Washer Reservoir

FLUID RECOMMENDATIONS AND LEVEL CHECK

The windshield washer pump fluid reservoir is a plastic container usually found on the side of the engine compartment near the wiper motor. The reservoir should be filled to the top of the container using a wiper fluid solution which can be found at most automotive stores. Do not further dilute the solution (unless it is sold in concentrate, then follow the manufacturer's instructions), as this will adversely affect its ability to keep from freezing at low temperatures. Also, never place another fluid, such as ethylene glycol antifreeze in the reservoir as other fluids could damage pump seals.

Chassis Greasing

Chassis greasing should be performed every 6 months or 7,500 miles for trucks used in normal/light service. More frequent greasing is recommended for trucks in heavy/severe usage; about every 3 months or 3,000 miles. Greasing can be performed with a commercial pressurized grease gun or at home by using a hand-operated grease gun. Wipe the grease fittings clean before greasing in order to prevent the possibility of forcing any dirt into the component.

The four wheel drive front driveshaft requires special attention for lubrication. The large constant velocity joint at the front of the transfer case has a special grease fitting in the centering ball. A special needle nose adapter for a flush type fitting is required, as well as a special lubricant (GM part No. 1052497). You can only get at this fitting when it is facing up toward the floorboard, so you need a flexible hose, too.

Water resistant EP chassis lubricant (grease) conforming to GM specification 6031-M (GM part No. 1052497) should be used for all chassis grease points.

Every year or 7500 miles (12,067 km) the front suspension ball joints, both upper and lower on each side of the truck, must be greased. Most trucks covered in this guide should be equipped with grease nipples on the ball joints, although some may have plugs which must be removed and nipples fitted.

⁂WARNING

Do not pump so much grease into the ball joint that excess grease squeezes out of the rubber boot. This destroys the watertight seal.

1. Raise up the front end of the truck and safely support it with jackstands. Block the rear wheels and firmly apply the parking brake.
2. If the truck has been parked in temperatures below 20°F (-7°C) for any length of time, park it in a heated garage for an hour or so until the ball joints loosen up enough to accept the grease.
3. Depending on which front wheel you work on first, turn the wheel and tire outward, either full-lock right or full-lock left. You now have the ends of the upper and lower suspension control arms in front of you; the grease nipples are visible pointing up (top ball joint) and down (lower ball joint) through the end of each control arm.
4. If the nipples are not accessible enough, remove the wheel and tire.
5. Wipe all dirt and crud from the nipples or from around the plugs (if installed). If plugs are on the truck, remove them and install grease nipples in the holes (nipples are available in various thread sizes at most auto parts stores).
6. Using a hand operated, low pressure grease gun loaded with a quality chassis grease, grease the ball joint only until the rubber joint boot begins to swell out.

The steering linkage should be greased at the same interval as the ball joints. Grease nipples are installed on the steering tie rod ends on most models.

7. Wipe all dirt and crud from around the nipples at each tie rod end.
8. Using a hand operated, low pressure grease gun loaded with a suitable chassis grease, grease the linkage until the old grease begins to squeeze out around the tie rod ends.
9. Wipe off the nipples and any excess grease. Also grease the nipples on the steering idler arms.

Use chassis grease on the parking brake cable where it contacts the cable guides, levers and linkage.

Apply a small amount of clean engine oil to the kickdown and shift linkage points at 7500 mile (12,000 km) intervals.

Body Lubrication And Maintenance

LOCK CYLINDERS

Apply graphite lubricant sparingly through the key slot. Insert the key and operate the lock several times to be sure that the lubricant is worked into the lock cylinder.

HOOD LATCH AND HINGES

Clean the latch surfaces and apply clean engine oil to the latch pilot bolts and the spring anchor. Also lubricate the hood hinges with engine oil. Use a chassis grease to lubricate all the pivot points in the latch release mechanism.

DOOR HINGES

The gas tank filler door and truck doors should be wiped clean and lubricated with clean engine oil once a year. The door lock cylinders and latch mechanisms should be lubricated periodically with a few drops of graphite lock lubricant or a few shots of silicone spray.

BODY DRAIN HOLES

Be sure that the drain holes in the doors and rocker panels are cleared of obstruction. A small punch, screwdriver or unbent wire coat hanger can be used to clear them of any debris.

Front Wheel Bearings

➧ **See Figure 182**

Only the front wheel bearings on 2WD models require periodic maintenance. A premium high melting point grease meeting GM specification 6031-M must be used. Long fiber type greases must not be used. This service is recommended at the intervals in the Maintenance Intervals Chart or whenever the truck has been driven in water up to the hubs.

Before handling the bearings, there are a few things that you should remember to do and not to do.

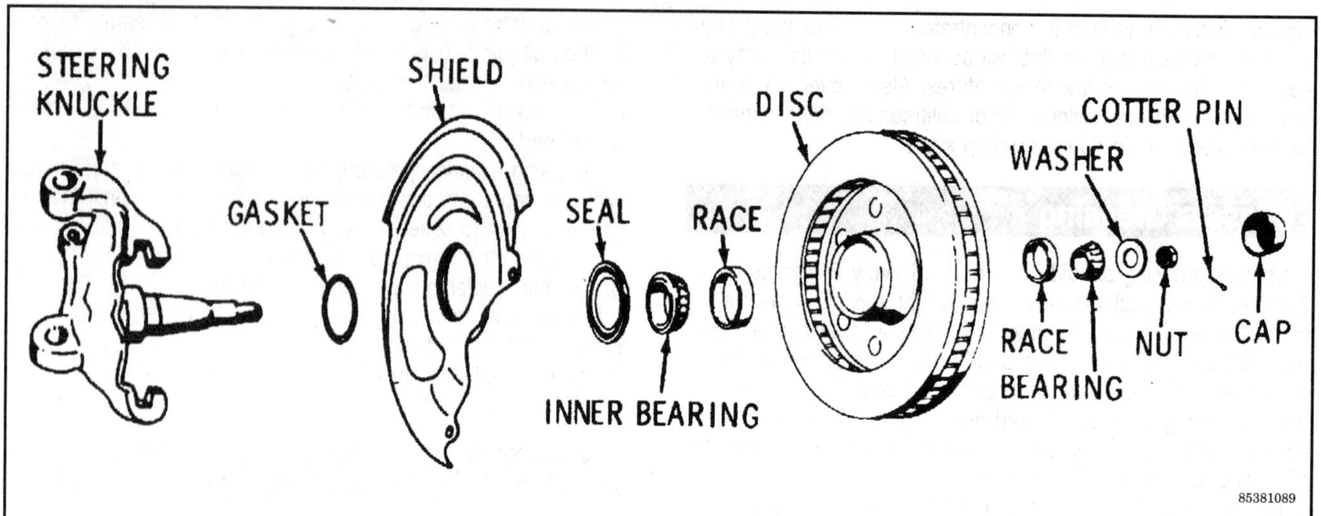

Fig. 182 Exploded view of a common 2WD front hub and bearing assembly

Remember to do the following:

- Remove all outside dirt from the housing before exposing the bearing.
- Treat a used bearing as gently as you would a new one.
- Work with clean tools in clean surroundings.
- Use clean, dry canvas gloves, or at least clean, dry hands.
- Clean solvents and flushing fluids are a must.
- Use clean paper when laying out the bearings to dry.
- Protect disassembled bearings from rust and dirt. Cover them up.
- Use clean rags to wipe bearings.
- Keep the bearings in oil-proof paper when they are to be stored or are not in use.
- Clean the inside of the housing before replacing the bearing.

Do not do the following:

- Don't work in dirty surroundings.
- Don't use dirty, chipped or damaged tools.
- Try not to work on wooden work benches or use wooden mallets.
- Don't handle bearings with dirty or moist hands.
- Do not use gasoline for cleaning; use a safe solvent.
- Do not spin-dry bearings with compressed air. They will be damaged.
- Do not spin dirty bearings.
- Avoid using cotton waste or dirty cloths to wipe bearings.
- Try not to scratch or nick bearing surfaces.
- Do not allow the bearing to come in contact with dirt or rust at any time.

REMOVAL, PACKING & INSTALLATION

➡Sodium-based grease is not compatible with lithium-based grease. Read the package labels and be careful not to mix the two types. If there is any doubt as to the type of grease used, completely clean the old grease from the bearing and hub before replacing.

2-Wheel Drive Models

➧ See Figures 183, 184, 185, 186, 187, 188, 189, 190, 191, 192, 193, 194, 195 and 196

1. Raise and support the front of the vehicle safely using jackstands.
2. Remove the tire and wheel assembly.
3. Remove the brake caliper mounting bolts and carefully remove the caliper (along with the brake pads) from the rotor. Do not disconnect the brake line; instead wire the caliper out of the way with the line still connected. Refer to Section 9 of this manual for this procedure.
4. Carefully pry out the grease cap, then remove the cotter pin, spindle nut, and washer.
5. Remove the hub, being careful not to drop the outer wheel bearings. As the hub is pulled forward, the outer wheel bearings will often fall forward and they may easily be removed at this time.
6. If not done already, remove the outer roller bearing assembly from the hub. The inner bearing assembly will remain in the hub and may be removed from the rear of the hub after

Fig. 183 Pry the dust cap from the hub, taking care not to distort or damage its flange

TCCS8025

Fig. 184 Once the bent ends are cut, grasp the cotter pin and pull or pry it free of the spindle

TCCS8026

Fig. 185 If difficulty is encountered, gently tap on the pliers with a hammer to help free the cotter pin

TCCS8027

Fig. 186 Loosen and remove the castellated nut from the spindle

TCCS8028

Fig. 187 Remove the washer from the spindle

TCCS8029

Fig. 188 With the nut and washer out of the way, the outer bearing may be removed from the hub

TCCS8030

Fig. 189 Pull the hub and inner bearing assembly from the spindle

TCCS8031

Fig. 190 Use a small prytool to remove the old inner bearing seal

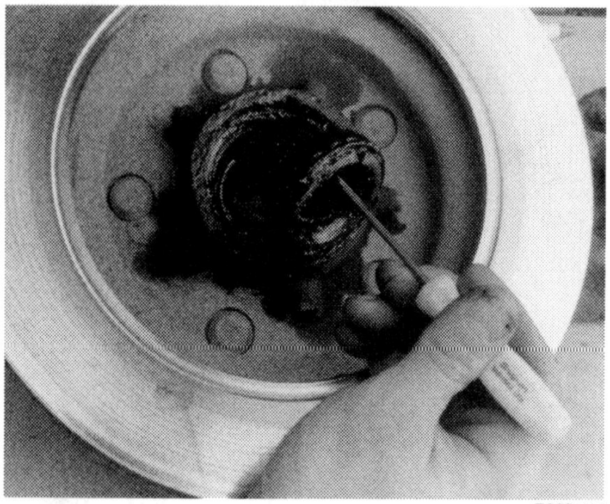

TCCS8032

Fig. 191 With the seal removed, the inner bearing may be withdrawn from the hub

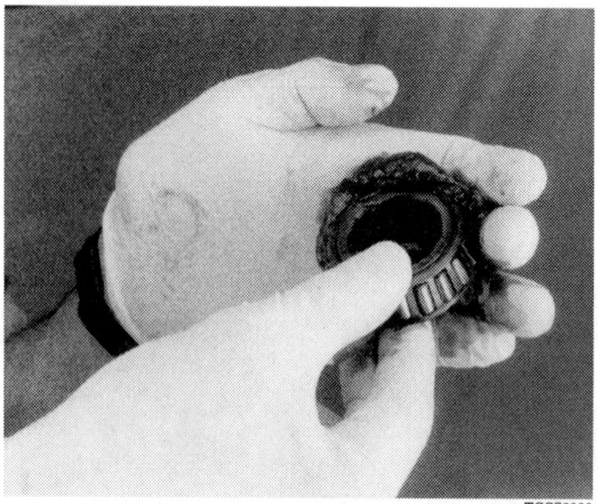

TCCS8033

Fig. 192 Thoroughly pack the bearing with fresh, high temperature wheel-bearing grease before installation

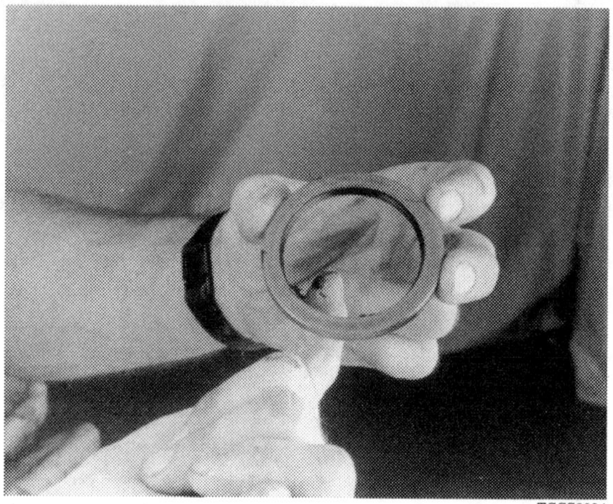

TCCS8034

Fig. 193 Apply a thin coat of fresh grease to the new inner bearing seal lip

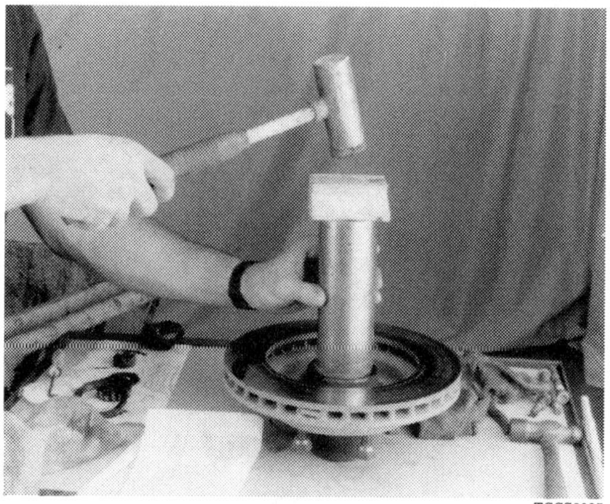

TCCS8035

Fig. 194 Use a suitably sized driver to install the inner bearing seal to the hub

TCCS8036

Fig. 195 Tighten the nut to specifications while gently spinning the wheel, then adjust the bearing

TCCS8037

Fig. 196 After the bearings are adjusted, install the dust cap by gently tapping on its flange

prying out the inner seal with a small prybar. Discard the seal after removal.

To install:

7. Clean all parts in a non-flammable solvent and let them air dry. Never spin-dry a bearing with compressed air! Check for excessive wear and damage.

➡DO NOT remove the bearing races from the hub, unless they show signs of damage.

8. If it is necessary to remove the wheel bearing races, use the GM front bearing race removal tool No. J-29117 or equivalent, to drive the races from the hub/disc assembly. A hammer and drift may be used to drive the races from the hub, but the race removal tool is quicker.
9. If the bearing races were removed, place the replacement races in the freezer for a few minutes and then install them to the hub:
   a. Lightly lubricate the inside of the hub/disc assembly using wheel bearing grease.
   b. Using the GM seal installation tools No. J-8092 and J-8850 or equivalent, drive the inner bearing race into the hub/disc assembly until it seats. Make sure the race is properly seated against the hub shoulder and is not cocked.

➡When installing the bearing races, be sure to support the hub/disc assembly with GM tool No. J-9746-02 or equivalent.

   c. Using the GM seal installation tools No. J-8092 and J-8457 or equivalent, drive the outer race into the hub/disc assembly until it seats.
10. Pack both wheel bearings using high melting point wheel bearing grease for disc brakes. Ordinary grease will melt and ooze out ruining the pads. Bearings should be packed using a cone-type wheel bearing greaser tool. If one is not available they may be packed by hand as follows:
   a. Place a healthy glob of grease in the palm of one hand.
   b. Force the edge of the bearing into it so that the grease fills the bearing. Do this until the whole bearing is packed.
11. Place the inner bearing in the hub, then apply a thin coating of grease to the sealing lip and install a new inner seal, making sure the seal flange faces the bearing cup.

➡Although a seal installation tool is preferable, a section of pipe with a smooth edge or a suitably sized socket may be used to drive the seal into position. Make sure the seal is flush with the outer surface of the hub assembly.

12. Carefully install the wheel hub over the spindle.
13. Using your hands, firmly press the outer bearing into the hub.
14. Loosely install the spindle washer and nut, but do not install the cotter pin or dust cap at this time.
15. Install the brake caliper.
16. Install the tire and wheel assembly.
17. Properly adjust the wheel bearings, then install a new cotter pin and the dust cap.
18. Install the wheel/hub cover, then remove the supports and carefully lower the vehicle.

4-Wheel Drive Models

These axles have integral hub/bearing assemblies. No periodic service is required. See Section 7 for disassembly details.

ADJUSTMENT

1. Raise and support the vehicle safely using a jackstand under the lower control arm.
2. If equipped, remove the wheel/hub cover for access, then remove the dust cap from the hub.
3. Remove the cotter pin and loosen the spindle nut.
4. Spin the wheel forward by hand and tighten the nut to 12 ft. lbs. (16 Nm) in order to fully seat the bearings and remove any burrs from the threads.
5. Back off the nut until it is just loose, then finger-tighten the nut.
6. Loosen the nut $1/4$-$1/2$ turn until either hole in the spindle lines up with a slot in the nut, then install a new cotter pin. This may appear to be too loose, but it is the correct adjustment.

➡Proper adjustment creates 0.001-0.005 in. (0.025-0.127mm) end-play.

TRAILER TOWING

➧ See Figure 197

General Recommendations

It is important to remember that towing a trailer will place additional loads on your vehicle's engine, drive train, steering, braking and other systems. However, if you decide to tow a trailer, using the proper equipment is a must.

Local laws may require specific equipment such as trailer brakes or fender mounted mirrors. Check your local laws.

Trailer Weight

The weight of the trailer is the most important factor. A good weight-to-horsepower ratio is about 35:1, 35 lbs. of Gross Combined Weight (GCW) for every horsepower your engine develops. Multiply the engine's rated horsepower by 35 and subtract the weight of the vehicle passengers and luggage. The number remaining is the approximate ideal maximum weight you should tow, although a numerically higher axle ratio can help compensate for heavier weight.

Hitch (Tongue) Weight

Calculate the hitch weight in order to select a proper hitch. The weight of the hitch is usually 9-11% of the trailer gross weight and should be measured with the trailer loaded. Hitches fall into various categories: those that mount on the frame and rear bumper, the bolt-on type, or the weld-on distribution type used for larger trailers. Axle mounted or clamp-on bumper hitches should never be used.

Check the gross weight rating of your trailer. Tongue weight is usually figured as 10% of gross trailer weight. Therefore, a trailer with a maximum gross weight of 2000 lbs. will have a maximum tongue weight of 200 lbs. Class I trailers fall into this category. Class II trailers are those with a gross weight rating of 2000-3000 lbs., while Class III trailers fall into the 3500-6000 lbs. category. Class IV trailers are those over 6000 lbs. and are for use with fifth wheel trucks, only.

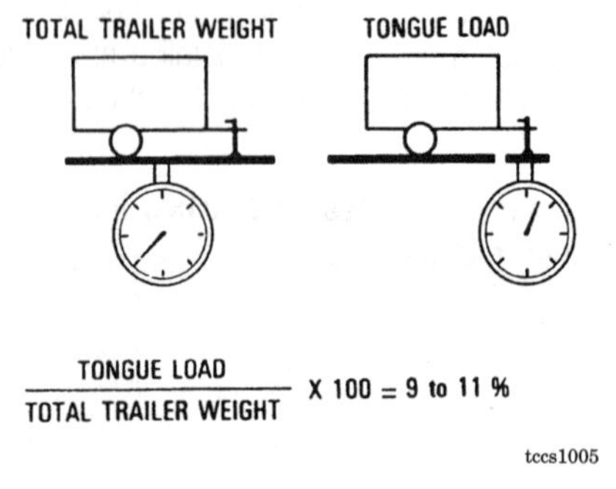

Fig. 197 Calculating proper tongue weight for your trailer

When you've determined the hitch that you'll need, follow the manufacturer's installation instructions, exactly, especially when it comes to fastener torques. The hitch will subjected to a lot of stress and good hitches come with hardened bolts. Never substitute an inferior bolt for a hardened bolt.

Cooling

ENGINE

Overflow Tank

One of the most common, if not THE most common, problems associated with trailer towing is engine overheating. If you have a cooling system without an expansion tank, you'll definitely need to get an aftermarket expansion tank kit, preferably one with at least a 2 quart capacity. These kits are easily installed on the radiator's overflow hose, and come with a pressure cap designed for expansion tanks.

Flex Fan

Another helpful accessory for vehicles using a belt-driven radiator fan is a flex fan. These fans are large diameter units designed to provide more airflow at low speeds, by using fan blades that have deeply cupped surfaces. The blades then flex, or flatten out, at high speed, when less cooling air is needed. These fans are far lighter in weight than stock fans, requiring less horsepower to drive them. Also, they are far quieter than stock fans. If you do decide to replace your stock fan with a flex fan, note that if your vehicle has a fan clutch, a spacer will be needed between the flex fan and water pump hub.

Oil Cooler

Aftermarket engine oil coolers are helpful for prolonging engine oil life and reducing overall engine temperatures. Both of these factors increase engine life. While not absolutely necessary in towing Class I and some Class II trailers, they are recommended for heavier Class II and all Class III towing. Engine oil cooler systems usually consist of an adapter, screwed on in place of the oil filter, a remote filter mounting and a multi-tube, finned heat exchanger, which is mounted in front of the radiator or air conditioning condenser.

TRANSMISSION

An automatic transmission is usually recommended for trailer towing. Modern automatics have proven reliable and, of course, easy to operate, in trailer towing. The increased load of a trailer, however, causes an increase in the temperature of the automatic transmission fluid. Heat is the worst enemy of an automatic transmission. As the temperature of the fluid increases, the life of the fluid decreases.

It is essential, therefore, that you install an automatic transmission cooler. The cooler, which consists of a multi-tube, finned heat exchanger, is usually installed in front of the radiator or air conditioning compressor, and hooked in-line with the transmission cooler tank inlet line. Follow the cooler manufacturer's installation instructions.

Select a cooler of at least adequate capacity, based upon the combined gross weights of the vehicle and trailer.

Cooler manufacturers recommend that you use an aftermarket cooler in addition to, and not instead of, the present cooling tank in your radiator. If you do want to use it in place of the radiator cooling tank, get a cooler at least two sizes larger than normally necessary.

➡A transmission cooler can, sometimes, cause slow or harsh shifting in the transmission during cold weather, until the fluid has a chance to come up to normal operating temperature. Some coolers can be purchased with or retrofitted with a temperature bypass valve which will allow fluid flow through the cooler only when the fluid has reached above a certain operating temperature.

Handling A Trailer

Towing a trailer with ease and safety requires a certain amount of experience. It's a good idea to learn the feel of a trailer by practicing turning, stopping and backing in an open area such as an empty parking lot.

TOWING THE VEHICLE

General Information

2-WHEEL DRIVE

Chevrolet and GMC Pick-ups can be towed on all four wheels (flat towed) at speeds of less than 35 mph (56 kph), for distances less than 50 miles (80 kph), providing that the axle, driveline and engine/transmission are normally operable. The transmission should be in Neutral, the engine off, the steering unlocked, and the parking brake released.

The rear wheels must be raised off the ground or the driveshaft disconnected when the transmission if not operating properly, or when speeds of over 35 mph (56 kph) will be used or when towing more than 50 miles. (80 kph).

Do not attach chains to the bumpers or bracketing. All attachments must be made to the structural members. Safety chains should be used. It should also be remembered that power steering and brake assists will not be working with the engine off.

4-WHEEL DRIVE

Remember that the power steering and power brakes will not have their power assist with the engine off. The only safe way to tow is with a tow bar. The steering column must be unlocked and the parking brake released. Attachments should be made to the frame and to the bumper or its brackets. Safety chains are also required.

JUMP STARTING A DEAD BATTERY

➧ See Figure 198

Whenever a vehicle is jump started, precautions must be followed in order to prevent the possibility of personal injury. Remember that batteries contain a small amount of explosive hydrogen gas which is a by-product of battery charging. Sparks should always be avoided when working around batteries, especially when attaching jumper cables. To minimize the possibility of accidental sparks, follow the procedure carefully.

✲✲CAUTION

NEVER hook the batteries up in a series circuit or the entire electrical system will go up in smoke, including the starter!

Vehicles equipped with a diesel engine may utilize two 12 volt batteries. If so, the batteries are connected in a parallel circuit (positive terminal to positive terminal, negative terminal to negative terminal). Hooking the batteries up in parallel circuit increases battery cranking power without increasing total battery voltage output. Output remains at 12 volts. On the other hand, hooking two 12 volt batteries up in a series circuit (positive terminal to negative terminal, positive terminal to negative terminal) increases total battery output to 24 volts (12 volts plus 12 volts).

Jump Starting Precautions

- Be sure that both batteries are of the same voltage. Vehicles covered by this manual and most vehicles on the road today utilize a 12 volt charging system.
- Be sure that both batteries are of the same polarity (have the same terminal, in most cases NEGATIVE grounded).
- Be sure that the vehicles are not touching or a short could occur.
- On serviceable batteries, be sure the vent cap holes are not obstructed.
- Do not smoke or allow sparks anywhere near the batteries.
- In cold weather, make sure the battery electrolyte is not frozen. This can occur more readily in a battery that has been in a state of discharge.
- Do not allow electrolyte to contact your skin or clothing.

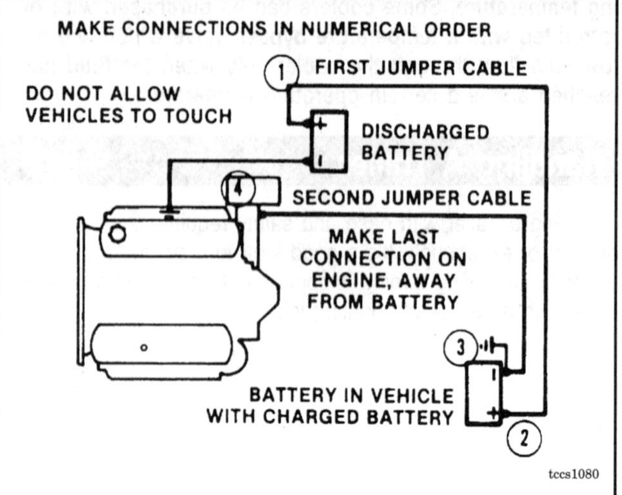

Fig. 198 Connect the jumper cables to the batteries and engine in the order shown

Jump Starting Procedure

1. Make sure that the voltages of the 2 batteries are the same. Most batteries and charging systems are of the 12 volt variety.
2. Pull the jumping vehicle (with the good battery) into a position so the jumper cables can reach the dead battery and that vehicle's engine. Make sure that the vehicles do NOT touch.
3. Place the transmissions/transaxles of both vehicles in **Neutral** (MT) or **P** (AT), as applicable, then firmly set their parking brakes.

➡If necessary for safety reasons, the hazard lights on both vehicles may be operated throughout the entire procedure without significantly increasing the difficulty of jumping the dead battery.

4. Turn all lights and accessories OFF on both vehicles. Make sure the ignition switches on both vehicles are turned to the **OFF** position.
5. Cover the battery cell caps with a rag, but do not cover the terminals.
6. Make sure the terminals on both batteries are clean and free of corrosion or proper electrical connection will be impeded. If necessary, clean the battery terminals before proceeding.
7. Identify the positive (+) and negative (-) terminals on both batteries.
8. Connect the first jumper cable to the positive (+) terminal of the dead battery, then connect the other end of that cable to the positive (+) terminal of the booster (good) battery.
9. Connect one end of the other jumper cable to the negative (-) terminal on the booster battery and the final cable clamp to an engine bolt head, alternator bracket or other solid, metallic point on the engine with the dead battery. Try to pick a ground on the engine that is positioned away from the battery in order to minimize the possibility of the 2 clamps touching should one loosen during the procedure. DO NOT connect this clamp to the negative (-) terminal of the bad battery.

⁂CAUTION

Be very careful to keep the jumper cables away from moving parts (cooling fan, belts, etc.) on both engines.

10. Check to make sure that the cables are routed away from any moving parts, then start the donor vehicle's engine. Run the engine at moderate speed for several minutes to allow the dead battery a chance to receive some initial charge.
11. With the donor vehicle's engine still running slightly above idle, try to start the vehicle with the dead battery. Crank the engine for no more than 10 seconds at a time and let the starter cool for at least 20 seconds between tries. If the vehicle does not start in 3 tries, it is likely that something else is also wrong or that the battery needs additional time to charge.
12. Once the vehicle is started, allow it to run at idle for a few seconds to make sure that it is operating properly.
13. Turn ON the headlights, heater blower and, if equipped, the rear defroster of both vehicles in order to reduce the severity of voltage spikes and subsequent risk of damage to the vehicles' electrical systems when the cables are disconnected. This step is especially important to any vehicle equipped with computer control modules.
14. Carefully disconnect the cables in the reverse order of connection. Start with the negative cable that is attached to the engine ground, then the negative cable on the donor battery. Disconnect the positive cable from the donor battery and finally, disconnect the positive cable from the formerly dead battery. Be careful when disconnecting the cables from the positive terminals not to allow the alligator clips to touch any metal on either vehicle or a short and sparks will occur.

JACKING

See Figures 199, 200 and 201

Your vehicle was supplied with a jack for emergency road repairs. This jack is fine for changing a flat tire or other short term procedures not requiring you to go beneath the vehicle. If it is used in an emergency situation, carefully follow the instructions provided either with the jack or in your owner's manual. Do not attempt to use the jack on any portions of the vehicle other than specified by the vehicle manufacturer. Always block the diagonally opposite wheel when using a jack.

A more convenient way of jacking is the use of a garage or floor jack. You may use the floor jack to raise your Pick-up.

Never place the jack under the radiator, engine or transmission components. Severe and expensive damage will result when the jack is raised. Additionally, never jack under the floorpan or bodywork; the metal will deform.

Whenever you plan to work under the vehicle, you must support it on jackstands or ramps. Never use cinder blocks or stacks of wood to support the vehicle, even if you're only going to be under it for a few minutes. Never crawl under the

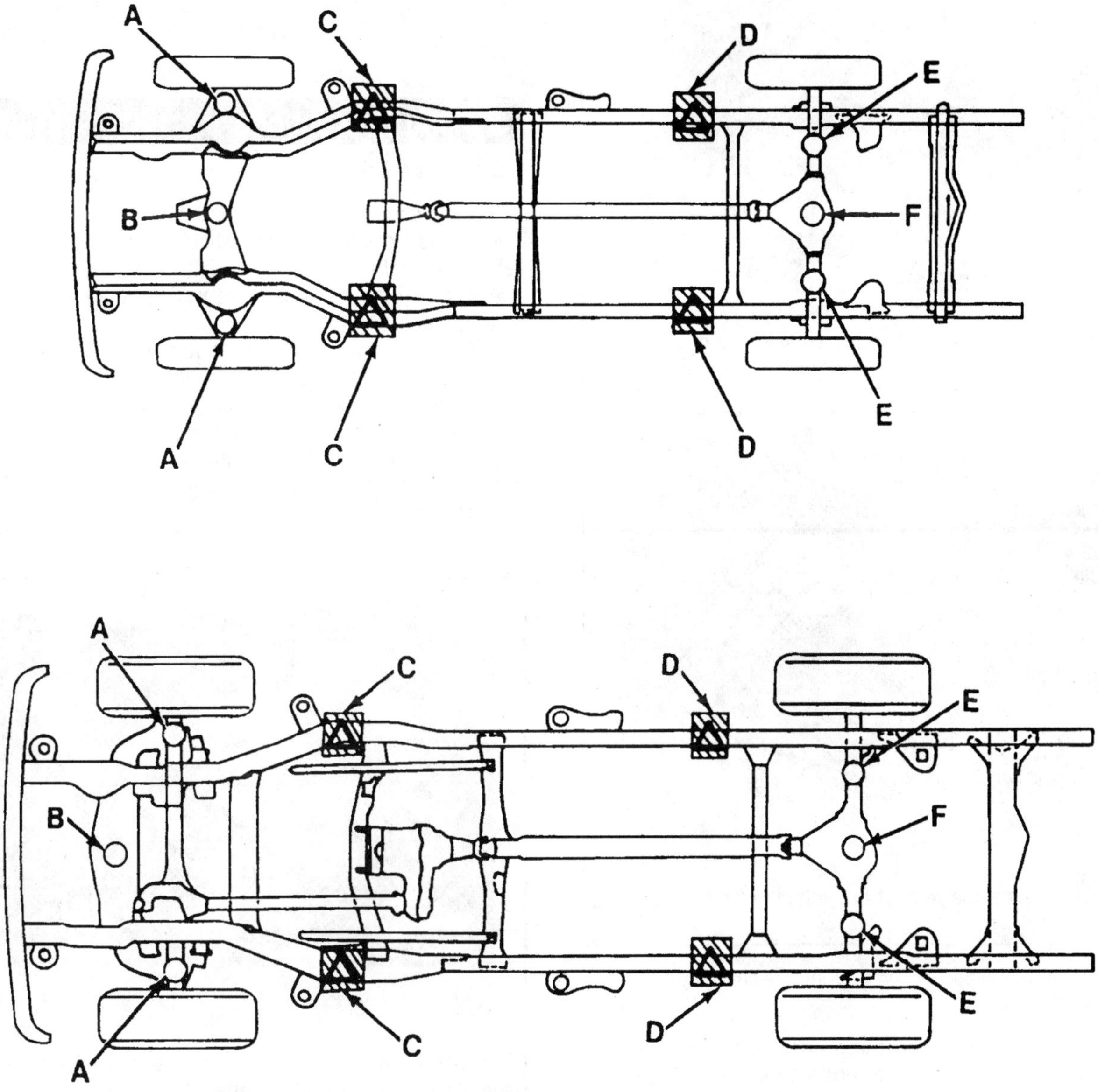

A. Lower Control Arm; Inboard of the Lower Ball Joint
B. Front Suspension Crossmember: Center
C. Frame; at Second Crossmember
D. Rear Spring; at Forward Spring Hanger
E. Axle; Inboard of Shock Absorber Hanger
F. Differential; at Center

△ Vehicle Jack or Floor Jack
○ Floor Jack
▨ Hoist

88451g03

Fig. 199 Recommended vehicle jacking and lifting points. Note that floor jacks may be used on the lined areas, but it is advisable to protect the vehicle's frame using a block of wood

Fig. 200 Raising the front of the vehicle using a hydraulic jack

Fig. 201 Raising the rear of the vehicle using a hydraulic jack

vehicle when it is supported only by the tire-changing jack or other floor jack.

➥Always position a block of wood or small rubber pad on top of the jack or jackstand to protect the lifting point's finish when lifting or supporting the vehicle.

Small hydraulic, screw, or scissors jacks are satisfactory for raising the vehicle. Drive-on trestles or ramps are also a handy and safe way to both raise and support the vehicle. Be careful though, some ramps may be too steep to drive your vehicle onto without scraping the front bottom panels. Never support the vehicle on any suspension member (unless specifically instructed to do so by a repair manual) or by an underbody panel.

Jacking Precautions

See Figure 202

The following safety points cannot be overemphasized:

- Always block the opposite wheel or wheels to keep the vehicle from rolling off the jack.
- When raising the front of the vehicle, firmly apply the parking brake.
- When the drive wheels are to remain on the ground, leave the vehicle in gear to help prevent it from rolling.
- Always use jackstands to support the vehicle when you are working underneath. Place the stands beneath the vehicle's jacking brackets. Before climbing underneath, rock the vehicle a bit to make sure it is firmly supported.

Fig. 202 Always use jackstands to support the vehicle when you are working underneath

HOW TO BUY A USED VEHICLE

Many people believe that a two or three year old used car or truck is a better buy than a new vehicle. This may be true as most new vehicles suffer the heaviest depreciation in the first two years and, at three years old, a vehicle is usually not old enough to present a lot of costly repair problems. But keep in mind, when buying a non-warranted automobile, there are no guarantees. Whatever the age of the used vehicle you might want to purchase, this section and a little patience should increase your chances of selecting one that is safe and dependable.

Tips

1. First decide what model you want, and how much you want to spend.
2. Check the used car lots and your local newspaper ads. Privately owned vehicles are usually less expensive, however, you may not get a warranty that, in many cases, comes with a used vehicle purchased from a lot. Of course, some aftermarket warranties may not be worth the extra money, so

this is a point you will have to debate and consider based on your priorities.

3. Never shop at night. The glare of the lights make it easy to miss faults on the body caused by accident or rust repair.

4. Try to get the name and phone number of the previous owner. Contact him/her and ask about the vehicle. If the owner of a lot refuses this information, look for a vehicle somewhere else.

A private seller can tell you about the vehicle and maintenance. But remember, there's no law requiring honesty from private citizens selling used vehicles. There is a law that forbids tampering with or turning back the odometer mileage. This includes both the private citizen and the lot owner. The law also requires that the seller or anyone transferring ownership of the vehicle must provide the buyer with a signed statement indicating the mileage on the odometer at the time of transfer.

5. You may wish to contact the National Highway Traffic Safety Administration (NHTSA) to find out if the vehicle has ever been included in a manufacturer's recall. Write down the year, model and serial number before you buy the vehicle, then contact NHTSA (there should be a 1-800 number that your phone company's information line can supply). If the vehicle was listed for a recall, make sure the needed repairs were made.

6. Refer to the Used Vehicle Checklist in this section and check all the items on the vehicle you are considering. Some items are more important than others. Only you know how much money you can afford for repairs, and depending on the price of the vehicle, may consider performing any needed work yourself. Beware, however, of trouble in areas that will affect operation, safety or emission. Problems in the Used Vehicle Checklist break down as follows:

- Numbers 1-8: Two or more problems in these areas indicate a lack of maintenance. You should beware.
- Numbers 9-13: Problems here tend to indicate a lack of proper care, however, these can usually be corrected with a tune-up or relatively simple parts replacement.
- Numbers 14-17: Problems in the engine or transmission can be very expensive. Unless you are looking for a project, walk away from any vehicle with problems in 2 or more of these areas.

7. If you are satisfied with the apparent condition of the vehicle, take it to an independent diagnostic center or mechanic for a complete check. If you have a state inspection program, have it inspected immediately before purchase, or specify on the bill of sale that the sale is conditional on passing state inspection.

8. Road test the vehicle — refer to the Road Test Checklist in this section. If your original evaluation and the road test agree — the rest is up to you.

USED VEHICLE CHECKLIST

See Figure 203

➡The numbers on the illustrations refer to the numbers on this checklist.

1. Mileage: Average mileage is about 12,000-15,000 miles per year. More than average mileage may indicate hard usage or could indicate many highway miles (which could be less detrimental than half as many tough around town miles).

2. Paint: Check around the tailpipe, molding and windows for overspray indicating that the vehicle has been repainted.

3. Rust: Check fenders, doors, rocker panels, window moldings, wheelwells, floorboards, under floormats, and in the trunk for signs of rust. Any rust at all will be a problem. There is no way to permanently stop the spread of rust, except to replace the part or panel.

➡If rust repair is suspected, try using a magnet to check for body filler. A magnet should stick to the sheet metal parts of the body, but will not adhere to areas with large amounts of filler.

4. Body appearance: Check the moldings, bumpers, grille, vinyl roof, glass, doors, trunk lid and body panels for general overall condition. Check for misalignment, loose hold-down clips, ripples, scratches in glass, welding in the trunk, severe misalignment of body panels or ripples, any of which may indicate crash work.

5. Leaks: Get down and look under the vehicle. There are no normal leaks, other than water from the air conditioner evaporator.

6. Tires: Check the tire air pressure. One old trick is to pump the tire pressure up to make the vehicle roll easier. Check the tread wear, open the trunk and check the spare too. Uneven wear is a clue that the front end may need an alignment.

7. Shock absorbers: Check the shock absorbers by forcing downward sharply on each corner of the vehicle. Good shocks will not allow the vehicle to bounce more than once after you let go.

8. Interior: Check the entire interior. You're looking for an interior condition that agrees with the overall condition of the vehicle. Reasonable wear is expected, but be suspicious of new seat covers on sagging seats, new pedal pads, and worn armrests. These indicate an attempt to cover up hard use. Pull back the carpets and look for evidence of water leaks or flooding. Look for missing hardware, door handles, control knobs, etc. Check lights and signal operations. Make sure all accessories (air conditioner, heater, radio, etc.) work. Check windshield wiper operation.

9. Belts and Hoses: Open the hood, then check all belts and hoses for wear, cracks or weak spots.

10. Battery: Low electrolyte level, corroded terminals and/or cracked case indicate a lack of maintenance.

11. Radiator: Look for corrosion or rust in the coolant indicating a lack of maintenance.

12. Air filter: A severely dirty air filter would indicate a lack of maintenance.

13. Ignition wires: Check the ignition wires for cracks, burned spots, or wear. Worn wires will have to be replaced.

14. Oil level: If the oil level is low, chances are the engine uses oil or leaks. Beware of water in the oil (there is probably a cracked block or bad head gasket), excessively thick oil (which is often used to quiet a noisy engine), or thin, dirty oil with a distinct gasoline smell (this may indicate internal engine problems).

15. Automatic Transmission: Pull the transmission dipstick out when the engine is running. The level should read FULL, and the fluid should be clear or bright red. Dark brown or black fluid that has distinct burnt odor, indicates a transmission in need of repair or overhaul.

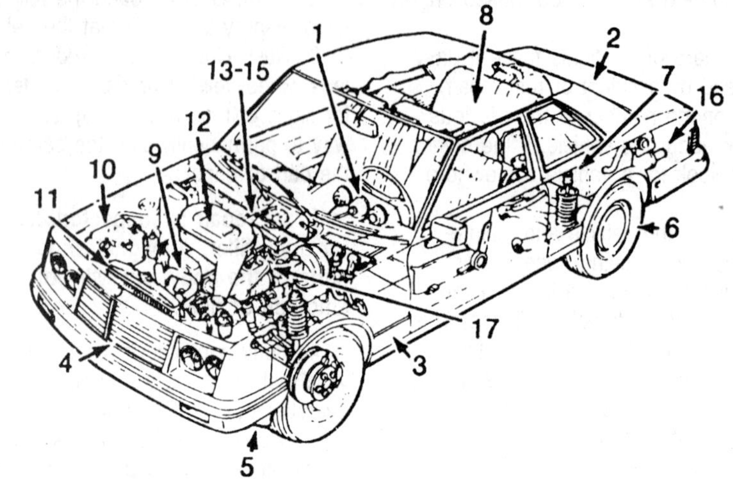

Fig. 203 Each of the numbered items should be checked when purchasing a used vehicle

16. Exhaust: Check the color of the exhaust smoke. Blue smoke indicates, among other problems, worn rings. Black smoke can indicate burnt valves or carburetor problems. Check the exhaust system for leaks; it can be expensive to replace.

17. Spark Plugs: Remove one or all of the spark plugs (the most accessible will do, though all are preferable). An engine in good condition will show plugs with a light tan or gray deposit on the firing tip.

ROAD TEST CHECKLIST

1. Engine Performance: The vehicle should be peppy whether cold or warm, with adequate power and good acceleration. It should respond smoothly through the gears.

2. Brakes: They should provide quick, firm stops with no noise, pulling or brake fade.

3. Steering: Sure control with no binding harshness, or looseness and no shimmy in the wheel should be expected. Noise or vibration from the steering wheel when turning the vehicle means trouble.

4. Clutch (Manual Transmission/Transaxle): Clutch action should give quick, smooth response with easy shifting. The clutch pedal should have free-play before it disengages the clutch. Start the engine, set the parking brake, put the transmission in first gear and slowly release the clutch pedal. The engine should begin to stall when the pedal is $\frac{1}{2}$-$\frac{3}{4}$ of the way up.

5. Automatic Transmission/Transaxle: The transmission should shift rapidly and smoothly, with no noise, hesitation, or slipping.

6. Differential: No noise or thumps should be present. Differentials have no normal leaks.

7. Driveshaft/Universal Joints: Vibration and noise could mean driveshaft problems. Clicking at low speed or coast conditions means worn U-joints.

8. Suspension: Try hitting bumps at different speeds. A vehicle that bounces excessively has weak shock absorbers or struts. Clunks mean worn bushings or ball joints.

9. Frame/Body: Wet the tires and drive in a straight line. Tracks should show two straight lines, not four. Four tire tracks indicate a frame/body bent by collision damage. If the tires can't be wet for this purpose, have a friend drive along behind you and see if the vehicle appears to be traveling in a straight line.

CAPACITIES

Year	Model	Engine ID/VIN	Engine Displacement Liters (cc)	Engine Oil with Filter (qts.)	Transmission (pts.) 4-Spd	5-Spd	Auto.	Transfer Case (pts.)	Drive Axle Front (pts.)	Rear (pts.)	Fuel Tank (gal.)	Cooling System (qts.)
1994	S Pick-up	4	2.2 (2189)	4.5	-	4.4	10.0 ①	-	-	4.0	20.0	11.5
	S/T Pick-up	W	4.3 (4293)	4.5	-	4.4	10.0 ①	2.2	2.6	4.0	20.0	12.1
	S/T Pick-up	Z	4.3 (4293)	4.5	-	4.4	10.0 ①	2.2	2.6	4.0	20.0	12.1
	Sonoma	4	2.2 (2189)	4.5	-	4.4	10.0 ①	-	-	4.0	20.0	11.5
	Sonoma	Z	4.3 (4293)	4.5	-	4.4	10.0 ①	2.2	2.6	4.0	20.0	12.1
	Sonoma	W	4.3 (4293)	4.5	-	4.4	10.0 ①	2.2	2.6	4.0	20.0	12.1
1995	S Pick-up	4	2.2 (2189)	4.5	-	4.4	10.0 ①	-	-	4.0	20.0	11.5
	S/T Pick-up	W	4.3 (4293)	4.5	-	4.4	10.0 ①	2.2	2.6	4.0	20.0	12.1
	S/T Pick-up	Z	4.3 (4293)	4.5	-	4.4	10.0 ①	2.2	2.6	4.0	20.0	12.1
	Sonoma	4	2.2 (2189)	4.5	-	4.4	10.0 ①	-	-	4.0	20.0	11.5
	Sonoma	Z	4.3 (4293)	4.5	-	4.4	10.0 ①	2.2	2.6	4.0	20.0	12.1
	Sonoma	W	4.3 (4293)	4.5	-	4.4	10.0 ①	2.2	2.6	4.0	20.0	12.1
1996	S Pick-up	4	2.2 (2189)	4.5	-	4.4	10.0 ①	-	-	4.0	19.0	11.5
	S/T Pick-up	W	4.3 (4293)	4.5	-	4.4	10.0 ①	②	2.6	4.0	19.0	11.9 ③
	S/T Pick-up	X	4.3 (4293)	4.5	-	4.4	10.0 ①	②	2.6	4.0	19.0	11.9 ③
	Sonoma	4	2.2 (2189)	4.5	-	4.4	10.0 ①	-	-	4.0	19.0	11.5
	Sonoma	W	4.3 (4293)	4.5	-	4.4	10.0 ①	②	2.6	4.0	19.0	11.9 ③
	Sonoma	X	4.3 (4293)	4.5	-	4.4	10.0 ①	②	2.6	4.0	19.0	11.9 ③
1997	S Pick-up	4	2.2 (2189)	4.5	-	4.4	10.0 ①	-	-	4.0	19.0	11.5
	S/T Pick-up	W	4.3 (4293)	4.5	-	4.4	10.0 ①	②	2.6	4.0	19.0	11.9 ③
	S/T Pick-up	X	4.3 (4293)	4.5	-	4.4	10.0 ①	②	2.6	4.0	19.0	11.9 ③
	Sonoma	4	2.2 (2189)	4.5	-	4.4	10.0 ①	-	-	4.0	19.0	11.5
	Sonoma	W	4.3 (4293)	4.5	-	4.4	10.0 ①	②	2.6	4.0	19.0	11.9 ③
	Sonoma	X	4.3 (4293)	4.5	-	4.4	10.0 ①	②	2.6	4.0	19.0	11.9 ③

① Figure shown is for pan removal only. For complete overhaul use 22 pts.

② With Borg Warner: 2.6 pts.
With New Venture Gear: 2.5 pts.

③ Figure shown is for manual transmission vehicles.
With automatic transmission use 11.7 qts.

88451C07

TO BE SERVICED	TYPE OF SERVICE	VEHICLE MILEAGE INTERVAL (x1000)							
		7.5	15	22.5	30	37.5	45	52.5	60
Change engine oil	R	✓	✓	✓	✓	✓	✓	✓	✓
Change oil filter	R	✓	✓	✓	✓	✓	✓	✓	✓
Lubricate chassis	S/I	✓	✓	✓	✓	✓	✓	✓	✓
Rotate tires	S/I	✓	✓	✓	✓	✓	✓	✓	✓
Service drive axle	S/I		✓		✓		✓		✓
Cooling system	S/I				✓				✓
Front wheel bearing repack (2WD)	S/I				✓				✓
Clutch fork pivot ball stud (4.3L)	S/I				✓				✓
PCV system	S/I				✓				✓
Spark plug wires	S/I				✓				✓
Fuel tank/cap/lines	S/I				✓				✓
Accessory drive belts	S/I				✓				✓
Evaporative control system	S/I				✓				✓
Differential fluid	S/I				✓				✓
Engine coolant	R				✓				✓
PCV filter	R				✓				✓
Air cleaner	R				✓				✓
Spark plugs	R				✓				✓
Fuel filter	R				✓				✓
Automatic transmission fluid & filter	R				✓				✓

R – Replace
S/I – Service or Inspect
NOTE: For complete warranty coverage, consult individual vehicle manufacturer's warranty maintenance guide.

FREQUENT OPERATION MAINTENANCE (SEVERE SERVICE)

Oil and filter change – change oil and filter every 3 months or 3000 miles
Chassis lubrication – at every other oil change, lubricate chassis
Lubrication points – transaxle shift linkage, parking brake cable guides, underbody contact points and linkage
Automatic transmission – change fluid and filter every 15,000 miles
Manual transmission – no fluid changes required
Drive axle service – at first oil change, replace locking differential fluid
at each subsequent oil change, check fluid level and add as necessary
standard differential does not require initial replacement
replace differential fluid every 15,000 miles if operating in dusty conditions
more frequent lubrication maybe required for off-road operation

88451C10

ENGLISH TO METRIC CONVERSION: MASS (WEIGHT)

Current mass measurement is expressed in pounds and ounces (lbs. & ozs.). The metric unit of mass (or weight) is the kilogram (kg). Even although this table does not show conversion of masses (weights) larger than 15 lbs, it is easy to calculate larger units by following the data immediately below.

To convert ounces (oz.) to grams (g): multiply th number of ozs. by 28
To convert grams (g) to ounces (oz.): multiply the number of grams by .035

To convert pounds (lbs.) to kilograms (kg): multiply the number of lbs. by .45
To convert kilograms (kg) to pounds (lbs.): multiply the number of kilograms by 2.2

lbs	kg	lbs	kg	oz	kg	oz	kg
0.1	0.04	0.9	0.41	0.1	0.003	0.9	0.024
0.2	0.09	1	0.4	0.2	0.005	1	0.03
0.3	0.14	2	0.9	0.3	0.008	2	0.06
0.4	0.18	3	1.4	0.4	0.011	3	0.08
0.5	0.23	4	1.8	0.5	0.014	4	0.11
0.6	0.27	5	2.3	0.6	0.017	5	0.14
0.7	0.32	10	4.5	0.7	0.020	10	0.28
0.8	0.36	15	6.8	0.8	0.023	15	0.42

ENGLISH TO METRIC CONVERSION: TEMPERATURE

To convert Fahrenheit (°F) to Celsius (°C): take number of °F and subtract 32; multiply result by 5; divide result by 9
To convert Celsius (°C) to Fahrenheit (°F): take number of °C and multiply by 9; divide result by 5; add 32 to total

Fahrenheit (F) °F	Celsius (C) °C	Celsius (C) °C	Fahrenheit (F) °F	Fahrenheit (F) °F	Celsius (C) °C	Celsius (C) °C	Fahrenheit (F) °F	Fahrenheit (F) °F	Celsius (C) °C	Celsius (C) °C	Fahrenheit (F) °F
−40	−40	−38	−36.4	80	26.7	18	64.4	215	101.7	80	176
−35	−37.2	−36	−32.8	85	29.4	20	68	220	104.4	85	185
−30	−34.4	−34	−29.2	90	32.2	22	71.6	225	107.2	90	194
−25	−31.7	−32	−25.6	95	35.0	24	75.2	230	110.0	95	202
−20	−28.9	−30	−22	100	37.8	26	78.8	235	112.8	100	212
−15	−26.1	−28	−18.4	105	40.6	28	82.4	240	115.6	105	221
−10	−23.3	−26	−14.8	110	43.3	30	86	245	118.3	110	230
−5	−20.6	−24	−11.2	115	46.1	32	89.6	250	121.1	115	239
0	−17.8	−22	−7.6	120	48.9	34	93.2	255	123.9	120	248
1	−17.2	−20	−4	125	51.7	36	96.8	260	126.6	125	257
2	−16.7	−18	−0.4	130	54.4	38	100.4	265	129.4	130	266
3	−16.1	−16	3.2	135	57.2	40	104	270	132.2	135	275
4	−15.6	−14	6.8	140	60.0	42	107.6	275	135.0	140	284
5	−15.0	−12	10.4	145	62.8	44	112.2	280	137.8	145	293
10	−12.2	−10	14	150	65.6	46	114.8	285	140.6	150	302
15	−9.4	−8	17.6	155	68.3	48	118.4	290	143.3	155	311
20	−6.7	−6	21.2	160	71.1	50	122	295	146.1	160	320
25	−3.9	−4	24.8	165	73.9	52	125.6	300	148.9	165	329
30	−1.1	−2	28.4	170	76.7	54	129.2	305	151.7	170	338
35	1.7	0	32	175	79.4	56	132.8	310	154.4	175	347
40	4.4	2	35.6	180	82.2	58	136.4	315	157.2	180	356
45	7.2	4	39.2	185	85.0	60	140	320	160.0	185	365
50	10.0	6	42.8	190	87.8	62	143.6	325	162.8	190	374
55	12.8	8	46.4	195	90.6	64	147.2	330	165.6	195	383
60	15.6	10	50	200	93.3	66	150.8	335	168.3	200	392
65	18.3	12	53.6	205	96.1	68	154.4	340	171.1	205	401
70	21.1	14	57.2	210	98.9	70	158	345	173.9	210	410
75	23.9	16	60.8	212	100.0	75	167	350	176.7	215	414

tccs1c01

ENGLISH TO METRIC CONVERSION: LENGTH

To convert inches (ins.) to millimeters (mm): multiply number of inches by 25.4

To convert millimeters (mm) to inches (ins.): multiply number of millimeters by .04

Inches	Decimals	Milli-meters	Inches to millimeters inches	mm	Inches	Decimals	Milli-meters	Inches to millimeters inches	mm
1/64	0.051625	0.3969	0.0001	0.00254	33/64	0.515625	13.0969	0.6	15.24
1/32	0.03125	0.7937	0.0002	0.00508	17/32	0.53125	13.4937	0.7	17.78
3/64	0.046875	1.1906	0.0003	0.00762	35/64	0.546875	13.8906	0.8	20.32
1/16	0.0625	1.5875	0.0004	0.01016	9/16	0.5625	14.2875	0.9	22.86
5/64	0.078125	1.9844	0.0005	0.01270	37/64	0.578125	14.6844	1	25.4
3/32	0.09375	2.3812	0.0006	0.01524	19/32	0.59375	15.0812	2	50.8
7/64	0.109375	2.7781	0.0007	0.01778	39/64	0.609375	15.4781	3	76.2
1/8	0.125	3.1750	0.0008	0.02032	5/8	0.625	15.8750	4	101.6
9/64	0.140625	3.5719	0.0009	0.02286	41/64	0.640625	16.2719	5	127.0
5/32	0.15625	3.9687	0.001	0.0254	21/32	0.65625	16.6687	6	152.4
11/64	0.171875	4.3656	0.002	0.0508	43/64	0.671875	17.0656	7	177.8
3/16	0.1875	4.7625	0.003	0.0762	11/16	0.6875	17.4625	8	203.2
13/64	0.203125	5.1594	0.004	0.1016	45/64	0.703125	17.8594	9	228.6
7/32	0.21875	5.5562	0.005	0.1270	23/32	0.71875	18.2562	10	254.0
15/64	0.234375	5.9531	0.006	0.1524	47/64	0.734375	18.6531	11	279.4
1/4	0.25	6.3500	0.007	0.1778	3/4	0.75	19.0500	12	304.8
17/64	0.265625	6.7469	0.008	0.2032	49/64	0.765625	19.4469	13	330.2
9/32	0.28125	7.1437	0.009	0.2286	25/32	0.78125	19.8437	14	355.6
19/64	0.296875	7.5406	0.01	0.254	51/64	0.796875	20.2406	15	381.0
5/16	0.3125	7.9375	0.02	0.508	13/16	0.8125	20.6375	16	406.4
21/64	0.328125	8.3344	0.03	0.762	53/64	0.828125	21.0344	17	431.8
11/32	0.34375	8.7312	0.04	1.016	27/32	0.84375	21.4312	18	457.2
23/64	0.359375	9.1281	0.05	1.270	55/64	0.859375	21.8281	19	482.6
3/8	0.375	9.5250	0.06	1.524	7/8	0.875	22.2250	20	508.0
25/64	0.390625	9.9219	0.07	1.778	57/64	0.890625	22.6219	21	533.4
13/32	0.40625	10.3187	0.08	2.032	29/32	0.90625	23.0187	22	558.8
27/64	0.421875	10.7156	0.09	2.286	59/64	0.921875	23.4156	23	584.2
7/16	0.4375	11.1125	0.1	2.54	15/16	0.9375	23.8125	24	609.6
29/64	0.453125	11.5094	0.2	5.08	61/64	0.953125	24.2094	25	635.0
15/32	0.46875	11.9062	0.3	7.62	31/32	0.96875	24.6062	26	660.4
31/64	0.484375	12.3031	0.4	10.16	63/64	0.984375	25.0031	27	690.6
1/2	0.5	12.7000	0.5	12.70					

ENGLISH TO METRIC CONVERSION: TORQUE

To convert foot-pounds (ft. lbs.) to Newton-meters: multiply the number of ft. lbs. by 1.3

To convert inch-pounds (in. lbs.) to Newton-meters: multiply the number of in. lbs. by .11

in lbs	N-m	in lbs	N-m	in lbs	N-m	in lbs	N-m	in lbs	N-m
0.1	0.01	1	0.11	10	1.13	19	2.15	28	3.16
0.2	0.02	2	0.23	11	1.24	20	2.26	29	3.28
0.3	0.03	3	0.34	12	1.36	21	2.37	30	3.39
0.4	0.04	4	0.45	13	1.47	22	2.49	31	3.50
0.5	0.06	5	0.56	14	1.58	23	2.60	32	3.62
0.6	0.07	6	0.68	15	1.70	24	2.71	33	3.73
0.7	0.08	7	0.78	16	1.81	25	2.82	34	3.84
0.8	0.09	8	0.90	17	1.92	26	2.94	35	3.95
0.9	0.10	9	1.02	18	2.03	27	3.05	36	4.07

tccs1c02

ENGLISH TO METRIC CONVERSION: TORQUE

Torque is now expressed as either foot-pounds (ft./lbs.) or inch-pounds (in./lbs.). The metric measurement unit for torque is the Newton-meter (Nm). This unit—the Nm—will be used for all SI metric torque references, both the present ft./lbs. and in./lbs.

ft lbs	N-m	ft lbs	N-m	ft lbs	N-m	ft lbs	N-m
0.1	0.1	33	44.7	74	100.3	115	155.9
0.2	0.3	34	46.1	75	101.7	116	157.3
0.3	0.4	35	47.4	76	103.0	117	158.6
0.4	0.5	36	48.8	77	104.4	118	160.0
0.5	0.7	37	50.7	78	105.8	119	161.3
0.6	0.8	38	51.5	79	107.1	120	162.7
0.7	1.0	39	52.9	80	108.5	121	164.0
0.8	1.1	40	54.2	81	109.8	122	165.4
0.9	1.2	41	55.6	82	111.2	123	166.8
1	1.3	42	56.9	83	112.5	124	168.1
2	2.7	43	58.3	84	113.9	125	169.5
3	4.1	44	59.7	85	115.2	126	170.8
4	5.4	45	61.0	86	116.6	127	172.2
5	6.8	46	62.4	87	118.0	128	173.5
6	8.1	47	63.7	88	119.3	129	174.9
7	9.5	48	65.1	89	120.7	130	176.2
8	10.8	49	66.4	90	122.0	131	177.6
9	12.2	50	67.8	91	123.4	132	179.0
10	13.6	51	69.2	92	124.7	133	180.3
11	14.9	52	70.5	93	126.1	134	181.7
12	16.3	53	71.9	94	127.4	135	183.0
13	17.6	54	73.2	95	128.8	136	184.4
14	18.9	55	74.6	96	130.2	137	185.7
15	20.3	56	75.9	97	131.5	138	187.1
16	21.7	57	77.3	98	132.9	139	188.5
17	23.0	58	78.6	99	134.2	140	189.8
18	24.4	59	80.0	100	135.6	141	191.2
19	25.8	60	81.4	101	136.9	142	192.5
20	27.1	61	82.7	102	138.3	143	193.9
21	28.5	62	84.1	103	139.6	144	195.2
22	29.8	63	85.4	104	141.0	145	196.6
23	31.2	64	86.8	105	142.4	146	198.0
24	32.5	65	88.1	106	143.7	147	199.3
25	33.9	66	89.5	107	145.1	148	200.7
26	35.2	67	90.8	108	146.4	149	202.0
27	36.6	68	92.2	109	147.8	150	203.4
28	38.0	69	93.6	110	149.1	151	204.7
29	39.3	70	94.9	111	150.5	152	206.1
30	40.7	71	96.3	112	151.8	153	207.4
31	42.0	72	97.6	113	153.2	154	208.8
32	43.4	73	99.0	114	154.6	155	210.2

tccs1c03

ENGLISH TO METRIC CONVERSION: FORCE

Force is presently measured in pounds (lbs.). This type of measurement is used to measure spring pressure, specifically how many pounds it takes to compress a spring. Our present force unit (the pound) will be replaced in SI metric measurements by the Newton (N). This term will eventually see use in specifications for electric motor brush spring pressures, valve spring pressures, etc.

To convert pounds (lbs.) to Newton (N): multiply the number of lbs. by 4.45

lbs	N	lbs	N	lbs	N	oz	N
0.01	0.04	21	93.4	59	262.4	1	0.3
0.02	0.09	22	97.9	60	266.9	2	0.6
0.03	0.13	23	102.3	61	271.3	3	0.8
0.04	0.18	24	106.8	62	275.8	4	1.1
0.05	0.22	25	111.2	63	280.2	5	1.4
0.06	0.27	26	115.6	64	284.6	6	1.7
0.07	0.31	27	120.1	65	289.1	7	2.0
0.08	0.36	28	124.6	66	293.6	8	2.2
0.09	0.40	29	129.0	67	298.0	9	2.5
0.1	0.4	30	133.4	68	302.5	10	2.8
0.2	0.9	31	137.9	69	306.9	11	3.1
0.3	1.3	32	142.3	70	311.4	12	3.3
0.4	1.8	33	146.8	71	315.8	13	3.6
0.5	2.2	34	151.2	72	320.3	14	3.9
0.6	2.7	35	155.7	73	324.7	15	4.2
0.7	3.1	36	160.1	74	329.2	16	4.4
0.8	3.6	37	164.6	75	333.6	17	4.7
0.9	4.0	38	169.0	76	338.1	18	5.0
1	4.4	39	173.5	77	342.5	19	5.3
2	8.9	40	177.9	78	347.0	20	5.6
3	13.4	41	182.4	79	351.4	21	5.8
4	17.8	42	186.8	80	355.9	22	6.1
5	22.2	43	191.3	81	360.3	23	6.4
6	26.7	44	195.7	82	364.8	24	6.7
7	31.1	45	200.2	83	369.2	25	7.0
8	35.6	46	204.6	84	373.6	26	7.2
9	40.0	47	209.1	85	378.1	27	7.5
10	44.5	48	213.5	86	382.6	28	7.8
11	48.9	49	218.0	87	387.0	29	8.1
12	53.4	50	224.4	88	391.4	30	8.3
13	57.8	51	226.9	89	395.9	31	8.6
14	62.3	52	231.3	90	400.3	32	8.9
15	66.7	53	235.8	91	404.8	33	9.2
16	71.2	54	240.2	92	409.2	34	9.4
17	75.6	55	244.6	93	413.7	35	9.7
18	80.1	56	249.1	94	418.1	36	10.0
19	84.5	57	253.6	95	422.6	37	10.3
20	89.0	58	258.0	96	427.0	38	10.6

tccs1c04

ENGLISH TO METRIC CONVERSION: LIQUID CAPACITY

Liquid or fluid capacity is presently expressed as pints, quarts or gallons, or a combination of all of these. In the metric system the liter (l) will become the basic unit. Fractions of a liter would be expressed as deciliters, centiliters, or most frequently (and commonly) as milliliters.

To convert pints (pts.) to liters (l): multiply the number of pints by .47
To convert liters (l) to pints (pts.): multiply the number of liters by 2.1
To convert quarts (qts.) to liters (l): multiply the number of quarts by .95

To convert liters (l) to quarts (qts.): multiply the number of liters by 1.06
To convert gallons (gals.) to liters (l): multiply the number of gallons by 3.8
To convert liters (l) to gallons (gals.): multiply the number of liters by .26

gals	liters	qts	liters	pts	liters
0.1	0.38	0.1	0.10	0.1	0.05
0.2	0.76	0.2	0.19	0.2	0.10
0.3	1.1	0.3	0.28	0.3	0.14
0.4	1.5	0.4	0.38	0.4	0.19
0.5	1.9	0.5	0.47	0.5	0.24
0.6	2.3	0.6	0.57	0.6	0.28
0.7	2.6	0.7	0.66	0.7	0.33
0.8	3.0	0.8	0.76	0.8	0.38
0.9	3.4	0.9	0.85	0.9	0.43
1	3.8	1	1.0	1	0.5
2	7.6	2	1.9	2	1.0
3	11.4	3	2.8	3	1.4
4	15.1	4	3.8	4	1.9
5	18.9	5	4.7	5	2.4
6	22.7	6	5.7	6	2.8
7	26.5	7	6.6	7	3.3
8	30.3	8	7.6	8	3.8
9	34.1	9	8.5	9	4.3
10	37.8	10	9.5	10	4.7
11	41.6	11	10.4	11	5.2
12	45.4	12	11.4	12	5.7
13	49.2	13	12.3	13	6.2
14	53.0	14	13.2	14	6.6
15	56.8	15	14.2	15	7.1
16	60.6	16	15.1	16	7.6
17	64.3	17	16.1	17	8.0
18	68.1	18	17.0	18	8.5
19	71.9	19	18.0	19	9.0
20	75.7	20	18.9	20	9.5
21	79.5	21	19.9	21	9.9
22	83.2	22	20.8	22	10.4
23	87.0	23	21.8	23	10.9
24	90.8	24	22.7	24	11.4
25	94.6	25	23.6	25	11.8
26	98.4	26	24.6	26	12.3
27	102.2	27	25.5	27	12.8
28	106.0	28	26.5	28	13.2
29	110.0	29	27.4	29	13.7
30	113.5	30	28.4	30	14.2

tccs1c05

ENGLISH TO METRIC CONVERSION: PRESSURE

The basic unit of pressure measurement used today is expressed as pounds per square inch (psi). The metric unit for psi will be the kilopascal (kPa). This will apply to either fluid pressure or air pressure, and will be frequently seen in tire pressure readings, oil pressure specifications, fuel pump pressure, etc.

To convert pounds per square inch (psi) to kilopascals (kPa): multiply the number of psi by 6.89

Psi	kPa	Psi	kPa	Psi	kPa	Psi	kPa
0.1	0.7	37	255.1	82	565.4	127	875.6
0.2	1.4	38	262.0	83	572.3	128	882.5
0.3	2.1	39	268.9	84	579.2	129	889.4
0.4	2.8	40	275.8	85	586.0	130	896.3
0.5	3.4	41	282.7	86	592.9	131	903.2
0.6	4.1	42	289.6	87	599.8	132	910.1
0.7	4.8	43	296.5	88	606.7	133	917.0
0.8	5.5	44	303.4	89	613.6	134	923.9
0.9	6.2	45	310.3	90	620.5	135	930.8
1	6.9	46	317.2	91	627.4	136	937.7
2	13.8	47	324.0	92	634.3	137	944.6
3	20.7	48	331.0	93	641.2	138	951.5
4	27.6	49	337.8	94	648.1	139	958.4
5	34.5	50	344.7	95	655.0	140	965.2
6	41.4	51	351.6	96	661.9	141	972.2
7	48.3	52	358.5	97	668.8	142	979.0
8	55.2	53	365.4	98	675.7	143	985.9
9	62.1	54	372.3	99	682.6	144	992.8
10	69.0	55	379.2	100	689.5	145	999.7
11	75.8	56	386.1	101	696.4	146	1006.6
12	82.7	57	393.0	102	703.3	147	1013.5
13	89.6	58	399.9	103	710.2	148	1020.4
14	96.5	59	406.8	104	717.0	149	1027.3
15	103.4	60	413.7	105	723.9	150	1034.2
16	110.3	61	420.6	106	730.8	151	1041.1
17	117.2	62	427.5	107	737.7	152	1048.0
18	124.1	63	434.4	108	744.6	153	1054.9
19	131.0	64	441.3	109	751.5	154	1061.8
20	137.9	65	448.2	110	758.4	155	1068.7
21	144.8	66	455.0	111	765.3	156	1075.6
22	151.7	67	461.9	112	772.2	157	1082.5
23	158.6	68	468.8	113	779.1	158	1089.4
24	165.5	69	475.7	114	786.0	159	1096.3
25	172.4	70	482.6	115	792.9	160	1103.2
26	179.3	71	489.5	116	799.8	161	1110.0
27	186.2	72	496.4	117	806.7	162	1116.9
28	193.0	73	503.3	118	813.6	163	1123.8
29	200.0	74	510.2	119	820.5	164	1130.7
30	206.8	75	517.1	120	827.4	165	1137.6
31	213.7	76	524.0	121	834.3	166	1144.5
32	220.6	77	530.9	122	841.2	167	1151.4
33	227.5	78	537.8	123	848.0	168	1158.3
34	234.4	79	544.7	124	854.9	169	1165.2
35	241.3	80	551.6	125	861.8	170	1172.1
36	248.2	81	558.5	126	868.7	171	1179.0

tccs1c06

2

ENGINE ELECTRICAL

BASIC ELECTRICAL THEORY

Understanding Electricity

For any electrical system to operate, there must be a complete circuit. This simply means that the power flow from the battery must make a full circle. When an electrical component is operating, power flows from the battery to the components, passes through the component (load) causing it to function, and returns to the battery through the ground path of the circuit. This ground may be either another wire or a metal part of the vehicle (depending upon how the component is designed).

BASIC CIRCUITS

See Figures 1 and 2

Perhaps the easiest way to visualize a circuit is to think of connecting a light bulb (with two wires attached to it) to the battery. If one of the two wires was attached to the negative post (-) of the battery and the other wire to the positive post (+), the circuit would be complete and the light bulb would illuminate. Electricity could follow a path from the battery to the bulb and back to the battery. It's not hard to see that with longer wires on our light bulb, it could be mounted anywhere on the vehicle. Further, one wire could be fitted with a switch so that the light could be turned on and off. Various other items could be added to our primitive circuit to make the light flash, become brighter or dimmer under certain conditions, or advise the user that it's burned out.

Ground

Some automotive components are grounded through their mounting points. The electrical current runs through the chassis of the vehicle and returns to the battery through the ground (-) cable; if you look, you'll see that the battery ground cable connects between the battery and the body of the vehicle.

Load

Every complete circuit must include a "load" (something to use the electricity coming from the source). If you were to connect a wire between the two terminals of the battery (DON'T do this, but take our word for it) without the light bulb, the battery would attempt to deliver its entire power supply from one pole to another almost instantly. This is a short circuit. The electricity is taking a short cut to get to ground and is not being used by any load in the circuit. This sudden and uncontrolled electrical flow can cause great damage to other components in the circuit and can develop a tremendous amount of heat. A short in an automotive wiring harness can develop sufficient heat to melt the insulation on all the surrounding wires and reduce a multiple wire cable to one sad lump of plastic and copper. Two common causes of shorts are broken insulation (thereby exposing the wire to contact with surrounding metal surfaces or other wires) or a failed switch (the pins inside the switch come out of place and touch each other).

Switches and Relays

Some electrical components which require a large amount of current to operate also have a relay in their circuit. Since these circuits carry a large amount of current (amperage or amps), the thickness of the wire in the circuit (wire gauge) is also greater. If this large wire were connected from the load to the control switch on the dash, the switch would have to carry the high amperage load and the dash would be twice as large to accommodate wiring harnesses as thick as your wrist. To prevent these problems, a relay is used. The large wires in the circuit are connected from the battery to one side of the relay and from the opposite side of the relay to the load. The relay is normally open, preventing current from passing through the circuit. An additional, smaller wire is connected from the relay to the control switch for the circuit. When the control switch is turned on, it grounds the smaller wire to the relay and completes its circuit. The main switch inside the relay closes, sending power to the component without routing the main

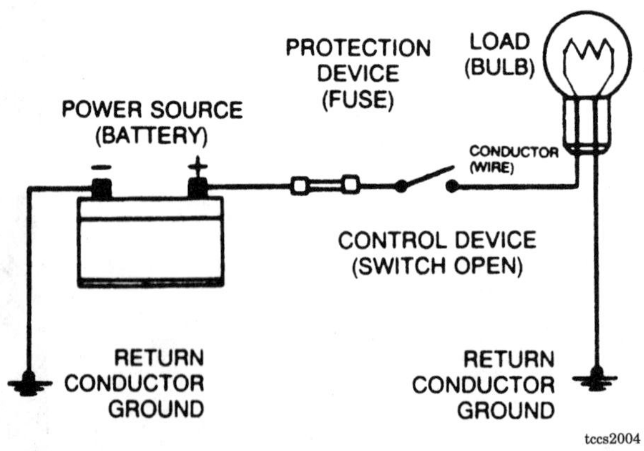

Fig. 1 Here is an example of a simple automotive circuit. When the switch is closed, power from the positive battery terminal flows through the fuse, the switch and then the load (light bulb). The light illuminates and the circuit is completed through the return conductor and the vehicle ground. If the light did not work, the tests could be made with a voltmeter or test light at the battery, fuse, switch or bulb socket

tccs2003

Fig. 2 Damaged insulation can allow wires to break (causing an open circuit) or touch (causing a short circuit)

power through the inside of the vehicle. Some common circuits which may use relays are the horn, headlights, starter and rear window defogger systems.

Protective Devices

It is possible for larger surges of current to pass through the electrical system of your vehicle. If this surge of current were to reach the load in the circuit, it could burn it out or severely damage it. To prevent this, fuses, circuit breakers and/or fusible links are connected into the supply wires of the electrical system. These items are nothing more than a built-in weak spot in the system. It's much easier to go to a known location (the fuse box) to see why a circuit is inoperative than to dissect 15 feet of wiring under the dashboard, looking for what happened.

When an electrical current of excessive power passes through the fuse, the fuse blows (the conductor melts) and breaks the circuit, preventing the passage of current and protecting the components.

A circuit breaker is basically a self repairing fuse. It will open the circuit in the same fashion as a fuse, but when either the short is removed or the surge subsides, the circuit breaker resets itself and does not need replacement.

A fuse link (fusible link or main link) is a wire that acts as a fuse. One of these is normally connected between the starter relay and the main wiring harness under the hood. Since the starter is usually the highest electrical draw on the vehicle, an internal short during starting could direct about 130 amps into the wrong places. Consider the damage potential of introducing this current into a system whose wiring is rated at 15 amps and you'll understand the need for protection. Since this link is very early in the electrical path, it's the first place to look if nothing on the vehicle works, but the battery seems to be charged and is properly connected.

TROUBLESHOOTING

See Figures 3, 4 and 5

Electrical problems generally fall into one of three areas:

- The component that is not functioning is not receiving current.
- The component is receiving power but is not using it or is using it incorrectly (component failure).
- The component is improperly grounded.

The circuit can be can be checked with a test light and a jumper wire. The test light is a device that looks like a pointed screwdriver with a wire on one end and a bulb in its handle. A jumper wire is simply a piece of wire with alligator clips or special terminals on each end. If a component is not working,

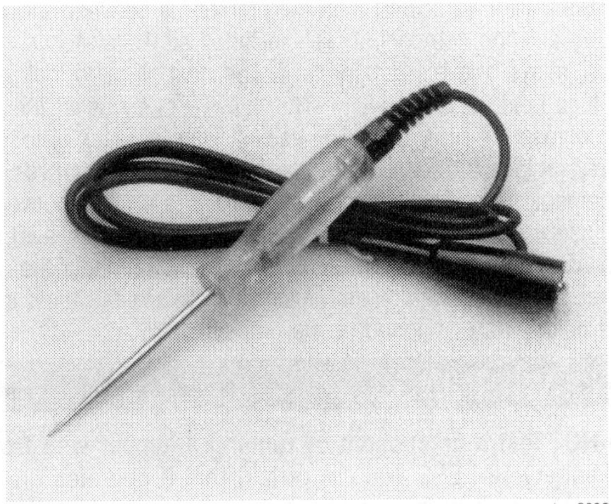

tccs2006

Fig. 3 A 12 volt test light is useful when checking parts of a circuit for power

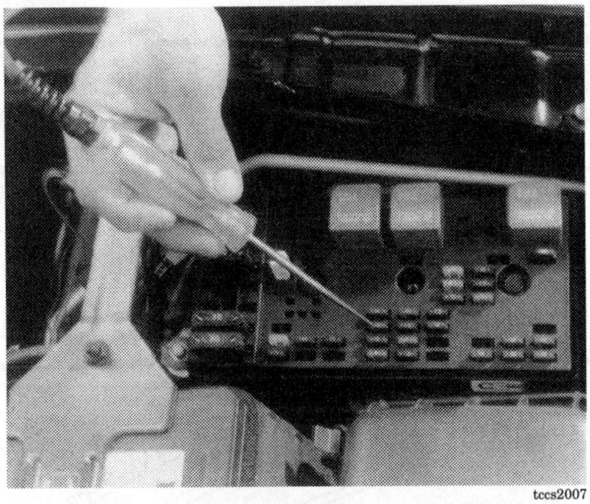

tccs2007

Fig. 4 Here, someone is checking a circuit by making sure there is power to the component's fuse you must follow a systematic plan to determine which of the three causes is the villain.

1. Turn ON the switch that controls the item not working.

➡**Some items only work when the ignition switch is turned ON.**

2. Disconnect the power supply wire from the component.
3. Attach the ground wire of a test light or a voltmeter to a good metal ground.
4. Touch the end probe of the test light (or the positive lead of the voltmeter) to the power wire; if there is current in the wire, the light in the test light will come on (or the voltmeter will indicate the amount of voltage). You have now established that current is getting to the component.
5. Turn the ignition or dash switch **OFF** and reconnect the wire to the component.

If there was no power, then the problem is between the battery and the component. This includes all the switches, fuses, relays and the battery itself. The next place to look is the fuse box; check carefully either by eye or by using the test light across the fuse clips. The easiest way to check is to simply replace the fuse. If the fuse is blown, and upon replacement, immediately blows again, there is a short between the fuse and the component. This is generally (not always) a sign of an internal short in the component. Disconnect the power wire at the component again and replace the fuse; if the fuse holds, the component is the problem.

****WARNING**

DO NOT test a component by running a jumper wire from the battery UNLESS you are certain that it operates on 12 volts. Many electronic components are designed to operate with less voltage and connecting them to 12 volts could destroy them. Jumper wires are best used to bypass a portion of the circuit (such as a stretch of wire or a switch) that DOES NOT contain a resistor and is suspected to be bad.

If all the fuses are good and the component is not receiving power, find the switch for the circuit. Bypass the switch with the jumper wire. This is done by connecting one end of the jumper to the power wire coming into the switch and the other end to the wire leaving the switch. If the component comes to life, the switch has failed.

****WARNING**

Never substitute the jumper for the component. The circuit needs the electrical load of the component. If you bypass it, you will cause a short circuit.

Checking the ground for any circuit can mean tracing wires to the body, cleaning connections or tightening mounting bolts for the component itself. If the jumper wire can be connected to the case of the component or the ground connector, you can ground the other end to a piece of clean, solid metal on the vehicle. Again, if the component starts working, you've found the problem.

A systematic search through the fuse, connectors, switches and the component itself will almost always yield an answer. Loose and/or corroded connectors, particularly in ground circuits, are becoming a larger problem in modern vehicles. The computers and on-board electronic (solid state) systems are highly sensitive to improper grounds and will change their function drastically if one occurs.

Remember that for any electrical circuit to work, ALL the connections must be clean and tight.

➡**For more information on Understanding and Troubleshooting Electrical Systems, please refer to Section 6 of this manual.**

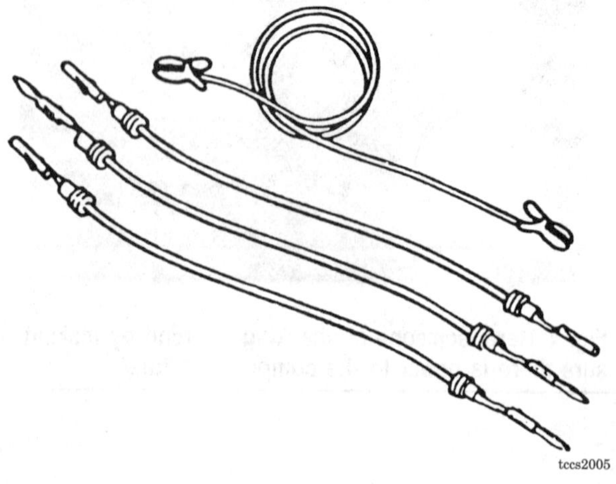

tccs2005

Fig. 5 Jumper wires with various connectors are handy for quick electrical testing

Battery, Starting and Charging Systems

BASIC OPERATING PRINCIPLES

Battery

The battery is the first link in the chain of mechanisms which work together to provide cranking of the automobile engine. In most modern vehicles, the battery is a lead/acid electrochemical device consisting of six 2v subsections (cells) connected in series so the unit is capable of producing approximately 12v of electrical pressure. Each subsection consists of a series of positive and negative plates held a short distance apart in a solution of sulfuric acid and water.

The two types of plates are of dissimilar metals. This sets-up a chemical reaction, and it is this reaction which produces current flow from the battery when its positive and negative terminals are connected to an electrical accessory such as a lamp or motor. The continued transfer of electrons would eventually convert the sulfuric acid to water, and make the two plates identical in chemical composition. As electrical energy is removed from the battery, its voltage output tends to drop. Thus, measuring battery voltage and battery electrolyte composition are two ways of checking the ability of the unit to supply power. During engine cranking, electrical energy is removed from the battery. However, if the charging circuit is in good condition and the operating conditions are normal, the power removed from the battery will be replaced by the alternator which will force electrons back through the battery, reversing the normal flow, and restoring the battery to its original chemical state.

Starting System

The battery and starting motor are linked by very heavy electrical cables designed to minimize resistance to the flow of current. Generally, the major power supply cable that leaves the battery goes directly to the starter, while other electrical system needs are supplied by a smaller cable. During starter operation, power flows from the battery to the starter and is grounded through the vehicle's frame/body or engine and the battery's negative ground strap.

The starter is a specially designed, direct current electric motor capable of producing a great amount of power for its size. One thing that allows the motor to produce a great deal of power is its tremendous rotating speed. It drives the engine through a tiny pinion gear (attached to the starter's armature), which drives the very large flywheel ring gear at a greatly reduced speed. Another factor allowing it to produce so much power is that only intermittent operation is required of it. Thus, little allowance for air circulation is necessary, and the windings can be built into a very small space.

The starter solenoid is a magnetic device which employs the small current supplied by the start circuit of the ignition switch. This magnetic action moves a plunger which mechanically engages the starter and closes the heavy switch connecting it to the battery. The starting switch circuit usually consists of the starting switch contained within the ignition switch, a neutral safety switch or clutch pedal switch, and the wiring necessary to connect these in series with the starter solenoid or relay.

The pinion, a small gear, is mounted to a one way drive clutch. This clutch is splined to the starter armature shaft. When the ignition switch is moved to the **START** position, the solenoid plunger slides the pinion toward the flywheel ring gear via a collar and spring. If the teeth on the pinion and flywheel match properly, the pinion will engage the flywheel immediately. If the gear teeth butt one another, the spring will be compressed and will force the gears to mesh as soon as the starter turns far enough to allow them to do so. As the solenoid plunger reaches the end of its travel, it closes the contacts that connect the battery and starter, then the engine is cranked.

As soon as the engine starts, the flywheel ring gear begins turning fast enough to drive the pinion at an extremely high rate of speed. At this point, the one-way clutch begins allowing the pinion to spin faster than the starter shaft so that the starter will not operate at excessive speed. When the ignition switch is released from the starter position, the solenoid is de-energized, and a spring pulls the gear out of mesh interrupting the current flow to the starter.

Some starters employ a separate relay, mounted away from the starter, to switch the motor and solenoid current on and off. The relay replaces the solenoid electrical switch, but does not eliminate the need for a solenoid mounted on the starter used to mechanically engage the starter drive gears. The relay is used to reduce the amount of current the starting switch must carry.

Charging System

The automobile charging system provides electrical power for operation of the vehicle's ignition system, starting system and all electrical accessories. The battery serves as an electrical surge or storage tank, storing (in chemical form) the energy originally produced by the engine driven generator. The system also provides a means of regulating output to protect the battery from being overcharged and to avoid excessive voltage to the accessories.

The storage battery is a chemical device incorporating parallel lead plates in a tank containing a sulfuric acid/water solution. Adjacent plates are slightly dissimilar, and the chemical reaction of the two dissimilar plates produces electrical energy when the battery is connected to a load such as the starter motor. The chemical reaction is reversible, so that when the generator is producing a voltage (electrical pressure) greater than that produced by the battery, electricity is forced into the battery, and the battery is returned to its fully charged state.

Newer automobiles use alternating current generators or alternators, because they are more efficient, can be rotated at higher speeds, and have fewer brush problems. In an alternator, the field usually rotates while all the current produced passes only through the stator winding. The brushes bear against continuous slip rings. This causes the current produced to periodically reverse the direction of its flow. Diodes (electrical one way valves) block the flow of current from traveling in the wrong direction. A series of diodes is wired together to permit the alternating flow of the stator to be rectified back to 12 volts DC for use by the vehicle's electrical system.

The voltage regulating function is performed by a regulator. The regulator is often built in to the alternator; this system is termed an integrated or internal regulator.

DISTRIBUTORLESS IGNITION SYSTEM

General Information

➧ See Figure 6

The distributorless Electronic Ignition (EI) system is used only on the 2.2L (VIN 4) engine. This electronic system is designed to provide spark for air/fuel combustion in response to timing commands from the Powertrain Control Module (PCM, often referred to in the past as the ECM). System components include the PCM, the Ignition Control Module (ICM) which contains 2 coil packs and the Crankshaft Position (CKP) sensor. Each coil pack is made up of 2 spark towers. Spark plug wires deliver voltage from the towers to the spark plugs located in the cylinder head bores. The ICM receives inputs from the crankshaft position sensor in order to monitor engine position and rotation. The module provides output signals, based on the CKP signal, which are used by the PCM to determine engine timing.

The crankshaft position sensor is mounted in the side of the engine block and protrudes within approximately 0.050 in. (1.27mm) of the crankshaft reluctor ring. The reluctor is a special wheel which is cast into the crankshaft with seven slots that are machined into it. Six of the slots are evenly spaced (60 degrees apart) while a seventh slot is spaced 10 degrees from one of the other slots. As the reluctor rotates with the crankshaft, the slots change the magnetic field of the sensor,

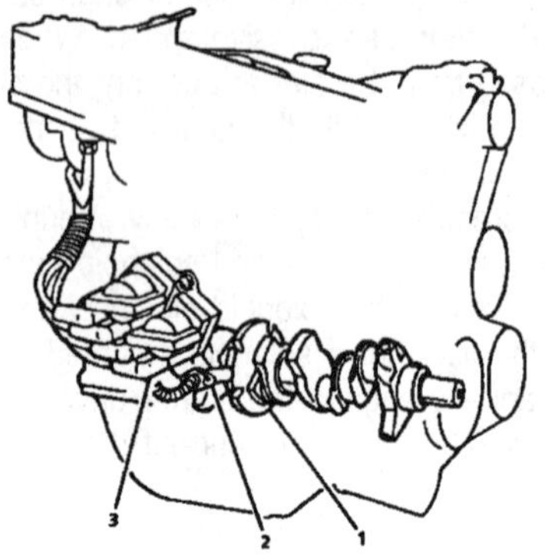

Fig. 6 Crankshaft sensor-to-crankshaft reluctor relationship

creating an induced voltage pulse. The unevenly spaced slot is used as a reference point so the ICM can tell the PCM what cylinder is next approaching TDC.

A distributorless ignition system such as this one operates based on the "waste spark" method of spark distribution. Each cylinder is paired with the cylinder that is opposite it (1 and 4 or 2 and 3) in the firing order. The spark occurs simultaneously in the cylinder coming up on the compression stroke and in the cylinder coming up on the exhaust stroke. Since the cylinder on the exhaust stroke requires very little of the available energy to fire the spark plug, most of the voltage will go to fire the cylinder on compression. As the process is repeated, the cylinders reverse roles.

When the ignition is switched to the **ON** (or **RUN**) position, battery voltage is applied to the ICM but no spark occurs because the CKP sensor shows no engine rotation. When the engine begins to rotate and reference signals are received, the ICM will control spark by triggering each of the 2 ignition coils at a pre-determined interval based only on engine speed. This ignition operation during engine cranking is known as bypass timing mode.

Once engine speed rises above 400 rpm, the PCM will take over control of the ignition control circuit in order to compensate for all driving conditions. This is known as Ignition Control (IC) mode. During normal engine operation in IC mode, the PCM will control spark timing advance or retard according to various sensor inputs, in order to obtain optimum performance. In IC mode the PCM will rely on the following information:

- Engine load (as determined by manifold pressure/vacuum)
- Atmospheric pressure
- Engine temperature
- Manifold air temperature
- Crankshaft position
- Engine speed (rpm)

PCM control of the ignition timing will continue unless a problem occurs and the bypass timing mode is again entered, during which the ICM module will determine engine timing based on preset values. If the vehicle stalls, the engine will cease rotation thus ending CKP reference pulses. The PCM and ICM will cut the ignition. Should this occur, the ICM will not resume plug firing until engine rotation resumes.

Diagnosis

Before beginning any diagnosis and testing procedures, visually inspect the components of the ignition system and engine control systems. Check for the following:

- Discharged battery
- Damaged or loose connections
- Damaged electrical insulation
- Poor coil and spark plug connections
- Ignition module connections
- Blown fuses
- Damaged vacuum hoses
- Damaged spark plugs

Check the spark plug wires and boots for signs of poor insulation that could cause crossfiring. Make sure the battery is fully charged and that all accessories are off during diagnosis and testing. Make sure the idle speed is within specification.

If an open or ground in the Ignition Control (IC) circuit occurs during engine operation, then engine will continue to run, but using a back-up timing mode (controlled by the ICM) based on preset timing values. The Malfunction Indicator Lamp (MIL) or SERVICE ENGINE SOON light will not illuminate at the first appearance of a break in the circuit. However, if the IC fault is still present once the engine is restarted, Code 42 will set in the PCM and the MIL will illuminate. Poor performance and fuel economy may be noticed while the engine is running under back-up timing.

When attempting to search for ignition troubles, keep in mind the various sensor inputs which the PCM uses to calculate timing may affect engine performance. The PCM will alter timing based on sensor inputs as follows:

- Low MAP output voltage = More spark advance
- Cold engine = More spark advance
- High MAP output voltage = Less spark advance
- Hot engine = Less spark advance

With this in mind, DETONATION could be caused by low MAP output or high resistance in the coolant sensor circuit. POOR PERFORMANCE could be caused by a high MAP output or low resistance in the coolant sensor circuit.

Ignition Coil Pack

REMOVAL & INSTALLATION

See Figure 7

1. Disconnect the negative battery cable.
2. Tag and disconnect the spark plug wiring from the coil(s).
3. Remove the coil retaining screws (there are 2 screws per coil).
4. Separate the coil from the ignition module.

To install:

5. Install the coil to the ignition module assembly.
6. Install the coil retaining screws and tighten to 40 inch lbs. (4.5 Nm).
7. Engage the spark plug wire to the coil(s) and noted during removal.
8. Connect the negative battery cable.

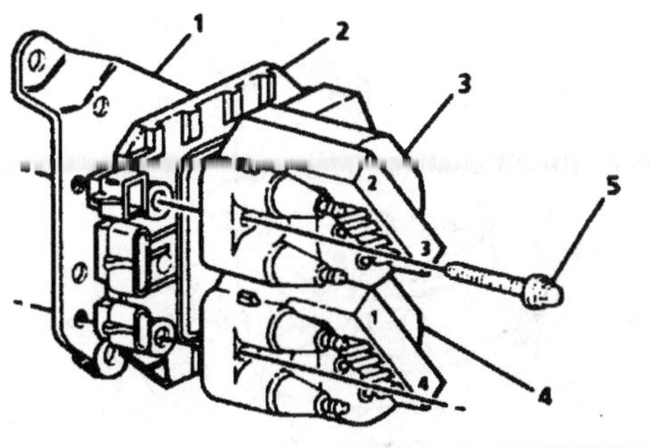

Fig. 7 Exploded view of the ignition coils and ignition module assembly

TESTING

1. Remove the ignition coil(s).
2. Using an ohmmeter, check the resistance between the primary terminals on the underside of the coil. The resistance should be 0.50-0.90 ohms.
3. Check the resistance between the secondary terminals. It should be 5000-10,000 ohms.
4. If the coil failed either test, replace the coil.

Ignition Control Module

REMOVAL & INSTALLATION

➧ See Figure 8

1. Disconnect the negative battery cable.
2. Disengage the module electrical connectors.
3. Tag and disconnect the spark plug wiring from the coils.
4. Remove the 3 ignition module/coil assembly-to-block retaining bolts, then remove the assembly from the engine.
5. Remove the coils from the ignition module, then separate the module from the assembly plate bracket.

To install:

6. Install the module to the assembly plate bracket, then install the ignition coils.
7. Install the module/coil assembly to the engine block and tighten the retaining bolts to 15-22 ft. lbs. (20-30 Nm).
8. Engage the spark plug cables to the proper coil towers, as noted during removal.
9. Engage the module electrical connectors.
10. Connect the negative battery cable.

Crankshaft Position Sensor

For information on the crankshaft position sensor, please refer to Section 4.

Camshaft Position Sensor

For information on the camshaft position sensor, please refer to Section 4.

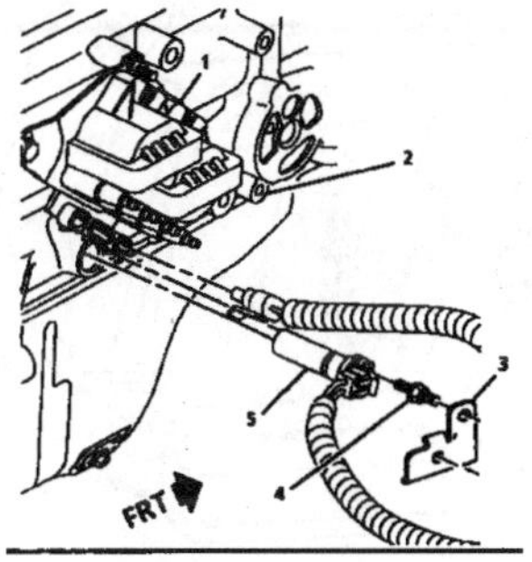

Fig. 8 The ignition coil and module assembly is mounted on the side of the engine, just above the crankshaft position sensor

HIGH VOLTAGE SWITCH (HVS) IGNITION SYSTEM

Description & Operation

➧ See Figures 9, 10, 11, 12 and 13

The High Voltage Switch (HVS) ignition system is used only on the 1995 4.3L (VIN W) engine. The ignition system is controlled by the Vehicle Control Module (VCM-A). The VCM-A obtains information from various engine sensors, then uses it to compute the desired spark timing, as well as control the dwell and firing of the ignition coil by way of an ignition control line to the coil driver. The High Voltage Switch (HVS) assembly resembles a distributor, containing both a cap and rotor. But, unlike a distributor ignition system, ignition timing is preset and cannot be adjusted because the HVS is mounted in a fixed position (it cannot be rotated). The HVS provides spark at exactly the right time to ignite the air/fuel mixture producing peak performance and fuel economy. The HVS system is comprised of the following parts:

- Vehicle Control Module (VCM-A)
- Crankshaft Position Sensor
- Ignition Coil Driver Module
- Ignition Coil
- High Voltage Switch

The Vehicle Control Module (VCM-A, often referred to in the past as an ECM) is located on the right-hand side fenderwell of the vehicle. It is the control center for fuel emissions, automatic transmission control functions and the anti-lock brake system. The VCM-A constantly monitors information from sensors in the engine and controls the component systems. It is designed to process the various input information, then send

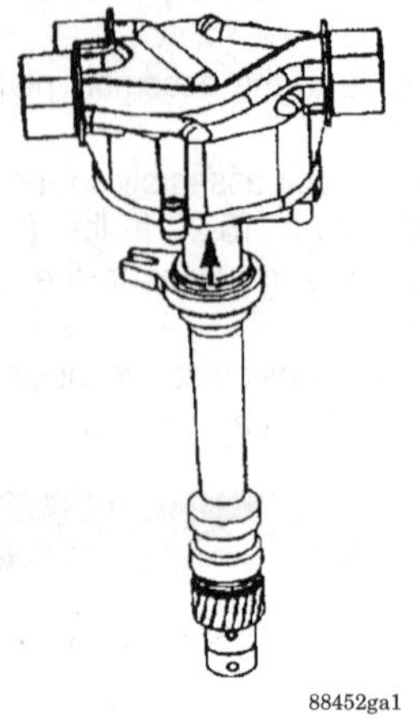

Fig. 9 High voltage switch — 1995 4.3L (VIN W) Engine

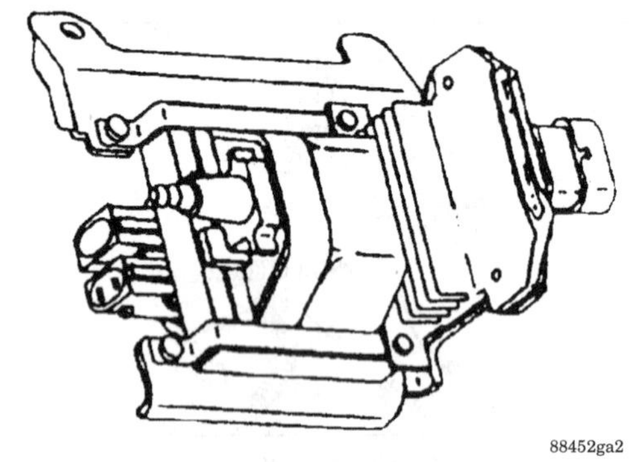

Fig. 10 HVS ignition coil — 1995 4.3L (VIN W) Engine

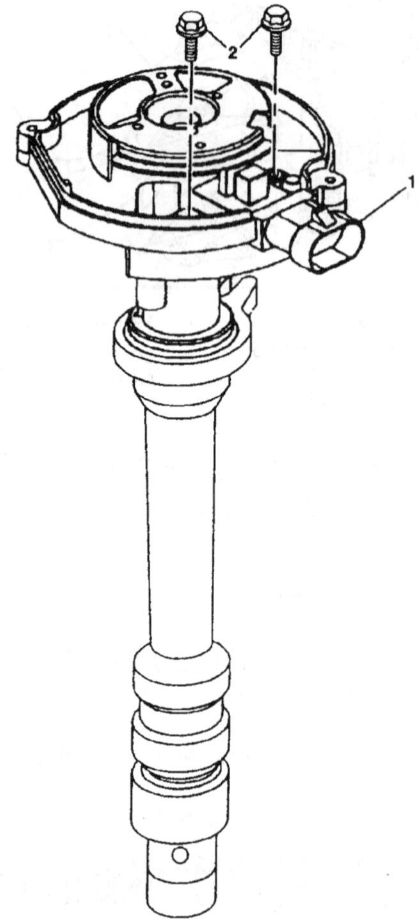

Fig. 11 HVS camshaft position sensor location

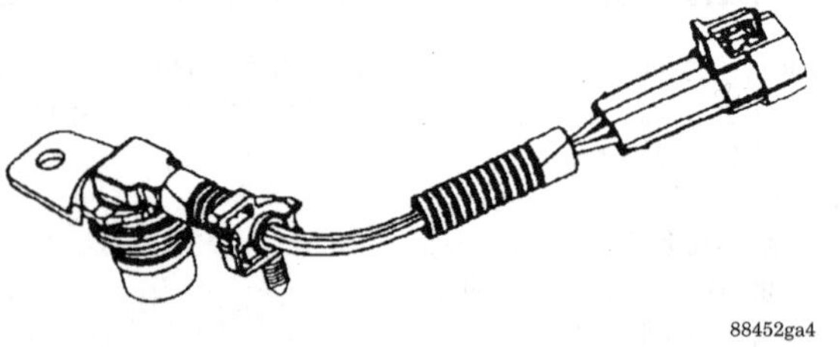

Fig. 12 Crankshaft position sensor

the necessary electrical responses. The ignition module that is used on the Distributor Ignition (DI) system is not used. All Ignition Control (IC) and Bypass functions are controlled by the VCM-A.

The Crankshaft Position Sensor (CKP) is a digital sensor that provides reference information to the VCM-A for spark and fuel delivery. It is located in the front timing chain cover and is perpendicular to the crankshaft target wheel. There is an air gap between the sensor and the target wheel which is not adjustable. The target wheel has three slots 60° apart and is keyed to the crankshaft. As the target wheel rotates, the slots passing by the sensor create a change in the magnetic field of the sensor which results in an induced voltage pulse. One revolution of the crankshaft results in three pulses (3x signal). From these pulses, the VCM-A is able to determine crankshaft position and engine speed. The VCM-A then activates the fuel injector and provides spark to the High Voltage Switch. There is a very important relationship between the crankshaft position sensor and the target wheel in that the sensor must be perpendicular to the target wheel and have the precise air gap.

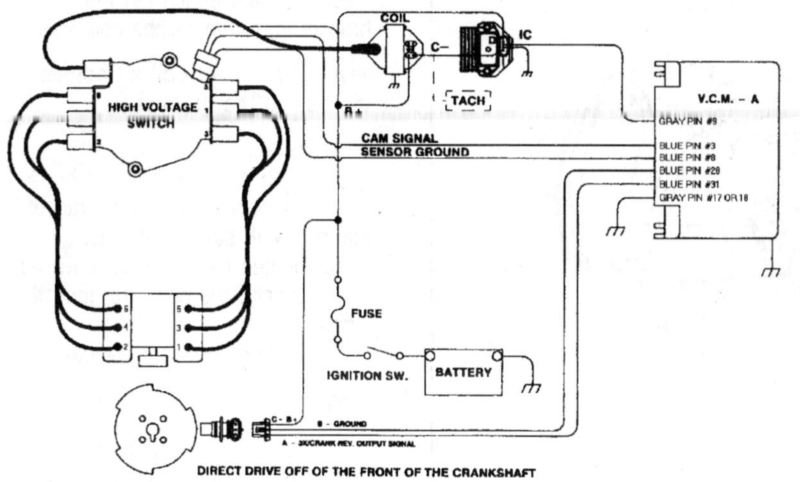

Fig. 13 High Voltage Switch (HVS) system operational schematic

The Ignition Coil Driver (ICD) Module is mounted on a bracket next to the ignition coil. The ICD controls the communication between the ignition coil and the VCM-A. The VCM-A sends a signal to the ICD commanding it to turn current ON and OFF to the ignition coil at the proper times.

The High Voltage Switch is an assembly that looks similar to a distributor. It contains the Camshaft Position (CMP) sensor, cap, rotor and shaft. The High Voltage Switch shaft is driven by the camshaft and rotates like a distributor providing spark to the correct cylinder using the cap and rotor.

The Camshaft Position (CMP) sensor is located within the HVS. It's operation is very similar to the Crankshaft Position (CKP) sensor, but it provides one pulse per camshaft revolution (1x signal). The VCM-A uses this signal along with the crankshaft position to determine which cylinder(s) are misfiring. It connects to the VCM-A through the primary engine harness and provides cylinder identification. The VCM-A controls the dwell and firing of the ignition coil through an ignition control line to the coil driver.

➡The Camshaft Position sensor does not have any effect on driveability. It's only purpose is to provide the VCM-A with cylinder identification and other needed information for misfire diagnostic trouble codes.

HVS SERVICE PRECAUTIONS

- When making compression checks, disconnect the HVS electrical connector to disable the ignition and fuel injection system. Refer to Section 3 for compression check procedures.
- No periodic lubrication of the high voltage switch is required. Engine oil lubricates the lower bushing and the upper bushing is prelubricated and sealed.
- There is no manual dwell adjustment.
- The spark plug wires are made of a material which is very pliable and soft. It is very important to route the spark plug wires correctly to prevent chafing or cutting.

Inspection & Testing

HIGH VOLTAGE SWITCH INSPECTION

1. Visually inspect the HVS cap for cracks or tiny holes. Replace the cap if it is damaged or worn.
2. Check the metal terminals in the cap for corrosion. If any corrosion is found, scrape the terminals clean with a suitable scraping tool or replace the cap.
3. Inspect the HVS rotor for wear or burning at the outer terminal. A build-up of carbon on the terminal means the rotor has worn and needs to be replaced.
4. Check HVS shaft for shaft-to-bushing looseness. Place the shaft in the housing. If the shaft wobbles, replace the housing and/or shaft.
5. Visually inspect the HVS housing for cracks or damage.

IGNITION COIL TEST

▶ See Figure 14

If the trouble has been narrowed down to one of the components in the ignition system, the following test can help pinpoint the problem. An ohmmeter with both high and low ranges should be used. This test is made with the negative battery cable disconnected.

1. Disconnect the high voltage switch lead and the wiring from the ignition coil.
2. Set the ohmmeter to the HIGH scale, then connect it to the coil, as shown in Step 1 of the illustration. The reading should be infinite. If not, verify a proper test connection to be assured of a true test result and if still not infinite, replace the coil.
3. Set the ohmmeter to the LOW scale, then connect it as shown in Step 2 of the illustration. The reading should be very low or zero. If not, verify a proper test connection and replace the coil.
4. Set the ohmmeter on the HIGH scale, then connect it to the coil as shown in Step 3 of the illustration. The ohmmeter

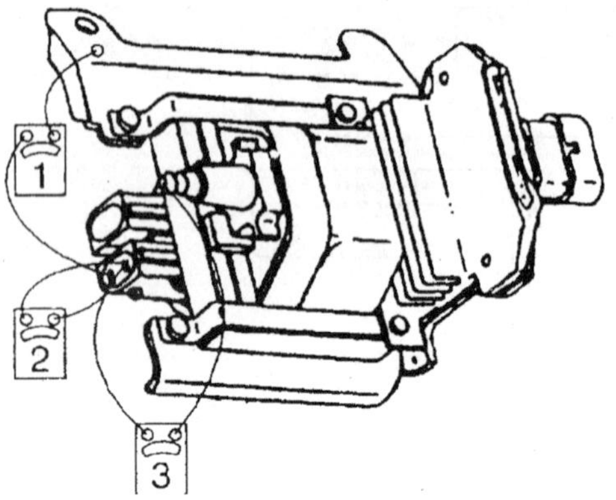

Fig. 14 HVS ignition coil testing — 1995 4.3L (VIN W) Engine

should NOT read infinite. If it does, verify the connection and replace the coil.

5. Reconnect the high voltage switch lead and wiring to the coil.

Component Replacement

REMOVAL & INSTALLATION

Ignition Coil

1. Disconnect the negative battery cable.
2. Disengage the wiring connectors from the side of the coil.
3. Disconnect the coil wire.
4. Disconnect the nuts holding the coil bracket and coil to the engine bracket or manifold.
5. Drill and punch out the two rivets holding the coil to the bracket then remove the coil bracket and the coil.

➡A replacement coil kit comes with two screws to attach the coil to the bracket.

To install:

6. Connect the coil to the bracket with two screws.
7. Connect the coil and bracket to the engine bracket or manifold with studs and nuts.
8. Tighten the coil hold-down nuts to 27 Nm (20 ft. lbs.).
9. Engage the coil wire, then the wiring connectors at the side of the coil.
10. Connect the negative battery cable.

HVS Cap

1. Disconnect the negative battery cable.
2. Remove the retainer and spark plug wires from the cap. If there is no wire retainer, be sure to tag all of the spark plug wires before disconnecting them from the cap. This will ease cap installation and ensure the correct firing order.
3. Loosen the two retaining screws holding the cap to the HVS assembly and remove the cap.

To install:

4. Install the cap to the HVS assembly and secure the two retaining screws.
5. Install the spark plug wires and wire retainer to the cap. If no retainer was used, be sure to connect the wires as tagged during removal.
6. Connect the negative battery cable.

Rotor

1. Disconnect the negative battery cable.
2. Remove the cap from the HVS housing assembly.
3. Remove the rotor attaching screws and note the position of the rotor (and also note what holes the screws were removed from), then remove the rotor.

To install:

4. Install the rotor in the position noted earlier, then secure the rotor using the attaching screws.
5. Install the cap to the HVS housing assembly.
6. Connect the negative battery cable.

DISTRIBUTOR IGNITION (DI) SYSTEM

General Information

The Distributor Ignition (DI) system consists of the distributor, hall effect switch (camshaft position sensor), ignition coil, secondary wires, spark plugs, knock sensor and the crankshaft position sensor. The system is controlled by the Vehicle Control Module (VCM). The VCM, using information from various engine sensors, controls the spark timing, dwell, and the firing of the ignition coil. It is used on some 4.3L models.

Diagnosis and Testing

The symptoms of a defective component within the DI system are exactly the same as those you would encounter in a conventional or HEI system. Some of these symptoms are:

- Hard or no Starting
- Rough Idle
- Fuel Poor Economy
- Engine misses under load or while accelerating

If you suspect a problem in the ignition system, there are certain preliminary checks which you should carry out before you begin to check the electronic portions of the system. First, it is extremely important to make sure the vehicle battery is in a good state of charge. A defective or poorly charged battery will cause the various components of the ignition system to read incorrectly when they are being tested. Second, make sure all wiring connections are clean and tight, not only at the battery, but also at the distributor cap, ignition coil, and at the electronic control module.

1. Check the cap for tiny holes and carbon tracks as follows.
   a. Remove the cap and place an ohmmeter lead on the cap terminal.
   b. Use the other lead to probe all the other terminals and the center carbon ball.
2. If the readings are not infinite, the cap must be replaced.

SECONDARY SPARK TEST

It is imperative to check the secondary ignition circuit first. If the secondary circuit checks out properly, then the engine condition is probably not the fault of the ignition system. To check the secondary ignition system, perform a simple spark test.

1. Remove one of the plug wires and insert some sort of extension in the plug socket. An old spark plug with the ground electrode removed makes a good extension.
2. Hold the wire and extension about 1/4 in. (0.25mm) away from the block and crank the engine.
3. If a normal spark occurs, then the problem is most likely not in the ignition system. Check for fuel system problems, or fouled spark plugs.
4. If, however, there is no spark or a weak spark, then test the ignition coil and the camshaft and crankshaft position sensors. For testing the camshaft and crankshaft position sensors, refer to Section 4.

Ignition Coil

TESTING

See Figure 15

Make sure the ignition switch is OFF

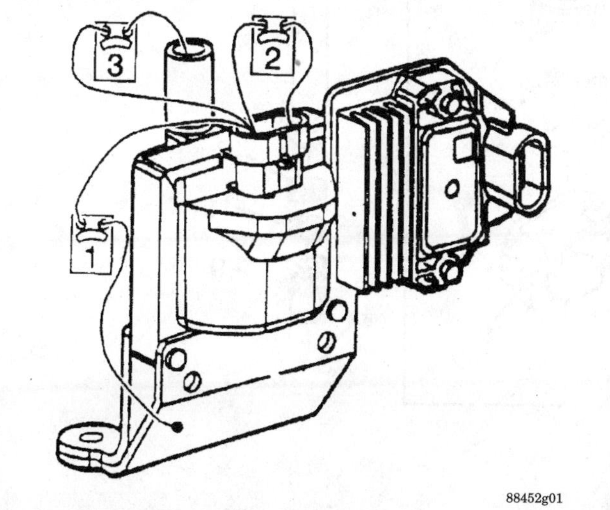

Fig. 15 Ignition coil testing points

1. Tag and disconnect the wires from the ignition coil.
2. Using a digital ohmmeter set on the high scale, probe the ignition coil as shown in Step 1 of the accompanying illustration.
3. The reading should be infinite. If not replace the coil.
4. Using the low scale of the ohmmeter, probe the ignition coil as shown in Step 2 of the accompanying illustration. The reading should be 0.2-0.5 ohms, if not replace the coil.
5. Using the high scale of the ohmmeter, probe the ignition coil as shown in Step 3 of the accompanying illustration. The reading should be 5k-25k ohms, if not replace the coil.
6. Reconnect the wires to the ignition coil.

REMOVAL & INSTALLATION

See Figure 16

1. Tag and disengage the wiring connectors from the coil and the coil wire.
2. Unfasten the retainers securing the coil bracket and coil to the manifold.
3. Remove the coil and bracket and drill out the two rivets securing the coil to the bracket.
4. Remove the coil from the bracket.

To install:

The replacement coil kit may come with the two screws to attach the coil to the bracket. If not, you must supply your own screws.

5. Fasten the coil to the bracket using two screws.
6. Fasten the coil and bracket to the manifold. Tighten the retainers to 20 ft. lbs. (27 Nm).
7. Engage the coil wire and the wiring connectors to the coil.

Ignition Module

REMOVAL & INSTALLATION

1994-95 Models

See Figure 17

1. Disconnect the negative battery cable.
2. Remove the distributor cap and rotor.
3. Tag and disengage the connectors from the sealed connectors.
4. Unfasten the module retainers and remove the module.

To install:

5. Coat the base of the base of the replacement module prior to installation.

Neglecting to coat the base of the module with heat-sink silicone grease can lead to repeated module failure.

6. Install the module and fasten the retainers.
7. Engage the module electrical connections.
8. Install the distributor rotor and cap.
9. Connect the negative battery cable.

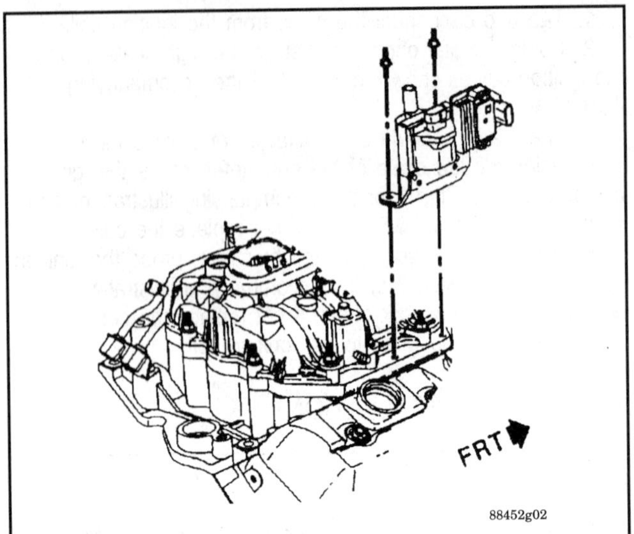

Fig. 16 Removing the ignition coil — 4.3L engine

1996-97 Models

➧ See Figure 18

1. Disconnect the negative battery cable.
2. Tag and disengage the electrical connections.
3. Unfasten the module retaining bolts, then remove the module.

To install:

4. Install the ignition module and tighten the retainers.
5. Engage the electrical connections.
6. Connect the negative battery cable.
7. Start the engine and check for proper operation.

Distributor

REMOVAL

➧ See Figures 19, 20, 21 and 22

1. Disconnect the negative battery cable.

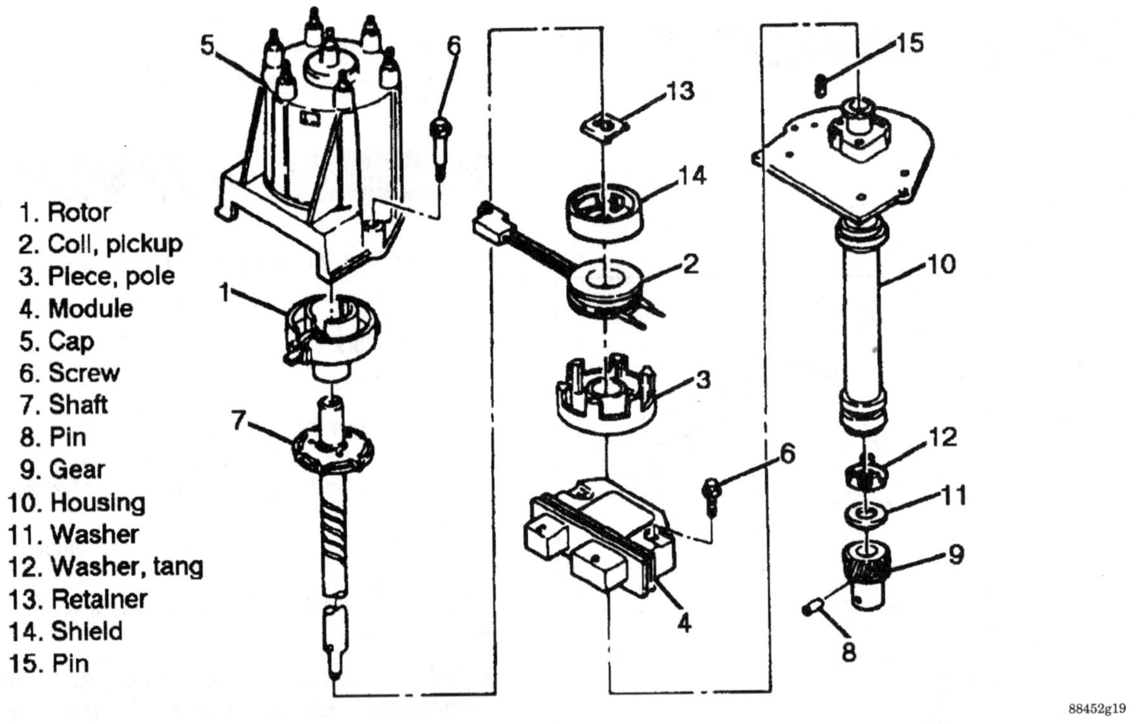

Fig. 17 Exploded view of the distributor and related components — 1994-95 4.3L engines

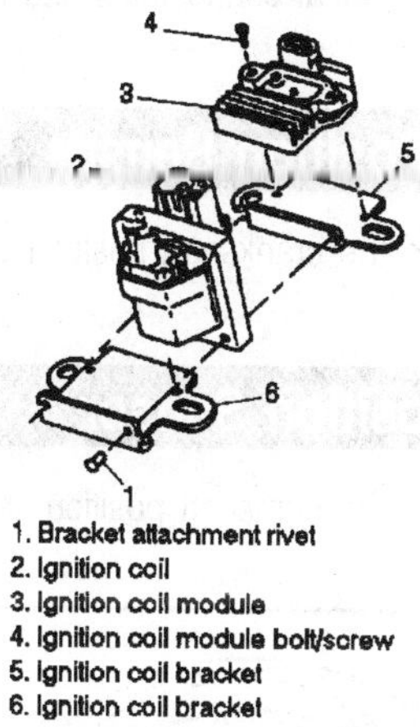

Fig. 18 Exploded view of the ignition coil and module — 1996-97 4.3L engines

2. Tag and remove the spark plug wires and the coil leads from the distributor.
3. Disengage the electrical connector at the base of the distributor.
4. Loosen the distributor cap fasteners and remove the cap.
5. Using a marker, matchmark the rotor-to-housing and housing-to-engine block positions so that they can be matched during installation.
6. Loosen and remove the distributor hold-down bolt.
7. Remove the distributor from the engine.

INSTALLATION

Engine Not Disturbed

1. Install the distributor in the engine making sure that the matchmarks are properly aligned.
2. Install the hold-down bolt and tighten the bolt to 20 ft. lbs. (27 Nm).

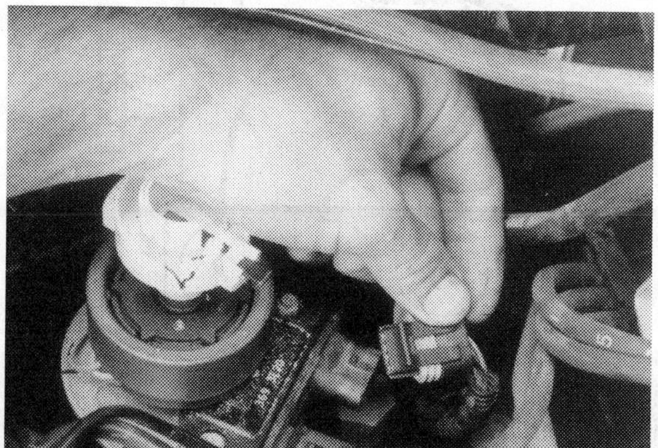

Fig. 19 Disengage the electrical connector from the distributor

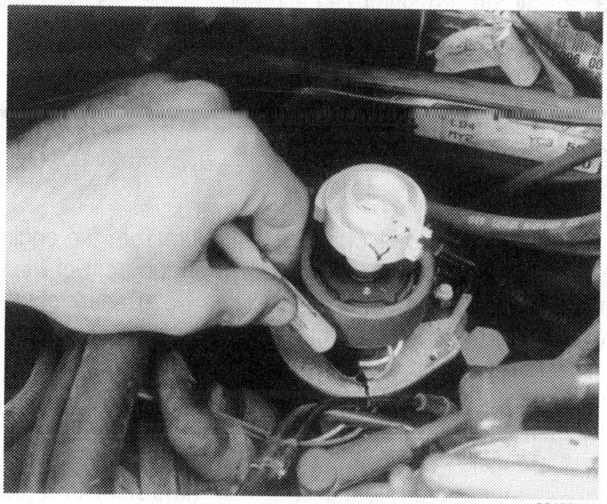

Fig. 20 Matchmark the rotor-to-housing and housing-to-engine block positions to aid in installation

Fig. 21 Using a distributor wrench, remove the distributor hold-down bolt

Fig. 22 Remove the distributor from the engine

3. Install the distributor cap and engage the electrical connector at the base of the distributor.
4. Install the spark plug wires and coil leads.
5. Connect the negative battery cable.

Engine Disturbed

See Figure 23

1. Remove the No. 1 cylinder spark plug. Turn the engine using a socket wrench on the large bolt on the front of the crankshaft pulley. Place a finger near the No. 1 spark plug hole and turn the crankshaft until the piston reaches Top Dead Center (TDC). As the engine approaches TDC, you will feel air being expelled by the No. 1 cylinder. If the position is not being met, turn the engine another full turn (360 degree). Once the engine's position is correct, install the spark plug.
2. Align the pre-drilled indent hole in the distributor driven gear with the white painted alignment line on the lower portion of the shaft housing.
3. Using a long screwdriver, align the oil pump drive shaft in the engine in the mating drive tab in the distributor.
4. Install the distributor in the engine.
5. When the distributor is fully seated, the rotor segment should be aligned with the pointer cast in the distributor base. The pointer will have a "6" or "8" cast into it indicating a 6 or 8 cylinder engine. If the rotor segment is not within a few degrees of the pointer, the distributor gear may be off a tooth or more. If this is the case repeat the process until the rotor aligns with the pointer.
6. Install the cap and fasten the mounting screws.
7. Tighten the distributor mounting bolt to 20 ft. lbs. (27 Nm).
8. Engage the electrical connections and the spark plug wires.

Crankshaft Position Sensor

For information on the crankshaft position sensor, please refer to Section 4.

Camshaft Position Sensor

For information on the camshaft position sensor, please refer to Section 4.

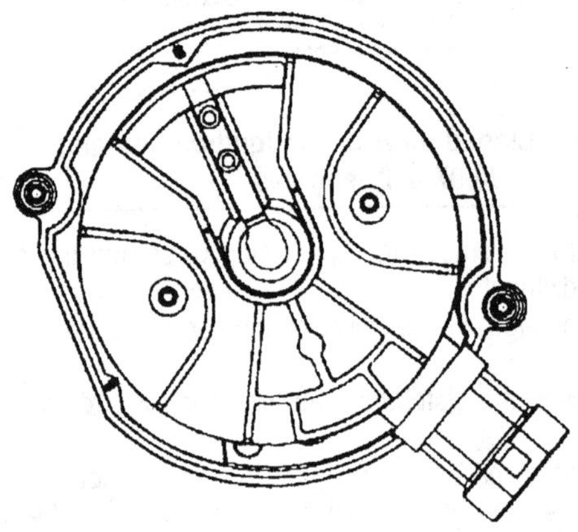

Fig. 23 The rotor segment should be aligned with the pointer cast in the distributor base, when the distributor is fully seated

FIRING ORDERS

See Figures 24, 25 and 26

➡To avoid confusion, replace spark plug wires one at a time.

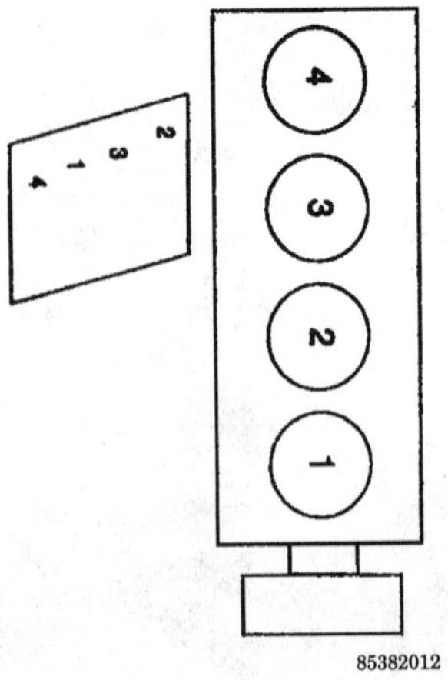

Fig. 24 2.2L Engine
Firing order: 1-3-4-2
Distributorless electronic ignition

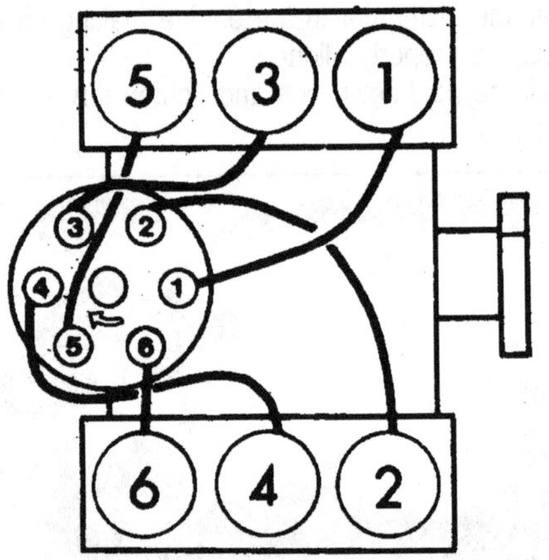

Fig. 25 4.3L Engine — non-HVS distributor
Firing order: 1-6-5-4-3-2
Distributor rotation: clockwise

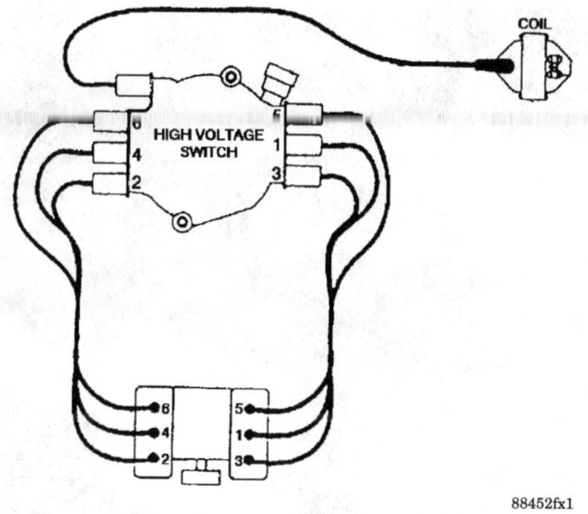

Fig. 26 4.3L Engine — HVS distributor
Firing order: 1-6-5-4-3-2
Distributor rotation: clockwise

CHARGING SYSTEM

General Information

The charging system provides electrical power for operation of the vehicle's ignition and starting systems and all the electrical accessories. The battery serves as an electrical surge or storage tank, storing (in chemical form) the energy originally produced by the engine driven generator. The system also provides a means of regulating generator output to protect the battery from being overcharged and to avoid excessive voltage to the accessories.

Alternator Precautions

To prevent damage to the alternator and regulator, the following precautionary measures must be taken when working with the electrical system.

- Never reverse the battery connections. Always check the battery polarity visually. This is to be done before any connections are made to ensure that all of the connections correspond to the battery ground polarity of the car
- Booster batteries must be connected properly. Make sure the positive cable of the booster battery is connected to the positive terminal of the battery which is getting the boost
- Disconnect the battery cables before using a fast charger; the charger has a tendency to force current through the diodes in the opposite direction for which they were designed.
- Never use a fast charger as a booster for starting the vehicle
- Never disconnect the voltage regulator while the engine is running, unless as noted for testing purposes.
- Do not ground the alternator output terminal
- Do not operate the alternator on an open circuit with the field energized
- Do not attempt to polarize the alternator
- Disconnect the battery cables and remove the alternator before using an electric arc welder on the car
- Protect the alternator from excessive moisture. If the engine is to be steam cleaned, cover or remove the alternator

Alternator

TESTING

➧ **See Figure 27**

1. Check drive belt(s) for wear and tension. Check wiring for obvious damage.
2. Go to Step 7 for vehicles without a charge indicator lamp.

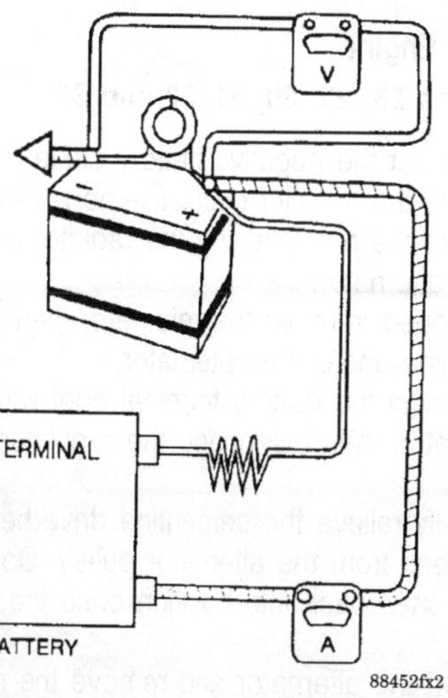

Fig. 27 Proper connections for alternator testing

3. With the ignition switch **ON** and the engine stopped, the lamp should be ON. If not, detach the wiring harness at the generator and ground the "L" terminal lead.

4. If the lamp illuminates, replace the alternator. If the lamp does not illuminate, locate the open circuit between the grounding lead and the ignition switch. Check the lamp, it may be open.

5. With the ignition switch **ON** and the engine running at moderate speed, the lamp should be OFF. If not, stop the engine, then turn the switch **ON** and detach the wiring harness at the alternator.

6. If the lamp goes out, replace the alternator. If the lamp stays ON, check for a grounded "L" terminal wire in the harness.

7. Determine if the battery is undercharged or overcharged.

- An undercharged battery is evidenced by slow cranking or a dark hydrometer.
- An overcharged battery is evidenced by excessive spewing of electrolyte from the vents.

8. Detach the wiring harness connector from the alternator.

9. With the ignition switch **ON**, and the engine not running, connect a voltmeter from ground to the "L" terminal in the wiring harness, and to the "I" terminal, if used.

10. A zero reading indicates an open circuit between the terminal and the battery. Repair the circuit as necessary.

11. Connect the harness connector to the alternator and run the engine at moderate speed with accessories OFF.

12. Measure the voltage across the battery. If above 16 volts, replace the alternator.

13. Connect an ammeter at the alternator output terminal, run the engine at moderate speed, turn ON all the accessories and load the battery with a carbon pile to obtain maximum amperage. Maintain voltage at 13 volts or above.

14. If the output is within 15 amps of the rated output of the alternator (stamped on the alternator case), the alternator is good. If the output is not within 15 amps, replace the alternator.

REMOVAL & INSTALLATION

Except 2.2L Engine

See Figures 28, 29, 30, 31, 32 and 33

1. Disconnect the negative battery cable.
2. Remove the air inlet duct assembly, if necessary.
3. Remove the nut retaining the radiator hose brace to the back on the alternator.
4. If equipped, remove the retainers, then remove the brace from the engine and/or the alternator.
5. Disconnect the battery terminal boot wiring from the back of the alternator, then disengage the regulator wiring connector.
6. Carefully relieve the serpentine drive belt tension, then remove the belt from the alternator pulley. Do not allow the tensioner to snap back into position once the belt is off the pulley.
7. Support the alternator and remove the mounting bolts (usually 2) from either side of the alternator, then remove the alternator from the vehicle.

88452p06

Fig. 28 Remove the air inlet duct assembly

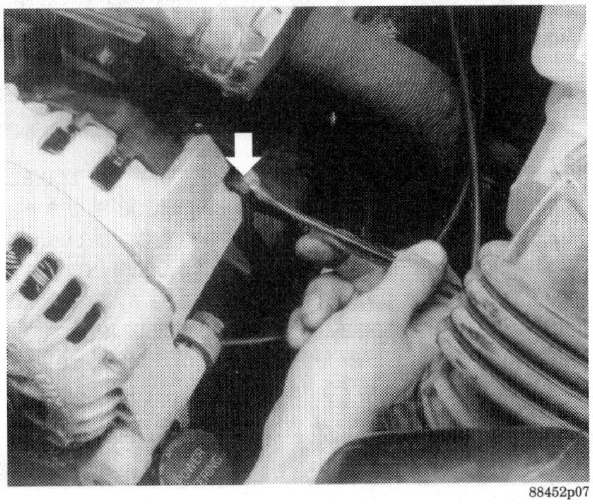

88452p07

Fig. 29 Unfasten the nut retaining the radiator hose brace to the back on the alternator

88452p08

Fig. 30 Remove the electrical wire from the rear of the alternator, . . .

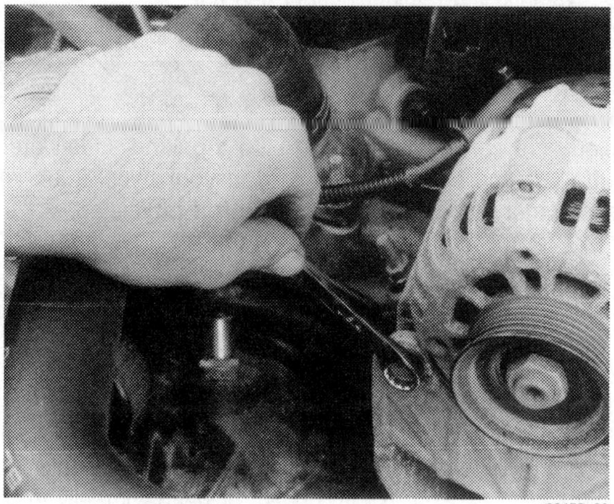

88452p09

Fig. 31 . . . then remove the alternator's mounting bolts . . .

88452p10

Fig. 32 . . . and remove the alternator from the vehicle

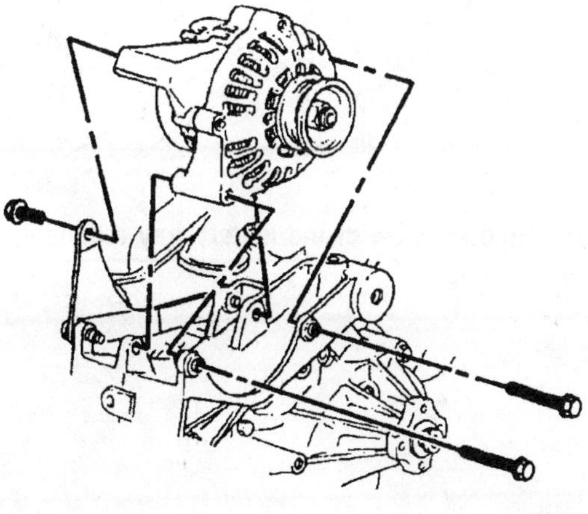

88452g05

Fig. 33 Alternator mounting — 4.3L engine

To install:

8. Position the alternator in the vehicle and loosely install using the mounting bolts.
9. If equipped, loosely install the brace to the engine and/or alternator.
10. Tighten the left or front alternator retaining bolts to 36 ft. lbs. (50 Nm), the right or rear alternator bolt to 18 ft. lbs. (25 Nm), the brace bolt to 18 ft. lbs. (25 Nm) and/or the brace nut (4.3L engines only) to 22 ft. lbs. (30 Nm), as applicable.
11. Connect and secure the alternator wiring.
12. Carefully relieve the serpentine drive belt tension and position the belt over the alternator pulley, then slowly release the tensioner into position.
13. If equipped, install the air inlet duct assembly.
14. Connect the negative battery cable.

2.2L Engine

➧ **See Figure 34**

1. Disconnect the negative battery cable.
2. Raise and support the front of the vehicle, then remove the tire and wheel assembly for access through the wheel well.

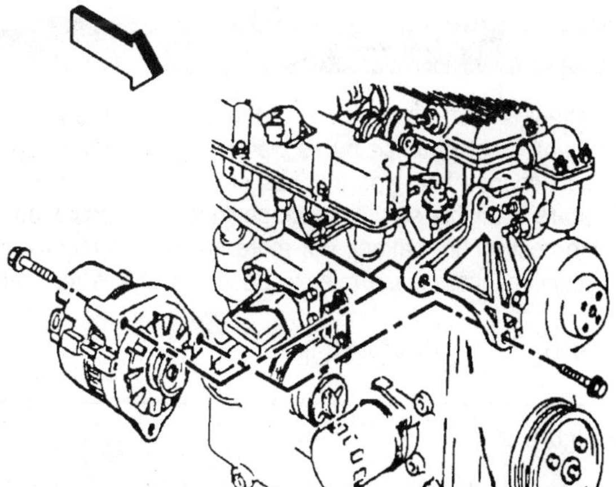

88452g06

Fig. 34 Alternator mounting — 2.2L engine

3. Working through the wheel well, unfasten the alternator brace-to-block bolt, then remove the brace-to-intake nut.
4. Carefully release the serpentine belt tension and remove the belt from the alternator pulley. Do not allow the tensioner to snap back into position once the belt is off the pulley.
5. Disengage the alternator wiring connector, then remove the battery terminal nut and wire.
6. Loosen the alternator retaining bolts, then support the alternator and remove the fasteners. Remove the alternator from the vehicle.

To install:

7. Position the alternator in the vehicle and loosely install the retaining bolts.
8. Tighten the left alternator bolt to 22 ft. lbs. (30 Nm) and the right bolt to 32 ft. lbs. (43 Nm).
9. Install the battery terminal wire and tighten the retaining nut, then engage the alternator wiring connector.
10. Install the alternator brace, then tighten the retaining nuts and bolts to 22 ft. lbs. (30 Nm).
11. Hold the serpentine drive belt tensioner, back off the belt while slipping the belt over the alternator pulley. Gradually lower the tensioner into contact with the belt, then check for proper alignment and tension.
12. Connect the negative battery cable.

Regulator

All vehicles covered in this manual were equipped with alternators which have built-in solid state voltage regulators. The regulator is in the end frame (inside) of the alternator. No adjustments are necessary or required on GM internal regulators.

Battery

The battery is normally mounted in the front of the engine compartment. Most of these trucks were originally equipped with a maintenance free type that has side mounted terminals. Adapters are available so your truck could also be equipped with a top post mount battery. For more information regarding battery maintenance, please refer to Section 1 of this manual.

REMOVAL & INSTALLATION

See Figure 35

1. Disconnect the negative battery cable terminal and then the positive cable terminal.

➡To avoid sparks, always disconnect the negative battery cable first, and reconnect it last.

2. Remove the retainer battery and nut.
3. Remove the battery, being careful not to spill the acid.

✱✱CAUTION

Spilled acid can be neutralized with a baking soda/water solution. If you somehow get acid in your eyes, flush with lots of water and immediately consult a physician.

To install:

4. Clean the cable terminals of any corrosion, using a wire brush tool or an old jackknife inside and out.
5. Install the battery. Position the retainer and nut, tighten it to 13 ft. lbs. (17 Nm).
6. Connect the positive and then the negative cable terminal. Do not hammer them in place. The terminals should be coated lightly (externally) with grease or petroleum jelly to prevent corrosion. Tighten them to 11 ft. lbs. (15 Nm).

✱✱WARNING

Make absolutely sure that the battery is connected properly before you start the engine! Reversed polarity can destroy your alternator and regulator in a matter of seconds!

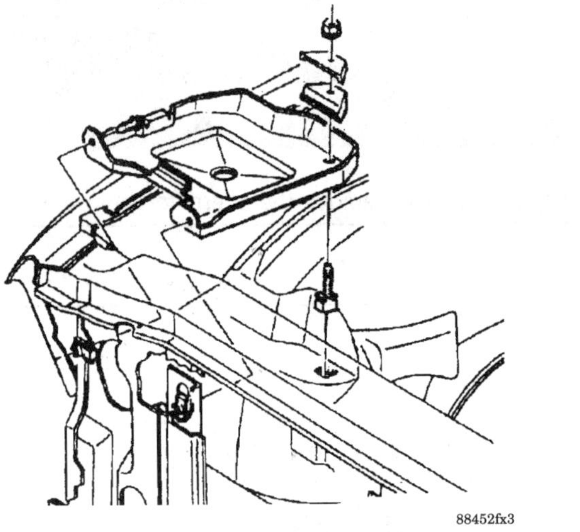

Fig. 35 Exploded view of the battery tray mounting

STARTING SYSTEM

Starter

The starting motor is a specially designed, direct current electric motor capable of producing a great amount of power for its size. One thing that allows the motor to produce a great deal of power is its tremendous rotating speed. It drives the engine through a tiny pinion gear (attached to the starter's armature), which drives the very large flywheel ring gear at a greatly reduced speed. Another factor allowing it to produce so much power is that only intermittent operation is required of it. Thus, little allowance for air circulation is required, and the windings can be built into a very small space.

The starter is usually located on the lower right-side (4.3L engines) or on the lower left-side (2.2L engines).

TESTING

Before removing the starter for repair or replacement, check the condition of all circuit wiring for damage. Inspect all connection to the starter motor, solenoid, ignition switch, and battery, including all ground connections. Clean and tighten all connections as required.

Check all switches to determine their condition. Vehicles equipped with manual transmission have a clutch safety switch attached to the clutch pedal bracket which closes when the clutch is depressed. Vehicles equipped with automatic transmissions have a manual interlock in the steering column which does not allow the ignition switch to turn to the start position unless the transmission is in the Park or Neutral position.

Check the battery to ensure that it is fully charged. For more information on battery service, please refer to Section 1 of this manual.

Check the battery cables for excessive resistance as follows:

CAUTION

To prevent possible injury from a moving vehicle or operating engine, engage the parking brakes, block the drive wheels, place the manual transmission in Neutral or the automatic transmission in Park, and disconnect the battery feed at the distributor before performing these tests.

- Check the voltage drop between the negative battery terminal and the vehicle frame by placing one lead of a voltmeter on the grounded battery post (not the cable clamp) and the other lead on the frame. Turn the ignition key to the START position and note the voltage drop.
- Check the voltage drop between the positive battery terminal (not the cable clamp) and the starter terminal stud. Turn the ignition key to the START position and note the voltage drop.
- Check the voltage drop between the starter housing and the frame. Turn the ignition key to the START position and note the voltage drop.
- If the voltage drop in any of the above is more than 1.0 volts, there is excessive resistance in the circuit. Clean and retest all cables not within specification. Replace as necessary.

No Load Test

See Figure 36

Make the test connections as shown in the illustration. Close the switch and compare the rpm, current and voltage readings with the specification found on the chart located later in this section.

- Current draw and no load speed within specifications indicates normal condition of the starter motor.
- Low free speed and high current draw indicates worn bearings, a bent armature shaft, a shorted armature or grounded armature fields
- Failure to operate with high current draw indicates a direct ground in the terminal or fields, or frozen bearings.
- Failure to operate with no current draw indicates an open field circuit, open armature coils, broken brush springs, worn brushes or other causes which would prevent good contact between the commutator and the brushes.
- A low no load speed and low current draw indicates high internal resistance due to poor connections, defective leads or a dirty commutator.
- High free speed and high current draw usually indicate shorted fields or a shorted armature.

REMOVAL & INSTALLATION

Two Wheel Drive

1994 MODELS

1. Disconnect the negative battery cable.
2. Raise and support the front of the truck safely using jackstands.
3. Remove the cover in order to provide access to the flywheel.
4. Tag and disconnect the solenoid wiring.
5. For the 2.2L engine, remove the attaching bracket-to-engine mount bolt.

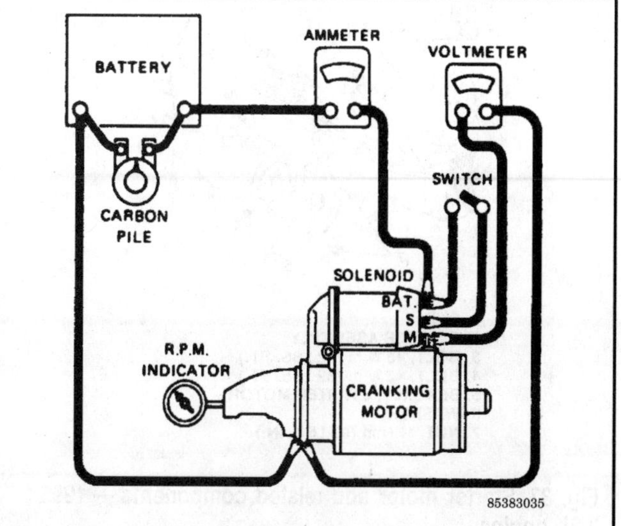

Fig. 36 Proper connections for the starter no-load test

6. Remove the starter-to-engine block bolts. When removing the last bolt, be sure to support the starter to keep it from falling and possibly injuring you.
7. Carefully lower the starter and shims (if equipped) from the vehicle.
8. If necessary, remove the bracket (2.2L engine) or the shield (4.3L engine) from the starter assembly.

To install:

9. If removed, install the bracket or shield to the starter, as applicable. Tighten the bracket nuts to 97 inch lbs. (11 Nm) or the shield nuts to 106 inch lbs. (12 Nm).
10. Carefully raise the starter and shims (if equipped) into position in the vehicle and thread one of the retaining bolts to hold it in position.
11. On the 2.2L engine, loosely install the bracket-to-engine mount bolt.
12. Install the remaining starter mounting bolt, then tighten all mounting fasteners to 32 ft. lbs. (43 Nm).
13. Engage the wiring to the solenoid as noted during removal.
14. Install the flywheel cover.
15. Remove the jackstands and carefully lower the truck.
16. Connect the negative battery cable.

1995-97 MODELS

See Figures 37 and 38

1. Disconnect the negative battery cable.
2. Raise and support the front of the truck safely using jackstands.
3. Disconnect the front exhaust pipe.
4. On the 2.2L engine, remove the brace rod from the front of the engine and the bell housing.
5. Disengage the wires from the starter solenoid.
6. On the 2.2L engine, remove the attaching bracket-to-engine mount bolt.
7. Remove the starter-to-engine block bolts. When removing the last bolt, be sure to support the starter to keep it from falling and possibly injuring you.
8. Carefully lower the starter and shims (if equipped) from the vehicle.

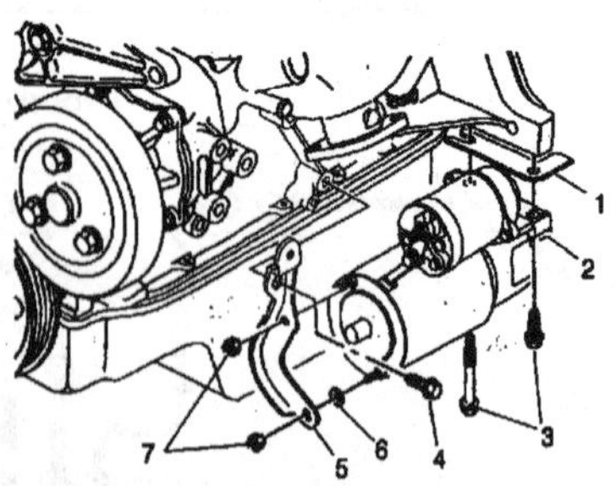

Fig. 37 Starter motor and related components — 1996 2.2L engine

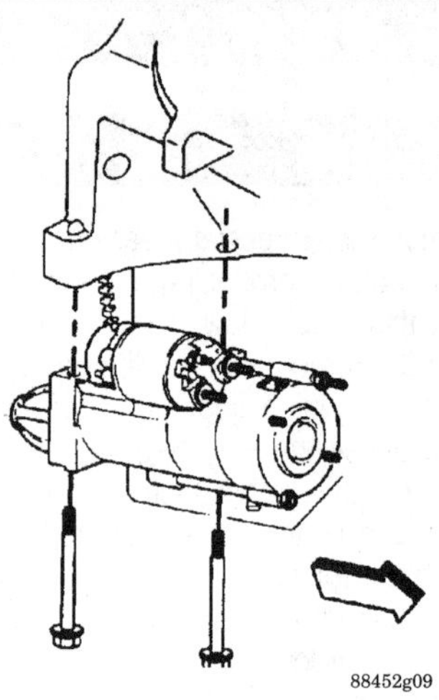

Fig. 38 Starter motor and related components — 1996 4.3L engine

9. If necessary, remove the bracket (2.2L engine) or the shield (4.3L engine) from the starter assembly.

To install:

10. If removed, install the bracket or shield to the starter, as applicable. Tighten the bracket nuts to 97 inch lbs. (11 Nm) or the shield nuts to 106 inch lbs. (12 Nm).
11. Carefully raise the starter and shims (if equipped) into position in the vehicle and thread one of the retaining bolts to hold it in position.
12. On the 2.2L engine, loosely install the bracket-to-engine mount bolt.
13. Install the remaining starter mounting bolt, then tighten all mounting fasteners to 32 ft. lbs. (43 Nm).
14. Engage the wiring to the solenoid as noted during removal.
15. On the 2.2L engine, install the brace rod and tighten the retainers.
16. Install the front exhaust pipe and tighten the fasteners.
17. Remove the jackstands and carefully lower the truck.
18. Connect the negative battery cable.

Four Wheel Drive

1. Disconnect the negative battery cable.
2. Unbolt the engine mounts, then raise and support the engine using a suitable lifting device.
3. Unbolt the transmission mount and support the transmission assembly.
4. Remove the starter-to-engine bolts and support the starter.
5. Rotate the starter as necessary for access, then tag and disconnect the solenoid wiring.
6. Carefully lower the starter and shims (if equipped) from the vehicle. Note the location of any shims for installation purposes.
7. If necessary, remove the shield from the starter assembly.

To install:

8. Raise the starter into position in the vehicle along with any shims (making sure they are in their original positions), then tighten the mounting bolts to 32 ft. lbs. (43 Nm).

9. If removed, install the shield to the starter assembly and tighten the retaining nuts to 106 inch lbs. (12 Nm).

10. Engage the wiring to the solenoid as noted during removal.

11. Install the transmission mount and remove the supports.

12. Lower the engine and secure the engine mounts, then remove the lifting device.

13. Connect the negative battery cable.

SHIMMING THE STARTER

See Figures 39 and 40

Starter noise during cranking and after the engine fires is often a result of too much or tool little distance between the starter pinion gear and the flywheel. A high pitched whine during cranking (before the engine fires) can be caused by the pinion and flywheel being too far apart. Likewise, a whine after the engine starts (as the key is released) is often a result of the pinion-flywheel relationship being too close. In both cases flywheel damage can occur. Shims are available in various sizes to properly adjust the starter on its mount. In order to check and adjust the shims, you will also need a flywheel turning tool, available at most auto parts stores or from any auto tool store or salesperson.

If your car's starter emits the above noises, follow the shimming procedure below:

1. Disconnect the negative battery cable.
2. Raise and support the vehicle safely using jackstands.
3. Remove the torque converter/flywheel cover from the bottom of the bell housing.
4. Using the flywheel turning tool, turn the flywheel and examine the flywheel teeth. If damage is evident, the flywheel should be replaced.

➡Most starters are equipped with an access hole in which a small screwdriver or prybar may be inserted to push the starter pinion outward into contact with the flywheel.

5. Move the starter pinion and clutch assembly so the pinion and flywheel teeth mesh. If necessary, rotate the flywheel so that a pinion tooth is directly in the center of the two

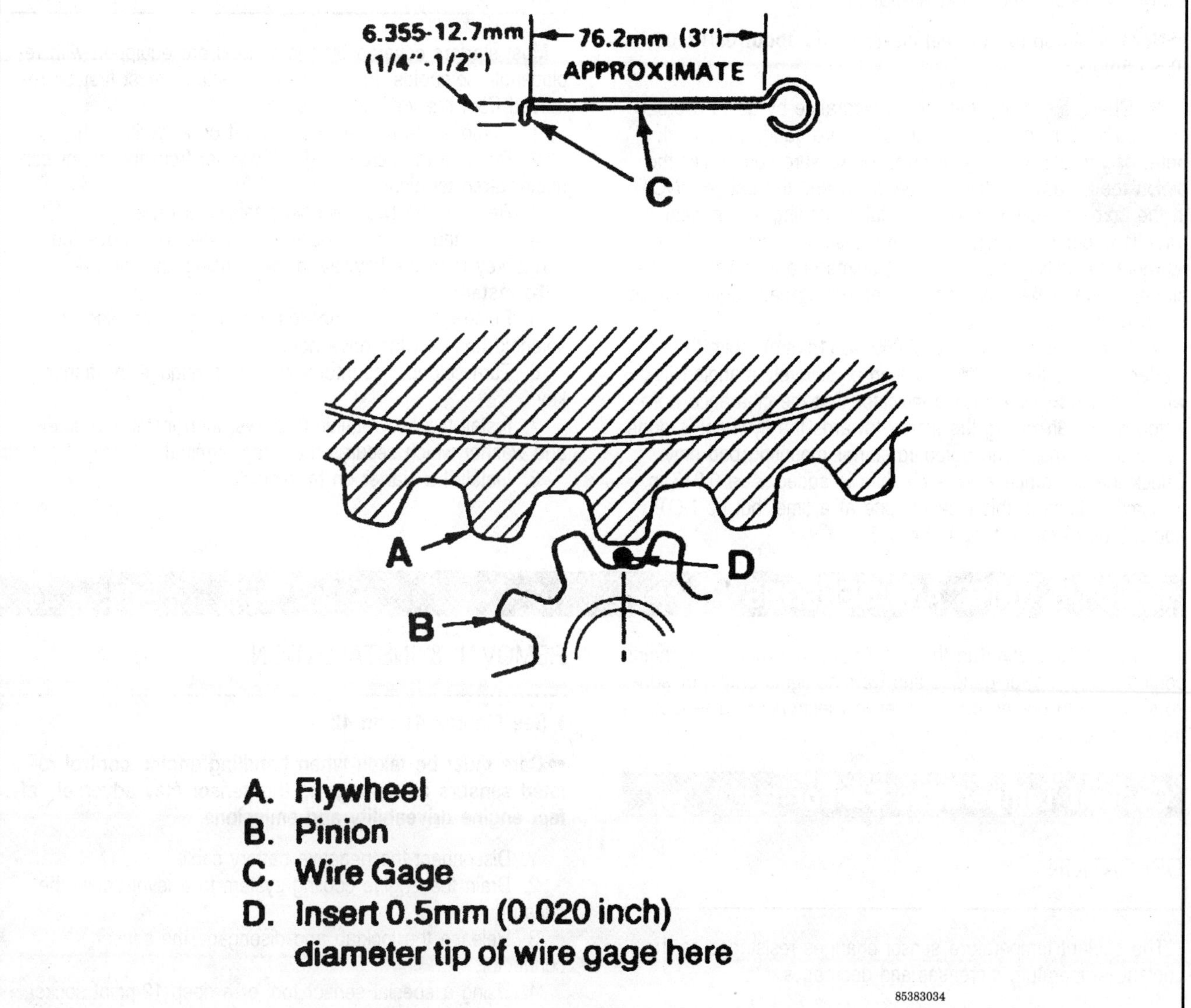

Fig. 39 Checking the gap between the starter pinion and flywheel

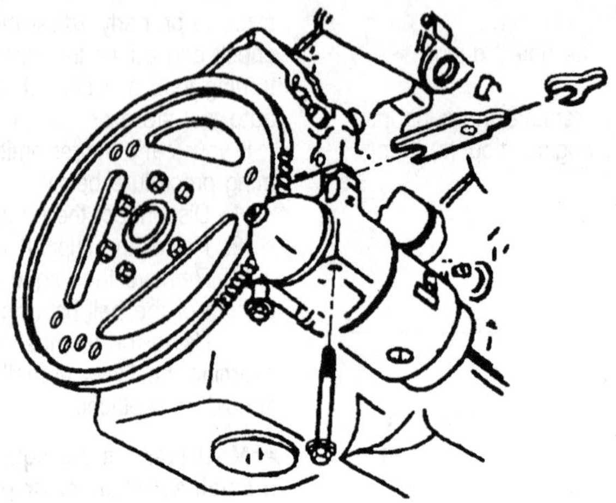
88452g10

Fig. 40 Shimming the starter motor

flywheel teeth and on the centerline of the two gears, as shown in the accompanying illustration.

➡Normal pinion-to-flywheel clearance is about 0.01-0.06 in. (0.5-1.5mm).

6. Check the pinion-to-flywheel clearance by using a 0.020 in. (0.5mm) wire gauge (a spark plug wire gauge may work here, or you can make your own). Make sure you center the pinion tooth between the flywheel teeth and the gauge - NOT in the corners, as you may get a false reading. If the clearance is under this minimum, shim the starter away from the flywheel by adding 0.04 in. (1mm) shims one at a time to the starter mount. Check clearance after adding each shim, but do not use more than 2 shims.
7. If the clearance is over 0.060 in. (1.5mm), shim the starter towards the flywheel. Broken or severely mangled flywheel teeth are also a good indicator that the clearance here is too great. Shimming the starter towards the flywheel is done by adding shims to the outboard starter mounting pad only. Check the clearance after each shim is added. Add 0.013 in. (0.33mm) shims at this location, one at a time, but do NOT add a total of more than 4 shims.

SOLENOID REPLACEMENT

Most starters covered by this manual are equipped with replaceable solenoids. In all cases, the starter must first be removed from the vehicle for access.

1. Remove the starter and place it on a workbench.
2. Remove the screw and the washer from the motor connector strap terminal.
3. Remove the two solenoid retaining screws.
4. Twist the solenoid housing clockwise to remove the flange key from the keyway in the housing and remove.

To install:

5. Place the return spring on the plunger and place the solenoid body on the drive housing.
6. Turn solenoid counterclockwise to engage the flange key.
7. Install the two retaining screws, then install the screw and washer which secures the strap terminal.
8. Install the starter on the vehicle.

SENDING UNITS AND SENSORS

The sensors covered in this section are not related to engine control. They are for gauges and warning lights only. For sensors related to engine control refer to Electronic Engine Controls in Section 4.

Coolant Temperature Sensor

OPERATION

The coolant temperature sensor changes resistance as the coolant temperature increases and decreases.

REMOVAL & INSTALLATION

See Figures 41 and 42

➡Care must be taken when handling engine control related sensors as damage to the sensor may adversely affect engine driveability and emissions.

1. Disconnect the negative battery cable.
2. Drain the engine cooling system to a level below the sensor.
3. Release the locktab and disengage the sensor connector.
4. Using a special sensor tool or a deep 12-point socket, loosen the sensor, then carefully unthread and remove it from the engine.

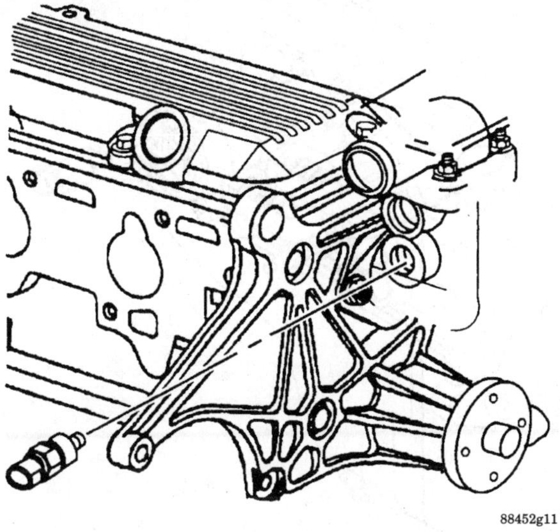
Fig. 41 Coolant temperature sensor location — 1996 2.2L engine

To install:

5. Thread the sensor into the engine by hand, then tighten using the socket or tool. If a replacement sensor came with instructions use a torque wrench to assure proper tightening.

➡On the 4.3L engine, the manufacturer suggests coating the coolant sensor threads with a sealant such as 1052080, or equivalent.

6. Engage the sensor wiring harness.
7. Connect the negative battery cable.
8. Properly refill the engine cooling system, then run the engine and check for leaks.

Oil Pressure Sender

OPERATION

The oil pressure sender relays to the dash gauge the oil pressure in the engine. The sensor is usually located on the top left side of the engine on the 2.2L engine and on the top left side near the distributor/high voltage switch on the 4.3L engine.

REMOVAL & INSTALLATION

See Figures 43 and 44

1. Disconnect the negative battery cable and drain the engine oil.
2. Disconnect the sensor electrical lead and unscrew the sensor.

To install:

3. Coat the first two or three threads with sealer. Install the sensor and tighten until snug. Engage the electrical lead.
4. Connect the battery cable and fill the engine with oil.

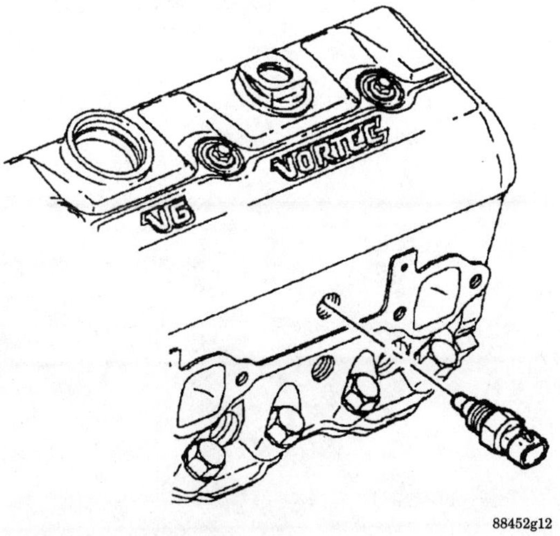

Fig. 42 Coolant temperature sensor location — 1996 4.3L engine

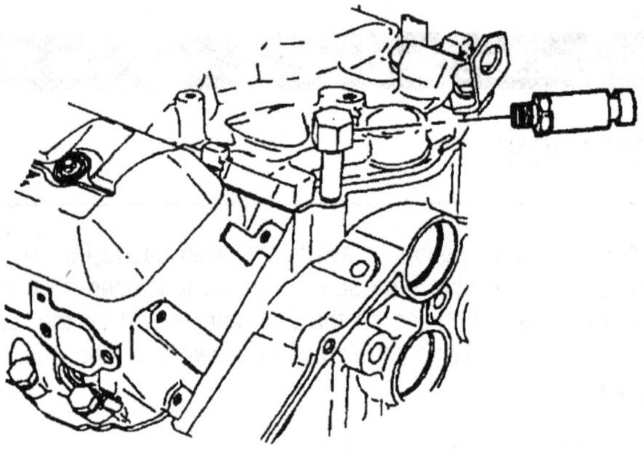

Fig. 43 Oil pressure sender location — 1996 4.3L engine

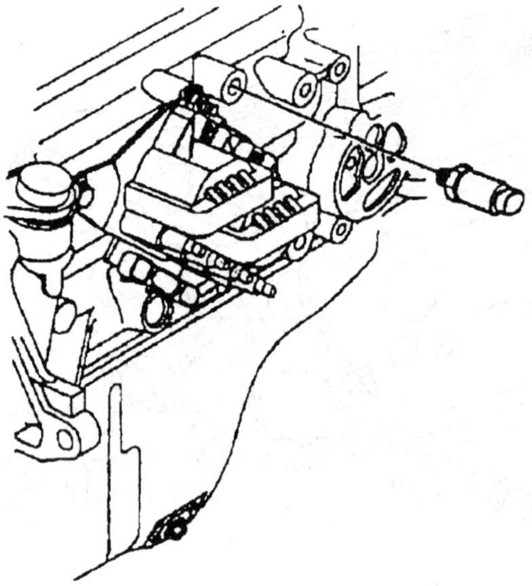

Fig. 44 Oil pressure sender location — 1996 2.2L engine

Troubleshooting Basic Starting System Problems

Problem	Cause	Solution
Starter motor rotates engine slowly	• Battery charge low or battery defective	• Charge or replace battery
	• Defective circuit between battery and starter motor	• Clean and tighten, or replace cables
	• Low load current	• Bench-test starter motor. Inspect for worn brushes and weak brush springs.
	• High load current	• Bench-test starter motor. Check engine for friction, drag or coolant in cylinders. Check ring gear-to-pinion gear clearance.
Starter motor will not rotate engine	• Battery charge low or battery defective	• Charge or replace battery
	• Faulty solenoid	• Check solenoid ground. Repair or replace as necessary.
	• Damaged drive pinion gear or ring gear	• Replace damaged gear(s)
	• Starter motor engagement weak	• Bench-test starter motor
	• Starter motor rotates slowly with high load current	• Inspect drive yoke pull-down and point gap, check for worn end bushings, check ring gear clearance
	• Engine seized	• Repair engine
Starter motor drive will not engage (solenoid known to be good)	• Defective contact point assembly	• Repair or replace contact point assembly
	• Inadequate contact point assembly ground	• Repair connection at ground screw
	• Defective hold-in coil	• Replace field winding assembly
Starter motor drive will not disengage	• Starter motor loose on flywheel housing	• Tighten mounting bolts
	• Worn drive end busing	• Replace bushing
	• Damaged ring gear teeth	• Replace ring gear or driveplate
	• Drive yoke return spring broken or missing	• Replace spring
Starter motor drive disengages prematurely	• Weak drive assembly thrust spring	• Replace drive mechanism
	• Hold-in coil defective	• Replace field winding assembly
Low load current	• Worn brushes	• Replace brushes
	• Weak brush springs	• Replace springs

tccs2c01

Troubleshooting Basic Charging System Problems

Problem	Cause	Solution
Noisy alternator	• Loose mountings • Loose drive pulley • Worn bearings • Brush noise • Internal circuits shorted (High pitched whine)	• Tighten mounting bolts • Tighten pulley • Replace alternator • Replace alternator • Replace alternator
Squeal when starting engine or accelerating	• Glazed or loose belt	• Replace or adjust belt
Indicator light remains on or ammeter indicates discharge (engine running)	• Broken belt • Broken or disconnected wires • Internal alternator problems • Defective voltage regulator	• Install belt • Repair or connect wiring • Replace alternator • Replace voltage regulator/alternator
Car light bulbs continually burn out—battery needs water continually	• Alternator/regulator overcharging	• Replace voltage regulator/alternator
Car lights flare on acceleration	• Battery low • Internal alternator/regulator problems	• Charge or replace battery • Replace alternator/regulator
Low voltage output (alternator light flickers continually or ammeter needle wanders)	• Loose or worn belt • Dirty or corroded connections • Internal alternator/regulator problems	• Replace or adjust belt • Clean or replace connections • Replace alternator/regulator

tccs2c02

3 ENGINE AND ENGINE OVERHAUL

ENGINE MECHANICAL

Engine Overhaul Tips

Most engine overhaul procedures are fairly standard. In addition to specific parts replacement procedures and specifications for your individual engine, this section is also a guide to acceptable rebuilding procedures. Examples of standard rebuilding practice are given and should be used along with specific details concerning your particular engine.

Competent and accurate machine shop services will ensure maximum performance, reliability and engine life. In most instances it is more profitable for the do-it-yourself mechanic to remove, clean and inspect the component, buy the necessary parts and deliver these to a shop for actual machine work.

On the other hand, much of the rebuilding work (crankshaft, block, bearings, piston rods, and other components) is well within the scope of the do-it-yourself mechanic's tools and abilities. You will have to decide for yourself the depth of involvement you desire in an engine repair or rebuild.

TOOLS

The tools required for an engine overhaul or parts replacement will depend on the depth of your involvement. With a few exceptions, they will be the tools found in a mechanic's tool kit (see Section 1 of this manual). More in-depth work will require some or all of the following:

- A dial indicator (reading in thousandths) mounted on a universal base
- Micrometers and telescope gauges
- Jaw and screw-type pullers
- Scraper
- Valve spring compressor
- Ring groove cleaner
- Piston ring expander and compressor
- Ridge reamer
- Cylinder hone or glaze breaker
- Plastigage®
- Engine stand

The use of most of these tools is illustrated in this chapter. Many can be rented for a one-time use from a local parts jobber or tool supply house specializing in automotive work.

Occasionally, the use of special tools is called for. See the information on Special Tools and the Safety Notice in the front of this book before substituting another tool.

INSPECTION TECHNIQUES

Procedures and specifications are given in this chapter for inspecting, cleaning and assessing the wear limits of most major components. Other procedures such as Magnaflux® and Zyglo® can be used to locate material flaws and stress cracks. Magnaflux® is a magnetic process applicable only to ferrous materials. The Zyglo® process coats the material with a fluorescent dye penetrant and can be used on any material.

Checking for suspected surface cracks can be more readily made using spot check dye. The dye is sprayed onto the suspected area, wiped off and the area sprayed with a developer. Cracks will show up brightly.

OVERHAUL TIPS

Aluminum has become extremely popular for use in engines, due to its low weight. Observe the following precautions when handling aluminum parts:

- Never hot tank aluminum parts (the caustic hot tank solution will eat the aluminum.
- Remove all aluminum parts (identification tag, etc.) from engine parts prior to the tanking.
- Always coat threads lightly with engine oil or anti-seize compounds before installation, to prevent seizure.
- Never overtorque bolts or spark plugs especially in aluminum threads.

Stripped threads in any component can be repaired using any of several commercial repair kits (Heli-Coil®, Microdot®, Keenserts®, etc.).

When assembling the engine, any parts that will be exposed to frictional contact must be prelubed to provide lubrication at initial start-up. Any product specifically formulated for this purpose can be used, but engine oil is not recommended as a prelube in most cases.

When semi-permanent (locked, but removable) installation of bolts or nuts is desired, threads should be cleaned and coated with Loctite® or another similar, commercial non-hardening sealant.

REPAIRING DAMAGED THREADS

See Figures 1, 2, 3, 4 and 5

Several methods of repairing damaged threads are available. Heli-Coil® (shown here), Keenserts® and Microdot® are among the most widely used. All involve basically the same principle — drilling out stripped threads, tapping the hole and installing a prewound insert — making welding, plugging and oversize fasteners unnecessary.

Two types of thread repair inserts are usually supplied: a standard type for most inch coarse, inch fine, metric course and metric fine thread sizes and a spark lug type to fit most spark plug port sizes. Consult the individual tool manufacturer's catalog to determine exact applications. Typical thread repair kits will contain a selection of prewound threaded inserts, a tap (corresponding to the outside diameter threads of the insert) and an installation tool. Spark plug inserts usually differ because they require a tap equipped with pilot threads and a combined reamer/tap section. Most manufacturers also supply blister-packed thread repair inserts separately in addition to a master kit containing a variety of taps and inserts plus installation tools.

Before attempting to repair a threaded hole, remove any snapped, broken or damaged bolts or studs. Penetrating oil can be used to free frozen threads. The offending item can usually be removed with locking pliers or using a screw/stud extractor. After the hole is clear, the thread can be repaired,

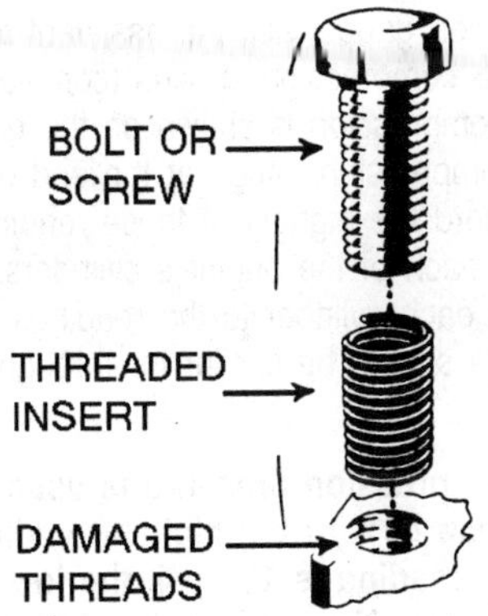

Fig. 1 Damaged bolt hole threads can be replaced with thread repair inserts

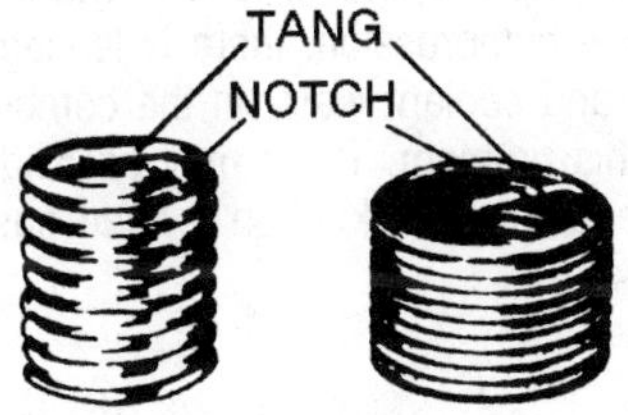

Fig. 2 Standard thread repair insert (left), and spark plug thread insert

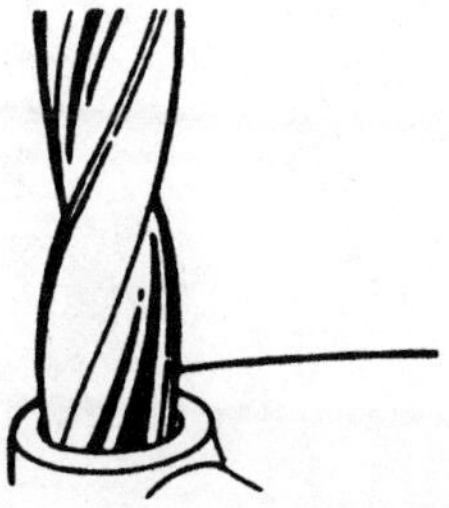

Fig. 3 Drill out the damaged threads with the specified size bit. Be sure to drill completely through the hole or to the bottom of a blind hole

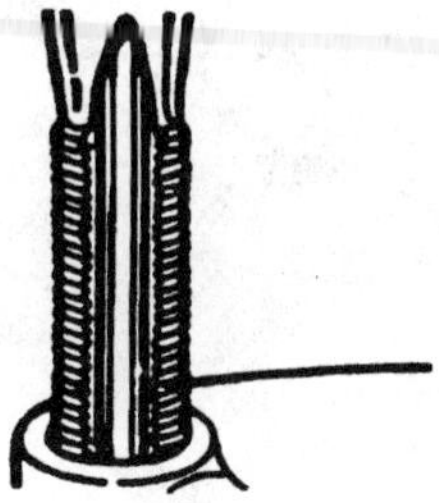

Fig. 4 Using the kit, tap the hole in order to receive the thread insert. Keep the tap well oiled and back it out frequently to avoid clogging the threads

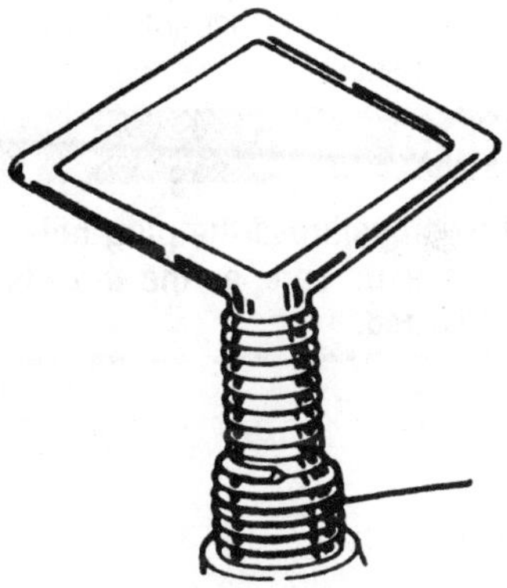

Fig. 5 Screw the insert onto the installer tool until the tang engages the slot. Thread the insert into the hole until it is 1/4-1/2 turn below the top surface, then remove the tool and break off the tang using a punch

as shown in the series of accompanying illustrations and in the kit manufacturer's instructions.

Checking Engine Compression

➧ **See Figure 6**

A noticeable lack of engine power, excessive oil consumption and/or poor fuel mileage measured over an extended period are all indicators of internal engine wear. Worn piston rings, scored or worn cylinder bores, blown head gaskets, sticking or burnt valves and worn valve seats are all possible culprits here. A check of each cylinder's compression will help you locate the problems.

As mentioned under Tools and Equipment in Section 1 of this manual, a screw-in type compression gauge is more accurate than the type you simply hold against the spark plug hole. Although it takes slightly longer to use, it's worth it to obtain a more accurate reading. Follow the procedures below.

1. Warm up the engine to normal operating temperature.
2. Remove all the spark plugs.

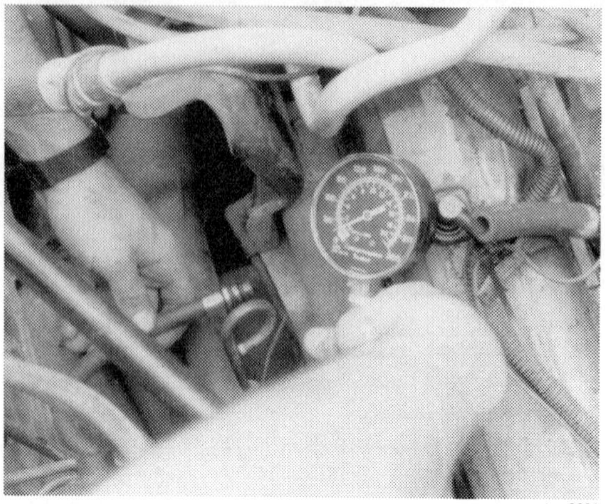

tccs3801

Fig. 6 A screw-in type compression gauge is more accurate and easier to use without an assistant

3. Disconnect the high tension lead from the ignition coil.

4. Screw the compression gauge into the No. 1 spark plug hole until the fitting is snug.

WARNING

Be careful not to crossthread the plug hole. On aluminum cylinder heads use extra care, as the threads in these heads are easily ruined.

5. Ask an assistant to depress the accelerator pedal fully on both carbureted and fuel injected vehicles. Then, while you read the compression gauge, ask the assistant to crank the engine through 4-5 compression strokes (complete revolutions) until the highest compression is shown on the gauge.

6. Read the compression gauge at the end of each series of cranks, and record the highest of these readings. Repeat this procedure for each of the engine's cylinders. Compare the highest reading of each cylinder to the readings on the other cylinders. Readings should be similar for throughout the engine.

➡A cylinder's compression pressure is usually acceptable if it is not less than 80% of the highest reading. For example, if the highest reading is 150 psi, the lowest should be no lower than 120 psi. No cylinder should be less than 100 psi.

7. If a cylinder is unusually low, pour a tablespoon of clean engine oil into the cylinder through the spark plug hole and repeat the compression test. If the compression comes up after adding the oil, it appears that the cylinder's piston rings or bore are damaged or worn. If the pressure remains low, the valves may not be seating properly (a valve job is needed), or the head gasket may be blown near that cylinder. If compression in any two adjacent cylinders is low, and if the addition of oil doesn't help the compression, there is leakage past the head gasket. Oil and coolant water in the combustion chamber can result from this problem. There may be evidence of water droplets on the engine dipstick when a head gasket has blown.

GENERAL ENGINE SPECIFICATIONS

Year	Engine ID/VIN	Engine Displacement Liters (cc)	Fuel System Type	Net Horsepower @ rpm	Net Torque @ rpm (ft. lbs.)	Bore x Stroke (in.)	Com-pression Ratio	Oil Pressure @ rpm
1994	4	2.2 (2189)	MFI	118@5200	130@2800	3.50x3.46	9.0:1	56@3000
	W	4.3 (4293)	CMFI	195@4500	260@3600	4.00x3.48	9.1:1	25-50@1200
	Z	4.3 (4293)	TBI	165@4000	235@2400	4.00x3.48	9.1:1	18@2000
1995	4	2.2 (2189)	MFI	118@5200	130@2800	3.50x3.46	9.0:1	56@3000
	W	4.3 (4293)	CMFI	191@4500	260@3400	4.00x3.48	9.1:1	18@2000
	Z	4.3 (4293)	TBI	155@4000	235@2400	4.00x3.48	9.1:1	18@2000
1996	4	2.2 (2189)	SFI	118@5200	130@2800	3.50x3.46	9.0:1	56@3000
	W	4.3 (4293)	CSFI	①	②	4.00x3.48	9.2:1	18@2000
	X	4.3 (4293)	CSFI	③	240@2800	4.00x3.48	9.2:1	18@2000
1997	4	2.2 (2189)	SFI	118@5200	130@2800	3.50x3.46	9.0:1	56@3000
	W	4.3 (4293)	CSFI	①	②	4.00x3.48	9.2:1	18@2000
	X	4.3 (4293)	CSFI	③	240@2800	4.00x3.48	9.2:1	18@2000

MFI - Multi-port Fuel Injection
SFI - Sequential Fuel Injection
TBI - Throttle Body Fuel Injection

CMFI - Central Multi-port Fuel Injection
CSFI - Central Sequential Fuel Injection

① 2WD: 180@4400
4WD: 190@4400

② 2WD: 245@2800
4WD: 250@2800

③ 2WD: 175@4400
4WD: 180@4400

88453C01

VALVE SPECIFICATIONS

Year	Engine ID/VIN	Engine Displacement Liters (cc)	Seat Angle (deg.)	Face Angle (deg.)	Spring Test Pressure (lbs. @ in.)	Spring Installed Height (in.)	Stem-to-Guide Clearance (in.)		Stem Diameter (in.)	
							Intake	Exhaust	Intake	Exhaust
1994	4	2.2 (2189)	46	45	220-236@ 1.278	1.71	0.0010-0.0027	0.0010-0.0030	NA	NA
	W	4.3 (4293)	46	45	194-206@ 1.25	1.69-1.71	0.0010-0.0027	0.0010-0.0027	NA	NA
	Z	4.3 (4293)	46	45	194-206@ 1.25	1.69-1.71	0.0010-0.0027	0.0010-0.0027	NA	NA
1995	4	2.2 (2189)	46	45	220-236@ 1.278	1.71	0.0010-0.0027	0.0010-0.0030	NA	NA
	W	4.3 (4293)	46	45	194-206@ 1.25	1.69-1.71	0.0010-0.0027	0.0010-0.0027	NA	NA
	Z	4.3 (4293)	46	45	194-206@ 1.25	1.69-1.71	0.0010-0.0027	0.0010-0.0027	NA	NA
1996	4	2.2 (2189)	46	45	220-236@ 1.278	1.71	0.0010-0.0027	0.0010-0.0030	NA	NA
	W	4.3 (4293)	46	45	187-203@ 1.27	1.69-1.71	0.0010-0.0027	0.0011-0.0027	NA	NA
	X	4.3 (4293)	46	45	187-203@ 1.27	1.69-1.71	0.0010-0.0027	0.0011-0.0027	NA	NA
1997	4	2.2 (2189)	46	45	220-236@ 1.278	1.71	0.0010-0.0027	0.0010-0.0030	NA	NA
	W	4.3 (4293)	46	45	187-203@ 1.27	1.69-1.71	0.0010-0.0027	0.0011-0.0027	NA	NA
	X	4.3 (4293)	46	45	187-203@ 1.27	1.69-1.71	0.0010-0.0027	0.0011-0.0027	NA	NA

NA - Not Available

88453C02

CAMSHAFT SPECIFICATIONS

All measurements given in inches.

Year	Engine ID/VIN	Engine Displacement Liters (cc)	Journal Diameter 1	2	3	4	5	Elevation In.	Ex.	Bearing Clearance	Camshaft End Play
1994	4	2.2 (2189)	1.8682-1.8692	1.8682-1.8692	1.8682-1.8692	1.8682-1.8692	1.8682-1.8692	0.2880	0.2880	0.0010-0.0039	0.0015-0.0050
	W	4.3 (4293)	1.8682-1.8692	1.8682-1.8692	1.8682-1.8692	1.8682-1.8692	-	0.2880	0.2940	NA	0.0010-0.0090
	Z	4.3 (4293)	1.8682-1.8692	1.8682-1.8692	1.8682-1.8692	1.8682-1.8692	-	0.2340	0.2570	NA	0.0040-0.0120
1995	4	2.2 (2189)	1.8682-1.8692	1.8682-1.8692	1.8682-1.8692	1.8682-1.8692	1.8682-1.8692	0.2880	0.2880	0.0010-0.0039	0.0015-0.0050
	W	4.3 (4293)	1.8682-1.8692	1.8682-1.8692	1.8682-1.8692	1.8682-1.8692	-	0.2880	0.2940	NA	0.0010-0.0090
	Z	4.3 (4293)	1.8682-1.8692	1.8682-1.8692	1.8682-1.8692	1.8682-1.8692	-	0.2340	0.2570	NA	0.0040-0.0120
1996	4	2.2 (2189)	1.8682-1.8692	1.8682-1.8692	1.8682-1.8692	1.8682-1.8692	1.8682-1.8692	0.2880	0.2880	0.0010-0.0039	0.0015-0.0050
	W	4.3 (4293)	1.8682-1.8692	1.8682-1.8692	1.8682-1.8692	1.8682-1.8692	-	0.2763	0.2763	NA	0.0010-0.0090
	X	4.3 (4293)	1.8682-1.8692	1.8682-1.8692	1.8682-1.8692	1.8682-1.8692	-	0.2763	0.2763	NA	0.0010-0.0090
1997	4	2.2 (2189)	1.8682-1.8692	1.8682-1.8692	1.8682-1.8692	1.8682-1.8692	1.8682-1.8692	0.2880	0.2880	0.0010-0.0039	0.0015-0.0050
	W	4.3 (4293)	1.8682-1.8692	1.8682-1.8692	1.8682-1.8692	1.8682-1.8692	-	0.2860-0.2900	0.2920-0.2960	NA	0.0010-0.0090
	X	4.3 (4293)	1.8682-1.8692	1.8682-1.8692	1.8682-1.8692	1.8682-1.8692	-	0.2860-0.2900	0.2920-0.2960	NA	0.0010-0.0090

NA - Not Available

88453C03

CRANKSHAFT AND CONNECTING ROD SPECIFICATIONS

All measurements are given in inches.

		Engine	Crankshaft				Connecting Rod		
Year	Engine ID/VIN	Displacement Liters (cc)	Main Brg. Journal Dia.	Main Brg. Oil Clearance	Shaft End-play	Thrust on No.	Journal Diameter	Oil Clearance	Side Clearance
1994	4	2.2 (2189)	2.4945-2.4954	0.0006-0.0019	0.0020-0.0070	4	1.9983-1.9994	0.0010-0.0031	0.0039-0.0149
	W	4.3 (4293)	①	③	0.0020-0.0070	4	2.2487-2.2497	0.0013-0.0035	0.0060-0.0140
	Z	4.3 (4293)	②	③	0.0020-0.0060	4	2.2487-2.2497	0.0013-0.0035	0.0060-0.0140
1995	4	2.2 (2189)	2.4945-2.4954	0.0006-0.0019	0.0020-0.0070	4	1.9983-1.9994	0.0010-0.0031	0.0039-0.0149
	W	4.3 (4293)	①	③	0.0050-0.0180	4	2.2487-2.2497	0.0013-0.0035	0.0150-0.0460
	Z	4.3 (4293)	②	③	0.0050-0.0180	4	2.2487-2.2497	0.0013-0.0035	0.0150-0.0460
1996	4	2.2 (2189)	2.4945-2.4954	0.0006-0.0019	0.0020-0.0070	4	1.9983-1.9994	0.0010-0.0031	0.0039-0.0149
	W	4.3 (4293)	①	④	0.0020-0.0080	4	2.2487-2.2497	0.0010-0.0030	0.0060-0.0170
	X	4.3 (4293)	①	④	0.0020-0.0080	4	2.2487-2.2497	0.0010-0.0030	0.0060-0.0170
1997	4	2.2 (2189)	2.4945-2.4954	0.0006-0.0019	0.0020-0.0070	4	1.9983-1.9994	0.0010-0.0031	0.0039-0.0149
	W	4.3 (4293)	①	⑤	0.0020-0.0080	4	2.2487-2.2497	0.0010-0.0030	0.0060-0.0170
	X	4.3 (4293)	①	⑤	0.0020-0.0080	4	2.2487-2.2497	0.0010-0.0030	0.0060-0.0170

① No. 1: 2.4488-2.4495
Nos. 2-3: 2.4485-2.4494
No. 4: 2.4480-2.4489

② No. 1: 2.4484-2.4493
Nos. 2-3: 2.4481-2.4490
No. 4: 2.4479-2.4488

③ No. 1: 0.0008-0.0020
Nos. 2-3: 0.0011-0.0023
No. 4: 0.0017-0.0032

④ No. 1: 0.0010-0.0015
Nos. 2-3: 0.0010-0.0025
No. 4: 0.0025-0.0035

⑤ No. 1: 0.0008 - 0.0020
Nos. 2-4: 0.0009 - 0.0024

88453C04

PISTON AND RING SPECIFICATIONS

All measurements are given in inches.

		Engine		Ring Gap			Ring Side Clearance		
Year	Engine ID/VIN	Displacement Liters (cc)	Piston Clearance	Top Compression	Bottom Compression	Oil Control	Top Compression	Bottom Compression	Oil Control
1994	4	2.2 (2189)	0.0007-0.0017	0.010-0.020	0.010-0.020	0.010-0.050	0.0019-0.0027	0.0019-0.0027	0.0019-0.0082
	W	4.3 (4293)	0.0007-0.0017	0.010-0.020	0.018-0.026	0.015-0.055	0.0014-0.0032	0.0014-0.0032	0.0020-0.0070 ③
	Z	4.3 (4293)	0.0007-0.0017	0.010-0.020	0.010-0.025	0.015-0.055	0.0012-0.0032	0.0012-0.0032	0.0020-0.0070 ③
1995	4	2.2 (2189)	0.0007-0.0017	0.010-0.020	0.010-0.020	0.010-0.050	0.0019-0.0027	0.0019-0.0027	0.0019-0.0082
	W	4.3 (4293)	0.0007-0.0017 ①	0.010-0.020	0.018-0.026	0.015-0.055	0.0014-0.0032	0.0014-0.0032	0.0020-0.0070 ③
	Z	4.3 (4293)	0.0007-0.0017 ①	0.010-0.020	0.010-0.025	0.015-0.055	0.0012-0.0032	0.0012-0.0032	0.0020-0.0070 ③
1996	4	2.2 (2189)	0.0007-0.0017	0.010-0.020	0.010-0.020	0.010-0.050	0.0019-0.0027	0.0019-0.0027	0.0019-0.0082
	W	4.3 (4293)	①	②	②	0.065 MAX	0.0042 MAX	0.0042 MAX	0.0080 MAX
	X	4.3 (4293)	①	②	②	0.065 MAX	0.0042 MAX	0.0042 MAX	0.0080 MAX
1997	4	2.2 (2189)	0.0007-0.0017	0.010-0.020	0.010-0.020	0.010-0.030	0.0019-0.0027	0.0019-0.0027	0.0019-0.0082
	W	4.3 (4293)	0.0007-0.0017 ①	0.010-0.016 ②	0.018-0.026 ②	0.065 MAX	0.0042 MAX	0.0042 MAX	0.0020-0.0070 ③
	X	4.3 (4293)	0.0007-0.0017 ①	0.010-0.016 ②	0.018-0.026 ②	0.065 MAX	0.0042 MAX	0.0042 MAX	0.0020-0.0070 ③

MAX - Maximum ① 0.0024 MAX ② 0.035 MAX ③ 0.0080 MAX

88453C05

TORQUE SPECIFICATIONS

All readings in ft. lbs.

Year	Engine ID/VIN	Engine Displacement Liters (cc)	Cylinder Head Bolts	Main Bearing Bolts	Rod Bearing Bolts	Crankshaft Damper Bolts	Flywheel Bolts	Manifold Intake	Manifold Exhaust	Spark Plugs	Lug Nut
1994	4	2.2 (2189)	①	70	38	77	55	⑤	10	②	95
	W	4.3 (4293)	⑨	78	③	70	74	⑩	④	11	95
	Z	4.3 (4293)	⑨	81	③	70	74	35	④	11	95
1995	4	2.2 (2189)	①	70	38	77	55	⑤	10	13	95
	W	4.3 (4293)	⑨	81	③	70	74	⑩	④	11	95
	Z	4.3 (4293)	⑨	81	③	70	74	35	④	11	95
1996	4	2.2 (2189)	①	70	38	77	55	⑤	10	13	95
	W	4.3 (4293)	⑥	77	③	74	74	⑧	⑦	15	95
	X	4.3 (4293)	⑥	77	③	74	74	⑧	⑦	15	95
1997	4	2.2 (2189)	①	70	38	77	55	⑤	10	13	95
	W	4.3 (4293)	⑥	77	③	74	74	⑧	⑦	15	95
	X	4.3 (4293)	⑥	77	③	74	74	⑧	⑦	15	95

① Step 1: Long bolts 1,4,5,8,9: 46 ft. lbs.
Short bolts 2,3,6,7,10: 43 ft. lbs.
(Tighten bolts in numerical sequence)
Step 2: Plus 90 degrees for all bolts

② 1st-time installation (new head): 20 ft. lbs.
All other installations: 12 ft. lbs.

③ 20 ft. lbs. plus 70 degrees

④ Two center bolts: 26 ft. lbs.
All others: 20 ft. lbs.

⑤ Lower intake manifold nuts: 24 ft. lbs.
Lower intake manifold studs: 89 inch lbs.
Upper intake manifold bolts: 22 ft. lbs.

⑥ 1st pass: 22 ft. lbs.
Final pass:
Short bolt: Plus 55 degrees
Medium bolt: Plus 65 degrees
Long bolt: Plus 75 degrees

⑦ 1st pass: 11 ft. lbs.
Final pass: 22 ft. lbs.

⑧ Lower intake manifold:
1st pass: 27 inch lbs.
2nd pass: 106 inch lbs.
Final pass: 11 ft. lbs.
Upper manifold bolts:
1st pass: 44 inch lbs.
Final pass: 88 inch lbs.

⑨ Step 1: 25 ft. lbs.
Step 2: 45 ft. lbs.
Step 3: 65 ft. lbs.

⑩ Lower manifold bolts: 35 ft. lbs.
Upper manifold bolts and studs: 88 inch lbs.

88453C06

Engine

REMOVAL & INSTALLATION

➧ See Figure 7

In the process of removing the engine, you will come across a number of steps which call for the removal of a separate component or system, such as "disconnect the exhaust system" or "remove the radiator." In most instances, a detailed removal procedure can be found elsewhere in this manual.

It is virtually impossible to list each individual wire and hose which must be disconnected, simply because so many different model and engine combinations have been manufactured. Careful observation and common sense are the best possible additions to any repair procedure. Be absolutely sure to tag the wire or hose before it is disconnected, so that you can be assured of proper reconnection during installation.

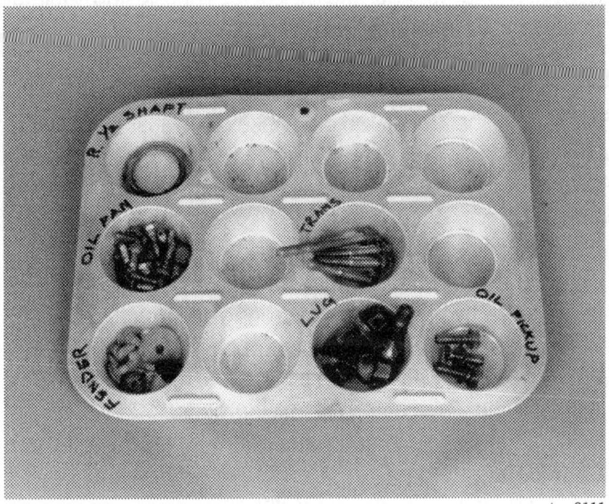

tccs3111

Fig. 7 When removing nuts, bolts and other parts, place them in a tray or similar container

4.3L Engines

See Figures 8, 9, 10 and 11

1. Disconnect the negative battery cable and properly relieve the fuel system pressure.
2. Disconnect the vacuum reservoir and/or the underhood light from the hood (as equipped), then remove the outer cowl vent grilles.
3. Matchmark and remove the hood from the vehicle.
4. Raise and support the front of the vehicle safely using jackstands. It will be most convenient if the truck can be supported so underhood access is still possible. Otherwise, the truck will have to be raised and lowered multiple times during the procedure for the necessary access.
5. Drain the engine cooling system and the engine oil into separate drain pans.
6. Disconnect the oxygen sensor and/or wiring.
7. Disconnect the exhaust at the manifolds and loosen the hanger at the catalytic converter. This is necessary to remove the rear catalytic converter cushion mounts for removal of the exhaust assembly.

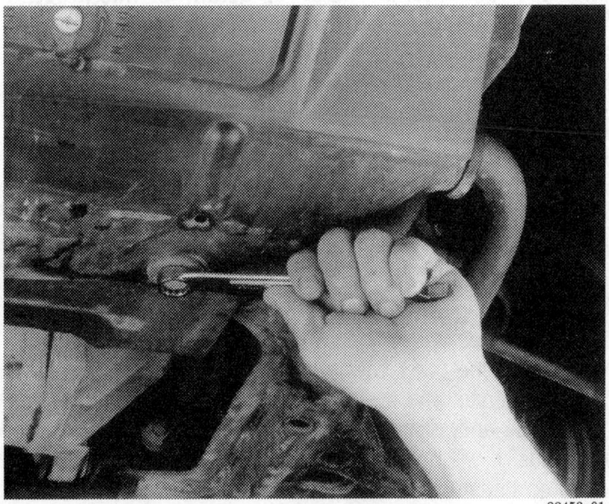

88453p01

Fig. 8 Unfasten the skid plate retaining bolts

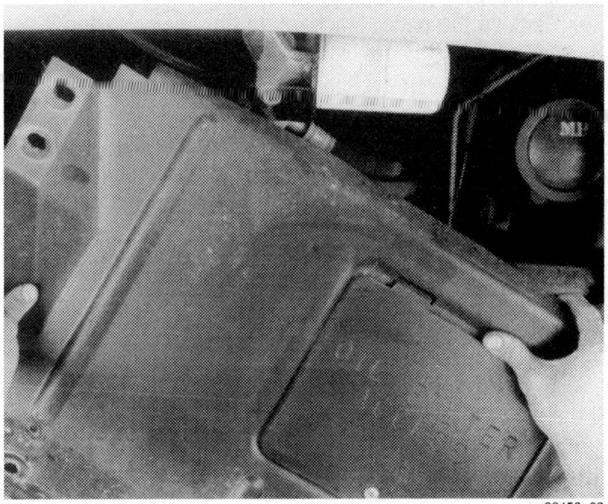

88453p02

Fig. 9 Remove the skid plate from the vehicle

88453p03

Fig. 10 Remove the air cleaner assembly

88453p04

Fig. 11 Relieve the belt tension, then remove the serpentine belt

8. If equipped, remove the skid plate.
9. Remove the pencil braces from the engine to the transmission.
10. If equipped, remove the slave cylinder and position aside.
11. Disconnect the line clamp at the bellhousing.
12. Tag and disengage the wiring from the starter, remove the flywheel cover and remove the starter from the vehicle.
13. Remove the oil filter.
14. Remove the engine mount through-bolts and unfasten all of the bellhousing bolts, except the upper left.
15. Disconnect the battery ground (negative) cable from the engine.
16. On 4WD vehicles, remove the front drive axle bolts and roll the axle downward.
17. Remove the air cleaner assembly and duct work.
18. Remove the upper radiator shroud, then remove the fan assembly.
19. Remove the multi-ribbed serpentine drive belt, then remove the water pump pulley.
20. Disconnect the upper radiator hose, then remove the A/C compressor (if equipped) and position aside with the lines intact.
21. Disconnect the lower radiator hose, then disconnect the oil cooler and overflow lines from the radiator. Plug the cooler line openings to prevent system contamination or excessive fluid loss.
22. Remove the radiator from the vehicle, then remove the lower radiator shroud.
23. Disconnect the power steering hoses from the steering gear, then cap the openings to prevent system contamination or excessive fluid loss.
24. Disconnect the heater hoses from the intake manifold and the water pump.
25. Tag, disconnect and remove the wiring harness and vacuum lines from the engine
26. Disconnect the throttle cables, then remove the distributor cap.
27. Remove the remaining bolt from the bellhousing.
28. Disconnect the fuel lines and remove the bracket.
29. Remove the ground strap(s) from the rear of the cylinder head.
30. On 4WD vehicles, loosen the front body mount bolts.
31. Support the transmission using a jack.
32. Install a suitable lifting device and carefully lift the engine from the vehicle. Pause several times while lifting the engine to make sure no wires or hoses have become snagged.

To install:

33. Carefully lower the engine into the vehicle.
34. On 4WD vehicles, tighten the front body mount bolts.
35. Install the ground strap(s) to the rear of the cylinder head.
36. Connect the fuel lines and install the bracket.
37. Install the upper left bellhousing bolt.
38. Install the distributor cap and wires.
39. Connect the throttle cables.
40. Engage the vacuum lines and wiring harness connectors as noted during removal.
41. Engage the heater hoses, then uncap and connect the power steering hoses.
42. Install the lower shroud, then install the radiator.
43. Uncap and connect the oil cooler lines to the radiator, then connect the overflow hose.
44. Connect the lower radiator hose, then if equipped, reposition and secure the A/C compressor to the engine.
45. Engage the upper radiator hose, then install the water pump pulley.
46. Install the serpentine drive belt, then install the fan assembly.
47. Install the upper radiator shroud.
48. Install the air cleaner and ducts.
49. For 4WD vehicles, roll the front axle up into position, then install and tighten the retaining bolts.
50. Connect the battery ground strap to the engine block.
51. Install the remaining bellhousing bolts.
52. Install the engine mount through-bolts and tighten to 49 ft. lbs. (66 Nm).
53. Install a new oil filter.
54. Install the starter motor.
55. Install the line clamp at the bellhousing.
56. Install the flywheel cover.
57. If equipped, reposition and secure the clutch slave cylinder.
58. Install the pencil brace and the skid plate, as equipped.
59. Install the catalytic converter Y-pipe assembly and hangers.
60. Remove the jackstands and carefully lower the truck.
61. Align the marks made during removal and install the hood.
62. Install the outer cowl vent grilles, then connect the vacuum reservoir and/or the underhood light to the hood (as equipped).
63. Check all powertrain fluid levels and add, as necessary. Be sure to properly fill the engine crankcase with clean engine oil.
64. Connect the negative battery cable and properly fill the engine cooling system.
65. Start and run the engine, then check for leaks.

2.2L (VIN 4) Engine

1994-95 MODELS

➡The manufacturer recommends the discharge and recovery of the A/C system R-134a refrigerant for this procedure. DO NOT attempt this without the proper equipment. R-134a should NOT be mixed with R-12 refrigerant and, depending on your local laws, attempting to service this system could be illegal.

1. Have the refrigerant recovered from the A/C system by a facility equipped with an approved recovery station.
2. Disconnect the negative battery cable and properly relieve the fuel system pressure.
3. Disconnect the vacuum reservoir and/or the underhood light from the hood (as equipped).
4. Disconnect the windshield washer line from the hood, then remove the outer cowl vent grilles.
5. Matchmark and remove the hood from the vehicle.
6. Raise and support the front of the vehicle safely using jackstands. It will be most convenient if the truck can be supported so underhood access is still possible. Otherwise, the truck will have to be raised and lowered multiple times during the procedure for the necessary access.

7. Drain the engine cooling system and the engine oil into separate drain pans.
8. Disconnect the oxygen sensor and/or wiring.
9. Disconnect the exhaust at the manifolds and loosen the hanger at the catalytic converter.
10. Remove the pencil braces from the engine to the transmission.
11. Remove the inspection cover.
12. Tag and disengage the wiring from the starter, then remove the starter from the vehicle.
13. Remove the engine mount through-bolts.
14. Remove the bellhousing bolts.
15. Remove the battery from the vehicle, then disconnect the battery ground (negative cable) from the engine.
16. Remove the air cleaner assembly and duct work.
17. Remove the upper and fan shroud.
18. Remove the engine cooling fan.
19. Remove the multi-ribbed serpentine drive belt.
20. Remove the water pump assembly.
21. Disconnect the upper radiator hose, then remove the A/C compressor (if equipped) and position aside.
22. Disconnect the lower radiator hose, then remove the radiator and lower fan shroud from the vehicle.
23. Disconnect the power steering hoses from the pump, then cap the openings to prevent system contamination or excessive fluid loss.
24. Disengage the heater hose from the intake manifold, then disconnect the ground straps at the rear of the engine.
25. Tag, disconnect and remove the wiring harness and vacuum lines from the engine.
26. Disengage the throttle cable, then disconnect the fuel lines from the fuel rail and engine.
27. Support the transmission using a floor jack.
28. Install a suitable lifting device and carefully lift the engine from the vehicle. Pause several times while lifting the engine to make sure no wires or hoses have become snagged.

To install:

29. Carefully lower the engine into the vehicle, then remove the floor jack and engine lifting device.
30. Connect the fuel lines and install the bracket(s).
31. Connect the throttle cable.
32. Engage the vacuum lines and wiring harness connectors as noted during removal.
33. Engage the wiring harness clips and connect the ground straps to the rear of the engine.
34. Engage the heater hose, then uncap and connect the power steering hoses.
35. Install the lower shroud.
36. Install the radiator.
37. Reposition and secure the A/C compressor to the engine.
38. Install the upper radiator hose.
39. Install the water pump.
40. Install the serpentine drive belt.
41. Install the fan assembly.
42. Install the upper radiator shroud.
43. Install the air cleaner and ducts.
44. Connect the battery ground strap to the engine block.
45. Install the bellhousing bolts.
46. Install the engine mount through-bolts.
47. Install the starter motor.
48. Install the flywheel cover.
49. Install the pencil braces.
50. Install the catalytic converter pipe assembly and hangers.
51. Remove the jackstands and carefully lower the truck.
52. Align the marks made during removal and install the hood.
53. Install the outer cowl vent grilles, then connect the vacuum reservoir and/or the underhood light to the hood (as equipped).
54. Connect the windshield washer hoses.
55. Check all powertrain fluid levels and add, as necessary. Be sure to properly fill the engine crankcase with clean engine oil.
56. Connect the negative battery cable and properly fill the engine cooling system.
57. Start and run the engine, then check for leaks.

1996-97 MODELS

✱✱CAUTION

When draining engine coolant, keep in mind that cats and dogs are attracted to ethylene glycol antifreeze and could drink any that is left in an uncovered container or in puddles on the ground. This will prove fatal in sufficient quantity. Always drain coolant into a sealable container. Coolant should be reused unless it is contaminated or is several years old.

1. Have the refrigerant recovered from the A/C system by a facility equipped with an approved recovery station.
2. Disconnect the negative battery cable and properly relieve the fuel system pressure.
3. Drain the engine cooling system and the engine oil into separate drain pans.
4. Matchmark and remove the hood from the vehicle.
5. Raise and support the front of the vehicle safely using jackstands. It will be most convenient if the truck can be supported so underhood access is still possible. Otherwise, the truck will have to be raised and lowered multiple times during the procedure for the necessary access.
6. Disengage the transmission from the engine. Refer to Section 7 in this manual for this procedure.
7. Support the engine with a hydraulic jack, then unfasten and remove the engine mount through bolts.
8. Remove the upper radiator shroud.
9. Tag and disconnect the hoses and transmission coolant lines engaged to the radiator, then remove the radiator and lower fan shroud from the vehicle.
10. Tag and disengage the air conditioning line from the evaporator core to the accumulator, then remove the support at the center of the bulkhead.
11. Disengage the air conditioning line to the compressor at the accumulator.
12. Tag and disengage the heater hoses from the heater core in the bulkhead.
13. Disengage the throttle cable, the remove the multi-ribbed serpentine drive belt.
14. Remove the power steering pump and bracket.
15. Tag and disengage all electrical connections and wiring harnesses.
16. Tag and disengage all vacuum lines.

17. Install a suitable lifting device and carefully lift the engine from the vehicle. Pause several times while lifting the engine to make sure no wires or hoses have become snagged.

To install:

18. Carefully lower the engine into the vehicle.
19. Engage all vacuum lines, electrical connections and wiring harnesses that were tagged and disconnected during the removal process.
20. Install the power steering pump and bracket.
21. Install the serpentine drive belt, then the throttle cable.
22. Engage the heater hoses to the heater core.
23. Connect the air conditioning hose to the compressor at the accumulator.
24. Engage the air conditioning support at the bulkhead, then connect the air conditioning line from the evaporator core to the accumulator.
25. Install the air conditioner condenser and the radiator.
26. Engage all hoses and transmission cooling lines to the radiator, then connect the radiator shroud(s).
27. Install and tighten the engine mount through bolts.
28. Engage the transmission to the engine.
29. Remove the jackstands and carefully lower the truck.
30. Align the marks made during removal and install the hood.
31. Check all powertrain fluid levels and add, as necessary. Be sure to properly fill the engine crankcase with clean engine oil.
32. Connect the negative battery cable and properly fill the engine cooling system.
33. Start and run the engine, then check for leaks.

Rocker Arm (Valve) Cover

REMOVAL & INSTALLATION

2.2L Engine

➧ **See Figure 12**

1. Disconnect the negative battery cable and disconnect the air duct from the inlet.
2. Disconnect the throttle cable and remove the cable support linkage.
3. Disconnect the power brake booster vacuum hose.
4. Remove the PCV valve and pipe assembly.
5. Loosen and remove the rocker cover retaining bolts, then remove the cover from the engine.

➡DO NOT pry on the cover to remove it. If it sticks, use your palm or a rubber mallet to bump it rearwards, from the front.

6. Using a putty knife, carefully clean the gasket mounting surfaces. Keep debris out of the engine.

To install:

7. Install the rocker arm cover to the engine using a new gasket, then tighten the retainers to 89 inch lbs. (10 Nm). Be careful not to overtighten the fasteners and either distort the valve cover (causing and leak) or break the fastener (causing more work).
8. Install the PCV valve and pipe assembly.

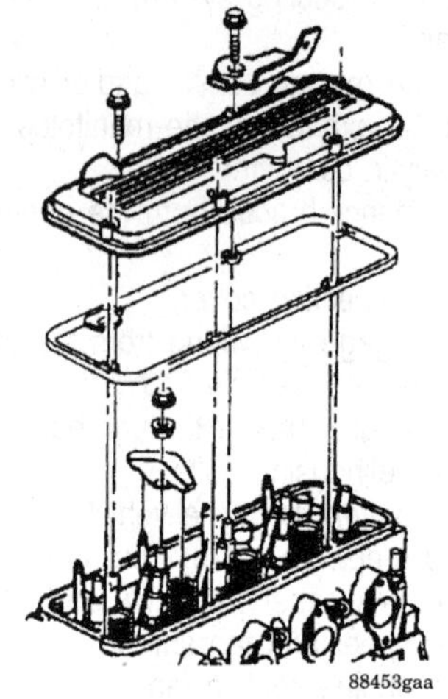

Fig. 12 View of the rocker arm cover — 1996 2.2L model shown

9. Connect the brake booster vacuum hose.
10. Connect the throttle cable and secure the cable support linkage. Tighten the bracket bolts to 10 ft. lbs. (25 Nm) and the bracket nut to 22 ft. lbs. (30 Nm).
11. Connect the air duct to the inlet, then connect the negative battery cable.

4.3L Engine

RIGHT SIDE — 1994-95

➧ **See Figures 13, 14, 15 and 16**

1. Disconnect the negative battery cable.
2. Remove the air cleaner.
3. On 1995 (VIN W) engines, remove the PCV valve and pipe assembly.
4. On 1995 (VIN W) engines, remove the coil with the bracket and lay to one side.
5. Remove the EGR controller and MAP sensor bracket.
6. Tag and disconnect the necessary vacuum lines.
7. Remove the wiring harness from the retaining clips and lay it aside.

Fig. 13 Tag and disengage the necessary electrical connections and vacuum lines

Fig. 14 Unfasten the rocker arm cover bolts

Fig. 15 Remove the rocker arm cover from the engine

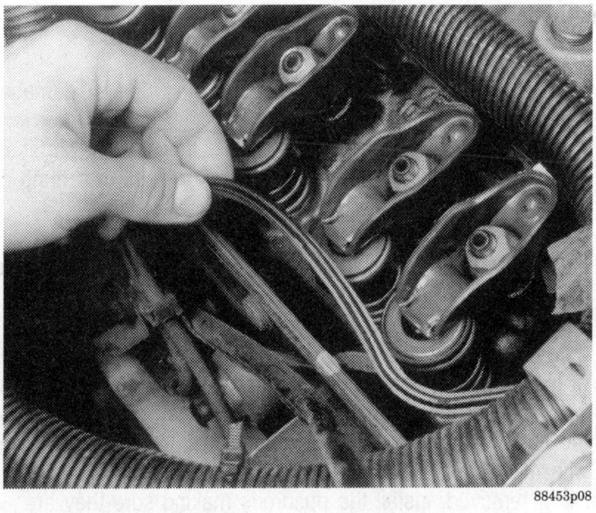

Fig. 16 Remove the old rocker arm cover gasket

8. Remove the rocker arm cover bolts, then remove the cover from the cylinder head.

➡DO NOT pry on the cover to remove it. If it sticks, use your palm or a rubber mallet to bump it rearwards, from the front.

9. Using a putty knife, carefully clean the gasket mounting surfaces. Keep debris out of the engine.

To install:

10. Install the rocker arm cover to the engine using a new gasket, then tighten the retainers to 89 inch lbs. (10 Nm). Be careful not to overtighten the fasteners and either distort the valve cover (causing and leak) or break the fastener (causing more work).
11. Install the EGR controller and MAP sensor bracket.
12. Connect the vacuum lines as noted during removal.
13. On 1995 (VIN W) engines, install the coil with the bracket.
14. On 1995 (VIN W) engines, install the PCV valve and pipe assembly.
15. Position and secure electrical wiring harness in the retaining clips.
16. Install the air cleaner.
17. Connect the negative battery cable.

RIGHT SIDE — 1995 (VIN W)

1. Disconnect the negative battery cable and disconnect the air duct from the inlet.
2. Remove the PCV valve and pipe assembly.
3. Remove the coil with the bracket and lay to one side.
4. Unfasten the rocker arm cover colts.
5. Remove the rocker arm cover and gasket.

➡DO NOT pry on the cover to remove it. If it sticks, use your palm or a rubber mallet to bump it rearwards, from the front.

6. Using a putty knife, carefully clean the gasket mounting surfaces. Keep debris out of the engine.

To install:

7. Install the rocker arm cover to the engine using a new gasket, then tighten the retainers to 89 inch lbs. (10 Nm). Be careful not to overtighten the fasteners and either distort the valve cover (causing and leak) or break the fastener (causing more work).
8. Install the coil and bracket.
9. Install the PCV valve and pipe assembly.
10. Connect the negative battery cable.

LEFT SIDE — 1994-95 (VINS W AND Z)

1. Disconnect the negative battery cable.
2. Remove the air cleaner assembly.
3. Remove the pencil brace, then disconnect the power brake vacuum line at the booster.
4. Remove the rocker arm cover bolts, then remove the cover.

➡DO NOT pry on the cover to remove it. If it sticks, use your palm or a rubber mallet to bump it rearwards, from the front.

5. Using a putty knife, carefully clean the gasket mounting surfaces. Keep debris out of the engine.

CAUTION

The EPA warns that prolonged contact with used engine oil may cause a number of skin disorders, including cancer! You should make every effort to minimize you exposure to used engine oil. Protective gloves should be worn when changing the oil. Wash your hands and any other exposed skin areas as soon as possible after exposure to used engine oil. Soap and water, or waterless hand cleaner should be used.

To install:

6. Install the rocker arm cover to the engine using a new gasket, then tighten the retainers to 89 inch lbs. (10 Nm). Be careful not to overtighten the fasteners and either distort the valve cover (causing and leak) or break the fastener (causing more work).
7. Connect the power brake booster vacuum line to the booster.
8. Install the pencil brace.
9. Install the air cleaner assembly.
10. Connect the negative battery cable.

LEFT SIDE — 1995 (VIN W)

1. Disconnect the negative battery cable.
2. Remove the crankcase ventilation pipe.
3. Unfasten the rocker arm cover bolts.
4. Remove the rocker arm cover and gasket.
5. Using a putty knife, carefully clean the gasket mounting surfaces. Keep debris out of the engine.

To install:

6. Install the rocker arm cover to the engine using a new gasket, then tighten the retainers to 89 inch lbs. (10 Nm). Be careful not to overtighten the fasteners and either distort the valve cover (causing and leak) or break the fastener (causing more work).
7. Install the crankcase ventilation pipe.
8. Connect the negative battery cable.

RIGHT SIDE — 1996-97 (VINS W, Z AND X)

1. Disconnect the negative battery cable.
2. Tag and disconnect the spark plug wires.
3. Remove the vent tube.
4. Disconnect the wiring bracket at the generator bracket.
5. Unfasten the oil level dipstick tube brace bolt, then move the heater hoses aside
6. Unfasten the rocker arm cover bolts.
7. Remove the rocker arm cover and gasket.
8. Using a putty knife, carefully clean the gasket mounting surfaces. Keep debris out of the engine.

To install:

9. Install the rocker arm cover to the engine using a new gasket, then tighten the retainers to 106 inch lbs. (12 Nm). Be careful not to overtighten the fasteners and either distort the valve cover (causing and leak) or break the fastener (causing more work).
10. Engage the wiring bracket to the generator bracket.
11. Install the vent tube and engage the spark plug wires.
12. Connect the negative battery cable.

LEFT SIDE — 1996-97 (VINS W, Z AND X)

1. Disconnect the negative battery cable and disconnect the air duct from the inlet.
2. Disengage the A/C compressor and bracket and move the compressor to one side.
3. Remove the PCV valve and pipe assembly.
4. Tag and disconnect the spark plug wires.
5. Unfasten the rocker arm cover bolts.
6. Remove the rocker arm cover and gasket.
7. Using a putty knife, carefully clean the gasket mounting surfaces. Keep debris out of the engine.

To install:

8. Install the rocker arm cover to the engine using a new gasket, then tighten the retainers to 106 inch lbs. (12 Nm). Be careful not to overtighten the fasteners and either distort the valve cover (causing and leak) or break the fastener (causing more work).
9. Connect the spark plug wires.
10. Install the A/C compressor bracket and compressor.
11. Install the PCV valve and pipe assembly.
12. Engage the air duct to the inlet and connect the negative battery cable.

Rocker Arms and Pushrods

REMOVAL & INSTALLATION

2.2L Engine

1. Remove the rocker arm cover from the cylinder head.
2. Remove the rocker arm retaining nut, then remove the arm and ball. If necessary, withdraw the pushrod form the cylinder head.

➡Valve train components which are to be reused MUST be installed in their original positions. If removed, be sure to tag or arrange all rocker arms and pushrods to assure proper installation.

To install:

3. Inspect the rocker arms, balls and pushrods for damage or wear and replace, as necessary:
   a. Check the rocker arms, balls and their mating surfaces. Make sure the surfaces are smooth and free from scoring or other damage.
   b. Check the rocker arm areas that contact the valve stems and the sockets that contact the pushrods, make sure these areas are smooth and free of both damage and wear.
   c. Make sure the pushrods are not bent; this can be determined by rolling them on a flat surface. Check the ends of the pushrods for scoring or roughness
   d. Inspect the rocker arm bolts for thread damage. Check the rocker arm bolts in the shoulder area for contact damage with the rocker arm.
4. If removed, install the pushrods making sure they are seated within the lifters.

5. If installing new rocker arms and balls, coat the friction surfaces using Dri-Slide Molykote® or an equivalent pre-lube.

➡When tightening the rocker arm retainers, make sure the lifter for that valve is resting on the base circle of the camshaft NOT on the lobe. DO NOT overtighten the retainers.

6. Install the rocker arms and ball, then tighten the retaining nuts to 22 ft. lbs. (30 Nm).

➡Valve lash is NOT adjustable on the 2.2L gasoline engine.

7. Install the rocker arm cover, then start and run the engine to check for leaks.

4.3L Engine

See Figures 17, 18, 19, 20 and 21

1. Remove the rocker arm cover(s) from the cylinder head.
2. Remove the rocker arm nut, the rocker arm and the ball washer.

➡If only the pushrod is to be removed, loosen the rocker arm nut, swing the rocker arm to the side and remove the pushrod.

3. Valve train components which are to be reused MUST be installed in their original positions. If removed, be sure to tag or arrange all rocker arms and pushrods to assure proper installation.
4. Withdraw the pushrod from the cylinder head.

To install:

5. Inspect and replace components if worn or damaged.
6. Coat the bearing surfaces of the rocker arms and the rocker arm ball washers with Molykote® or equivalent pre-lube.
7. Install the pushrods making sure that they seat properly in the lifter.
8. Install the rocker arms, ball washers and the nuts.
9. For the 4.3L engines which are equipped with screw-in type rocker arm studs with positive stop shoulders, tighten the rocker arm adjusting nuts against the stop shoulders to 20 ft. lbs. (27 Nm). No further adjustment is necessary, or possible.

88453p09

Fig. 17 Unfasten the rocker arm nut

88453p10

Fig. 18 Remove the ball washer . . . .

88453p11

Fig. 19 . . . . then remove the rocker arm

88453p12

Fig. 20 Remove the pushrod from the cylinder head

88453p13

Fig. 21 A piece of cardboard may be used to hold the pushrods in order

10. For most 4.3L engines which are not equipped with screw-in type rocker arm studs and positive stop shoulders, properly adjust the valve lash. For details on valve lash adjustment, please refer to the procedure in this section.
11. Install the rocker arm cover(s) to the cylinder head.
12. Start and run the engine, then check for leaks and for proper ignition timing adjustment.

Valve Lash

ADJUSTMENT

2.2L (VIN 4) Engine

This engine utilizes hydraulic valve lifters which means that a valve adjustment is NOT a regular maintenance item.

4.3L Engine

The 4.3L engines may be equipped with either of 2 rocker arm retaining systems. If your engine utilizes screw-in type rocker arm studs with positive stop shoulders, no valve lash adjustment is necessary or possible. If however, you engine utilizes the pressed-in rocker arm studs, use the following procedure to tighten the rocker arm nuts and properly center the pushrod on the hydraulic lifter:

1. To prepare the engine for valve adjustment, rotate the crankshaft until the mark on the damper pulley aligns with the 0° mark on the timing plate and the No. 1 cylinder is on the compression stroke. You will know when the No. 1 piston is on it's compression stroke because both the intake and exhaust valves will remain closed as the crankshaft damper mark approaches the timing scale.

➡Another method to tell when the piston is coming up on the compression stroke is by removing the spark plug and placing your thumb over the hole, you will feel the air being forced out of the spark plug hole. Stop turning the crankshaft when the TDC timing mark on the crankshaft pulley is directly aligned with the timing mark pointer or the zero mark on the scale.

The valve arrangement is as follows:

- E — I — I — E — I — E (right bank — front-to-rear)
- E — I — E — I — I — E (left bank — front-to-rear)

2. With the engine on the compression stroke, adjust the exhaust valves of cylinders No. 1, 5 & 6 and the intake valves of cylinders No. 1, 2 & 3 by performing the following procedures:
   a. Back out the adjusting nut until lash can be felt at the pushrod.
   b. While rotating the pushrod, turn the adjusting nut inward until all of the lash is removed.
   c. When the play has disappeared, turn the adjusting nut inward 1¾ additional turns.
3. Rotate the crankshaft one complete revolution and align the mark on the damper pulley with the 0° mark on the timing plate; the engine is now positioned on the No. 4 firing position. This time the No. 4 cylinder valves remain closed as the timing mark approaches the scale. Adjust the exhaust valves of cylinders No. 2, 3 & 4 and the intake valves of cylinders No. 4, 5 & 6, by performing the following procedures:
   a. Back out the adjusting nut until lash can be felt at the pushrod.
   b. While rotating the pushrod, turn the adjusting nut inward until all of the lash is removed.
   c. When the play has disappeared, turn the adjusting nut inward 1¾ additional turn.
4. Install the remaining components, then start the engine and check for oil leaks.

Thermostat

DIAGNOSIS

Make an operational check of the thermostat by hanging the it on a hook in a pot of warm water. Insert a thermometer into the water (neither the thermostat or thermometer should touch the metal sides or bottom of the pot) and heat the water to the thermostat opening temperature (stamped on the top of the thermostat). With the temperature within 10° of the opening temperature, the thermostat should open. If not, replace the thermostat.

REMOVAL & INSTALLATION

2.2L Engine

➧ See Figure 22

The thermostat is located in a housing protruding from the front of the engine, just above the water pump assembly.

CAUTION

When draining engine coolant, keep in mind that cats and dogs are attracted to ethylene glycol antifreeze and could drink any that is left in an uncovered container or in puddles on the ground. This will prove fatal in sufficient quantity. Always drain coolant into a sealable container. Coolant should be reused unless it is contaminated or is several years old.

1. Drain the engine cooling system to a level just below the thermostat.
2. Remove the water outlet retaining nuts, then lift the outlet from the housing.
3. Remove the thermostat from the housing, noting the orientation for installation purposes.

To install:

4. Carefully clean the all traces of the old gasket or sealer from the housing and outlet.
5. Install the thermostat to the housing, oriented as noted during removal, then position a new gasket (if used).
6. Place a 1/8 in. (3mm) bead of RTV sealant in the groove on the water outlet sealing surface, then install the outlet while the sealer is still wet.
7. Install the outlet retainers and tighten to 18 ft. lbs. (25 Nm) on 1994 models and 89 inch lbs. (10 Nm) on 1995-97 models.
8. Properly fill the engine cooling system and check for leaks.

4.3L Engine

➧ See Figures 23, 24 and 25

The thermostat is located between the water outlet and a housing built into the intake manifold.

CAUTION

When draining engine coolant, keep in mind that cats and dogs are attracted to ethylene glycol antifreeze and could drink any that is left in an uncovered container or in puddles on the ground. This will prove fatal in sufficient quantity. Always drain coolant into a sealable container. Coolant should be reused unless it is contaminated or is several years old.

1. Disconnect the negative battery cable.
2. Drain the cooling system to a level below the thermostat.
3. Remove the thermostat outlet-to-engine retainers (usually either 2 bolts or 1 bolt and 1 stud), then remove outlet from the intake manifold.

88453p14

Fig. 23 Unfasten the thermostat outlet-to-engine bolts

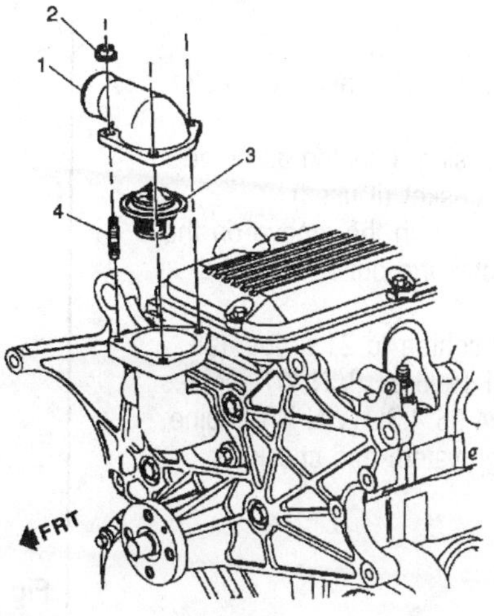

88453gab

Fig. 22 View of the thermostat and related components — 1996 2.2L engine

Fig. 24 Remove the outlet from the intake manifold

Fig. 25 Remove the thermostat from the housing

4. Remove the thermostat from the housing, noting the orientation for installation purposes.

To install:

5. Carefully clean the all traces of the old gasket or sealer from the housing and outlet.
6. Install the thermostat to the housing, oriented as noted during removal, then position a new gasket (if used).
7. Place a 1/8 in. bead of RTV sealant in the groove on the water outlet sealing surface, then install the outlet while the sealer is still wet.
8. Install the outlet retainers and tighten to 21 ft. lbs. (28 Nm) for the 4.3L (VIN Z and X) and 1996-97 (VIN W) engines or to 14 ft. lbs. (19 Nm) for the 1994-95 4.3L (VIN W) engine.
9. Properly fill the engine cooling system and check for leaks.

Intake Manifold

REMOVAL & INSTALLATION

2.2L Engine

➧ See Figures 26 and 27

The 2.2L (VIN 4) engine was introduced in 1994 and utilizes a Multi-Port Fuel Injection (MFI) system. The intake manifold is an assembly of separate components, an upper and a lower manifold.

1. Properly release the fuel system pressure (if the lower manifold assembly is being removed) and disconnect the negative battery cable.
2. Remove the air cleaner duct work.
3. Disconnect the throttle cable support and cable from the manifold.

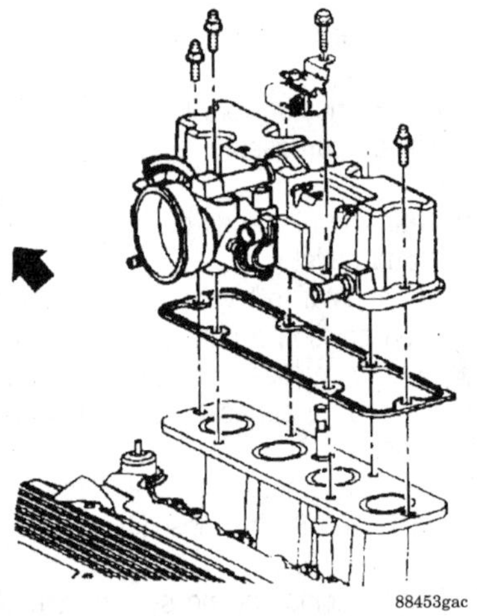

Fig. 26 View of the upper intake manifold — 1996 2.2L engine

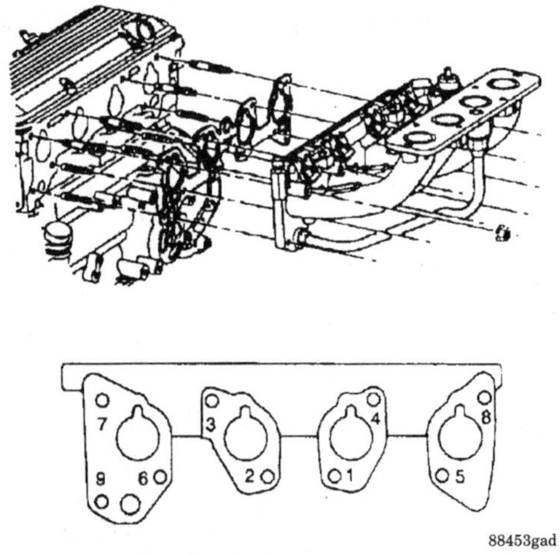

Fig. 27 View of the lower intake manifold — 1996 2.2L engine

4. Remove the MAP sensor and the EGR solenoid valve from the upper intake manifold and engine (if the upper manifold is not being replaced, simply disengage the wiring and hoses).

5. Tag and disengage all wiring and vacuum hoses from the upper intake manifold.

6. Loosen the retainers, then remove the upper intake manifold from the engine and lower manifold assembly.

7. Disconnect the fuel lines.

8. If applicable, disconnect the heater hose on the right side of the intake manifold.

9. Remove the EGR inlet pipe, if applicable.

10. Tag and disconnect the spark plug wires from the EI coil pack.

11. Remove the lower intake manifold retaining nuts, then remove the lower intake manifold and gasket.

To install:

12. Carefully remove all traces of gasket material from the mating surfaces. Check the EGR passage to be sure it is free of excessive carbon deposits and clean, as necessary.

13. Install the lower intake manifold using a new gasket, then tighten the retaining nut to 24 ft. lbs. (33 Nm) using the proper sequence.

14. Connect the spark plug wires to the EI coil pack and noted during removal.

15. If removed, install the EGR inlet pipe.

16. If applicable, connect the heater hose on the right side of the intake manifold.

17. Connect the fuel lines.

18. Install the upper intake manifold using a new gasket, then tighten the retainers to 22 ft. lbs (30 Nm).

19. Engage the wiring connectors and vacuum hoses to the upper intake manifold assembly.

20. Install the MAP sensor and EGR solenoid valve.

21. Install and secure the throttle cable support and cable. Tighten the cable bracket bolts to 18 ft. lbs. (25 Nm).

22. Install the air cleaner duct work.

23. Connect the negative battery cable, then start and run the engine to check for leaks.

4.3L Engine

1994-95 VIN Z

See Figures 28 and 29

CAUTION

When draining engine coolant, keep in mind that cats and dogs are attracted to ethylene glycol antifreeze and could drink any that is left in an uncovered container or in puddles on the ground. This will prove fatal in sufficient quantity. Always drain coolant into a sealable container. Coolant should be reused unless it is contaminated or is several years old.

1. Disconnect the negative battery cable and properly relieve the fuel system pressure.

2. Drain the cooling system.

3. Remove the air cleaner and heat stove tube.

4. Remove the two braces at the rear of the serpentine drive belt tensioner.

5. Disconnect the upper radiator hose.

6. Remove the emissions relays along with the bracket, then disengage the wiring harness from the retaining clips and position aside. Disconnect the ground cable from the intake manifold stud.

7. Remove the power brake vacuum pipe, then disconnect the heater hose pipe at the manifold and fuel lines at the TBI unit.

8. Remove the ignition coil, then disengage the electrical connectors at the sensors on the manifold.

9. Matchmark and remove the distributor from the engine. For details, please refer to the procedure in Section 2.

For ease of installation, DO NOT crank the engine with the distributor removed.

10. Tag and disengage the wires and hoses from the TBI unit.

11. Disconnect the the EGR hose, then disengage the throttle, TVS and cruise control cables (as equipped).

12. Unfasten the intake manifold retaining studs and/or bolts, then remove the manifold and gaskets.

To install:

CAUTION

The EPA warns that prolonged contact with used engine oil may cause a number of skin disorders, including cancer! You should make every effort to minimize you exposure to used engine oil. Protective gloves should be worn when changing the oil. Wash your hands and any other exposed skin areas as soon as possible after exposure to used engine oil. Soap and water, or waterless hand cleaner should be used.

13. Using a putty knife, carefully clean the gasket mounting surfaces. Be sure to inspect the manifold for warpage and/or cracks; if necessary, replace it.

14. Position the gaskets to the cylinder head with the port blocking plates to the rear, then apply a 3/16 in. (5mm) bead of RTV sealant to the front and rear of the engine block at the block-to-manifold mating surface. Extend the bead 1/2 in. (13mm) up each cylinder head to seal and retain the gaskets.

15. Install the intake manifold taking care not to disturb the gaskets, then tighten the manifold retainers to 35 ft. lbs. (48 Nm) using the proper torque sequence.

16. Engage the TVS, cruise control and/or throttle cables, as equipped.

17. Connect the EGR hose then engage the wires and hoses at the TBI unit as noted during removal

18. Align and install the distributor assembly.

19. Install the ignition coil, then connect the fuel pipes.

20. Connect the heater hose pipe and the power brake vacuum pipe.

21. Connect the ground cable to the intake manifold stud, then position and secure the wiring harness using the clips.

22. Install the emissions relays along with their bracket, then connect the upper radiator hose.

23. Install the brace at the rear of the drive belt tensioner, then install the air cleaner and heat stove tube.

24. Connect the negative battery cable, then properly refill the engine cooling system.

25. Run the engine and check for leaks.

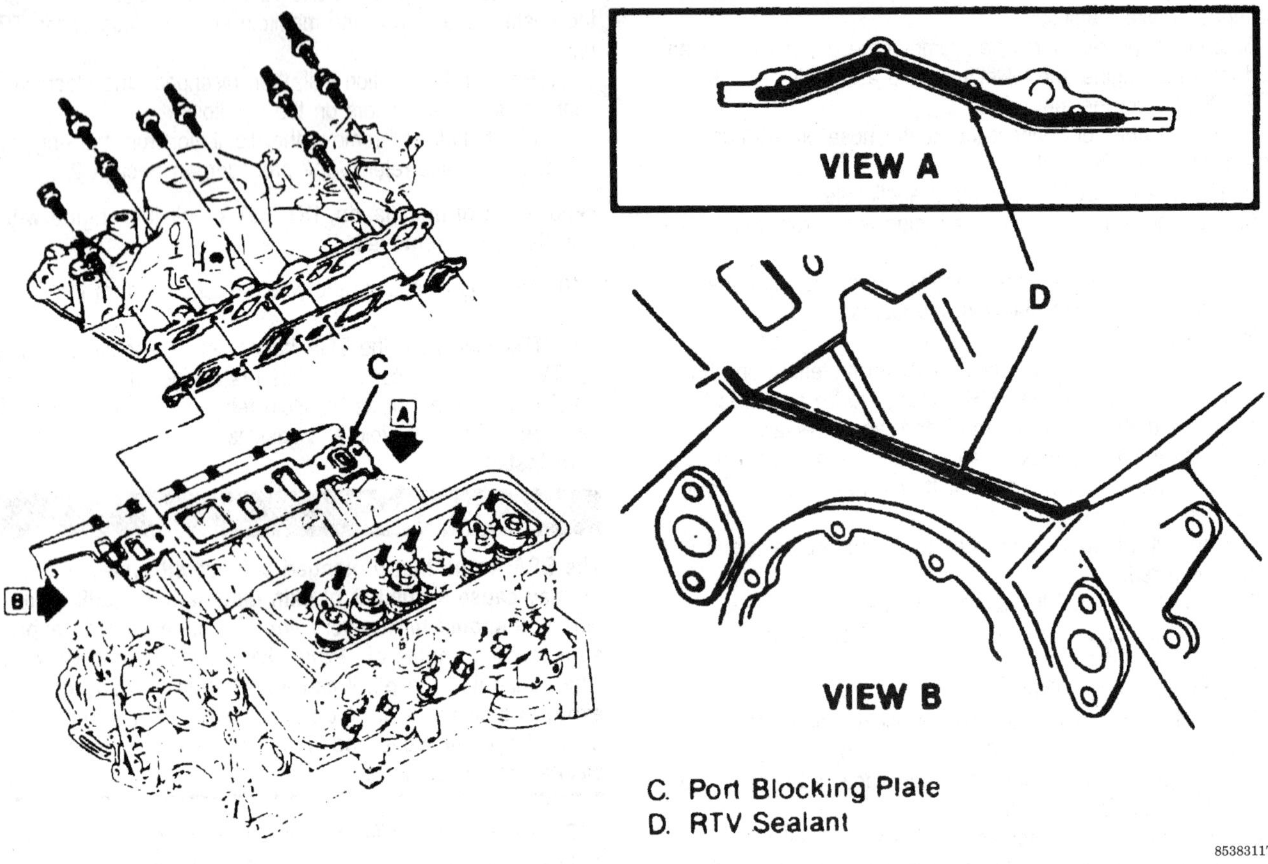

Fig. 28 Intake manifold mounting — 1994 4.3L (VIN Z) engine; note the bolt/stud usage may vary

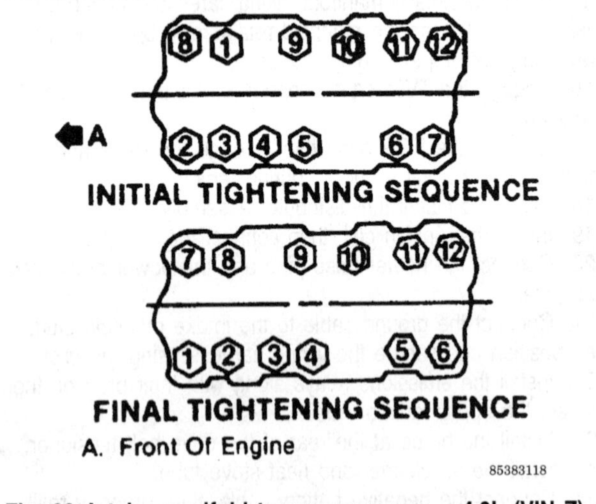

Fig. 29 Intake manifold torque sequence — 4.3L (VIN Z) engine

1994-95 VIN W

See Figures 30, 31, 32, 33, 34, 35, 36 and 37

CAUTION

When draining engine coolant, keep in mind that cats and dogs are attracted to ethylene glycol antifreeze and could drink any that is left in an uncovered container or in puddles on the ground. This will prove fatal in sufficient quantity. Always drain coolant into a sealable container. Coolant should be reused unless it is contaminated or is several years old.

If only the upper intake manifold is being removed, the fuel system pressure does not need to be released. ALWAYS release the pressure before disconnecting any fuel lines.

1. Remove the plastic cover, then properly relieve the fuel system pressure and disconnect the negative battery cable.
2. Drain the engine cooling system, then remove the air cleaner and air inlet duct.

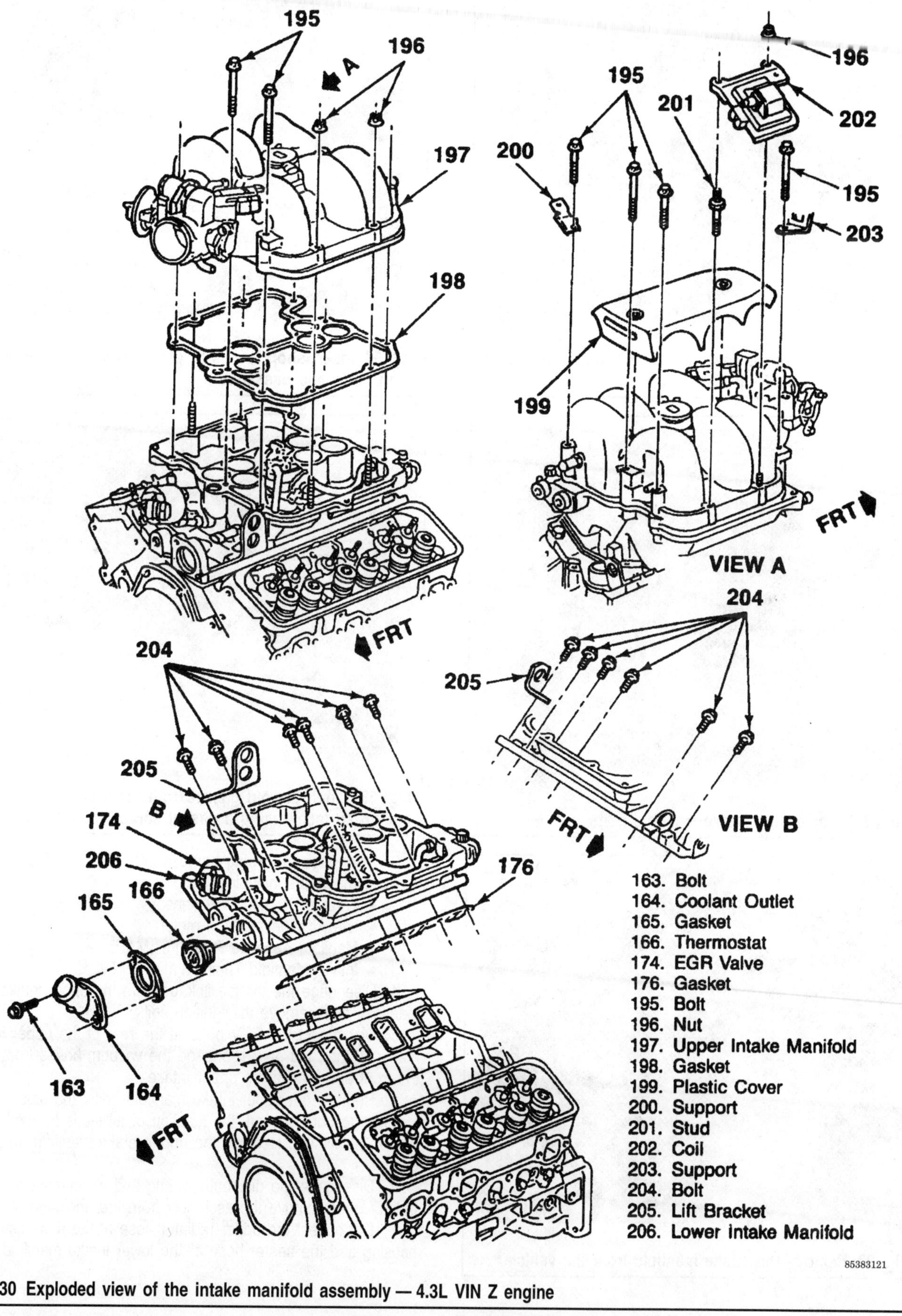

Fig. 30 Exploded view of the intake manifold assembly — 4.3L VIN Z engine

88453p17

Fig. 31 Matchmark the rotor and distributor-to-engine location. This will aid in installation

88453p18

Fig. 32 Unfasten the intake manifold bolts

88453p19

Fig. 33 Remove the intake manifold from the vehicle

88453p20

Fig. 34 Insert shop towels to prevent dirt from entering open ports and passages

88453p21

Fig. 35 Clean the old gasket from the intake manifold mating surfaces using a gasket scraper or putty knife

3. Disengage the wiring harness from the necessary upper intake components including:

- Throttle Position (TP) sensor
- Idle Air Control (IAC) motor
- Manifold Absolute Pressure (MAP) sensor
- Intake Manifold Tuning Valve (IMTV)

4. Disengage the throttle linkage from the upper intake manifold, then remove the ignition coil.

5. Disconnect the PCV hose at the rear of the upper intake manifold, then tag and disengage the vacuum hoses from both the front and rear of the upper intake.

6. Remove the upper intake manifold bolts and studs, making sure to note or mark the location of all studs to assure proper installation. Remove the upper intake manifold from the engine.

7. Disengage the distributor wiring and matchmark the distributor, then remove the assembly from the engine.

8. Disconnect the upper radiator hose at the thermostat housing and the heater hose at the lower intake manifold.

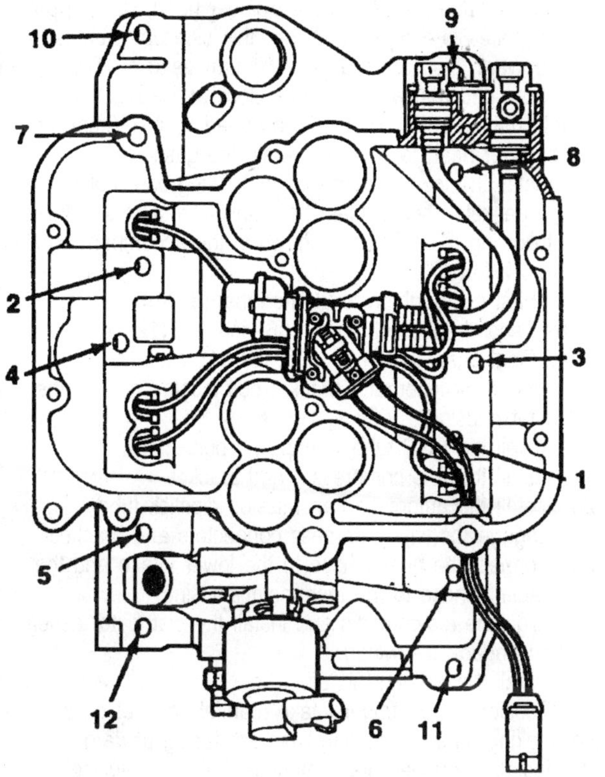

Fig. 36 Lower intake manifold torque sequence — 4.3L VIN Z engine

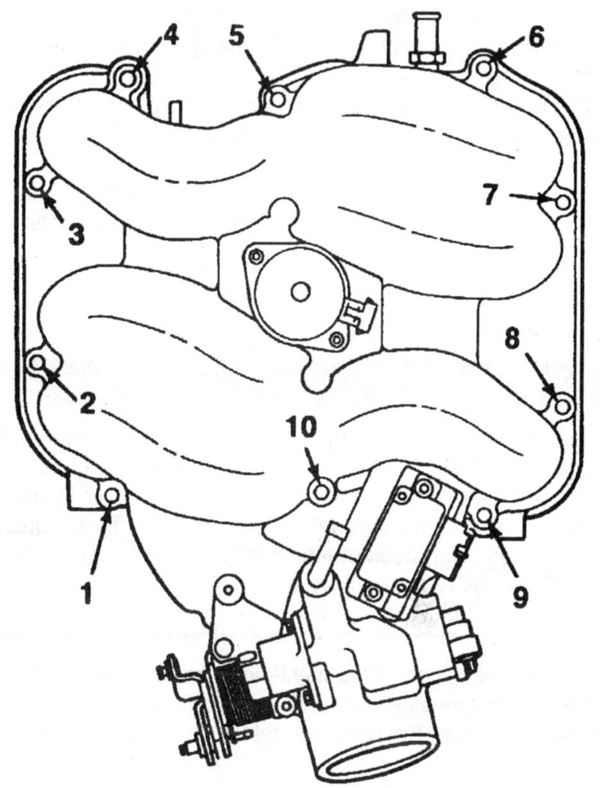

Fig. 37 Upper intake manifold torque sequence — 4.3L VIN Z engine

9. Disconnect the fuel supply and return lines at the rear of the lower intake manifold.
10. Remove the pencil brace (A/C compressor bracket-to-lower intake manifold).
11. Disengage the wiring harness connectors from the necessary lower intake components including:

- Fuel injector
- Exhaust Gas Recirculation (EGR) valve
- Engine Coolant Temperature (ECT) sensor

12. Remove the lower intake manifold retaining bolts, then remove the manifold from the engine.

To install:

13. Using a putty knife, carefully clean the gasket mounting surfaces. Be sure to inspect the manifold for warpage and/or cracks; if necessary, replace it.
14. Position the gaskets to the cylinder head with the port blocking plates to the rear and the "this side up" stamps facing upward, then apply a $^3/_{16}$ in. (5mm) bead of RTV sealant to the front and rear of the engine block at the block-to-manifold mating surface. Extend the bead $^1/_2$ in. (13mm) up each cylinder head to seal and retain the gaskets.
15. Install the lower intake manifold taking care not to disturb the gaskets, then tighten the manifold retainers to 35 ft. lbs. (48 Nm) using the proper torque sequence.
16. Engage the wiring harness to the lower manifold components, including the injector, EGR valve and ECT sensor.
17. Install the pencil brace to the A/C compressor bracket and the lower intake manifold.
18. Connect the fuel supply and return lines to the rear of the lower intake. Temporarily reconnect the negative battery cable, then pressurize the fuel system (by cycling the ignition without starting the engine) and check for leaks. Disconnect the negative battery cable and continue installation.
19. Connect the heater hose to the lower intake and the upper radiator hose to the thermostat housing.
20. Align the matchmarks and install the distributor assembly, then engage the wiring.
21. Position a new upper intake manifold gasket on the engine, making sure the green sealing lines are facing upward.
22. Install the upper intake manifold being careful not to pinch the fuel injector wires between the manifolds.

23. Install the manifold retainers, making sure the studs are properly positioned, then tighten them using the proper sequence to 124 inch lbs. (14 Nm).
24. Connect the PCV hose to the rear of the upper intake manifold and the vacuum hoses to both the front and rear of the manifold assembly.
25. Connect the throttle linkage to the upper intake, then install the ignition coil.
26. Engage the necessary wiring to the upper intake components including the TP sensor, IAC motor, MAP sensor and the IMTV.
27. Install the plastic cover, the air cleaner and air inlet duct.
28. Connect the negative battery cable, then properly refill the engine cooling system.

1996-97 VINS W AND X

See Figures 38 and 39

CAUTION

When draining engine coolant, keep in mind that cats and dogs are attracted to ethylene glycol antifreeze and could drink any that is left in an uncovered container or in puddles on the ground. This will prove fatal in sufficient quantity. Always drain coolant into a sealable container. Coolant should be reused unless it is contaminated or is several years old.

If only the upper intake manifold is being removed, the fuel system pressure does not need to be released. ALWAYS release the pressure before disconnecting any fuel lines.

1. Disconnect the negative battery cable and properly relieve the fuel system pressure.
2. Drain the cooling system.
3. Remove the air intake duct.
4. Tag and disengage the wiring harness connectors and move to one side.
5. Disconnect the throttle cable and support.
6. Disengage the fuel lines from the rear of the lower intake.
7. Disconnect the brake booster vacuum hose from the upper manifold, then remove the ignition coil and bracket.
8. Remove the purge solenoid and bracket, then unfasten the upper intake manifold bolts and studs. Mark the location of the studs to aid in installation.
9. Remove the upper intake manifold.
10. Disengage the distributor wiring and matchmark the distributor, then remove the assembly from the engine.
11. Disconnect the upper radiator hose at the thermostat housing and the heater hose at the lower intake manifold.
12. On automatic transmission equipped vehicles, disconnect the transmission dipstick tube.
13. Remove the EGR tube, clamp and bolt.
14. Disengage the A/C compressor and bracket and move it to one side.
15. Remove the alternator bracket bolt located next to the thermostat housing.
16. Remove the lower intake manifold retaining bolts, then remove the manifold from the engine.
17. Using a putty knife, carefully clean the gasket mounting surfaces. Be sure to inspect the manifold for warpage and/or cracks; if necessary, replace it.
18. Position the gaskets to the cylinder head with the port blocking plates to the rear and the "this side up" stamps facing upward, then apply a 3/16 in. (5mm) bead of RTV sealant to the front and rear of the engine block at the block-to-manifold mating surface. Extend the bead 1/2 in. (13mm) up each cylinder head to seal and retain the gaskets.
19. Install the lower intake manifold taking care not to disturb the gaskets, then tighten the manifold retainers in three steps following the sequence shown in the accompanying illustration as follows.
    a. First pass tighten to 26 inch lbs. (3 Nm)
    b. Second pass tighten to 106 inch lbs. (12 Nm)
    c. Final pass tighten to 11 ft. lbs. (15 Nm)
20. Fasten the alternator bracket bolt located next to the thermostat housing.
21. Install the EGR tube, clamp and bolt.
22. Install the A/C compressor and bracket.
23. Install the automatic transmission dipstick tube.
24. Engage the wiring harness connectors and brackets.
25. Connect the heater hose to the lower intake and the upper radiator hose to the thermostat housing.
26. Align the matchmarks and install the distributor assembly, then engage the wiring.
27. Install the vacuum hoses.
28. Position a new upper intake manifold gasket on the engine, making sure the sealing lines are facing upward.
29. Install the upper intake manifold being careful not to pinch the fuel injector wires between the manifolds.
30. Install the manifold retainers, making sure the studs are properly positioned, then tighten them using the proper sequence to 88 inch lbs. (10 Nm).
31. Install the purge solenoid and bracket.
32. Install the ignition coil and bracket and the brake booster vacuum hose.
33. Install the fuel lines and the throttle linkage and bracket.
34. Engage the wiring harness connectors and brackets.
35. Install the air cleaner intake duct, then connect the negative battery cable.
36. Start the vehicle and check for leaks.

Exhaust Manifold

CAUTION

ALWAYS use extreme caution when working around the exhaust system. Make sure the engine has had time to thoroughly cool or personal injury from exhaust system burns may occur. Also, be sure to wear safety goggles when working on exhaust parts and they are likely to rust and loose particle will be falling from them during the procedure.

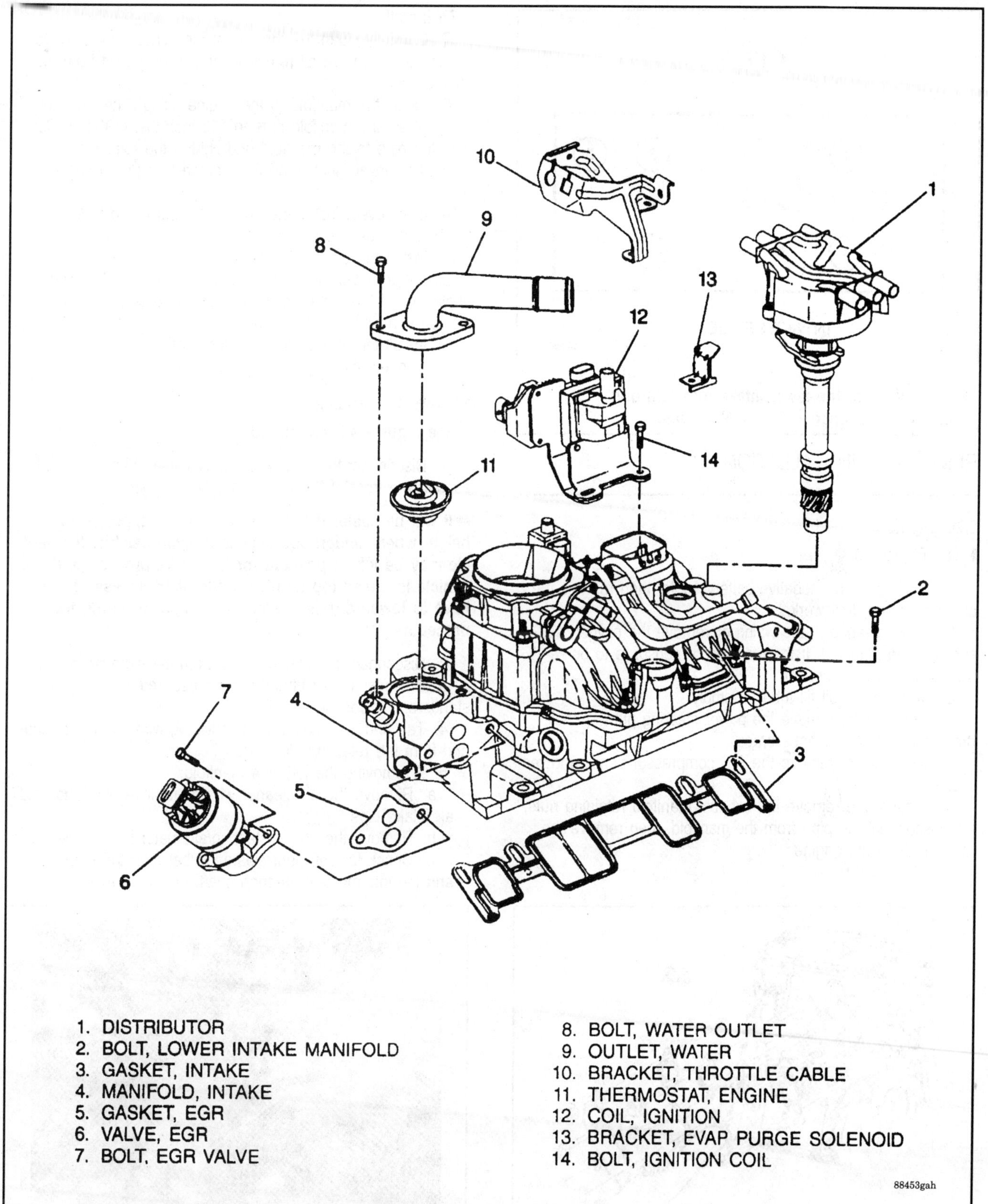

Fig. 38 View of the upper intake manifold and related components — 1996 4.3L engine

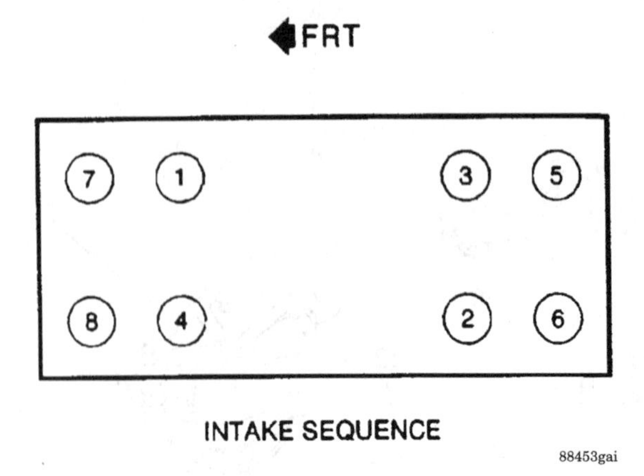

Fig. 39 View of the lower intake manifold bolt tightening sequence — 1996 4.3L engine

REMOVAL & INSTALLATION

2.2L Engine

See Figure 40

1. Disconnect the negative battery cable, then remove the air cleaner and duct work.
2. Either disengage the wiring or remove the oxygen sensor from the manifold. If the manifold or sensor is to be replaced, remove the sensor.
3. Remove the oil fill tube assembly.
4. If applicable, remove the power steering pump pencil brace and the heater hose brace.
5. If applicable, remove the A/C compressor pencil and rear brace.
6. Loosen and remove the exhaust manifold retaining nuts, first disconnect the pipe from the manifold, then remove the manifold from the engine.

To install:

7. Carefully clean the threads of the exhaust manifold retainers, then remove all remaining traces of gasket from the mating surfaces.
8. Install the manifold to the engine using a new gasket, then tighten the manifold nuts to 115 inch lbs. (13 Nm). Connect the pipe to the manifold and tighten the retainers.
9. If removed, install the A/C compressor pencil and rear brace.
10. If removed, install the power steering pump brace and the heater hose brace.
11. Install the oil fill tube assembly.
12. Either install the oxygen sensor or engage the wiring, as applicable. If the sensor or manifold was replaced, tighten the oxygen sensor to 31 ft. lbs. (42 Nm).
13. Install the air cleaner and duct work.
14. Connect the negative battery cable.

1994-95 4.3L Engine

See Figures 41, 42 and 43

1. Disconnect the negative battery cable, then raise and support the front of the vehicle safely using jackstands.

It will be easier if the vehicle is only supported to a height where underhood access is still possible, the vehicle may be left in position for the entire procedure. If the vehicle is raised too high for underhood access, it will have to lowered, raised and lowered again during the procedure.

2. Disconnect the exhaust pipe from the exhaust manifold.
3. If necessary for underhood access, remove the jackstands and lower the vehicle.
4. Tag and disconnect the spark plug wires from the plugs and from the retaining clips.
5. If removing the left side manifold:
   a. Remove the air cleaner with heat stove pipe and cold air intake pipe.
   b. Remove the power steering/alternator rear bracket.
   c. Check for sufficient clearance between the manifold and the intermediate steering shaft. On some models it will

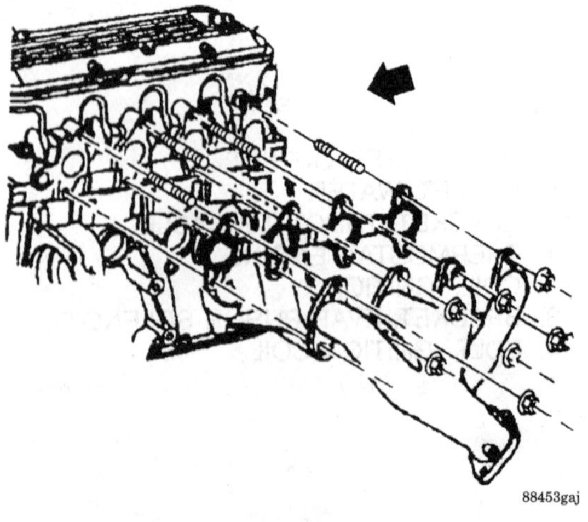

Fig. 40 View of the exhaust manifold and related components — 1996 2.2L engine

Fig. 41 Unfasten the exhaust manifold retaining bolts and studs then . . .

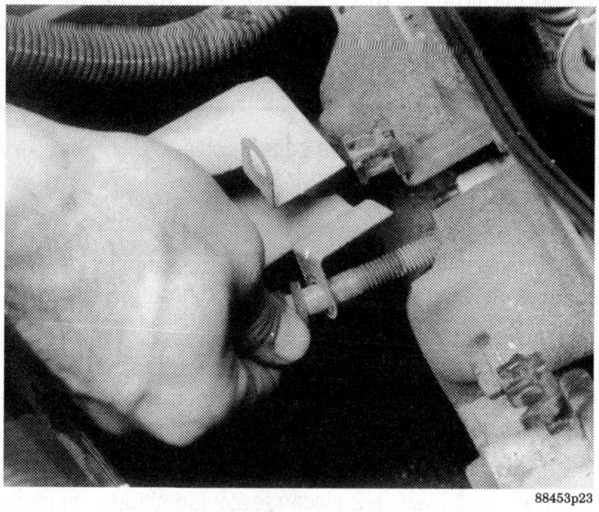

Fig. 42 . . . remove the bolts and studs

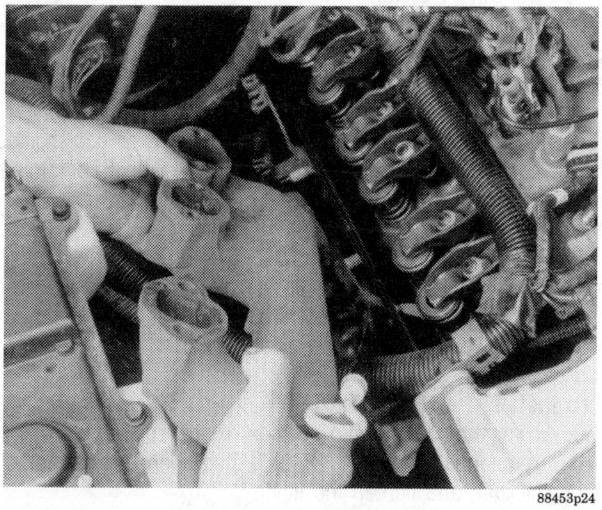

Fig. 43 Remove the exhaust manifold from the engine

be necessary to disconnect the intermediate shaft from the steering gear in order to reposition the shaft for clearance.

6. If necessary when removing the right side manifold, unbolt the A/C compressor and bracket, then position the assembly aside. DO NOT disconnect the lines or allow them to become kinked or otherwise damaged.

7. If necessary for the right side manifold, remove the spark plugs, dipstick tube and wiring.

8. Unbend the locktangs then unfasten the exhaust manifold retaining bolts, washers and tab washers.

9. Disengage the exhaust manifold, then remove and discard the old gaskets.

To install:

10. Using a putty knife, clean the gasket mounting surfaces. Inspect the exhaust manifold for distortion, cracks or damage; replace if necessary.

11. Install the exhaust manifold to the cylinder using a new gasket, then tighten the exhaust manifold-to-cylinder head bolts to 26 ft. lbs. (36 Nm) on the center exhaust tube and to 20 ft. lbs. (28 Nm) on the front and rear exhaust tubes. Once the bolts are tightened, bend the tabs on the washers back over the heads of all bolts in order to lock them in position.

12. If removed on the right side, install the spark plugs, dipstick tube and wiring.

13. If unbolted, reposition and secure the A/C compressor and bracket assembly.

14. If the left manifold was removed:

a. If unbolted, reconnect the intermediate shaft to the steering gear.

b. Install the power steering/alternator rear bracket.

c. Install the air cleaner along with the heat stove pipe and cold air intake pipe.

15. Connect the spark plug wires to the retainer clips and to the plugs as noted during removal.

16. If lowered for underhood access, raise and support the front of the vehicle again using the jackstands.

17. Connect the exhaust pipe to the manifold.

18. Remove the jackstands and carefully lower the vehicle, then connect the negative battery cable.

1996-97 4.3L Engine

See Figures 44 and 45

1. Disconnect the negative battery cable, then raise and support the front of the vehicle safely using jackstands.

➡It will be easier if the vehicle is only supported to a height where underhood access is still possible, the vehicle may be left in position for the entire procedure. If the vehicle is raised too high for underhood access, it will have to lowered, raised and lowered again during the procedure.

2. Disconnect the exhaust pipe from the exhaust manifold. It may be necessary to remove the tires to gain access to the rear manifold bolts.

3. Remove the EGR inlet pipe from the left side manifold, if necessary.

4. Unbend the locktangs then remove the exhaust manifold retaining bolts, washers and tab washers. Remove the heat shields.

5. Remove the exhaust manifold, then remove and discard the old gaskets.

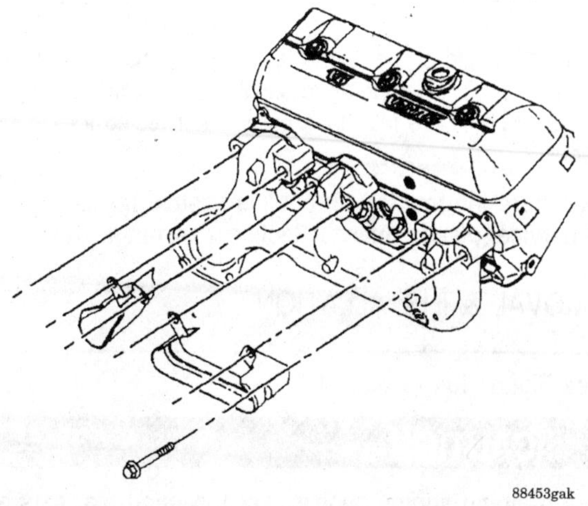

Fig. 44 View of the exhaust manifold heat shields — 1996 4.3L engine

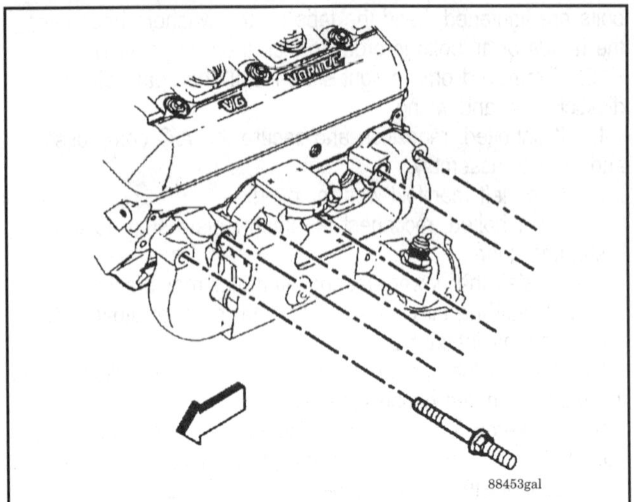

Fig. 45 View of the exhaust manifold — 1996 4.3L engine

To install:

6. Using a putty knife, clean the gasket mounting surfaces. Inspect the exhaust manifold for distortion, cracks or damage; replace if necessary.
7. Install the exhaust manifold to the cylinder using a new gasket, then tighten the bolts to 22 ft. lbs. (30 Nm). Once the bolts are tightened, bend the tabs on the washers back over the heads of all bolts in order to lock them in position.
8. If removed, install the EGR inlet pipe.
9. Install and tighten the rear manifold bolts through the front wheel opening.
10. Install the front tires.
11. Engage the exhaust pipe to the manifold and lower the vehicle.
12. Connect the negative battery cable.

Radiator

DIAGNOSIS

Test for restrictions in the radiator by warming the engine to operating temperature and then turning the engine off. Feel the radiator, it should be hot along the left side and warm along the right side. The temperature should rise evenly from right to left. If cold spots are felt, have the radiator tested for clogged sections.

➡For more information on cooling system maintenance and service, please refer to Section 1 of this manual.

REMOVAL & INSTALLATION

▸ See Figure 46

⁂CAUTION

When draining engine coolant, keep in mind that cats and dogs are attracted to ethylene glycol antifreeze and could drink any that is left in an uncovered container or in puddles on the ground. This will prove fatal in sufficient quantity. Always drain coolant into a sealable container. Coolant should be reused unless it is contaminated or is several years old.

1. Disconnect the negative battery cable.
2. Drain the engine cooling system.
3. Disconnect the overflow hose from the radiator, then disconnect the upper and lower radiator hoses.
4. If equipped with A/C, it may be necessary to remove the A/C hose retaining clip and reposition the hose for shroud and/or radiator removal. DO NOT disconnect any refrigerant fittings.

➡If equipped with a 1 piece shroud, then shroud may be unbolted from the radiator support and pushed back over the cooling fan instead of removing it completely.

5. If equipped with a 2 piece radiator/fan shroud, remove the upper fan shroud-to-radiator support bolts and the upper fan shroud-to-lower fan shroud retainers. Remove the upper shroud from the vehicle.
6. If equipped with an A/T, disconnect and plug the fluid cooler lines at the radiator. Plug all openings to prevent system contamination or excessive fluid loss.
7. If equipped with a factory engine oil cooler which is integral to the radiator, disconnect and plug the oil cooler lines at the radiator. Plug all openings to prevent system contamination or excessive fluid loss. Plug all openings to prevent system contamination or excessive fluid loss.
8. Lift the radiator straight upward from the supports and from the vehicle. Be careful to lift the radiator straight upward and not to tilt it excessively as the radiator will still contain a significant amount of coolant and, if applicable, transmission fluid/engine oil.

To install:

9. Lower the radiator into position on the supports.
10. If equipped, remove the plugs, then connect the engine oil cooler lines and tighten the fittings.
11. If equipped with an A/T, remove the plugs, then connect the transmission fluid cooler lines and tighten the fittings.
12. Install the upper fan shroud and secure using the support and lower shroud retainers.
13. If applicable, reposition the A/C refrigerant hose and secure using the retaining clip.
14. Connect the overflow hose, upper and lower radiator hoses.
15. Connect the negative battery cable.
16. Properly refill the engine cooling system.

Engine Oil Cooler & Adapter

Some of the vehicles covered by this manual may be equipped with an original equipment oil cooler and adapter. On these vehicles the oil cooler is usually built into the left side of the radiator, while the adapter is mounted between the engine block and oil filter. The following procedure may be used to service these parts. But, your vehicle might instead be equipped with an aftermarket cooler and adapter. Although the adapter for most aftermarket kits will be removed and installed in the same manner as the OEM adapter, aftermarket coolers are usually not integral with the radiator. If equipped,

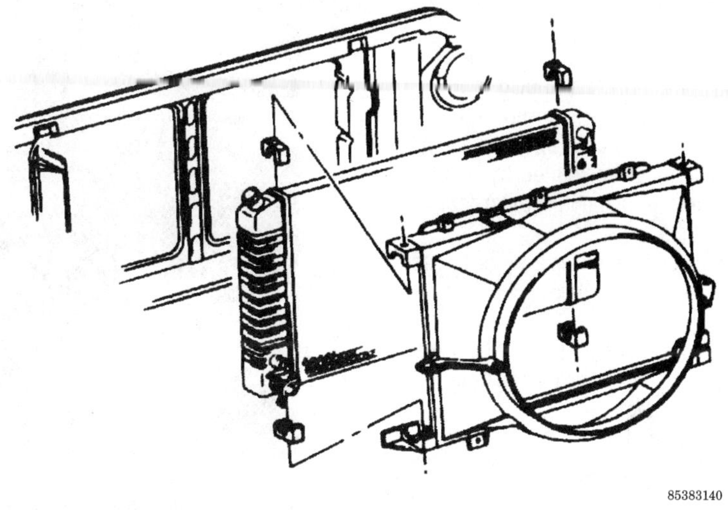

Fig. 46 Exploded view of a common radiator and shroud assembly

aftermarket coolers are usually separate radiator units mounted near the truck's radiator. When dealing with an aftermarket unit, follow the manufacturer's instructions.

REMOVAL & INSTALLATION

See Figures 47 and 48

1. Disconnect the negative battery cable.
2. Remove the oil filter from the adapter.
3. Disconnect the oil cooler lines from the oil cooler adapter.
4. Unfasten oil cooler adapter retaining bolt, then remove the adapter from the engine block.
5. If necessary, remove the radiator from the vehicle to service or replace the engine oil cooler tank. The radiator may be taken to a repair shop if the tank is to be replaced.

To install:

6. If removed, install the radiator to the vehicle. For details, please refer to the procedure earlier in this section.

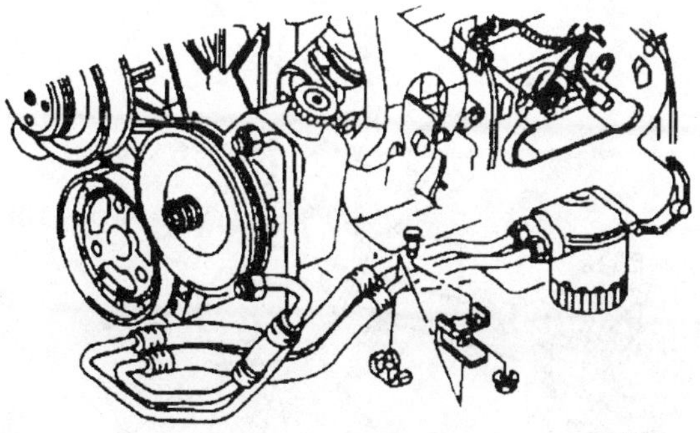

Fig. 47 View of the engine oil cooler and lines — 1996 2WD models

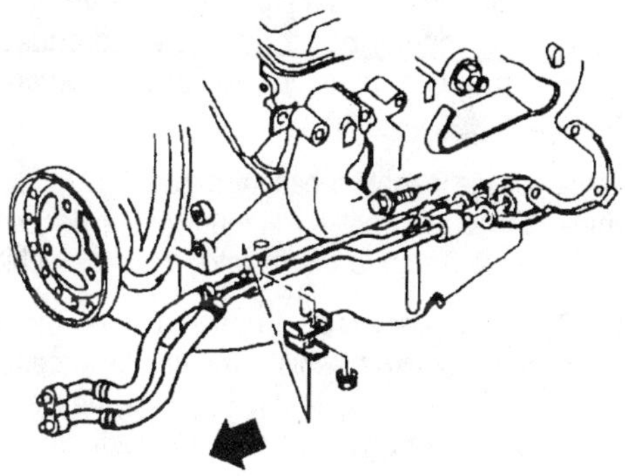

Fig. 48 View of the engine oil cooler and lines — 1996 4WD models

7. Install the oil cooler adapter to the engine block and secure using the retaining bolt.
8. Connect the oil cooler lines to the adapter.
9. Install a new oil filter. (Remember it is inexpensive and worth the extra protection).
10. Connect the negative battery cable, then start and run the engine to normal operating temperature. Check for leaks.

Engine Cooling Fan/Clutch Fan

The vehicles covered by this manual are either equipped with a standard cooling fan (early models) or a clutch fan assembly (most later model vehicles). Standard cooling fans are simply bolted to the water pump hub, while on clutch fans, the fan blade assembly is bolted to a clutch assembly which is secured to water pump hub studs. Both fans are removed in a similar manner, but the clutch assembly requires a little more effort.

CLUTCH FAN DIAGNOSIS

Start the engine and listen for fan noise. Fan noise is usually evident during the first few minutes after start-up and when the clutch is engaged for maximum cooling (during idle). If fan noise is excessive, the fan cannot be rotated by hand while the engine is stopped or there is a rough grating feel as the fan is turned, replace the clutch.

Check a loose fan assembly for wear and replace as necessary. Under certain conditions, the fan may flex up to 1/4 in. This is not cause for replacement.

The fan clutch is not affected by small fluid leaks which may occur in the area around the bearing assembly. If leakage appears excessive, replace the fan clutch.

If the fan clutch free-wheels with no drag (revolves more than five times when spun by hand), replace the clutch.

88453p26

Fig. 50 . . . then remove the fan and clutch assembly from the vehicle

REMOVAL & INSTALLATION

See Figures 49, 50, 51 and 52

DO NOT use or repair a damaged fan assembly. An unbalanced fan assembly could fly apart and cause personal injury or property damage. Replace damaged assemblies with new ones.

1. Disconnect the negative battery cable.
2. Remove the upper radiator shroud and, if desired for additional clearance, remove the radiator from the vehicle.

Although it is not necessary in most cases, the radiator may be removed from the vehicle for easier access to the fan retainers. If the radiator is left in place, use extra caution to prevent damage to the fragile radiator fins.

3. Remove the fan assembly attaching nuts (clutch type) or bolts (standard type), then remove the fan assembly from the engine.

Some vehicles use a space between the fan and the water pump pulley. If used, be sure to retain the spacer for installation.

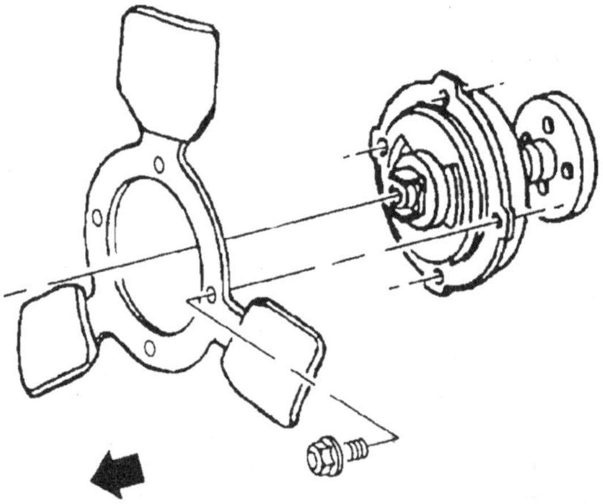
88453gao

Fig. 51 View of the fan-to-fan clutch mounting — 1996 2.2L engine without A/C

88453p25

Fig. 49 Unfasten the cooling fan retaining bolts. . . .

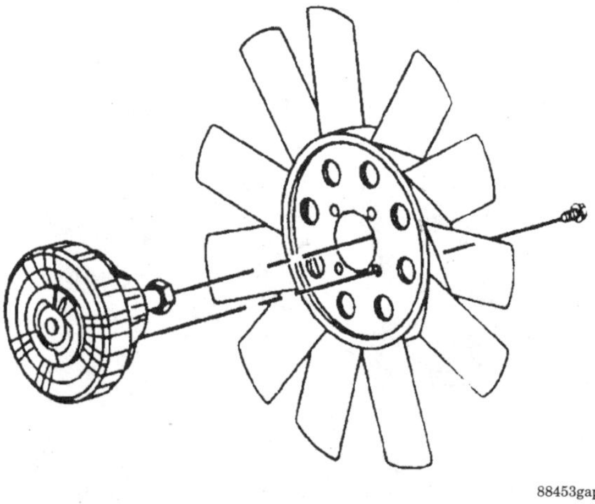
88453gap

Fig. 52 View of the fan-to-fan clutch mounting — 1996 4.3L engine with A/C

4. If necessary, the clutch may be removed from the fan by removing the attaching nuts or bolts (as applicable).

To install:

5. If removed, install the fan to the clutch and secure using the fasteners.
6. Position the spacer (if used) and fan assembly to the water pump pulley and secure using the fasteners.
7. If removed for clearance, install the radiator.
8. Install the upper fan shroud.
9. Connect the negative battery cable.
10. If the radiator was removed, properly refill the engine cooling system.

Water Pump

DIAGNOSIS

Check the water pump operation by running the engine while squeezing the upper radiator hose. When the engine warms (thermostat opens) a pressure surge should be felt. Check for a plugged vent hole at the pump snout.

REMOVAL & INSTALLATION

See Figures 53, 54, 55, 56, 57 and 58

CAUTION

When draining engine coolant, keep in mind that cats and dogs are attracted to ethylene glycol antifreeze and could drink any that is left in an uncovered container or in puddles on the ground. This will prove fatal in sufficient quantity. Always drain coolant into a sealable container. Coolant should be reused unless it is contaminated or is several years old.

1. Disconnect the negative battery cable, then drain the engine cooling system.
2. Relieve the belt tension, then remove the drive belt.
3. Remove the upper fan shroud, then remove the fan or fan and clutch assembly, as applicable.
4. Remove the water pump pulley.
5. Loosen the clamp and disconnect the coolant hose(s) from the water pump.
6. Unfasten the retainers, then remove the water pump from the engine. Note the positions of all retainers as some engines will utilize different length fasteners in different locations and/or bolts and studs in different locations.

To install:

7. Using a putty knife, carefully clean the gasket mounting surfaces.

The water pumps on some of the engines covered by this manual, may have been installed using sealer only, no gasket, at the factory. If a gasket is supplied with the replacement part, it should be used. Otherwise, a 1/8 in. (.125mm) bead of RTV sealer should be used around the sealing surface of the pump.

88453p27

Fig. 53 After removing the cooling fan assembly, remove the water pump pulley

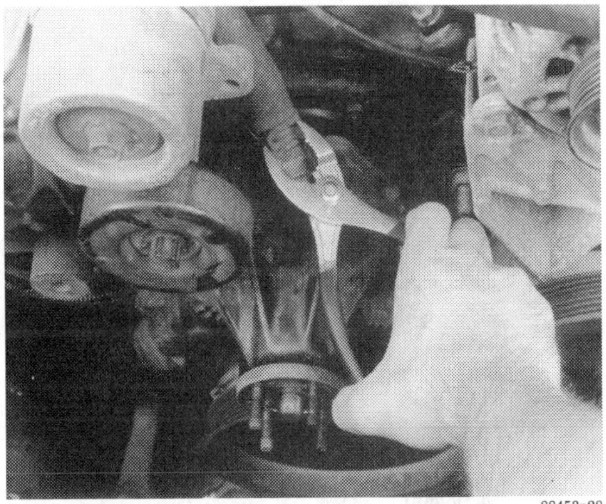

88453p28

Fig. 54 Disengage all hoses connected to the water pump assembly

88453p29

Fig. 55 Unfasten and remove the water pump retaining bolts

Fig. 56 Remove the water pump from the vehicle

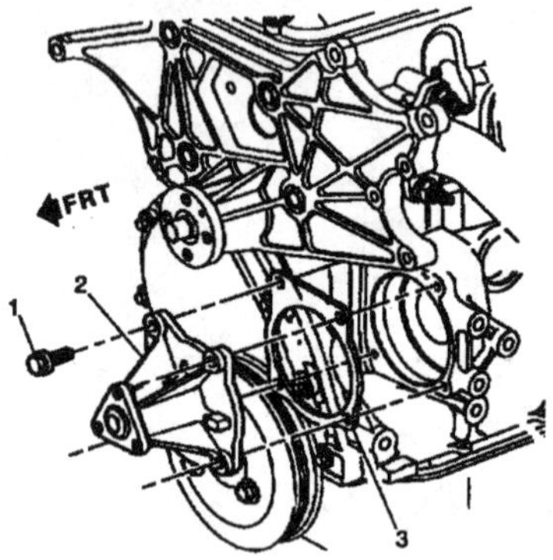

Fig. 57 Water pump mounting — 2.2L gasoline engine

8. Apply 1052080 or an equivalent sealant to the threads of the water pump retainers. Install the water pump to the engine using a new gasket, then thread the retainers in order to hold it in position.
9. Tighten the water pump retainers to specification:
   a. For the 2.2L engines tighten the water pump-to-engine retainers to 18 ft. lbs. (25 Nm).
   b. For the 4.3L engine, tighten the bolts and studs to 30 ft. lbs. (41 Nm).
10. Connect the coolant hose(s) and secure using the retaining clamp(s).
11. Install the water pump pulley, then install the fan or fan and clutch assembly.
12. Position the serpentine belt over the pulleys, then carefully allow the tensioner back into contact with the belt.
13. Install the upper fan shroud, then connect the negative battery cable.
14. Properly refill the engine cooling system, then run the engine and check for leaks.

Cylinder Head

REMOVAL & INSTALLATION

2.2L Engine

➧ See Figure 59

1994-95 MODELS

✻✻CAUTION

When draining engine coolant, keep in mind that cats and dogs are attracted to ethylene glycol antifreeze and could drink any that is left in an uncovered container or in puddles on the ground. This will prove fatal in sufficient quantity. Always drain coolant into a sealable container. Coolant should be reused unless it is contaminated or is several years old.

1. Properly relieve the fuel system pressure, then disconnect the negative battery cable.
2. Drain the engine cooling system, then disconnect the air duct from the air inlet.
3. Disconnect the upper radiator hose, then remove the upper fan shroud.
4. Remove the radiator assembly, then remove the lower fan shroud.
5. Remove the fan assembly, then remove the serpentine drive belt.
6. Remove the water pump pulley.
7. Disconnect the heater hose from the intake manifold and the thermostat housing, then remove the thermostat housing.
8. Remove the alternator support brace and disengage the alternator wiring.
9. If equipped, remove the A/C compressor with brackets, then position them aside. DO NOT disconnect the refrigerant lines, but be careful not to kink and damage them.
10. Disconnect and reposition the accessory bracket along with the alternator and P/S pump still attached. Be careful not to damage the steering pump lines.
11. Disconnect the throttle cable and cable support linkage, then disconnect the heater hose from the water pump.
12. Remove the oil fill tube, then disconnect the exhaust pipe and the oxygen sensor.
13. Unfasten the exhaust manifold bolts, then remove the manifold.
14. Tag and disconnect both the electrical wiring and the vacuum hoses from the upper intake manifold.
15. Remove the upper intake manifold, then tag and disconnect the wiring from the lower intake manifold.
16. Disconnect the fuel lines, then tag and disengage the spark plug wires.
17. Remove the lower intake manifold from the engine.
18. Remove the rocker arm cover from the cylinder head.
19. Remove the rocker arms and pushrods.
20. Disconnect the engine lift bracket from the rear of the engine.
21. Remove the cylinder head bolts and studs, then carefully lift the cylinder head from the engine.

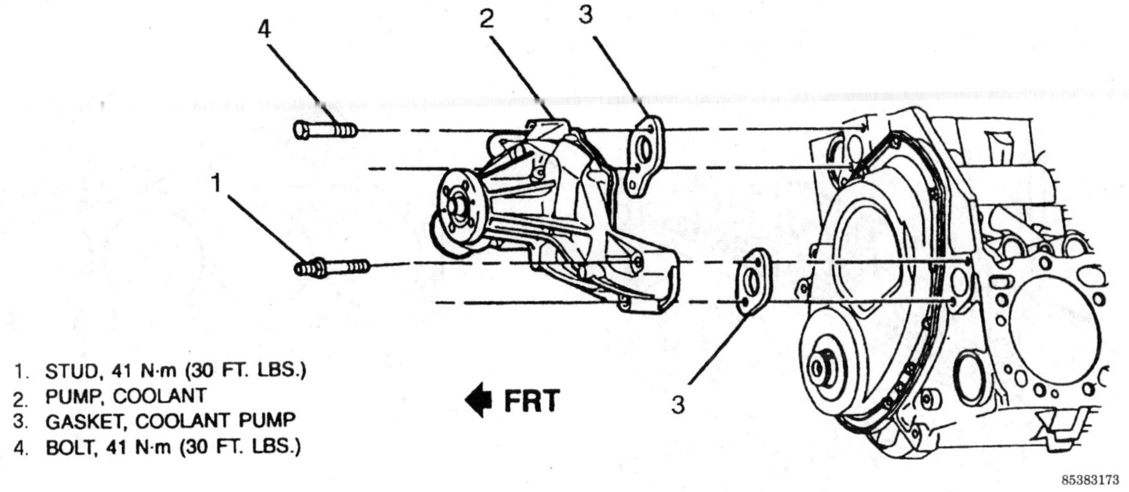

Fig. 58 Water pump mounting — 4.3L engine (note that stud locations may vary)

To install:

22. Carefully clean and inspect the gasket mounting surfaces.

➡The gasket surfaces on both the head and block must be clean of any foreign matter and free of nicks or heavy scratches. The cylinder bolt threads in the block and thread on the bolts must be cleaned (dirt will affect the bolt torque).

23. Place a new gasket over the dowel pins (DO NOT use any sealer on the gasket), then position the cylinder head over the gasket and dowels.
24. Apply a coating of 1052080 or equivalent sealer to the cylinder head bolt threads. Install the cylinder head bolts (within 15 minutes of sealer application), then tighten them in the proper sequence first to a torque of 46 ft. lbs. (63 Nm) for long bolts or to 43 ft. lbs. (58 Nm) for short bolts and then tighten all bolts an additional 90 degree turn using a torque angle meter.
25. Install the engine lift bracket.
26. Install the rocker arms and pushrods.
27. Install the rocker arm cover.
28. Install the lower intake manifold. Refer to the procedure earlier in this section for specifications.
29. Connect the spark plug wires and the fuel lines.
30. Engage the wiring to the lower intake manifold.
31. Install the upper intake manifold. Refer to the procedure earlier in this section for specifications.
32. Connect the vacuum hoses and electrical wiring to the upper intake, as tagged during removal.
33. Install the oil fill tube assembly.
34. Install the exhaust manifold, then connect the exhaust pipe and oxygen sensor.
35. Connect the heater hose to the water pump, then connect the throttle cable support and throttle cable.
36. Install the accessory support bracket and components.
37. If equipped, reposition and secure the A/C compressor.
38. Install the power steering support brace and the alternator support brace. Engage the alternator wiring.
39. Install the thermostat housing, then connect the heater hose to the housing.
40. Install the water pump pulley and the serpentine drive belt.
41. Install the fan assembly, then engage the radiator and the lower fan shroud.
42. Install the upper fan shroud, then connect the upper radiator hose.
43. Engage the air inlet duct work, then connect the negative battery cable.
44. Properly refill the engine cooling system and check for leaks.

1996-97 MODELS

✲✲✲CAUTION

When draining engine coolant, keep in mind that cats and dogs are attracted to ethylene glycol antifreeze and could drink any that is left in an uncovered container or in puddles on the ground. This will prove fatal in sufficient quantity. Always drain coolant into a sealable container. Coolant should be reused unless it is contaminated or is several years old.

1. Properly relieve the fuel system pressure, then disconnect the negative battery cable.
2. Drain the engine cooling system.
3. Remove the upper and lower intake manifolds. Refer to the procedures outlined in this section.
4. Unfasten the exhaust manifold bolts, then remove the manifold.
5. Remove the fan assembly, then remove the serpentine drive belt.
6. Remove the water pump pulley.
7. Disconnect the heater hose from the intake manifold and the thermostat housing.
8. Disengage the electrical connection from the temperature sensor.
9. Disconnect the upper radiator hose.
10. Remove the thermostat housing.
11. Remove the radiator assembly, then remove the lower fan shroud.
12. Disengage the alternator electrical connectors.

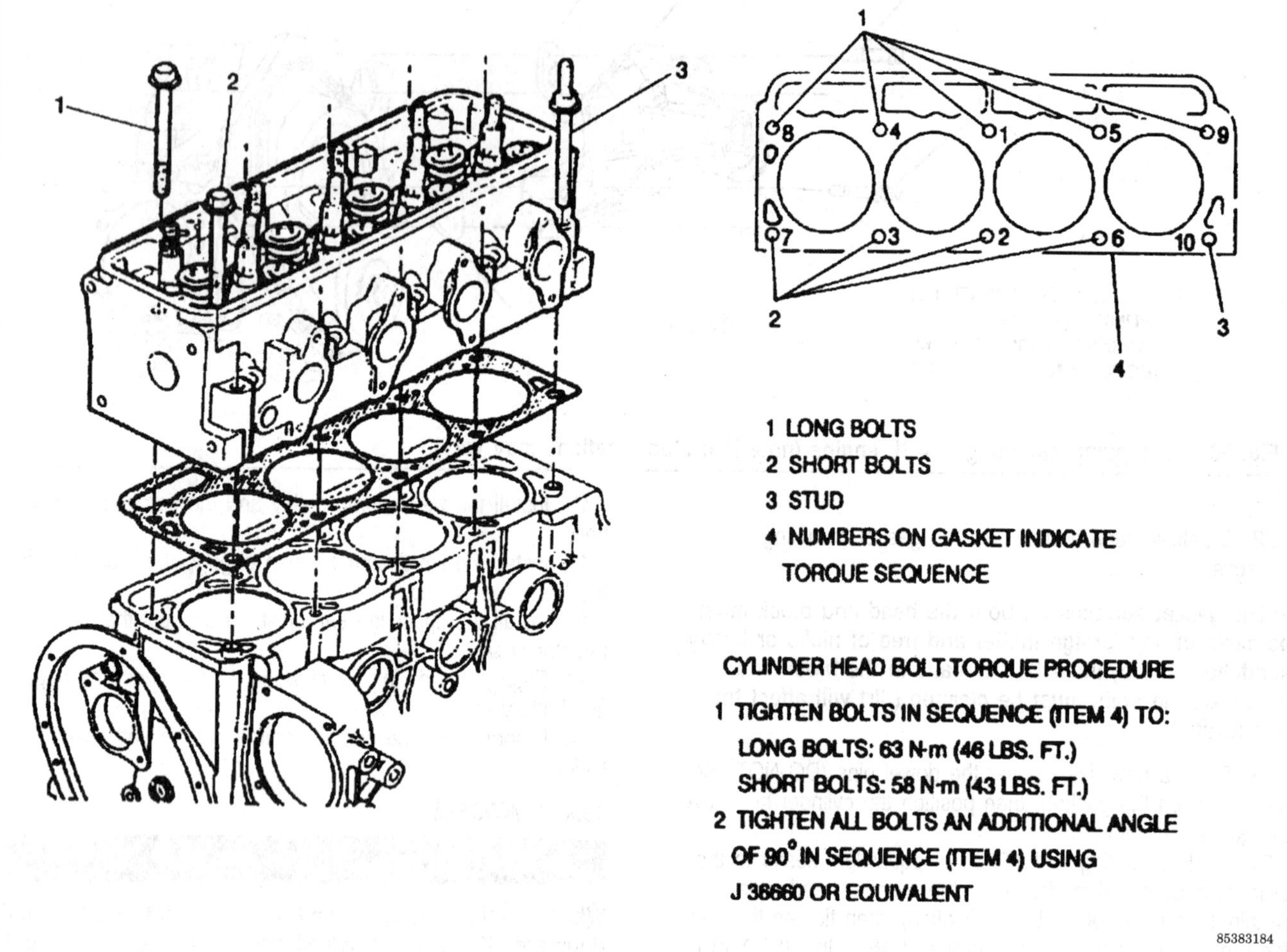

Fig. 59 Cylinder head bolt torque sequence — 2.2L engine

13. If equipped, remove the A/C compressor with brackets, then position them aside. DO NOT disconnect the refrigerant lines, but be careful not to kink and damage them.
14. Disconnect and reposition the accessory bracket along with the alternator and P/S pump still attached. Be careful not to damage the steering pump lines.
15. Remove the rocker arm cover from the cylinder head.
16. Remove the rocker arms and pushrods.
17. Disconnect the engine lift bracket from the rear of the engine.
18. Remove the cylinder head bolts and studs, then carefully lift the cylinder head from the engine.

To install:

19. Carefully clean and inspect the gasket mounting surfaces.

➡The gasket surfaces on both the head and block must be clean of any foreign matter and free of nicks or heavy scratches. The cylinder bolt threads in the block and thread on the bolts must be cleaned (dirt will affect the bolt torque).

20. Place a new gasket over the dowel pins (DO NOT use any sealer on the gasket), then position the cylinder head over the gasket and dowels.
21. Apply a coating of 1052080 or equivalent sealer to the cylinder head bolt threads. Install the cylinder head bolts (within 15 minutes of sealer application), then tighten them in the proper sequence first to a torque of 46 ft. lbs. (63 Nm) for long bolts or to 43 ft. lbs. (58 Nm) for short bolts and then tighten all bolts an additional 90 degree turn using a torque angle meter.
22. Install the engine lift bracket.
23. Install the rocker arms and pushrods.
24. Install the power steering support brace and the alternator support brace. Engage the alternator wiring.
25. Install the rocker arm cover.
26. If equipped, reposition and secure the A/C compressor.
27. Install the thermostat housing assembly, then engage the electrical connection to the temperature sensor.
28. Install the upper radiator hose, then engage the heater hoses to the heater core and the thermostat.

29. Install the water pump pulley and the serpentine drive belt.
30. Install the fan assembly.
31. Install the exhaust manifold.
32. Install the upper and lower intake manifolds. Refer to the procedure earlier in this section for specifications.
33. Connect the negative battery cable.
34. Properly refill the engine cooling system and check for leaks.

4.3L Engine

1994-95 MODELS

See Figures 60, 61, 62, 63, 64 and 65

CAUTION

When draining engine coolant, keep in mind that cats and dogs are attracted to ethylene glycol antifreeze and could drink any that is left in an uncovered container or in puddles on the ground. This will prove fatal in sufficient quantity. Always drain coolant into a sealable container. Coolant should be reused unless it is contaminated or is several years old.

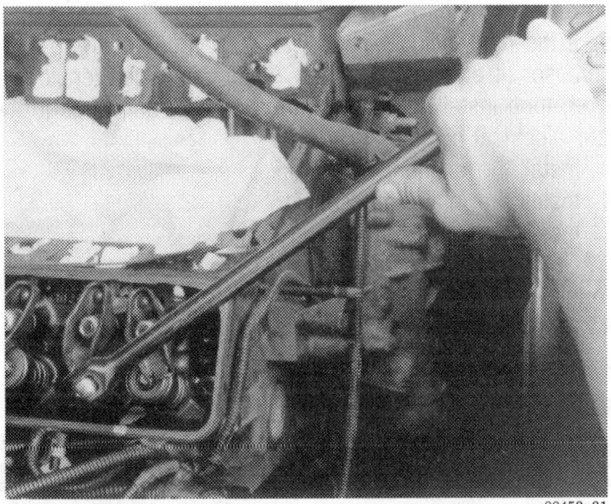

88453p31

Fig. 60 Loosen the cylinder head bolts in the reverse order of the torque sequence

88453p32

Fig. 61 Remove the cylinder head from the engine

88453p33

Fig. 62 Remove and discard the old cylinder head gasket

1. Properly relieve the fuel system pressure, then disconnect the negative battery cable.
2. Drain the engine cooling system.
3. Remove the rocker arm cover.
4. Remove the intake manifold.
5. Remove the exhaust manifold.
6. If removing the right cylinder head, remove or disconnect:
   - Electrical connector at the sensor.
   - Dipstick tube at the cylinder head bracket.
   - Air conditioning compressor (position it aside with the refrigerant lines attached), if equipped.
   - A/C compressor (if equipped)/belt tensioner bracket.
7. If removing the left cylinder head, remove or disconnect:
   - Alternator (position it aside).
   - Left side engine accessory bracket with power steering pump (position the pump aside with the lines attached) and brackets, if equipped.
8. Tag and disconnect the wiring from the spark plugs. If necessary, remove the spark plugs from the cylinder head.
9. Loosen the rocker arms and remove the pushrods.

If valve train components, such as the rocker arms or pushrods, are to be reused, they must be tagged or arranged to insure installation in their original locations.

10. Unfasten the cylinder head bolts by loosening them in the reverse of the torque sequence, then carefully remove the cylinder head.

To install:

11. Carefully clean and inspect the gasket mounting surfaces.

The gasket surfaces on both the head and block must be clean of any foreign matter and free of nicks or heavy scratches. The cylinder bolt threads in the block and thread on the bolts must be cleaned (dirt will affect the bolt torque).

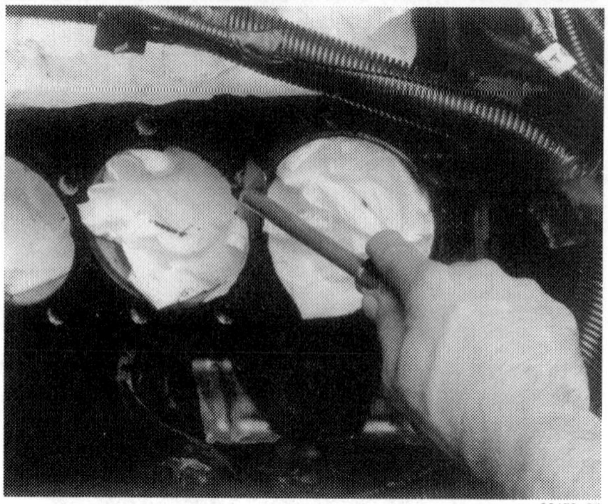
88453p34

Fig. 63 Place rags or shop towels in the combustion chambers before cleaning the old gasket from the block

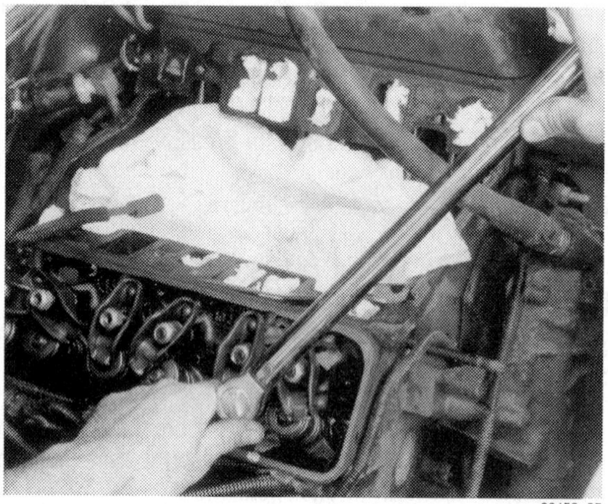
88453p35

Fig. 64 Tighten the cylinder head bolts in sequence using a torque wrench

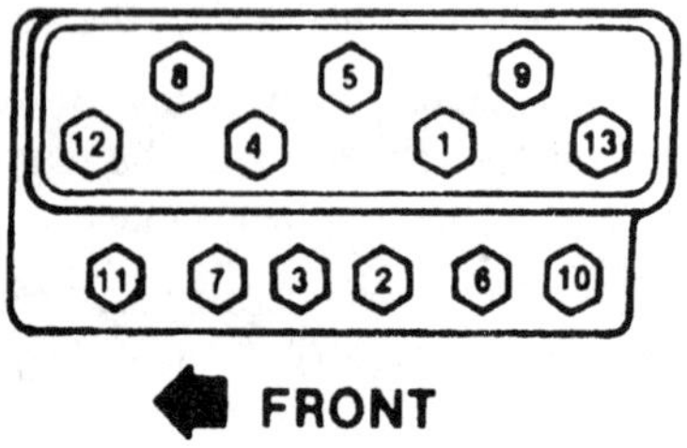

85383187

Fig. 65 Cylinder head bolt torque sequence — 4.3L engine

➡DO NOT apply sealer to composition steel-asbestos gaskets.

12. If using a steel only gasket, apply a thin and even coat of sealer to both sides of the gaskets.
13. Place a new gasket over the dowel pins with the bead or the words "This Side Up" facing upwards (as applicable), then carefully lower the cylinder head into position over the gasket and dowels.
14. Apply a coating of 1052080 or equivalent sealer to the threads of the cylinder head bolts, then thread the bolts into position until finger-tight. Using the proper torque sequence, tighten the bolts in 3 steps:
    - First, tighten the bolts to 25 ft. lbs. (34 Nm).
    - Next, tighten the bolts to 45 ft. lbs. (61 Nm).
    - Finally, tighten the bolts to 65 ft. lbs. (90 Nm).
15. Install the pushrods, secure the rocker arms and adjust the valves.
16. If removed, install the spark plugs. Engage the spark plug wires.
17. If the left cylinder head was removed, reposition and secure the engine accessory bracket with the power steering pump and brackets, as equipped. Install the alternator.
18. If the right cylinder head was removed, install the A/C compressor (if equipped) and A/C compressor/belt tensioner bracket, then install the dipstick tube bracket and engage the sensor electrical connector.
19. Install the exhaust manifold.
20. Install the intake manifold.
21. Install the rocker arm cover.
22. Connect the negative battery cable, then properly refill the engine cooling system.
23. Run the engine to check for leaks, then check and/or adjust the ignition timing.

1996-97 MODELS

✻✻CAUTION

Relieve the pressure on the fuel system before disconnecting any fuel line connection. Please refer to Section 5 of this manual for the proper procedures.

1. Properly relieve the fuel system pressure, then disconnect the negative battery cable.
2. Drain the engine cooling system.
3. Remove the intake manifold.
4. Remove the exhaust manifold.
5. If removing the right cylinder head, remove the alternator and bracket.
6. If removing the left cylinder head, remove the air conditioning compressor (position it aside with the refrigerant lines attached), if equipped.
7. Tag and disengage the wiring harness and clip from the rear of the cylinder head.
8. Disconnect the coolant sensor wire.
9. Tag and disconnect the wiring from the spark plugs. If necessary, remove the spark plugs from the cylinder head.
10. Remove the rocker arm cover.

11. Loosen the rocker arms and remove the pushrods.

➡If valve train components, such as the rocker arms or pushrods, are to be reused, they must be tagged or arranged to insure installation in their original locations.

12. Unfasten the cylinder head bolts by loosening them in the reverse of the torque sequence, then carefully remove the cylinder head.

To install:

13. Carefully clean and inspect the gasket mounting surfaces.

➡The gasket surfaces on both the head and block must be clean of any foreign matter and free of nicks or heavy scratches. The cylinder bolt threads in the block and thread on the bolts must be cleaned (dirt will affect the bolt torque).

➡DO NOT apply sealer to composition steel-asbestos gaskets.

14. If using a steel only gasket, apply a thin and even coat of sealer to both sides of the gaskets.
15. Place a new gasket over the dowel pins with the bead or the words "This Side Up" facing upwards (as applicable), then carefully lower the cylinder head into position over the gasket and dowels.
16. Apply a coating of 12346004 or equivalent sealer to the threads of the cylinder head bolts, then thread the bolts into position until finger-tight.
17. Install the bolts in sequence to 22 ft. lbs. (30 Nm). The bolts must then be tightened again in sequence in the following order:
    a. Short length bolts: (11, 7, 3, 2, 6, 10) 55 degrees
    b. Medium length bolts: (12, 13) 65 degrees
    c. Long length bolts: (1, 4, 8, 5, 9) 75 degrees
18. Install the pushrods, secure the rocker arms and adjust the valves.
19. Install the rocker arm cover.
20. If removed, install the spark plugs. Engage the spark plug wires.
21. If the left cylinder head was removed, reposition and secure the air conditioning compressor and bracket.
22. If the right cylinder head was removed, install the alternator and bracket.
23. Engage the wiring harness and clip from the rear of the cylinder head.
24. Connect the coolant sensor wire.
25. Install the exhaust manifold.
26. Install the intake manifold.
27. Connect the negative battery cable, then properly refill the engine cooling system.
28. Run the engine to check for leaks.

CLEANING & INSPECTION

➧ See Figures 66, 67, 68 and 69

1. With the valves installed to protect the valve seats, remove carbon deposits from the combustion chambers and valve heads with a drill-mounted wire brush. Be careful not to damage the cylinder head gasket surface. If the head is to be

tccs3133

Fig. 66 An electric drill equipped with a wire wheel will expedite complete gasket removal

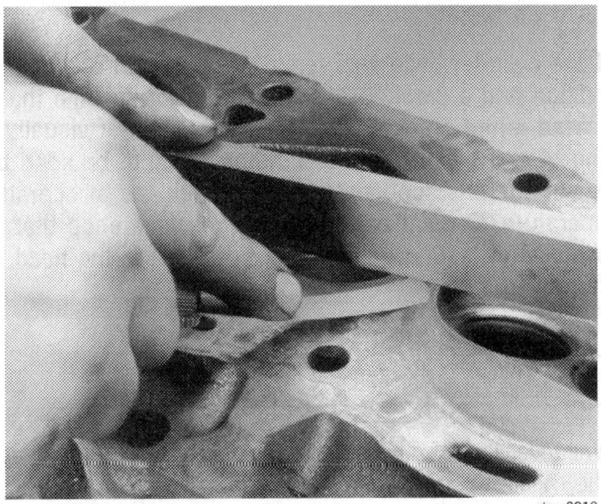

tccs3918

Fig. 67 Check the cylinder head for flatness across the head surface

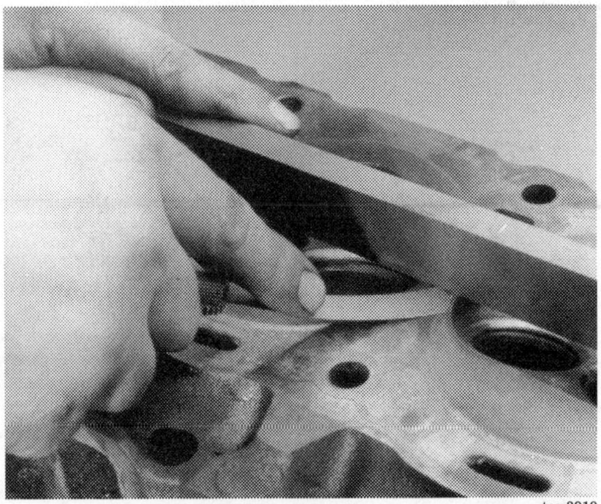

tccs3919

Fig. 68 Checks should be made both straight across the head and a both diagonals

disassembled, proceed to Step 3. If the head is not to be disassembled, proceed to Step 2.

2. Remove all dirt, oil and old gasket material from the cylinder head with solvent. Clean the bolt holes and the oil passage. Be careful not to get solvent on the valve seals as the solvent may damage them. If available, dry the cylinder head with compressed air. Check the head for cracks or other damage, and check the gasket surface for burrs, nicks and flatness. If you are in doubt about the head's serviceability, consult a reputable automotive machine shop.

3. Remove the valves, springs and retainers, then clean the valve guide bores with a valve guide cleaning tool. Remove all dirt, oil and old gasket material from the cylinder head with solvent. Clean the bolt holes and the oil passage.

4. Remove all deposits from the valves with a wire brush or buffing wheel. Inspect the valves as described later in this section.

5. Check the head for cracks using a dye penetrant in the valve seat area and ports, head surface and top. Check the gasket surface for burrs, nicks and flatness. If you are in doubt about the head's serviceability, consult a reputable automotive machine shop.

➡If the cylinder head was removed due to an overheating condition and a crack is suspected, do not assume that the head is not cracked because a crack is not visually found. A crack can be so small that it cannot be seen by eye, but can pass coolant when the engine is at operating temperature. Consult an automotive machine shop that has pressure testing equipment to make sure the head is not cracked.

RESURFACING

Whenever the cylinder head is removed, check the flatness of the cylinder head gasket surface as follows:

1. Make sure all dirt and old gasket material has been cleaned from the cylinder head. Any foreign material left on the head gasket surface can cause a false measurement.

2. Place a straightedge straight across and diagonally across the gasket surface of the cylinder head (in the positions shown in the figures). Using feeler gauges, determine the clearance at the center of the straightedge.

3. If warpage exceeds the 0.004 in. (0.10mm) then the cylinder head should likely be resurfaced or replaced. Contact a reputable machine shop for machining service and recommendations.

➡When resurfacing the cylinder head(s), the intake manifold mounting position is altered and must be corrected by machining a proportionate amount from the intake manifold flange.

Valves

REMOVAL & INSTALLATION

➧ See Figures 70, 71, 72, 73, 74, 75, 76 and 77

New valve seals must be installed when the valve train is put back together. Certain seals slip over the valve stem and guide boss, while others require that the boss be machined. In some applications Teflon guide seals are available. Check with a machinist and/or automotive parts store for a suggestion on the proper seals to use.

1. Remove the cylinder head(s), and place on a clean surface.

2. Using a suitable spring compressor (either a leverage or jawed type that is designed for pushrod overhead valve engines), compress the valve spring and remove the valve spring cap key. Carefully release the spring compressor and remove the valve spring and cap (and valve rotator on some engines).

➡Use care in removing the keys; they are easily lost.

3. Remove the valve seals and the spring seat (if applicable) from the valve guides. Throw these old seals away, as you'll be installing new seals during reassembly.

4. Slide the valves out of the head from the combustion chamber side.

5. Make a holder for the valves out of a piece of wood with drilled holes or cardboard. Make sure you number each

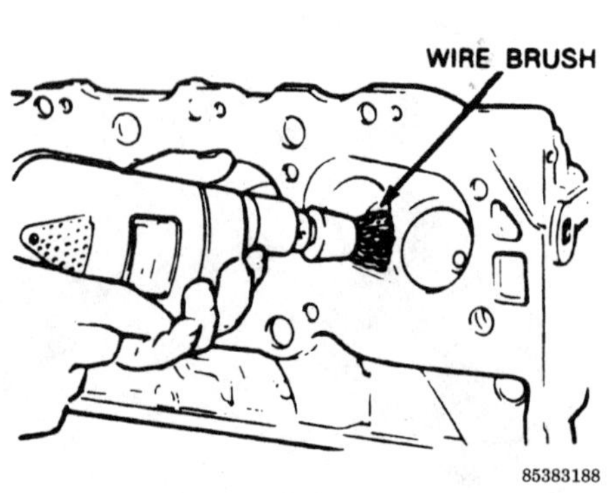

Fig. 69 Clean the combustion chamber using a drill-mounted wire brush

Fig. 70 Use a valve spring compressor tool to relieve spring tension from the valve caps

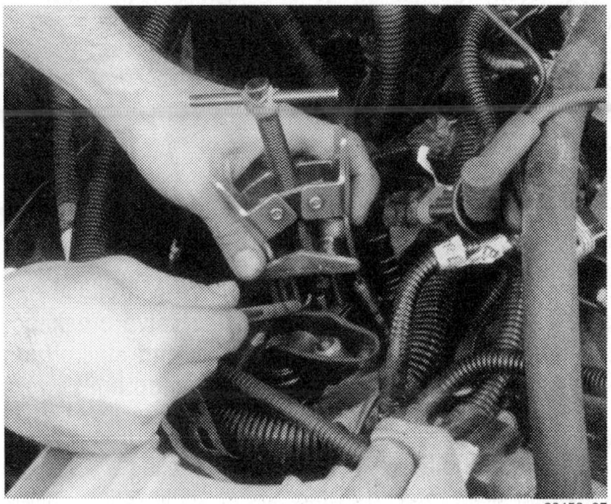

88453p37

Fig. 71 A magnet may be helpful in removing the valve keepers

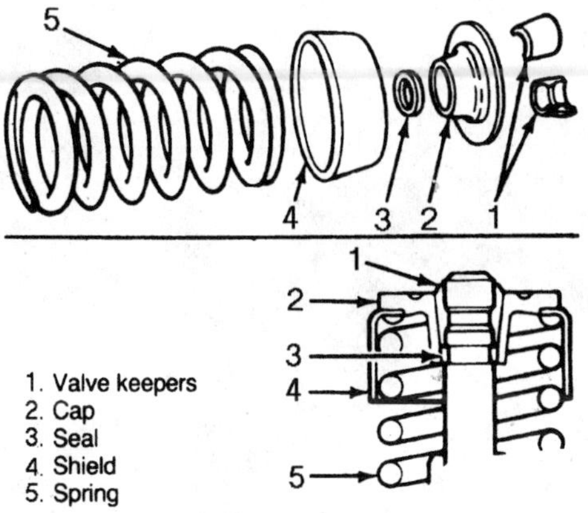

85383201

Fig. 74 Exploded and cross-sectional view of a common valve component assembly

88453p38

Fig. 72 Remove the spring from the valve stem

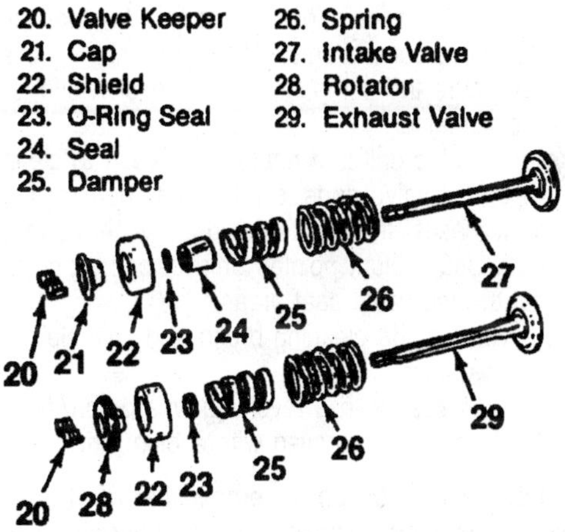

85383202

Fig. 75 Exploded view of the 4.3L engine valves and components

88453p39

Fig. 73 Remove the valve stem seal from the cylinder head

tccs3141

Fig. 76 Invert the cylinder head and withdraw the valve from the cylinder head bore

tccs3802

Fig. 77 A wire wheel may be used to clean the combustion chambers of carbon deposits

hole in the holder to keep the valves in proper order; they MUST be installed in their original locations. Another method of sorting the valve components is to use numbered containers, and make sure the components from each valve is stored in a separate container.

6. Use an electric drill and rotary wire brush to clean the intake and exhaust valve ports, combustion chamber and valve seats. In some cases, the carbon build-up will have to be chipped away. Use a blunt pointed drift for carbon chipping, being careful around valve seat areas.
7. Use a valve guide cleaning brush and suitable solvent to clean the valve guides.
8. Clean the valves with a revolving wire brush. Heavy carbon deposits may be removed with a blunt drift.

➡When using a wire brush to remove carbon from the cylinder head or valves, make sure the deposits are actually removed and not just burnished.

9. Wash and clean all valve springs, retainers etc., in safe solvent. Remember to keep parts from each valve separate.
10. Check the cylinder head for cracks. Cracks usually start around the exhaust valve seat because it is the hottest part of the combustion chamber. If a crack is suspected but cannot be detected visually, have the area checked by pressure testing, with a dye penetrant or other method by an automotive machine shop.
11. Inspect the valves, guides, springs and seats and machine or replace parts, as necessary.

To install:

12. Lubricate the valve stems with clean engine oil.
13. Install the valves in the cylinder head, one at a time, as numbered.
14. Lubricate and position the spring seats (if applicable), new seals and valve springs, again one valve at a time.
15. Install the spring caps, and compress the springs.
16. With the valve key groove exposed above the compressed valve spring, wipe some wheel bearing grease around the groove. This will retain the keys as you release the spring compressor.
17. Using needle nose pliers (or your fingers), carefully place the keys in the key grooves. The grease should hold the keys in place. Slowly release the spring compressor; the valve cap or rotator will raise up as the compressor is released, retaining the key.
18. Install the cylinder head(s).

INSPECTION

➧ See Figures 78, 79, 80, 81, 82 and 83

➡Excessive valve stem-to-bore clearance will cause excessive oil consumption and may cause valve breakage. Insufficient clearance will result in noisy and sticky functioning of the valve and disturb engine smoothness.

Inspect the valve faces and seats (in the head) for pits, burned spots and other evidence of poor seating. Valves that are pitted must be refaced to the proper angle (45°). Valves that are warped excessively must be replaced. When a valve head that is warped excessively is refaced, a knife edge will be ground on part or all of the valve head due to the amount

tccs3142

Fig. 78 A dial gauge may be used to check valve stem-to-guide clearance

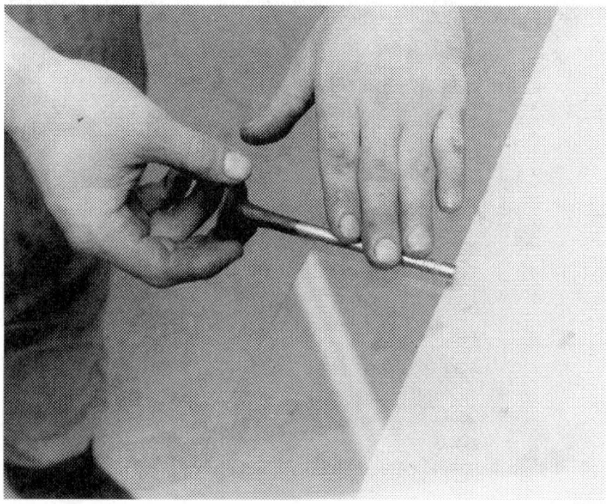

tccs3144

Fig. 79 Valve stems may be rolled on a flat surface to check for bends

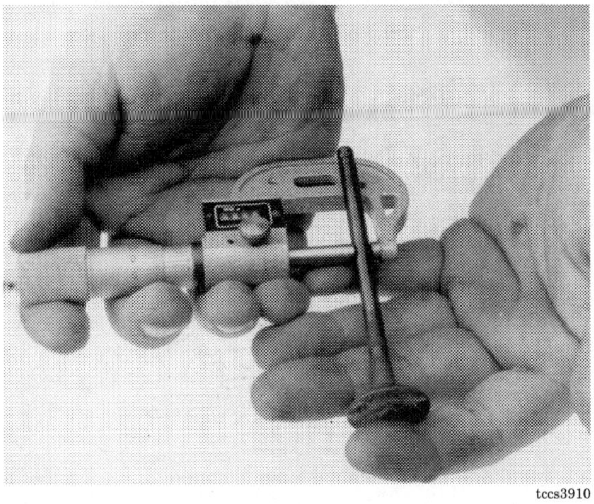

Fig. 80 Use a micrometer to check the valve stem diameter

of material that must be removed to completely reface the valve. Knife edges lead to breakage, burning or preignition due to heat localizing on the knife edge. If the edge of the valve head is less than $^1/_{32}$ in. (.093mm) after machining, replace the valve. We recommend that all machine work be performed by a reputable machine shop.

Make sure the valve stem is not bent. The valve may be rolled on a flat surface such as a mirror or glass. An even better indication of valve stem bending can be determined by carefully chocking the stem into an electric drill. Use the drill the spin the stem while you watch the valve head. A bent stem will be obvious by the wobbling of the head. Be very careful if this method is used. If the valve stem is not properly chocked in position it could come flying out of the drill and cause injury.

Some of the engines covered in this guide are equipped with valve rotators, which double as valve spring caps. In normal operation the rotators put a certain degree of wear on the tip of the valve stem; this wear appears as concentric rings on the stem tip. However, if the rotator is not working properly, the wear may appear as straight notches or **X** patterns across the valve stem tip. Whenever the valves are removed from the cylinder head, the tips should be inspected for improper pattern, which could indicate valve rotator problems. Valve stem tips will have to be ground flat if rotator patterns are severe.

Check the valve stem for scoring and burned spots. If not noticeably scored or damaged, clean the valve stem with solvent to remove all gum and varnish. Clean the valve guides using solvent and an expanding wire type valve guide cleaner. Check the valve stem-to-guide clearance in one or more of the following manners, but do not rely on the visual inspection alone:

1. A visual inspection can give you a fairly good idea if the guide, valve stem or both are worn. Insert the valve into the guide until the valve head is slightly away from the valve seat. Wiggle the valve sideways. A small amount of wobble is normal, excessive wobble means a worn guide and/or valve stem.

➡If a dial indicator and micrometer are not available to you, take your cylinder head and valves to a reputable machine shop of inspection.

2. If a dial indicator is on hand, mount the indicator so that gauge stem is 90° to the valve stem as close to the top of the valve guide as possible. Move the valve from the seat, and measure the valve guide-to-stem clearance by rocking the stem back and forth to actuate the dial indicator. Measure the valve stem using a micrometer and compare to specifications to determine whether stem or guide is causing excessive clearance.

3. If both a ball gauge and a micrometer are available, first, measure the inside diameter of the valve guide bushing at three locations using the ball gauge. Second, use the micrometer to measure the stem diameter. Finally, subtract the valve stem diameter from the corresponding valve guide inside diameter to arrive at the valve clearance. If clearance is greater than specification, the valve and guide bushing must be replaced.

The valve guide, if worn, must be repaired before the valve seats can be resurfaced. A new valve guide should be installed or, in some cases, knurled. Consult an automotive machine shop.

If the valve guide is okay, measure the valve seat concentricity using a runout gauge. Follow the manufacturers instructions. If runout is excessive, reface or replace the valve and machine or replace the valve seat.

➡Valves and seats must always be machined together. Never use a refaced valve on a valve seat that has not been machined; never use a valve that has not been refaced on a machined valve seat.

REFACING

Valve refacing should only be handled by a reputable machine shop, as the experience and equipment needed to do the job are beyond that of the average owner/mechanic. During the course of a normal valve job, refacing is necessary when simply lapping the valves into their seats will not correct the seat and face wear. When the valves are reground (resurfaced), the valve seats must also be recut, again requiring special equipment and experience.

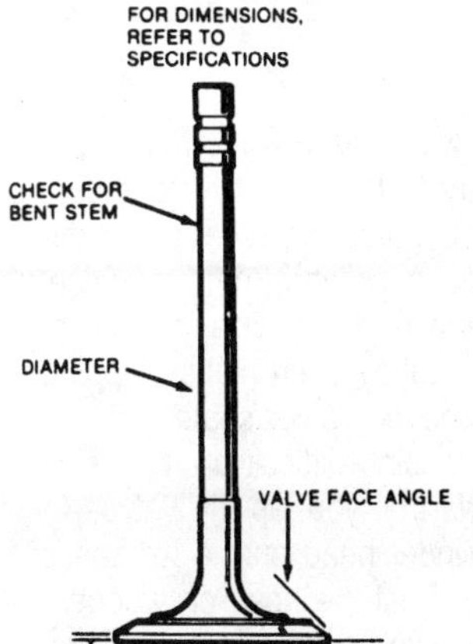

Fig. 81 Valve inspection and measurement

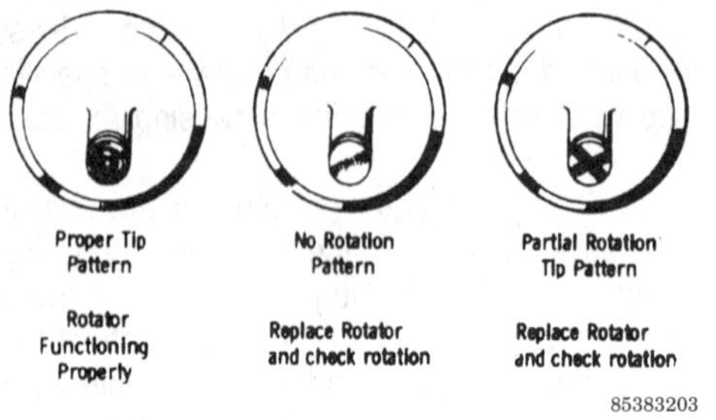

Fig. 82 Valve stem wear patterns on engines equipped with rotator cups

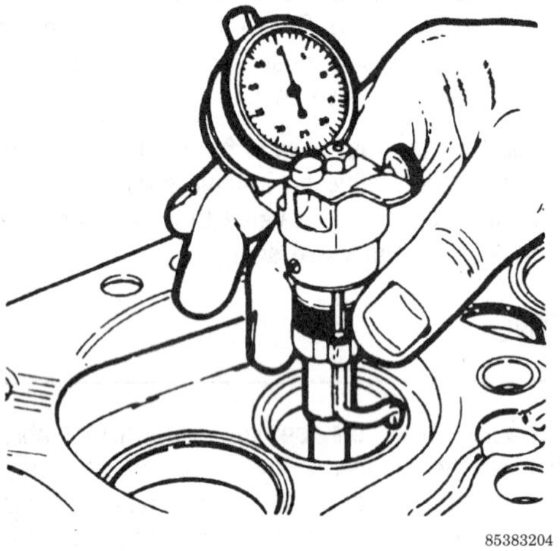

Fig. 83 A run-out (dial) gauge is used to check valve seat concentricity

VALVE LAPPING

See Figure 84

After machine work has been performed on the valves, it may be necessary to lap the valve to assure proper contact. For this, you should first contact your machine shop to determine if lapping is necessary. Some machine shops will perform this for you as part of the service, but the precision machining which is available today often makes lapping unnecessary. Additionally, the hardened valves/seats used in modern automobiles may make lapping difficult or impossible. If your machine shop recommends that you lap the valves, proceed as follows:

1. Set the cylinder head on the workbench, combustion chamber side up. Rest the head on wooden blocks on either end, so there are two or three inches between the tops of the valve guides and the bench.
2. Lightly lube the valve stem with clean engine oil. Coat the valve seat completely with valve grinding compound. Use just enough compound that the full width and circumference of the seat are covered.

Fig. 84 Lapping the valves by hand

3. Install the valve in its proper location in the head. Attach the suction cup end of the valve lapping tool to the valve head. It usually helps to put a small amount of saliva into the suction cup to aid it sticking to the valve.
4. Rotate the tool between the palms, changing position and lifting the tool often to prevent grooving. Lap the valve in until a smooth, evenly polished seat and valve face are evident.
5. Remove the valve from the head. Wipe away all traces of grinding compound from the valve face and seat. Wipe out the port with a solvent soaked rag, and swab out the valve guide with a piece of solvent soaked rag to make sure there are no traces of compound grit inside the guide. This cleaning is important.
6. Proceed through the remaining valves, one at a time. Make sure the valve faces, seats, cylinder ports and valve guides are clean before reassembling the valve train.

Valve Stem Seals

REPLACEMENT

Cylinder Head Installed

The valve stem seals on most engines covered by this manual may be replaced with the cylinder head either on or off the engine. The removal procedure with the cylinder head installed utilizes compressed air in the cylinder to hold the valve in place and keep it from dropping into the cylinder once the valve key, cap and spring are removed.

➡If air pressure is lost while the valve keepers are removed, the valve will drop into the cylinder. If this happens, the cylinder head must be removed in order to recover the valve.

1. Disconnect the negative battery cable.

2. Remove the rocker arm cover.

➡**The cylinder must be on at TDC of it's compression stroke in order to follow this procedure. On the compression stroke, the cylinder's valves will be closed allowing the air pressure to hold the valve in position. The engine must therefore be turned slightly for each cylinder's valve seals.**

3. Remove the rocker arm and pushrod assemblies from the cylinders on which the valves are being serviced.
4. Remove the spark plug from the cylinder which is on it's compression stroke and install a spark plug air fitting adapter such as tool J-23590 or its equivalent, with an in-line gauge set between the adapter and air compressor. Apply compressed air to hold the valve in place.
5. Compress the valve spring using a suitable compressor tool and remove the valve key. Carefully release the spring tension, then remove the valve cap and spring.

➡**If the air pressure has forced the piston to the bottom of the cylinder, any removal of air pressure will allow the valves to fall into the cylinder. A rubber band, tape or string wrapped around the end of the valve stem will prevent this.**

6. Remove the old seal using a suitable removal tool.

To install:

7. Install the new seal using the valve stem seal tool.
8. Install the valve spring and cap, then compress the spring and install the valve key.
9. When the valve springs are properly installed, release the air pressure from the cylinder using the gauge set, then remove the spark plug adapter.
10. Install the spark plug and turn the engine sufficiently to work on the next cylinder. Repeat the above steps until all seals are replaced.
11. Install the rocker arm and pushrod assemblies, then install the rocker cover and connect the negative battery cable.

Cylinder Heads Removed

The valve stem oil seals are replaced as a part of normal valve service any time the valve stems are removed from the cylinder head. Refer to the valve procedure in this section for seal removal and installation when the cylinder head has been removed from the vehicle.

Valve Springs

REMOVAL & INSTALLATION

See Figures 85 and 86

Removal or installation of the valve springs requires use of the following tools:

- Valve Spring Compressor tool (leverage type) No. J-5892-C, J-5892-D or their equivalents
- GM Air Adapter tool No. J-23590 or equivalent to retain the valves if the cylinder head is to remain installed

The valve springs are removed and installed as part of the valve procedure found earlier in this section. If only a spring replacement is required, refer to the valve stem seal procedure with the cylinder head installed. The same air pressure method may be used to retain the valve while only a spring is replaced.

INSPECTION

See Figures 87, 88 and 89

1. Place the valve spring on a flat, clean surface next to a square.
2. Measure the height of the spring, and rotate it against the edge of the square to measure distortion (out-of-roundness). If spring height varies between springs by more than $^1/_{16}$ in. (.062mm) or if the distortion exceeds $^1/_{16}$ in. (.062mm), replace the spring.

A valve spring tester is needed to test spring test pressure, so the valve springs must usually be taken to a professional machine shop for this test. Spring pressure at the installed and/or compressed heights is checked, depending on the specification.

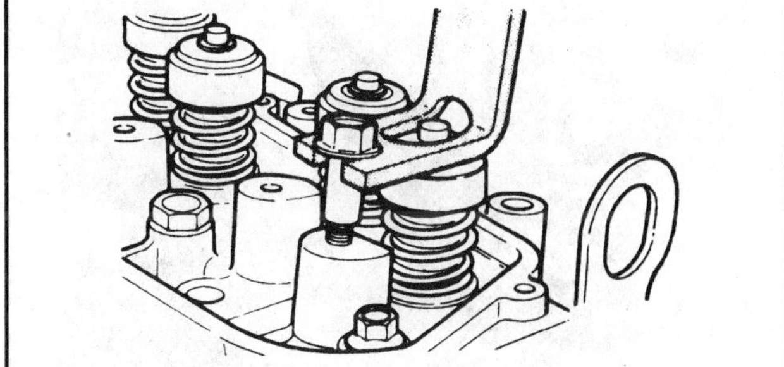

85383211

Fig. 85 Leverage type valve spring compressor tool — 2.2L and 4.3L engines

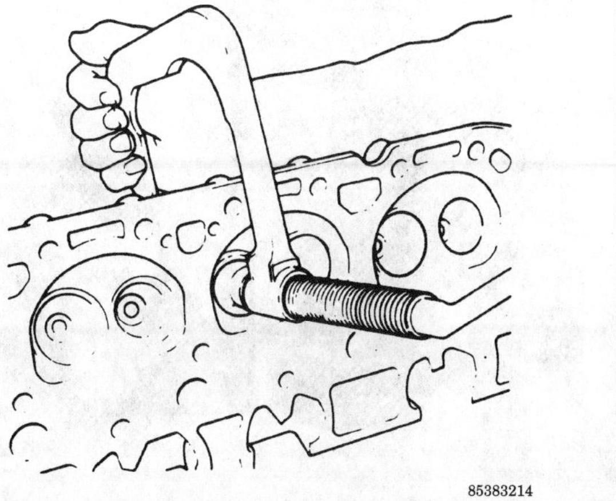

85383214

Fig. 86 On most engines a C-clamp type spring may be used if the cylinder head is removed from the engine

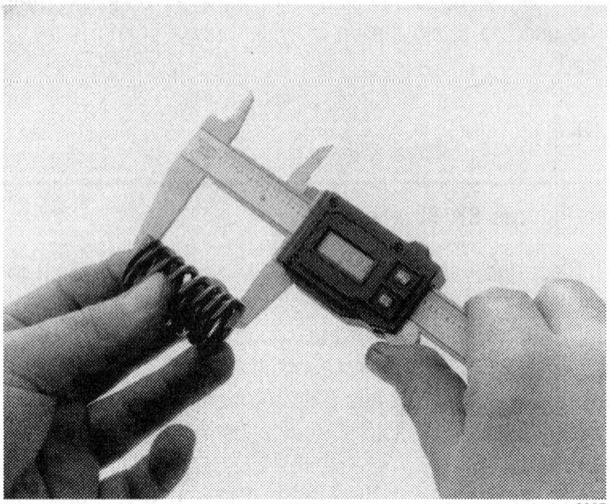
tccs3907

Fig. 87 Use a caliper gauge to check the valve spring free-length

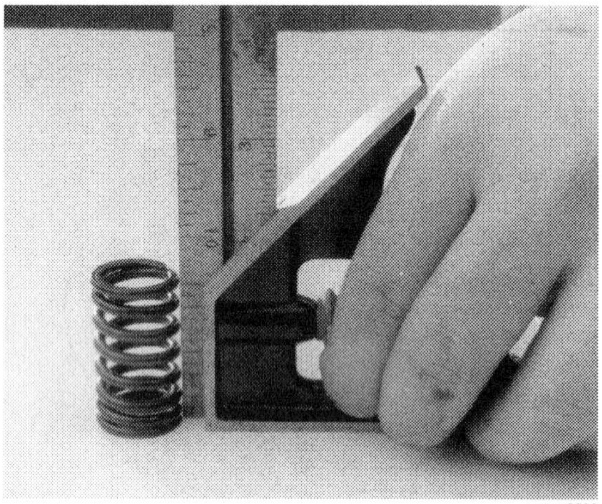
tccs3908

Fig. 88 Check the valve spring for squareness on a flat service; a carpenter's square can be used

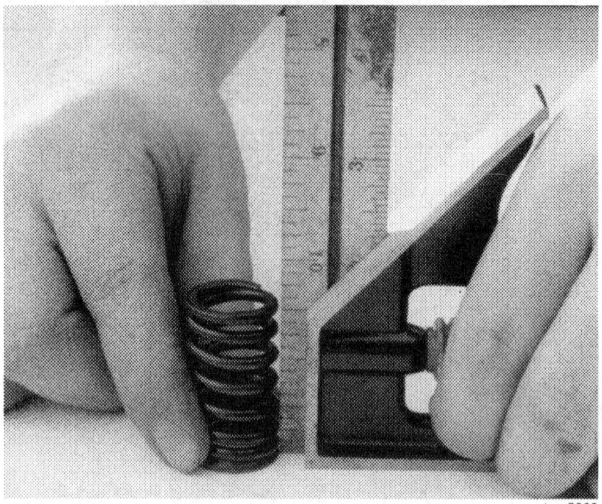
tccs3909

Fig. 89 The valve spring should be straight up and down when placed like this

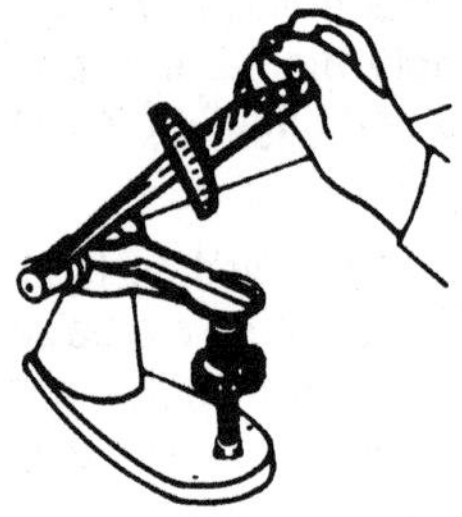
85383218

Fig. 90 If a spring pressure testing tool is not available, have the spring checked professionally

Valve Seats

REMOVAL & INSTALLATION

Due to the high degree of precision and special equipment required, valve seat replacement should be left to an automotive machine shop. Seat replacement procedures vary depending on whether the engine is equipped with cast iron or aluminum heads. Iron heads use a valve seat which is originally an integral part of the head. To replace these, a bore must be cut in the head which will accept an insert. The bore must be drilled to exacting specifications for the insert to work.

Aluminum cylinder heads are already equipped with valve seat inserts. There are various methods to replace these inserts, and although most are similar, the specifications are unique to each cylinder head application. The following procedure can be construed as what is generally acceptable for aluminum cylinder heads; the actual method employed should be the decision of the machinist.

The replaceable inserts can be removed by cutting them out to within a few thousandths of their outside diameter and then collapsing the remainder. Another method sometimes used to remove aluminum head seat inserts is to heat the head to a high temperature and drive the seat out.

Upon installation, the new seat may be installed with the aluminum cylinder head heated to a high temperature, then the seat, which is at room temperature or slightly chilled, is pressed into the head. The aluminum head is then allowed to cool and as it does, it contracts and grips the seat. In certain applications, the new seat may be driven in with both the head and seat at room temperature. The calculated press-fit interference will then retain the seat in the head.

Valve Guides

REMOVAL & INSTALLATION

See Figure 91

The 2.2L and 4.3L engines use integral valve guides; that is, they are a part of the cylinder head and cannot be replaced. The guides can, however, be reamed oversize if they are found to be worn past an acceptable limit. Occasionally, a valve guide bore will be oversize as manufactured. These are marked on the inboard side of the cylinder heads on the machined surface just above the intake manifold.

If the guides must be reamed (this service is available at most machine shops) then valves with oversize stems must be fitted. Valves are usually available in 0.001 in. (.025mm), 0.003 in. (.076mm) and 0.005 in. (.127mm) stem oversizes for most applications. Valve guides which are not excessively worn or distorted may, in some cases, be knurled rather than reamed.

Knurling is a process which the metal on the valve guide bore is displaced and raised, thereby reducing clearance. Knurling also provides excellent oil control. The option of knurling rather than reaming valve guides should be discussed with a reputable machinist or engine specialist.

Valve Lifter

REMOVAL & INSTALLATION

2.2L Engine

See Figure 92

When installing new lifters, a pre-lube should always be applied to the lifter body. It is also a good idea to prime hydraulic lifters by submerging them in clean engine oil and depressing the plunger using an old pushrod. This allows the internal components of the hydraulic lifter to coat with oil before initial operation in the engine. All lifters should be replaced when a new camshaft is installed.

➡If any valve train components (lifters, pushrods, rocker arms) are to be reused, they must be tagged or arranged during removal to assure installation in their original locations.

1. Remove the rocker arm cover.
2. Remove the cylinder head assembly from the engine.
3. Remove the bolts retaining the lifter anti-rotation brackets, then remove the brackets.
4. Remove the hydraulic roller lifters from the bores.

To install:

➡If installing a new lifter, coat the lifter body with a suitable camshaft pre-lube

5. Install each hydraulic lifter to its bore being careful to align the flat sides (top) of the lifters with the flat sides of the anti-rotation brackets. When properly installed the flat sides of each lifter are aligned parallel to the anti-rotation bracket. The roller at the bottom of the lifter is parallel to the camshaft lobe.

➡Make sure to properly align and install each lifter as improper installation of the lifters or brackets could result in engine damage.

6. Install the anti-rotation bracket retaining bolts and tighten to 97 inch lbs. (11 Nm).
7. Install the cylinder head.
8. Install the rocker arm cover.

4.3L Engine

See Figures 93, 94, 95, 96 and 97

1. Remove the rocker arm cover.
2. Remove the intake manifold assembly.

➡If any valve train components (lifters, pushrods, rocker arms) are to be reused, they must be tagged or arranged during removal to assure installation in their original locations.

3. Remove the rocker arm and pushrod assemblies.

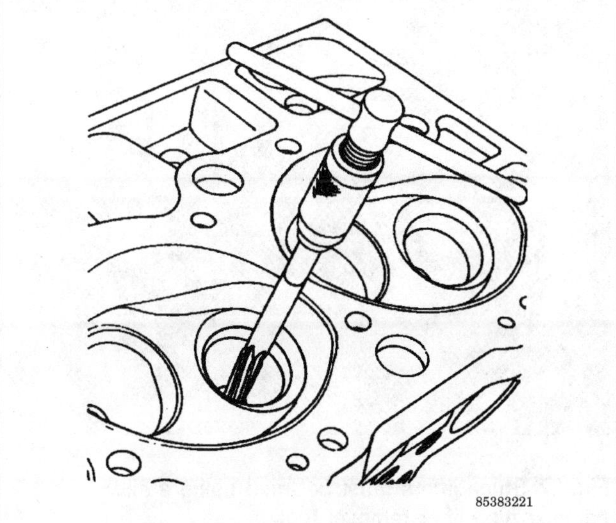

Fig. 91 Reaming the valve guides

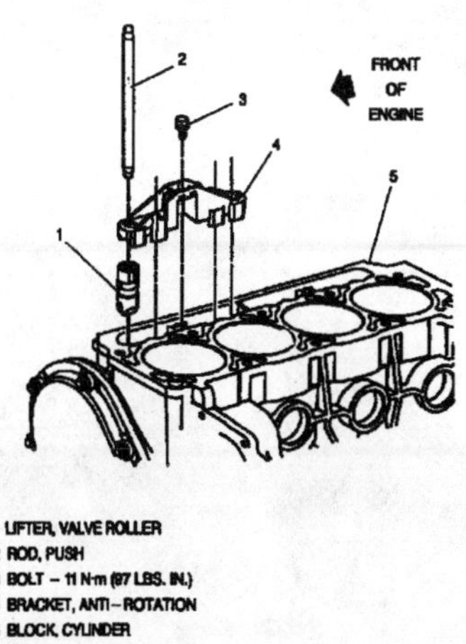

Fig. 92 Removing the hydraulic roller lifter from the 2.2L engine

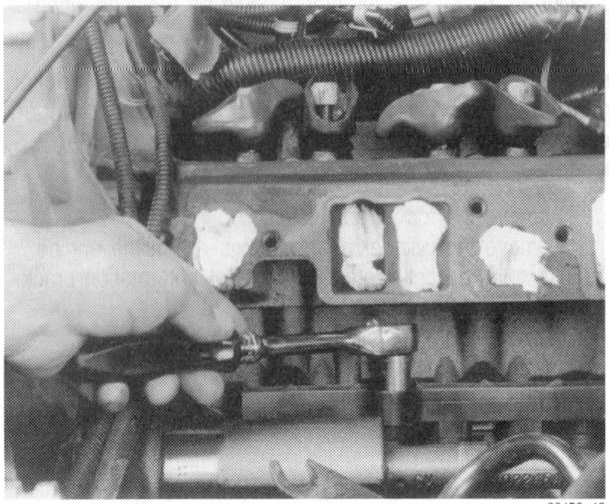
88453p43

Fig. 93 Unfasten the lifter retainer bolts

88453p44

Fig. 94 Remove the lifter retainer

88453p45

Fig. 95 Remove the lifter from its bore

tccs3812

Fig. 96 A magnet is useful in removing lifters from their bores

tccs3813

Fig. 97 Stuck lifters must be freed using a slide hammer type lifter removal tool

4. Remove the hydraulic lifter retainer bolts, them remove the retainers or retainers and restrictors, as equipped.
5. Remove the lifters from the engine.

To install:

6. Inspect the lifter and lifter bore for wear and scuffing. Examine the roller for freedom of movement and/or flat spots on the roller surface.
7. If new lifters are being installed, lubricate the lifters using a suitable pre-lube and add GM engine oil supplement or an equivalent additive to the crankcase.
8. Install the hydraulic lifters along with the restrictors and/or retainers. Secure the retainers using the bolts and tighten to 12 ft. lbs. (16 Nm).
9. Install the pushrods and rocker arm assemblies, then adjust the valve lash.
10. Install the intake manifold assembly.
11. Install the rocker arm covers.

Oil Pan

Pan removal is possible with the engine in the vehicle on some of the powertrain combinations covered by this manual. If it is possible, it will often require the removal or repositioning of components including, the steering linkage assembly, the forward drive axle and crossmember (4WD) and/or the engine mounts. It is a difficult and tedious task to remove the oil pan with the engine in the vehicle. The chances of contaminating the bearing surfaces or damaging other internal engine components is great. Also, working under the vehicle with the engine jacked up in the frame puts you at great risk for great personal injury. Therefore, it is desirable in most cases to remove the engine in order to gain access to the oil pan.

REMOVAL & INSTALLATION

2.2L Engine

See Figure 98

1. Remove the engine assembly from the vehicle.
2. If equipped, remove the clutch pressure plate and disc from the engine.
3. Remove the flywheel.
4. Remove the oil pan nuts and bolts, then remove the pan from the bottom of the block.

To install:

5. Carefully clean the gasket mating surfaces of any remaining old gasket or sealer material.
6. Position a new gasket and seal onto the oil pan. Use a thin bead of sealant at either side of the sealer (as shown in the illustration).
7. Install the oil pan and tighten the retaining bolts to 89 inch. lbs. (10 Nm).
8. Install the flywheel.
9. If equipped, install the pressure plate and disc.
10. Install the engine to the vehicle.

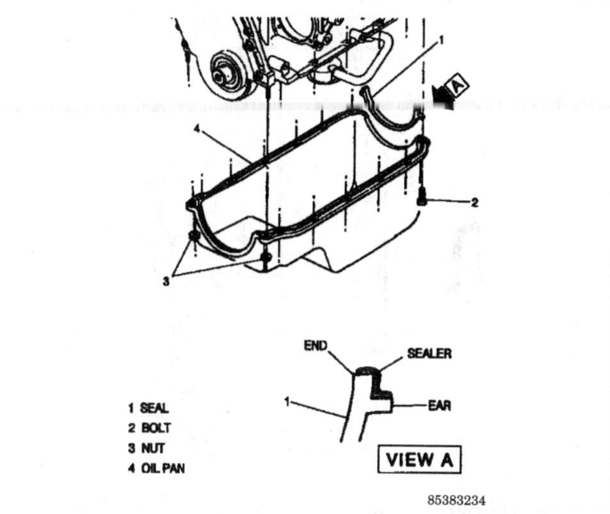

Fig. 98 Oil pan and gasket installation — 2.2L engine

4.3L Engine

2-WHEEL DRIVE

1. Remove the engine from the vehicle.
2. Remove the oil pan retainers (nuts, studs and/or bolts) and rail reinforcements, if equipped.
3. Remove the rubber bell housing plugs, if equipped.
4. Remove the oil pan from the block.

To install:

5. Using a putty knife, clean the gasket mounting surfaces. Make sure that all sealing surfaces are clean and free of oil.
6. Apply 1052080 or an equivalent sealant to the oil pan rail where it contacts the timing cover-to-block joint (front) and the crankshaft rear seal retainer-to-block joint (rear). Continue the bead of sealant about 1 in. (25mm) in both directions from each of the four corners.
7. Using a new gasket, install the oil pan, reinforcements (if equipped) and retainers. Tighten the retainers to specification:

On 1994-95 models.

- Bolts: 100 inch lbs. (11 Nm).
- Nuts at corners: 17 ft. lbs. (23 Nm)

On 1996-97 models.

- Bolts and studs: 18 ft. lbs. (25 Nm)

8. Install the engine into the vehicle. Refill the crankcase with fresh oil. Start the engine, establish normal operating temperatures and check for leaks.

4-WHEEL DRIVE VEHICLES

See Figures 99, 100, 101 and 102

1. Disconnect the negative battery cable.
2. Remove the dipstick tube.
3. Raise and support the front of the vehicle safely using jackstands.
4. Remove the drive belt splash shield, the front axle shield, and the transfer case shield.
5. Remove the front skid plate and drain the engine crankcase oil, then remove the flywheel cover.
6. If applicable, disengage the wiring harness bracket at the right side of the oil pan.
7. Remove the left and right motor mount through-bolts.

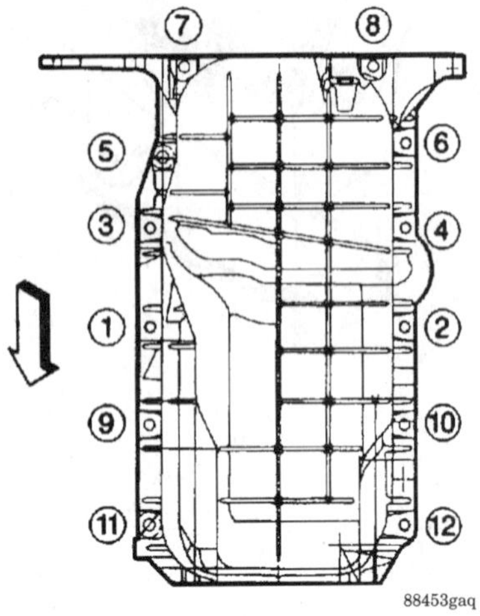

Fig. 99 Oil pan bolt tightening sequence — 1996 4.3L engine

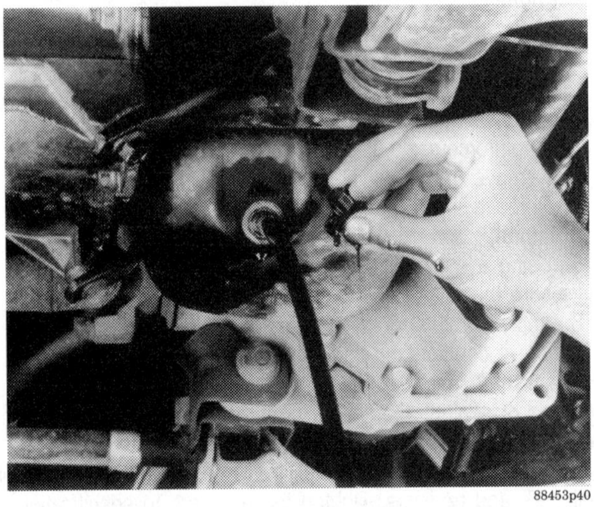

Fig. 100 Drain the engine oil from the crankcase

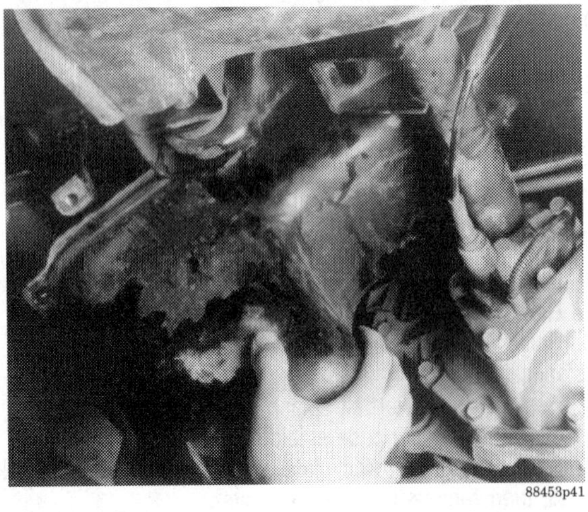

Fig. 101 After unfastening the oil pan bolts remove the oil pan

Fig. 102 Remove and discard the old oil pan gasket

8. Raise the engine using a suitable lifting device and block in position. This may be accomplished using large wooden blocks between the motor mounts and brackets.

➡Use extreme caution when blocking the engine in position. Get out from underneath the truck and rock the engine slightly once the blocks are in place to be sure the engine is properly supported.

9. Disconnect the oil cooler line, then remove the oil filter adapter.
10. Remove the pitman arm bolt, then disconnect the pitman arm.
11. Remove the idler arm bolts, then disconnect the idler arm.
12. Remove the front differential through-bolts, then disconnect or remove the front driveshaft (as necessary).
13. Roll the differential assembly forward for clearance.
14. Remove the starter motor retaining bolts, then lower the starter and either remove it from the vehicle or suspend it out of the way using mechanic's wire.
15. Remove the oil pan bolts, nuts and reinforcements, then lower the oil pan and gasket from the vehicle.

To install:

16. Using a putty knife, clean the gasket mounting surfaces. Make sure that all sealing surfaces are clean and free of oil.
17. Apply 1052080, or an equivalent sealant to the oil pan rail where it contacts the timing cover-to-block joint (front) and the crankshaft rear seal retainer-to-block joint (rear). Continue the bead of sealant about 1 in. (25mm) in both directions from each of the four corners.
18. Using a new gasket, install the oil pan, reinforcements and retainers. Tighten the bolts to 100 inch lbs. (11 Nm) and

the nuts at the corners to 17 ft. lbs. (23 Nm) on 1994-95 models and 18 ft. lbs. (25 Nm) on 1996-97 models.

✱✱CAUTION

Use a feeler gauge to check the clearance between the three oil pan-to-transmission bell housing contact points. if the clearance exceeds 0.010 in. (0.254mm) at any of the points, move the pan until the clearance is within specifications.

19. Install the starter motor and secure using the mounting bolts.
20. Roll the differential back into position, then install/connect the front driveshaft. Install the front differential through-bolts.
21. Connect the idler arm and secure using the retaining bolts, then connect the pitman arm and secure using the bolts.
22. Install the transfer case shield.
23. Install the flywheel cover, then install the front skid plate.
24. Install the front axle shield, then install the drive belt splash shield.
25. If applicable, engage the wiring harness bracket at the right side of the oil pan.
26. Remove the jackstands and carefully lower the truck.
27. Install the dipstick, then properly refill the engine crankcase.
28. Connect the negative battery cable.
29. Start the engine, establish normal operating temperatures and check for leaks.

Oil Pump

REMOVAL & INSTALLATION

➧ See Figures 103 and 104

1. Remove the oil pan.
2. Remove the oil pump attaching bolt and, if equipped, the pickup tube nut/bolt then remove the pump along with the pickup tube and shaft, as necessary.

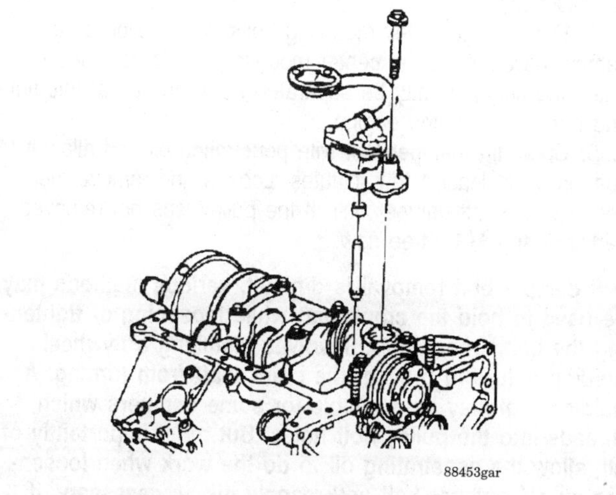

Fig. 103 Exploded view of a common oil pump mounting — 4.3L engine shown

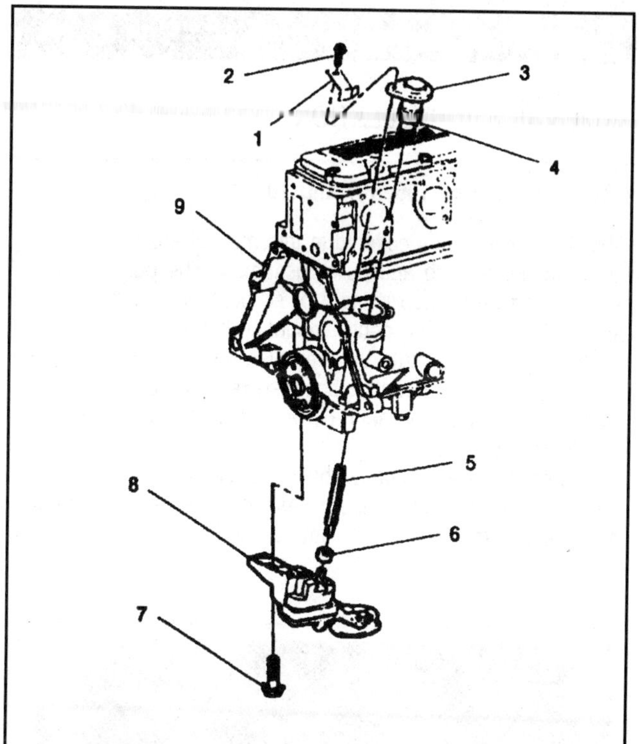

Fig. 104 Exploded view of a common oil pump mounting — 2.2L engine shown

3. If necessary for the 2.2L engine, remove the extension shaft and retainer (being careful not the crack the retainer) from the pump.

To install:

4. For the 2.2L engine, if the extension shaft was removed, heat the extension shaft retainer in hot water, then install the shaft and retainer to the oil pump. Make sure the retainer does not crack during installation.
5. Ensure that the pump pickup tube is tight in the pump body. If the tube should come loose, oil pressure will be lost and oil starvation will occur. If the pickup tube is loose it should be replaced.
6. Install the pump aligning the pump shaft with the distributor drive gear as necessary. Tighten oil pump/pickup tube retainer(s) to specification:
   - 2.2L engine: 32 ft. lbs. (44 Nm)
   - 4.3L engine: 65 ft. lbs. (90 Nm)
7. Install the oil pan and refill the engine crankcase. Start the engine and make sure oil pressure builds immediately or engine damage could occur.

Crankshaft Damper/Pulley

REMOVAL & INSTALLATION

See Figures 105, 106, 107 and 108

Most of the engines covered in this manual are equipped with a crankshaft hub and pulley assembly. The pulley is usually mounted to the hub using 3 or so bolts around the inner circle of the pulley. The center mounting bolt is used to retain the hub to the crankshaft, but may also be used to retain the pulley. If the center mounting bolt also retains the pulley, a washer can normally be seen between the bolt head and the inner lip of the pulley.

1. Disconnect the negative battery cable.
2. Loosen and remove the accessory drive belts or serpentine drive belt from the crankshaft damper.

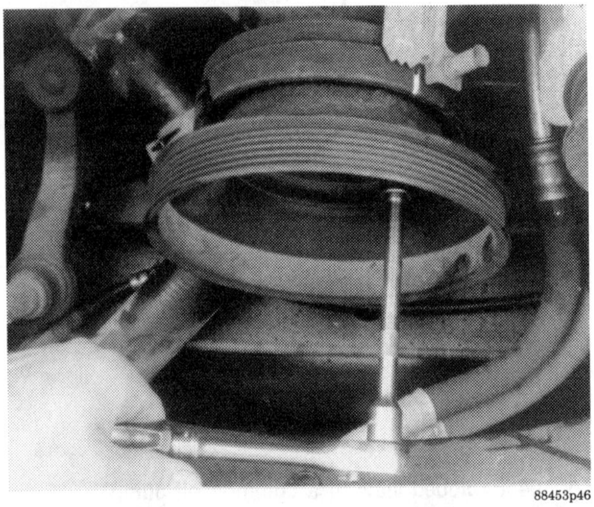

Fig. 105 Unfasten the pulley mounting bolts

Fig. 106 Unfasten the center pulley bolts and remove the pulley from the vehicle

Fig. 107 Using a suitable puller, disengage the damper from the crankshaft

Fig. 108 Remove the damper from the vehicle

3. If necessary for access on certain models, remove the fan assembly.
4. Remove the pulley mounting bolts from the pulley and damper assembly. If the center mounting bolt is not used to retain the pulley, it may be separated from the hub at this time and removed from the engine.
5. Spray the damper bolt with penetrating oil and allow it to soak in for at least a few minutes. Loosen and remove the center crankshaft damper bolt. If the pulley was not removed earlier, it should be free now.

➡If damper bolt removal is difficult, various methods may be used to hold the crankshaft while loosening or tightening the bolt. One method involves installing a flywheel holding fixture to prevent the crankshaft from turning. A holding tool may be available for some dampers which threads into the pulley bolt holes. But most importantly of all, allow the penetrating oil to do the work when loosening an old damper bolt and reapply oil, as necessary. If you have the time, you might even want the oil to sit overnight.

6. Remove the damper from the end of the crankshaft using a suitable threaded damper puller, NOT a jawed-type puller which would most likely destroy dampers with bonded hubs.

⁂WARNING

The use of any other type of puller, such as a universal claw type which pulls on the outside of the hub, can destroy the balancer on some of these engines. Many of the vehicles covered in this manual use a balancer, the outside ring of which is bonded in rubber to the hub. Pulling on the outside will break the bond.

To install:

7. If removal of the damper was difficult, check the damper inner diameter and the crankshaft outer diameter for corrosion. A small amount of corrosion may be removed using steel wool, then the surface may be lubricated lightly using clean engine oil.

8. Coat the front cover seal contact edge of the damper lightly with clean engine oil, then apply a small amount of RTV sealant to the keyway in the damper hub. Install the damper on the end of the crankshaft (along with the pulley if the share the center retaining bolt), but DO NOT hammer it into position, instead use a damper installation tool to slowly draw the hub into position. If the damper can be positioned far enough over the end of the crankshaft, the damper bolt may be used to draw it into position, but be careful that sufficient threads are in contact to prevent stripping the bolt or crankshaft.

9. Once the damper is fully seated, install and tighten the retaining bolt to specification.

10. If not done earlier, install the pulley and secure using the outer retaining bolts.

11. If removed for access, install the fan assembly.

12. Install the drive belt(s) to the crankshaft pulley.

13. Connect the negative battery cable.

Timing Chain Cover and Seal

REMOVAL & INSTALLATION

2.2L Engine

1994-95 MODELS

1. Disconnect the negative battery cable.

2. Remove the power steering fluid reservoir from the radiator shroud, then disengage the upper fan shroud.

3. Carefully release the belt tension, then remove the serpentine drive belt.

4. Remove the alternator and brackets from the engine, then position them aside.

5. Remove the crankshaft pulley and hub. For details, please refer to the procedure located earlier in this section.

6. As necessary, disconnect the lower radiator hose clamp at the water pump, then loosen and/or remove the oil pan.

➡There may be bolts attaching the front of the oil pan to the timing cover. If so, make sure they are removed before attempting to remove the cover.

7. Unfasten the crankcase (timing) front cover bolts, then disengage cover from the engine. Make sure all bolts are removed and be careful not to force and damage the cover.

8. Carefully remove the old crankshaft seal from the cover using a suitable prytool. Be very careful not to distort the front cover or to score the end of the crankshaft.

To install:

9. Carefully remove all traces of gasket or sealant from the mating surfaces.

10. Lubricate the lips of a new seal with clean engine oil, then use a seal centering tool (such as J-35468 or equivalent) to install the seal to the front cover. Leave the tool in position in the seal until the cover is installed.

11. Apply a 3/8 in. (10mm) wide by 5/16 (5mm) thick bead of RTV sealer to the oil pan at the front crankcase cover sealing surface. Then apply a 1/4 in. (6mm) by 1/8 in. (3mm) thick bead of RTV to the crankcase front cover at the block sealing surface.

12. Install the crankcase front cover to the engine using the seal tool to assure it is properly centered and prevent damage to the hub. Tighten the cover retaining bolts to 97 inch lbs. (11 Nm), then remove the seal centering tool.

13. Install the lower radiator hose clamp at the water pump, then install and secure the oil pan, as applicable.

14. If removed, install the oil pan.

15. Install the crankshaft pulley and hub.

16. Reposition and secure the alternator with brackets.

17. Install the serpentine drive belt, then install the upper fan shroud.

18. Reposition and secure the power steering reservoir.

19. Connect the negative battery cable.

1996-97 MODELS

➧ See Figure 109

1. Disconnect the negative battery cable.

2. Carefully release the belt tension, then remove the serpentine drive belt.

3. Remove the crankshaft pulley and hub. For details, please refer to the procedure located earlier in this section.

4. Remove the cooling fan assembly and pulley.

5. Remove the belt tensioner/idler pulley assembly.

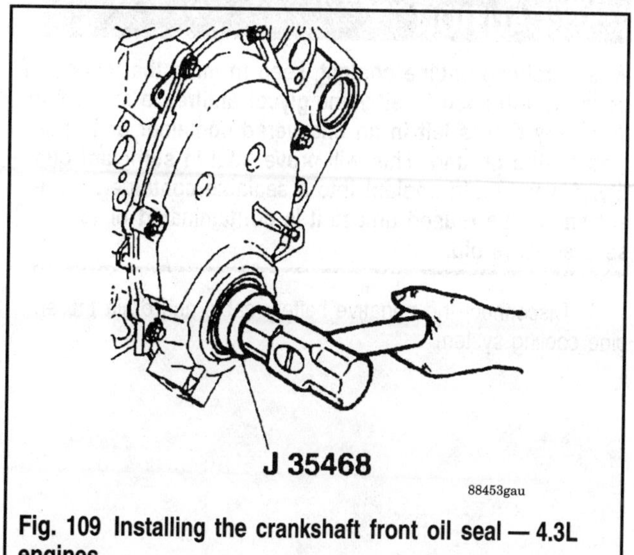

Fig. 109 Installing the crankshaft front oil seal — 4.3L engines

6. Unfasten the front oil pan nuts and studs.
7. Remove the starter. Refer to the procedure outlined in Section 2.
8. If necessary, remove the alternator and brackets from the engine, then position them aside.
9. As necessary, loosen and/or remove the oil pan.
10. Unfasten the crankcase (timing) front cover bolts, then disengage cover from the engine. Make sure all bolts are removed and be careful not to force and damage the cover.
11. Carefully remove the old crankshaft seal from the cover using a suitable prytool. Be very careful not to distort the front cover or to score the end of the crankshaft.

To install:

12. Carefully remove all traces of gasket or sealant from the mating surfaces.
13. Lubricate the lips of a new seal with clean engine oil, then use a seal centering tool (such as J-35468 or equivalent) to install the seal to the front cover. Leave the tool in position in the seal until the cover is installed.
14. Apply a 3/8 in. (10mm) wide by 5/16 (5mm) thick bead of RTV sealer to the oil pan at the front crankcase cover sealing surface. Then apply a 1/4 in. (6mm) by 1/8 in. (3mm) thick bead of RTV to the crankcase front cover at the block sealing surface.
15. Install the crankcase front cover to the engine using the seal tool to assure it is properly centered and prevent damage to the hub. Tighten the cover retaining bolts to 97 inch lbs. (11 Nm), then remove the seal centering tool.
16. Install and secure the oil pan, as applicable.
17. Install the starter. Refer to the procedure outlined in Section 2.
18. If removed, reposition and secure the alternator with brackets.
19. Install the belt tensioner/idler pulley assembly.
20. Install the belt assembly.
21. Install the cooling fan assembly and pulley.
22. Install the crankshaft pulley and hub.
23. Connect the negative battery cable.

4.3L Engine

See Figures 110 and 111

****CAUTION**

When draining engine coolant, keep in mind that cats and dogs are attracted to ethylene glycol antifreeze and could drink any that is left in an uncovered container or in puddles on the ground. This will prove fatal in sufficient quantity. Always drain coolant into a sealable container. Coolant should be reused unless it is contaminated or is several years old.

1. Disconnect the negative battery cable and drain the engine cooling system.

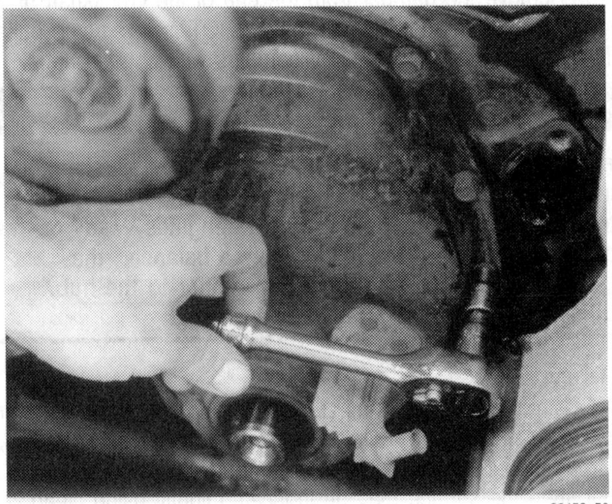
88453p50

Fig. 110 Remove the timing cover retaining bolts

88453p51

Fig. 111 Remove the timing cover from the vehicle

2. Remove the crankshaft pulley and damper. For details, please refer to the procedure earlier in this section.

****WARNING**

The outer ring (weight) of the torsional damper is bonded to the hub with rubber. The damper must be removed with a puller which acts on the inner hub only. Pulling on the outer portion of the damper will break the rubber bond or destroy the tuning of the unit.

3. Remove the water pump assembly.
4. Loosen the oil pan.
5. If applicable, remove the crankshaft position sensor.
6. Remove the front cover bolts and, if equipped, the reinforcements, then remove the front cover from the engine.
7. Pry the seal out of the front cover using a small prytool. Be very careful not to distort the front cover or to score the end of the crankshaft.

To install:

➡On 1995-97 models, anytime the front cover is removed, the cover must be replaced upon reassembly. If you reuse the old cover, oil leaks may develop.

8. Clean the gasket mating surfaces of the engine and cover of all remaining gasket or sealer material. Be careful not to score or damage the surfaces.

➡The manufacturer suggests you wait until the front cover is mounted to the engine before you install the replacement crankshaft oil seal. This assures the cover is properly supported.

9. Lightly coat the lips of the replacement crankshaft seal with clean engine oil, then position the seal with the open end facing inward the engine. Use a suitable seal installation driver to position the seal in the front cover.
10. Position a new front cover gasket to the engine or cover using gasket cement to hold it in position. Lubricate the front of the oil pan seal with engine oil to aid in reassembly.
11. Install the front cover to the engine. Take care while engaging the front of the oil pan seal with the bottom of the cover.
12. Install front cover retaining bolts and tighten to 124 inch lbs. (14 Nm) on 1994-95 models and 106 inch. lbs. (12 Nm) on 1996-97 models.
13. If removed, install the crankshaft position sensor.
14. Secure the oil pan.
15. Install the water pump.
16. Install the crankshaft damper and pulley.
17. Connect the negative battery cable, then properly refill the engine cooling system.
18. Run the engine until normal operating temperature has been reached, then check for leaks.

Timing Chain

REMOVAL & INSTALLATION

2.2L Engine

➧ **See Figures 112 and 113**

1. Disconnect the negative battery cable.
2. Remove the crankcase (timing) front cover from the engine.
3. Turn the crankshaft until the timing marks on the sprockets are in alignment. The marks should also be in alignment with the tabs on the tensioner.
4. Remove the tensioner retaining bolts.
5. Unfasten the camshaft sprocket retaining bolts, then remove the sprocket and timing chain and tensioner at the same time.
6. If applicable, remove the crankshaft position sensor.
7. If necessary, remove the camshaft sprocket using J-22888-20 or an equivalent puller.

To install:

8. If removed, install the crankshaft sprocket using a suitable installer. Make sure the sprocket is fully seated against the crankshaft.

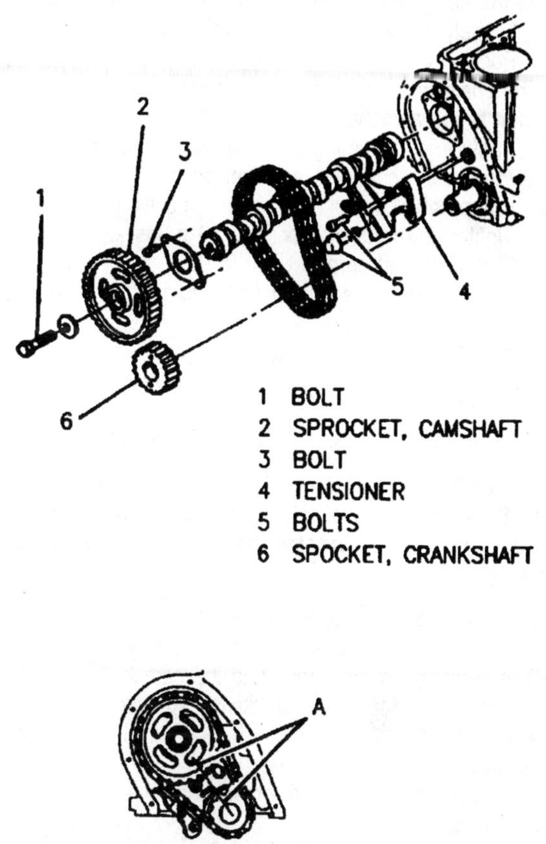

Fig. 112 Timing chain, sprocket and camshaft mounting — 2.2L engine

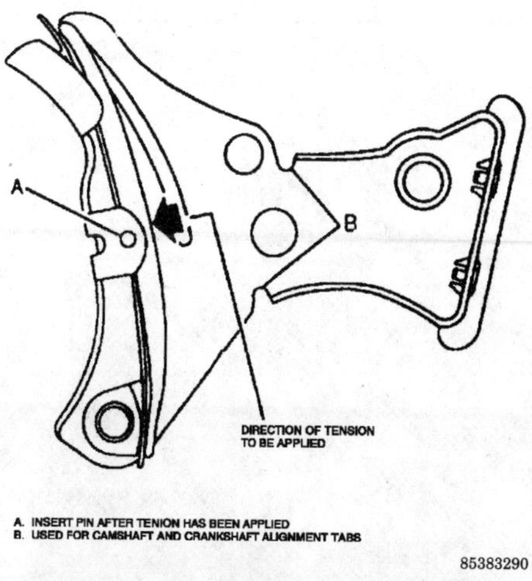

Fig. 113 Locking the timing chain tensioner into position for chain installation — 2.2L engine

9. Compress the tensioner spring and insert a cotter pin or nail in the hole provided to hold the tensioner in position.
10. Loosely install the tensioner retaining bolts.
11. Position the camshaft sprocket in the timing chain, position the chain under the crankshaft sprocket and the camshaft sprocket to the camshaft.
12. Verify that the timing marks are all properly aligned, then loosely install the camshaft sprocket bolt.
13. If applicable, install the camshaft position sensor.
14. Tighten the tensioner bolts to 18 ft. lbs. (24 Nm), then tighten the camshaft sprocket bolt to 96 ft. lbs. (130 Nm).
15. Remove the cotter pin or nail holding the tensioner in position off the chain.
16. Install the timing cover to the engine.

4.3L Engine

See Figures 114, 115, 116, 117, 118 and 119

The following procedure requires the use of the Crankshaft Sprocket Removal tool No. J-5825-A or equivalent, and the Crankshaft Sprocket Installation tool No. J-5590 or equivalent.

1. Remove the timing cover from the engine.
2. Rotate the crankshaft until the No. 4 cylinder is on the TDC of its compression stroke and the camshaft sprocket mark aligns with the mark on the crankshaft sprocket (facing each other at a point closest together in their travel) and in line with the shaft centers.
3. If applicable, remove the crankshaft position sensor reluctor ring.
4. Remove the camshaft sprocket-to-camshaft nut and/or bolts, then remove the camshaft sprocket (along with the timing chain). If the sprocket is difficult to remove, use a plastic mallet to bump the sprocket from the camshaft.

The camshaft sprocket (located by a dowel) is lightly pressed onto the camshaft and should come off easily. The chain comes off with the camshaft sprocket.

5. If necessary use J-5825-A or an equivalent crankshaft sprocket removal tool to free the timing sprocket from the crankshaft.

88453p52

Fig. 114 Make sure the marks camshaft and crankshaft sprockets are aligned

88453p53

Fig. 115 Unfasten the camshaft sprocket retainers

88453p54

Fig. 116 Remove the camshaft sprocket and the timing chain together

88453p55

Fig. 117 Using a suitable puller, remove the crankshaft sprocket

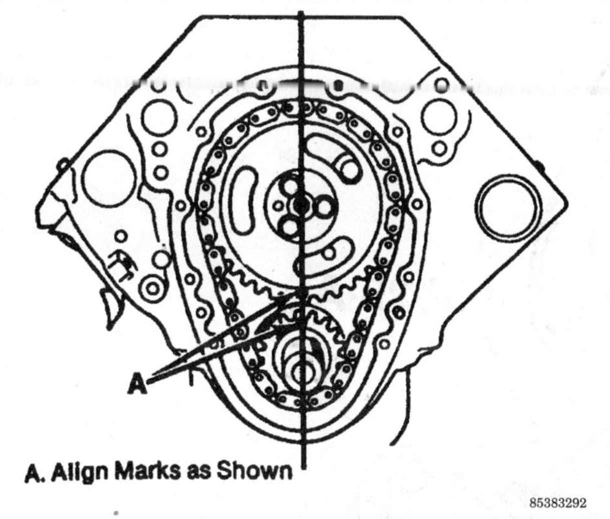

Fig. 118 Timing mark alignment — 4.3L engine

6. If necessary, remove the crankshaft sprocket key.

To install:

7. Inspect the timing chain and the timing sprockets for wear or damage, replace the damaged parts as necessary.
8. Using a putty knife, clean the gasket mounting surfaces. Using solvent, clean the oil and grease from the gasket mounting surfaces.
9. If removed, install the crankshaft sprocket key.
10. If removed, use J-5590, or an equivalent crankshaft sprocket installation tool and a hammer to drive the crankshaft sprocket onto the crankshaft, without disturbing the position of the engine.

➡During installation, coat the thrust surfaces lightly with Molykote® or an equivalent pre-lube.

11. Position the timing chain over the camshaft sprocket. Arrange the camshaft sprocket in such a way that the timing marks will align between the shaft centers and the camshaft locating dowel will enter the dowel hole in the cam sprocket.
12. Position the chain under the crankshaft sprocket, then place the cam sprocket, with the chain still mounted over it, in position on the front of the camshaft. Install and tighten the camshaft sprocket-to-camshaft retainers to 21 ft. lbs. (28 Nm) on 1994-96 models and 18 ft. lbs. (25 Nm) on 1997 models.
13. With the timing chain installed, turn the crankshaft two complete revolutions, then check to make certain that the timing marks are in correct alignment between the shaft centers.
14. If applicable, install the crankshaft position sensor reluctor ring.
15. Install the timing cover.

Camshaft and Bearings

REMOVAL & INSTALLATION

On all engines equipped with lifters, a complete new set of lifters must be installed whenever the camshaft is replaced in order to prolong the new camshaft's service life.

2.2L Engine

➧ See Figure 120

✱✱CAUTION

When draining engine coolant, keep in mind that cats and dogs are attracted to ethylene glycol antifreeze and could drink any that is left in an uncovered container or in puddles on the ground. This will prove fatal in sufficient quantity. Always drain coolant into a sealable container. Coolant should be reused unless it is contaminated or is several years old.

1. If equipped, have the air conditioning system discharged by a qualified technician using a proper refrigerant recovery/recycling station.
2. Properly relieve the fuel system pressure, then disconnect the negative battery cable.
3. Drain the engine cooling system and the engine oil.
4. Remove the upper radiator shroud, then disengage the oil and transmission cooler lines at the radiator.
5. Tag and disengage all hoses from the radiator.
6. Remove the radiator and air conditioning condenser from the vehicle.
7. Remove the rocker arm cover.
8. Remove the cylinder head.
9. Unfasten the anti-rotation bracket bolts and brackets, then remove the valve lifters.
10. Unfasten the oil pump drive retaining bolt, then remove the drive by lifting and twisting.
11. Remove the crankshaft pulley and hub.
12. Remove the serpentine drive belt idler pulley.
13. Remove the timing cover from the engine.
14. Remove the timing chain and camshaft sprocket.
15. Unfasten the camshaft thrust plate retaining bolts, then remove the plate from the block.
16. Pull the camshaft straight out of the engine, turning slightly as it is withdrawn and taking care not to damage the bearings.
17. If removal of camshaft bearings is necessary, use the following procedure:
    a. Install a camshaft bearing removal/installation tool with the shoulder toward the bearing. Ensure that enough threads are engaged.
    b. Using two wrenches, hold the puller screw while turning the nut. When the bearing has been released from the bore, remove the tool.
    c. Assemble the tool on the driver to remove the front and rear bearings.
    d. Install the bearings so that the oil holes in the block and the bearing align.
    e. Install a fresh camshaft bearing rear cover using sealant.

To install:

18. Inspect the camshaft, journals and lobes for wear and replace, if necessary.
19. Inspect the bearings for scratches, pits or a loose fit in their bores and replace, if necessary.
20. Coat the camshaft lobes and journals with a high viscosity oil with zinc such as No. 12345501, or equivalent.
21. Carefully insert the camshaft in the engine, turning it slightly from side to side and it is inserted.

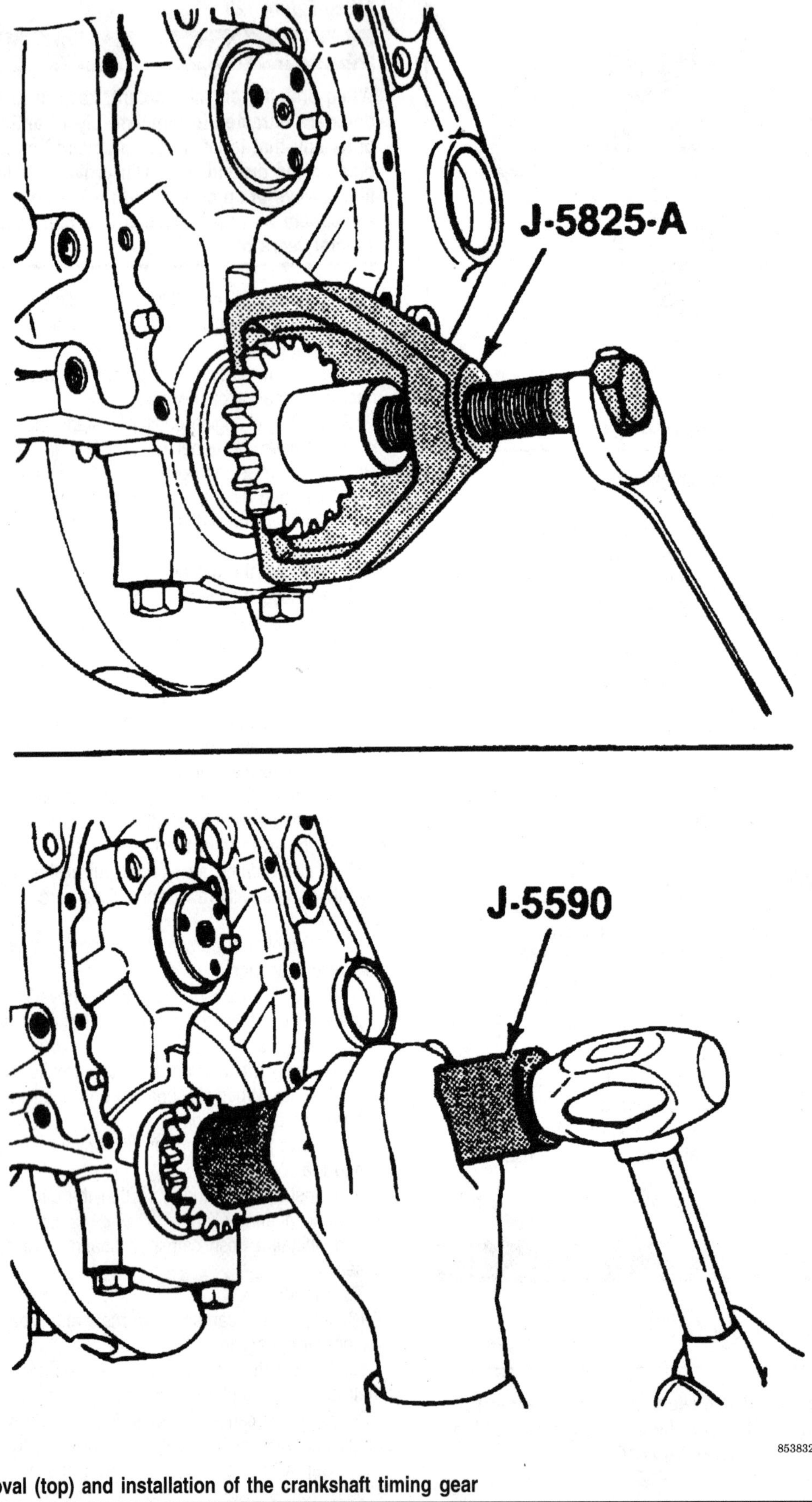

Fig. 119 Removal (top) and installation of the crankshaft timing gear

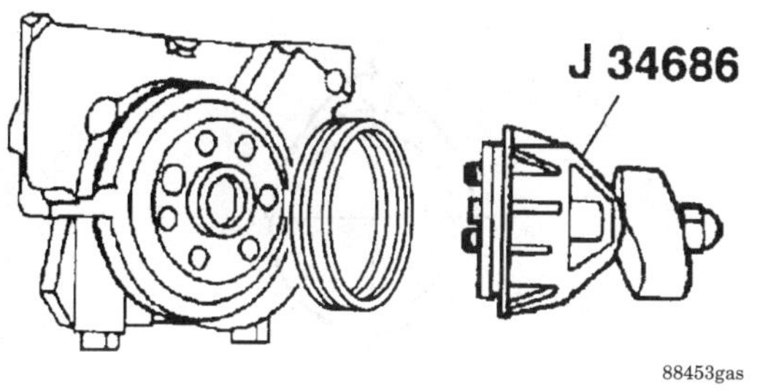

Fig. 120 Exploded view of the camshaft and related components — 2.2L engine

22. Install the thrust plate and tighten the retaining bolts to 106 inch lbs. (12 Nm).
23. Install the timing chain and camshaft sprocket.
24. Install the timing cover to the engine.
25. Install the serpentine drive belt idler pulley.
26. Install the crankshaft pulley and hub.
27. Install the oil pump drive by inserting while twisting, then install the retaining bolt and tighten to 18 ft. lbs. (25 Nm).
28. Install the valve lifters and the anti-rotation brackets.
29. Install the cylinder head.
30. Install the rocker arm cover.
31. Install the air conditioning condenser and the radiator assemblies. Engage all hoses removed from the radiator.
32. Engage the oil and transmission cooler lines at the radiator, then install the radiator shroud.
33. Engage the air cleaner assembly and connect the negative battery cable.
34. Fill the crankcase with the correct grade and amount of oil.
35. Fill the cooling system with coolant.
36. Connect the negative battery cable.
37. Have the air conditioning system charged by a qualified technician using a proper refrigerant recovery/recycling station.

4.3L Engines

See Figures 121, 122 and 123

CAUTION

When draining engine coolant, keep in mind that cats and dogs are attracted to ethylene glycol antifreeze and could drink any that is left in an uncovered container or in puddles on the ground. This will prove fatal in sufficient quantity. Always drain coolant into a sealable container. Coolant should be reused unless it is contaminated or is several years old.

1. Properly relieve the fuel system pressure, then disconnect the negative battery cable.
2. Disconnect the air intake duct, if applicable.
3. Drain the engine cooling system.
4. Remove the radiator from the vehicle.
5. Remove the rocker arm covers from the engine.
6. Remove the intake manifold assembly.
7. Remove the rocker arms, pushrods and lifters.
8. Remove the crankshaft pulley and hub.
9. Remove the engine front (timing) cover.
10. Align the timing marks on the crankshaft and camshaft sprockets.
11. Remove the camshaft sprocket and timing chain.
12. If necessary, remove the crankshaft position sensor reluctor ring and sprocket.
13. Remove the thrust plate screws, then remove the thrust plate.
14. Install the sprocket bolts or longer bolts of the same thread into the end of the camshaft as a handle, then remove the camshaft front the front of the engine while turning slightly from side to side, as necessary. Take care not to damage the camshaft bearings when removing the camshaft.
15. If removal of camshaft bearings is necessary, use the following procedure:
    a. Install a camshaft bearing removal/installation tool with the shoulder toward the bearing. Ensure that enough threads are engaged.
    b. Using two wrenches, hold the puller screw while turning the nut. When the bearing has been released from the bore, remove the tool.
    c. Assemble the tool on the driver to remove the front and rear bearings.
    d. Install the bearings so that the oil holes in the block and the bearing align.
    e. Install a fresh camshaft bearing rear cover using sealant.

To install:

16. Lubricate the camshaft journals with clean engine oil or a suitable pre-lube, then install the camshaft into the block being extremely careful not to contact the bearings with the cam lobes.
17. Install the camshaft thrust plate and tighten the bolts to 106 inch lbs. (12 Nm).
18. Install the timing chain and camshaft sprocket.
19. Install the engine front (timing) cover.
20. Install the crankshaft pulley and hub.

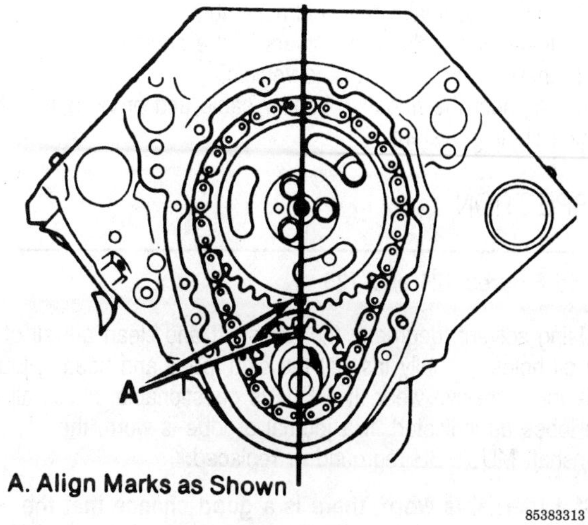

Fig. 121 Aligning the timing marks — 4.3L engine

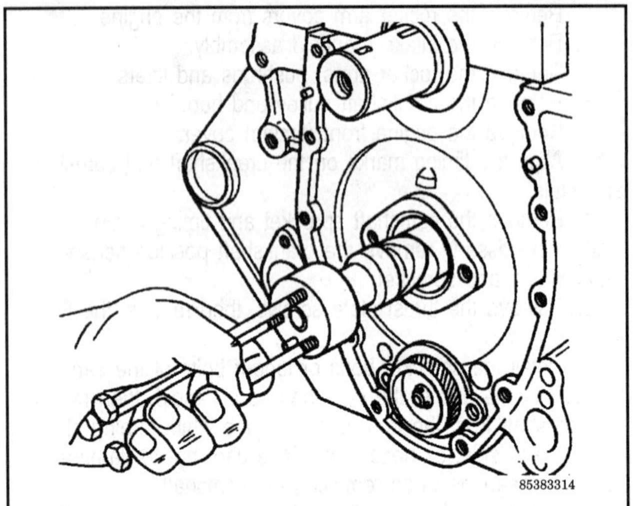

Fig. 122 Use bolts as a handle to help remove the camshaft

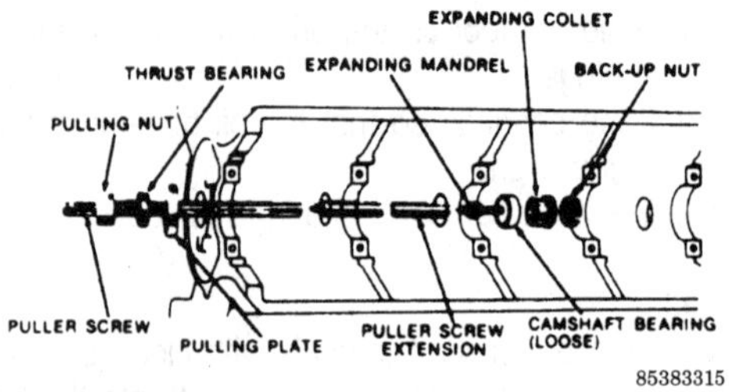

Fig. 123 Common camshaft bearing removal tool — OHV engines

21. Install the valve lifters, then install the pushrods and rocker arms. Properly adjust the valve clearance.
22. Install the intake manifold assembly.
23. Install the rocker arm covers to the engine.
24. Install the radiator to the vehicle.
25. Connect the negative battery cable and properly refill the engine cooling system.

INSPECTION

See Figures 124 and 125

Using solvent, degrease the camshaft and clean out all of the oil holes. Visually inspect the cam lobes and bearing journals for excessive wear. If a lobe is questionable, check all of the lobes as indicated. If a journal or lobe is worn, the camshaft MUST BE reground or replaced.

If a journal is worn, there is a good chance that the bearings are worn and need replacement.

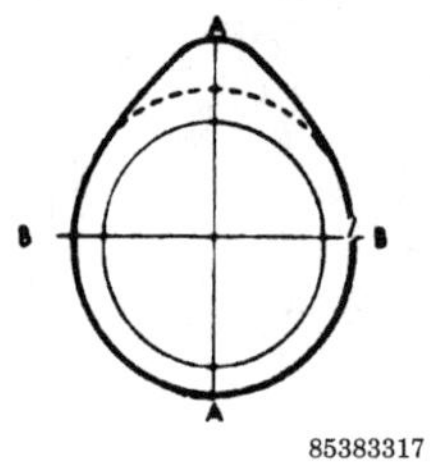

Fig. 125 Measuring camshaft lobe lift

If the lobes and journals appear intact, place the front and rear journals in V-blocks and rest a dial indicator on the center journal. Rotate the camshaft to check the straightness. If deviation exceeds 0.001 in. (0.0254mm), the camshaft should likely be replaced.

On most engines lobe lift can be measured with the camshaft still installed. Simply remove the rocker cover and rocker arm, then use a dial gauge on the end of the pushrod. When the pushrod is at the bottom of its travel, set the dial gauge to "0" then turn the engine and note the gauge's highest reading.

Check the camshaft lobes with a micrometer, by measuring the across the lobe centerline from the nose to the base and again at the centerline across the diameter at 90° from the first measurement (see illustration). The lobe lift is determined by subtracting the second measurement (diameter) from the first (diameter plug lobe lift). If the lobes vary from specification, the camshaft must be reground or replace.

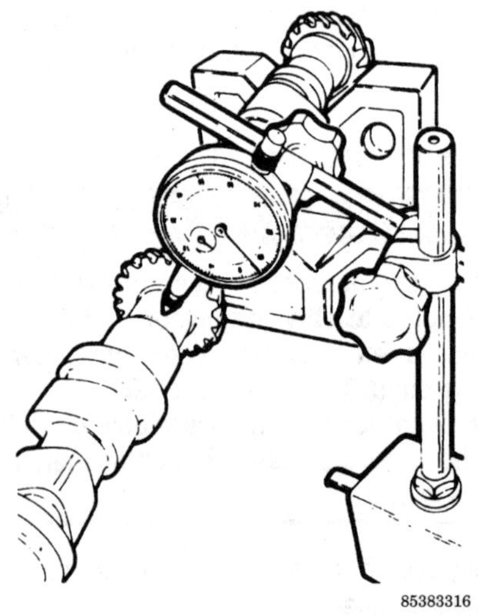

Fig. 124 Checking the camshaft for straightness

Balance Shaft

REMOVAL & INSTALLATION

See Figures 126, 127, 128 and 129

CAUTION

When draining engine coolant, keep in mind that cats and dogs are attracted to ethylene glycol antifreeze and could drink any that is left in an uncovered container or in puddles on the ground. This will prove fatal in sufficient quantity. Always drain coolant into a sealable container. Coolant should be reused unless it is contaminated or is several years old.

1. Have the air conditioning system discharged by a qualified technician using a proper refrigerant recovery/recycling station.

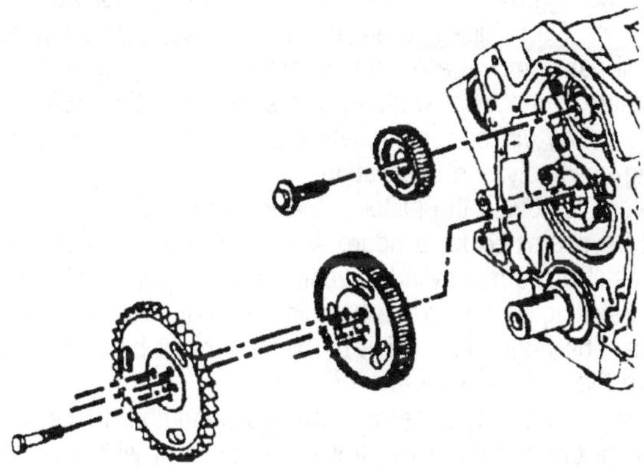

Fig. 126 View of the balance shaft drive and driven gears

Fig. 127 View of the balance shaft location — 1994 4.3L engine

Fig. 128 Unfasten the balance shaft gear bolt . . .

Fig. 129 . . . then remove the gear

2. Properly relieve the fuel system pressure, then disconnect the negative battery cable.
3. Disconnect the air cleaner intake duct.
4. Drain the engine cooling system.
5. Remove the upper radiator shroud, then disengage the oil and transmission cooler lines at the radiator.
6. Tag and disengage all hoses from the radiator.
7. Remove the radiator and air conditioning condenser from the vehicle.
8. Remove the fan assembly.
9. Carefully release the belt tension, then remove the serpentine drive belt.
10. If equipped, unfasten the pencil brace at the coolant pump, then remove the coolant pump.
11. Remove the crankshaft pulley and damper. For details, please refer to the procedure in this section.
12. If necessary, remove the flywheel inspection cover.
13. Remove the front cover. For details, please refer to the procedure in this section.

14. Remove the timing chain and sprockets. For details, please refer to the procedure in this section.
15. Unfasten the balance shaft gear bolt, then remove the gear.
16. Remove the balance shaft retainer.
17. Remove the intake manifold assembly. For details, please refer to the procedure in this section.
18. Remove the lifter retainer.
19. Remove the balance shaft and front bearing by gently driving them out using a soft faced mallet.
20. Using tool J-38834 or its equivalent, remove the balance shaft rear bearing.

➡The balance shaft and drive and driven gears are serviced only as a set, including the gear bolt. The balance shaft and front bearing are serviced as a package.

⁂WARNING

The front bearing must not be removed from the balance shaft

To install:

21. Inspect the balance shaft gears for damage, such as nicks and burrs.
22. Using a putty knife, clean the gasket mounting surfaces. Using solvent, clean the oil and grease from the gasket mounting surfaces.
23. Lubricate the balance shaft rear bearing with clean engine oil, then install the bearing using tool J-38834 or its equivalent.
24. Lubricate the balance shaft with clean engine oil, then install the balance shaft into the block.
25. Install the balance shaft bearing retainer and bolts. Tighten the bolts to 120 inch. lbs. (14 Nm).
26. Install the balance shaft driven gear and bolt. Tighten the bolt to 15 ft. lbs. (20 Nm) plus an additional 35 degrees using a torque/angle meter.
27. Install the lifter retainer, then rotate the balance shaft by hand and check that there is clearance between the balance shaft and the lifter retainer.
28. Temporarily install the balance shaft drive gear so that the timing mark on the gear points straight up, then remove the drive gear, turn the balance shaft so the timing mark on the driven gear is facing straight down.
29. Install the drive gear and make sure the timing marks on both gears line up (dot-to-dot).
30. Install the drive gear retaining bolt and tighten to 12 ft. lbs. (16 Nm).
31. Install the intake manifold assembly. For details, please refer to the procedure in this section.
32. Install the timing chain and sprocket assemblies. For details, please refer to the procedure in this section.
33. Install the front cover, seal, bolts and the oil pan assembly. For details, please refer to the procedure in this section.
34. Install the flywheel inspection cover, then using tool J-39046 or its equivalent engage the crankshaft pulley and damper. For details, please refer to the procedure in this section.
35. Install the coolant pump, then engage the pencil brace to the pump.
36. Install the serpentine drive belt.
37. Install the fan assembly.
38. Install the air conditioning condenser and the radiator assemblies. Engage all hoses removed from the radiator.
39. Engage the oil and transmission cooler lines at the radiator, then install the radiator shroud.
40. Install the air cleaner assembly and connect the negative battery cable.
41. Fill the crankcase with the correct grade and amount of oil.
42. Fill the cooling system with coolant.
43. Start the vehicle and check for leaks.
44. Have the air conditioning system charged by a qualified technician using a proper refrigerant recovery/recycling station.

Pistons and Connecting Rods

REMOVAL

➧ See Figures 130, 131, 132, 133, 134, 135 and 136

Although in some cases the pistons and connecting rods may be removed with the engine still in the vehicle, it is rarely worth the aggravation, especially when you are not working with a lift. On vehicles where this is possible (cylinder head and oil pan removal are both possible with the engine installed and there is sufficient working clearance) take EXTREME care to assure no dirt or contamination is allowed into the cylinders during assembly and installation.

Before removing the pistons, the top of the cylinder bore must be examined for a ridge. A ridge at the top of the bore is the result of normal cylinder wear, caused by the piston rings only traveling so far up the bore in the course of the piston stroke. The ridge can be felt by hand; it must be removed before the pistons are removed.

A ridge reamer is necessary for this operation. Place the piston at the bottom of its stroke, and cover it with a rag. Cut the ridge away with the ridge reamer, using extreme care to avoid cutting too deeply. Remove the rag, and remove the cuttings that remain on the piston with a magnet and a rag soaked in clean oil. Make sure the piston top and cylinder bore are absolutely clean before moving the piston. For more

tccs3803

Fig. 130 Place rubber hose over the connecting rod studs to protect the crankshaft and cylinders from damage

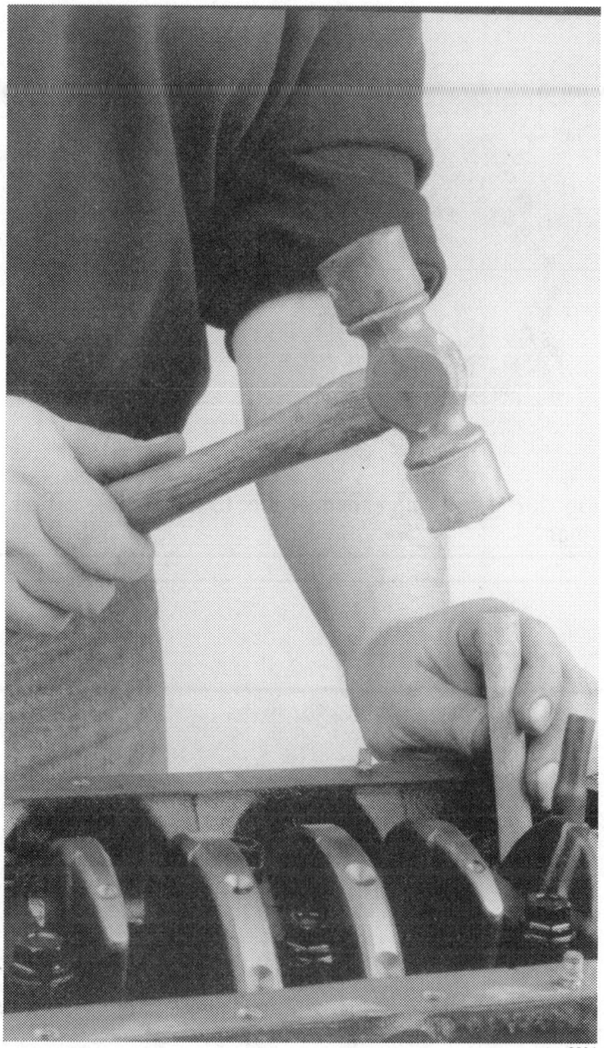

Fig. 131 Carefully tap the piston out of the bore using a wooden dowel

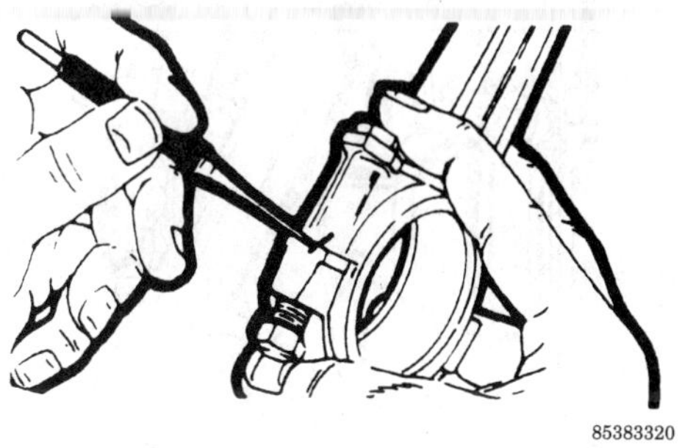

Fig. 133 Match connecting rods to their caps using a scribe mark

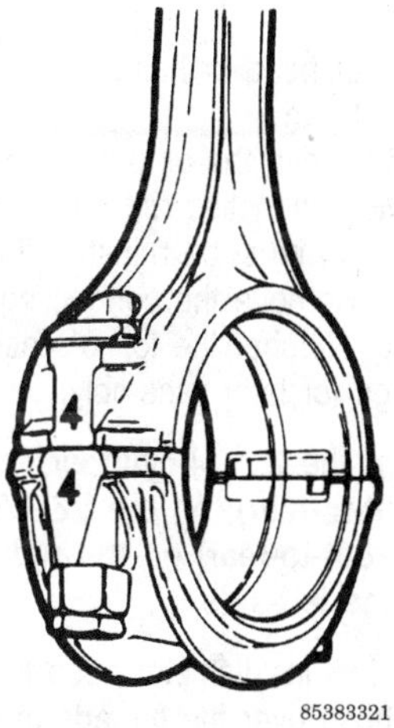

Fig. 134 Match the connecting rods to their cylinders using a number stamp

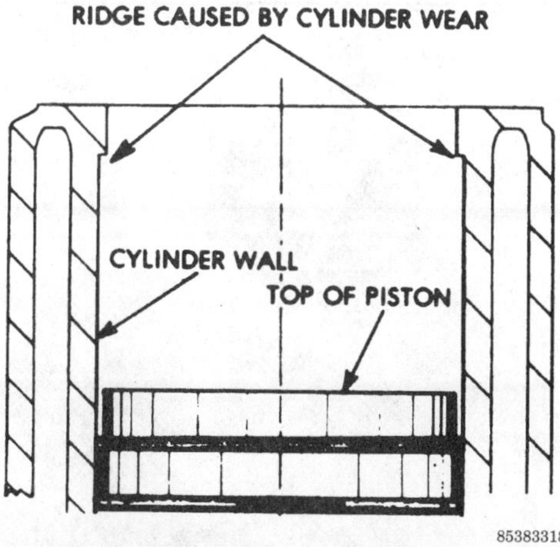

Fig. 132 If present, the cylinder ridge must be removed before the pistons are removed from the block

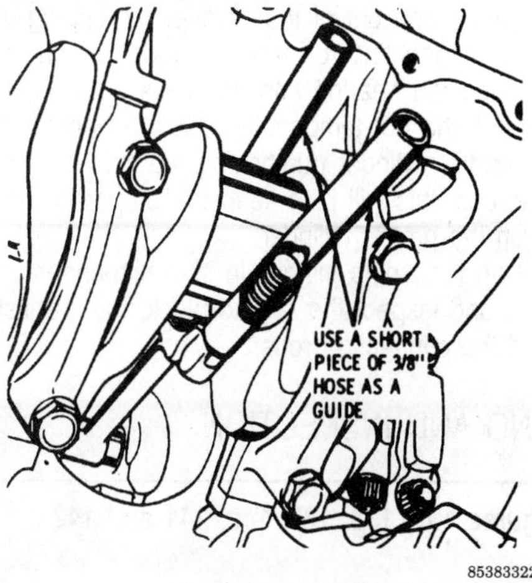

Fig. 135 Cut lengths of rubber hose for connecting rod bolt guides

Fig. 136 Carefully tap the piston and rod assembly out using a wooden hammer handle

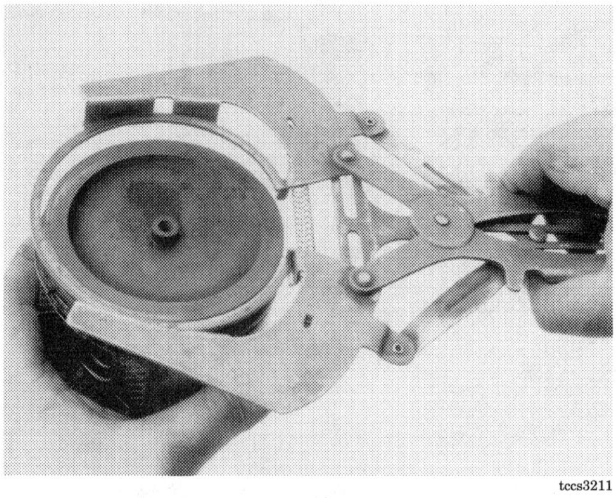

Fig. 137 Use a ring expander tool to remove the piston rings

details, refer to the ridge removal and honing procedures outlined in this section.

1. Remove cylinder head or heads.
2. Remove the oil pan.
3. If necessary, remove the oil pump assembly.
4. Matchmark the connecting rod cap to the connecting rod with a scribe; each cap must be reinstalled on its proper rod in the proper direction. Remove the connecting rod bearing cap and the rod bearing. Number the top of each piston with silver paint or a felt-tip pen for later assembly.

➡The cylinders on the 2.2L 4-cylinder engine are numbered 1-2-3-4 (front-to-rear); on the V6 4.3L engine, are numbered 1-3-5 (front-to-rear) on the right-side and 2-4-6 (front-to-rear) on the left-side.

5. Cut lengths of $^3/_8$ in. diameter hose to use as rod bolt guides. Install the hose over the threads of the rod bolts, to prevent the bolt threads from damaging the crankshaft journals and cylinder walls when the piston is removed.
6. Squirt some clean engine oil onto the cylinder wall from above, until the wall is coated. Carefully push the piston and rod assembly up and out of the cylinder by tapping on the bottom of the connecting rod with a wooden hammer handle.
7. Place the rod bearing and cap back on the connecting rod, and install the nut temporarily. Using a number stamp or punch, stamp the cylinder number on the side of the connecting rod and cap; this will help keep the proper piston and rod assembly on the proper cylinder.
8. Remove remaining pistons in similar manner.
9. Clean and inspect the engine block, the crankshaft, the pistons and the connecting rods.

Fig. 138 Clean the piston grooves using a ring groove cleaner

CLEANING AND INSPECTION

➧ See Figures 137, 138, 139, 140, 141 and 142

Pistons

A piston ring expander is necessary for removing piston rings without damaging them; any other method (screwdriver blades, pliers, etc.) usually results in the ring being bent,

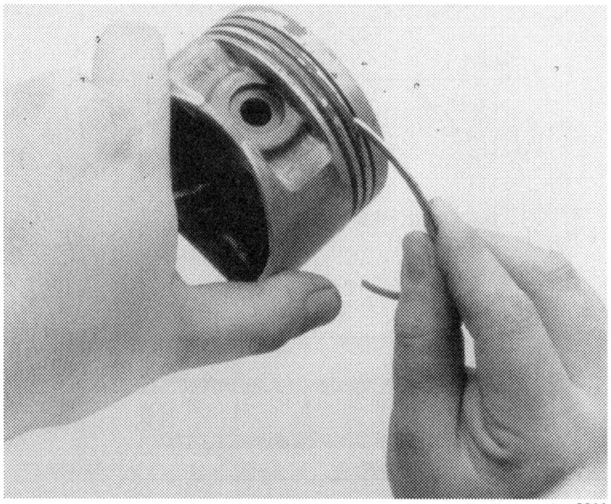

Fig. 139 You can use a piece of an old ring to clean the piston grooves, BUT be careful, the ring is sharp

tccs3210

Fig. 140 Measure the piston's outer diameter using a micrometer

scratched or distorted, or the piston itself being damaged. When the rings are removed, clean the piston grooves using an appropriate ring groove cleaning tool, using care not to cut too deeply. Thoroughly clean all carbon and varnish from the piston with solvent.

✲✲WARNING

Do not use a wire brush or caustic solvent (acids, etc.) on piston. Inspect the pistons for scuffing, scoring, cranks, pitting, or excessive ring groove wear. If these are evident, the piston must be replaced.

Clean the varnish from the piston skirts and pins with a cleaning solvent. DO NOT WIRE BRUSH ANY PART OF THE PISTON. Clean the ring grooves with a groove cleaner and make sure that the oil ring holes and slots are clean.

Inspect the piston for cracked ring lands, scuffed or damaged skirts, eroded areas at the top of the piston. Replace the pistons that are damaged or show signs of excessive wear.

Inspect the grooves for nicks of burrs that might cause the rings to hang up.

Measure the piston in relation to cylinder diameter. Refer to the cylinder bore cleaning and inspection procedures later in this section.

Connecting Rods

Wash the connecting rods in cleaning solvent and dry with compressed air. Check for twisted or bent rods and inspect for nicks or cracks. Replace the connecting rods that are damaged.

Cylinder Bores

➧ See Figure 143

The piston should also be checked in relation to the cylinder diameter. Using a telescoping gauge and micrometer, or a dial gauge, measure the cylinder bore diameter perpendicular (90 degrees) to the piston pin, about 1-2½ in. below the cylinder block deck (surface where the block mates with the heads). Then, with the micrometer, measure the piston perpendicular to

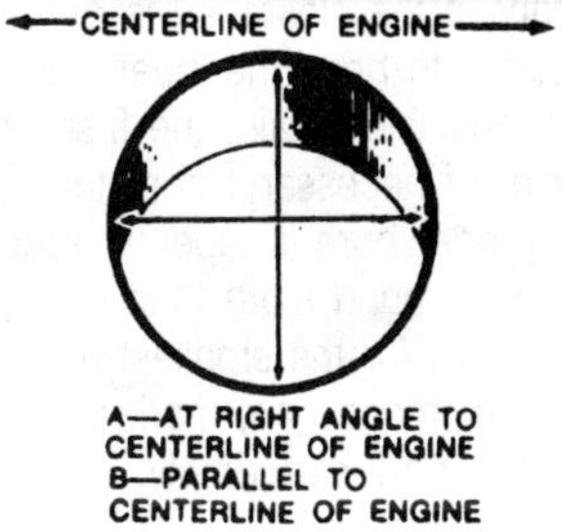

85383329

Fig. 142 Cylinder bore measuring points

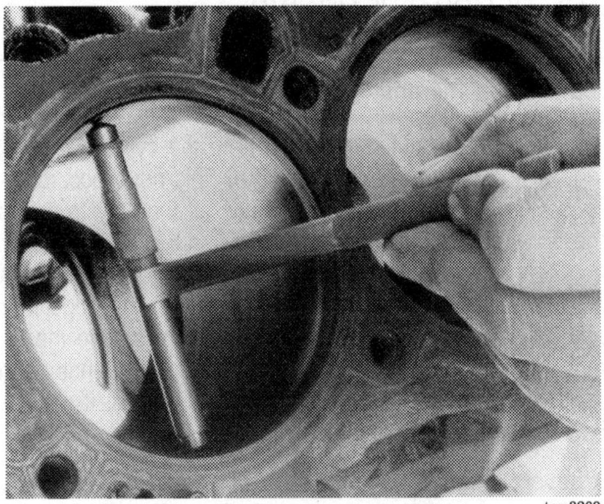
tccs3209

Fig. 143 A telescoping gauge may be used to measure the cylinder bore diameter

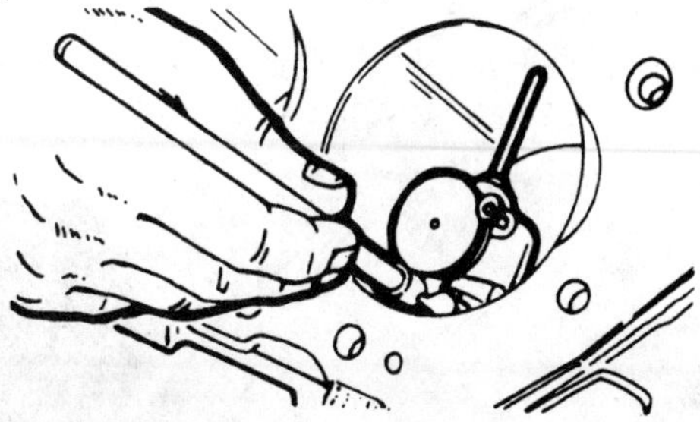
85383328

Fig. 141 The cylinder bore may also be measured using a dial gauge

its wrist pin on the skirt. The difference between the two measurements is the piston clearance.

If the clearance is within specifications or slightly below (after the cylinders have been bored or honed), finish honing is all that is necessary, If the clearance is excessive, try to obtain a slightly larger piston to bring the clearance within specifications. If this is not possible obtain, the first oversize piston and hone the cylinder or (if necessary) bore the cylinder to size. Generally, if the cylinder bore is tapered more than 0.005 in. (0.127mm) or is out-of-round more than 0.003 in. (0.0762mm), it is advisable to rebore for the smallest possible oversize piston and rings. After measuring, mark the pistons with a felt-tip pen for reference and for assembly.

➡Boring of the cylinder block should be performed by a reputable machine shop with the proper equipment. In some cases, clean-up honing can be done with the cylinder block in the vehicle, but most excessive honing and all cylinder boring MUST BE done with the block stripped and removed from the vehicle.

RIDGE REMOVAL & HONING

See Figures 144 and 145

1. Before the piston is removed from the cylinder, check for a ridge at the top of the cylinder bore. This ridge occurs because the piston ring does not travel all the way to the top of the bore, thereby leaving an unworn portion of the bore.
2. Clean away any carbon buildup at the top of the cylinder with sand paper, in order to see the extent of the ridge more clearly. If the ridge is slight, it will be safe to remove the pistons without damaging the rings or piston ring lands. If the ridge is severe, and easily catches your fingernail, it will have to be removed using a ridge reamer.

➡A severe ridge is an indication of excessive bore wear. Before removing the piston, check the cylinder bore diameter with a bore gauge, as explained in the cleaning and inspection procedure. Compare your measurement with engine specification. If the bore is excessively worn, the cylinder will have to bored oversize and the piston and rings replaced.

tccs3213

Fig. 144 Removing cylinder glazing using a flexible hone

tccs3216

Fig. 145 A properly cross-hatched cylinder bore

3. Install the ridge removal tool in the top of the cylinder bore. Carefully follow the manufacturers instructions for operation. Only remove the amount of material necessary to remove the ridge. Place the piston at the bottom of its stroke, and cover it with a rag. Cut the ridge away with the ridge reamer, using extreme care to avoid cutting too deeply. Remove the rag and cuttings that remain on the piston with a magnet and a rag soaked in clean oil. Make sure the piston top and cylinder bore are absolutely clean before moving the piston.

****WARNING**

Be very careful if you are unfamiliar with operating a ridge reamer. It is very easy to remove more cylinder bore material than you want, possibly requiring a cylinder overbore and piston replacement that may not have been necessary.

4. After the piston and connecting rod assembly have been removed, check the clearances as explained earlier in this section under the cleaning and inspection procedure, to determine whether boring and honing or just light honing are required. If boring is necessary, consult an automotive machine shop. If light honing is all that is necessary, proceed with the next step.
5. Honing is best done with the crankshaft removed, to prevent damage to the crankshaft and to make post-honing cleaning easier, as the honing process will scatter metal particles. However, if you do not want to remove the crankshaft, position the connecting rod journal for the cylinder being honed as far away from the bottom of the cylinder bore as possible, and wrap a shop cloth around the journal.
6. Honing can be done either with a flexible glaze breaker type hone or with a rigid hone that has honing stones and guide shoes. The flexible hone removes the least amount of metal, and is especially recommended if your piston-to-cylinder bore clearance is on the loose side. The flexible hone is useful to provide a finish on which the new piston rings will seat. A

rigid hone will remove more material than the flexible hone and requires more operator skill.

7. Regardless of which type of hone you use, carefully follow the manufacturers instructions for operation.

8. The hone should be moved up and down the bore at sufficient speed to obtain a uniform finish. A rigid hone will provide a definite cross-hatch finish; operate the rigid hone at a speed to obtain a 45-65 degree for 4.3L engine, or a 45 degree for the 2.2L engine included angle in the cross-hatch. The finish marks should be clean but not sharp, free from embedded particles and torn or folded metal.

9. Periodically during the honing procedure, thoroughly clean the cylinder bore and check the piston-to-bore clearance with the piston for that cylinder.

10. After honing is completed, thoroughly wash the cylinder bores and the rest of the engine with hot water and detergent. Scrub the bores well with a stiff bristle brush and rinse thoroughly with hot water. Thorough cleaning is essential, for if any abrasive material is left in the cylinder bore, it will rapidly wear the new rings and the cylinder bore. If any abrasive material is left in the rest of the engine, it will be picked up by the oil and carried throughout the engine, damaging bearings and other parts.

11. After the bores are cleaned, wipe them down with a clean cloth coated with light engine oil, to keep them from rusting.

PISTON PIN REPLACEMENT

➧ **See Figures 146 and 147**

✻✻WARNING

Do not use a wire brush or caustic solvent (acids, etc.) on pistons. Inspect the pistons for scuffing, scoring, cracks, pitting, or excessive ring groove wear. If these are evident, the piston must be replaced.

Most engines covered by this manual utilize a piston and pin assembly which are pressed together. Disassembly will require an arbor press, a suitable support and the proper drivers.

➡The following procedure requires the use of the GM fixture/support assembly tool No. J-24086-20, GM piston pin removal tool No. J-24086-8, and the GM piston pin installation tool No. J-24086-9 or the equivalents.

Use care at all times when handling and servicing the connecting rods and pistons. To prevent possible damage to these units, DO NOT clamp the rod or piston in a vise since they may become distorted. DO NOT allow the pistons to strike one another, against hard objects or bench surfaces, since distortion of the piston contour or nicks in the soft aluminum material may result.

1. Using an arbor press, the GM fixture/support assembly tool No. J-24086-20 or equivalent, and the GM piston pin removal tool No. J-24086-8 or equivalent, place the piston assembly in the fixture/support tool and press the pin from the piston assembly.

➡The piston and the piston pin are a matched set which are not serviced separately.

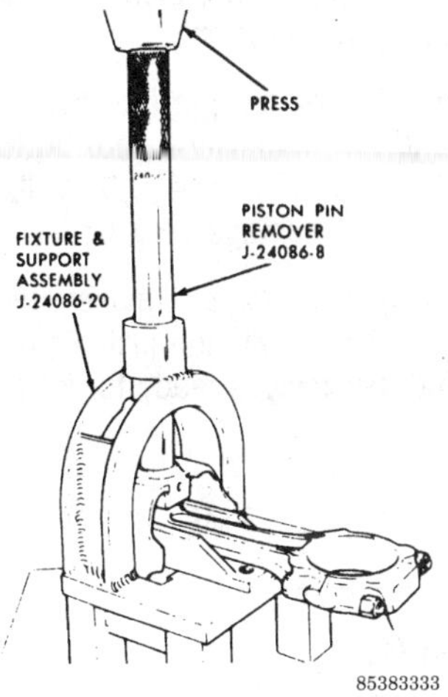

Fig. 146 Removing the piston pin from the assembly — press fit pistons assemblies

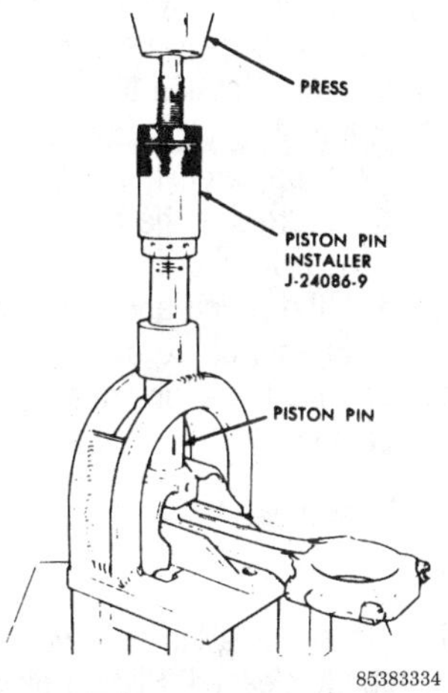

Fig. 147 Installing the piston pin — press fit piston assemblies

2. Using a suitable solvent, wash the varnish and oil from the parts, then inspect the parts for scuffing or wear.

3. Using a micrometer, measure the diameter of the piston pin. Using a inside micrometer or a dial bore gauge, measure the diameter of the piston bore.

➡If the piston pin-to-piston clearance is in excess of 0.001 in. (0.0254mm), replace the piston and piston pin assembly.

To install:

4. Lubricate the piston pin and the piston bore with engine oil.

5. Install the piston pin into the piston assembly, use an arbor press, the GM fixture/support assembly tool No. J-24086-20 or equivalent, and the GM piston pin installation

tool No. J-24086-9 or equivalent, then press the piston pin into the piston/connecting rod assembly.

➡When installing the piston pin into the piston/connecting rod assembly and the installation tool bottoms onto the support assembly, DO NOT exceed 5000 lbs. (22240 N) of pressure or structural damage may occur to the tool.

6. After installing the piston pin, make sure that the piston has freedom of movement with the piston pin. The piston/connecting rod assembly is ready for installation into the engine block.

PISTON RING REPLACEMENT

Piston Ring End Gap

Piston ring end-gap should be checked while the rings are removed from the pistons. Incorrect end-gap indicates the wrong size rings are being used; ring breakage could occur and engine damage could result.

Squirt clean engine oil into the cylinder, then carefully compress and insert the piston rings to be used in a cylinder, one at a time, into that cylinder. Position the rings approximately 1 in. below the deck of the block at a point where bore diameter is smallest. The ring can be carefully positioned using the top of the piston, this will assure that the ring is properly squared to the cylinder walls. Measure the ring end-gap with a feeler gauge, and compare to the piston and ring chart in this chapter. Carefully pull the ring out of the cylinder and, if a larger clearance is necessary, file the ends squarely with a fine file to obtain the proper clearance.

Piston Ring Side Clearance

▶ See Figure 148

Check the pistons to see that the ring grooves and oil return holes have been properly cleaned. Slide a piston ring into its groove, and check the side clearance with a feeler gauge. On used pistons, make sure you insert the gauge between the ring and its lower land (lower edge of the groove), because any wear that occurs forms a step at the inner portion of the lower land. If the piston grooves have worn to the extent that relatively high steps exist on the lower land, the piston should be replaced, because these will interfere with the operation of the new rings and ring clearance will be excessive. Piston rings are not furnished in oversize widths to compensate for ring groove wear.

Ring Installation

▶ See Figures 149, 150, 151 and 152

Install the rings on the piston, lowest ring first, using a piston ring expander. There is a high risk of breaking or distorting the rings, or scratching the piston, if the rings are installed by hand or other means.

Position the rings on the piston as illustrated; spacing of the various piston ring gaps is crucial to proper oil retention and even cylinder wear. When installing new rings, refer to the installation diagram furnished with the new parts.

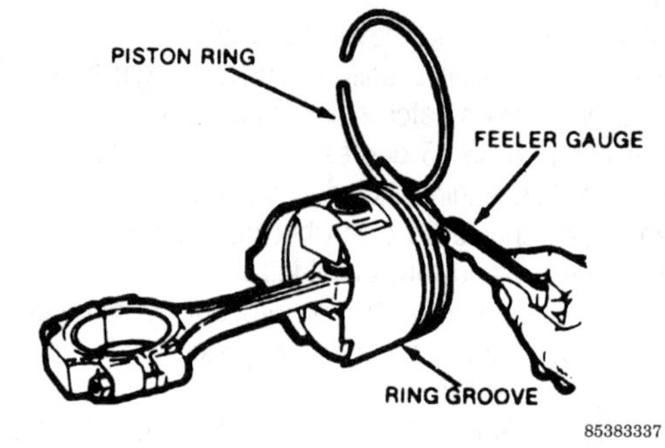

Fig. 148 Checking ring side clearance on a used piston

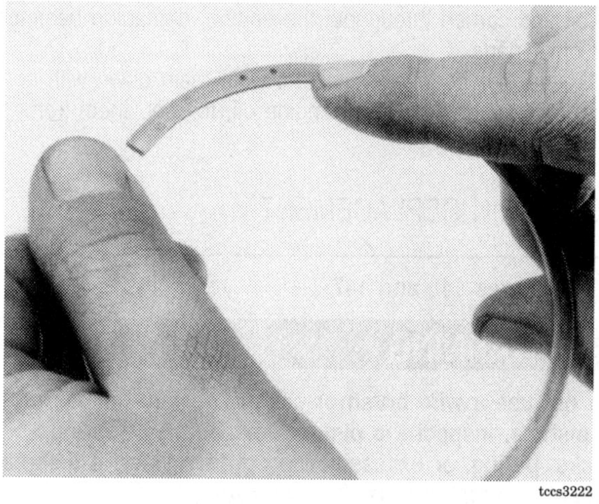

Fig. 149 Most rings are marked to show which side should face upward

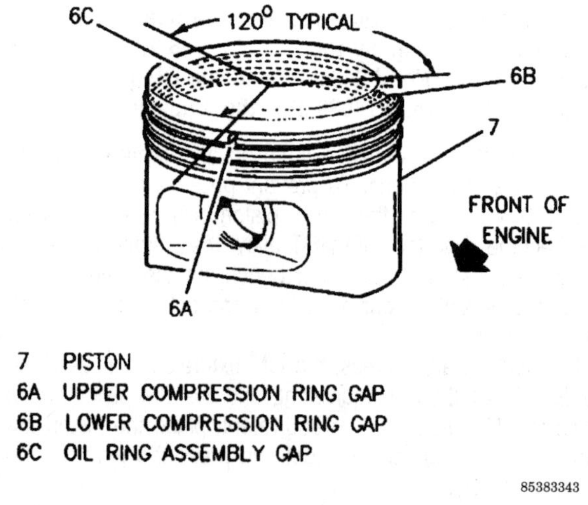

Fig. 150 Piston ring gap location — 2.2L engine

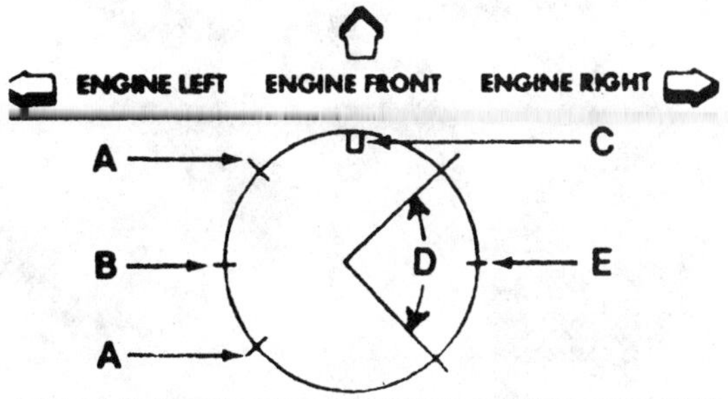

A. Oil Ring Rail Gaps
B. 2nd Compression Ring Gap
C. Notch In Piston
D. Oil Ring Spacer Gap
(Tang In Hole Or Slot With Arc)
E Top Compression Ring Gap

85383344

Fig. 151 Piston ring gap location — 4.3L engines

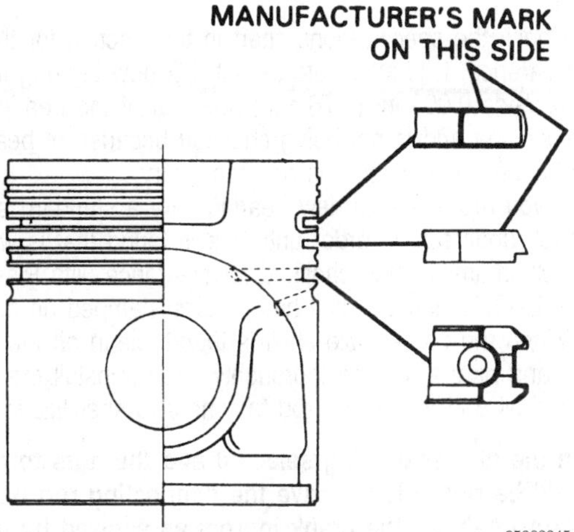

Fig. 152 Common piston ring installation

CONNECTING ROD BEARING REPLACEMENT

▶ **See Figures 153 and 154**

Connecting rod bearings for the engines covered in this guide consist of two halves or shells which are usually interchangeable in the rod and cap. When the shells are placed in position, the ends extend slightly beyond the rod and cap surfaces so that when the rod bolts are torqued the shells will be clamped tightly in place to insure positive seating and to prevent turning. A tang holds the shells in place.

➡The ends of the bearing shells must never be filed flush with the mating surface of the rod and cap.

If a rod bearing becomes noisy or is worn so that its clearance on the crank journal is sloppy, a new bearing of the correct undersize must be selected and installed since there is no provision for adjustment.

✲✲WARNING

Under no circumstances should the rod end or cap be filed to adjust the bearing clearance, nor should shims of any kind be used.

Inspect the rod bearings while the rod assemblies are out of the engine. If the shells are scored or show flaking, they should be replaced. If they are in good shape check for proper clearance on the crank journal (see below). Any scoring or ridges on the crank journal means the crankshaft must be replaced, or reground and fitted with undersized bearings.

Checking Bearing Clearance and Replacing Bearings

▶ **See Figures 155 and 156**

➡Make sure connecting rods and their caps are kept together, and that the caps are installed in the proper direction.

Replacement bearings are available in standard size, and in undersizes for reground crankshaft. Connecting rod-to-crankshaft bearing clearance is checked using Plastigage® or an equivalent gauging material at either the top or bottom of each crank journal. The Plastigage® has a range of 0.001-0.003 in. (0.0254-0.0762mm).

1. Remove the rod cap with the bearing shell. completely clean the bearing shell and the crank journal, then blow any oil from the oil hole in the crankshaft; Plastigage® is soluble in oil.
2. Place a piece of Plastigage® lengthwise along the bottom center of the lower bearing shell, then install the cap with shell and torque the bolt or nuts to specification. DO NOT turn the crankshaft with Plastigage® in the bearing.
3. Remove the bearing cap with the shell. The flattened Plastigage® will be found sticking to either the bearing shell or crank journal. Do not remove it yet.
4. Use the scale printed on the Plastigage® envelope to measure the flattened material to its widest point. The number within the scale which most closely corresponds to the width of

A. Place Gaging Plastic
Parallel to Crankshaft

85383346

Fig. 153 Apply a strip of gauging material to the connecting rod journal or the bearing

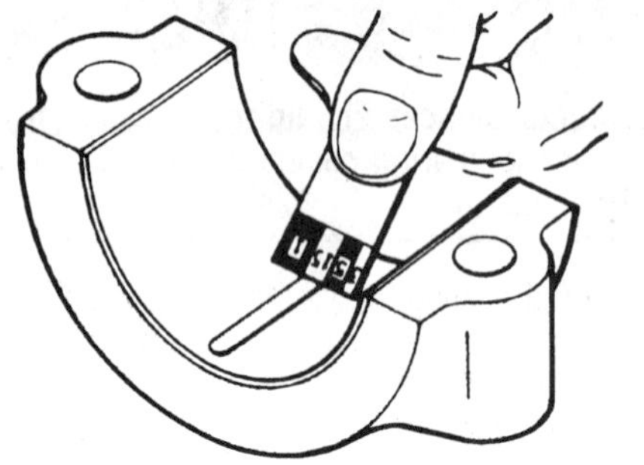

Fig. 154 Remove the bearing cap and compare the gauging material to the scale provided with the package (check the journal if the material was applied there)

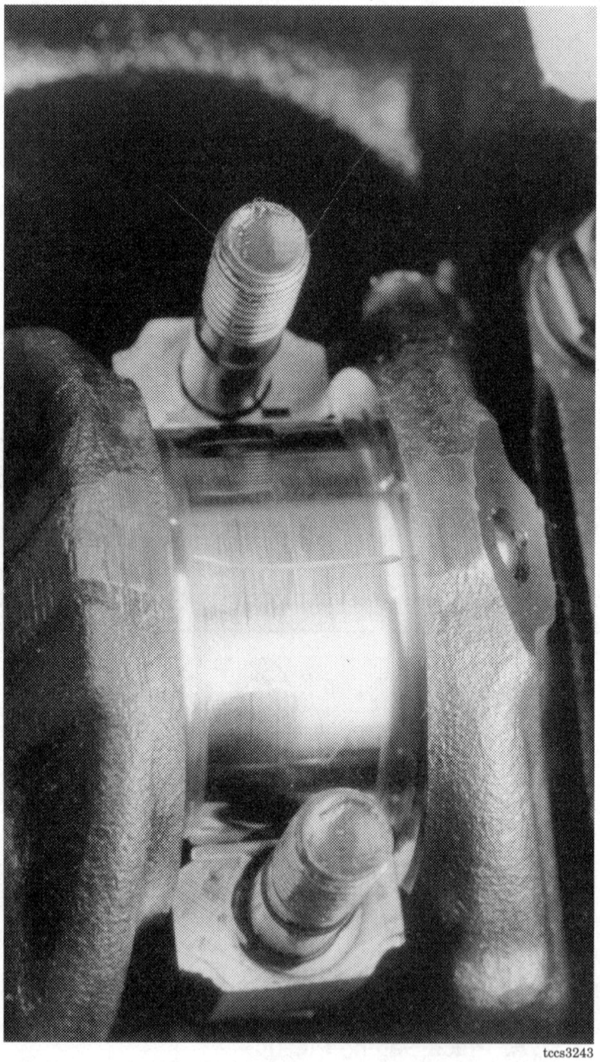

Fig. 155 Apply a strip of gauging material to the bearing journal, then install and torque the cap

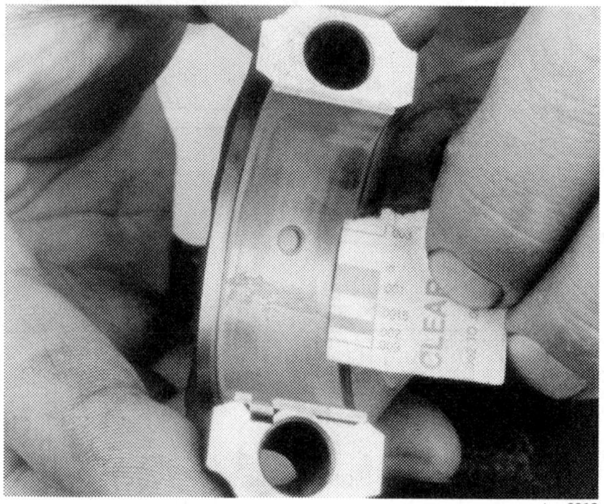

Fig. 156 After the cap is removed again, use the scale supplied with the gauge material to check clearances

the Plastigage® indicates bearing clearance in thousandths of an inch.

5. Check the specifications chart in this section for the desired clearance. It is advisable to install a new bearing if clearance exceeds 0.003 in. (.076mm); however, if the bearing is in good condition and is not being checked because of bearing noise, bearing replacement is not necessary.

6. If you are installing new bearings, try a standard size, then each undersize in order until one is found that is within the specified limits when checked for clearance with Plastigage®. Each undersize shell has its size stamped on it.

7. When the proper size shell is found, clean off the Plastigage® and oil the bearing thoroughly, then reinstall the cap with its shell and torque the rod fasteners to specification.

➡With the proper bearing selected and the nuts torqued, it should be possible to move the connecting rod back and forth freely on the crank journal as allowed by the specified connecting rod end clearance. If the rod cannot be moved, either the rod bearing is too far undersize or the rod is misaligned.

INSTALLATION

➧ See Figures 157, 158, 159 and 160

➡The following procedure requires the use of a ring compressor tool such as J-8037 or equivalent, and the ring expander (removal/installation) tool mentioned earlier.

Assemble the piston, connecting rod and rings as detailed earlier in this section.

1. Make sure that the connecting rod big-end bearings (including the end cap) are of the correct size and are properly installed.

2. Fit rubber hoses over the connecting rod bolts to protect the crankshaft journals, as done during removal. Coat the rod bearings with clean oil.

➡It is a good idea to lightly coat the walls of the cylinder bore with clean engine oil during assembly.

tccs3814

Fig. 157 Most pistons are marked to indicate positioning in the engine (usually a mark means the side facing front)

tccs3914

Fig. 158 Installing the piston into the block using a ring compressor and the handle of a hammer

tccs3917

Fig. 159 The notch on the the side of the bearing cap matches the groove on the bearing insert

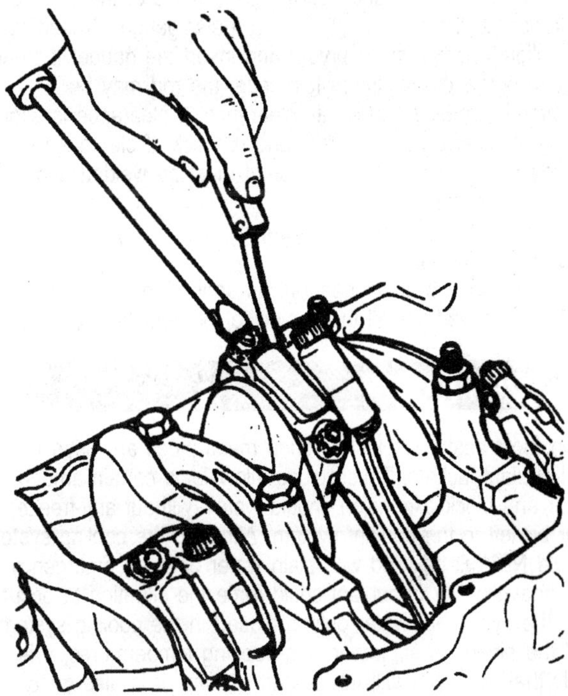

85383352

Fig. 160 Check the connecting rod side clearance using a feeler gauge. A small prybar should be used to carefully spread the connecting rods.

3. Using the proper ring compressor, compress the rings around the piston head, then insert the piston assembly into the cylinder so that the notch (or other mark) in the top of the piston faces the front of the engine. This assumes that the dimple(s) or other markings on the connecting rods are in correct relation to the piston marking(s). The marks made during disassembly should serve as a guide here.

4. From beneath the engine, coat each crank journal with clean oil. Pull the connecting rod, with the bearing shell in place, into position against the crank journal.

5. Remove the rubber hoses from the studs. Install the bearing cap (with bearing shell) onto the connecting rod and the cap nuts. Tighten the connecting rod cap nuts to the following:

- 2.2L engine: 38 ft. lbs. (52 Nm)
- 4.3L engine: 20 ft. lbs. (27 Nm), plus a 70 degree additional turn

➡When more than one rod and piston assembly is being installed, the connecting rod cap attaching nuts should only be tightened enough to keep each rod in position until all have been installed. This will ease the installation of the remaining piston assemblies.

6. Check the clearance between the sides of the connecting rods and the crankshaft using a feeler gauge. Spread the rods slightly with a small prybar and insert the gauge. If clearance is below the minimum tolerance, the rod may be machined to provide adequate clearance. If clearance is excessive, substitute an unworn rod, and recheck. If clearance is still outside specifications, the crankshaft must be welded and reground, or replaced.
7. If removed, install the oil pump
8. Install the oil pan.
9. Install the cylinder head(s), as applicable.
10. If removed, install the engine to the vehicle.

Freeze Plugs

On most cast iron blocks, round metal plugs are used to seal coolant jackets. These plugs allow for a certain amount of water and block expansion should water (without anti-freeze) ever be left in the coolant system. Although the cooling system should NEVER be filled with plain water only, an emergency and unavailability of coolant could force the situation to occur.

In the event that water only is placed in the cooling system and the engine is subject to sub-freezing temperatures, it is likely that the water will freeze and expand. It is also quite possible that the block will expand and crack. If you are lucky though, the expansion may only cause freeze plugs to become dislodged.

During engine block overhaul, it is often standard procedure to remove and replace all of the freeze plugs.

REMOVAL & INSTALLATION

➧ See Figures 161 and 162

1. Disconnect the negative battery cable, then properly drain the engine cooling system.
2. If equipped, remove the engine coolant drain plugs (located at the bottom of the block usually near the oil pan rail) and drain the coolant from the block. If the engine is not equipped with coolant drain plugs, drill a small hole in the leaking freeze plug and allow any remaining coolant to drain.
3. Remove any components that restrict access to the freeze plug or, if necessary, remove the engine from the vehicle for access to the freeze plug(s).

⁂CAUTION

Always wear proper eye protection when using a chisel, especially when attempting to dislodge a freeze plug.

4. Using a chisel, tap the bottom edge of the freeze plug to cock it in the bore. Remove the plug using pliers, but be careful not to score the block or the new freeze plug may not fit well. An alternate method is to drill an 1/8 in. (.125mm) hole in the plug and remove it using a dent puller.

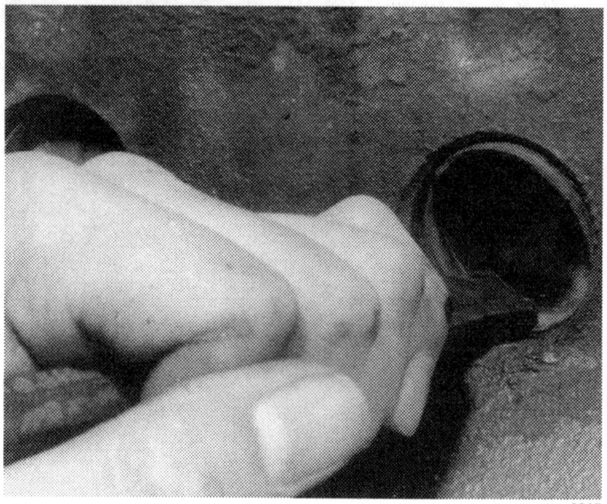

tccs3905

Fig. 161 Using a punch and hammer, the freeze plug can be loosened in the block

tccs3906

Fig. 162 Once the freeze plug has been loosened, it can be removed from the block

To install:

5. Clean the bore of any debris and make sure it is free of any deep scratches which could cause a leak.

➡Some auto part stores may offer easy to install freeze plugs consisting of a grommet with metal plates and an adjustment bolt. These plugs are positioned, then the bolt is tightened to expand the grommet sealing the block bore. Although these might be handy to get the vehicle home quickly, they should not be installed as a permanent fix.

6. Freeze plugs are interference fitted to the block. Make sure you have the proper plug size and an equalled sized driver. The proper sized driver will ease the installation process by preventing the plug from cocking in the bore as it is driven into position.
7. Coat the plug with sealant, then position it to the bore and drive it into position.
8. Install the interfering components or the engine, as applicable.

9. Connect the negative battery cable and properly refill the engine cooling system, then check for leaks.

Block Heater

REMOVAL & INSTALLATION

1. Disconnect the negative battery cable, then properly drain the engine cooling system.
2. If equipped, remove the engine coolant drain plugs (located at the bottom of the block near the oil pan rail) and drain the coolant from the block. If the engine is not equipped with coolant drain plugs, be ready to catch the coolant that will likely drain from the block when the block heater is removed.
3. Disconnect the block heater electrical connector.
4. Loosen the block heater retaining screw and remove the block heater from the engine.

To install:

5. Coat the block heater O-ring with engine oil and clean the block heater hole of rust.
6. Install the block heater and tighten the retaining screw.
7. Connect the negative battery cable and properly refill the engine cooling system, then check for leaks.

Rear Main Oil Seal

Replacing a rear main seal is a formidable task. Before replacing the seal, care should be taken in determining the exact source of the leak. Various manufacturers produce a fluorescent die oil additive which can be added to your crankcase. The engine is run, allowing the dyed oil to leak from the same source, then a black light is used to illuminate the leak so it can be traced.

REPLACEMENT

2.2L Engines

➧ See Figures 163 and 164

➡The following procedure requires the use of a seal installation tool such as J-34686 or equivalent.

1. Remove the transmission assembly.
2. Remove the flywheel and verify the rear main seal is leaking.
3. Remove the seal by inserting a small prybar through the dust lip at an angle and prying the seal out. Be careful not to score the crankshaft sealing surface.

To install:

4. Check the crankshaft and seal bore for nicks or damage. Repair as necessary.
5. Lightly coat the inner diameter of the seal with clean engine oil.
6. Position the seal over the mandrel of the J-34686 or an equivalent installation tool. Make sure the dust lip (back of seal) is bottomed squarely against the collar of the tool.
7. Lightly coat the outer diameter of the seal using clean engine oil, then position the tool to the crankshaft while aligning the tool dowel pin with the crankshaft dowel pin hole.

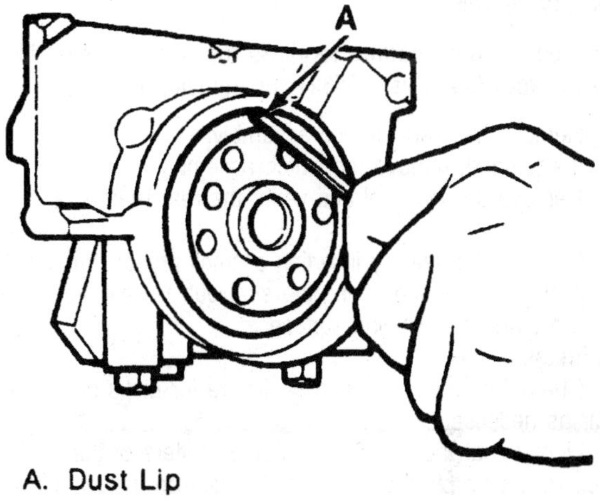

Fig. 163 Prying out the rear main seal — 2.2L engines

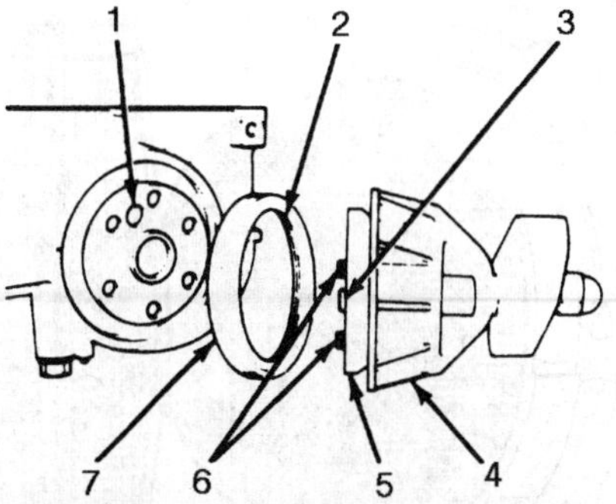

Fig. 164 Installing the rear main seal

Tighten the screws to attach the tool and assure proper seal installation.

8. Turn the handle of the tool until the collar is tight against the case and the seal has been completely seated.
9. Turn the handle of the tool out until it stops, then remove the tool and verify that the is seated squarely in the bore.
10. Install the flywheel.
11. Install the transmission assembly.

4.3L Engine

See Figure 165

The following procedure requires the use of a seal installation tool (such as J-35621) or equivalent.

1. Remove the transmission assembly.
2. If equipped, remove the clutch assembly.
3. Remove the flywheel and verify the rear main seal is leaking.
4. Remove the seal by inserting a small prybar through the dust lip at an angle and prying the seal out. Be careful not to score the crankshaft sealing surface.

To install:

5. Check the crankshaft and seal bore for nicks or damage. Repair as necessary.
6. Lightly coat the inner and outer diameters of the seal with clean engine oil, then position the seal on the installation tool.
7. Position the tool to the crankshaft and thread the tool's screws into the tapped holes. Tighten the screws securely using a screwdriver to attach the tool and assure proper seal installation.
8. Turn the handle of the tool until it bottoms and the seal has been completely seated.
9. Turn the handle of the tool out until it stops, then remove the tool and verify that the is seated squarely in the bore.
10. Install the flywheel to the engine.
11. If equipped, install the clutch assembly.
12. Install the transmission assembly.

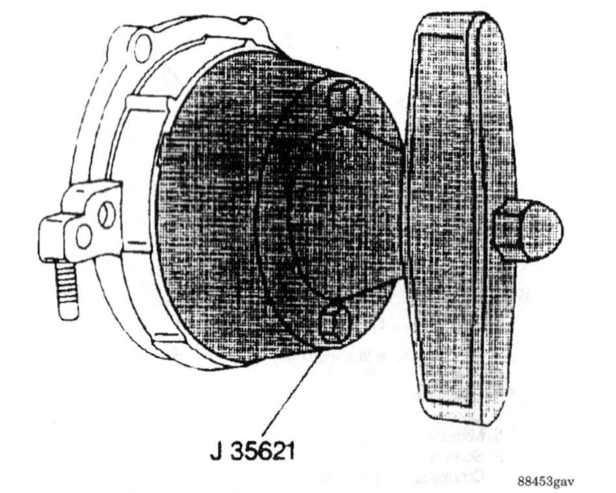

Fig. 165 Installing the rear oil seal using seal installation tool J-35621

Crankshaft and Main Bearings

REMOVAL & INSTALLATION

See Figures 166, 167, 168, 169 and 170

1. Drain the crankcase oil and remove the engine from the truck.
2. Remove the flywheel and mount the engine on a work stand in a suitable working area. Invert the engine, so the oil pan is facing up.

If the cylinder heads are not being removed, the spark plugs should be removed in order to release engine compression and allow for easier rotation of the crankshaft when necessary.

3. Remove the engine front (timing) cover.
4. Align the timing marks, then remove the timing chain and gears.

After removing the timing gear or sprocket from the crankshaft, be sure to remove the woodruff key from the crankshaft.

5. Remove the oil pan.
6. If necessary, remove the oil pump assembly.
7. Inspect the connecting rods and bearing caps for identification marks (numbers). If there are none, stamp the cylinder number on the machined surfaces of the bolt bosses of the connecting rods and caps for identification when reinstalling. If the pistons are to be removed eventually from the connecting rod, mark the cylinder number on the pistons with silver paint or felt-tip pen for proper cylinder identification and cap-to-rod location.
8. Remove the connecting rod nuts and caps, then store them in the order of removal. Place short pieces of rubber hose on the connecting rod studs to prevent damaging the crankshaft bearing surfaces.
9. Check the main bearing caps for identification marks (if not identified, mark them). Remove the main bearing caps and

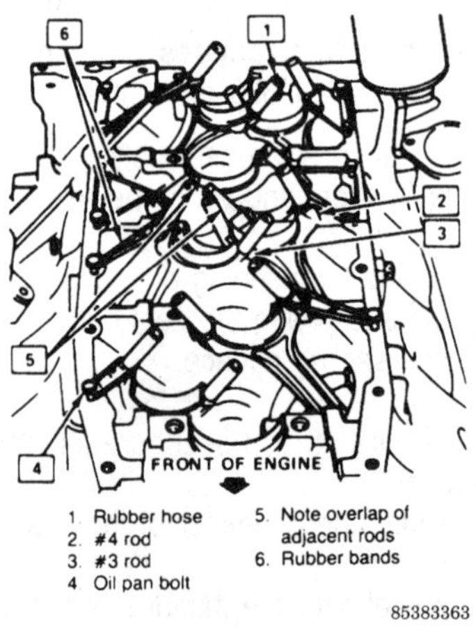

Fig. 166 Support the connecting rods with rubber bands and install rubber rod bolt caps to protect the crankshaft during removal and installation

store them in order, for reassembly purposes; the caps must be reinstalled in their original position.

10. If equipped, remove the 1-piece rear main seal retainer from the engine.

11. Install rubber bands between a bolt on each connecting rod and oil pan bolts that have been reinstalled in the block (see illustration). This will keep the rods from banging on the block when the crank is removed.

12. Carefully lift the crankshaft out of the block. The rods will pivot to the center of the engine when the crank is removed.

To install:

13. Clean and inspect all parts for damage. Repair or replace, as necessary.

14. Install new bearing shell inserts and check the bearing clearances.

➡If necessary, deliver the crankshaft to an automotive machine shop, have the crankshaft journals ground and new bearing shells matched.

15. Lubricate all of the parts and oil seals with clean engine oil.

16. Using a feeler gauge and a medium prybar, move the crankshaft forward-and-rearward. Check the crankshaft end-play by inserting a feeler gauge between the crankshaft and the thrust bearing shell. An alternate method is to use a dial indicator at the crankshaft snout. Install the indicator, move the crankshaft rearward, zero the indicator and then move the crankshaft forward. the dial indicator will read the end-play. Thrust bearing location varies with the engine is No. 4

17. Tighten main bearing caps (in three steps) to specification:

- 2.2L engine: 70 ft. lbs. (95 Nm)
- 4.3L engine: 80 ft. lbs. (108 Nm)

18. Remove the rubber hoses from the studs. Install the bearing cap (with bearing shell) onto the connecting rod and the cap nuts. Tighten the connecting rod cap nuts to the following:

- 2.2L engine: 38 ft. lbs. (52 Nm)
- 4.3L engine: 45 ft. lbs. 20 ft. lbs. (27 Nm), plus a 70 degree additional turn

➡When more than one rod and piston assembly is being installed, the connecting rod cap attaching nuts should only be tightened enough to keep each rod in position until all have been installed. This will ease the installation of the remaining piston assemblies.

19. Check connecting rod side clearance by inserting a feeler gauge between the side of the rod and the crankshaft. If not within specification, repair as necessary.

20. If necessary, install the pump assembly.

21. Install the oil pan.

22. Make sure the woodruff key is installed in the end of the crankshaft, then install the timing chain and gears.

23. Install the engine front (timing) cover.

24. Remove the engine from the work stand, then install the flywheel.

25. Refill the crankcase and install the engine to the truck.

CLEANING AND INSPECTION

➧ See Figures 171, 172 and 173

1. Clean the crankshaft with solvent and a brush. Clean the oil passages with a suitable brush, then blow them out with compressed air.

2. Inspect the crankshaft for obvious damage or wear. Check the main and connecting rod journals for cracks, scratches, grooves or scores. Inspect the crankshaft oil seal surface for nicks, sharp edges or burrs that could damage the oil seal or cause premature seal wear.

3. If the crankshaft passes a visual inspection, check journal runout using a dial indicator. Support the crankshaft in V-blocks as shown in the figure and check the runout as shown. Compare to specifications.

4. Measure the main and connecting rod journals for wear, out-of-roundness or taper, using a micrometer. Measure in at least 4 places around each journal and compare your findings with the journal diameter specifications.

5. If the crankshaft fails any inspection for wear or damage, it must be reground or replaced.

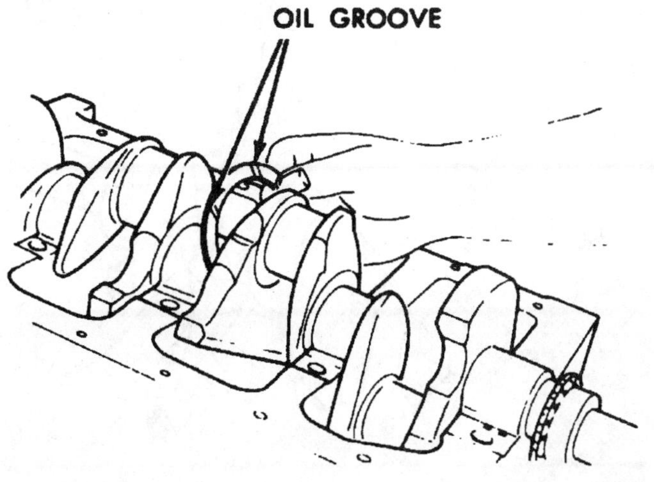

Fig. 167 Thrust bearing location

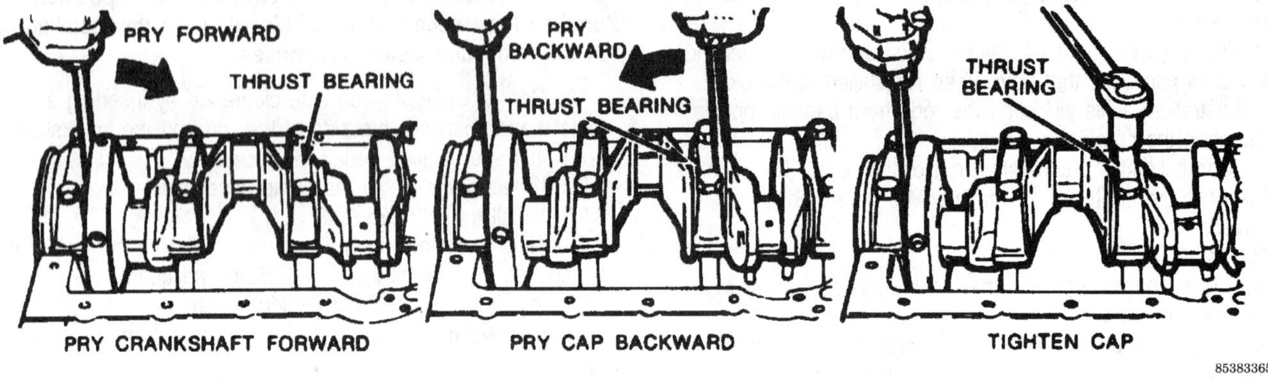

Fig. 168 Aligning the thrust bearings and tightening the main caps

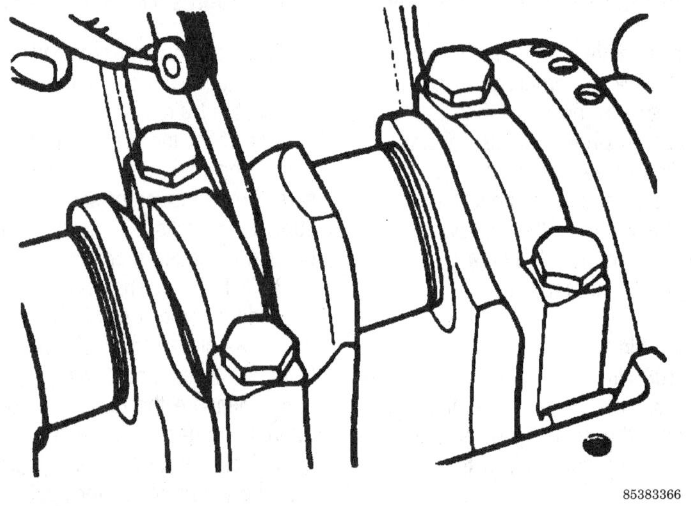

Fig. 169 Checking crankshaft end-play using a feeler gauge

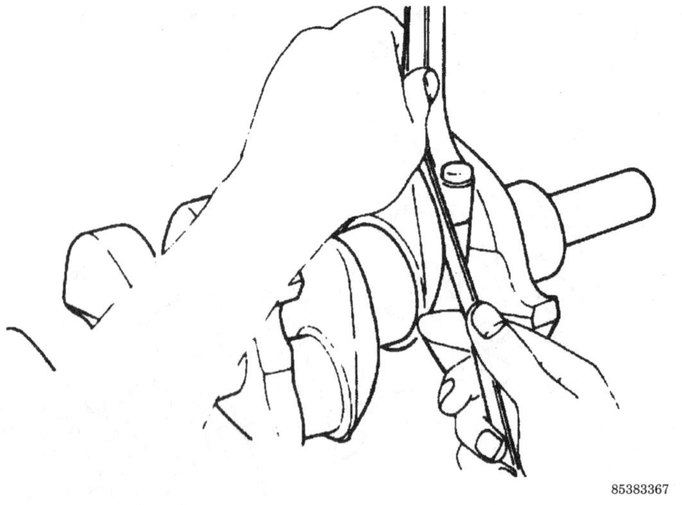

Fig. 170 Measuring the connecting rod side clearance

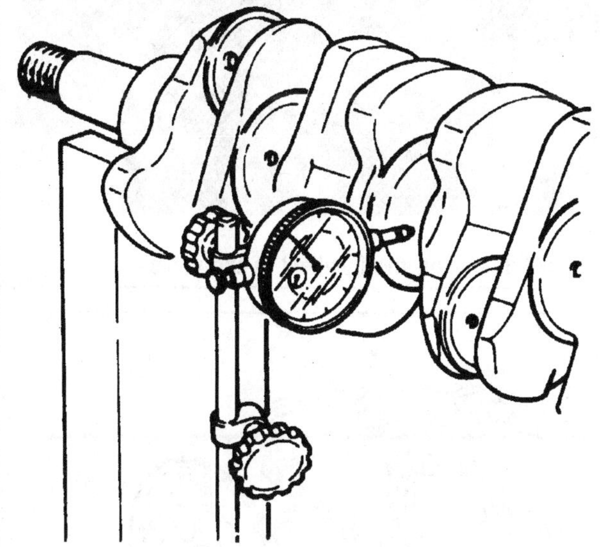
85383368

Fig. 171 Checking the crankshaft for excessive runout

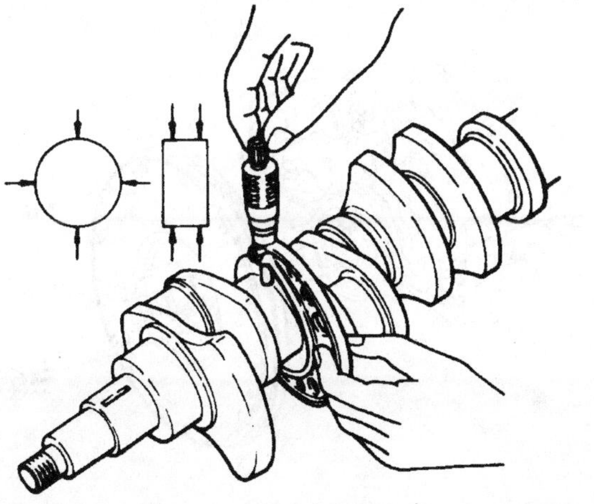
85383369

Fig. 172 Checking the main bearing journal using a micrometer

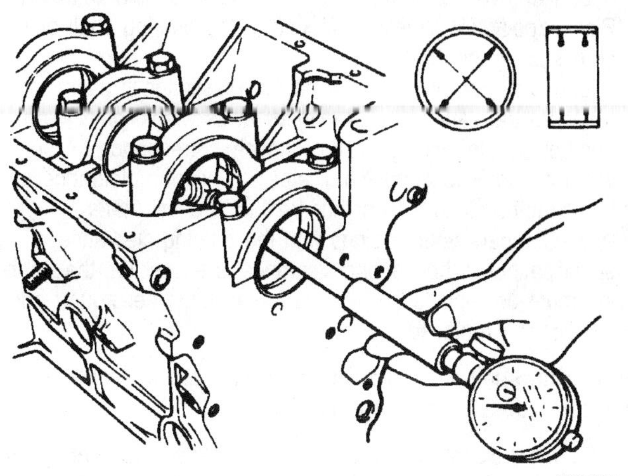
85383370

Fig. 173 Checking main bearing bore diameter with bearings installed

BEARING REPLACEMENT

➡The following procedure requires the use of Plastigage® or a micrometer set consisting of inside and outside micrometers, and a dial indicator.

1. Inspect the bearings for scoring, chipping or other wear.
2. Inspect the crankshaft journals as detailed in the Cleaning and Inspection procedure.
3. If the crankshaft journals appear usable, clean them and the bearing shells until they are completely free of oil. Blow any oil from the oil hole in the crankshaft.
4. To check the crankshaft/rod bearing clearances using a micrometer, perform the following procedures:
    a. Set the crankshaft on V-blocks. Using a dial indicator set on the center bearing journal, check the crankshaft runout. Repair or replace the crankshaft if out of specification.
    b. Using an outside micrometer, measure the crankshaft bearing journals for diameter and out-of-round conditions; if necessary, regrind the bearing journals.
    c. Install the bearings and caps and torque the nuts/bolts to specifications. Using an inside micrometer, check the bearing bores in the engine block. If out of specification, regrind the bearing bores to the next largest oversize.
    d. The difference between the two readings is the bearing clearance. If out of specification, inspect for the cause and repair as necessary.
5. To inspect the main bearing surfaces, using the Plastigage® method, perform the following procedures:

➡NOTE:The journal surfaces and bearing shells must be completely free of oil to get an accurate reading with Plastigage®.

   a. Place a strip of Plastigage® lengthwise along the bottom center of the lower bearing shell, then install the cap with the shell and tighten the connecting rod nuts or main cap bolts to specification.

➡When the Plastigage® material is installed on the bearing surfaces, DO NOT rotate the crankshaft.

b. Remove the bearing cap with the shell. The flattened Plastigage® will either be sticking to the bearing shell or the crankshaft journal.

c. Using the printed scale on the Plastigage® package, measure the flattened Plastigage® at its widest point. The number on the scale that most closely corresponds to the width of the Plastigage® indicates the bearing clearance in thousandths of an inch or hundredths of a millimeter.

d. Compare your findings with the bearing clearance specification. If the bearing clearance is excessive, the bearing must be replaced or the crankshaft must be ground and the bearing replaced.

➡Bearing shell sets over standard size are available to correct excessive bearing clearance.

e. After clearance measuring is completed, be sure to remove the Plastigage® from the crankshaft and/or bearing shell.

f. For final bearing shell installation, make sure the connecting rod and rod cap and/or cylinder block and main cap bearing saddles are clean and free of nicks or burrs. Install the bearing shells in the bearing saddles, making sure the bearing shell tangs are seated in the notches.

➡Be careful when handling any plain bearings. Your hands and the working area should be clean. Dirt is easily embedded in the bearing surface and the bearings are easily scratched or damaged.

Flywheel

On most of the engines covered by this manual the flywheel and the ring gear are machined from one piece of metal and cannot be separated. On some of the 4.3L engines the ring gear is a separate piece and can be driven from the flywheel once the gear is heated using a torch.

REMOVAL & INSTALLATION

➧ See Figures 174, 175 and 176

1. Remove the transmission assembly from the vehicle.
2. If equipped with a manual transmission, remove the clutch and pressure plate assembly.
3. Remove the flywheel-to-crankshaft bolts, then remove the flywheel from the engine.

To install:

4. Inspect the flywheel for cracks, and inspect the ring gear for burrs or worn teeth. Replace the flywheel if any damage is apparent. Remove burrs with a mill file.
5. Install the flywheel. Most flywheels will only attach to the crankshaft in one position, as the bolt holes are unevenly spaced and/or the crankshaft is fitted with a dowel pin. Install the bolts and torque to specification using a crisscross pattern.
6. If equipped, install the clutch and pressure plate assembly.
7. Install the transmission assembly.

Fig. 174 Installing the flywheel in the vehicle

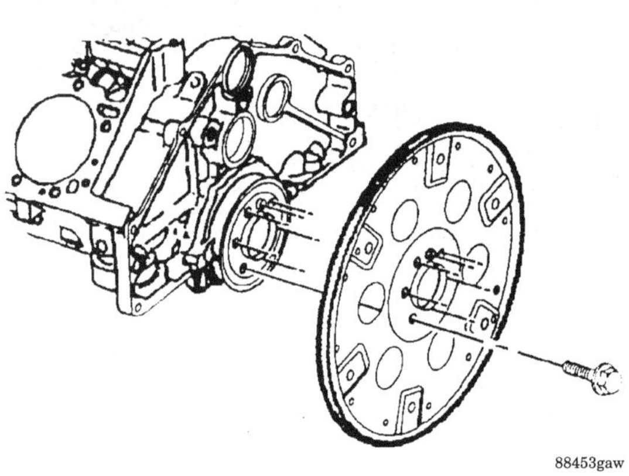

Fig. 175 View of the flywheel and related components (automatic transmission)

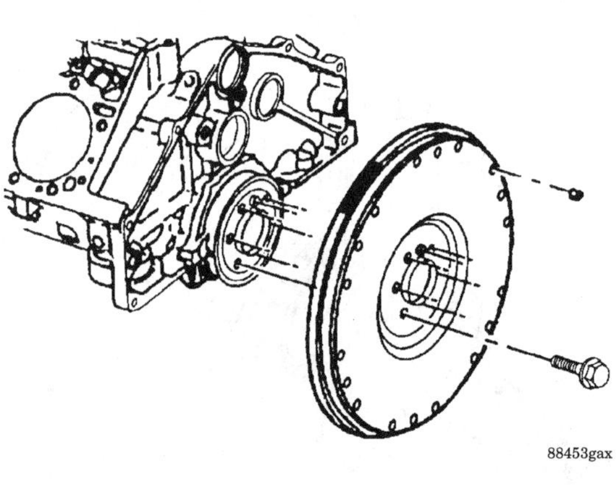

Fig. 176 View of the flywheel and related components (manual transmission)

RING GEAR REPLACEMENT

1. Remove the flywheel from the vehicle. Refer to the procedure outlined in this section.
2. Make certain that the ring gear is a separate piece, then using a torch, uniformly heat it around the entire circumference. DO NOT heat the gear until it is red hot as this will change the metal structure.
3. When the ring gear is hot enough, drive it off the flywheel using a hammer.

To install:

4. Using a torch, heat the ring gear uniformly until it expands enough to be installed on the flywheel.

****CAUTION**

Never heat the ring gear to a temperature above 400°F (204°C) as this will weaken the structure of the metal.

5. When the ring gear and flywheel have cooled sufficiently, install the flywheel on the vehicle.

EXHAUST SYSTEM

General Information

See Figures 177, 178, 179, 180 and 181

➡Safety glasses should be worn at all times when working on or near the exhaust system. Older exhaust systems will almost always be covered with loose rust particles which will shower you when disturbed. These particles are more than a nuisance and could injure your eye.

Whenever working on the exhaust system always keep the following in mind:

- Check the complete exhaust system for open seams, holes loose connections, or other deterioration which could permit exhaust fumes to seep into the passenger compartment.
- The exhaust system is usually supported by free-hanging rubber mountings which permit some movement of the exhaust system, but does not permit transfer of noise and vibration into the passenger compartment. Do not replace the rubber mounts with solid ones.
- Before removing any component of the exhaust system, ALWAYS squirt a liquid rust dissolving agent onto the fasteners for ease of removal. A lot of knuckle skin will be saved by following this rule. It may even be wise to spray the fasteners and allow them to sit overnight.

****CAUTION**

Allow the exhaust system to cool sufficiently before spraying a solvent exhaust fasteners. Some solvents are highly flammable and could ignite when sprayed on hot exhaust components.

- Annoying rattles and noise vibrations in the exhaust system are usually caused by misalignment of the parts. When aligning the system, leave all bolts and nuts loose until all parts are properly aligned, then tighten, working from front to rear.
- When installing exhaust system parts, make sure there is enough clearance between the hot exhaust parts and pipes and hoses that would be adversely affected by excessive heat. Also make sure there is adequate clearance from the floor pan to avoid possible overheating of the floor.
- Two types of pipe connections are used on most exhaust systems, they are: the ball joint (to allow angular movement for alignment purposes) and the slip joint. Gaskets are used only with the ball joint type connections.

As with many areas of service on your truck, the exhaust system presents it's own dangers. Always follow the safety precautions carefully during exhaust system service.

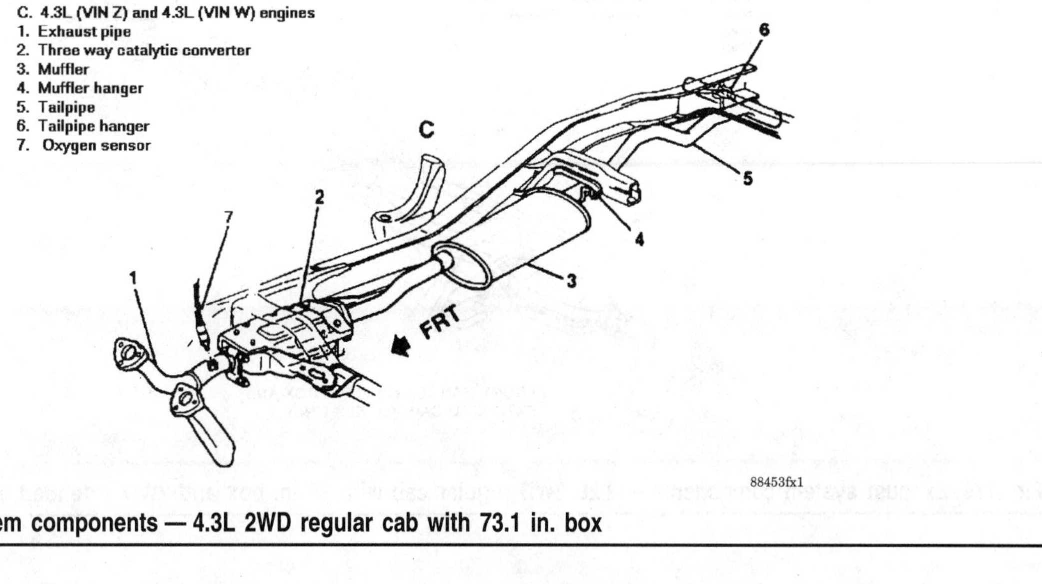

Fig. 177 Exhaust system components — 4.3L 2WD regular cab with 73.1 in. box

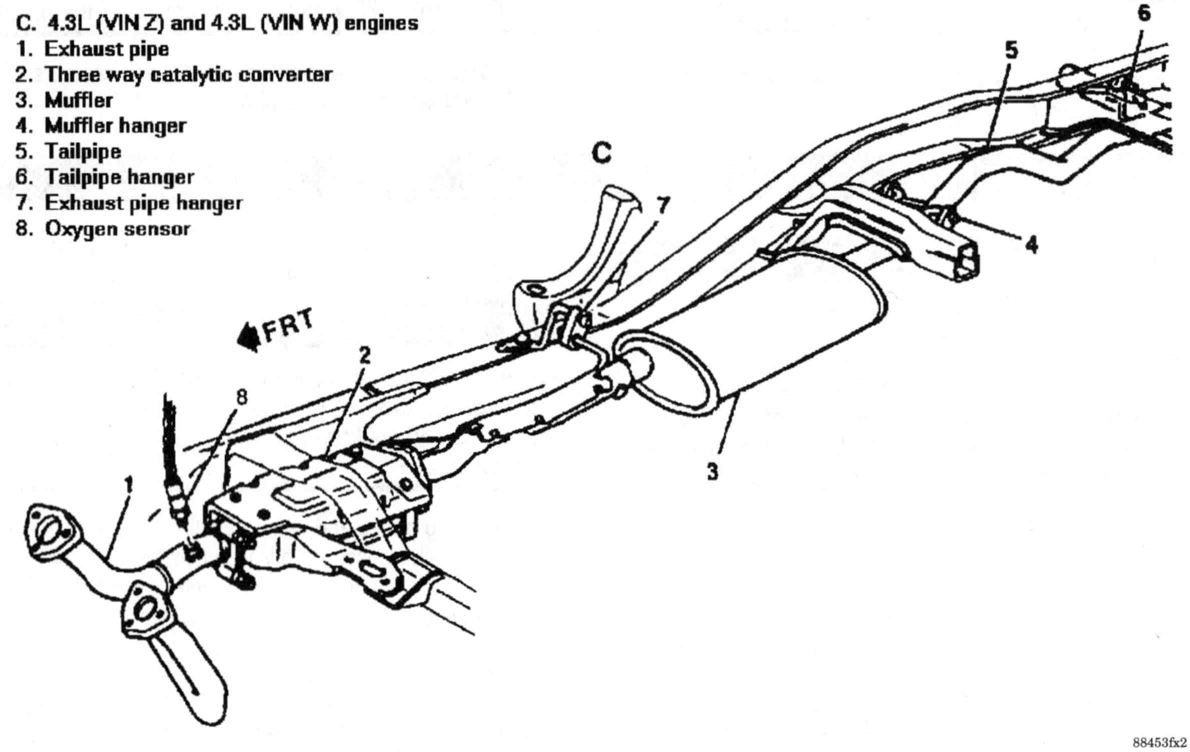

Fig. 178 Exhaust system components — 4.3L 2WD regular cab with 89 in. box and 2WD extended cab

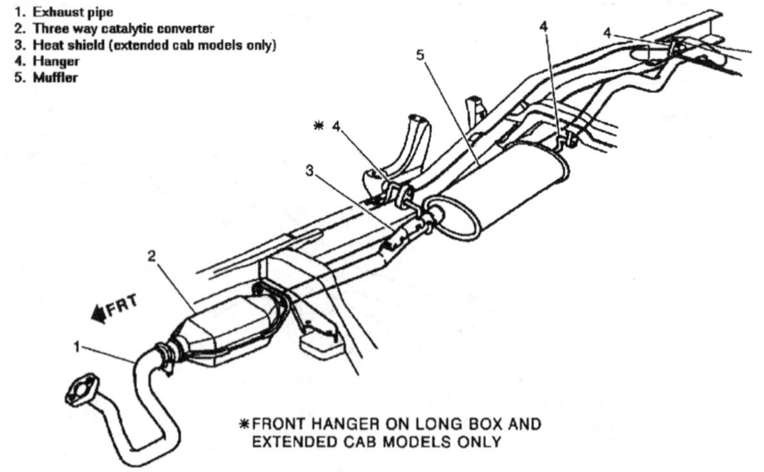

Fig. 179 Exhaust system components — 2.2L 2WD regular cab with 89 in. box and 2WD extended cab

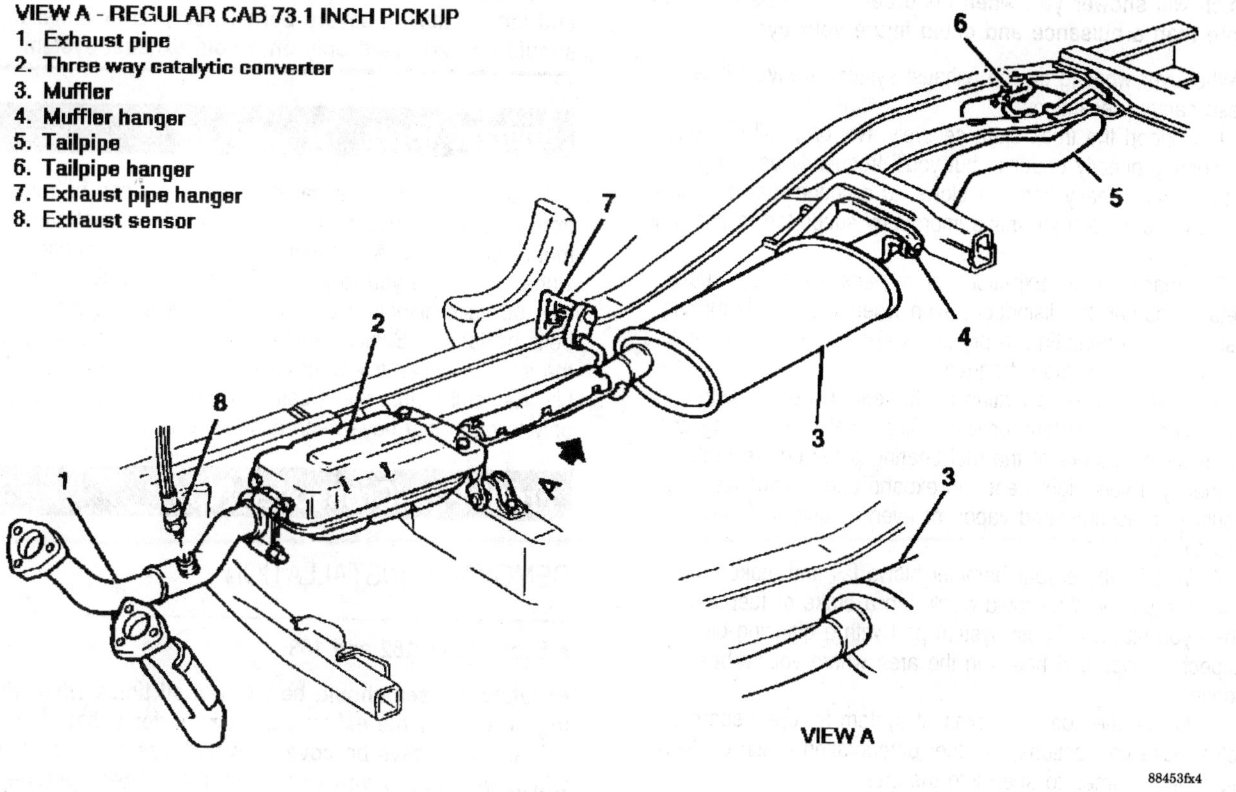

Fig. 180 Exhaust system components — 4WD with 5 speed transmission

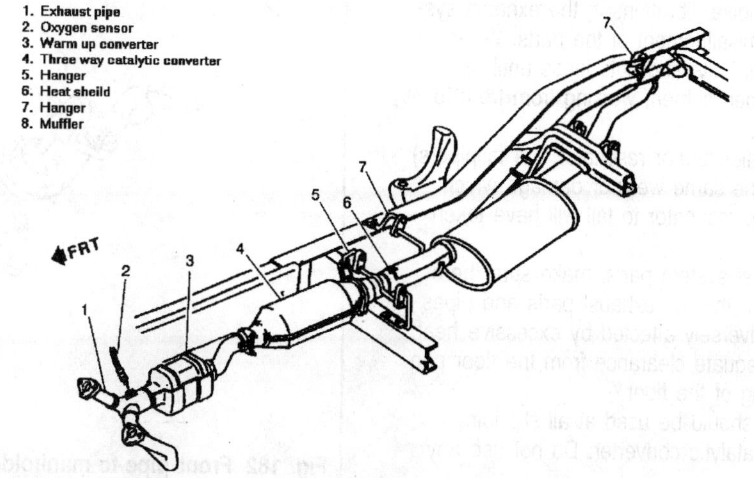

Fig. 181 Exhaust system components — 4WD with automatic transmission

Safety Precautions

➡Safety glasses should be worn at all times when working on or near the exhaust system. Older exhaust systems will almost always be covered with loose rust particles which will shower you when disturbed. These particles are more than a nuisance and could injure your eye.

Whenever working on the exhaust system always follow these safety precautions:

1. Support the truck extra securely. Not only will you often be working directly under it, but you'll frequently be using a lot of force, say, heavy hammer blows, to dislodge rusted parts. This can cause a truck that's improperly supported to shift and possibly fall.
2. Wear goggles. Exhaust system parts are always rusty. Metal chips can be dislodged, even when you're only turning rusted bolts. Attempting to pry pipes apart with a chisel makes the chips fly even more frequently.
3. If you're using a cutting torch, keep it a great distance from either the fuel tank or lines. Stop what you're doing and feel the temperature of the fuel bearing pipes on the tank frequently. Even slight heat can expand and/or vaporize fuel, resulting in accumulated vapor, or even a liquid leak, near your torch.
4. Watch where your hammer blows fall and make sure you hit squarely. You could easily tap a brake or fuel line when you hit an exhaust system part with a glancing blow. Inspect all lines and hoses in the area where you've been working.
5. Check the complete exhaust system for open seams, holes loose connections, or other deterioration which could permit exhaust fumes to seep into the cab.
6. The exhaust system is supported by free-hanging rubber mountings which permits some movement of the exhaust system, but does not permit transfer of noise and vibration into the cab. Do not replace the rubber mounts with solid ones.
7. Before removing any component of the exhaust system, ALWAYS squirt a liquid rust dissolving agent onto the fasteners for ease of removal. A lot of knuckle skin will be saved by following this rule.
8. Annoying rattles and noise vibrations in the exhaust system are usually caused by misalignment of the parts. When aligning the system, leave all bolts and nuts loose until all parts are properly aligned, then tighten, working from front to rear.
9. When replacing a muffler and/or resonator, the tailpipe(s) should be checked. Often, the same wear or damage which caused a vehicle's muffler or resonator to fail will have taken the same toll on the tailpipe.
10. When installing exhaust system parts, make sure there is enough clearance between the hot exhaust parts and pipes and hoses that would be adversely affected by excessive heat. Also make sure there is adequate clearance from the floor pan to avoid possible overheating of the floor.
11. Exhaust pipe sealers should be used at all slip joint connections except at the catalytic converter. Do not use any sealers at the converter as the sealer will not withstand converter temperatures.

✲✲CAUTION

Be very careful when working on or near the catalytic converter. External temperatures can reach 1,500°F (816°C) and more, causing severe burns. Removal or installation should be performed only on a cold exhaust system.

Special Tools

A number of special exhaust system tools can be rented from auto supply houses or local rental stores that carry automotive equipment. A common one is a tailpipe expander, designed to enable you to join pipes of identical diameter. It may also be quite helpful to use solvents designed to loosen rusted bolts or flanges. Soaking rusted parts the night before you do the job can speed the work of freeing rusted parts considerably. Remember that these solvents are often flammable. Apply only to parts that have been allowed to cool!

Front Pipe/Crossover Pipe

REMOVAL & INSTALLATION

➧ See Figures 182 and 183

➡Safety glasses should be worn at all times when working on or near the exhaust system. Older exhaust systems will almost always be covered with loose rust particles which will shower you when disturbed. These particles are more than a nuisance and could injure your eye.

1. Raise and support the front of the truck safely using jackstands.
2. Spray all fasteners which are to be disconnected using a penetrating oil.

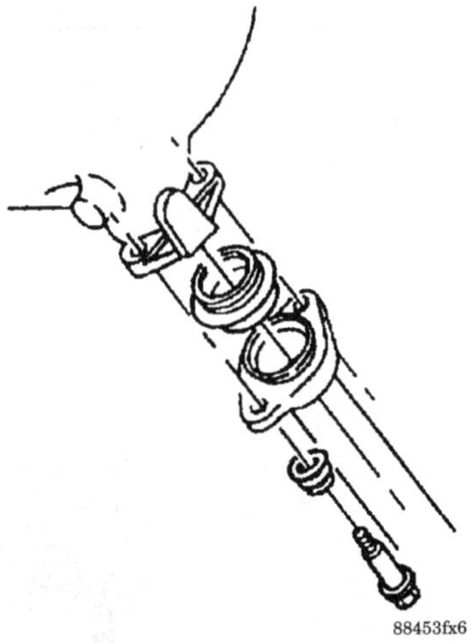

Fig. 182 Front pipe-to-manifold connection — 2.2L engines

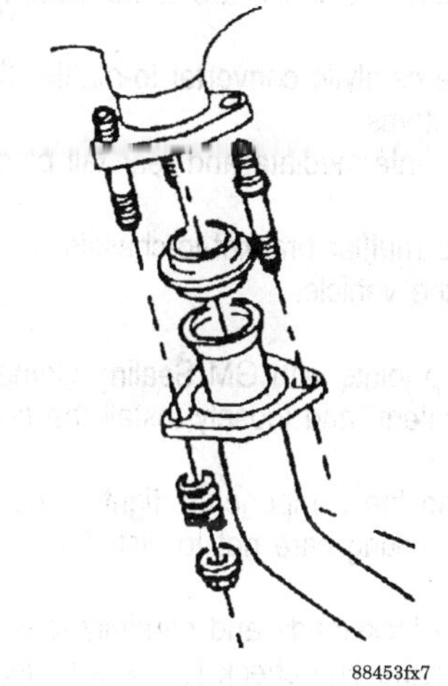

Fig. 183 Front pipe-to-manifold connection — 4.3L engines

3. Remove the front pipe(s)-to-manifold(s) nuts and separate (pry, if necessary) the front pipe (usually a ball joint fitting) from the exhaust manifold(s).

4. At the catalytic converter, loosen the front pipe-to-converter clamp nuts, then slide the clamp away from the converter and separate the front pipe from the converter.

➡Use a twisting motion to separate the front pipe-to-converter slip joint connection. If the front pipe cannot be removed from the catalytic converter, use a hammer (to loosen the connection) or wedge tool to separate the connection.

5. Inspect the pipe for holes, damage or deterioration; if necessary, replace the front pipe.

To install:

6. Engage the front pipe to the converter and install the clamp.

7. Engage the front pipe to the exhaust manifold(s). Finger-tighten the nuts.

➡Be sure to use a sealing compound such as 1051249 or equivalent, at the slip joint connection.

8. Lubricate the front pipe-to-manifold(s) studs/nuts and the front pipe-to-converter clamp threads. Torque the front pipe-to-exhaust manifold bolts to 15 ft. lbs. (20 Nm) and the front pipe-to-converter clamp nuts to 35 ft. lbs. (47 Nm).

9. Start the engine and check for exhaust leaks.

Catalytic Converter

The catalytic converter is an emission control device added to the exhaust system to reduce the emission of hydrocarbon and carbon monoxide pollutants.

REMOVAL & INSTALLATION

▶ See Figure 184

➡Safety glasses should be worn at all times when working on or near the exhaust system. Older exhaust systems will almost always be covered with loose rust particles which will shower you when disturbed. These particles are more than a nuisance and could injure your eye.

1. Raise and support the front of the truck safely using jackstands.

2. Spray all fasteners which are to be disconnected using a penetrating oil.

3. Remove the catalytic converter-to-muffler bolts and separate the muffler from the converter.

➡The connection between the converter and the muffler is usually a ball joint type, which can be easily separated.

4. Remove the catalytic converter-to-front pipe clamp nuts and move the clamp forward.

5. Remove the converter-to-mounting bracket bolts, then twist the converter to separate it from the front pipe.

6. Inspect the condition of the catalytic converter for physical damage, replace it, if necessary.

To install:

➡When installing the catalytic converter, be sure that it is installed with adequate clearance from the floor pan, to prevent overheating of the vehicle floor.

7. Engage the converter to the front pipe, then install the catalytic converter-to-mounting bracket bolts.

8. Install the catalytic converter-to-front pipe clamp and tighten the nuts.

9. Engage the muffler to the catalytic converter and install the converter-to-muffler bolts.

➡Be sure to use a sealing compound such as 1051249 or equivalent, at the slip joint connection.

10. Tighten the fasteners taking care not to damage the pipe sealing surfaces when tightening the retaining clamps.

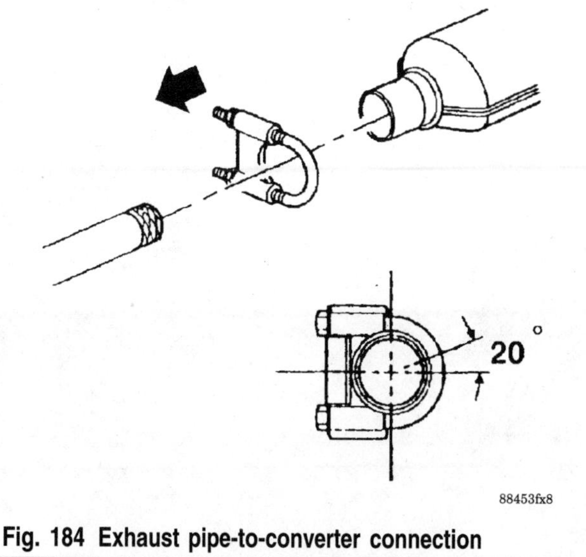

Fig. 184 Exhaust pipe-to-converter connection

11. Remove the jackstands and carefully lower the truck.
12. Start the engine and check for exhaust leaks.

Muffler

REMOVAL & INSTALLATION

➡Safety glasses should be worn at all times when working on or near the exhaust system. Older exhaust systems will almost always be covered with loose rust particles which will shower you when disturbed. These particles are more than a nuisance and could injure your eye.

1. Raise and support the front of the truck safely using jackstands.
2. Spray all fasteners which are to be disconnected using a penetrating oil.
3. Remove the catalytic converter-to-muffler flange bolts and separate the items.
4. Remove the intermediate and rear tail pipe-to-bracket clamp nuts/bolts.
5. Remove the muffler bracket-to-chassis bolts and lower the muffler from the vehicle.

To install:

6. Coat the slip joints with GM Sealing Compound No. 1051249 or equivalent, and loosely install the components onto the vehicle.
7. After aligning the components, tighten the connecting bolts and clamps, taking care not to distort the sealing surfaces.
8. Remove the jackstands and carefully lower the vehicle.
9. Start the engine and check for exhaust leaks.

ENGINE REBUILDING SPECIFICATIONS

Component	US	Metric
Camshaft		
Intake Lobe lift		
2.2L Engines		
1994-97	0.288 in.	7.315mm
1994-95 (VIN Z)	0.234 in.	5.94mm
1994-95 (VIN W)	0.288 in.	7.315mm
1996	0.2763 in.	7.018mm
1997	0.286-0.290 in.	0.0726-0.0736mm
Exhaust Lobe lift		
1994-95 (VIN Z)	0.257 in.	6.53mm
1994-95 (VIN W)	0.294 in.	0.746mm
1996	0.2763 in.	0.7018mm
1997	0.292-0.296 in.	0.0741-0.0751mm
Journal Diameter		
2.2L Engines		
1994-97	1.8682-1.8692 in.	47.45-47.48mm
4.3L Engines		
1994-95	1.8682-1.8692 in.	47.45-47.48mm
1996	1.8677-1.8697 in.	47.44-47.48mm
1997	1.8682-1.8692 in.	47.45-47.47mm
Endplay		
2.2L Engines		
1994-97	0.0015-0.005 in.	0.0381-0.0127mm
4.3L Engines		
1994-97	0.001-0.009 in.	0.0254-0.022mm
Crankshaft/Connecting Rods		
Journal Diameter		
2.2L Engines		
1994-97	2.495-2.4954 in.	63.373-63.383mm
4.3L Engines		
1994-95 (VIN Z)		
#1	2.4484-2.4493 in.	62.19-62.21mm
#2, #3	2.4481-2.4490 in.	62.18-62.20mm
#4	2.2979-2.2994 in.	58.37-58.40mm
1994-97 (VINS W and X)		
#1	2.4488-2.4495 in.	62.19-62.21mm
#2, #3	2.4485-2.4494 in.	62.19-62.21mm
#4	2.24480-2.4489 in.	62.18-62.20mm
Bearing Oil Clearance		
4.3L Engines		
1994-95		
#1	0.0008-0.0020 in.	0.02-0.05mm
#2, #3	0.0011-0.0023 in.	0.03-0.06mm
#4	0.0017-0.0032 in.	0.04-0.08mm
1996		
#1	0.0010-0.0015 in.	0.0254-0.0381mm
#2, #3	0.0010-0.0025 in.	0.0254-0.0635mm
#4	0.0025-0.0035 in.	0.0635-0.0889mm
1997		
#1	0.0010-0.0015 in.	0.0254-0.0381mm
#2, #3, #4	0.0010-0.0025 in.	0.0254-0.0635mm

88453C07

ENGINE REBUILDING SPECIFICATIONS

Component	US	Metric
Endplay		
2.2L Engines		
1994-97	0.002-0.007 in.	0.050-0.17mm
4.3L Engines		
1994-97	0.002-0.006 in.	0.05-0.15mm
Runout		
4.3L Engines	0.001 in (max)	0.03mm (max)
Crankpin Diameter		
2.2L Engines	1.9983-1.9994 in.	50.756-50.784mm
4.3L Engines	2.2487-2.2497 in.	57.12-57.14 mm
Connecting Rod Bearing Clearance		
2.2L Engines		
1994-97	0.00098-0.0031 in.	0.0248-0.0787mm
4.3L Engines		
1994-95	0.0013-0.0035 in.	0.03-0.09mm
1996-97	0.0010-0.0030 in.	0.0254-0.0762mm
Connecting Rod Side Clearance		
2.2L Engines	0.0039-0.0149 in.	0.10-0.38mm
1994-97		
4.3L Engines		
1994	0.006-0.014 in.	0.16-0.35mm
1995	0.015-0.046 in.	0.38-1.16mm
1996-97	0.006-0.017 in.	0.16-0.43mm
Cylinder Bore		
Diameter		
2.2L Engines		
1994-97	3.5036-3.5043 in.	88.991-89.009mm
4.3L Engines		
1994-97	4.0007-4.0017 in.	101.62-101.64mm
Out-of-Round		
2.2L Engines		
1994-97	0.005 in.	0.013mm
4.3L Engines		
1994-97	0.001 in. (max)	0.03mm (max)
Pistons/Rings		
Piston Clearance		
4.3L Engines	0.0007-0.0017 in.	0.018-0.043mm
Ring Groove Clearance		
2.2L Engines		
1994-97		
1st	0.0019-0.0027 in.	0.05-0.068mm
2nd	0.0019-0.0027 in.	0.05-0.068mm
Oil	0.0019-0.0082 in.	0.05-0.20mm
4.3L Engines		
1994-95		
1st	0.0012-0.0032 in.	0.03-0.08mm
2nd	0.0010-0.0020 in.	0.0254-0.05mm
Oil	0.002-0.007 in.	0.05-0.17mm
1996-97		
1st	0.02-0.06 in.	0.050-0.15mm
2nd	0.04-0.08 in.	0.10-0.20mm
Oil	0.002-0.007 in.	0.050-0.17mm
Piston Pin Diameter		
2.2L Engines		
1994-97	0.08000-0.8002 in.	20.320-20.325mm
4.3L Engines		
1994-95	0.9270-0.9271 in.	23.545-23.553mm
1996-97	0.9267-0.9271 in.	23.538-23.553mm
Piston Pin Clearance		
2.2L Engines		
1994-96	0.0004-0.0009 in.	0.0101-0.0228mm

88453C08

ENGINE REBUILDING SPECIFICATIONS

Component	US	Metric
1997	0.0003-0.0007 in.	0.008-0.018mm
4.3L Engines		
1994-97	0.0002-0.0007 in.	0.005-0.017mm
Piston Pin Fit		
2.2L Engines		
1994-97	0.00098-0.0017 in.	0.025-0.045mm
4.3L Engines		
1994-97	0.0008-00.0016 in. (interference)	0.008-0.031mm
Valves		
Face angle		
2.2L Engines		
1994-97	45°	
4.3L Engines		
1994-97	45°	
Seat Angle		
All Engines	46°	
Seat Runout		
All Engines	0.002 in. (max)	0.05mm
Stem Clearance		
Intake Valve		
All Engines	0.0010-0.0027 in.	0.025-0.068mm
Exhaust Valve		
2.2L Engines	0.001-0.003 in.	0.025-0.076mm
4.3L Engines		
1994-95	0.0010-0.0027 in.	0.025-0.068mm
1996-97	0.002 in. (Max)	0.05mm
Spring Free Length		
2.2L Engines	1.94	49.27mm
4.3L Engines		
1994	1.86 in.	47.24mm
1995-97	2.03 in.	49.28mm
Spring Pressure		
Closed		
2.2L Engines	78 lbs. @ 1.70 in.	352 N @ 43mm
4.3L Engines	76-84 lbs. @ 1.78 in.	338-373 N @ 43mm
Open		
2.2L Engines	220-236 lbs. @ 1.278	979-1049 N @ 32.47mm
4.3L Engines		
1994-95	194-206 lbs. @ 1.25 in.	832-903 N @ 32mm
1996-97	187-203 lb. @ 1.27 in.	756-801N @ 35.56mm
Spring Installed Height		
4.3L Engines	1.690-1.710 in.	42.92-43.43mm

88453C09

TORQUE SPECIFICATIONS

Component	US	Metric
Exhaust Manifold		
2.2L Engine		
1994-97		
nuts	115 inch lbs.	13 Nm
studs	89 inch lbs.	10 Nm
4.3L Engine		
1994-95		
Center Bolts	26 ft. lbs.	36 Nm
All Other Bolts	20 ft. lbs	28 Nm
1996-97		
Stud and Bolt		
First Pass	11 ft. lbs.	15 Nm
Final Pass	22 ft. lbs.	30 Nm
Intake Manifold		
2.2L Engine		
1994-97		
lower manifold Nuts	24 ft. lbs.	33 Nm
lower manifold Studs	89 inch lbs.	10 Nm
upper manifold bolts	22 ft. lbs.	30 Nm
4.3L Engine		
1994-95		
manifold bolts (VIN Z)	35 ft. lbs.	47 Nm
lower manifold bolts (VIN W)	35 ft. lbs.	47 Nm
1996-97		
lower manifold bolts		
first pass	27 inch lbs.	3 Nm
second pass	106 inch lbs.	12 Nm
final pass	11 ft. lbs	15 Nm
upper manifold bolts		
first pass	44 inch lbs.	5 Nm
final pass	88 inch lbs.	10 Nm
Oil Pan		
2.2L Engine		
1994-97		
All fasteners	89 inch lbs.	10 Nm
4.3L Engine		
1994-95		
Nuts	17 ft. lbs.	23 Nm
Bolts	97 inch lbs.	11 Nm
1996-97		
Nuts	17 ft. lbs.	23 Nm
Bolts	18 ft. lbs.	25 Nm
Oil Pump		
2.2L Engine		
1994-97	32 ft. lbs.	43 Nm
4.3L Engine		
1994-97	65 ft. lbs	90 Nm

88453C10

TORQUE SPECIFICATIONS

Component	US	Metric
Rocker Arm/Valve Cover		
2.2L Engine		
1994-97	89 inch lbs.	10 Nm
4.3L Engine		
1994-95	89 inch lbs.	10 Nm
1996-97	106 inch lbs.	12 Nm
Rocker Arms		
2.2L Engine		
1994-97	22 ft. lbs.	30 Nm
4.3L Engine		
1994-95		
Nuts	20 ft. lbs.	27 Nm
Studs	35 ft. lbs.	47 Nm
1996-97		
Nuts	20 ft. lbs.	25 Nm
Thermostat Housing		
2.2L Engine		
1994-97	89 inch lbs.	10 Nm
4.3L Engine		
1994-95		
(VIN Z)	21 ft. lbs.	28 Nm
(VIN W)	14 ft. lbs.	19 Nm
1996-97	21 ft. lbs.	28 Nm
Timing Chain Front Cover		
2.2L Engine		
1994-97	97 inch. lbs	11 Nm
4.3L Engine		
1994-95	124 inch lbs.	14 Nm
1996-97	106 inch lbs.	12 Nm
Water Pump		
2.2L Engine		
1994-97		
Bolts	18 ft. lbs.	25 Nm
4.3L Engine		
1994-95	30 ft. lbs.	41 Nm
1996-97	33 ft. lbs.	45 Nm

88453C11

USING A VACUUM GAUGE

White needle = steady needle ***Dark needle = drifting needle***

The vacuum gauge is one of the most useful and easy-to-use diagnostic tools. It is inexpensive, easy to hook up, and provides valuable information about the condition of your engine.

Indication: ***Normal engine in good condition***

Gauge reading: ***Steady, from 17–22 in./Hg.***

Indication: ***Sticking valve or ignition miss***

Gauge reading: ***Needle fluctuates from 15–20 in./Hg. at idle***

Indication: ***Late ignition or valve timing, low compression, stuck throttle valve, leaking carburetor or manifold gasket.***

Gauge reading: ***Low (15–20 in./Hg.) but steady***

Indication: ***Improper carburetor adjustment, or minor intake leak at carburetor or manifold***

NOTE: Bad fuel injector O-rings may also cause this reading.

Gauge reading: ***Drifting needle***

Indication: ***Weak valve springs, worn valve stem guides, or leaky cylinder head gasket (vibrating excessively at all speeds).***

NOTE: A plugged catalytic converter may also cause this reading.

Gauge reading: ***Needle fluctuates as engine speed increases***

Indication: ***Burnt valve or improper valve clearance. The needle will drop when the defective valve operates.***

Gauge reading: ***Steady needle, but drops regularly***

Indication: ***Choked muffler or obstruction in system. Speed up the engine. Choked muffler will exhibit a slow drop of vacuum to zero.***

Gauge reading: ***Gradual drop in reading at idle***

Indication: ***Worn valve guides***

Gauge reading: ***Needle vibrates excessively at idle, but steadies as engine speed increases***

tccs3c01

Troubleshooting Engine Mechanical Problems

Problem	Cause	Solution
External oil leaks	• Cylinder head cover RTV sealant broken or improperly seated	• Replace sealant; inspect cylinder head cover sealant flange and cylinder head sealant surface for distortion and cracks
	• Oil filler cap leaking or missing	• Replace cap
	• Oil filter gasket broken or improperly seated	• Replace oil filter
	• Oil pan side gasket broken, improperly seated or opening in RTV sealant	• Replace gasket or repair opening in sealant; inspect oil pan gasket flange for distortion
	• Oil pan front oil seal broken or improperly seated	• Replace seal; inspect timing case cover and oil pan seal flange for distortion
	• Oil pan rear oil seal broken or improperly seated	• Replace seal; inspect oil pan rear oil seal flange; inspect rear main bearing cap for cracks, plugged oil return channels, or distortion in seal groove
	• Timing case cover oil seal broken or improperly seated	• Replace seal
	• Excess oil pressure because of restricted PCV valve	• Replace PCV valve
	• Oil pan drain plug loose or has stripped threads	• Repair as necessary and tighten
	• Rear oil gallery plug loose	• Use appropriate sealant on gallery plug and tighten
	• Rear camshaft plug loose or improperly seated	• Seat camshaft plug or replace and seal, as necessary
Excessive oil consumption	• Oil level too high	• Drain oil to specified level
	• Oil with wrong viscosity being used	• Replace with specified oil
	• PCV valve stuck closed	• Replace PCV valve
	• Valve stem oil deflectors (or seals) are damaged, missing, or incorrect type	• Replace valve stem oil deflectors
	• Valve stems or valve guides worn	• Measure stem-to-guide clearance and repair as necessary
	• Poorly fitted or missing valve cover baffles	• Replace valve cover
	• Piston rings broken or missing	• Replace broken or missing rings
	• Scuffed piston	• Replace piston
	• Incorrect piston ring gap	• Measure ring gap, repair as necessary
	• Piston rings sticking or excessively loose in grooves	• Measure ring side clearance, repair as necessary
	• Compression rings installed upside down	• Repair as necessary
	• Cylinder walls worn, scored, or glazed	• Repair as necessary

tccs3c02

Troubleshooting Engine Mechanical Problems

Problem	Cause	Solution
Excessive oil consumption (cont.)	• Piston ring gaps not properly staggered • Excessive main or connecting rod bearing clearance	• Repair as necessary • Measure bearing clearance, repair as necessary
No oil pressure	• Low oil level • Oil pressure gauge, warning lamp or sending unit inaccurate • Oil pump malfunction • Oil pressure relief valve sticking • Oil passages on pressure side of pump obstructed • Oil pickup screen or tube obstructed • Loose oil inlet tube	• Add oil to correct level • Replace oil pressure gauge or warning lamp • Replace oil pump • Remove and inspect oil pressure relief valve assembly • Inspect oil passages for obstruction • Inspect oil pickup for obstruction • Tighten or seal inlet tube
Low oil pressure	• Low oil level • Inaccurate gauge, warning lamp or sending unit • Oil excessively thin because of dilution, poor quality, or improper grade • Excessive oil temperature • Oil pressure relief spring weak or sticking • Oil inlet tube and screen assembly has restriction or air leak • Excessive oil pump clearance • Excessive main, rod, or camshaft bearing clearance	• Add oil to correct level • Replace oil pressure gauge or warning lamp • Drain and refill crankcase with recommended oil • Correct cause of overheating engine • Remove and inspect oil pressure relief valve assembly • Remove and inspect oil inlet tube and screen assembly. (Fill inlet tube with lacquer thinner to locate leaks.) • Measure clearances • Measure bearing clearances, repair as necessary
High oil pressure	• Improper oil viscosity • Oil pressure gauge or sending unit inaccurate • Oil pressure relief valve sticking closed	• Drain and refill crankcase with correct viscosity oil • Replace oil pressure gauge • Remove and inspect oil pressure relief valve assembly
Main bearing noise	• Insufficient oil supply • Main bearing clearance excessive • Bearing insert missing • Crankshaft end-play excessive • Improperly tightened main bearing cap bolts • Loose flywheel or drive plate • Loose or damaged vibration damper	• Inspect for low oil level and low oil pressure • Measure main bearing clearance, repair as necessary • Replace missing insert • Measure end-play, repair as necessary • Tighten bolts with specified torque • Tighten flywheel or drive plate attaching bolts • Repair as necessary

tccs3c03

Troubleshooting Engine Mechanical Problems

Problem	Cause	Solution
Connecting rod bearing noise	• Insufficient oil supply	• Inspect for low oil level and low oil pressure
	• Carbon build-up on piston	• Remove carbon from piston crown
	• Bearing clearance excessive or bearing missing	• Measure clearance, repair as necessary
	• Crankshaft connecting rod journal out-of-round	• Measure journal dimensions, repair or replace as necessary
	• Misaligned connecting rod or cap	• Repair as necessary
	• Connecting rod bolts tightened improperly	• Tighten bolts with specified torque
Piston noise	• Piston-to-cylinder wall clearance excessive (scuffed piston)	• Measure clearance and examine piston
	• Cylinder walls excessively tapered or out-of-round	• Measure cylinder wall dimensions, rebore cylinder
	• Piston ring broken	• Replace all rings on piston
	• Loose or seized piston pin	• Measure piston-to-pin clearance, repair as necessary
	• Connecting rods misaligned	• Measure rod alignment, straighten or replace
	• Piston ring side clearance excessively loose or tight	• Measure ring side clearance, repair as necessary
	• Carbon build-up on piston is excessive	• Remove carbon from piston
Valve actuating component noise	• Insufficient oil supply	• Check for: (a) Low oil level (b) Low oil pressure (c) Wrong hydraulic tappets (d) Restricted oil gallery (e) Excessive tappet to bore clearance
	• Rocker arms or pivots worn	• Replace worn rocker arms or pivots
	• Foreign objects or chips in hydraulic tappets	• Clean tappets
	• Excessive tappet leak-down	• Replace valve tappet
	• Tappet face worn	• Replace tappet; inspect corresponding cam lobe for wear
	• Broken or cocked valve springs	• Properly seat cocked springs; replace broken springs
	• Stem-to-guide clearance excessive	• Measure stem-to-guide clearance, repair as required
	• Valve bent	• Replace valve
	• Loose rocker arms	• Check and repair as necessary
	• Valve seat runout excessive	• Regrind valve seat/valves
	• Missing valve lock	• Install valve lock
	• Excessive engine oil	• Correct oil level

tccs3c04

Troubleshooting Engine Performance

Problem	Cause	Solution
Hard starting (engine cranks normally)	• Faulty engine control system component	• Repair or replace as necessary
	• Faulty fuel pump	• Replace fuel pump
	• Faulty fuel system component	• Repair or replace as necessary
	• Faulty ignition coil	• Test and replace as necessary
	• Improper spark plug gap	• Adjust gap
	• Incorrect ignition timing	• Adjust timing
	• Incorrect valve timing	• Check valve timing; repair as necessary
Rough idle or stalling	• Incorrect curb or fast idle speed	• Adjust curb or fast idle speed (If possible)
	• Incorrect ignition timing	• Adjust timing to specification
	• Improper feedback system operation	• Refer to Chapter 4
	• Faulty EGR valve operation	• Test EGR system and replace as necessary
	• Faulty PCV valve air flow	• Test PCV valve and replace as necessary
	• Faulty TAC vacuum motor or valve	• Repair as necessary
	• Air leak into manifold vacuum	• Inspect manifold vacuum connections and repair as necessary
	• Faulty distributor rotor or cap	• Replace rotor or cap (Distributor systems only)
	• Improperly seated valves	• Test cylinder compression, repair as necessary
	• Incorrect ignition wiring	• Inspect wiring and correct as necessary
	• Faulty ignition coil	• Test coil and replace as necessary
	• Restricted air vent or idle passages	• Clean passages
	• Restricted air cleaner	• Clean or replace air cleaner filter element
Faulty low-speed operation	• Restricted idle air vents and passages	• Clean air vents and passages
	• Restricted air cleaner	• Clean or replace air cleaner filter element
	• Faulty spark plugs	• Clean or replace spark plugs
	• Dirty, corroded, or loose ignition secondary circuit wire connections	• Clean or tighten secondary circuit wire connections
	• Improper feedback system operation	• Refer to Chapter 4
	• Faulty ignition coil high voltage wire	• Replace ignition coil high voltage wire (Distributor systems only)
	• Faulty distributor cap	• Replace cap (Distributor systems only)
Faulty acceleration	• Incorrect ignition timing	• Adjust timing
	• Faulty fuel system component	• Repair or replace as necessary
	• Faulty spark plug(s)	• Clean or replace spark plug(s)
	• Improperly seated valves	• Test cylinder compression, repair as necessary
	• Faulty ignition coil	• Test coil and replace as necessary

tccs3c05

Troubleshooting Engine Performance

Problem	Cause	Solution
Faulty acceleration (cont.)	• Improper feedback system operation	• Refer to Chapter 4
Faulty high speed operation	• Incorrect ignition timing	• Adjust timing (if possible)
	• Faulty advance mechanism	• Check advance mechanism and repair as necessary (Distributor systems only)
	• Low fuel pump volume	• Replace fuel pump
	• Wrong spark plug air gap or wrong plug	• Adjust air gap or install correct plug
	• Partially restricted exhaust manifold, exhaust pipe, catalytic converter, muffler, or tailpipe	• Eliminate restriction
	• Restricted vacuum passages	• Clean passages
	• Restricted air cleaner	• Cleaner or replace filter element as necessary
	• Faulty distributor rotor or cap	• Replace rotor or cap (Distributor systems only)
	• Faulty ignition coil	• Test coil and replace as necessary
	• Improperly seated valve(s)	• Test cylinder compression, repair as necessary
	• Faulty valve spring(s)	• Inspect and test valve spring tension, replace as necessary
	• Incorrect valve timing	• Check valve timing and repair as necessary
	• Intake manifold restricted	• Remove restriction or replace manifold
	• Worn distributor shaft	• Replace shaft (Distributor systems only)
	• Improper feedback system operation	• Refer to Chapter 4
Misfire at all speeds	• Faulty spark plug(s)	• Clean or relace spark plug(s)
	• Faulty spark plug wire(s)	• Replace as necessary
	• Faulty distributor cap or rotor	• Replace cap or rotor (Distributor systems only)
	• Faulty ignition coil	• Test coil and replace as necessary
	• Primary ignition circuit shorted or open intermittently	• Troubleshoot primary circuit and repair as necessary
	• Improperly seated valve(s)	• Test cylinder compression, repair as necessary
	• Faulty hydraulic tappet(s)	• Clean or replace tappet(s)
	• Improper feedback system operation	• Refer to Chapter 4
	• Faulty valve spring(s)	• Inspect and test valve spring tension, repair as necessary
	• Worn camshaft lobes	• Replace camshaft
	• Air leak into manifold	• Check manifold vacuum and repair as necessary
	• Fuel pump volume or pressure low	• Replace fuel pump
	• Blown cylinder head gasket	• Replace gasket
	• Intake or exhaust manifold passage(s) restricted	• Pass chain through passage(s) and repair as necessary
Power not up to normal	• Incorrect ignition timing	• Adjust timing
	• Faulty distributor rotor	• Replace rotor (Distributor systems only)

tccs3c06

Troubleshooting Engine Performance

Problem	Cause	Solution
Power not up to normal (cont.)	• Incorrect spark plug gap	• Adjust gap
	• Faulty fuel pump	• Replace fuel pump
	• Faulty fuel pump	• Replace fuel pump
	• Incorrect valve timing	• Check valve timing and repair as necessary
	• Faulty ignition coil	• Test coil and replace as necessary
	• Faulty ignition wires	• Test wires and replace as necessary
	• Improperly seated valves	• Test cylinder compression and repair as necessary
	• Blown cylinder head gasket	• Replace gasket
	• Leaking piston rings	• Test compression and repair as necessary
	• Improper feedback system operation	• Refer to Chapter 4
Intake backfire	• Improper ignition timing	• Adjust timing
	• Defective EGR component	• Repair as necessary
	• Defective TAC vacuum motor or valve	• Repair as necessary
Exhaust backfire	• Air leak into manifold vacuum	• Check manifold vacuum and repair as necessary
	• Faulty air injection diverter valve	• Test diverter valve and replace as necessary
	• Exhaust leak	• Locate and eliminate leak
Ping or spark knock	• Incorrect ignition timing	• Adjust timing
	• Distributor advance malfunction	• Inspect advance mechanism and repair as necessary (Distributor systems only)
	• Excessive combustion chamber deposits	• Remove with combustion chamber cleaner
	• Air leak into manifold vacuum	• Check manifold vacuum and repair as necessary
	• Excessively high compression	• Test compression and repair as necessary
	• Fuel octane rating excessively low	• Try alternate fuel source
	• Sharp edges in combustion chamber	• Grind smooth
	• EGR valve not functioning properly	• Test EGR system and replace as necessary
Surging (at cruising to top speeds)	• Low fuel pump pressure or volume	• Replace fuel pump
	• Improper PCV valve air flow	• Test PCV valve and replace as necessary
	• Air leak into manifold vacuum	• Check manifold vacuum and repair as necessary
	• Incorrect spark advance	• Test and replace as necessary
	• Restricted fuel filter	• Replace fuel filter
	• Restricted air cleaner	• Clean or replace air cleaner filter element
	• EGR valve not functioning properly	• Test EGR system and replace as necessary
	• Improper feedback system operation	• Refer to Chapter 4

tccs3c07

Troubleshooting the Serpentine Drive Belt

Problem	Cause	Solution
Tension sheeting fabric failure (woven fabric on outside circumference of belt has cracked or separated from body of belt)	• Grooved or backside idler pulley diameters are less than minimum recommended	• Replace pulley(s) not conforming to specification
	• Tension sheeting contacting (rubbing) stationary object	• Correct rubbing condition
	• Excessive heat causing woven fabric to age	• Replace belt
	• Tension sheeting splice has fractured	• Replace belt
Noise (objectional squeal, squeak, or rumble is heard or felt while drive belt is in operation)	• Belt slippage	• Adjust belt
	• Bearing noise	• Locate and repair
	• Belt misalignment	• Align belt/pulley(s)
	• Belt-to-pulley mismatch	• Install correct belt
	• Driven component inducing vibration	• Locate defective driven component and repair
	• System resonant frequency inducing vibration	• Vary belt tension within specifications. Replace belt.
Rib chunking (one or more ribs has separated from belt body)	• Foreign objects imbedded in pulley grooves	• Remove foreign objects from pulley grooves
	• Installation damage	• Replace belt
	• Drive loads in excess of design specifications	• Adjust belt tension
	• Insufficient internal belt adhesion	• Replace belt
Rib or belt wear (belt ribs contact bottom of pulley grooves)	• Pulley(s) misaligned	• Align pulley(s)
	• Mismatch of belt and pulley groove widths	• Replace belt
	• Abrasive environment	• Replace belt
	• Rusted pulley(s)	• Clean rust from pulley(s)
	• Sharp or jagged pulley groove tips	• Replace pulley
	• Rubber deteriorated	• Replace belt
Longitudinal belt cracking (cracks between two ribs)	• Belt has mistracked from pulley groove	• Replace belt
	• Pulley groove tip has worn away rubber-to-tensile member	• Replace belt
Belt slips	• Belt slipping because of insufficient tension	• Adjust tension
	• Belt or pulley subjected to substance (belt dressing, oil, ethylene glycol) that has reduced friction	• Replace belt and clean pulleys
	• Driven component bearing failure	• Replace faulty component bearing
	• Belt glazed and hardened from heat and excessive slippage	• Replace belt
"Groove jumping" (belt does not maintain correct position on pulley, or turns over and/or runs off pulleys)	• Insufficient belt tension	• Adjust belt tension
	• Pulley(s) not within design tolerance	• Replace pulley(s)
	• Foreign object(s) in grooves	• Remove foreign objects from grooves

tccs3c09

Troubleshooting the Serpentine Drive Belt

Problem	Cause	Solution
"Groove jumping" (belt does not maintain correct position on pulley, or turns over and/or runs off pulleys)	• Excessive belt speed • Pulley misalignment • Belt-to-pulley profile mismatched • Belt cordline is distorted	• Avoid excessive engine acceleration • Align pulley(s) • Install correct belt • Replace belt
Belt broken (Note: identify and correct problem before replacement belt is installed)	• Excessive tension • Tensile members damaged during belt installation • Belt turnover • Severe pulley misalignment • Bracket, pulley, or bearing failure	• Replace belt and adjust tension to specification • Replace belt • Replace belt • Align pulley(s) • Replace defective component and belt
Cord edge failure (tensile member exposed at edges of belt or separated from belt body)	• Excessive tension • Drive pulley misalignment • Belt contacting stationary object • Pulley irregularities • Improper pulley construction • Insufficient adhesion between tensile member and rubber matrix	• Adjust belt tension • Align pulley • Correct as necessary • Replace pulley • Replace pulley • Replace belt and adjust tension to specifications
Sporadic rib cracking (multiple cracks in belt ribs at random intervals)	• Ribbed pulley(s) diameter less than minimum specification • Backside bend flat pulley(s) diameter less than minimum • Excessive heat condition causing rubber to harden • Excessive belt thickness • Belt overcured • Excessive tension	• Replace pulley(s) • Replace pulley(s) • Correct heat condition as necessary • Replace belt • Replace belt • Adjust belt tension

tccs3c10

Troubleshooting the Cooling System

Problem	Cause	Solution
High temperature gauge indication—overheating	• Coolant level low	• Replenish coolant
	• Improper fan operation	• Repair or replace as necessary
	• Radiator hose(s) collapsed	• Replace hose(s)
	• Radiator airflow blocked	• Remove restriction (bug screen, fog lamps, etc.)
	• Faulty pressure cap	• Replace pressure cap
	• Ignition timing incorrect	• Adjust ignition timing
	• Air trapped in cooling system	• Purge air
	• Heavy traffic driving	• Operate at fast idle in neutral intermittently to cool engine
	• Incorrect cooling system component(s) installed	• Install proper component(s)
	• Faulty thermostat	• Replace thermostat
	• Water pump shaft broken or impeller loose	• Replace water pump
	• Radiator tubes clogged	• Flush radiator
	• Cooling system clogged	• Flush system
	• Casting flash in cooling passages	• Repair or replace as necessary. Flash may be visible by removing cooling system components or removing core plugs.
	• Brakes dragging	• Repair brakes
	• Excessive engine friction	• Repair engine
	• Antifreeze concentration over 68%	• Lower antifreeze concentration percentage
	• Missing air seals	• Replace air seals
	• Faulty gauge or sending unit	• Repair or replace faulty component
	• Loss of coolant flow caused by leakage or foaming	• Repair or replace leaking component, replace coolant
	• Viscous fan drive failed	• Replace unit
Low temperature indication—undercooling	• Thermostat stuck open	• Replace thermostat
	• Faulty gauge or sending unit	• Repair or replace faulty component
Coolant loss—boilover	• Overfilled cooling system	• Reduce coolant level to proper specification
	• Quick shutdown after hard (hot) run	• Allow engine to run at fast idle prior to shutdown
	• Air in system resulting in occasional "burping" of coolant	• Purge system
	• Insufficient antifreeze allowing coolant boiling point to be too low	• Add antifreeze to raise boiling point
	• Antifreeze deteriorated because of age or contamination	• Replace coolant
	• Leaks due to loose hose clamps, loose nuts, bolts, drain plugs, faulty hoses, or defective radiator	• Pressure test system to locate source of leak(s) then repair as necessary

tccs3c11

Troubleshooting the Cooling System (cont.)

Problem	Cause	Solution
Coolant loss—boilover	• Faulty head gasket • Cracked head, manifold, or block • Faulty radiator cap	• Replace head gasket • Replace as necessary • Replace cap
Coolant entry into crankcase or cylinder(s)	• Faulty head gasket • Crack in head, manifold or block	• Replace head gasket • Replace as necessary
Coolant recovery system inoperative	• Coolant level low • Leak in system • Pressure cap not tight or seal missing, or leaking • Pressure cap defective • Overflow tube clogged or leaking • Recovery bottle vent restricted	• Replenish coolant to FULL mark • Pressure test to isolate leak and repair as necessary • Repair as necessary • Replace cap • Repair as necessary • Remove restriction
Noise	• Fan contacting shroud • Loose water pump impeller • Glazed fan belt • Loose fan belt • Rough surface on drive pulley • Water pump bearing worn • Belt alignment	• Reposition shroud and inspect engine mounts (on electric fans inspect assembly) • Replace pump • Apply silicone or replace belt • Adjust fan belt tension • Replace pulley • Remove belt to isolate. Replace pump. • Check pulley alignment. Repair as necessary.
No coolant flow through heater core	• Restricted return inlet in water pump • Heater hose collapsed or restricted • Restricted heater core • Restricted outlet in thermostat housing • Intake manifold bypass hole in cylinder head restricted • Faulty heater control valve • Intake manifold coolant passage restricted	• Remove restriction • Remove restriction or replace hose • Remove restriction or replace core • Remove flash or restriction • Remove restriction • Replace valve • Remove restriction or replace intake manifold

NOTE: *Immediately after shutdown, the engine enters a condition known as heat soak. This is caused by the cooling system being inoperative while engine temperature is still high. If coolant temperature rises above boiling point, expansion and pressure may push some coolant out of the radiator overflow tube. If this does not occur frequently it is considered normal.*

tccs3c12

4

DRIVEABILITY AND EMISSION CONTROLS

AIR POLLUTION

The earth's atmosphere, at or near sea level, consists approximately of 78 percent nitrogen, 21 percent oxygen and 1 percent other gases. If it were possible to remain in this state, 100 percent clean air would result. However, many varied sources allow other gases and particulates to mix with the clean air, causing our atmosphere to become unclean or polluted.

Some of these pollutants are visible while others are invisible, with each having the capability of causing distress to the eyes, ears, throat, skin and respiratory system. Should these pollutants become concentrated in a specific area and under certain conditions, death could result due to the displacement or chemical change of the oxygen content in the air. These pollutants can also cause great damage to the environment and to the many man made objects that are exposed to the elements.

To better understand the causes of air pollution, the pollutants can be categorized into 3 separate types, natural, industrial and automotive.

Natural Pollutants

Natural pollution has been present on earth since before man appeared and continues to be a factor when discussing air pollution, although it causes only a small percentage of the overall pollution problem. It is the direct result of decaying organic matter, wind born smoke and particulates from such natural events as plain and forest fires (ignited by heat or lightning), volcanic ash, sand and dust which can spread over a large area of the countryside.

Such a phenomenon of natural pollution has been seen in the form of volcanic eruptions, with the resulting plume of smoke, steam and volcanic ash blotting out the sun's rays as it spreads and rises higher into the atmosphere. As it travels into the atmosphere the upper air currents catch and carry the smoke and ash, while condensing the steam back into water vapor. As the water vapor, smoke and ash travel on their journey, the smoke dissipates into the atmosphere while the ash and moisture settle back to earth in a trail hundreds of miles long. In some cases, lives are lost and millions of dollars of property damage result.

Industrial Pollutants

Industrial pollution is caused primarily by industrial processes, the burning of coal, oil and natural gas, which in turn produce smoke and fumes. Because the burning fuels contain large amounts of sulfur, the principal ingredients of smoke and fumes are sulfur dioxide and particulate matter. This type of pollutant occurs most severely during still, damp and cool weather, such as at night. Even in its less severe form, this pollutant is not confined to just cities. Because of air movements, the pollutants move for miles over the surrounding countryside, leaving in its path a barren and unhealthy environment for all living things.

Working with Federal, State and Local mandated regulations and by carefully monitoring emissions, big business has greatly reduced the amount of pollutant introduced from its industrial sources, striving to obtain an acceptable level. Because of the mandated industrial emission clean up, many land areas and streams in and around the cities that were formerly barren of vegetation and life, have now begun to move back in the direction of nature's intended balance.

Automotive Pollutants

The third major source of air pollution is automotive emissions. The emissions from the internal combustion engines were not an appreciable problem years ago because of the small number of registered vehicles and the nation's small highway system. However, during the early 1950's, the trend of the American people was to move from the cities to the surrounding suburbs. This caused an immediate problem in transportation because the majority of suburbs were not afforded mass transit conveniences. This lack of transportation created an attractive market for the automobile manufacturers, which resulted in a dramatic increase in the number of vehicles produced and sold, along with a marked increase in highway construction between cities and the suburbs. Multi-vehicle families emerged with a growing emphasis placed on an individual vehicle per family member. As the increase in vehicle ownership and usage occurred, so did pollutant levels in and around the cities, as suburbanites drove daily to their businesses and employment, returning at the end of the day to their homes in the suburbs.

It was noted that a smoke and fog type haze was being formed and at times, remained in suspension over the cities, taking time to dissipate. At first this "smog," derived from the words "smoke" and "fog," was thought to result from industrial pollution but it was determined that automobile emissions shared the blame. It was discovered that when normal automobile emissions were exposed to sunlight for a period of time, complex chemical reactions would take place.

It is now known that smog is a photo chemical layer which develops when certain oxides of nitrogen (NOx) and unburned hydrocarbons (HC) from automobile emissions are exposed to sunlight. Pollution was more severe when smog would become stagnant over an area in which a warm layer of air settled over the top of the cooler air mass, trapping and holding the cooler mass at ground level. The trapped cooler air would keep the emissions from being dispersed and diluted through normal air flows. This type of air stagnation was given the name "Temperature Inversion."

TEMPERATURE INVERSION

In normal weather situations, surface air is warmed by heat radiating from the earth's surface and the sun's rays. This causes it to rise upward, into the atmosphere. Upon rising it will cool through a convection type heat exchange with the cooler upper air. As warm air rises, the surface pollutants are carried upward and dissipated into the atmosphere.

When a temperature inversion occurs, we find the higher air is no longer cooler, but is warmer than the surface air, causing the cooler surface air to become trapped. This warm air blanket can extend from above ground level to a few hundred or even a few thousand feet into the air. As the surface air is trapped, so are the pollutants, causing a severe smog condition. Should this stagnant air mass extend to a few thousand feet high, enough air movement with the inversion takes place to allow the smog layer to rise above ground level but the pollutants still cannot dissipate. This inversion can remain for days over an area, with the smog level only rising or lowering from ground level to a few hundred feet high. Meanwhile, the pollutant levels increase, causing eye irritation, respiratory problems, reduced visibility, plant damage and in some cases, even disease.

This inversion phenomenon was first noted in the Los Angeles, California area. The city lies in terrain resembling a basin and with certain weather conditions, a cold air mass is held in the basin while a warmer air mass covers it like a lid.

Because this type of condition was first documented as prevalent in the Los Angeles area, this type of trapped pollution was named Los Angeles Smog, although it occurs in other areas where a large concentration of automobiles are used and the air remains stagnant for any length of time.

HEAT TRANSFER

Consider the internal combustion engine as a machine in which raw materials must be placed so a finished product comes out. As in any machine operation, a certain amount of wasted material is formed. When we relate this to the internal combustion engine, we find that through the input of air and fuel, we obtain power during the combustion process to drive the vehicle. The by-product or waste of this power is, in part, heat and exhaust gases with which we must dispose.

The heat from the combustion process can rise to over 4000°F (2204°C). The dissipation of this heat is controlled by a ram air effect, the use of cooling fans to cause air flow and a liquid coolant solution surrounding the combustion area to transfer the heat of combustion through the cylinder walls and into the coolant. The coolant is then directed to a thin-finned, multi-tubed radiator, from which the excess heat is transferred to the atmosphere by 1 of the 3 heat transfer methods, conduction, convection or radiation.

The cooling of the combustion area is an important part in the control of exhaust emissions. To understand the behavior of the combustion and transfer of its heat, consider the air/fuel charge. It is ignited and the flame front burns progressively across the combustion chamber until the burning charge reaches the cylinder walls. Some of the fuel in contact with the walls is not hot enough to burn, thereby snuffing out or quenching the combustion process. This leaves unburned fuel in the combustion chamber. This unburned fuel is then forced out of the cylinder and into the exhaust system, along with the exhaust gases.

Many attempts have been made to minimize the amount of unburned fuel in the combustion chambers due to quenching, by increasing the coolant temperature and lessening the contact area of the coolant around the combustion area. However, design limitations within the combustion chambers prevent the complete burning of the air/fuel charge, so a certain amount of the unburned fuel is still expelled into the exhaust system, regardless of modifications to the engine.

AUTOMOTIVE EMISSIONS

Before emission controls were mandated on internal combustion engines, other sources of engine pollutants were discovered along with the exhaust emissions. It was determined that engine combustion exhaust produced approximately 60 percent of the total emission pollutants, fuel evaporation from the fuel tank and carburetor vents produced 20 percent, with the final 20 percent being produced through the crankcase as a by-product of the combustion process.

Exhaust Gases

The exhaust gases emitted into the atmosphere are a combination of burned and unburned fuel. To understand the exhaust emission and its composition, we must review some basic chemistry.

When the air/fuel mixture is introduced into the engine, we are mixing air, composed of nitrogen (78 percent), oxygen (21 percent) and other gases (1 percent) with the fuel, which is 100 percent hydrocarbons (HC), in a semi-controlled ratio. As the combustion process is accomplished, power is produced to move the vehicle while the heat of combustion is transferred to the cooling system. The exhaust gases are then composed of nitrogen, a diatomic gas (N_2), the same as was introduced in the engine, carbon dioxide (CO_2), the same gas that is used in beverage carbonation, and water vapor (H_2O). The nitrogen (N_2), for the most part, passes through the engine unchanged, while the oxygen (O_2) reacts (burns) with the hydrocarbons (HC) and produces the carbon dioxide (CO_2) and the water vapors (H_2O). If this chemical process would be the only process to take place, the exhaust emissions would be harmless. However, during the combustion process, other compounds are formed which are considered dangerous. These pollutants are hydrocarbons (HC), carbon monoxide (CO), oxides of nitrogen (NOx) oxides of sulfur (SOx) and engine particulates.

HYDROCARBONS

Hydrocarbons (HC) are essentially fuel which was not burned during the combustion process or which has escaped into the atmosphere through fuel evaporation. The main sources of incomplete combustion are rich air/fuel mixtures, low engine temperatures and improper spark timing. The main sources of hydrocarbon emission through fuel evaporation on most vehicles used to be the vehicle's fuel tank and carburetor float bowl.

To reduce combustion hydrocarbon emission, engine modifications were made to minimize dead space and surface area in the combustion chamber. In addition, the air/fuel mixture was made more lean through the improved control which feedback carburetion and fuel injection offers and by the addition of external controls to aid in further combustion of the hydrocarbons outside the engine. Two such methods were the addition of air injection systems, to inject fresh air into the exhaust manifolds and the installation of catalytic converters, units that are able to burn traces of hydrocarbons without affecting the internal combustion process or fuel economy.

To control hydrocarbon emissions through fuel evaporation, modifications were made to the fuel tank to allow storage of the fuel vapors during periods of engine shut-down. Modifications were also made to the air intake system so that at specific times during engine operation, these vapors may be purged and burned by blending them with the air/fuel mixture.

CARBON MONOXIDE

Carbon monoxide is formed when not enough oxygen is present during the combustion process to convert carbon (C) to carbon dioxide (CO_2). An increase in the carbon monoxide (CO) emission is normally accompanied by an increase in the hydrocarbon (HC) emission because of the lack of oxygen to completely burn all of the fuel mixture.

Carbon monoxide (CO) also increases the rate at which the photo chemical smog is formed by speeding up the conversion of nitric oxide (NO) to nitrogen dioxide (NO_2). To accomplish this, carbon monoxide (CO) combines with oxygen (O_2) and nitric oxide (NO) to produce carbon dioxide (CO_2) and nitrogen dioxide (NO_2). ($CO + O_2 + NO = CO_2 + NO_2$).

The dangers of carbon monoxide, which is an odorless and colorless toxic gas are many. When carbon monoxide is inhaled into the lungs and passed into the blood stream, oxygen is replaced by the carbon monoxide in the red blood cells, causing a reduction in the amount of oxygen supplied to the many parts of the body. This lack of oxygen causes headaches, lack of coordination, reduced mental alertness and, should the carbon monoxide concentration be high enough, death could result.

NITROGEN

Normally, nitrogen is an inert gas. When heated to approximately 2500°F (1371°C) through the combustion process, this gas becomes active and causes an increase in the nitric oxide (NO) emission.

Oxides of nitrogen (NOx) are composed of approximately 97-98 percent nitric oxide (NO). Nitric oxide is a colorless gas but when it is passed into the atmosphere, it combines with oxygen and forms nitrogen dioxide (NO_2). The nitrogen dioxide then combines with chemically active hydrocarbons (HC) and when in the presence of sunlight, causes the formation of photo-chemical smog.

Ozone

To further complicate matters, some of the nitrogen dioxide (NO_2) is broken apart by the sunlight to form nitric oxide and oxygen. (NO_2 + sunlight = NO + O). This single atom of oxygen then combines with diatomic (meaning 2 atoms) oxygen (O_2) to form ozone (O_3). Ozone is one of the smells associated with smog. It has a pungent and offensive odor, irritates the eyes and lung tissues, affects the growth of plant life and causes rapid deterioration of rubber products. Ozone can be formed by sunlight as well as electrical discharge into the air.

The most common discharge area on the automobile engine is the secondary ignition electrical system, especially when inferior quality spark plug cables are used. As the surge of high voltage is routed through the secondary cable, the circuit builds up an electrical field around the wire, which acts upon the oxygen in the surrounding air to form the ozone. The faint glow along the cable with the engine running that may be visible on a dark night, is called the "corona discharge." It is the result of the electrical field passing from a high along the cable, to a low in the surrounding air, which forms the ozone gas. The combination of corona and ozone has been a major cause of cable deterioration. Recently, different and better quality insulating materials have lengthened the life of the electrical cables.

Although ozone at ground level can be harmful, ozone is beneficial to the earth's inhabitants. By having a concentrated ozone layer called the "ozonosphere," between 10 and 20 miles (16-32 km) up in the atmosphere, much of the ultra violet radiation from the sun's rays are absorbed and screened. If this ozone layer were not present, much of the earth's surface would be burned, dried and unfit for human life.

OXIDES OF SULFUR

Oxides of sulfur (SOx) were initially ignored in the exhaust system emissions, since the sulfur content of gasoline as a fuel is less than $^{1}/_{10}$ of 1 percent. Because of this small amount, it was felt that it contributed very little to the overall pollution problem. However, because of the difficulty in solving the sulfur emissions in industrial pollutions and the introduction of catalytic converter to the automobile exhaust systems, a change was mandated. The automobile exhaust system, when equipped with a catalytic converter, changes the sulfur dioxide (SO_2) into the sulfur trioxide (SO_3).

When this combines with water vapors (H_2O), a sulfuric acid mist (H_2SO_4) is formed and is a very difficult pollutant to handle since it is extremely corrosive. This sulfuric acid mist that is formed, is the same mist that rises from the vents of an automobile battery when an active chemical reaction takes place within the battery cells.

When a large concentration of vehicles equipped with catalytic converters are operating in an area, this acid mist may rise and be distributed over a large ground area causing land, plant, crop, paint and building damage.

PARTICULATE MATTER

A certain amount of particulate matter is present in the burning of any fuel, with carbon constituting the largest percentage of the particulates. In gasoline, the remaining particulates are the burned remains of the various other compounds used in its manufacture. When a gasoline engine is in good internal condition, the particulate emissions are low but as the engine wears internally, the particulate emissions increase. By visually inspecting the tail pipe emissions, a determination can be made as to where an engine defect may exist. An engine with light gray or blue smoke emitting from the tail pipe normally indicates an increase in the oil consumption through burning due to internal engine wear. Black smoke would indicate a defective fuel delivery system, causing the engine to operate in a rich mode. Regardless of the color of the smoke, the internal part of the engine or the fuel delivery system should be repaired to prevent excess particulate emissions.

Diesel and turbine engines emit a darkened plume of smoke from the exhaust system because of the type of fuel used. Emission control regulations are mandated for this type of emission and more stringent measures are being used to prevent excess emission of the particulate matter. Electronic components are being introduced to control the injection of the fuel at precisely the proper time of piston travel, to achieve the optimum in fuel ignition and fuel usage. Other particulate after-burning components are being tested to achieve a cleaner emission.

Good grades of engine lubricating oils should be used, which meet the manufacturers specification. Cut-rate oils can contribute to the particulate emission problem because of their low flash or ignition temperature point. Such oils burn prematurely during the combustion process causing emission of particulate matter.

The cooling system is an important factor in the reduction of particulate matter. The optimum combustion will occur, with the cooling system operating at a temperature specified by the manufacturer. The cooling system must be maintained in the same manner as the engine oiling system, as each system is required to perform properly in order for the engine to operate efficiently for a long time.

Crankcase Emissions

Crankcase emissions are made up of water, acids, unburned fuel, oil fumes and particulates. These emissions are classified as hydrocarbons (HC) and are formed by the small amount of unburned, compressed air/fuel mixture entering the crankcase from the combustion area (between the cylinder walls and piston rings) during the compression and power strokes. The head of the compression and combustion help to form the remaining crankcase emissions.

Since the first engines, crankcase emissions were allowed into the atmosphere through a road draft tube, mounted on the lower side of the engine block. Fresh air came in through an open oil filler cap or breather. The air passed through the crankcase mixing with blow-by gases. The motion of the vehicle and the air blowing past the open end of the road draft tube caused a low pressure area (vacuum) at the end of the tube. Crankcase emissions were simply drawn out of the road draft tube into the air.

To control the crankcase emission, the road draft tube was deleted. A hose and/or tubing was routed from the crankcase to the intake manifold so the blow-by emission could be burned with the air/fuel mixture. However, it was found that intake manifold vacuum, used to draw the crankcase emissions into the manifold, would vary in strength at the wrong time and not allow the proper emission flow. A regulating valve was needed to control the flow of air through the crankcase.

Testing, showed the removal of the blow-by gases from the crankcase as quickly as possible, was most important to the longevity of the engine. Should large accumulations of blow-by gases remain and condense, dilution of the engine oil would occur to form water, soots, resins, acids and lead salts, resulting in the formation of sludge and varnishes. This condensation of the blow-by gases occurs more frequently on vehicles used in numerous starting and stopping conditions, excessive idling and when the engine is not allowed to attain normal operating temperature through short runs.

Evaporative Emissions

Gasoline fuel is a major source of pollution, before and after it is burned in the automobile engine. From the time the fuel is refined, stored, pumped and transported, again stored until it is pumped into the fuel tank of the vehicle, the gasoline gives off unburned hydrocarbons (HC) into the atmosphere. Through the redesign of storage areas and venting systems, the pollution factor was diminished, but not eliminated, from the refinery standpoint. However, the automobile still remained the primary source of vaporized, unburned hydrocarbon (HC) emissions.

Fuel pumped from an underground storage tank is cool but when exposed to a warmer ambient temperature, will expand. Before controls were mandated, an owner might fill the fuel tank with fuel from an underground storage tank and park the vehicle for some time in warm area, such as a parking lot. As the fuel would warm, it would expand and should no provisions or area be provided for the expansion, the fuel would spill out of the filler neck and onto the ground, causing hydrocarbon (HC) pollution and creating a severe fire hazard. To correct this condition, the vehicle manufacturers added overflow plumbing and/or gasoline tanks with built in expansion areas or domes.

However, this did not control the fuel vapor emission from the fuel tank. It was determined that most of the fuel evaporation occurred when the vehicle was stationary and the engine not operating. Most vehicles carry 5-25 gallons (19-95 liters) of gasoline. Should a large concentration of vehicles be parked in one area, such as a large parking lot, excessive fuel vapor emissions would take place, increasing as the temperature increases.

To prevent the vapor emission from escaping into the atmosphere, the fuel systems were designed to trap the vapors while the vehicle is stationary, by sealing the system from the atmosphere. A storage system is used to collect and hold the fuel vapors from the carburetor (if equipped) and the fuel tank when the engine is not operating. When the engine is started, the storage system is then purged of the fuel vapors, which are drawn into the engine and burned with the air/fuel mixture.

ENGINE EMISSION CONTROLS

See Figures 1 and 2

There are three sources of automotive pollutants: Crankcase fumes, exhaust gases and gasoline evaporation. The pollutants formed from these substances can be grouped into three categories: unburned hydrocarbons (HC), carbon monoxide (CO) and oxides of nitrogen (NO_x). The equipment that is used to limit these pollutants is commonly called emission control equipment.

Positive Crankcase Ventilation

OPERATION

See Figure 3

The Positive Crankcase Ventilation (PCV) system is used to evacuate the crankcase vapors. Outside vehicle air is routed through the air cleaner to the crankcase where it mixes with the blow-by gases and is passed through the PCV valve. It is then routed into the intake manifold. The PCV valve meters the air flow rate which varies under engine operation depending on manifold vacuum. In order to maintain idle quality, the PCV valve limits the air flow when intake manifold vacuum is high. If abnormal operating conditions occur, the system will allow excessive blow-by gases to back flow through the crankcase vent tube into the air cleaner. These blow-by gases will then be burned by normal combustion.

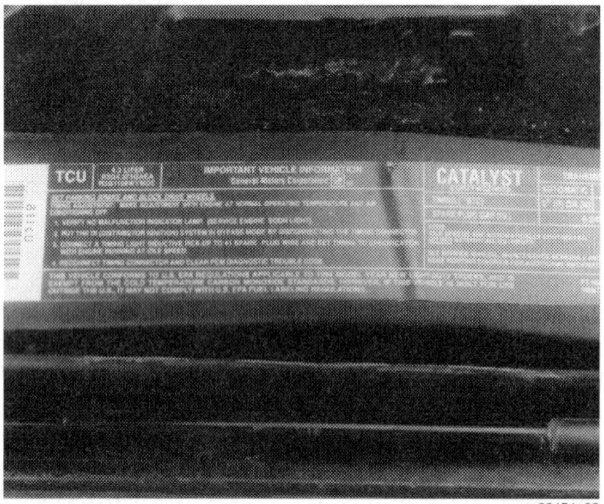

88454p02

Fig. 1 Some vehicle emission control labels show engine control system adjustment information . . . .

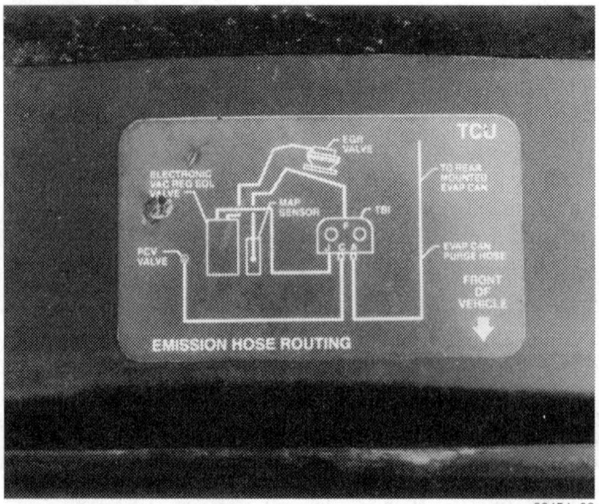

88454p03

Fig. 2 . . . . while other labels show vacuum routing diagrams

A plugged PCV valve or hose may cause rough idle, stalling or slow idle speed, oil leaks, oil in the air cleaner or sludge in the engine. A leaking PCV valve or hose could cause rough idle, stalling or high idle speed.

Other than checking and replacing the PCV valve and associated hoses, there is no service required. Engine operating conditions that would direct suspicion to the PCV system are rough idle, oil present in the air cleaner, oil leaks and excessive oil sludging or dilution. If any of the above conditions exist, remove the PCV valve and shake it. A clicking sound indicates that the valve is free. If no clicking sound is heard, replace the valve. Inspect the PCV breather in the air cleaner. Replace the breather if it is so dirty that it will not allow gases to pass through. Check all the PCV hoses for condition and tight connections. Replace any hoses that have deteriorated.

TESTING

See Figure 4

1. Remove the PCV valve from the rocker arm cover, but leave the vacuum hose attached.
2. Operate the engine at idle speed.
3. Place your thumb over the end of the valve to check for vacuum. If no vacuum exists, check the valve, the hoses or the manifold port for a plugged condition.
4. Remove the valve from the hose(s), then shake it and listen for a rattling of the check needle (inside the valve); the rattle means the valve is working. If no rattle is heard the valve is stuck, and should be replaced.

REMOVAL & INSTALLATION

See Figures 5, 6 and 7

PCV Valve

The large end of the valve is inserted into a rubber grommet in the valve cover. At the narrow end, it is inserted into a hose and usually clamped.

1. Gently pull the valve out of the valve cover, then open the clamp with a pair of pliers. Hold the clamp open while sliding it an inch or two down the hose (away from the valve), and then remove the valve.

To install:

2. If the end of the hose is hard or cracked where it holds the valve, it may be feasible to cut the end off if there is plenty of extra hose. Otherwise, replace the hose.
3. Replace the grommet in the valve cover if it is cracked or hard.
4. Replace the clamp if it is broken or weak.
5. In replacing the valve, make sure it is fully inserted in the hose, that the clamp is moved over the ridge on the valve so that the valve will not slip out of the hose, and that the valve is fully inserted into the grommet in the valve cover.

PCV Breather

Most breathers are located inside the air cleaner assembly, though they may be mounted directly to a valve cover. Al-

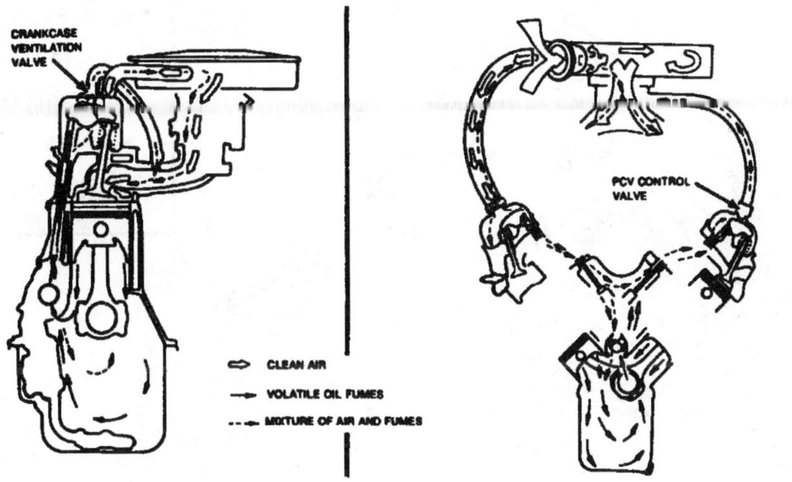

85384002

Fig. 3 Positive Crankcase Ventilation (PCV) system schematic

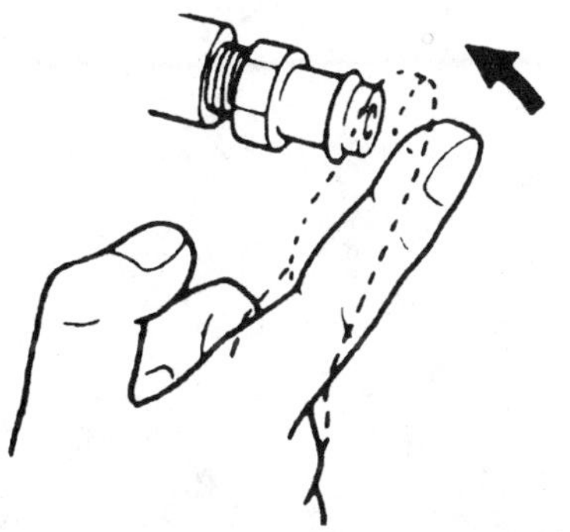

tccs4p05

Fig. 4 Check the PCV valve for vacuum at idle

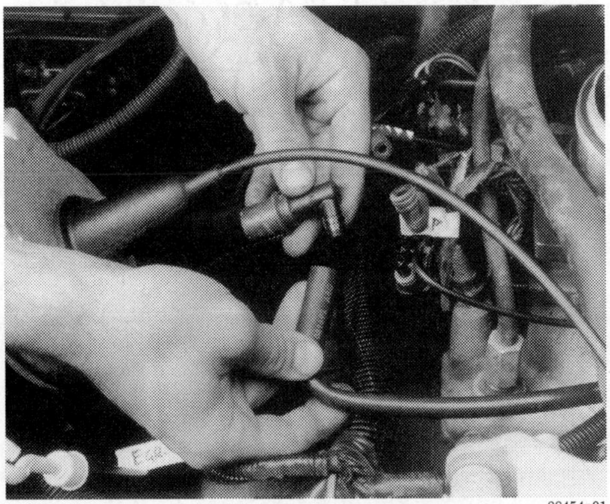

88454p01

Fig. 5 Removing the PCV valve from the hose

though a breather may in some cases be removed and cleaned, it is an inexpensive part and it is wise to replace it if dirty. Breathers which are mounted directly to the valve cover may be simply grasped and pulled from the cover grommet. For breathers which are mounted inside the air cleaner follow the procedure listed below.

1. Loosen the wing nut or release the retainers, then remove the top of the air cleaner assembly.
2. Slide the rubber coupling that joins the tube coming from the valve cover to the breather off the breather nipple.
3. Slide the spring clamp off the breather nipple (if equipped) which is protruding from the air cleaner housing, then withdraw the breather from inside the air cleaner assembly.
4. Inspect the rubber grommet in the valve cover and the rubber coupling for brittleness or cracking. Replace parts as necessary.

To install:

5. Insert the new PCV breather through the hole in the air cleaner with the open portion of the breather upward. Make sure that the breather is fully seated in the air cleaner housing.
6. If equipped, install a new spring clamp onto the nipple. Make sure the clamp goes under the ridge on the breather nipple all the way around.
7. Reconnect the rubber coupling.
8. Install the air cleaner cover and secure.

Evaporative Emission Control System (EECS)

OPERATION

The Evaporative Emission Control System (EECS) is designed to prevent fuel tank vapors from being emitted into the atmosphere. Gasoline vapors are absorbed and stored by a fuel vapor charcoal canister. The charcoal canister absorbs the gasoline vapors and stores them until certain engine conditions are met, then the vapors are purged and burned in the combustion process.

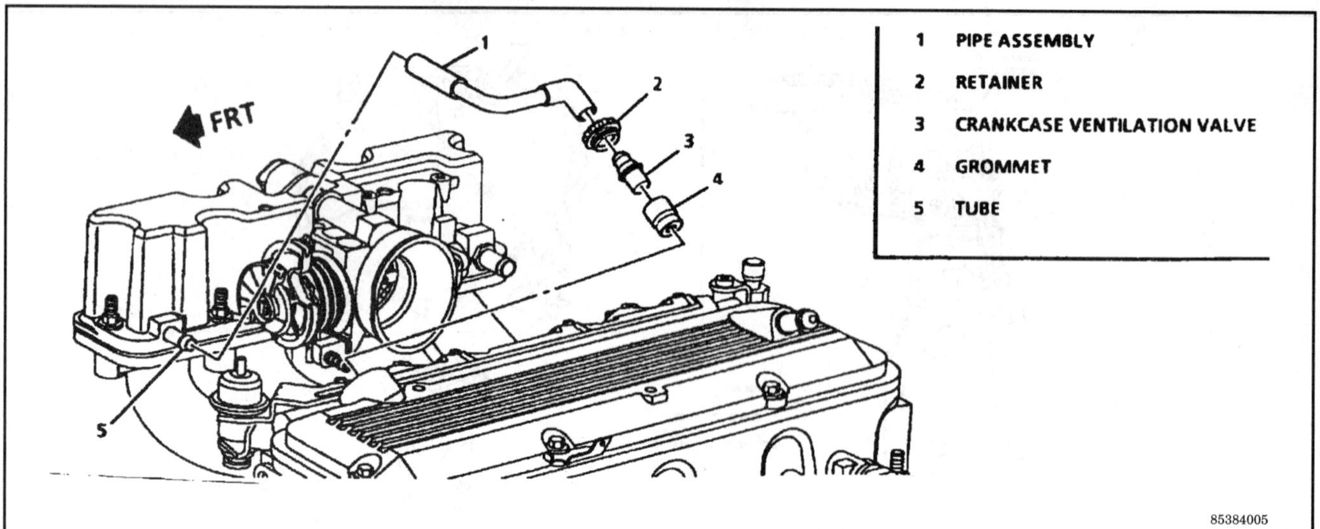

Fig. 6 PCV valve location and mounting — 2.2L engine

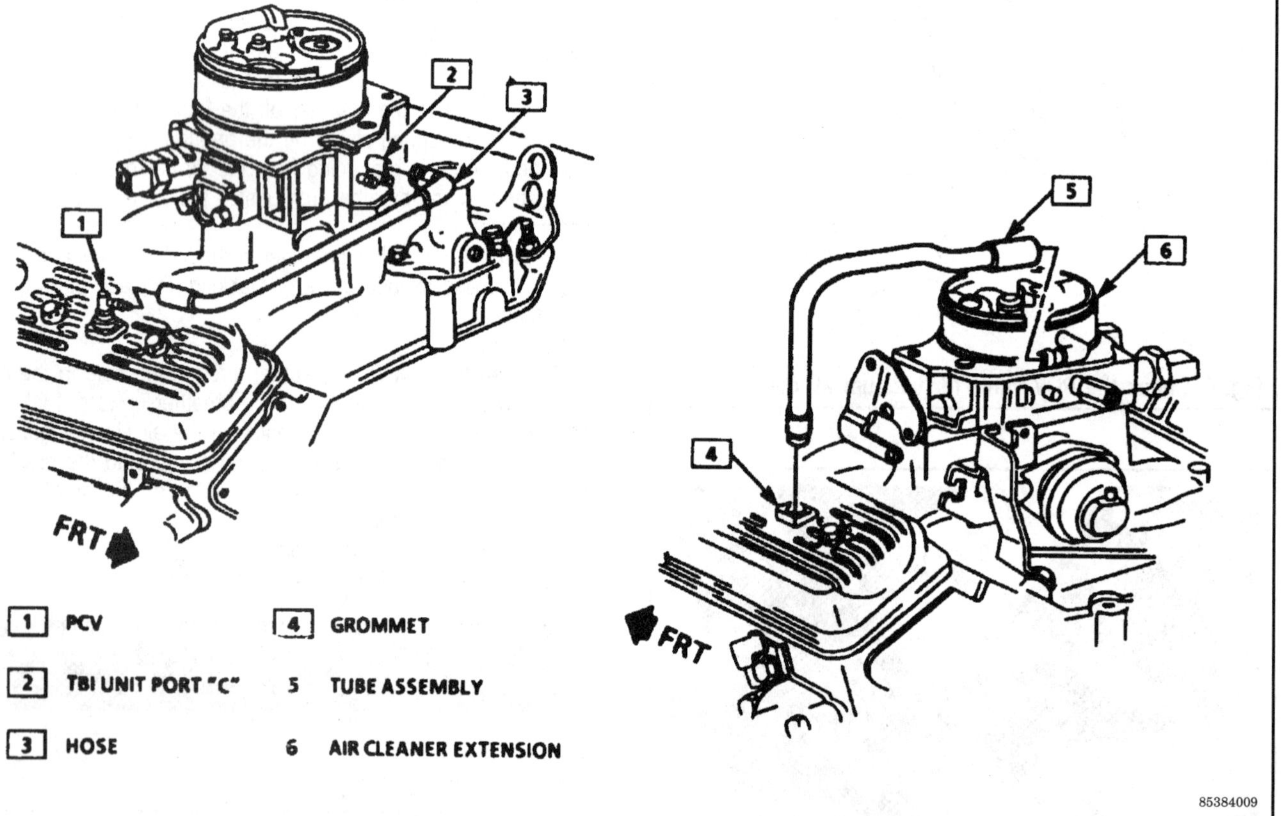

Fig. 7 PCV system — 4.3L (VIN Z), VIN W similar

The charcoal canister purge cycle is normally controlled either by a thermostatic vacuum switch or by a timed vacuum source, though some models may use electronic regulation in the form of a purge control solenoid. The thermostatic vacuum switch is installed in a coolant passage and prevents canister purge when engine operating temperature is below approximately 115°F (46°C). A timed vacuum source uses a manifold vacuum-controlled diaphragm to control canister purge. When the engine is running, full manifold vacuum is applied to the top tube of the purge valve which lifts the valve diaphragm and opens the valve. If equipped with a purge solenoid, under proper engine operating conditions the ECM will signal the solenoid which will then open the vacuum line allowing manifold vacuum to control the purge diaphragm. Most solenoids used on these vehicles are normally closed and will open when the ECM provides a ground signal energizing the solenoid.

➡Remember that the fuel tank filler cap is an integral part of the system in that it is designed to seal in fuel vapors. If it is lost or damaged, make sure the replacement is of the correct size and fit so a proper seal can be obtained.

A vent, located in the fuel tank, allows fuel vapors to flow to the charcoal canister. A tank pressure control valve, used on high altitude applications, prevents canister purge when the engine is not running. The fuel tank cap does not normally vent to the atmosphere but is designed to provide both vacuum and pressure relief.

Poor engine idle, stalling and poor driveability can be caused by a damaged canister or split, damaged or improperly connected hoses.

Evidence of fuel loss or fuel vapor odor can be caused by a liquid fuel leak; a cracked or damaged vapor canister; disconnected, misrouted, kinked or damaged vapor pipe or canister hoses; a damaged air cleaner or improperly seated air cleaner gasket.

TESTING

➧ See Figures 8 and 9

Charcoal Canister and Purge Valve

The fuel vapor canister is used to absorb and store fuel vapors from the fuel tank. Vacuum sources are generally ported, either through an internal or remote mounted purge control valve. Engines employing the timed vacuum source purge system usually use a canister purge valve which is integral to the vapor canister. The valve consists of a housing and tube molded into the canister cover, valve assembly, diaphragm and valve spring. The diaphragm cover has a built-in control vacuum signal tube.

1. Remove the vacuum hose from the lower tube of the purge valve and install a short length of tube, then try to blow through it (little or no air should pass, though a small amount may pass if the vehicles is equipped with a constant purge hole).
2. Using a vacuum source such as a hand vacuum pump, apply 15 in. Hg (51 kPa) to the upper tube of the purge valve. The diaphragm should hold the vacuum for at least 20 seconds, if not replace the purge valve (remote mounted) or canister (internal mounted valve), as applicable.
3. While holding the vacuum on the upper tube, blow through the lower tube (an increased volume of air should now pass); if not, replace the valve or canister, as necessary.

➡When testing valves by blowing air through them, be careful that you are blowing in the proper direction of flow. Many valves are designed to only allow air to flow in one direction and a proper working valve may seem defective if it is tested with air flow only in the wrong direction.

Thermostatic Vacuum Switch (TVS)

➧ See Figure 10

➡The number stamped on the base of the switch (valve) is the calibration temperature.

1. With engine temperature below 100°F (38°C), apply vacuum to the manifold side of the switch. The switch should hold vacuum.
2. As the engine temperature increases above 122°F (50°C), vacuum should drop off.

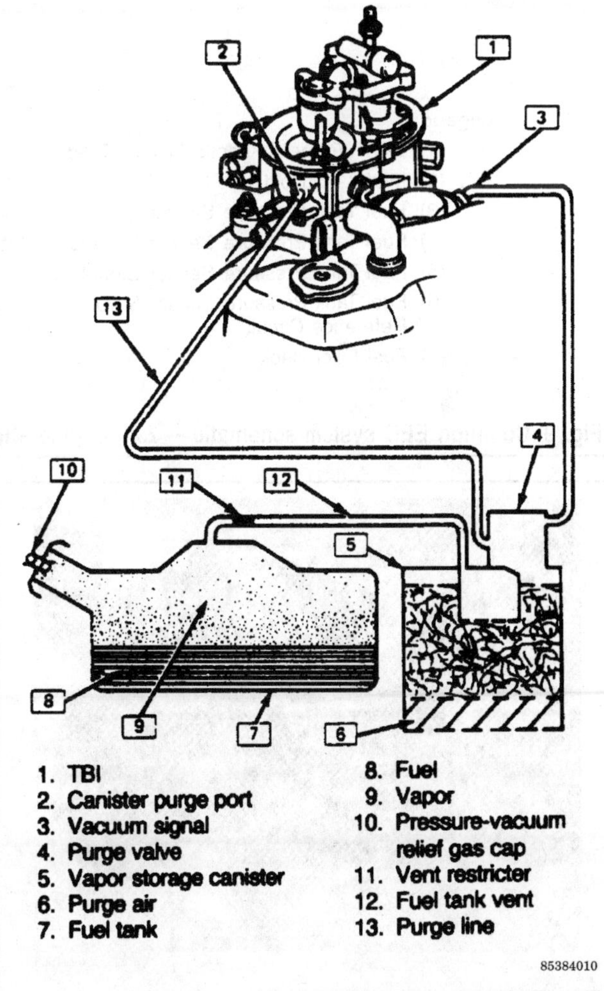

Fig. 8 Common EEC system schematic — 4.3L (VIN Z) engines shown

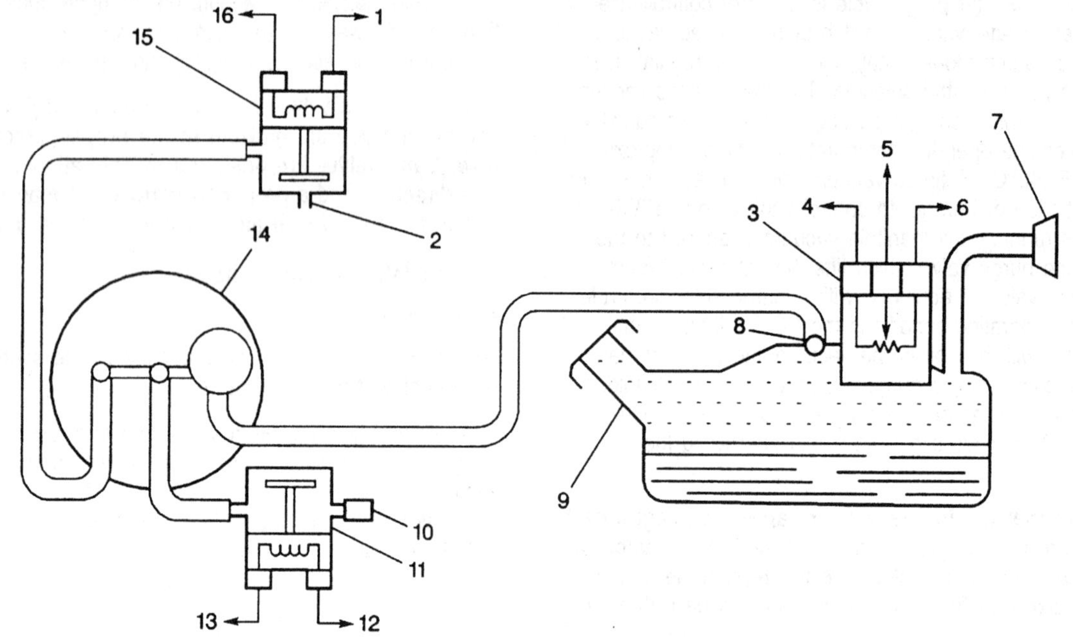

Legend

(1) EVAP Purge Solenoid Ignition Feed
(2) Intake Manifold
(3) Fuel Tank Pressure Sensor
(4) Fuel Tank Pressure Sensor Ground Circuit
(5) Fuel Tank Pressure Sensor Signal Circuit
(6) Fuel Tank Pressure Sensor 5 Volt Reference Circuit
(7) Fuel Filler Neck
(8) Rollover Valve
(9) Fuel Tank
(10) EVAP Vent Valve Filter
(11) EVAP Vent Valve
(12) EVAP Vent Valve Control Circuit
(13) EVAP Valve Ignition Feed
(14) EVAP Canister
(15) EVAP Purge Solenoid
(16) EVAP Purge Solenoid Control Circuit

88454g01

Fig. 9 Common EEC system schematic — 2.2L engine shown

tccs4p03

Fig. 10 Disconnecting the hoses from the thermal vacuum valve

3. Replace the switch if it fails either test.

➡A leakage of up to 2 in. Hg (13 kPa)/2 min. is allowable and does not mean that the valve is defective.

Canister Purge Control Solenoid

➧ See Figure 11

As stated earlier, most solenoids found on these vehicles use a normally closed solenoid valve. This means that when the solenoid is de-energized it is closed or, when it is energized it will open allowing vacuum to pass. On most vehicles equipped with this solenoid, fused ignition voltage is applied to the solenoid through one of it's terminals. When the ECM recognizes proper engine operating conditions, it will provide a ground through the other solenoid terminal in order to energize the solenoid.

To test a normally closed solenoid valve, try blowing air through the valve fittings when the engine is **OFF**, air should not flow. When the engine is running the solenoid should de-energize during engine warm-up and energize once it has

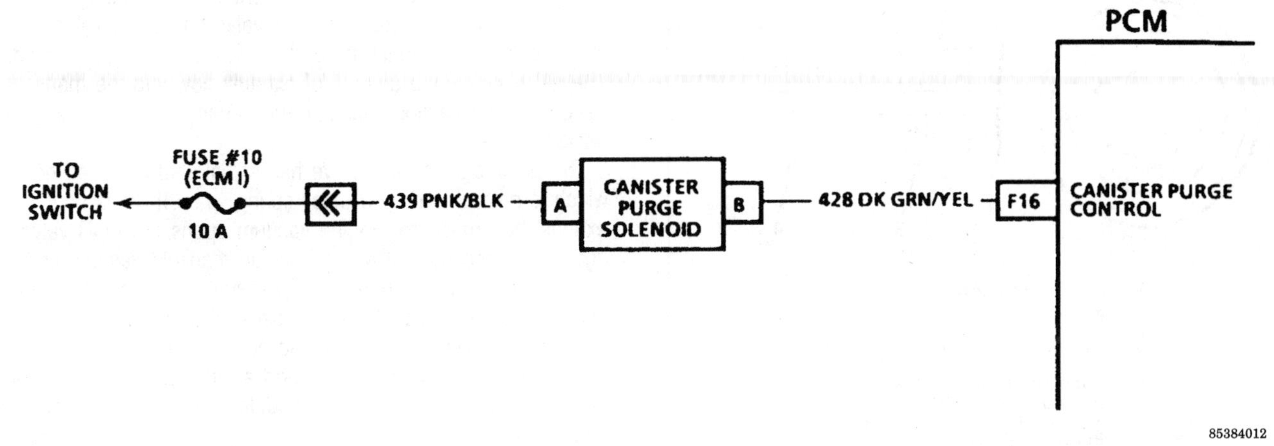

Fig. 11 Normally closed canister purge solenoid schematic — normally found on California emissions vehicles

reached normal operating temperature and proper running conditions.

REMOVAL & INSTALLATION

Charcoal Canister

1. Tag and disconnect them from the canister assembly.

➡If access to the vapor hoses is difficult with the canister installed, wait until the canister is released from the bracket or mounting, then reposition the canister for better access.

2. Loosen the screw(s) fastening the canister retaining bracket to the vehicle.
3. Carefully remove the canister or canister and bracket assembly, as applicable.

To install:

4. Position the canister in the vehicle.
5. If the hoses cannot be accessed once the canister is secured, connect them now as tagged during removal.
6. Install the canister to the retaining bracket and secure using the retaining screw(s).
7. If not done earlier, connect the lines to the canister assembly as tagged during removal.

Thermostatic Vacuum Switch (TVS)

➧ See Figure 12

The TVS is located near the engine coolant outlet housing.

1. Drain the engine cooling system to a level below the TVS.
2. Disconnect the vacuum hose manifold from the TVS. If the hoses are not connected to a single manifold, be sure to tag them before removal to assure proper installation.
3. Using a wrench, unthread and remove the TVS from the engine.

To install:

4. Apply a soft setting sealant to the TVS threads.

➡DO NOT apply sealant to the sensor end of the TVS.

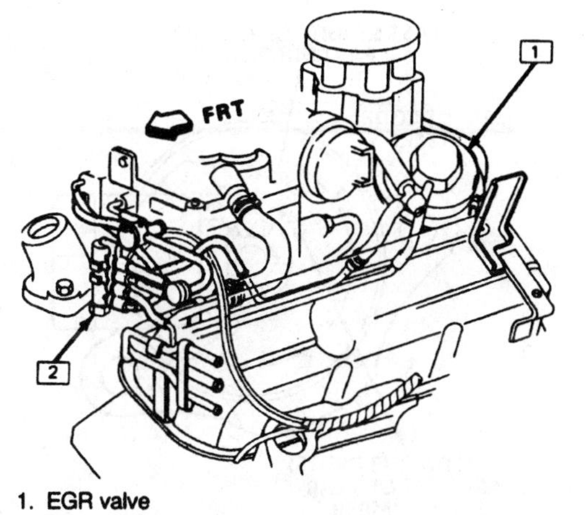

Fig. 12 Common TVS mounting

5. Install and tighten the TVS.
6. Reconnect the vacuum hoses.
7. Properly refill the engine cooling system, then run the engine and check for leaks.

Exhaust Gas Recirculation (EGR)

OPERATION

➧ See Figures 13, 14 and 15

The EGR system's purpose is to control oxides of nitrogen which are formed during the peak combustion temperatures. The end products of combustion are relatively inert gases derived from the exhaust gases which are directed into the EGR valve to help lower peak combustion temperatures.

The port EGR valve is controlled by a flexible diaphragm which is spring loaded to hold the valve closed. Vacuum applied to the top side of the diaphragm overcomes the spring

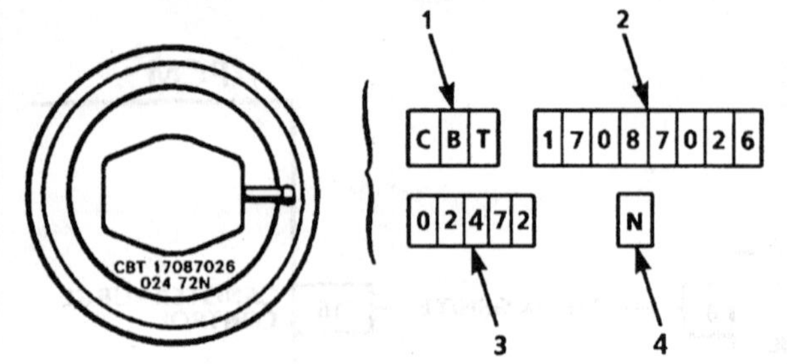

Fig. 13 EGR valve identification

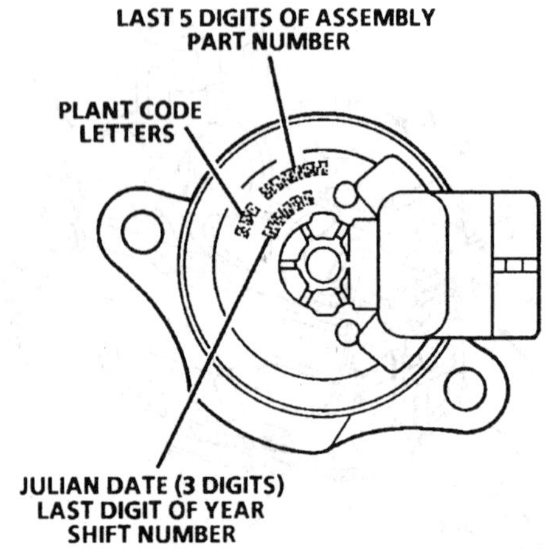

Fig. 14 Linear EGR valve identification

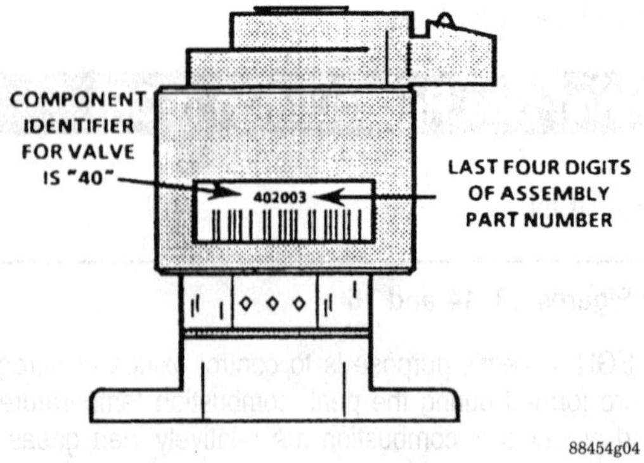

Fig. 15 Linear EGR valve part identification label

pressure and opens the valve which allows exhaust gas to be pulled into the intake manifold and enter the engine cylinders.

The negative backpressure EGR valve has bleed valve spring below the diaphragm, and the valve is normally closed. The valve varies the amount of exhaust flow into the manifold depending on manifold vacuum and variations in exhaust backpressure.

The diaphragm on this valve has an internal air bleed hole which is held closed by a small spring when there is no exhaust backpressure. Engine vacuum opens the EGR valve against the pressure of a large. When manifold vacuum combines with negative exhaust backpressure, the vacuum bleed hole opens and the EGR valve closes. This valve will open if vacuum is applied with the engine not running.

The linear EGR valve is operated exclusively by the control module command. The control module monitors various engine parameters:

- Throttle Position Sensor (TPS)
- Manifold Absolute Pressure (MAP)
- Engine Coolant Temperature (ECT) sensor
- Pintle position sensor

Output messages are then sent to the EGR system indicating the proper amount of exhaust gas recirculation necessary to lower combustion temperatures.

Refer to the accompanying illustrations to identify the EGR valve used in your vehicle.

TESTING

See Figures 16, 17, 18, 19, 20, 21 and 22

Refer to the appropriate chart for diagnosis the EGR system. On linear EGR systems, an OBD-II compliant scan tool will be needed.

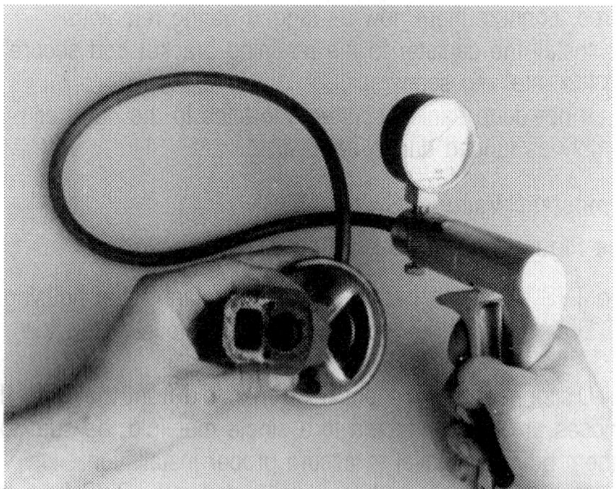

Fig. 16 Some EGR valves may be tested using a vacuum pump by watching for diaphragm movement

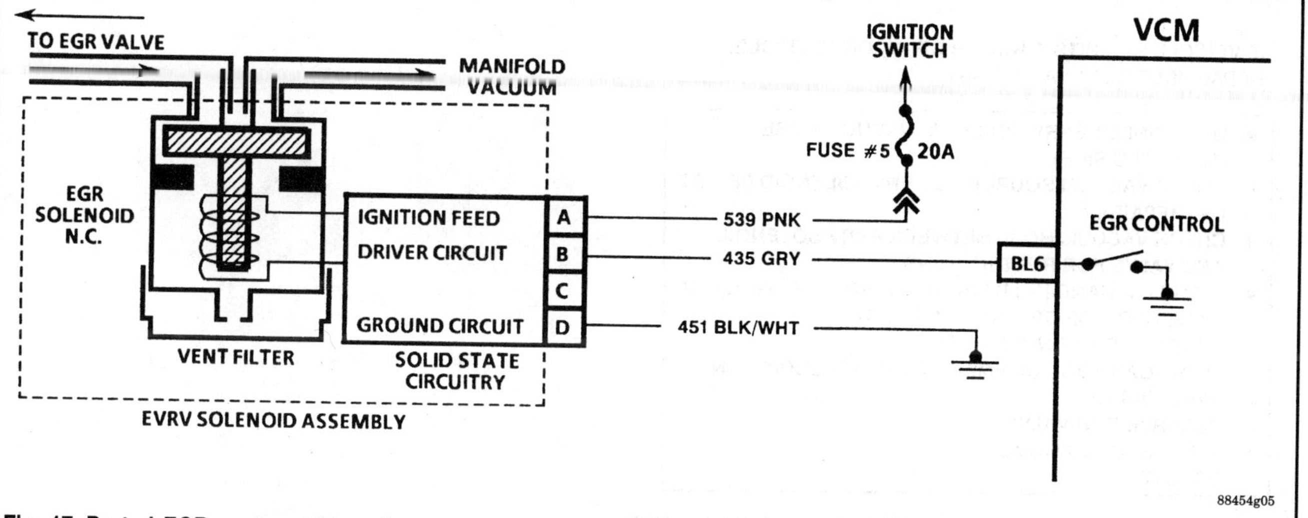

Fig. 17 Ported EGR system wiring diagram

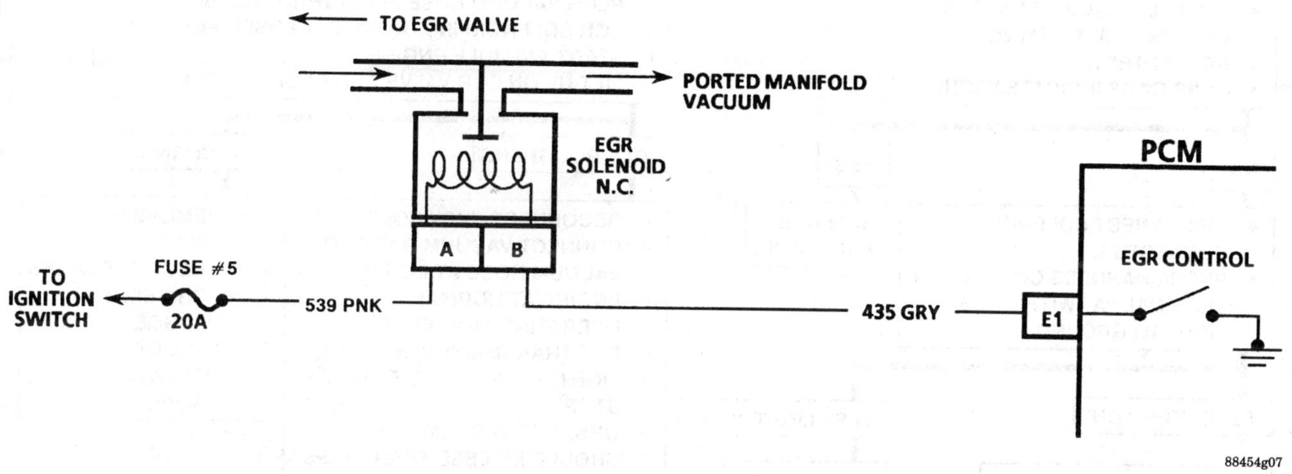

Fig. 18 Negative EGR system wiring diagram

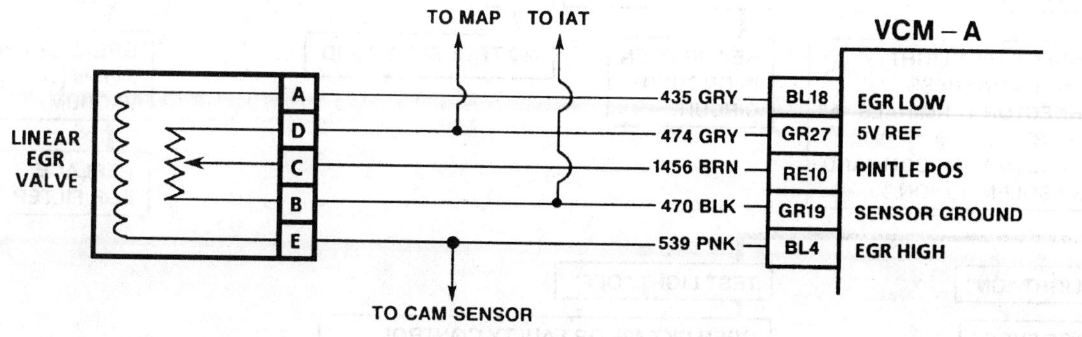

Fig. 19 Linear EGR system wiring diagram

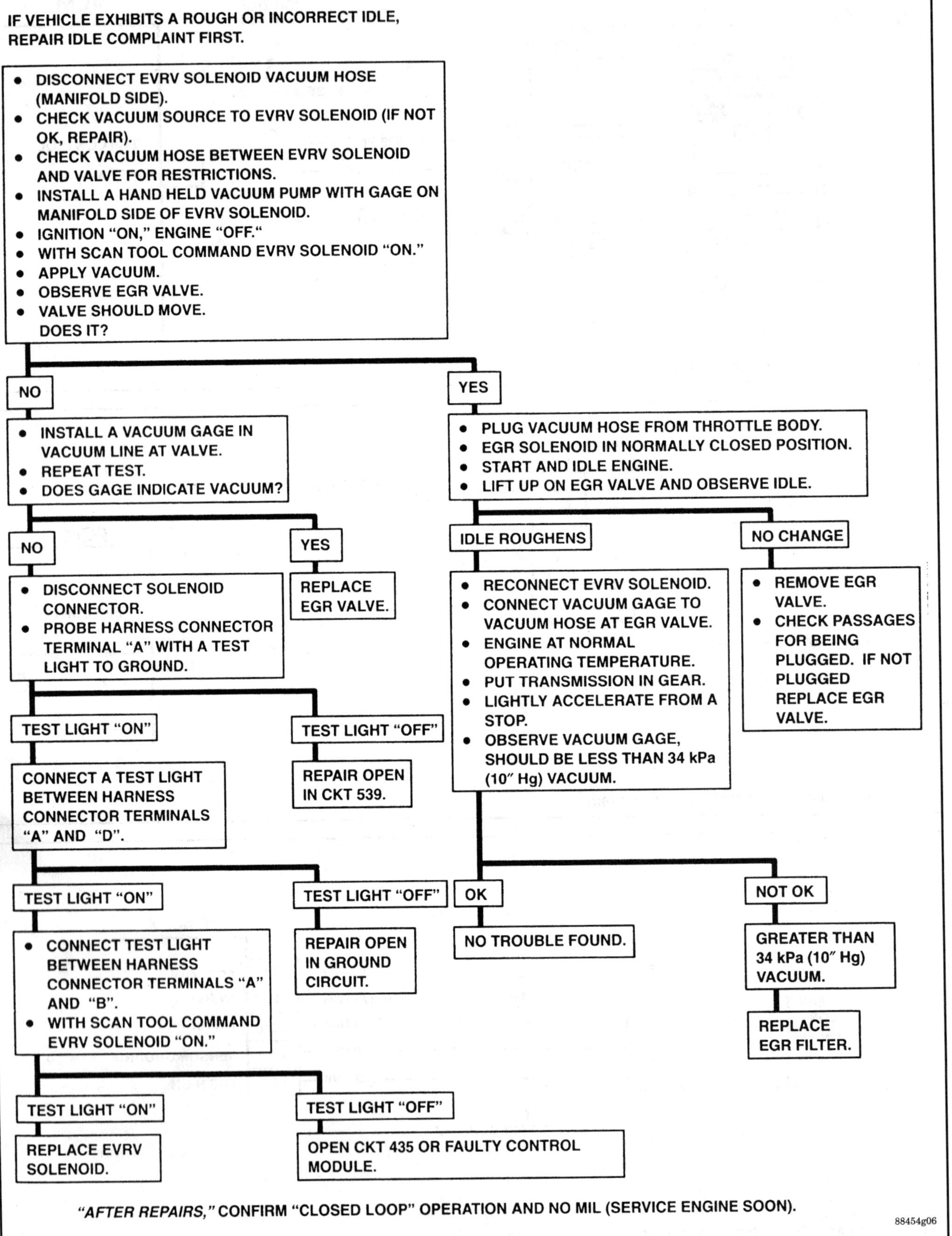

Fig. 20 Ported EGR system check

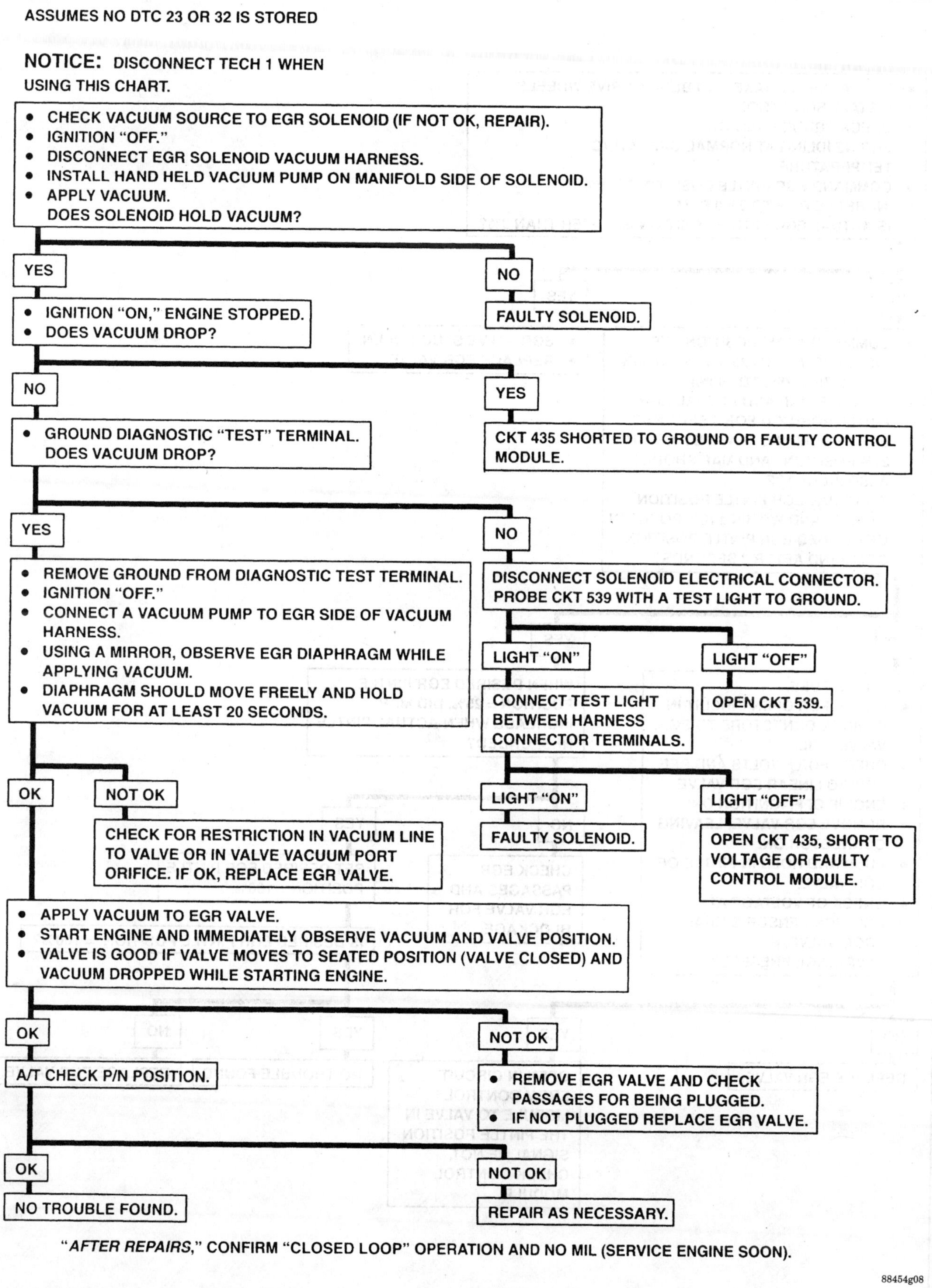

Fig. 21 Negative backpressure EGR system test

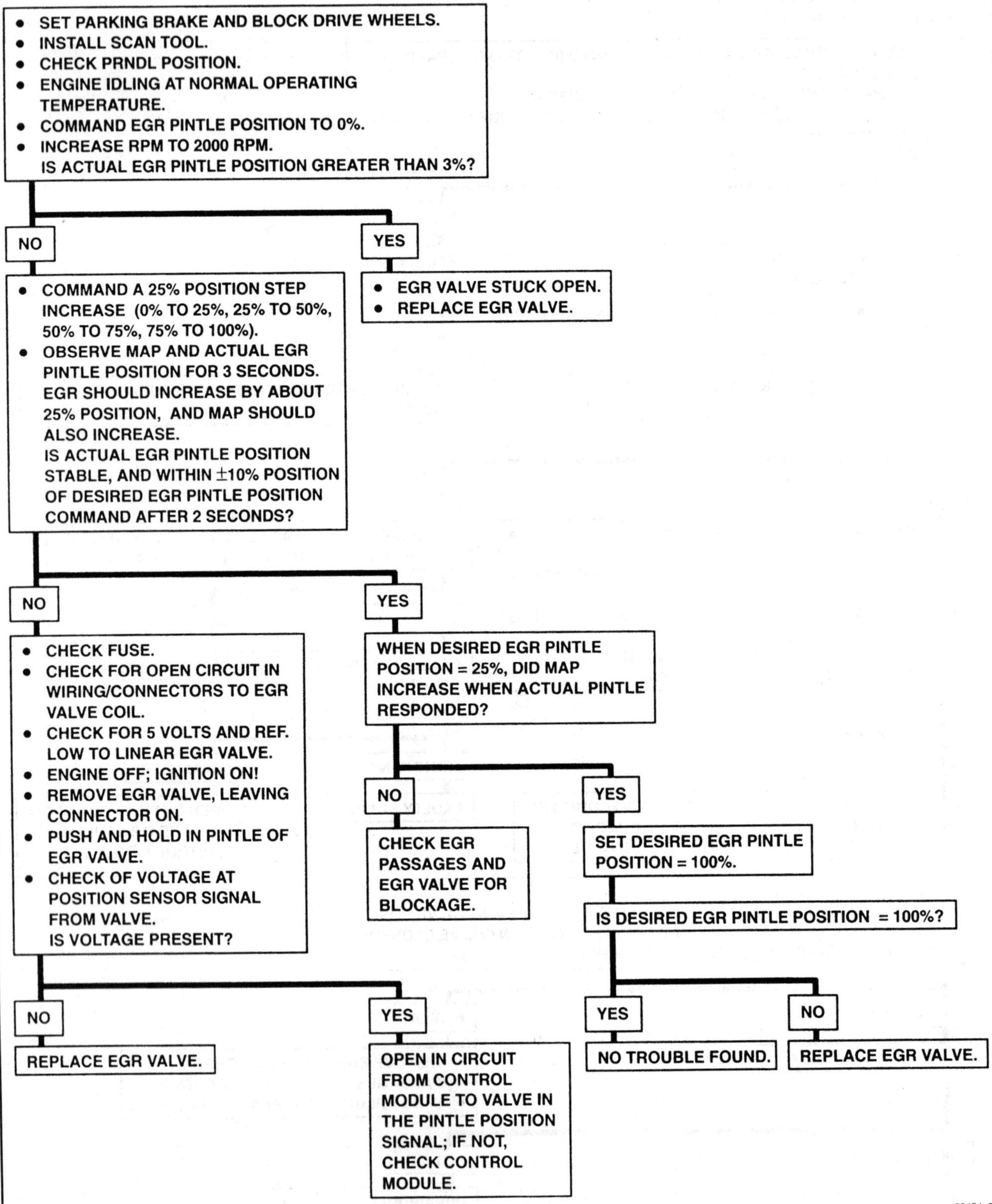

88454g09

Fig. 22 Linear EGR system test

REMOVAL & INSTALLATION

EGR Valve

➧ See Figures 23 and 24

1. Disconnect the negative battery cable.
2. Remove the air cleaner assembly from the engine.
3. Remove the EGR valve vacuum tube from the valve.
4. Remove the EGR bolts and/or nuts and remove the EGR valve and gasket.

To install:

5. Install a new gasket to the EGR valve and install the EGR valve to the manifold.
6. Install the nuts and/or bolts. Tighten the bolts to 17 ft. lbs. (24 Nm) and the nuts to 15 ft. lbs. (20 Nm).
7. Connect the vacuum tube to the EGR valve.
8. Install the air cleaner and connect the negative battery cable.

88454p04

Fig. 23 Unfasten the EGR valve retaining bolts. . .

88454p05

Fig. 24 . . . then remove the EGR valve from the vehicle

EGR Solenoid

1. Disconnect the negative battery cable.
2. Remove the air cleaner, as required.
3. Unplug the electrical connector at the solenoid.
4. Disconnect the vacuum hoses.
5. Remove the retaining bolts and the solenoid.
6. Remove the filter, as required.

To install:

7. If removed, install the filter.
8. Install the solenoid and retaining bolts.
9. Connect the vacuum hoses.
10. Engage the electrical connector.
11. If removed, install the air cleaner.
12. Connect the negative battery cable.

Catalytic Converter

OPERATION

The catalytic converter is a muffler-like container built into the exhaust system to aid in the reduction of exhaust emissions. The catalyst element is coated with a noble metal such as platinum, palladium, rhodium or a combination of them. When the exhaust gases come into contact with the catalyst, a chemical reaction occurs which reduces the pollutants into harmless substances such as water and carbon dioxide.

There are two types of catalytic converters: an oxidizing type and a three-way type. Both are used on Chevrolet/GMC full size trucks. The oxidizing catalyst requires the addition of oxygen to spur the catalyst into reducing the engine's HC and CO emissions into H_2O and CO_2.

PRECAUTIONS

1. Use only unleaded fuel.
2. Avoid prolonged idling; the engine should run no longer than 20 min. at curb idle and no longer than 10 min. at fast idle.
3. Don't disconnect any of the spark plug leads while the engine is running. If any engine testing procedure requires disconnecting or bypassing a control component, perform the procedure as quickly as possible. A misfiring engine can overheat the catalyst and damage the oxygen sensor.
4. Make engine compression checks as quickly as possible.
5. Whenever under the vehicle or around the catalytic converter, remember that it has a very high outside or skin temperature. During operation, the catalyst must reach very high temperatures to work efficiently. Be very wary of burns, even after the engine has been shut off for a while. Additionally, because of the heat, never park the vehicle on or over flammable materials, particularly dry grass or leaves. Inspect the heat shields frequently and correct any bends or damage.
6. In the unlikely event that the catalyst must be replaced, DO NOT dispose of the old one where anything containing grease, gas or oil can come in contact with it. The catalytic action with these substances will result in heat which may start a fire.

ELECTRONIC ENGINE CONTROLS

Vehicle Control Module (VCM)

OPERATION

➡When the term Vehicle Control Module (VCM) is used in this manual it will refer to the engine control computer regardless that it may be a Electronic Control Module (ECM), Powertrain Control Module (PCM) or Vehicle Control Module (VCM).

The Vehicle Control Module (VCM) is required to maintain the exhaust emissions at acceptable levels. The module is a small, solid state computer which receives signals from many sources and sensors; it uses these data to make judgments about operating conditions and then control output signals to the fuel and emission systems to match the current requirements.

Engines coupled to electronically controlled transmissions employ a Powertrain Control Module (PCM) or Vehicle Control Module (VCM) to oversee both engine and transmission operation. The integrated functions of engine and transmission control allow accurate gear selection and improved fuel economy.

In the event of an VCM failure, the system will default to a pre-programmed set of values. These are compromise values which allow the engine to operate, although at a reduced efficiency. This is variously known as the default, limp-in or backup mode. Driveability is almost always affected when the VCM enters this mode.

REMOVAL & INSTALLATION

See Figure 25

1. Disconnect the negative battery cable.
2. Disengage the connectors from the VCM.
3. Unfasten and remove the retainers.

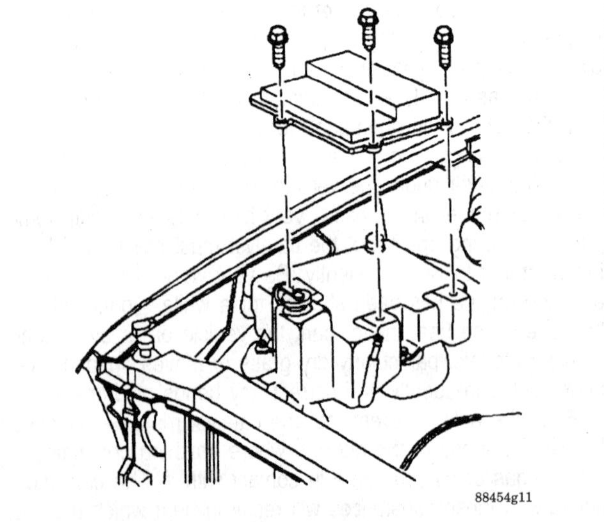

Fig. 25 Removing the Vehicle Control Module (VCM)

4. Remove the VCM.

To install:

5. Install the VCM.
6. Fasten the retainers and engage the electrical connectors.
7. Connect the negative battery cable.

Oxygen Sensor

OPERATION

See Figure 26

There are two types of oxygen sensor's used in these vehicles. They are the single wire oxygen sensor (02S) and the heated oxygen sensor (H02S). The oxygen sensor is a spark plug shaped device that is screwed into the exhaust manifold. It monitors the oxygen content of the exhaust gases and sends a voltage signal to the Vehicle Control Module (VCM). The VCM monitors this voltage and, depending on the value of the received signal, issues a command to the mixture control solenoid to adjust for rich or lean conditions.

The heated oxygen sensor has a heating element incorporated into the sensor to aid in the warm up to the proper operating temperature and to maintain that temperature.

The proper operation of the oxygen sensor depends upon four basic conditions:

1. Good electrical connections. Since the sensor generates low currents, good clean electrical connections at the sensor are a must.
2. Outside air supply. Air must circulate to the internal portion of the sensor. When servicing the sensor, do not restrict the air passages.
3. Proper operating temperatures. The VCM will not recognize the sensor's signals until the sensor reaches approximately 600°F (316°C).

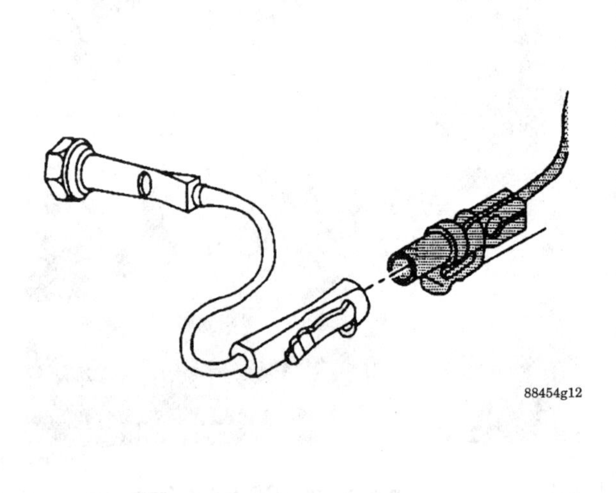

Fig. 26 View of a heated oxygen sensor used on the 2.2L engine

4. Non-leaded fuel. The use of leaded gasoline will damage the sensor very quickly.

TESTING

Single Wire Sensor

➧ See Figure 27

1. Start the engine and bring it to normal operating temperature, then run the engine above 1200 rpm for two minutes.
2. Backprobe with a high impedance averaging voltmeter (set to the DC voltage scale) between the oxygen sensor (02S) and battery ground.
3. Verify that the 02S voltage fluctuates rapidly between 0.40-0.60 volts.
4. If the 02S voltage is stabilized at the middle of the specified range (approximately 0.45-0.55 volts) or if the 02S voltage fluctuates very slowly between the specified range (02S signal crosses 0.5 volts less than 5 times in ten seconds), the 02S may be faulty.
5. If the 02S voltage stabilizes at either end of the specified range, the VCM is probably not able to compensate for a mechanical problem such as a vacuum leak or a faulty pressure regulator. These types of mechanical problems will cause the 02S to sense a constant lean or constant rich mixture. The mechanical problem will first have to be repaired and then the 02S test repeated.
6. Pull a vacuum hose located after the throttle plate. Voltage should drop to approximately 0.12 volts (while still fluctuating rapidly). This tests the ability of the 02S to detect a lean mixture condition. Reattach the vacuum hose.
7. Richen the mixture using a propane enrichment tool. Voltage should rise to approximately 0.90 volts (while still fluctuating rapidly). This tests the ability of the 02S to detect a rich mixture condition.
8. If the 02S voltage is above or below the specified range, the 02S and/or the O2S wiring may be faulty. Check the wiring for any breaks, repair as necessary and repeat the test.

Heated Oxygen Sensor

➧ See Figure 28

1. Start the engine and bring it to normal operating temperature, then run the engine above 1200 rpm for two minutes.
2. Turn the ignition **OFF** and disengage the H02S harness connector.
3. Connect a test light between harness terminals **A** and **B**. With the ignition switch **ON** and the engine off, verify that the test light is lit. If the test light is not lit, either the supply voltage to the H02S heater or the ground circuit of the H02S heater is faulty. Check the H02S wiring and the fuse.
4. Next, connect a high impedance ohmmeter between the H02S terminals **B** and **A** and verify that the resistance is 3.5-14.0 ohms.
5. If the H02S heater resistance is not as specified, the H02S may be faulty.
6. Start the engine and bring it to normal operating temperature, then run the engine above 1200 rpm for two minutes.
7. Backprobe with a high impedance averaging voltmeter (set to the DC voltage scale) between the oxygen sensor (02S) and battery ground.
8. Verify that the 02S voltage fluctuates rapidly between 0.40-0.60 volts.
9. If the 02S voltage is stabilized at the middle of the specified range (approximately 0.45-0.55 volts) or if the 02S voltage fluctuates very slowly between the specified range (02S signal crosses 0.5 volts less than 5 times in ten seconds), the 02S may be faulty.
10. If the 02S voltage stabilizes at either end of the specified range, the VCM is probably not able to compensate for a mechanical problem such as a vacuum leak or a faulty fuel pressure regulator. These types of mechanical problems will cause the 02S to sense a constant lean or constant rich mixture. The mechanical problem will first have to be repaired and then the 02S test repeated.
11. Pull a vacuum hose located after the throttle plate. Voltage should drop to approximately 0.12 volts (while still fluctuating rapidly). This tests the ability of the 02S to detect a lean mixture condition. Reattach the vacuum hose.
12. Richen the mixture using a propane enrichment tool. Voltage should rise to approximately 0.90 volts (while still fluc-

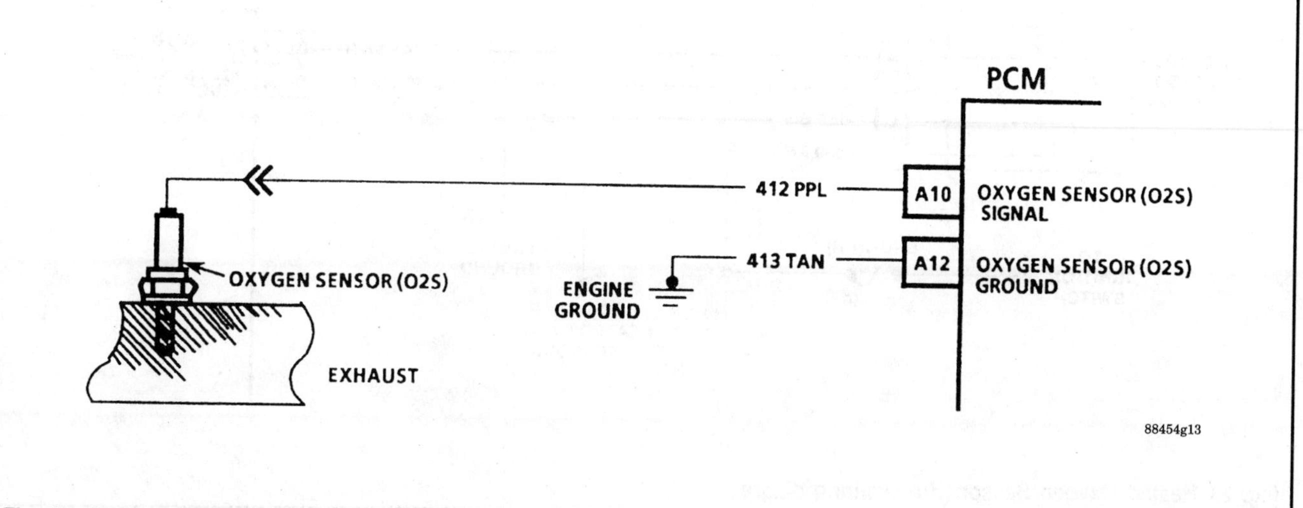

Fig. 27 Oxygen sensor (02S) wiring diagram

tuating rapidly). This tests the ability of the 02S to detect a rich mixture condition.

13. If the 02S voltage is above or below the specified range, the 02S and/or the O2S wiring may be faulty. Check the wiring for any breaks, repair as necessary and repeat the test.

REMOVAL & INSTALLATION

See Figure 29

WARNING

The sensor uses a permanently attached pigtail and connector. This pigtail should not be removed from the sensor. Damage or removal of the pigtail or connector could affect the proper operation of the sensor. Keep the electrical connector and louvered end of the sensor clean and free of grease. NEVER use cleaning solvents of any type on the sensor! The oxygen sensor may be difficult to remove when the temperature of the engine is below 120°F (49°C). Excessive force may damage the threads in the exhaust manifold or exhaust pipe.

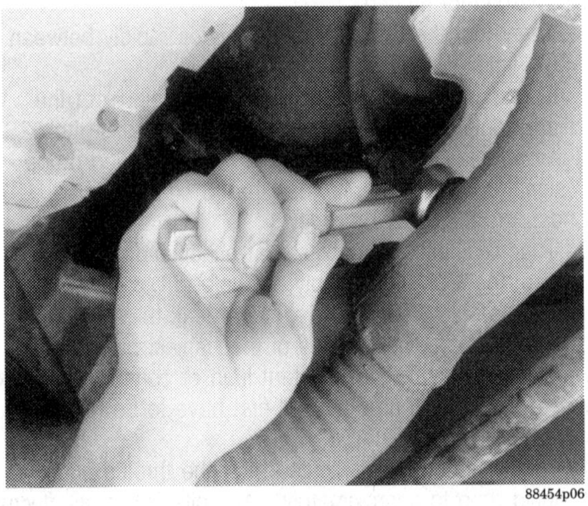

Fig. 29 Removing the oxygen sensor from the exhaust pipe

1. Disconnect the negative battery cable.
2. Unplug the electrical connector and any attaching hardware.
3. Remove the sensor.

To install:

4. Coat the threads of the sensor with a GM anti-seize compound, part number 5613695, or its equivalent, before installation. New sensors are precoated with this compound.

The GM anti-seize compound is NOT a conventional anti-seize paste. The use of a regular paste may electrically insulate the sensor, rendering it useless. The threads MUST be coated with the proper electrically conductive anti-seize compound.

5. Install the sensor and tighten to 30 ft. lbs. (40 Nm). Use care in making sure the silicone boot is in the correct position to avoid melting it during operation.
6. Engage the electrical connector.
7. Connect the negative battery cable.

Crankshaft Position (CKP) Sensor

OPERATION

The Crankshaft Position (CKP) sensor provides a signal through the ignition module which the VCM uses as a reference to calculate rpm and crankshaft position.

TESTING

See Figure 30

1. Disconnect the CKP sensor harness. Connect an LED test light between battery ground and CKP harness terminal **A**.

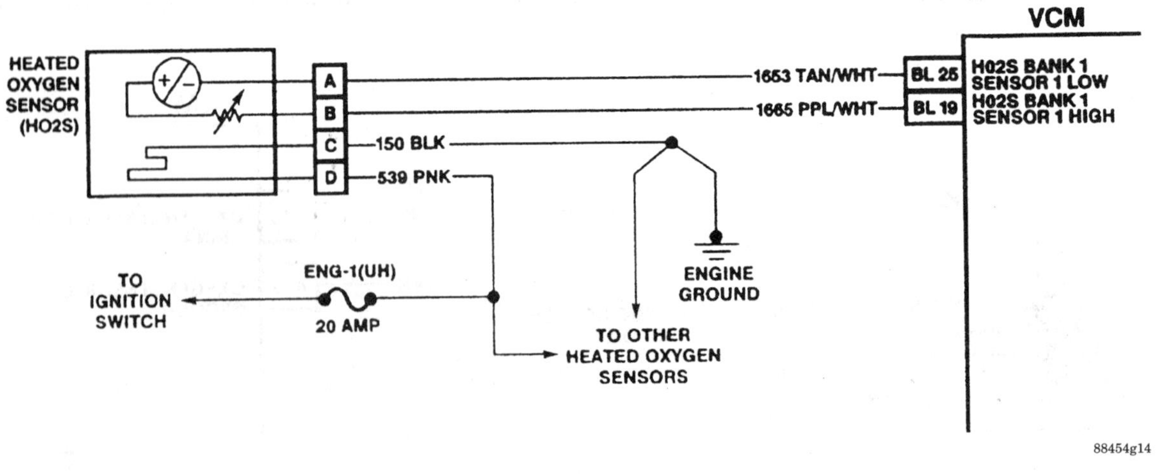

Fig. 28 Heated Oxygen Sensor (H02S) wiring diagram

2. With the ignition **ON** and the engine off, verify that the test light illuminates.
3. If not as specified, repair or replace the fuse and/or wiring.
4. Carefully connect the test light between CKP harness terminal **A** and **B**. Verify that the test light illuminates.
5. If not as specified, repair the CKP harness ground circuit (terminal **B**).
6. Turn the ignition **OFF** and disconnect the test light.
7. Next, connect suitable jumper wires between the CKP sensor and CKP sensor harness. Connect a duty cycle meter to the jumper wire corresponding to CKP terminal **C** and battery ground.
8. Crank the engine and verify that the duty cycle signal is between 40-60%.
9. If it is not as specified, the CKP sensor may be faulty.
10. Next, connect a AC volt meter to the jumper wire corresponding to CKP terminal **C** and battery ground.
11. Crank the engine and verify that the AC voltage signal is at least 10.0 volts.
12. If not as specified the CKP sensor may be faulty.

REMOVAL & INSTALLATION

See Figures 31 and 32

1. Disconnect the negative battery cable.
2. Detach the sensor harness connector at the sensor.
3. Unfasten the retaining bolt, then remove the sensor from the front cover. Inspect the sensor O-ring for wear, cracks or leakage and replace if necessary.

To install:

4. Lubricate the O-ring with clean engine oil, then place on the sensor. Install the sensor into the front cover.
5. Install the sensor and tighten the retaining bolt.
6. Attach the sensor harness connector.
7. Connect the negative battery cable.

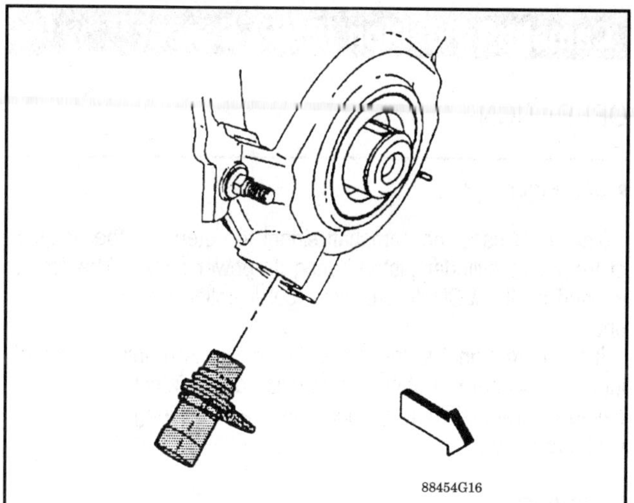

Fig. 31 View of the Crankshaft Position Sensor (CKP) location — 1996 4.3L engine

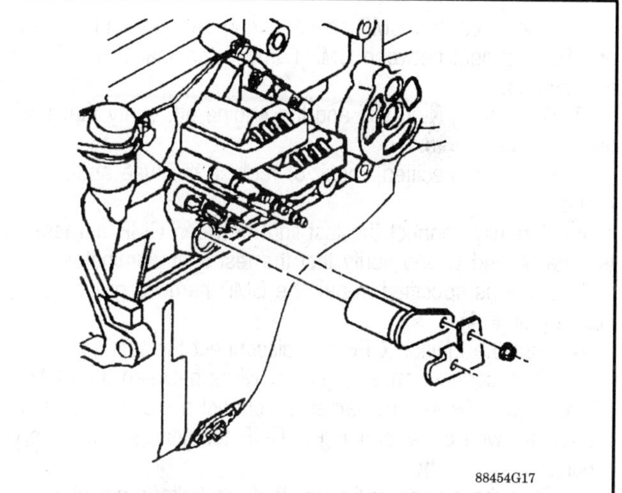

Fig. 32 View of the Crankshaft Position Sensor (CKP) location — 1996 2.2L engine

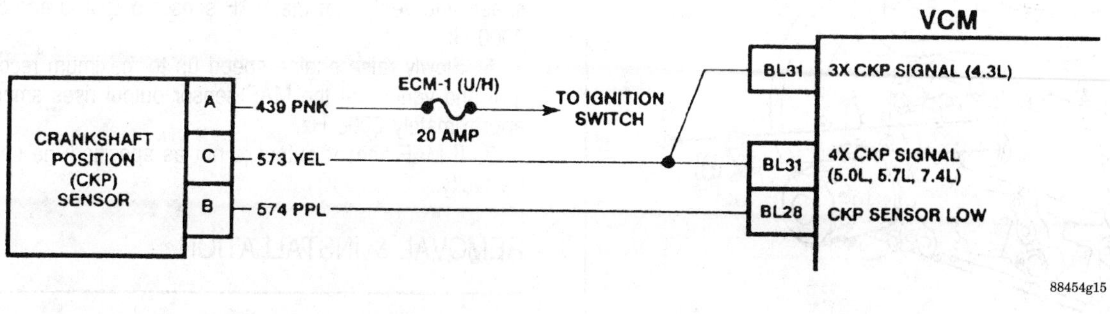

Fig. 30 Crankshaft Position (CKP) sensor wiring diagram

Camshaft Position (CMP) Sensor

OPERATION

➧ **See Figure 33**

The VCM uses the camshaft signal to determine the position of the No. 1 cylinder piston during its power stroke. The signal is used by the VCM to calculate fuel injection mode of operation.

If the cam signal is lost while the engine is running, the fuel injection system will shift to a calculated fuel injected mode based on the last fuel injection pulse, and the engine will continue to run.

TESTING

➧ **See Figure 34**

1. Disconnect the CMP sensor wiring harness and connect an LED test light between CMP harness terminal **C** and battery ground.
2. With the ignition **ON** and the engine off, verify that the test light illuminates.
3. If not as specified, repair or replace the fuse and/or wiring.
4. Carefully connect the test light between CMP harness terminal **A** and **C** and verify that the test light illuminates.
5. If not as specified, repair the CMP harness ground circuit (terminal **A**).
6. Turn the ignition **OFF** and disconnect the test light.
7. Next, connect suitable jumper wires between the CMP sensor and CMP sensor harness. Connect a DC volt meter to the jumper wire corresponding to CMP terminal **B** and battery ground.
8. Start the engine and verify that the voltage signal is 5-7 volts.
9. If it is not as specified, the CMP sensor may be faulty.

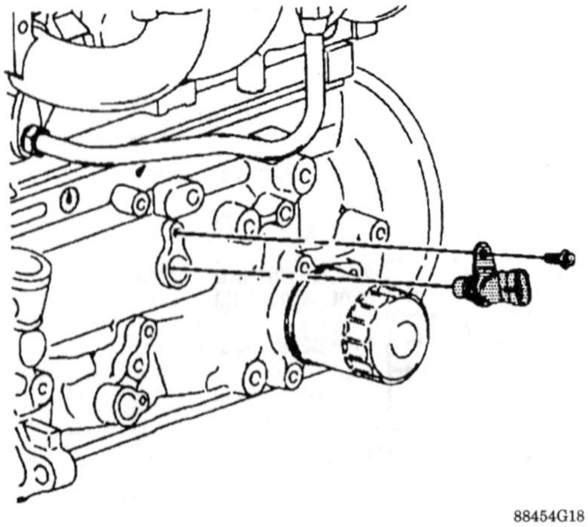

Fig. 33 Camshaft Position (CMP) sensor location — 1996 2.2L engine

REMOVAL & INSTALLATION

1. Disconnect the negative battery cable.
2. Detach the sensor harness connector at the sensor.
3. Unfasten the retaining bolt, then remove the sensor from the camshaft housing. Inspect the sensor O-ring for wear, cracks or leakage and replace if necessary.

To install:

4. Lubricate the O-ring with clean engine oil, then place on the sensor. Install the sensor into the camshaft housing.
5. Install the CMP sensor retaining bolt, then tighten to 88 inch lbs. (10 Nm).
6. Attach the sensor harness connector.
7. Connect the negative battery cable.

Mass Air Flow (MAF) Sensor

OPERATION

➧ **See Figure 35**

The Mass Air Flow (MAF) Sensor measures the amount of air entering the engine during a given time. The VCM uses the mass airflow information for fuel delivery calculations. A large quantity of air entering the engine indicates an acceleration or high load situation, while a small quantity of air indicates deceleration or idle.

TESTING

➧ **See Figure 36**

1. Backprobe with a high impedance voltmeter between MAF sensor terminals **C** and **B**.
2. With the ignition **ON** engine off, verify that battery voltage is present.
3. If the voltage is not as specified, either the wiring to the MAF sensor, fuse or the VCM may be faulty. Correct any wiring or VCM faults before continuing test.
4. Disconnect the voltmeter and backprobe with a frequency meter between MAF sensor terminals **A** and **B**.
5. Start the engine and wait until it reaches normal idle speed and verify that the MAF sensor output is approximately 2000 Hz.
6. Slowly raise engine speed up to maximum recommended rpm and verify that the MAF sensor output rises smoothly to approximately 8000 Hz.
7. If MAF sensor output is not as specified the sensor may be faulty.

REMOVAL & INSTALLATION

1. Disconnect the negative battery cable.
2. Unplug the electrical connector.
3. Remove the air intake hoses from the sensor, then remove its attaching bolts.
4. Installation is the reverse of removal.

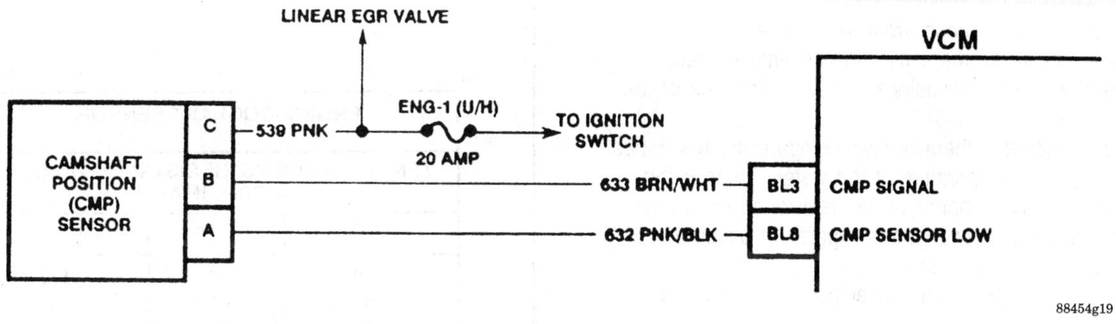

Fig. 34 Camshaft Position (CMP) wiring schematic

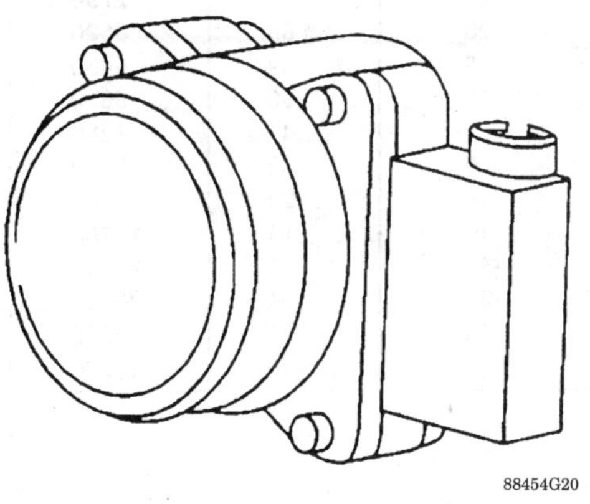

Fig. 35 View of the Mass Air Flow (MAF) sensor

Engine Coolant Temperature (ECT) Sensor

OPERATION

The Engine Coolant Temperature (ECT) sensor is mounted in the intake manifold and sends engine temperature information to the VCM. The VCM supplies 5 volts to the coolant temperature sensor circuit. The sensor is a thermistor which changes internal resistance as temperature changes. When the sensor is cold (internal resistance high), the VCM monitors a high signal voltage which it interprets as a cold engine. As the sensor warms (internal resistance low), the VCM monitors a low signal voltage which it interprets as warm engine.

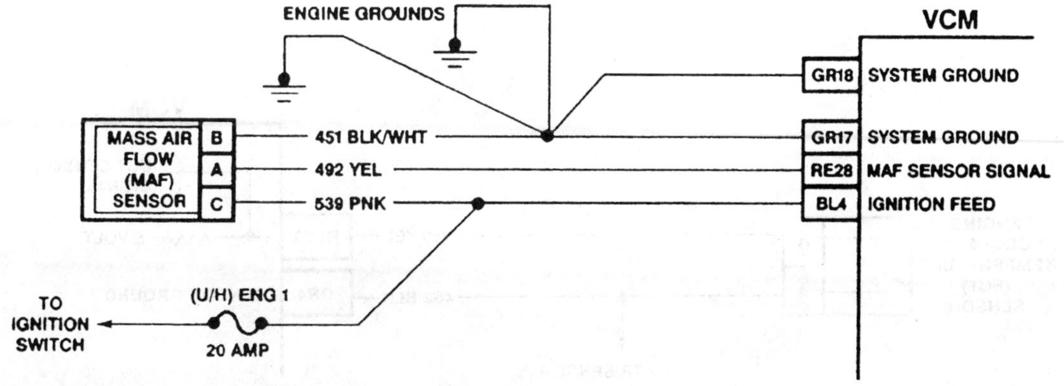

Fig. 36 Mass Airflow (MAF) sensor wiring diagram

TESTING

See Figures 37 and 38

1. Remove the ECT sensor from the vehicle.
2. Immerse the tip of the sensor in container of water.
3. Connect a digital ohmmeter to the two terminals of the sensor.
4. Using a calibrated thermometer, compare the resistance of the sensor to the temperature of the water. Refer to the engine coolant sensor temperature vs. resistance illustration.
5. Repeat the test at two other temperature points, heating or cooling the water as necessary.
6. If the sensor does not met specification, it must be replaced.

REMOVAL & INSTALLATION

See Figures 39 and 40

1. Disconnect the negative battery cable.
2. Drain the cooling system below the level of the sensor and disengage the sensor electrical connection.
3. Remove the coolant sensor.

To install:

4. Install the sensor and engage the electrical connector.
5. Refill the cooling system and connect the negative battery cable.

Intake Air Temperature (IAT) Sensor

OPERATION

The Intake Air Temperature (IAT) sensor is a thermistor which changes value based on the temperature of the air entering the engine. Low temperature produces a high resistance, while a high temperature causes a low resistance. The VCM supplies a 5 volt signal to the sensor through a resistor in the VCM and measures the voltage. The voltage will be high when

ENGINE COOLANT SENSOR		
TEMPERATURE VS. RESISTANCE VALUES (APPROXIMATE)		
°C	°F	OHMS
100	212	177
90	194	241
80	176	332
70	158	467
60	140	667
50	122	973
45	113	1188
40	104	1459
35	95	1802
30	86	2238
25	77	2796
20	68	3520
15	59	4450
10	50	5670
5	41	7280
0	32	9420
-5	23	12300
-10	14	16180
-15	5	21450
-20	-4	28680
-30	-22	52700
-40	-40	100700

88454G25

Fig. 38 Engine Coolant Temperature (ECT) sensor temperature vs. resistance values

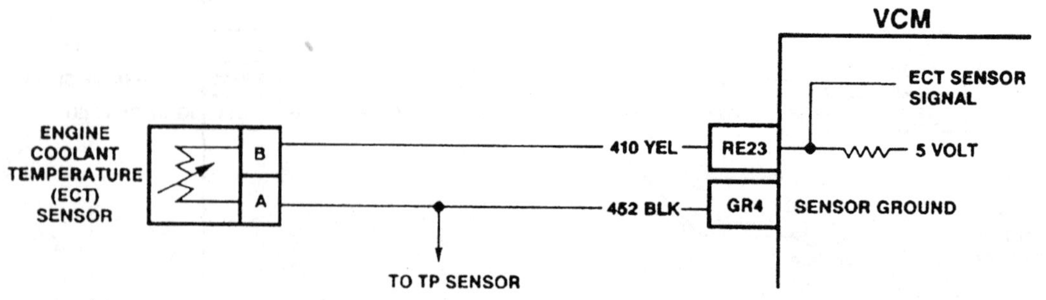

Fig. 37 Engine Coolant Temperature (ECT) sensor wiring diagram

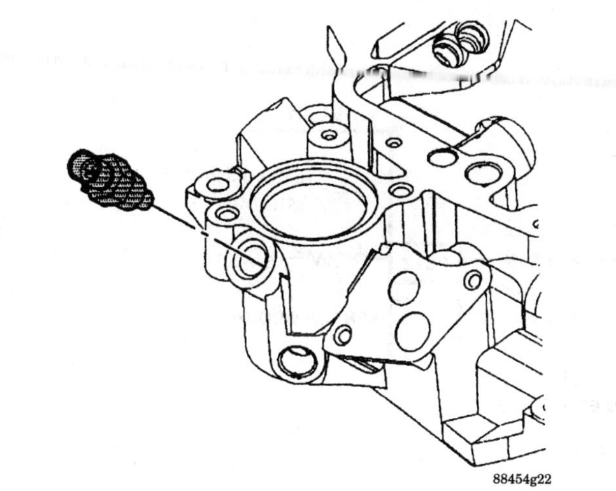

Fig. 39 Engine Coolant Temperature (ECT) sensor location — 4.3L engine

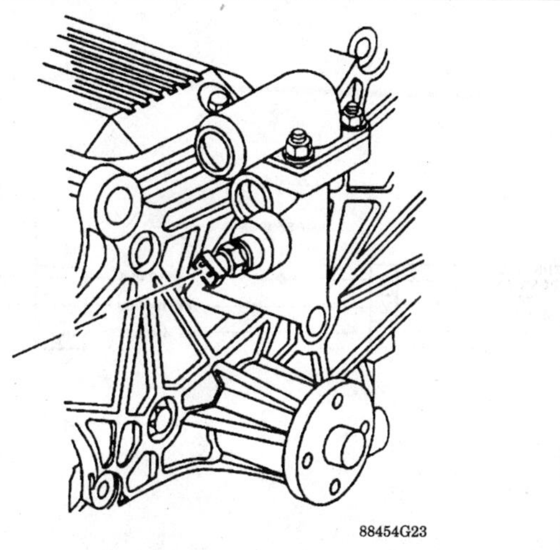

Fig. 40 Engine Coolant Temperature (ECT) sensor location — 2.2L engine

the incoming air is cold, and low when the air is hot. By measuring the voltage, the VCM calculates the incoming air temperature.

the IAT sensor signal is used to adjust spark timing according to incoming air density.

TESTING

See Figures 41 and 42

1. Remove the Intake Air Temperature (IAT) sensor.
2. Connect a digital ohmmeter to the two terminals of the sensor.
3. Using a calibrated thermometer, compare the resistance of the sensor to the temperature of the ambient air. Refer to the temperature vs. resistance illustration.
4. Repeat the test at two other temperature points, heating or cooling the air as necessary with a hair dryer or other suitable tool.
5. If the sensor does not meet specification, it must be replaced.

REMOVAL & INSTALLATION

See Figure 43

1. Disconnect the negative battery cable.
2. Disengage the sensor electrical connection.
3. Loosen and remove the IAT sensor.
4. Installation is the reverse of removal.

Throttle Position Sensor (TPS)

OPERATION

The Throttle Position Sensor (TPS) is connected to the throttle shaft on the throttle body. It is a potentiometer with one end connected to 5 volts from the VCM and the other to ground.

A third wire is connected to the VCM to measure the voltage from the TPS. As the throttle valve angle is changed (accelerator pedal moved), the output of the TPS also changes. At a closed throttle position, the output of the TPS is low (approximately 0.5 volts). As the throttle valve opens, the output increases so that, at wide-open throttle, the output voltage should be approximately 4.5 volts.

By monitoring the output voltage from the TPS, the VCM can determine fuel delivery based on throttle valve angle (driver demand).

TESTING

See Figure 44

1. Backprobe with a high impedance voltmeter at TPS terminals **A** and **B**.
2. With the key **ON** and engine off, the voltmeter reading should be approximately 5.0 volts.
3. If the voltage is not as specified, either the wiring to the TPS or the VCM may be faulty. Correct any wiring or VCM faults before continuing test.
4. Backprobe with a high impedance voltmeter at terminals **C** and **B**.
5. With the key **ON** and engine off and the throttle closed, the TPS voltage should be approximately 0.5-1.2 volts.
6. Verify that the TPS voltage increases or decreases smoothly as the throttle is opened or closed. Make sure to open and close the throttle very slowly in order to detect any abnormalities in the TPS voltage reading.
7. If the sensor voltage is not as specified, replace the sensor.

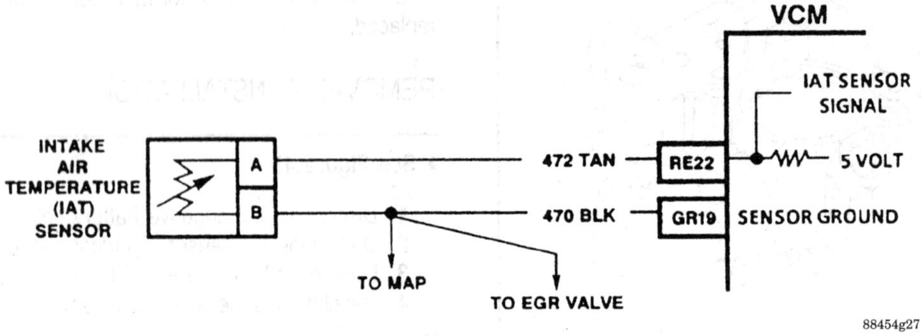

Fig. 41 Intake Air Temperature (IAT) sensor wiring diagram

INTAKE AIR SENSOR

TEMPERATURE VS. RESISTANCE VALUES (APPROXIMATE)

°C	°F	OHMS
100	212	177
90	194	241
80	176	332
70	158	467
60	140	667
50	122	973
45	113	1188
40	104	1459
35	95	1802
30	86	2238
25	77	2796
20	68	3520
15	59	4450
10	50	5670
5	41	7280
0	32	9420
-5	23	12300
-10	14	16180
-15	5	21450
-20	-4	28680
-30	-22	52700
-40	-40	100700

88454G28

Fig. 42 Intake Air Temperature (IAT) sensor temperature vs. resistance values

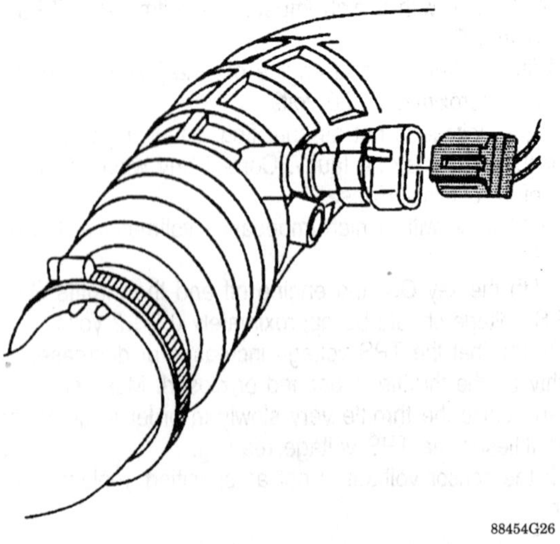

Fig. 43 Intake Air Temperature (IAT) sensor location

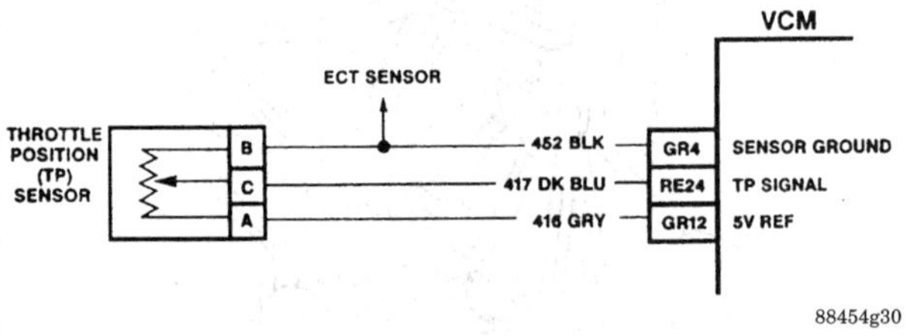

Fig. 44 Throttle Position Sensor (TPS) wiring diagram

REMOVAL & INSTALLATION

▶ See Figure 45

1. Disconnect the negative battery cable and remove the air cleaner and gasket.
2. Disengage the electrical connector.
3. Unfasten the two TPS attaching screw assemblies.
4. Remove the TPS from the throttle body assembly.
5. Remove the TPS seal.

To install:

6. Install the TPS seal over the throttle shaft.
7. With the throttle valve closed, install the TPS on the throttle shaft. Rotate it counterclockwise, to align the mounting holes.
8. Install the two TPS attaching screw assemblies.
9. Engage the electrical connector.
10. Install the air cleaner and gasket.
11. Connect the negative battery cable.

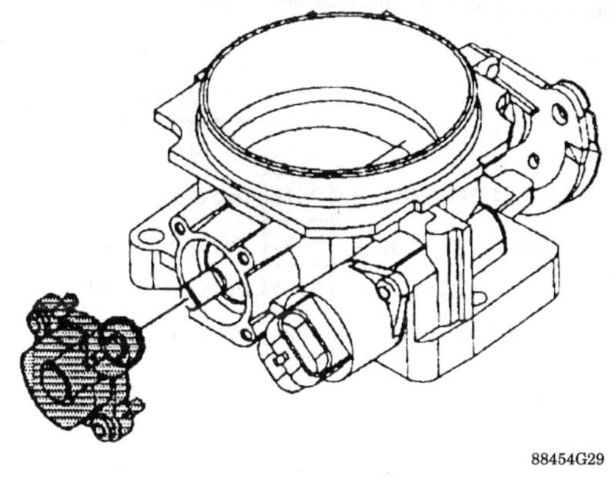

Fig. 45 Common Throttle Position Sensor (TPS)

Idle Air Control (IAC) Valve

OPERATION

The engine idle speed is controlled by the VCM through the Idle Air Control (IAC) valve mounted on the throttle body. The VCM sends voltage pulses to the IAC motor causing the IAC motor shaft and pintle to move in or out a given distance (number of steps) for each pulse, (called counts).

This movement controls air flow around the throttle plate, which in turn, controls engine idle speed, either cold or hot. IAC valve pintle position counts can be seen using a scan tool. Zero counts corresponds to a fully closed passage, while 140 or more counts (depending on the application) corresponds to full flow.

TESTING

See Figure 46

1. Disengage the IAC electrical connector.
2. Using an ohmmeter, measure the resistance between IAC terminals **A** and **B**. Next measure the resistance between terminals **C** and **D**.
3. Verify that the resistance between both sets of IAC terminals is 20-80 ohms. If the resistance is not as specified, the IAC may be faulty.
4. Measure the resistance between IAC terminals **B** and **C**. Next measure the resistance between terminals **A** and **D**.
5. Verify that the resistance between both sets of IAC terminals is infinite. If the resistance is not infinite, the IAC may be faulty.
6. Also, with a small mirror, inspect IAC air inlet passage and pintle for debris. Clean as necessary, as this can cause IAC malfunction.

REMOVAL & INSTALLATION

See Figures 47 and 48

1. Disconnect the negative battery cable.
2. Disengage the electrical connection.
3. Remove the IAC valve. On thread-mounted units, use $1^1/_4$ in. (32mm) wrench and on flange-mounted units, remove the screw assemblies.
4. Remove the IAC valve gasket or O-ring and discard it.

To install:

5. Clean the old gasket material from the surface of the throttle body assembly on the thread mounted valve. On the flange-mounted valve clean the surface to ensure proper O-ring sealing
6. Install the valve with a new gasket or O-ring. Tighten the thread mounted assembly 13 ft. lbs. (18 Nm) and tighten the flange mounted attaching screws to 28 inch. lbs. (3 Nm).
7. Engage the electrical connector to the IAC valve.
8. Connect the negative battery cable.

Manifold Absolute Pressure (MAP) Sensor

OPERATION

The Manifold Absolute Pressure (MAP) sensor measures the changes in intake manifold pressure, which result from the engine load and speed changes, and converts this to a voltage output.

A closed throttle on engine coastdown will produce a low MAP output, while a wide-open throttle will produce a high output. This high output is produced because the pressure inside the manifold is the same as outside the manifold, so 100 percent of the outside air pressure is measured.

The MAP sensor reading is the opposite of what you would measure on a vacuum gauge. When manifold pressure is high, vacuum is low. The MAP sensor is also used to measure barometric pressure under certain conditions, which allows the VCM to automatically adjust for different altitudes.

The VCM sends a 5 volt reference signal to the MAP sensor. As the manifold pressure changes, the electrical resistance of the sensor also changes. By monitoring the sensor output voltage, the VCM knows the the manifold pressure. A higher pressure, low vacuum (high voltage) requires more fuel, while a lower pressure, higher vacuum (low voltage) requires less fuel.

The VCM uses the MAP sensor to control fuel delivery and ignition timing.

TESTING

See Figure 49

1. Backprobe with a high impedance voltmeter at MAP sensor terminals **A** and **C**.
2. With the key **ON** and engine off, the voltmeter reading should be approximately 5.0 volts.

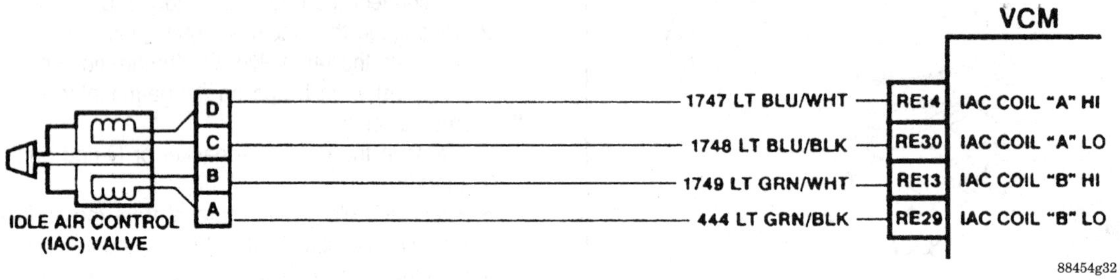

Fig. 46 Idle Air Control (IAC) valve wiring and terminal identification

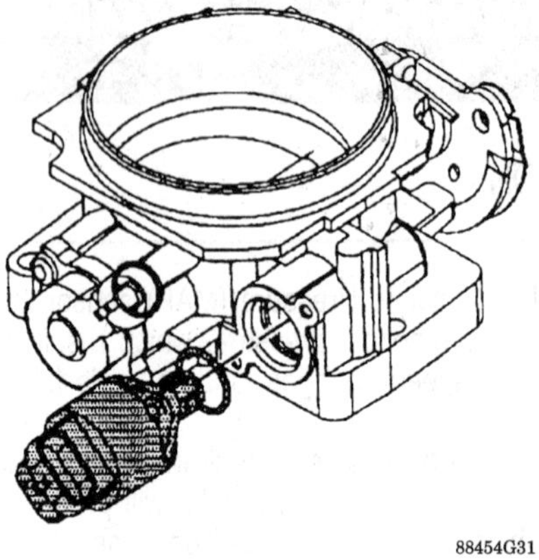

Fig. 47 The IAC valve can be on the throttle body, usually next to the throttle position sensor — 1996 4.3L engine shown

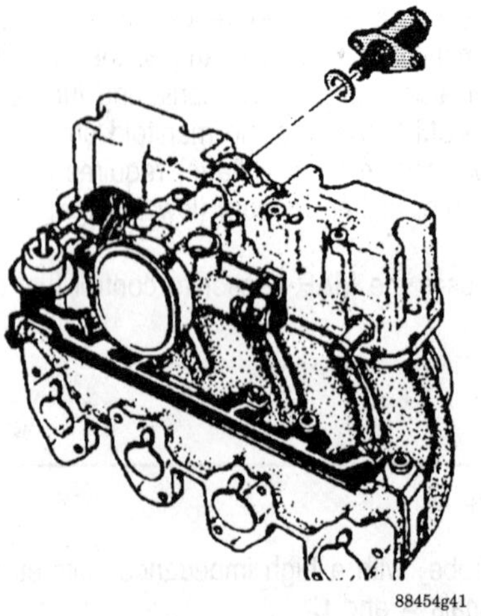

Fig. 48 Location of the IAC valve — 1996 2.2L engine shown

3. If the voltage is not as specified, either the wiring to the MAP sensor or the VCM may be faulty. Correct any wiring or VCM faults before continuing test.
4. Backprobe with the high impedance voltmeter at MAP sensor terminals **B** and **A**.
5. Verify that the sensor voltage is approximately 0.5 volts with the engine not running (at sea level).
6. Record MAP sensor voltage with the key **ON** and engine off.
7. Start the vehicle.
8. Verify that the sensor voltage is greater than 1.5 volts (above the recorded reading) at idle.
9. Verify that the sensor voltage increases to approximately 4.5. volts (above the recorded reading) at Wide Open Throttle (WOT).
10. If the sensor voltage is as specified, the sensor is functioning properly.
11. If the sensor voltage is not as specified, check the sensor and the sensor vacuum source for a leak or a restriction. If no leaks or restrictions are found, the sensor may be defective and should be replaced.

REMOVAL & INSTALLATION

See Figures 50 and 51

1. Disconnect the negative battery cable.
2. Tag and disconnect the vacuum harness assembly.
3. Disengage the electrical connector.
4. Release the locktabs, unfasten the bolts and remove the sensor.
5. Installation is the reverse of removal.

Vehicle Speed Sensor (VSS)

OPERATION

The vehicle speed sensor is made up of a coil mounted on the transmission and a tooth rotor mounted to the output shaft

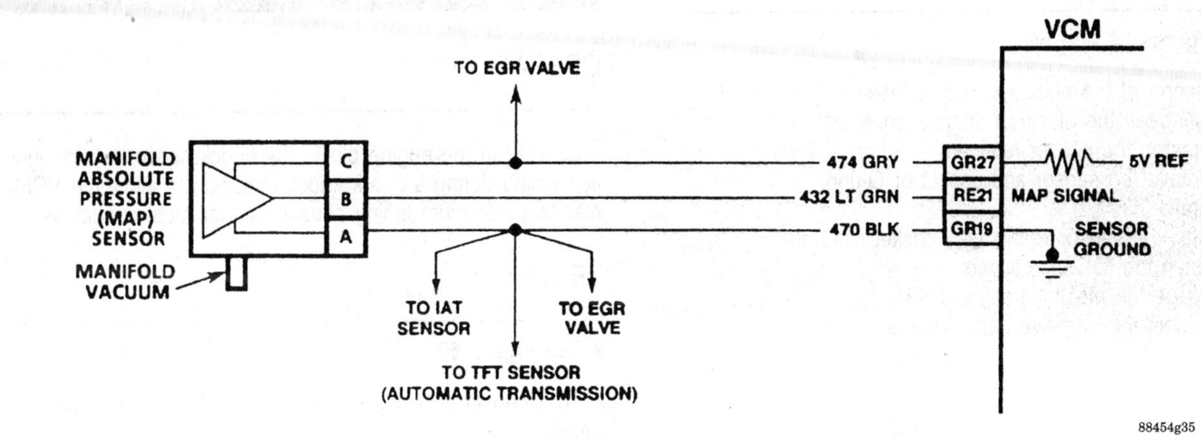

Fig. 49 Manifold Absolute Pressure (MAP) sensor wiring diagram

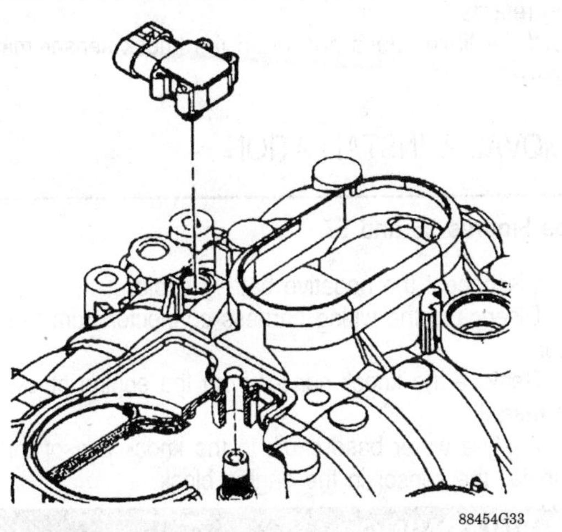

Fig. 50 Manifold Absolute Pressure (MAP) sensor location — 1996 4.3L engine

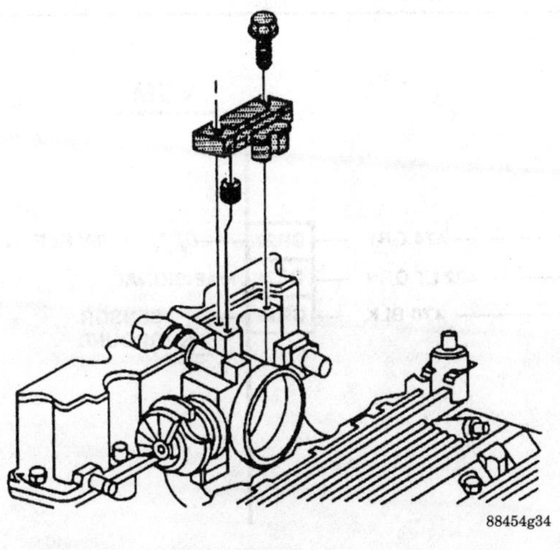

Fig. 51 Manifold Absolute Pressure (MAP) sensor location — 1996 2.2L engine

of the transmission. As each tooth nears the coil, the coil produces an AC voltage pulse. As the vehicle speed increases the number of voltage pulses per second increases.

TESTING

See Figure 52

1. To test the VSS, backprobe the VSS terminals with a high impedance voltmeter (set at the AC voltage scale).
2. Safely raise and support the entire vehicle using jackstands. Make absolutely sure the vehicle is stable.
3. Start the vehicle and place it in gear.
4. Verify that the VSS voltage increases as the drive shaft speed increases.
5. If the VSS voltage is not as specified the VSS may be faulty.

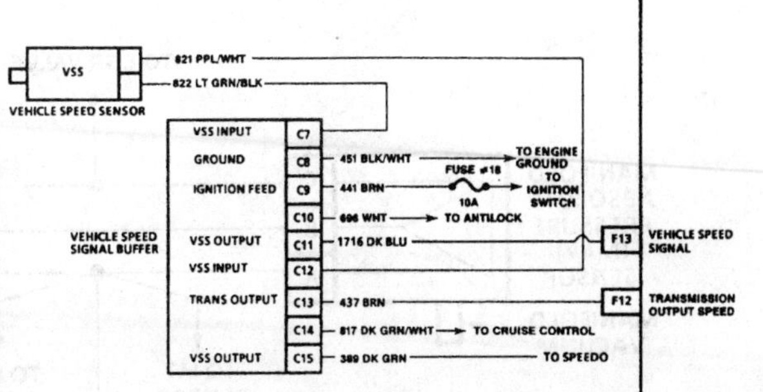

Fig. 52 Vehicle Speed Sensor (VSS) and vehicle speed signal buffer wiring diagram

REMOVAL & INSTALLATION

See Figures 53 and 54

1. Disconnect the negative battery cable.
2. Disengage the electrical connection.
3. Unfasten the sensor retainers.
4. Remove the sensor and gasket or O-ring.

To install:

5. Install the sensor with a new gasket or O-ring.
6. Fasten the sensor retainers.
7. Engage the electrical connections.
8. Connect the negative battery cable.

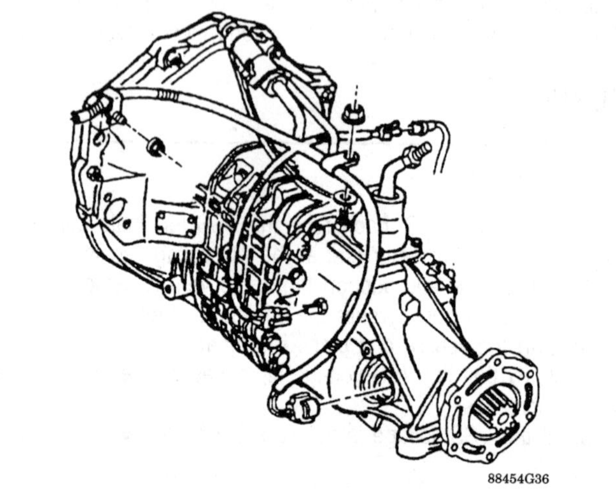

Fig. 54 Vehicle Speed Sensor (VSS) location — manual transmission equipped vehicles

Knock Sensor

OPERATION

Located in the engine block, the knock sensor retards ignition timing during a spark knock condition to allow the VCM to maintain maximum timing advance under most conditions.

TESTING

See Figure 55

1. Connect a timing light to the vehicle and start the engine.
2. Check that the timing is correct before testing knock sensor operation.
3. If timing is correct, tap on the front of the engine block with a metal object while observing the timing to see if the timing retards.
4. If the timing does not retard the knock sensor may be defective.

REMOVAL & INSTALLATION

See Figures 56 and 57

1. Disconnect the negative battery cable.
2. Disengage the wiring harness connector from the knock sensor.
3. Remove the knock sensor from the engine block.

To install:

4. Apply a water base caulk to the knock sensor threads and install the sensor in the engine block.

****WARNING**

Do not use silicon tape to coat the knock sensor threads as this will insulate the sensor from the engine block.

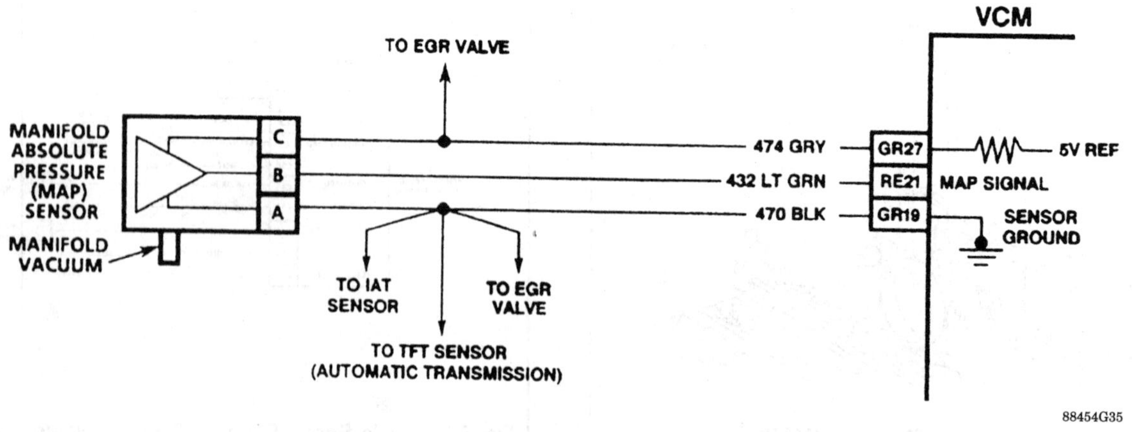

Fig. 53 Vehicle Speed Sensor (VSS) location — automatic transmission equipped vehicles

5. Engage the wiring harness connector.
6. Connect the negative battery cable.

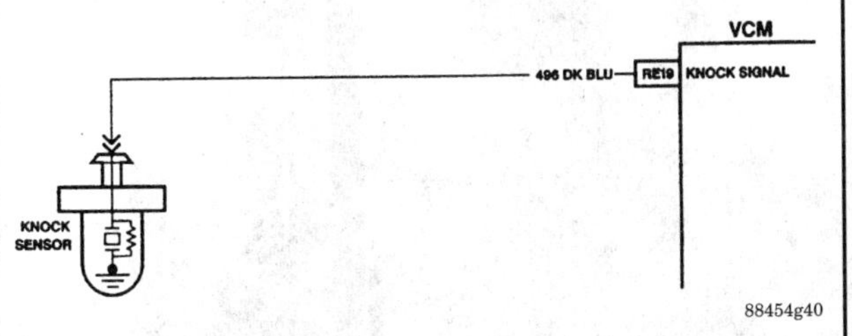

Fig. 55 Knock Sensor (KS) wiring diagram

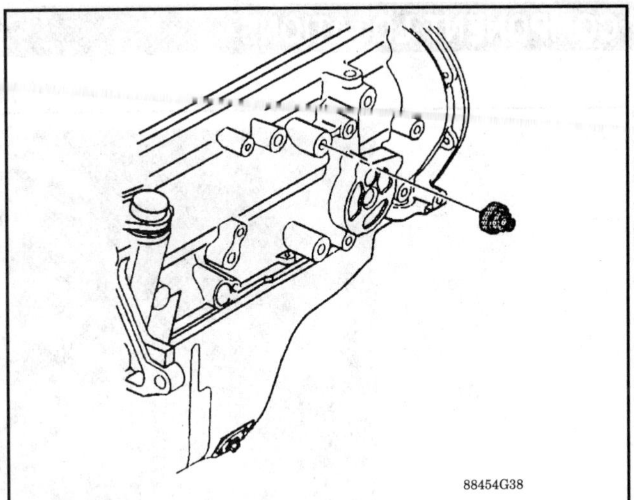

Fig. 56 View of the knock sensor location — 2.2L engine

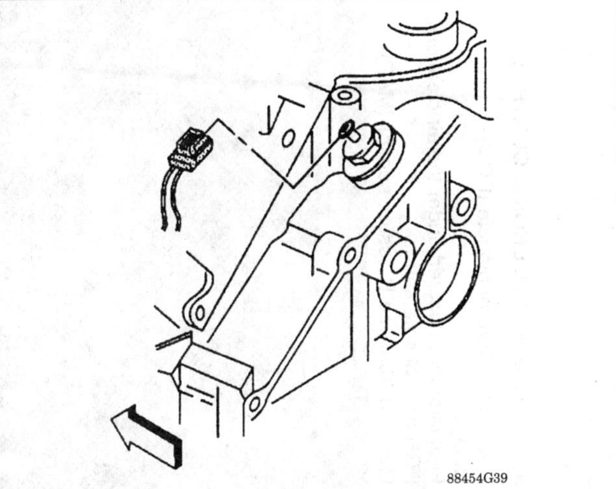

Fig. 57 View of the knock sensor location — 4.3L engine

COMPONENT LOCATIONS

1994 CHEVY/GMC 4.3L ENGINE CONTROLS

1. Powertrain Control Module (PCM)
2. Relays
3. Fuel injectors (located under the air cleaner)
4. EGR control solenoid
5. Manifold Absolute Pressure sensor (MAP)

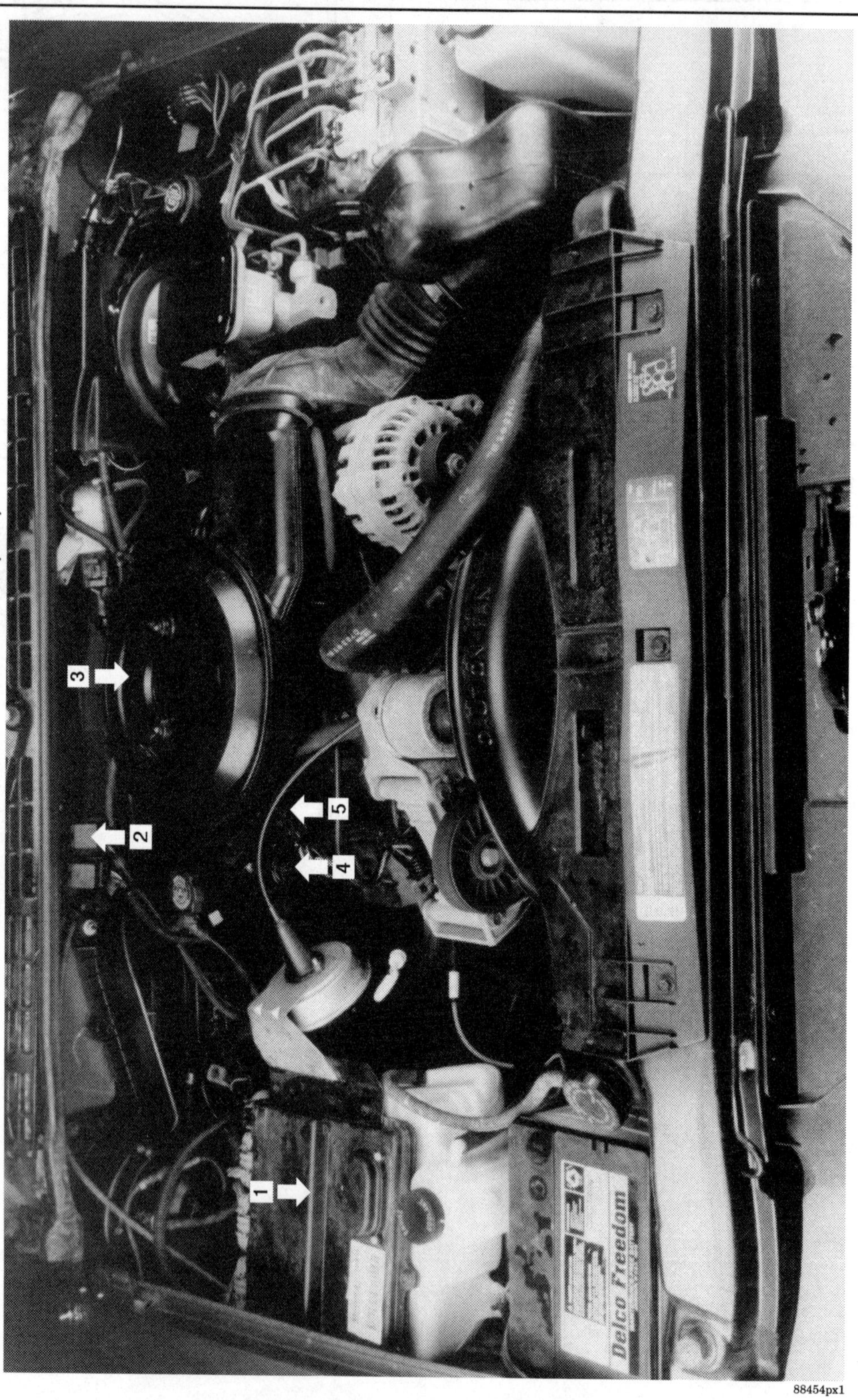

88454px1

Fig. 58 Electronic engine control component locations — 4.3L TBI engines (1994 shown)

1996 CHEVY/GMC 4.3L ENGINE CONTROLS

1. Powertrain Control Module (PCM)
2. Relays
3. Intake Air Temperature Sensor (IAT)
4. Mass Airflow Sensor (MAF)
5. EGR solenoid
6. Idle Air Control (IAC)
7. Ignition Control Module
8. Camshaft Position Sensor (Located in the distributor)
9. Fuel injectors (located under the air cleaner)

88454px2

Fig. 59 Electronic engine control component locations — 4.3L CSFI engines (1996 shown)

'S' SERIES RPO:LN2 ENGINE CODE:4 2.2L L4

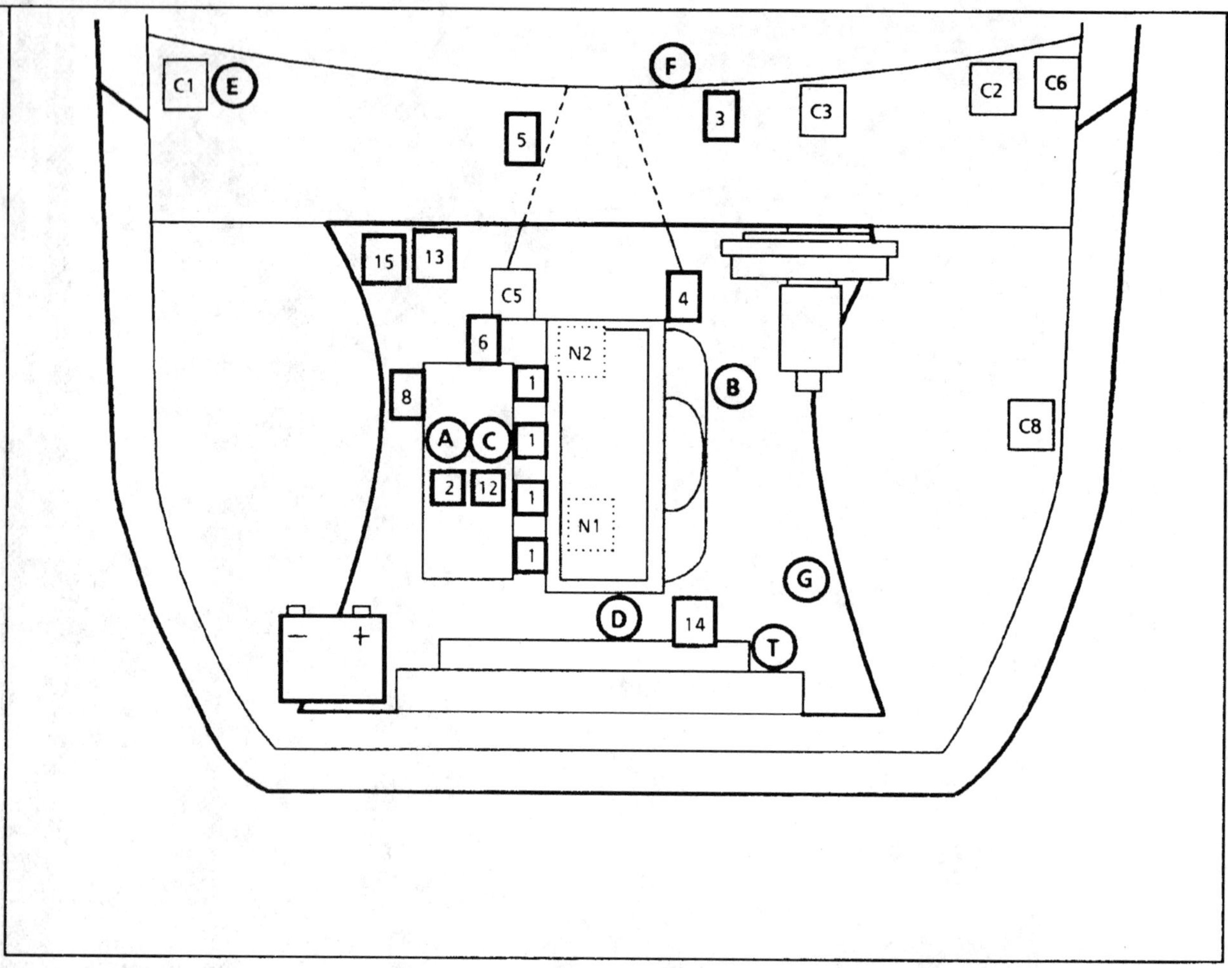

CONTROL MODULE SYSTEM

- C1 Powertrain Control Module (PCM)
- C2 Data Link Connector (DLC)
- C3 Malfunction Indicator Lamp (MIL)
- C5 PCM harness ground
- C6 Fuse block
- C8 Fuel pump test connector

PCM CONTROLLED COMPONENTS

- 1 Fuel injectors
- 2 Idle Air Control (IAC)
- 3 Fuel pump relay (located in convenience center)
- 4 EGR valve
- 5 Transmission connector
- 6 Ignition coil assembly
- 8 Oil pressure switch
- 12 Exhaust Gas Recirculation (EGR) vacuum solenoid
- 13 Air conditioning (A/C relay)
- 14 A/C High pressure cut-out switch
- 15 A/C Low pressure cut-out switch

PCM INFORMATION SENSORS

- A Manifold Absolute Pressure (MAP) sensor
- B Oxygen Sensor (O2S)
- C Throttle Position (TP) sensor
- D Engine Coolant Temperature (ECT) sensor
- E VSS buffer
- F Vehicle Speed Sensor (VSS)
- G Power Steering Pressure (PSP) switch
- T Intake Air Temperature (IAT) sensor (in air intake system)

EMISSION COMPONENTS (NOT PCM CONTROLLED)

- N1 Crankcase vent valve
- Fuel vapor canister (located at driver's rear of vehicle above rear axle).
- N2 Canister purge vacuum control valve

88454x01

Fig. 60 Component locations — 1994 2.2L (VIN 4) engine with automatic and manual transmissions

'S/T' SERIES RPO:LB4 ENGINE CODE:Z 4.3L V6

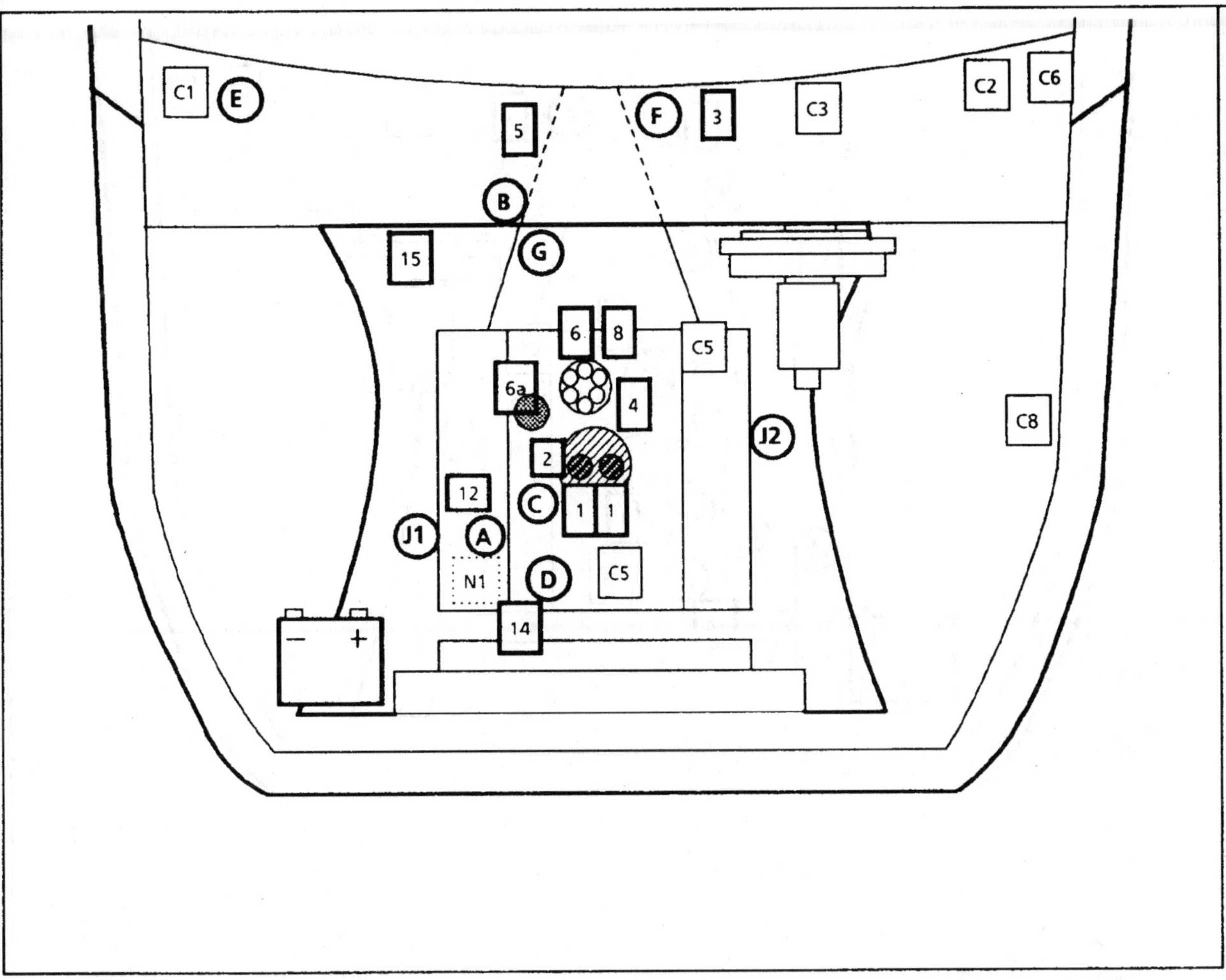

□ COMPUTER COMMAND CONTROL

- C1 Powertrain Control Module (PCM)
- C2 Data Link Connector (DLC)
- C3 MIL (Service Engine Soon)
- C5 PCM harness ground
- C6 Fuse block
- C8 Fuel pump test connector

□ PCM CONTROLLED COMPONENTS

- 1 Fuel injectors
- 2 Idle Air Control (IAC)
- 3 Fuel pump relay (located in convenience center)
- 4 EGR valve
- 5 Transmission connector
- 6 Ignition Control (IC) distributor
- 6a Remote ignition coil
- 8 Oil pressure switch
- 12 (EVRV) vacuum solenoid
- 14 A/C High pressure cut-out switch
- 15 A/C Low Pressure cut-out switch (Pressure cycling)

○ PCM INFORMATION SENSORS

- A Manifold Absolute Pressure (MAP)
- B Heated Oxygen Sensor (HO2S)
- C Throttle Position (TP) sensor
- D Engine Coolant Temperature (ECT) sensor
- E VSS Buffer
- F Vehicle Speed Sensor (VSS)
- G A/C delay relay
- J1 Knock Sensor (KS) (1 of 2)
- J2 Knock Sensor (KS) (2 of 2)

EMISSION COMPONENTS (NOT PCM CONTROLLED)

- N1 Crankcase vent valve
- Fuel vapor canister (Located at drivers rear of vehicle above rear axle).

88454x02

Fig. 61 Component locations — 1994 4.3L (VIN Z) engine with automatic transmission

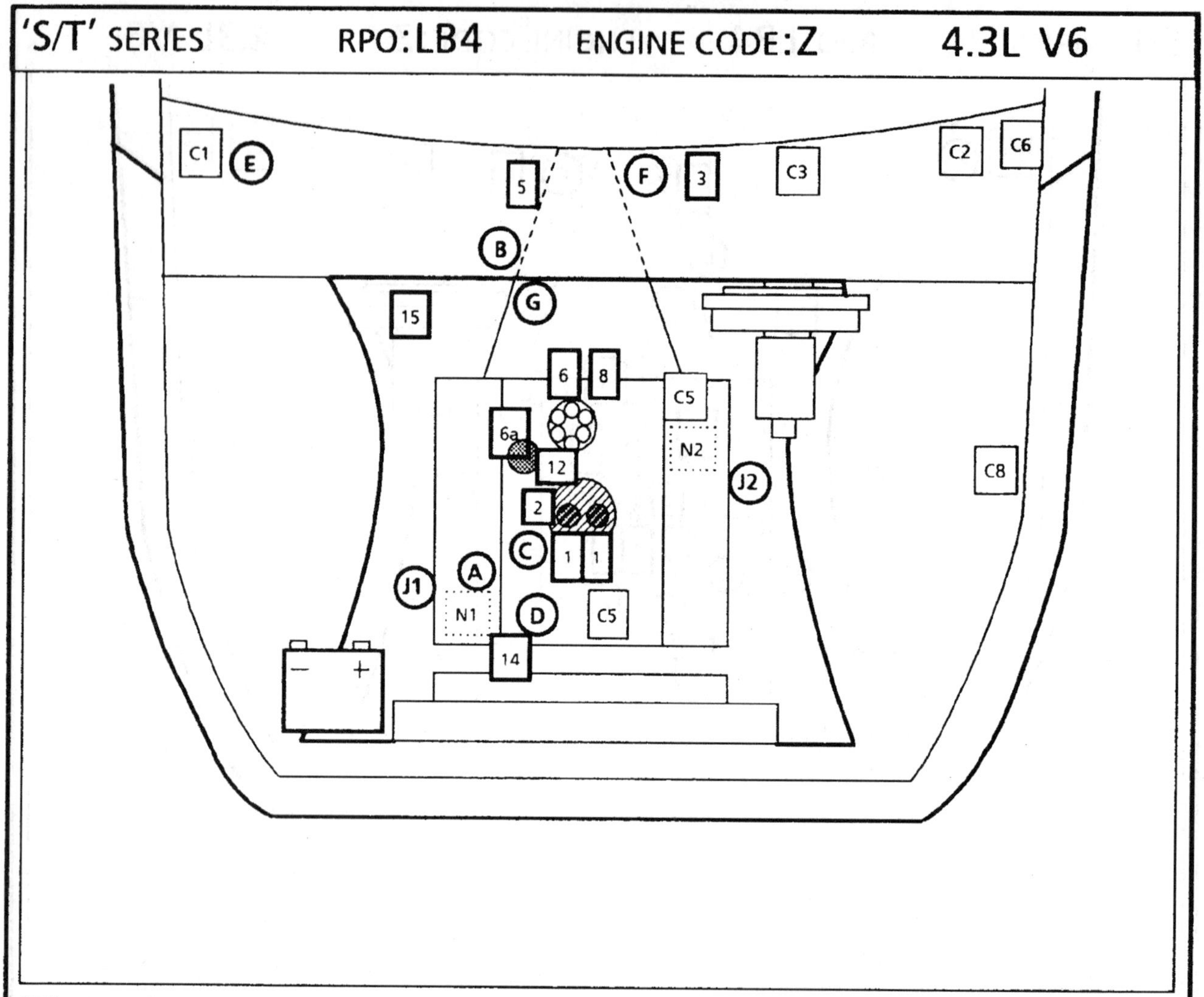

COMPUTER COMMAND CONTROL

- C1 Powertrain Control Module (PCM)
- C2 Data Link Connector (DLC)
- C3 MIL (Service Engine Soon)
- C5 PCM harness ground
- C6 Fuse block
- C8 Fuel pump test connector

PCM CONTROLLED COMPONENTS

- 1 Fuel injectors
- 2 Idle Air Control (IAC)
- 3 Fuel pump relay (located in convenience center)
- 5 Transmission connector
- 6 Ignition Control (IC) distributor
- 6a Remote ignition coil
- 8 Oil pressure switch
- 12 Linear Exhaust Gas Recirculation (EGR) valve
- 14 A/C High pressure cut-out switch
- 15 A/C Low pressure cut-out switch (Pressure cycling)

PCM INFORMATION SENSORS

- A Manifold Absolute Pressure (MAP)
- B Heated Oxygen Sensor (HO2S)
- C Throttle Position (TP) sensor
- D Engine Coolant Temperature (ECT) sensor
- E VSS buffer
- F Vehicle Speed Sensor (VSS)
- G A/C delay relay
- J1 Knock Sensor (KS) (1 of 2)
- J2 Knock Sensor (KS) (2 of 2)

EMISSION COMPONENTS (NOT PCM CONTROLLED)

- N1 Crankcase vent valve
  Fuel vapor canister (Located at drivers rear of vehicle above rear axle).
- N2 Vapor canister purge solenoid

88454x03

Fig. 62 Component locations — 1994 4.3L (VIN Z) engine with automatic transmission (California emissions)

'S/T' SERIES RPO:LB4 ENGINE CODE:Z 4.3L V6

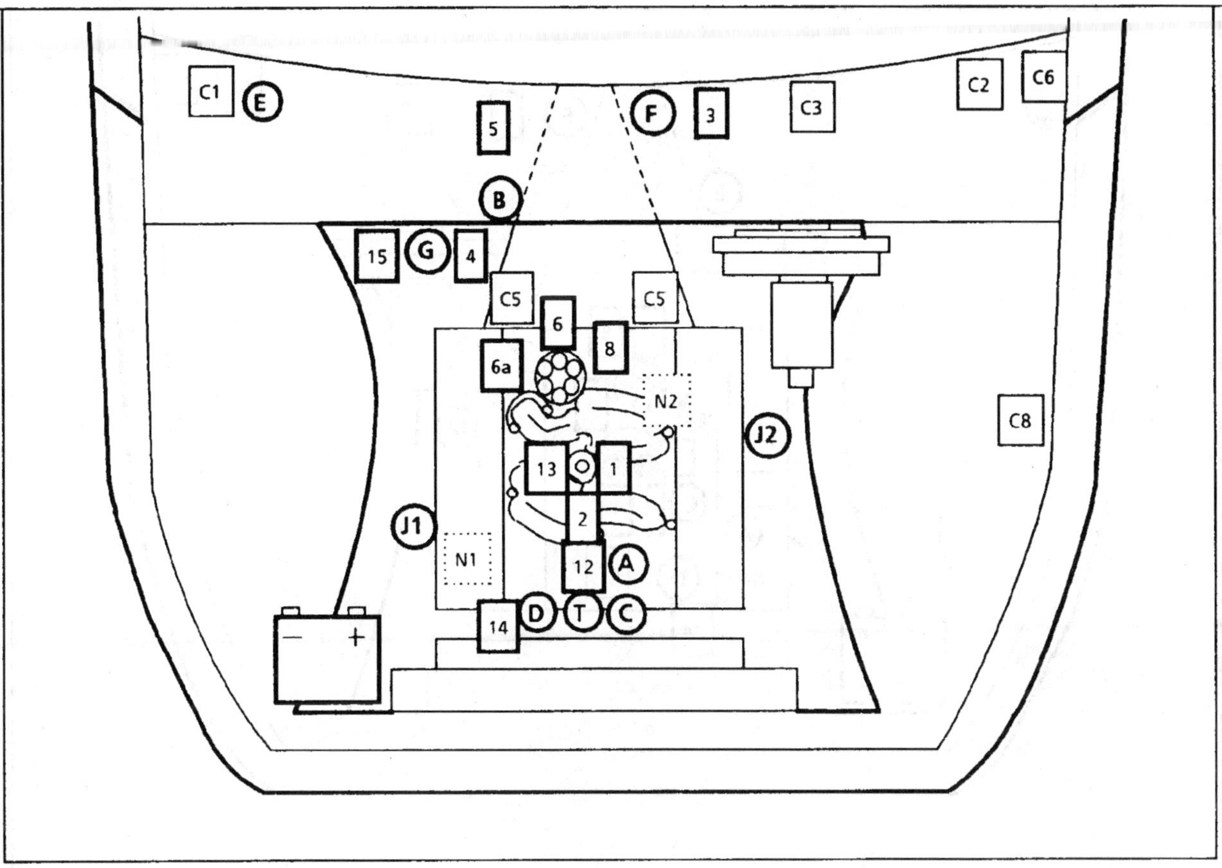

CONTROL MODULE SYSTEM

- C1 Powertrain Control Module (PCM)
- C2 Data Link Connector (DLC)
- C3 Malfunction Indicator Lamp (MIL)
- C5 PCM harness ground
- C6 Fuse block
- C8 Fuel pump test connector

□ PCM CONTROLLED COMPONENTS

- 1 Intake Manifold Tuning Valve (IMTV)
- 2 Idle Air Control (IAC)
- 3 Fuel pump relay (located in convenience center)
- 4 Intake Manifold Tuning Valve (IMTV) relay
- 5 Transmission connector
- 6 Ignition Control (IC) distributor
- 6a Remote ignition coil
- 8 Oil pressure switch
- 12 Linear Exhaust Gas Recirculation (EGR)
- 13 Central Multi-Port Fuel Injection (CMFI) injector assembly (internal)
- 14 A/C High pressure cut-out switch
- 15 A/C Low pressure cut-out switch (Pressure cycling)

○ PCM INFORMATION SENSORS

- A Manifold Absolute Pressure (MAP) sensor
- B Heated Oxygen Sensor (HO2S)
- C Throttle Position (TP) sensor
- D Engine Coolant Temperature (ECT) sensor
- E VSS Buffer
- F Vehicle Speed Sensor (VSS)
- G A/C delay relay
- J1 Knock Sensor (KS) (1 of 2)
- J2 Knock Sensor (KS) (2 of 2)
- T Intake Air Temperature (IAT) sensor

EMISSION COMPONENTS (NOT PCM CONTROLLED)

- N1 Crankcase vent valve
- Fuel vapor canister (Located at drivers rear of vehicle above rear axle).
- N2 Canister purge vacuum control valve

88454x04

Fig. 63 Component locations — 1994 4.3L (VIN W) engine with automatic transmission

'S/T' SERIES RPO:LB4 ENGINE CODE:Z 4.3L V6

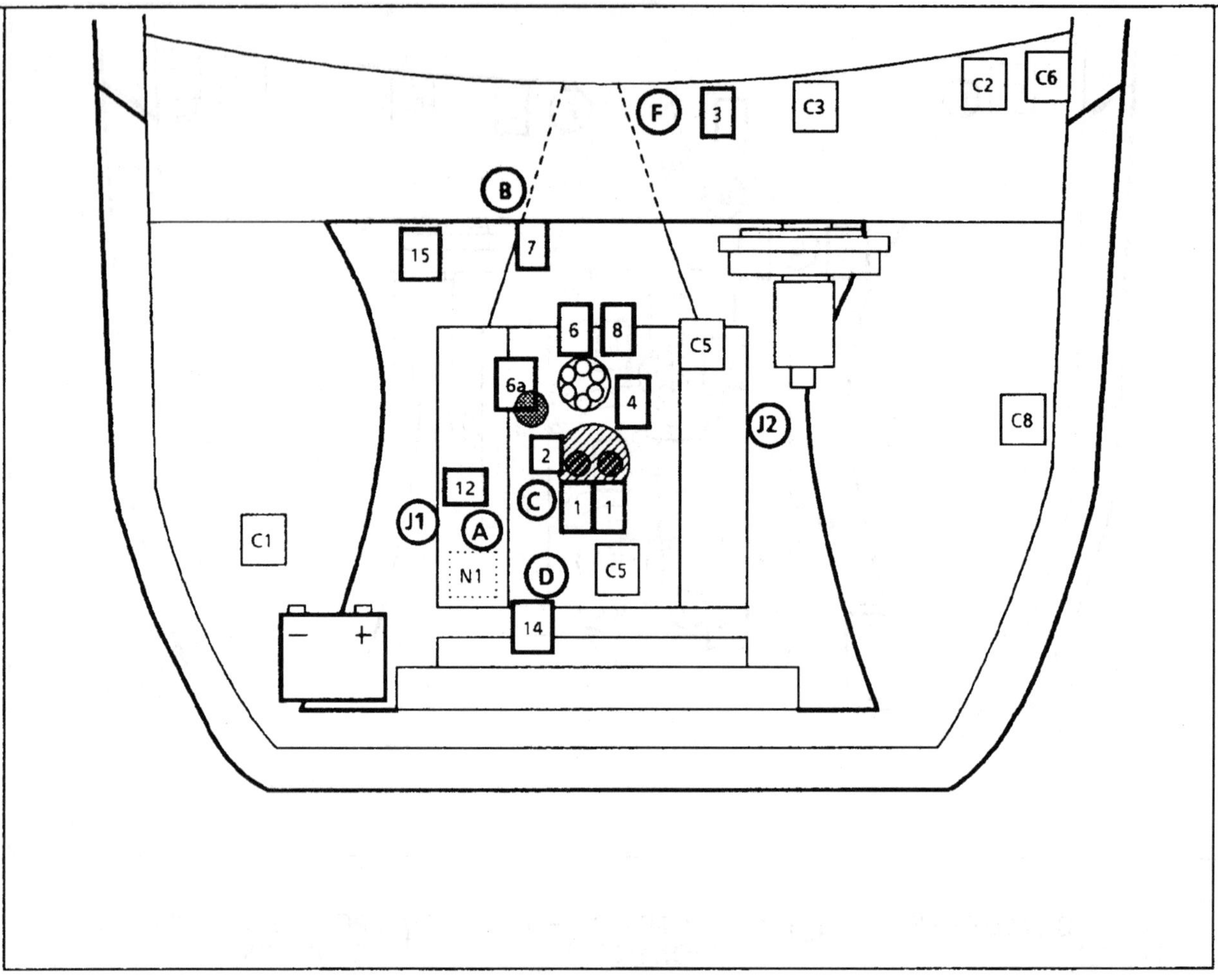

COMPUTER COMMAND CONTROL

C1 Vehicle Control Module (VCM)
C2 Data Link Connector (DLC)
C3 MIL (Service Engine Soon)
C5 VCM harness ground
C6 Fuse block
C8 Fuel pump test connector

VCM CONTROLLED COMPONENTS

1 Fuel injectors
2 Idle Air Control (IAC)
3 Fuel pump relay (located in convenience center)
4 EGR valve
6 Ignition Control (IC) distributor
6a Remote ignition coil
7 A/C relay
8 Oil pressure switch
12 (EVRV) vacuum solenoid
14 A/C High pressure cut-out switch
15 A/C Low pressure cut-out switch

EMISSION COMPONENTS (NOT PCM CONTROLLED)

N1 Crankcase vent valve
Fuel vapor canister (Located at drivers rear of vehicle above rear axle).

VCM INFORMATION SENSORS

A Manifold Absolute Pressure (MAP)
B Heated Oxygen Sensor (HO2S)
C Throttle Position (TP) sensor
D Engine Coolant Temperature (ECT) sensor
F Vehicle Speed Sensor (VSS)
J1 Knock Sensor (KS) (1 of 2)
J2 Knock Sensor (KS) (2 of 2)

88454x05

Fig. 64 Component locations — 1994 4.3L (VIN Z) engine with manual transmission

'S/T' SERIES RPO:L35 ENGINE CODE:W 4.3L V6

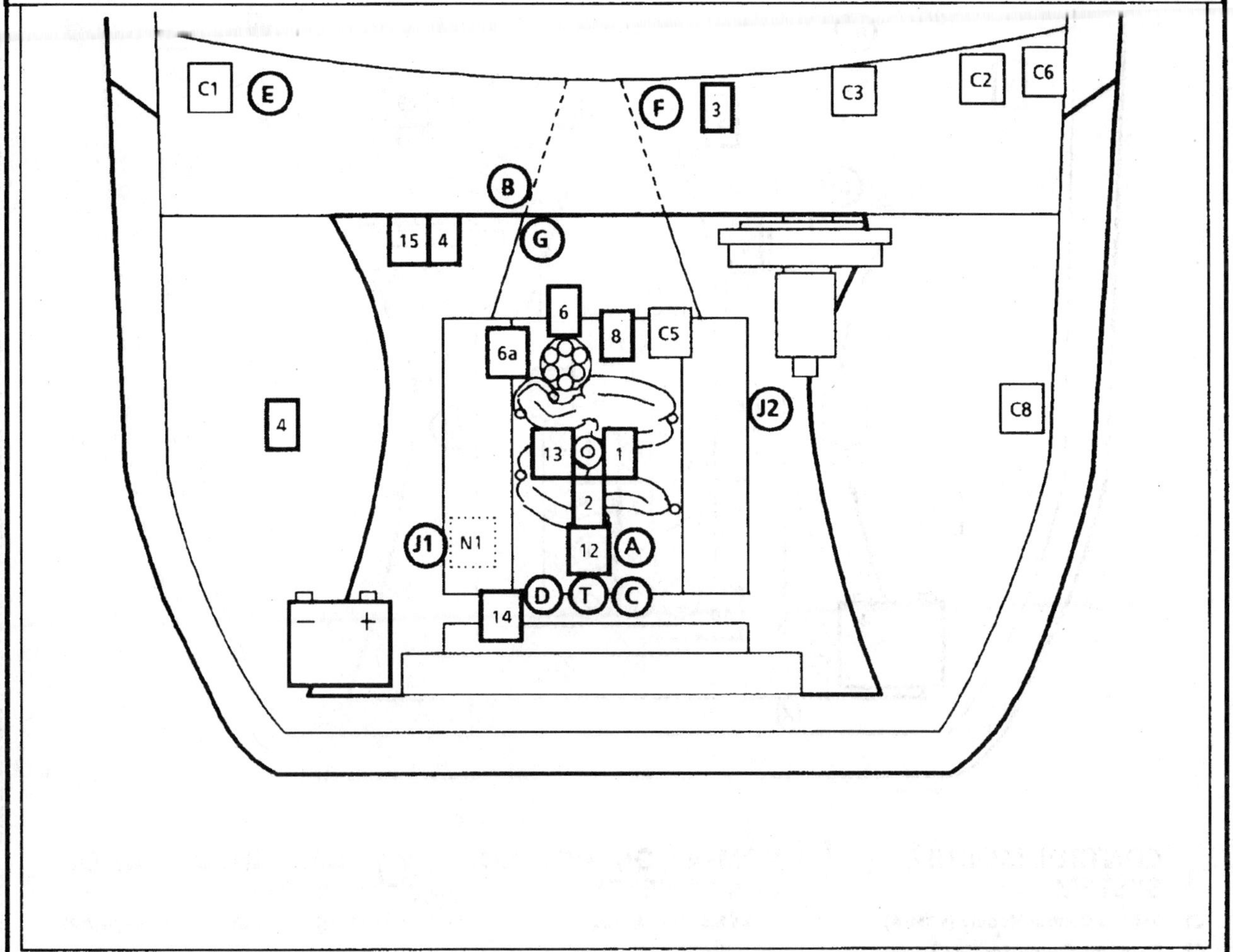

☐ **CONTROL MODULE SYSTEM**

- C1 Engine Control Module (ECM)
- C2 Data Link Connector (DLC)
- C3 Malfunction Indicator Lamp (MIL)
- C5 ECM harness ground
- C6 Fuse block
- C8 Fuel pump test connector

☐ **ECM CONTROLLED COMPONENTS**

- 1 Intake Manifold Tuning Valve (IMTV)
- 2 Idle Air Control (IAC)
- 3 Fuel pump relay (located in convenience center)
- 4 Intake Manifold Tuning Valve (IMTV) relay
- 6 Ignition Control (IC) distributor
- 6a Remote ignition coil
- 8 Oil pressure switch
- 12 Linear Exhaust Gas Recirculation (EGR)
- 13 Central Multi-Port Fuel Injection (CMFI) injector assembly (internal)
- 14 A/C High pressure cut-out switch
- 15 A/C Low pressure cut-out switch (Pressure cycling)

○ **ECM INFORMATION SENSORS**

- A Manifold Absolute Pressure (MAP) sensor
- B Heated Oxygen Sensor (HO2S)
- C Throttle Position (TP) sensor
- D Engine Coolant Temperature (ECT) sensor
- E VSS Buffer
- F Vehicle Speed Sensor (VSS)
- G A/C delay relay
- J1 Knock Sensor (KS) (1 of 2)
- J2 Knock Sensor (KS) (2 of 2)
- T Intake Air Temperature (IAT) sensor

EMISSION COMPONENTS (NOT ECM CONTROLLED)

- N1 Crankcase vent valve
- Fuel vapor canister (Located at drivers rear of vehicle above rear axle)
- N2 Canister purge vacuum control valve

88454x06

Fig. 65 Component locations — 1994 4.3L (VIN W) engine with manual transmission

'S/T' SERIES RPO:L35 ENGINE CODE:W 4.3L V6

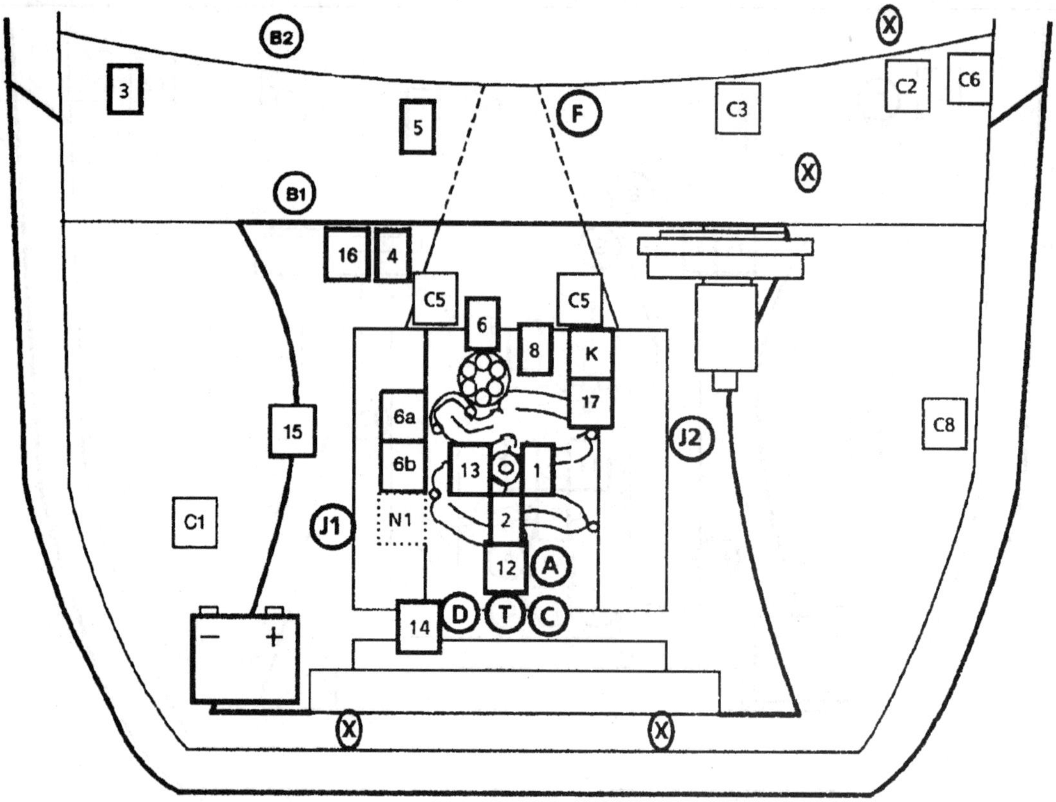

CONTROL MODULE SYSTEM

- C1 Vehicle Control Module (VCM-A)
- C2 Data Link Connector (DLC)
- C3 Malfunction Indicator Lamp (MIL)
- C5 VCM-A harness ground
- C6 Fuse block
- C8 Fuel pump test connector

Ⓧ SIR SYSTEM COMPONENTS

□ VCM-A CONTROLLED COMPONENTS

- 1 Intake Manifold Tuning Valve (IMTV)
- 2 Idle Air Control (IAC)
- 3 Fuel pump relay (located in glove box)
- 4 Intake Manifold Tuning Valve (IMTV) relay
- 5 Transmission connector
- 6 Ignition Control (IC) High Voltage Switch
- 6a Remote ignition coil
- 6b Coil Driver Module
- 8 Oil pressure switch
- 12 Linear Exhaust Gas Recirculation (EGR)
- 13 Central Multi-Port Fuel Injection (Central MFI) injector assembly (internal)
- 14 A/C High pressure cut-out switch
- 15 A/C Low pressure cut-out switch (Pressure cycling)
- 16 A/C Relay
- 17 Evap Canister Purge Solenoid

○ VCM-A INFORMATION SENSORS

- A Manifold Absolute Pressure (MAP) sensor
- B1 Heated Oxygen Sensor (HO2S) Bank 1 Sensor 1
- B2 Heated Oxygen Sensor (HO2S) Bank 1 Sensor 2
- C Throttle Position (TP) sensor
- D Engine Coolant Temperature (ECT) sensor
- F Vehicle Speed Sensor (VSS)
- J1 Knock Sensor (KS) (1 of 2)
- J2 Knock Sensor (KS) (2 of 2)
- K Evap Canister Vacuum Switch
- T Intake Air Temperature (IAT) sensor

⬚ EMISSION COMPONENTS (NOT VCM-A CONTROLLED)

- N1 Crankcase vent valve
- Evap canister (Located at driver's rear of vehicle behind rear axle).

88454x07

Fig. 66 Component locations — 1995 4.3L (VIN W) engine with manual transmission

'S/T' SERIES RPO: L35 ENGINE CODE: W 4.3L V6

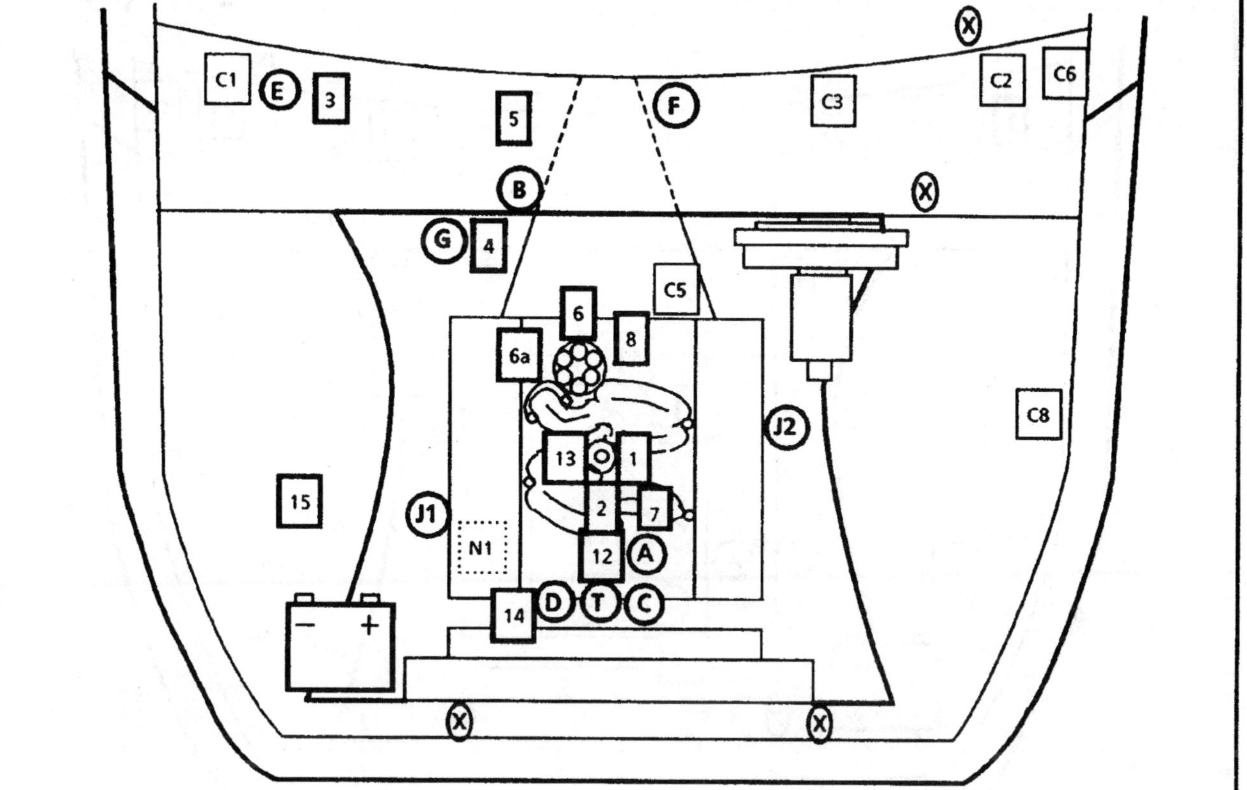

CONTROL MODULE SYSTEM

- C1 Powertrain Control Module (PCM)
- C2 Data Link Connector (DLC)
- C3 Malfunction Indicator Lamp (MIL)
- C5 PCM harness ground
- C6 Fuse block
- C8 Fuel pump test connector

⊗ SIR SYSTEM COMPONENTS

□ PCM CONTROLLED COMPONENTS

- 1 Intake Manifold Tuning Valve (IMTV)
- 2 Idle Air Control (IAC)
- 3 Fuel pump relay (located in glove box).
- 4 Intake Manifold Tuning Valve (IMTV) relay
- 5 Transmission connector
- 6 Ignition Control (IC) distributor
- 6a Remote ignition coil
- 7 Canister Purge Solenoid
- 8 Oil pressure switch
- 12 Linear Exhaust Gas Recirculation (EGR)
- 13 Central Multi-Port Fuel Injection (CMFI) injector assembly (internal)
- 14 A/C High pressure cut-out switch
- 15 A/C Low pressure cut-out switch (Pressure cycling)

○ PCM INFORMATION SENSORS

- A Manifold Absolute Pressure (MAP) sensor
- B Heated Oxygen Sensor (HO2S)
- C Throttle Position (TP) sensor
- D Engine Coolant Temperature (ECT) sensor
- E VSS Buffer
- F Vehicle Speed Sensor (VSS)
- G A/C delay relay
- J1 Knock Sensor (KS) (1 of 2)
- J2 Knock Sensor (KS) (2 of 2)
- T Intake Air Temperature (IAT) sensor

EMISSION COMPONENTS (NOT PCM CONTROLLED)

- N1 Crankcase vent valve
- Fuel vapor canister (Located at drivers rear of vehicle behind rear axle).

88454x08

Fig. 67 Component locations — 1995 4.3L (VIN W) engine with automatic transmission

'S/T' SERIES RPO:LB4 ENGINE CODE:Z 4.3L V6

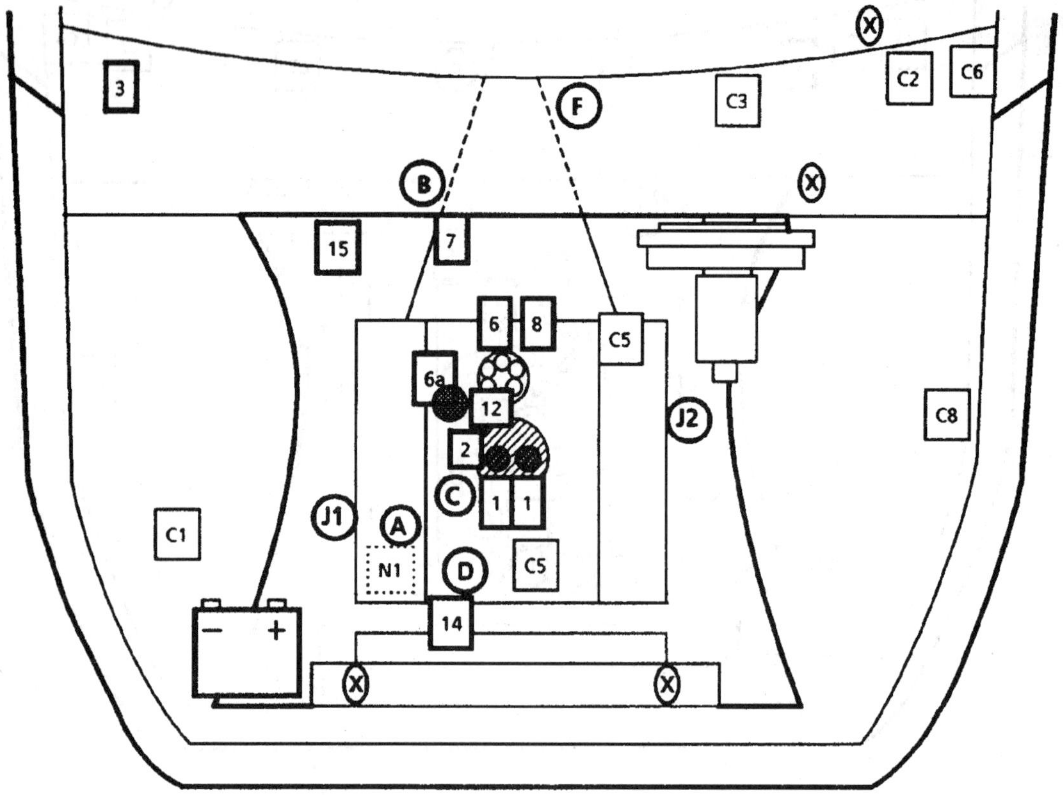

☐ COMPUTER COMMAND CONTROL

- C1 Vehicle Control Module (VCM)
- C2 Data Link Connector (DLC)
- C3 MIL (Service Engine Soon)
- C5 VCM harness ground
- C6 Fuse block
- C8 Fuel pump test connector

ⓧ SIR SYSTEM COMPONENTS

☐ VCM CONTROLLED COMPONENTS

- 1 Fuel injectors
- 2 Idle Air Control (IAC)
- 3 Fuel pump relay (located in glove box)
- 6 Ignition Control (IC) distributor
- 6a Remote ignition coil
- 7 A/C relay
- 8 Oil pressure switch
- 12 Linear EGR valve
- 14 A/C High pressure cut-out switch
- 15 A/C Low pressure cut-out switch

EMISSION COMPONENTS (NOT PCM CONTROLLED)

- N1 Crankcase vent valve
- Fuel vapor canister (Located at drivers rear of vehicle above rear axle).

○ VCM INFORMATION SENSORS

- A Manifold Absolute Pressure (MAP)
- B Heated Oxygen Sensor (HO2S)
- C Throttle Position (TP) sensor
- D Engine Coolant Temperature (ECT) sensor
- F Vehicle Speed Sensor (VSS)
- J1 Knock Sensor (KS) (1 of 2)
- J2 Knock Sensor (KS) (2 of 2)

88454x09

Fig. 68 Component locations — 1995 4.3L (VIN Z) engine with manual transmission

'S/T' SERIES RPO: LB4 ENGINE CODE: Z 4.3L V6

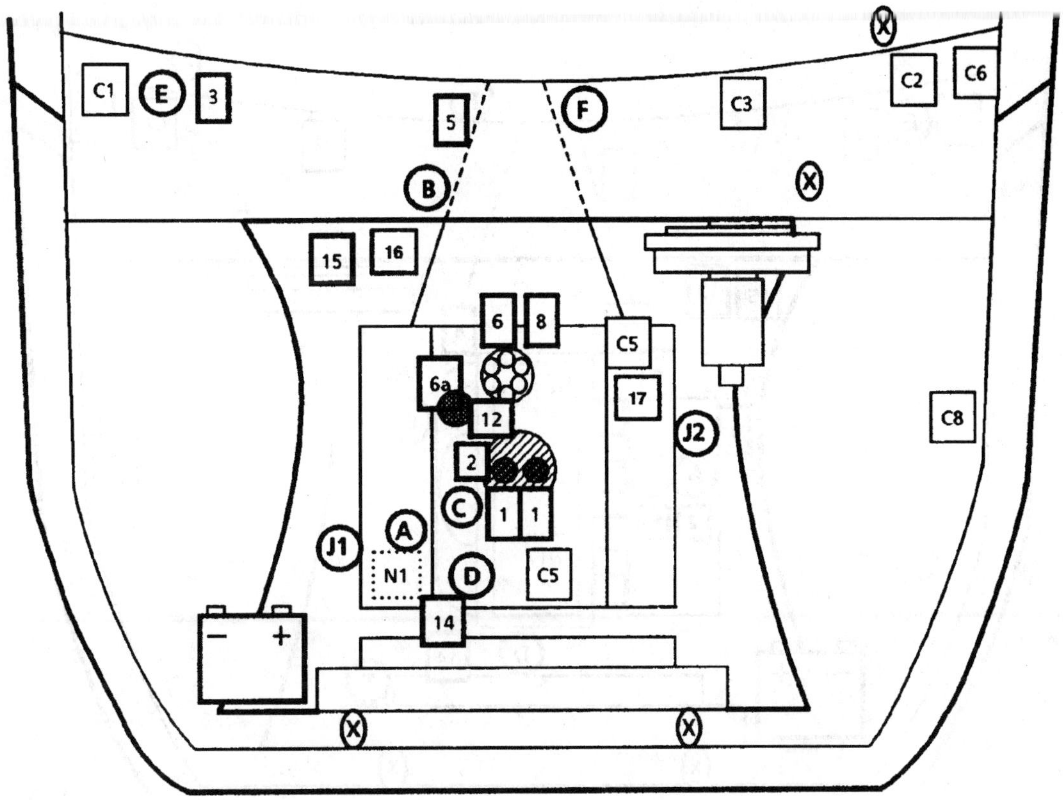

☐ COMPUTER COMMAND CONTROL

- C1 Powertrain Control Module (PCM)
- C2 Data Link Connector (DLC)
- C3 MIL (Service Engine Soon)
- C5 PCM harness ground
- C6 Fuse block
- C8 Fuel pump test connector

Ⓧ SIR SYSTEM COMPONENTS

PCM CONTROLLED COMPONENTS

- 1 Fuel injectors
- 2 Idle Air Control (IAC)
- 3 Fuel pump relay (located in glove box)
- 5 Transmission connector
- 6 Ignition Control (IC) distributor
- 6a Remote ignition coil
- 8 Oil pressure switch
- 12 Linear Exhaust Gas Recirculation (EGR) valve
- 14 A/C High pressure cut-out switch
- 15 A/C Low pressure cut-out switch (Pressure cycling)
- 16 A/C delay relay
- 17 Evap canister purge solenoid

○ PCM INFORMATION SENSORS

- A Manifold Absolute Pressure (MAP)
- B Heated Oxygen Sensor (HO2S)
- C Throttle Position (TP) sensor
- D Engine Coolant Temperature (ECT) sensor
- E VSS buffer
- F Vehicle Speed Sensor (VSS)
- J1 Knock Sensor (KS) (1 of 2)
- J2 Knock Sensor (KS) (2 of 2)

EMISSION COMPONENTS (NOT PCM CONTROLLED)

- N1 Crankcase vent valve
- Evap canister (Located at drivers rear of vehicle above rear axle).

88454x10

Fig. 69 Component locations — 1995 4.3L (VIN Z) engine with automatic transmission

"S" SERIES RPO:LN2 ENGINE CODE:4 2.2L L4

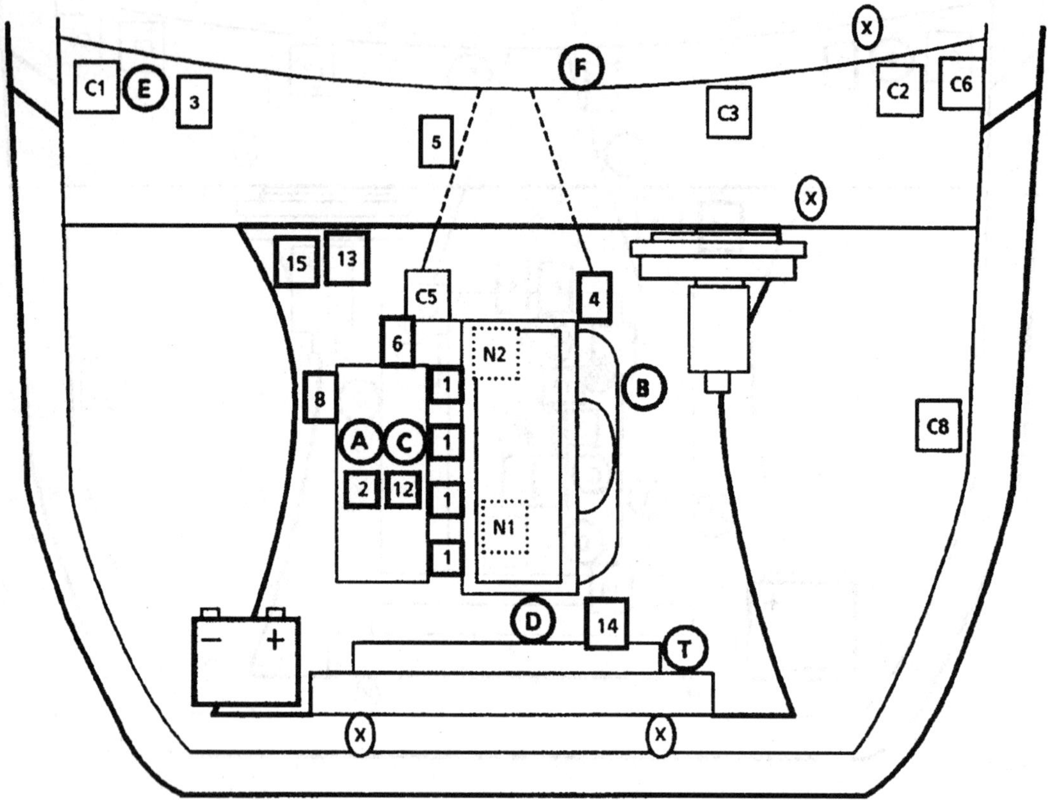

☐ CONTROL MODULE SYSTEM

- C1 Powertrain Control Module (PCM)
- C2 Data Link Connector (DLC)
- C3 Malfunction Indicator Lamp (MIL)
- C5 PCM harness ground
- C6 Fuse block
- C8 Fuel pump test connector

(X) SIR SYSTEM COMPONENTS

☐ PCM CONTROLLED COMPONENTS

- 1 Fuel injectors
- 2 Idle Air Control (IAC)
- 3 Fuel pump relay (located in glove box)
- 4 EGR valve
- 5 Transmission connector
- 6 Ignition coil assembly
- 8 Oil pressure switch
- 12 Exhaust Gas Recirculation (EGR) vacuum solenoid
- 13 Air conditioning (A/C relay)
- 14 A/C High pressure cut-out switch
- 15 A/C Low pressure cut-out switch

○ PCM INFORMATION SENSORS

- A Manifold Absolute Pressure (MAP) sensor
- B Oxygen Sensor (O2S)
- C Throttle Position (TP) sensor
- D Engine Coolant Temperature (ECT) sensor
- E VSS buffer
- F Vehicle Speed Sensor (VSS)
- T Intake Air Temperature (IAT) sensor (in air intake system)

⋯ EMISSION COMPONENTS (NOT PCM CONTROLLED)

- N1 Crankcase vent valve
  Evap canister (located at driver's rear of vehicle above rear axle).
- N2 Evap canister purge vacuum control valve

88454x11

Fig. 70 Component locations — 1995 2.2L (VIN 4) engine with manual and automatic transmission

TROUBLE CODES

General Information

Since the control module is programmed to recognize the presence and value of electrical inputs, it will also note the lack of a signal or a radical change in values. It will, for example, react to the loss of signal from the vehicle speed sensor or note that engine coolant temperature has risen beyond acceptable (programmed) limits. Once a fault is recognized, a numeric code is assigned and held in memory. The dashboard warning lamp: CHECK ENGINE or SERVICE ENGINE SOON (SES), will illuminate to advise the operator that the system has detected a fault. This lamp is also known as the Malfunction Indicator Lamp (MIL).

More than one code may be stored. Keep in mind not every engine uses every code. Additionally, the same code may carry different meanings relative to each engine or engine family.

In the event of an computer control module failure, the system will default to a pre-programmed set of values. These are compromise values which allow the engine to operate, although possibly at reduced efficiency. This is variously known as the default, limp-in or back-up mode. Driveability is almost always affected when the VCM enters this mode.

SCAN TOOLS

See Figures 71, 72 and 73

On most models, the stored codes may be read with only the use of a small jumper wire, however the use of a hand-held scan tool such as GM's TECH-1® or equivalent is recommended. On 1996-97 models, an OBD-II compliant scan tool must be used. There are many manufacturers of these tools; a purchaser must be certain that the tool is proper for the intended use. If you own a scan type tool, it probably came with comprehensive instructions on proper use. Be sure to follow

tccs4P06

Fig. 71 Used properly, a scan tool can be a powerful diagnostic aid

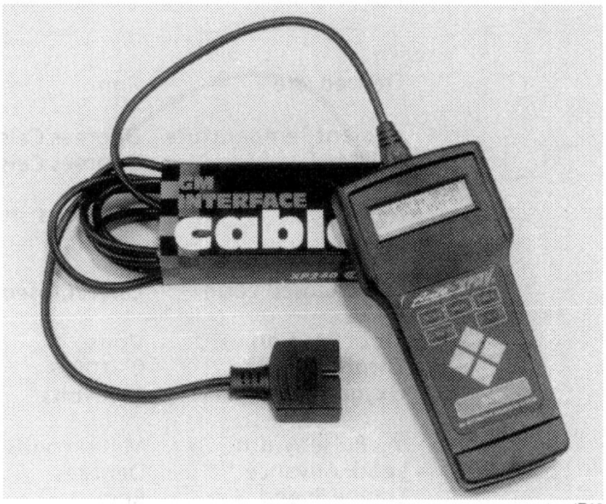

tccs4P12

Fig. 72 Some inexpensive scan tools, such as the Auto Xray®, can interface with GM vehicles

the instructions that came with your unit if they differ from what is given here; this is a general guide with useful information included.

The scan tool allows any stored codes to be read from the VCM or PCM memory. The tool also allows the operator to view the data being sent to the computer control module while the engine is running. This ability has obvious diagnostic advantages; the use of the scan tool is frequently required for component testing. The scan tool makes collecting information easier; the data must be correctly interpreted by an operator familiar with the system.

An example of the usefulness of the scan tool may be seen in the case of a temperature sensor which has changed its electrical characteristics. The VCM is reacting to an apparently warmer engine (causing a driveability problem), but the sensor's voltage has not changed enough to set a fault code. Connecting the scan tool, the voltage signal being sent to the VCM may be viewed; comparison to normal values or a known good vehicle reveals the problem quickly.

ELECTRICAL TOOLS

The most commonly required electrical diagnostic tool is the digital multimeter, allowing voltage, ohmage (resistance) and amperage to be read by one instrument. The multimeter must be a high-impedance unit, with 10 megohms of impedance in the voltmeter. This type of meter will not place an additional load on the circuit it is testing; this is extremely important in low voltage circuits. The multimeter must be of high quality in all respects. It should be handled carefully and protected from impact or damage. Replace batteries frequently in the unit.

Other necessary tools include an unpowered test light, a quality tachometer with an inductive (clip-on) pick up, and the proper tools for releasing GM's Metri-Pack, Weather Pack and Micro-Pack terminals as necessary. The Micro-Pack connectors are used at the VCM electrical connector. A vacuum

"SCAN" Position	Units Displayed	Typical Data Value
Engine Speed	Rpm	± 50 RPM from desired rpm in drive (A/T) ± 100 RPM from desired rpm in neutral (M/T)
Desired Idle	Rpm	ECM idle command (varies with temp.)
Coolant Temperature	Degrees Celsius	85° - 105°
IAT/MAT	Degrees Celsius	10° - 90° (varies with underhood temp. and sensor location)
MAP	kPa/Volts	29-48 kPa/1 - 2 volts (varies with manifold and barometric pressures)
Open/Closed Loop	Open/Closed	"Closed Loop" (may enter "Open Loop" with extended idle)
Throt Position	Volts	.30 - 1.33
Throttle Angle	0 - 100%	0
Oxygen Sensor	Millivolts	100 - 999 (varies continuously)
Inj. Pulse Width	Milliseconds	.8 - 3.0
Spark Advance	Degrees	Varies
Engine Speed	Rpm	± 50 RPM from desired rpm in drive (A/T) ± 100 RPM from desired rpm in neutral (M/T)
Fuel Integrator	Counts	110-145
Block Learn	Counts	118-138
Idle Air Control	Counts (steps)	1 - 50
P/N Switch	P-N and R-D-L	Park/Neutral (P/N)
MPH/KPH	0-255	0
TCC	"ON"/"OFF"	"OFF"
Crank Rpm	Rpm	) 796
Ign/Batt Voltage	Volts	13.5 - 14.5
Cooling Fan Relay	"ON"/"OFF"	"OFF" (coolant temperature below 102°C)
A/C Request	"YES"/"NO"	No
A/C Clutch	"ON"/"OFF"	"OFF"
Power Steering	Normal/High Pressure	Normal
Shift Light (M/T)	"ON"/"OFF"	"OFF"

88454g42

Fig. 73 Example of scan tool data and typical or baseline values

pump/gauge may also be required for checking sensors, solenoids and valves.

Diagnosis and Testing

Diagnosis of a driveablility and/or emissions problems requires attention to detail and following the diagnostic procedures in the correct order. Resist the temptation to perform any repairs before performing the preliminary diagnostic steps. In many cases this will shorten diagnostic time and often cure the problem without electronic testing.

The proper troubleshooting procedure for these vehicles is as follows:

VISUAL/PHYSICAL INSPECTION

This is possibly the most critical step of diagnosis and should be performed immediately after retrieving any codes. A detailed examination of connectors, wiring and vacuum hoses can often lead to a repair without further diagnosis. Performance of this step relies on the skill of the technician performing it; a careful inspector will check the undersides of hoses as well as the integrity of hard-to-reach hoses blocked by the air cleaner or other component. Wiring should be checked carefully for any sign of strain, burning, crimping, or terminal pull-out from a connector. Checking connectors at components or in harnesses is required; usually, pushing them together will reveal a loose fit.

INTERMITTENTS

If a fault occurs intermittently, such as a loose connector pin breaking contact as the vehicle hits a bump, the VCM will note the fault as it occurs and energize the dash warning lamp. If the problem self-corrects, as with the terminal pin again making contact, the dash lamp will extinguish after 10 seconds but a code will remain stored in the computer control module's memory.

When an unexpected code appears during diagnostics, it may have been set during an intermittent failure that self-corrected; the codes are still useful in diagnosis and should not be discounted.

CIRCUIT/COMPONENT REPAIR

The fault codes and the scan tool data will lead to diagnosis and checking of a particular circuit. It is important to note that the fault code indicates a fault or loss of signal in an VCM-controlled system, not necessarily in the specific component.

Refer to the appropriate Diagnostic Code chart to determine the codes meaning. The component may then be tested following the appropriate component test procedures found in this section. If the component is OK, check the wiring for shorts or opens. Further diagnoses should be left to an experienced driveability technician.

If a code indicates the VCM to be faulty and the VCM is replaced, but does not correct the problem, one of the following may be the reason:

• There is a problem with the VCM terminal connections: The terminals may have to be removed from the connector in order to check them properly.

• The VCM or PROM is not correct for the application: The incorrect VCM or PROM may cause a malfunction and may or may not set a code.

• The problem is intermittent: This means that the problem is not present at the time the system is being checked. In this case, make a careful physical inspection of all portions of the system involved.

• Shorted solenoid, relay coil or harness: Solenoids and relays are turned on and off by the VCM using internal electronic switches called drivers. Each driver is part of a group of four called Quad-Drivers. A shorted solenoid, relay coil or harness may cause an VCM to fail, and a replacement VCM to fail when it is installed. Use a short tester, J34696, BT 8405, or equivalent, as a fast, accurate means of checking for a short circuit.

• The Programmable Read Only Memory (PROM) may be faulty: Although the PROM rarely fails, it operates as part of the VCM. Therefore, it could be the cause of the problem. Substitute a known good PROM.

• The replacement VCM may be faulty: After the VCM is replaced, the system should be rechecked for proper operation. If the diagnostic code again indicates the VCM is the problem, substitute a known good VCM. Although this is a very rare condition, it could happen.

Reading Codes

1994-95 MODELS

See Figures 74 and 75

Listings of the trouble for the various engine control system covered in this manual are located in this section. Remember that a code only points to the faulty circuit NOT necessarily to a faulty component. Loose, damaged or corroded connections may contribute to a fault code on a circuit when the sensor or component is operating properly. Be sure that the components

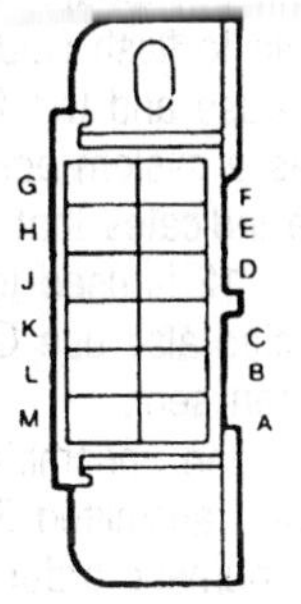

Fig. 74 ALDL connector — 1994 models

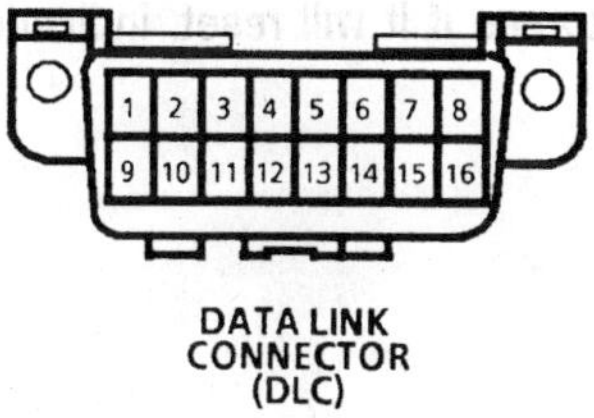

Fig. 75 ALDL connector — 1995 models

are faulty before replacing them, especially the expensive ones.

The Assembly Line Diagnostic Link (ALDL) connector or Data Link Connector (DLC) may be located under the dash and sometimes covered with a plastic cover labeled DIAGNOSTIC CONNECTOR.

1. The diagnostic trouble codes can be read by grounding test terminal **B**. The terminal is most easily grounded by connecting it to terminal **A** (internal ECM ground). This is the terminal to the right of terminal B on the top row of the ALDL connector.

2. Once the terminals have been connected, the ignition switch must be moved to the **ON** position with the engine not running.

3. The Service Engine Soon or Check Engine light should be flashing. If it isn't, turn the ignition **OFF** and remove the jumper wire. Turn the ignition **ON** and confirm that light is now on. If it is not, replace the bulb and try again. If the bulb still will not light, or if it does not flash with the test terminal

grounded, the system should be diagnosed by an experienced driveability technician. If the light is OK, proceed as follows.

4. The code(s) stored in memory may be read through counting the flashes of the dashboard warning lamp. The dash warning lamp should begin to flash Code 12. The code will display as one flash, a pause and two flashes. Code 12 is not a fault code. It is used as a system acknowledgment or handshake code; its presence indicates that the VCM can communicate as requested. Code 12 is used to begin every diagnostic sequence. Some vehicles also use Code 12 after all diagnostic codes have been sent.

5. After Code 12 has been transmitted 3 times, the fault codes, if any, will each be transmitted 3 times. The codes are stored and transmitted in numeric order from lowest to highest.

➡The order of codes in the memory does not indicate the order of occurrence.

6. If there are no codes stored, but a driveability or emissions problem is evident, the system should be diagnosed by an experienced driveability technician.

7. If one or more codes are stored, record them. Refer to the applicable Diagnostic Code chart in this section.

8. Switch the ignition **OFF** when finished with code retrieval or scan tool readings.

➡After making repairs, clear the trouble codes and operate the vehicle to see if it will reset, indicating further problems.

1996-97 MODELS

See Figures 76, 77, 78, 79 and 80

On 1996-97 models, an OBD-II compliant scan tool must be used to retrieve the trouble codes. Follow the scan tool manufacturer's instructions on how to connect the scan tool to the vehicle and how to retrieve the codes.

Clearing Codes

Stored fault codes may be erased from memory at any time by removing power from the VCM for at least 30 seconds. It may be necessary to clear stored codes during diagnosis to check for any recurrence during a test drive, but the stored codes must be written down when retrieved. The codes may still be required for subsequent troubleshooting. Whenever a repair is complete, the stored codes must be erased and the vehicle test driven to confirm correct operation and repair.

WARNING

The ignition switch must be OFF any time power is disconnected or restored to the VCM. Severe damage may result if this precaution is not observed.

Depending on the electrical distribution of the particular vehicle, power to the VCM may be disconnected by removing the VCM fuse in the fusebox, disconnecting the in-line fuse holder near the positive battery terminal or disconnecting the VCM power lead at the battery terminal. Disconnecting the negative battery cable to clear codes is not recommended as this will also clear other memory data in the vehicle such as radio presets.

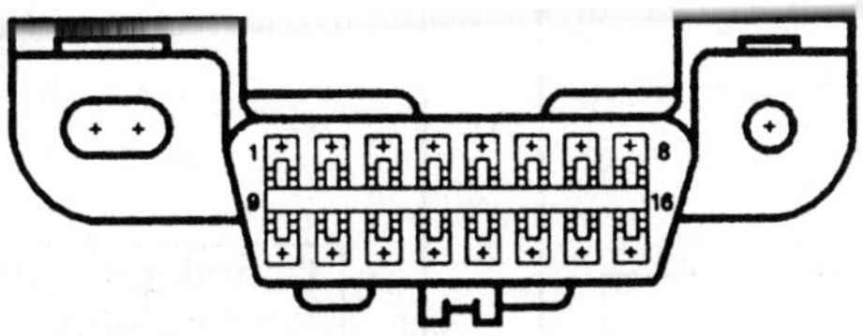

** Cavities which are not listed are not used.

CAVITY	WIRE COLOR	WIRE SIZE	CKT	DESCRIPTION
2	PPL	0.8	1807	SERIAL DATA SIGNAL - PRIMARY
4	BLK	0.8	150	GROUND
5	BLK/WHT	0.8	151	GROUND
8	BLK/WHT	0.8	1455	KEYLESS ENTRY PROGRAM ENABLE (EXCEPT BASE PICKUP)
9	TAN	0.8	800	SERIAL DATA SIGNAL - PRIMARY
12	TAN/WHT	0.8	799	ABS DIAGNOSTIC SIGNAL (PICKUP ONLY)
13	ORN	0.8	1568	TRANSFER CASE SHIFT CONTROL MODULE (W/ 4WD W/ ELECTRIC SHIFT NP1)
16	ORN	1	840	BATTERY - FUSED

88454g45

Fig. 76 ALDL connector — 1996 models

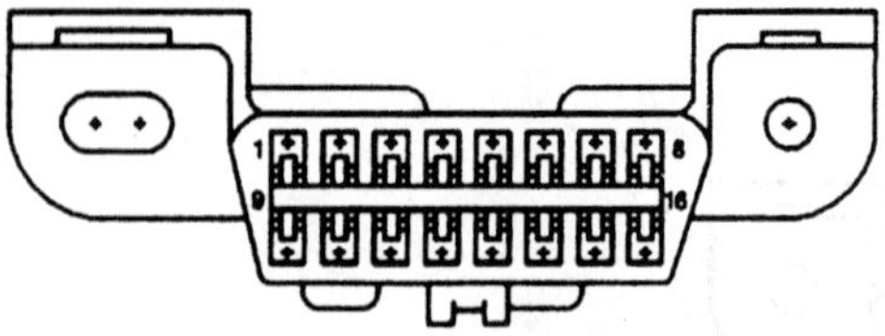

Connector Part Information	• 12110250 • 16 - Way F Metri-Pack 150 Series (Black)		
Pin	**Wire Color**	**Circuit No.**	**Function**
1	—	—	Not Used
2	PPL	1807	Serial data signal - Class II
3	—	—	Not Used
4	BLK	150	Ground
5	BLK/WHT	151	Ground
6	—	—	Not Used
7	—	—	Not Used
8	—	—	Not Used
9	TAN	800	Serial data signal - Primary (SIR)
10	—	—	Not Used
11	—	—	Not Used
12	TAN/WHT	799	Antilock Brake System diagnostic request
13	—	—	Not Used
14	—	—	Not Used
15	—	—	Not Used
16	ORN	840	Battery - fused

88454g46

Fig. 77 ALDL connector — 1997 base pickup models

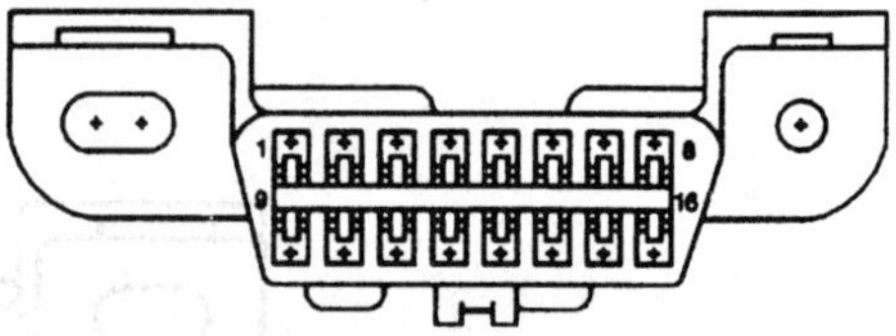

Connector Part Information	• 12110250 • 16 - Way F Metri-Pack 150 Series (Black)		
Pin	**Wire Color**	**Circuit No.**	**Function**
1	—	—	Not Used
2	PPL	1807	Serial data signal - Class II
3	—	—	Not Used
4	BLK	150	Ground
5	BLK/WHT	151	Ground
6	—	—	Not Used
7	—	—	Not Used
8	BLK/WHT	1455	Keyless entry program enable
9	TAN	800	Serial data signal - Primary (SIR)
10	—	—	Not Used
11	—	—	Not Used
12	TAN/WHT	799	Antilock Brake System diagnostic request
13	—	—	Not Used
14	—	—	Not Used
15	—	—	Not Used
16	ORN	840	Battery - fused

88454g47

Fig. 78 ALDL connector — 1997 non-base pickup with 2.2L engine

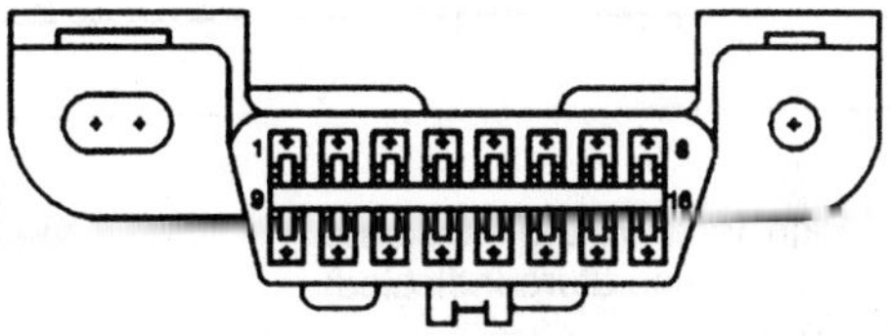

Connector Part Information		• 12110250 • 16 - Way F Metri-Pack 150 Series (Black)	
Pin	**Wire Color**	**Circuit No.**	**Function**
1	—	—	Not Used
2	PPL	1807	Serial data signal - Class II
3	—	—	Not Used
4	BLK	150	Ground
5	BLK/WHT	151	Ground
6	—	—	Not Used
7	—	—	Not Used
8	BLK/WHT	1455	Keyless entry program enable
9	TAN	800	Serial data signal - Primary (SIR)
10	—	—	Not Used
11	—	—	Not Used
12	TAN/WHT	799	Antilock Brake System diagnostic request
13	—	—	Not Used
14	—	—	Not Used
15	—	—	Not Used
16	ORN	840	Battery - fused

88454g48

Fig. 79 ALDL connector — 1997 4.3L engines without electric shift 4WD

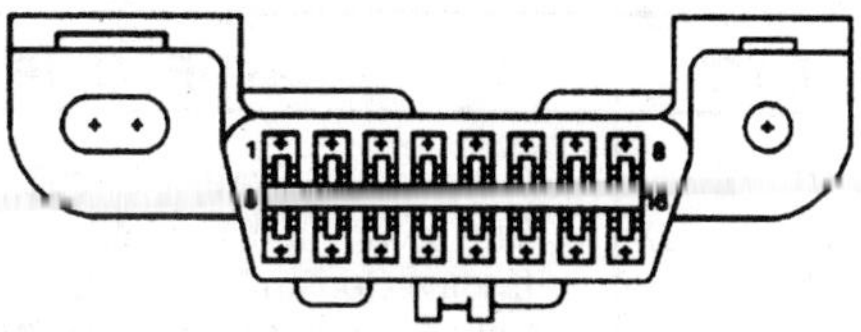

Connector Part Information		• 12110250 • 16 - Way F Metri-Pack 150 Series (Black)	
Pin	**Wire Color**	**Circuit No.**	**Function**
1	—	—	Not Used
2	PPL	1807	Serial data signal - Class II
3	—	—	Not Used
4	BLK	150	Ground
5	BLK/WHT	151	Ground
6	—	—	Not Used
7	—	—	Not Used
8	BLK/WHT	1455	Keyless entry program enable
9	TAN	800	Serial data signal - Primary (SIR)
10	—	—	Not Used
11	—	—	Not Used
12	TAN/WHT	799	Antilock Brake System diagnostic request
13	ORN	1568	Transfer Case Shift Control Module diagnostic request
14	—	—	Not Used
15	—	—	Not Used
16	ORN	840	Battery - fused

88454g49

Fig. 80 ALDL connector — 1997 4.3L engines with electric shift 4WD

DTC	DESCRIPTION
13	Oxygen Sensor (02S) Circuit (Open Circuit)
14	Engine Coolant Temperature (ECT) Sensor Circuit (High Temperature Indicated)
15	Engine Coolant Temperature (ECT) Sensor Circuit (Low Temperature Indicated)
21	Throttle Position (TP) Sensor Circuit (Signal Voltage High)
22	Throttle Position (TP) Sensor Circuit (Signal Voltage Low)
23	Intake Air Temperature (IAT) Sensor Circuit (Low Temperature Indicated)
24	Vehicle Speed Sensor (VSS)
25	Intake Air Temperature (IAT) Sensor Circuit (High Temperature Indicated)
32	Exhaust Gas Recirculation (EGR) System
33	Manifold Absolute Pressure (MAP) Sensor Circuit (Signal Voltage High-Low Vacuum)
34	Manifold Absolute Pressure (MAP) Sensor Circuit (Signal Voltage Low-High Vacuum)
35	Idle Air Control (IAC) System
42	Ignition Control (IC)
43	Knock Sensor (KS) Circuit
44	Oxygen Sensor (02S) Circuit (Lean Exhaust Indicated)
45	Oxygen Sensor (02S) Circuit (Rich Exhaust Indicated)
51	Faulty PROM (CAL-PAK)
53	System Over Voltage
54	Fuel Pump Circuit (Low Voltage)
55	Faulty ECM

88454g50

Fig. 81 DTC chart for 1994 ECM models

DTC	DESCRIPTION
13	Oxygen 02S Sensor Circuit (Open Circuit)
14	Engine Coolant Temperature (ECT) Sensor Circuit Low (High Temperature Indicated)
15	Engine Coolant Temperature (ECT) Sensor Circuit High (Low Temperature Indicated)
16	Vehicle Speed Signal (VSS) Buffer Fault (Vehicle Speed Signal)
21	Throttle Position (TP) Sensor Circuit High (Signal Voltage High)
22	Throttle Position (TP) Sensor Circuit Low (Signal Voltage Low)
23	Intake Air Temperature (IAT) Sensor Circuit High (Low Temperature Indicated)
24	Vehicle Speed Sensor (VSS) Circuit Low (Trans Output Speed Signal)
25	Intake Air Temperature (IAT) Sensor Circuit Low (High Temperature Indicated)
28	Transmission Range (TR) Pressure Switch Assembly
32	Exhaust Gas Recirculation (EGR) System
33	Manifold Absolute Pressure (MAP) Sensor Circuit High (Low Vacuum)
34	Manifold Absolute Pressure (MAP) Sensor Circuit Low (High Vacuum)
35	IAC Error
37	Brake Switch Stuck "ON"
38	Brake Switch Stuck "OFF"
41	IX Signal Error
42	Ignition Control (IC) Error
43	Knock Sensor (KS) Circuit
44	Lean Exhaust
45	Rich Exhaust
51	PROM Error (MEL-CAL)
52	System Voltage High Long
53	System Voltage High
54	Fuel Pump Relay Circuit (Low Voltage)
55	Faulty PCM
58	Transmission Fluid Temperature (TFT) Sensor Circuit Low (High Temperature Indicated)
59	Transmission Fluid Temperature (TFT) Sensor Circuit High (Low Temperature Indicated)
66	3-2 Control Solenoid Circuit Fault
67	Torque Converter Clutch (TCC) Solenoid Circuit Fault
69	Torque Converter Clutch (TCC) Stuck "ON"
72	Vehicle Speed Sensor (VSS) Circuit Loss (Trans Output Speed Signal)
73	Pressure Control Solenoid (PCS) Fault (Current Error)
75	System Voltage Low
79	Transmission Fluid Over Temp
81	2-3 Shift Solenoid Circuit Fault
82	1-2 Shift Solenoid Circuit Fault

88454g51

Fig. 82 DTC chart for 1994 PCM models

DTC	DESCRIPTION
P0107	Manifold Absolute Pressure (MAP) Sensor Circuit (Signal Voltage Low-High Vacuum)
P0108	Manifold Absolute Pressure (MAP) Sensor Circuit (Signal Voltage High-Low Vacuum)
P0117	Engine Coolant Temperature (ECT) Sensor Circuit High (Low Temperature Indicated)
P0118	Engine Coolant Temperature (ECT) Sensor Circuit Low (High Temperature Indicated)
P0122	Throttle Position (TP) Sensor Circuit Low (Signal Voltage Low)
P0123	Throttle Position (TP) Sensor Circuit High (Signal Voltage High)
P0139	Heated Oxygen Sensor (H02S) Circuit (Open Circuit)
P0171	Lean Exhaust
P0172	Rich Exhaust
P0320	Ignition Control (IC) Error
P0327	Knock Sensor (KS) Circuit Grounded
P0328	Knock Sensor (KS) Circuit Open
P0400	Exhaust Gas Recirculation (EGR) Error
P0500	Vehicle Speed Sensor (VSS) Error
P1222	Fuel Pump Relay Circuit (Low Voltage)
P1632	System Voltage High

88454g52

Fig. 83 DTC chart for 1994 — 95 VCM models

DTC	DESCRIPTION
13	Oxygen 02S Sensor Circuit (Open Circuit)
14	Engine Coolant Temperature (ECT) Sensor Circuit Low (High Temperature Indicated)
15	Engine Coolant Temperature (ECT) Sensor Circuit High (Low Temperature Indicated)
16	Vehicle Speed Signal (VSS) Buffer Fault (Vehicle Speed Signal)
21	Throttle Position (TP) Sensor Circuit High (Signal Voltage High)
22	Throttle Position (TP) Sensor Circuit Low (Signal Voltage Low)
23	Intake Air Temperature (IAT) Sensor Circuit High (Low Temperature Indicated)
24	Vehicle Speed Sensor (VSS) Circuit Low (Trans Output Speed Signal)
25	Intake Air Temperature (IAT) Sensor Circuit Low (High Temperature Indicated)
28	Transmission Range (TR) Pressure Switch Assembly
32	Exhaust Gas Recirculation (EGR) System
33	Manifold Absolute Pressure (MAP) Sensor Circuit High (Low Vacuum)
34	Manifold Absolute Pressure (MAP) Sensor Circuit Low (High Vacuum)
35	IAC Error
37	Brake Switch Stuck "ON"
38	Brake Switch Stuck "OFF"
41	IX Signal Error
42	Ignition Control (IC) Error
43	Knock Sensor (KS) Circuit
44	Lean Exhaust
45	Rich Exhaust
51	PROM Error (MEL-CAL)
52	System Voltage High Long
53	System Voltage High
54	Fuel Pump Relay Circuit (Low Voltage)
55	Faulty PCM
58	Transmission Fluid Temperature (TFT) Sensor Circuit Low (High Temperature Indicated)
59	Transmission Fluid Temperature (TFT) Sensor Circuit High (Low Temperature Indicated)
66	3-2 Control Solenoid Circuit Fault
67	Torque Converter Clutch (TCC) Solenoid Circuit Fault
69	Torque Converter Clutch (TCC) Stuck "ON"
72	Vehicle Speed Sensor (VSS) Circuit Loss (Trans Output Speed Signal)
73	Pressure Control Solenoid (PCS) Fault (Current Error)
75	System Voltage Low
79	Transmission Fluid Over Temp
81	2-3 Shift Solenoid Circuit Fault
82	1-2 Shift Solenoid Circuit Fault
83	TCC PWM SOL

88454g53

Fig. 84 DTC chart for 1995 PCM models

DTC	DESCRIPTION
P0106	Manifold Absolute Pressure (MAP) Sensor Circuit Range Problem
P0107	Manifold Absolute Pressure (MAP) Sensor Circuit - Low Input
P0108	Manifold Absolute Pressure (MAP) Sensor Circuit - High Input
P0112	Intake Air Temperature (IAT) Sensor Circuit - Low Input
P0113	Intake Air Temperature (IAT) Sensor Circuit - High Input
P0117	Engine Coolant Temperature (ECT) Sensor Circuit - Low Input
P0118	Engine Coolant Temperature (ECT) Sensor Circuit - High Input
P0121	Throttle Position (TP) Sensor Circuit Range/Performance Problem
P0122	Throttle Position (TP) Sensor Circuit - Low Input
P0123	Throttle Position (TP) Sensor Circuit - High Input
P0125	Engine Coolant Temperature (ECT) Sensor - Engine Coolant Temperature Excessive Time to "Closed Loop"
P0131	Heated Oxygen Sensor (H02S 1) Circuit Low Voltage (Bank 1, Sensor 1)
P0132	Heated Oxygen Sensor (H02S 1) Circuit High Voltage (Bank 1, Sensor 1)
P0133	H02S Circuit Slow Response (Bank 1, Sensor 1)
P0134	Heated Oxygen Sensor (H02S 1) Circuit No Activity Detected (Bank 1, Sensor 1)
P0135	H02S Heater Circuit Malfunction (Bank 1, Sensor 1)
P0137	H02S Circuit Low Voltage (Bank 1, Sensor 2) (Catalyst Monitor)
P0138	H02S Circuit High Voltage (Bank 1, Sensor 2) (Catalyst Monitor)
P0140	Heated Oxygen Sensor (H02S 2) Circuit - No Activity Detected (Bank 1, Sensor 2) (Catalyst Monitor)
P0141	H02S Heater Malfunction (Bank 1, Sensor 2) (Catalyst Monitor)
P0171	System Too Lean (Bank 1, Sensor 1) (1 of 2)
P0172	System Too Rich (Bank 1, Sensor 1) (1 of 2)
P0300	Random Misfire Detected
P0301	Cylinder 1 Misfire Detected
P0302	Cylinder 2 Misfire Detected
P0303	Cylinder 3 Misfire Detected
P0304	Cylinder 4 Misfire Detected
P0305	Cylinder 5 Misfire Detected
P0306	Cylinder 6 Misfire Detected
P0325	Knock Sensor (KS) Circuit Short or Open
P0326	Knock Sensor (KS) Circuit Range/Rationality
P0337	Crankshaft Position Sensor Circuit - Low Input
P0338	Crankshaft Position Sensor Circuit - High Imput
P0340	Camshaft Position Sensor Circuit Malfunction
P0341	Camshaft Position Sensor Circuit - Range/Rationality
P0401	Exhaust Gas Recirculation (EGR) Insufficient Flow Detected
P0420	Catalyst System - Efficiency Below Threshold (Bank 1)
P0441	Evaporative Emissions Control System Incorrect Purge Flow
P0500	Vehicle Speed Sensor (VSS) Error
P0506	Idle Speed Lower Than Expected
P0507	Idle Speed Higher Than Expected
P1106	Manifold Absolute Pressure (MAP) Sensor Circuit - Intermittent High Input
P1107	Manifold Absolute Pressure (MAP) Sensor Circuit - Intermittent Low Input
P1111	Intake Air Temperature (IAT) Circuit - Intermittent High Input
P1112	Intake Air Temperature (IAT) Sensor Circuit - Intermittent Low Input
P1114	Engine Coolant Temperature (ECT) Sensor Circuit - Intermittent Low Input
P1115	Engine Coolant Temperature (ECT) Sensor Circuit - Intermittent High Input
P1121	Throttle Position (TP) Sensor Circuit - Intermittent High Input
P1122	Throttle Position (TP) Sensor Circuit - Intermittent Low Input
P1133	H02S System Fault - Too Few Rich/Lean or Lean/Rich Transitions, Insufficient Activity (Bank 1, Sensor 1)
P1221	Fuel Pump Secondary System Circuit Low

88454g54

Fig. 85 DTC chart for 1995 VCM-A models

DTC	DESCRIPTION
P1345	Camshaft Sensor Misinstalled
P1351	EST Output High or Pulses Detected When Open
P1361	EST Not Toggling After Enable
P1406	Exhaust Gas Recirculation (EGR) System Pintle Position Error (1 of 2)
P1441	Evaporative Emissions System Continuous Open Purge Flow
P1442	Purge Solenoid Switch Static Test Malfunction
P1508	Idle Air Control Counts Low
P1509	Idle Air Control Counts High

88454g55

Fig. 86 DTC chart for 1995 VCM-A models

DTC	DESCRIPTION
P0101	Mass Air Flow System Performance
P0102	MAF Sensor Circuit Low Frequency
P0103	MAF Sensor Circuit High Frequency
P0106	MAP System Performance
P0107	MAP Sensor Circuit Low Voltage
P0108	MAP Sensor Circuit High Voltage
P0112	IAT Sensor Circuit Low Voltage
P0113	IAT Sensor Circuit High Voltage
P0117	ECT Sensor Circuit Low Voltage
P0118	ECT Sensor Circuit High Voltage
P0121	TP Sensor Performance
P0122	TP Sensor Circuit Low Voltage
P0123	TP Sensor Circuit High Voltage
P0125	ECT Excessive Time to Closed Loop
P0131	HO2S Circuit Low Voltage Sensor 1
P0132	H02S Circuit High Voltage Sensor 1
P0133	H02S Circuit Slow Response Sensor 1
P0134	H02S CKT Insufficient Activity Sensor 1
P0135	H02S Heater Circuit Sensor 1
P0137	H02S Circuit Low Voltage Sensor 2
P0138	H02S Circuit High Voltage Sensor 2
P0140	H02S CKT Insufficient Activity Sensor 2
P0141	H02S Heater Circuit Sensor 2
P0143	H02S Circuit Low Voltage Bank 1 Sensor 3
P0144	H02S Circuit High Voltage Bank 1 Sensor 3
P0146	H02S Insufficient Activity Bank 1 Sensor 3
P0147	H02S Heater Circuit Bank 1 Sensor 3
P0151	H02S Circuit Low Voltage Bank 2 Sensor 1
P0152	H02S Circuit High Voltage Bank 2 Sensor 1
P0153	H02S Slow Response Bank 2 Sensor 1
P0154	H02S Insufficient Activity Bank 2 Sensor 1
P0155	H02S Heater Circuit Bank 2 Sensor 1
P0171	Fuel Trim System Lean Bank 1
P0172	Fuel Trim System Rich Bank 1
P0174	Fuel Trim System Lean Bank 2
P0175	Fuel Trim System Rich Bank 2
P0300	Engine Misfire Detected
P0301	Cylinder 1 Misfire Detected
P0302	Cylinder 2 Misfire Detected
P0303	Cylinder 3 Misfire Detected
P0304	Cylinder 4 Misfire Detected
P0305	Cylinder 5 Misfire Detected
P0306	Cylinder 6 Misfire Detected
P0325	Knock Sensor Module Circuit
P0327	Knock Sensor Circuit Low Voltage
P0336	CKP Sensor Circuit Performance
P0337	CKP Sensor Circuit Low Frequency
P0338	CKP Sensor Circuit High Frequency
P0339	CKP Sensor Circuit Intermittent
P0340	CMP Sensor Circuit
P0341	CMP Sensor Circuit Performance
P0401	EGR System
P0420	TWC System Low Efficiency Bank 1
P0440	EVAP System

88454g56

Fig. 87 DTC chart for 1996-97 VCM models

DTC	DESCRIPTION
P0442	EVAP Control System Small Leak Detected
P0446	EVAP Canister Vent Blocked
P0461	Fuel Level Sensor Circuit Performance
P0463	Fuel Level Sensor Circuit High Voltage
P0500	Vehicle Speed Sensor Circuit
P0506	Idle Control System Low RPM
P0507	Idle Control System High RPM
P0704	Clutch Switch Circuit
P1106	MAP Sensor CKT Intermittent High Voltage
P1107	MAP Sensor CKT Intermittent Low Voltage
P1111	IAT Sensor CKT Intermittent High Voltage
P1112	IAT Sensor CKT Intermittent Low Voltage
P1114	ECT Sensor CKT Intermittent Low Voltage
P1115	ECT Sensor CKT Intermittent High Voltage
P1121	TP Sensor CKT Intermittent High Voltage
P1122	TP Sensor CKT Intermittent Low Voltage
P1133	H02S Insufficient Switching Bank 1 Sensor 1
P1134	H02S Transition Time Ratio Bank 1 Sensor 1
P1153	Insufficient Switching Bank 2 Sensor 1
P1154	H02S Transition Time Ratio Bank 2 Sensor 1
P1345	CKP/CMP Correlation
P1351	IC Circuit High Voltage
P1361	IC Circuit Not Toggling
P1380	EBCM DTC Rough Road Data Unstable
P1406	EGR Valve Pintle Position Circuit
P1441	EVAP System Flow During Non-Purge
P1508	IAC System Low RPM
P1509	IAC System High RPM

88454g57

Fig. 88 DTC chart for 1996-97 VCM models

VACUUM DIAGRAMS

Following is a listing of vacuum diagrams for many of the engine and emissions package combinations covered by this manual. Because vacuum circuits will vary based on various engine and vehicle options, always refer first to the vehicle emission control information label. Should the label be missing, or should the vehicle be equipped with a different engine from the original equipment, refer to the diagrams below for the same or similar configuration.

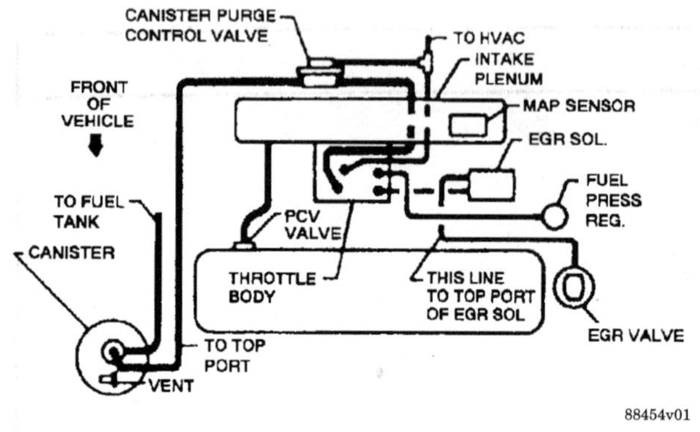

Fig. 89 Engine vacuum schematic — 1994 2.2L (VIN 4)

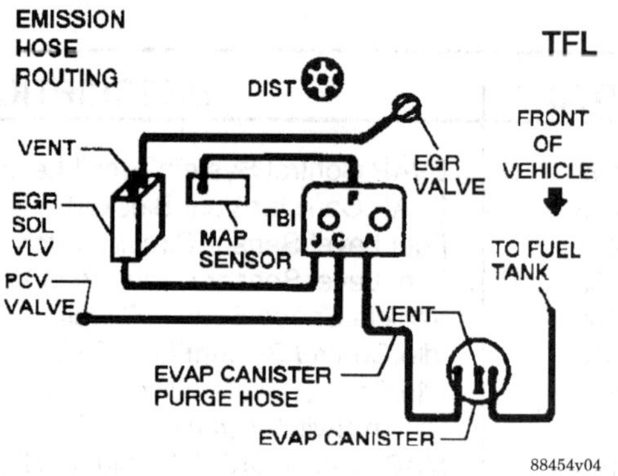

Fig. 92 Engine vacuum schematic — 1994 4.3L (VIN Z) engines, California models (Code TFL)

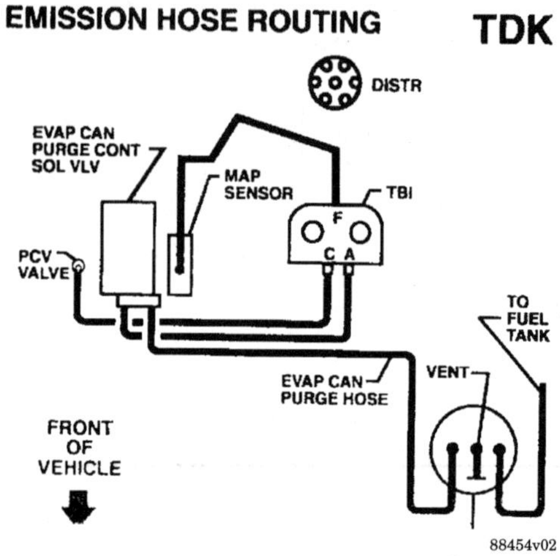

Fig. 90 Engine vacuum schematic — 1994 4.3L (VIN Z) engines, California models with a M/T (Code TDK)

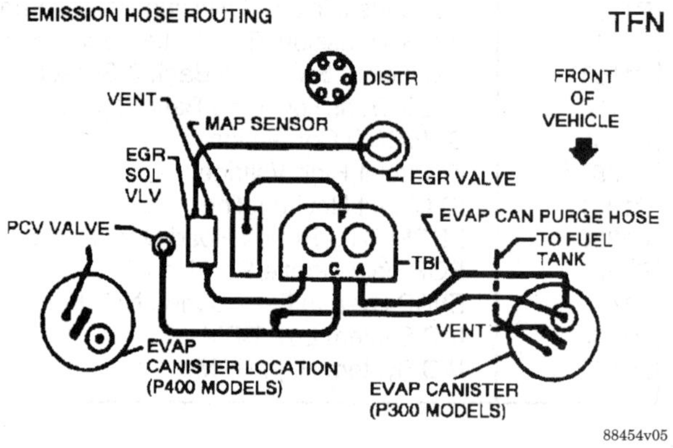

Fig. 93 Engine vacuum schematic — 1994 4.3L (VIN Z) engines (Code TFN)

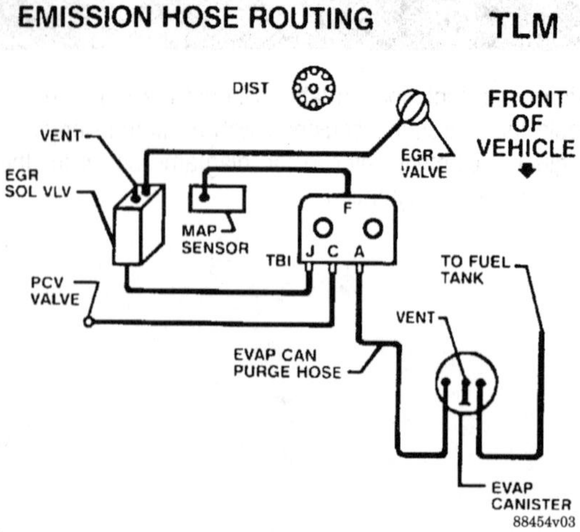

Fig. 91 Engine vacuum schematic — 1994 4.3L (VIN Z) engines, California models with M/T (Code TLM)

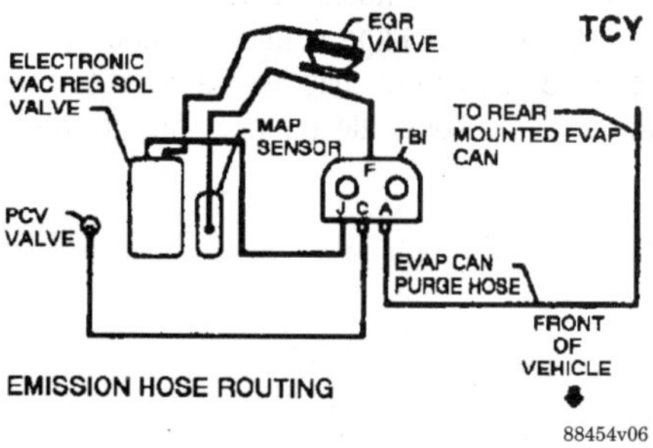

Fig. 94 Engine vacuum schematic — 1994 4.3L (VIN Z) engines, California models with M/T (Code TCY)

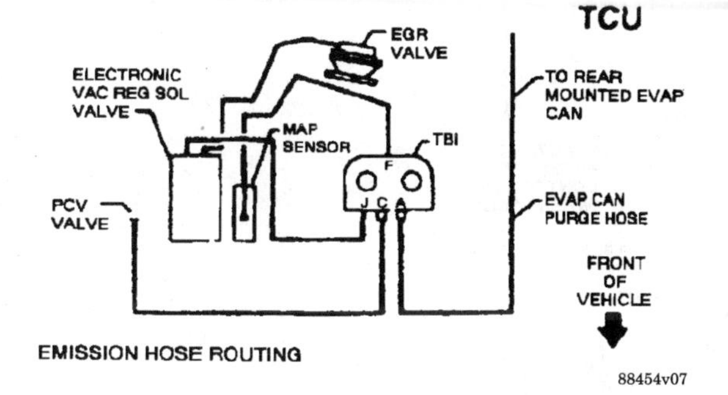

Fig. 95 Engine vacuum schematic — 1994 4.3L (VIN Z) engines (Code TCU)

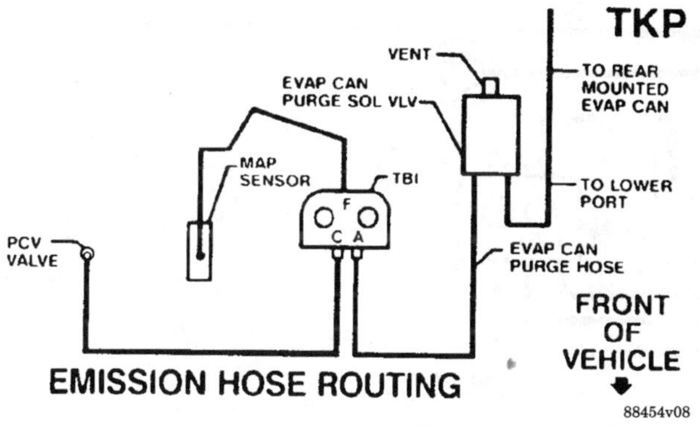

Fig. 96 Engine vacuum schematic — 1994 4.3L (VIN Z) engines, California models with A/T (Code TKP)

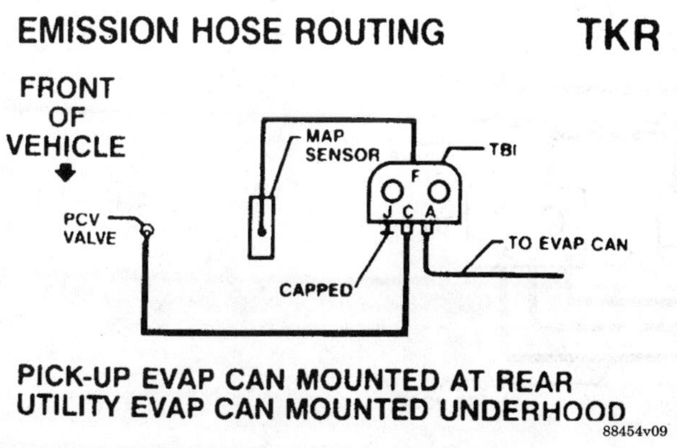

Fig. 97 Engine vacuum schematic — 1994 4.3L (VIN Z) engines (Code TKR)

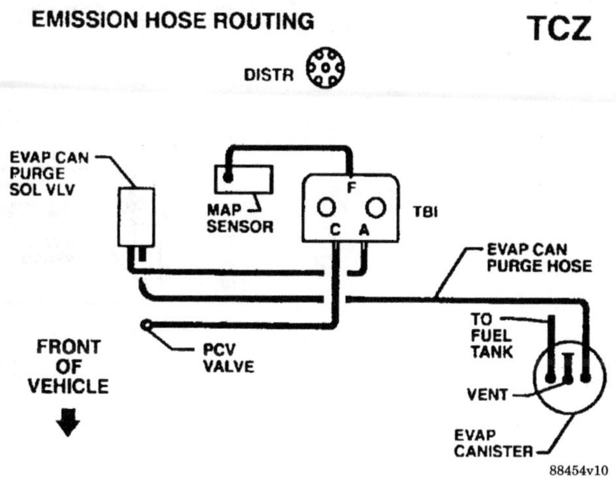

Fig. 98 Engine vacuum schematic — 1994 4.3L (VIN Z) engines with A/T (Code TCZ)

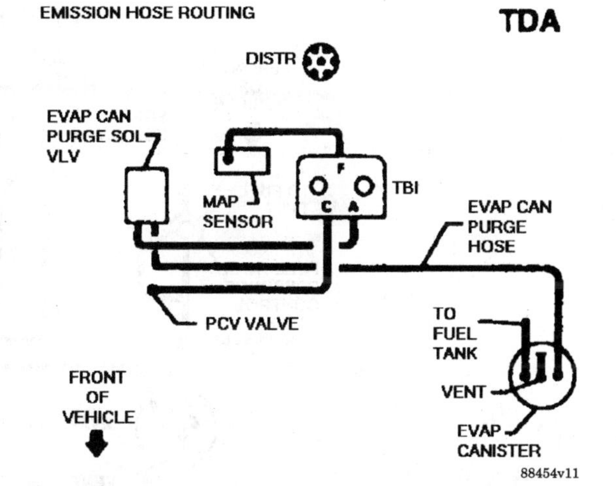

Fig. 99 Engine vacuum schematic — 1994 4.3L (VIN Z) engines, California models (Code TDA)

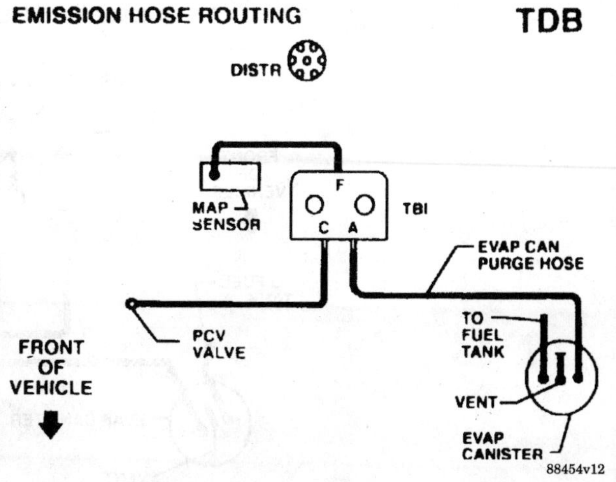

Fig. 100 Engine vacuum schematic — 1994 4.3L (VIN Z) engines, Export models (Code TDB)

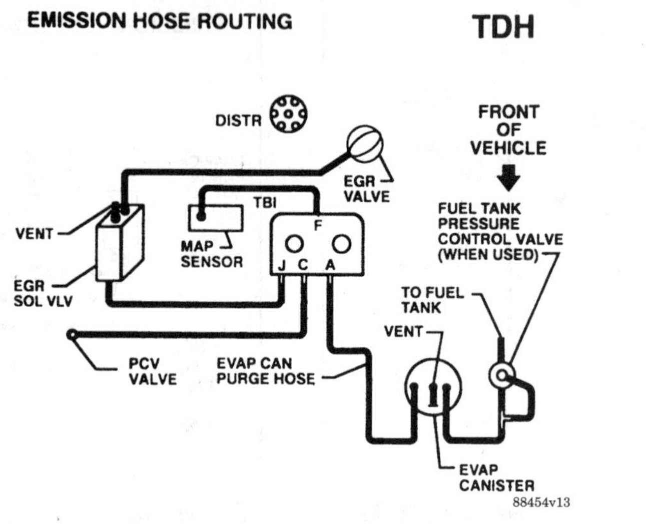

Fig. 101 Engine vacuum schematic — 1994 4.3L (VIN Z) engines (Code TDH)

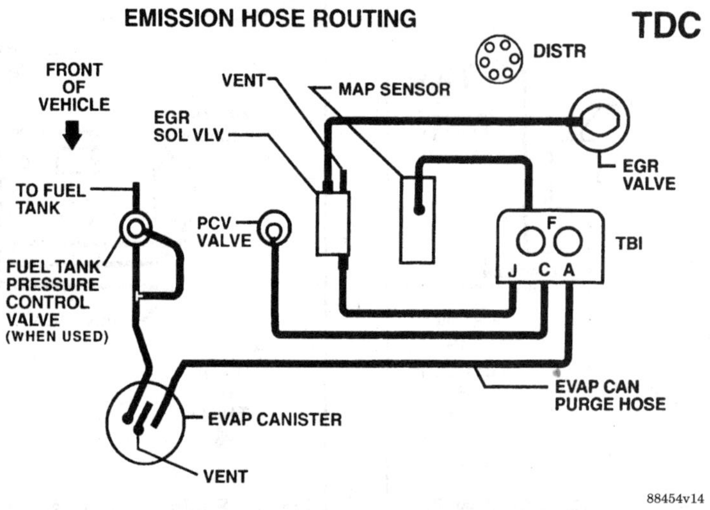

Fig. 102 Engine vacuum schematic — 1994 4.3L (VIN Z) engines with A/T (Code TDC)

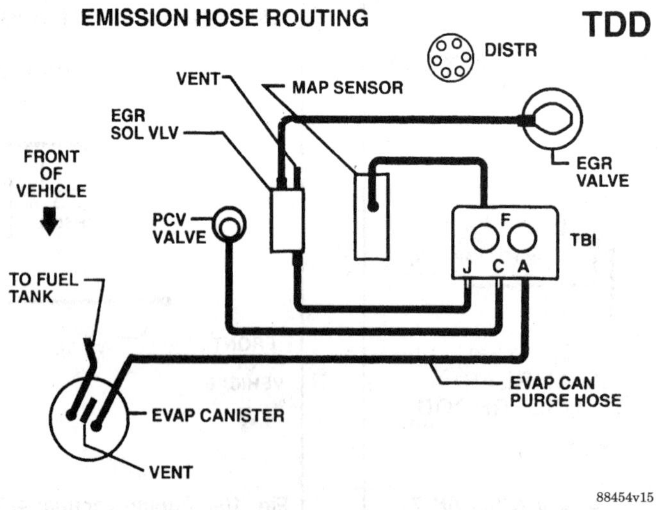

Fig. 103 Engine vacuum schematic — 1994 4.3L (VIN Z) engines, California models with A/T (Code TDD)

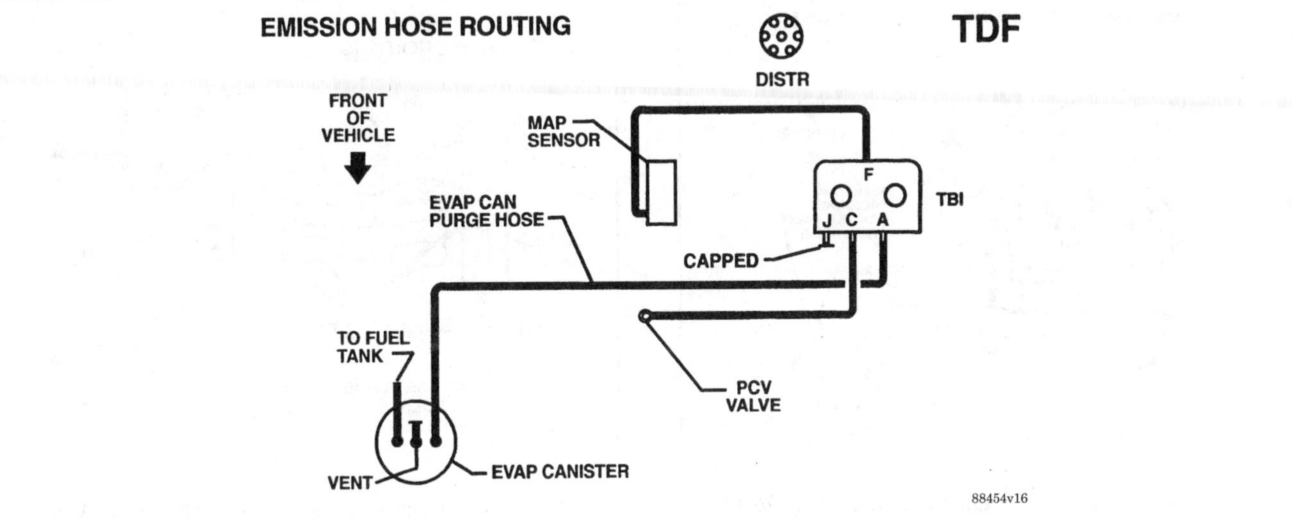

Fig. 104 Engine vacuum schematic — 1994 4.3L (VIN Z) engines with A/T (Code TDF)

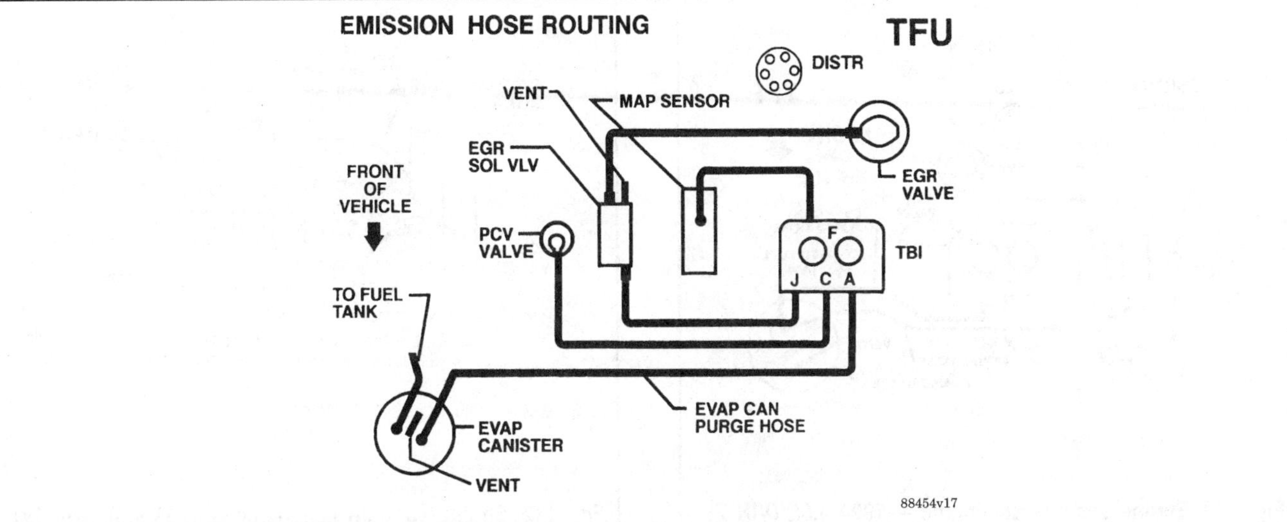

Fig. 105 Engine vacuum schematic — 1994 4.3L (VIN Z) engines with A/T (Code TFU)

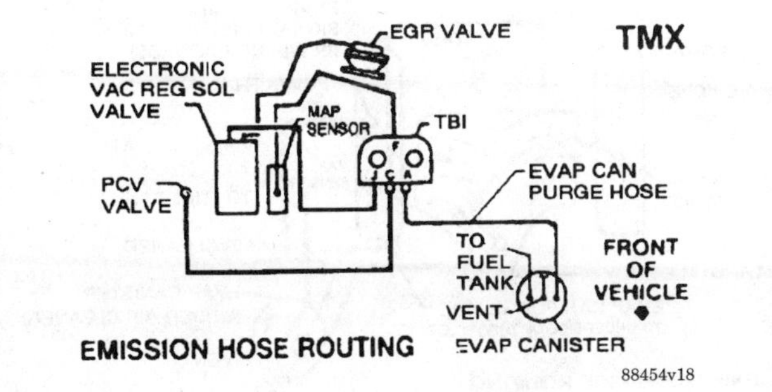

Fig. 106 Engine vacuum schematic — 1994 4.3L (VIN Z) engines with M/T (Code TMX)

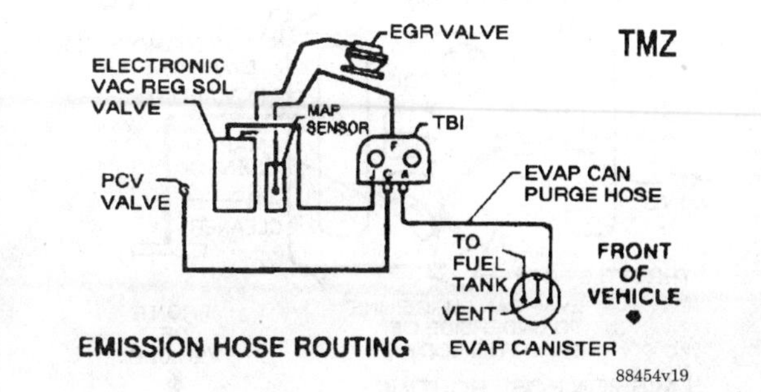

Fig. 107 Engine vacuum schematic — 1994 4.3L (VIN Z) engines with A/T (Code TMZ)

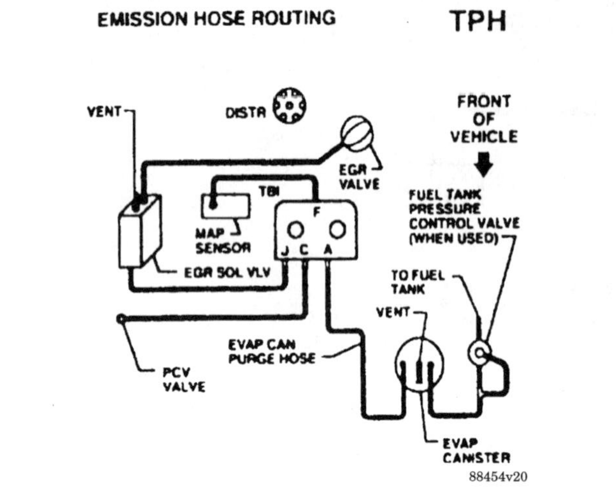

Fig. 108 Engine vacuum schematic — 1994 4.3L (VIN Z) engines (Code TPH)

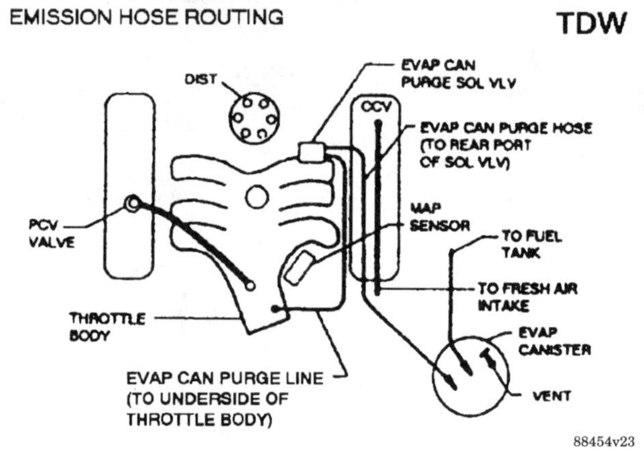

Fig. 111 Engine vacuum schematic — 1994 4.3L (VIN W) engines, California models with A/T (Code TDW)

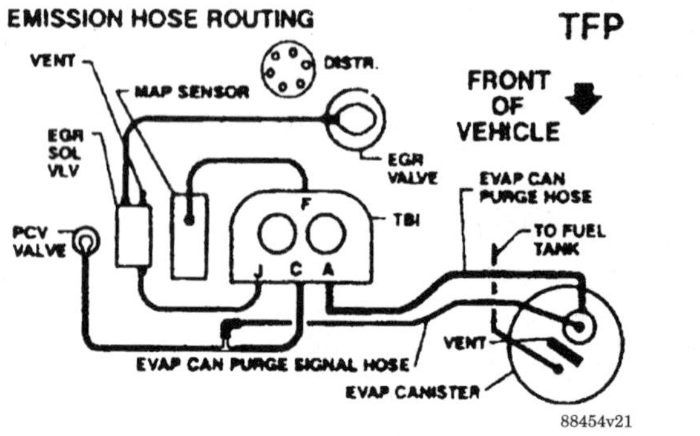

Fig. 109 Engine vacuum schematic — 1994 4.3L (VIN Z) engines (Code TFP)

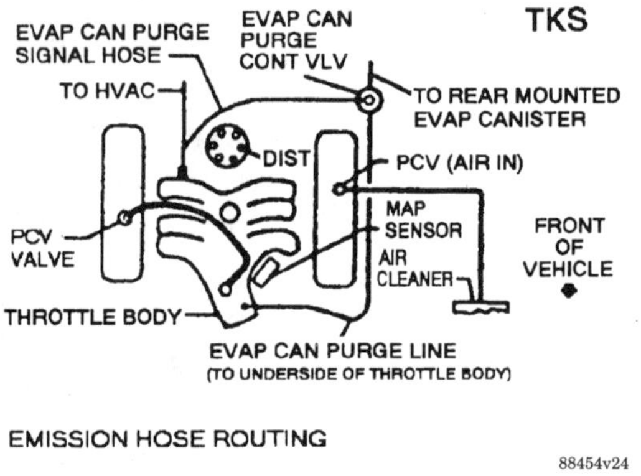

Fig. 112 Engine vacuum schematic — 1994 4.3L (VIN W) engines (Code TKS)

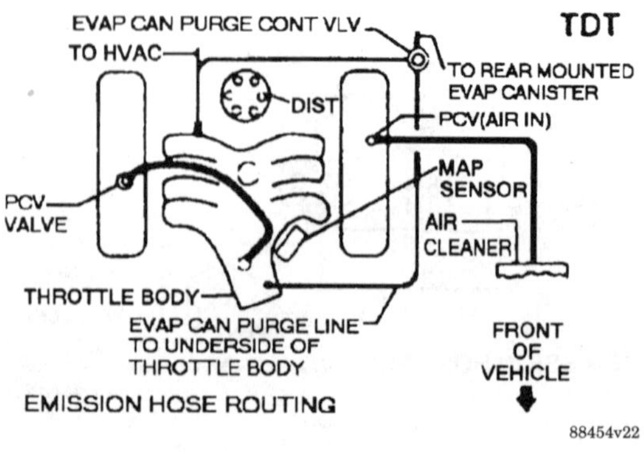

Fig. 110 Engine vacuum schematic — 1994 4.3L (VIN W) engines, California models with M/T (Code TDT)

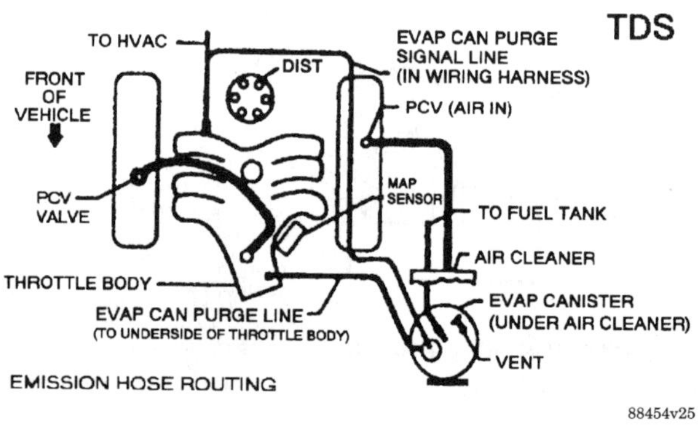

Fig. 113 Engine vacuum schematic — 1994 4.3L (VIN W) engines with A/T (Code TDS)

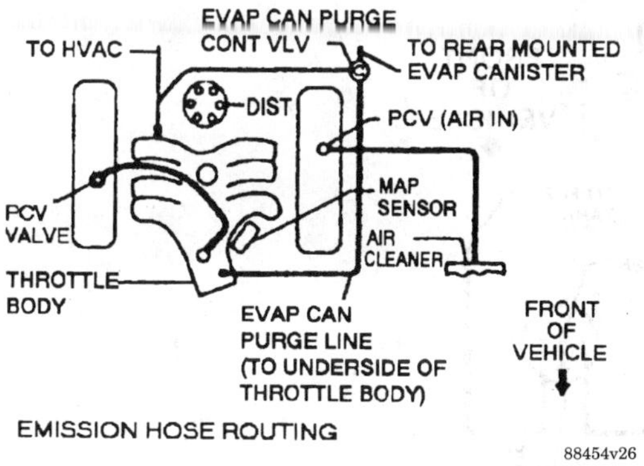

Fig. 114 Engine vacuum schematic — 1994 4.3L (VIN W) engines (Code TDM)

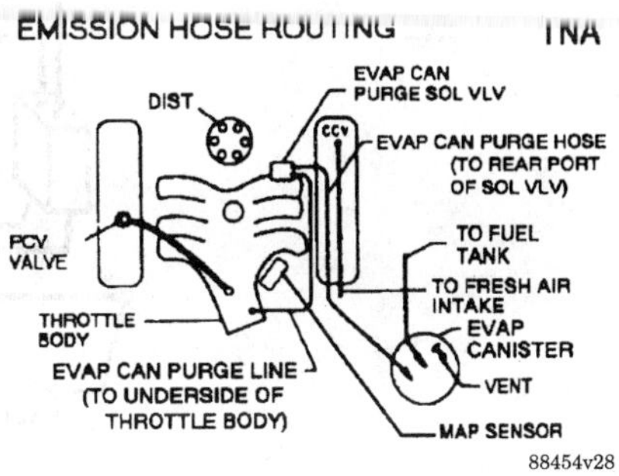

Fig. 116 Engine vacuum schematic — 1994 4.3L (VIN W) engines with A/T (Code TNA)

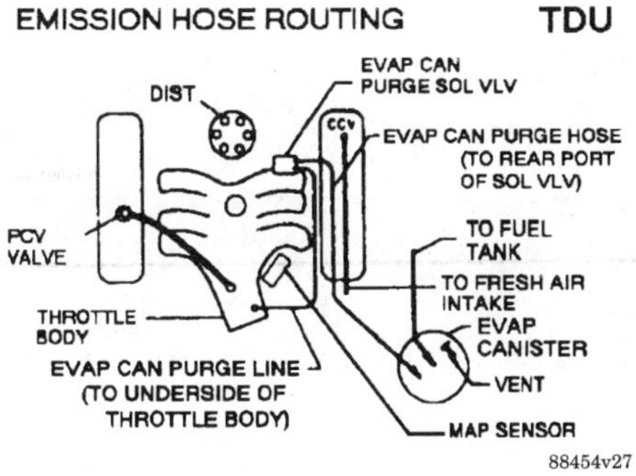

Fig. 115 Engine vacuum schematic — 1994 4.3L (VIN W) engines with A/T (Code TDU)

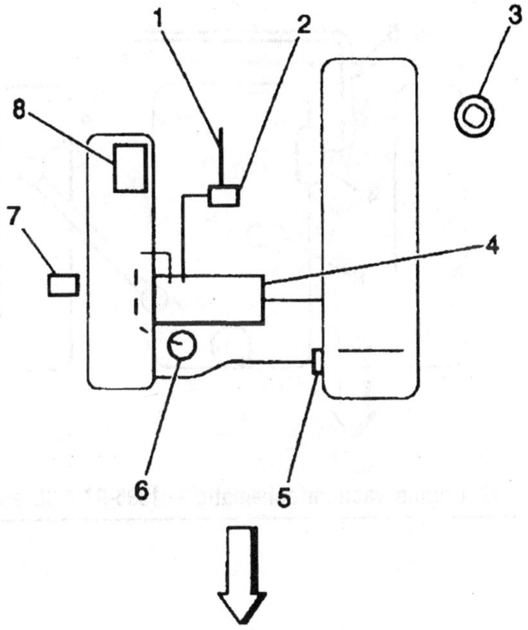

(1) To Rear Mounted EVAP Canister
(2) EVAP Canister Purge Solenoid
(3) EGR Valve
(4) Throttle Body
(5) PCV Valve
(6) Fuel Pressure Regulator Valve
(7) Service Port
(8) MAP Sensor

88454v29

Fig. 117 Engine vacuum schematic — 1995-97 2.2L (VIN 4) engines

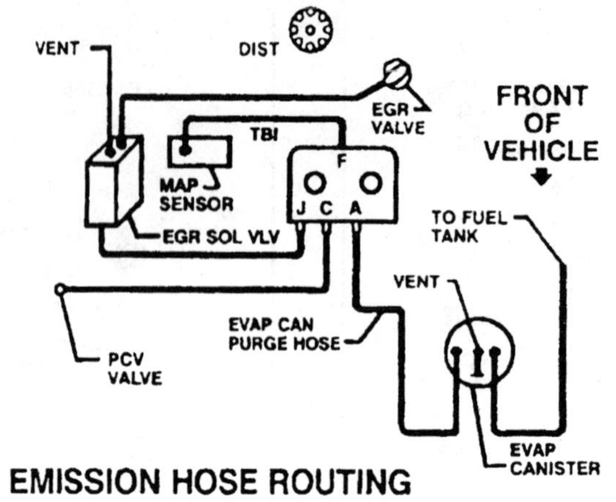

Fig. 118 Engine vacuum schematic — 1995 4.3L (VIN Z) engines

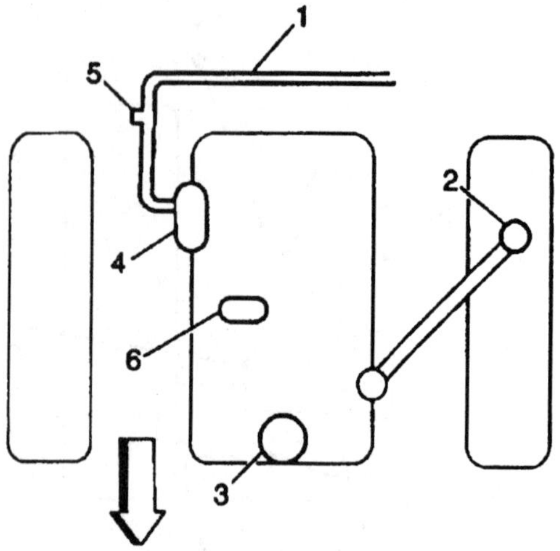

(1) EVAP purge vacuum hose (to EVAP canister).
(2) Positive Crankcase Ventilation (PCV) valve.
(3) Throttle Body.
(4) EVAP Purge Solenoid.
(5) EVAP Service Port.
(6) Manifold Absolute Pressure (MAP) sensor.

88454v31

Fig. 119 Engine vacuum schematic — 1996-97 4.3L engines

5

FUEL SYSTEMS

BASIC FUEL SYSTEM DIAGNOSIS

When there is a problem starting or driving a vehicle, two of the most important checks involve the ignition and the fuel systems. The two questions that mechanics attempt to answer first, "is there spark?" and "is there fuel?" will often lead to solving most basic problems. For ignition system diagnosis and testing, please refer to Section 2 of this manual. If the ignition system checks out (there is spark), then you must determine if the fuel system is operating properly (is there fuel?).

Precautions

Safety is the most important factor when performing not only fuel system maintenance, but any type of maintenance. Failure to conduct maintenance and repairs in a safe manner may result in serious personal injury or death. Maintenance and testing of the vehicle's fuel system components can be accomplished safely and effectively by adhering to the following rules and guidelines:

- To avoid the possibility of fire and personal injury, always disconnect the negative battery cable unless the repair or test procedure requires that battery voltage be applied.
- Always relieve the fuel system pressure prior to disconnecting any fuel system component (injector, fuel rail, pressure regulator, etc.), fitting or fuel line connection. Exercise extreme caution whenever relieving fuel system pressure to avoid exposing skin, face and eyes to fuel spray. Please be advised that fuel under pressure may penetrate the skin or any part of the body that it contacts.
- Always place a shop towel or cloth around the fitting or connection prior to loosening to absorb any excess fuel due to spillage. Ensure that all fuel spillage (should it occur) is quickly removed from engine surfaces. Ensure that all fuel soaked cloths or towels are deposited into a suitable waste container.
- Always keep a dry chemical (Class B) fire extinguisher near the work area.
- Do not allow fuel spray or fuel vapors to come into contact with a spark or open flame.
- Always use a backup wrench when loosening and tightening fuel line connection fittings. This will prevent unnecessary stress and torsion to fuel line piping. Always follow the proper torque specifications.
- Always replace worn fuel fitting O-rings with new ones. Do not substitute fuel hose or equivalent where fuel pipe is installed.
- Due to the possibility of a fire or explosion, never drain or store gasoline in an open container.

FUEL LINE FITTINGS

Quick-Connect Fittings

REMOVAL & INSTALLATION

See Figure 1

➡This procedure requires Tool Set J37088-A or its equivalent fuel line quick-connect separator.

1. Grasp both sides of the fitting. Twist the female connector ¼ turn in each direction to loosen any dirt within the fittings. Using compressed air, blow out the dirt from the quick-connect fittings at the end of the fittings.

CAUTION

Safety glasses MUST be worn when using compressed air to avoid eye injury due to flying dirt particles!

2. For plastic (hand releasable) fittings, squeeze the plastic retainer release tabs, then pull the connection apart.
3. For metal fittings, choose the correct tool from kit J37088-A or its equivalent for the size of the fitting to be disconnected. Insert the proper tool into the female connector, then push inward to release the locking tabs. Pull the connection apart.
4. If it is necessary to remove rust or burrs from the male tube end of a quick-connect fitting, use emery cloth in a radial motion with the tube end to prevent damage to the O-ring sealing surfaces. Using a clean shop towel, wipe off the male tube ends. Inspect all connectors for dirt and burrs. Clean and/or replace if required.

To install:

5. Apply a few drops of clean engine oil to the male tube end of the fitting.
6. Push the connectors together to cause the retaining tabs/fingers to snap into place.
7. Once installed, pull on both ends of each connection to make sure they are secure and check for leaks.

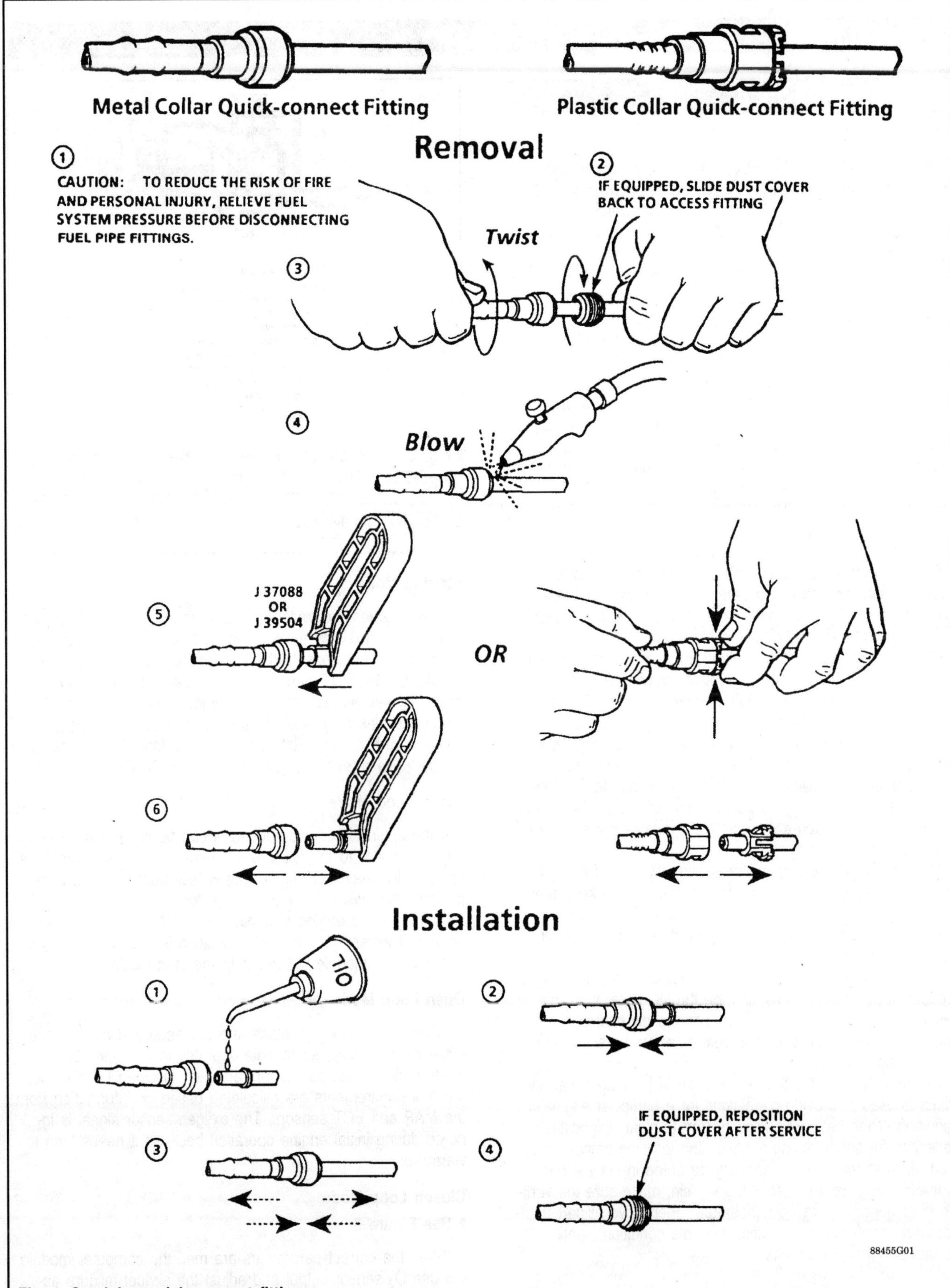

Fig. 1 Servicing quick connect fittings

THROTTLE BODY FUEL INJECTION SYSTEM

General Information

▶ **See Figure 2**

Some 1994-95 fuel injected vehicles were equipped with a Throttle Body Injection (TBI) system. The system uses a TBI unit mounted centrally on the intake manifold where a carburetor would normally be found on older vehicles. The throttle body assembly is equipped with electronic fuel injectors in order to supply fuel to regulate the air/fuel mixture. All fuel injection and ignition functions are controlled by the computer control module, which is sometimes also referred to as the ECM, PCM or VCM, depending on the application. It accepts inputs from various sensors and switches, calculates the optimum air/fuel mixture and operates the various output devices to provide peak performance within specific emissions limits. The module will attempt to maintain the ideal air/fuel mixture of 14.7:1 in order to optimize catalytic converter operation. If a system failure occurs that is not serious enough to stop the engine, the module will illuminate the CHECK ENGINE or SERVICE ENGINE SOON light (as applicable) and will continue to operate the engine, although it may need to operate in a backup or fail-safe mode.

Fuel is supplied to the injector(s) through an electric fuel pump assembly which is mounted in the vehicle's fuel tank. The module provides a signal to operate the fuel pump though the fuel pump relay and oil pressure switch.

Other system components include a pressure regulator, an Idle Air Control (IAC) valve, a Throttle Position (TP) sensor, Manifold Air Temperature (MAT) or Intake Air Temperature (IAT) sensor, Engine Coolant Temperature (ECT) sensor, a Manifold Absolute Pressure (MAP) sensor and an oxygen sensor. The fuel injectors are solenoid valves that the control module pulse on and off many times per second to promote proper fuel atomization. The pulse width determines how long an injector is **ON** each cycle and this regulates the amount of fuel supplied to the engine.

The system pressure regulator is normally part of the TBI unit fuel meter cover. The regulator is designed to keep fuel pressure constant at the injector regardless of engine rpm. This is accomplished by controlling the flow in the return line (a calibrated bypass).

The idle air control valve is a stepper motor that controls the amount of air allowed to bypass the throttle plate. With this valve the computer control module can closely control idle speed even when the engine is cold or when there is a high engine load at idle.

The module used on TBI vehicles has a learning capability which is used to provide corrections for a particular engine's condition. If the battery is disconnected to clear diagnostic codes, or for safety during a repair, the learning process must start all over again. A change may be noted in vehicle performance. In order to "teach" the vehicle, make sure the vehicle is at normal operating temperature, then drive at part throttle, under moderate acceleration and idle conditions, until normal performance returns.

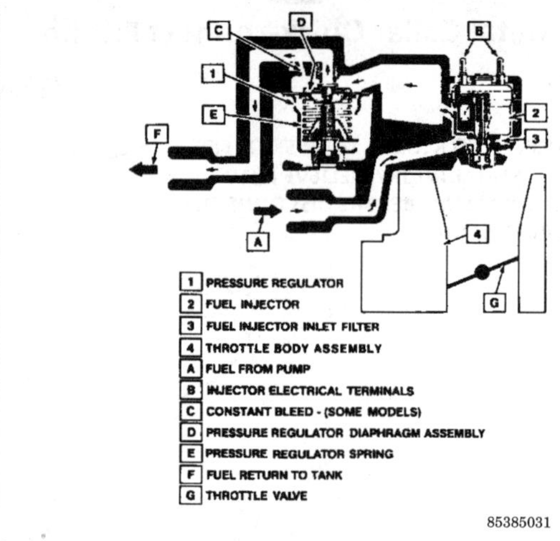

Fig. 2 A cross-sectional view of TBI unit operation — model 220 found on V6 engines

OPERATING MODES

Starting Mode

When the ignition switch is first turned **ON**, the fuel pump relay is energized by the module for 2 seconds in order to build system pressure. In the start mode, the computer module checks the ECT, TP sensor and crank signal in order to determine the best air/fuel ratio for starting. The modules on later model vehicles may also use the IAT or MAT (as equipped) and the MAP sensor. Ratios could range from 1.5:1 at approximately -33°F (-36°C), to 14.7:1 at 201°F (94°C).

Clear Flood Mode

If the engine becomes flooded, it can be cleared by opening the accelerator to the full throttle position. When the throttle is open all the way and engine rpm is less than 600, the computer module will pulse the fuel injector at an air/fuel ratio of 16.5:1 while the engine is turning over in order to clear the engine of excess fuel. If throttle position is reduced below 65 percent , the module will return to the start mode.

Open Loop Mode

When the engine first starts and engine speed rises above 400 rpm, the computer module operates in the Open Loop mode until specific parameters are met. In Open Loop mode, the fuel requirements are calculated based on information from the MAP and ECT sensors. The oxygen sensor signal is ignored during initial engine operation because it needs time to warm up.

Closed Loop Mode

▶ **See Figure 3**

When the correct parameters are met, the computer module will use O_2 sensor output and adjust the air/fuel mixture accordingly in order to maintain a narrow band of exhaust gas oxygen concentration. When the module is correcting and adjusting fuel mixture based on the oxygen sensor signal along with the other sensors, this is known as feedback air/fuel ratio control. The computer module will shift into this Closed Loop mode when:

- Oxygen sensor output voltage is varied, indicating that the sensor has warmed up to operating temperature
- The ECT shows an engine coolant temperature above a specified level.
- The engine has been operating for a programmed amount of time.

Acceleration Mode

If the throttle position and manifold pressure is quickly increased, the module will provide extra fuel for smooth acceleration.

Deceleration Mode

As the throttle closes and the manifold pressure decreases, fuel flow is reduced by the module. If both conditions remain for a specific number of engine revolutions indicating a very fast deceleration, the module may decide fuel flow is not needed and stop the flow by temporarily shutting off the injectors.

Highway Fuel Mode (Semi-Closed Loop)

On some vehicles, the computer control module is programmed to enter a special highway mode to improve fuel economy. If the module senses the correct ECT, ignition control, canister purge activity and a constant engine speed, it will enter highway mode. During this operation, there will be very little adjustment of the long and short term fuel trims, also, the oxygen sensor values will usually read below 100 millivolts.

Decel En-Leanment Mode

On some vehicles, the computer control module is programmed to further reduce emissions by leaning the fuel spray on deceleration. The module does this when a high MAP vacuum (low voltage or pressure) is sensed, BUT it should be noted that the module may do this when the vehicle is not moving.

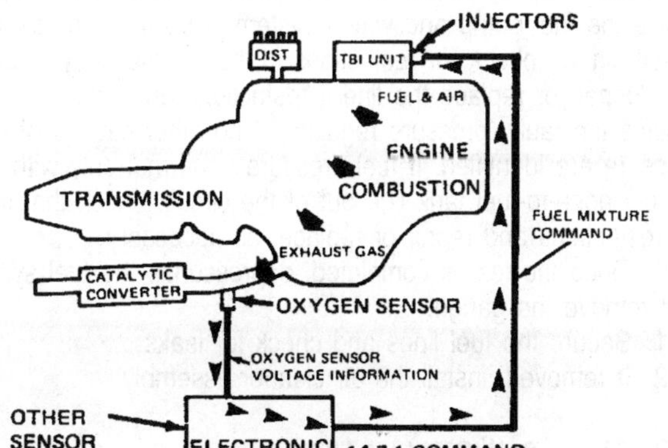

Fig. 3 Computer module fuel control schematic for common closed loop engine operation (same for PCMs and VCMs)

This mode of operation may be misdiagnosed as a lean condition. When diagnosing the control system using a scan tool with the transmission in Park, the oxygen sensor signal low (usually below 100 mV), and both fuel trim numbers around 128 counts, lower the engine speed to 1000 rpm. If the sensor and long term trim numbers respond normally, it is possible that the system was fooled into decel en-leanment operation. If the oxygen sensor and long term numbers do not respond at the lower rpm, there are other problems with the vehicle.

Battery Low Mode

If the computer module detects a low battery, it will increase injector pulse width to compensate for the low voltage and provide proper fuel delivery. It will also increase idle speed to increase alternate output and, in some cases, ignition dwell time to allow for proper engine operation.

Field Service Mode

When the diagnostic terminal of the test connector is grounded with the engine running, the computer control module will enter the Field Service Mode. If the engine is running in Open Loop Mode, the CHECK ENGINE or SERVICE ENGINE SOON Malfunction Indicator Lamp (MIL) will flash quickly, about 2½ times per second. When the engine is in Closed Loop Mode, the MIL will flash only about once per second. If the light stays OFF most of the time in Close Loop, the engine is running lean. If the light is ON most of the time, the engine is running rich.

While the engine continues to operate in Field Service Mode certain conditions will apply:

- The distributor operates with a fixed spark advance (some early model vehicles).
- New trouble codes cannot be stored in computer memory.
- The closed loop timer is bypassed.

➡For more information concerning the computer control module, self-diagnosis systems and other electronic engine controls, please refer to Section 4 of this manual.

Fuel Pressure Relief

Prior to servicing any component of the fuel injection system, the fuel pressure must relieved. If fuel pressure is not relieved, serious injury could result.

✲✲CAUTION

To reduce the chance of personal injury when disconnecting a fuel line, always cover the fuel line with cloth to collect escaping fuel, then place the cloth in an approved container.

1. Disconnect the negative battery cable.
2. Loosen fuel filler cap to relieve fuel tank pressure.
3. The internal constant bleed feature of the Model 220 TBI unit relieves fuel pump system pressure when the engine is turned **OFF**. Therefore, no further action is required.

➡Allow the engine to set for 5-10 minutes; this will allow the orifice (in the fuel system) to bleed off the pressure.

4. When fuel service is finished, tighten the fuel filler cap and connect the negative battery cable.

Electric Fuel Pump

See Figure 4

The electric fuel pump is attached to the fuel sending unit, located in the fuel tank.

TESTING

See Figures 5, 6 and 7

1. Properly relieve the fuel system pressure.
2. If necessary for access, remove the air cleaner assembly and plug the vacuum port(s).
3. Disconnect the flexible fuel supply line, located in the engine compartment between the fuel filter and throttle body.

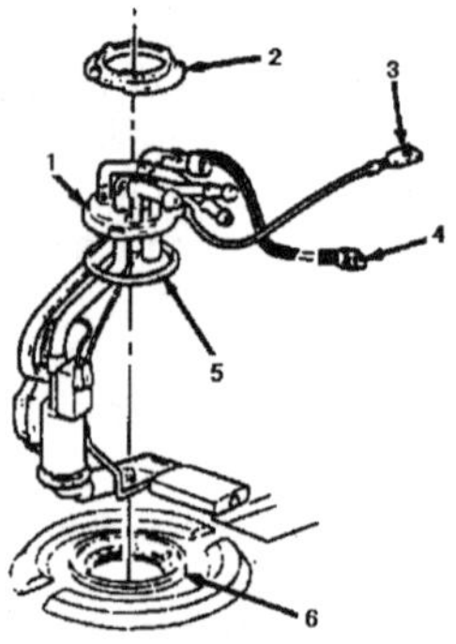

1. Fuel pump & sender
2. CAM
3. Ground wire
4. Electrical connector
5. Seal
6. Fuel tank

88455g02

Fig. 4 Exploded view of the fuel pump and related components used on TBI equipped models

tccs4p04

Fig. 5 Fuel pressure can be checked using an inexpensive pressure/vacuum gauge

4. Install a fuel pressure gauge, such as J-29658 or equivalent, inline in-line between the fuel filter and throttle body unit (between the steel line and flexible hose). If necessary use an adapter or T fitting in order to connect the gauge and complete the fuel circuit.

➡A T fitting may be fabricated for this purpose. Depending on the fuel pressure gauge, short lengths of steel tubing, appropriately sized flare nuts and a flare nut adapter may be used.

5. If the engine will run, start the engine and allow it to run at normal idle speed. The fuel pressure should be 9-13 psi (62-90 kPa).
6. If the engine does not run, turn the ignition **ON**, but do not attempt to start the engine. Listen for the fuel pump to run. Within 2 seconds of turning the ignition **ON** pressure should be 9-13 psi (62-90 kPa). If necessary, cycle the ignition **OFF**, then **ON** again, in order to build up system pressure.
7. If the fuel pump did not run or system pressure did not reach specification, locate the fuel pump test connector. The test connector is usually found on the driver's side of the engine compartment (on or near the fender), with a single wire (usually red) leading from the relay to the connector. Using a jumper wire, apply battery voltage to the test connector in order to energize and run the fuel pump. The pump should run and produce fuel pressure of 9-13 psi (62-90 kPa). If the pump does not run, check the relay and fuel pump wiring.
8. If the pump pressure was lower than specification, first check for a restricted fuel line or filter and replace, as necessary. If no restrictions can be found, restrict the fuel supply line between the pressure gauge and the TBI unit (a flexible hose may be temporarily clamped to produce the restriction), then apply voltage to the test connector again. If pressure is now above 13 psi (90 kPa), replace the faulty pressure regulator. If pressure remains below 9 psi (62 kPa), then the problem is located in the fuel tank (the fuel pump, coupling hose or inlet filter).
9. If during Step 7, the pressure was higher than specification, disengage the injector connector, then disconnect the fuel return line flexible hose which connects the line from the throttle body to the tank line. Attach a 5/16 ID flex hose to the fuel line from the throttle body and place the other end into an approved gasoline container. Cycle the ignition in order to energize the fuel pump and watch system pressure. If pressure is still higher, check for restrictions in the throttle body return line. Repair or replace the line if restrictions are found or replace the faulty pressure regulator if no other causes of high pressure are identified. If fuel pressure is normal only with the flexible hose-to-fuel tank line out of the circuit, check that line for restrictions and repair or replace, as necessary.
10. Once the test is completed, depressurize the fuel system and remove the gauge.
11. Secure the fuel lines and check for leaks.
12. If removed, install the air cleaner assembly.

REMOVAL & INSTALLATION

1. Properly relieve the fuel system pressure.

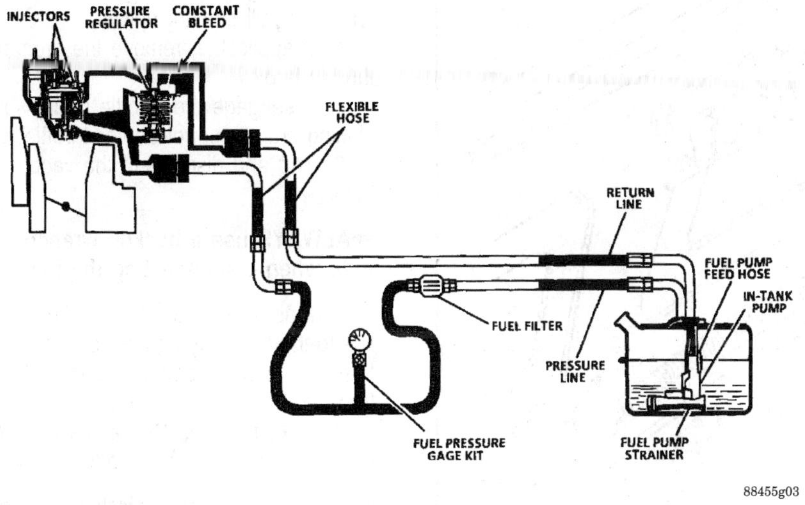

Fig. 6 Fuel system pressure testing

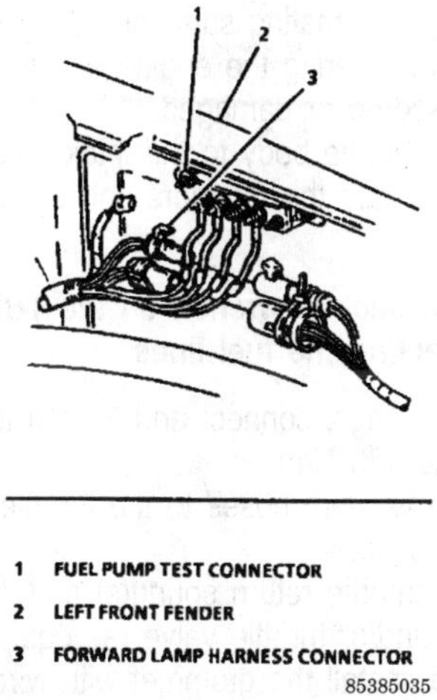

Fig. 7 The fuel pump test connector is normally found in the engine compartment, on the left fender

2. Connect the negative battery cable.

➡Be sure to keep a Class B (dry chemical) fire extinguisher nearby.

⁂CAUTION

Due to the possibility of fire or explosion, never drain or store gasoline in an open container.

3. Drain the fuel tank, then remove it from the vehicle. Refer to the procedure found later in this section for details.

4. Using the GM fuel gauge sending unit retaining cam tool No. J-24187, J-36608 (or equivalent) or a brass drift and a hammer, remove the cam locking ring (fuel sending unit) by twisting counterclockwise. With the locking ring released, carefully lift the sending unit from the fuel tank.

5. Remove the fuel pump from the fuel sending unit, by performing the following procedures:

a. Pull the fuel pump up into the mounting tube, while pulling outward (away) from the bottom support.

➡When removing the fuel pump from the sending unit, be careful not to damage the rubber insulator and the strainer.

b. When the pump assembly is clear of the bottom support, pull it out of the rubber connector.

To install:

6. Inspect the fuel pump hose and bottom sound insulator for signs of deterioration, then replace, as necessary.

7. Push the fuel pump onto the sending tube.

8. Using a new sending unit-to-fuel tank O-ring, carefully lower the sending unit/fuel pump assembly into the fuel tank.

➡When installing the sending unit, be careful not to fold or twist the fuel strainer or it may restrict the fuel flow.

9. Secure the sending unit by turning or driving the lockring clockwise and into position under the tabs.

10. Install the fuel tank assembly to the vehicle.

11. Connect the negative battery cable and check for proper pump operation.

Fuel Pump Relay

The fuel pump relay is normally found on a relay bracket which is mounted to the left front fender in the engine compartment. Positioning within the bracket will vary according to model and application. Check for loose electrical connections; no other service is possible, except replacement.

REMOVAL & INSTALLATION

▶ See Figure 8

1. Disconnect the negative battery cable.

2. Disengage the relay/electrical connector assembly from the bracket.

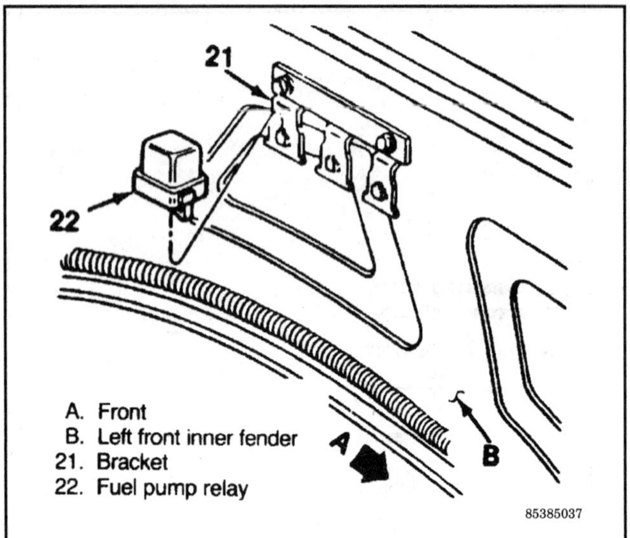

Fig. 8 Common fuel pump relay mounting

3. Pull the fuel pump relay from the electrical connector.
4. If necessary, use a new relay, then reverse the removal procedures.

Throttle Body

See Figure 9

The Model 220 throttle body assembly is used on the 4.3L engine. It consists of three major casting assemblies:

- Fuel pressure cover with pressure regulator.
- Fuel metering body with fuel injectors.
- Throttle body with an Idle Speed Control (IAC) valve and a Throttle Position (TP) sensor.

The Throttle Position (TP) sensor is a variable resistor used to convert the degree of throttle plate opening to an electrical signal to the computer control module. The module uses this signal as a reference point of throttle valve position. In addition, an Idle Air Control (IAC) assembly, mounted in the throttle body is used to control idle speeds. A cone-shaped valve in the IAC assembly is located in an air passage in the throttle body that leads from the point beneath the air cleaner to below the throttle valve. The module monitors idle speeds and, depending on engine load, moves the IAC cone in the air passage to increase or decrease air bypassing the throttle valve to the intake manifold for control of idle speeds.

The operation of all throttle bodies is basically the same. Each is constantly monitored by the computer control module in order to produce a 14.7:1 air/fuel ratio, which is vital to the catalytic converter operation.

REMOVAL & INSTALLATION

See Figures 10, 11, 12 and 13

1. Properly relieve the fuel system pressure, then disconnect the negative battery cable.
2. Remove the air cleaner assembly.
3. Disengage the electrical connectors from the idle air control valve, the throttle position sensor and the fuel injector(s). When disengaging the injector connectors, squeeze the plastic tabs and pull straight upward.
4. If applicable, remove the grommet with wires from the throttle body.
5. Disengage the throttle return spring(s) and linkage (including cruise control and/or throttle valve (as equipped).
6. Tag and disconnect the vacuum hoses from the throttle body.

➡ALWAYS use a backup wrench on the TBI fuel line inlet nuts when disconnecting the fuel lines.

7. Place a rag (to catch the excess fuel) under the fuel line-to-throttle body connection, then disengage the fuel lines from the throttle body. Remove and discard the old O-rings from the lines.
8. Unfasten the TBI unit-to-manifold attaching hardware, then remove the throttle body and discard the old gasket.

➡Be sure to place a cloth or plastic cover over the intake manifold opening to prevent dirt from entering the engine.

To install:

9. Clean the gasket mating surfaces taking great care to prevent debris from entering the engine and to make sure the surfaces are not scored or damaged.
10. Position the throttle body to the intake manifold using a new gasket, then thread the retainers and tighten to 12 ft. lbs. (16 Nm).

➡ALWAYS use a backup wrench on the TBI fuel line inlet nuts when connecting the fuel lines.

11. Using new O-rings, connect and tighten the fuel line fittings to 20 ft. lbs. (26 Nm).
12. Connect the vacuum hoses to the throttle body, as tagged during removal.
13. Engage the throttle return spring(s) and linkage (including cruise control and/or throttle valve (as equipped).
14. If applicable, install the grommet with wires to the throttle body.
15. Engage the electrical connectors to the idle air control valve, the throttle position sensor and the fuel injector(s).
16. Install the air cleaner assembly.
17. Connect the negative battery cable.
18. Depress the accelerator pedal to the floor and release it, to see if the pedal returns freely. Turn the ignition switch **ON** and check for fuel leaks.

Fuel Injector

REMOVAL & INSTALLATION

See Figures 14, 15, 16, 17, 18, 19 and 20

⁂CAUTION

When removing the injector(s), be careful not to damage the electrical connector pins (on top of the injector), the injector fuel filter and the nozzle. The fuel injector is serviced as a complete assembly ONLY, it is an electrical component and should not be immersed in any kind of cleaner.

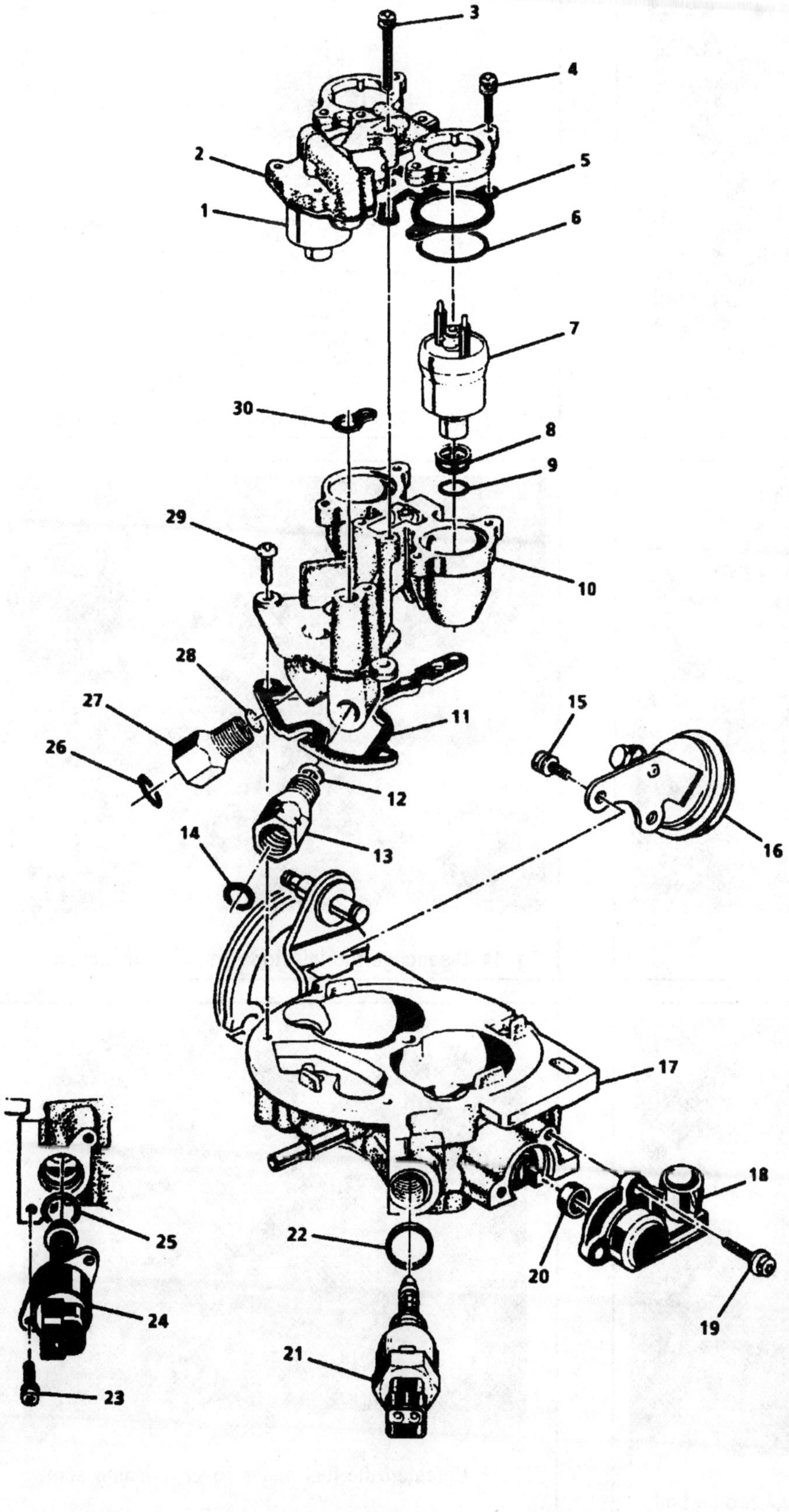

1	REGULATOR ASSEMBLY - FUEL PRESSURE
2	COVER ASSEMBLY - FUEL METER
3	SCREW - FUEL METER COVER ATTACHING - LONG
4	SCREW - FUEL METER COVER ATTACHING - SHORT
5	GASKET - FUEL METER COVER
6	O-RING - FUEL INJECTOR UPPER
7	INJECTOR ASSEMBLY - TBI FUEL
8	FILTER - FUEL INJECTOR INLET
9	O-RING - FUEL INJECTOR LOWER
10	BODY ASSEMBLY - FUEL METER
11	GASKET - THROTTLE BODY TO FUEL METER BODY
12	GASKET - FUEL OUTLET NUT
13	NUT - FUEL OUTLET
14	O-RING - FUEL RETURN LINE
15	SCREW - ISC ACTUATOR ASSEMBLY ATTACHING
16	ACTUATOR ASSEMBLY - IDLE SPEED CONTROL (ISC)
17	BODY ASSEMBLY - THROTTLE
18	SENSOR - THROTTLE POSITION (TP)
19	SCREW - TP SENSOR ATTACHING
20	SEAL - TP SENSOR
21	VALVE ASSEMBLY - IDLE AIR CONTROL (IAC) - THREAD MOUNTED
22	GASKET - IAC VALVE
23	SCREW - IAC VALVE ATTACHING
24	VALVE ASSEMBLY - IDLE AIR CONTROL (IAC) - FLANGE MOUNTED
25	O-RING - IAC VALVE
26	O-RING - FUEL INLET LINE
27	NUT - FUEL INLET
28	GASKET - FUEL INLET NUT
29	SCREW - FUEL METER BODY TO THROTTLE BODY ATTACHING
30	GASKET - FUEL METER OUTLET

85385040

Fig. 9 Exploded view of the model 220 TBI unit — 4.3L engines

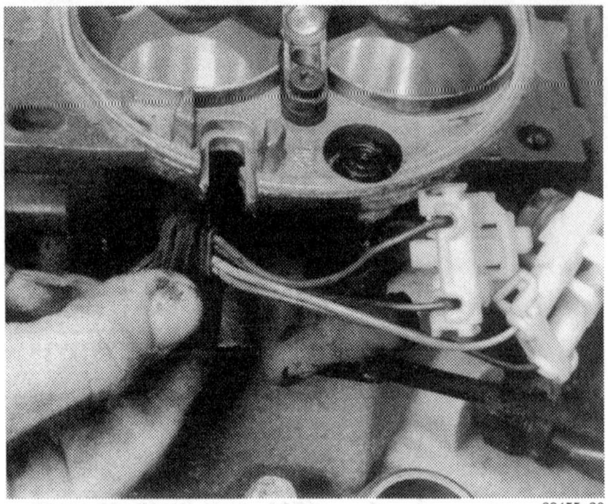

88455p20

Fig. 10 Unplug the injector connectors and remove the grommet with wires from the throttle body

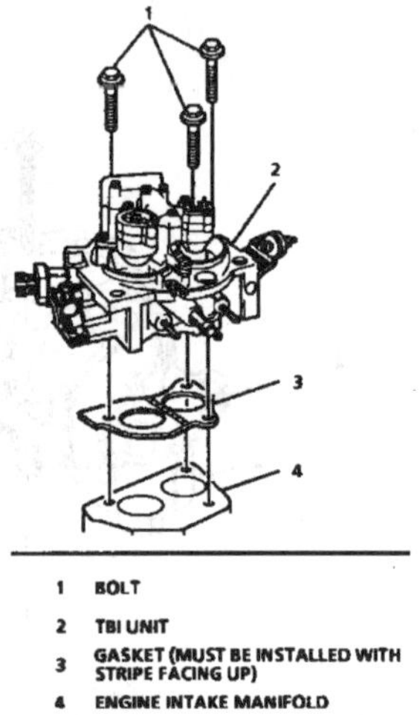

85385044

Fig. 13 Model 220 TBI unit mounting — 4.3L engine

88455p21

Fig. 11 Disconnect the throttle linkage

88455p24

Fig. 14 Disengage the injector electrical connection

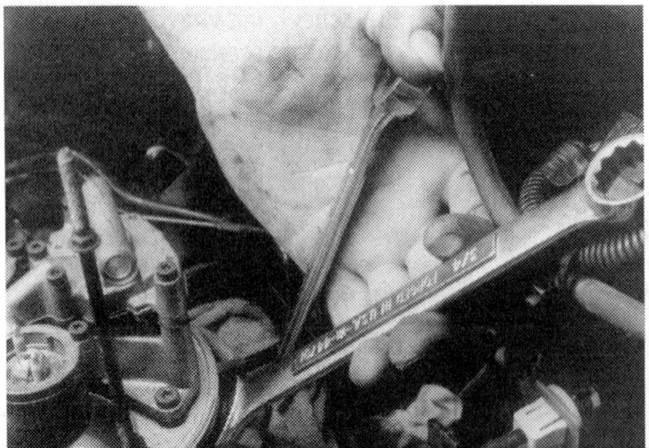

88455p22

Fig. 12 Disengage the fuel lines from the throttle body

88455p25

Fig. 15 Unfasten the fuel meter cover retaining screws . . .

88455p26

Fig. 16 . . . then remove the fuel meter cover

88455p27

Fig. 17 Using a metal dowel as a fulcrum and a prytool to remove the injectors from their bores

88455p28

Fig. 18 Remove the injectors . . .

88455p29

Fig. 19 Remove and discard the O-ring seals

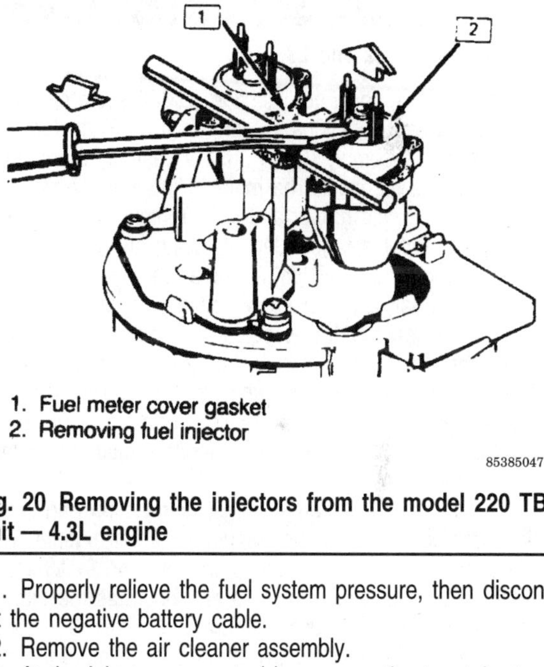

1. Fuel meter cover gasket
2. Removing fuel injector

85385047

Fig. 20 Removing the injectors from the model 220 TBI unit — 4.3L engine

1. Properly relieve the fuel system pressure, then disconnect the negative battery cable.
2. Remove the air cleaner assembly.
3. At the injector connector(s), squeeze the two tabs together and pull straight up to disengage connector from the injector.
4. Loosen the fuel meter cover retaining screws, then remove the cover from the fuel meter body, but leave the cover gasket in place.
5. Using a small pry bar and a round fulcrum, carefully pry the injector until it is free, then remove the injector from the fuel meter body.
6. Remove the small O-ring from the nozzle end of the injector. If equipped and removal is necessary, carefully rotate the injector's fuel filter back and forth to remove it from the base of the injector.
7. Remove and discard the fuel meter cover gasket.
8. Remove the large O-ring and back-up washer (if equipped) from the top of the counterbore of the fuel meter body injector cavity.

To install:

9. If removed, with the larger end of the filter facing the injector (so that the filter covers the raised rib of the injector base) install the filter by twisting it into position on the injector.

10. Lubricate the new O-rings with clean automatic transmission fluid, then install the small O-ring on the nozzle end of the injector. Be sure the O-ring is pressed up against the injector or injector filter (as applicable).

11. Install the steel backup washer (if equipped) in the top counterbore of the fuel meter body's injector cavity, then install the new large O-ring directly over the backup washer. Make sure the O-ring is properly seated in the cavity and is flush with the top of the fuel meter body casting surface.

➡**If the backup washer and large O-ring are not properly installed BEFORE the fuel injector, a fuel leak will likely result.**

12. Install the fuel injector into the cavity by aligning the raised lug on the injector base with the cast notch in the fuel meter body cavity. Once the injector is aligned, carefully push down on the injector by hand until it is fully seated in the cavity. When properly aligned and installed, the injector terminals will be approximately parallel to the throttle shaft.

13. Position a new fuel meter cover gasket, then install the cover to the body, making sure the gasket remains in position. Using a suitable threadlocking compound, install and tighten the cover retainers to 30 inch lbs. (4 Nm).

14. Engage the injector electrical connector(s).

15. Connect the negative battery cable, then turn the **ON** to pressurize the fuel system and check for leaks.

16. Install the air cleaner assembly, then start the engine and check for leaks.

CENTRAL MULTI-PORT FUEL INJECTION SYSTEM

General Information

See Figures 21, 22 and 23

The Central Multi-port Fuel Injection (CMFI) system, found on 1994-95 models, functions similarly to the TBI system in that an injection assembly (CMFI unit) is centrally mounted on the engine intake manifold. The major differences come in the incorporation of a split (upper and lower) intake manifold assembly with a variable tuned plenum (using an intake manifold tuning valve) and the CMFI unit's single fuel injector which feeds 6 poppet valves (1 for each individual cylinder).

The non-repairable CMFI assembly or injection unit consists of a fuel meter body, gasket seal, fuel pressure regulator, fuel injector and six poppet nozzles with fuel tubes. The assembly is housed in the lower intake manifold. Should a failure occur in the CMFI assembly, the entire component must be replaced as a unit.

As with other fuel injection systems, all injection and ignition functions are controlled by the computer control module. The module accepts inputs from various sensors and switches, calculates the optimum air/fuel mixture and operates the various output devices to provide peak performance within specific emissions limits. The module will attempt to maintain the ideal air/fuel mixture of 14.7:1 in order to optimize catalytic converter operation. If a system failure occurs that is not serious enough to stop the engine, the module will illuminate the SERVICE ENGINE SOON light and will continue to operate the engine, although it may need to operate in a backup or fail-safe mode.

Fuel is supplied to the injector through an electric fuel pump assembly which is mounted in the vehicle's fuel tank. The module provides a signal to operate the fuel pump though the fuel pump relay and oil pressure switch. The CMFI unit internal pressure regulator maintains a system pressure of approximately 55-61 psi (380-420 kPa). When the injector is energized by the control module, an armature lifts allowing pressurized fuel to travel down the 6 fuel tubes to the poppet valves. In the poppet valves, fuel pressure (working against the extension spring force) will cause the nozzle ball to open from its seat and fuel will flow from the nozzle. It takes approximately 51 psi (350 kPa) to force fuel from the poppet nozzle. Once the module de-energizes the injector, the armature will close, allowing fuel pressure in the tubes to drop and the spring force will close off fuel flow.

Other system components include a pressure regulator, an Idle Air Control (IAC) valve, a Throttle Position (TP) sensor, Intake Air Temperature (IAT) sensor, Engine Coolant Temperature (ECT) sensor, a Manifold Absolute Pressure (MAP) sensor and an oxygen sensor.

The idle air control valve is a stepper motor that controls the amount of air allowed to bypass the throttle plate. With this valve the computer control module can closely control idle speed even when the engine is cold or when there is a high engine load at idle.

The computer module used on CMFI vehicles has a learning capability which is used to provide corrections for a particular engine's condition. If the battery is disconnected to clear diagnostic codes, or for safety during a repair, the learning process must start all over again. A change may be noted in vehicle performance. In order to "teach" the vehicle, make sure the vehicle is at normal operating temperature, then drive at part throttle, under moderate acceleration and idle conditions, until normal performance returns.

OPERATING MODES

Starting Mode

When the ignition switch is first turned **ON**, the fuel pump relay is energized by the module for 2 seconds in order to build system pressure. In the start mode, the computer module checks the ECT, IAT, TP sensor, MAP and crank signal in order to determine the best air/fuel ratio for starting. Ratios could range from 1.5:1 at approximately -33°F (-36°C), to 14.7:1 at 201°F (94°C).

Clear Flood Mode

If the engine becomes flooded, it can be cleared by opening the accelerator to the full throttle position. When the throttle is open all the way and engine rpm is less than 600, the computer module will pulse the fuel injector at an air/fuel ratio of 16.5:1 while the engine is turning over in order to clear the

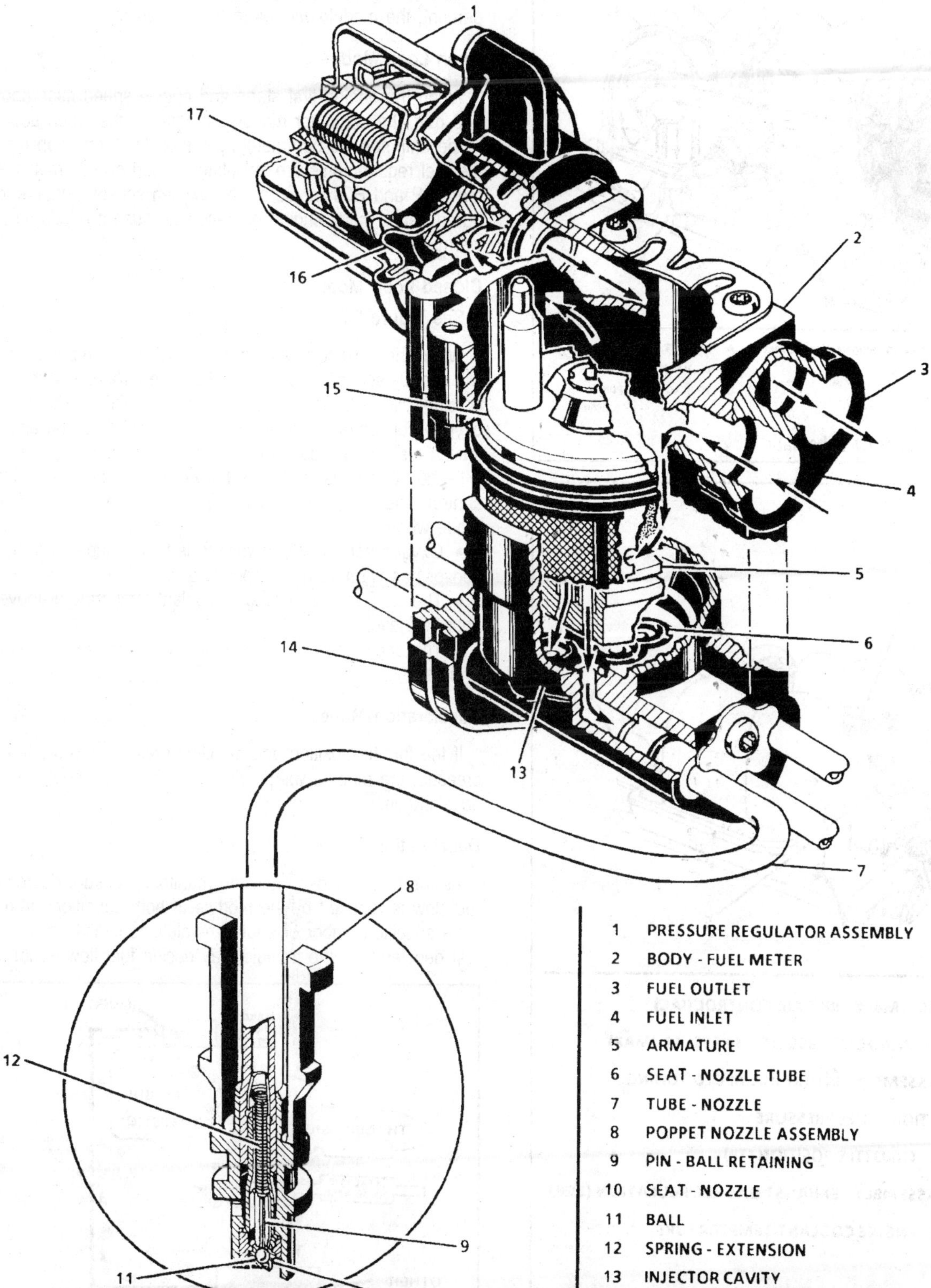

1 PRESSURE REGULATOR ASSEMBLY
2 BODY - FUEL METER
3 FUEL OUTLET
4 FUEL INLET
5 ARMATURE
6 SEAT - NOZZLE TUBE
7 TUBE - NOZZLE
8 POPPET NOZZLE ASSEMBLY
9 PIN - BALL RETAINING
10 SEAT - NOZZLE
11 BALL
12 SPRING - EXTENSION
13 INJECTOR CAVITY
14 SEAL - CMFI FUEL METER BODY
15 SOLENOID ASSEMBLY
16 DIAPHRAGM & VALVE ASSEMBLY
17 SPRING - PRESSURE REGULATOR

88455g05

Fig. 21 Cross-sectional view of CMFI assembly

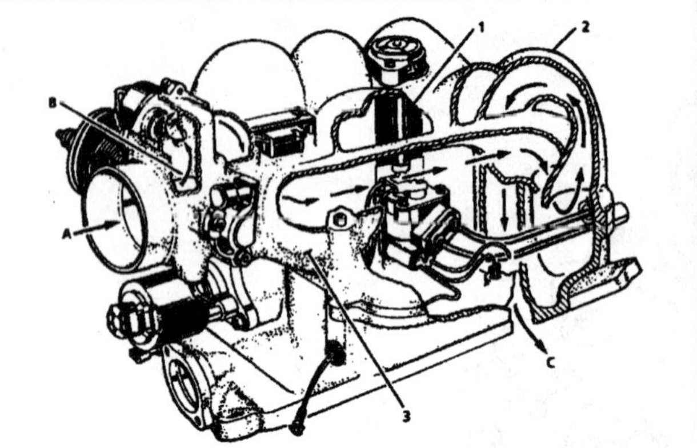

1 INTAKE MANIFOLD TUNING VALVE ASSEMBLY
2 TRI-LOBULAR RUNNER
3 ZIP TUBE
A AIR INLET
B IAC VALVE BYPASS AIR
C TO HEAD INTAKE PORT

85385053

Fig. 22 CMFI air flow schematic

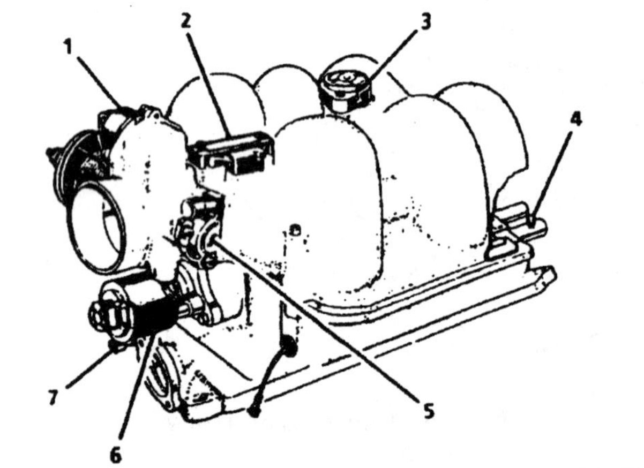

1 VALVE ASSEMBLY - IDLE AIR CONTROL (IAC)
2 SENSOR - MANIFOLD ABSOLUTE PRESSURE (MAP)
3 VALVE ASSEMBLY - INTAKE MANIFOLD TUNING
4 CONNECTION - FUEL PRESSURE
5 SENSOR - THROTTLE POSITION (TP)
6 VALVE ASSEMBLY - EXHAUST GAS RECIRCULATION (EGR)
7 SENSOR - ENGINE COOLANT TEMPERATURE

85385054

Fig. 23 Various CMFI engine components are mounted to the intake manifolds (the CMFI unit is located under the upper intake)

engine of excess fuel. If throttle position is reduced below 65 percent, the module will return to the start mode.

Open Loop Mode

When the engine first starts and engine speed rises above 400 rpm, the computer module operates in the Open Loop mode until specific parameters are met. In Open Loop mode, the fuel requirements are calculated based on information from the MAP and ECT sensors. The oxygen sensor signal is ignored during initial engine operation because it needs time to warm up.

Closed Loop Mode

➧ See Figure 24

When the correct parameters are met, the computer module will use O_2 sensor output and adjust the air/fuel mixture accordingly, in order to maintain a narrow band of exhaust gas oxygen concentration. When the module is correcting and adjusting fuel mixture based on the oxygen sensor signal along with the other sensors, this is known as feedback air/fuel ratio control. The computer module will shift into this Closed Loop mode when:

- Oxygen sensor output voltage is varied, indicating that the sensor has warmed up to operating temperature
- The ECT shows an engine coolant temperature above a specified level.
- The engine has been operating for a programmed amount of time.

Acceleration Mode

If the throttle position and manifold pressure is quickly increased, the module will provide extra fuel for smooth acceleration.

Deceleration Mode

As the throttle closes and the manifold pressure decreases, fuel flow is reduced by the module. If both conditions remain for a specific number of engine revolutions indicating a very fast deceleration, the module may decide fuel flow is not

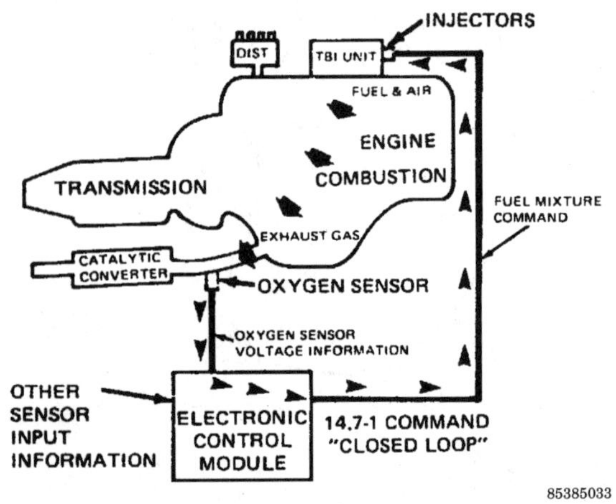

85385033

Fig. 24 Computer module fuel control schematic for common closed loop engine operation (note CMFI unit replaces the TBI on these engines)

needed and stop the flow by temporarily shutting off the injectors.

Highway Fuel Mode (Semi-Closed Loop)

The computer control module is programmed to enter a special highway mode to improve fuel economy. If the module senses the correct ECT, ignition control, canister purge activity and a constant engine speed, it will enter highway mode. During this operation, there will be very little adjustment of the long and short term fuel trims, also, the oxygen sensor values will usually read below 100 millivolts.

Decel En-Leanment Mode

The computer control module is programmed to further reduce emissions by leaning the fuel spray on deceleration. The module does this when a high MAP vacuum (low voltage or pressure) is sensed, BUT it should be noted that the module may do this when the vehicle is not moving. This mode of operation may be misdiagnosed as a lean condition. When diagnosing the control system using a scan tool with the transmission in Park, the oxygen sensor signal low (usually below 100 mV), and both fuel trim numbers around 128 counts, lower the engine speed to 1000 rpm. If the sensor and long term trim numbers respond normally, it is possible that the system was fooled into decel en-leanment operation. If the oxygen sensor and long term numbers do not respond at the lower rpm, there are other problems with the vehicle.

Battery Low Mode

If the computer module detects a low battery, it will increase injector pulse width to compensate for the low voltage and provide proper fuel delivery. It will also increase idle speed to increase alternate output and ignition dwell time to allow for proper engine operation.

Field Service Mode

When the diagnostic terminal of the test connector is grounded with the engine running, the computer module will enter the Field Service Mode. If the engine is running in Open Loop Mode, the SERVICE ENGINE SOON Malfunction Indicator Lamp (MIL) will flash quickly, about 2½ times per second. When the engine is in Closed Loop Mode, the MIL will flash only about once per second. If the light stays OFF most of the time in Close Loop, the engine is running lean. If the light is ON most of the time, the engine is running rich.

While the engine continues to operate in Field Service Mode certain conditions will apply:

- New trouble codes cannot be stored in computer memory.
- The closed loop timer is bypassed.

➡For more information concerning the computer control module, self-diagnosis systems and other electronic engine controls, please refer to Section 4 of this manual.

Fuel Pressure Relief

▸ See Figure 25

Prior to servicing any component of the fuel injection system, the fuel pressure must relieved. If fuel pressure is not relieved, serious injury could result.

A Schrader valve is provided on this fuel system in order to conveniently test or release the fuel system pressure. A fuel pressure gauge and adapter will be necessary to connect the gauge to the fitting. The CMFI system covered here uses a valve located on the inlet pipe fitting, immediately before it enters the CMFI assembly (towards the rear of the engine).

1. Disconnect the negative battery cable to assure the prevention of fuel spillage if the ignition switch is accidentally turned **ON** while a fitting is still disconnected.
2. Loosen the fuel filter cap to release the fuel tank pressure.
3. Make sure the release valve on the fuel gauge is closed, then connect the fuel gauge to the pressure fitting located on the inlet fuel pipe fitting.

➡When connecting the gauge to the fitting, be sure to wrap a rag around the fitting to avoid spillage. After repairs, place the rag in an approved container.

4. Install the bleed hose portion of the fuel gauge assembly into an approved container, then open the gauge release valve and bleed the fuel pressure from the system.
5. When the gauge is removed, be sure to open the bleed valve and drain all fuel from the gauge assembly.

Electric Fuel Pump

The electric pump is attached to the fuel sending unit, located in the fuel tank.

TESTING

▸ See Figure 26

1. Properly relieve the fuel system pressure.
2. Leave the gauge attached to the pressure fitting on the fuel inlet pipe.
3. If disconnected during the fuel pressure relief procedure, reconnect the negative battery terminal.
4. If the engine will run, start the engine and allow it to run at normal idle speed. The fuel pressure should be 55-61 psi (380-420 kPa). Once the engine is at normal operating temper-

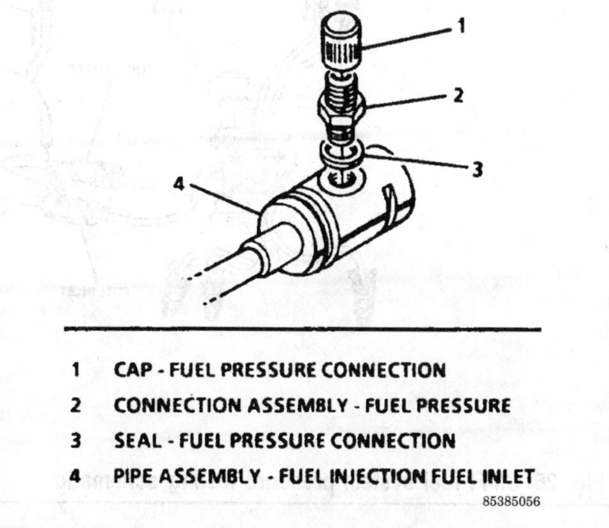

Fig. 25 Fuel pressure connection

ature, open the throttle quickly while noting fuel pressure; it should quickly approach 61 psi (40 kPa) if all components are operating properly (there is no need to proceed further). If the pressure was in specification before, but does not approach 61 psi (420 kPa) on acceleration, the pressure regulator in the CMFI unit is faulty and the assembly should be replaced.

5. If the engine does not run, turn the ignition **ON**, but do not attempt to start the engine. Listen for the fuel pump to run. Within 2 seconds of turning the ignition **ON** pressure should be 55-61 psi (380-420 kPa) while the pump is running. Once the pump stops, pressure may vary by several pounds, then it should hold steady. If the pressure does not hold steady, wait 10 seconds and repeat this step, but pinch the fuel pressure line flexible hose and watch if the pressure holds. If it still does not hold, the CMFI unit should be replaced. If the pressure holds with the pressure line pinched, check for a partially disconnected fuel dampener (pulsator) or faulty in-tank fuel pump.

6. If the fuel pump did not run or system pressure did not reach specification, locate the fuel pump test connector. The test connector is usually found on the driver's side of the engine compartment (on or near the fender), with a single wire (usually red) leading from the relay to the connector. Using a 10 amp fused jumper wire, apply battery voltage to the test connector in order to energize and run the fuel pump. The pump should run and produce fuel pressure of 55-61 psi (380-420 kPa). If the pump does not run, check the relay and fuel pump wiring.

7. If the pump pressure was lower than specification, first check for a restricted fuel line, filter or a disconnected fuel pulse dampener (pulsator) and repair/replace, as necessary. If no restrictions can be found, restrict the flexible fuel return line (by gradually pinching it) until the pressure rises above 61 psi (420 kPa), but DO NOT allow pressure to exceed 75 psi (517 kPa). If the fuel pressure rises above specification with the return line restricted, then the pressure regulator is faulty and the CMFI assembly should be replaced. If pressure still does not reach specification, check for a faulty fuel pump, partially disconnected fuel pulse dampener (pulsator), partially restricted pump strainer or an incorrect pump.

8. If during the previous steps, the fuel pressure was higher than specification, relieve the system pressure, then disconnect the engine compartment fuel return line. Attach a 5/16 ID flex hose to the fuel line from the throttle body and place the other end into an approved gasoline container. Cycle the ignition in order to energize the fuel pump and watch system pressure. If pressure is still higher, check for restrictions in the line between the pressure regulator and the point where it was disconnected. Repair or replace the line if restrictions are found or replace the CMFI assembly with the faulty internal pressure regulator if no other causes of high pressure are identified. If fuel pressure is normal only with the rest of the return line out of the circuit, check that remaining line for restrictions and repair or replace, as necessary.

9. Once the test is completed, depressurize the fuel system and remove the gauge.

REMOVAL & INSTALLATION

Removal and installation of the fuel pump and sending unit assembly is the same on CMFI vehicles as it is for TBI vehicles. Please refer to the TBI procedures earlier in this section for electric fuel pump replacement.

Fuel Pump Relay

For CMFI vehicles, the fuel pump relay is normally found in the convenience center, located under the center of the dashboard. If a problem is suspected, first check for loose electrical connections; no other service is possible, except replacement.

REMOVAL & INSTALLATION

➧ **See Figure 27**

1. Disconnect the negative battery cable.
2. Remove the retainer, if equipped.
3. Disengage the relay electrical connector.

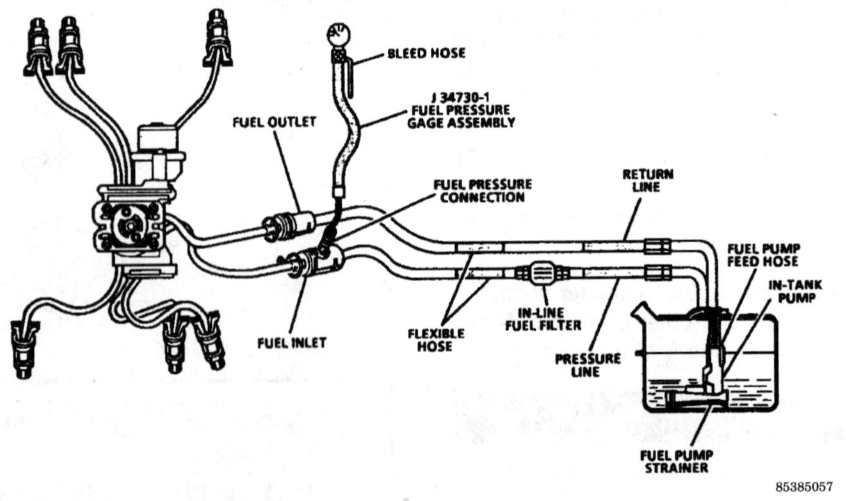

Fig. 26 CMFI fuel system pressure testing schematic

4. Remove the relay by depressing the bracket clip at the rear of the relay, or removing the bolts from the retaining bracket, as applicable.

5. If necessary, use a new relay, then reverse the removal procedures.

CMFI Assembly

REMOVAL & INSTALLATION

➧ **See Figures 28 and 29**

The CMFI assembly is mounted to the lower intake manifold. The upper intake manifold assembly must be removed for access. The CMFI assembly includes a fuel meter body, gasket seal, fuel pressure regulator, fuel injector and six poppet nozzles with fuel tubes. Should a failure occur in any components of the CMFI unit, the entire assembly must be replaced.

1. Remove the plastic cover and properly relieve the fuel system pressure.
2. Disconnect the negative battery cable, then remove the air cleaner and air inlet duct.
3. Disengage the wiring harness from the necessary upper intake components including:
   - Throttle Position (TP) sensor
   - Idle Air Control (IAC) motor
   - Manifold Absolute Pressure (MAP) sensor
   - Intake Manifold Tuning Valve (IMTV)
4. Disengage the throttle linkage from the upper intake manifold, then remove the ignition coil.
5. Disconnect the PCV hose at the rear of the upper intake manifold, then tag and disengage the vacuum hoses from both the front and rear of the upper intake.
6. Remove the upper intake manifold bolts and studs, making sure to note or mark the location of all studs to assure proper installation. Remove the upper intake manifold from the engine.
7. Disengage the injector wiring harness connector at the CMFI assembly.
8. Remove and discard the fuel fitting clip.

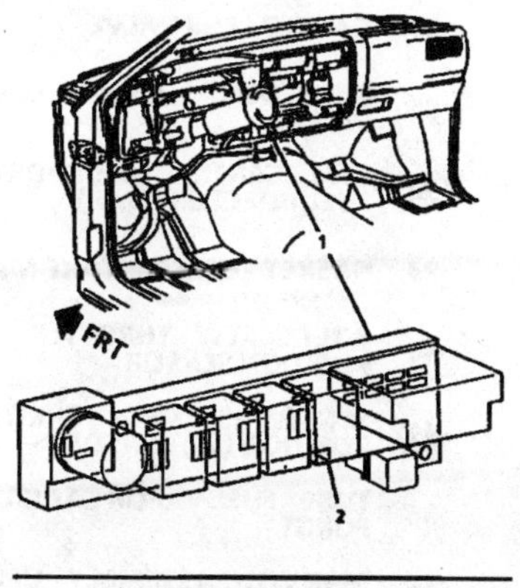

Fig. 27 Common fuel pump relay mounting — CMFI vehicles

9. Disconnect the fuel inlet and return tube and fitting assembly. Discard the old O-rings.
10. Squeeze the poppet nozzle locktabs together while lifting each nozzle out of the casting socket. Once all six nozzles are released, carefully lift the CMFI assembly out of the casting.

To install:

11. Align the CMFI assembly grommet with the casting grommet slots and push downward until it is seated in the bottom guide hole.

****CAUTION**

To reduce the risk of fire and personal injury, be ABSOLUTELY SURE that the poppet nozzles are firmly seated and locked into their casting sockets. An unlocked poppet nozzle could work loose from its socket resulting in a dangerous fuel leak.

12. Carefully insert the poppet nozzles into the casting sockets. Make sure they are FIRMLY SEATED and locked into the casting sockets.
13. Position new O-ring seals (lightly coated with clean engine oil), then connect the fuel inlet and return tube and fitting assembly.
14. Install a new fuel fitting clip.
15. Temporarily connect the negative battery cable, then pressurize the fuel system by cycling the ignition switch **ON** for 2 seconds, then **OFF** for 10 seconds and repeating, as necessary. Once the fuel system is pressurized, check for leaks.
16. Disconnect the negative battery cable.
17. Position a new upper intake manifold gasket on the engine, making sure the green sealing lines are facing upward.
18. Install the upper intake manifold being careful not to pinch the fuel injector wires between the manifolds.
19. Install the manifold retainers, making sure the studs are properly positioned, then tighten them using the proper sequence to 124 inch lbs. (14 Nm).
20. Connect the PCV hose to the rear of the upper intake manifold and the vacuum hoses to both the front and rear of the manifold assembly.
21. Connect the throttle linkage to the upper intake, then install the ignition coil.
22. Engage the necessary wiring to the upper intake components including the TP sensor, IAC motor, MAP sensor and the IMTV.
23. Install the plastic cover, the air cleaner and air inlet duct.
24. Connect the negative battery cable.

Intake Manifold Tuning Valve

➧ **See Figure 30**

The upper intake manifold on the CMFI engine is of a variable tuned split plenum design. The manifold using a centrally mounted tuning valve to equalize pressure in the side by side inlet plenums. The valve is electronically operated by the computer control module.

REMOVAL & INSTALLATION

1. Disconnect the negative battery cable.

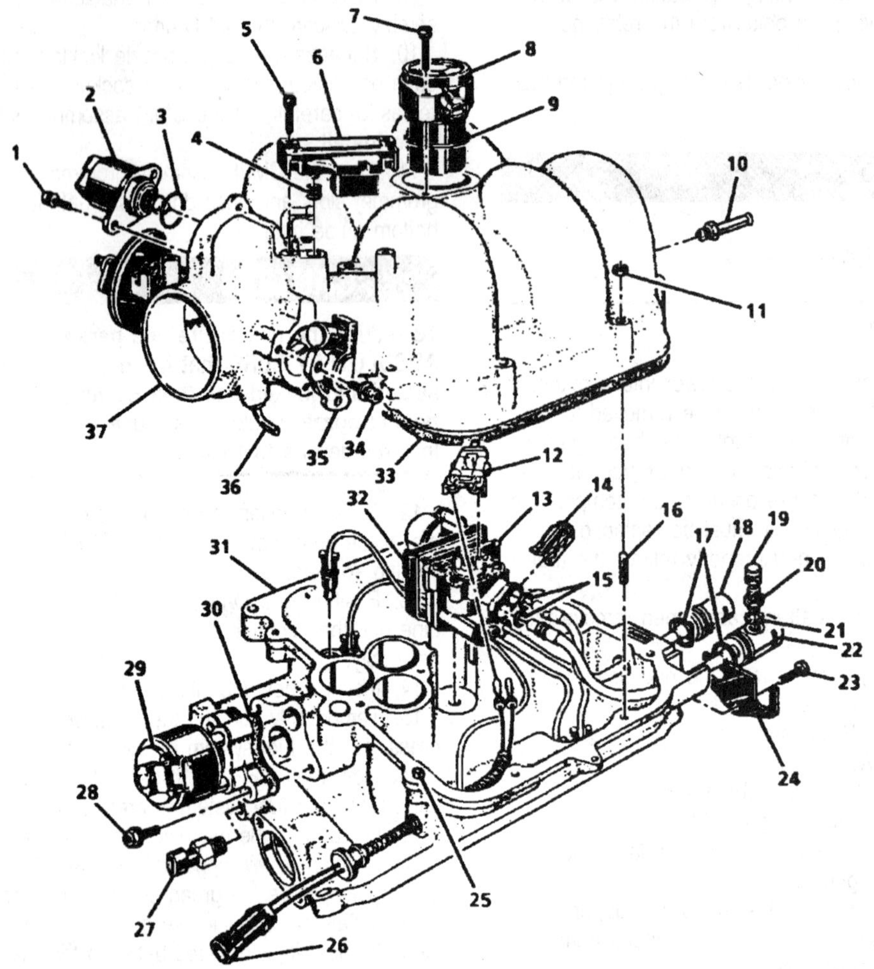

1	BOLT/SCREW - IDLE AIR CONTROL VALVE	14	CLIP - FUEL INJECTION FUEL FEED AND RETURN PIPE	26	HARNESS ASSEMBLY - CENTRAL MULTIPORT FUEL INJECTOR WIRING
2	VALVE ASSEMBLY - IDLE AIR CONTROL (IAC)	15	SEAL - FUEL INJECTION FUEL FEED AND RETURN PIPE (O-RING)	27	SENSOR ASSEMBLY - ENGINE COOLANT TEMPERATURE (ECT)
3	SEAL - IDLE AIR CONTROL VALVE (O-RING)	16	STUD - UPPER INTAKE MANIFOLD	28	BOLT/SCREW - EGR VALVE
4	SEAL - MAP SENSOR	17	SEAL - LOWER INTAKE MANIFOLD FUEL FEED AND RETURN PIPE (O-RING)	29	VALVE ASSEMBLY - EGR
5	BOLT/SCREW - MAP SENSOR	18	PIPE ASSEMBLY - FUEL INJECTION FUEL RETURN	30	GASKET - EGR VALVE
6	SENSOR ASSEMBLY - MANIFOLD ABSOLUTE PRESSURE (MAP)	19	CAP - FUEL PRESSURE CONNECTION	31	MANIFOLD ASSEMBLY - LOWER INTAKE
7	BOLT/SCREW - INTAKE MANIFOLD TUNING VALVE	20	FUEL PRESSURE CONNECTION ASSEMBLY	32	SEAL - CENTRAL MULTIPORT FUEL INJECTOR (CMFI)
8	VALVE ASSEMBLY - INTAKE MANIFOLD TUNING	21	SEAL - FUEL PRESSURE CONNECTION	33	GASKET - UPPER INTAKE MANIFOLD
9	SEAL - INTAKE MANIFOLD VALVE (O-RING)	22	PIPE ASSEMBLY - FUEL INJECTION FUEL FEED	34	BOLT/SCREW - THROTTLE POSITION SENSOR
10	FITTING - POWER BRAKE BOOSTER VACUUM	23	BOLT/SCREW - FUEL INJECTION FUEL FEED AND RETURN PIPE RETAINER	35	SENSOR ASSEMBLY - THROTTLE POSITION (TP) SENSOR
11	NUT - UPPER INTAKE MANIFOLD	24	RETAINER - FUEL INJECTION FUEL FEED AND RETURN PIPE	36	TUBE - FUEL VAPOR CANISTER PURGE
12	CONNECTOR ASSEMBLY - CENTRAL MULTIPORT FUEL INJECTOR WIRING HARNESS	25	PIN - UPPER INTAKE MANIFOLD LOCATING	37	MANIFOLD ASSEMBLY - UPPER INTAKE (WITH THROTTLE BODY)
13	INJECTOR ASSEMBLY - CENTRAL MULTIPORT FUEL INJECTOR (CMFI)				

85385059

Fig. 28 Exploded view of the upper and lower intake manifolds and the CMFI system components

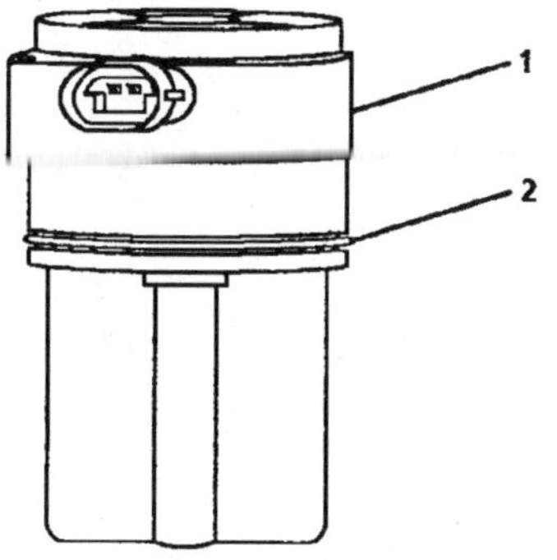

Fig. 30 View of a common intake manifold tuning valve used on Central MFI equipped vehicles

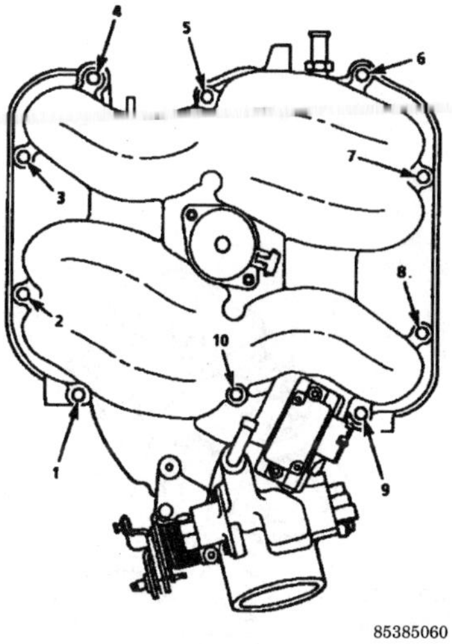

Fig. 29 Upper intake manifold torque sequence

2. Remove the tuning valve attaching screws.
3. Remove the tuning valve from the top of the upper intake manifold assembly.
4. Remove and discard the old O-ring seal.

To install:

5. Lubricate the new O-ring seal with clean engine oil.
6. Make sure the threads of the retaining screws are coated with Loctite®262, or an equivalent threadlocking compound.
7. Position the tuning valve to the upper intake manifold, then carefully thread the retaining screws.

➡To avoid breaking the valve mounting ears, alternately tighten the attaching screws until they engage the mounting ear surface, then carefully tighten the screws to specification.

8. Tighten the retaining screws to 18 inch lbs. (2 Nm).
9. Engage the valve electrical connector, then connect the negative battery cable.

CENTRAL SEQUENTIAL FUEL INJECTION (CSFI)

General Information

The 1996-97 trucks are equipped with the Central Sequential Fuel Injection (CSFI) system. Fuel is delivered to the engine by individual fuel injectors and poppet nozzles mounted in the intake manifold near each cylinder. Each is fired sequentially for accuracy and precise metering control.

Relieving Fuel System Pressure

➡Fuel pressure gauge J 34730-1A or its equivalent is required to perform this procedure

1. Disconnect the negative battery cable.
2. Loosen the fuel filler cap to relieve fuel tank pressure.
3. Engage the fuel pressure gauge to the fuel pressure connection. Wrap a shop towel around the fitting while connecting the gauge to prevent spillage.
4. Install the bleed hose into an approved container and open the valve to bleed the system. The system is now safe for servicing.
5. Drain any fuel remaining in the gauge into an approved container.

Electric Fuel Pump

➧ See Figure 31

All Chevrolet/GMC Central Sequential Fuel Injection (CSFI) fuel-injected vehicles are equipped with an electric fuel pump. For a fuel injection system to work properly, the pump must develop pressures well above those of a mechanical fuel pump. This high pressure is maintained within the lines even when the engine is **OFF**. Extreme caution must be used to safely release the pressurized fuel before any work is begun.

CAUTION

Always relieve the fuel pressure within the system before any work is begun on any fuel component. Failure to safely relieve the pressure may result in fire and/or serious injury.

TESTING

1. Turn the ignition **OFF** for 10 seconds, then turn the ignition **ON**. The pump should operate for 2 seconds.
2. If the pump does not operate, connect a 12 volt fused jumper wire to the fuel pump test terminal. The pump should operate.

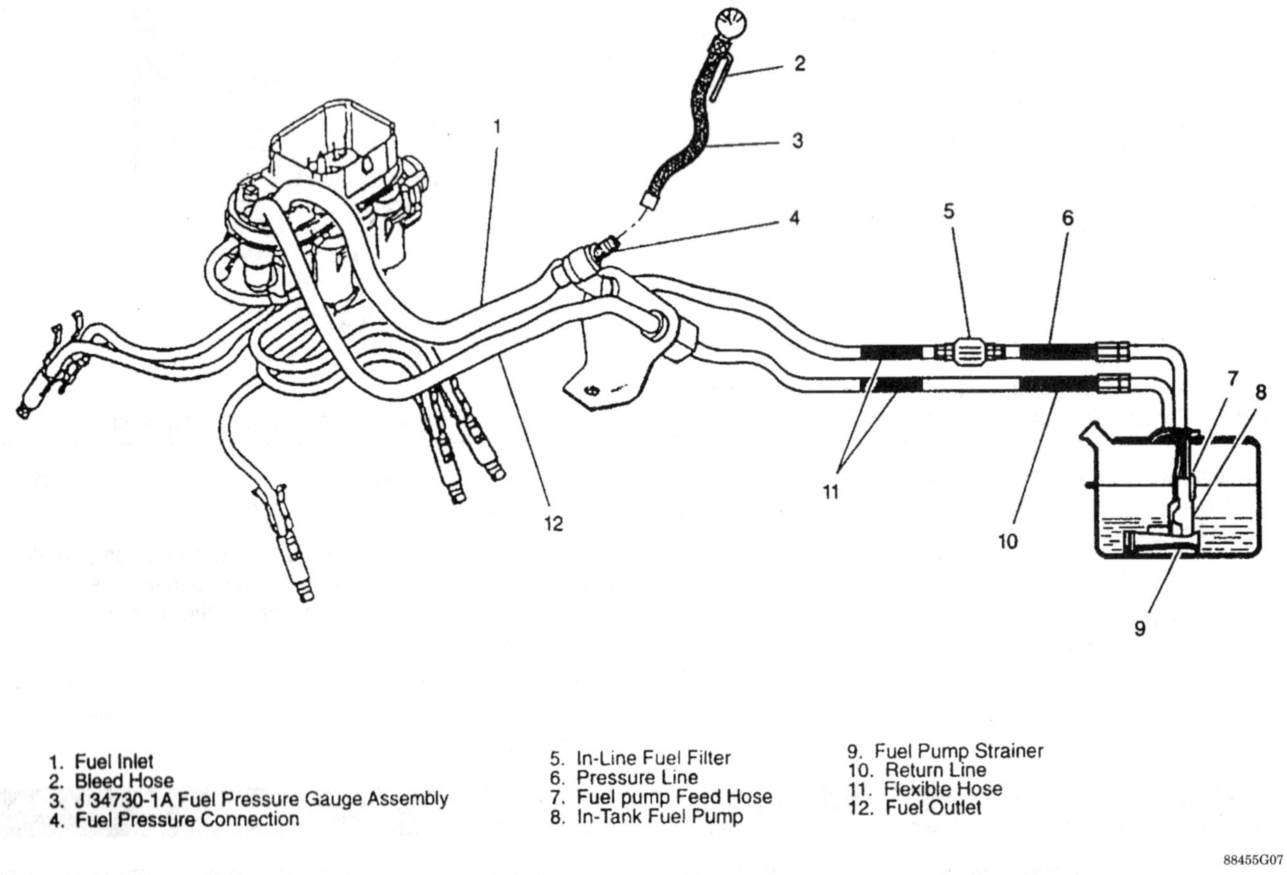

Fig. 31 Exploded view of the fuel supply system

3. If the pump does not operate, disengage the fuel pump harness connector at the tank.
4. Connect a 12 volt fused jumper wire to the fuel pump test terminal.
5. Using a test light connected to ground, probe the fuel pump feed circuit.
6. If the light does not illuminate, use a test light connected to the fuel pump ground (tank side) and probe the fuel pump feed circuit.
7. If the light illuminates the pump is defective and must be replaced.
8. If the pump does not light, their is an open between the fuel pump test terminal and the fuel pump feed circuit that must be repaired.

REMOVAL & INSTALLATION

See Figures 32, 33 and 34

Single Tank

1. Disconnect the negative battery cable.
2. Relieve the fuel system pressure. Refer to the fuel system relief procedure in this section.
3. Raise the vehicle and support it safely with jackstands.
4. Drain the fuel system and remove the fuel tank. Refer to the fuel tank removal procedure in this section.
5. Remove the fuel sender assembly turning it counterclockwise using tool J 36608 or its equivalent.
6. Remove the fuel pump from the sender assembly. Pull the pump up into the attaching hose while pulling outward from the bottom support. Do not damage the rubber insulator or the strainer.
7. Inspect the fuel pump attaching hose and the rubber sound insulation for signs of deterioration.
8. Inspect the strainer for blockage and damage.

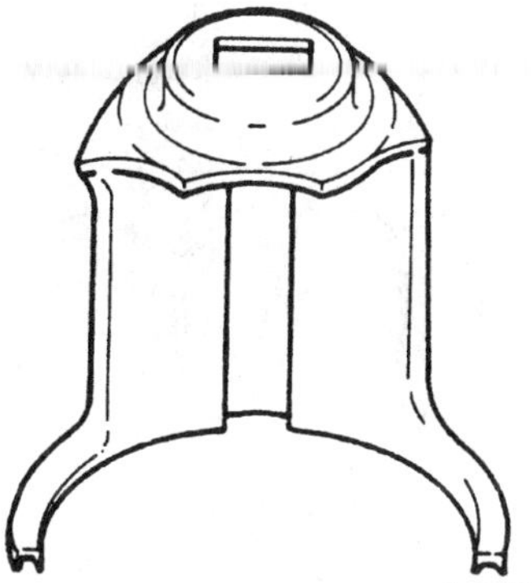
tccs5p06

Fig. 32 A special tool is usually available to remove or install the fuel pump locking cam

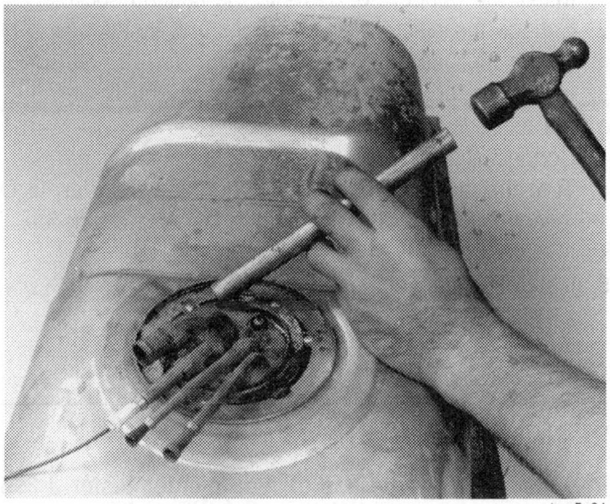
tccs5p04

Fig. 33 A brass drift and a hammer can be used to loosen the fuel pump locking cam

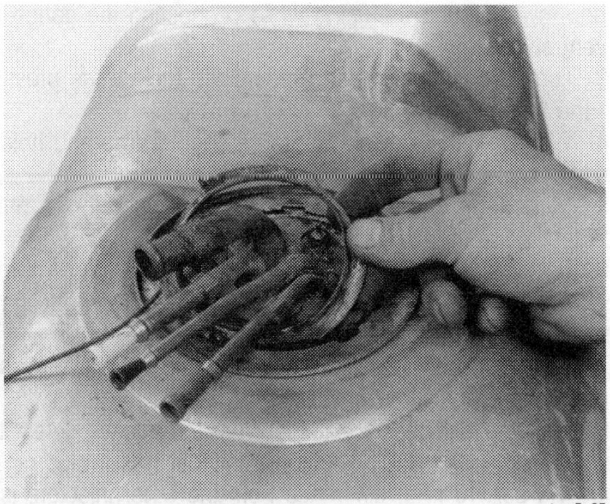
tccs5p05

Fig. 34 Once the locking cam is released it can be removed to free the fuel pump

To install:

9. Install the fuel pump assembly into the attaching hose.

➡Be careful not to bend or fold over the fuel strainer when installing the fuel sender as this will restrict fuel flow.

10. Install the fuel sender into the fuel tank. Insert a new o-ring seal.
11. Install the camlock assembly turning it clockwise to lock it.
12. Install the fuel tank. Refer to the fuel tank installation procedure in this section.
13. Connect the negative battery cable.

Dual Tanks

1. Disconnect the negative battery cable.
2. Loosen the filler cap(s) to relieve fuel tank pressure.
3. Disconnect the fuel pipes from the pump.
4. Slide the pump out of the bracket.

To install:

5. Install new fuel pipe O-rings.
6. Position the pump in the pump bracket.
7. Connect the fuel feed pipe and suction pipe to the fuel pump.
8. Using a backup wrench to stop the fuel pump from turning, tighten the fittings to 22 ft. lbs. (30 Nm).
9. Engage the electrical connector.
10. Connect the negative battery cable.
11. Turn the ignition switch **ON** for 2 seconds then turn the switch **OFF** for 10 seconds. Again, turn the ignition switch **ON** and check for leaks.

Throttle Body

REMOVAL & INSTALLATION

1. Disconnect the negative battery cable.
2. Remove the air inlet fastener and duct.
3. Disengage the Idle Air Control (IAC) valve and the Throttle Position Sensor (TPS) electrical connectors.
4. Disconnect the throttle and cruise control cables.
5. Disconnect the accelerator cable bracket bolts and nuts.
6. Disengage the wiring harness fastener nut.
7. Unfasten the throttle body retaining nuts and remove the throttle body.
8. Remove and discard the flange gasket.
9. Clean both gasket mating surfaces.

➡When cleaning the old gasket from the machined aluminum surfaces be careful as sharp tools may damage the sealing surfaces

To install:

10. Install the new flange gasket and the throttle body assembly.
11. Tighten the throttle body attaching nuts to 18 ft. lbs. (25 Nm).
12. Install the accelerator cable bracket bolts and nuts and tighten to 18 ft. lbs (25 Nm).
13. Connect the throttle and cruise control cables.

14. Engage the IAC valve and the TPS electrical connectors.
15. Install the air inlet fastener and duct. Connect the negative battery cable.

Fuel Injectors

REMOVAL & INSTALLATION

See Figures 35 and 36

1. Disconnect the negative battery cable.
2. Relieve the fuel system pressure. Refer to the fuel system relief procedure in this section.
3. Disengage the fuel meter body electrical connection and the fuel feed and return hoses from the engine fuel pipes.
4. Remove the upper manifold assembly.
5. Tag and remove the poppet nozzle out of the casting socket.
6. Remove the fuel meter body by releasing the locktabs.

Each injector is calibrated. When replacing the fuel injectors, be sure to replace it with the correct injector.

7. Disassemble the lower hold-down plate and nuts.
8. While pulling the poppet nozzle tube downward, push with a small screwdriver down between the injector terminals and remove the injectors.

To install:

9. Install the fuel meter body assembly into the intake manifold and tighten the fuel meter bracket retainer bolts to 88 inch. lbs. (10 Nm).

CAUTION

To reduce the risk of fire or injury ensure that the poppet nozzles are properly seated and locked in their casting sockets

10. Install the fuel meter body into the bracket and lock all the tabs in place.

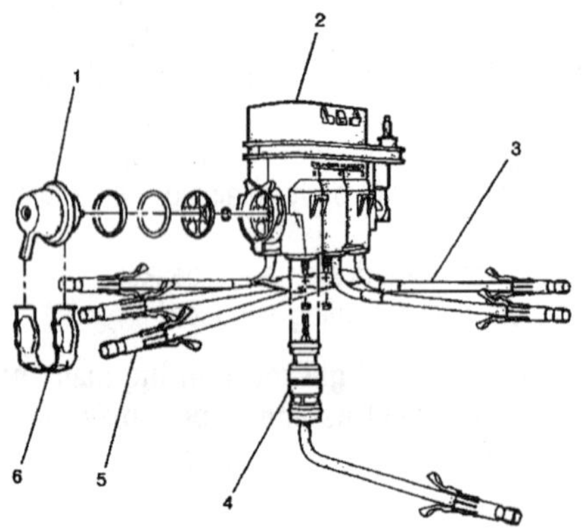

Fig. 35 Exploded view of the fuel meter body assembly

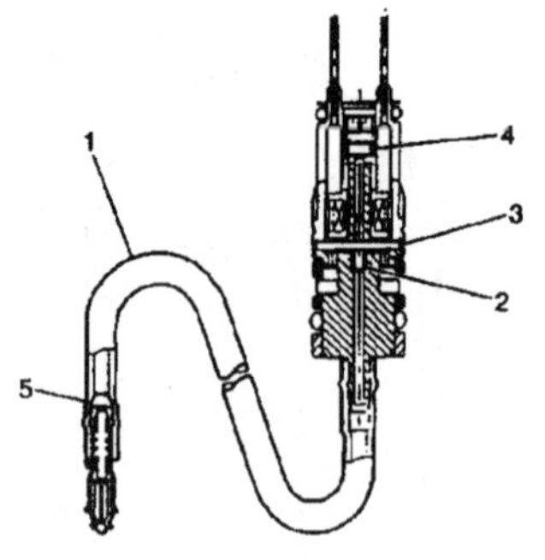

Fig. 36 Exploded view of the fuel injector assembly

11. Install the poppet nozzles into the casting sockets.
12. Engage the electrical connections and install new o-ring seals on the fuel return and feed hoses.
13. Install the fuel feed and return hoses and tighten the fuel pipe nuts to 22 ft. lbs. (30 Nm).
14. Connect the negative battery cable.
15. Turn the ignition **ON** for 2 seconds and then turn it **OFF** for 10 seconds. Again turn the ignition **ON** and check for leaks.
16. Install the manifold plenum.

TESTING

See Figure 37

This test requires the use of fuel injector tester J 39021 or its equivalent.

1. Disconnect the fuel injector harness and attach a noid light in order to test for injector pulse.
2. With the engine cool and the ignition turned **OFF**, install the fuel pressure gauge to the fuel pressure connection. Wrap a shop towel around the fitting while connecting the gauge to prevent spillage.
3. Turn **ON** the ignition and record the fuel gauge pressure with the pump running.
4. Turn **OFF** the ignition. Pressure should drop and hold steady at this point.
5. To perform this test, set the selector switch to the balance test 2.5 amp position.
6. Turn the injector **ON** by depressing the button on the injector tester. Note this pressure reading the instant the gauge needle stops.
7. Repeat the balance test on the remaining injectors and record the pressure drop on each.
8. Start the engine to clear fuel from the intake. Retest the injectors that appear faulty. Any injector that has a plus or minus 1.5 psi (10 kPa) difference from the other injectors is suspect.

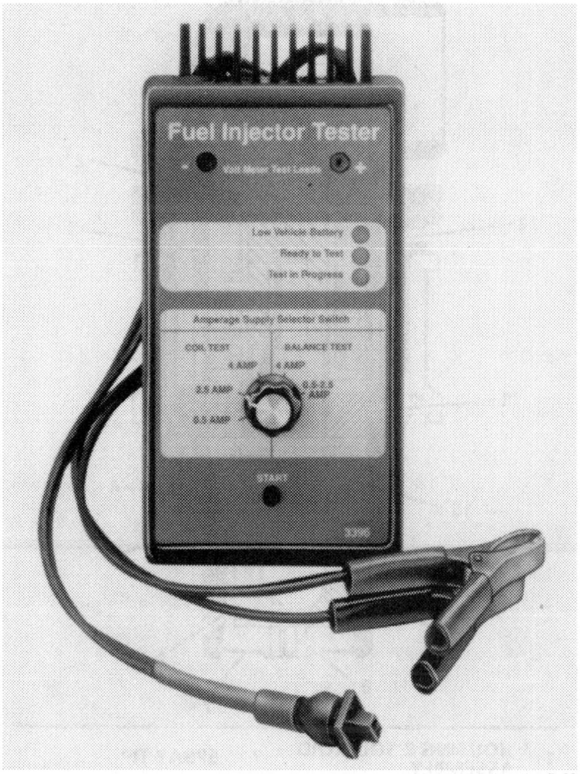

tccs5p03

Fig. 37 Fuel injector testers can be purchased or sometimes rented

Fuel Pressure Regulator

REMOVAL & INSTALLATION

1. Disconnect the negative battery cable.
2. Relieve the fuel system pressure. Refer to the fuel system relief procedure in this section.
3. Remove the upper manifold assembly.
4. Remove the fuel pressure regulator vacuum tube.
5. Disassemble the fuel pressure regulator snapring retainer.
6. Remove the fuel pressure regulator assembly and the O-rings. Discard the O-rings, filter and back-up O-rings.

To install:

7. Lubricate the O-rings with clean engine oil and install as an assembly.
8. Install the fuel pressure regulator, attach the vacuum tube.
9. Install the snapring retainer.
10. Install the upper manifold assembly.
11. Connect the negative battery cable.

Engine Fuel Pipes

REMOVAL & INSTALLATION

1. Disconnect the negative battery cable.
2. Relieve the fuel system pressure. Refer to the fuel system relief procedure in this section.
3. Remove the fuel lines at the rear of the intake manifold.
4. Remove the nuts and the retainer.
5. Loosen the injector fuel inlet and outlet pipes.
6. Remove the rear fuel line bracket.
7. Pull straight up on the fuel pipe to remove the pipes from the injector assembly.
8. Remove the O-rings from both ends of the fuel feed and return pipes.

To install:

9. Install the inlet and outlet of the fuel injector assembly.
10. Apply a few drops of clean engine oil to the male tube ends.
11. Install the fuel pipes to the fuel injector assembly.
12. Install the fuel pipe retainer and attaching nuts. After the pipes are secured, pull up on them gently to ensure that they are properly secured. Tighten the rear fuel line bracket bolt to 53 inch. lbs. (6 Nm) and the fuel pipe retainer nuts to 27 inch. lbs. (3 Nm).
13. Tighten the fuel pipe nuts to 22 ft. lbs. (30 Nm) and connect the negative battery cable.
14. Turn the ignition **ON** for 2 seconds and then turn it **OFF** for 10 seconds. Again turn the ignition **ON** and check for leaks.

Fuel Pressure Connection

The fuel pressure connection is non-replaceable, but is serviceable.

SERVICE

1. Disconnect the negative battery cable.
2. Relieve the fuel system pressure. Refer to the fuel system relief procedure in this section.
3. Remove the fuel pressure connection cap.
4. Using a valve core removal tool remove the valve core assembly and discard it.

To install:

5. Install a new valve core assembly using a valve core removal tool.
6. Connect the negative battery cable.
7. Turn the ignition **ON** for 2 seconds and then turn it **OFF** for 10 seconds. Again turn the ignition **ON** and check for leaks.
8. Install the fuel pressure connection cap.

MULTI-PORT FUEL INJECTION SYSTEM

General Information

See Figures 38 and 39

The MFI system functions with electronic engine control like most fuel injection systems. A throttle body is used to meter intake air (the throttle body is integral with the upper intake manifold on the 2.2L engine), but unlike TBI systems, the fuel is delivered further downstream of the air flow. The defining feature of a MFI system is that a separate fuel injector is used for each cylinder. A 2-piece intake manifold assembly is used. The "fuel rail" is incorporated into the lower intake manifold. Fuel is supplied through a passage in the lower intake to each of the bottom feed fuel injectors.

As with other fuel injection systems, all injection and ignition functions are controlled by the computer control module. The module accepts inputs from various sensors and switches, calculates the optimum air/fuel mixture and operates the various output devices to provide peak performance within specific emissions limits. The module will attempt to maintain the ideal air/fuel mixture of 14.7:1 in order to optimize catalytic converter operation. If a system failure occurs that is not serious enough to stop the engine, the module will illuminate the CHECK ENGINE OR SERVICE ENGINE SOON light (as equipped) and will continue to operate the engine, although it may need to operate in a backup or fail-safe mode.

Fuel is supplied to the injectors through an electric fuel pump assembly which is mounted in the vehicle's fuel tank. The module provides a signal to operate the fuel pump though the fuel pump relay and oil pressure switch. The fuel pressure regulator (mounted to the lower intake manifold on the 2.2L engine) maintains a constant system pressure by metering flow to the fuel return line. A spring diaphragm is capable of restricting flow until sufficient pressure is achieved, then preventing over-pressurization by allowing increased flow in the return line, as necessary. When the fuel injectors are energized by the control module, the ball valve will open to allow pressurized fuel through the nozzle. Fuel is sprayed in a conical pattern towards the intake valve.

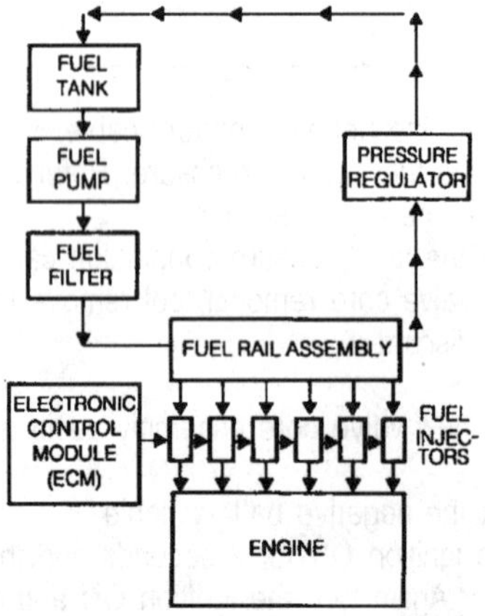

85385062

Fig. 38 Common fuel supply system schematic for a 6-cylinder engine (4-cylinder similar, but uses fewer injectors)

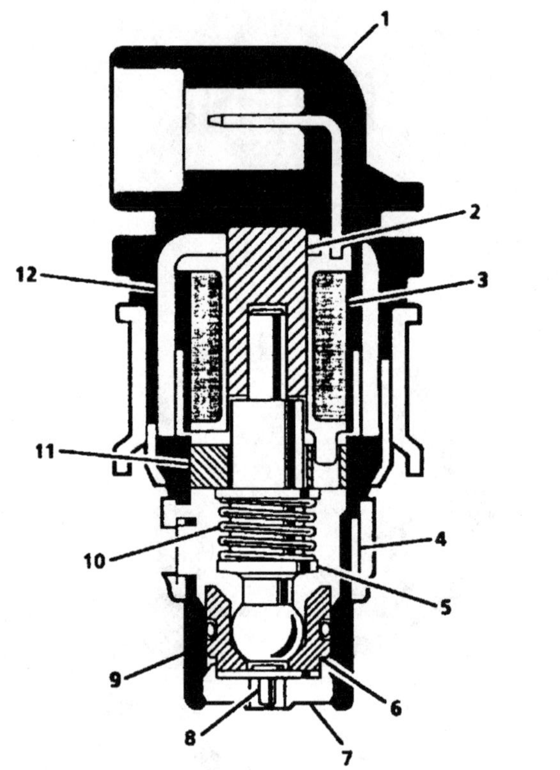

1	HOUSING & SOLENOID ASSEMBLY	7	SPRAY TIP
2	POLE PIECE	8	DIRECTOR
3	SOLENOID	9	HOUSING - SPRAY TIP
4	FILTER - FUEL INLET	10	SPRING - CORE
5	CORE ASSEMBLY	11	SCREW & GUIDE ASSEMBLY
6	CORE SEAT	12	SOLENOID BODY

85385063

Fig. 39 Cross-sectional view of a bottom feed fuel injector used on the 2.2L engine

Other system components include a pressure regulator, an Idle Air Control (IAC) valve, a Throttle Position (TP) sensor, Intake Air Temperature (IAT) sensor, Engine Coolant Temperature (ECT) sensor, a Manifold Absolute Pressure (MAP) sensor and an oxygen sensor.

The idle air control valve is a stepper motor that controls the amount of air allowed to bypass the throttle plate. With this valve the computer control module can closely control idle speed even when the engine is cold or when there is a high engine load at idle.

The computer module used on all MFI vehicles has a learning capability which is used to provide corrections for a particular engine's condition. If the battery is disconnected to clear diagnostic codes, or for safety during a repair, the learning process must start all over again. A change may be noted in vehicle performance. In order to "teach" the vehicle, make sure the vehicle is at normal operating temperature, then drive at part throttle, under moderate acceleration and idle conditions, until normal performance returns.

OPERATING MODES

Starting Mode

When the ignition switch is first turned **ON**, the fuel pump relay is energized by the module for 2 seconds in order to build system pressure. In the start mode, the computer module checks the ECT, IAT, TP sensor, MAP and crank signal in order to determine the best air/fuel ratio for starting. Ratios could range from 1.5:1 at approximately -33°F (-36°C), to 14.7:1 at 201°F (94°C).

Clear Flood Mode

If the engine becomes flooded, it can be cleared by opening the accelerator to the full throttle position. When the throttle is open all the way and engine rpm is less than 600, the computer module will pulse the fuel injector at an air/fuel ratio of 16.5:1 while the engine is turning over in order to clear the engine of excess fuel. If throttle position is reduced below 65 percent, the module will return to the start mode.

Open Loop Mode

When the engine first starts and engine speed rises above 400 rpm, the computer module operates in the Open Loop mode until specific parameters are met. In Open Loop mode, the fuel requirements are calculated based on information from the MAP and ECT sensors. The oxygen sensor signal is ignored during initial engine operation because it needs time to warm up.

Closed Loop Mode

See Figure 40

When the correct parameters are met, the computer module will use O_2 sensor output and adjust the air/fuel mixture accordingly in order to maintain a narrow band of exhaust gas oxygen concentration. When the module is correcting and adjusting fuel mixture based on the oxygen sensor signal along with the other sensors, this is known as feedback air/fuel ratio control. The computer module will shift into this Closed Loop mode when:

- Oxygen sensor output voltage is varied, indicating that the sensor has warmed up to operating temperature
- The ECT shows an engine coolant temperature above a specified level.
- The engine has been operating for a programmed amount of time.

Acceleration Mode

If the throttle position and manifold pressure is quickly increased, the module will provide extra fuel for smooth acceleration.

Deceleration Mode

As the throttle closes and the manifold pressure decreases, fuel flow is reduced by the module. If both conditions remain for a specific number of engine revolutions indicating a very fast deceleration, the module may decide fuel flow is not needed and stop the flow by temporarily shutting off the injectors.

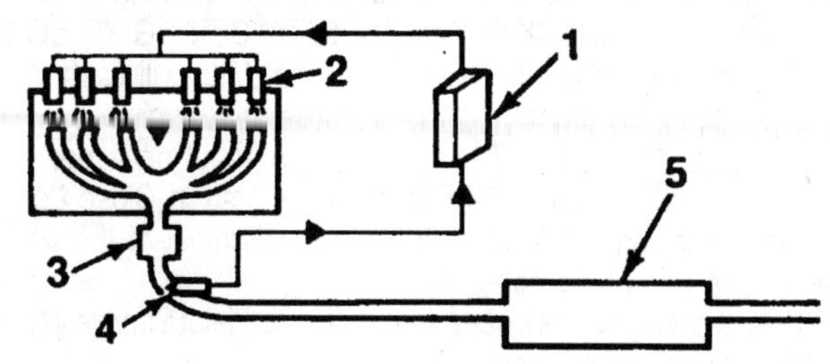

1. Electronic Control Module (ECM)
2. Fuel Injectors
3. Turbocharger
4. Exhaust Oxygen (O_2) Sensor
5. Catalytic Converter

85385064

Fig. 40 Closed loop operational schematic — 6-cylinder shown but 4-cylinder similar (just with fewer injectors)

Highway Fuel Mode (Semi-Closed Loop)

For the 2.2L engine, the computer control module is programmed to enter a special highway mode to improve fuel economy. If the module senses the correct ECT, ignition control, canister purge activity and a constant engine speed, it will enter highway mode. During this operation, there will be very little adjustment of the long and short term fuel trims, also, the oxygen sensor values will usually read below 100 millivolts.

Decel En-Leanment Mode

For the 2.2L engine, the computer control module is programmed to further reduce emissions by leaning the fuel spray on deceleration. The module does this when a high MAP vacuum (low voltage or pressure) is sensed, BUT it should be noted that the module may do this when the vehicle is not moving. This mode of operation may be misdiagnosed as a lean condition. When diagnosing the control system using a scan tool with the transmission in Park, the oxygen sensor signal low (usually below 100 mV), and both fuel trim numbers around 128 counts, lower the engine speed to 1000 rpm. If the sensor and long term trim numbers respond normally, it is possible that the system was fooled into decel en-leanment operation. If the oxygen sensor and long term numbers do not respond at the lower rpm, there are other problems with the vehicle.

Battery Low Mode

If the computer module detects a low battery, it will increase injector pulse width to compensate for the low voltage and provide proper fuel delivery. It will also increase idle speed to increase alternate output and ignition dwell time to allow for proper engine operation.

Field Service Mode

When the diagnostic terminal of the test connector is grounded with the engine running, the computer module will enter the Field Service Mode. If the engine is running in Open Loop Mode, the CHECK ENGINE or SERVICE ENGINE SOON (as applicable) Malfunction Indicator Lamp (MIL) will flash quickly, about 2½ times per second. When the engine is in Closed Loop Mode, the MIL will flash only about once per second. If the light stays OFF most of the time in Close Loop, the engine is running lean. If the light is ON most of the time, the engine is running rich.

While the engine continues to operate in Field Service Mode certain conditions will apply:

- New trouble codes cannot be stored in computer memory.
- The closed loop timer is bypassed.

➡For more information concerning the computer control module, self-diagnosis systems and other electronic engine controls, please refer to Section 4 of this manual.

Fuel Pressure Relief

Prior to servicing any component of the fuel injection system, the fuel pressure must be relieved. If fuel pressure is not relieved, serious injury could result.

A valve is provided on these fuel systems in order to conveniently test or release the fuel system pressure. A fuel pressure gauge and adapter will be necessary to connect to the fitting. The 2.2L system is equipped with a valve located on the fuel feed inlet fitting, on the opposite end of the lower intake from the pressure regulator.

1. Disconnect the negative battery cable to assure the prevention of fuel spillage if the ignition switch is accidentally turned **ON** while a fitting is still disconnected.
2. Loosen the fuel filter cap to release the fuel tank pressure.
3. Make sure the release valve on the fuel gauge is closed, then connect the fuel gauge to the pressure fitting located on the inlet fuel pipe fitting.

➡When connecting the gauge to the fitting, be sure to wrap a rag around the fitting to avoid spillage. After repairs, place the rag in an approved container.

4. Install the bleed hose portion of the fuel gauge assembly into an approved container, then open the gauge release valve and bleed the fuel pressure from the system.
5. When the gauge is removed, be sure to open the bleed valve and drain all fuel from the gauge assembly.

Electric Fuel Pump

The electric pump is attached to the fuel sending unit, located in the fuel tank.

TESTING

➧ See Figures 41, 42, 43, 44 and 45

1. Properly relieve the fuel system pressure.
2. Leave the gauge attached to the pressure fitting on the fuel inlet pipe.
3. If disconnected during the fuel pressure relief procedure, reconnect the negative battery terminal.
4. Turn the ignition **ON** and listen for the pump to run (is should run for 2 seconds). If necessary, cycle the ignition **OFF** for 10 seconds and then **ON** again in order to build maximum system pressure. Check that pressure is at specification:
   a. Note the fuel pressure with the pump RUNNING, it should be 41-47 psi (284-325 kPa). When the pump stops pressure may vary slightly, then should hold steady. If not, refer to the accompanying fuel system diagnosis charts.

REMOVAL & INSTALLATION

Removal and installation of the fuel pump and sending unit assembly is the same on MFI vehicles as it is for TBI vehicles. Please refer to the TBI procedures earlier in this section for electric fuel pump replacement.

Fuel Pump Relay

The fuel pump relay is normally found in the convenience center, located under the center of the dashboard. If a problem is suspected, first check for loose electrical connections; no other service is possible, except replacement.

REMOVAL & INSTALLATION

➧ See Figure 46

1. Disconnect the negative battery cable.
2. Remove the retainer, if equipped.
3. Disengage the relay electrical connector.
4. Remove the relay from the bracket and from the vehicle.
5. If necessary, use a new relay, then reverse the removal procedures.

Throttle Body

REMOVAL & INSTALLATION

On the 2.2L MFI engine, the throttle body is an integral part of the cast upper intake manifold assembly. For removal and installation procedures, please refer to Section 3 of this manual.

Fuel Injectors

REMOVAL & INSTALLATION

➧ See Figures 47 and 48

The bottom feed fuel injectors on the 2.2L MFI engine are installed to the lower intake manifold assembly. For access, the upper intake must first be removed.

➡Take care when servicing the lower intake and fuel injectors to prevent dirt or contaminants from entering the fuel system. ALL openings in the fuel lines and passages should be capped or plugged while disconnected.

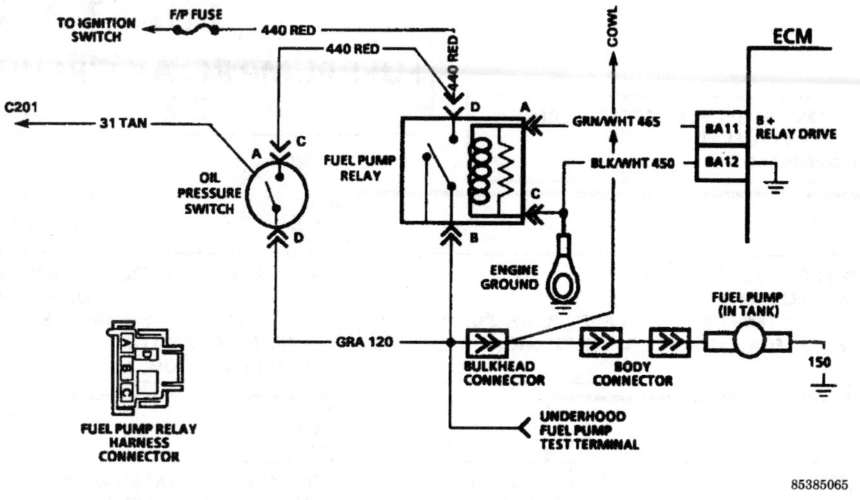

Fig. 41 Fuel pump relay circuit

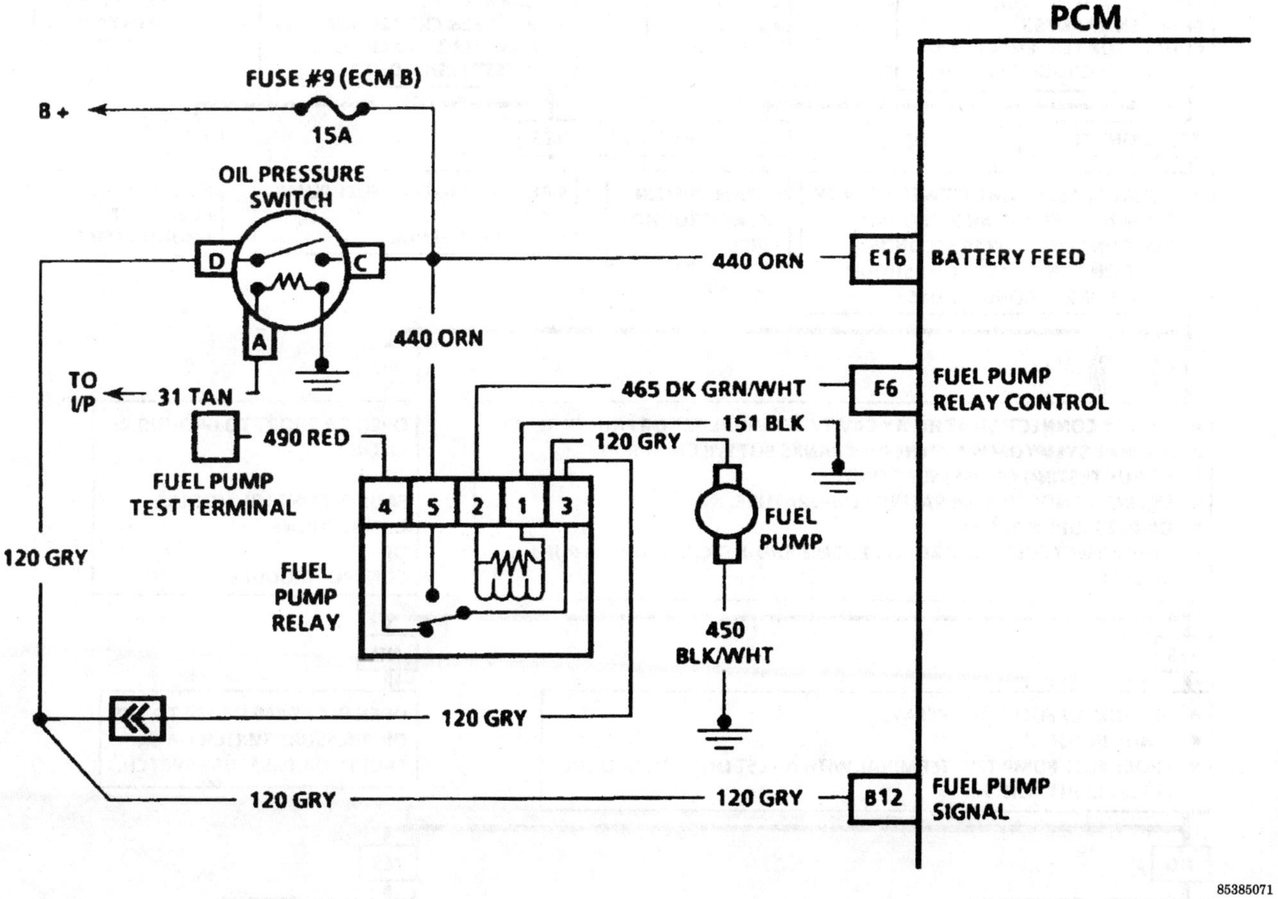

Fig. 42 Fuel pump circuit

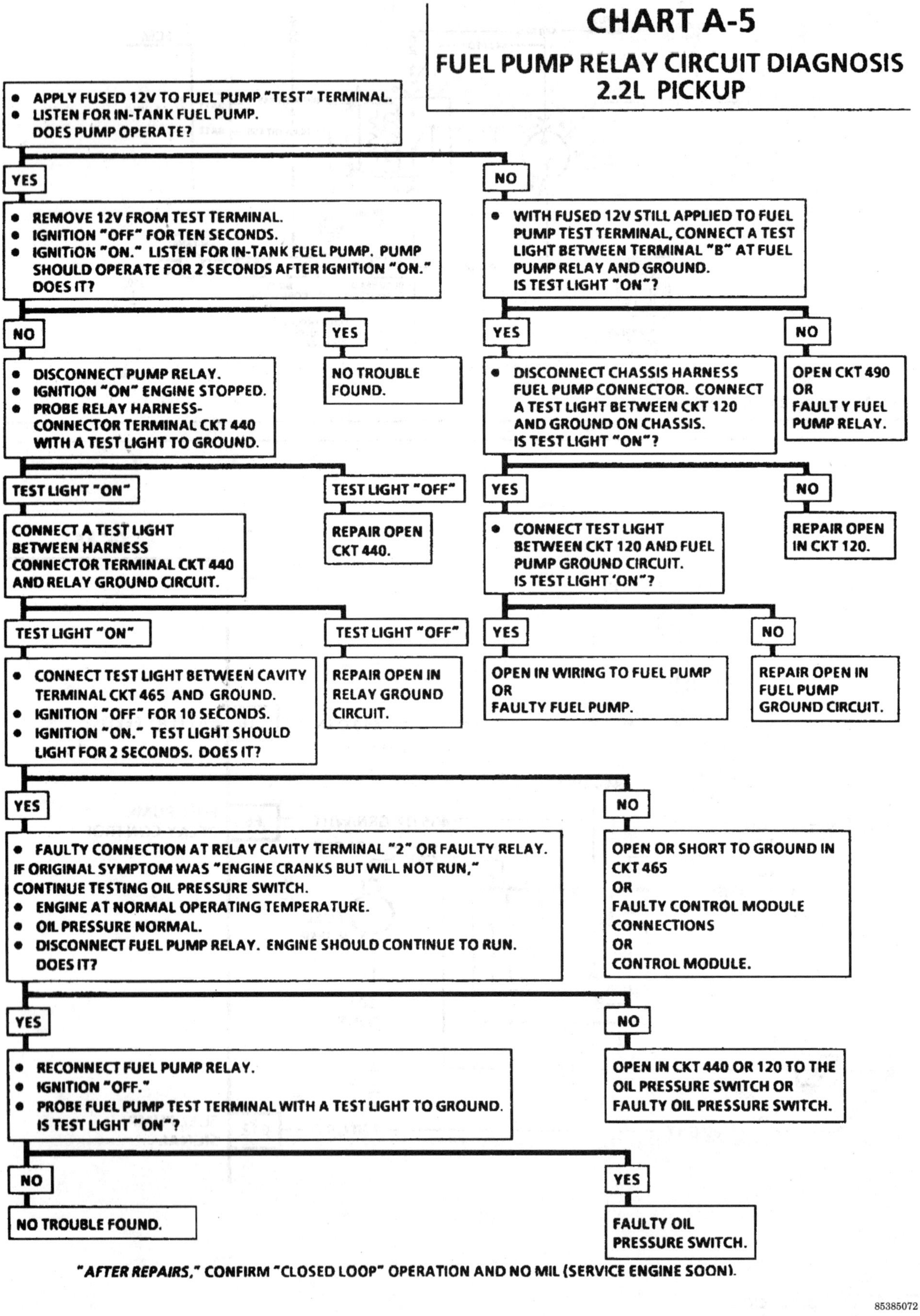

Fig. 43 Diagnostic chart

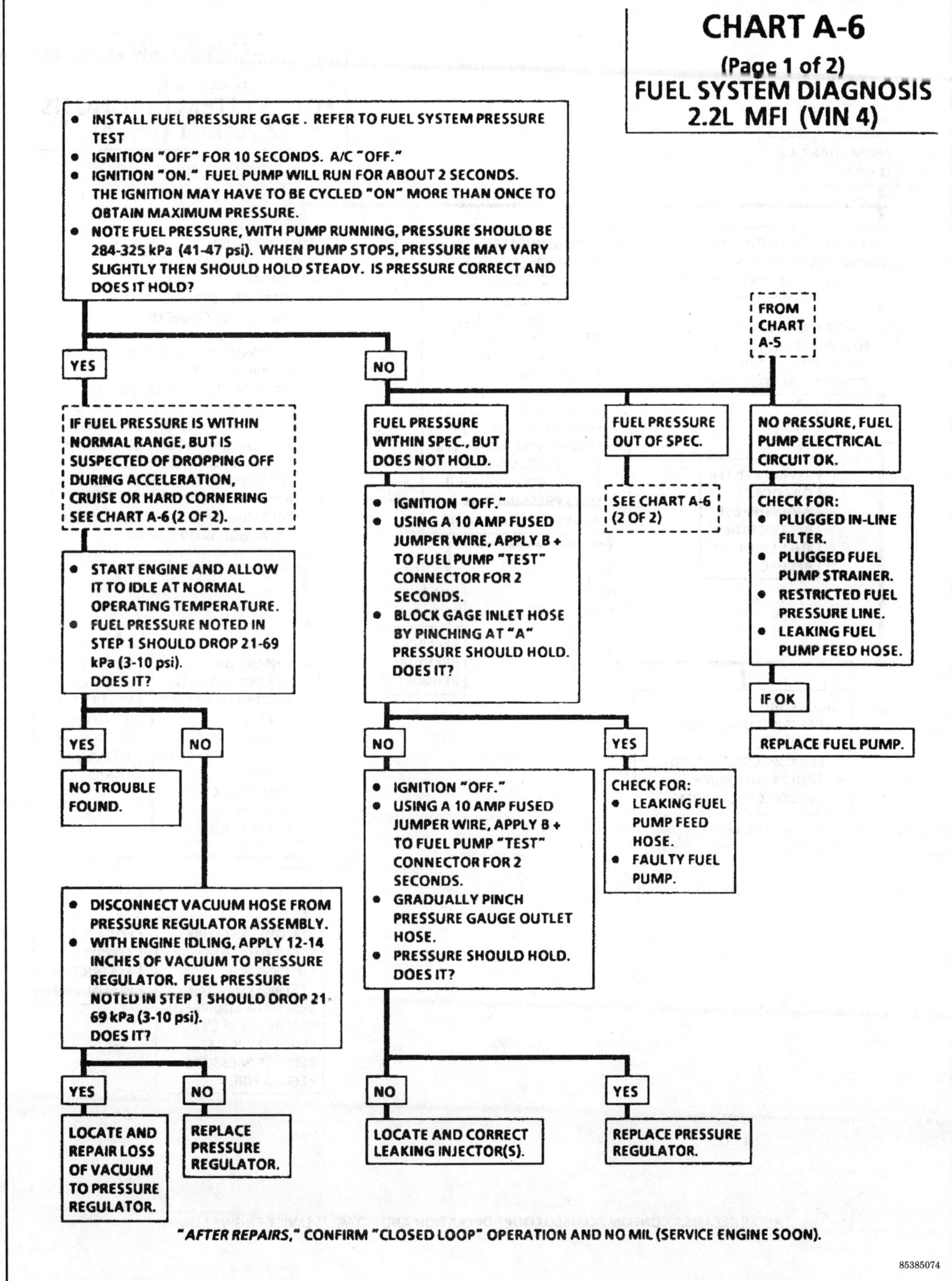

Fig. 44 Diagnostic chart

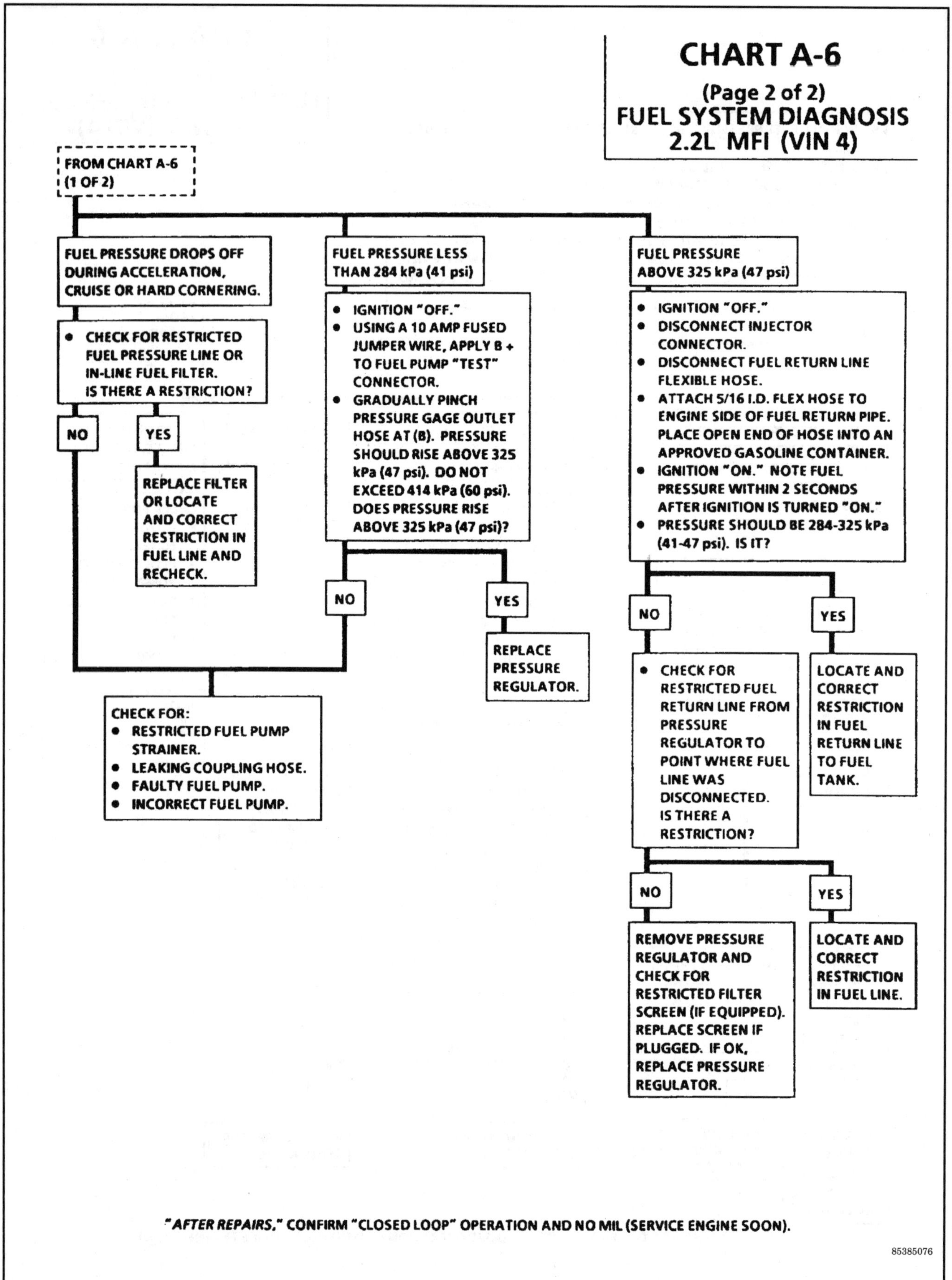

Fig. 45 Diagnostic chart

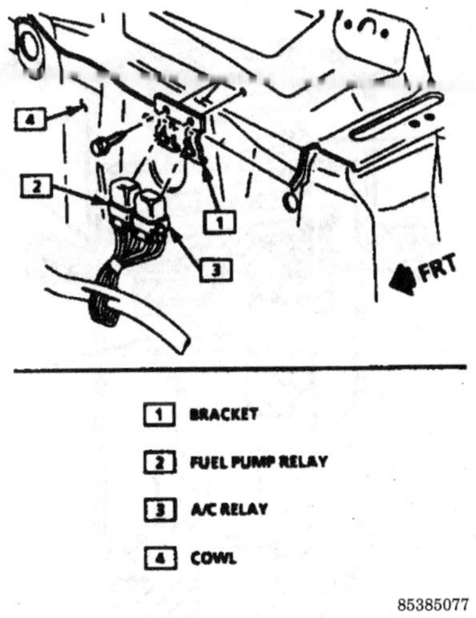

Fig. 46 Common fuel pump relay mounting

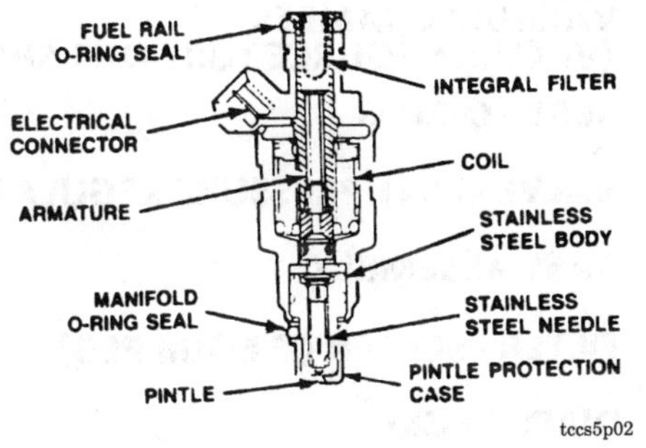

Fig. 47 Cross-sectional view of a typical MFI fuel injector

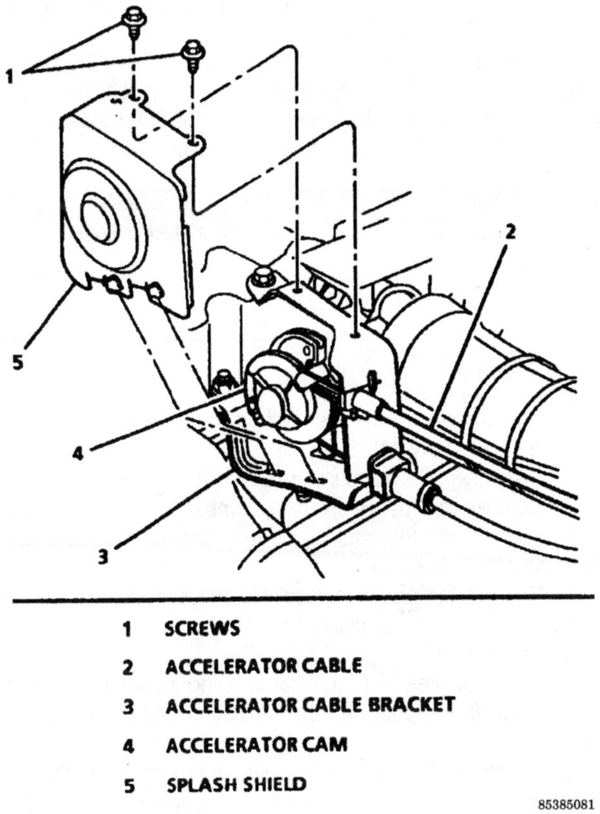

Fig. 48 Common accelerator cam splash shield

1. Properly relieve the fuel system pressure, then disconnect the negative battery cable.

2. Remove the accelerator bracket retaining bolts/nuts, then remove or reposition the bracket.

3. Remove the upper intake manifold assembly. For details, please refer to the intake manifold procedures found in Section 3 of this manual.

4. Remove the fuel return line bracket nut, then remove the return line retaining bracket and position it away from the pressure regulator.

5. Remove the fuel pressure regulator assembly. For details, please refer to the procedure later in this section.

➡DO NOT attempt to remove the injectors from their bores while lifting upward on the retaining bracket or damage may occur. DO NOT attempt to remove the bracket without first removing the pressure regulator.

6. Remove the fuel injector retainer bracket attaching screws, then remove the bracket by carefully sliding it off to clear the injector slots and regulator.

7. Tag and disengage the injector electrical connectors.

8. Remove the fuel injectors from the lower intake manifold assembly, then remove and discard the old O-rings.

To install:

➡Because each injector is calibrated for a specific flow rate, make sure you only replace fuel injectors using an IDENTICAL part number to the old injectors.

9. Lubricate the new O-ring seals with clean engine oil, then position them on the injectors.

10. Carefully install the injectors assemblies into the lower manifold sockets, making sure the electrical connectors are facing inward.

11. Position the injector bracket to the retaining slots and regulator are aligned with the bracket slots.

12. Engage the injector electrical connectors as tagged during removal.

13. Install the fuel pressure regulator assembly.

14. Make sure the threads of the injector retainer bracket screws are coated with a suitable threadlocking compound

such as Loctite®262 or equivalent, then install and tighten them to 31 inch lbs. (3.5 Nm).

15. Install the upper intake manifold assembly. Please refer to the procedure in Section 3 of this manual.
16. If not done already, install the accelerator cable bracket. Tighten the retaining nut to 22 ft. lbs. (30 Nm) and the retaining bolts to 18 ft. lbs. (25 Nm).
17. Connect the negative battery cable.
18. Pressurize the fuel system by cycling the ignition (without attempting to start the engine), then check for leaks.
19. If not done already, install the air inlet duct

Fuel Pressure Regulator

REMOVAL & INSTALLATION

➧ **See Figure 49**

1. Properly relieve the fuel system pressure and disconnect the negative battery cable.
2. Disconnect the vacuum hose form the regulator.
3. Remove the fuel return pipe clamp.
4. Remove the fuel return pipe from the regulator and discard the old O-ring.
5. Remove the pressure regulator attaching screw, then remove the regulator and discard the O-ring.

To install:

6. If the old pressure regulator is being installed, check the filter screen (if equipped) for contamination and replace, if necessary.
7. Lubricate the new O-rings with clean engine oil, then install them on the pressure regulator and fuel pipe.
8. Install the pressure regulator onto the manifold.
9. Make sure the regulator attaching screw threads are covered with Loctite®262 or an equivalent threadlocking compound, then install and tighten the screws to 31 inch lbs. (3.5 Nm).
10. Connect the vacuum hose to the regulator.
11. Make sure the new O-ring is in position, then connect the fuel return pipe to the pressure regulator and tighten to 22 ft. lbs. (30 Nm).
12. Install the fuel return pipe clamp and attaching nut to the lower intake manifold assembly.

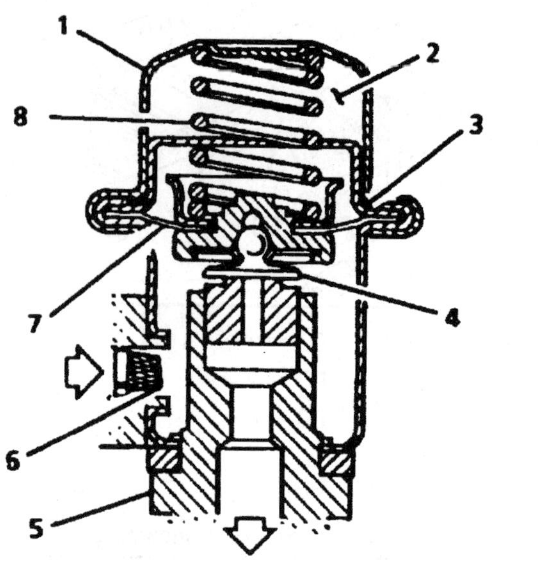

Fig. 49 Cross-sectional view of the fuel pressure regulator — 2.2L MFI engine

13. Connect the negative battery cable, then pressurize the fuel system by cycling the ignition (without attempting to start the engine) and check for leaks.

FUEL TANK

Service

DRAINING

1. Remove the tank filler cap in order to release vapor pressure in the tank.

➡**If the pump device is equipped with a static ground wire, be sure to connect it to a metal part of the gas tank before you begin draining the fuel.**

2. Use a hand operated pump device to remove fuel through the filler neck. If difficulty is encountered, disconnect the filler hose from the tank neck and insert the pump hose directly into the tank.
3. The hand pump may not be able to completely drain the tank, but do your best to remove as much as possible.
4. On vehicles equipped with an electric fuel pump, disconnect the feed line (somewhere between the tank and engine, wherever access is convenient), then connect a length of rubber hose to the feed line. Place the other end of the rubber hose in an approved container, then operate the fuel pump to further drain the tank. On most of these vehicles, the easiest method of energizing the fuel pump is to use a 10 amp fused jumper wire to apply battery voltage to the fuel pump test connector. The connector is usually located in the engine compartment, often on the left fender.

REMOVAL & INSTALLATION

➧ See Figures 50, 51, 52, 53, 54, 55 and 56

Except With Shield Package

1. Properly drain the fuel tank, then disconnect the negative battery cable.
2. If not done already, raise and support the rear of the truck safely using jackstands.
3. If equipped on late-model vehicles, loosen and remove the tank plastic shield.
4. Loosen the retaining clamp and disconnect the tank filler hose from the tank neck.

➡If fuel and vapor hoses or pump/sending unit wiring can be accessed at this time, they may be tagged and disconnected. If not, wait for the retaining straps to be loosened and lower the tank slightly for access.

5. Tag and disconnect and accessible wiring or hoses from the top of the fuel tank.
6. Have and assistant support the fuel tank, then remove the fuel tank-to-vehicle straps and, if equipped, the isolation strips. If no assistant is available, position a floor jack to support the tank while the straps are removed.
7. Lower the tank slightly, then remove the sending unit or sending unit/pump wires, hoses and ground strap. Be sure to label all connections to ease installation.
8. Carefully lower the fuel tank from the vehicle and store in a safe place.

To install:

9. Raise the tank partially into position in the vehicle. If you are working without an assistant, you may wish to loosely install one of the retaining straps and use a floor jack to support the tank at an angle so there is access to the sending unit or sending unit/pump assembly (as applicable).
10. Connect the fuel/vapor hoses and wiring to the top of the fuel tank, as tagged during removal.
11. Carefully raise the fuel tank so it is fully into position and loosely secure the retaining straps. Make sure the wires and hoses are not pinched or damaged when raising the tank. Also, be sure that the isolation strips (if used) are positioned between the retaining straps and the fuel tank.
12. It may be easier to connect the fuel filler hose to the tank neck at this time. If desired, connect the hose and secure the clamp.
13. Tighten the fuel tank retaining strap fasteners to specification. Tighten the strap nuts to 33 ft. lbs. (45 Nm).
14. If not done earlier, connect the tank filler hose to the tank neck and secure using the clamp.
15. If equipped, install and secure the tank plastic shield.
16. Remove the jackstands and carefully lower the rear of the truck.
17. Refill the fuel tank and install the filler cap, then check for leaks.
18. Connect the negative battery cable.

Equipped With Shield Package

1. Properly drain the fuel tank, then disconnect the negative battery cable.
2. Raise and support the rear of the truck safely using jackstands.
3. Remove the shield forward support and bracket.
4. While supporting the shield and tank assembly with the help of both an assistant and a floor jack, remove the remaining bolts holding the assembly to the frame, then lower it sufficiently for access to the hoses and wires.
5. Tag and disengage the hoses and wires from the sending unit assembly.
6. Carefully lower the fuel tank and shield from the vehicle, then if necessary for service or replacement, separate the tank from the shield.

To install:

7. If separated, install the tank to the shield.
8. Carefully raise the tank and shield assembly partially into position with the help of an assistant and a floor jack.
9. Connect the wiring and hoses to the sending unit assembly, as tagged during removal.
10. Raise the tank and shield assembly fully into position, then secure to the frame using the lower retaining bolts.
11. Install the shield forward support bracket.

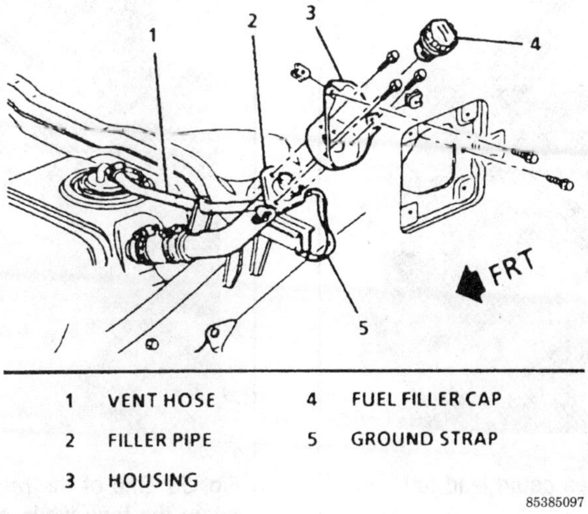

Fig. 50 Common fuel tank filler neck installation

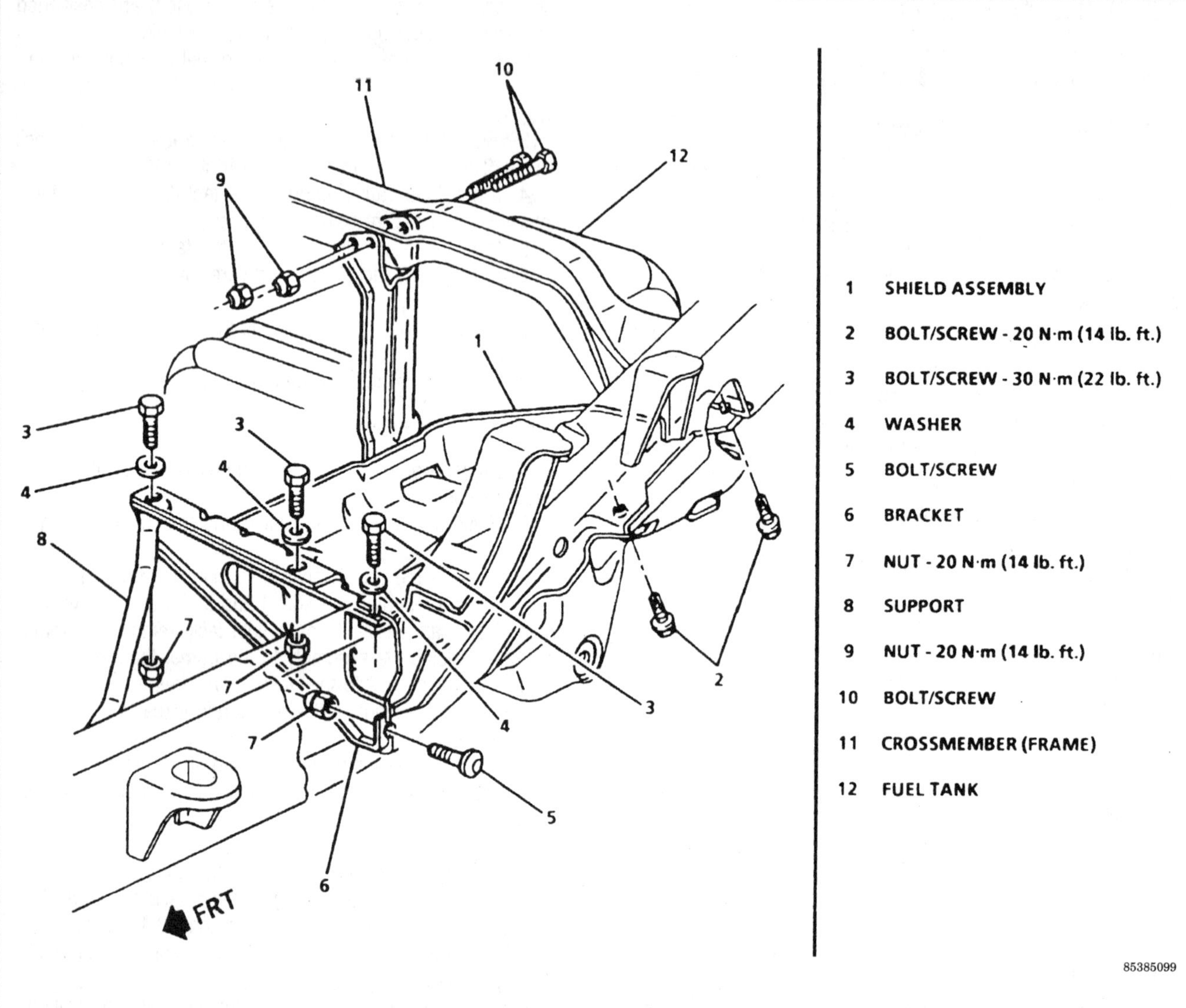

Fig. 51 Fuel tank mounting — vehicles equipped with shield package

Fig. 52 Failure to tag the fuel lines could lead to confusion during installation

Fig. 53 One of the retaining straps may be used to help retain the tank while connecting hoses and wires

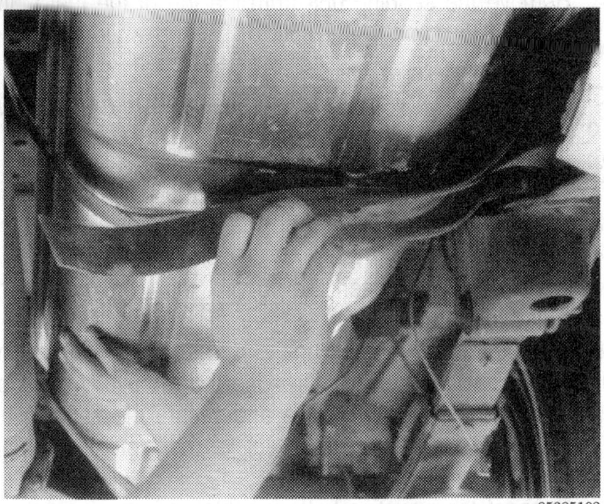
85385102

Fig. 54 If equipped, make sure the isolators are positioned between the straps and tank

85385103

Fig. 55 Secure the retaining straps using the fasteners

85385104

Fig. 56 Most tanks on these vehicles are retained using 2 straps

12. Remove the jackstands and carefully lower the rear of the truck.
13. Refill the fuel tank and install the filler cap, then check for leaks.
14. Connect the negative battery cable.

SENDING UNIT REPLACEMENT

See Figures 57, 58, 59, 60 and 61

1. Properly drain the fuel tank, then disconnect the negative battery cable.
2. Remove the fuel tank assembly from the truck.
3. Release the sending unit lockring cam using J-24187, or an equivalent locking tool to turn it counterclockwise. If no tool is available, a hammer and a brass drift may be used to CAREFULLY turn the lockring and release it from the tabs. DO NOT force the ring or tank/sending unit damage may occur.

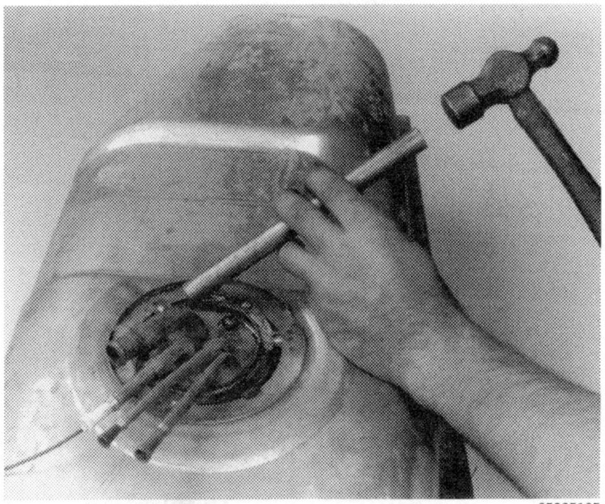
85385105

Fig. 57 Loosen the lockring by turning counterclockwise

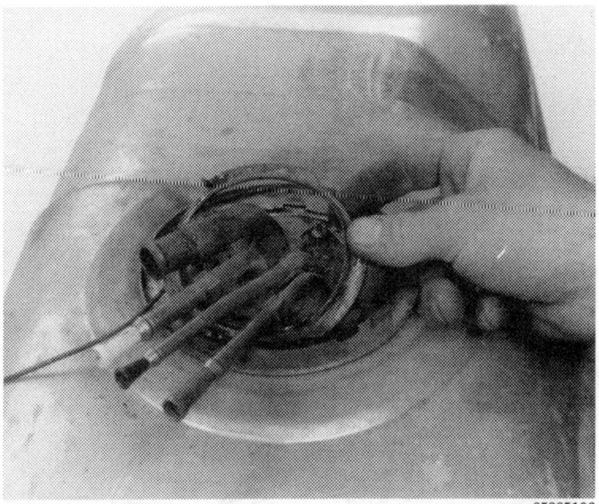
85385106

Fig. 58 Once the lockring is released, the sending unit is free to be removed from the tank

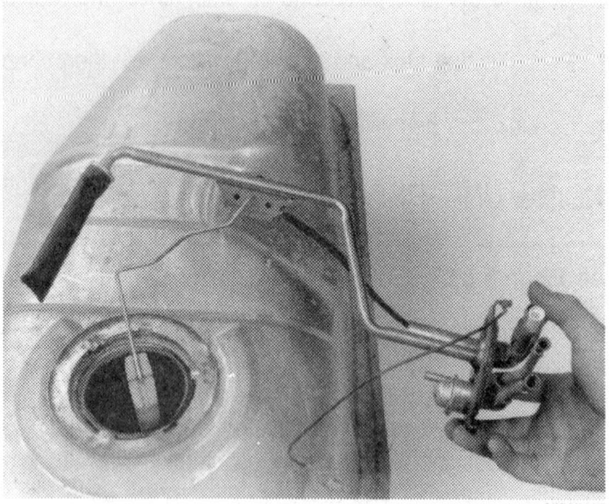
85385107

Fig. 59 Tilt the sending unit during removal in order to prevent damage to the float and pickup

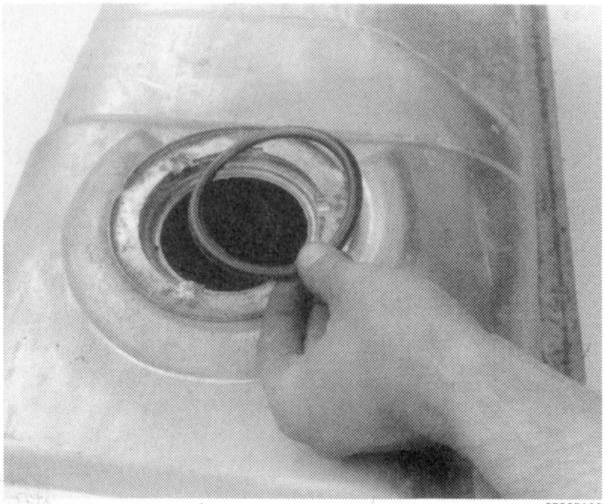
85385108

Fig. 60 ALWAYS replace the sending unit-to-tank O-ring

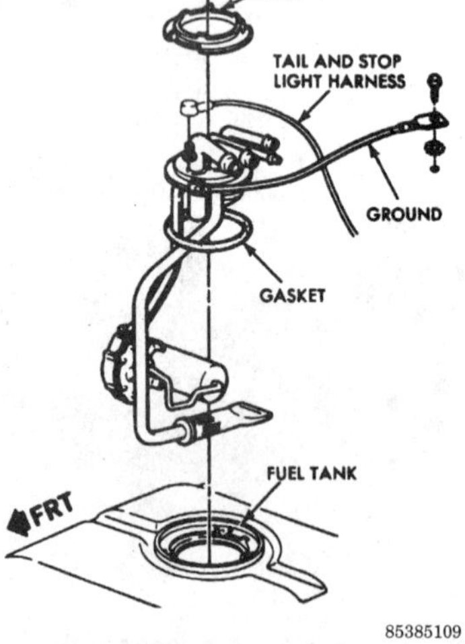

85385109

Fig. 61 Common sending unit mounting

4. Remove the sending unit from the top of the fuel tank. Be careful not to damage the float or pick-up while removing the unit.
5. Remove and discard the old sending unit-to-tank O-ring.

To install:

6. Position a new O-ring on the top of the tank opening.
7. Carefully insert the sending unit to the tank, making sure that the unit is properly aligned so the bottom or sides of the tank do not interfere with the float or pickup. If necessary, carefully tilt the unit to insert the bottom, then straighten it out as it is inserted into the tank.
8. Make sure the sending unit and O-ring are properly installed, then position the lockring. Use the removal/installation tool to turn the lockring clockwise and secure the sending unit.
9. Install the fuel tank to the vehicle, then refill it and check for leaks.
10. Connect the negative battery cable and check for proper sending unit operation.

6

CHASSIS ELECTRICAL

UNDERSTANDING AND TROUBLESHOOTING ELECTRICAL SYSTEMS

Over the years import and domestic manufacturers have incorporated electronic control systems into their production lines. In fact, electronic control systems are so prevalent that all new cars and trucks built today are equipped with at least one on-board computer. These electronic components (with no moving parts) should theoretically last the life of the vehicle, provided that nothing external happens to damage the circuits or memory chips.

While it is true that electronic components should never wear out, in the real world malfunctions do occur. It is also true that any computer-based system is extremely sensitive to electrical voltages and cannot tolerate careless or haphazard testing/service procedures. An inexperienced individual can literally cause major damage looking for a minor problem by using the wrong kind of test equipment or connecting test leads/connectors with the ignition switch **ON**. When selecting test equipment, make sure the manufacturer's instructions state that the tester is compatible with whatever type of system is being serviced. Read all instructions carefully and double check all test points before installing probes or making any test connections.

The following section outlines basic diagnosis techniques for dealing with automotive electrical systems. Along with a general explanation of the various types of test equipment available to aid in servicing modern automotive systems, basic repair techniques for wiring harnesses and connectors are also given. Read the basic information before attempting any repairs or testing. This will provide the background of information necessary to avoid the most common and obvious mistakes that can cost both time and money. Although the replacement and testing procedures are simple in themselves, the systems are not, and unless one has a thorough understanding of all components and their function within a particular system, the logical test sequence these systems demand cannot be followed. Minor malfunctions can make a big difference, so it is important to know how each component affects the operation of the overall system in order to find the ultimate cause of a problem without replacing good components unnecessarily. It is not enough to use the correct test equipment; the test equipment must be used correctly.

Safety Precautions

**CAUTION

Whenever working on or around any electrical or electronic systems, always observe these general precautions to prevent the possibility of personal injury or damage to electronic components.

- Never install or remove battery cables with the key **ON** or the engine running. Jumper cables should be connected with the key **OFF** to avoid power surges that can damage electronic control units. Engines equipped with computer controlled systems should avoid both giving and getting jump starts due to the possibility of serious damage to components from arcing in the engine compartment if connections are made with the ignition **ON**.
- Always remove the battery cables before charging the battery. Never use a high output charger on an installed battery or attempt to use any type of "hot shot" (24 volt) starting aid.
- Exercise care when inserting test probes into connectors to insure good contact without damaging the connector or spreading the pins. Always probe connectors from the rear (wire) side, NOT the pin side, to avoid accidental shorting of terminals during test procedures.
- Never remove or attach wiring harness connectors with the ignition switch **ON**, especially to an electronic control unit.
- Do not drop any components during service procedures and never apply 12 volts directly to any component (like a solenoid or relay) unless instructed specifically to do so. Some component electrical windings are designed to safely handle only 4 or 5 volts and can be destroyed in seconds if 12 volts are applied directly to the connector.
- Remove the electronic control unit if the vehicle is to be placed in an environment where temperatures exceed approximately 176°F (80°C), such as a paint spray booth or when arc/gas welding near the control unit location.

Understanding Basic Electricity

Understanding the basic theory of electricity makes electrical troubleshooting much easier. Several gauges are used in electrical troubleshooting to see inside the circuit being tested. Without a basic understanding, it will be difficult to understand testing procedures.

THE WATER ANALOGY

Electricity is the flow of electrons — hypothetical particles thought to constitute the basic stuff of electricity. Many people have been taught electrical theory using an analogy with water. In a comparison with water flowing in a pipe, the electrons would be the water. As the flow of water can be measured, the flow of electricity can be measured. The unit of measurement is amperes, frequently abbreviated amps. An ammeter will measure the actual amount of current flowing in the circuit.

Just as the water pressure is measured in units such as pounds per square inch, electrical pressure is measured in volts. When a voltmeter's two probes are placed on two live portions of an electrical circuit with different electrical pressures, current will flow through the voltmeter and produce a reading which indicates the difference in electrical pressure between the two parts of the circuit.

While increasing the voltage in a circuit will increase the flow of current, the actual flow depends not only on voltage, but on the resistance of the circuit. The standard unit for measuring circuit resistance is an ohm, measured by an ohmmeter. The ohmmeter is somewhat similar to an ammeter, but incorporates its own source of power so that a standard voltage is always present.

CIRCUITS

An actual electric circuit consists of four basic parts. These are: the power source, such as a generator or battery; a hot wire, which conducts the electricity under a relatively high voltage to the component supplied by the circuit; the load, such as a lamp, motor, resistor or relay coil; and the ground wire, which carries the current back to the source under very low voltage. In such a circuit the bulk of the resistance exists between the point where the hot wire is connected to the load, and the point where the load is grounded. In an automobile, the vehicle's frame or body, which is made of steel, is used as a part of the ground circuit for many of the electrical devices.

Remember that, in electrical testing, the voltmeter is connected in parallel with the circuit being tested (without disconnecting any wires) and measures the difference in voltage between the locations of the two probes; that the ammeter is connected in series with the load (the circuit is separated at one point and the ammeter inserted so it becomes a part of the circuit); and the ohmmeter is self-powered, so that all the power in the circuit should be off and the portion of the circuit to be measured contacted at either end by one of the probes of the meter.

For any electrical system to operate, it must make a complete circuit. This simply means that the power flow from the battery must make a complete circle. When an electrical component is operating, power flows from the battery to the component, passes through the component causing it to perform it to function (such as lighting a light bulb) and then returns to the battery through the ground of the circuit. This ground is usually (but not always) the metal part of the vehicle on which the electrical component is mounted.

Perhaps the easiest way to visualize this is to think of connecting a light bulb with two wires attached to it to your vehicle's battery. The battery in your vehicle has two posts (negative and positive). If one of the two wires attached to the light bulb was attached to the negative post of the battery and the other wire was attached to the positive post of the battery, you would have a complete circuit. Current from the battery would flow out one post, through the wire attached to it and then to the light bulb, where it would pass through causing it to light. It would then leave the light bulb, travel through the other wire, and return to the other post of the battery.

AUTOMOTIVE CIRCUITS

The normal automotive circuit differs from this simple example in two ways. First, instead of having a return wire from the bulb to the battery, the light bulb return the current to the battery through the chassis of the vehicle. Since the negative battery cable is attached to the chassis and the chassis is made of electrically conductive metal, the chassis of the vehicle can serve as a ground wire to complete the circuit. Secondly, most automotive circuits contain switches to turn components on and off.

Some electrical components which require a large amount of current to operate also have a relay in their circuit. Since these circuits carry a large amount of current, the thickness of the wire in the circuit (gauge size) is also greater. If this large wire were connected from the component to the control switch on the instrument panel, and then back to the component, a voltage drop would occur in the circuit. To prevent this potential drop in voltage, an electromagnetic switch (relay) is used. The large wires in the circuit are connected from the vehicle battery to one side of the relay, and from the opposite side of the relay to the component. The relay is normally open, preventing current from passing through the circuit. An additional, smaller wire is connected from the relay to the control switch for the circuit. When the control switch is turned on, it grounds the smaller wire from the relay and completes the circuit.

SHORT CIRCUITS

If you were to disconnect the light bulb (from the previous example of a light-bulb being connected to the battery by two wires) from the wires and touch the two wires together (please take our word for this; don't try it), the result will be a shower of sparks. A similar thing happens (on a smaller scale) when the power supply wire to a component or the electrical component itself becomes grounded before the normal ground connection for the circuit. To prevent damage to the system, the fuse for the circuit blows to interrupt the circuit — protecting the components from damage. Because grounding a wire from a power source makes a complete circuit — less the required component to use the power — the phenomenon is called a short circuit. The most common causes of short circuits are: the rubber insulation on a wire breaking or rubbing through to expose the current carrying core of the wire to a metal part of the car, or a shorted switch.

Some electrical systems on the vehicle are protected by a circuit breaker which is, basically, a self-repairing fuse. When either of the described events takes place in a system which is protected by a circuit breaker, the circuit breaker opens the circuit the same way a fuse does. However, when either the short is removed from the circuit or the surge subsides, the circuit breaker resets itself and does not have to be replaced as a fuse does.

Troubleshooting

When diagnosing a specific problem, organized troubleshooting is a must. The complexity of a modern automobile demands that you approach any problem in a logical, organized manner. There are certain troubleshooting techniques that are standard:

1. Establish when the problem occurs. Does the problem appear only under certain conditions? Were there any noises, odors, or other unusual symptoms?

2. Isolate the problem area. To do this, make some simple tests and observations; then eliminate the systems that are working properly. Check for obvious problems such as broken wires, dirty connections or split/disconnected vacuum hoses. Always check the obvious before assuming something complicated is the cause.

3. Test for problems systematically to determine the cause once the problem area is isolated. Are all the components functioning properly? Is there power going to electrical switches and motors? Is there vacuum at vacuum switches and/or actuators? Is there a mechanical problem such as bent linkage

or loose mounting screws? Performing careful, systematic checks will often turn up most causes on the first inspection without wasting time checking components that have little or no relationship to the problem.

4. Test all repairs after the work is done to make sure that the problem is fixed. Some causes can be traced to more than one component, so a careful verification of repair work is important in order to pick up additional malfunctions that may cause a problem to reappear or a different problem to arise. A blown fuse, for example, is a simple problem that may require more than another fuse to repair. If you don't look for a problem that caused a fuse to blow, a shorted wire (for example) may go undetected.

Experience has shown that most problems tend to be the result of a fairly simple and obvious cause, such as loose or corroded connectors or air leaks in the intake system. This makes careful inspection of components during testing essential to quick and accurate troubleshooting.

BASIC TROUBLESHOOTING THEORY

Electrical problems generally fall into one of three areas:

- The component that is not functioning is not receiving current.
- The component itself is not functioning.
- The component is not properly grounded.

Problems that fall into the first category are by far the most complicated. It is the current supply system to the component which contains all the switches, relay, fuses, etc.

The electrical system can be checked with a test light and a jumper wire. A test light is a device that looks like a pointed screwdriver with a wire attached to it. It has a light bulb in its handle. A jumper wire is a piece of insulated wire with an alligator clip attached to each end.

If a light bulb is not working, you must follow a systematic plan to determine which of the three causes is the villain.

1. Turn on the switch that controls the inoperable bulb.
2. Disconnect the power supply wire from the bulb.
3. Attach the ground wire to the test light to a good metal ground.
4. Touch the probe end of the test light to the end of the power supply wire that was disconnected from the bulb. If the bulb is receiving current, the test light will go on.

➡If the bulb is one which works only when the ignition key is turned on (turn signal), make sure the key is turned on.

If the test light does not go on, then the problem is in the circuit between the battery and the bulb. As mentioned before, this includes all the switches, fuses, and relays in the system. Turn to a wiring diagram and find the bulb on the diagram. Follow the wire that runs back to the battery. The problem is an open circuit between the battery and the bulb. If the fuse is blown and, when replaced, immediately blows again, there is a short circuit in the system which must be located and repaired. If there is a switch in the system, bypass it with a jumper wire. This is done by connecting one end of the jumper wire to the power supply wire into the switch and the other end of the jumper wire to the wire coming out of the switch. If the test light illuminates with the jumper wire installed, the switch or whatever was bypassed is defective.

➡Never substitute the jumper wire for the bulb, as the bulb is the component required to use the power from the power source.

5. If the bulb in the test light goes on, then the current is getting to the bulb that is not working in the car. This eliminates the first of the three possible causes. Connect the power supply wire and connect a jumper wire from the bulb to a good metal ground. Do this with the switch which controls the bulb works with jumper wire installed, then it has a bad ground. This is usually caused by the metal area on which the bulb mounts to the vehicle being coated with some type of foreign matter.

6. If neither test located the source of the trouble, then the light bulb itself is defective.

The above test procedure can be applied to any of the components of the chassis electrical system by substituting the component that is not working for the light bulb. Remember that for any electrical system to work, all connections must be clean and tight.

TEST EQUIPMENT

➡Pinpointing the exact cause of trouble in an electrical system can sometimes only be accomplished by the use of special test equipment. The following describes different types of commonly used test equipment and explains how to use them in diagnosis. In addition to the information covered below, the tool manufacturer's instructions booklet (provided with the tester) should be read and clearly understood before attempting any test procedures.

Jumper Wires

Jumper wires are simple, yet extremely valuable, pieces of test equipment. They are basically test wires which are used to bypass sections of a circuit. The simplest type of jumper wire is a length of multi-strand wire with an alligator clip at each end. Jumper wires are usually fabricated from lengths of standard automotive wire and whatever type of connector (alligator clip, spade connector or pin connector) that is required for the particular vehicle being tested. The well equipped tool box will have several different styles of jumper wires in several different lengths. Some jumper wires are made with three or more terminals coming from a common splice for special purpose testing. In cramped, hard-to-reach areas it is advisable to have insulated boots over the jumper wire terminals in order to prevent accidental grounding, sparks, and possible fire, especially when testing fuel system components.

Jumper wires are used primarily to locate open electrical circuits, on either the ground (-) side of the circuit or on the hot (+) side. If an electrical component fails to operate, connect the jumper wire between the component and a good ground. If the component operates only with the jumper installed, the ground circuit is open. If the ground circuit is good, but the component does not operate, the circuit between the power feed and component may be open. By moving the jumper wire successively back from the lamp toward the power source, you can isolate the area of the circuit where the open is located. When the component stops functioning, or the power is cut off, the open is in the segment of wire between the jumper and the point previously tested.

You can sometimes connect the jumper wire directly from the battery to the hot terminal of the component, but first make sure the component uses 12 volts in operation. Some electrical components, such as fuel injectors, are designed to operate on about 4 volts and running 12 volts directly to the injector terminals can cause damage.

By inserting an in-line fuse holder between a set of test leads, a fused jumper wire can be used for bypassing open circuits. Use a 5 amp fuse to provide protection against voltage spikes. When in doubt, use a voltmeter to check the voltage input to the component and measure how much voltage is normally being applied.

CAUTION

Never use jumpers made from wire that is of lighter gauge than that which is used in the circuit under test. If the jumper wire is of too small a gauge, it may overheat and possibly melt. Never use jumpers to bypass high resistance loads in a circuit. Bypassing resistances, in effect, creates a short circuit. This may, in turn, cause damage and fire. Jumper wires should only be used to bypass lengths of wire.

Unpowered Test Lights

The 12 volt test light is used to check circuits and components while electrical current is flowing through them. It is used for voltage and ground tests. Twelve volt test lights come in different styles but all have three main parts; a ground clip, a probe, and a light. The most commonly used 12 volt test lights have pick-type probes. To use a 12 volt test light, connect the ground clip to a good ground and probe wherever necessary with the pick. The pick should be sharp so that it can be probed into tight spaces.

CAUTION

Do not use a test light to probe electronic ignition spark plug or coil wires. Never use a pick-type test light to probe wiring on computer controlled systems unless specifically instructed to do so. Any wire insulation that is pierced by the test light probe should be taped and sealed with silicone after testing.

Like the jumper wire, the 12 volt test light is used to isolate opens in circuits. But, whereas the jumper wire is used to bypass the open to operate the load, the 12 volt test light is used to locate the presence of voltage in a circuit. If the test light glows, you know that there is power up to that point; if the 12 volt test light does not glow when its probe is inserted into the wire or connector, you know that there is an open circuit (no power). Move the test light in successive steps back toward the power source until the light in the handle does glow. When it glows, the open is between the probe and point which was probed previously.

➡The test light does not detect that 12 volts (or any particular amount of voltage) is present; it only detects that some voltage is present. It is advisable before using the test light to touch its terminals across the battery posts to make sure the light is operating properly.

Self-Powered Test Lights

The self-powered test light usually contains a 1.5 volt penlight battery. One type of self-powered test light is similar in design to the 12 volt unit. This type has both the battery and the light in the handle, along with a pick-type probe tip. The second type has the light toward the open tip, so that the light illuminates the contact point. The self-powered test light is a dual purpose piece of test equipment. It can be used to test for either open or short circuits when power is isolated from the circuit (continuity test). A powered test light should not be used on any computer controlled system or component unless specifically instructed to do so. Many engine sensors can be destroyed by even this small amount of voltage applied directly to the terminals.

Voltmeters

A voltmeter is used to measure voltage at any point in a circuit, or to measure the voltage drop across any part of a circuit. It can also be used to check continuity in a wire or circuit by indicating current flow from one end to the other. Analog voltmeters usually have various scales on the meter dial and a selector switch to allow the selection of different voltages. The voltmeter has a positive and a negative lead. To avoid damage to the meter, always connect the negative lead to the negative (-) side of the circuit (to ground or nearest the ground side of the circuit) and connect the positive lead to the positive (+) side of the circuit (to the power source or the nearest power source). Note that the negative voltmeter lead will always be black and that the positive voltmeter will always be some color other than black (usually red).

Depending on how the voltmeter is connected into the circuit, it has several uses. A voltmeter can be connected either in parallel or in series with a circuit and it has a very high resistance to current flow. When connected in parallel, only a small amount of current will flow through the voltmeter current path; the rest will flow through the normal circuit current path and the circuit will work normally. When the voltmeter is connected in series with a circuit, only a small amount of current can flow through the circuit. The circuit will not work properly, but the voltmeter reading will show if the circuit is complete or not.

Ohmmeters

The ohmmeter is designed to read resistance (which is measured in ohms or Ω) in a circuit or component. Although there are several different styles of ohmmeters, all analog meters will usually have a selector switch which permits the measurement of different ranges of resistance (usually the selector switch allows the multiplication of the meter reading by 10, 100, 1000, and 10,000). A calibration knob allows the meter to be set at zero for accurate measurement. Since all ohmmeters are powered by an internal battery, the ohmmeter can be used as a self-powered test light. When the ohmmeter is connected, current from the ohmmeter flows through the circuit or component being tested. Since the ohmmeter's internal resistance and voltage are known values, the amount of current flow through the meter depends on the resistance of the circuit or component being tested.

The ohmmeter can be used to perform a continuity test for opens or shorts (either by observation of the meter needle or as a self-powered test light), and to read actual resistance in a circuit. It should be noted that the ohmmeter is used to check the resistance of a component or wire while there is no voltage applied to the circuit. Current flow from an outside voltage source (such as the vehicle battery) can damage the ohmmeter, so the circuit or component should be isolated from the vehicle electrical system before any testing is done. Since the ohmmeter uses its own voltage source, either lead can be connected to any test point.

➡When checking diodes or other solid state components, the ohmmeter leads can only be connected one way in order to measure current flow in a single direction. Make sure the positive (+) and negative (-) terminal connections are as described in the test procedures to verify the one-way diode operation.

In using the meter for making continuity checks, do not be concerned with the actual resistance readings. Zero resistance, or any ohm reading, indicates continuity in the circuit. Infinite resistance indicates an open in the circuit. A high resistance reading where there should be none indicates a problem in the circuit. Checks for short circuits are made in the same manner as checks for open circuits except that the circuit must be isolated from both power and normal ground. Infinite resistance indicates no continuity to ground, while zero resistance indicates a dead short to ground.

Ammeters

An ammeter measures the amount of current flowing through a circuit in units called amperes or amps. Amperes are units of electron flow which indicate how fast the electrons are flowing through the circuit. Since Ohms Law dictates that current flow in a circuit is equal to the circuit voltage divided by the total circuit resistance, increasing voltage also increases the current level (amps). Likewise, any decrease in resistance will increase the amount of amps in a circuit. At normal operating voltage, most circuits have a characteristic amount of amperes, called "current draw" which can be measured using an ammeter. By referring to a specified current draw rating, measuring the amperes, and comparing the two values, one can determine what is happening within the circuit to aid in diagnosis. An open circuit, for example, will not allow any current to flow so the ammeter reading will be zero. More current flows through a heavily loaded circuit or when the charging system is operating.

An ammeter is always connected in series with the circuit being tested. All of the current that normally flows through the circuit must also flow through the ammeter; if there is any other path for the current to follow, the ammeter reading will not be accurate. The ammeter itself has very little resistance to current flow and therefore will not affect the circuit, but it will measure current draw only when the circuit is closed and electricity is flowing. Excessive current draw can blow fuses and drain the battery, while a reduced current draw can cause motors to run slowly, lights to dim and other components to not operate properly. The ammeter can help diagnose these conditions by locating the cause of the high or low reading.

Multimeters

Different combinations of test meters can be built into a single unit designed for specific tests. Some of the more common combination test devices are known as Volt/Amp testers, Tach/Dwell meters, or Digital Multimeters. The Volt/Amp tester is used for charging system, starting system or battery tests and consists of a voltmeter, an ammeter and a variable resistance carbon pile. The voltmeter will usually have at least two ranges for use with 6, 12 and/or 24 volt systems. The ammeter also has more than one range for testing various levels of battery loads and starter current draw. The carbon pile can be adjusted to offer different amounts of resistance. The Volt/Amp tester has heavy leads to carry large amounts of current and many later models have an inductive ammeter pickup that clamps around the wire to simplify test connections. On some models, the ammeter also has a zero-center scale to allow testing of charging and starting systems without switching leads or polarity. A digital multimeter is a voltmeter, ammeter and ohmmeter combined in an instrument which gives a digital readout. These are often used when testing solid state circuits because of their high input impedance (usually 10 megohms or more).

The tach/dwell meter that combines a tachometer and a dwell (cam angle) meter is a specialized kind of voltmeter. The tachometer scale is marked to show engine speed in rpm and the dwell scale is marked to show degrees of distributor shaft rotation. In most electronic ignition systems, dwell is determined by the control unit, but the dwell meter can also be used to check the duty cycle (operation) of some electronic engine control systems. Some tach/dwell meters are powered by an internal battery, while others take their power from the vehicle battery in use. The battery powered testers usually require calibration (much like an ohmmeter) before testing.

TESTING

Open Circuits

To use the self-powered test light or a multimeter to check for open circuits, first isolate the circuit from the vehicle's 12 volt power source by disconnecting the battery or wiring harness connector. Connect the test light or ohmmeter ground clip to a good ground and probe sections of the circuit sequentially with the test light. (start from either end of the circuit). If the light is out/or there is infinite resistance, the open is between the probe and the circuit ground. If the light is on/or the meter shows continuity, the open is between the probe and end of the circuit toward the power source.

Short Circuits

By isolating the circuit both from power and from ground, and using a self-powered test light or multimeter, you can check for shorts to ground in the circuit. Isolate the circuit from power and ground. Connect the test light or ohmmeter ground clip to a good ground and probe any easy-to-reach test point in the circuit. If the light comes on or there is continuity, there is a short somewhere in the circuit. To isolate the short, probe a test point at either end of the isolated circuit (the light should be on/there should be continuity). Leave the test light probe engaged and open connectors, switches, remove parts, etc., sequentially, until the light goes out/continuity is broken. When the light goes out, the short is between the last circuit component opened and the previous circuit opened.

➡The battery in the test light and does not provide much current. A weak battery may not provide enough power to illuminate the test light even when a complete circuit is made (especially if there are high resistances in the circuit). Always make sure that the test battery is strong. To check the battery, briefly touch the ground clip to the probe; if the light glows brightly the battery is strong enough for testing. Never use a self-powered test light to perform checks for opens or shorts when power is applied to the electrical system under test. The 12 volt vehicle power will quickly burn out the light bulb in the test light.

Available Voltage Measurement

Set the voltmeter selector switch to the 20V position and connect the meter negative lead to the negative post of the battery. Connect the positive meter lead to the positive post of the battery and turn the ignition switch **ON** to provide a load. Read the voltage on the meter or digital display. A well charged battery should register over 12 volts. If the meter reads below 11.5 volts, the battery power may be insufficient to operate the electrical system properly. This test determines voltage available from the battery and should be the first step in any electrical trouble diagnosis procedure. Many electrical problems, especially on computer controlled systems, can be caused by a low state of charge in the battery. Excessive corrosion at the battery cable terminals can cause a poor contact that will prevent proper charging and full battery current flow.

Normal battery voltage is 12 volts when fully charged. When the battery is supplying current to one or more circuits it is said to be "under load." When everything is off the electrical system is under a "no-load" condition. A fully charged battery may show about 12.5 volts at no load; will drop to 12 volts under medium load; and will drop even lower under heavy load. If the battery is partially discharged the voltage decrease under heavy load may be excessive, even though the battery shows 12 volts or more at no load. When allowed to discharge further, the battery's available voltage under load will decrease more severely. For this reason, it is important that the battery be fully charged during all testing procedures to avoid errors in diagnosis and incorrect test results.

Voltage Drop

When current flows through a resistance, the voltage beyond the resistance is reduced (the larger the current, the greater the reduction in voltage). When no current is flowing, there is no voltage drop because there is no current flow. All points in the circuit which are connected to the power source are at the same voltage as the power source. The total voltage drop always equals the total source voltage. In a long circuit with many connectors, a series of small, unwanted voltage drops due to corrosion at the connectors can add up to a total loss of voltage which impairs the operation of the normal loads in the circuit. The maximum allowable voltage drop under load is critical, especially if there is more than one high resistance problem in a circuit because all voltage drops are cumulative. A small drop is normal due to the resistance of the conductors.

INDIRECT COMPUTATION OF VOLTAGE DROPS

1. Set the voltmeter selector switch to the 20 volt position.
2. Connect the meter negative lead to a good ground.
3. While operating the circuit, probe all loads in the circuit with the positive meter lead and observe the voltage readings. A drop should be noticed after the first load. But, there should be little or no voltage drop before the first load.

DIRECT MEASUREMENT OF VOLTAGE DROPS

1. Set the voltmeter switch to the 20 volt position.
2. Connect the voltmeter negative lead to the ground side of the load to be measured.
3. Connect the positive lead to the positive side of the resistance or load to be measured.
4. Read the voltage drop directly on the 20 volt scale.

Too high a voltage indicates too high a resistance. If, for example, a blower motor runs too slowly, you can determine if perhaps there is too high a resistance in the resistor pack. By taking voltage drop readings in all parts of the circuit, you can isolate the problem. Too low a voltage drop indicates too low a resistance. Take the blower motor for example again. If a blower motor runs too fast in the MED and/or LOW position, the problem might be isolated in the resistor pack by taking voltage drop readings in all parts of the circuit to locate a possibly shorted resistor.

HIGH RESISTANCE TESTING

1. Set the voltmeter selector switch to the 4 volt position.
2. Connect the voltmeter positive lead to the positive post of the battery.
3. Turn on the headlights and heater blower to provide a load.
4. Probe various points in the circuit with the negative voltmeter lead.
5. Read the voltage drop on the 4 volt scale. Some average maximum allowable voltage drops are:
   - FUSE PANEL: 0.7 volts
   - IGNITION SWITCH: 0.5 volts
   - HEADLIGHT SWITCH: 0.7 volts
   - IGNITION COIL (+): 0.5 volts
   - ANY OTHER LOAD: 1.3 volts

➡Voltage drops are all measured while a load is operating; without current flow, there will be no voltage drop.

Resistance Measurement

The batteries in an ohmmeter will weaken with age and temperature, so the ohmmeter must be calibrated or "zeroed" before taking measurements. To zero the meter, place the selector switch in its lowest range and touch the two ohmmeter leads together. Turn the calibration knob until the meter needle is exactly on zero.

➡All analog (needle) type ohmmeters must be zeroed before use, but some digital ohmmeter models are automatically calibrated when the switch is turned on. Self-calibrating digital ohmmeters do not have an adjusting knob, but its a good idea to check for a zero readout before use by touching the leads together. All computer controlled systems require the use of a digital ohmmeter with at least 10 megohms impedance for testing. Before any test procedures are attempted, make sure the ohmmeter used is compatible with the electrical system or damage to the on-board computer could result.

To measure resistance, first isolate the circuit from the vehicle power source by disconnecting the battery cables or the harness connector. Make sure the key is **OFF** when disconnecting any components or the battery. Where necessary, also isolate at least one side of the circuit to be checked in order to avoid reading parallel resistances. Parallel circuit resistances will always give a lower reading than the actual resistance of either of the branches. When measuring the resistance of parallel circuits, the total resistance will always be lower than the smallest resistance in the circuit. Connect the meter leads to both sides of the circuit (wire or component) and read the actual measured ohms on the meter scale. Make sure the selector switch is set to the proper ohm scale for the circuit being tested to avoid misreading the ohmmeter test value.

✲✲WARNING

Never use an ohmmeter with power applied to the circuit. Like the self-powered test light, the ohmmeter is designed to operate on its own power supply. The normal 12 volt automotive electrical system current could damage the meter!

Wiring Harnesses

The average automobile contains about ½ mile of wiring, with hundreds of individual connections. To protect the many wires from damage and to keep them from becoming a confusing tangle, they are organized into bundles, enclosed in plastic or taped together and called wiring harnesses. Different harnesses serve different parts of the vehicle. Individual wires are color coded to help trace them through a harness where sections are hidden from view.

Automotive wiring or circuit conductors can be in any one of three forms:

1. Single strand wire
2. Multi-strand wire
3. Printed circuitry

Single strand wire has a solid metal core and is usually used inside such components as alternators, motors, relays and other devices. Multi-strand wire has a core made of many small strands of wire twisted together into a single conductor. Most of the wiring in an automotive electrical system is made up of multi-strand wire, either as a single conductor or grouped together in a harness. All wiring is color coded on the insulator, either as a solid color or as a colored wire with an identification stripe. A printed circuit is a thin film of copper or other conductor that is printed on an insulator backing. Occasionally, a printed circuit is sandwiched between two sheets of plastic for more protection and flexibility. A complete printed circuit, consisting of conductors, insulating material and connectors for lamps or other components is called a printed circuit board. Printed circuitry is used in place of individual wires or harnesses in places where space is limited, such as behind instrument panels.

Since automotive electrical systems are very sensitive to changes in resistance, the selection of properly sized wires is critical when systems are repaired. A loose or corroded connection or a replacement wire that is too small for the circuit will add extra resistance and an additional voltage drop to the circuit. A ten percent voltage drop can result in slow or erratic motor operation, for example, even though the circuit is complete. The wire gauge number is an expression of the cross-section area of the conductor. The most common system for expressing wire size is the American Wire Gauge (AWG) system.

Gauge numbers are assigned to conductors of various cross-section areas. As gauge number increases, area decreases and the conductor becomes smaller. A 5 gauge conductor is smaller than a 1 gauge conductor and a 10 gauge is smaller than a 5 gauge. As the cross-section area of a conductor decreases, resistance increases and so does the gauge number. A conductor with a higher gauge number will carry less current than a conductor with a lower gauge number.

➡Gauge wire size refers to the size of the conductor, not the size of the complete wire. It is possible to have two wires of the same gauge with different diameters because one may have thicker insulation than the other.

12 volt automotive electrical systems generally use 10, 12, 14, 16 and 18 gauge wire. Main power distribution circuits and larger accessories usually use 10 and 12 gauge wire. Battery cables are usually 4 or 6 gauge, although 1 and 2 gauge wires are occasionally used. Wire length must also be considered when making repairs to a circuit. As conductor length increases, so does resistance. An 18 gauge wire, for example, can carry a 10 amp load for 10 feet without excessive voltage drop; however if a 15 foot wire is required for the same 10 amp load, it must be a 16 gauge wire.

An electrical schematic shows the electrical current paths when a circuit is operating properly. It is essential to understand how a circuit works before trying to figure out why it doesn't. Schematics break the entire electrical system down into individual circuits and show only one particular circuit. In a schematic, no attempt is made to represent wiring and components as they physically appear on the vehicle; switches and other components are shown as simply as possible. Face views of harness connectors show the cavity or terminal locations in all multi-pin connectors to help locate test points.

If you need to backprobe a connector while it is on the component, the order of the terminals must be mentally reversed. The wire color code can help in this situation, as well as a keyway, lock tab or other reference mark.

WIRING REPAIR

Soldering is a quick, efficient method of joining metals permanently. Everyone who has the occasion to make wiring repairs should know how to solder. Electrical connections that are soldered are far less likely to come apart and will conduct electricity much better than connections that are only "pig-tailed" together. The most popular (and preferred) method of soldering is with an electrical soldering gun. Soldering irons are available in many sizes and wattage ratings. Irons with higher wattage ratings deliver higher temperatures and recover lost heat faster. A small soldering iron rated for no more than 50 watts is recommended, especially on electrical systems where excess heat can damage the components being soldered.

There are three ingredients necessary for successful soldering; proper flux, good solder and sufficient heat. A soldering flux is necessary to clean the metal of tarnish, prepare it for soldering and to enable the solder to spread into tiny crevices. When soldering, always use a rosin core solder which is non-corrosive and will not attract moisture once the job is finished. Other types of flux (acid core) will leave a residue that will attract moisture and cause the wires to corrode. Tin is a unique metal with a low melting point. In a molten state, it dissolves and alloys easily with many metals. Solder is made by mixing tin with lead. The most common proportions are 40/60, 50/50 and 60/40, with the percentage of tin listed first. Low priced solders usually contain less tin, making them very difficult for a beginner to use because more heat is required to melt the solder. A common solder is 40/60 which is well suited for all-around general use, but 60/40 melts easier and is preferred for electrical work.

Soldering Techniques

Successful soldering requires that the metals to be joined be heated to a temperature that will melt the solder, usually 360-460°F (182-238°C). Contrary to popular belief, the purpose of the soldering iron is not to melt the solder itself, but to heat the parts being soldered to a temperature high enough to melt the solder when it is touched to the work. Melting flux-cored solder on the soldering iron will usually destroy the effectiveness of the flux.

➡Soldering tips are made of copper for good heat conductivity, but must be "tinned" regularly for quick transference of heat to the project and to prevent the solder from sticking to the iron. To "tin" the iron, simply heat it and touch the flux-cored solder to the tip; the solder will flow over the hot tip. Wipe the excess off with a clean rag, but be careful as the iron will be hot.

After some use, the tip may become pitted. If so, simply dress the tip smooth with a smooth file and "tin" the tip again. Flux-cored solder will remove oxides but rust, bits of insulation and oil or grease must be removed with a wire brush or emery cloth. For maximum strength in soldered parts, the joint must start off clean and tight. Weak joints will result in gaps too wide for the solder to bridge.

If a separate soldering flux is used, it should be brushed or swabbed on only those areas that are to be soldered. Most solders contain a core of flux and separate fluxing is unnecessary. Hold the work to be soldered firmly. It is best to solder on a wooden board, because a metal vise will only rob the piece to be soldered of heat and make it difficult to melt the solder. Hold the soldering tip with the broadest face against the work to be soldered. Apply solder under the tip close to the work, using enough solder to give a heavy film between the iron and the piece being soldered, while moving slowly and making sure the solder melts properly. Keep the work level or the solder will run to the lowest part and favor the thicker parts, because these require more heat to melt the solder. If the soldering tip overheats (the solder coating on the face of the tip burns up), it should be retinned. Once the soldering is completed, let the soldered joint stand until cool. Tape and seal all soldered wire splices after the repair has cooled.

Wire Harness Connectors

Most connectors in the engine compartment or that are otherwise exposed to the elements are protected against moisture and dirt which could create oxidation and deposits on the terminals.

These special connectors are weather-proof. All repairs require the use of a special terminal and the tool required to service it. This tool is used to remove the pin and sleeve terminals. If removal is attempted with an ordinary pick, there is a good chance that the terminal will be bent or deformed. Unlike standard blade type terminals, these weather-proof terminals cannot be straightened once they are bent. Make certain that the connectors are properly seated and all of the sealing rings are in place when connecting leads. On some models, a hinge-type flap provides a backup or secondary locking feature for the terminals. Most secondary locks are used to improve connector reliability by retaining the terminals if the small terminal lock tangs are not positioned properly.

Molded-on connectors require complete replacement of the connection. This means splicing a new connector assembly into the harness. All splices should be soldered to insure proper contact. Use care when probing the connections or replacing terminals in them as it is possible to short between opposite terminals. If this happens to the wrong terminal pair, it is possible to damage certain components. Always use jumper wires between connectors for circuit checking and never probe through weatherproof seals.

Open circuits are often difficult to locate by sight because corrosion or terminal misalignment are hidden by the connectors. Merely wiggling a connector on a sensor or in the wiring harness may correct the open circuit condition. This should always be considered when an open circuit or a failed sensor is indicated. Intermittent problems may also be caused by oxidized or loose connections. When using a circuit tester for diagnosis, always probe connections from the wire side. Be careful not to damage sealed connectors with test probes.

All wiring harnesses should be replaced with identical parts, using the same gauge wire and connectors. When signal wires are spliced into a harness, use wire with high temperature insulation only. It is seldom necessary to replace a complete harness. If replacement is necessary, pay close attention to insure proper harness routing. Secure the harness with suitable plastic wire clamps to prevent vibrations from causing the harness to wear in spots or contact any hot components.

➡Weatherproof connectors cannot be replaced with standard connectors. Instructions are provided with replacement connector and terminal packages. Some wire harnesses have mounting indicators (usually pieces of colored tape) to mark where the harness is to be secured.

In making wiring repairs, its important that you always replace damaged wires with wiring of the same gauge as the wire being replaced. The heavier the wire, the smaller the gauge number. Wires are color-coded to aid in identification and whenever possible the same color coded wire should be used for replacement. A wire stripping and crimping tool is necessary to install solderless terminal connectors. Test all crimps by pulling on the wires; it should not be possible to pull the wires out of a good crimp.

Wires which are open, exposed or otherwise damaged are repaired by simple splicing. Where possible, if the wiring harness is accessible and the damaged place in the wire can be located, it is best to open the harness and check for all possible damage. In an inaccessible harness, the wire must be bypassed with a new insert, usually taped to the outside of the old harness.

When replacing fusible links, be sure to use fusible link wire, NOT ordinary automotive wire. Make sure the fusible segment is of the same gauge and construction as the one being replaced and double the stripped end when crimping the terminal connector for a good contact. The melted (open) fusible link segment of the wiring harness should be cut off as close to the harness as possible, then a new segment spliced in as described. In the case of a damaged fusible link that feeds two harness wires, the harness connections should be replaced with two fusible link wires so that each circuit will have its own separate protection.

➡Most of the problems caused in the wiring harness are due to bad ground connections. Always check all vehicle ground connections for corrosion or looseness before performing any power feed checks to eliminate the chance of a bad ground affecting the circuit.

Hard-Shell Connectors

Unlike molded connectors, the terminal contacts in hard-shell connectors can be replaced. Weatherproof hard-shell connectors with the leads molded into the shell have non-replaceable terminal ends. Replacement usually involves the use of a special terminal removal tool that depresses the locking tangs (barbs) on the connector terminal and allows the connector to be removed from the rear of the shell. The connector shell should be replaced if it shows any evidence of burning, melting, cracks, or breaks. Replace individual terminals that are burnt, corroded, distorted or loose.

➡The insulation crimp must be tight to prevent the insulation from sliding back on the wire when the wire is pulled. The insulation must be visibly compressed under the crimp tabs, and the ends of the crimp should be turned in for a firm grip on the insulation.

The wire crimp must be made with all wire strands inside the crimp. The terminal must be fully compressed on the wire strands with the ends of the crimp tabs turned in to make a firm grip on the wire. Check all connections with an ohmmeter to insure a good contact. There should be no measurable resistance between the wire and the terminal when connected.

Add-On Electrical Equipment

The electrical system in your vehicle is designed to perform under reasonable operating conditions without interference between components. Before any additional electrical equipment is installed, it is recommended that you consult your dealer or a reputable repair facility that is familiar with the vehicle and its systems.

If the vehicle is equipped with mobile radio equipment and/or mobile telephone, it may have an effect upon the operation of any on-board computer control modules. Radio Frequency Interference (RFI) from the communications system can be picked up by the vehicle's wiring harnesses and conducted into the control module, giving it the wrong messages at the wrong time. Although well shielded against RFI, the computer should be further protected by taking the following measures:

- Install the antenna as far as possible from the control module. For instance, if the module is located behind the center console area, then the antenna should be mounted at the rear of the vehicle.
- Keep the antenna wiring a minimum of eight inches away from any wiring running to control modules and from the module itself. NEVER wind the antenna wire around any other wiring.
- Mount the equipment as far from the control module as possible. Be very careful during installation not to drill through any wires or short a wire harness with a mounting screw.
- Insure that the electrical feed wire(s) to the equipment are properly and tightly connected. Loose connectors can cause interference.
- Make certain that the equipment is properly grounded to the vehicle. Poor grounding can damage expensive equipment.

SUPPLEMENTAL INFLATABLE RESTRAINT SYSTEM

General Information

➧ See Figure 1

The Supplemental Inflatable Restraint (SIR) system offers protection in addition to that provided by the driver's seat belt by deploying an air bag from the center of the steering wheel. The air bag deploys when the vehicle is involved in a frontal crash of sufficient force up to 30° off the centerline of the vehicle. To further absorb the crash energy, there is also a knee bolster located beneath the instrument panel in the driver's area and the steering wheel is collapsible.

The system has an energy reserve, which can store a large enough electrical charge to deploy the air bag(s) for up to ten minutes after the battery has been disconnected or damaged. The system **MUST** be disabled before any service is performed on or around SIR components or SIR wiring.

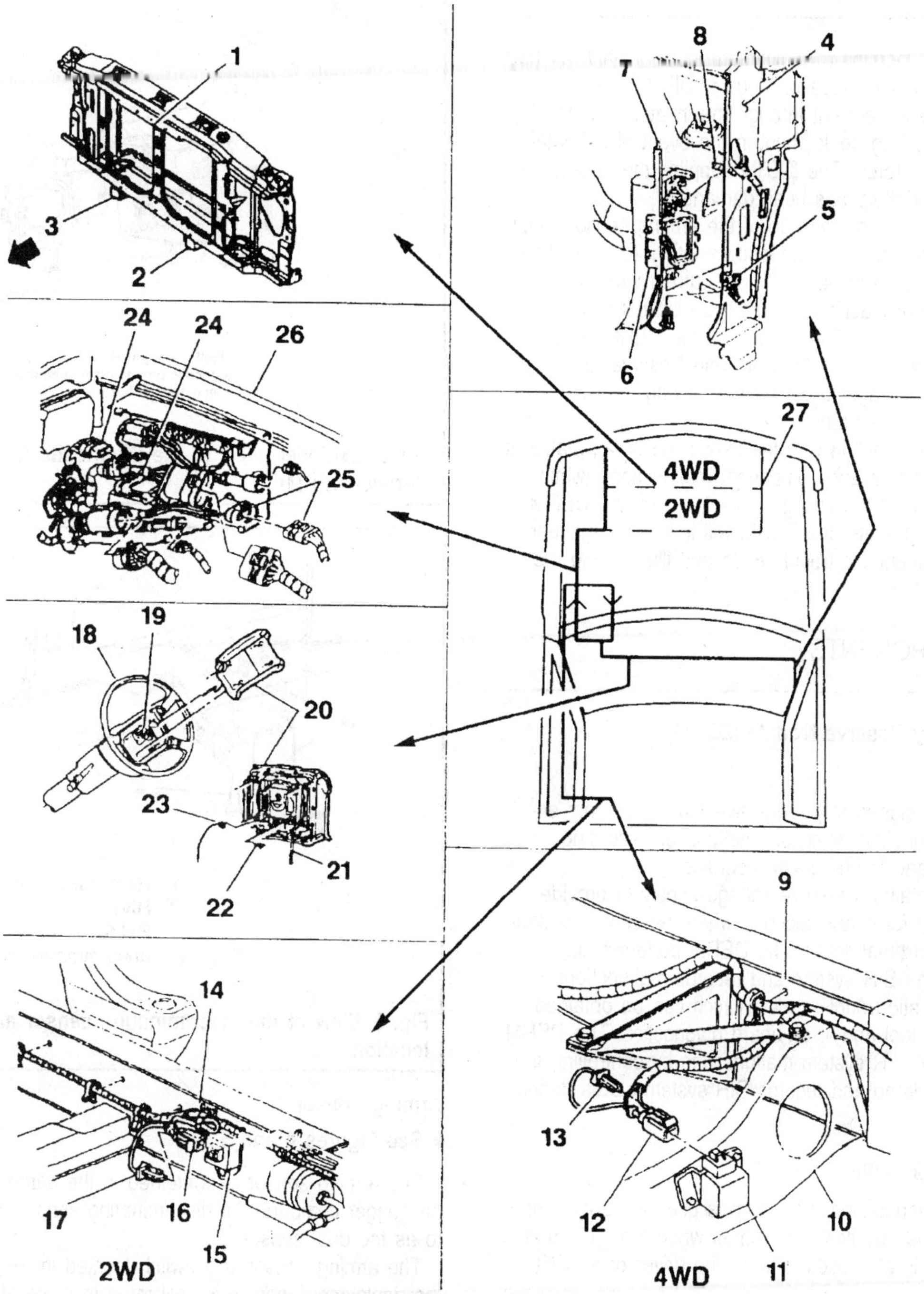

1. Radiator support
2. LH forward discriminating sensor
3. RH forward discriminating sensor
4. Cowl side panel
5. Derm connector
6. Derm
7. RH cowl side trim plate
8. Sir wiring harness
9. LH frame rail
10. Cross member
11. Arming sensor
12. Arming sensor harness connector
13. Connector position assurance
14. LH frame rail
15. Arming sensor
16. Arming sensor harness connector
17. Connector position assurance
18. Steering wheel
19. Sir coil assembly
20. Inflator module
21. Horn wire assembly
22. Connector position assurance
23. Sir coil assembly connector
24. Arming sensor jumper harness connector
25. Discriminating sensor intermediate harness connector
26. LH fender
27. Sir wiring harness

88456g01

Fig. 1 Supplemental Inflatable Restraint (SIR) system component and wiring locations

SYSTEM OPERATION

The SIR system contains a deployment loop for each air bag and a Diagnostic Energy Reserve Module (DERM). The deployment loop supplies current through the inflator module which will cause air bag deployment in the event of a frontal collision of sufficient force. The DERM supplies the necessary power, even if the battery has been damaged.

The deployment loop is made up of the arming sensors, coil assembly, inflator module and the discriminating sensors. The inflator module is only supplied sufficient current when the arming sensor and at least one of the two discriminating sensors close simultaneously. The function of the DERM is to supply the deployment loop a 36 Volt Loop Reserve (36VLR) to assure sufficient voltage to deploy the air bag if ignition voltage is lost in a frontal crash.

The DERM, in conjunction with the sensor resistors, makes it possible to detect circuit and component malfunctions within the deployment loop. If the voltages monitored by the DERM fall outside expected limits, the DERM will indicate a malfunction by storing a diagnostic trouble code and illuminating the AIR BAG lamp.

SYSTEM COMPONENTS

Diagnostic Energy Reserve Module (DERM)

See Figure 2

The DERM is designed to perform five main functions: energy reserve, malfunction detection, malfunction recording, driver notification and frontal crash recording.

The DERM maintains a reserve voltage supply to provide deployment energy for a few seconds when the vehicle voltage is low or lost in a frontal crash. The DERM performs diagnostic monitoring of the SIR system and records malfunctions in the form of diagnostic trouble codes, which can be obtained from a hand scan tool and/or on-board diagnostics. The DERM warns the driver of SIR system malfunctions by controlling the AIR BAG warning lamp and records SIR system status during a frontal crash.

AIR BAG Warning Lamp

The AIR BAG warning/indicator lamp is used to verify lamp and DERM operation by flashing 7 times when the ignition is first turned **ON**. It is also used to warn the driver of an SIR system malfunction.

Discriminating Sensors

See Figure 3

Vehicles equipped with driver's side air bag only, have two discriminating sensors. The forward discriminating sensor is located in front of the radiator. The passenger compartment discriminating sensor is located behind the right side of the instrument panel.

The discriminating sensor consists of a sensing element, diagnostic resistor and normally open switch contacts. The sensing element closes the switch contact when vehicle velocity changes are severe enough to warrant air bag deployment.

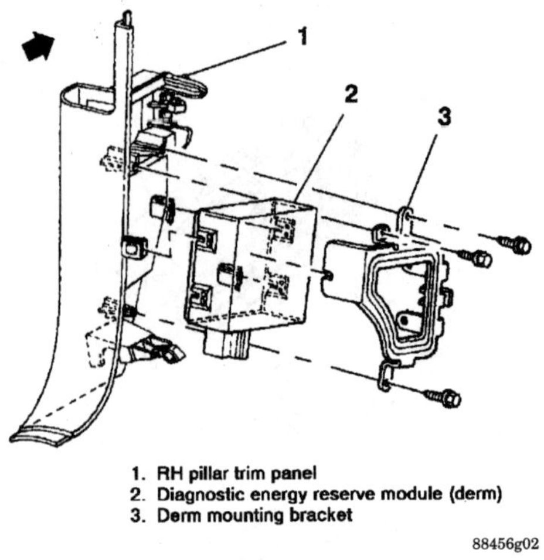

Fig. 2 Exploded view of the Diagnostic Energy Reserve Module (DERM)

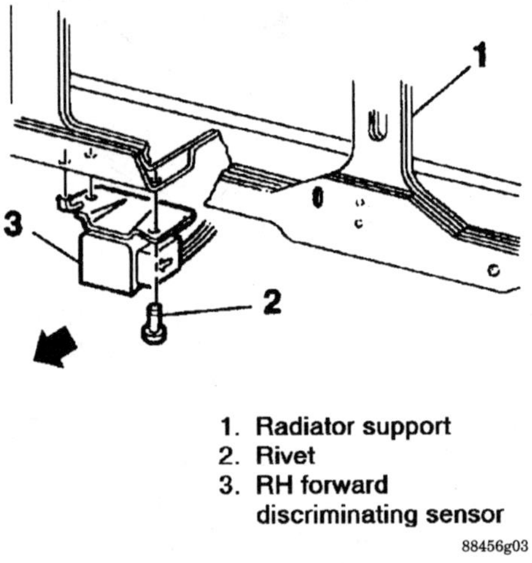

Fig. 3 View of the discriminating sensor and its location

Arming Sensor

See Figures 4 and 5

The arming sensor is contained in the same housing as the passenger compartment discriminating sensor and is referred to as the dual sensor.

The arming sensor is a switch located in the power side of the deployment loop. It is calibrated to close at low level velocity changes (lower than the discriminating sensors), assuring that the inflator module is connected directly to the 36VLR output of the DERM or Ignition 1 voltage when any discriminating sensor closes.

SIR Coil Assembly

See Figure 6

The SIR coil assembly consists of two current carrying coils. They are attached to the steering column and allow rotation of the steering wheel while maintaining continuous deployment loop contact through the inflator module.

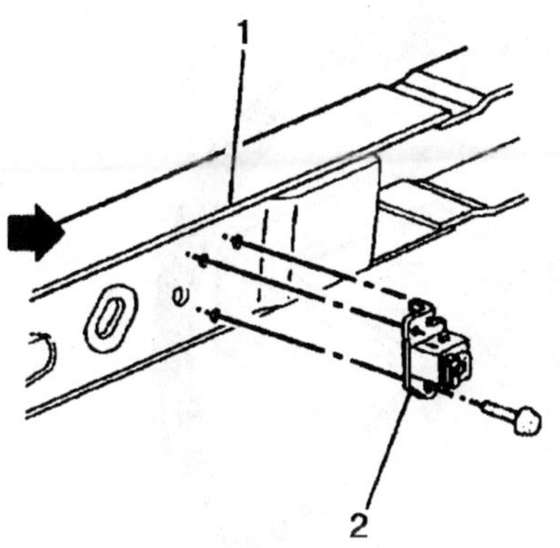

Fig. 4 View of the arming sensor and its location — 2.2L models

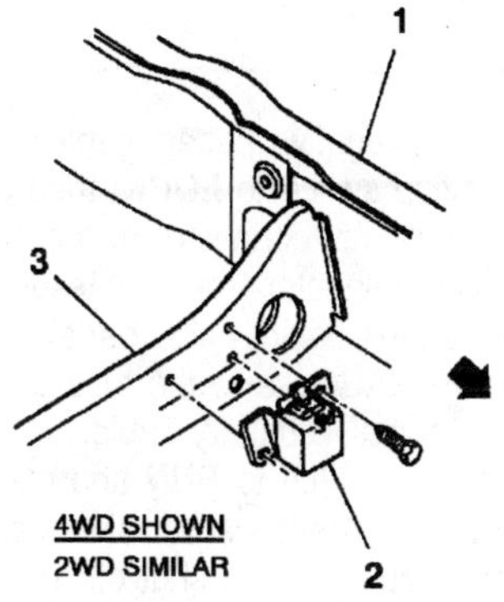

Fig. 5 View of the arming sensor and its location — 4.3L models

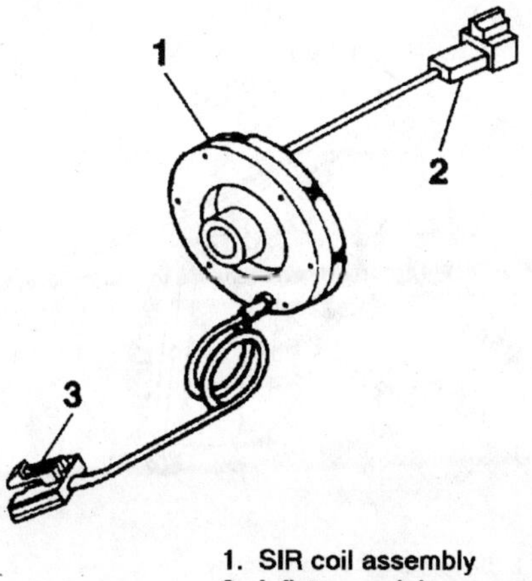

Fig. 6 SIR coil assembly and electrical connections

There is a shorting bar on the lower steering column connector that connects the SIR coil to the SIR wiring harness. The shorting bar shorts the circuit when the connector is disengaged. The circuit to the inflator module is shorted in this way to prevent unwanted air bag deployment when servicing the steering column or other SIR components.

Inflator Module

➧ **See Figure 7**

The inflator module consists of an inflatable bag and an inflator (a canister of gas-generating material and an initiating device). When the vehicle is in a frontal crash of sufficient force to close the arming sensor and at least one discriminating sensor simultaneously, current flows through the deployment loop. Current passing through the initiator ignites the material in the inflator module, causing a reaction which produces a gas that rapidly inflates the air bag.

All vehicles are equipped with an inflator module located in the steering wheel.

SERVICE PRECAUTIONS

➧ **See Figure 8**

- When performing service around the SIR system components or wiring, the SIR system **MUST** be disabled. Failure to do so could result in possible air bag deployment, personal injury or unneeded SIR system repairs.
- When carrying a live inflator module, make sure that the bag and trim cover are pointed away from you. Never carry the inflator module by the wires or connector on the underside of the module. In case of accidental deployment, the bag will then deploy with minimal chance of injury.
- When placing a live inflator module on a bench or other surface, always face the bag and trim cover up, away from the surface.

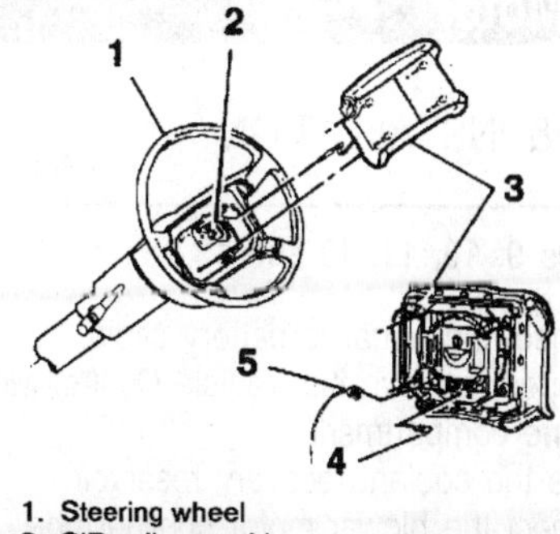

Fig. 7 Exploded view of the inflator module and its related components

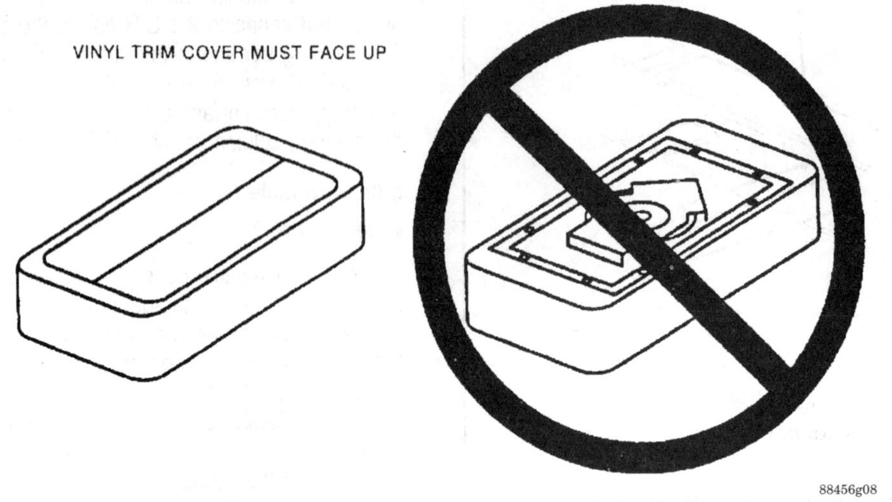

Fig. 8 When storing an inflator module, ensure that the vinyl cover faces up

DISABLING THE SYSTEM

1. Turn the steering wheel so that the vehicle's wheels are pointing straight ahead.
2. Turn the ignition switch to **LOCK**, remove the key, then disconnect the negative battery cable.
3. Remove the AIR BAG fuse from the fuse block.
4. Remove the steering column filler panel.
5. Disengage the Connector Position Assurance (CPA) and yellow two way connector at the base of the steering column.
6. Connect the negative battery cable.

➡With the AIR BAG fuse removed, the battery cable connected and the ignition in the ON position, the AIR BAG warning lamp will be ON. This is normal and does not indicate a system malfunction.

ENABLING THE SYSTEM

1. Disconnect the negative battery cable.
2. Turn the ignition switch to **LOCK**, then remove the key.
3. Engage the two way connector at the base of the steering column and the Connector Position Assurance (CPA).
4. Install the steering column filler panel.
5. Install the AIR BAG fuse to the fuse block.
6. Connect the negative battery cable.
7. Turn the ignition switch to **RUN** and make sure that the AIR BAG warning lamp flashes seven times and then shuts off. If the warning lamp does not shut off, make sure that the wiring is properly connected. If the light remains on, take the vehicle to a reputable repair facility for service.

HEATER

Blower Motor

REMOVAL & INSTALLATION

See Figures 9, 10, 11, 12 and 13

1. Disconnect the negative battery cable.
2. If equipped, remove the Vehicle Control Module (VCM) from the engine compartment.
3. Remove the coolant recovery reservoir.
4. Disconnect the blower motor cooling tube.
5. Disengage the electrical connector(s) from the blower motor, as necessary.
6. Remove the blower motor-to-case screws, then carefully withdraw the blower motor from the case.

To install:

7. Install the blower motor to the case and secure using the retaining screws.
8. Engage the electrical connector(s) to the motor, as necessary.

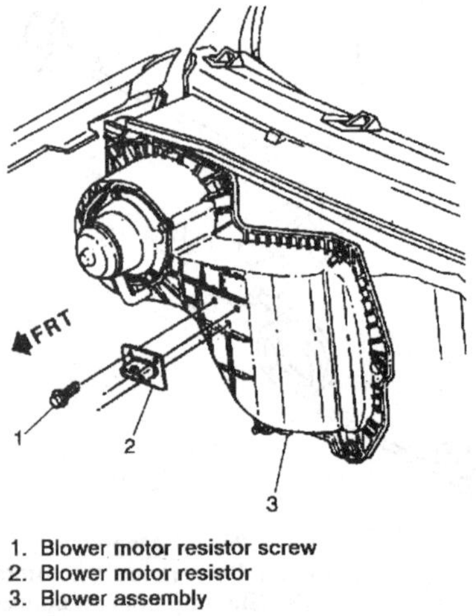

Fig. 9 Blower motor assembly and resistor locations

88456p01

Fig. 10 Remove the VCM from the engine compartment

88456p02

Fig. 11 Disengage the blower motor electrical connection

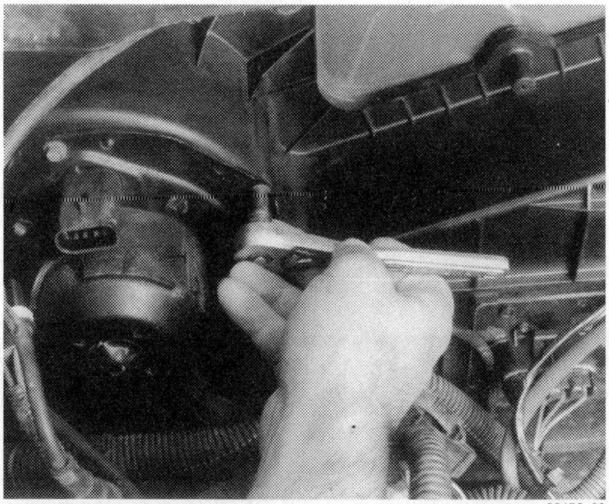
88456p03

Fig. 12 Unfasten and remove the blower motor retainers

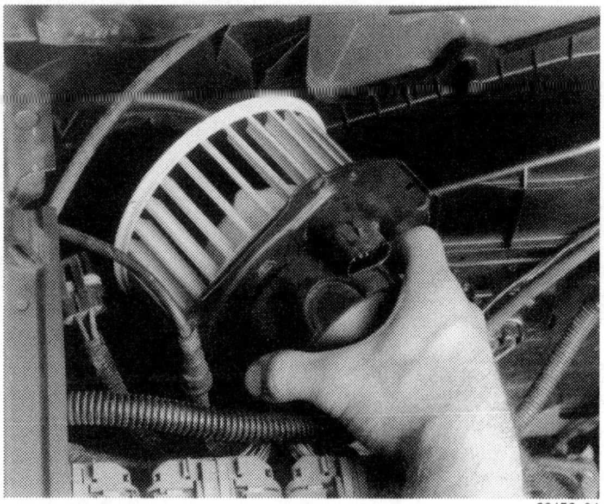
88456p04

Fig. 13 Remove the blower motor from the housing assembly

9. If moved on early model vehicles, reposition and secure the A/C vacuum tank.
10. Connect the blower motor cooling tube.
11. Install the coolant recovery reservoir, then if equipped, install the VCM.
12. Connect the negative battery cable.

Heater Core

The heater core is removable from under the right side of the instrument panel.

REMOVAL & INSTALLATION

1994 Vehicles

See Figure 14

1. Disconnect the negative battery cable and properly drain the engine cooling system to a level below the heater core.
2. Disconnect the heater hoses from the core tubes near the cowl.

The instrument panel carrier is designed not only to provide access to parts through removal of the carrier components, but the carrier will also tilt downward as a complete assembly to allow access from the top. If this is desired, remove the retainer screws along the top and bottom of the carrier assembly (refer to the figure). The instrument panel will then tilt as an assembly into the cab. It is necessary to unbolt and lower the steering column from the carrier to allow for maximum movement of the instrument panel.

3. The instrument panel must be removed or repositioned for access to the heater core case. Unbolt and either tilt the instrument panel forward or disengage the instrument panel components and remove the panel from the vehicle. In most cases, tilting the panel forward should be sufficient for the necessary access, but if necessary remove the panel refer to Section 10 in this manual.

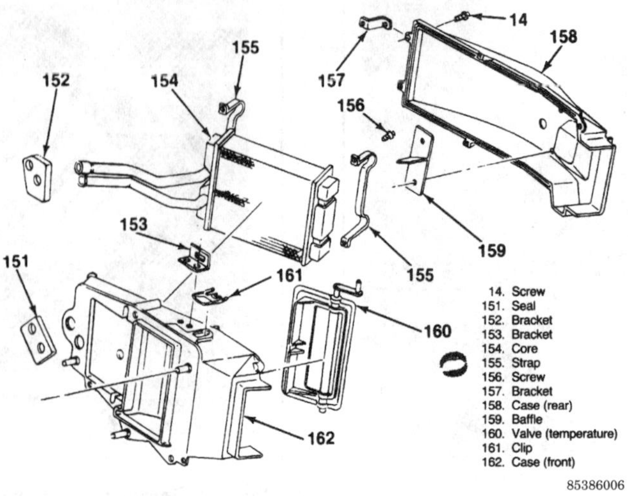

Fig. 14 Exploded view of a common heater core and case assembly

4. Unfasten the heater core rear case retaining screws, then remove the rear case for access to the heater core.
5. Loosen the retainers and remove the heater core retaining straps.
6. Remove the heater core and seals.

To install:

7. Install the heater core and seals, taking care not to damage the core tubes when inserting them through the cowl.
8. Install and secure the core retaining straps.
9. Install the rear case and secure using the screws.
10. Reposition and secure the instrument panel and components. Tighten the cowl screws to 17 inch lbs. (1.9 Nm) and the lower instrument panel screws to 66 inch lbs. (7.5 Nm).
11. Connect the heater hoses to the core tubes.
12. Connect the negative battery cable, then properly refill the engine cooling system.
13. Run the engine at normal operating temperature, then check for leaks.

Control Panel and Blower Switch

REMOVAL & INSTALLATION

See Figures 15, 16 and 17

1. Disconnect the negative battery cable.
2. Remove the instrument panel trim plate.

Most dash trim plates on these vehicles are retained by screws and/or snap fasteners. Make sure all screws are removed before attempting to remove the trim plate. If retained by snap fasteners, it may be necessary to pry the plate loose, BUT take care not to force and break the usually fragile plastic pieces.

3. Remove the control panel-to-instrument panel screws, then pull the control panel from the instrument panel.
4. Disengage the vacuum hoses and electrical connectors from the control panel. Make sure each connection may be only made 1 way, or tag hoses/wires and cables before removal.

Fig. 15 Remove the trim plate from the instrument panel

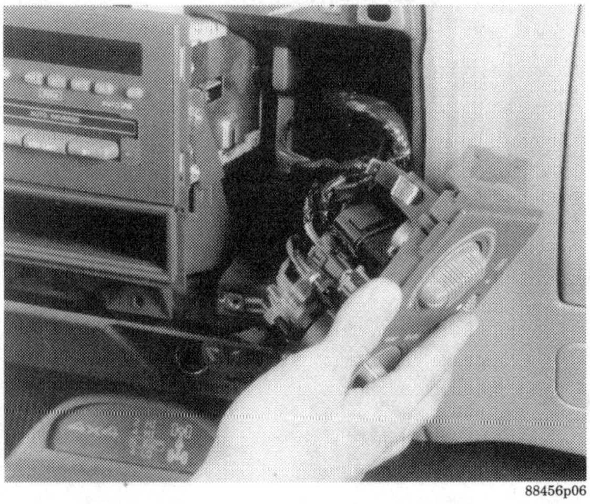

Fig. 16 Unfasten the retainers and remove the control head from the instrument panel

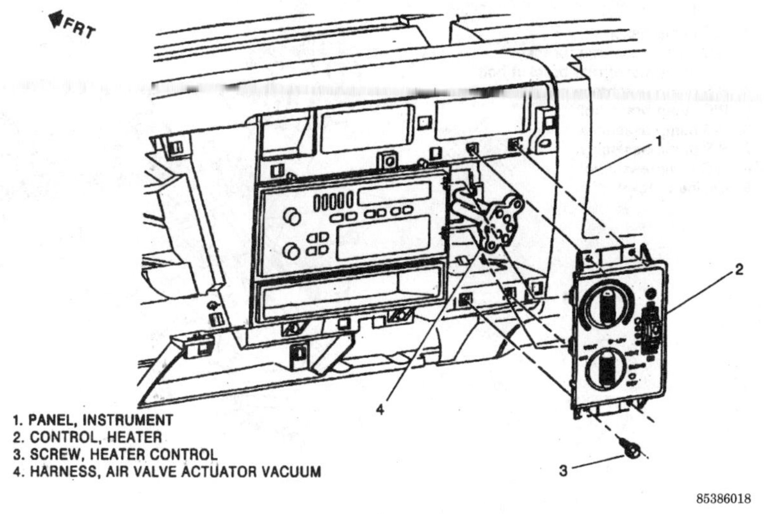

Fig. 17 Common control head assembly

5. Remove the control panel assembly from the vehicle.

To install:

6. Engage the electrical connections and vacuum lines to the control panel.
7. Install the control panel and fasten the retaining screws.
8. Install the trim plate by either fastening the retaining screws or snapping the clips back into place.
9. Connect the negative battery cable and check for proper panel operation.

AIR CONDITIONER

➡Be sure to consult the laws in your area before servicing the air conditioning system. In most areas, it is illegal to perform repairs involving refrigerant unless the work is done by a certified technician. Also, it is quite likely that you will not be able to purchase refrigerant without proof of certification.

Discharging, evacuating and charging the air conditioning system must be performed by a properly trained and certified mechanic in a facility equipped with refrigerant recovery/recycling equipment that meets SAE standards for the type of system to be serviced.

If you don't have access to the necessary equipment, we recommend that you take your vehicle to a reputable service station to have the work done. If you still wish to perform repairs on the vehicle, have them discharge the system, then take your vehicle home and perform the necessary work. When you are finished, return the vehicle to the station for evacuation and charging. Just be sure to cap ALL A/C system fittings immediately after opening them and keep them protected until the system is recharged.

Compressor

REMOVAL & INSTALLATION

See Figures 18, 19 and 20

1. Disconnect the negative battery cable. Discharge and recover the refrigerant from the air conditioning system.
2. Remove the drive belt.
3. Disconnect the refrigerant lines at the compressor. Cap all openings!
4. Disengage the electrical connections.
5. Disconnect the compressor and condenser hose assembly.
6. Remove the mounting bolts and nuts and lift the compressor from the bracket.
7. Drain and measure the compressor oil.

To install:

8. Replace the compressor oil as detailed later and position the compressor on the bracket. Tighten the bolts to 24 ft. lbs. (33 Nm) on the 4.3L engine and on the 2.2L engine tighten the compressor bolts to 37 ft. lbs. (50 Nm) and the rear bracket bolts to 23 ft. lbs. (31 Nm).
9. Engage the compressor and condenser hose assembly.
10. Connect the electrical leads and the refrigerant lines.
11. Install and adjust the belt.
12. Connect the battery cable. Evacuate and charge the air conditioning system.

Condenser

REMOVAL & INSTALLATION

See Figures 21, 22 and 23

1. Disconnect the negative battery cable. Discharge and recover the refrigerant from the air conditioning system.
2. Remove the upper fan shroud.
3. Remove the radiator.
4. Disconnect the compressor and condenser hose assembly from the condenser.

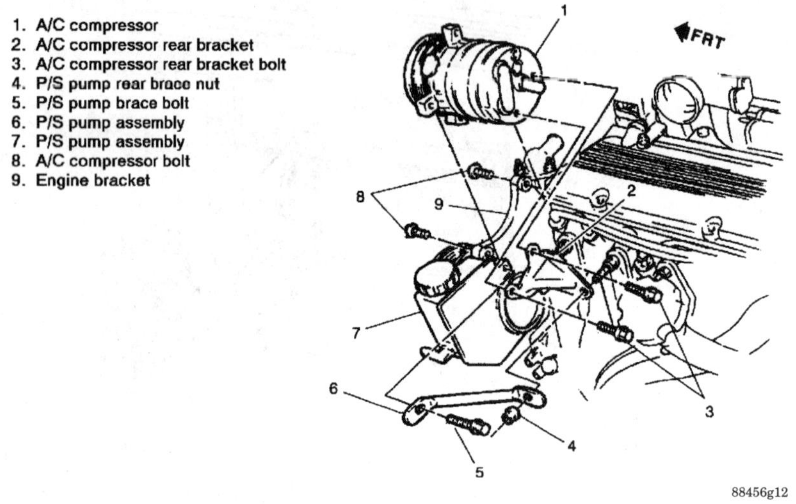

Fig. 18 Common compressor mounting — 2.2L engine shown

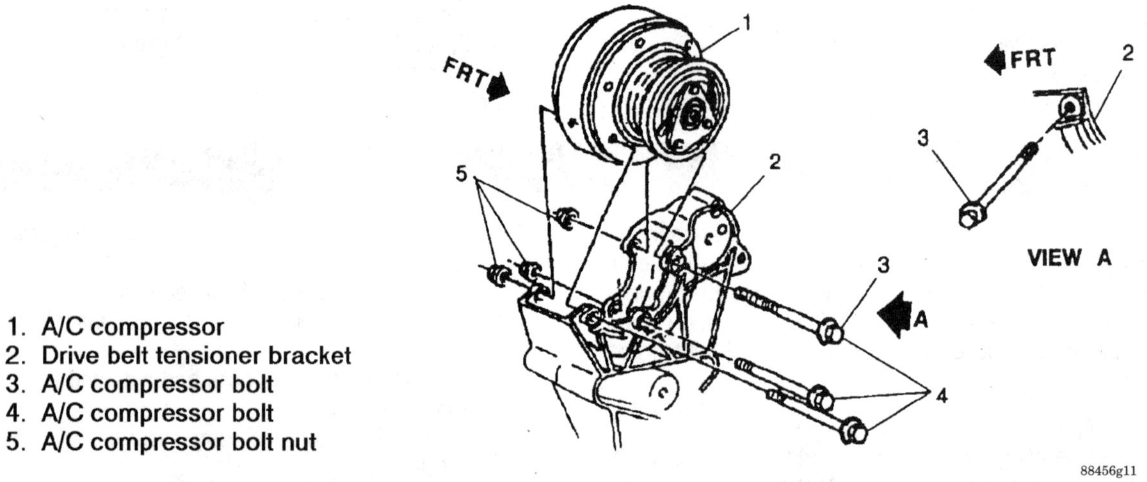

Fig. 19 Common compressor mounting — 1994-95 4.3L engine shown

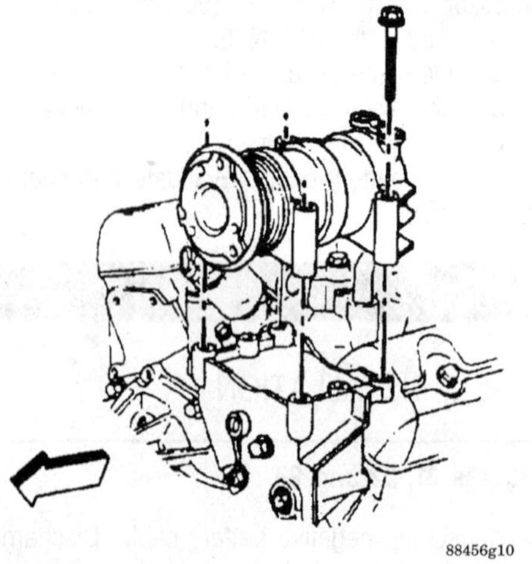

Fig. 20 Common compressor mounting — 1996 4.3L engine shown

5. Disengage the evaporator tube from the condenser.

6. Unfasten the insulator retainer bolts and remove the upper insulator retainers.

7. Remove the condenser from the vehicle.

To install:

8. Install the condenser and the upper insulator retainers and bolts. Tighten the bolts to 21 inch lbs. (2.4 Nm).

9. Engage the evaporator tube and the compressor and condenser hoses to the condenser.

10. Install the radiator and the upper fan shroud.

11. Connect the battery cable. Evacuate and charge the air conditioning system.

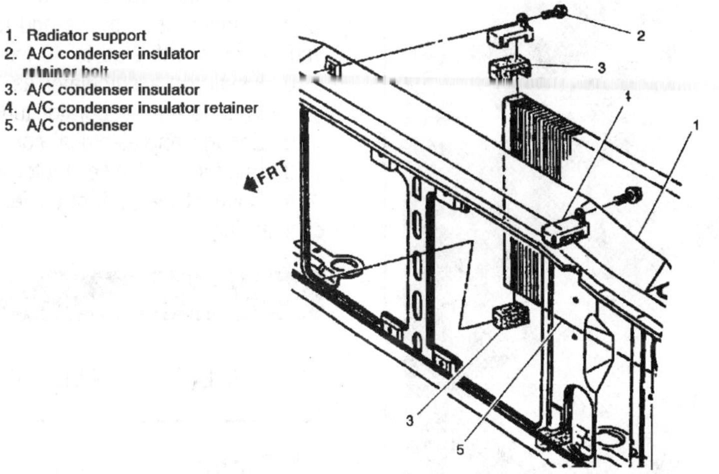

88456g13

Fig. 21 View of a common condenser assembly

88456p07

Fig. 22 Remove the upper radiator cover

Evaporator Core

REMOVAL & INSTALLATION

➧ **See Figures 24, 25, 26 and 27**

1. Disconnect the negative battery cable. Discharge and recover the refrigerant from the air conditioning system.
2. Disengage the blower motor resistor.
3. Tag and disengage any electrical connections that are in the way.
4. Disconnect the evaporator tube from the evaporator.
5. Remove the accumulator as outlined in this section.
6. Remove the evaporator and blower module screws, nuts and the evaporator and blower module.
7. Remove the screws and separate the case sections, then remove the core.

To install:

8. Install the core, engage the case sections and fasten the screws.

88456p08

Fig. 23 Removing the condenser assembly from the vehicle

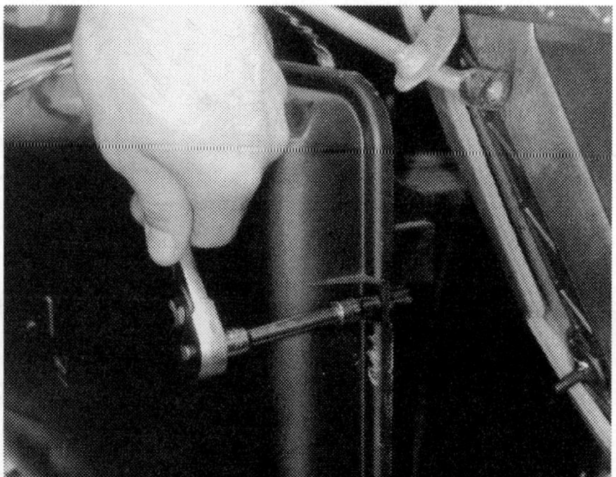

88456p19

Fig. 24 Unfasten the evaporator case's retaining screws . . .

Fig. 25 . . . then separate the case sections

Fig. 26 Loosen and remove the evaporator core retainers, then remove the core

9. Install the evaporator and blower assembly into the vehicle and tighten the screws and nuts to 22 inch. lbs. (2.5 Nm) and the bolts and stud to 40 inch. lbs. (4.5 Nm).
10. Install the accumulator as outlined in this section.
11. Engage the evaporator tube to the evaporator.
12. Engage any electrical connections that were unplugged.
13. Engage the blower motor resistor.
14. Connect the battery cable. Evacuate and charge the air conditioning system.

Accumulator

REMOVAL & INSTALLATION

2.2L Engines

➧ See Figure 28

1. Disconnect the negative battery cable. Discharge and recover the refrigerant from the air conditioning system.
2. Disengage the compressor and condenser hoses from the accumulator, then disengage the evaporator and accumulator hoses from the accumulator.
3. Unfasten the accumulator clamp bolt, then remove the accumulator from the clamp and vehicle.

To install:

4. Install the accumulator into the clamp and tighten the clamp bolt to 88 inch lbs. (10 Nm).
5. Engage the evaporator and accumulator and the compressor and condenser hoses to the accumulator.
6. Connect the battery cable. Evacuate and charge the air conditioning system.

4.3L Engines

1. Disconnect the negative battery cable. Discharge and recover the refrigerant from the air conditioning system.
2. Disconnect the evaporator from the accumulator.
3. Disengage the compressor hose from the accumulator, then remove the O-ring seals and cap or plug the open lines.

1. A/C evaporator and blower module gasket
2. A/C evaporator and blower module stud
3. Heater screw
4. Dash and cowl panel
5. A/C evaporator and blower module nut
6. A/C evaporator and blower module nut
7. A/C evaporator and blower module bolt
8. A/C evaporator and blower module

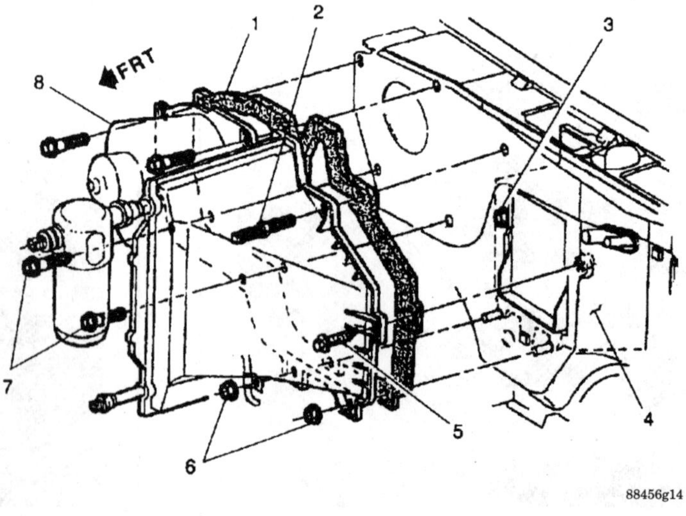

Fig. 27 Exploded view of the evaporator and blower module

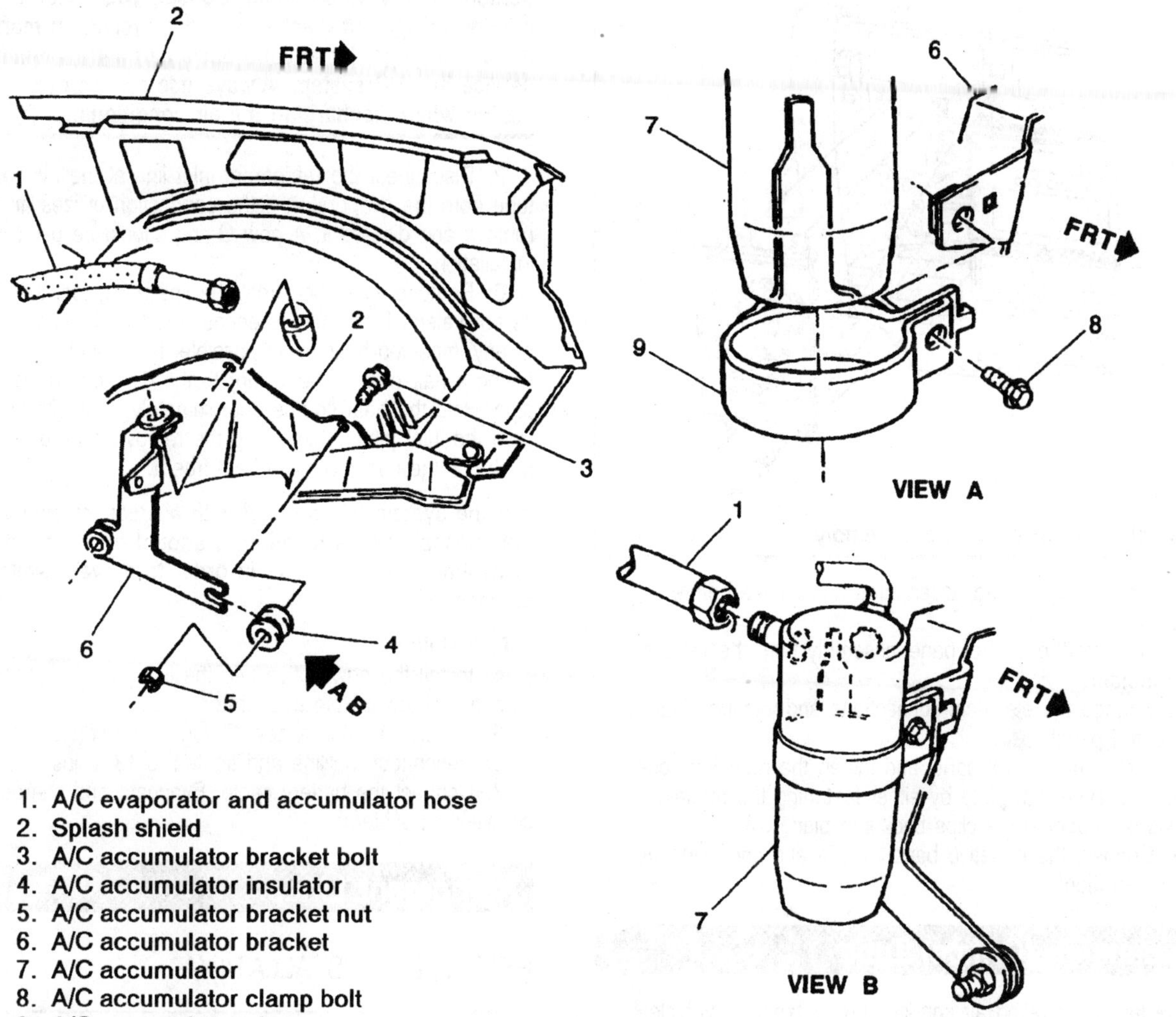

1. A/C evaporator and accumulator hose
2. Splash shield
3. A/C accumulator bracket bolt
4. A/C accumulator insulator
5. A/C accumulator bracket nut
6. A/C accumulator bracket
7. A/C accumulator
8. A/C accumulator clamp bolt
9. A/C accumulator clamp
10. Left front fender

Fig. 28 View of the accumulator assembly — 2.2L engines

4. Tag and disengage any electrical connections that are in the way.
5. Remove the screw bracket and the accumulator. Install caps if the accumulator is not being replaced.

To install:

6. Install the accumulator, bracket and screw.
7. Engage any electrical connections that were unplugged during removal.
8. Install new O-ring seal and engage the compressor hose to the accumulator. Tighten the hose to 30 ft. lbs. (41 Nm).
9. Engage the evaporator to the accumulator and tighten the evaporator to 30 ft. lbs. (41 Nm).
10. Connect the battery cable. Evacuate and charge the air conditioning system.

Control Panel and Blower Switch

REMOVAL & INSTALLATION

See Figure 29

1. Disconnect the negative battery cable.
2. Remove the instrument panel trim plate.

➡Most dash trim plates on these vehicles are retained by screws and/or snap fasteners. Make sure all screws are removed before attempting to remove the trim plate. If retained by snap fasteners, it may be necessary to pry the plate loose, BUT take care not to force and break the usually fragile plastic pieces.

3. Remove the control panel-to-instrument panel screws, then pull the control panel from the instrument panel.
4. Disengage the vacuum hoses and electrical connectors from the control panel. Make sure each connection may be

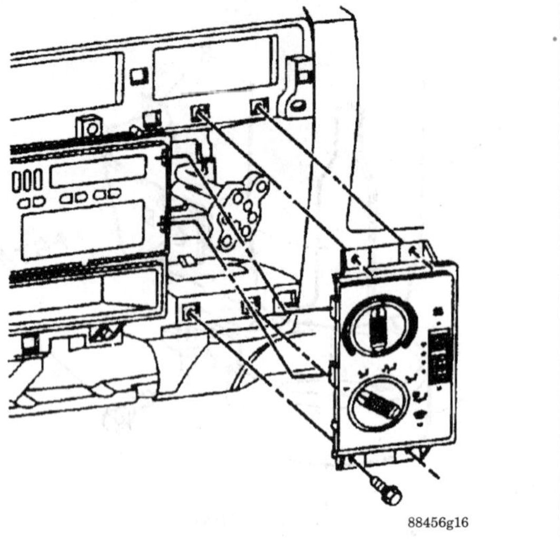

Fig. 29 View of the control assembly

only made 1 way, or tag hoses/wires and cables before removal.

5. Remove the control panel assembly from the vehicle.

To install:

6. Engage the electrical connections and vacuum lines to the control panel.
7. Install the control panel and fasten the retaining screws.
8. Install the trim plate by either fastening the retaining screws or snapping the clips back into place.
9. Connect the negative battery cable and check for proper panel operation.

Expansion (Orifice) Tube

The factory installed air conditioning systems for vehicles covered by this manual utilize an expansion (orifice) tube. The orifice is used to regulate the flow of refrigerant to the evaporator, so is placed somewhere in-line between the condenser and the evaporator. It is designed to ensure that the evaporator remains as full of liquid refrigerant, as possible without allowing any liquid to pass into the compressor suction line. The orifice is usually found in the evaporator inlet, often at the liquid line connection.

REMOVAL & INSTALLATION

See Figure 30

➡An orifice tube removal and installation tool (J-26549) is required to perform this procedure.

1. Disconnect the negative battery cable. Discharge and recover the refrigerant from the air conditioning system.

✲✲CAUTION

Please refer to Section 1 of this manual before discharging/recovering the A/C system or disconnecting air conditioning lines. Damage to the air conditioning system or personal injury could result. Consult your local laws concerning refrigerant discharge and recycling. In many areas it may be illegal for anyone but a certified technician to service the A/C system. Always use an approved recovery station when discharging the air conditioning.

2. Disconnect the refrigerant inlet line at the evaporator tube from the evaporator. If the connection utilizes an O-ring, remove and discard it. A new O-ring should be used during installation.
3. Remove the orifice from the line using tool J-26549 or its equivalent. If difficulty is encountered, first remove as much of any impacted residue as possible, then carefully apply heat (using a hair drier or heat gun) to the dimples on the inlet pipe. Hold the heat source approximately 1/4 in. (7mm) away from the inlet pipe, while using the removal tool to twist and push-pull the component to help free it.

➡If the system is equipped with a pressure switch near the expansion tube location, it should be removed PRIOR to heating the connection in order to prevent switch damage.

To install:

4. Install the new orifice into the line with the shorter screen end toward the evaporator.
5. If used, position a new O-ring to the connection.
6. Reconnect the line and tighten to 13 ft. lbs. (17 Nm).
7. Connect the battery cable. Evacuate and charge the air conditioning system.

Refrigerant Lines

REMOVAL & INSTALLATION

See Figures 31 and 32

1. Disconnect the negative battery cable. Discharge and recover the refrigerant from the air conditioning system.

➡For some vehicles it may be necessary to remove the radiator grille for access to the lines.

2. Remove the banjo bolt or loosen the fitting, depending on the application, then disconnect the line at either end. Immediately plug all openings in the system to prevent system contamination and damage.
3. Remove any clips attaching the pipe to the vehicle, then remove the pipe assembly.

To install:

4. Position the pipe in the vehicle, then remove the plug from 1 end and secure the fitting right away to minimize atmospheric exposure. Remove the plug from the other end and secure that fitting. Make sure the fittings or banjo bolts are properly tightened.
5. Install any clips attaching the pipe.
6. If removed install the radiator grille.
7. Connect the battery cable. Evacuate and charge the air conditioning system.

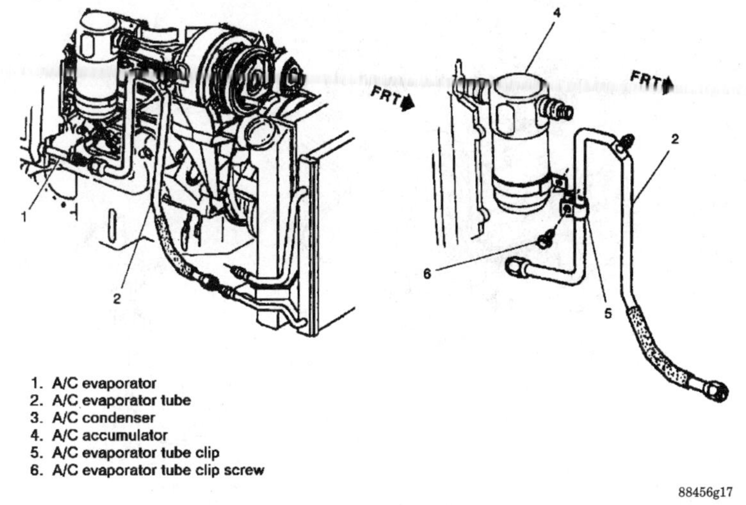

Fig. 30 View of the evaporator tube and related components

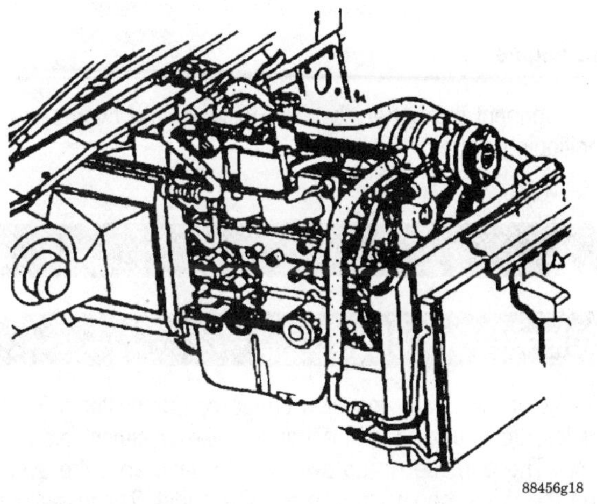

Fig. 31 View of the compressor and condenser hose routing — 2.2L engine

Temperature Valve Actuator

REMOVAL & INSTALLATION

The temperature valve actuator is located on top of the heater case.

1. Disconnect the negative battery cable.
2. Remove the instrument panel. Refer to Section 10 in this manual for this procedure.
3. Disengage the electrical connectors.
4. Unfasten the retaining screws and remove the temperature valve actuator.

To Install:

5. Install the temperature valve actuator and tighten the retaining screws.
6. Engage the electrical connectors.
7. Install the instrument panel. Refer to Section 10 in this manual for this procedure.
8. Connect the negative battery cable.

Center Outlet Duct and Defroster Valve Vacuum Actuator

REMOVAL & INSTALLATION

1. Disconnect the negative battery cable.
2. Remove the instrument panel. Refer to Section 10 in this manual for this procedure.
3. Disengage the vacuum hose connector(s) at the center outlet duct actuator and/or defroster valve actuator, by sliding the tab of the connector past the L-shaped bend in the actuator vacuum tube, then slide the hose connector off the tube while continuing to hold the connector tab.
4. Remove the outlet duct actuator and/or defroster valve actuator and disengage the linkage.

To install:

5. Install the outlet duct actuator and/or defroster valve actuator and engage the linkage.
6. Engage the vacuum hose connection(s).
7. Install the instrument panel. Refer to Section 10 in this manual for this procedure.
8. Connect the negative battery cable.

Cycling Clutch Switch

REMOVAL & INSTALLATION

1. Disconnect the negative battery cable. Discharge and recover the refrigerant from the air conditioning system.
2. Detach the electrical connector from the switch in the rear head of the compressor.
3. Remove the switch from the compressor. Remove the O-ring seal from the switch cavity.

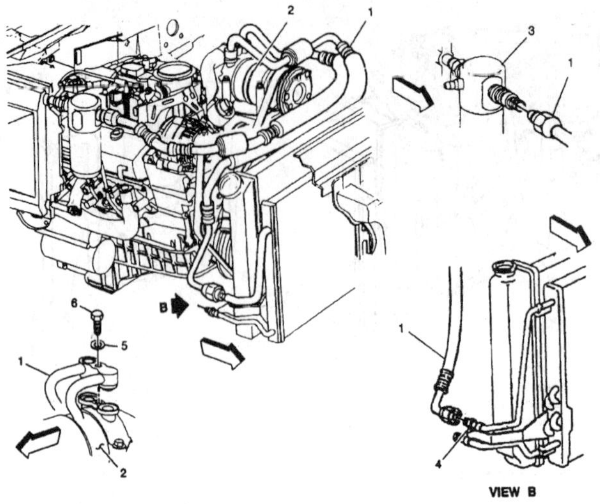

Fig. 32 View of the compressor and condenser hose routing — 4.3L engine

To install:

4. Install the switch using new O-ring seals, then engage the electrical connections.

5. Connect the battery cable. Evacuate and charge the air conditioning system.

CRUISE CONTROL

Cruise Control Actuator Switch

REMOVAL & INSTALLATION

The cruise control actuator switch on most S/T vehicles with factory or dealer installed systems is part of the multi-function lever located on the steering column.

1. Disconnect the negative battery cable.
2. Unsnap and remove the housing cover cap from the steering column for access to the wiring.
3. Disengage the cruise control wiring connectors from the column wiring harness.

➡Before removing the lever from the column, make sure the turn signal switch is in the OFF/center position.

4. Grasp the lever and remove it from the steering column by pulling straight outward and from the turn signal switch.

To install:

5. With the switch in the center/OFF position, carefully push the lever into the turn signal switch on the column.
6. Engage the cruise control wiring connectors to the column wiring.
7. Snap the housing cover cap into position on the column.
8. Connect the negative battery cable and check for proper operation.

Release Switches

All factory or dealer installed cruise control systems for these vehicles are equipped with either a brake or clutch release switch. The purpose of the switch is to deactivate the system when the driver begins to depress the pedal. These switches are self-adjusting when installed properly. The switch used on these vehicles is bolted into position, so no adjustment is necessary or possible.

REMOVAL & INSTALLATION

➧ See Figure 33

1. Disconnect the negative battery cable.
2. Disengage the necessary electrical connector(s).
3. Remove the bracket bolt, then remove the switch from the pedal bracket.

To install:

4. Install the switch to the bracket and secure using the retaining bolt. Tighten the bolt to 13 ft. lbs. (17 Nm).
5. Engage the necessary electrical connector(s).
6. Connect the negative battery cable and verify proper switch operation.

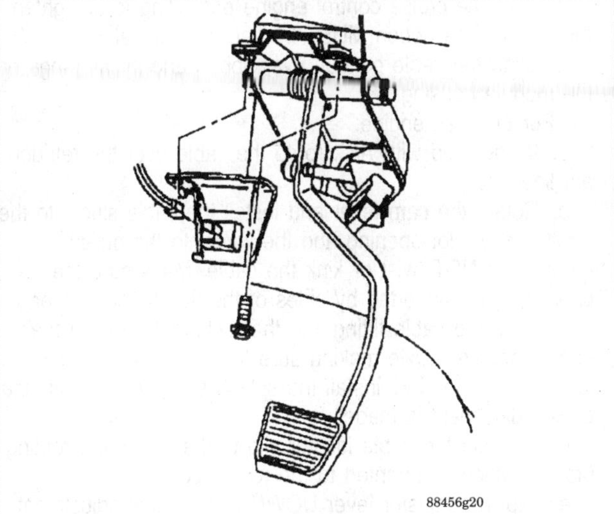

Fig. 33 View of the release switch location

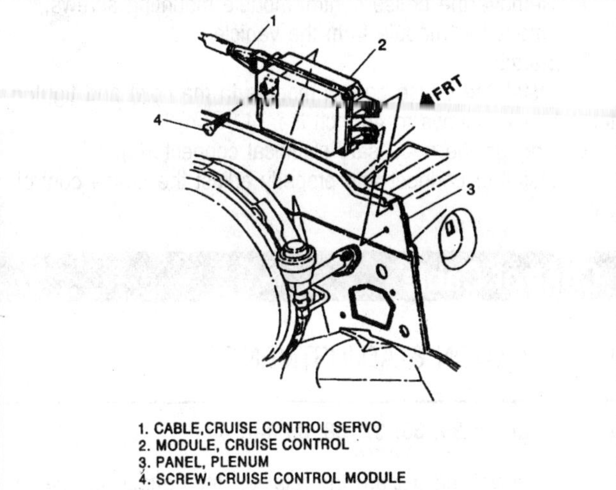

Fig. 34 Cruise control module mounting

Vehicle Speed Sensor (VSS)

REMOVAL & INSTALLATION

1. Disconnect the negative battery cable.
2. Raise and safely support the vehicle.
3. Detach the VSS electrical lead from the transmission.
4. Unfasten the retaining bolts, then remove the sensor from the housing. Remove and discard the sensor O-ring.

To install:

5. Insert a new O-ring, then install the sensor and tighten the bolts.
6. Engage the electrical connection, then lower the vehicle.
7. Connect the negative battery cable.

Cruise Control Module

REMOVAL & INSTALLATION

See Figures 34, 35, 36, 37, 38, 39 and 40

The S/T series trucks are equipped with a fully electronic cruise control system (no vacuum servo or switches). The center of the system is the cruise control module which is mounted to the left side of the cowl, near the brake booster. The module includes an electronic controller and a stepper motor to control throttle position through manipulation of the cruise control cable.

1. Disconnect the negative battery cable.
2. Disconnect or remove the cruise control cable.
3. Disengage the necessary electrical connector(s).

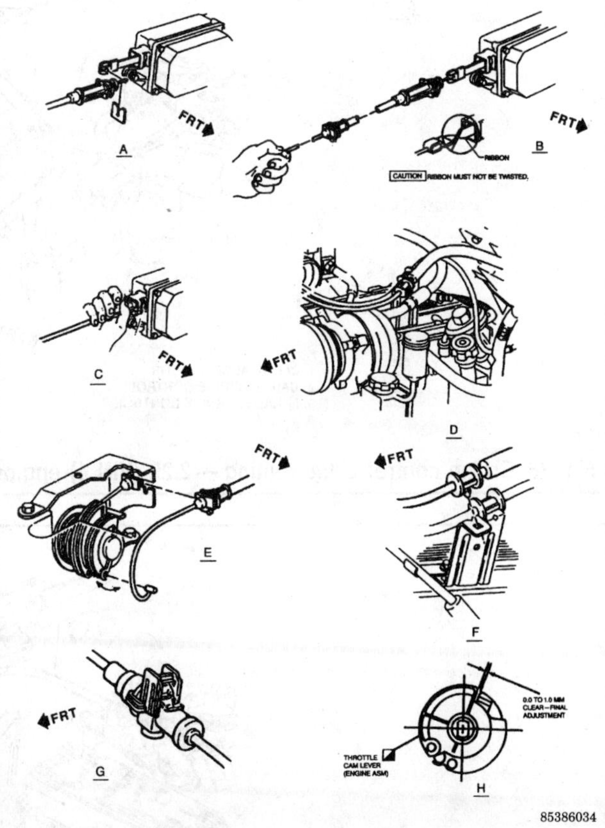

Fig. 35 Cruise control cable installation and adjustment — 2.2L (VIN 4) engine

4. Remove the cruise control module mounting screws, then remove the module from the vehicle.

To install:

5. Install the cruise control module to the cowl and tighten the retaining screws to 40 inch lbs. (4.5 Nm).
6. Engage the necessary electrical connector(s).
7. Install or connect and properly adjust the cruise control cable.

Control Cable

INSTALLATION & ADJUSTMENT

See Figures 35, 36, 37, 38, 39 and 40

1. Remove and discard the retainer, then attach the cable bead to the module ribbon end fitting.
2. For the 4.3L (VINS W and X) engine:
   a. Snap the cruise cable fitting over ferrule on end of conduit until an audible "snap" is heard.
   b. Pull the cruise control cable engine end fitting until the cable is taut.
   c. Turn the cruise control engine end fitting to straighten the ribbon. The ribbon MUST be flat and vertical.
   d. Slide the cable conduit over ribbon and install tangs on the module housing.
3. For the 2.2L engine:
   a. If equipped with A/C, route the cable over the refrigerant line.
   b. Rotate the cam lever and install the cable slug into the throttle lever slot opening and the wire into the pulley groove. Do NOT twist or kink the cable. Make sure the cable slug is supported by sides of the throttle cam lever.
   c. Slide the cable fitting into the rectangular slot in the engine bracket, while making sure the tab snaps into the locking slot. Do NOT install the splash shield cover until final cable adjustment is made.
   d. Connect the cable locator clip to the top of the routing bracket which is mounted to the rocker cover.
   e. Flip the adjuster lever DOWN to lock final adjustment to the cable.
   f. Adjustment should result in a clearance of 0-0.39 in. (0-10mm) at the throttle cam lever. Refer to the illustration for details.

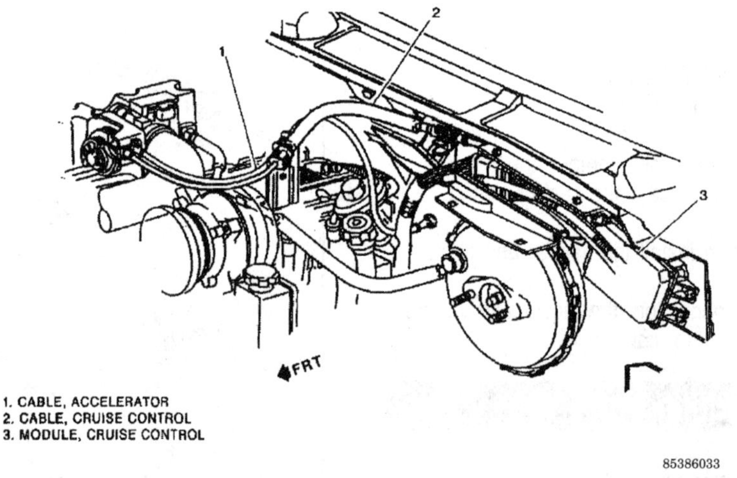

Fig. 36 Cruise control cable routing — 2.2L (VIN 4) engine

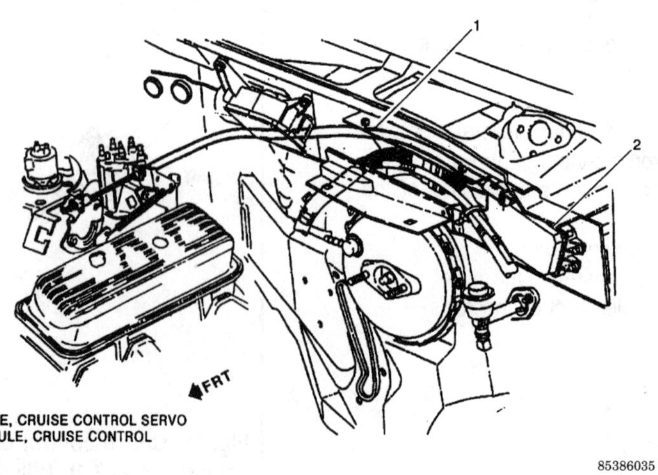

Fig. 37 Cruise control cable routing — 4.3L (VIN Z) engine

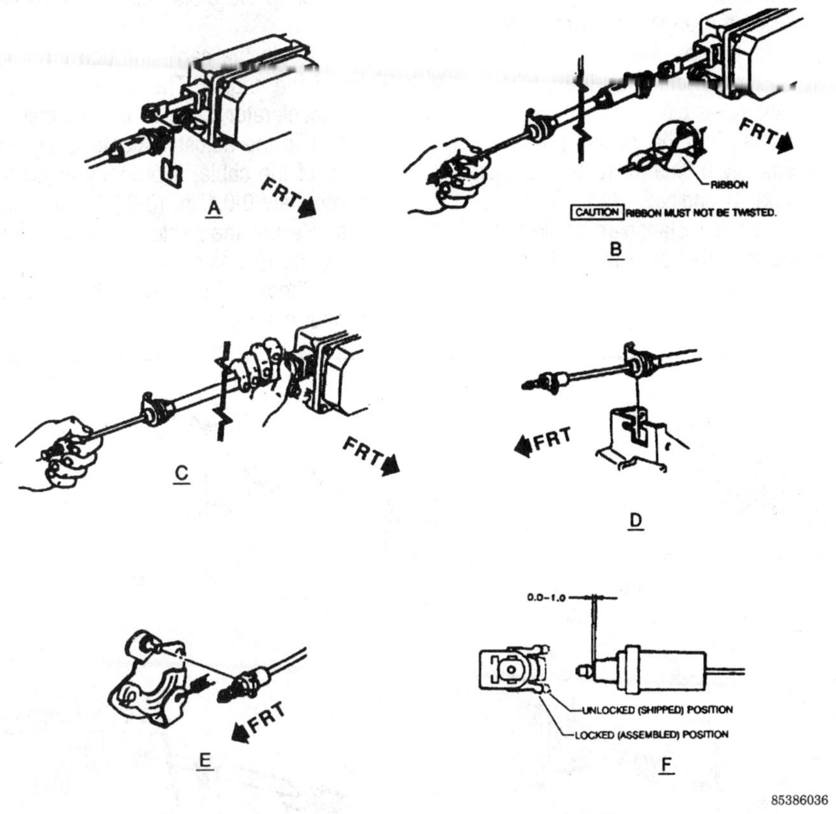

Fig. 38 Cruise control cable installation and adjustment — 4.3L (VIN Z) engine

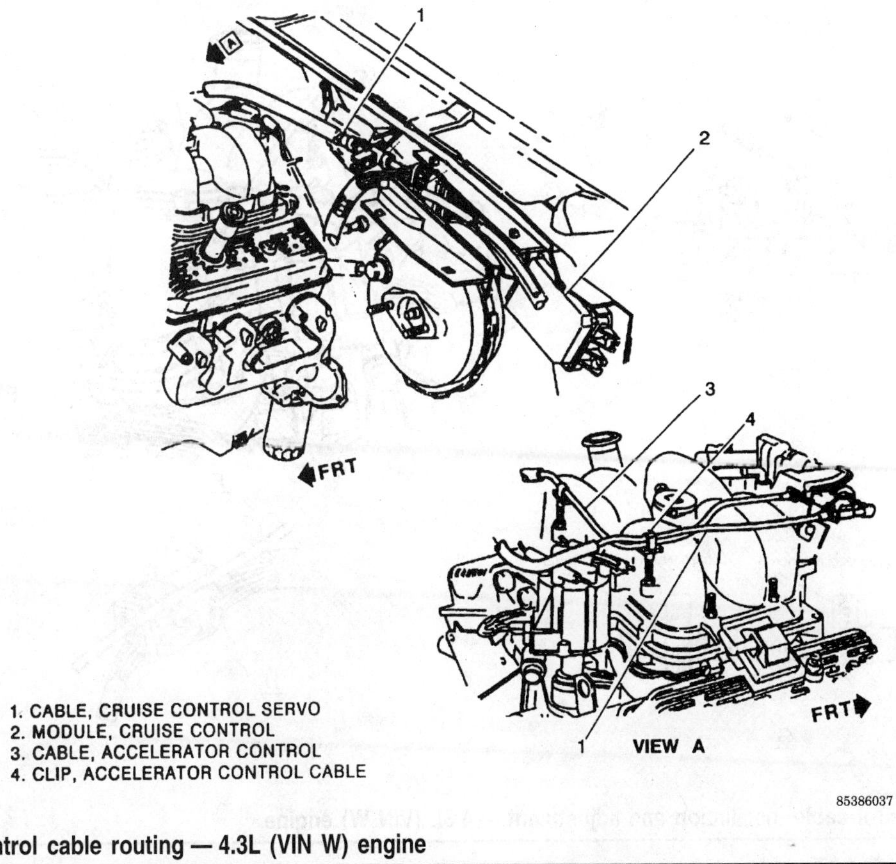

Fig. 39 Cruise control cable routing — 4.3L (VIN W) engine

4. For the 4.3L (VIN Z) engine:
   a. Install the cable conduit in the engine bracket, then press firmly until the tang locks into position.
   b. Rotate the cam lever rearward and snap the cable fitting securely over the throttle lever pin.
   c. Push the cable adjuster tab into the locking position. Check the cable for approximately 0-0.39 in. (0-10mm) lash.
5. For the 4.3L (VINS W and X) engine:
   a. Slide the cable fitting into the rectangular slot in the engine bracket, while making sure the tab snaps into the locking slot.
   b. Snap the cruise control cable fitting over the throttle lever pin.
   c. Route the cable through the retainer on right rear corner of the engine. The cruise control cable must route above the accelerator cable in the retainer.
   d. Flip the adjuster toggle lever in order to lock adjustment of the cable. If properly adjusted, there should be approximately 0-0.1 in. (0-0.25mm) of clearance.
   e. Secure the cable to the electrical junction connector using the retaining strap.
   f. Check to be sure all throttle linkage operates freely, without binding.

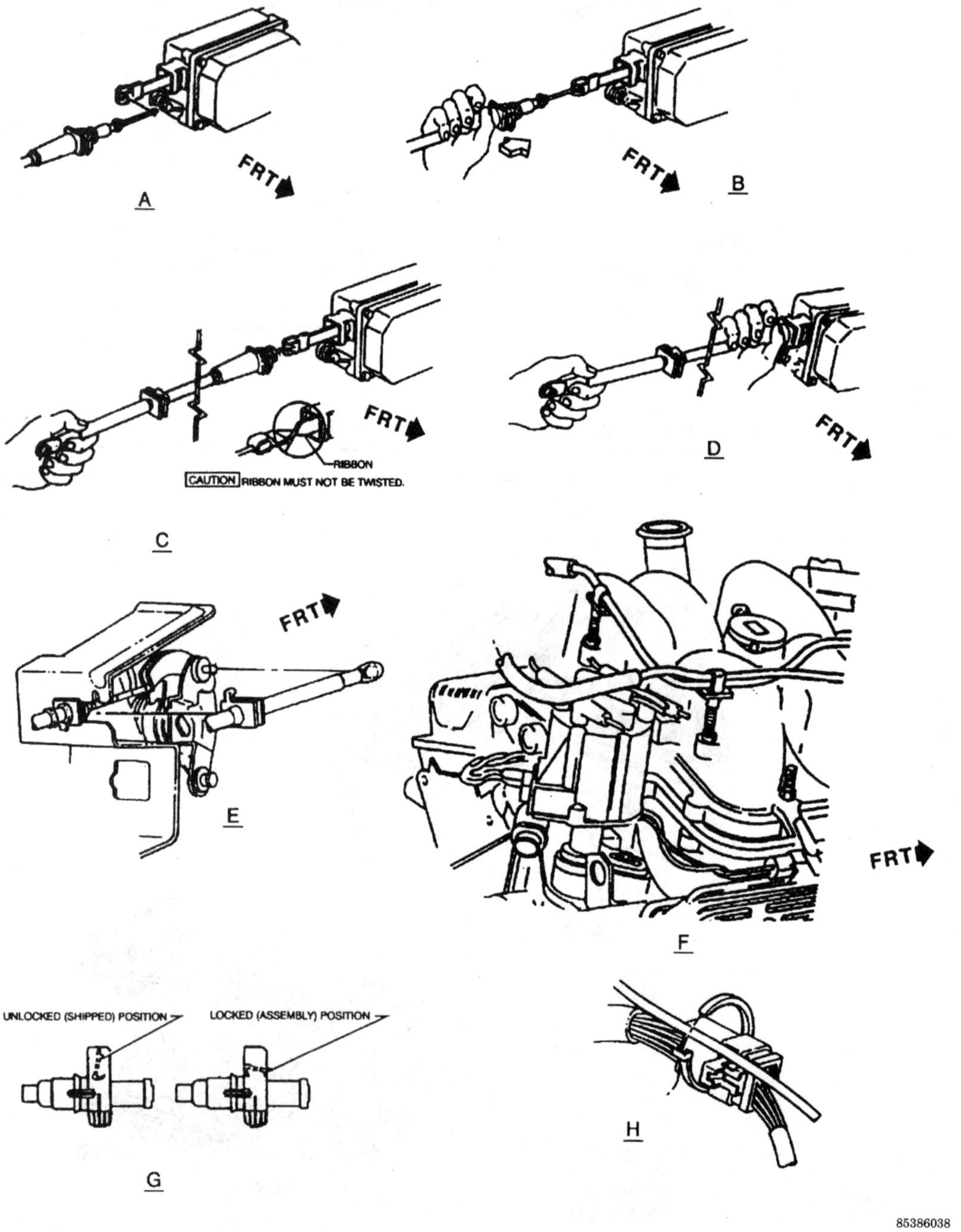

Fig. 40 Cruise control cable installation and adjustment — 4.3L (VIN W) engine

ENTERTAINMENT SYSTEMS

Radio

REMOVAL & INSTALLATION

➧ See Figures 41, 42 and 43

1. Disconnect the negative battery cable.
2. Remove the accessory trim plate.

➡Most dash trim plates on these vehicles are retained by screws and/or snap fasteners. Make sure all screws are removed before attempting to remove the trim plate. If retained by snap fasteners, it may be necessary to pry the plate loose, BUT take care not to force and break the usually fragile plastic pieces.

88456p05

Fig. 41 Remove the trim plate from the instrument panel

88456p09

Fig. 42 Unfasten and remove the radio retainers

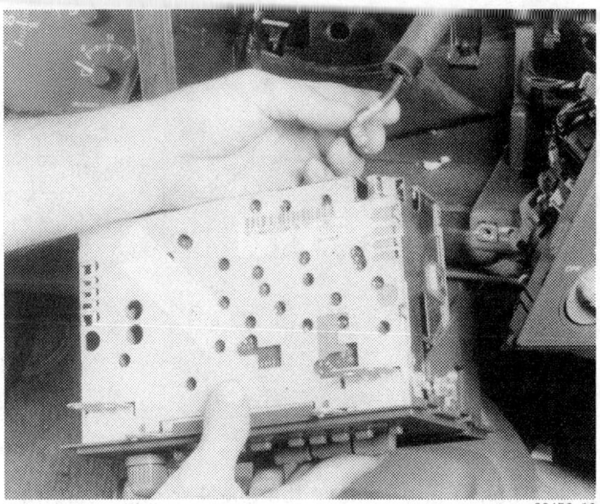
88456p10

Fig. 43 Slide the radio forward, then disengage the electrical connections and the antenna

3. Remove the heating/air conditioning control head. For details, please refer to the procedure in this section.
4. Remove the radio bracket-to-instrument panel bracket screws or nuts, then carefully pull the instrument panel center compartment forward with the radio.
5. Disengage the antenna lead and electrical connectors, as necessary.
6. Remove the radio from the vehicle.
7. Remove the radio retaining nuts and separate the radio from the instrument panel center compartment.

To install:

8. Install the radio to the instrument panel center compartment.
9. Position the radio in front of the instrument panel, then engage the necessary electrical connectors and antenna lead.
10. Insert the radio into the dash, then secure using the retainers.
11. Install the climate control head.
12. Install the accessory trim plate.

➡In order to prevent damage to the receiver, always connect the speaker wire to the receiver before applying power to it.

13. Connect the negative battery cable and enjoy the tunes.

Speakers

REMOVAL & INSTALLATION

Front

INSTRUMENT PANEL MOUNTED

➧ See Figures 44, 45, 46, 47, 48 and 49

1. Disconnect the negative battery cable

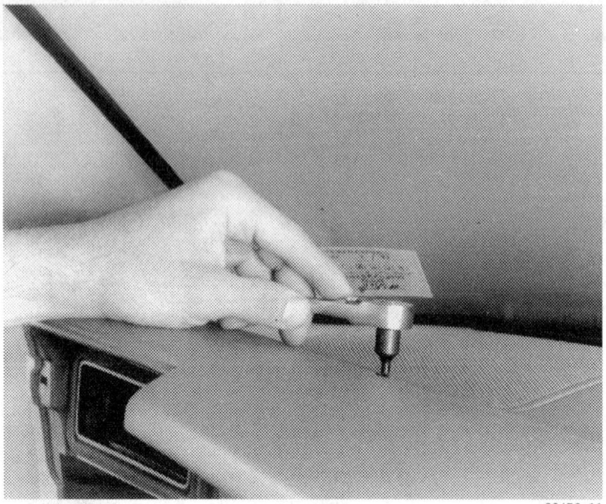

88456p11

Fig. 44 Loosen and remove the speaker grille screws

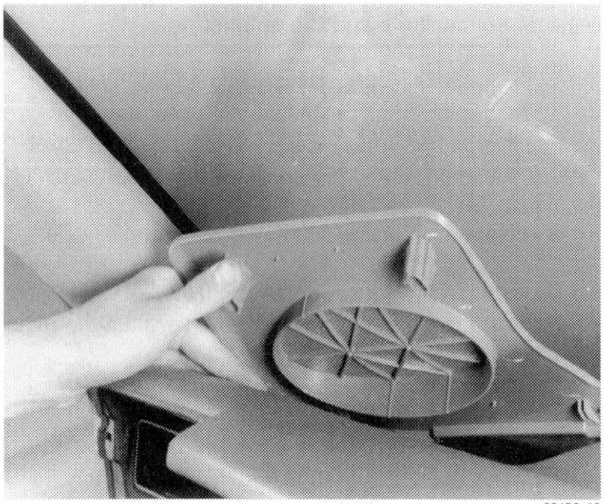

88456p12

Fig. 45 Remove the speaker grille

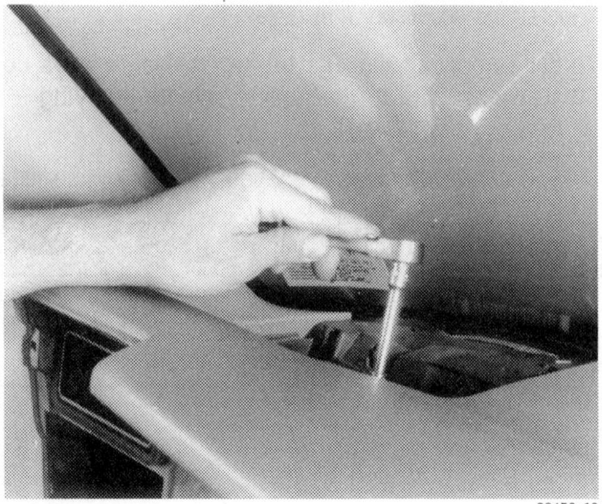

88456p13

Fig. 46 Remove the speaker-to-instrument panel retainers

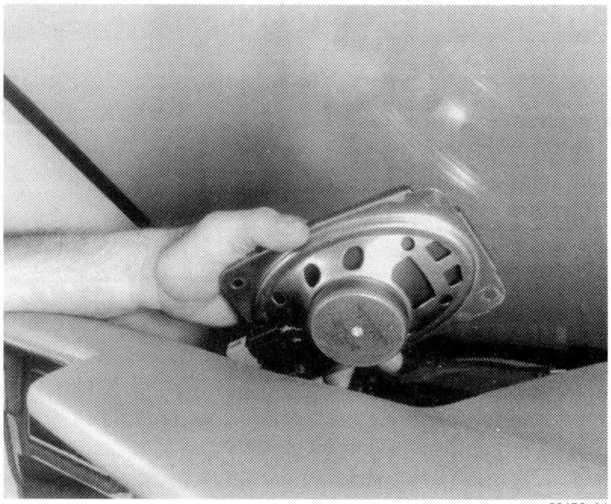

88456p14

Fig. 47 Lift the speaker from the instrument panel . . .

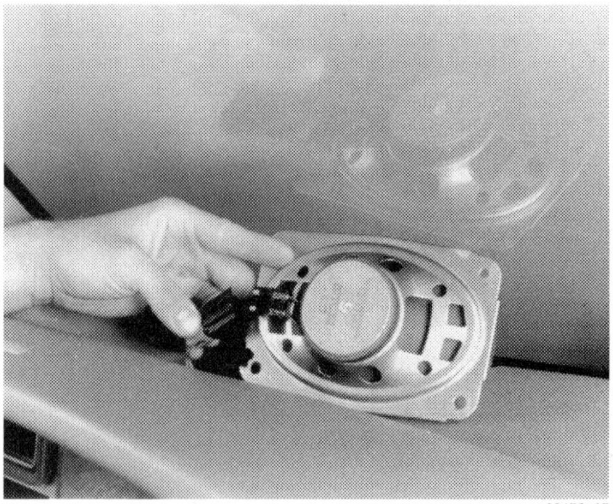

88456p15

Fig. 48 . . . then disengage the electrical connection and remove the speaker

2. Remove the front speaker grille screws, then lift and remove the grille.

➡On some models, the grille screws also retain the speaker. Always check to make sure that no additional fasteners are hidden under the grilles.

3. If equipped, remove the speaker-to-instrument panel retainers.
4. Lift the speaker and disengage the electrical connection(s), then remove the speaker from the vehicle.

To install:

5. Engage the speaker electrical connection(s), then install the speaker in the vehicle.
6. If equipped, install the speaker-to-instrument panel screws.
7. Install the speaker grille and tighten the screws.
8. Connect the negative battery cable.

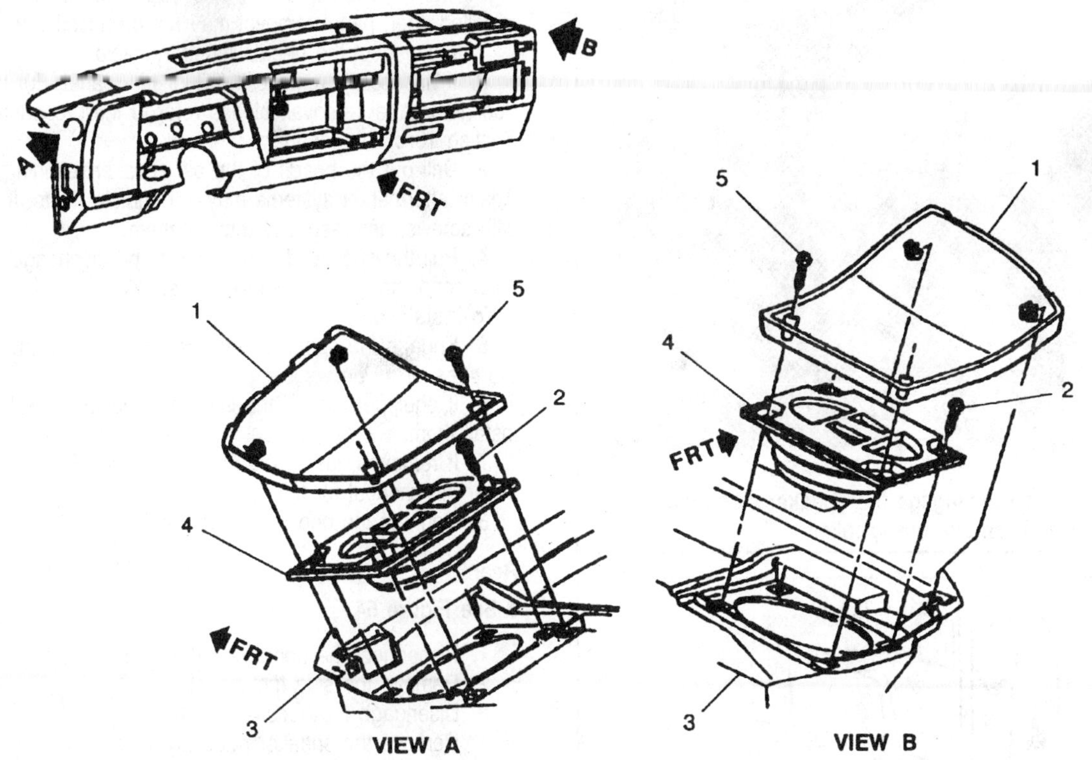

Fig. 49 Exploded view of the front (instrument panel) speaker mounting

DOOR MOUNTED

See Figures 50, 51, 52 and 53

Some trucks may be equipped with door mounted radio speakers. Access to factory mounted speakers on some vehicles usually requires removal of inner door trim panel. Aftermarket speakers may be mounted in a variety of ways, but will often not require trim panel removal. In order to save time, be sure removal of the panel is necessary before start-

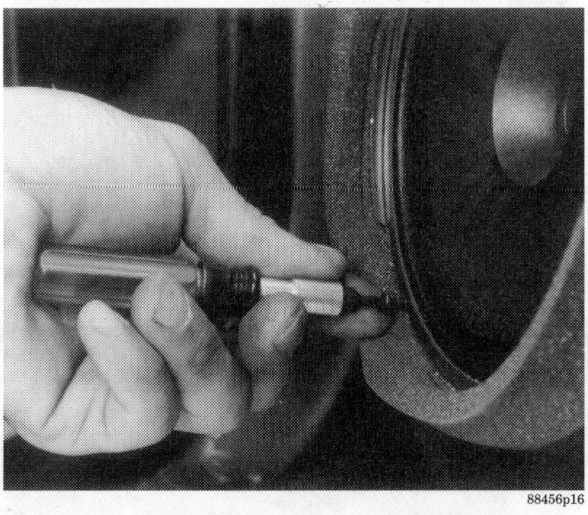

Fig. 50 Remove the speaker retaining screws

Fig. 51 Slide the speaker forward . . .

Fig. 52 . . . then disengage the speaker electrical connection and remove the speaker

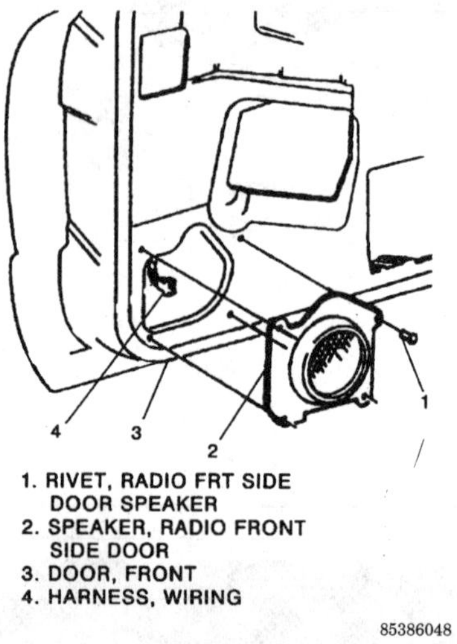

Fig. 53 View of the door panel mounted speakers

ing. If the grille fasteners are accessible with the trim panel installed, then panel removal may not be necessary.

1. Disconnect the negative battery cable
2. If necessary, remove the door trim panel. For details on door trim panel removal, please refer to the procedures in Section 10 of this manual.
3. Drill out the heads of the old speaker retaining rivets. Again, aftermarket systems may not contain rivets. If equipped with screws, unthread and remove them.
4. Pull the speaker from the door and disengage the electrical connectors, then remove the speaker from the vehicle.

To install:

5. Engage the speaker electrical connections, then install the speaker in the vehicle.
6. If equipped, install the screws. If equipped with rivets, install them.
7. If removed, install the door trim panel. Refer to Section 10 of this manual for this procedure.
8. Connect the negative battery cable.

Rear

See Figure 54

1. Disconnect the negative battery cable
2. Remove the side trim panel.
3. Disengage the necessary wiring.
4. Remove the speaker retaining nuts.
5. Remove the speaker from the vehicle.

To install:

6. Install the speaker and fasten retaining nuts to 11 inch lbs. (1.2 Nm).
7. Engage the speaker electrical connections.
8. Install the trim panel, then connect the negative battery cable.

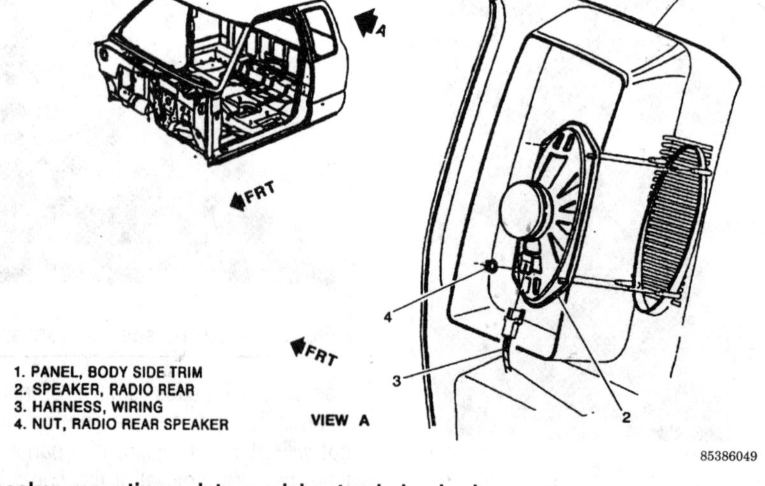

Fig. 54 Common rear speaker mounting — late model extended cab shown

WINDSHIELD WIPERS AND WASHERS

Windshield Wiper Blade and Arm

REMOVAL & INSTALLATION

Wiper Blade

1. Lift the wiper arm up into the serviceable position.
2. Press down on the locking tab of the blade assembly, then pull the assembly forward to disengage it from the wiper arm.

To install:

3. Install the new blade in the wiper arm assembly and make sure it engages properly.
4. Place the wiper arm back in its normal position.

Wiper Arm

See Figures 55, 56, 57 and 58

1. To aid in installation, use a non-permanent marker and mark the position of the wiper arm assembly on the windshield.
2. Remove the cover from the wiper assembly.
3. Unfasten the arm retaining nut, then remove the arm.

To install:

4. Install the arm assembly and tighten the retaining nut to 17 ft. lbs. (23 Nm).
5. Install the wiper arm cover and check the wiper operation.

Windshield Wiper Motor

REMOVAL & INSTALLATION

See Figures 59, 60, 61, 62, 63 and 64

1. Disconnect the negative battery cable.

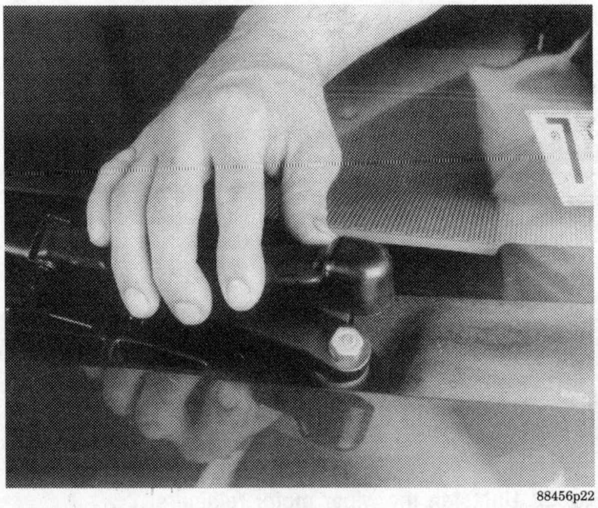

88456p22

Fig. 55 Remove the cover from the wiper assembly

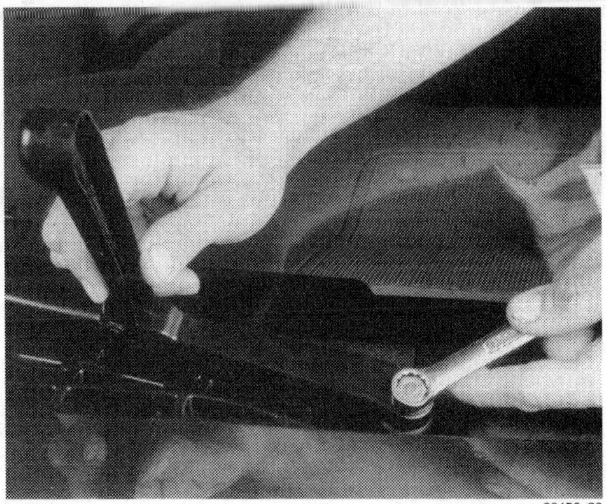

88456p23

Fig. 56 Unfasten and remove the wiper arm retainer

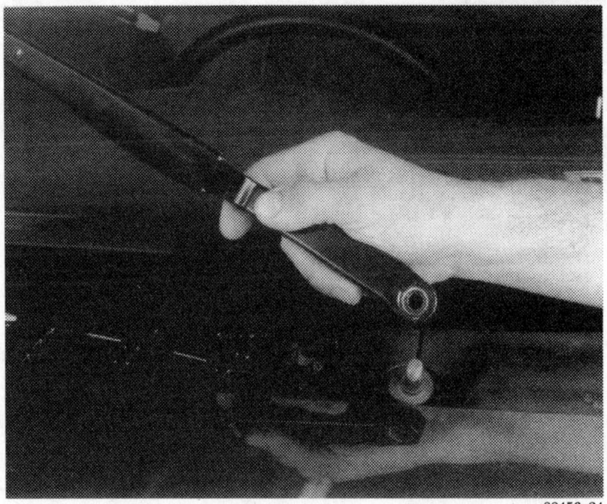

88456p24

Fig. 57 Remove the wiper arm from the vehicle

2. Remove the wiper arms from the linkage so the cowl may be removed.
3. Remove the cowl vent grille and screen. On some vehicles, the windshield washer hose may be connected to a hard plastic fitting located under the cowl grille. If the hose connection is very tight it may make removing the cowl grille difficult. Take your time if difficulty is encountered. If possible, reach underneath the grille to disconnect the hose from the fitting.
4. Remove the wiper transmission from the wiper motor drive link using J-39232 or an equivalent tool.
5. Disengage the wiring from the wiper motor.
6. Remove the wiper motor-to-cowl screws. Carefully rotate the motor and guide the drive link from the hole in the cowl, then remove the motor from the vehicle.

To install:

7. Guide the motor drive link through the hole in the cowl, then install the motor and secure using the retainers.

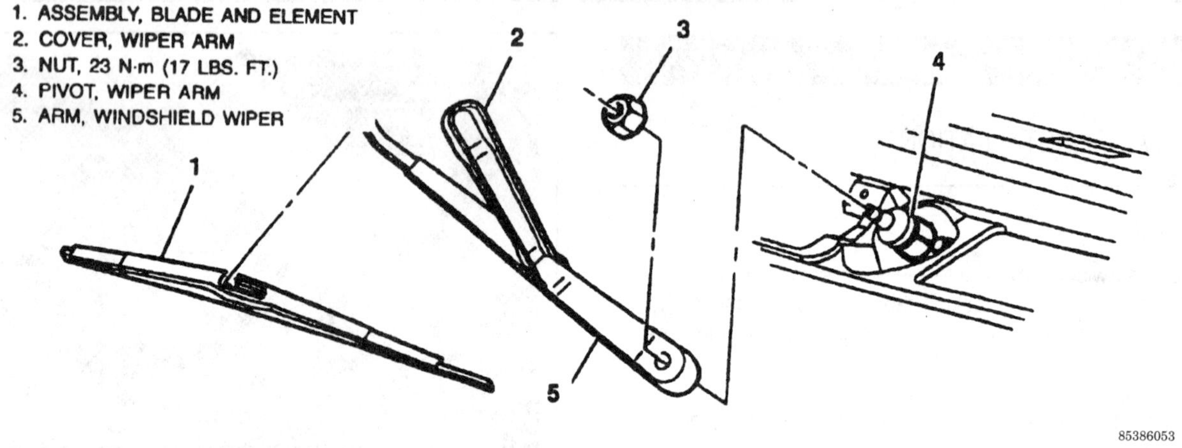

Fig. 58 Exploded view of the wiper arm assembly mounting

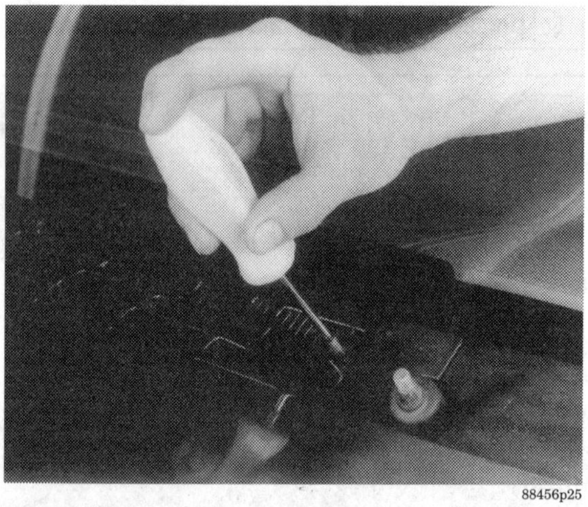

Fig. 59 Remove the cowl vent grille and screen retainers

Fig. 61 Disengage the wiper linkage from the wiper transmission

Fig. 60 Remove the cowl vent grille and screen from the vehicle

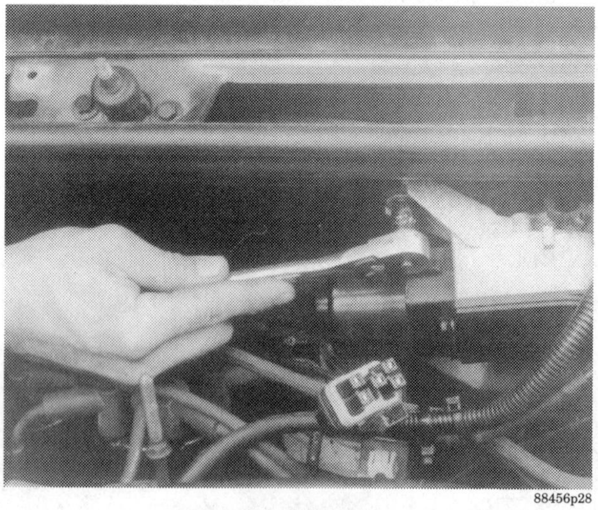

Fig. 62 Unfasten the wiper motor retainers . . .

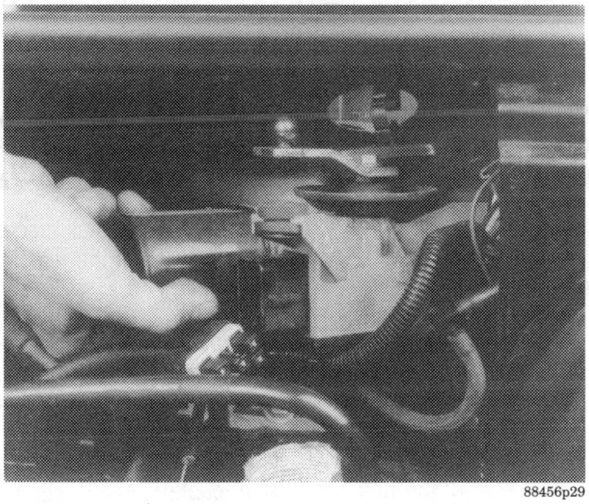

Fig. 63 . . . then remove the wiper motor from the vehicle

8. Install the drive link socket onto the crank arm ball using J-39529 or an equivalent tool. The wiper transmission assembly must be installed to the crank arm PAST the 2nd detent so that the seal is compressed to a maximum height of 1 in. (25.5mm)
9. Engage the wiring to the wiper motor.
10. Install the cowl vent grille and screen. On vehicles equipped with a plastic fitting attached to the cowl grille, the washer hose should be connected as the grille is positioned. Make sure the hose is not pinched or damaged as the grille is fastened.
11. Install the wiper arm and blade assemblies to the transmission linkage.
12. Connect the negative battery cable and verify proper operation.

Wiper Linkage

REMOVAL & INSTALLATION

➧ See Figures 65, 66 and 67

1. Disconnect the negative battery cable.
2. Remove the wiper arms from the linkage so the cowl may be removed.
3. Remove the cowl vent grille and screen. On some vehicles, the a windshield washer hose may be connected to a hard plastic fitting located under the cowl grille. If the hose connection is very tight it may make removing the cowl grille difficult. Take your time if difficulty is encountered, if possible, reach underneath the grille to disconnect the hose from the fitting.
4. Remove the wiper transmission from the wiper motor drive link using J-39232 or an equivalent tool.

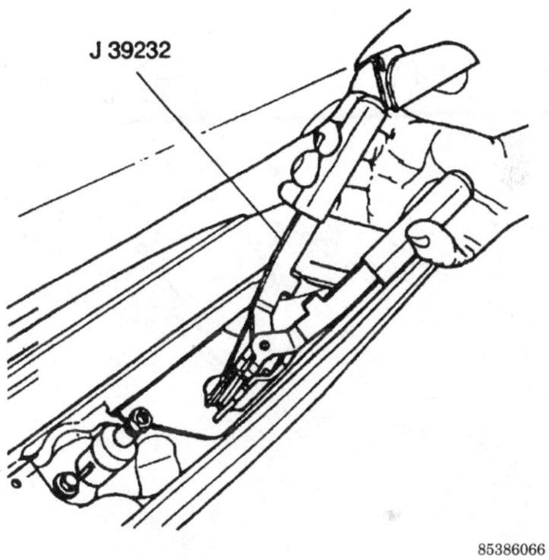

Fig. 65 Disconnecting the wiper transmission from the motor crank arm ball

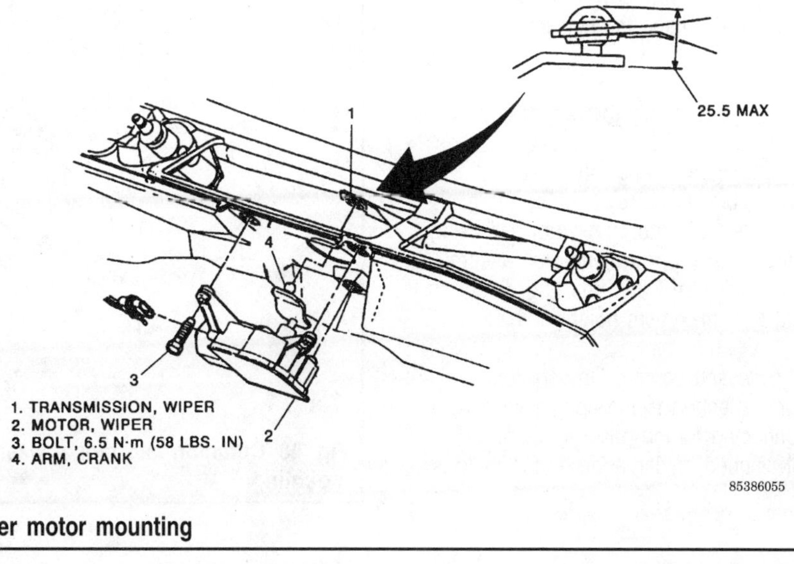

Fig. 64 Windshield wiper motor mounting

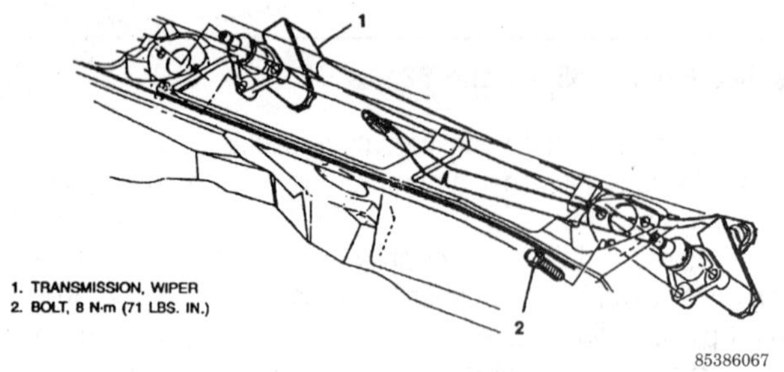

Fig. 66 Wiper transmission assembly mounting

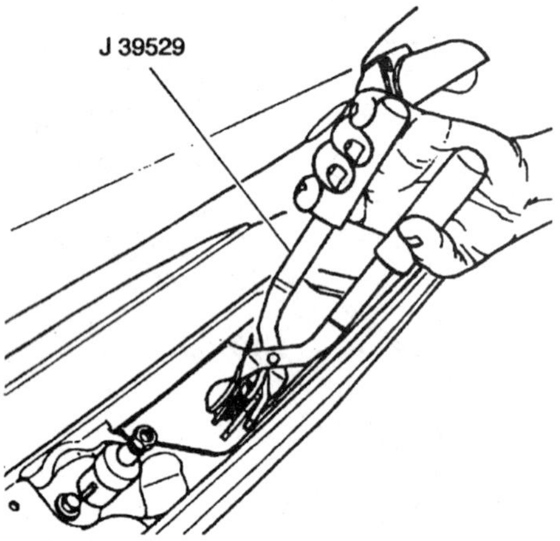

Fig. 67 Connecting the wiper transmission and the motor crank arm ball

5. Remove the transmission linkage-to-cowl retaining screws, then carefully remove the linkage through the top of the cowl.

To install:

6. Carefully guide the linkage assembly through the opening in the top of the cowl.
7. Secure the transmission linkage using the retainers. Tighten the fasteners securely, but do not overtighten them.
8. Install the drive link socket onto the crank arm ball using J-39529 or an equivalent tool. The wiper transmission assembly must be installed to the crank arm PAST the 2nd detent so that the seal is compressed to a maximum height of 1 in. (25.5mm)
9. Install the cowl vent grille and screen. On vehicles equipped with a plastic fitting attached to the cowl grille, the washer hose should be connected as the grille is positioned. Make sure the hose is not pinched or damaged as the grille is fastened.
10. Install the wiper arm and blade assemblies to the transmission linkage.
11. Connect the negative battery cable and verify proper wiper operation.

Wiper Fluid Reservoir and Washer Motor

The vehicles covered by this manual utilize a small electric washer pump which is mounted to the bottom of the washer reservoir.

REMOVAL & INSTALLATION

See Figure 68

1. Disconnect the negative battery cable.
2. Use a siphon or hand pump to drain the washer fluid from the reservoir. If you are using a siphon, be careful not to inhale or swallow the fluid. The stuff tastes nasty, and like with most fluids in your truck, can be harmful if swallowed.
3. Disengage the electrical connector and washer hose from the pump.
4. Unfasten the washer fluid reservoir mounting screws, then remove the reservoir from the vehicle.
5. Remove the washer pump from the reservoir.

To install:

6. Install the washer pump to the reservoir. Make sure the pump is fully inserted into the washer reservoir seal.
7. Install the reservoir to the vehicle and secure using the retaining screws.
8. Engage the washer hose and electrical connector to the pump.
9. Refill the reservoir with fluid. Add just a little at first, and check for leaks. Refill the reservoir when you are certain the pump seal is secure.
10. Connect the negative battery cable and check for proper pump operation.

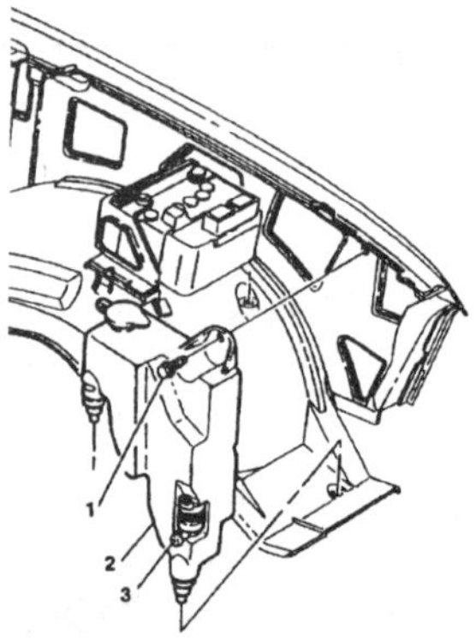

Fig. 68 Common late model washer pump and reservoir mounting

INSTRUMENTS AND SWITCHES

✲✲WARNING

Many solid state electrical components utilized in these vehicles can be damaged by Electrostatic Discharge (ESD). Some of these components will display a label informing you that they will be damaged by (ESD) and some will not have labels, but they may be damaged also. To avoid the possible damage to any of these components, follow the steps outlined in Handling Electrostatic Discharge (ESD) sensitive parts in this section.

Handling Electrostatic Discharge (ESD) Sensitive Parts

➧ See Figure 69

1. Body movement produces an electrostatic charge. To discharge personal static electricity, touch a ground point (metal) on the vehicle. This should be performed any time you:
   - slide across the vehicle seat
   - sit down or get up
   - do any walking
2. Do not touch any exposed terminals on components or connectors with your fingers or any tools.
3. Never use jumper wires, ground a terminal on a component, use test equipment on any component or terminal unless instructed to in a diagnosis or testing procedure. When using test equipment, always connect the ground lead first.
4. If installing a new component, never remove the replacement component from its protective packaging until you are ready to install it.
5. Always touch the component package to ground before opening it.
6. Solid state components may also be damaged if the are dropped, bumped, laid on any metal work bench or laid near any components that operate electrically such as a TV, radio, or an oscilloscope.

88456g21

Fig. 69 Electrostatic Discharge (ESD) label

Instrument Cluster

REMOVAL & INSTALLATION

1994 Vehicles

➧ See Figures 70, 71 and 72

1. Disconnect the negative battery cable.
2. Remove the instrument cluster trim bezel. Since the light switch assembly is mounted to the bezel, once the bezel is released, pull it forward in order to disengage the wiring, then the bezel may be removed.
3. If equipped disengage the shift indicator cable from the lower shift bowl.

88456p30

Fig. 70 Common instrument panel — 1994 model

88456p31

Fig. 71 Remove the trim plate to gain access to the instrument cluster retainers

4. Remove the 4 cluster-to-instrument panel retaining screws.

5. Carefully pull the cluster forward and from the multi-pin connector, then remove the cluster from the vehicle.

To install:

6. Carefully position the cluster in the vehicle, then firmly seat it onto the connector.

7. Install the cluster retaining screws and tighten to 17 inch lbs. (1.9 Nm).

8. If equipped, connect the shift indicator cable to the lower shift bowl and adjust, as necessary.

9. Install the instrument cluster bezel.

10. Connect the negative battery cable.

1995-97 Vehicles

See Figure 73

1. Disconnect the negative battery cable.
2. Remove the sound insulators/trim panels.
3. Unfasten the steering column nuts, then lower the column for access.
4. Remove the instrument cluster bezel.
5. Unfasten the screws retaining the instrument cluster to the instrument panel, disengage any electrical connections from the rear of the cluster, then remove the cluster.

To install:

6. Engage the electrical connections to the instrument cluster and then install the cluster to the instrument panel and tighten the fasteners to 17 inch. lbs. (1.9 Nm).
7. Install the instrument cluster panel bezel.
8. Re-position the steering column and tighten retaining nuts to 20 ft. lbs. (27 Nm).
9. Install the sound insulators/trim panels.
10. Connect the negative battery cable.

Windshield Wiper Switch

The windshield wiper switch is located deep inside the steering column assembly and is actuated by the multi-function lever on the left of the steering column. For details concerning

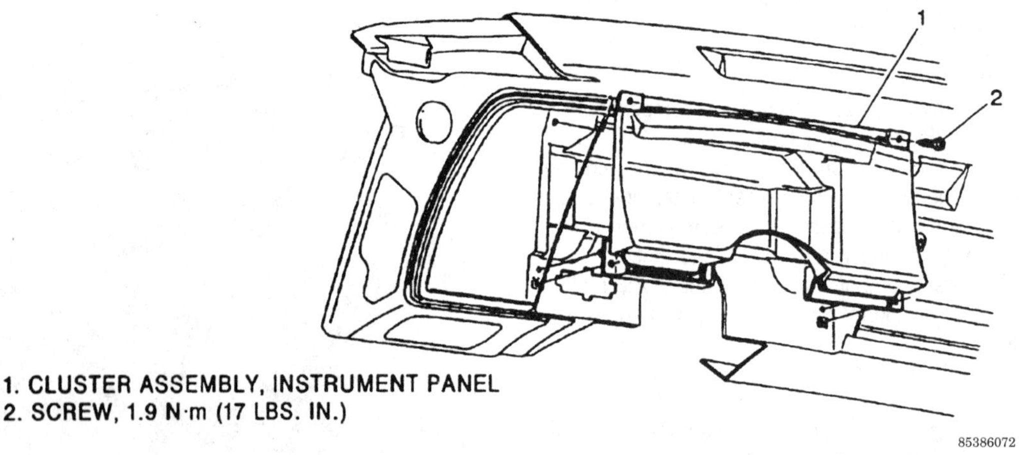

Fig. 72 Instrument cluster mounting — 1994 vehicles

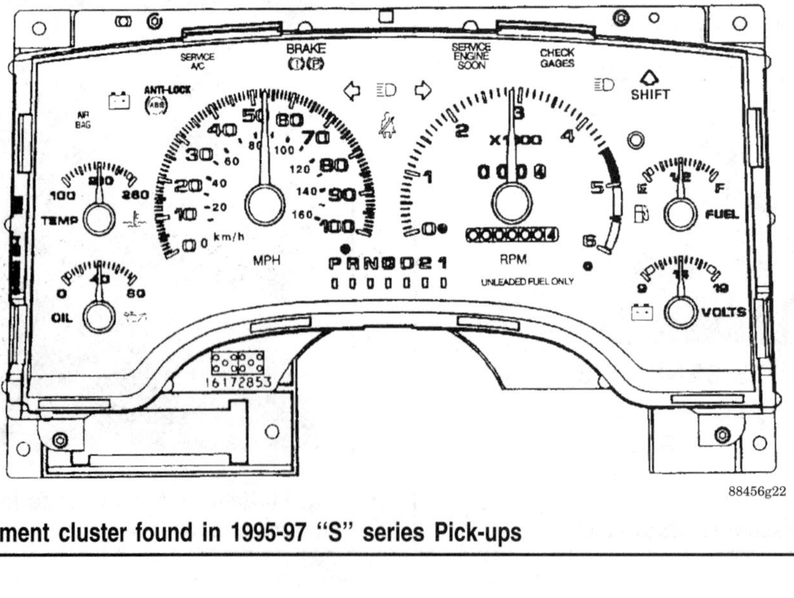

Fig. 73 Common instrument cluster found in 1995-97 "S" series Pick-ups

removal and installation, please refer to the steering column procedures located in Section 8 of this manual.

Headlight Switch

See Figure 74

The headlight switch is located on the left side of the instrument panel. A rheostat dial, usually located just above the headlight/parking light switch, is used to control the illumination of the instrument panel lighting.

A dimmer switch is mounted on the lower back of the steering column (near the ignition switch) and is actuated by the multi-function lever. For dimmer switch removal and installation, please refer to the steering column procedures located in Section 8 of this manual.

REMOVAL & INSTALLATION

See Figure 75

1. Disconnect the negative battery cable.
2. Remove the instrument cluster trim bezel.
3. Disengage the electrical connector.
4. Remove the switch-to-bezel retaining screws.
5. Remove the switch from the bezel.

To install:

6. Engage the switch to the bezel and tighten the switch-to-bezel retaining screws.
7. Engage the electrical connector.
8. Install the instrument cluster trim panel.
9. Connect the negative battery cable.
10. Check the switch for proper operation.

88456p32

Fig. 74 Headlight switch location (arrow) — 1994 model

Fog Lamp Switch

REMOVAL & INSTALLATION

See Figure 76

The fog lamp switch is located in the instrument cluster trim bezel assembly near the headlight switch.

1. Disconnect the negative battery cable.
2. Remove the instrument cluster trim bezel.
3. Disengage the wiring harness connector.
4. Remove the switch by squeezing the tabs, then pushing the switch through the bezel.

To install:

5. Engage the switch to the bezel by inserting it from the front. Ensure the switch retainers are fully seated.
6. Engage the electrical connection.
7. Install the instrument cluster bezel.
8. Connect the negative battery cable.

Back-Up Light/Neutral Safety Switch

REMOVAL & INSTALLATION

Automatic Transmission

The back-up light switch on automatic transmission vehicles also acts as the neutral safety switch. The switch will activate the reverse lights when the gear shift lever is placed in the Reverse position, and it will prevent the engine from starting unless the shifter is in Neutral or Park. The switch is mounted to the steering column on most vehicles covered by this manual.

COLUMN MOUNTED SWITCH

See Figures 77 and 78

Two type of switches are generally found on these vehicles. Some early models will be equipped with adjustable switches which are bolted into position. Most vehicles covered by this manual should be equipped with ratcheting self-adjusting switches.

1. Disconnect the negative battery cable.
2. If necessary for access, remove the steering column insulator/filler panel for access to the switch.
3. Disengage the electrical harness connector from the switch.
4. Remove the switch by grasping and pulling it straight out of the steering column jacket.

To install:

5. If equipped with an early model switch which is bolted into position, the switch should be equipped with a gauge hole for adjustment. If equipped, loosely install the switch to the column and adjust following the procedures in the illustration.
6. Most vehicles covered by this manual utilize a self-adjusting (ratcheting) switch. To adjust:
   a. Align the actuator on the switch with the holes in the shift tube.

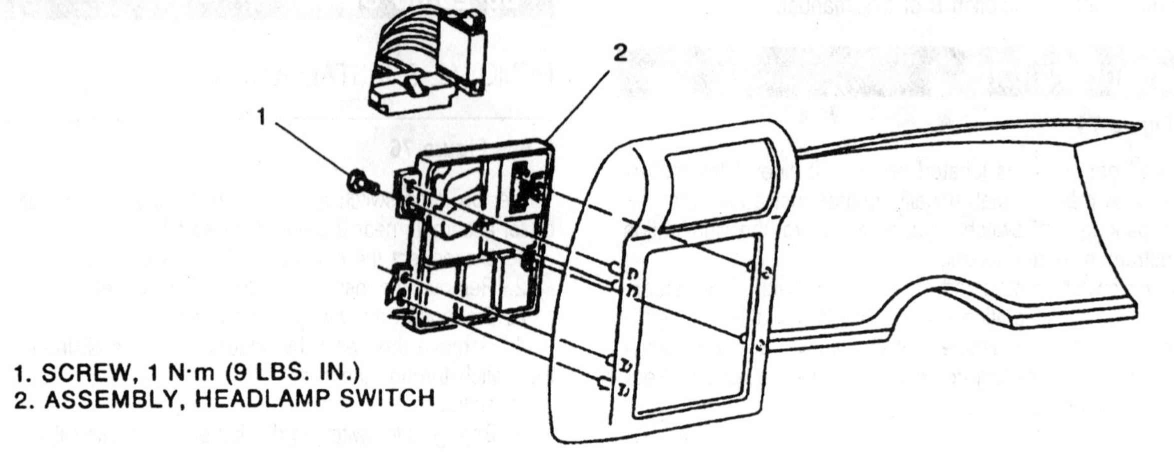

Fig. 75 Exploded view of the headlight switch-to-bezel mounting

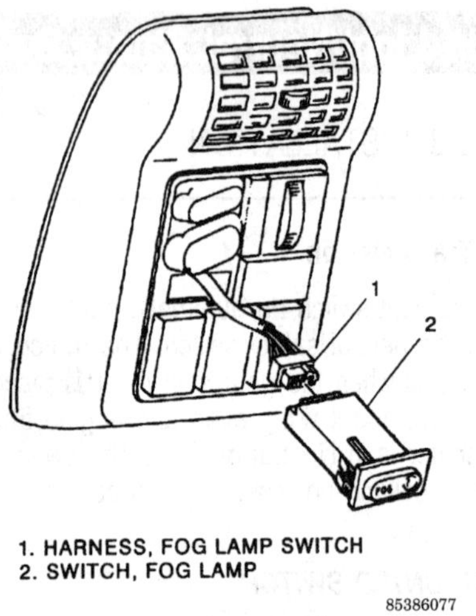

Fig. 76 Fog lamp switch mounting

b. Set the parking brake and place the gear selector in Neutral.

c. Press down on the front of the switch until the tangs snap into the rectangular holes in the steering column jacket.

d. Adjust the switch by moving the gear selector to **P**. The main housing and the housing back should ratchet, providing the proper switch adjustment.

7. Engage the harness connector to the switch.
8. Connect the negative battery cable, then verify proper switch operation. Make sure the reverse lights work and that the ignition will only work in the **N** or **P** positions. If necessary, readjust the switch. For ratcheting type switches, move the gear selector all the way to the **L** position, then repeat the adjustment.
9. If applicable, install the steering column insulator/filler panel.

FLOOR CONSOLE MOUNTED SWITCH

1. Disconnect the negative battery cable.
2. Remove the center console for access to the switch assembly.

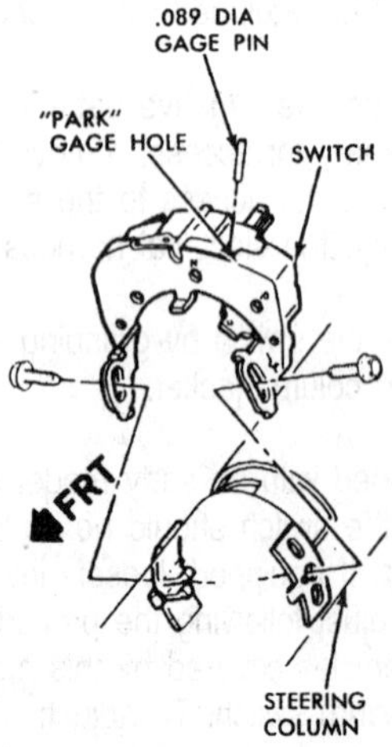

Fig. 77 Installation and adjustment of the early model bolt-on back-up lamp/neutral safety switch

3. Disengage the switch electrical connector.
4. Remove the retaining nuts, then remove the switch from the vehicle.
5. If necessary, remove the gauge pin from the switch.
6. If installing a new switch:
   a. Place the shift control lever in **N**.
   b. Align the carrier tang on the back-up lamp/neutral safety switch with the slot on the shifter.

➡Replacement switches are pinned in the N position to ease installation. If the switch has been rotated or the switch is broken, install the switch using the "old switch" installation and adjustment procedure.

   c. Tighten the switch retaining nuts to 30 inch lbs. (3.4 Nm), then engage the switch connector.
   d. Move the shift control lever out of Neutral in order to shear the plastic pin, then remove the accessible piece(s) of the gauge pin.
7. If installing an old switch, install and adjust the switch to assure proper operation:
   a. Place the shift control lever in **N**.
   b. Align the carrier tang on the switch with the slot on the shifter.
   c. Loosely install the retaining switch nuts and engage the wiring connector.
   d. Rotate the switch to align the service adjustment hole with the carrier tang hold, then use a 0.09 in. (2.34mm) gauge pin to complete adjustment. Insert the pin in the service adjustment hole and rotate the switch until it drops to a depth of 0.59 in. (15mm). Hold the switch in this position and tighten the retaining nuts to 30 inch lbs. (3.4 Nm).
8. Install the center console.
9. Connect the negative battery cable.
10. Verify proper switch operation.

Manual Transmission

On manual transmissions, the back-up light switch is normally mounted to the transmission. The safety switch is replaced by a clutch switch which is mounted to the clutch pedal. For replacement procedures, please refer to Section 7 of this manual.

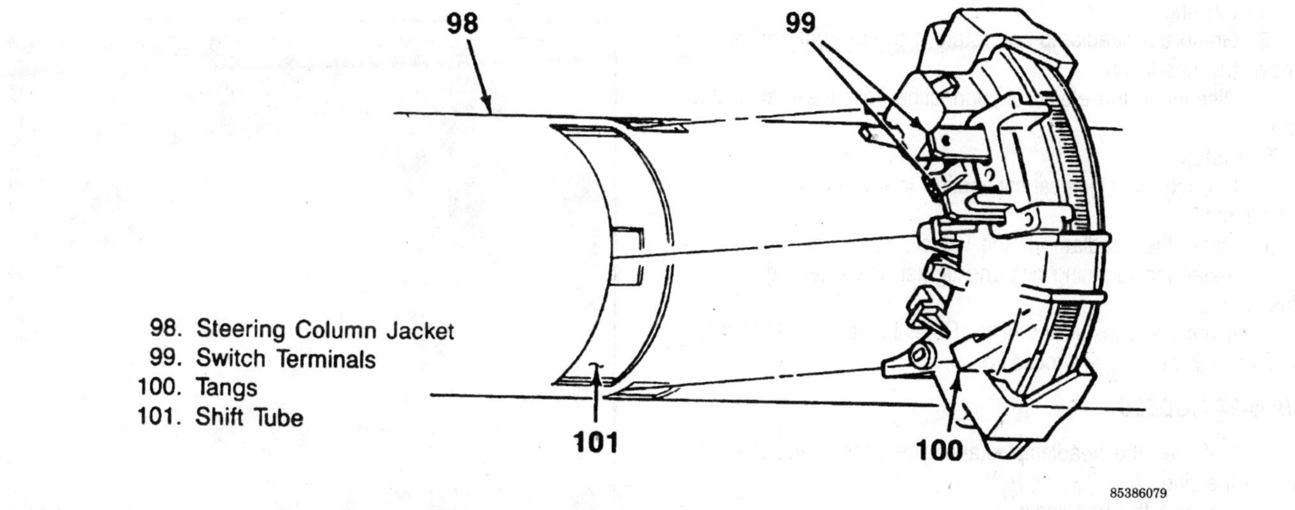

Fig. 78 Ratcheting type back-up lamp/neutral safety switch mounting

LIGHTING

Headlights

REMOVAL & INSTALLATION

Sealed Beam

➧ See Figure 79

➡If some or all of the headlight bulbs being replaced still operate, refer to the headlight aiming procedure later in this section to ease checking or adjustment of the headlights after installation.

1994-95 MODELS

➧ See Figures 80, 81 and 82

1. If necessary, remove the grille from the vehicle. Refer to Section 10 of this manual for the proper procedure.
2. Unfasten the headlamp retaining ring fasteners, then remove the ring.
3. Grasp the headlamp and rotate it to the right and remove the headlamp.
4. Disengage the electrical connection from the rear of the lamp.

To install:

5. Engage the electrical connection to the rear of the headlamp.
6. Install the headlamp in the vehicle.
7. Install the retaining ring and tighten the retaining fasteners.
8. If removed, install the grille. Refer to Section 10 of this manual for the proper procedure.

1996-97 MODELS

1. Unfasten the headlamp retaining ring fasteners, then remove the ring.
2. Remove the headlamp.

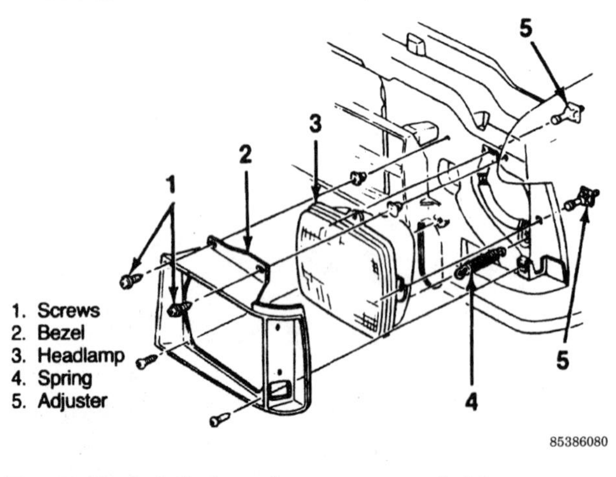

Fig. 79 Exploded view of a common sealed beam headlight mounting (with separate headlight bezel shown)

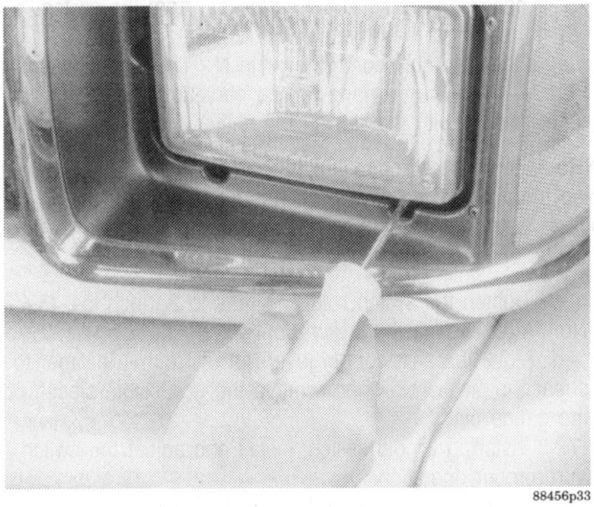

Fig. 80 Loosen the retaining ring fasteners . . .

Fig. 81 . . . then remove the retaining ring

3. Disengage the electrical connection from the rear of the lamp.

To install:

4. Engage the electrical connection to the rear of the headlamp.
5. Install the headlamp in the vehicle.
6. Install the retaining ring and tighten the retaining fasteners.

Composite Beam

➧ See Figure 83

Some vehicles covered by this manual were equipped with composite headlight assemblies. The composite headlight assembly houses the headlamp and side marker lamp bulbs. In most cases, the assembly is bolted in a fixed position so no adjustment is necessary or possible. Also, due to space constraints, no access may be provided to withdraw the bulbs, so

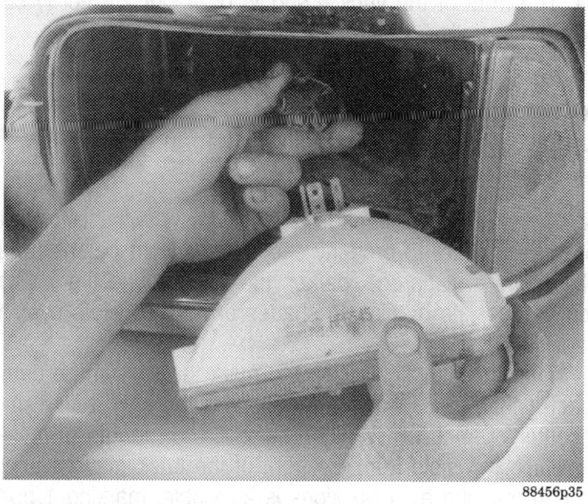

Fig. 82 Slide the headlamp forward and disengage the electrical connection

the replacement usually requires removal of the composite assembly.

➡The composite headlight assemblies use Halogen bulbs which contain a gas under pressure. Handling a bulb improperly could cause it to shatter into flying glass fragments. To help avoid personal injury follow the precautions closely.

Whenever handling Halogen bulb ALWAYS follow these precautions:

- Turn the lamp switch OFF and allow the bulb to cool before changing it. Leave the switch OFF until the change is complete.
- ALWAYS wear eye protection when changing a Halogen bulb.
- DO NOT drop or scratch the bulb. Keep moisture away.
- Place the used bulb in the new bulb's carton and dispose of it properly.

1994-95 MODELS

1. Disconnect the negative battery cable.
2. If replacing the right side bulb, remove the battery from the vehicle.
3. If replacing the left side bulb, remove the intake air box.
4. Remove the grille from the front of the vehicle.
5. Remove the retaining screw from the engine side of the radiator support, then remove the headlight capsule-to-radiator support screws.
6. Pull the composite headlight assembly forward slightly, then disengage the headlamp and side marker lamp wiring connectors.
7. Remove the headlight assembly from the vehicle. Remove the necessary bulb(s) from the assembly.

To install:

8. Install new bulbs, as necessary to the composite headlight assembly.
9. Position the assembly to the vehicle and engage the connectors.
10. Install the assembly retaining screws and tighten to 62 inch lbs. (7 Nm).
11. Install the grille to the front of the vehicle.
12. Install the air intake box and/or battery, as applicable.
13. Connect the negative battery cable and verify proper lamp operation.

1996-97 MODELS

1. Unfasten and remove the headlamp mounting retainers.
2. Disengage the headlamp and side marker lamp connectors.
3. Remove the headlamp assembly from the vehicle.
4. Remove the bulbs from the headlamp assembly.

To install:

5. Install the bulbs in the headlamp assembly.
6. Engage the electrical connectors for the headlamp and side marker assemblies.
7. Install and tighten the headlamp mounting screws to 62 inch. lbs. (7 Nm).

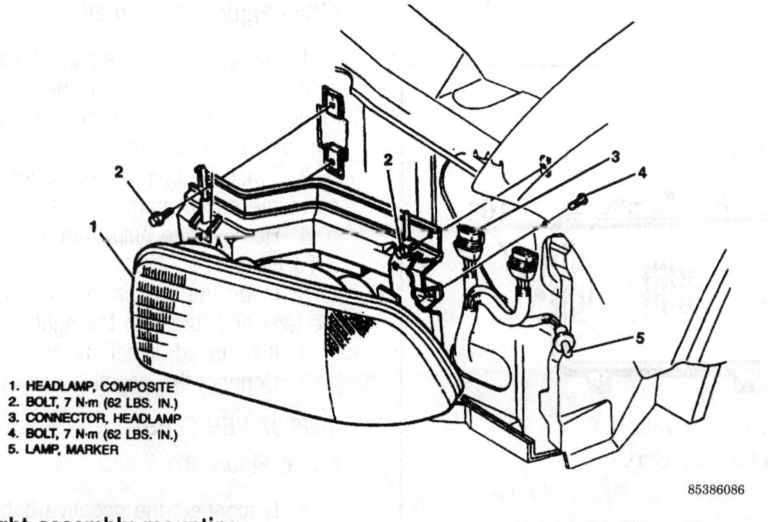

Fig. 83 Composite headlight assembly mounting

HEADLIGHT AIMING

See Figure 84

The headlights must be properly aimed to provide the best, safest road illumination. The lights should be checked for proper aim and adjusted as necessary. Certain state and local authorities have requirements for headlight aiming; these should be checked before adjustment is made.

Headlight adjustment may be temporarily made using a wall, as described below, or on the rear of another vehicle. When adjusted, the lights should not glare in oncoming car or truck windshields, nor should they illuminate the passenger compartment of vehicles driving in front of you. These adjustments are rough and should always be fine-tuned by a repair shop which is equipped with headlight aiming tools. Improper adjustments may be both dangerous and illegal.

For most S/T vehicles, horizontal and vertical aiming of each sealed beam unit is provided by two adjusting screws which move the retaining ring and adjusting plate against the tension of a coil spring. There is no adjustment for focus; this is done during headlight manufacturing.

➡Because the composite headlight assembly is bolted into position, no adjustment should be necessary or possible. Some applications however may be bolted to an adjuster plate or may be retained used adjusting screws. If so, follow this procedure when adjusting the lights, BUT always have the adjustment checked by a reputable shop.

Before removing the headlight bulb or disturbing the headlamp in any way, note the current settings in order to make adjusting the headlights upon reassembly easier. If the high or low beam setting of the old lamp still works, this can be done using the wall of a garage or a building:

1. Park the truck on a level surface, with the fuel tank no more than ½ full and with the vehicle empty of all extra cargo (unless normally carried). The vehicle should be facing a wall which is no less the 6 feet (1.82 m) high and 12 feet (3.96 m) wide. The front of the vehicle should be about 25 feet (7.62 m) from the wall.

➡The truck's fuel tank should be about half full when adjusting the headlights. Tires should be properly inflated, and if a heavy load is normally carried in the bed, it should remain there.

2. If this is be performed outdoors, it is advisable to wait until dusk in order to properly see the headlight beams on the wall. If done in a garage, darken the area around the wall as much as possible by closing shades or hanging cloth over the windows.
3. Turn the headlights **ON** and mark the wall at the center of each light's low beam, then switch on the brights and mark the center of each light's high beam. A short length of masking tape which is visible from the front of the truck may be used. Although marking all 4 positions is advisable, marking 1 position from each light should be sufficient.
4. If neither beam on 1 side of the vehicle is working, park another like-sized truck in the exact spot where the truck was and mark the beams using the same side light on that truck. Then switch the trucks so the S/T is back in the original spot. The truck must be parked no closer to or farther away from the wall than the second vehicle.
5. Perform the necessary repairs, but make sure the truck is not moved or is returned to the exact spot from which the lights were marked. Turn the headlights **ON** and adjust the beams to match the marks on the wall.
6. Have the headlight adjustment checked as soon as possible by a reputable repair shop.

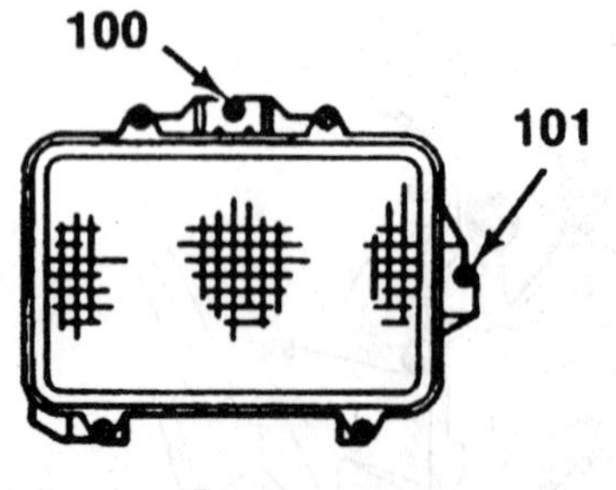

Fig. 84 Headlight adjustment screw locations for most sealed beam headlight adjusting plates

Signal and Marker Lights

REMOVAL & INSTALLATION

Front Turn Signal and Parking Lights

1994-95 VEHICLES

See Figures 85 and 86

1. Disconnect the negative battery cable.
2. Check for access to the rear of the lens. If none can be found, remove the grille from the front of the vehicle. Then remove the front bumper.
3. Twist the bulb socket to the left to release it, then remove the socket from the lens.
4. Remove the bulb from the socket.

To install:

5. Insert the bulb in the socket, then install the socket in the lens and turn it to the right to engage it.
6. If removed, install the front bumper and lens.
7. Connect the negative battery cable.

1996-97 VEHICLES

See Figure 87

1. Disconnect the negative battery cable.
2. Unfasten the lens retaining screws, then remove the lens.
3. Turn the bulb twist socket ¼ turn to the left and remove the socket from the lamp housing.

88456p40

Fig. 85 Twist and remove the bulb socket from the rear of the lens housing . . .

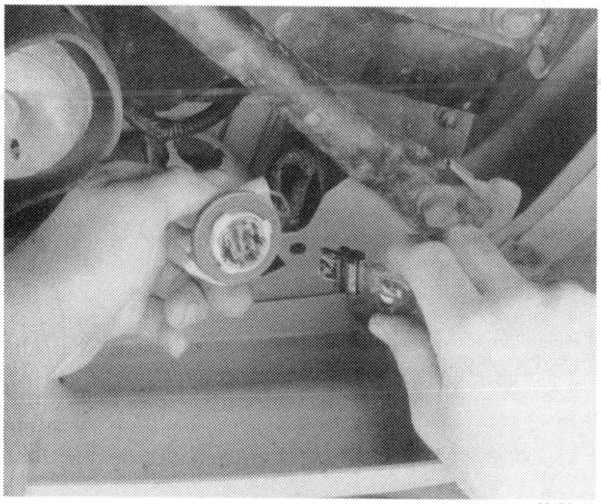

88456p41

Fig. 86 . . . then pull the bulb from the socket

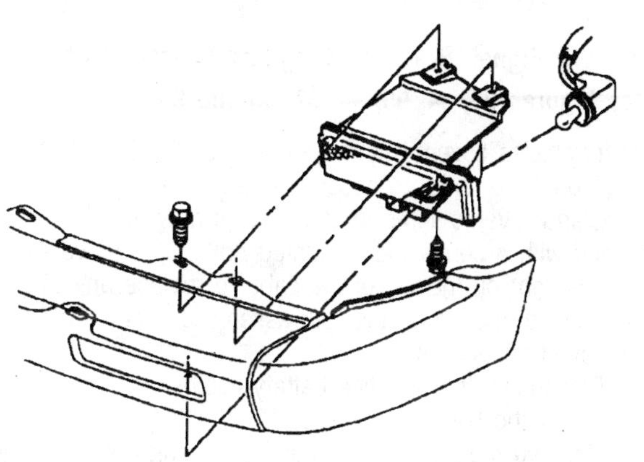

88456g23

Fig. 87 Exploded view of the front parking lamp assembly — 1996-97 models

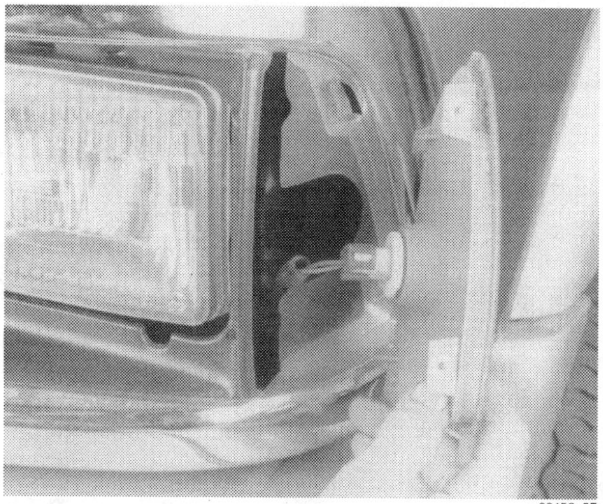

88456p37

Fig. 89 Remove the lens from its housing . . .

88456p36

Fig. 88 Remove the side marker lens retaining screws

4. Remove the bulb from the socket.

To install:

5. Insert the bulb in the socket, then install the socket in the lamp housing and turn it 1/4 turn to the left to engage it properly.
6. Install the lens and tighten the retaining screws.
7. Connect the negative battery cable.

Front Marker Lights

1994-95 VEHICLES

See Figures 88, 89, 90, 91 and 92

➡On vehicles equipped with composite headlights, the front marker light bulb is mounted in the composite assembly. Please refer to the headlight procedure earlier in this section for marker bulb replacement on these vehicles.

Vehicles equipped with sealed beam headlights use a similar marker lens assembly. The difference comes in that the lens screws are easily accessible with the grille/bezel assembly in-

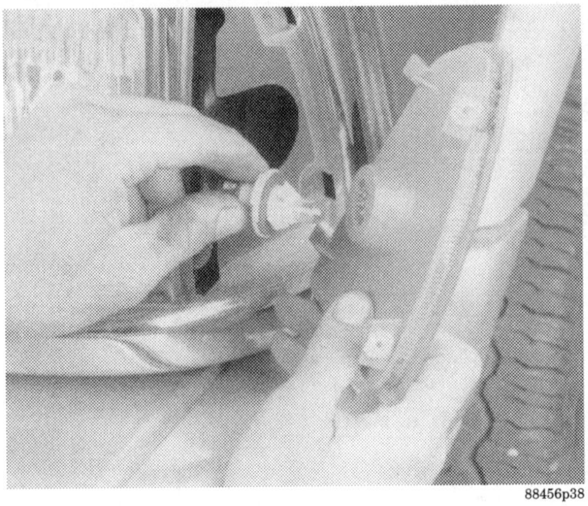

Fig. 90 . . . then twist the socket 1/4 turn to the left and remove the socket from the lamp housing

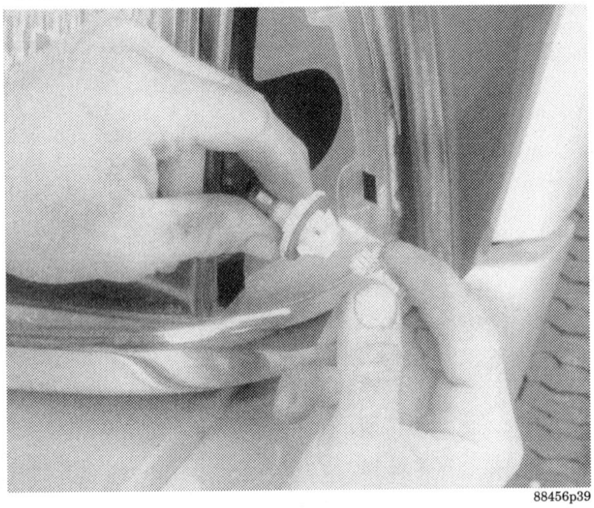

Fig. 91 Remove the bulb from the socket

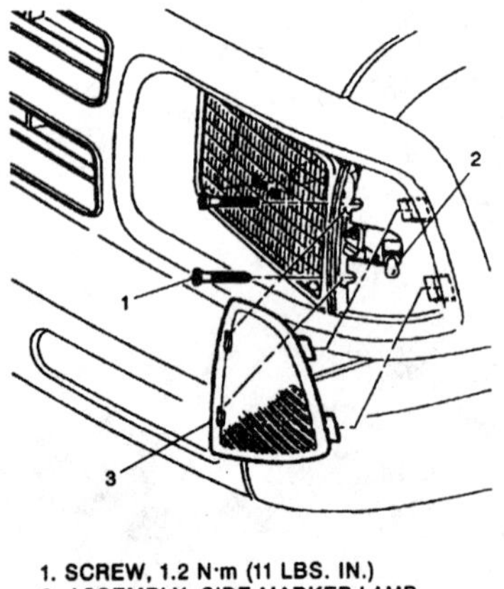

Fig. 92 Front marker light lens mounting — 1994 vehicles

stalled. To replace marker lights on these vehicles, use the following procedure. Composite headlight vehicles should refer to that procedure located earlier in this section.

1. Disconnect the negative battery cable.
2. Remove the retaining screws from the marker light lens.
3. Carefully pull the lens forward from the grille/bezel assembly for access to the bulb. Turn the twist socket 1/4 turn to left in order to release it.
4. Remove the bulb from the socket and replace, if necessary, with a new bulb.
5. Installation is the reverse of removal.

1996-97 VEHICLES

1. Disconnect the negative battery cable.
2. Remove the bulb socket from the lens by twisting it to the left.
3. Remove the bulb from the socket.

To install:

4. Install the bulb in the socket.
5. Install the bulb socket in the lens and turn it to the right to properly engage it.
6. Connect the negative battery cable.

Rear Turn Signal, Brake, Parking and Reverse Lights

▸ See Figures 93, 94, 95, 96, 97, 98 and 99

Most vehicles covered by this manual us 2 tail light assemblies (1 on either side) to house the rear turn signal, brake, parking and reverse lights. A few models may also be equipped with a center high-mounted brake light (covered later in this section) on the top of the cab. To replace any of the bulbs housed in the rear tail light assemblies, then lens must be removed for access.

1. Disconnect the negative battery cable.
2. Lower the tailgate.
3. Remove the rear lamp assembly-to-vehicle screws, then carefully pull the lamp housing away from the vehicle for access to the bulb twist sockets. On most vehicles, lamp screws can be found on the outer edge of the lamp and behind the tailgate. Make sure all screws are removed and DO NOT force the lens.

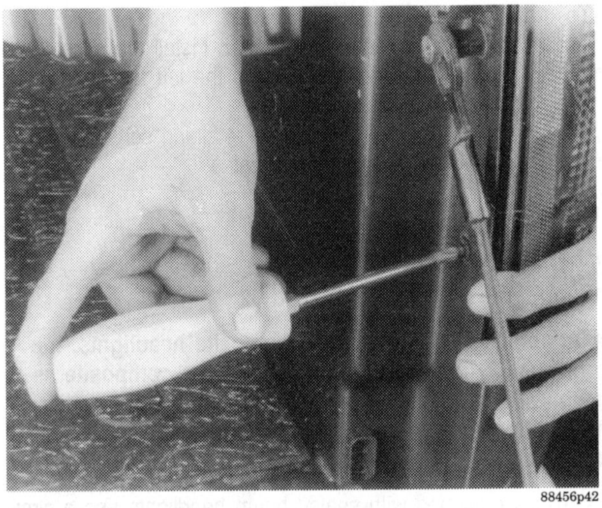

Fig. 93 Unfasten the rear lens retaining screws

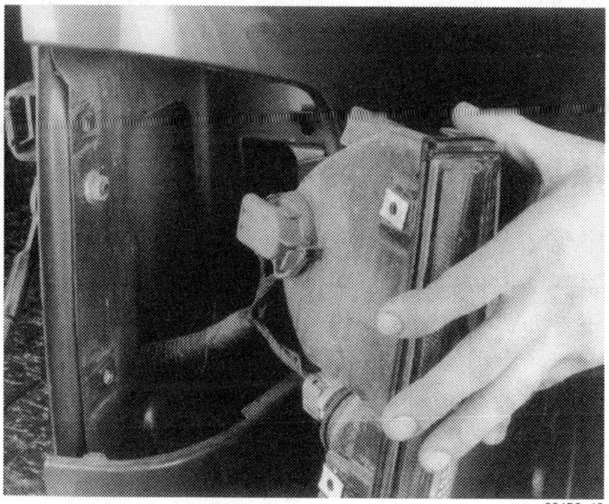

88456p43

Fig. 94 Carefully remove the lens from its housing

88456p46

Fig. 97 Removing the reverse lamp socket from the lens

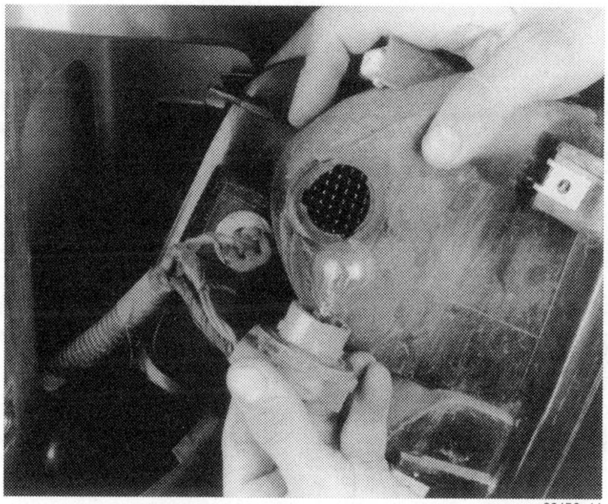

88456p44

Fig. 95 Removing the brake lamp socket from the lens

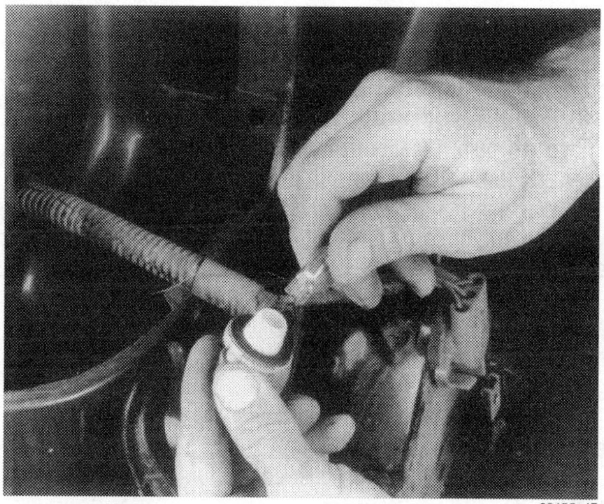

88456p47

Fig. 98 Removing the reverse lamp bulb from its socket

88456p45

Fig. 96 Removing the brake lamp bulb from its socket

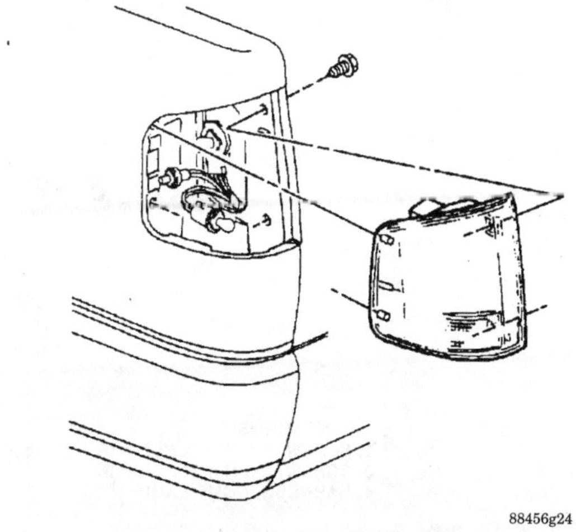

88456g24

Fig. 99 Exploded view of a common tail light assembly mounting

4. Turn the bulb twist socket ¼ turn to the left and remove the socket from the lamp housing.
5. Remove the bulb from the bulb socket; if necessary, replace the bulb.

To install:

6. Insert the bulb in the socket.
7. Install the bulb twist socket in the lamp housing and turn it¼ turn to the right to engage it properly.
8. Install the lamp assembly and tighten the retaining screws.
9. Close the tail gate assembly.
10. Connect the negative battery cable and check for proper lamp operation.

Center High-Mount Brake Light

REMOVAL & INSTALLATION

See Figure 100

1. Disconnect the negative battery cable.
2. Remove the outer high-mount brake lens retaining screws.
3. From inside the cab, remove the dome lamp lens, then remove the bulb. Disengage the dome lamp connectors by squeezing and sliding them out of the dome lamp assembly.
4. With the dome lamp components out of the way, remove the 4 dome lamp-to-high mount lens screws from inside the vehicle.
5. Disengage the wiring connector from the dome lamp harness.
6. Remove the center high-mount lamp from the vehicle.

To install:

7. Install the dome lamp and center high-mount lamp assembly to the vehicle.
8. Install the dome lamp bulb connectors to the lamp housing.
9. Engage the connector to the dome lamp harness.
10. Install the inner and outer lens retaining screws and tighten to 22 inch lbs. (2.5 Nm).
11. Connect the negative battery cable and verify proper operation.

Dome Light

REMOVAL & INSTALLATION

See Figures 101, 102 and 103

1. Remove the lens assembly.
2. Remove the bulb by pulling it gently from the connector.

To install:

3. Install a new bulb in the connector.
4. Install the lens assembly.

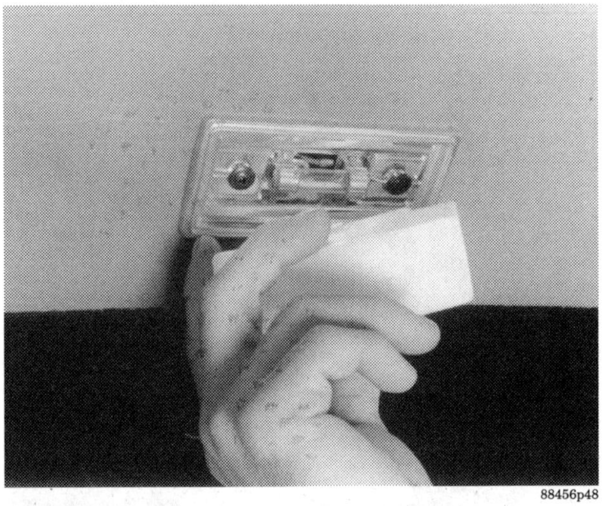

Fig. 101 Remove the dome light cover

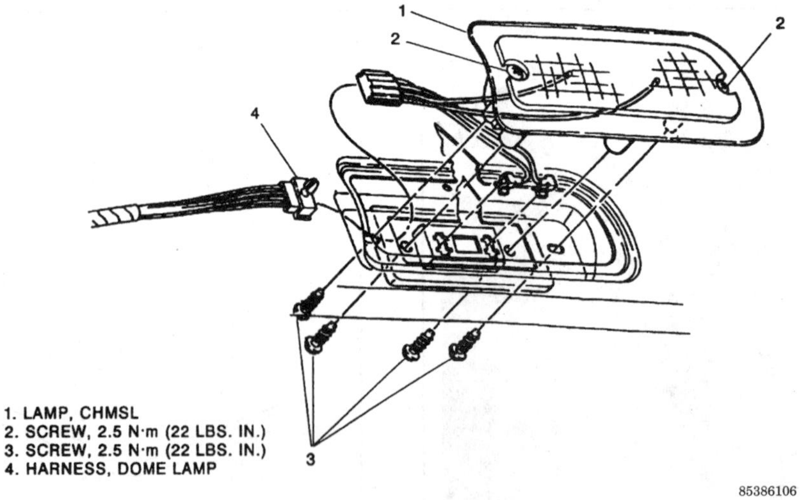

Fig. 100 Exploded view of the center high-mounted brake light assembly

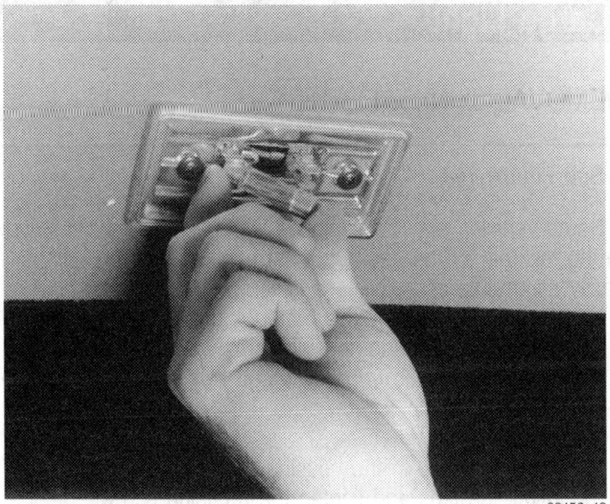

Fig. 102 Remove the bulb from the dome light

License Plate Light

REMOVAL & INSTALLATION

Step Bumper Models

➧ See Figure 104

1. Disconnect the negative battery cable.
2. Remove the step bumper pads.
3. Remove the bumper bolts, then rotate the bumper for access. An assistant to steady the bumper will be helpful here.
4. Disengage the electrical wiring connector.
5. Remove the lamp-to-bumper screws, then remove the lamp from the vehicle.

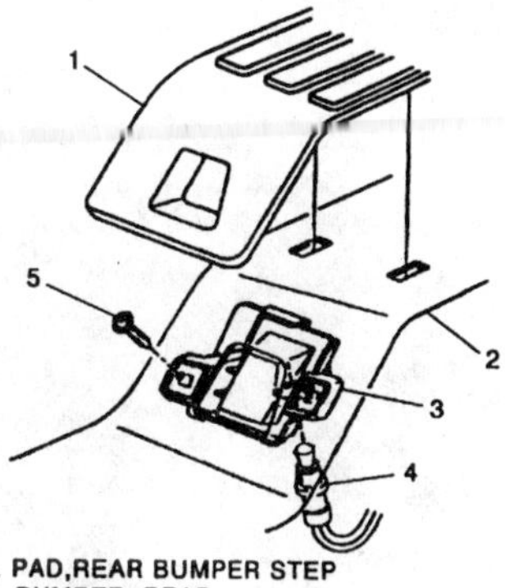

Fig. 104 License plate lamp mounting on vehicles with a step bumper

To install:

6. Install the lamp to the bumper, then tighten the retaining screws to 14 inch lbs. (1.6 Nm).
7. Engage the wiring connector.
8. Install the bumper and step pad to the vehicle.
9. Connect the negative battery cable.

Except Step Bumper Models

➧ See Figures 105, 106 and 107

1. Disconnect the negative battery cable.
2. Remove the socket from the lens by turning it 1/4 turn to the left.
3. Remove the bulb from the socket.

To install:

4. Install the bulb in the socket.
5. Install the socket in the lens and engage it by turning it a 1/4 turn to the right.
6. Connect the negative battery cable.

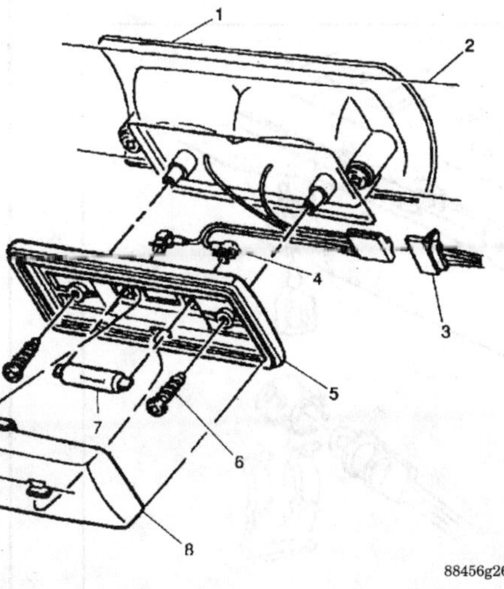

Fig. 103 Exploded view of a common dome lamp assembly

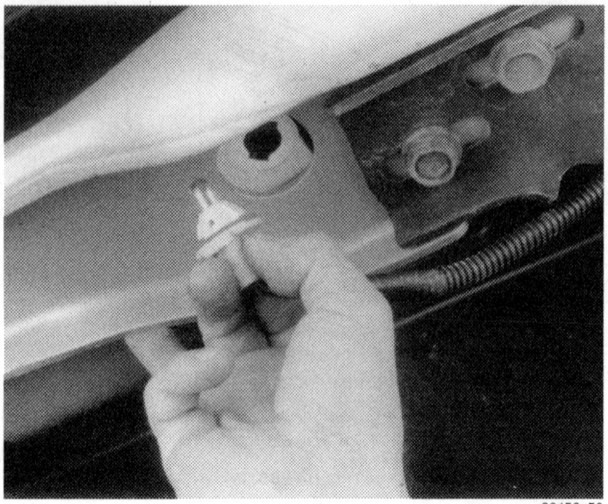
88456p50

Fig. 105 Remove the socket from the lens by turning it slightly to the left

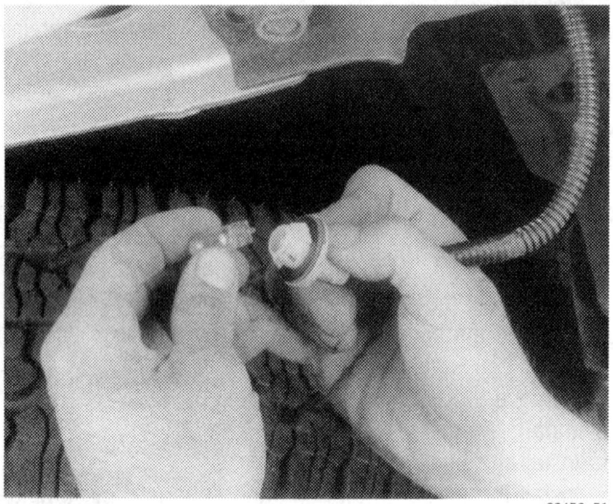
88456p51

Fig. 106 Remove the license plate light bulb from its socket

88456g25

Fig. 107 License plate lamp mounting on vehicles without a step bumper

Cargo Light

REMOVAL & INSTALLATION

➧ **See Figure 108**

Some vehicles may be equipped with a cargo light mounted to the top rear of the cab. On most applications, the bulb is easily accessible once the lens is removed.

1. Disconnect the negative battery cable.
2. Remove the lens-to-housing screws and the lens.
3. Remove the bulb from the cargo light housing; if necessary, replace the bulb.

To install:

4. Install the bulb in the housing.
5. Install the lens and tighten the retaining screws.
6. Connect the negative battery cable.

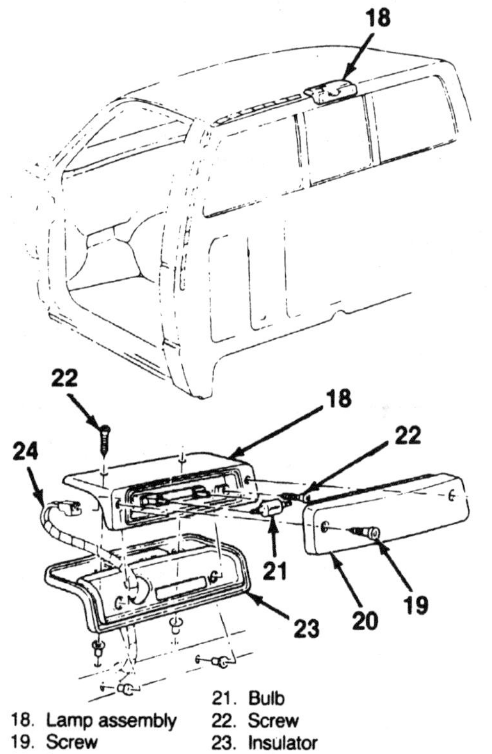

Fig. 108 Exploded view of a common cargo lamp assembly

Fog Lamps

REMOVAL & INSTALLATION

➧ See Figure 109

➡If removing or replacing the fog lamps (not just the bulb) and 1 or both of the fog lamps still operate, refer to the aiming procedure later in this section to ease checking or adjustment of the fog lamps after installation.

Most fog lamp bulbs are easily replaced by removing the lens cover (standard bulbs) or lens trim panels (halogen bulbs) for access. Most later model vehicles are equipped with Halogen bulbs which require extra care. Handling a Halogen bulb improperly could cause it to shatter into flying glass fragments. To help avoid personal injury follow the precautions closely.

Whenever handling Halogen bulb ALWAYS follow these precautions:

- Turn the lamp switch OFF and allow the bulb to cool before changing it. Leave the switch OFF until the change is complete.
- ALWAYS wear eye protection when changing a Halogen bulb.
- DO NOT drop or scratch the bulb. Keep moisture away.
- Place the use bulb in the new bulb's carton and dispose of it properly.

1. Disconnect the negative battery cable.
2. Remove the lens trim panel screws from the front of the lamp, then pull the lamp and lens assembly forward from the case and turn it over.
3. Disengage the white wire connector inside the braided insulator (leave the ground wire connected). Note the position of the wire clip at the lamp and lens assembly, then squeeze the edges of the clip together and remove it.
4. Lift out the wire and the halogen bulb assembly.

To install:

5. Install the white wire connector to the wiring in the brained insulator.
6. Install the bulb into the back of the lamp and lens assembly.
7. Install the wire clip to hold the bulb in place. Make sure the clip is firmly in position and the bulb is not loose.
8. Install the lens and lamp assembly into the case, then secure the trim panels using the retaining screws.
9. Connect the negative battery cable and check for proper operation.

INSTALLING AFTERMARKET AUXILIARY LIGHTS

➡Before installing any aftermarket light, make sure it is legal for road use. Most acceptable lights will have a DOT approval number. Also check your local and regional inspection regulations. In certain areas, aftermarket lights must be installed in a particular manner or they may not be legal for inspection.

1. Disconnect the negative battery cable.
2. Unpack the contents of the light kit purchased. Place the contents in an open space where you can easily retrieve a piece if needed.
3. Choose a location for the lights. If you are installing fog lights, below the bumper and apart from each other is desirable. Most fog lights are mounted below or very close to the headlights. If you are installing driving lights, above the bumper and close together is desirable. Most driving lights are mounted between the headlights.
4. Drill the needed hole(s) to mount the light. Install the light, and secure using the supplied retainer nut and washer. Tighten the light mounting hardware, but not the light adjustment nut or bolt.
5. Install the relay that came with the light kit in the engine compartment, in a rigid area, like a fender. Always install the relay with the terminals facing down. This will prevent water from entering the relay assembly.
6. Using the wire supplied, locate the ground terminal, or terminal with the number 85 next to it on the relay, and connect a length of wire from this terminal to a good ground source. You can drill a hole and screw this wire to an inside

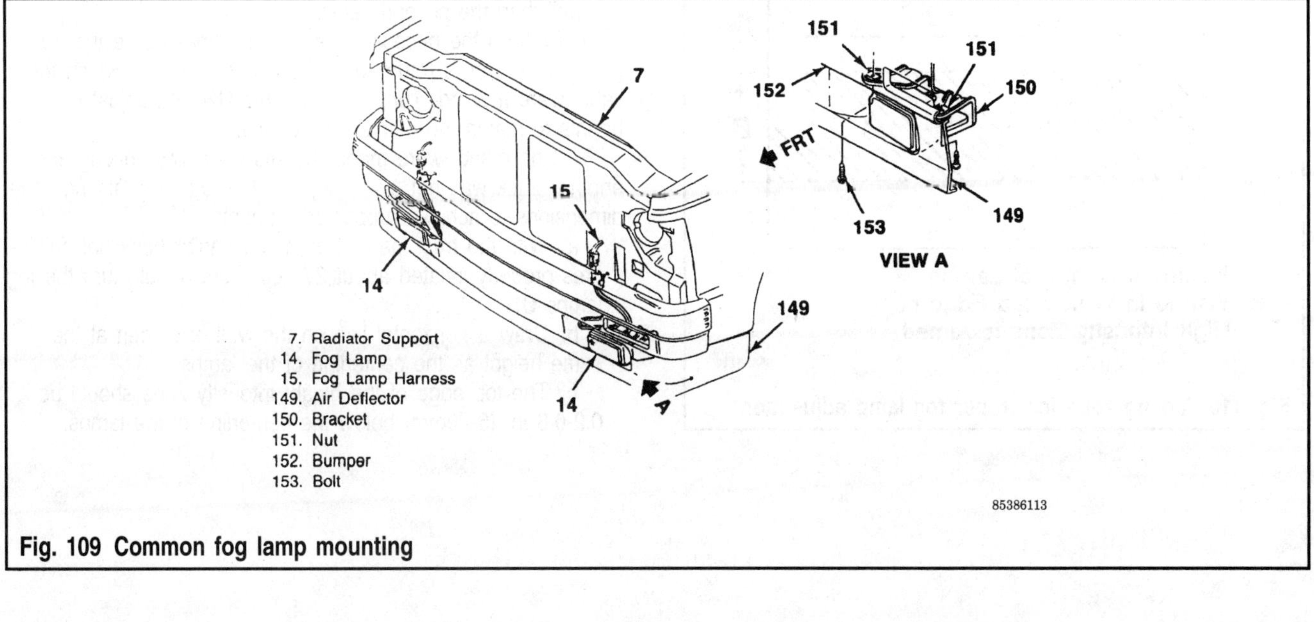

Fig. 109 Common fog lamp mounting

piece of metal; just scrape the paint away from the hole to ensure a good connection.

7. Locate the light terminal, or terminal with the number 87 next to it on the relay; and attach a length of wire between this terminal and the fog/driving lamps.

8. Locate the ignition terminal, or terminal with the number 86 next to it on the relay, and connect a length of wire between this terminal and the light switch.

9. Find a suitable mounting location for the light switch and install. Some examples of mounting areas are a location close to the main light switch, auxiliary light position in the dash panel, if equipped, or in the center of the dash panel.

10. Depending on local and regional regulations, the other end of the switch can be connected to a constant power source like the battery, an ignition opening in the fuse panel, or a parking or headlight wire.

11. Locate the power terminal, or terminal with the No. 30 next to it on the relay, and connect a wire with a fuse of at least 10 amperes in it between the terminal and the battery.

12. With all the wires connected and tied up neatly, connect the negative battery cable.

13. Turn the lights **ON** and adjust the light pattern if needed.

AIMING

➧ **See Figure 110**

The fog lights must be properly aimed to provide the best, safest road illumination. The lights should be checked for proper aim and adjusted as necessary. Certain state and local authorities have requirements for for fog light aiming; these should be checked before adjustment is made.

Fog light adjustment may be temporarily made using a wall, as described below, or on the rear of another vehicle. When adjusted, the lights should not glare in oncoming car or truck windshields, nor should they illuminate the passenger compartment of vehicles driving in front of you. Fog lights should NOT be adjusted to match the beams of the headlights either. They are designed to illuminate the road in a different manner and because of their lower mounting an attempt to match the headlight beams would likely result in blinding oncoming traffic. Improper adjustments may be both dangerous and illegal.

For most factory installed fog lamps, the beam may be adjusted upward and downward using the adjusting screw provided below the lens assembly. No horizontal adjustment is provided for on factory installed lamps. On many aftermarket lamps however, aiming is achieved by physically adjusting the housing. Most aftermarket applications do not use adjustment screws, instead the mounting bolts are loosened, the housing is repositioned slightly and the retainers are tightened again.

Before removing the fog lamp assembly or disturbing the lamp in any way, note the current settings in order to make adjusting the headlights upon reassembly easier. This can be done using the wall of a garage or a building:

1. Park the truck on a level surface, with the fuel tank no more than 1/2 full and with the vehicle empty of all extra cargo (unless normally carried). The vehicle should be facing a wall or screen which is 2 1/5 feet from the front of the truck.

➡The truck's fuel tank should be about half full when adjusting the fog lamps. Tires should be properly inflated, and if a heavy load is normally carried in the bed, it should remain there.

2. If this is be performed outdoors, it is advisable to wait until dusk in order to properly see the fog light beams on the wall. If done in a garage, darken the area around the wall as much as possible by closing shades or hanging cloth over the windows.

3. Turn the fog lamps **ON** and mark the wall at the center of each light's beam. A short length of masking tape which is visible from the front of the truck may be used.

4. If the beam on 1 side of the vehicle is not working, park another like-sized truck in the exact spot where the truck was and mark the beams using the same side light on that truck. Then switch the trucks so the S/T is back in the original spot. The truck must be parked no closer to or farther away from the wall than the second vehicle.

5. Perform the necessary repairs, but make sure the truck is not moved or is returned to the exact spot from which the lights were marked. Turn the fog lights **ON** and adjust the beams to match the marks on the wall.

6. If no marks were made (beams were not working and another truck was not available) use the fog lamp aiming zone dimensions to achieve proper adjustment:

a. With the truck parked as noted earlier (tank half full, tires properly inflated about 2 1/5 feet from a wall) turn the fog lamps **ON**.

b. Draw a horizontal line on the wall or screen at the same height as the centerline of the lamps.

c. The top edge of the height intensity zone should be 0.2-0.8 in. (5-20mm) below the centerline of the lamps.

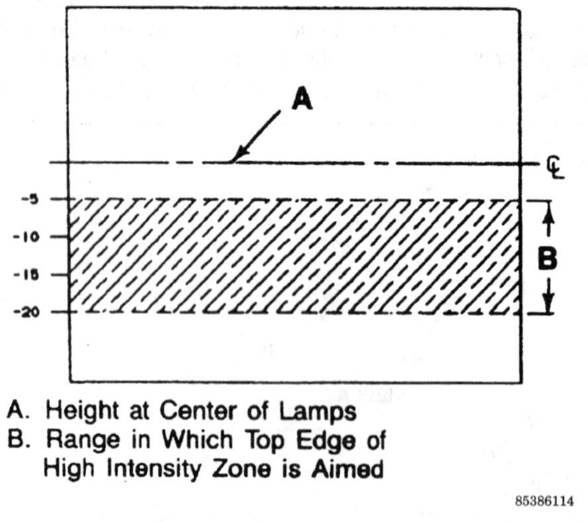

Fig. 110 Aiming zone for proper fog lamp adjustment

TRAILER WIRING

Wiring the vehicle for towing is fairly easy. There are a number of good wiring kits available and these should be used, rather than trying to design your own.

All trailers will need brake lights and turn signals as well as tail lights and side marker lights. Most areas require extra marker lights for overwide trailers. Also, most areas have recently required back-up lights for trailers, and most trailer manufacturers have been building trailers with back-up lights for several years.

Additionally, some Class I, most Class II and just about all Class III trailers will have electric brakes. Add to this number an accessories wire, to operate trailer internal equipment or to charge the trailer's battery, and you can have as many as seven wires in the harness.

Determine the equipment on your trailer and buy the wiring kit necessary. The kit will contain all the wires needed, plus a plug adapter set which includes the female plug, mounted on the bumper or hitch, and the male plug, wired into, or plugged into the trailer harness.

When installing the kit, follow the manufacturer's instructions. The color coding of the wires is usually standard throughout the industry. One point to note: some domestic vehicles, and most imported vehicles, have separate turn signals. On most domestic vehicles, the brake lights and rear turn signals operate with the same bulb. For those vehicles with separate turn signals, you can purchase an isolation unit so that the brake lights won't blink whenever the turn signals are operated, or, you can go to your local electronics supply house and buy four diodes to wire in series with the brake and turn signal bulbs. Diodes will isolate the brake and turn signals. The choice is yours. The isolation units are simple and quick to install, but far more expensive than the diodes. The diodes, however, require more work to install properly, since they require the cutting of each bulb's wire and soldering in place of the diode.

One, final point, the best kits are those with a spring loaded cover on the vehicle mounted socket. This cover prevents dirt and moisture from corroding the terminals. Never let the vehicle socket hang loosely; always mount it securely to the bumper or hitch.

CIRCUIT PROTECTION

Fuse Block and Fuses

See Figure 111

The fuse block on most models covered by this manual is located on the side of the instrument panel to the left of the steering column. If the panel is not visible, check for a removable compartment door or trim panel which may be used on later models to hide the block.

Each fuse block uses miniature fuses (normally plug-in blade terminal type for these vehicles) which are designed for increased circuit protection and greater reliability. The compact plug-in or blade terminal design allows for fingertip removal and replacement.

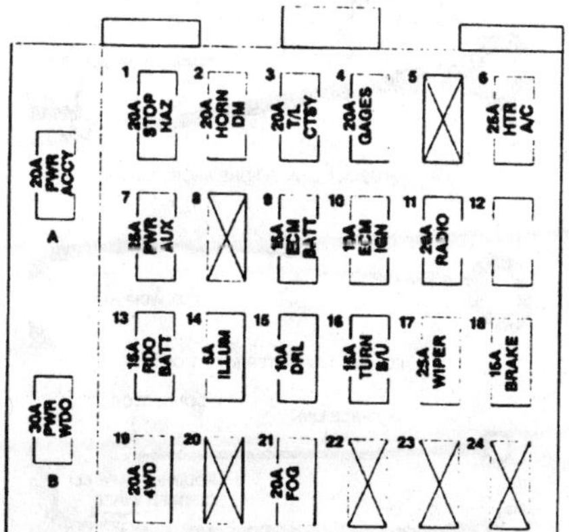

Fig. 111 Example of a common fuse block

Although most fuses are interchangeable in size, the amperage values are not. Should you install a fuse with too high a value, damaging current could be allowed to destroy the component you were attempting to protect by using a fuse in the first place. The plug-in type fuses have a bold number molded on them and are color coded for easy identification. Be sure to only replace a fuse with the proper amperage rated substitute.

A blown fuse can easily be checked by visual inspection or by continuity checking.

FUSE REPLACEMENT

See Figures 112, 113 and 114

1. Pull the fuse from the fuse block.
2. Inspect the fuse element (through the clear plastic body) to the blade terminal for defects.

When replacing the fuse, DO NOT use one of a higher amperage.

3. Once repairs are completed, install a replacement fuse of the same amperage.

Fusible Links

A fusible link is a protective device used in an electrical circuit and acts very much like a standard fuse. The major difference lies in that fusible links are larger and capable of conducting a higher amperage than most fuses. When the current increases beyond the rated amperage for a given link, the fusible metal of the wire link will melt, thus breaking the electrical circuit and preventing further damage to any other components or wiring. Whenever a fusible link is melted because of a short circuit, correct the cause before installing a

88456p52

Fig. 112 Remove the fuse panel cover or trim panel (note the spare fuses and fuse puller on the cover)

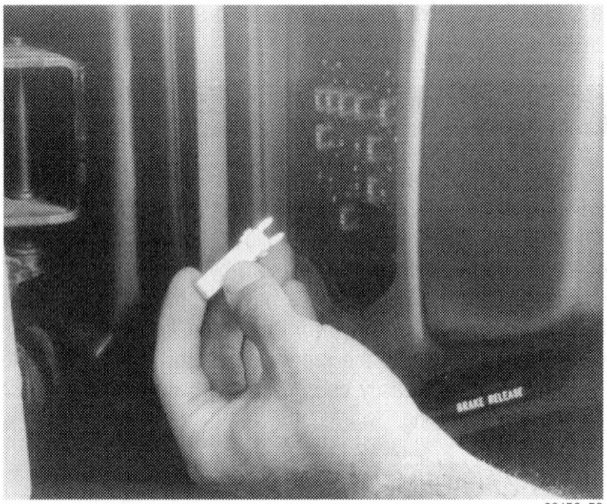
88456p53

Fig. 113 Removing a fuse using the fuse puller

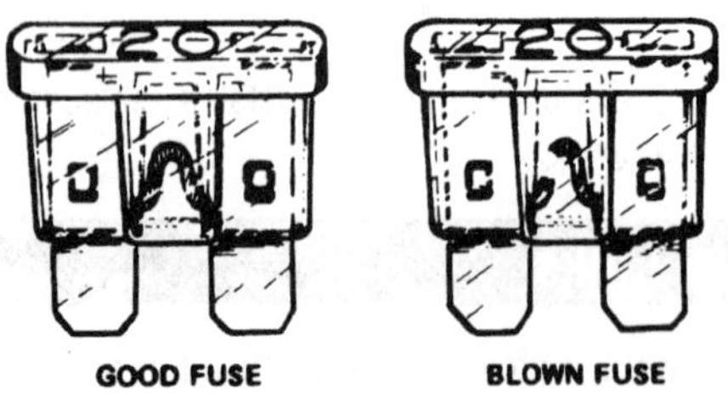

85386119

Fig. 114 Visual examination will reveal a blown fuse, but it should not be replaced until repairs are made

new one. There are 4 different gauge sizes commonly used and they are usually color coded so that they may be easily installed in their original positions.

REPLACING FUSIBLE LINKS

See Figure 115

1. Disconnect the negative battery cable, followed by the positive cable.
2. Locate the burned out link.
3. If both ends of the link are ring terminal connectors which are easily accessed:
   a. Measure the installed length necessary for the new link.
   b. Unbolt and remove the link and connector pieces.
   c. Obtain a suitable length of link, then strip the insulation off the harness wire back 1/2 in (12.7mm) to allow soldering of the new connectors.
   d. Position the new connector around the new link and crimp it securely. Then, solder the connection, using rosin core solder and sufficient heat to guarantee a good connection. Repeat for the remaining connection.

Whenever splicing a new wire, always bond the splice with rosin core solder, then cover with electrical tape. Using acid core solder may cause corrosion.

4. If the ends of the connector are not easily accessed, repair the length in the vehicle.
   a. Strip away the melted insulation and cut the burned link ends from the wire.
   b. Strip the wire back 1/2 in. (12.7mm) to allow soldering of the new link.
   c. Using a new fusible link of appropriate gauge and length, solder it into the circuit.
5. Tape all exposed wiring with electrical tape and seal with silicone or use a heat shrink tube, if available to weatherproof the repair.
6. If removed from the vehicle, install the link and secure the connectors.

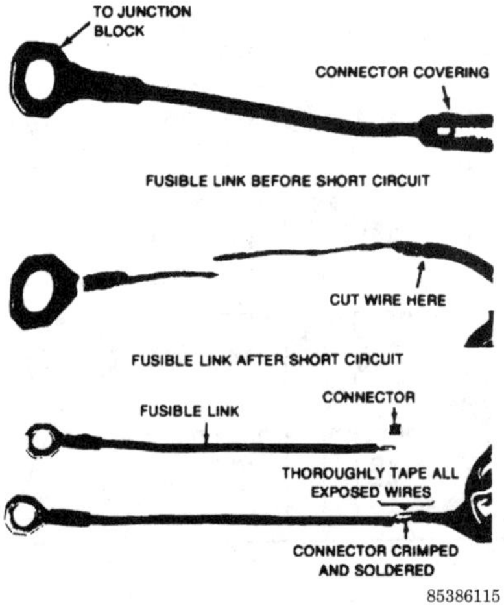

85386115

Fig. 115 Fusible links may be repaired by soldering a new link into the wire

7. Reconnect the positive, followed by the negative battery cables.

Circuit Breakers

One device used to protect electrical components from burning out due to excessive current is a circuit breaker. Circuit breakers open and close the flow path for the electricity rapidly in order to protect the circuit if current is excessive. A circuit breaker is used on components which are more likely to draw excessive current such as a breaker often found in the light switch that protects the headlight circuit. Circuit breakers may be found in various locations on the vehicle including on/in the protected component, on a firewall bracket, the convenience center and/or the fuse block.

Convenience Center

See Figures 116 and 117

The convenience center is used to centrally locate various buzzers, relays, flashers and/or circuit breakers. The turn signal and hazard flasher units are usually located in the convenience center located just below the instrument panel on the drivers side. Replace the flasher by unplugging the old one and plugging in the new one. Confirm proper flasher operation.

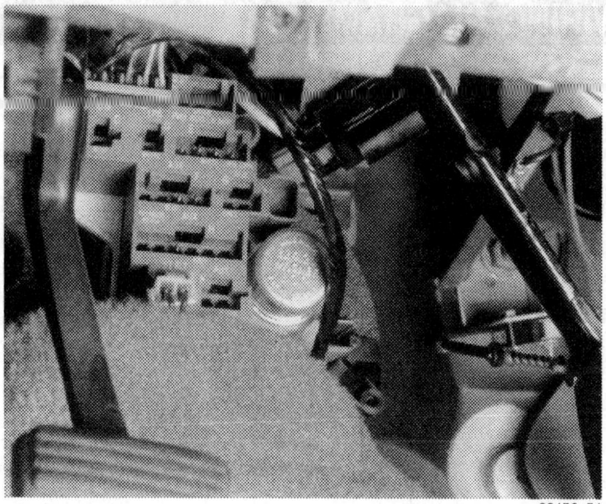

Fig. 116 The convenience center is usually located just below the instrument panel on the driver's side

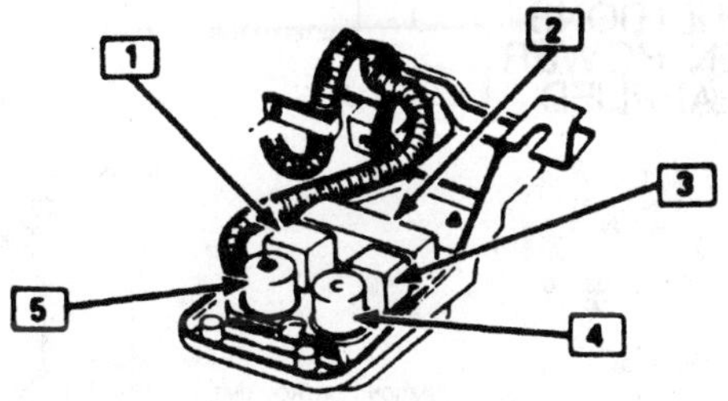

Fig. 117 Common swing-down type convenience center

WIRING DIAGRAMS

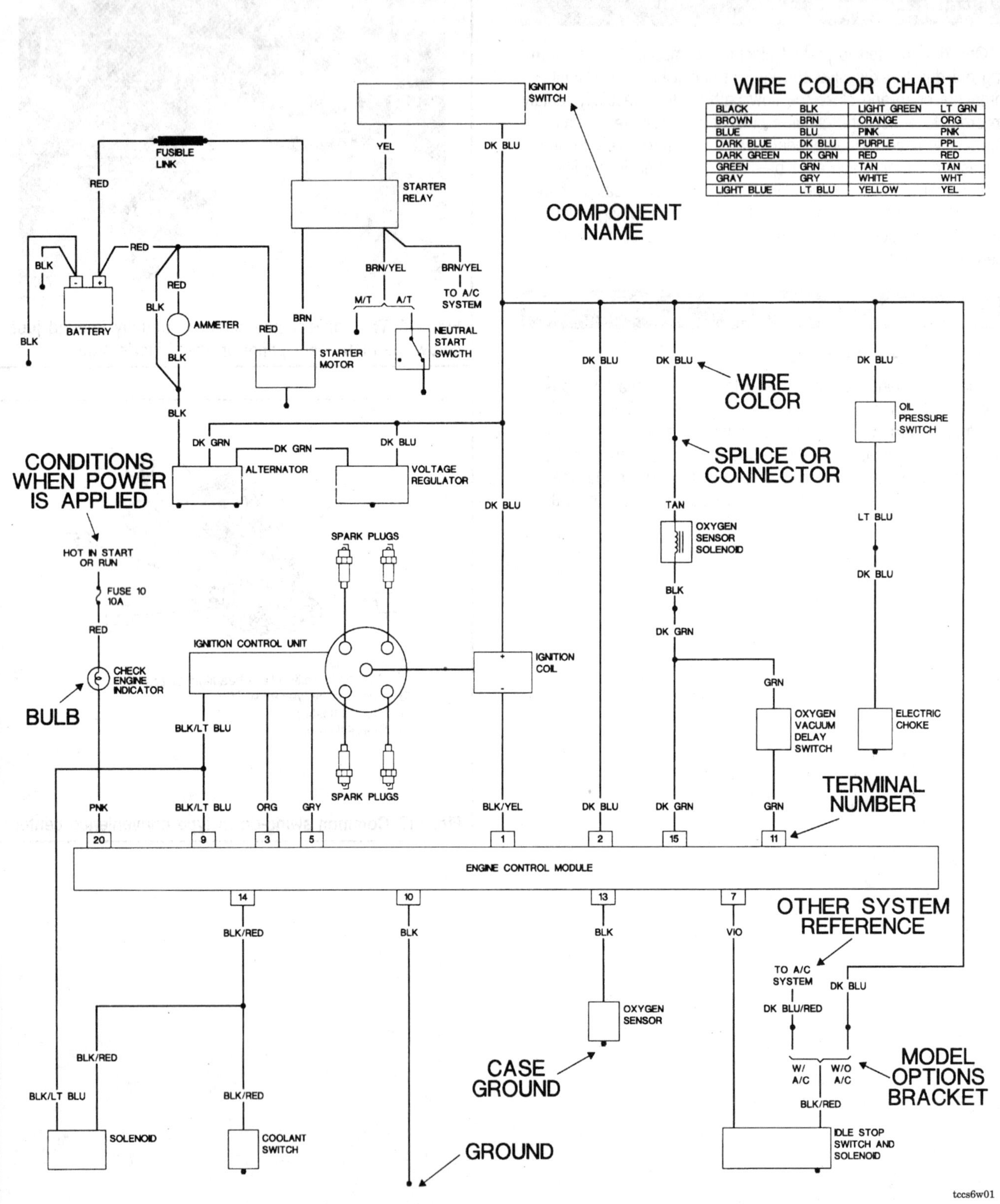

BLACK	BLK	LIGHT GREEN	LT GRN
BROWN	BRN	ORANGE	ORG
BLUE	BLU	PINK	PNK
DARK BLUE	DK BLU	PURPLE	PPL
DARK GREEN	DK GRN	RED	RED
GREEN	GRN	TAN	TAN
GRAY	GRY	WHITE	WHT
LIGHT BLUE	LT BLU	YELLOW	YEL

Fig. 118 Sample diagram — how to read and interpret wiring

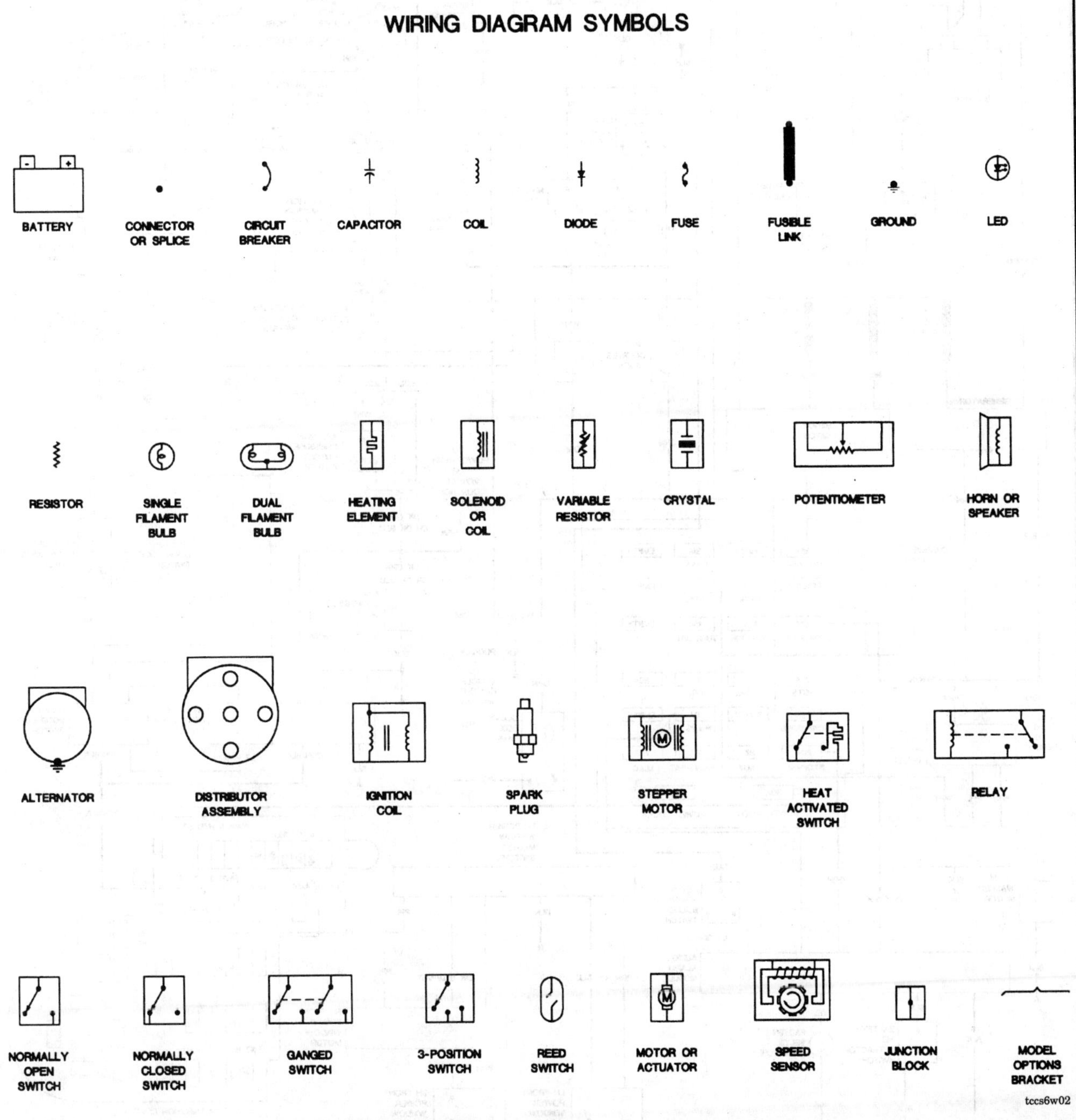

Fig. 119 Common wiring diagram symbols

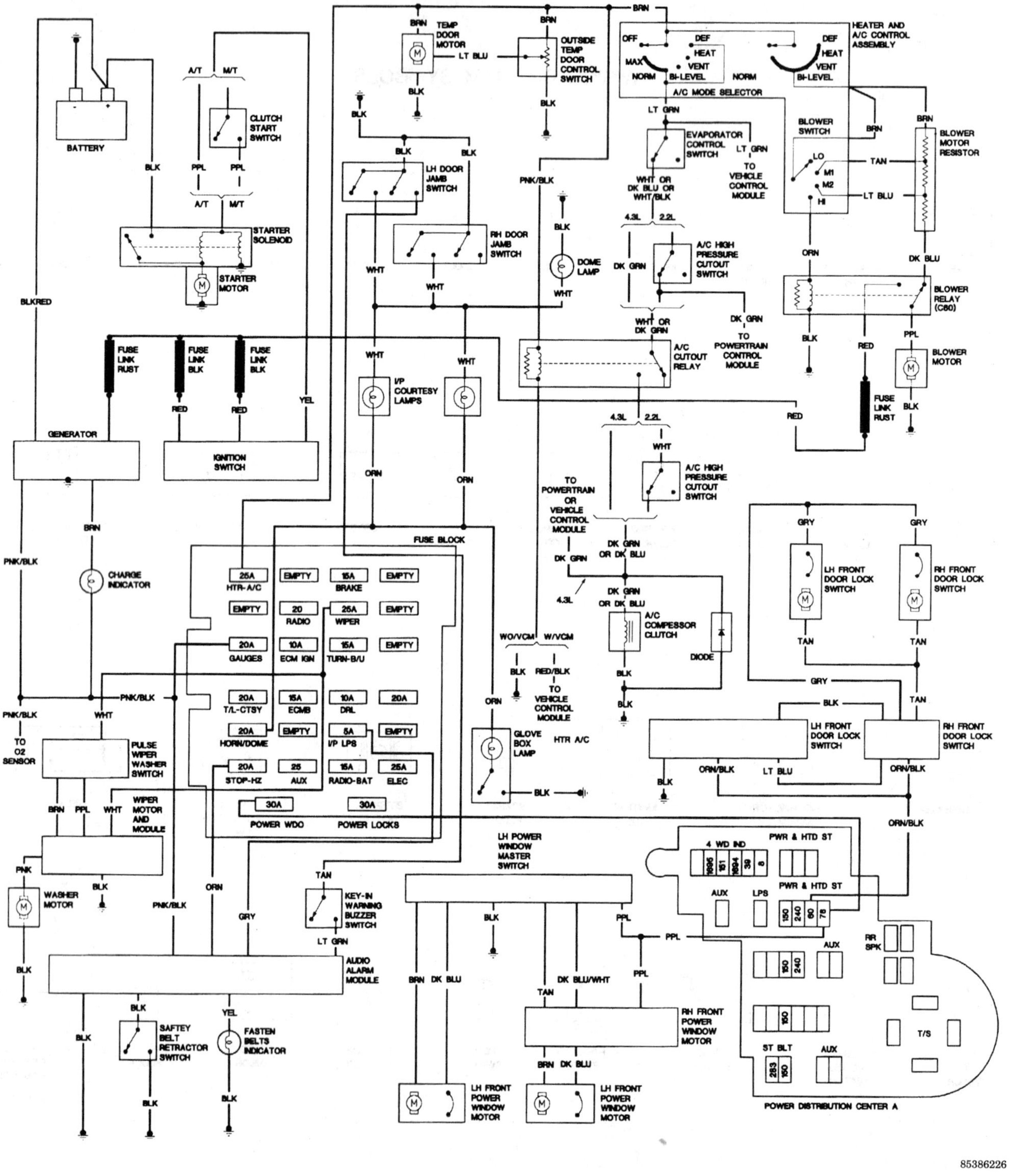

Fig. 120 Chassis wiring — 1994 models

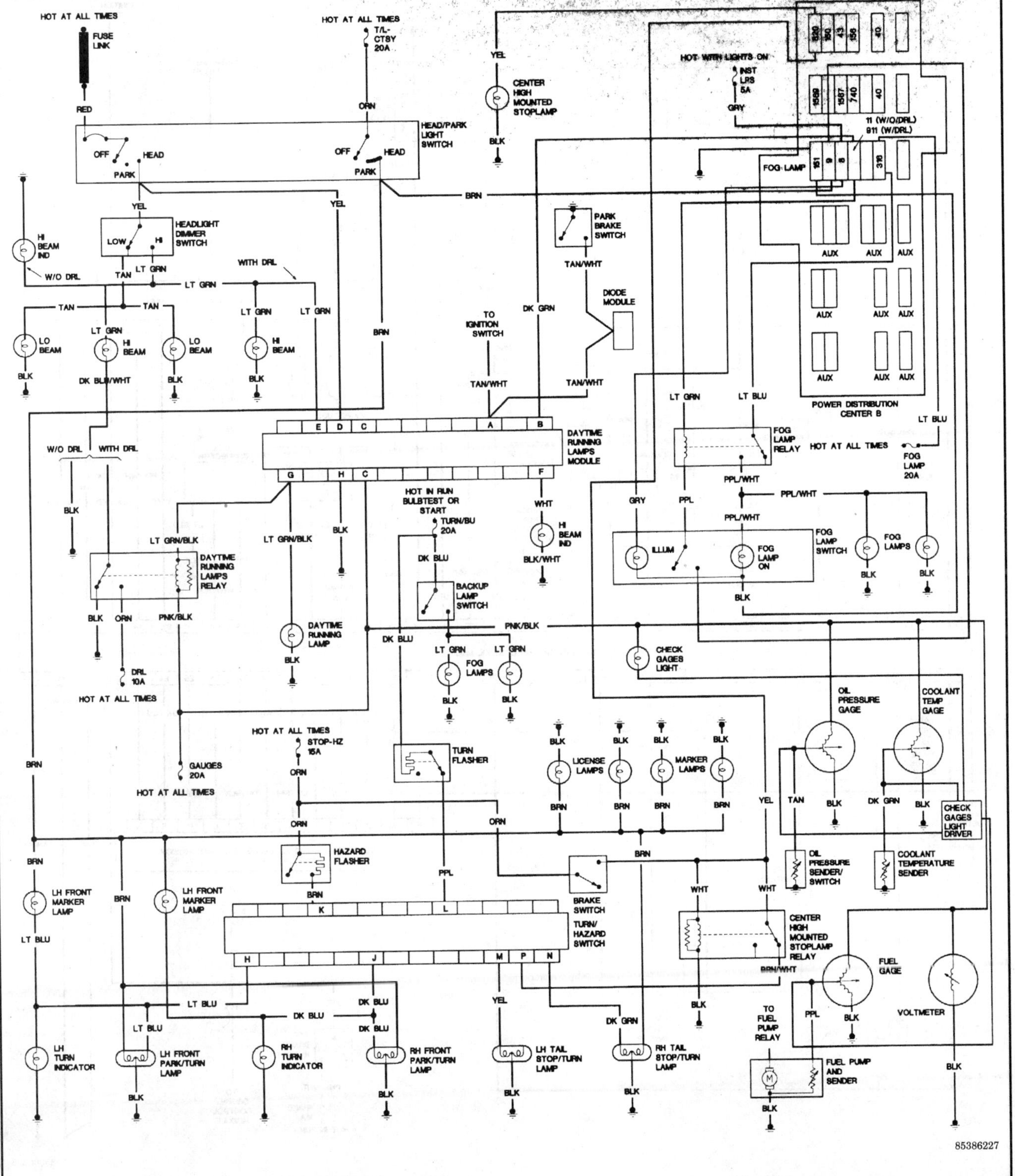

Fig. 121 Chassis wiring — 1994 models (continued)

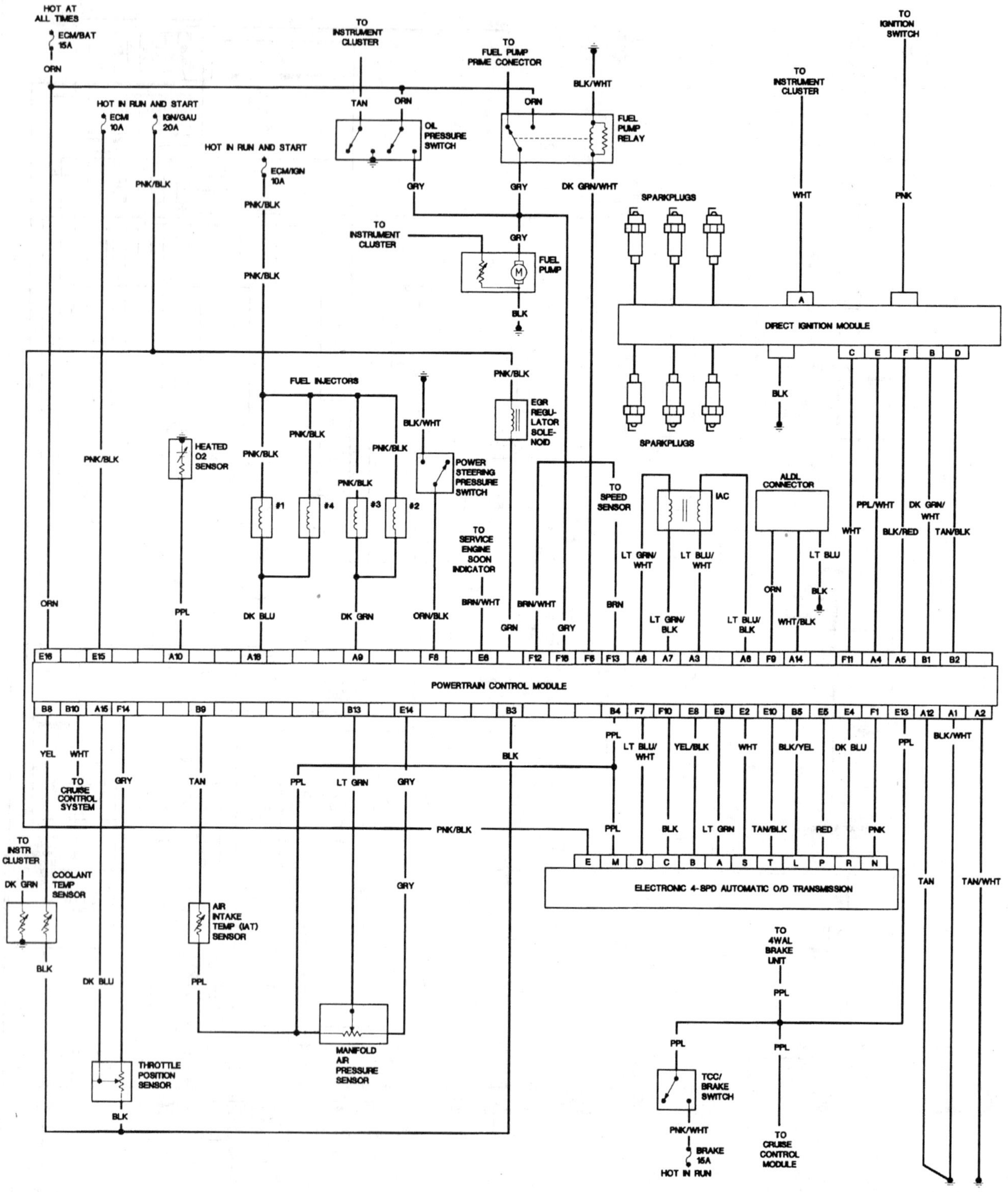

85386228

Fig. 122 2.2L engine wiring — 1994 models

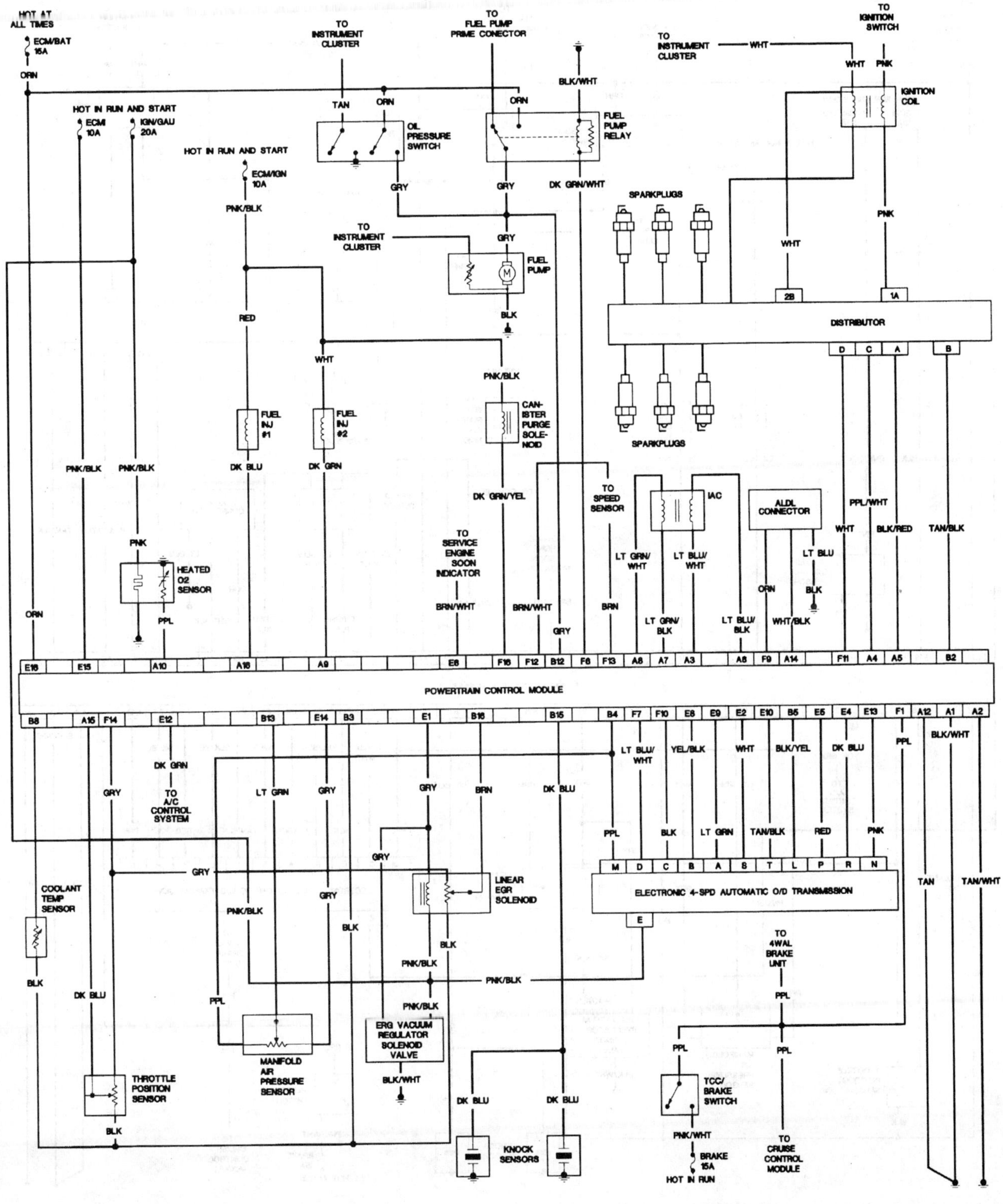

Fig. 123 4.3L (VIN Z) engine wiring — 1994 PCM equipped models

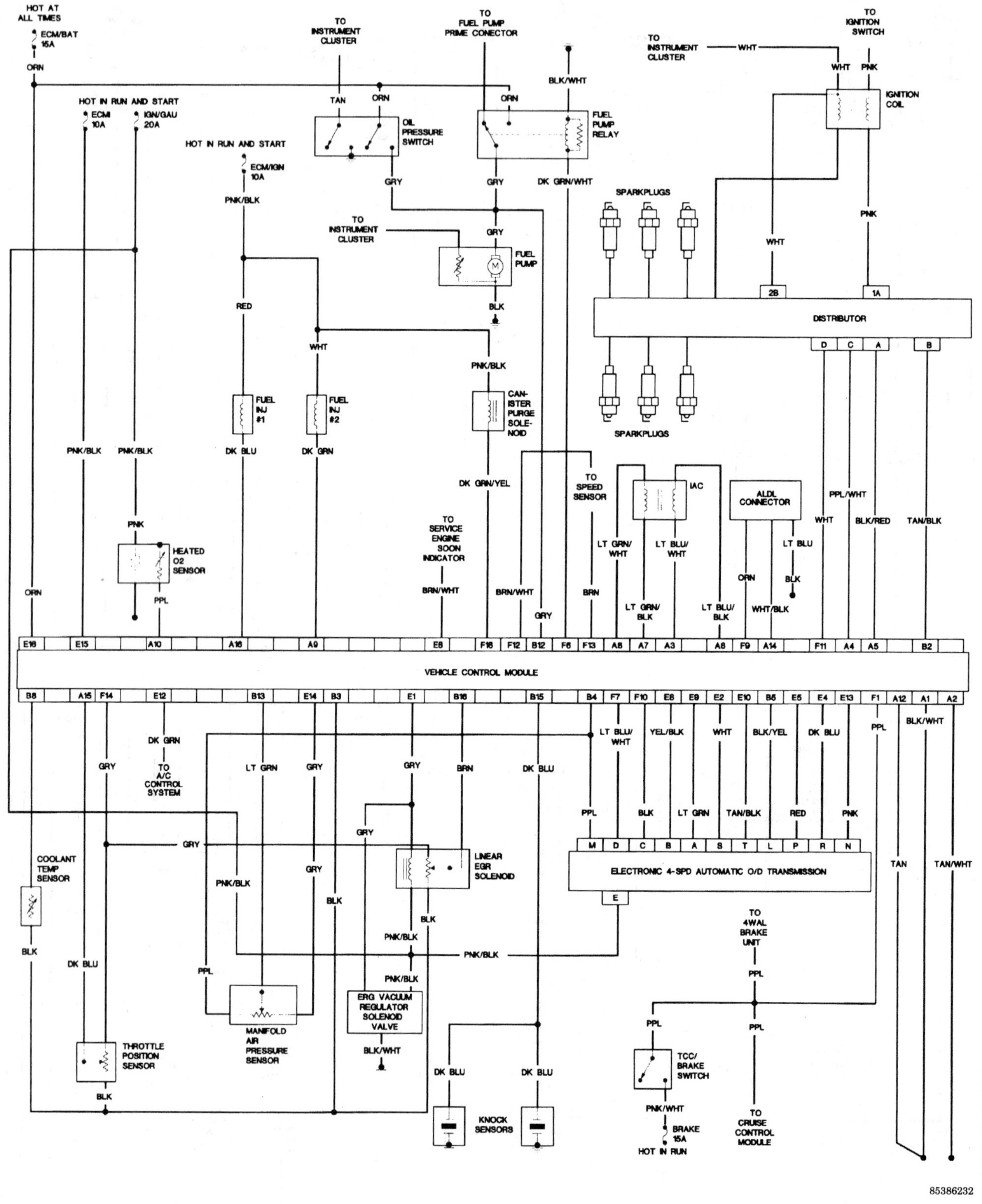

Fig. 124 4.3L (VIN Z) engine wiring — 1994 VCM equipped models

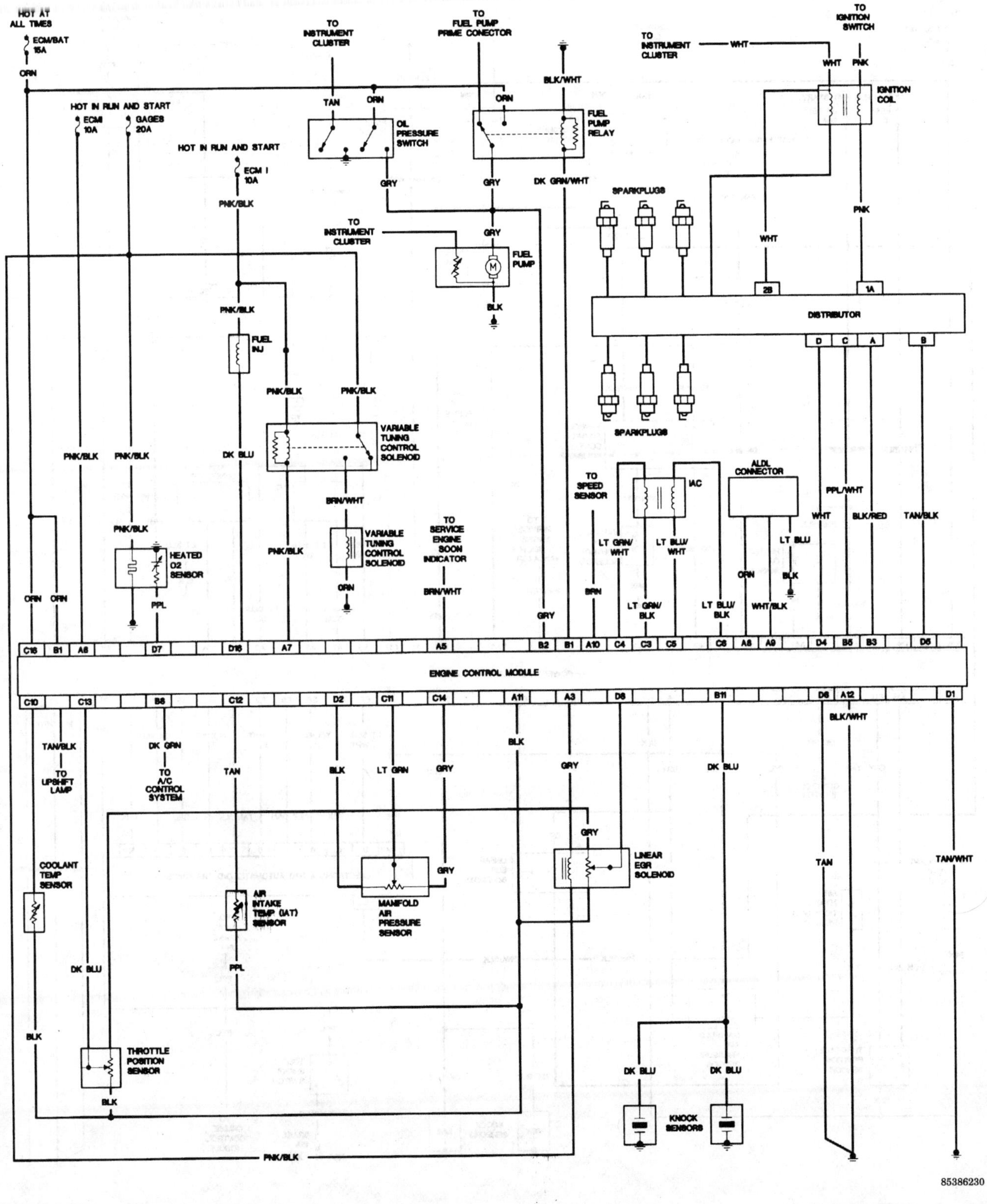

Fig. 125 4.3L (VIN W) engine wiring — 1994 ECM equipped models with manual transmission

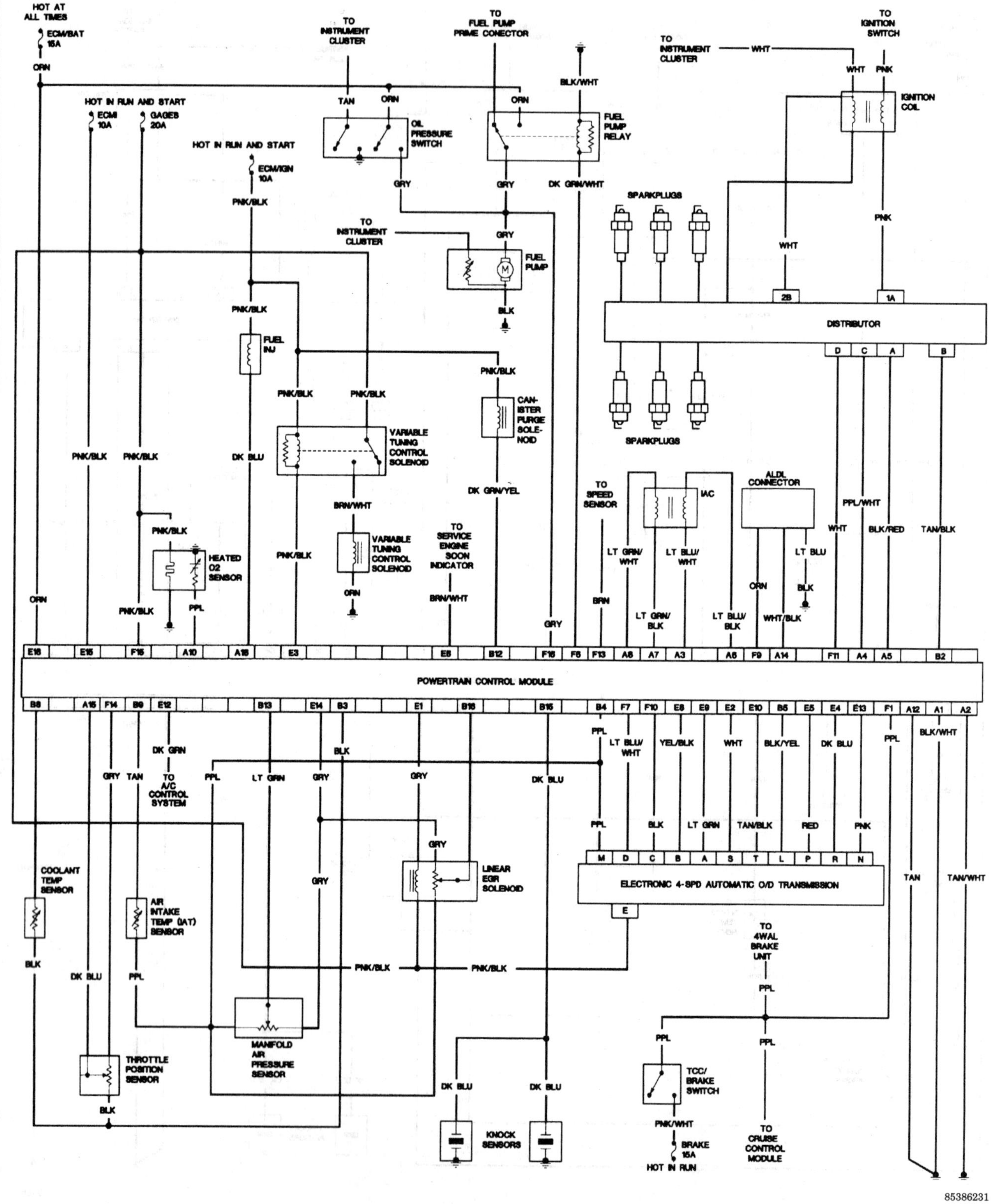

Fig. 126 4.3L (VIN W) engine wiring — 1994 PCM equipped models with automatic transmission

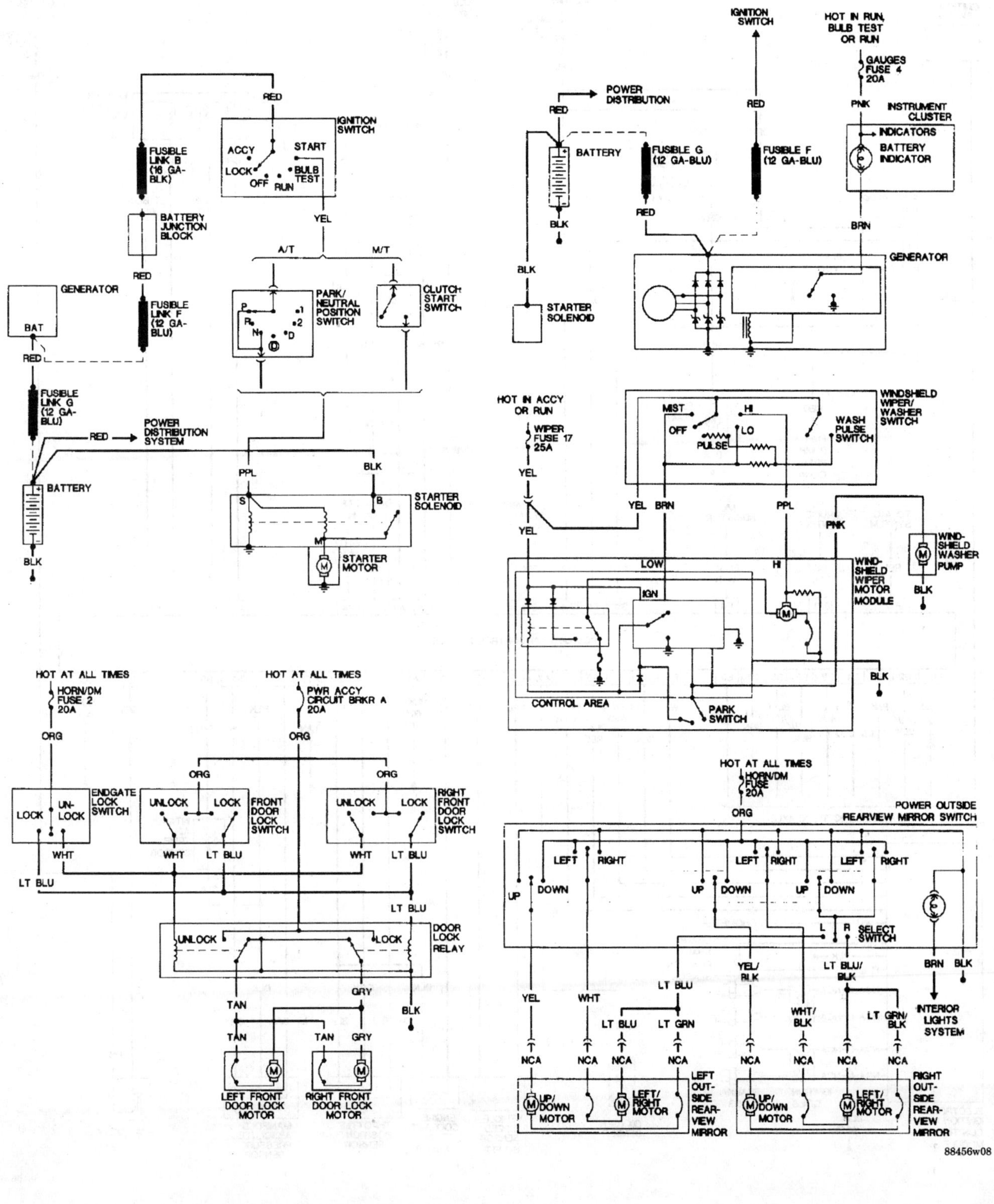

Fig. 127 Chassis wiring — 1995 models

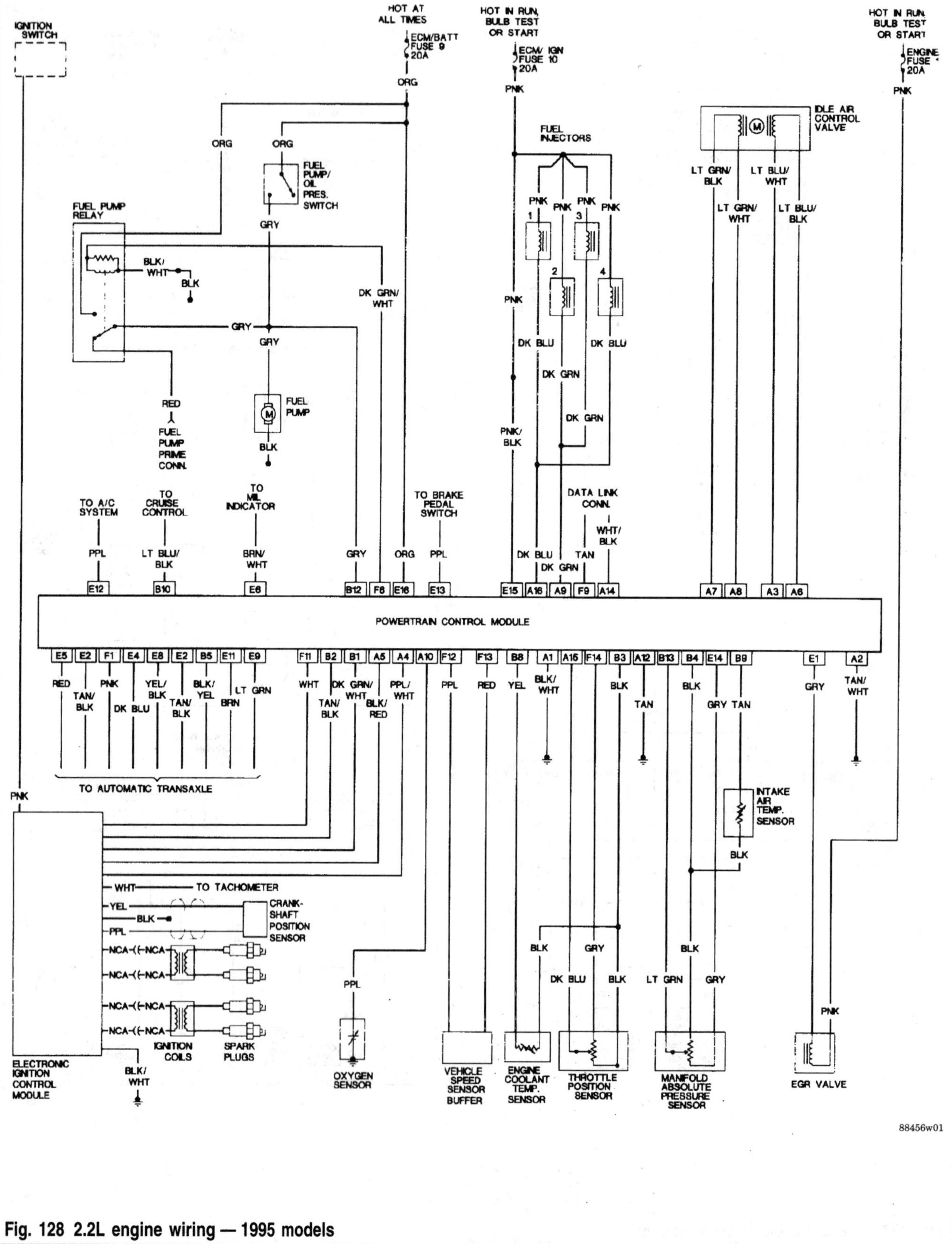

Fig. 128 2.2L engine wiring — 1995 models

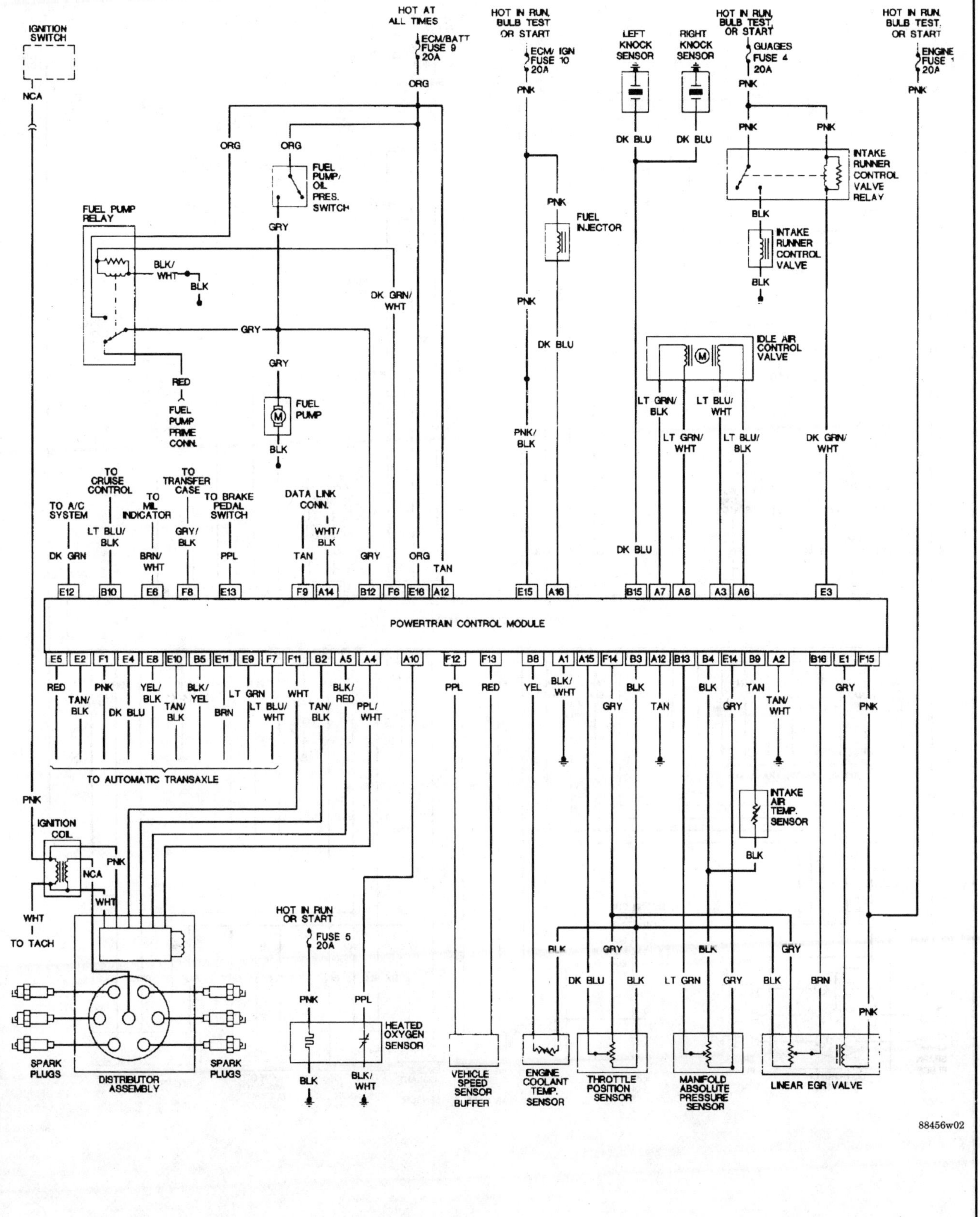

Fig. 129 4.3L (VIN W) engine wiring — 1995 PCM equipped models

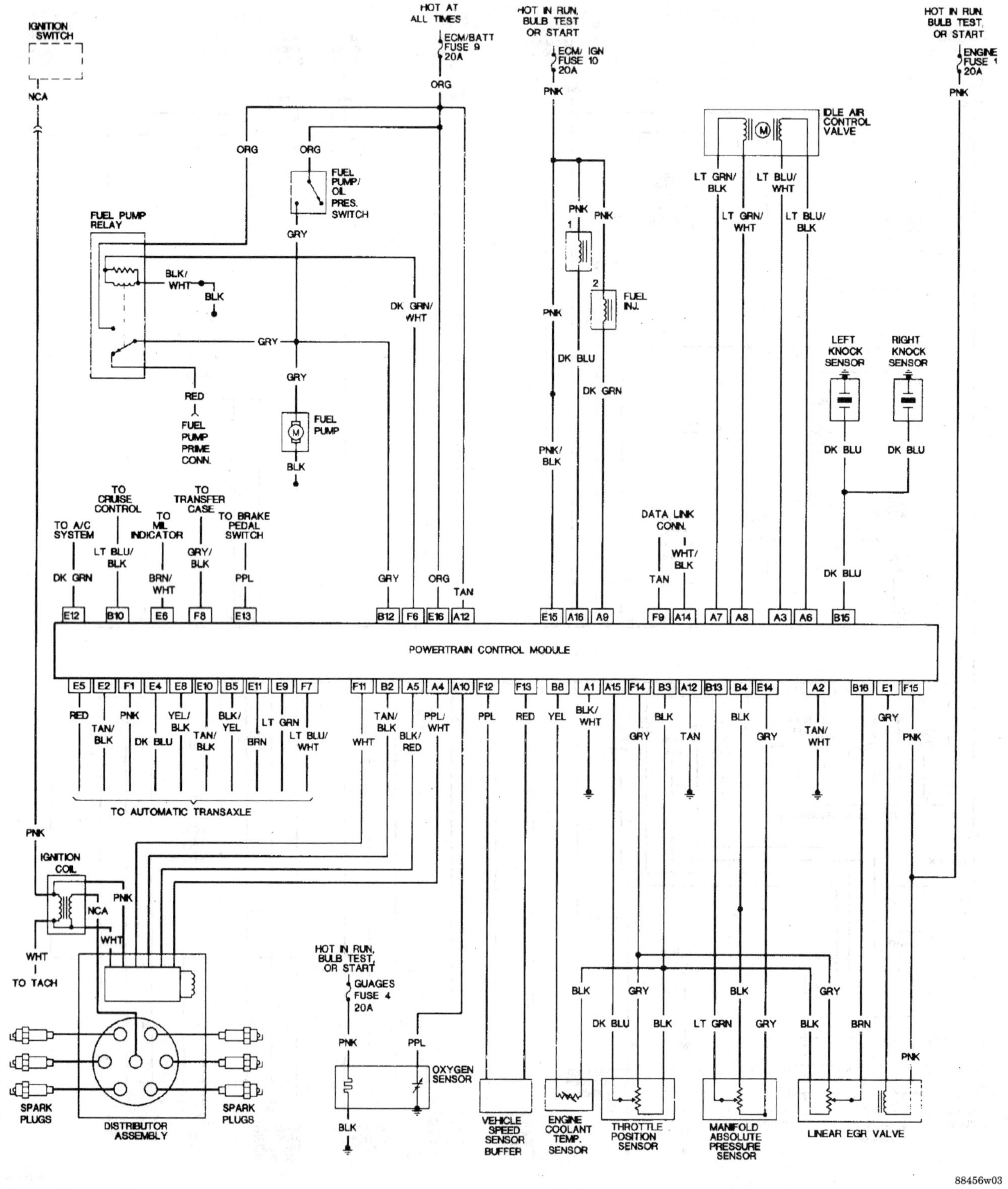

Fig. 130 4.3L (VIN Z) engine wiring — 1995 PCM equipped models

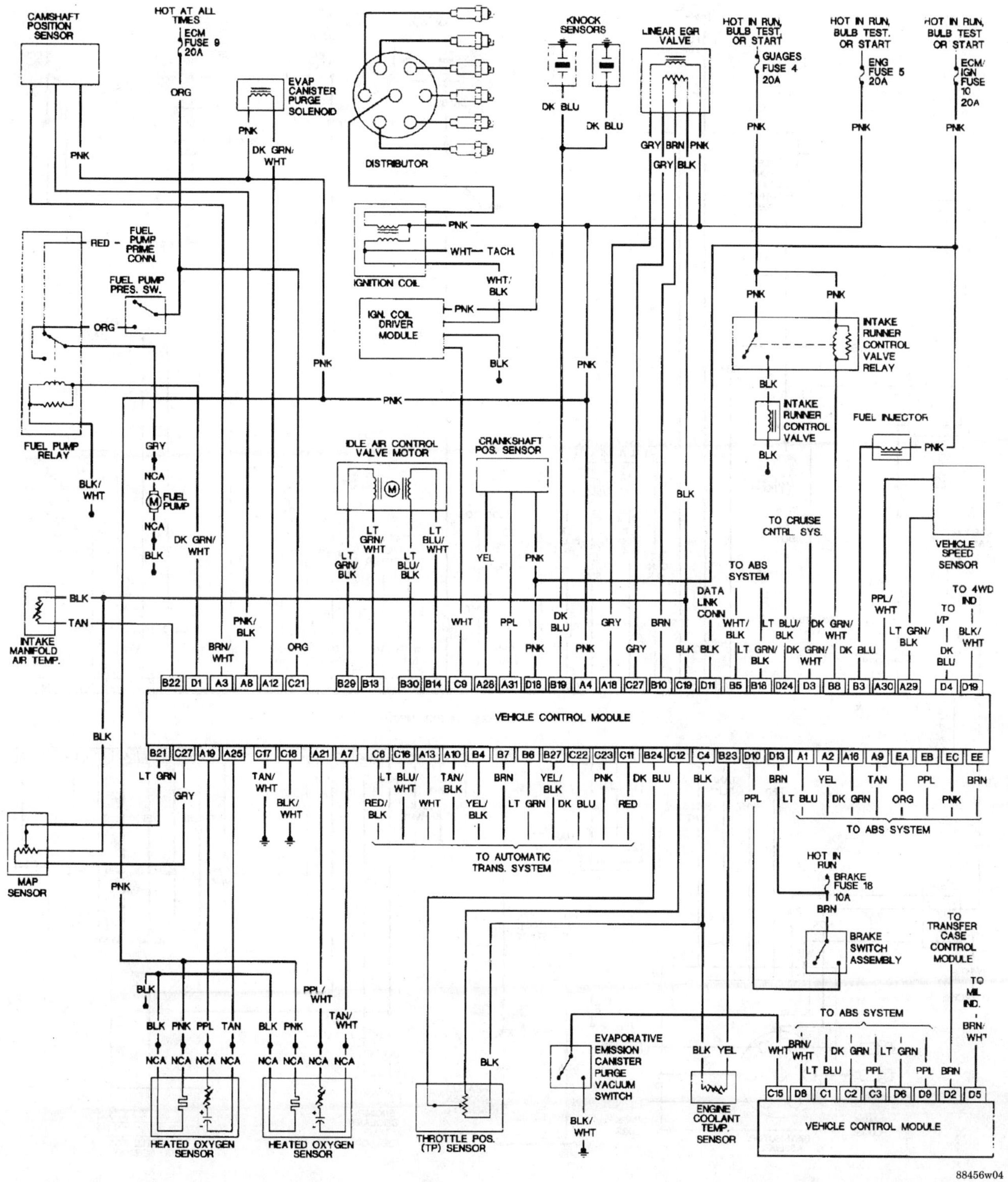

88456w04

Fig. 131 4.3L (VIN W) engine wiring — 1995 VCM equipped models

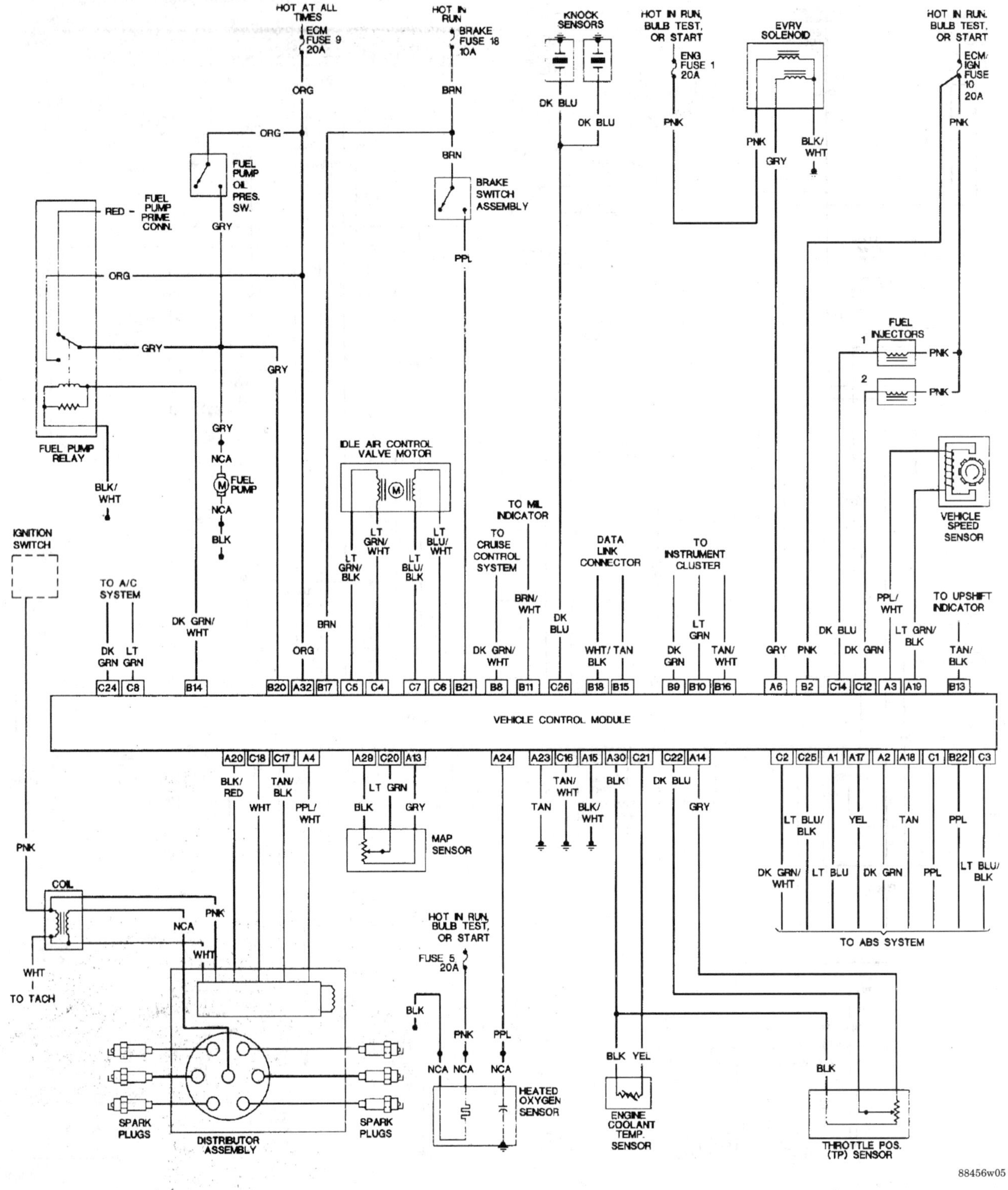

Fig. 132 4.3L (VIN Z) engine wiring — 1995 VCM equipped models (only available with manual transmission)

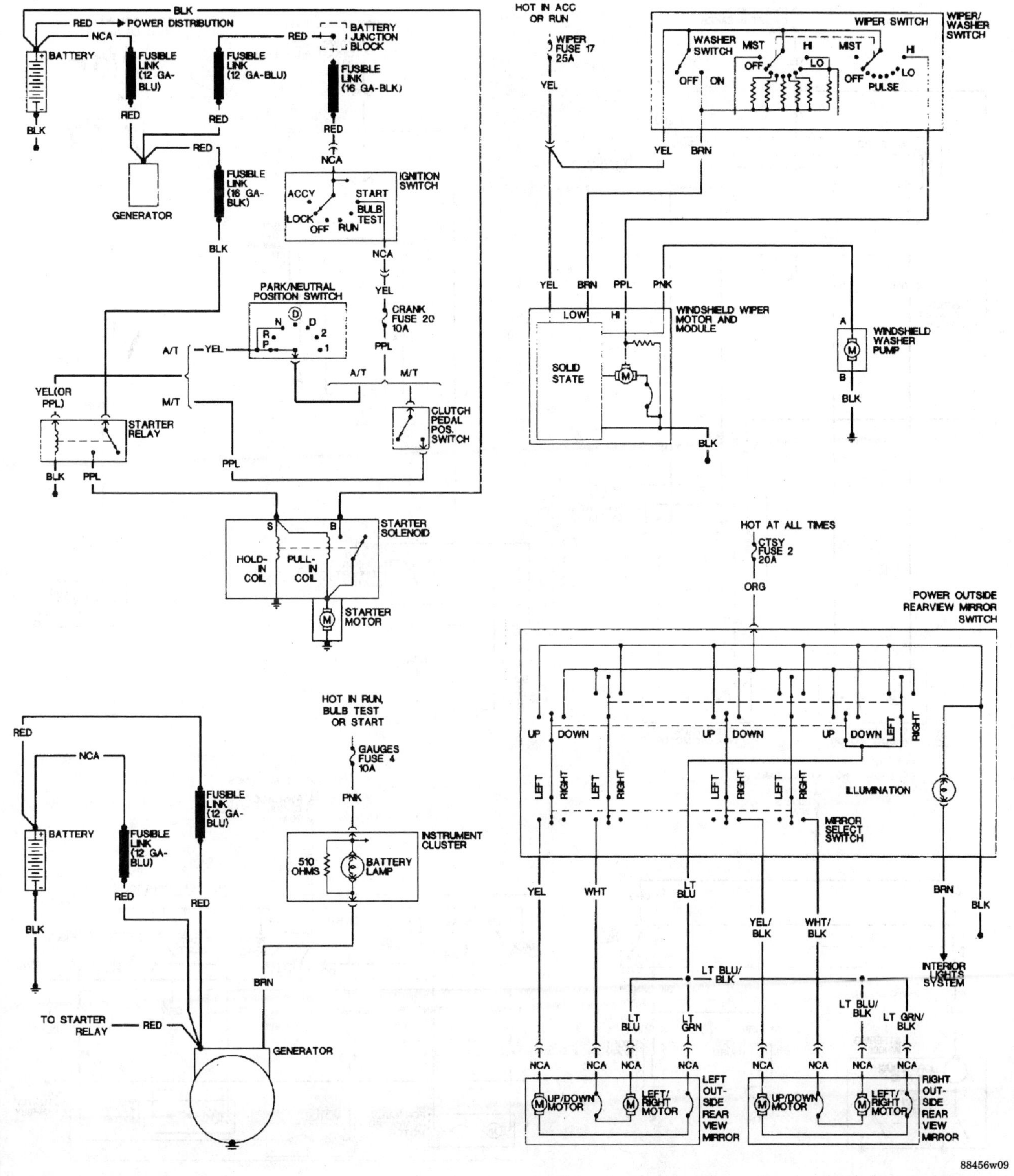

Fig. 133 Chassis wiring — 1996-97 models

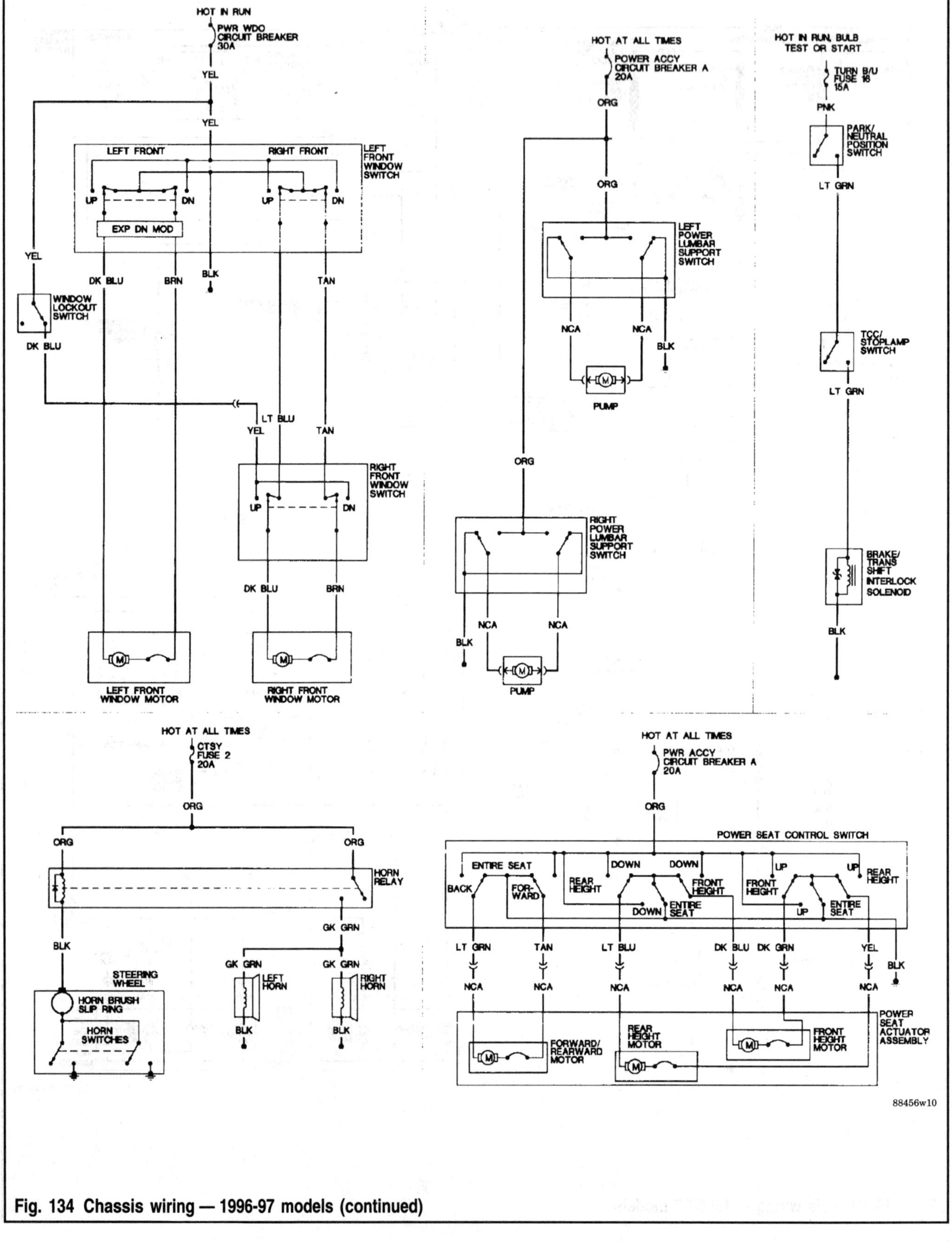

Fig. 134 Chassis wiring — 1996-97 models (continued)

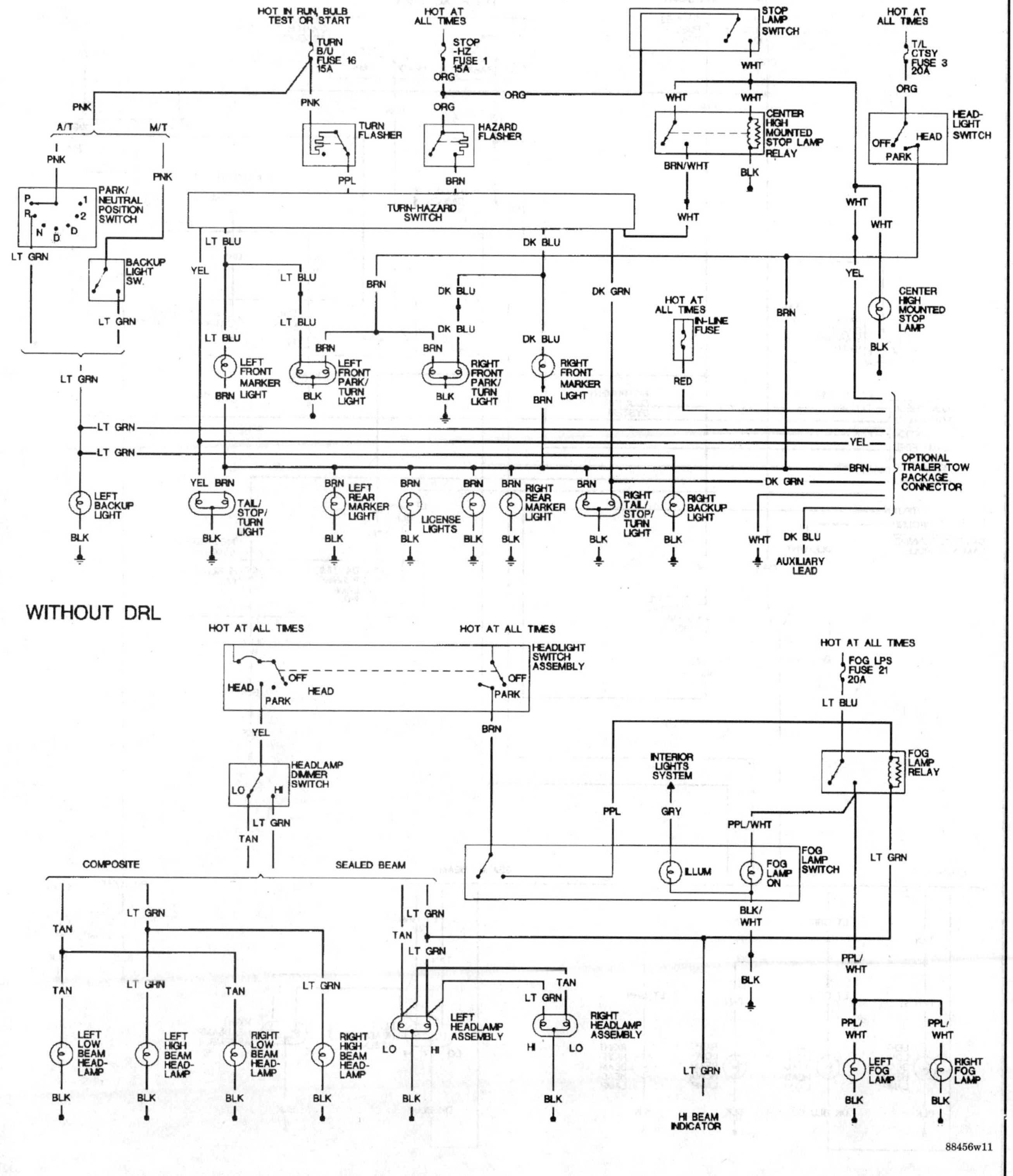

88456w11

Fig. 135 Chassis wiring — 1996-97 models (continued)

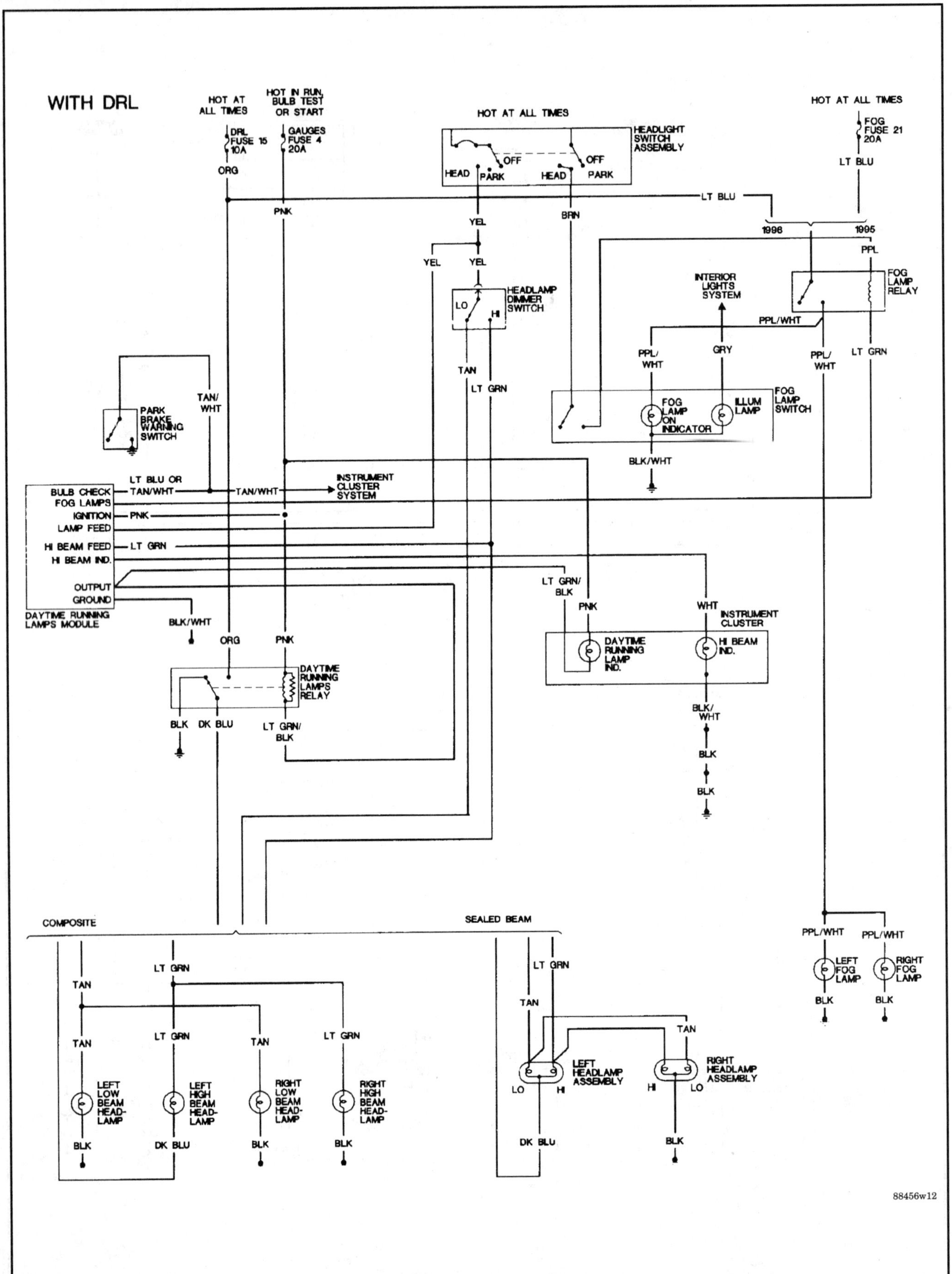

Fig. 136 Chassis wiring — 1996-97 models (continued)

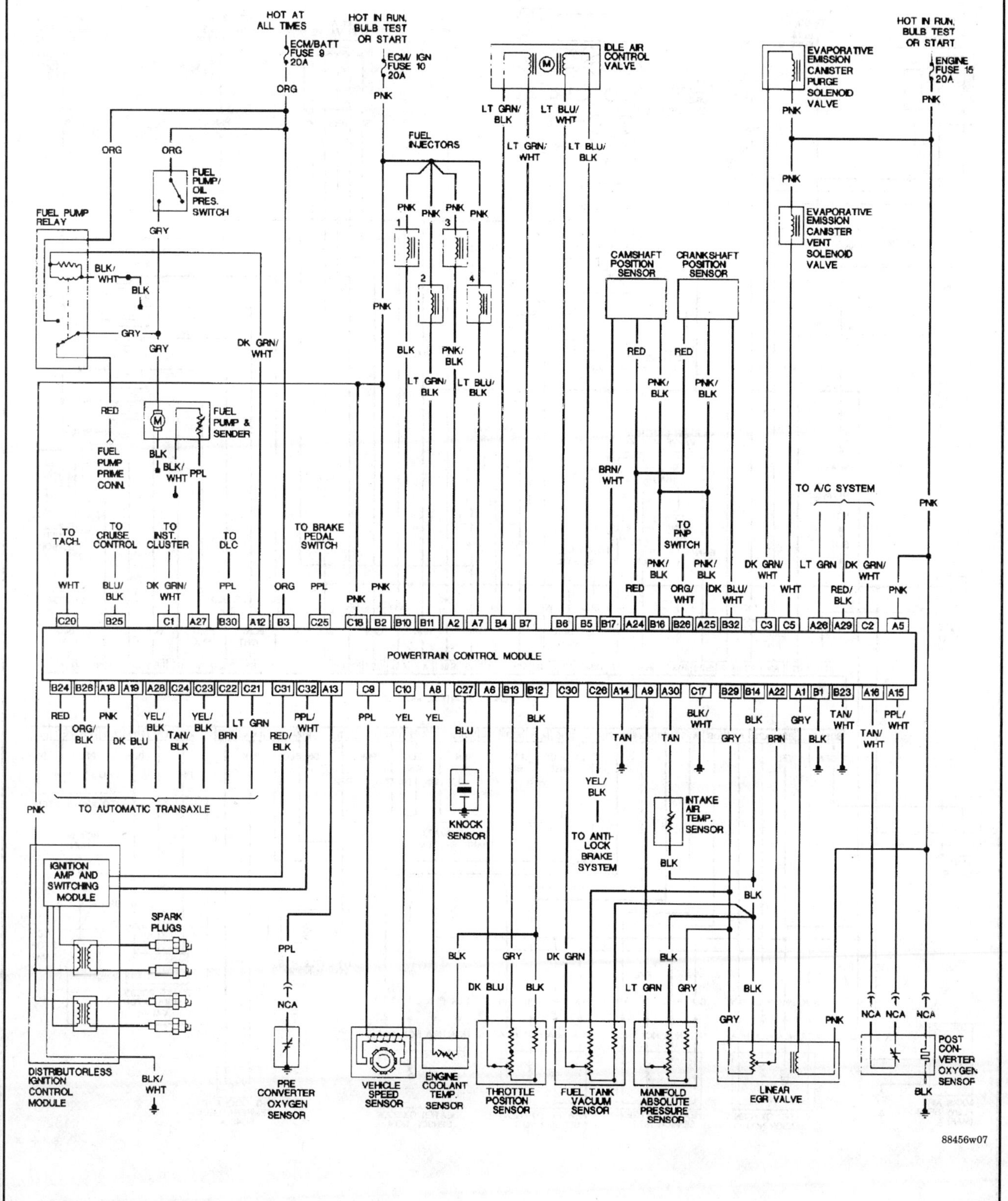

Fig. 137 2.2L engine wiring — 1996-97 models

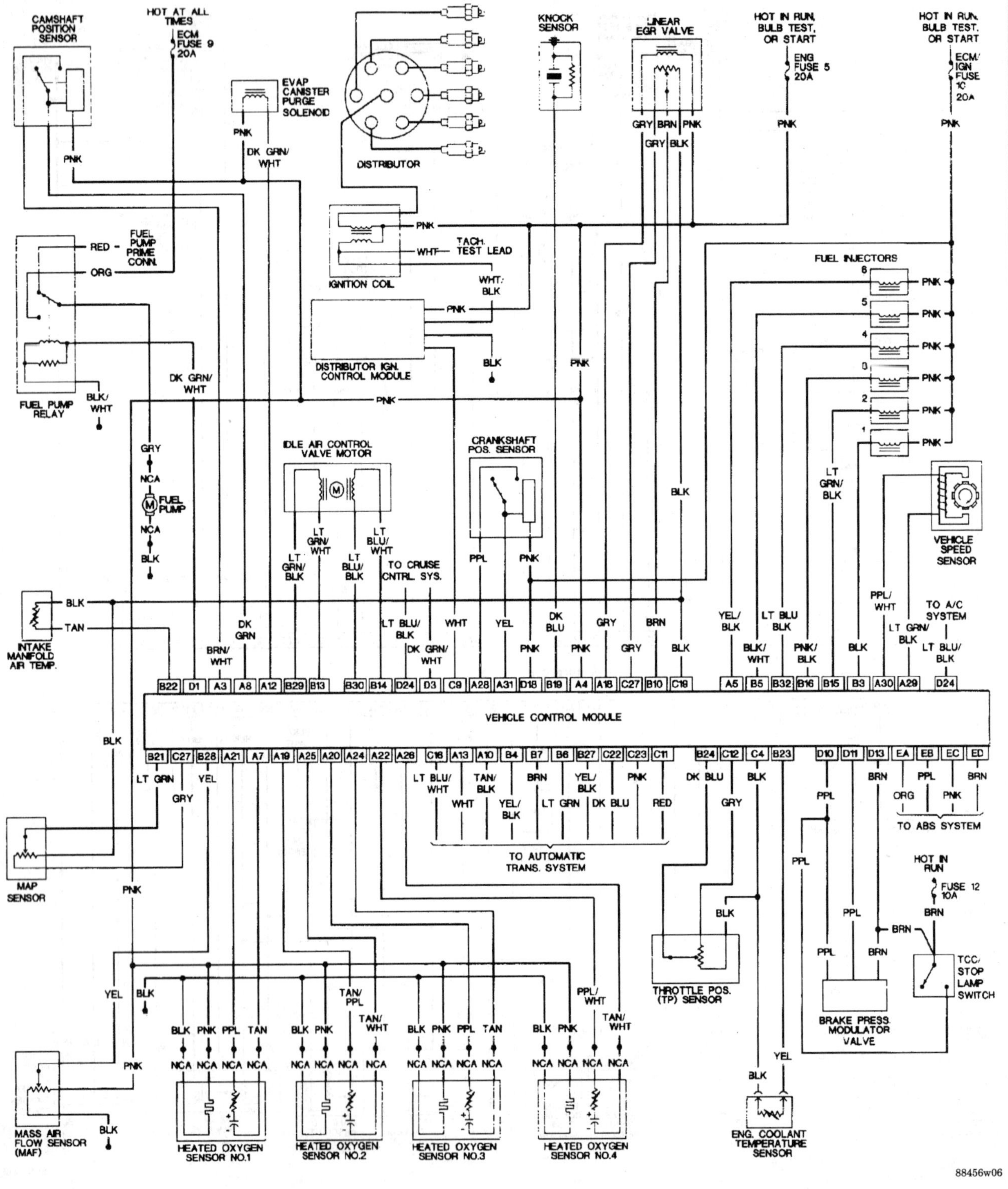

Fig. 138 4.3L engine wiring — 1996-97 models

7 DRIVE TRAIN

MANUAL TRANSMISSION

Understanding the Manual Transmission and Clutch

Because of the way an internal combustion gasoline engine breathes, it can produce torque, or twisting force, only within a narrow speed range. Most engine covered by this manual must turn somewhere between 2000-4000 rpm to produce their peak torque. By 4,500 rpm they are producing so little torque that continued increases in engine speed produce no power increases.

The transmission and clutch are employed to vary the relationship between engine speed and the speed of the wheels so that adequate engine power can be produced under all circumstances. The clutch allows engine torque to be applied to the transmission input shaft gradually, due to mechanical slippage. The truck can, consequently, be started smoothly from a full stop.

The transmission is used to change the ratio between the rotating speeds of the engine and the wheels by the use of gears. 4-speed or 5-speed transmissions are used on these vehicles. The lower gears allow full engine power to be applied to the rear wheels during acceleration at low speeds.

The clutch driven plate is a thin disc, the center of which is splined to the transmission input shaft. Both sides of the disc are covered with a layer of material which is similar to brake lining and which is capable of allowing slippage without roughness or excessive noise.

The clutch cover in bolted to the engine flywheel and incorporates a diaphragm spring which provides the pressure to engage the clutch. The cover also houses the pressure plate. The clutch driven disc is sandwiched between the pressure plate and the smooth surface of the flywheel when the clutch pedal is released, thus forcing it to turn at the same speed as the engine crankshaft.

The transmission housing contains a mainshaft which passes all the way through the transmission, from the clutch to the driveshaft. This shaft is separated at one point, so that front and rear portions can turn at different speeds. Power is transmitted by a countershaft in the lower gears and in reverse. The gears of the countershaft mesh with gears on the mainshaft, allowing power to be carried from one to the other and then back again to the rear half of the mainshaft. All the countershaft gears are integral with that shaft, while several of the mainshaft gears can either rotate independently of the shaft or be locked to it. Shifting from one gear to the next causes one of the gears to be freed from rotating with the shaft, and locks another to it. Gears are locked and unlocked by internal dog clutches which slide between the center of the gear and the shaft. The forward gears usually employ synchronizers: friction members which smoothly bring gear and shaft to the same speed before the toothed dog clutches are engaged. The clutch is operating properly if:

1. It will stall the engine when released with the vehicle held stationary.
2. The shift lever can be moved freely between 1st and reverse gears when the engine is running, the vehicle is stationary and the clutch disengaged (the pedal held downward).

A clutch pedal free-play adjustment is incorporated in the linkage. If there is about 1-2 in. (25-50mm) of motion before the pedal begins to release the clutch, it is adjusted properly. Inadequate free-play wears all parts of the clutch releasing mechanisms and may cause slippage. Excessive free-play may cause inadequate release and hard shifting of gears.

Identification

➡For more information concerning manual transmission identification, please refer to Section 1 of this manual.

Manual transmissions are officially identified by using the following descriptions:

The number of forward gears.

The measured distance between the center lines of the mainshaft and the countergear.

For 1994-95 models, 2 transmissions were available. The MW1 (Borg-Warner T5 transmission) is used on 4-cylinder engines, while the MW2 (New Venture Gear 3500) manual transmission was available for 6-cylinder engine. The last year the MW1 was used was 1995 and preceded by the MW2 (New Venture Gear 1500) in 1996. In 1996 the New Venture Gear 3500 can be identified by RPO code (M50) for 4WD vehicles and (MG5) for rear wheel drive vehicles. Both of these transmissions are similar to the 5-speed 77mm model used earlier, except only the MW1 utilizes a detachable bell housing. For the MW2, the bell housing-to-engine bolts must be removed in order to remove the transmission assembly from the engine.

Adjustments

SHIFTER

Because the shifter on manual transmissions covered by this manual is bolted directly to the top of the transmission housing, no shifter/linkage adjustments should be necessary or possible. If shift trouble is encountered, check for a worn clutch or a damaged shifter assembly.

CLUTCH SWITCH

▶ See Figures 1 and 2

A clutch switch is located under the instrument panel and attached to the top of the clutch pedal. Its function is to prevent starter operation unless the clutch pedal is depressed. Some vehicles may be equipped with a separate cruise control release clutch switch or the switch may be combined with the starter safety switch, depending on the model and application.

Vehicles covered by this manual, the clutch (starter safety) switch is mounted in position by clips. No adjustment is necessary or possible.

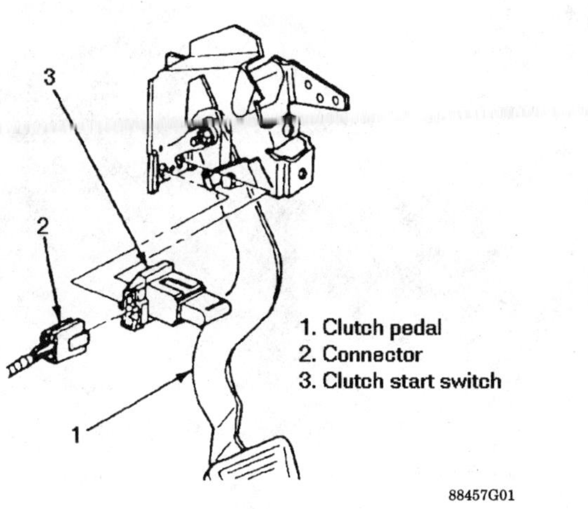

Fig. 1 Non-adjustable clutch safety switch mounting — 1994-95 vehicles

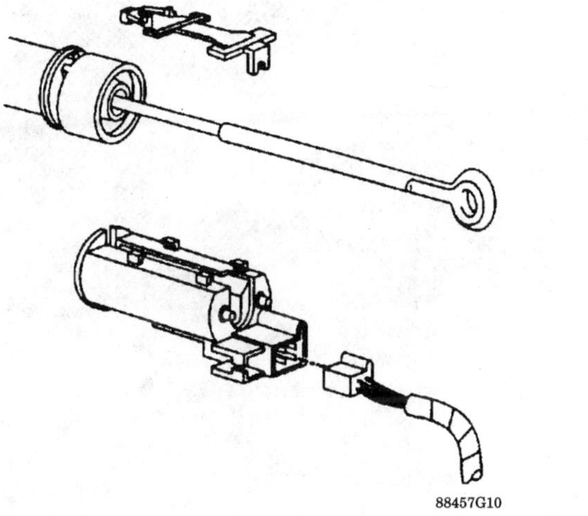

Fig. 2 Non-adjustable clutch safety switch — 1996-97 vehicles

Shift Handle

REMOVAL & INSTALLATION

See Figures 3, 4, 5, 6, 7, 8, 9, 10 and 11

Most vehicles covered by this manual utilize a 2-piece shift lever assembly. The upper portion of the shift lever is threaded to the lower portion and locked in position using a jamnut. If equipped, the upper portion may removed without unbolting the rest of the shifter lever/housing from the top of the transmission housing. In fact, on most later model vehicles, the shift lever housing cannot or should not be removed with transmission installed. On some transmissions, such as the New Venture Gear 3500, the shift lever is retained to a shift lever socket inside the transmission using a roll pin.

1. Position the transmission in Neutral, this will prevent stressing the internal shift forks when working on the shift lever components.

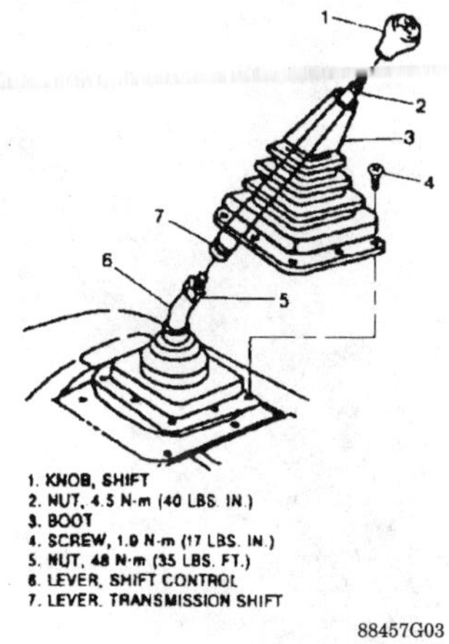

Fig. 3 View of the shifter lever mounting

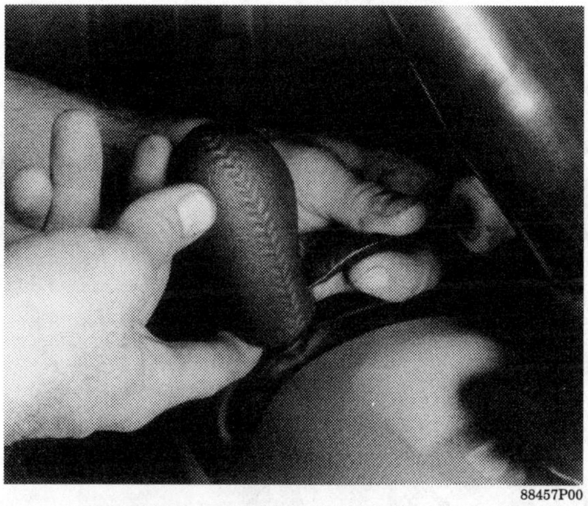

Fig. 4 Use an appropriate tool to locate the shift knob retainer clip — 4WD vehicles

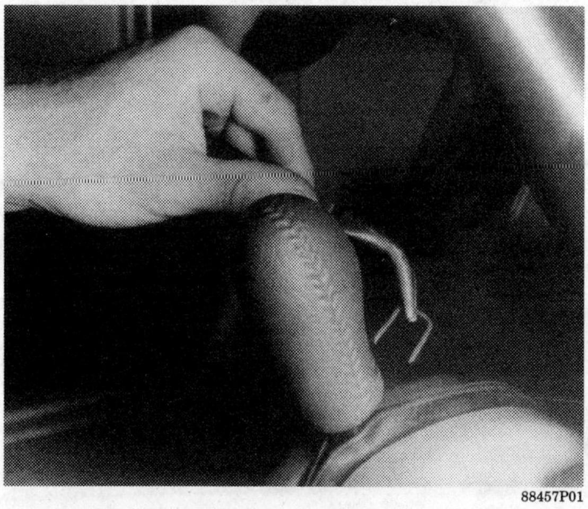

Fig. 5 After the retainer clip is removed, the knob can be removed

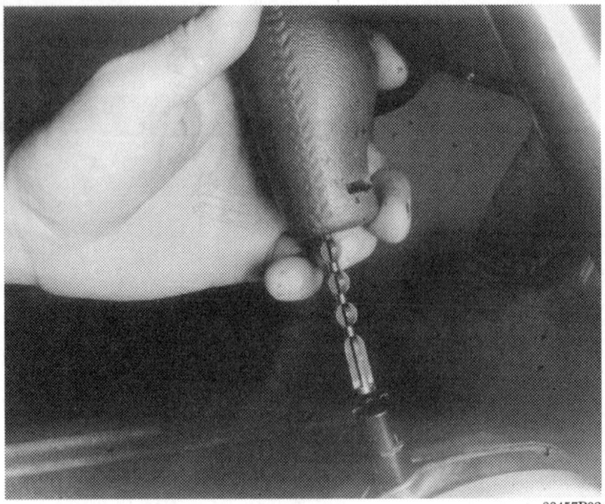

88457P02

Fig. 6 Pull the knob up and off

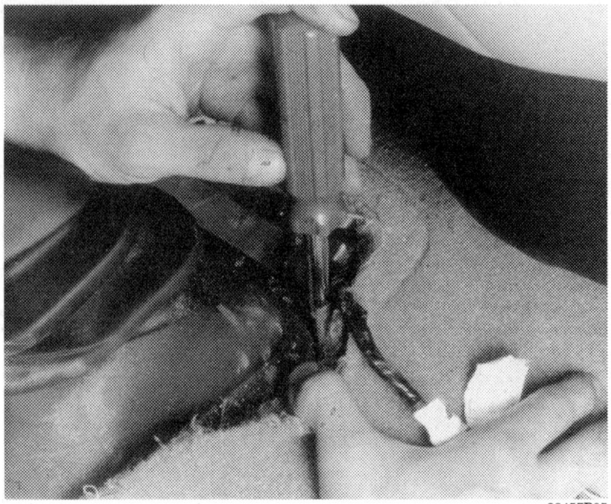

88457P05

Fig. 9 Remove the shifter boot retainer screws

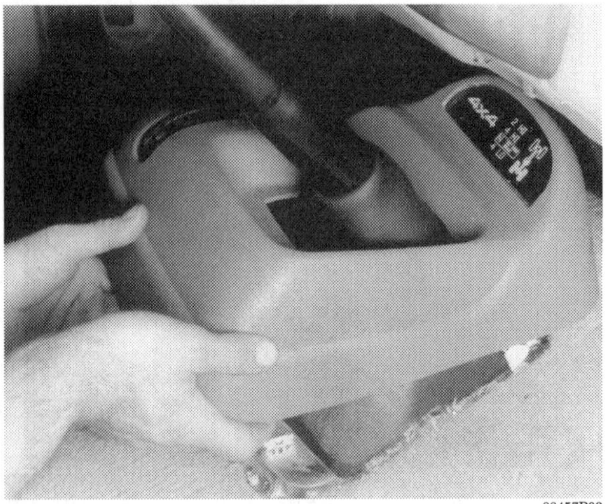

88457P03

Fig. 7 Remove the shifter cover

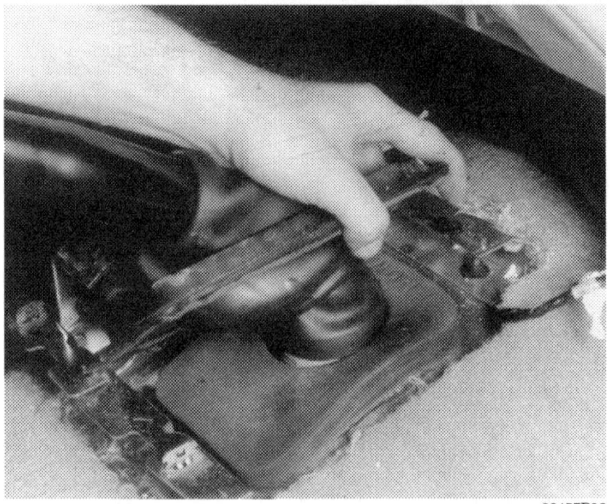

88457P06

Fig. 10 Pull the shifter boot cover over the shifter and remove

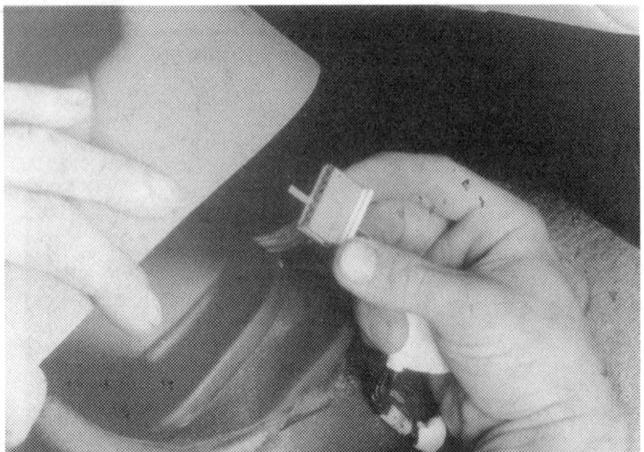

88457P04

Fig. 8 Disengage the electrical harness

88457P07

Fig. 11 Once the boot is out of the way the shifter lever can be removed

2. Unthread the shift knob and nut (if equipped) from the top of the shift lever. The nut is usually used as a jamnut to hold the shift knob in position. Knob removal may be easier if you turn the nut slightly to ease tension from the knob before attempting to unthread it. This will most likely mean turning the nut clockwise to thread it further down on the top of the shift lever.
3. If equipped with a shifter boot retainer, loosen and remove the retaining screws.
4. Remove the shifter boot along with the retainer (if equipped).

➡On most models covered by this manual there is a locknut (jamnut) at the base of the shift lever (where the lower portion of the shift lever enters the transmission housing. This locknut is used on 2 piece shift levers, if removal of only the upper portion is desired, it may be unthreaded from the lower portion at this time.

5. On models equipped with a 2-piece shift lever, hold the lower locknut from turning and use the wrench slots in the base of the upper shift lever to unthread and remove it from the vehicle. If removal is difficult it is advised that you back the nut off of the upper lever by turning it clockwise, then unthread the lever by turning it (the lever) counterclockwise.

To install:

6. Thread the locknut all the way on to the base of the lower shift lever (do not tighten it), then thread the upper shift lever to the lower portion. Secure the upper lever by holding the lever using the wrench slots and tightening the locknut up against the base of the upper lever Tighten the locknut to 35 ft. lbs. (48 Nm).
7. Install the shifter boot along with the retainer (if equipped). On vehicles equipped with a boot retainer, install and tighten the bolts.
8. If equipped with an upper locknut, thread the nut all of the way onto the top of the upper shift lever, but do not tighten it. Thread the shift knob onto the lever, then turn the knob as necessary to align the shift pattern. Hold the knob aligned as desired and tighten the knob jamnut against the knob to retain the position.

Back-Up Light Switch

REMOVAL & INSTALLATION

➧ See Figure 12

1. Disconnect the negative battery cable.
2. Locate the switch on the left or right rear of the transmission housing (depending on the application), the back-up light switch is threaded into the transmission case. The speed sensor is held in with a separate bracket. Disengage the electrical connector from the back-up light switch.
3. Remove the back-up light switch from the transmission.
4. To install, reverse the removal procedures.
5. With the engine NOT running (for safety), place the gear shift lever in the reverse position and check the back-up lights work.

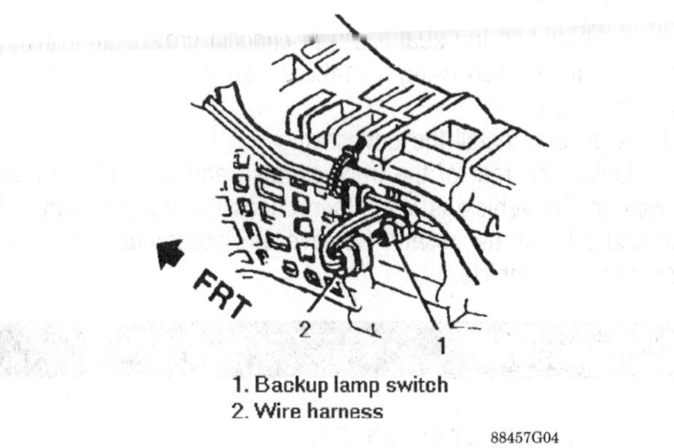

Fig. 12 Location of the back-up light switch

Extension Housing Seal

➧ See Figure 13

The extension housing seal (located in the tail section of the transmission assembly) controls oil leakage around the driveshaft. Continued failure of this seal usually indicates a worn output shaft bushing. If so, there will be signs of the same wear on the driveshaft, at the point where it contacts the seal and bushing. The seal is a fairly simple component to install, but it requires the proper driver tool to assure proper installation and prevent the danger of component damage.

1. Raise and support the rear of the truck safely using jackstands. If the rear of the vehicle is supported sufficiently, transmission oil loss will be minimized during the procedure. Keep a drain pan handy though, just to be sure.
2. Matchmark and remove the driveshaft from the truck. Refer to the procedure later in this section for details.
3. Pry the seal out of the transmission extension housing. Be careful not to score and damage the housing sealing surface when removing the seal.

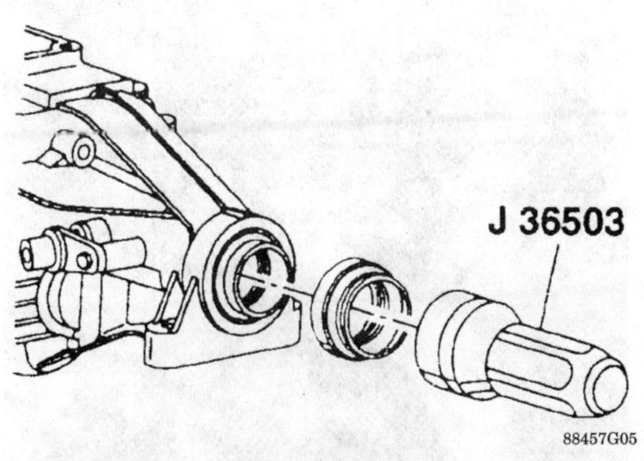

Fig. 13 Using a special tool to install the extension housing seal

To install:

4. Coat the outside of the replacement seal using a suitable locking compound.
5. Fill between the seal lips with chassis grease and drive the seal into position using J-21426, or an equivalent seal installation tool.
6. Align and install the driveshaft.
7. Lower the rear of the truck or raise and support the front as well so the vehicle is level, then check the transmission fluid and add, as necessary. Remove the jackstands and carefully lower the vehicle.

Transmission

REMOVAL & INSTALLATION

See Figures 14, 15, 16, 17, 18, 19, 20, 21, 22, 23, 24 and 25

Manual transmission removal on most vehicles covered by this manual can be done through the following, fairly straightforward procedures. In most cases, the Borg Warner T-5 transmission can be removed leaving the bell housing and the clutch assembly in position. The bell housing on the NV1500/3500 (New Venture Gear) 5-speeds is integral with the transmission casing and therefore must be unbolted in order to remove the transmission assembly. Of course, if the transmission is being removed for clutch replacement, the bell housing must be removed anyway.

On many of the vehicles covered by this manual, the upper bell housing-to-engine bolts (especially the upper left) may be difficult to access and withdraw due to the close proximity of the cowl sheet metal. Even if a wrench fits over the bolt, there may be insufficient room to fully unthread it. The factory recommended procedure to access these bolts is to remove the left body mount bolt(s) from under the cab and loosen the radiator support mounting, then carefully jack the body up off the frame until sufficient clearance exists. Place wooden blocks between the body and frame to support the body (this is to prevent damage and for SAFETY) during service. In some

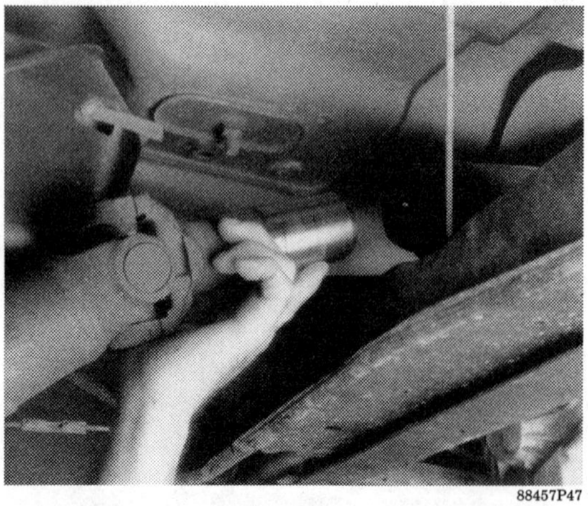

Fig. 14 Once the driveshaft has been disconnected at the rear differential, slide the shaft from the transmission tailshaft

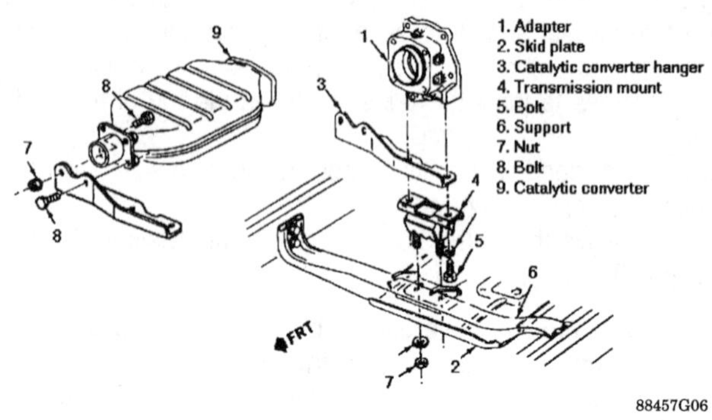

Fig. 15 Catalytic converter hanger assembly under the transmission — common application

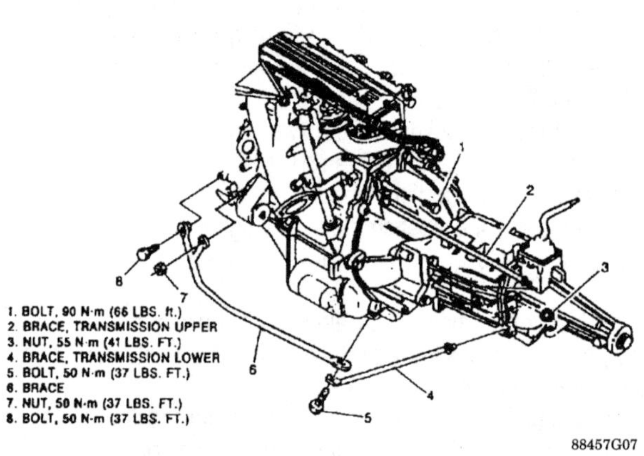

Fig. 16 Common brace mounting — left side of the 2.2L gasoline engine shown

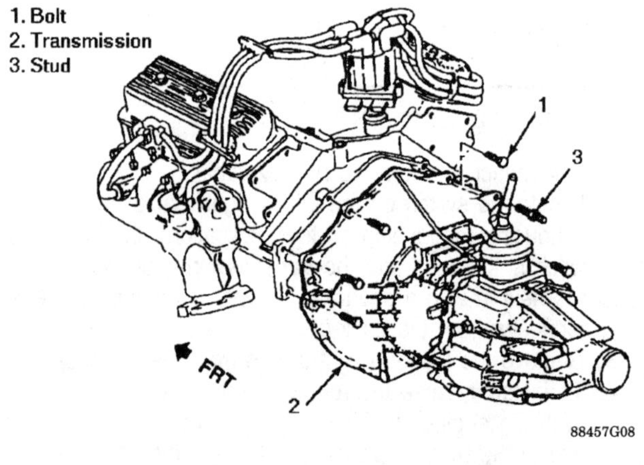

Fig. 17 Common transmission-to-engine mounting — New Venture Gear 3500 model shown

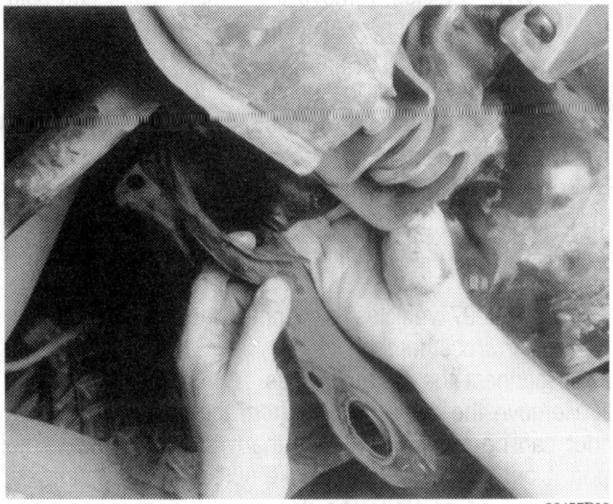

88457P08

Fig. 18 Move the starter motor back out of the way so that inspection over can be removed

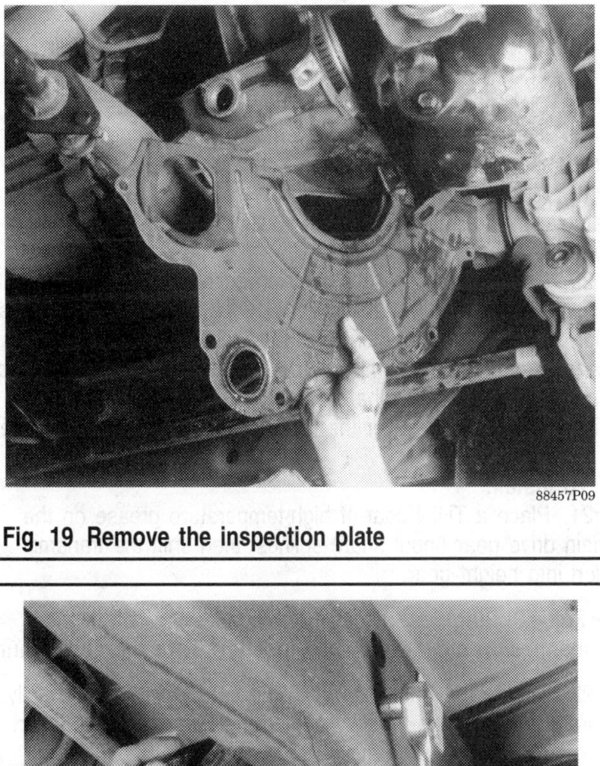

88457P09

Fig. 19 Remove the inspection plate

88457P10

Fig. 20 With the transmission supported securely with a jack, remove the crossmember-to-frame bolts

88457P11

Fig. 21 With the transmission supported securely with a jack, remove the mount-to-frame bolts

88457P12

Fig. 22 With the transmission supported securely with a jack, the crossmember can be safely removed

88457P13

Fig. 23 Remove the remaining section of the exhaust system

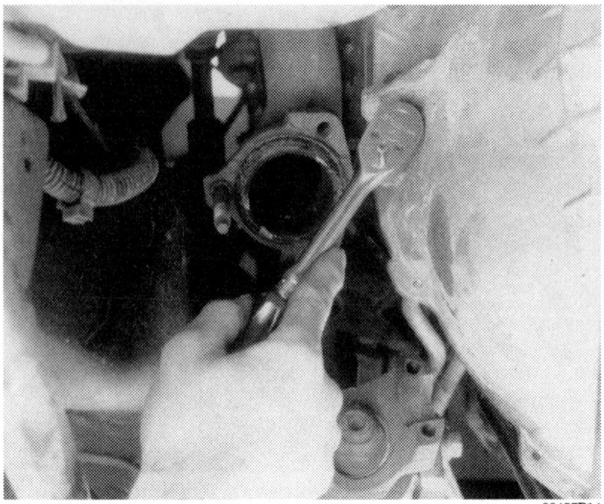
88457P14

Fig. 24 Loosen and remove the bell housing bolts

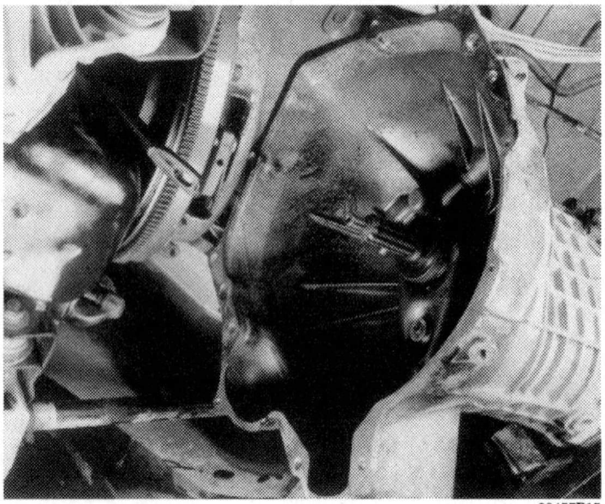
88457P15

Fig. 25 Carefully pull the transmission away from the engine to clear the input shaft and lower it down

cases, this may be unnecessary if the engine will pivot downward sufficiently on the motor mount to allow bolt access or if the motor mounts are removed and the engine is supported using a lifting device. BUT DO NOT try this if it appears that the mounts will be damaged by the stress. Also, be sure the engine is properly supported at ALL times and that no components will be damaged. Watch that the distributor does not contact the cowl and that the cooling fan remains clear of the radiator and shroud assembly. When in doubt, unbolt and raise the body for access.

1. Disconnect the negative battery cable.
2. Remove the shift lever. For details, please refer to the procedure earlier in this section.
3. Raise and support the vehicle safely using jackstands.
4. Disconnect the parking brake cable for clearance. Before disconnecting the cable, you may want to measure the adjustment or scribe marks to ease adjustment after installation.
5. Matchmark and remove the driveshaft. For details, please refer to the procedure later in this section.
6. If equipped, remove the skid plate.
7. On 4WD vehicles, remove the transfer case and shift lever. For details, please refer to the procedure later in this section.
8. Tag and disengage the necessary wiring connectors, including the reverse (backup) light switch and Vehicle Speed Sensor (VSS) connectors.
9. For 1994-95 4.3L engines properly relieve the fuel system pressure, then disconnect the fuel lines at the engine.
10. For 1994-95 2.2L engines, disconnect the fuel lines from the top cover.
11. For 1996-97 vehicles, disconnect the fuel line retainers from the rear crossmember.
12. Disconnect the exhaust pipes.
13. Remove the slave cylinder from the transmission. If the cylinder can be repositioned with the hydraulics intact, simply support it out of the way, but make sure the line is not stretched, kinked or otherwise damaged. If necessary, disconnect the line and remove the cylinder completely.
14. Support the transmission carefully using a floor jack. If possible, secure the transmission to the jack to keep it from shifting suddenly and falling.
15. Remove the transmission mount retainers.
16. If necessary, remove the catalytic converter support hanger.
17. Disconnect or remove the necessary support braces.
18. If necessary, unbolt and remove the transmission crossmember.
19. Make sure the transmission is properly supported, then remove the transmission-to-bell housing or transmission-to-engine bolts, as necessary.
20. Carefully pull the transmission assembly, straight back to disengage the input shaft splines, DO NOT allow the transmission to hang on the clutch. For 4.3L engines it may be necessary to rotate the transmission counterclockwise, then pull back and disengage it from the engine. Once the transmission is disengaged, slowly lower the jack and transmission to remove it from the vehicle.

To install:

21. Place a THIN coat of high-temperature grease on the main drive gear (input shaft) splines, then shift the transmission into height gear.

➡For 4.3L engines, it may be necessary to rotate the transmission clockwise while inserting it to the clutch hub.

22. Secure the transmission to the floor jack, then carefully raise it into position, directly behind the engine. Slowly insert the input shaft through the clutch. Rotate the output shaft slowly to engage the splines of the input shaft into the clutch while pushing the transmission forward into place. DO NOT force the transmission into position, the transmission will easily fall into place when everything is properly aligned.
23. Once the transmission is properly positioned, install the retaining bolts and tighten to 55 ft. lbs. (75 Nm).
24. If removed, install the crossmember to the vehicle.
25. Install or connect the necessary support braces.
26. If removed, install the catalytic converter support hanger.
27. Install the transmission mount bolts and tighten to 37 ft. lbs. (50 Nm).
28. Install the slave cylinder to the transmission. If the hydraulic line was disconnected, the system will have to be bled of air.
29. Connect the exhaust pipes.

30. For 1994-95 2.2L engines, connect the fuel lines to the top cover.
31. For 1996-97 vehicles, connect the fuel line retainers from the rear crossmember.
32. Engage the necessary wiring harness connectors, including the reverse light switch and the VSS.
33. For 4WD vehicles, install the transfer case.
34. If equipped, install the skid plate.
35. Align and install the driveshaft.
36. Connect and adjust the parking brake cable.
37. Remove the jackstands and carefully lower the vehicle.
38. Install the shift lever.
39. Connect the negative battery cable.

CLUTCH

Understanding the Clutch

See Figure 26

CAUTION

The clutch driven disc may contain asbestos, which has been determined to be a cancer causing agent. Never clean clutch surfaces with compressed air! Avoid inhaling any dust from any clutch surface! When cleaning clutch surfaces, use a commercially available brake cleaning fluid.

The transmission varies the gear ratio between the engine and rear wheels. It can be shifted to change engine speed as driving conditions and loads change. The transmission and clutch allows disengaging and reversing power from the engine to the wheels.

The purpose of the clutch is to smoothly connect and disconnect engine power from the transmission. A truck at rest requires a lot of engine torque to get all that weight moving. An internal combustion engine does not develop a high starting torque (unlike steam engines), so it must be allowed to operate without any load until it builds up enough torque to move the truck. Torque increases with engine rpm, to a certain point, then torque will level or fall off. The clutch allows the engine to build up torque by physically disconnecting the engine from the transmission, relieving the engine of any load or resistance. The transfer of engine power to the transmission (the load) must be smooth and gradual; if it weren't, drive line components would wear out or break quickly. This gradual power transfer is made possible by gradually releasing the clutch pedal. The clutch disc and pressure plate are the connecting link between the engine and transmission. When the clutch pedal is released, the disc and plate contact each other (clutch engagement), physically joining the engine and transmission. When the pedal is pushed in, the disc and plate separate (the clutch is disengaged), disconnecting the engine from the transmission.

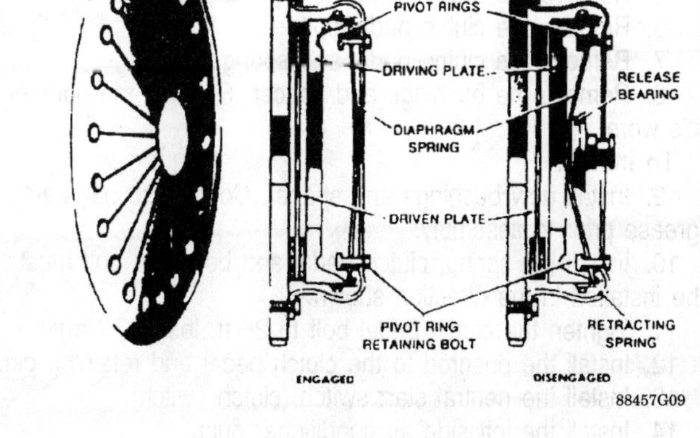

Fig. 26 Operation of the diaphragm spring clutch

The clutch assembly consists of the flywheel, clutch disc, clutch pressure plate, throwout bearing and fork, the clutch pedal and the actuating linkage or clutch master and slave cylinder (as applicable). The flywheel and clutch pressure plate (driving members) are connected to the engine crankshaft and rotate with it. The clutch disc is located between the flywheel and pressure plate, and is splined to the transmission shaft. A driving member is one that is attached to the engine and transfers engine power to a driven member (clutch disc) on the transmission shaft. A driving member (pressure plate) rotates (drives) a driven member (clutch disc) on contact and, in so doing, turns the transmission shaft. There is a circular diaphragm spring within the pressure plate cover (transmission side). In a relaxed state (when the clutch pedal is fully released), this spring is convex; that is, it is dished outward toward the transmission. Pushing in the clutch pedal actuates an attached linkage rod or hydraulic slave cylinder. Connected to the other end of this rod or slave cylinder is the throwout bearing fork. When the clutch pedal is depressed, the clutch linkage/slave cylinder pushes the fork and bearing forward to contact the diaphragm spring of the pressure plate. The outer edges of the spring are secured to the pressure plate and are pivoted on rings so that when the center of the spring is compressed by the throwout bearing, the outer edges bow outward and, by so doing, pull the pressure plate in the same direction — away from the clutch disc. This action separates the disc from the plate, disengaging the clutch and allowing the transmission to be shifted into another gear. On linkage equipped vehicles, a coil type clutch return spring attached to the clutch pedal arm helps eliminate slop and makes sure the pedal returns fully to the upward position. Releasing the pedal allows this coil spring to pull the throwout bearing away from the diaphragm spring resulting in a reversal of spring position. The hydraulic actuating system works similarly, but differences are described later in this section. As bearing pressure is gradually released from the spring center, the outer edges of the spring bow outward, pushing the pressure plate into closer contact with the clutch disc. As the disc and plate move closer together, friction between the two increases and slippage is reduced until, when full diaphragm spring pressure is applied (by fully releasing the pedal), The speed of the disc and plate are the same. This stops all slipping, creating a direct connection between the plate and disc which results in the transfer of power from the engine to the transmission. The clutch disc is now rotating with the pressure plate at engine speed and, because it is splined to the transmission shaft, the shaft now turns at the same engine speed. Understanding clutch operation can be rather difficult at first; if you're still confused after reading this, consider the following analogy. The action of the diaphragm spring can be compared to that of an oil can bottom. The bottom of an oil can is shaped very much like the clutch diaphragm spring and pushing in on the can bottom and then releasing it produces a similar effect. As mentioned earlier, the clutch pedal return spring permits full release of the pedal and reduces slack due to wear on linkage systems. As the clutch wears on linkage systems, clutch free-pedal travel will increase, while free-travel will decrease as the clutch wears. Free-travel is actually throwout bearing lash.

HYDRAULIC CLUTCH SYSTEM

See Figure 27

The trucks covered by this manual use a hydraulic clutch system (partially described earlier) which consists of a master cylinder and slave cylinder. When pressure is applied to the clutch pedal (pedal depressed), the pushrod contacts the plunger and pushes it up the bore of the master cylinder. In the first 1/32 in. (0.8mm) of movement, the center valve seal closes the port to the fluid reservoir tank and as the plunger continues to move up the bore of the cylinder, the fluid is forced through the outlet line to the slave cylinder mounted on the clutch housing. As fluid is pushed down the pipe from the master cylinder, this in turn forces the piston in the slave cylinder outward. A pushrod is connected to the slave cylinder and rides in the pocket of the clutch fork. As the slave cylinder piston moves rearward the pushrod forces the clutch fork and the release bearing to disengage the pressure plate from the clutch disc. On the return stroke (pedal released), the plunger moves back as a result of the return pressure of the clutch. Fluid returns to the master cylinder and the final movement of the plunger lifts the valve seal off the seat, allowing an unrestricted flow of fluid between the system and the reservoir.

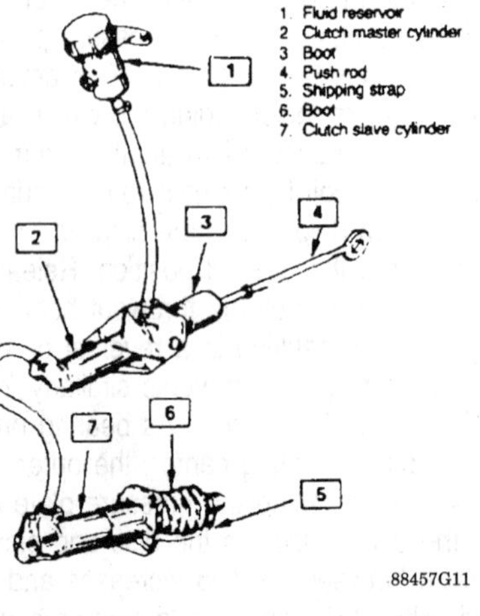

Fig. 27 Components of a common hydraulic clutch system

A piston return spring in the slave cylinder preloads the clutch linkage and assures contact of the release bearing with the clutch release fingers at all times. As the driven disc wears, the diaphragm spring fingers move rearward forcing the release bearing, fork and pushrod to move. This movement forces the slave cylinder piston forward in its bore, displacing hydraulic fluid up into the master cylinder reservoir, thereby providing the self-adjusting feature of the hydraulic clutch linkage system.

Before attempting to repair the clutch, transmission, hydraulic system or related linkages for any reason other than an obvious failure, the problem and probable cause should be identified. A large percentage of clutch and manual transmission problems are manifested by shifting difficulties such as high shift effort, gear clash and grinding or transmission block out. When any of these problems occur, a careful analysis of these difficulties should be made, then the basic checks and adjustments performed before removing the clutch or transmission for repairs. Run the engine at a normal idle with the transmission in Neutral (clutch engaged). Disengage the clutch, wait about 10 seconds and shift the transmission into Reverse (no grinding noise should be heard). A grinding noise indicates incorrect clutch travel, lost motion, clutch misalignment or internal problems such as failed dampers, facings, cushion springs, diaphragm spring fingers, pressure plate drive straps, pivot rings or etc.

Adjustment

Since the hydraulic system provides automatic clutch adjustment, no adjustment of the clutch linkage or pedal height is required on vehicles equipped with the master and slave cylinder actuator system.

Clutch Pedal

REMOVAL & INSTALLATION

See Figures 28, 29 and 30

1. Disconnect the negative battery cable.
2. Remove the steering column lower covers.
3. Remove the left side air conditioner duct.
4. Remove the neutral start switch (clutch switch).
5. Remove the pushrod retaining pin and washer.
6. Remove the clutch pedal bolt.
7. Remove the clutch pedal and spring.
8. Remove the bushings and spacer. Replace the bumper if it's worn.

To install:

9. Install new bushings and spacer. Coat these parts with grease prior to assembly.
10. Install the spring, clutch pedal and bolt. The bolt must be installed in the direction shown.
11. Tighten the clutch pedal bolt to 26 ft. lbs. (37 Nm).
12. Install the pushrod to the clutch pedal and retaining pin.
13. Install the neutral start switch (clutch switch).
14. Install the left side air conditioner duct.
15. Connect the negative battery cable.

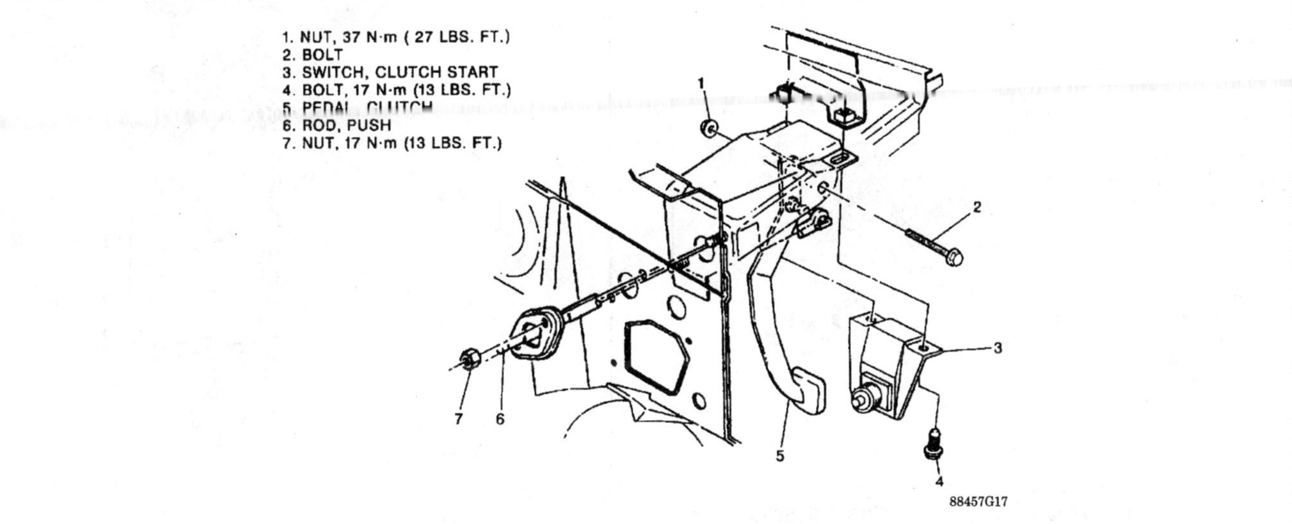

Fig. 28 Clutch pedal components — 1995 vehicles

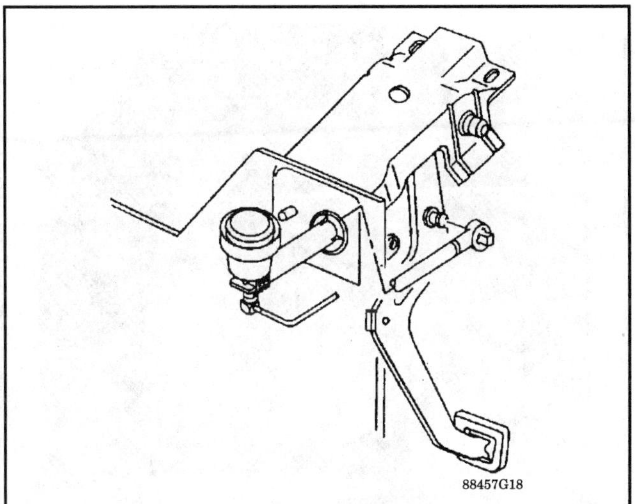

Fig. 29 Removing the clutch pushrod from the pedal assembly

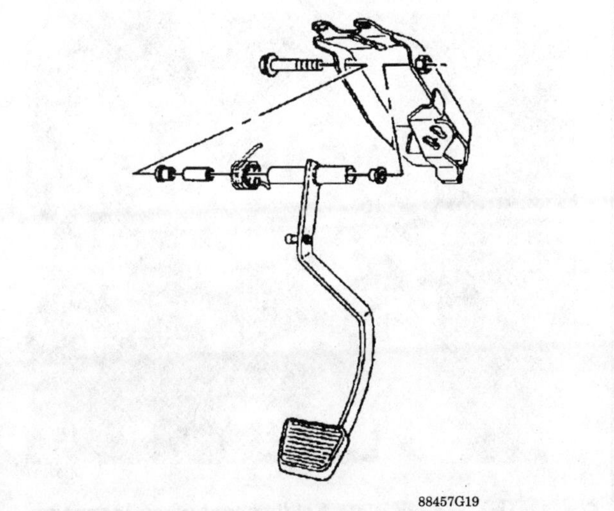

Fig. 30 Clutch pedal components — 1996-97 vehicles

Clutch Disc and Pressure Plate

REMOVAL & INSTALLATION

➧ **See Figures 31, 32, 33, 34, 35, 36, 37, 38, 39, 40, 41, 42, 43, 44, 45, 46, 47 and 48**

✱✱CAUTION

The clutch plate may contain asbestos, which has been determined to be a cancer causing agent. Never clean the clutch surfaces with compressed air! Avoid inhaling any dust from any clutch surface! When cleaning clutch surfaces, use a commercially available brake cleaning fluid. If a spray cleaning fluid is not available, use a water dampened (NOT SOAKED) cloth to wipe away dust from the assembly.

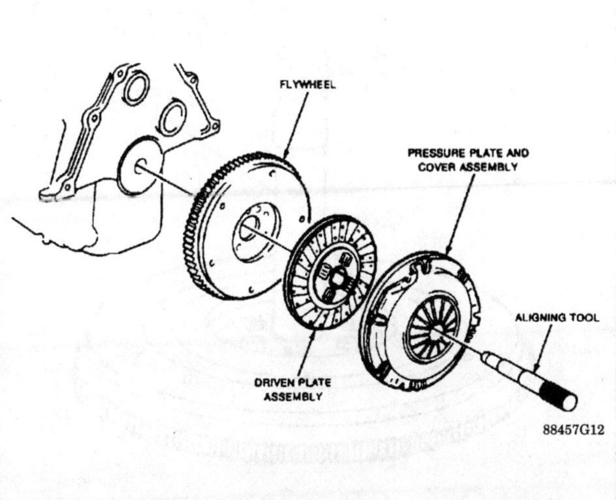

Fig. 31 A clutch alignment tool (or used clutch drive gear) is necessary to remove/install the clutch assembly

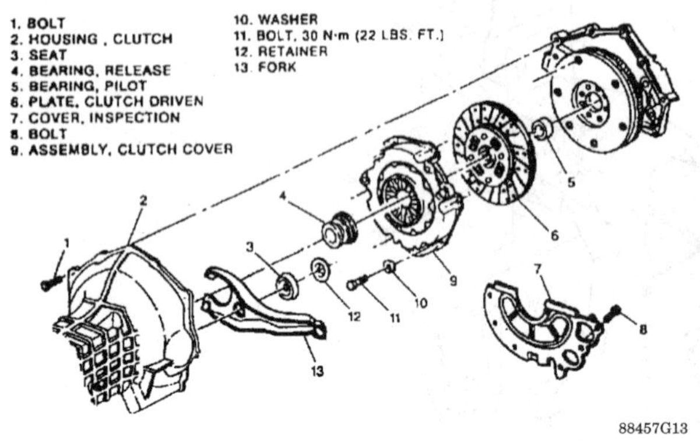

Fig. 32 Exploded view of a common clutch assembly — New Venture Gear transmission shown

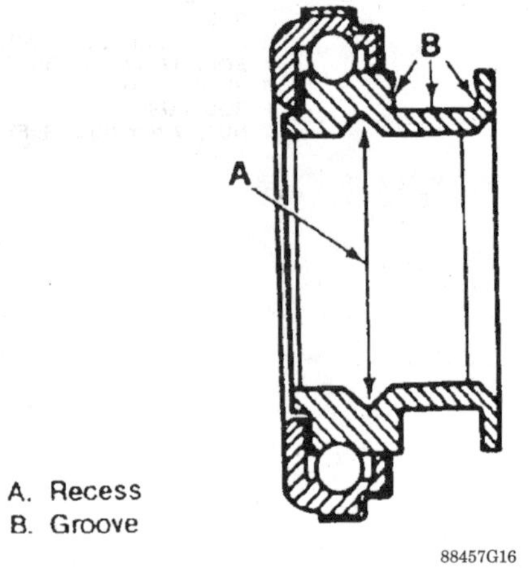

Fig. 35 Release bearing lubrication points

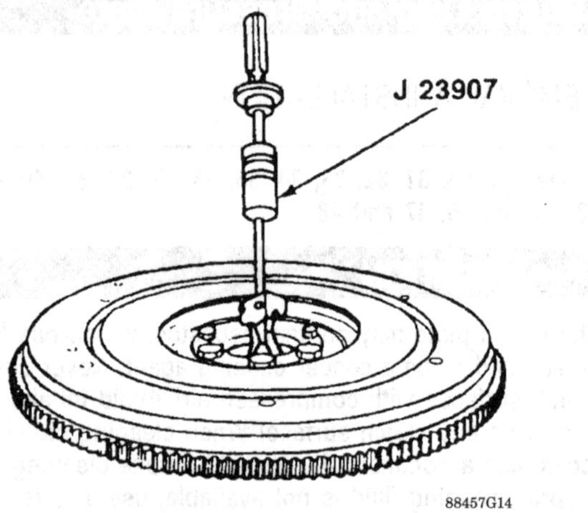

Fig. 33 Using a slide-hammer puller tool to remove the pilot bearing from the flywheel

Fig. 36 View of the clutch assembly with the transmission removed

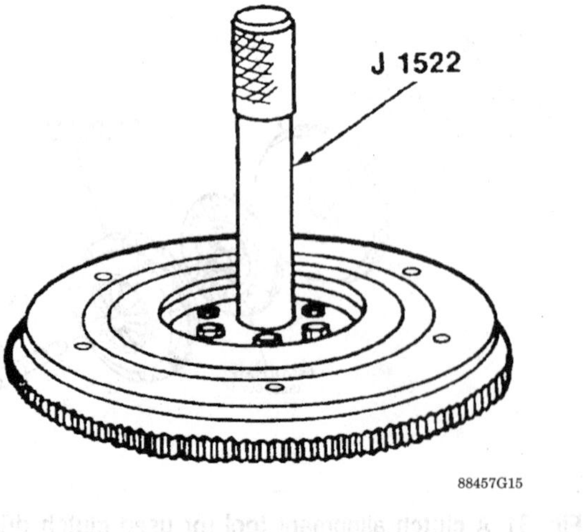

Fig. 34 Installing the pilot bearing

Fig. 37 Use a drive plate holding tool when loosening the pressure plate bolts

88457P18

Fig. 38 Take care not to allow the disc to slip down when removing the plate assembly

88457P19

Fig. 39 Inspect the clutch disc and drive plate and replace as required

88457P20

Fig. 40 Remove the driveplate-to-crankshaft retainer bolts

88457P21

Fig. 41 Remove the driveplate for machining or further inspection

88457P22

Fig. 42 Examine the rear seal for leakage

88457P23

Fig. 43 If necessary, remove the rear crankshaft seal . . .

Fig. 44 . . . then replace the rear crank seal with a new one

Fig. 45 Always use a pilot alignment tool to properly align the clutch disc

Fig. 46 Using the driveplate holding tool, be sure to use a torque wrench to tighten the bolts

Fig. 47 Disengage the clutch cable from release lever

Fig. 48 Prior to installing the transmission, remove the release bearing lever and replace the release bearing

1. Remove the manual transmission assembly from the vehicle. For details, refer to the procedures located earlier in this section.

2. If not performed for transmission removal, disconnect the slave cylinder from the clutch release fork and move it aside.

3. If the bell housing was not removed with the transmission, remove the inspection cover (if equipped), then loosen the retaining bolts and remove the bell housing from the rear of the engine assembly.

4. Remove the clutch fork from the ball stud (by carefully prying it free) and the dust boot (if applicable). Except for vehicles equipped with a New Venture Gear transmission, carefully pry the retainer out of the clutch fork (if it is not damaged). If necessary, remove the ball stud.

➡A used clutch drive gear may be used as an alignment tool. This may be available inexpensively from a junk yard or a transmission rebuilding shop.

5. Insert a clutch alignment tool such as No. J-33169, into the crankshaft pilot bearing to support the clutch assembly.

6. Check for an "X" or other painted mark on the pressure plate and flywheel. If no marks are readily visible, matchmark the flywheel, clutch cover and pressure plate lug for installation purposes.

7. Loosen the pressure plate-to-flywheel bolts, evenly and alternately, a little at a time, until the spring tension is released. Remove the pressure plate, driven clutch plate and alignment tool.

To install:

8. Check the flywheel for cracks, wear, scoring or other damage. Check the pilot bearing for wear. If necessary, replace the bearing by removing it with a slide-type bearing puller and driving in a new one with a wood or plastic hammer. Lubricate the new pilot bearing with a few drops of machine oil.

9. If available, check the driven plate for run-out using a dial gauge. Run-out should not exceed 0.02 in. (5.08mm).

10. Using the clutch alignment tool to support the clutch, align and install the clutch plate and cover assembly. If a new clutch is being installed align the manufacturer's marks as directed.

11. Install the washers and bolts, then tighten each bolt one turn at a time to avoid warping the clutch cover. If spring washers were used, new ones should be installed. Once the bolts are fully threaded, tighten each one to 28-33 ft. lbs. (38-45 Nm). Refer to torque specification chart for correct application. Remove the clutch alignment tool.

12. If removed, install the ball stud. Pack the seat and coat the rounded end of the ball stud with high temperature (wheel-bearing) grease.

➡The clutch release bearing used on most vehicles covered by this manual is permanently packed with lubricant and should NOT be soaked in cleaning solvent as this will dissolve the lubricant.

13. Install the release bearing and the clutch fork. Pack the inside recess (A) and coat the outside groove (B) of the release bearing with high-temperature wheel-bearing grease. Please refer to the illustration for lubrication points.

14. If separate, install the flywheel housing and install the retaining bolts.

15. If removed, install the inspection cover.

16. For vehicles equipped with a hydraulic clutch system (and the flywheel housing is already installed), reposition and secure the slave cylinder.

17. For vehicles equipped with a clutch cable (and the flywheel housing is already installed), install and adjust the clutch cable.

18. Install the manual transmission assembly. For details, please refer to the procedures located earlier in this section.

Master Cylinder and Reservoir

The clutch master cylinder is located in the engine compartment, on the left-side of the firewall, above or near the steering column.

REMOVAL & INSTALLATION

▶ See Figure 49

➡On the 2.2L engine, individual components of the clutch actuating system (master cylinder/slave cylinder) may not be available for service. If so it is recommended that a complete, pre-filled and pre-bled unit should be installed and NO attempts should be made to disconnect the hydraulic lines.

1. Disconnect the negative battery cable.
2. Remove lower filler panel from under the dash.
3. If necessary, remove the lower left A/C duct.
4. Remove the pushrod retainer, then disconnect pushrod from clutch pedal.

➡To expedite the hydraulic clutch bleeding, loose as little fluid as possible when disconnecting hydraulic lines. All openings should be immediately capped or plugged to prevent system contamination or excessive fluid loss.

5. Disconnect the slave cylinder hydraulic line from the master cylinder. Drive out the retaining pin holding the hydraulic tube to the master cylinder using a $^{7}/_{64}$ in. (3mm) punch.
6. Remove the master cylinder from the cowl panel by grasping the cylinder body and rotating it about 45 degrees clockwise, then withdrawing it from the opening.

To install:

7. Hold the master cylinder assembly at a 45 degree angle (as during removal), then install the master cylinder to the cowl by inserting and twisting counterclockwise 45 degrees. Be sure not to over rotate the cylinder assembly or damage will occur.

➡Use a new retaining pin and quad seal during hydraulic line installation.

8. Remove the caps, then connect the slave cylinder hydraulic line to the master cylinder assembly.
9. Connect the pushrod to the pedal and secure using the retainer.
10. If removed, install the lower left A/C duct.
11. Install the lower filler panel.
12. Connect the negative battery cable.

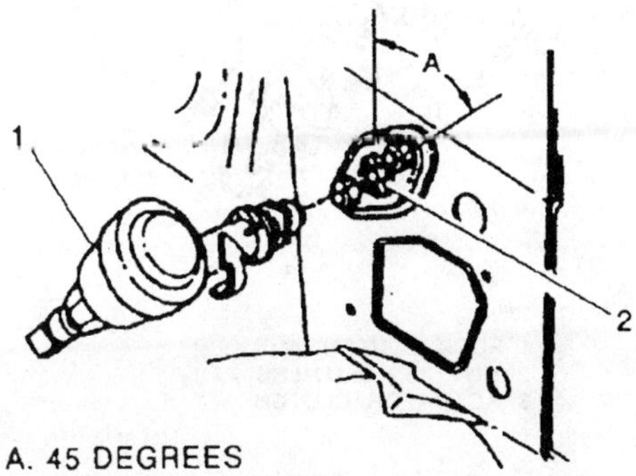

A. 45 DEGREES
1. CYLINDER, MASTER
2. ROD, PUSH

88457G20

Fig. 49 Clutch master cylinder mounting

13. Properly refill the master cylinder reservoir, then bleed the system of air and check for fluid leaks.

Slave (Secondary) Cylinder

On 1994-95 vehicles the slave cylinder is a conventional hydraulic actuator. It is located on the left side of the bell housing and controls the clutch release fork operation.

On 1996-97 vehicles the slave cylinder is called a concentric slave cylinder. It is located on the inside of the transmission bell housing on the input shaft. Removal of the transmission is required to replace it. It directly engages the clutch release bearing. For more information, please refer to understanding the clutch, earlier in this section.

REMOVAL & INSTALLATION

1994-95 Vehicles

See Figures 50 and 51

On the 2.2L engine, individual components of the clutch actuating system (master cylinder/slave cylinder) may not be available for service. If so it is recommended that a complete, pre-filled and pre-bled unit should be installed and NO attempts should be made to disconnect the hydraulic lines.

1. Disconnect the master cylinder pushrod from the clutch pedal assembly.

The master cylinder pushrod should be disconnected to protect the slave cylinder while it is removed from the bell housing. If not, any attempt to depress the clutch pedal while the slave cylinder is withdrawn from the bell housing will cause permanent damage to the slave cylinder assembly.

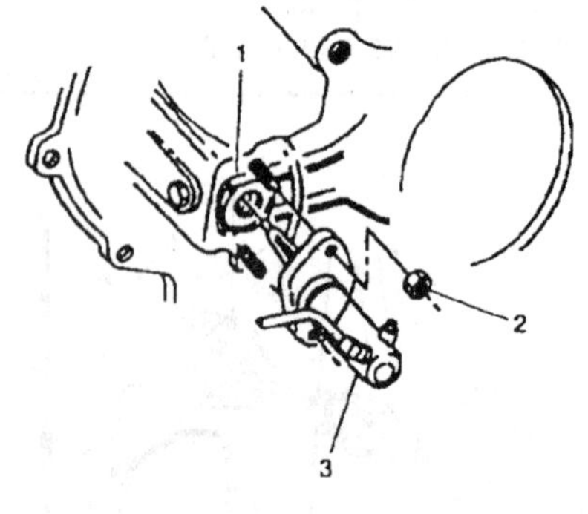

Fig. 50 Slave cylinder mounting — 1994-95 vehicles equipped with the Borg-Warner transmission

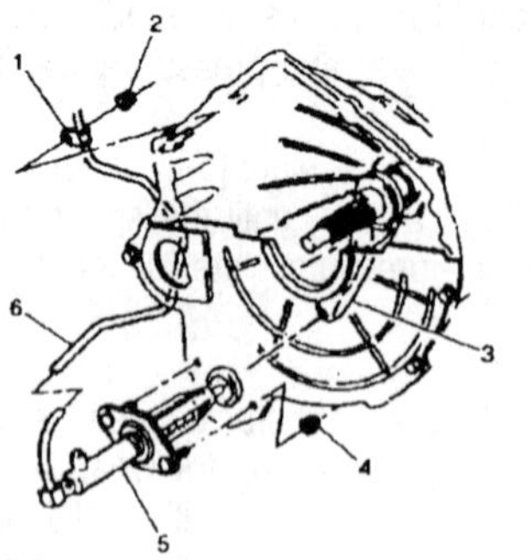

Fig. 51 Slave cylinder mounting — 1994-95 vehicles equipped with the New Venture Gear transmission

2. Using a 7/64 in. (3mm) punch to drive out the roll pin, disconnect the hydraulic line from the slave cylinder assembly. Immediately cap or plug all openings to prevent system contamination or excessive fluid loss.

To expedite the hydraulic clutch bleeding process, loose as little fluid as possible.

3. Remove the slave cylinder-to-bell housing retaining nuts.
4. Remove the slave cylinder from the bell housing and from the vehicle.

To install:

5. Install the slave cylinder to the bell housing, then tighten the retaining nuts to 18 ft. lbs. (24 Nm).
6. Uncover the hydraulic line openings, then connect the hydraulic line to the slave cylinder using a new O-ring (lightly lubricated with fluid) and a new roll pin.
7. Connect the master cylinder pushrod to the clutch pedal assembly.
8. Properly bleed the hydraulic system, then check for leaks.

1996-97 Vehicles

See Figure 52

1. Remove the transmission. Refer to the procedure in this section.
2. Remove the clutch assembly. Refer to the procedure in this section.
3. Remove the 2 bolts securing the concentric slave cylinder to the transmission and input shaft.
4. Remove the concentric slave cylinder from the input shaft.

To install:

5. Install the concentric slave cylinder over the transmission input shaft and install 2 bolts.
6. Tighten the bolts to 80 inch lbs. (9 Nm).
7. Install the clutch assembly.
8. Install the transmission.
9. Bleed the clutch hydraulic system.

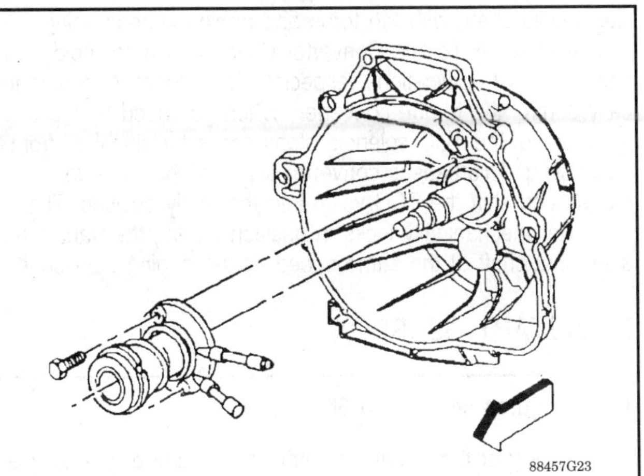

Fig. 52 Concentric slave cylinder mounting — 1996-97 vehicles equipped with the New Venture Gear transmission

HYDRAULIC SYSTEM BLEEDING

Bleeding air from the hydraulic clutch system is necessary whenever any part of the system has been disconnected or the fluid level (in the reservoir) has been allowed to fall so low, that air has been drawn into the master cylinder.

1. Fill master cylinder reservoir with new brake fluid conforming to DOT 3 specifications. Check manufactures recommendations for each vehicle.

****CAUTION**

Never, under any circumstances, use fluid which has been bled from a system to fill the reservoir as it may be aerated, have too much moisture content and possibly be contaminated.

2. Raise and safely support the vehicle high enough to work comfortable under it.
3. Have an assistant fully depress and hold the clutch pedal, then open the bleeder screw of the slave cylinder or concentric cylinder.
4. Close the bleeder screw and have your assistant release the clutch pedal.
5. Repeat the procedure until all of the air is evacuated from the system. Check and refill master cylinder reservoir as required to prevent air from being drawn through the master cylinder.

➡Never release a depressed clutch pedal with the bleeder screw open or air will be drawn into the system.

6. Lower the vehicle and test clutch operation.
7. If the previous steps do not result in satisfactory pedal feel, remove the reservoir cap and pump the clutch pedal very fast for 30 seconds. Stop to let the air escape, then repeat the procedure as necessary to purge all remaining air.

AUTOMATIC TRANSMISSION

Understanding Automatic Transmissions

The automatic transmission allows engine torque and power to be transmitted to the rear wheels within a narrow range of engine operating speeds. The transmission will allow the engine to turn fast enough to produce plenty of power and torque at very low speeds, while keeping it at a sensible rpm at high vehicle speeds. The transmission performs this job entirely without driver assistance. The transmission uses a light fluid as the medium for the transmission of power. This fluid also works in the operation of various hydraulic control circuits and as a lubricant. Because the transmission fluid performs all three of these functions, trouble within the unit can easily travel from one part to another. For this reason, and because of the complexity and unusual operating principles of the transmission, a very sound understanding of the basic principles of operation is necessary for troubleshooting.

TORQUE CONVERTER

➧ See Figure 53

The torque converter replaces the conventional clutch. It has three functions:

1. It allows the engine to idle with the vehicle at a standstill, even with the transmission in gear by effectively disconnecting the engine from the transmission at these times.
2. It allows the transmission to shift from range to range smoothly, without requiring that the driver close the throttle during the shift.
3. It multiplies engine torque to an increasing extent as vehicle speed drops and throttle opening is increased. This has the effect of making the transmission more responsive and reduces the amount of shifting required.

The torque converter is a metal case which is shaped like a sphere that has been flattened on opposite sides. It is bolted to the rear end of the engine's crankshaft. Generally, the entire metal case rotates at engine speed and serves as the engine's flywheel.

The case contains three sets of blades. One set is attached directly to the case. This set forms the torus or pump. Another set is directly connected to the output shaft, and forms the turbine. The third set is mounted on a hub which, in turn, is

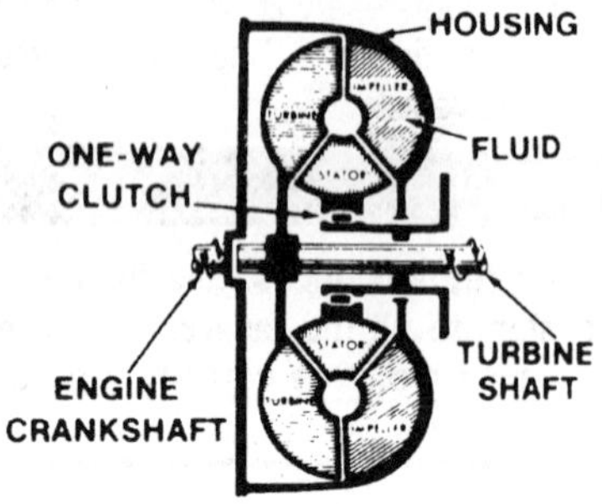

Fig. 53 The torque converter housing is rotated by the engine's crankshaft, and turns the impeller — The impeller then spins the turbine, which gives motion to the turbine shaft, driving the gears

mounted on a stationary shaft through a one-way clutch. This third set is known as the stator.

A pump, which is driven by the converter hub at engine speed, keeps the torque converter full of transmission fluid at all times. Fluid flows continuously through the unit to provide cooling.

Under low speed acceleration, the torque converter functions as follows:

The torus is turning faster than the turbine. It picks up fluid at the center of the converter and, through centrifugal force, slings it outward. Since the outer edge of the converter moves faster than the portions at the center, the fluid picks up speed.

The fluid then enters the outer edge of the turbine blades. It then travels back toward the center of the converter case along the turbine blades. In impinging upon the turbine blades, the fluid loses the energy picked up in the torus.

If the fluid were now to immediately be returned directly into the torus, both halves of the converter would have to turn at approximately the same speed at all times, and torque input and output would both be the same.

In flowing through the torus and turbine, the fluid picks up two types of flow, or flow in two separate directions. It flows through the turbine blades, and it spins with the engine. The stator, whose blades are stationary when the vehicle is being accelerated at low speeds, converts one type of flow into another. Instead of allowing the fluid to flow straight back into the torus, the stator's curved blades turn the fluid almost 90° toward the direction of rotation of the engine. Thus the fluid does not flow as fast toward the torus, but is already spinning when the torus picks it up. This has the effect of allowing the torus to turn much faster than the turbine. This difference in speed may be compared to the difference in speed between the smaller and larger gears in any gear train. The result is that engine power output is higher, and engine torque is multiplied.

As the speed of the turbine increases, the fluid spins faster and faster in the direction of engine rotation. As a result, the ability of the stator to redirect the fluid flow is reduced. Under cruising conditions, the stator is eventually forced to rotate on its one-way clutch in the direction of engine rotation. Under these conditions, the torque converter begins to behave almost like a solid shaft, with the torus and turbine speeds being almost equal. A Torque Converter Clutch (TCC) solenoid is used on most applications (especially late model) to electronically control the torque converter. When grounded by the control module, the TCC solenoid stops converter signal oil from exhausting. This causes converter signal oil pressure to increase and shift the TCC valve into the apply position. The converter mechanically locks in position turning the transmission input shaft at the same speed as the engine crankshaft.

PLANETARY GEARBOX

See Figures 54, 55 and 56

The ability of the torque converter to multiply engine torque is limited. Also, the unit tends to be more efficient when the turbine is rotating at relatively high speeds. Therefore, a planetary gearbox is used to carry the power output of the turbine to the driveshaft.

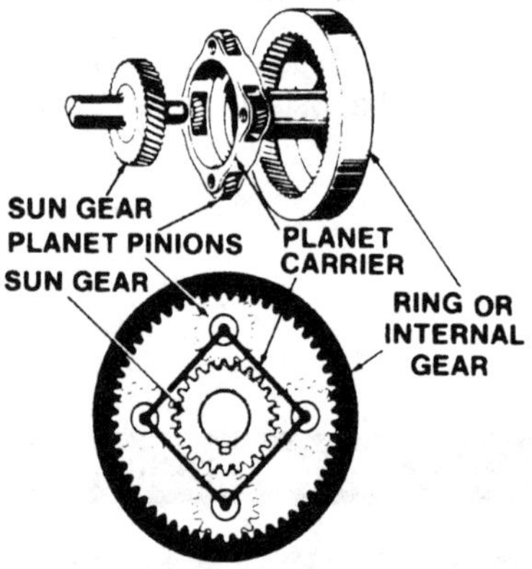

Fig. 54 Planetary gears work in a similar fashion to manual transmission gears, but are composed of three parts

Fig. 55 Planetary gears in the maximum reduction (low) range. The ring gear is held and a lower gear ratio is obtained

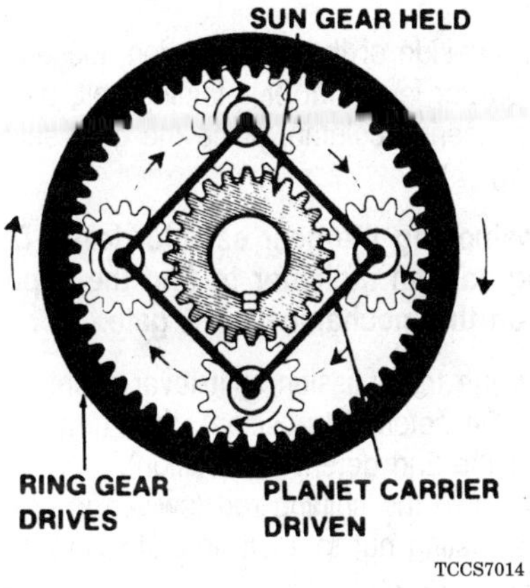

Fig. 56 Planetary gears in the minimum reduction (drive) range. The ring gear is allowed to revolve, providing a higher gear ratio

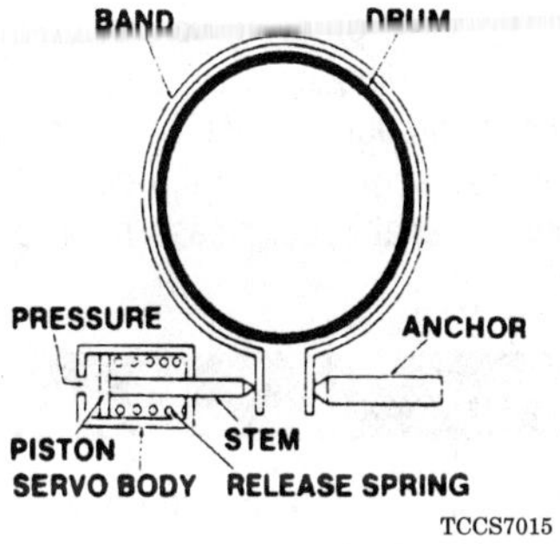

Fig. 57 Servos, operated by pressure, are used to apply or release the bands, to either hold the ring gear or allow it to rotate

Planetary gears function very similarly to conventional transmission gears. However, their construction is different in that three elements make up one gear system, and, in that all three elements are different from one another. The three elements are: an outer gear that is shaped like a hoop, with teeth cut into the inner surface; a sun gear, mounted on a shaft and located at the very center of the outer gear; and a set of three planet gears, held by pins in a ring-like planet carrier, meshing with both the sun gear and the outer gear. Either the outer gear or the sun gear may be held stationary, providing more than one possible torque multiplication factor for each set of gears. Also, if all three gears are forced to rotate at the same speed, the gearset forms, in effect, a solid shaft.

Most modern automatics use the planetary gears to provide either a single reduction ratio of about 1.8:1, or two reduction gears: a low of about 2.5:1, and an intermediate of about 1.5:1. Bands and clutches are used to hold various portions of the gearsets to the transmission case or to the shaft on which they are mounted. Shifting is accomplished, then, by changing the portion of each planetary gearset which is held to the transmission case or to the shaft.

SERVOS AND ACCUMULATORS

➧ **See Figure 57**

The servos are hydraulic pistons and cylinders. They resemble the hydraulic actuators used on many familiar machines, such as bulldozers. Hydraulic fluid enters the cylinder, under pressure, and forces the piston to move to engage the band or clutches.

The accumulators are used to cushion the engagement of the servos. The transmission fluid must pass through the accumulator on the way to the servo. The accumulator housing contains a thin piston which is sprung away from the discharge passage of the accumulator. When fluid passes through the accumulator on the way to the servo, it must move the piston against spring pressure, and this action smooths out the action of the servo.

HYDRAULIC CONTROL SYSTEM

The hydraulic pressure used to operate the servos comes from the main transmission oil pump. This fluid is channeled to the various servos through the shift valves. There is generally a manual shift valve which is operated by the transmission selector lever, and an automatic shift valve for each automatic upshift the transmission provides: i.e., 2-speed automatics have a low/high shift valve, while 3-speeds have a 1-2 valve, and a 2-3 valve. Late model vehicles are equipped with an electronically controlled transmission on which the standard shift valves have been replaced by electronic solenoid valves.

There are two pressures which affect the operation of the standard shift valves. One is the governor pressure which is affected by vehicle speed. The other is the modulator pressure which is affected by intake manifold vacuum or throttle position. Governor pressure rises with an increase in vehicle speed and modulator pressure rises as the throttle is opened wider. By responding to these two pressures, the shift valves cause the upshift points to be delayed with increased throttle opening to make the best use of the engine's power output.

Most transmissions also make use of an auxiliary circuit for downshifting. This circuit may be actuated by the throttle linkage or the vacuum line which actuates the modulator, or by a cable or solenoid. It applies pressure to a special downshift surface on the shift valve or valves.

The transmission modulator also governs the line pressure, used to actuate the servos. In this way, the clutches and bands will be actuated with a force matching the torque output of the engine.

ELECTRONIC CONTROL SYSTEM

Late model engines are often equipped with the 4L60-E, electronically controlled automatic transmission. Although hydraulic fluid is still used by these systems, the fluid is controlled by the Powertrain Control Module (PCM) through shift solenoid valves. The PCM receives information regarding fluid pressure through a pressure switch assembly (made up of 5 switches) mounted on the valve body. The pressure switch uses this information to determine actual manual valve position. The throttle valve found on older transmissions is replaced by a transmission pressure control solenoid. The PCM is equipped with a self-diagnostic system and is capable of relaying fault codes through the use of a scan tool or flash diagnosis. For more information on the computer control module's self-diagnostic capabilities, please refer to Section 4 of this manual.

Identification

The Hydra-Matic 4L60-E transmission is an electronically controlled fully automatic transmission which provides 4 forward gears and a reverse gear. Oil pressure and shifting points are controlled by the PCM through a series of solenoid valves and sensors.

➡For more information regarding serial number and transmission identification, please refer to Section 1 of this manual.

Adjustments

SHIFT LINKAGE

1994 Vehicles

➧ See Figures 58, 59 and 60

The shift linkage should be adjusted so that transmission is in the proper gear when the selector is in the shift gate. The shift indicator position should not be relied on, instead, make sure the shifter properly engages each gate position when the transmission is shifted to each gear. After adjustment, check the back-up light/neutral safety switch adjustment to be sure the engine will only start when the transmission is in the **P** or **N** positions.

1. Firmly apply the parking brake and chock the rear wheels.

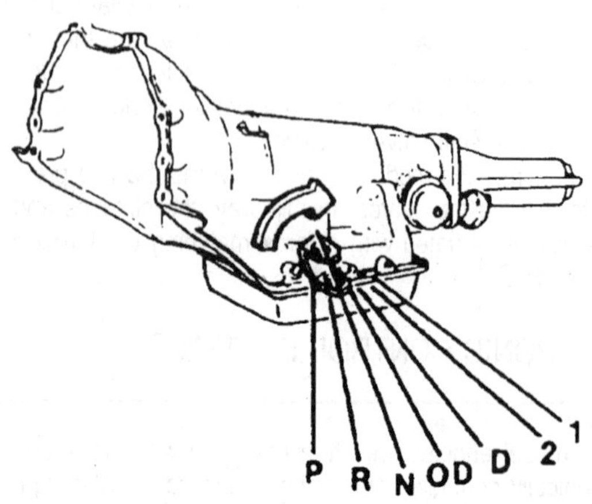

Fig. 58 Transmission shift positions

2. Raise and safely support the front of the vehicle on jackstands.
3. At the left-side of the transmission, loosen the shift rod swivel-to-equalizer lever nut or retaining bolt, as equipped.
4. At the steering column, place the gear selector lever into the **N** position.

➡When positioning the gear selector lever, DO NOT use the steering column indicator to find the N position. Instead rely on the mechanical shift gate.

5. Rotate the transmission shift lever counterclockwise (forward) to the 1st detent (**P** position), then turn it clockwise (rearward) to the 2nd detent (**N** position).
6. Tightly, hold the shifting rod (swivel) in position, then tighten the adjusting nut to 11 ft. lbs. (15 Nm) or the bolt to 18 ft. lbs. (25 Nm), as applicable.
7. Place the gear selector lever (on the steering column) in the **P** position and check the adjustment. Move the gear selector lever into the various positions; the engine must start in the **P** and the **N** positions.

➡If the engine will not start in the N and/or P positions (or will start in gear), refer to back-up light switch adjustment procedures in Section 6 of this manual, then properly adjust the switch.

⁂CAUTION

With the gear selector lever in the P position, the parking pawl should engage the rear internal gear lugs or output ring gear lugs to prevent the vehicle from rolling and possibly causing personal injury.

8. Align the gear selector lever indicator, if necessary. Remove the jackstands and carefully lower the vehicle.

SHIFT CABLE

1995-97 Vehicles

➧ See Figures 61 and 62

The shift cable should be adjusted so that transmission is in the proper gear when the selector is in the shift gate. The shift indicator position should not be relied on, instead, make sure the shifter properly engages each gate position when the transmission is shifted to each gear. After adjustment, check the back-up light/neutral safety switch adjustment to be sure the engine will only start when the transmission is in the Park or Neutral positions.

1. Firmly apply the parking brake and chock the rear wheels.
2. At the steering column, place the gear selector lever into the **N** position.

➡When positioning the gear selector lever, DO NOT use the steering column indicator to find the N position. Instead rely on the mechanical shift gate.

3. Raise and safely support the front of the vehicle on jackstands.
4. If 4WD, remove the transfer case shield to gain access to the shift cable.

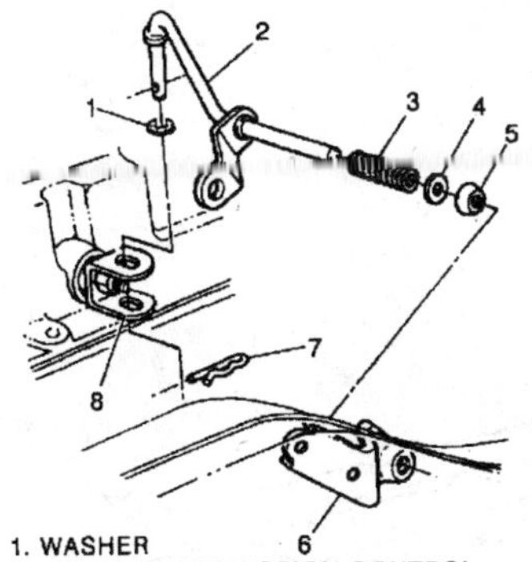

Fig. 59 Shift linkage — 2WD vehicles

5. Remove the retainer securing the shift cable to the transmission bracket.
6. Squeeze the cable retainers while pulling the cable towards the rear of the vehicle.
7. Remove the shift cable end from the transmission control ball stud. This is accomplished by pressing the locking tab on the shaft cable in and pulling the shift cable back through the bracket.
8. Rotate the transmission shift lever clockwise (forward) to the 1st detent (**P** position), then turn it counterclockwise (rearward) to the 2nd detent (**N** position).
9. Install the shift cable to the shift cable bracket by pulling the shift cable through the bracket while pressing in the locking tab until the shift cable is locked into place on the bracket.
10. Install the shift cable end to the transmission control lever ball stud.
11. Install the retainer securing the shift cable to the transmission bracket.
12. If 4WD, install the transfer case shield.
13. Remove the jackstands and carefully lower the vehicle.
14. With the park brake engage and the engine running, test the transmission and shift control for proper operation.
15. Place the gear selector lever (on the steering column) in the **P** position and check the adjustment. Move the gear selector lever into the various positions; the engine must start in the **P** and the **N** positions.

➡If the engine will not start in the N and/or P positions (or will start in gear), refer to back-up light switch adjustment procedures in Section 6 of this manual, then properly adjust the switch.

⁂CAUTION

With the gear selector lever in the P position, the parking pawl should engage the rear internal gear lugs or output ring gear lugs to prevent the vehicle from rolling and possibly causing personal injury.

16. Align the gear selector lever indicator, if necessary.

Back-Up Lamp/Neutral Safety Switch

The back-up lamp/neutral safety switch assembly is mounted either on the steering column or on the floor shifter assembly, under the console, depending on the vehicle and application. Most models utilize a steering column mounted shifter for the automatic transmission, therefore the switch will be found on the steering column for most vehicles covered by this manual. For the removal, installation and adjustment procedures, please refer to the back-up lamp/neutral safety switch procedures in Section 6, of this manual.

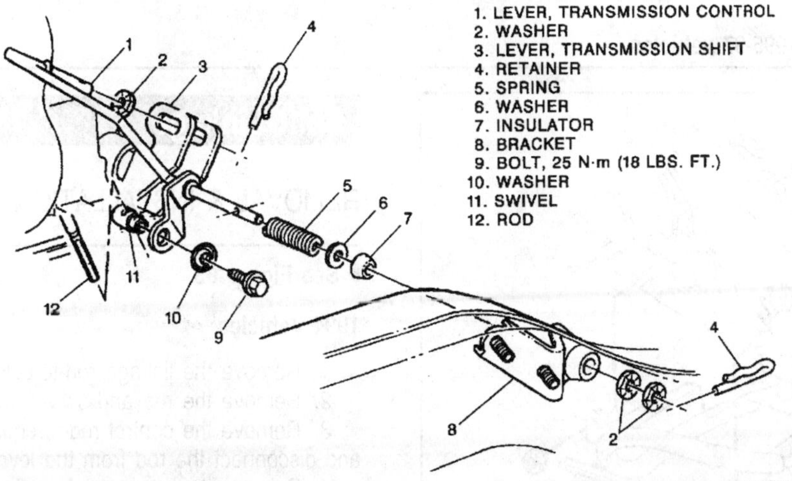

Fig. 60 Shift linkage — 4WD vehicles

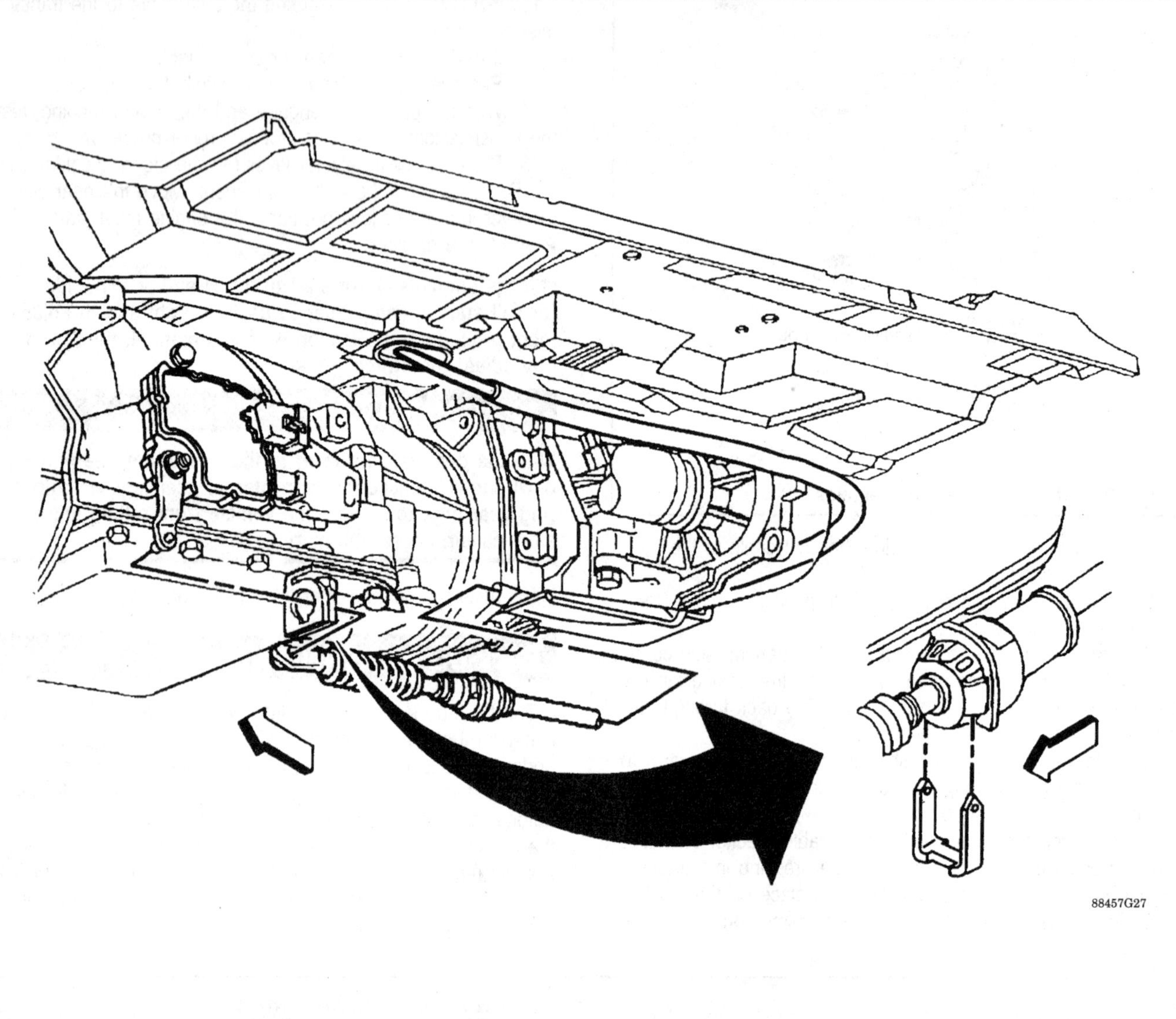

Fig. 61 Shift cable — 1995-97 vehicles

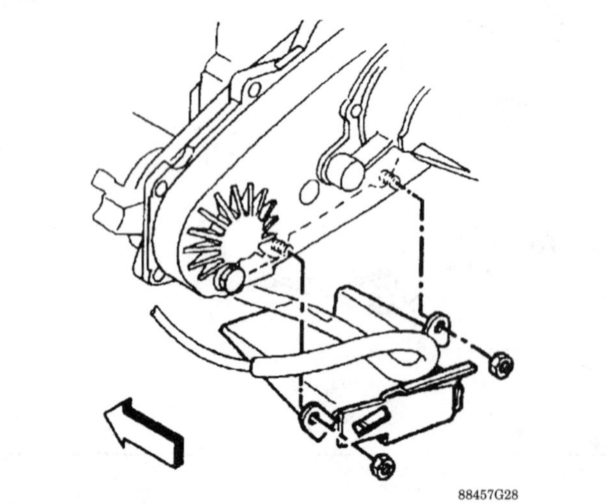

Fig. 62 Remove the transfer case shield

Shift Linkage

REMOVAL & INSTALLATION

➧ See Figure 63

1994 Vehicles

1. Remove the linkage rod-to-column bolt and washer.
2. Remove the rod and swivel from the column.
3. Remove the control rod-to-equalizer lever retaining pin and disconnect the rod from the lever.
4. Remove the intermediate rod-to-transmission lever retaining pin and remove the rod and equalizer lever assembly. Don't loose the spring and bushing.

To install:

5. Install the transmission control lever into the holes of the shift lever.
6. Install a new retainer pin in the control lever.
7. Install the shift rod to the control lever.

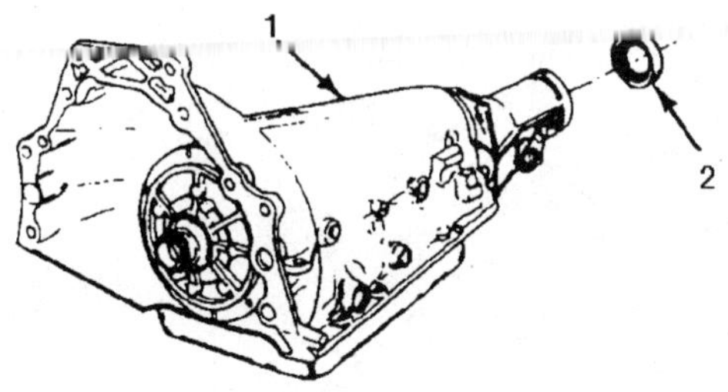

Fig. 63 Rear extension housing oil seal

8. Install the spring washer and bolt. Adjust the linkage.
9. Tighten the bolt to 18 ft. lbs. (25 Nm).

Shift Cable

REMOVAL & INSTALLATION

See Figures 61, 62 and 64

1995-97 Vehicles

1. Disconnect the negative battery cable.
2. Firmly apply the parking brake and chock the rear wheels.
3. At the steering column, place the gear selector lever into the **N** position.
4. Remove the steering column cover panel.
5. Remove the door sill trim and cowl side trim panels.
6. Remove the driver side seat.
7. Remove the retainer securing the shift cable to steering column.
8. Remove the shift cable end from the steering column shift bracket lower ball stud.
9. Remove the nut securing the shift cable and clip to the pedal bracket.
10. Remove the grommet and tape securing the shift cable to the floor panel.
11. Raise and support the vehicle safely using jackstands.
12. Remove the retainer securing the shift cable to the transmission bracket. This is accomplished by squeezing the cable retainers while pulling the cable towards the rear of the vehicle.
13. Remove the shift cable from the transmission control lever ball stud.
14. If the vehicle is equipped with 4WD:
    a. Remove the 2 nuts securing the transfer case shield to the transfer case.
    b. Remove the nut securing the shift cable to the transfer case upper clip.
15. Lower the vehicle.
16. Lift the carpet on the drivers side and pull the grommet and cable into the vehicle.

To install:

Ensure that the transmission control lever and steering column selector are in their mechanical neutral position. To accomplish this, move the shift lever to the full clockwise position and then turn the shift lever back 2 detents counterclockwise.

Lift the carpet and feed the cable through the floor panel.

17. Install the grommet and tape securing the shift cable to the floor panel.
18. Install the nut securing the shift cable and clip to the pedal bracket.
19. Shift the cable end to the steering column shaft bracket lower ball stud.
20. Install the retainer securing the shift cable to the steering column.
21. Raise and support the vehicle safely using jackstands.
22. Position the locking tab at the transmission end of the shift cable out, to release the shift cable adjuster.
23. Shift the cable end to the transmission control lever ball stud.
24. Press and push the locking tab of the shift cable in. Do not contact the shift cable while pushing the locking tab in.
25. Install the retainer securing the shift cable to the transmission bracket.
26. On vehicles equipped with 4WD:
    a. Install the nut securing the shift cable to the transfer case upper clip.
    b. Install the nut securing the shift cable to the transfer case lower clip.
    c. Install the 2 nuts securing the transfer case shield to the transfer case.
27. Lower the vehicle.
28. Install the steering column cover panel.
29. Install the cowl side trim panel and door sill trim panel.
30. Install the driver side seat.
31. Connect the negative battery cable.

Extension Housing Seal

REMOVAL & INSTALLATION

See Figures 63 and 65

1. Raise and support the vehicle safely using jackstands. If the rear of the vehicle is supported significantly higher than the front of the truck, the transmission fluid may not have to be drained for this service.
2. Remove the transmission fluid pan and drain the fluid from the vehicle. This step is recommended, but may not be necessary if the rear of the vehicle is held higher than the front. What is important is that the sealing surface in the extension housing may be cleaned of fluid and debris before installing the new seal. If fluid continues to run out of the housing once the old seal is removed, then the fluid should be drained to allow for proper seal installation.
3. Matchmark and remove the driveshaft. Most vehicles covered in this manual should be equipped with a slip yoke and the front of the driveshaft. In order to remove the shaft,

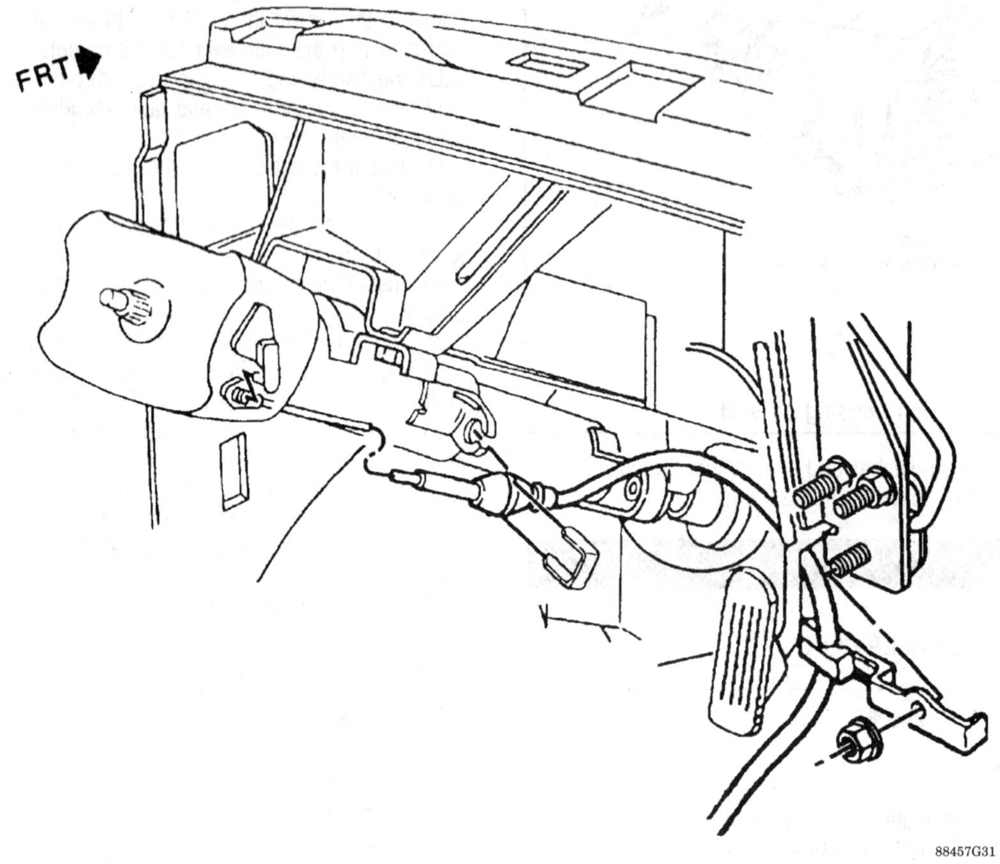

Fig. 64 Removing the shift cable at the steering column end

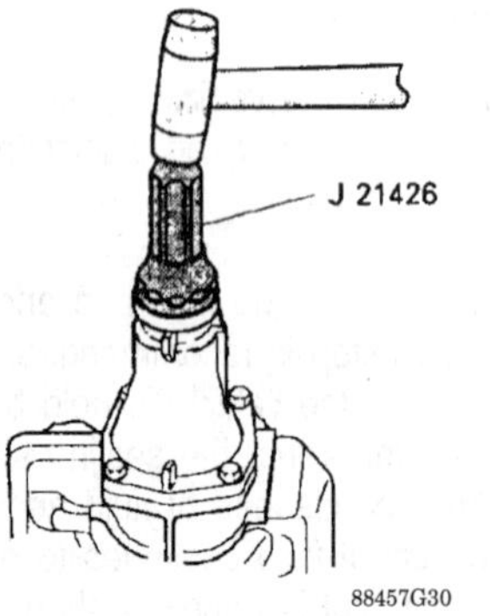

Fig. 65 Installing the rear extension housing seal

disconnect it from the rear axle, then carefully withdraw the splined yoke from the rear of the transmission.

4. Carefully distort the seal using a punch, then pry the seal from the rear of the transmission housing. Be careful not to damage the sealing surface of the housing.

To install:

5. Clean and DRY the sealing surface in the rear of the transmission housing.

6. Coat the outside of the new seal with a non-hardening sealing compound.

7. Carefully drive the new seal into position using a proper seal installation tool. Be careful not to damage the housing or the transmission output shaft upon installation.

8. Align and install the driveshaft assembly.

9. Remove the jackstands and carefully lower the vehicle.

10. Immediately check and, if necessary, add fresh transmission fluid. Please refer to Section 1 of this manual for details concerning proper methods and type of automatic transmission fluid.

Transmission

REMOVAL & INSTALLATION

On many of the vehicles covered by this manual, the upper transmission-to-engine bolts (especially the upper left) may be difficult to access and withdraw due to the close proximity of the cowl sheet metal. Even if a wrench fits over the bolt, there may be insufficient room to fully unthread it. The factory recommended procedure to access these bolts is to remove the left body mount bolt(s) from under the cab and loosen the radiator support mounting, then carefully jack the body up off the frame until sufficient clearance exists. Place wooden blocks between the body and frame to support the body (this is to prevent damage and for SAFETY) during service. In some cases, this may be unnecessary if the engine will pivot downward sufficiently on the motor mount to allow bolt access or if the motor mounts are removed and the engine is supported using a lifting device. BUT DO NOT try this if it appears that the mounts will be damaged by the stress. Also, be sure the engine is properly supported at ALL times and that no components will be damaged. Watch that the distributor does not contact the cowl and that the cooling fan remains clear of the radiator and shroud assembly. When in doubt, unbolt and raise the body for access.

1994-95 Vehicles

See Figure 66

1. Properly relieve the fuel system pressure, then disconnect the negative battery cable.
2. Raise and support the vehicle safely using jackstands.
3. Drain the transmission fluid. For details, please refer to the pan procedure located in Section 1 of this manual.
4. On 1994 vehicles, disconnect the shift linkage from the transmission.
5. On 1995 vehicles, disconnect the shift cable from the transmission.
6. Matchmark and remove the rear driveshaft. For details, please refer to the procedure located later in this section.
7. For 4WD vehicles, remove the transfer case assembly. For details, please refer to the procedure located later in this section.
8. Disconnect the fuel lines.
9. Remove the transmission crossmember-to-frame retaining bolts and member-to-transmission retainer(s), then remove the crossmember from the vehicle. Take care not to stretch or damage any cables or wiring when attempting to remove the crossmember.
10. Disconnect the exhaust pipe(s) from the manifold(s).
11. Remove the flywheel inspection cover and matchmark the flywheel-to-torque converter relationship, then remove the flywheel-to-torque converter bolts.
12. Remove the fuel lines and wiring harness from the transmission.
13. Make sure the transmission is properly supported by a floor jack, then remove the transmission-to-engine bolts. Note the positioning of any brackets, clips or harnesses as they are removed.
14. Remove the dipstick tube and seal, then plug or cover the opening in the transmission housing in order to prevent system contamination.
15. Disconnect the cooler lines. Plug or cover all openings in order to prevent system contamination or excessive fluid spillage.
16. Support the engine using a jackstand and a block of wood.
17. Using the floor jack to support the transmission, pull it straight back and disengage it from the engine. Carefully lower the transmission and remove it from the vehicle. If possible, install a torque converter retaining strap before attempting to lower the transmission. This will prevent the converter from possibly falling and causing damage and/or personal injury.

To install:

18. Make sure the torque converter is properly seated and a retaining strap is installed.
19. Using the floor jack, carefully raise the transmission into position in the vehicle, then remove the converter retaining strap. Slide the transmission straight onto the locating pins while aligning the marks on the flywheel and torque converter.

➡The converter must be flush on the flywheel and rotate freely by hand.

20. Install the transmission-to-engine retainers, taking care to properly reposition all brackets, clips and harness, as noted during removal. Do NOT install the dipstick tube or transmission support brace screws at this time.
21. Tighten the transmission-to-engine retainers to 23 ft. lbs. (32 Nm).
22. Connect the transmission cooler lines.
23. Remove the plug from the opening, then position a new seal to the transmission and install the dipstick tube.
24. If equipped, install the transfer case support rods to the transmission housing.
25. Install the wiring harness and fuel lines to the transmission housing.
26. Make sure the matchmarks are aligned, then install and finger-tighten the flywheel-to-converter bolts. Once the converter is properly seated by finger-tightening the bolts, tighten them to 46 ft. lbs. (63 Nm).
27. Hook the edge of the flywheel inspection cover under the lip of the engine oil pan, then install and secure the cover.
28. Connect the exhaust pipe(s) to the manifold(s).
29. Install the transmission crossmember to the vehicle. Tighten the member-to-frame bolts to 56 ft. lbs. (77 Nm).
30. On 4WD vehicles, install the transfer case assembly. Remove the floor jack.
31. Align and install the rear driveshaft.
32. On 1994 vehicles, connect the shift linkage then check and adjust, as necessary.
33. On 1995 vehicles, connect the shift cable then check and adjust, as necessary.
34. Refill the transmission using fresh fluid. Refer to Section 1 of this manual for fluid recommendations, capacities and level checking.
35. Remove the jackstands and carefully lower the vehicle.
36. Connect the negative battery cable, then check for proper operation.

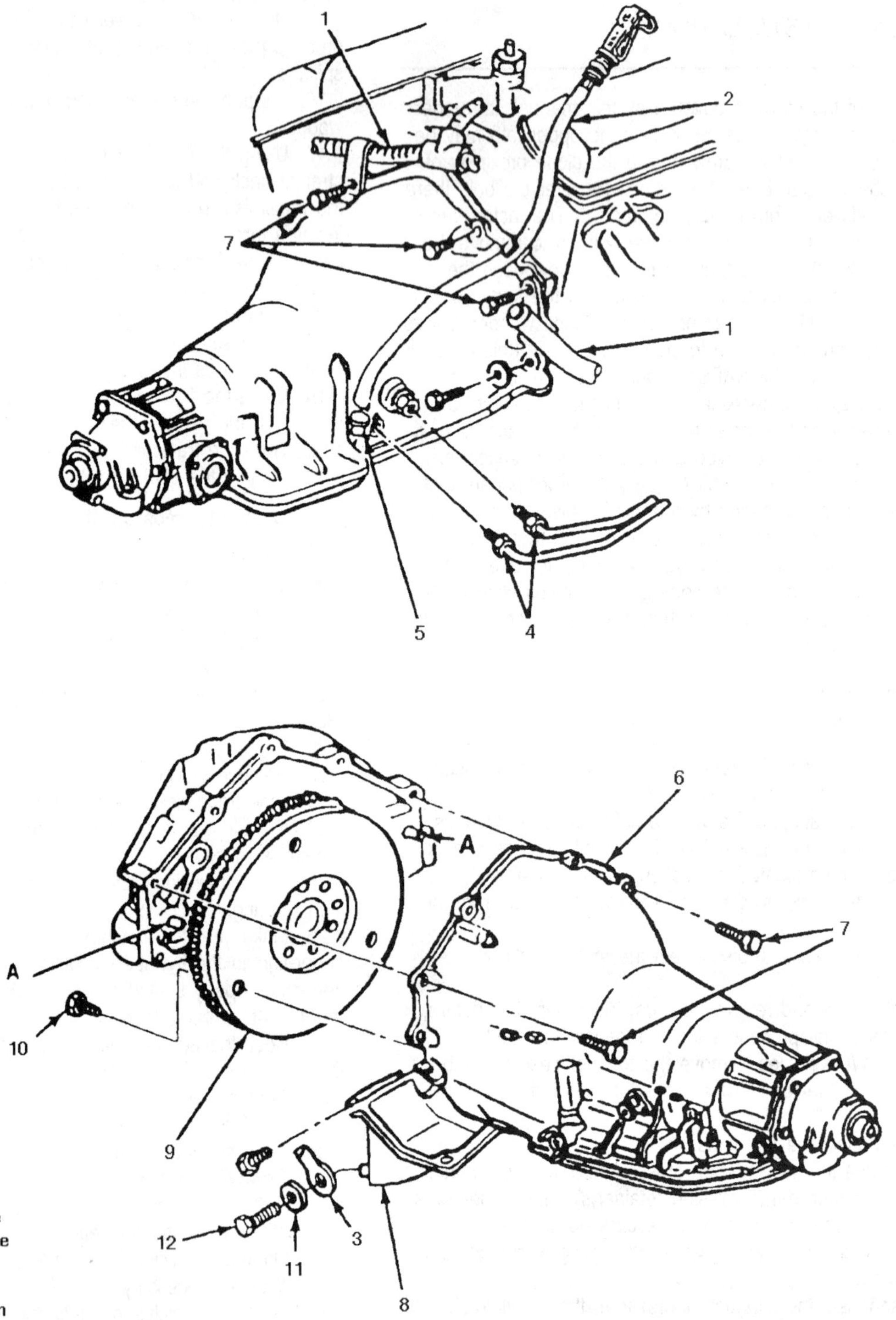

1. Harness
2. Dipstick tube
3. Support brace
4. Cooler lines
5. Seal
6. Transmission
7. Transmission to engine screws
8. Converter housing cover
9. Flywheel
10. Flywheel to torque converter screw
11. Washer
12. Screw

88457G32

Fig. 66 Transmission mounting and components — 1994 4L60-E shown

1996-97 Vehicles

▶ See Figures 67 and 68

1. Disconnect the negative battery cable.
2. Raise and support the vehicle safely using jackstands.
3. Drain the transmission fluid. For details, please refer to the pan procedure located in Section 1 of this manual.
4. Remove the driveshaft from the transmission (2WD) and transfer case, if equipped (4WD).
5. Support the transmission with a suitable transmission jack.
6. Remove the shift cable from the transmission control lever and bracket.
7. Remove the nut and washer securing the transmission mount to the crossmember.
8. Remove the bolts and washers securing the mount to the transmission.
9. Disconnect the exhaust pipe from the exhaust manifold(s).
10. Remove the 6 bolts securing the converter pan cover to the transmission on 2.2L equipped models only.
11. Remove the 3 bolts securing the torque converter to the flywheel.
12. Remove the bolt, clip, and strap securing the three fuel lines and transmission vent hose to the transmission case.
13. Remove the 5 bolts and nut securing the transmission to the engine on 2.2L equipped models only.
14. Remove the 9 bolts securing the transmission to the engine on 4.3L equipped models only.
15. Remove the oil filler tube and seal from the transmission.
16. Disconnect the transmission cooler lines from the transmission. Plug the lines and the ports in the transmission.
17. Remove the wiring harness connectors from the transmission.
18. Inspect for any other wiring, brackets etc. which may interfere with the removal of the transmission.
19. Since the transmission acts as a rear engine mount, properly support the rear of the engine with an underbody support of other suitable support before attempting to remove the transmission. Otherwise the rear of the engine may pitch downward and components on the rear of the engine and on the firewall may be damaged.
20. Remove the transmission from the engine by pulling the transmission rearward to disengage it from the locator dowel pins on the back of the block. Carefully lower the transmission from the vehicle. Use care that the torque converter does not fall out of the front of the transmission.

➡Use converter holding strap tool No. J-21366, or equivalent, to secure the torque converter to the transmission during removal and installation procedures.

To install:

21. Make sure the torque converter is fully seated in the pump drive. If not, the transmission will not fit tightly to the rear of the engine block.
22. Raise the transmission into position and remove the torque converter holding strap and carefully. Slide the transmission forward until the dowel pins are engaged.
23. The torque converter should be flush with the flywheel and turn freely by hand.
24. Install the transmission-to-engine bolts. Tighten the bolts to 66 ft. lbs. (90 Nm) for 2.2L equipped vehicles and to 34 ft. lbs. (47 Nm) for 4.3L equipped vehicles.
25. Engage the wiring harness connectors to the transmission.
26. Install any other wiring, brackets etc. which were removed prior to the removal of the transmission.
27. Install the transmission cooler lines.
28. Install the transmission oil filler tube and seal.
29. Install the bolt, clip, and strap to secure the three fuel lines and transmission vent hose to the transmission case.
30. Install the 3 bolts securing the torque converter to the flywheel. Tighten each bolt finger-tight to ensure proper converter seating. Final tighten the bolts to 46 ft. lbs. (63 Nm).
31. Install the 6 bolts to secure the converter pan cover to the transmission on 2.2L equipped vehicles only. Tighten the bolts to 37 ft. lbs. (50 Nm)
32. Connect the exhaust pipe to the exhaust manifold(s).
33. Install the bolts and washers securing the transmission mount. Tighten the bolts to 35 ft. lbs. (47 Nm).

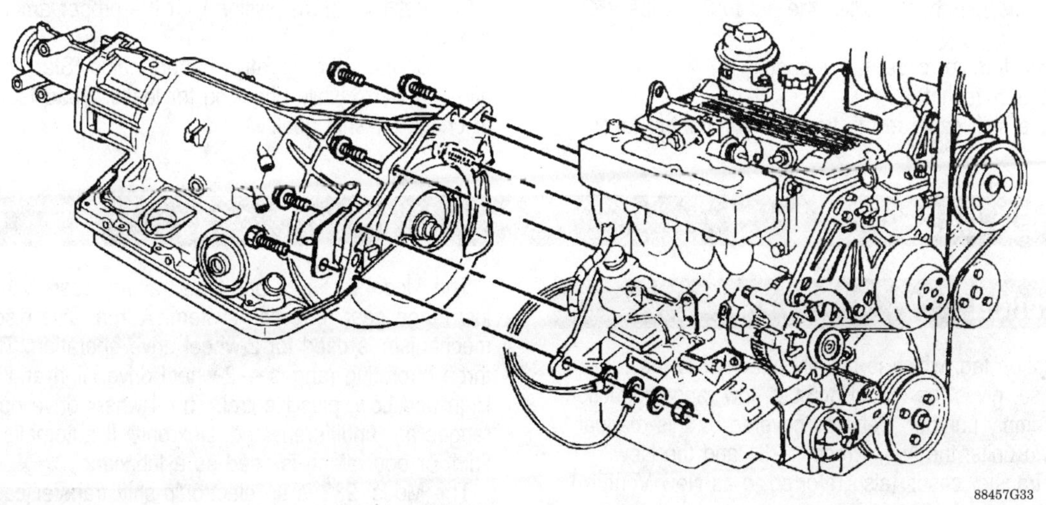

Fig. 67 Transmission mounting on 1996-97 2.2L engines

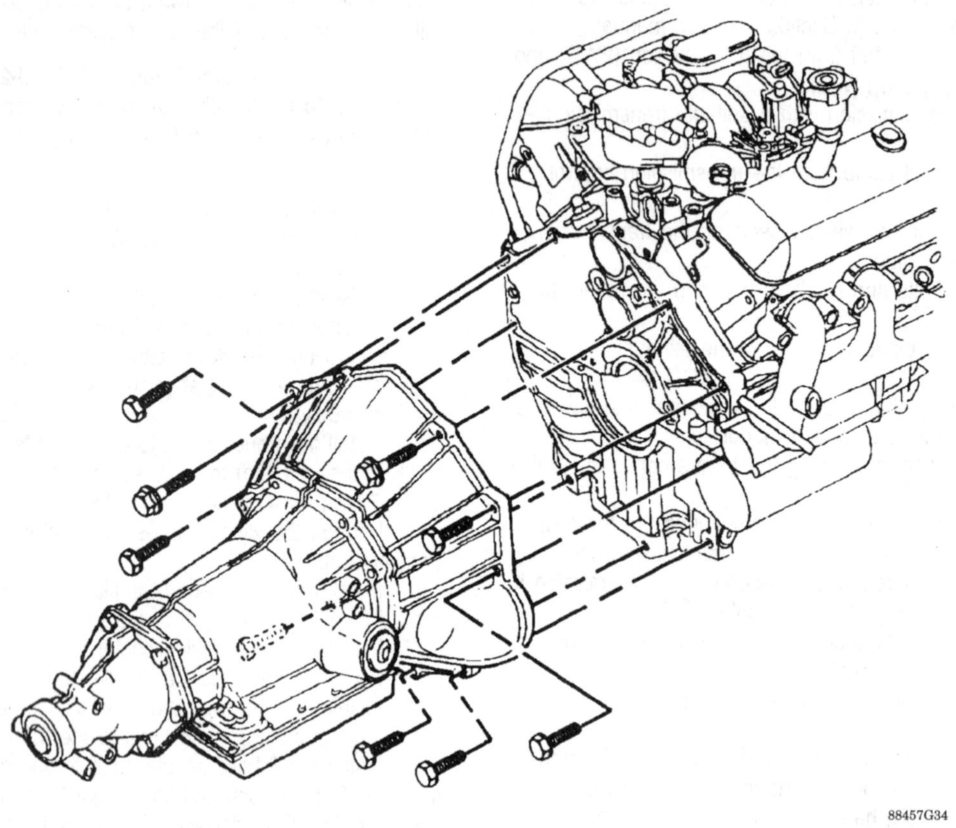

Fig. 68 Transmission mounting on 1996-97 4.3L engines

34. Install the nut and washer securing the transmission mount to the crossmember. Tighten the nut to 38 ft. lbs. (52 Nm).
35. Install the transfer case, if equipped.
36. Install the driveshaft.
37. Install the shift cable to the transmission control lever and bracket.
38. Lower the vehicle.
39. Refill the transmission with the proper amount and type of fluid.
40. Connect the negative battery cable. Start the vehicle and allow to warm while checking for leaks. Road test the vehicle to check for shift quality.

TRANSFER CASE

Identification

An identification tag, which is usually attached to the rear half of the case, gives the model number, low range reduction ratio and assembly number. Vehicles covered by this manual use one of two units: the New Process 231 and the New Process 233 transfer cases (also referred to as New Venture). A floor mounted transfer case shifter are equipped with the 231, while the New Process 233 is an electronic shift transfer case and does not use a shifter.

The Model 231 is a part-time transfer case with a built in low range gear reduction system. A front axle disconnect mechanism is used for 2-wheel drive operation. The 231 has three operating ranges — 2-wheel drive High and 4-wheel drive High and Low, plus Neutral. The 4-wheel drive operating ranges are undifferentiated. Dexron® II automatic transmission fluid, or equivalent, is used as a lubricant.

The Model 233 is an electronic shift transfer case that has 3 modes of operation: 2WD range, 4WD High, and 4WD Low. Gear reduction for low range is provided by a planetary gear set. The floor mounted shifter has been replaced by a dash mounted switch for these units.

Adjustments

SHIFT LEVER/LINKAGE

See Figures 69, 70, 71, 72 and 73

Only the 231 model transfer case is equipped with a shift lever. In order to adjust the lever/linkage assembly, then floor console must be removed for access.

1. Remove the floor shift lever knob retainer, then remove the shift lever knob.
2. Remove the front floor console.
3. Place the shift lever in Neutral.
4. Pull the control cable from the shift lever, then loosen the control cable locknut.

Fig. 70 Removing the transfer case cable retainer nut

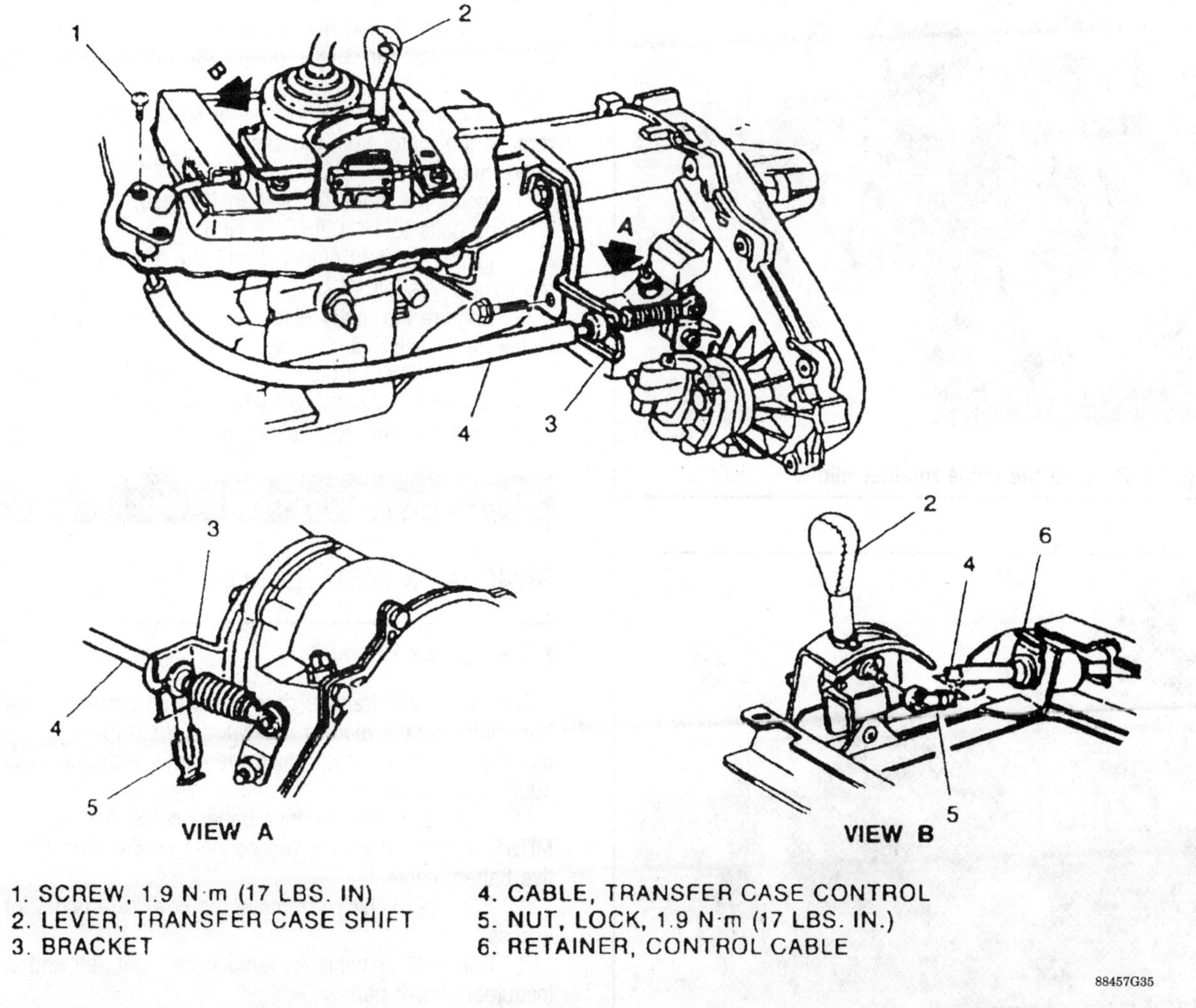

Fig. 69 Transfer case shift adjustment

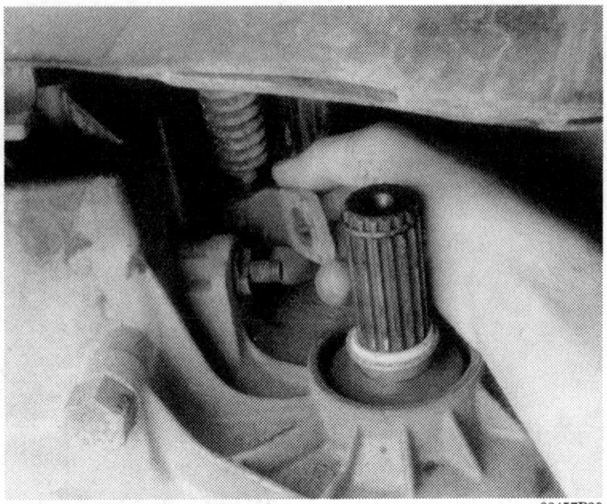

Fig. 71 Remove the transfer case shift linkage from the shaft

Fig. 72 Remove the cable retainer clip

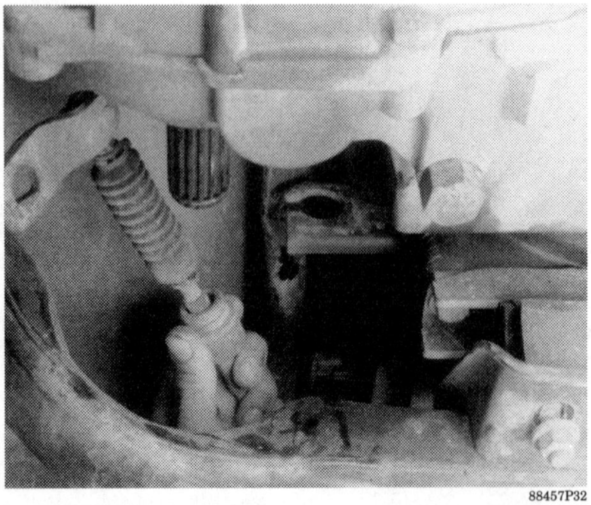

Fig. 73 Remove the cable assembly from the vehicle

5. Verify that the transfer case and the floor shift lever are both in Neutral. Turn the shift lever end of the cable in or out, as necessary, until it is aligned with the shifter.
6. Install the control cable to the shift lever.
7. Tighten the control cable locknut to 17 inch lbs. (1.9 Nm).
8. Verify proper shift operation.
9. Install the front floor console.
10. Install the shift lever knob and retainer.

Shift Motor

REMOVAL & INSTALLATION

See Figure 74

The Model 233 transfer case utilizes an electronic shifter. The motor is attached to the lower side of the transfer case.

1. Disconnect the negative battery cable.
2. Raise and support the vehicle safely using jackstands.
3. If equipped, remove the transfer case shield for access.
4. Disengage the motor electrical connector.
5. Matchmark and remove the front driveshaft and the output shaft yoke. For details, please refer to the procedure later in this section.
6. Remove the motor-to-transfer case retaining bolts, then remove the motor from the case.

To install:

7. Install the motor to the transfer case, then tighten the retaining bolts to 13 ft. lbs. (18 Nm).
8. Install the front output shaft yoke, then align and install the front driveshaft.
9. Engage the motor electrical connector, then if equipped, install the transfer case shield.
10. Remove the jackstands and carefully lower the vehicle.
11. Connect the negative battery cable.
12. Verify proper motor operation.

Shift Motor Control Module

REMOVAL & INSTALLATION

See Figures 75 and 76

The Model 233 transfer case utilizes an electronic shifter. The motor control module is located behind the right side cowl panel on 1994 pickups, behind the center instrument panel on 1995-97 pickups.

1. Disconnect the negative battery cable. The ignition MUST be **OFF** whenever you connect or disconnect the negative battery cable.
2. For 1994 vehicles, remove the cowl side panel for access.
3. For 1995-97 vehicles, remove the right, left and center instrument lower panels.
4. On all vehicles, disengage the electrical wiring from the module.
5. Remove the retainers, then remove the module from the vehicle.

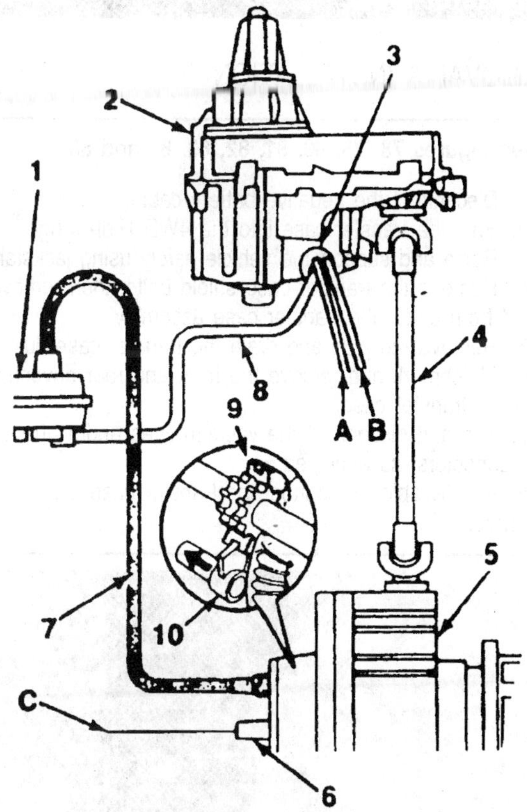

VACUUM ACTUATED

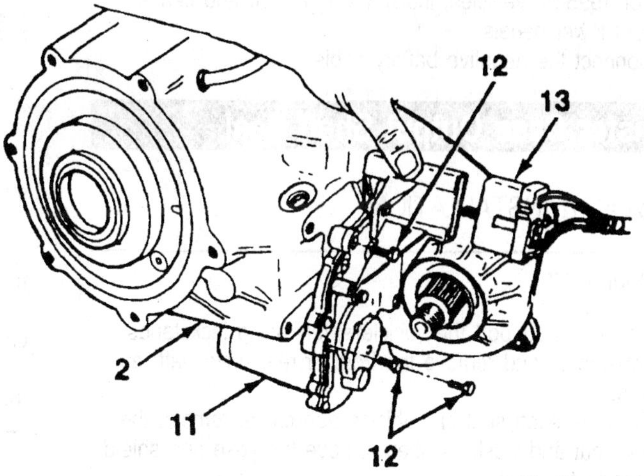

ELECTRONIC ACTUATED

A. Hose to Engine Vacuum
B. Vent Hose to Atmosphere
C. Wire to Front Axle Indicator Lamp
1. Vacuum Actuator
2. Transfer Case
3. Vacuum Switch
4. Front Propeller Shaft
5. Front Axle
6. Front Axle Switch
7. Actuator Cable
8. Vacuum Hose
9. Connector Sleeve
10. Shift Fork
11. Electric Motor
12. Bolt
13. Electric Motor Connection

88457G36

Fig. 74 Electronically actuated shift motor

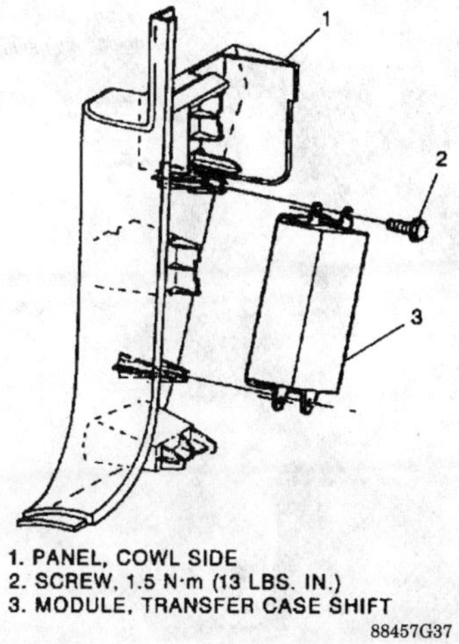

1. PANEL, COWL SIDE
2. SCREW, 1.5 N·m (13 LBS. IN.)
3. MODULE, TRANSFER CASE SHIFT

88457G37

Fig. 75 Shift motor control module mounting — 1994 pickup shown

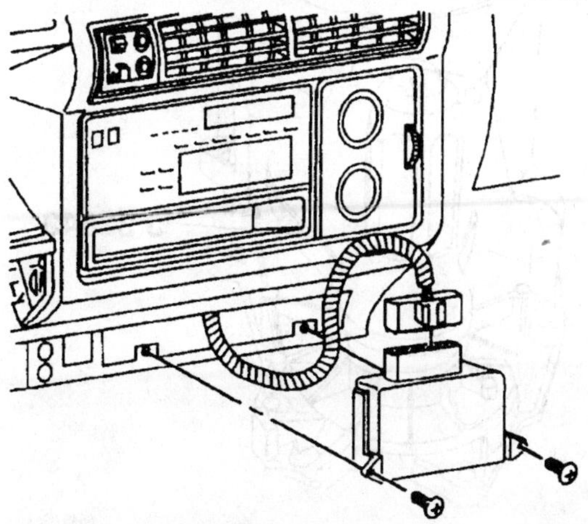

88457G38

Fig. 76 Shift motor control module mounting — 1995 pickup shown

To install:

6. Engage the electrical connector to the module.
7. Install the module in mounting position and install retainers.
8. For 1994 vehicles, install the cowl side panel.
9. For 1995-97 vehicles, install the right, left and center instrument lower panels.
10. Connect the negative battery cable.

Transfer Case Output Shaft Seal

REMOVAL & INSTALLATION

See Figure 77

1. Raise and support the vehicle safely using jackstands.
2. Matchmark and remove the front or rear driveshaft, as applicable.
3. For front shaft seal on vehicles applicable, remove the shaft yoke nut and washers, then remove the yoke and shield for access to the seal.
4. Pry out the old seal using a small suitable prytool. Be careful not to damage the seal bore.

To install:

5. Lubricate the lips of the new seal using automatic transmission fluid or petroleum jelly, whichever is at hand.
6. Position the seal and carefully drive it into position using a suitable seal installer tool.
7. On NV231 and NV233 transfer cases, install the front seal using tool J-33834 and tool J-33843, or equivalent tools for the rear seal
8. As applicable, install the shield and shaft yoke, then install the washers and yoke nut. On 1994 vehicles, tighten the nut to 110 ft. lbs. (149 Nm). On 1995-97 vehicles, tighten the nut to 80 ft. lbs. (108 Nm).
9. Align and install the driveshaft to the vehicle.
10. Remove the jackstands and carefully lower the vehicle.

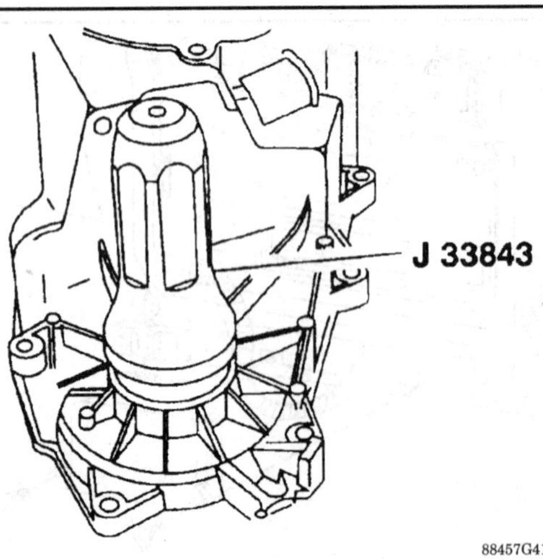

Fig. 77 Install the shaft seal using a suitable installation tool or driver — NV231 and NV233 shown

Transfer Case

REMOVAL & INSTALLATION

See Figures 78, 79, 80, 81, 82, 83, 84 and 85

1. Disconnect the negative battery cable.
2. Shift the transfer case into the 4WD High range.
3. Raise and support the vehicle safely using jackstands.
4. Remove the transfer case shield bolts, then remove the shield from under the transfer case assembly.
5. Remove the plug and drain the transfer case fluid.
6. Matchmark and remove the front and rear driveshafts from the transfer case.
7. Tag and disconnect the vacuum lines and/or the electrical connectors, as equipped.
8. If applicable, disconnect the transfer case shift rod from the case.

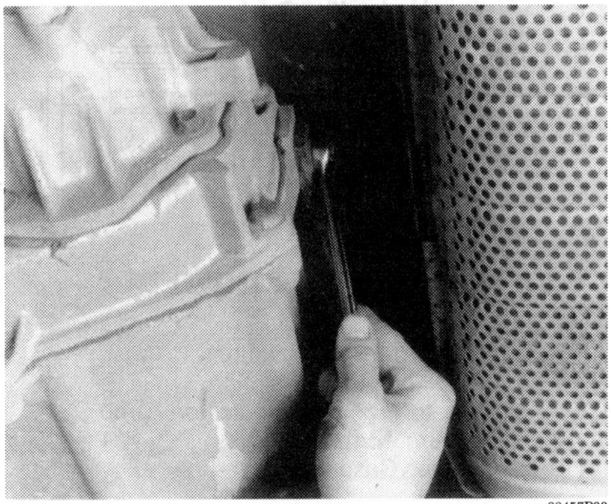

Fig. 78 If equipped, disconnect the shift cable linkage

Fig. 79 Disengage the vacuum harness

Fig. 80 With the transfer case supported, remove the transfer case retainer bolts

Fig. 81 Carefully lower the transfer case from the vehicle on a transmission jack

Fig. 82 Prior to installation, remove the old gasket from the mating surfaces

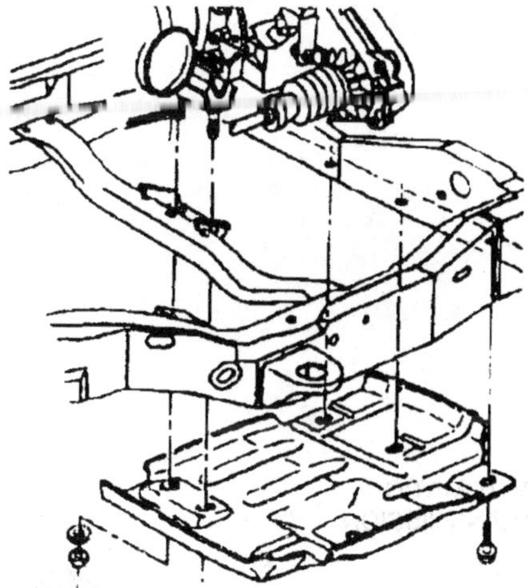

Fig. 83 View of the transfer case shield

9. If applicable, remove the support brace-to-transfer case bolts.
10. Support the transfer case using a floor jack, then remove the transfer case-to-transmission retaining bolts
11. Slide the transfer case rearward and off the transmission output shaft, then careful lower it from the vehicle.
12. Remove all traces of old gasket material from the mating surfaces.

To install:

13. Using the floor jack, carefully raise the transfer case into position behind the transmission. Position a new gasket, using sealer to hold it in position, then slide the transfer case onto the transmission output shaft.
14. Install the transfer case-to-transmission retaining bolts, then tighten to 24 ft. lbs. (33 Nm) on 1994 vehicles, or 41 ft. lbs. (55 Nm) on 1995-97 vehicles.
15. If equipped, install the right and left side support brace bolts and tighten to 35 ft. lbs. (47 Nm) on 1994-95 vehicles, or 37 ft. lbs. (50 Nm) on 1996-97 vehicles.
16. Remove the floor jack from the transfer case.
17. If equipped, connect the shift rod to the case.
18. Engage the vacuum lines and/or electrical connections, as necessary.
19. Align and install the front and rear driveshafts.
20. Make sure the truck is level, then properly refill the transfer case through the filler plug. For details, please refer to Section 1 of this manual.
21. Install the transfer case shield. Tighten the transfer shield retainer bolts to 25 ft. lbs. (34 Nm).
22. If not done already, remove the jackstands and carefully lower the vehicle.
23. Connect the negative battery cable.

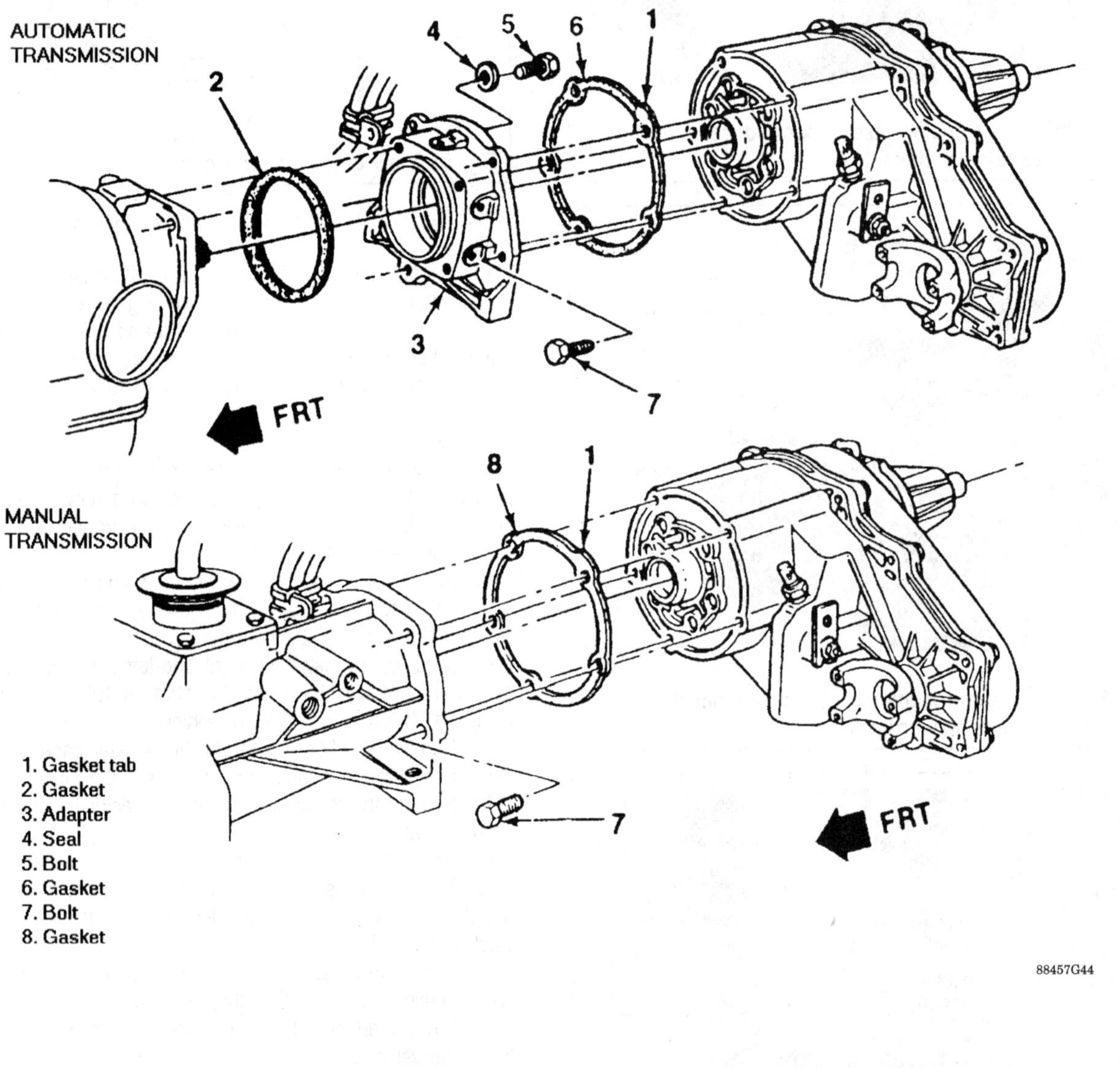

Fig. 84 Transfer case mounting to automatic and manual transaxle

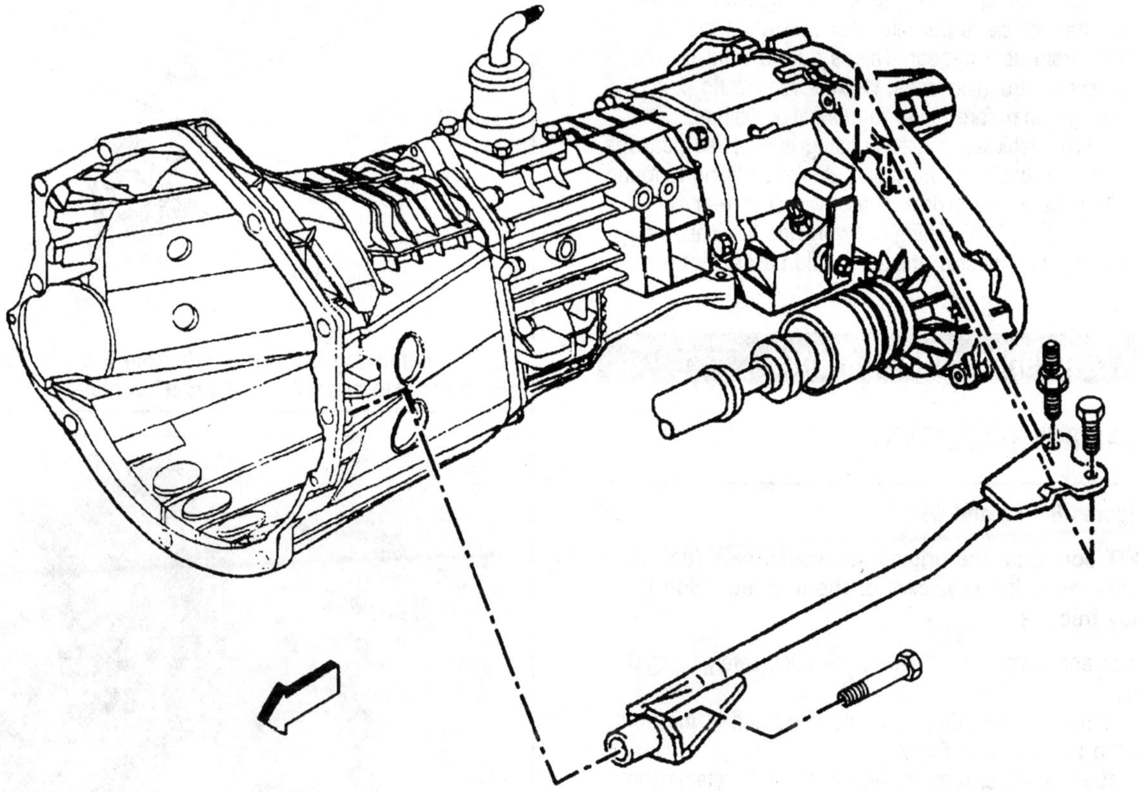

Fig. 85 Removing the left side support brace from the transmission/transfer case assembly — manual unit shown

DRIVELINE

On all models covered by this manual, conventional, open type driveshafts are used. Located at either end of the driveshaft is a universal joint (U-joint), which allows the driveshaft to move up and down (within designed limits) in order to match the motion of the rear axle. The shaft is designed and built with yoke lugs (ears) in line with each other in order to produce the smoothest possible running shaft. Because some vehicles covered by this manual utilize 2-pieces shafts and splined yokes, it may be possible to reinstall the shaft incorrectly or "out of the phase" which would cause vibration. Many of these vehicles will utilize a keyed slip yoke to prevent this, but DO NOT risk improper installation. ALWAYS matchmark the shaft ends to the yokes before removal or installation.

Since the truck can be obtained in either 2WD or 4WD and in various cab/bed combinations (long and short beds, standard and extended cabs), four types of driveshafts may be employed. Some models will be equipped with a one-piece rear driveshaft, while others have a two-piece rear driveshaft which uses a center support bearing. Most 4WD vehicles are equipped with a front shaft which is a two piece telescopic type with internal splines.

On the front of the rear one or two-piece driveshafts, the U-joints connect the driveshaft to a slip-jointed yoke. This yoke is internally splined and allows the driveshaft to move in and out on the transmission splines (one-piece) or the shaft splines (two-piece). On the rear of the one or two-piece driveshaft, the U-joint is clamped to the rear axle pinion. It is usually attached to the rear axle pinion by use of bolted straps.

For the front driveshaft on 4WD vehicles, the U-joints are secured to the transfer case and the front differential by the use of bolted straps. Located in the center of the driveshaft is a slip-joint, which allows the driveshaft to move in and out on its own splines.

On production U-joints, nylon is injected through a small hole in the yoke during manufacture and flows along a circular groove between the U-joint and the yoke, creating a non-metallic snapring. Since plastic retaining rings must be sheared for removal and no snapring grooves are supplied, the production joints must be replaced as an assembly whenever they are removed from the shaft.

Bad U-joints, requiring replacement, will produce a clunking sound when the vehicle is put into gear and when the transmission shifts from gear-to-gear. This is due to worn needle bearings or scored trunnion ends. U-joints require no periodic maintenance and therefore have no lubrication fittings.

On many 4WD vehicles, a grease fitting is supplied near the front (axle end) of the front driveshaft. A similar fitting is found near the slip yoke at the middle of the two-piece rear driveshaft assemblies. This fitting is to provide lubrication for the center slip joint. Chassis grease should be used at this fitting.

Front Driveshaft and U-Joints

REMOVAL & INSTALLATION

See Figures 86, 87 and 88

DO NOT pound on the original driveshaft ears (unless the U-joints are being replaced) or the injected nylon U-joints may fracture.

1. Raise and support the front of the truck safely using jackstands.
2. Matchmark the relationship of the driveshaft to the front axle and the transfer case flanges.
3. On 1994 vehicles, remove the driveshaft-to-retainer bolts and the retainers, first from the transfer case, then from the front axle.
4. On 1995-97 vehicles, remove the driveshaft-to-retainer bolts and the retainers front axle yoke.
5. On 1994 vehicles, collapse the driveshaft so it may be disengaged from the transfer case flange then from the front axle.

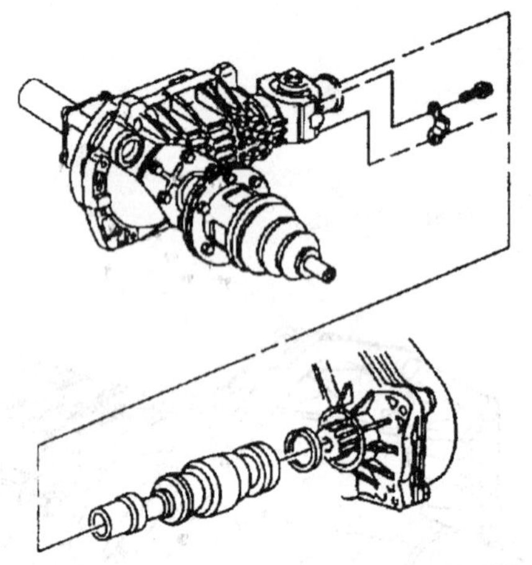
88457G47

Fig. 87 Removing the driveshaft from the transfer case and front axle assembly — 1995-97 vehicles

88457P38

Fig. 88 It may be necessary to use a mallet to loosen the driveshaft from the transfer case shaft

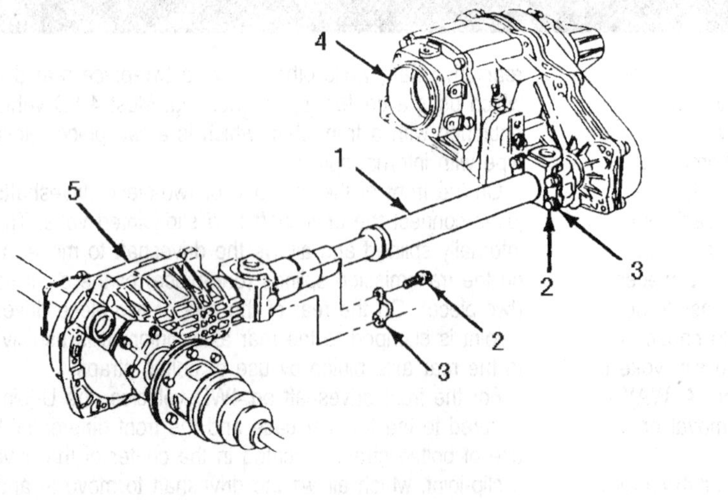

88457G46

Fig. 86 Front axle and driveline assembly — 1994 vehicles

6. On 1995-97 vehicles, collapse the driveshaft and tilt it downward away from front axle end, then slide it out from the transfer case shaft.

➡Use care when handling the driveshaft to avoid dropping the U-joint cap assemblies and loosing portions of the bearing assemblies.

7. Wrap a length of tape around the loose caps to hold them in place.

To install:

8. Carefully insert the driveshaft into position in the vehicle.
9. Align the matchmarks made earlier, then remove the tape from the U-joints cap assemblies and position them to the flanges. Loosely install the retainers to hold the shaft in position.
10. Verify that the marks are properly aligned then tighten the retainers as follows:
    - On 1994 vehicles, tighten the transfer case flange bolts and to 92 ft. lbs. (125 Nm) and the front axle flange bolts to 53 ft. lbs. (72 Nm).
    - On 1995 vehicles, tighten the front axle flange bolts to 55 ft. lbs. (75 Nm).
    - On 1996-97 vehicles, tighten the front axle flange bolts to 15 ft. lbs. (20 Nm).
11. Remove the jackstands and carefully lower the vehicle.

U-JOINT REPLACEMENT

With the exception of the size socket/pipe which must be used to support the trunnion yoke on some driveshafts, U-joint replacement is identical between the front and rear driveshaft assemblies. Please refer to the procedure found later for the rear driveshaft to service the U-joints. Make sure an appropriately sized socket is used as a support. These driveshafts require a 1⅛ in. socket used by most front and rear driveshafts.

Rear Driveshaft and U-Joints

REMOVAL & INSTALLATION

➧ **See Figures 89, 90 and 91**

➡DO NOT pound on the original propeller shaft yoke ears (unless the U-joints are being replaced) or the injected nylon joints may fracture.

1. Raise and support the rear of the truck safely using jackstands.
2. Matchmark relationship of the driveshaft-to-pinion flange and the slip yoke-to-front driveshaft or transmission/transfer case housing, as necessary. ALL shaft components which are being removed should be installed in their original positions, this includes slip yokes and U-joints ears. Disconnect the rear universal joint by removing retainers. If the bearing caps are loose, tape them together to prevent dropping and loss of bearing rollers.

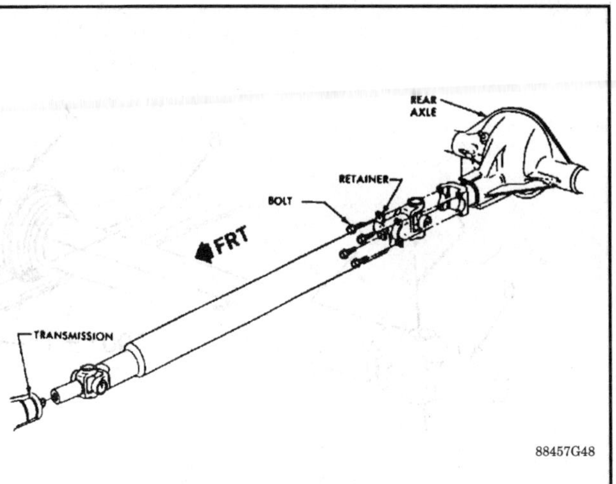

Fig. 89 One-piece rear driveshaft

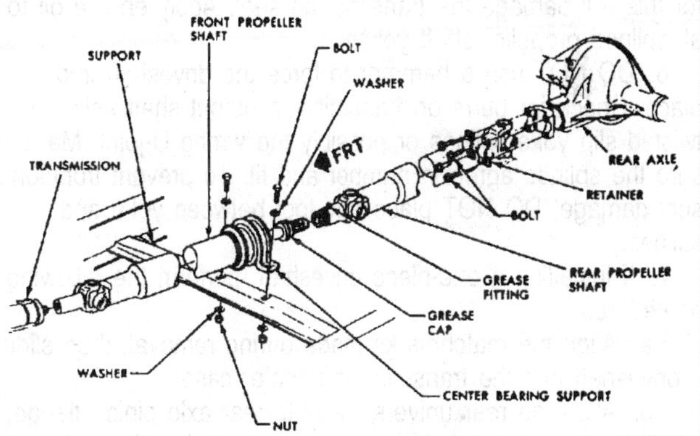

Fig. 90 Two-piece rear driveshaft with center bearing

3. If equipped with a one-piece driveshaft, perform the following procedures:
    a. Slide the driveshaft forward to disengage it from the rear axle flange.
    b. Move the driveshaft rearward to disengage it from the transmission slip-joint, passing it under the axle housing.
4. If equipped with a two piece driveshaft, perform the following procedures:
    a. Slide the rear driveshaft half forward to disengage it from the rear axle flange.
    b. Slide the driveshaft rearward to disengage it from slip-joint of the front driveshaft half passing it under the axle housing.
    c. Remove the center bearing support nuts and bolts.
    d. Slide the front driveshaft half rearward to disengage it from the transfer case/transmission slip-joint.

➡DO NOT allow the driveshaft to drop or allow the universal joints to bend to extreme angles, as this might fracture injected joint internally. Support propeller shaft during removal.

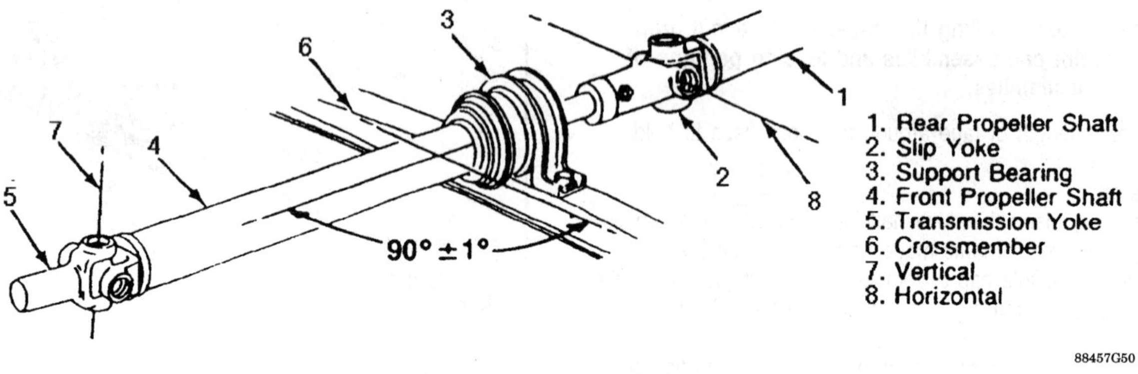

Fig. 91 Center bearing alignment or phasing to prevent vibrations

To install:

5. Inspect the slip-joint splines for damage, burrs or wear, for this will damage the transmission seal. Apply engine oil to all splined propeller shaft yokes.
6. DO NOT use a hammer to force the driveshaft into place. Check for burrs on transmission output shaft spline, twisted slip yoke splines or possibly the wrong U-joint. Make sure the splines agree in number and fit. To prevent trunnion seal damage, DO NOT place any tool between yoke and splines.
7. If installing a one-piece driveshaft, perform the following procedures:
   a. Align the matchmarks made during removal, then slide driveshaft into the transmission/transfer case.
   b. Align the rear universal joint-to-rear axle pinion flange, make sure the bearings are properly seated in the pinion flange yoke.
   c. Install the rear driveshaft-to-pinion fasteners and verify all marks are aligned. Tighten the fasteners to 15 ft. lbs. (20 Nm).
8. If installing a two-piece driveshaft, perform the following procedures:
   a. Install the front driveshaft half into the transmission/transfer case (aligning the marks made during removal) and bolt the center bearing support in position. Tighten the center bearing to support nuts and bolts to 25 ft. lbs. (34 Nm).

➡In most cases, the yoke on the front driveshaft half must be bottomed out in the transmission (fully forward) before installation to the support.

   b. Rotate the shaft as necessary so the front U-joint trunnion is in the correct position to align the matchmarks for the rear driveshaft half.

➡Before installing the rear driveshaft, align the U-joint trunnions using the matchmarks made earlier (in some cases a "key" in the output spline of the front driveshaft half will align with a missing spline in the rear yoke).

   c. Attach the rear U-joint to the axle, then tighten the retainers to 15 ft. lbs. (20 Nm).
9. Remove the jackstands and carefully lower the vehicle.
10. Road test the vehicle.

U-JOINT REPLACEMENT

➧ See Figures 92, 93, 94, 95, 96, 97 and 98

As mentioned earlier in this section, these vehicles utilize 2 different types of U-joint assemblies. At the factory, most vehicles are equipped with a nylon injected assembly. Because these assemblies contain no snapring grooves, and the very action of removing them destroys their retainers, they cannot be reused. Once removed, nylon injected U-joints should be discarded. If your vehicle has already received U-joint service, then it will be equipped with a snapring retained assembly. Once properly removed, these assemblies may be reused if they are in good condition.

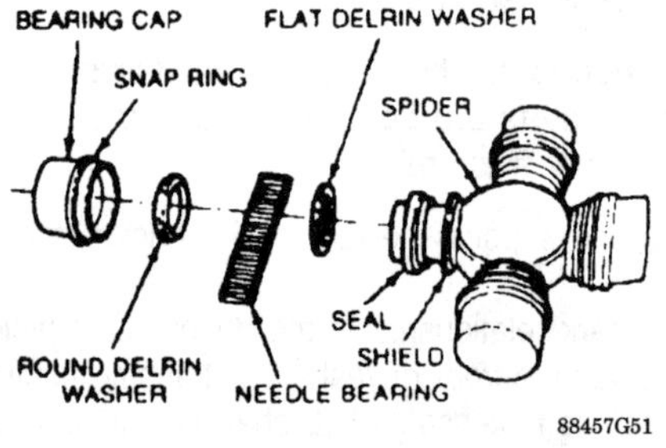

Fig. 92 Exploded view of a replacement U-joint assembly — internal snapring type

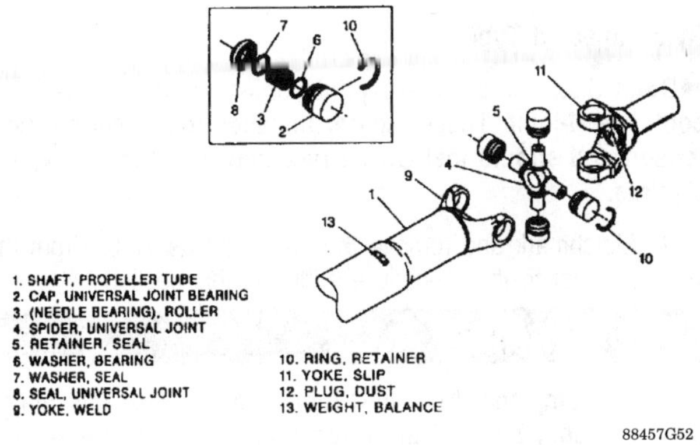

Fig. 93 Exploded view of a replacement U-joint assembly — external snapring type

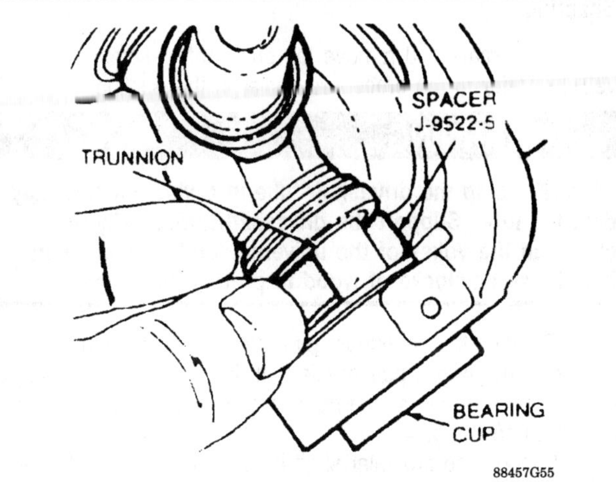

Fig. 96 Positioning the spacer tool to assist in bearing cap removal

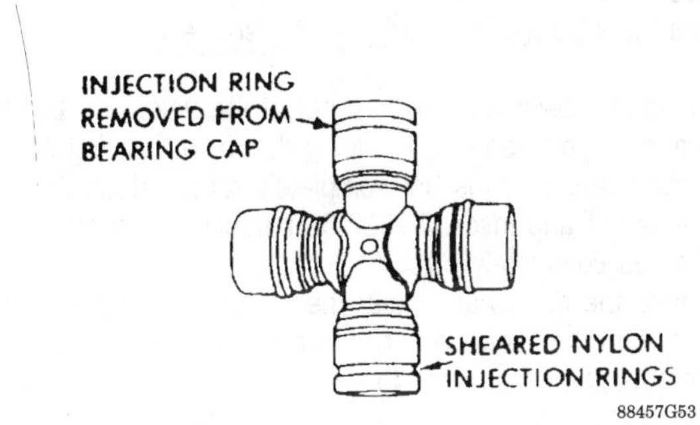

Fig. 94 Production nylon type U-joint

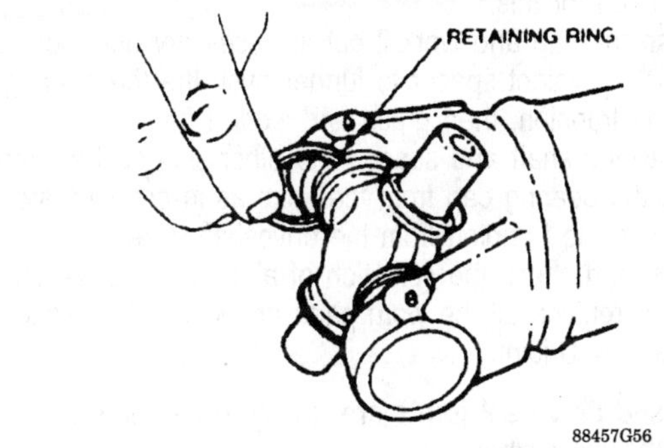

Fig. 97 Installing the snaprings

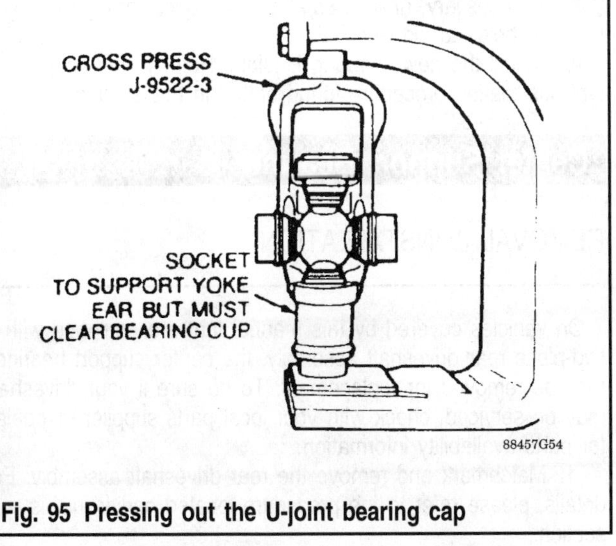

Fig. 95 Pressing out the U-joint bearing cap

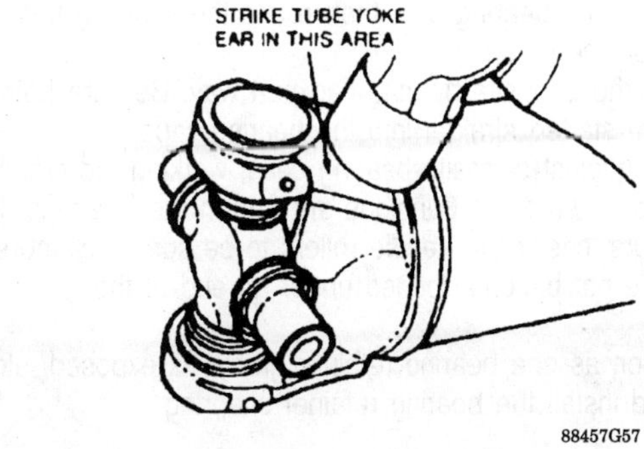

Fig. 98 Tapping the yoke in order to seat the retaining clip

Snapring Type

1. Matchmark and remove the driveshaft assembly from the vehicle. Refer to the procedure earlier in this section.

****WARNING**

NEVER clamp the driveshaft tube in a vise, for this may dent the tube. Support the driveshaft horizontally and clamp on the yokes of the universal joints using a soft-jawed vise or blocks of wood to protect the yokes.

2. Remove the snaprings from the yoke by pinching the ends together with a pair of pliers. If the snapring is difficult to remove, tap the end of the bearing cap lightly to relieve pressure from snapring.
3. Support the propeller shaft horizontally in line with the base plate of a bench vise, but never clamp the driveshaft tube.
4. Place the universal joint so the lower ear of the yoke is supported on a 1$^{1}/_{8}$ inch socket (or ID pipe), depending on the application. Most driveshafts require the 1$^{1}/_{8}$ in. support. Press the trunnion bearing against the socket/pipe in order to partially press it from the yoke. A cross press such as tool J-9522-3 should be used for this.
5. Grasp the cap and work it out, if necessary use tool J-9522-5 or equivalent spacer to further push the the bearing cap from the trunnion, then grasp and work it free.
6. Rotate the shaft and support the other side of the yoke, then press the bearing cap from the yoke as in previous steps.
7. Remove the trunnion from the driveshaft yoke.
8. Clean and check the condition of all parts. Use U-joint repair kits to replace all the worn parts or replace the assembly using a new U-joint.

➡If the used universal joints are going to be reinstalled, repack with new grease.

To install:

9. Repack the bearings with chassis grease and replace the trunnion dust seals after any operation that requires disassembly of the U-joint. Be sure the lubricant reservoir at the end of the trunnion is full of lubricant. Fill the reservoirs with lubricant from the bottom.
10. Partially insert the cross into the yoke so one trunnion seats freely in the bearing cap, then rotate the shaft so this trunnion is on the bottom.
11. Install the opposite bearing cap part way. Be sure both trunnions are started straight into the bearing caps.
12. Press against opposite bearing caps, working the cross constantly to be sure the trunnions are free in the bearings. If binding occurs, check the needle rollers to be sure 1 or more needles have not become lodged under an end of the trunnion.
13. As soon as one bearing retainer groove is exposed, stop pressing and install the bearing retainer snapring.

➡It may be necessary to strike the yoke with a hammer to align the seating of the bearing retainers.

14. Continue to press until the opposite bearing retainer can be installed. If difficulty installing the snaprings is encountered, tap the yoke with a hammer to spring the yoke ears slightly.
15. Once the driveshaft and U-joints are properly assembled, align the matchmarks and install the driveshaft to the vehicle.

Nylon Injected Type

➡Don't disassemble these joints unless replacing the complete U-joint. These factory installed joints cannot be reused and should instead be replaced by snapring type U-joints.

1. Matchmark and remove the driveshaft assembly from the vehicle. Refer to the procedure earlier in this section.

****WARNING**

NEVER clamp the driveshaft tube in a vise, for this may dent the tube. Support the driveshaft horizontally and clamp on the yokes of the universal joints using a soft-jawed vise or blocks of wood to protect the yokes.

2. Support the propeller shaft horizontally in line with the base plate of a bench vise, but never clamp the driveshaft tube.
3. Place the universal joint so the lower ear of the yoke is supported on a 1$^{1}/_{8}$ inch socket (or ID pipe), depending on the application. Most driveshafts driveshafts require the 1$^{1}/_{8}$ in support.
4. Press the lower bearing cap out of the yoke ear, this will shear the nylon injected ring retaining the lower bearing cap.
5. If the bearing cap is not completely removed, lift the cross (J-9522-3) and insert J-9522-5 or equivalent spacer, then press the cap completely out.
6. Rotate the driveshaft, shear the opposite plastic retainer, and press the other bearing cap out in the same manner.
7. Remove the cross from the yoke.

➡Production U-joints cannot be reassembled. There are no bearing retainer grooves in the caps. Discard all parts that were removed and substitute those in the overhaul kit.

8. If the front U-joint is being removed, separate the bearing caps from the slip yoke in the same manner.
9. Remove the sheared plastic bearing retainer from the yoke. If necessary, drive a small pin or punch through the injection holes to aid removal.
10. Install the new snapring U-joints. Refer to the snapring type installation procedure found earlier in this section.

Center Support Bearing

REMOVAL & INSTALLATION

On vehicles covered by this manual that are equipped with a two-piece rear driveshaft assembly, the center support bearing may be removed for replacement. To be sure if your driveshaft may be serviced, check with your local parts supplier or dealer for parts availability information.

1. Matchmark and remove the rear driveshaft assembly. For details, please refer to the procedure located earlier in this section.

2. Remove the strap retaining the rubber cushion from the bearing support.
3. Pull the support bracket from the rubber cushion and the cushion from the bearing.
4. Press the bearing assembly from the halfshaft.

To install:

5. Assemble the center support bearing to the driveshaft:
   a. If removed, install the inner deflector onto the front shaft half and prick punch the deflector at 2 opposite points to make sure it is tight on the shaft.
   b. Fill the space between the inner dust shield and bearing with lithium soap grease.
   c. Start the bearing and slinger assembly straight onto the shaft journal. Support the shaft and using a length of pipe over the splined end of the shaft, press the bearing and inner slinger against the shoulder of the front shaft half.
   d. Install the bearing retainer, the rubber cushion onto bearing, the bracket onto the cushion and the retaining strap.
6. Align and install the driveshaft assembly to the vehicle.

FRONT DRIVE AXLE

Identification

The front axle assembly used on most 4WD models covered by this manual utilizes a central disconnect type front axle/transfer case system which allows shifting in and out of 4WD when the vehicle is moving under most driving conditions. The axle has an aluminum carrier which includes a vacuum activated center lock feature.

The drive axles employ completely flexible assemblies which consist of inner and outer constant velocity (CV) joints connected by an axle shaft. The inner CV joint is a "tri-pot" design, which is completely flexible and can move in and out. The outer CV joint is a "Rzeppa" design which is also flexible but cannot move in or out.

➡For more information on front axle identification, please refer to Section 1 of this manual.

Halfshafts (Drive Axle)

REMOVAL & INSTALLATION

See Figures 99, 100, 101, 102, 103, 104, 105 and 106

1. Disconnect the negative battery cable.
2. Unlock the steering column so the linkage is free to move, then raise and support the front of the vehicle safely using jackstands.
3. If equipped, remove the front skid plate for access
4. Remove the tire and wheel assembly.
5. Insert a drift through the brake caliper into one of the brake rotor vanes to prevent the drive axle from turning.
6. Remove the cotter pin and retainer from the hub end of the shaft. Hold the hub from turning and loosen the axle nut. Once the nut is loosened unthread it and remove the washer.
7. Matchmark the inner shaft flange, then loosen (but DO NOT remove) the bolts retaining the inner joint flange to the output shaft companion flange.
8. Remove the brake line support bracket from the upper control arm in order to allow for additional knuckle travel. If necessary, remove the brake caliper and support aside.
9. Remove the cotter pin and nut from the outer tie rod end, then disengage the tie rod at the steering knuckle using J-24319-B, or an equivalent jawed tie rod puller. Push the linkage out toward the opposite side of the vehicle, then support the outer tie rod out of the way to provide the necessary clearance for shaft removal.

88457P48

Fig. 99 Remove the cotter pin from the hub end of the shaft

88457P48

Fig. 100 Remove the retainer for access to the end nut

10. Remove the lower shock absorber retainers, then compress the shock and secure it out of the way using safety wire.
11. Position a jackstand between the spring seat and lower control arm ball joint for maximum leverage, then use the vehicle's weight to relieve the spring tension on the upper control arm.

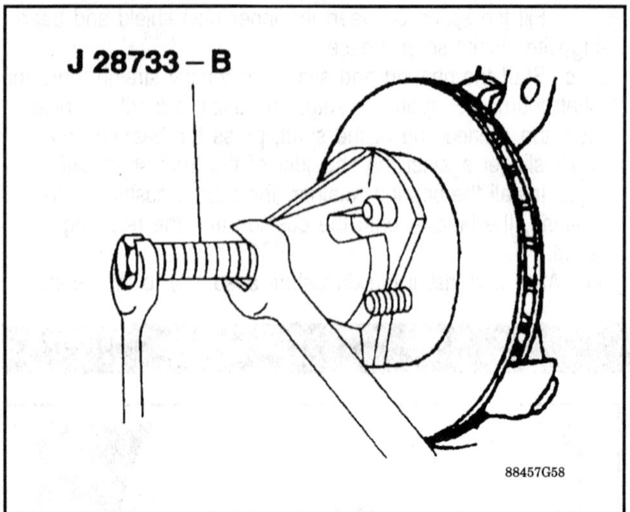

Fig. 101 Use a suitable axle shaft removal tool to drive the shaft from the hub

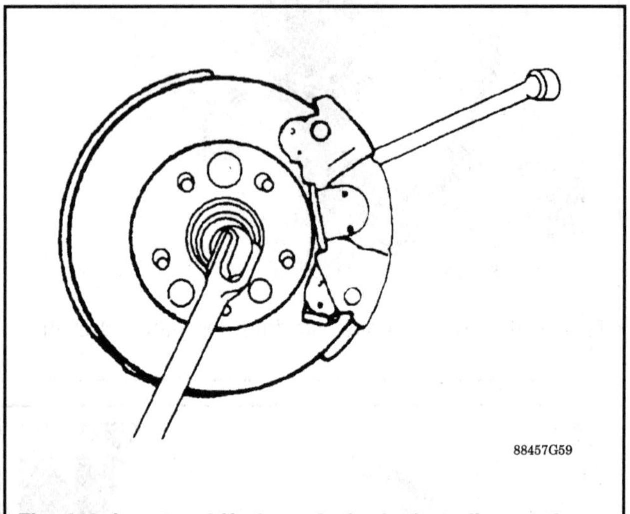

Fig. 102 Insert a drift through the brake caliper and rotor vane to prevent turning

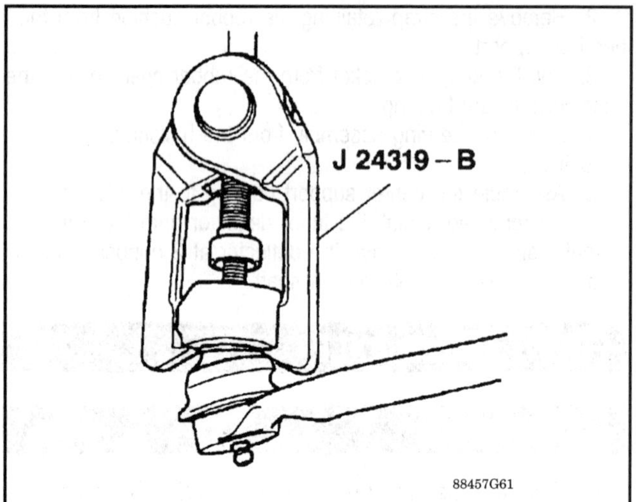

Fig. 104 Separating the tie rod from the steering knuckle

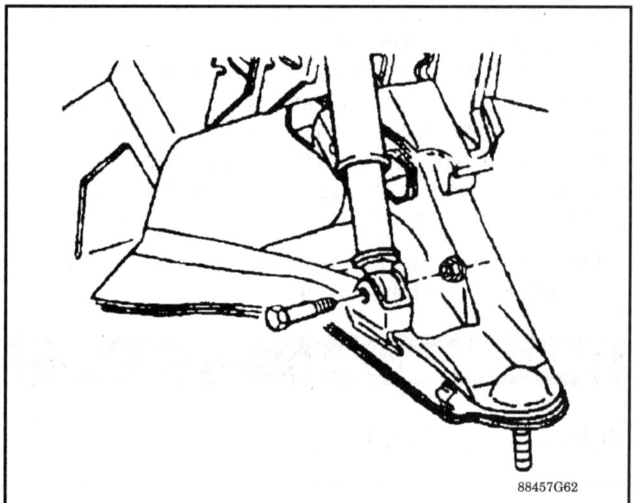

Fig. 105 Disconnecting the lower shock mount

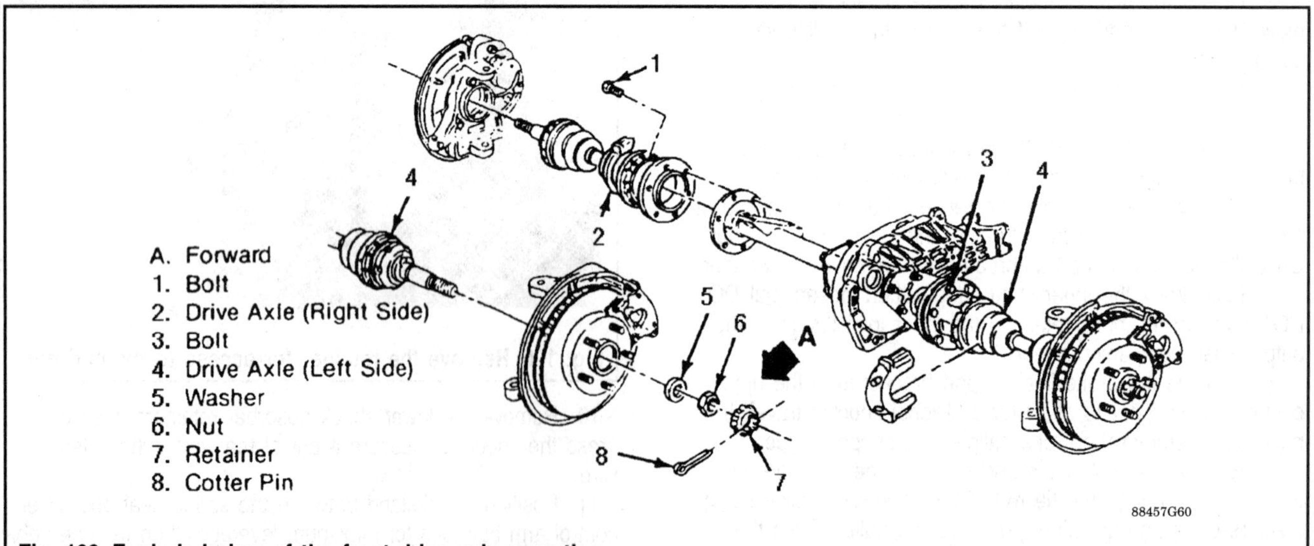

Fig. 103 Exploded view of the front drive axle mounting

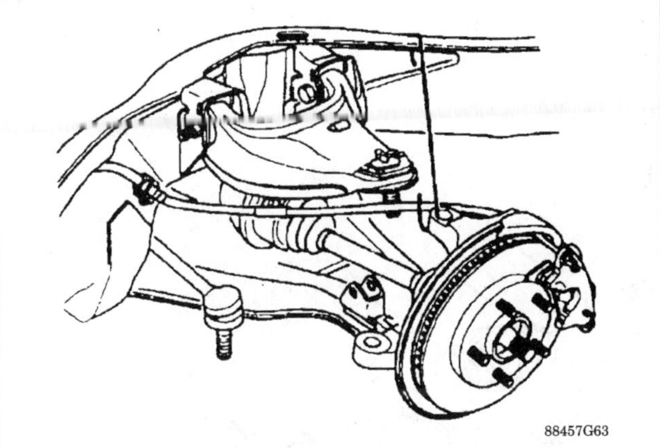

Fig. 106 Once the upper ball joint is disconnected, support the knuckle from the upper control arm or frame to prevent damage to the brake line and/or lower ball joint

12. Remove the cotter pin and retainer, then loosen and remove the upper ball joint stud nut away from the knuckle. Tip the knuckle out and toward the rear of the vehicle. Suspend the knuckle from the upper control arm or frame in order to prevent straining and damaging the brake line.
13. Using a suitable axle remover such as J-28733-B or equivalent, drive the axle shaft from the hub.
14. Remove the inboard flange bolts which were removed earlier.
15. Remove the axle from the vehicle. If the boots are not being serviced, take care not to damage or rip the CV-boots during removal.

CAUTION

DO NOT allow the vehicle's weight to load the front wheels or attempt to operate the vehicle when the drive axle(s) or hub nut(s) are removed. To do so may cause the front wheel bearing inner races to separate resulting in damage to the front brake and suspension components and/or personal injury.

To install:

16. Prior to shaft installation, cover the shock mounting bracket, lower control arm ball stud and ALL other sharp edges with a cloth or rag to help protect the boot.
17. Install the axle to the vehicle taking care not to damage the CV-boots. Insert the shaft end into the hub making sure to properly align the shaft splines.
18. Install the washer and retaining nut, if the nut can be fully threaded, it may be used to help draw the shaft into position in the hub.
19. Align the inboard flange to the output shaft companion flange, then loosely install the retainers.

➡Neither the flange retainers or the axle end nut should be fully tightened at this time. Thread the retainers to hold the axle shaft in position and reassemble the other components.

20. Install the upper ball joint to the steering knuckle, then install the nut and tighten to 61 ft. lbs. (83 Nm). Install a new cotter pin, but DO NOT back of the specified torque. Lube the ball joint until grease appears at the seals, then remove the support from underneath the lower control arm.
21. Reposition and secure the lower shock absorber fasteners. Tighten the nut and bolt to 47 ft. lbs. (64 Nm).
22. Install the tie rod end to the steering knuckle, then tighten the nut to 35 ft. lbs. (47 Nm). Align the cotter pin hole by rotating the retainer, DO NOT back off the specified torque OR exceed specification in order to install the cotter pin. Install the new cotter pin once the retainer is aligned.
23. Install the brake line support bracket and tighten the retainer(s) to 13 ft. lbs. (17 Nm). Make sure the brake hose is not twisted, kinked or otherwise damaged before securing the bracket.
24. Insert a drift through the brake caliper to prevent the drive axle from turning, then tighten the inboard flange bolts to 60 ft. lbs. (80 Nm).
25. Tighten the hub nut on the end of the axle to 180 ft. lbs. (245 Nm), then install the retainer and a new cotter pin. Rotate the retainer, as necessary to install the cotter pin. DO NOT back off or exceed specification to install the cotter pin.
26. If removed, reposition and secure the caliper.
27. Install the tire and wheel assembly.
28. If applicable, install the skid plate.
29. Remove the jackstands and carefully lower the vehicle.
30. Make sure the ignition is **OFF**, then connect the negative battery cable.

CV-JOINT OVERHAUL

Outer CV-Joint

➧ See Figures 107, 108, 109, 110, 111, 112, 113, 114, 115, 116 and 117

1. Remove the drive axle from the vehicle.
2. Place the axle in a vise using a protective covering on the vise jaws to prevent axle damage.

CAUTION

Because the retaining clamps are under tension, use care when cutting and removing them. Wear gloves and safety goggles to protect you should the clamp spring loose upon releasing the tension.

3. Cut and remove the CV-boot retaining clamps. If the boot is not being replaced, use care not to cut or damage the boot.

➡Some vehicles are equipped with a swage ring. In order to remove the ring, use a hand grinder to cut through the ring. Take care not to damage the outer race while cutting the swage ring free.

4. Once the clamps are removed, reposition the boot and wipe the grease away in order to locate the snapring.
5. Remove the snapring using a suitable pair of snapring pliers, such as J-8059 or equivalent.
6. Remove the joint assembly from the axle shaft.
7. Using a brass drift and hammer, tap the cage until it tilts sufficiently to remove the first ball, remove the remaining balls in the same manner.

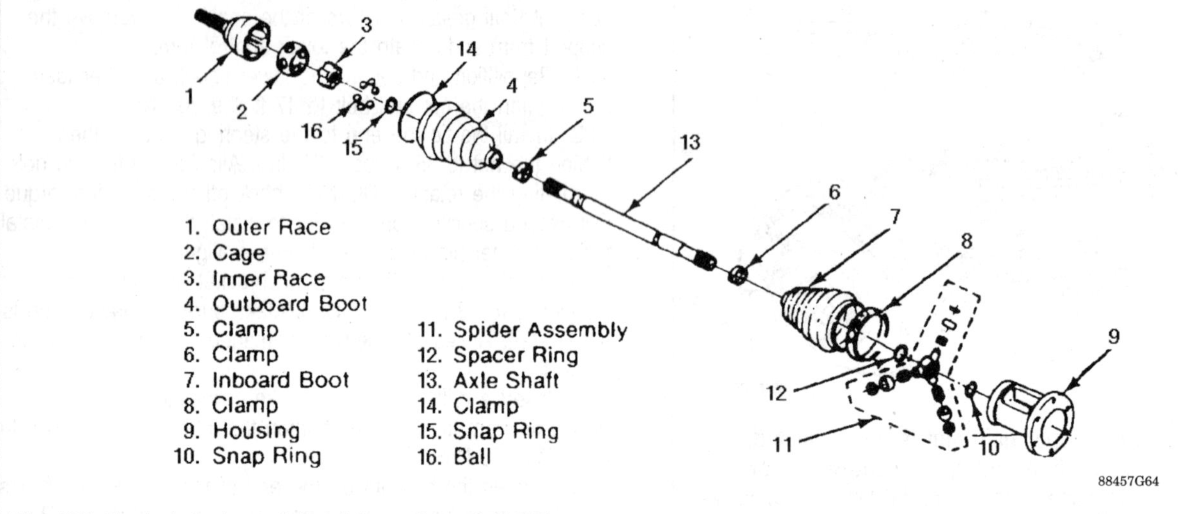

Fig. 107 Exploded view of the drive axle and CV-joints

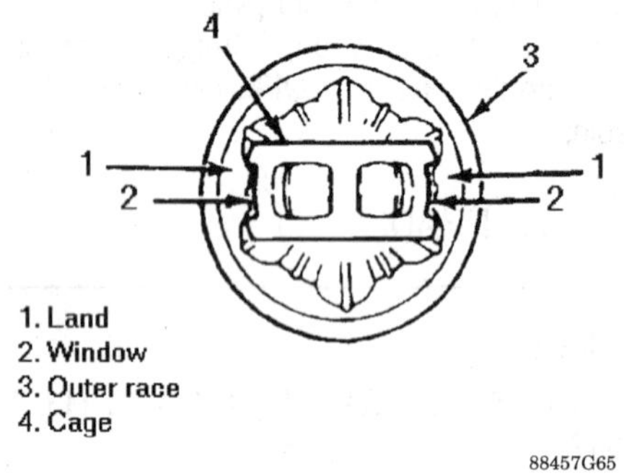

Fig. 108 Aligning the cage windows with the outer race lands so the cage (and inner race) may be removed

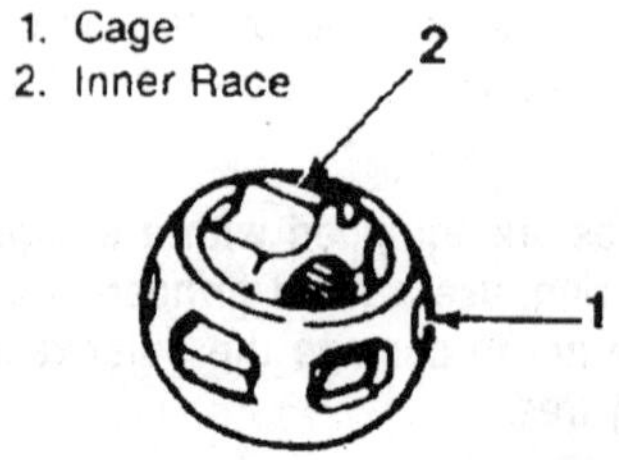

Fig. 109 Rotating the inner race up and out of the cage

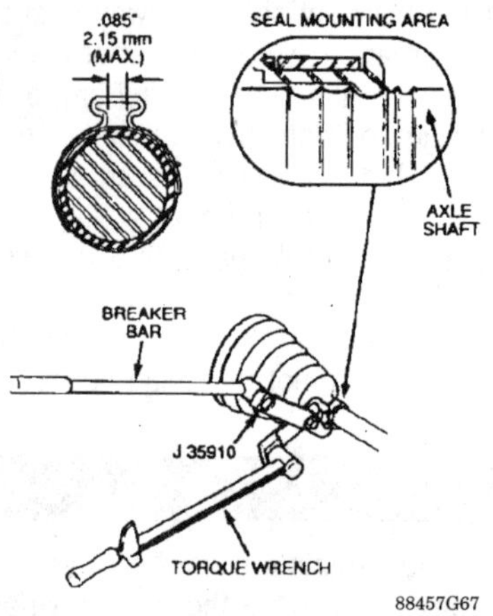

Fig. 110 Small retaining clamp installation and ear dimension

8. Pivot the cage so the inner race is 90 degrees to the centerline of the outer race, then align the cage windows with the outer race lands and lift the cage (along with the inner race) from the outer race. Please refer to the illustration for clarification.

9. Rotate the inner race up and out of the cage.

10. Thoroughly clean all parts in an approved solvent, then check for wear or damage and replaces, as necessary.

To install:

11. Apply a suitable grease to the ball grooves of the inner and outer races.

12. Install the inner race to the cage by inserting and rotating.

13. Align the cage windows with the outer race lands, then install the cage (along with the inner race) to the outer race. Make sure the retaining ring side of the inner race faces outward.

14. Use the brass drift to tap the cage to a tilted position, then install the balls.

15. Pack the joint using a suitable grease.

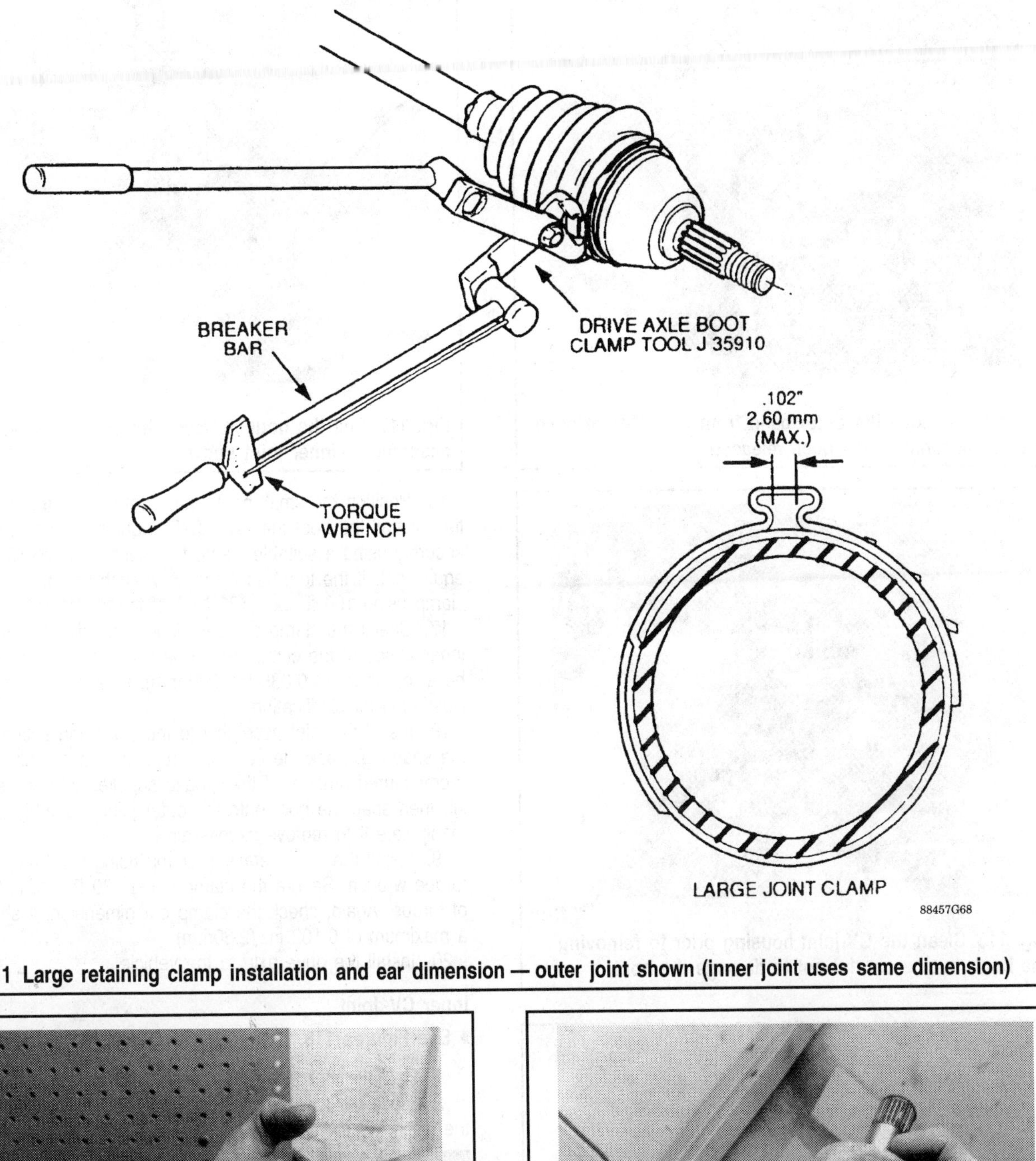

Fig. 111 Large retaining clamp installation and ear dimension — outer joint shown (inner joint uses same dimension)

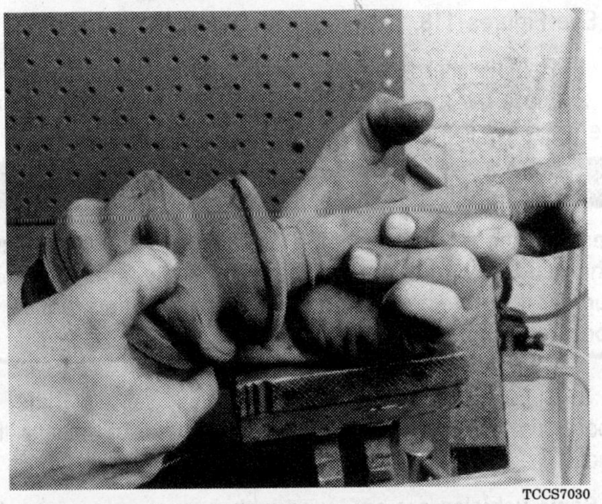

Fig. 112 Before removal check the CV-boot for wear or damage

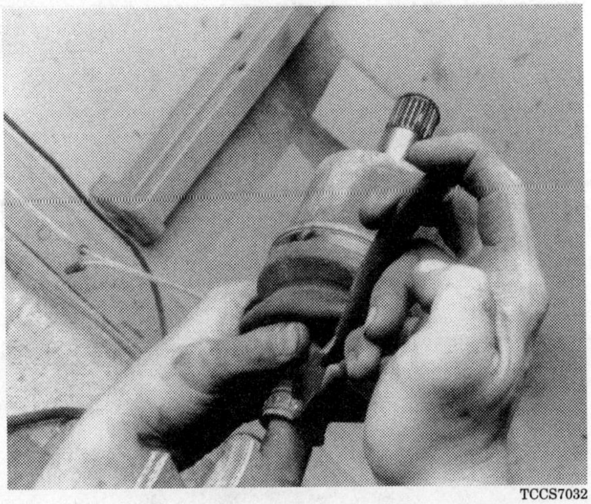

Fig. 113 In most cases, use a pair of side cutters to release clamp tension — inner band shown

TCCS7031

Fig. 114 Remove the outer band from the CV-boot once the clamp tension has been released

TCCS7034

Fig. 115 Clean the CV-joint housing prior to removing the boot, but be careful not to damage the boot

TCCS7033

Fig. 116 With the clamps removed, carefully pull the CV-boot from the joint housing

TCCS7035

Fig. 117 Pull the housing from the spider and shaft assembly — inner joint shown

16. Position the small boot clamp onto the outboard boot, then install the boot the axle shaft. Tighten the small clamp securely using a suitable clamp tool such as J-35910 or equivalent. If the tool has a torque wrench fitting, secure the clamp using 100 ft. lbs. (136 Nm) of torque.
17. Check the clamp ear gap dimension (distance that the inner bends of the crimp should be from each other), it should be a maximum of 0.085 in. (2.15mm). Please refer to the illustration for clarification.
18. Install the joint assembly to the shaft and secure using the snapring. Pack the boot and outer joint assembly with the premeasured amount of the grease supplied with the service kit, then snap the boot onto the outer joint assembly and manipulate it to remove excess air.
19. Install the large retaining clamp using the clamp tool and torque wrench. Secure the clamp using 130 ft. lbs. (176 Nm) of torque. Again, check the clamp ear dimension, it should be a maximum of 0.102 in. (2.60mm)
20. Install the drive axle to the vehicle.

Inner CV-Joint

See Figures 118, 119, 120, 121, 122, 123, 124 and 125

1. Remove the drive axle from the vehicle.
2. Place the axle in a vise using a protective covering on the vise jaws to prevent axle damage.

****CAUTION**

Because the retaining clamps are under tension, use care when cutting and removing them. Wear gloves and safety goggles to protect you should the clamp spring loose upon releasing the tension.

3. Cut and remove the CV-boot retaining clamps. If the boot is not being replaced, use care not to cut or damage the boot.

Some vehicles are equipped with a swage ring. In order to remove the ring, use a hand grinder to cut through the ring. Take care not to damage the outer race while cutting the swage ring free.

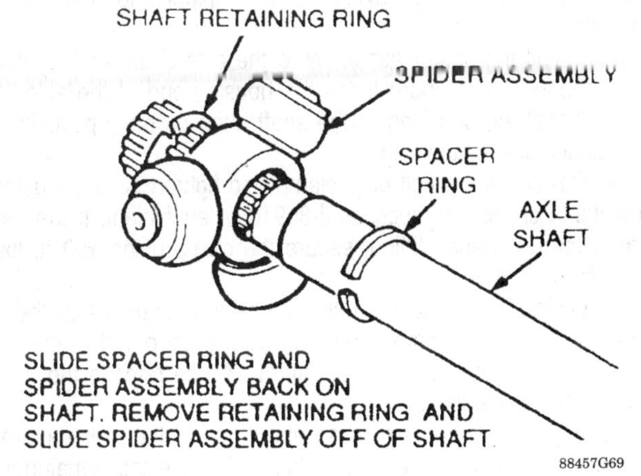

Fig. 118 Snapring and spider removal

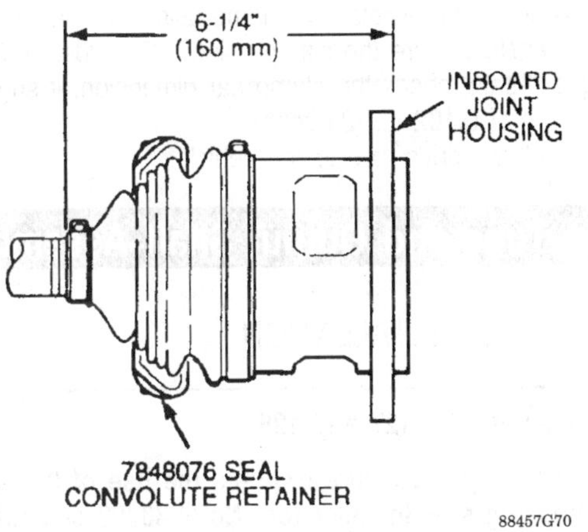

Fig. 119 Proper inboard boot and housing positioning

Fig. 120 On the inner CV-joint, be careful not to loose the spider assembly components

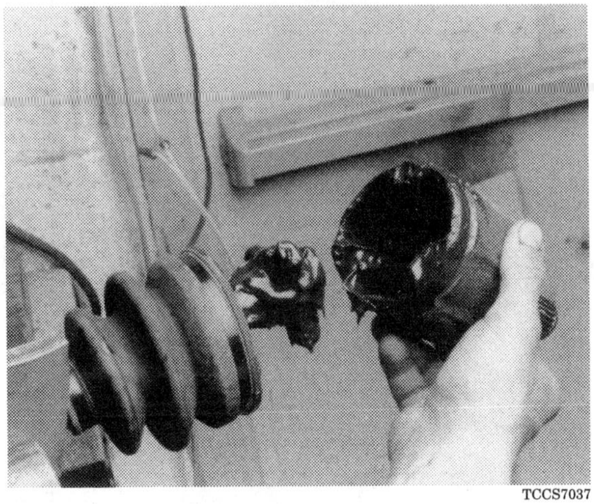

Fig. 121 Remove the CV-joint housing and check for wear or damage

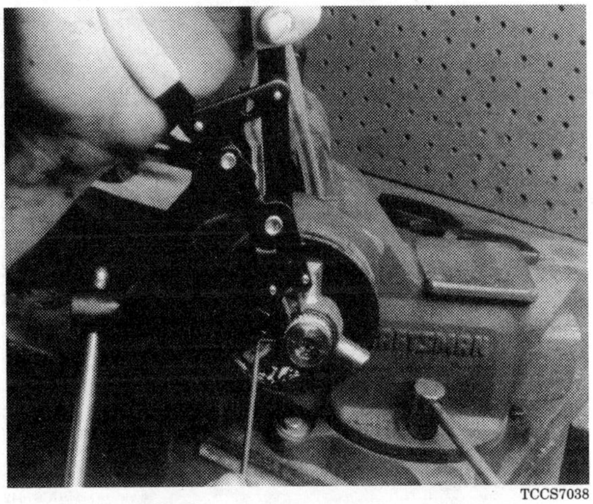

Fig. 122 With the spacer and spider pushed back, grasp the snapring using a pair of snapring pliers

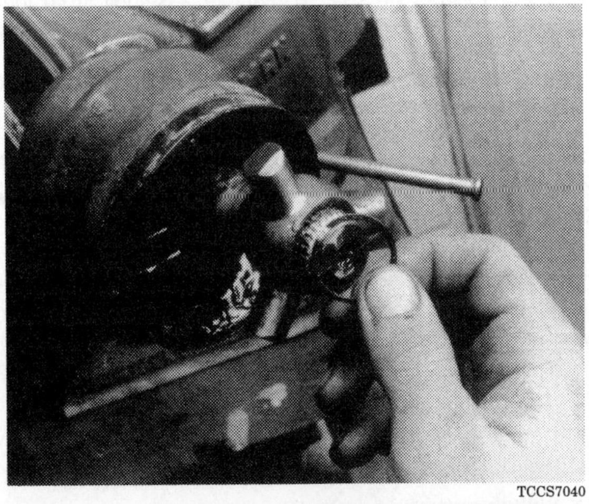

Fig. 123 Remove the snapring from the shaft so the spider assembly may be removed

TCCS7041

Fig. 124 With the snapring removed, the spider is free to be pulled from the shaft

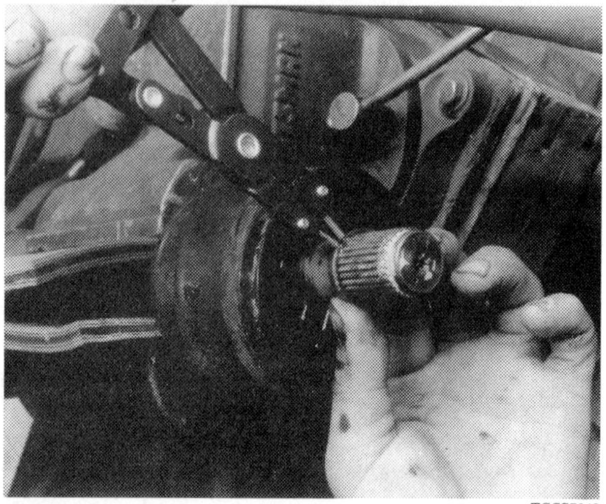
TCCS7042

Fig. 125 If necessary, remove the spacer ring from the shaft

4. Remove the axle shaft with spider assembly from the housing.

➡Handle the spider assembly with care. The tripot needle rollers may separate from the spider trunnions.

5. Grasp the space ring using J-8059, or an equivalent pair of snapring pliers, then slide the ring back on the axle shaft in order to provide clearance to move the spider assembly.
6. Move the spider assembly back on the shaft in order to expose the retaining snapring.
7. Remove the snapring using a suitable pair of snapring pliers, such as J-8059 or equivalent.
8. Remove the spider assembly.
9. Thoroughly clean all grease from the housing. Check for rust at the boot mounting grooves, if found remove with a wire brush.

To install:

10. Install the small boot clamp and inboard boot to the axle shaft.
11. If the spacer ring was removed, make sure it is positioned up on the shaft leaving room for spider and snapring installation.
12. Install the spider assembly to the axle shaft, making sure the snapring counterbore faces the housing end of the axle.
13. Install the snapring to the shaft, then properly position the spider and space ring.
14. Position the small boot clamp and tighten securely using a suitable clamp tool such as J-35910 or equivalent. If the tool has a torque wrench fitting, secure the clamp using 100 ft. lbs. (136 Nm) of torque.
15. Check the clamp ear gap dimension (distance that the inner bends of the crimp should be from each other), it should be a maximum of 0.085 in. (2.15mm). Please refer to the illustration for clarification.
16. Repack the housing using about half of the premeasured grease supplied with the service kit, then place the remainder of grease in the boot. Coat the inside of the boot sealing lips with grease.
17. Make sure the joint/boot are assembled to the proper dimension of 6 1/4 in. (160mm) between the clamps. Please refer to the illustration for clarification.
18. Install the large retaining clamp using the clamp tool and torque wrench. Secure the clamp using 130 ft. lbs. (176 Nm) of torque. Again, check the clamp ear dimension, it should be a maximum of 0.102 in. (2.60mm).
19. Install the drive axle to the vehicle.

Axle Tube and Output Shaft Assembly

REMOVAL & INSTALLATION

➧ See Figures 126, 127 and 128

➡The following procedure requires the use of the shift cable housing seal Installer tool No. J-33799 or equivalent.

1. Disconnect the negative battery cable.
2. Disconnect the shift cable from the vacuum actuator by disengaging the locking spring. Then push the actuator diaphragm in to release the cable.

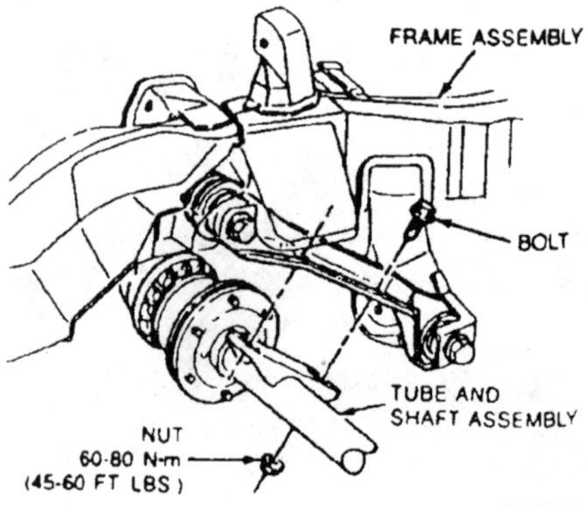

88457G71

Fig. 126 Tube-to-frame attachment

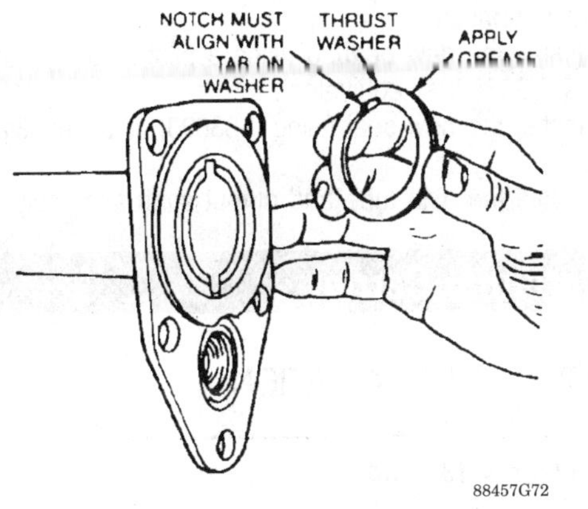

Fig. 127 Apply grease to hold it in position, then install the thrust washer to the output shaft tube

3. Unlock the steering wheel at steering column so the linkage is free to move.
4. Raise and support the front of the truck safely using jackstands.
5. Remove the front wheel assemblies.
6. If equipped, remove the front axle skid plate.
7. If necessary, remove the right side caliper and support using safety wire.
8. Place a support under right-side lower control arm and disconnect right-side upper ball joint, then remove the support so the control arm will hang free.

➡To keep the axle from turning, insert a drift through the opening in the top of the brake caliper, into the corresponding vane of the brake rotor.

9. Matchmark the right-side drive axle to the output shaft. Remove the right-side drive axle shaft-to-tube assembly bolts and separate the drive axle from the tube assembly, then remove the drift from the brake caliper and rotor.
10. Disengage the 4WD indicator lamp electrical connector from the switch.
11. Remove the three bolts securing the cable and switch housing-to-carrier and pull the housing away to gain access to the cable locking spring. DO NOT unscrew the cable coupling nut unless the cable is being replaced.
12. Disconnect the cable from the shift fork shaft by lifting the spring over the slot in the shift fork.
13. Remove the 2 bolts securing the tube bracket to the frame.
14. Remove the remaining 2 upper bolts securing the tube assembly to the carrier. The other 3 were removed with the shift cable housing.
15. Remove the tube assembly by working around the drive axle. Be careful not to allow the sleeve, thrust washers, connector and output shaft to fall out of carrier or be damaged when removing the tube.

To install:

16. Apply a bead of sealant on the tube-to-carrier mating surface.
17. Make sure the sleeve, thrust washers, connector and output shaft are in position in the carrier. Apply grease to the thrust washer to hold it in place during assembly, then position the washer to the tube.
18. Install the tube and shaft assembly-to-carrier, then thread and finger-tighten a bolt at one o'clock position but DO NOT torque. Pull the assembly down, then install the cable/switch housing and the remaining bolts. Tighten the bolts to 36 ft. lbs. (48 Nm).
19. Install the tube-to-frame nuts/bolts and tighten to 55 ft. lbs. (75 Nm).
20. Using the hub engagement tool No. J-33798 or equivalent, check the operation of the 4WD mechanism. Insert tool into the shift fork and check for the rotation of the axle shaft.
21. Remove the engagement tool, then install the shift cable switch housing by pushing the cable through into fork shaft hole. The cable will automatically snap into place. Please refer to shift cable replacement, later in this section for details.
22. Engage the 4WD indicator light wiring connector to the switch.

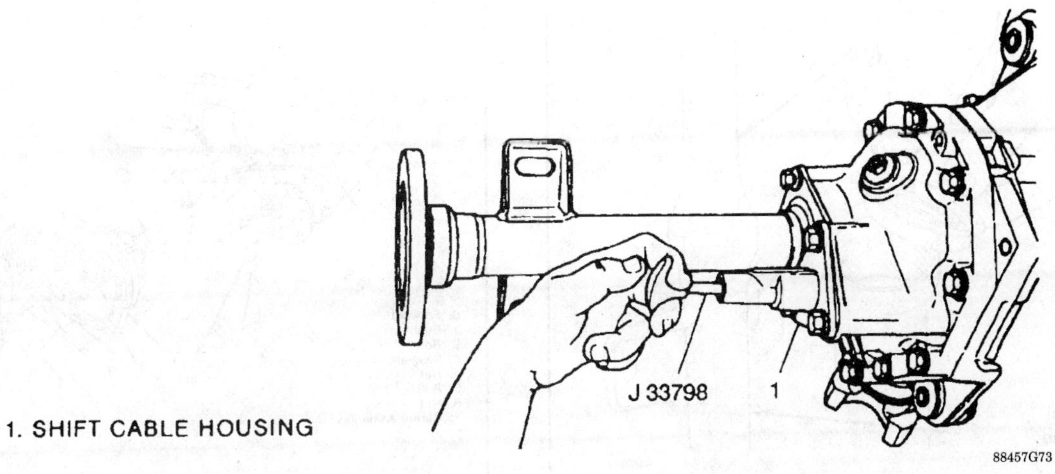

Fig. 128 Checking the shift mechanism

23. Install the support under the right-side lower control arm to raise arm and connect upper ball joint. For details, please refer to Section 8 of this manual.
24. Align and install right-side drive axle to the axle tube output shaft by installing one bolt first, then, rotate the axle to install and finger-tighten the remaining bolts. Tighten the bolts to 60 ft. lbs. (80 Nm).

➡To hold the axle from turning, insert a drift through the opening in the top of the brake caliper into the corresponding vane of the brake rotor. If the caliper was removed, either temporarily install it or use a prybar across 2 installed lug nuts.

25. If removed, reposition and secure the right side caliper.
26. If equipped, install the front axle skid plate.
27. Install the front wheel assemblies.
28. Remove the jackstands and carefully lower the vehicle.
29. Connect the shift cable-to-vacuum actuator by pushing the cable end into the vacuum actuator shaft hole. The cable will snap into place, automatically. For details, please refer to shift cable replacement, late in this section.
30. Make sure the ignition is **OFF**, then connect the negative battery cable.

Output Shaft Pilot Bearing

REMOVAL & INSTALLATION

See Figure 129

➡The following procedures requires the use of the pilot bearing remover tool No. J-34011 and the pilot bearing installer tool No. J-33842, or equivalents.

1. Remove the axle tube and output shaft assembly from the vehicle. For details, please refer to the procedure located earlier in this section.
2. Remove the pilot bearing from the tube using J-34011 or an equivalent pilot bearing remover tool.

To install:

3. Lubricate the new seal lips and the new bearing using fresh axle lubricant.
4. Install the new bearing using a pilot bearing installer tool such as J-33842, or equivalent.
5. Install the new seal using J-33893, or an equivalent seal installer.
6. Install the axle tube and output shaft assembly.

Differential Carrier

REMOVAL & INSTALLATION

See Figures 130 and 131

1. Unlock the steering column so the linkage is free to move.
2. Remove the battery and battery tray from the vehicle.
3. Disconnect the shift cable from the vacuum actuator. For details, please refer to the procedure located later in this section.
4. Raise and support the front of the vehicle safely using jackstands, then remove the front wheels.
5. If equipped, remove the skid plate.
6. Remove the drain plug and flat washer, then drain the fluid from the carrier.
7. Remove the right lower shock retainer, then push the shock upward and wire it out of the way for access to the output shaft bolts.
8. Disengage the wire from the indicator switch.
9. Disconnect the shift cable housing and/or shift cable from the carrier housing, as necessary. Refer to the shift cable procedure later in this section for details.
10. Disconnect the vent hose.
11. Remove the steering relay rod from the idler arm and pitman arm, then pull the linkage forward for access.
12. Align the drive axles to their flanges. Hold the drive axles from turning by inserting a brass drift through the calipers into the rotor vanes, then remove the drive axle to output shaft retaining bolts.

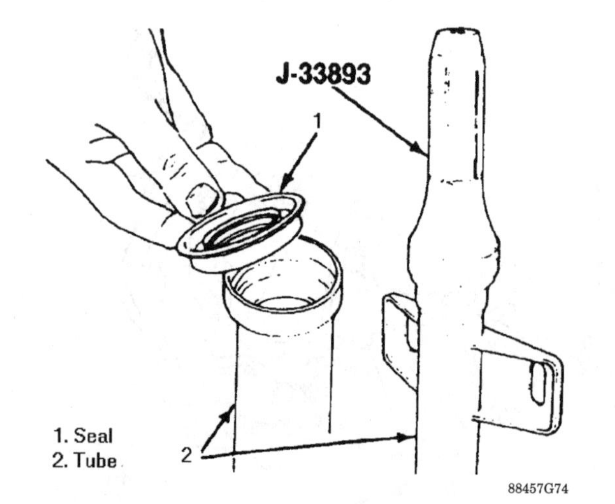

Fig. 129 Installing a new output shaft seal

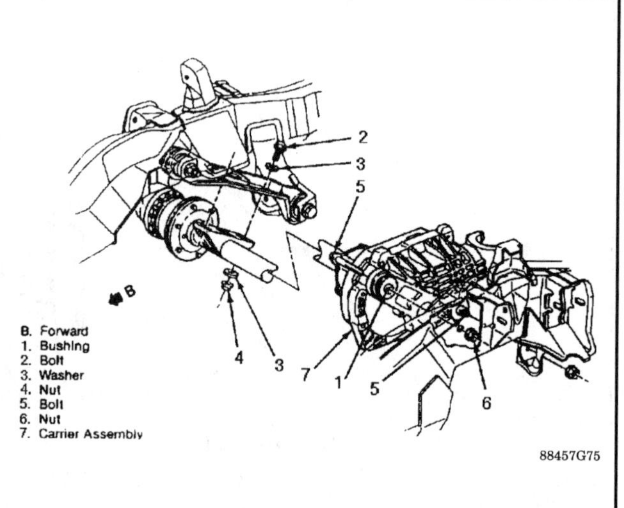

Fig. 130 Carrier assembly installation

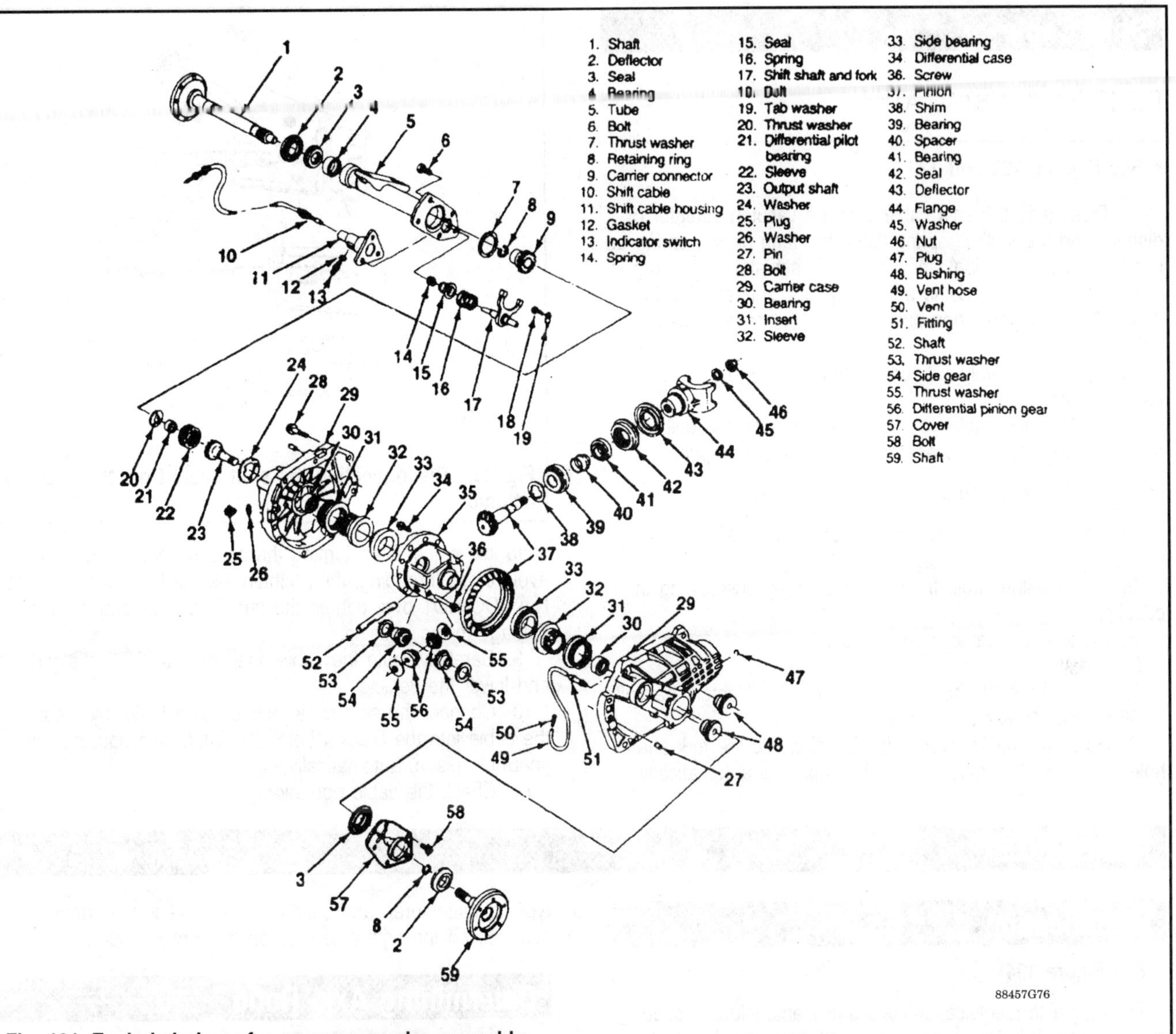

Fig. 131 Exploded view of a common carrier assembly

13. Remove the nuts and washers holding the axle tube to the frame.
14. Matchmark and remove the front driveshaft.
15. Support both lower control arms using jackstands at the edge of the stabilizer shaft. Lower the vehicle until the font weight is resting on the stands.
16. Remove the bolts and nuts retaining the carrier assembly to the vehicle. Use an 18mm wrench inserted through the frame to keep the upper nut from turning.
17. Roll the carrier assembly counterclockwise while lifting upward to gain the necessary clearance from the mounting ears and remove the carrier from the vehicle.

To install:

18. Install the carrier assembly to the vehicle and secure using the retaining nuts and bolts. Tighten the bolts to 65 ft. lbs. (90 Nm) and the nuts to 55 ft. lbs. (75 Nm).
19. Install the nuts and washers holding the axle tube to the frame, then tighten to 36 ft. lbs. (48 Nm).
20. Matchmark and install the front driveshaft assembly.
21. Align and install the drive axles to the carrier/output shaft flanges.
22. Connect the vent hose.
23. Connect the idler and pitman arms to the steering relay rod. For more information, please refer to Section 8 of this manual.
24. Connect the shift cable housing and/or cable, as applicable.
25. Engage the indicator switch wiring.
26. Remove the safety wire, then reposition and secure the shock.
27. If not done already, install the drain plug and flat washer, then check the fluid level and add as necessary. Remember that the vehicle must be level when checking or adding fluid.
28. If equipped, install the skid plate.
29. Install the front wheels, then remove the jackstands and carefully lower the vehicle.
30. Connect the shift cable to the vacuum actuator.
31. Install the battery tray and the battery to the vehicle.

Shift Cable

REMOVAL & INSTALLATION

See Figures 132 and 133

1. Disengage the shift cable from the vacuum actuator by disengaging the locking spring (bend the tang on the spring as shown in the illustration), then, push the actuator diaphragm in to release the cable. Using a pair of pliers, squeeze the two cable locking fingers, then pull the cable out of the bracket hole.
2. Raise and safely support the front of the truck safely using jackstands.
3. Remove the cable housing-to-carrier bolts and pull the housing away to gain access to the cable locking spring.

➡DO NOT unscrew the coupling nut at this time.

4. Disconnect the cable from the shift fork shaft by lifting the spring over shift fork slot.
5. Unscrew the cable from the housing by unscrewing the coupling nut.
6. Remove the cable from the truck.

To install:

7. Install the cable housing-to-carrier bolts. Tighten the bolts to 36 ft. lbs. (48 Nm).
8. Guide the cable through the housing into the fork shaft hole and push the cable inward; the cable will automatically snap into place. Start turning the coupling nut by hand, to avoid cross threading, then tighten the nut to 90 inch lbs. (10 Nm). DO NOT over tighten the nut as this will cause thread damage to the housing.
9. Carefully route the cable, then remove the jackstands and lower the vehicle.
10. Connect the shift cable-to-vacuum actuator by pressing the cable into the bracket hole. The cable and housing will snap into place, automatically.
11. Check the cable operation.

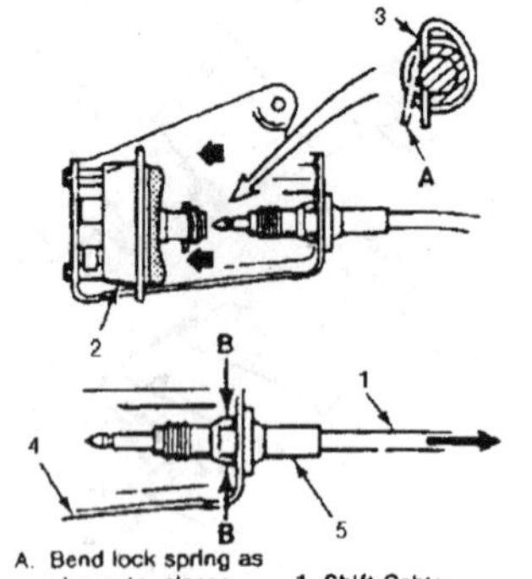

Fig. 132 Disconnecting the shift cable from the vacuum actuator

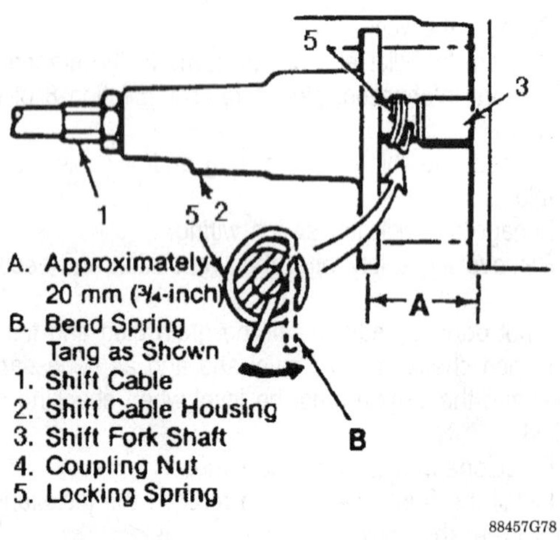

Fig. 133 Disconnecting the shift cable from the housing mounted to the carrier

REAR AXLE

Identification

See Figure 134

The rear axle identification code and manufacturer's code must be known before attempting to adjust or repair axle shafts or rear axle case assembly. Rear axle ratio, differential type, manufacturer, and build date information is normally stamped on the right axle tube on the forward side.

Determining Axle Ratio

An axle ratio is obtained by dividing the number of teeth on the drive pinion gear into the number of teeth on the ring gear.

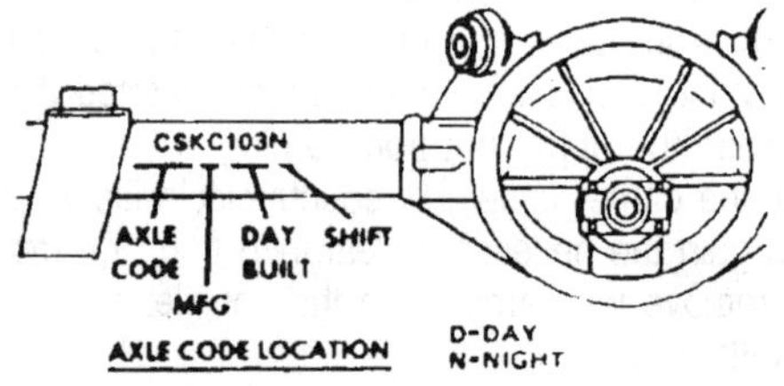

Fig. 134 Rear axle identification codes are normally stamped on the front of the right axle tube

For instance, on a 4.11 ratio, the driveshaft will turn 4.11 times for every turn of the rear wheel. The most accurate way to determine the axle ratio is to drain the differential, remove the cover and count the number of teeth on the ring and pinion.

An easier method is to jack and support the vehicle so that both rear wheels are off the ground. make a chalk mark on the rear wheel and the driveshaft. Block the front wheels and put the transmission in Neutral. Turn the rear wheel one complete revolution and count the number of turns made by the driveshaft. The number of driveshaft rotations is the axle ratio. More accuracy can be obtained by going more than one tire revolution and dividing the result by the number of tire rotations.

➡In order to rotate the driveshaft, 4WD vehicles must have their transfer cases set in Neutral or 2WD.

The axle ratio is also identified by the axle serial number prefix on the axle; the axle ratios are listed in dealer's parts books according to prefix number. Some axles have a tag on the cover.

Axle Shaft, Bearing and Seal

REMOVAL & INSTALLATION

See Figures 135, 136, 137, 138, 139, 140, 141, 142 and 143

Although the axle shaft is easily removed using common hand tools, special tools are required if the bearings are also to be serviced.

1. Raise and support the rear of the vehicle safely using jackstands.

88457P39

Fig. 135 Loosen pinion shaft lockscrew

88457P41

Fig. 136 Remove the lockscrew in order to free the pinion shaft

88457P42

Fig. 137 Once the shaft is freed, withdraw it from the differential

88457P43

Fig. 138 Push the axle shaft to expose the C-lock, then remove the lock in order to free the axle shaft

Fig. 139 Remove the shaft by pulling it straight back and from the housing tube

Fig. 140 Remove the old seal, but be careful not to damage the sealing surface

Fig. 141 Install a new seal using a suitable installation tool or driver

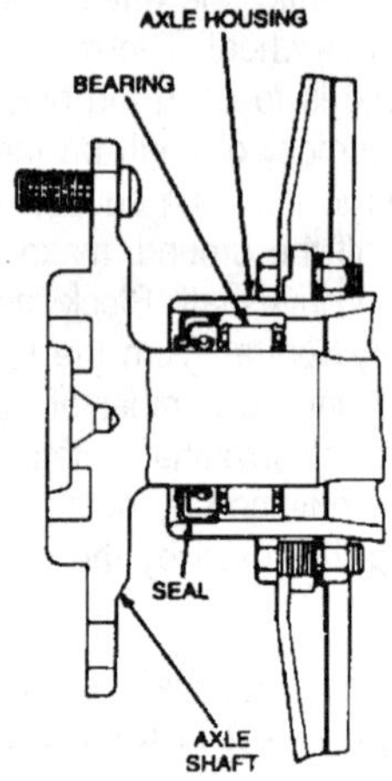

Fig. 142 Cross-sectional view of a common axle bearing and seal assembly

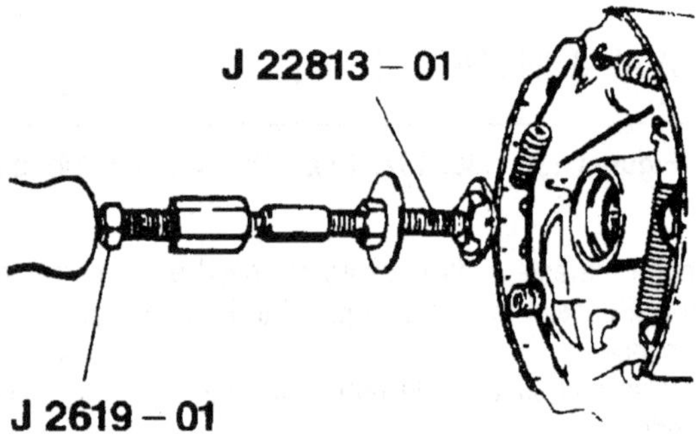

Fig. 143 Use a slide hammer, bearing puller and adapter to remove the old axle bearing

2. Remove the rear wheel and brake drum.

✱✱CAUTION

Brake shoes may contain asbestos, which has been determined to be a cancer causing agent. Never clean the brake surfaces with compressed air! Avoid inhaling any dust from any brake surface! When cleaning brake surfaces, use a commercially available brake cleaning fluid.

3. Using a wire brush, clean the dirt/rust from around the rear axle cover. This should be done to help prevent foreign material from entering the rear axle and possibly damaging the differential.

4. Place a catch pan under the differential, then unscrew the retaining bolts and remove the rear cover. When removing the cover, a small prytool may be used at the base of the cover to gently pry it back from the axle housing, breaking the gasket seal and allowing the lubricant to drain out into the container. Be careful not to use excessive force and damage the cover or housing.

5. Remove the rear pinion shaft lockbolt and the pinion shaft from the differential.

6. Push the axle shaft inward, then remove the C-lock from the button end of the axle shaft.

7. Remove the axle shaft from the axle housing by pulling straight back on the shaft hub, be careful not to damage the oil seal with the shaft splines.

➡It is recommended, when the axle shaft is removed, to replace the oil seal.

8. If the bearing and/or oil seal is being replaced, use a medium pry bar to carefully pry the old oil seal from the end of the rear axle housing. DO NOT score or damage the housing oil seal surface.

9. If the wheel bearing is being removed, use the GM slide hammer tool No. J-2619, along with adapter No. J-2619-4 and the axle bearing puller No. J-22813-01, or the equivalent tools to pull the bearing from the tube. Be sure to install the tool assembly so that the tangs engage the outer race of the bearing, then use the action of the slide hammer to withdraw the wheel bearing from the axle housing.

To install:

10. Clean and inspect the axle tube housing.

11. If the bearing was removed, thoroughly clean the wheel bearing using solvent, then blow dry with compressed air. DO NOT spin the bearing with the compressed air or damage may occur. Inspect the wheel bearing for excessive wear or damage. If it feels rough, replace it.

12. With a new or the reused bearing, place a blob of heavy grease in the palm of your hand, then work the bearing into the grease until it is thoroughly lubricated. Using an axle shaft bearing installer such as No. J-34974, J-23765 or equivalents, drive the bearing into the axle housing until it bottoms against the seat.

13. If the bearing and/or seal was removed, use an axle shaft seal installer tool such as No. J-33782, J-23771 or equivalents to drive the new seal into the housing until it is flush with the axle tube. If a seal installer is not available, a suitably sized driver or socket may be used, just make sure the surface in contact with the seal is smooth so that it won't damage the seal.

14. Using gear oil, lubricate the new seal lips.

15. Using a putty knife, clean the gasket mounting surfaces on the housing and cover. Take care to keep material out of the differential housing. If necessary, place a rag or paper towels over the differential while cleaning the housing flange.

➡When installing the axle shaft(s), be careful not to cut the oil seal lips.

16. Slide the axle shaft into the rear axle housing, taking care not to damage the seal, then engage the splines of the axle shaft with the splines of the rear axle side gear.

17. Install the C-lock retainer on the axle shaft button end. After the C-lock is installed, pull the axle shaft outward to seat the C-lock retainer in the counterbore of the side gears.

18. Install the pinion shaft through the case and the pinions, then install a new pinion shaft lockbolt. Tighten the new lockbolt to 25 ft. lbs. (34 Nm) except for 1994 vehicles on which the lockbolt should be tightened to 27 ft. lbs. (36 Nm).

➡When adding oil to the rear axle, be aware that some locking differentials require the use of a special gear lubricant additive.

19. Install the rear cover using a new gasket and sealant. Tighten the retaining bolts using a crosswise pattern to 20 ft. lbs. (27 Nm).

➡Make sure the vehicle is level before attempting to add fluid to the rear axle or an incorrect fluid level will result.

20. Refill the rear axle housing using the proper grade and quantity of lubricant as detailed in Section 1 of this manual. Install the filler plug, operate the vehicle and check for any leaks.

Pinion Oil Seal

REPLACEMENT

See Figures 144, 145 and 146

➡The following procedure requires the use of the pinion holding tool No. J-8614-10 or equivalent, the pinion flange removal tool No. J-8614-1, J-8614-2, J-8614-3 or equivalent, and the pinion oil seal installation tool No. J-23911 or equivalent.

1. Matchmark the driveshaft and pinion flange to assure they are reassembled in the same position.

2. Disconnect the driveshaft from rear axle pinion flange and support the shaft up in body tunnel by wiring the driveshaft to the exhaust pipe. If the U-joint bearings are not retained by a retainer strap, use a piece of tape to hold bearings on their journals.

3. Mark the position of the pinion stem, flange and nut for reference.

4. Use an inch lbs. torque wrench to measure the amount of torque necessary to turn the pinion, then note this measure-

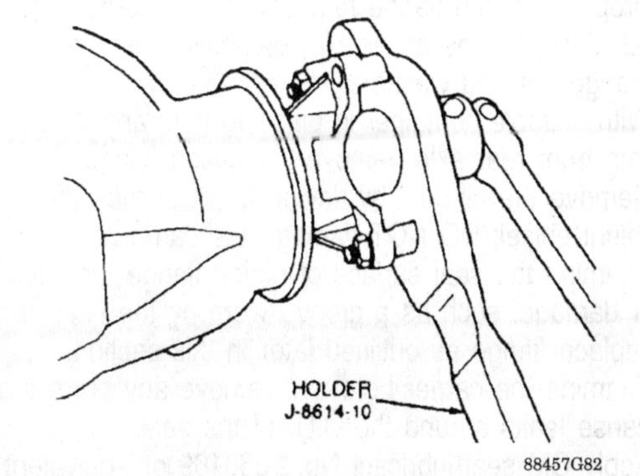

Fig. 144 Removing the pinion nut using a pinion holding fixture tool

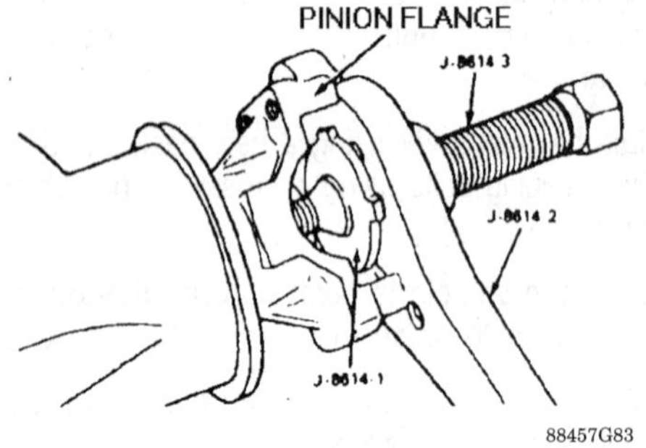

Fig. 145 A puller and adapter should be used to withdraw the pinion from the housing

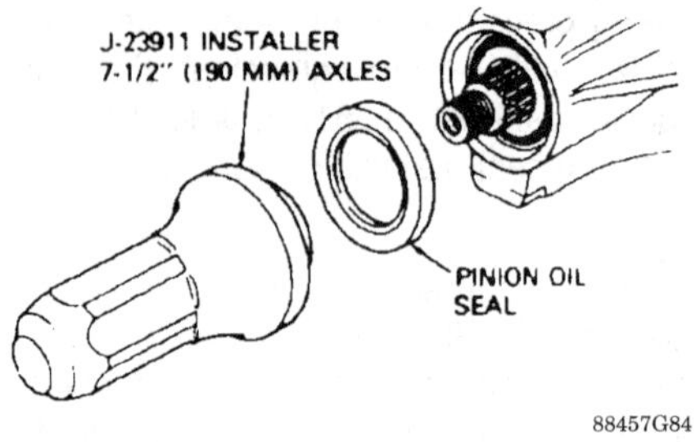

Fig. 146 Use the appropriately sized installation tool to drive the new seal into position.

ment as it is the combined pinion bearing, seal, carrier bearing, axle bearing and seal preload.

5. Using a pinion holding tool such as No. J-8614-10, and the appropriate pinion flange removal tool No. J-8614-1, J-8614-2, J-8614-3 (as applicable) or equivalents, remove the pinion flange nut and washer.

6. With suitable container in place to hold any fluid that may drain from rear axle, remove the pinion flange.

7. Remove the oil seal by driving it out of the differential with a blunt chisel; DO NOT damage the carrier.

8. Examine the seal surface of pinion flange for tool marks, nicks or damage, such as a groove worn by the seal. If damaged, replace flange as outlined later in this section.

9. Examine the carrier bore and remove any burrs that might cause leaks around the O.D. of the seal.

10. Apply GM seal lubricant No. 1050169 or equivalent to the outside diameter of the pinion flange and sealing lip of new seal. Drive the new seal into place using a correctly sized installation tool.

11. Install the pinion flange and tighten nut to the same position as marked in Step 3. Tighten the nut a little at a time and turn the pinion flange several times after each tightening in order to set the rollers.

12. Measure the torque necessary to turn the pinion and compare this to the reading taken during removal. Tighten the nut additionally, as necessary to achieve the same preload as measured earlier.

➡If fluid was lost from the differential housing during this procedure, be sure to check and add additional fluid, as necessary. For details, please refer to Section 1 of this manual.

13. Remove the support then align and secure the driveshaft assembly to the pinion flange. The original matchmarks MUST be aligned to assure proper shaft balance and prevent vibration.

Pinion Flange Replacement

REMOVAL & INSTALLATION

1. Raise and safely support the rear of the truck safely using jackstands.

2. Remove both rear wheels and drums.

3. Matchmark the driveshaft and pinion flange, then disconnect the rear U-joint and support the driveshaft out of the way. If the U-joint bearings are not retained by a retainer strap, use a piece of tape to hold bearing caps on their journals.

4. The pinion rides against a tapered roller bearing. Check the pre-load by reading how much torque is required to turn the pinion. Use an inch pound torque wrench on the pinion flange nut and record the reading. This will give combined pinion bearing, carrier bearing, axle bearing and seal pre-load.

5. Remove pinion flange nut and washer. A suitable pinion holding tool should be used keep the flange from turning when loosening the nut.

6. With a suitable container in place to hold any fluid that may drain from the rear axle, remove the pinion flange.

To install:

7. Apply GM seal lubricant No. 1050169 or equivalent, to the outside diameter of the new pinion flange, then install the pinion flange.

➡DO NOT hammer on the pinion flange in order to install it to the stem.

8. Install the washer and a new pinion flange nut finger-tight.

9. While holding the pinion flange, tighten the nut a little at a time and turn the drive pinion several revolutions after each tightening to set the rollers. Check the pre-load of bearings each time with an inch pound torque wrench until the same pre-load is achieved as the reading that was obtained in Step 4.

10. Remove the support then align and secure the driveshaft assembly to the pinion flange. The original matchmarks MUST

be aligned to assure proper shaft balance and prevent vibration.

➡If fluid was lost from the differential housing during this procedure, be sure to check and add additional fluid, as necessary. For details, please refer to Section 1 of this manual.

11. Install the rear drums and wheels.
12. Remove the jackstands and carefully lower the vehicle.

Axle Housing

REMOVAL & INSTALLATION

See Figure 147

1. Raise and support the rear of the vehicle safely using jackstands under the frame. Position a floor jack or a second set of jackstands to support the rear axle housing. If a floor jack is being used, take care when removing the U-bolts to keep the axle from suddenly dislodging.
2. Remove the rear wheels and drums for clearance and to remove some weight from the axle housing.
3. Matchmark and remove the rear driveshaft from the pinion flange. Either remove the shaft completely from the vehicle or support it aside from the undercarriage using safety wire, but DO NOT allow the shaft to hang from the slip joint.

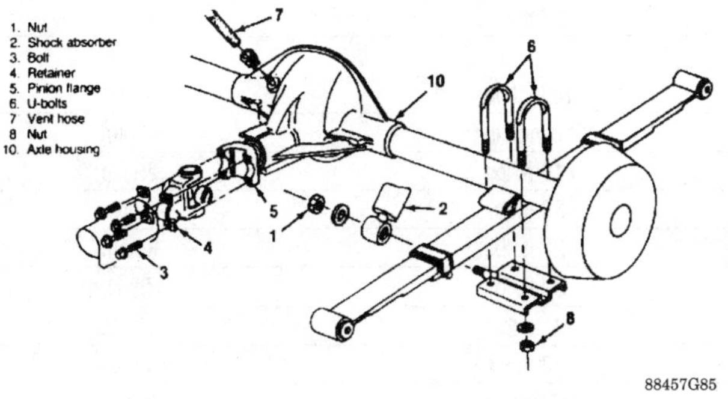

Fig. 147 Exploded view of the rear axle mounting

4. Remove the shock absorber-to-axle housing retainers, then swing the shock absorbers away from the axle housing.
5. Disconnect the brake lines from the axle housing clips and the backing plates (wheel cylinders).

➡When disconnecting the brake lines from the wheel cylinders, immediately plug or cap the lines to prevent system contamination or excessive fluid loss.

6. If applicable, disengage the speed sensor connectors at the junction block.
7. For 1994 vehicles or as necessary, disconnect the parking brake cable(s).
8. Disconnect the axle housing-to-spring U-bolt nuts, washers. U-bolts and the anchor plates.
9. Remove the vent hose from the top of the axle housing.
10. Remove the axle with the help of an assistant by moving it to clear the leaf spring, or if desired, the leaf springs can be disconnected from the frame at the rear end to lower the axle down and back, but first refer to the leaf spring procedures for information regarding spring installation and removal.

To install:

11. With the help of an assistant, carefully position the rear axle into the vehicle.
12. Connect the vent hose to the axle housing.
13. Be sure the housing is properly positioned on the leaf spring, then loosely install the U-bolts, anchor plates, washers and nuts.
14. Tighten the U-bolt nuts in a cross pattern to 18 ft. lbs. (25 Nm) to made sure everything is evenly seated. Then tighten the nuts in steps to to 41 ft. lbs. (55 Nm), then to 85 ft. lbs. (115 Nm).
15. Remove the caps from the brakes lines then connect the lines and secure them to the axle housing.
16. If removed, connect the parking brake cable(s).
17. If applicable, engage the speed sensor connectors to the junction block.
18. Align and install the driveshaft assembly. Refer to the procedure earlier in this section for details.
19. Install the shock absorbers to the lower mounts, then tighten the mount nuts.
20. Install the brake drums and the tire/wheel assemblies.
21. Properly refill the brake master cylinder and bleed the hydraulic brake system.
22. Check the fluid level in the rear axle assembly and add, as necessary. Make sure the vehicle is level when checking and adding fluid.
23. Remove the jackstands and carefully lower the truck.

TORQUE SPECIFICATIONS

Component	US	Nm
Manual transmission:		
Brace-to-engine bolts (4.3L engine)	27 ft. lbs.	37 Nm
Crossmember-to-frame bolt	34 ft. lbs.	46 Nm
Crossmember-to-mount nut (1995)	33 ft. lbs.	45 Nm
Crossmember-to-mount nut (1994)	26 ft. lbs.	35 Nm
Crossmember reinforcement-to- frame bolt	15 ft. lbs.	21 Nm
Inspection cover bolts (2.2L engine)	62 inch lbs.	7 Nm
Inspection cover bolts (4.3L engine)	88 inch lbs.	10 Nm
Lower transmission brace bolts	37 ft. lbs.	50 Nm
Oil drain plug - 1994-97	①	①
Oil drain plug - (1996-97 NV1500)	27 ft. lbs.	37 Nm
Oil drain and fill plugs - (1996 NV1500/3500)	44 ft. lbs.	60 Nm
Oil fill plug - 1994-97	②	②
Shift knob nut	40 inch lbs.	4.5 Nm
Shift housing-to-transmission bolts (1996-97)	89 inch lbs.	10 Nm
Shift lever boot screws	17 inch lbs.	1.9 Nm
Shift lever nut	35 ft. lbs.	48 Nm
Speed sensor bolt	16 ft. lbs.	22 Nm
Transmission brace nuts-to-extension housing	41 ft. lbs.	55 Nm
Transmission brace-to-Engine bolts (2.2L) - 1996-97	35 ft. lbs.	48 Nm
Transmission brace-to-Engine bolts - 1996-97	37 ft. lbs.	50 Nm
Transmission brace-to-Engine Stud	35 ft. lbs.	48 Nm
Transmission mount bolts	37 ft. lbs.	50 Nm
Transmission-to-clutch housing bolts	55 ft. lbs.	75 Nm
Transmission-to-engine bolts	35 ft. lbs.	47 Nm
Upper transmission brace bolts - 1994-95	66 ft. lbs.	90 Nm
Lower transmission brace bolts - 1994-96	37 ft. lbs.	50 Nm
Transfer case:		
Control cable locknut	18 inch lbs.	2 Nm
Control cable floor screws	18 inch lbs.	2 Nm
Drain and fill plugs	18 ft. lbs.	25 Nm
Extension housing bolts (BW 4472)	30 ft. lbs.	42 Nm
Extension housing bolts (NV231 and NV233)	23 ft. lbs.	31 Nm
Front Output flange nut	80 ft. lbs.	108 Nm
Lever assembly floor nuts	9 ft. lbs.	12 Nm
Rear retainer housing bolts	23 ft. lbs.	31 Nm
Selector switch bracket screws	35 inch lbs.	4 Nm
Transfer case brace bolts and stud	35 ft. lbs.	47 Nm
Transfer case mount bolts	37 ft. lbs.	50 Nm
Transfer case shield bolts and nuts	24 ft. lbs.	33 Nm
Transfer case-to-transmission bolts	41 ft. lbs.	55 Nm
Vacuum switch	17 ft. lbs.	24 Nm
Clutch		
Actuator cylinder nuts (2.2L engine)	17 ft. lbs.	23 Nm
Actuator cylinder nuts (4.3L engine)	13 ft. lbs.	17 Nm
Actuator cylinder shield bolts (4.3L engine)	18 ft. lbs.	25 Nm
Clutch cover bolts	③	③
Clutch cover assembly bolts (4.3L engine)	29 ft. lbs.	40 Nm
Clutch fork inspection plug	70 inch lbs.	8 Nm
Clutch housing bolts and nuts	55 ft. lbs.	75 Nm
Clutch housing cover bolts (1997 NV3500)	62 inch lbs.	7 Nm

88457C01

TORQUE SPECIFICATIONS

Component	US	Nm
Clutch pedal bolt	27 ft. lbs.	37 Nm
Inspection cover bolts (2.2L engine)	62 inch lbs.	7 Nm
Inspection cover bolts (4.3L engine)	88 inch lbs.	10 Nm
Pushrod-to-cowl bolts	17 ft. lbs.	23 Nm

① 1994: All 20 ft.lbs. - 27 Nm
1995: All 17 ft.lbs. - 23 Nm
1996-97: NV1500: All 27 ft.lbs. - 37 Nm

② 1994: All 20 ft.lbs. - 27 Nm
1995: All 17 ft.lbs. - 23 Nm
1996-97: NV1500: All 17 ft.lbs. - 23 Nm

③ 1994: All 30 ft.lbs. - 40 Nm
1995: 2.2 28 ft.lbs. - 38 Nm
1996: 2.2 33 ft.lbs. - 45 Nm

88457C02

TORQUE SPECIFICATIONS

Component	US	Nm
Automatic transmission:		
Accumulator cover-to-case	97 inch lbs.	11 Nm
Auxiliary valve body-to-case	97 inch lbs.	11 Nm
Bracket-to-frame bolts (1996)	19 ft. lbs.	26 Nm
Case extension-to-case	25 ft. lbs.	34 Nm
Connector cooler pipe	28 ft. lbs.	38 Nm
Converter cover bolts (1996)	37 ft. lbs.	50 Nm
Converter cover bolts (1997)	89 inch lbs.	10 Nm
Converter housing cover	88 inch lbs.	10 Nm
Converter-to-flywheel	46 ft. lbs.	63 Nm
Cooler lines-to-radiator	18 ft. lbs.	24 Nm
Cooler lines-to-transmission	18 ft. lbs.	24 Nm
Crossmember-to-frame	56 ft. lbs.	77 Nm
Detent spring-to-valve body	16 ft. lbs.	22 Nm
Filler tube-to-engine	23 ft. lbs.	32 Nm
Floor shift control bolt (1997)	89 inch lbs.	10 Nm
Manual shaft-to-inside detent lever	23 ft. lbs.	31 Nm
Oil level indicator tube bolt (1997)	35 ft. lbs.	47 Nm
Oil pan-to-transmission case	97 inch lbs.	11 Nm
Oil passage cover-to-case	97 inch lbs.	11 Nm
Park/Neutral position switch bolts	21 ft. lbs.	28 Nm
Pressure plugs (1/8-27)	97 inch lbs.	11 Nm
Pressure plugs (1/4-18)	18 ft. lbs.	24 Nm
Pressure switches	97 inch lbs.	11 Nm
Speed sensor bolts	97 inch lbs.	11 Nm
Solenoid assembly-to-pump	97 inch lbs.	11 Nm
Shift linkage	20 ft. lbs.	28 Nm
Swivel-to-equalizer lever	20 ft. lbs.	28 Nm
Shift lever-to-transmission	22 ft. lbs.	30 Nm
Bracket-to-frame	19 ft. lbs.	26 Nm
TCC solenoid bolts	97 inch lbs.	11 Nm
Valve body-to-case	97 inch lbs.	11 Nm
Transmission rear mount-to-crossmember	38 ft. lbs.	52 Nm
Transmission converter-to flywheel bolts	46 ft. lbs.	63 Nm
Transmission support braces bolts	44 ft. lbs.	60 Nm
Transmission-to-engine (2.2L engine)	66 ft. lbs.	90 Nm
Transmission-to-engine (4.3L engine)	34 ft. lbs.	47 Nm
Valve body-to-case	97 inch lbs.	11 Nm
Transfer case:		
Control cable locknut	18 inch lbs.	2 Nm
Control cable floor screws	18 inch lbs.	2 Nm
Drain and fill plugs	18 ft. lbs.	25 Nm
Extension housing bolts (BW 4472)	30 ft. lbs.	42 Nm
Extension housing bolts (NV231 and NV233)	23 ft. lbs.	31 Nm
Front Output flange nut	80 ft. lbs.	108 Nm
Lever assembly floor nuts	9 ft. lbs.	12 Nm
Rear retainer housing bolts	23 ft. lbs.	31 Nm
Selector switch bracket screws	35 inch lbs.	4 Nm
Transfer case adapter bolts	41 ft. lbs.	55 Nm
Transfer case brace bolts and stud	35 ft. lbs.	47 Nm
Transfer case mount bolts	37 ft. lbs.	50 Nm
Transfer case shield bolts and nuts	24 ft. lbs.	33 Nm
Transmission adapter bolts	31 ft. lbs.	42 Nm
Vacuum switch	17 ft. lbs.	24 Nm

88457C03

8

SUSPENSION AND STEERING

WHEELS

Wheel Assembly

REMOVAL & INSTALLATION

➧ **See Figures 1 and 2**

The vehicles covered by this manual use a variety of wheel styles, but from the factory they are all one piece rims with 5 bolt holes in a bolt circle of 5 in. (127mm). Wheels are also available in a variety of standard sizes from 14 x 6 in. (355.6 x 152.4mm) to 15 x 7 in. (381 x 177.8mm). Most vehicles are equipped with a space saver spare, for EMERGENCY USE ONLY, which comes in a 16 x 4 in. (406.4mm x 101.6mm) and 15 x 4 in. (381 x 101.6mm) sizes.

1. Apply the parking brake and block the opposite wheel.
2. If equipped with an automatic transmission/transaxle, place the selector lever in **P**; with a manual transmission/transaxle, place the shifter in Reverse.
3. If equipped, remove the wheel cover or hub cap.
4. Break loose the lug nuts. If a nut is stuck, never use heat to loosen it or damage to the wheel and bearings may occur. If the nuts are seized, one or two heavy hammer blows directly on the end of the bolt head usually loosens the rust. Be careful as continued pounding will likely damage the brake drum or rotor.
5. Raise the vehicle until the tire is clear of the ground. Support the vehicle safely using jackstands.
6. Remove the lug nuts, then remove the tire and wheel assembly.

To install:

7. Make sure the wheel and hub mating surfaces, as well as the wheel lug studs, are clean and free of all foreign material. Always remove rust from the wheel mounting surfaces and the brake rotors/drums. Failure to do so may cause the lug nuts to loosen in service.
8. Position the wheel on the hub or drum and hand-tighten the lug nuts. Make sure that the coned ends face inward.

Fig. 1 Most trucks are equipped with a spare tire mounted to a hanger bracket under the bed

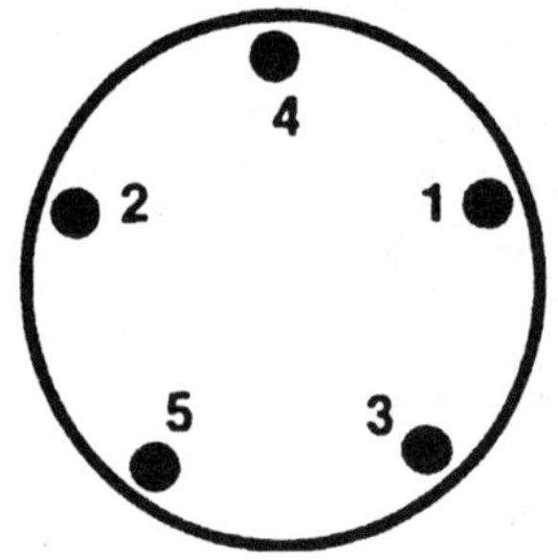

Fig. 2 Wheel lug tightening sequence for a 5-lug wheel

9. Tighten all the lug nuts, in a crisscross pattern, until they are snug.
10. Remove the supports, if any, and lower the vehicle. Tighten the lug nuts, in a crisscross pattern. Always use a torque wrench to achieve the proper lug nut torque which is 95 ft. lbs. (130 Nm).
11. Repeat the torque pattern to assure proper wheel tightening.
12. If equipped, install the hub cab or wheel cover.

INSPECTION

➧ **See Figures 3 and 4**

Check the wheels for any damage. They must be replaced if they are bent, dented, heavily rusted, have elongated bolt holes, or have excessive lateral or radial run-out. Wheels with excessive run-out may cause a high-speed vehicle vibration.

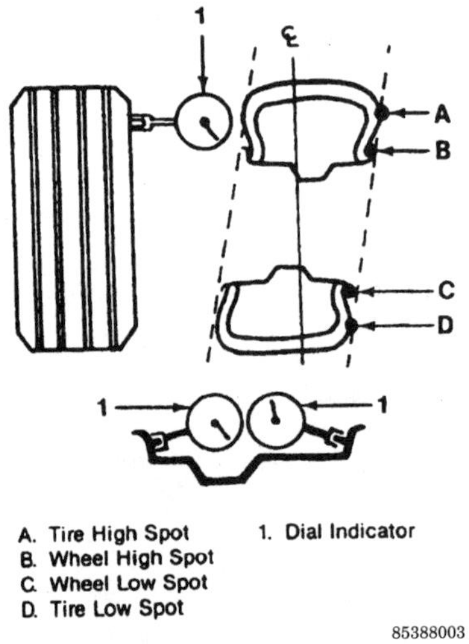

Fig. 3 Measuring lateral runout

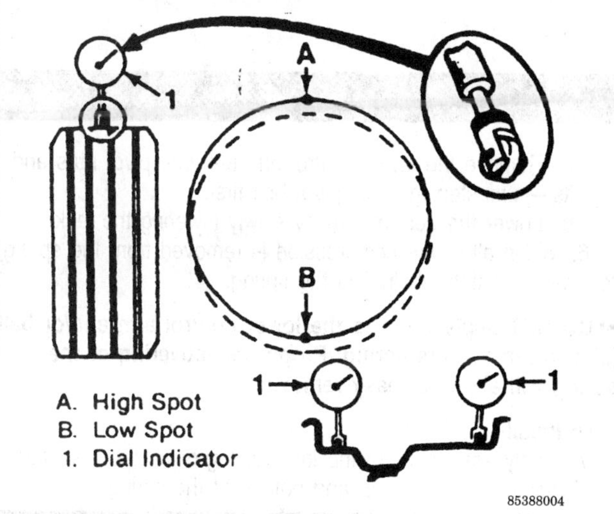

Fig. 4 Measuring radial runout

Replacement wheels must be of the same load capacity, diameter, width, offset and mounting configuration as the original wheels. Using the wrong wheels may affect wheel bearing life, ground and tire clearance, or speedometer and odometer calibrations.

Wheel Lug Studs

REMOVAL & INSTALLATION

Front Wheels on 2WD Vehicles

➧ See Figure 5

1. Raise and support the front of the vehicle safely using jackstands, then remove the wheel.
2. Remove the brake pads and caliper. Support the caliper aside using wire or a coat hanger. For details, please refer to Section 9 of this manual.
3. Remove the outer wheel bearing and lift the rotor off the axle. For details on removal, installation and adjustment, please refer to Section 1 of this manual.
4. Properly support the rotor using press bars, then drive the stud out using an arbor press.

To install:

5. Clean the stud hole with a wire brush and start the new stud with a hammer and drift pin. Do not use any lubricant or thread sealer.
6. Finish installing the stud with the press.
7. Install the rotor and adjust the wheel bearing.
8. Install the brake caliper and pads.
9. Install the tire, then remove the jackstands and carefully lower the vehicle.

Rear Wheels and Front Wheels on 4WD Vehicles

➧ See Figure 6

1. Raise and support the vehicle safely using jackstands, then remove the wheel.
2. On front wheels, remove the brake, caliper and rotor. Support the caliper from the suspension using wire or a coat hanger. For details, please refer to Section 9 of this manual.
3. On rear wheels, remove the brake drum.

➡**When replacing the front hub bolts on vehicles with 4 wheel anti-lock brakes, remove and replace only one wheel lug stud at a time to avoid misaligning the speed sensor exciter ring.**

4. Do not hammer the wheel stud to remove it. This will ruin the wheel bearing. Use the stud press tool such as J-6627A or equivalent to press the stud out of the hub.

To install:

5. Clean the hole with a wire brush and start the new stud into the hole. Do not use any lubricant or threadsealer.
6. Stack 4 or 5 washers onto the stud and then put the nut on. Tighten the nut to draw the stud into place.It should be easy to feel when the stud is seated.
7. Reinstall the rotor and caliper or drum, as applicable.

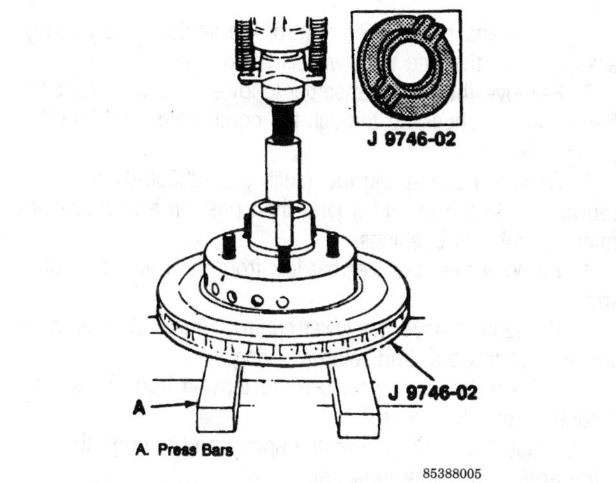

Fig. 5 Use an arbor press to drive the old stud from the rotor — front wheel of 2WD vehicles

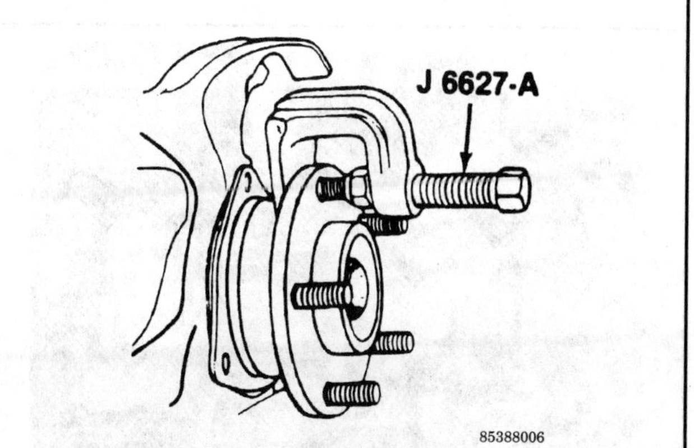

Fig. 6 On many vehicles a stud press tool may be used with the hub still installed on the vehicle

8. Install the tire, then remove the jackstands and carefully lower the vehicle.

FRONT SUSPENSION

➧ See Figure 7

Coil Spring

The 2WD vehicles covered by this manual use a coil spring support for the front suspension.

REMOVAL & INSTALLATION

➧ See Figures 8 and 9

➡The following procedure requires the use of a coil spring removal and installation tool such as No. J-23038-01 or equivalent.

1. Raise and support the front of the vehicle safely using jackstands so that the front wheels hang free.
2. Remove the shock absorber-to-lower control arm bolts, then push the shock up through the control arm and into the spring.
3. Secure a coil spring tool (such as J-23038-01 or equivalent), to the end of a jack, then position it to cradle the inner control arm bushings.
4. Remove the stabilizer bar link from the lower control arm.
5. Properly remove the lower control arm pivot bolts in order to pivot the arm and remove spring:
   a. Raise the jack to remove the tension from the lower control arm pivot bolts.
   b. Install a chain around the spring and through the control arm as a safety measure.

➡During removal, note the direction in which the pivot bolts are mounted.

   c. Remove the lower control arm-to-frame pivot nuts and bolts — unfasten the rear pivot bolt first.
   d. Lower the control arm by slowly lowering the jack.
6. When all of the compression is removed from the spring, remove the safety chain and the spring.

➡DO NOT apply force to the lower control arm and/or ball joint to remove the spring. Proper maneuvering of the spring will allow for easy removal.

To install:

7. Apply adhesive into the insulators groove, then position the insulators onto the top and bottom of the spring.

****CAUTION**

Use extreme care when installing and compressing the spring. Be sure the spring tool and jack and properly installed and the spring is securely seated.

8. Secure the coil spring tool, then position the coil spring and insulators on the lower control arm. Raise the control arm and spring assembly into position.
9. Install the pivot bolts, starting with the front bolt first, and secure using new nuts. Both bolts should be installed in the direction they were facing when removed, which usually means they are inserted from the front of the vehicle.
10. Install and secure the stabilizer bar link to the lower control arm.
11. Position and secure the shock absorber.
12. Remove the jackstands and carefully lower the vehicle.

Torsion Bar

Instead of the coil spring used on the front suspension of 2WD trucks, the 4WD vehicles covered by this manual are equipped with a torsion bar.

88458p02

Fig. 7 View of the 4WD front suspension — visible are the lower control arms and sway bar

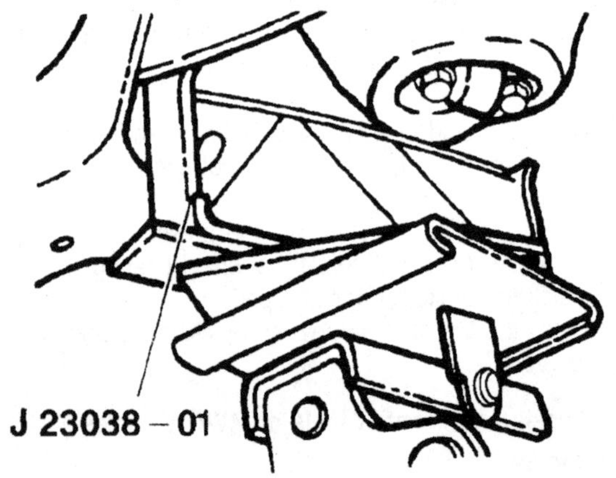

88458g02

Fig. 8 With the spring tool secured to a jack, raise the control arm in order to relieve tension from the control arm pivot bolts

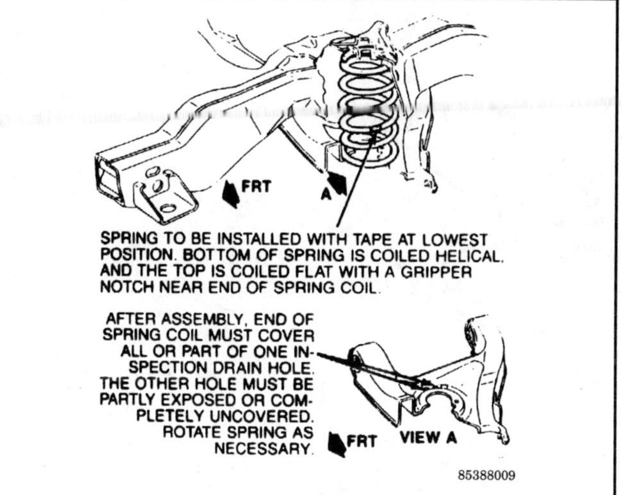

Fig. 9 The spring must be properly positioned during installation

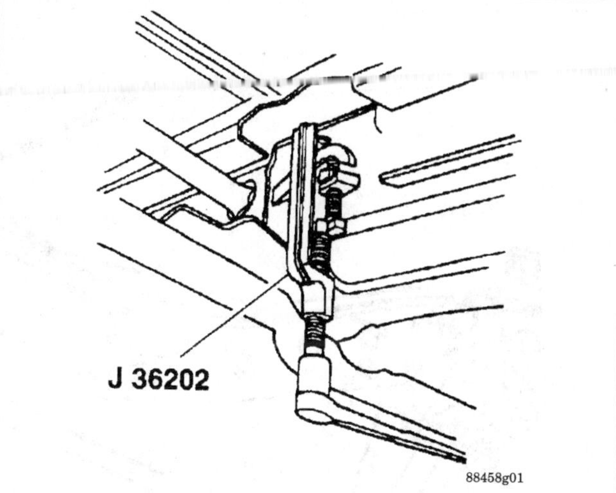

Fig. 11 Use the torsion bar unloader to ease tension so the adjuster bolt may be removed

REMOVAL & INSTALLATION

1994 Models

See Figures 10, 11 and 12

The following procedure requires the use of the torsion bar unloader tool J-22517-C or equivalent.

1. Raise and safely support the front of the vehicle safely using jackstands.
2. Install a torsion bar unloader tool to relax the tension on the torsion bar adjusting arm screw; record the number of turns necessary to properly install the tool. Remove the adjusting screw.
3. Remove the adjuster arms.
4. Unfasten the nut and square washer (raise the support out of the way) from the retainer, then remove the retainer bolts from underneath the frame.
5. Slide the insulator off the support and remove it from the vehicle.

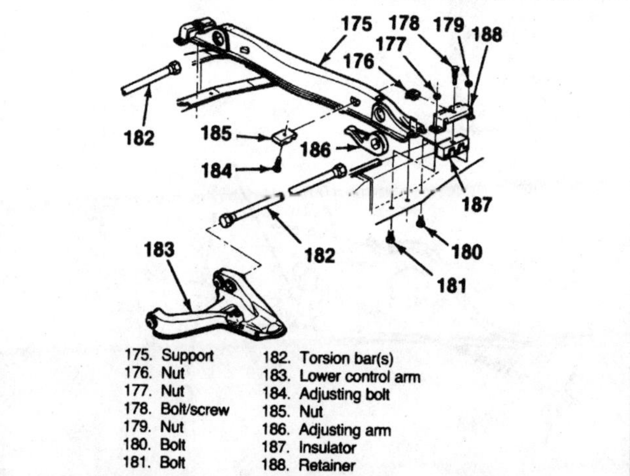

Fig. 10 Torsion bar front mounting — 4WD front suspension

6. Disconnect the muffler flange from the converter, loosen the rear exhaust hanger and lower the rear exhaust.
7. Remove the torsion support from the frame.
8. Remove the torsion bars from the lower control arms.

To install:

9. Position the torsion bars with the lower control arms. If installing a replacement component, be sure the tag is facing forward.
10. Install the support.
11. Install and secure the rear exhaust system to the proper height, then connect the muffler flange to the converter.
12. Install the insulator, making sure the mount studs are positioned through the support and the insulator locator tabs are indexed to the support (facing forward).
13. Install and finger-tighten the square washer and nut.
14. Install the insulator mounting retainers, then tighten the bolts to 26 ft. lbs. (35 Nm) and/or the nuts to 25 ft. lbs. (34 Nm).
15. Install the adjuster arms, then connect the torsion bars to the arms. With the torsion bars installed, check for an assembled clearance from the end of the bar to the support of 0.236 in. (6.0mm).
16. Lubricate the top of the adjusting arm and the adjusting bolt, then install the nuts and adjuster bolts.

1995-97 Models

The following procedure requires the use of the torsion bar unloader tool No. J-36202 or equivalent.

1. Raise and safely support the front of the vehicle safely using jackstands.
2. Remove the transmission shield, if equipped.
3. Install a torsion bar unloader tool to relax the tension on the torsion bar adjusting arm screw; record the number of turns necessary to properly install the tool. Remove the adjusting screw and the unloader tool.
4. Unfasten the lower link mount nut from one side, then disengage the torsion bars.

Note the direction of the forward end and side of the torsion bar being removed

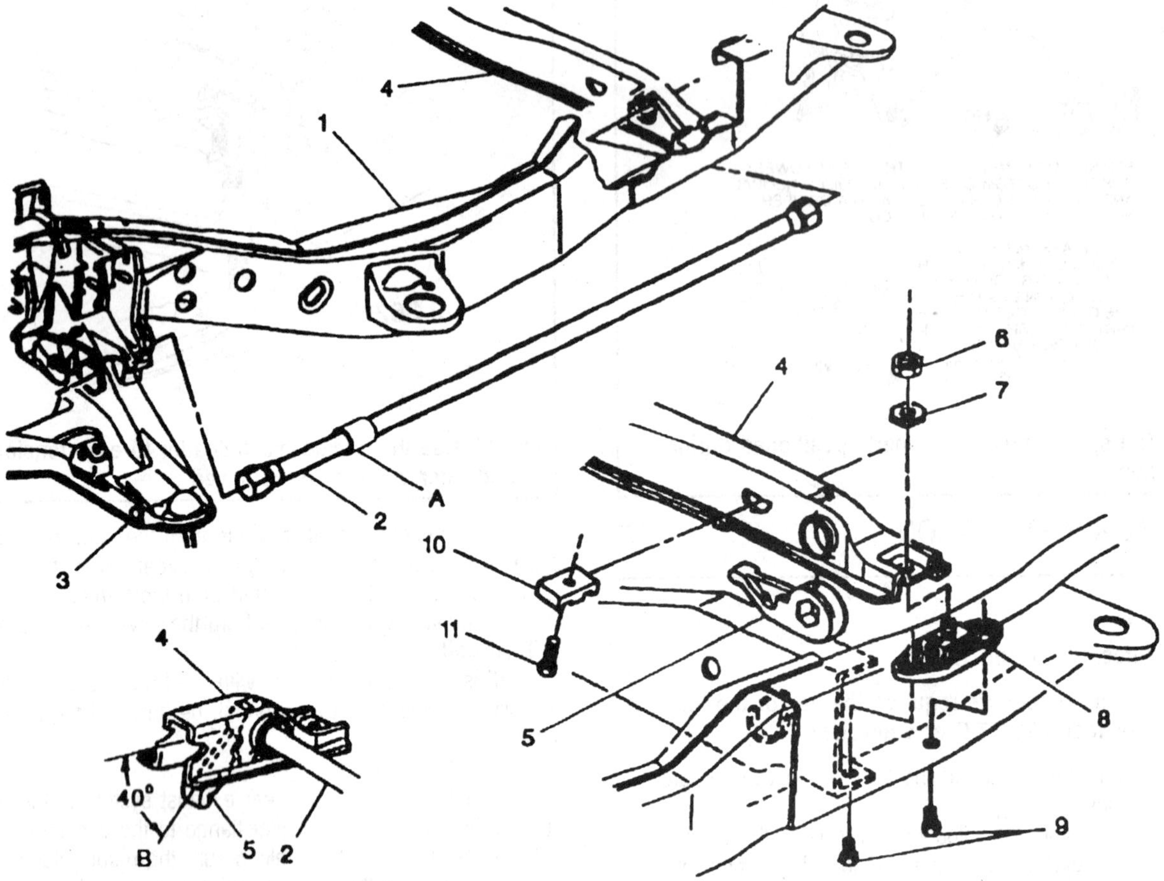

A. TAG MUST BE INSTALLED IN FORWARD POSITION OF VEHICLE
B. APPROXIMATE FREE POSITION OF ADJUSTMENT ARM WHEN LOWER CONTROL ARM IS RESTING ON JOUNCE BUMPER
C. INSULATOR MUST BE INSTALLED WITH TOP LOCATOR TAB TO FRONT OF VEHICLE
D. BOTTOM OFFSET IS INSTALLED TO REAR OF VEHICLE
E. GAP NOT TO EXCEED 6.0mm (0.25 IN.)
F. A 1.0mm (0.040 IN.) CLEARANCE MUST BE PROVIDED AFTER FINAL ADJUSTMENT
G. 25.0mm (1.0 IN.) ORIGINAL INSTALLATION POSITION FOR BOLT/SCREW FINAL POSITION ADJUSTED AFTER TRIM HEIGHT
1. FRAME
2. BAR, TORSION
3. ARM KIT, LOWER CONTROL
4. SUPPORT, TORSION BAR
5. ARM, TORSION BAR ADJUSTER
6. NUT
7. WASHER, SQUARE
8. INSULATOR
9. BOLT
10. NUT, TORSION BAR ADJUSTER
11. BOLT, TORSION BAR ADJUSTER

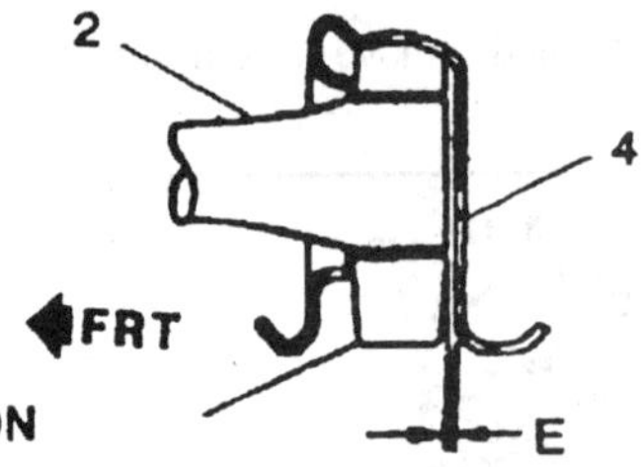

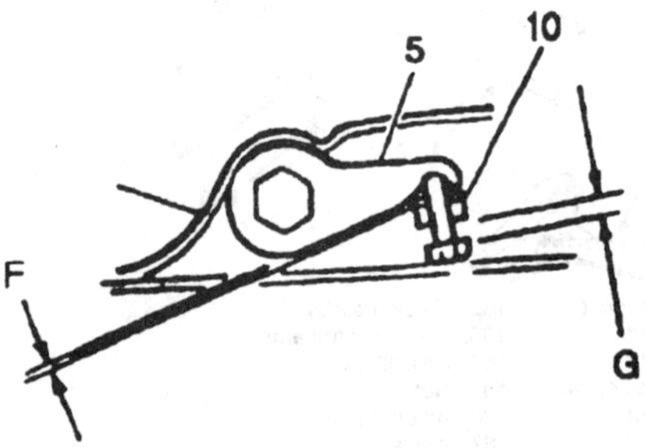

85388012

Fig. 12 Torsion bar and support mounting/alignment — 1994 vehicles

5. Remove the lower link nut from the opposite side.
6. Remove the lower link mount, upper link mount nut, upper link mount and then unfasten the torsion bar from the frame.

To install:

7. Install the torsion bar and support.
8. Install the upper link mount and mount nut. Tighten the nut to 33 ft. lbs. (45 Nm).
9. Place a jack under the torsion bar to release tension, then install the lower link mount bushing and nut. Tighten the nut to 13 ft. lbs. (18 Nm) on 1995 models and 50 ft. lbs. (68 Nm) on 1996-97 models.
10. Install the torsion bar unloader tool and tighten the tool against the adjusting arm the same number turns recorded earlier, then remove the tool. This loads the torsion bars.
11. Install the transmission shield, if removed.
12. Remove the jackstands and lower the vehicle.

Shock Absorbers

REMOVAL & INSTALLATION

2WD Vehicles

See Figure 13

1. Raise and support the front of the truck safely using jackstands.
2. Using an open end wrench, hold the shock absorber upper stem from turning, then remove the upper stem retaining nut, the retainer and rubber grommet.
3. Remove the shock absorber-to-lower control arm retaining bolts and lower the shock absorber assembly from the bottom of the control arm.
4. Inspect and test the shock absorber; replace it, if necessary.

To install:

5. Fully extend the shock absorber stem, then push it up through the lower control arm and spring so that the upper stem passes through the mounting hole in the upper control arm frame bracket.
6. Install the upper shock absorber nut and tighten to 100 inch. lbs. (11 Nm) on 1994-95 models and 54 ft. lbs. (73 Nm) on 1996-97 models. Be careful not to crush the rubber bushing.
7. Install the shock absorber-to-lower control arm retaining bolts and tighten to 20 ft. lbs. (27 Nm) on 1994-95 models and 54 ft. lbs. (73 Nm) on 1996-97 models.
8. Remove the jackstands and carefully lower the vehicle.

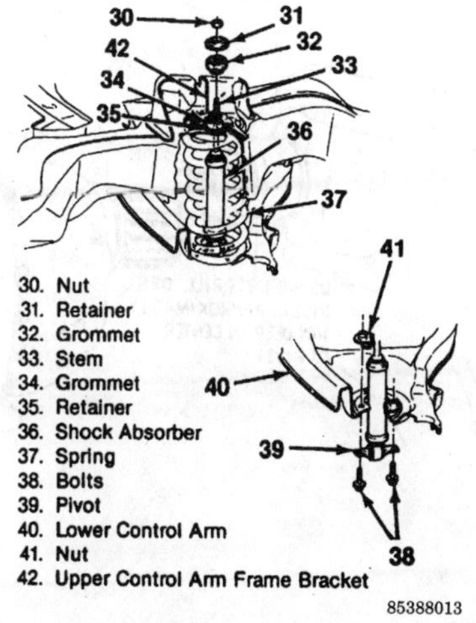

Fig. 13 Common front shock absorber mounting — 2WD vehicles

4WD Vehicles

See Figures 14 and 15

1. Raise and support the front of the truck safely using jackstands.
2. Remove the tire and wheel assembly to ease access.
3. Remove the shock absorber-to-lower control arm nut and bolt (using a backup wrench), then collapse the shock absorber.
4. Remove the upper shock absorber-to-frame nut and bolt (again, using a backup wrench).

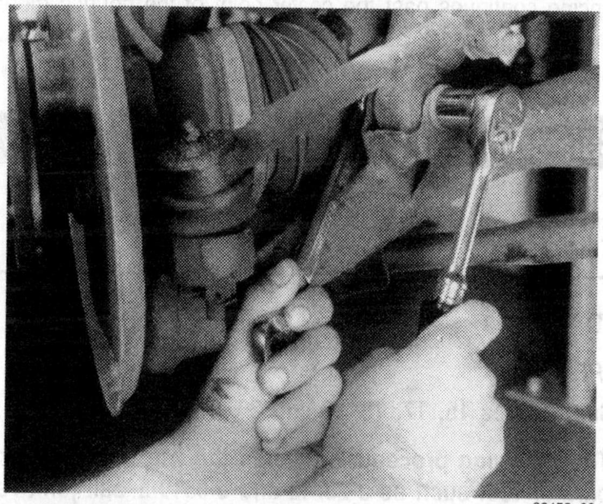

88458p03

Fig. 14 Loosen and remove the shock absorber lower mounting bolt

88458p04

Fig. 15 Then loosen the upper mounting bolt and remove the shock from the vehicle

5. Inspect and test the shock absorber; replace it, if necessary.

To install:

6. Position the shock absorber to the mounting brackets.
7. Install the upper and lower retaining bolts (inserted from the front of the vehicle).
8. Install the retaining nuts to the bolts, then tighten the retainers to 54 ft. lbs. (73 Nm).
9. Install the tire and wheel assembly, then remove the jackstands and carefully lower the vehicle.

TESTING

Visually inspect the shock absorber. If there is evidence of leakage and the shock absorber is covered with oil the shock is defective and should be replaced.

If there is no sign of excessive leakage (a small amount of weeping is normal) bounce the truck at one corner by pressing down on the bumper and releasing it. When you have the truck bouncing as much as you can, release the bumper. The truck should stop bouncing after the first rebound. If the bouncing continues past the center point of the bounce more than once, the shock absorbers are worn and should be replaced.

Ball Joints

REMOVAL & INSTALLATION

2WD Vehicles

UPPER

See Figures 16, 17, 18, 19 and 20

➡The following procedure requires the use of a ball joint separator tool such as J-23742 and J-9519-E ball joint remover and installer set or their equivalents.

1. Raise and support the front of the vehicle safely by placing jackstands securely under the lower control arms. Because the vehicle's weight is used to relieve spring tension on the upper control arm, the floor stands must be positioned between the spring seats and the lower control arm ball joints for maximum leverage.

CAUTION

With components unbolted, the jackstand is holding the lower control arm in place against the coil spring. Make sure the jackstand is firmly positioned and cannot move, or personal injury could result.

2. Remove the tire and wheel assembly.
3. Remove the brake caliper and support it from the vehicle using a coat hanger or wire. Make sure the brake line is not stretched or damaged and that the caliper's weight is not supported by the line.
4. Remove the cotter pin and retaining nut from the upper ball joint.
5. Position J-23742 or an equivalent ball joint separator tool between upper joint stud and the lower joint/control arm. Use the tool to separate the upper ball joint from the steering knuckle. Pull the steering knuckle free of the ball joint after removal.

➡After separating the steering knuckle from the upper ball joint, be sure to support the steering knuckle/hub assembly to prevent damaging the brake hose.

6. Remove the riveted upper ball joint from the upper control arm:
   a. Drill a 1/8 in. (3mm) hole, about 1/4 in. (6mm) deep into each rivet.
   b. Then use a 1/2 in. (13mm) drill bit, to drill off the rivet heads.
   c. Using a pin punch and the hammer, drive out the rivets in order to free the upper ball joint from the upper control arm assembly, then remove the upper ball joint.
7. Clean and inspect the steering knuckle hole. Replace the steering knuckle if the hole is out of round.

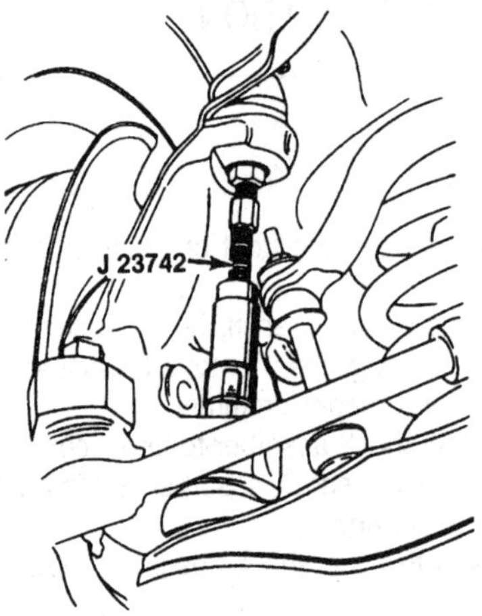

85388020

Fig. 16 Use a ball joint separator tool to drive the upper ball joint from the steering knuckle

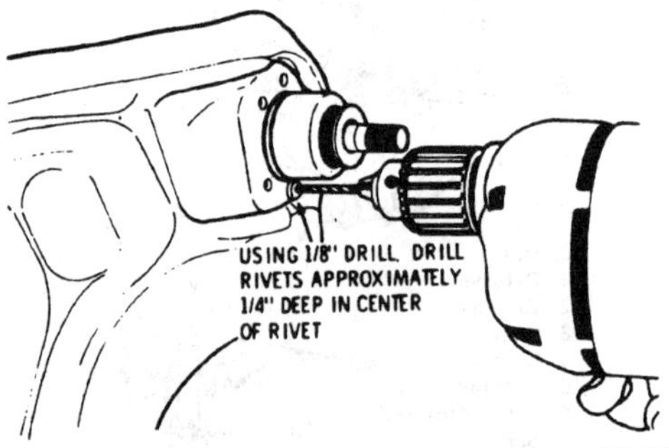

85388021

Fig. 17 Drill a small guide hole into each ball joint rivet

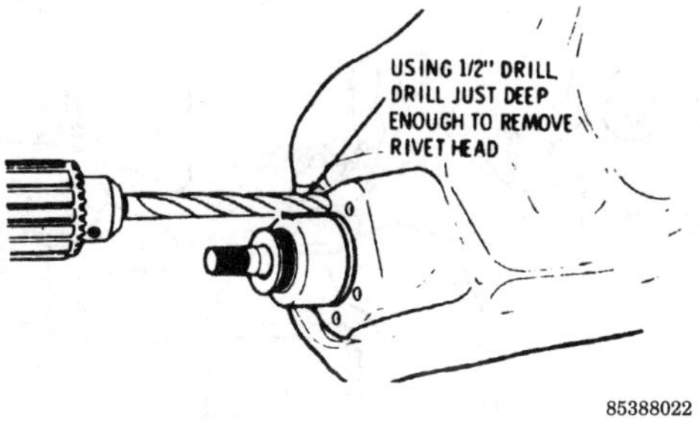

Fig. 18 Then drill off the rivet heads

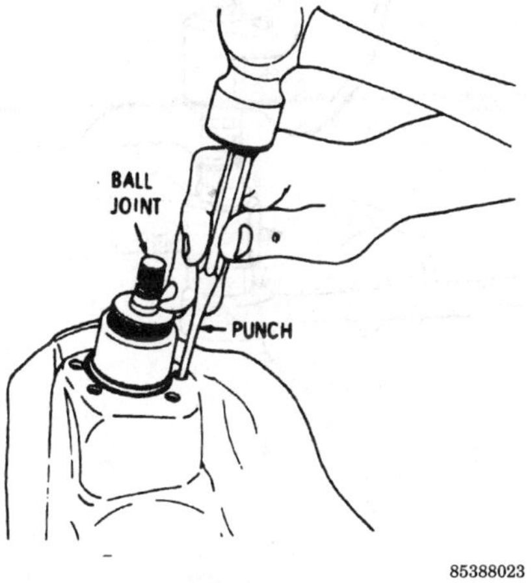

Fig. 19 Punch the rivets out and remove the ball joint

To install:

8. Position the joint in the upper control arm, then install the joint retaining nuts and bolts. Position the bolts threaded upward from under the control arm. Tighten the ball joint retainers to 17 ft. lbs. (23 Nm).

9. Remove the support from the steering knuckle, then install the ball joint to the knuckle. Make sure the joint is seated, then install the stud nut and tighten to 61 ft. lbs. (83 Nm). Insert a new cotter pin.

➡When installing the cotter pin, never loosen the castle nut to expose the cotter pin hole.

10. If not installed already, thread the grease fitting into the ball joint. Use a grease gun to lubricate the upper ball joint.
11. Reposition and secure the brake caliper.
12. Install the tire and wheel assembly.
13. Remove the jackstands and carefully lower the vehicle.
14. Check and adjust the front end alignment, as necessary.

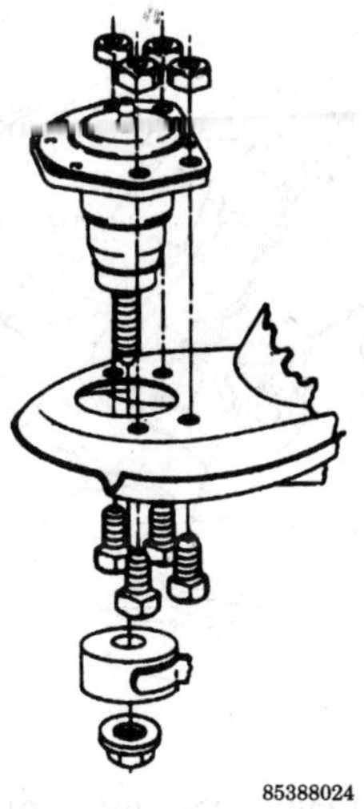

Fig. 20 Service ball joints are bolted to the control arm

LOWER

See Figures 21, 22 and 23

➡The following procedure requires the use of a ball joint remover/installer set (the particular set may vary upon application but must include a clamping-type tool with the appropriately sized adapters) and a ball joint separator tool, such as J-23742 or equivalent.

1. Raise and support the front of the vehicle safely using jackstands under the frame so the control arms hang free.
2. Remove the tire and wheel assembly.
3. Position a floor jack under the spring seat of the lower control arm, then raise the jack to support the arm.

➡The floor jack MUST remain under the lower control arm, during the removal and installation procedures, to retain the arm and spring positions. Make sure the jack is securely positioned and will not slip or release during the procedure or personal injury may result.

4. Remove the brake caliper and support it aside using a hanger or wire. Make sure the brake line is not stressed or damaged.
5. Remove and discard the lower ball joint cotter pin, then loosen and remove the stud nut.
6. Position J-23742 or an equivalent ball joint separator tool between lower joint stud and the upper joint/control arm. Use the tool to separate the lower ball joint from the steering knuckle.
7. Carefully guide the lower control arm out of the opening in the splash shield using a putty knife. Position a block of wood between the frame and upper control arm to keep the knuckle out of the way.
8. Remove the grease fitting from the control arm.
9. Use the ball joint remover set along with the appropriate adapters to drive the ball joint from the control arm.

To install:

10. Clean the tapered hole in the steering knuckle of any dirt or foreign matter, then check the hole to see if it is out of round, deformed or otherwise damaged. If a problem is found, then knuckle must be replaced.

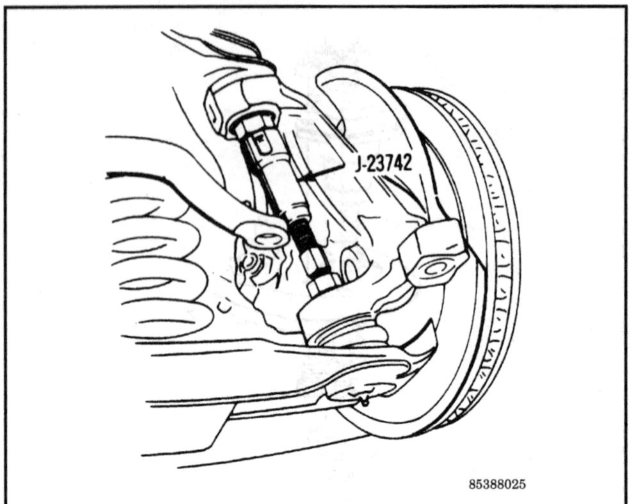

Fig. 21 Use a ball joint separator to drive the lower joint from the knuckle

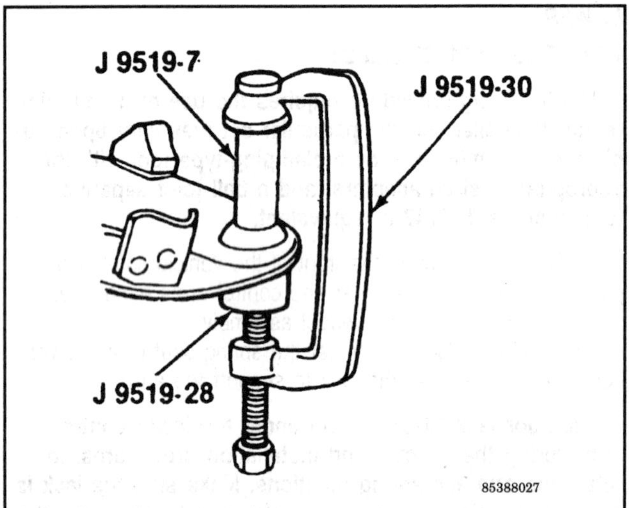

Fig. 22 Driving the lower joint from the control arm

11. Using a suitable installation set, press the new ball joint until it bottoms in the control arm. Make sure the grease seal is facing inboard.
12. Position the ball joint stud into the steering knuckle, then install the retaining nut and tighten to 83 ft. lbs. (113 Nm). Insert a new cotter pin.

➡When installing the cotter pin, never loosen the castle nut to expose the cotter pin hole.

13. If not installed already, thread the grease fitting into the ball joint, then use a grease gun to lubricate the joint.
14. Reposition and secure the brake caliper.
15. Install the tire and wheel assembly.
16. Remove the jackstands and carefully lower the vehicle.
17. Check and adjust the front end alignment, as necessary.

4WD Vehicles

See Figures 24, 25, 26 and 27

On 4WD vehicles both the upper and lower ball joints are removed in the same manner. Once the joint is separated from

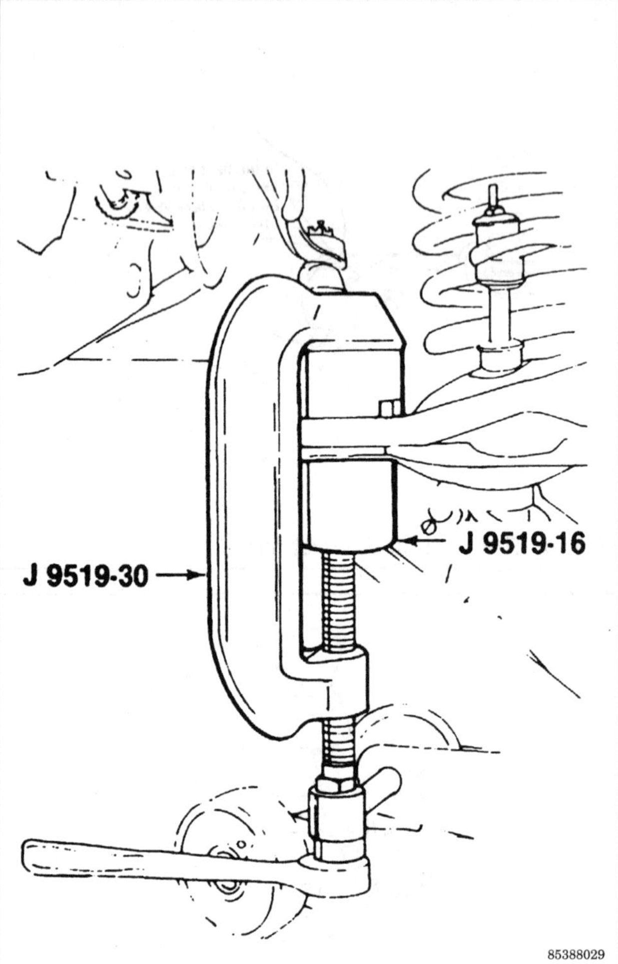

Fig. 23 Installing a new ball joint

Fig. 24 Remove the cotter pin from the ball joint . . .

88458p06

Fig. 25 . . . then unfasten the retaining nut

88458p07

Fig. 26 Position a suitable ball joint separator tool and carefully loosen the joint in the steering knuckle . . .

88458p08

Fig. 27 . . . then disengage the tool and the retaining nut, then remove the joint from the knuckle

the steering knuckle the rivets are drilled and punched to free the joint from the control arm. Service joints are bolted into position with the retaining bolts threaded upward from beneath the control arm. In this manner, the joint is replaced in an almost identical fashion to the upper joints on 2WD vehicles.

1. Raise and support the front of the vehicle safely using jackstands.
2. Remove the tire and wheel assembly.
3. Remove the cotter pin from the ball joint, then loosen the retaining nut.
4. Position a suitable ball joint separator tool such as J-36607, or equivalent, then carefully loosen the joint in the steering knuckle. Disengage the tool and the retaining nut, then remove the joint from the knuckle.

➡After separating the steering knuckle from the upper ball joint, be sure to support the steering knuckle/hub assembly to prevent damaging the brake hose.

5. Remove the riveted ball joint from the control arm:
   a. Drill a 1/8 in. (3mm) hole, about 1/4 in. (6mm) deep into each rivet.
   b. Then use a 1/2 in. (13mm) drill bit, to drill off the rivet heads.
   c. Using a pin punch and the hammer, drive out the rivets in order to free the ball joint from the control arm assembly, then remove the ball joint.

To install:

6. Position the joint in the control arm, then install the joint retaining nuts and bolts. Position the bolts threaded upward from under the control arm. Tighten the ball joint retainers to 17 ft. lbs. (23 Nm).
7. Remove the support from the steering knuckle, then install the ball joint to the knuckle. Make sure the joint is seated, then install the stud nut and tighten both nuts to 70 ft. lbs. (95 Nm) on 1994-95 models. On 1996-97 models tighten the lower nut to 79 ft. lbs. (108 Nm) and the upper nut to 61 ft. lbs. (83 Nm). Install a new cotter pin.

➡When installing the cotter pin, never loosen the castle nut to expose the cotter pin hole, but DO NOT tighten more than an additional 1/6 turn.

8. Use a grease gun to lubricate the upper ball joint.
9. Install the tire and wheel assembly.
10. Remove the jackstands and carefully lower the vehicle.
11. Check and adjust the front end alignment, as necessary.

INSPECTION

▶ See Figures 28, 29, 30 and 31

➡Before performing this inspection, make sure that the wheel bearings are adjusted correctly and that the control arm bushings are in good condition.

1. Make sure the vehicle is parked on a level surface.
2. Raise and support the front of the vehicle safely by placing jackstands under each lower control arm as close as possible to each lower ball joint (as far outboard as possible). Make sure that the vehicle is stable and the control arm bumpers are not contacting the frame.

3. Wipe the ball joints clean and check the seals for cuts or tears. If a seal is cut or torn, then the ball joint must be replaced.

4. If necessary on 2WD vehicles, adjust the wheel bearings before proceeding.

5. Check the ball joints for horizontal deflection (looseness):

a. Position a dial indicator against the lowest outboard point on the rim.

b. Grasp the tire (top and bottom), then pull outward on the top and push inward on the bottom; record the reading on the dial indicator.

c. Grasp the tire (top and bottom), then pull outward on the bottom and push inward on the top; record the reading on the dial indicator.

d. The difference in the dial indicator reading is the horizontal deflection of both joints. If the reading exceeds 0.125 in. (3.2mm), the lower ball joint should be checked for wear in order to determine what component(s) must be replaced.

➡The lower ball joints used on 2WD vehicles use wear indicators.

6. On 4WD vehicles (no wear indicators), check the lower ball joint for wear:

a. With the vehicle still supported by jackstands, place a dial indicator against the spindle in order to measure vertical movement.

➡DO NOT pry between the lower control arm and the drive axle seal or damage to the seal will result.

b. Pry between the lower control arm and the outer bearing race while reading the dial indicator. This reading will show vertical deflection (looseness).

c. The lower ball joint is not a pre-loaded joint and may show some looseness, but it should be replaced if movement exceeds 0.125 in. (3.2mm).

7. For 2WD vehicles check for lower ball joint wear using the indicators:

a. Visually inspect the positioning of the grease fitting on the ball joint. The fitting is threaded into a small housing nub which projects approximately 0.050 in. (1.27mm) beyond the surface of the ball joint cover on new parts. As the joint wears, the nub will slowly retreat inward. If the housing nub is visible above the cover, then the joint is still good.

b. If necessary, scrape a screwdriver or fingernail across the ball joint cover and feel for the housing nub. If the housing is flush or inside the cover surface, the joint is worn and should be replaced.

8. Finally, if the joints failed the initial combined test, but the lower joint is found good, the upper ball joint should be checked for looseness as it is probably the culprit:

a. Disconnect the upper ball joint from the steering knuckle.

b. Check for any looseness or if the stud can be twisted by hand. If so, the joint should be replaced.

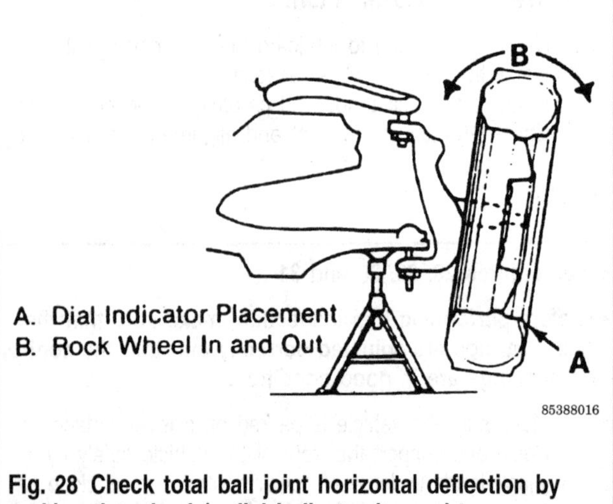

Fig. 28 Check total ball joint horizontal deflection by rocking the wheel (a dial indicator is used to measure play)

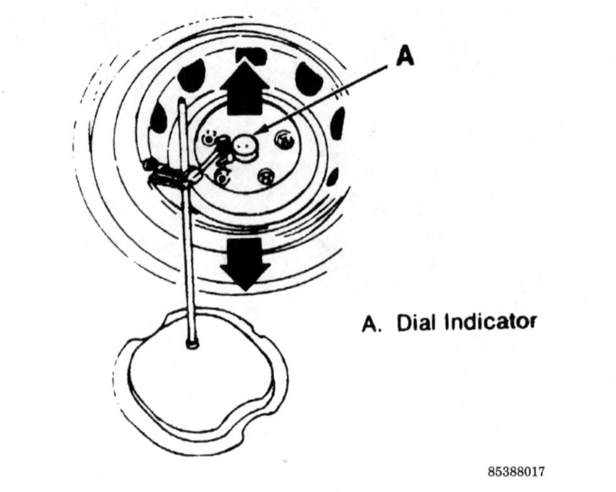

Fig. 29 A dial indicator may also be used to check lower joint vertical deflection

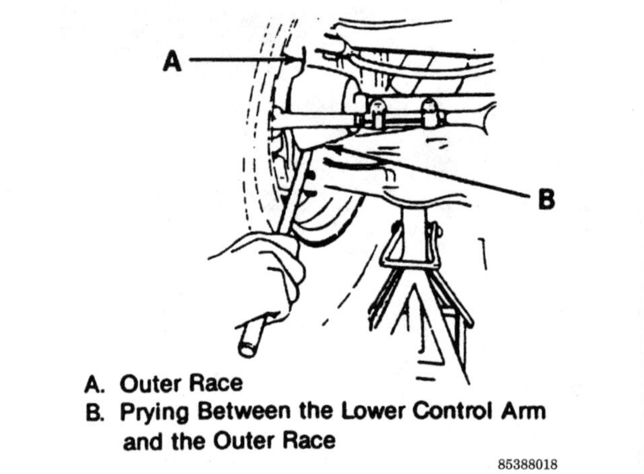

Fig. 30 Use a prybar to carefully pry between the lower control arm and outer race (NOT on the drive axle joint/seal)

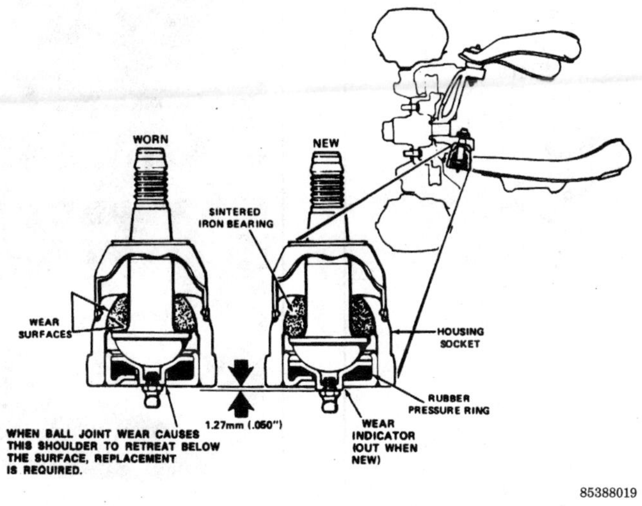

Fig. 31 The lower joints on late model 2WD vehicles are equipped with wear indicators

Stabilizer Bar

REMOVAL & INSTALLATION

2WD Vehicles

➧ See Figure 32

1. Raise and support the front of the vehicle safely using jackstands.
2. If necessary, remove the front wheels for additional access.
3. Loosen the nut from the top of one of the the link bolts, then remove the retainer and grommet so the stabilizer may be separated from the link bolt.
4. If necessary, remove the link bolt, washers and grommets, but make sure all components remain in order on the link bolt once it is removed in order to ease installation.

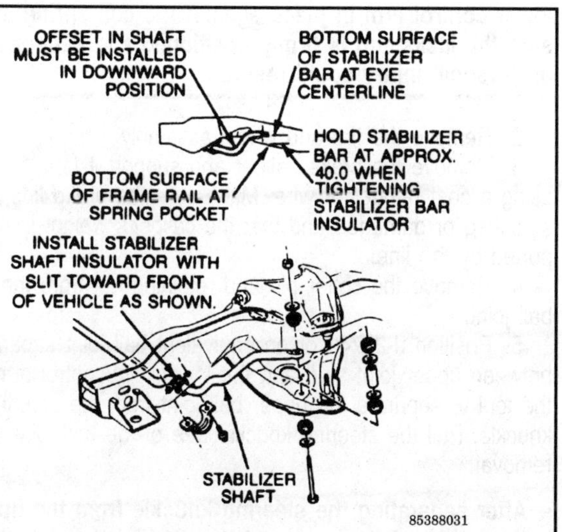

Fig. 32 Front stabilizer bar mounting — 2WD vehicles

5. Loosen the nut from the top of the other link bolt and separate it from the stabilizer in the same fashion. If the link bolt and components are completely removed, be sure to tag or arrange everything to assure installation on the same side.
6. Unfasten the bolts retaining the stabilizer brackets to the frame, then remove the stabilizer bar from the vehicle.
7. If necessary, remove the rubber bushings (insulators).

To install:

8. If removed, install the rubber bushings to the stabilizer bar, making sure they are positioned with the slits facing toward the front of the vehicle.
9. Position the stabilizer shaft, then install the brackets over the bushings to retain the shaft. Tighten the bracket bolts to 24 ft. lbs. (33 Nm).
10. Install the link bolts making sure the positioning of the grommets, retainers and washers is correct. If necessary, refer to the illustration for classification. But keep in mind the grommets are normally surrounded by washers/retainers or components (control arm or stabilizer).
11. Install the upper grommet, retainer and nut to the top of each link bolt, then tighten to 13 ft. lbs. (17 Nm).
12. If removed, install the front wheels.
13. Remove the jackstands and carefully lower the truck.

4WD Vehicles

➧ See Figures 33, 34 and 35

➡Installation of the stabilizer bar requires that the torsion bar be unloaded using a special unloader tool used during tension bar removal. Do not attempt this procedure without the unloader. For details on the unloader and its use, please refer to the torsion bar procedure found earlier in this section.

1. Raise and support the front of the vehicle safely using jackstands.
2. Remove the stabilizer bar clamp-to-control arm retaining bolts, then remove the clamps.
3. Remove the stabilizer bar clamp-to-frame retaining bolts/nuts, then remove the clamps and carefully lower the stabilizer bar from the vehicle.
4. If necessary remove the bushings (insulators).

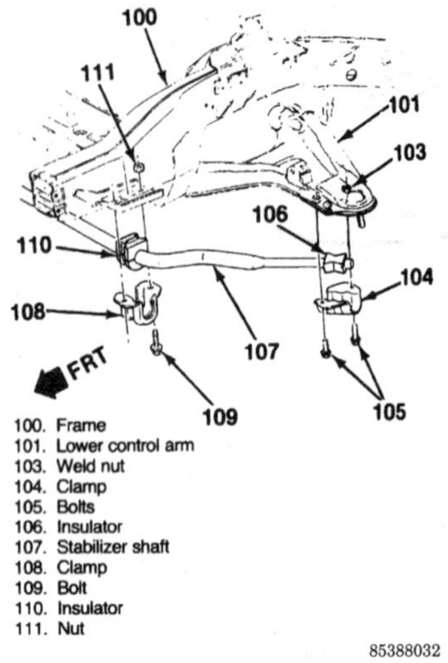

Fig. 33 Front stabilizer bar mounting — 4WD vehicles

To install:

5. Using a tension bar unloader tool, properly unload the tension bar.

6. If removed, install the insulators to the stabilizer bar, making sure the slits in the insulators face forward.

7. Position the stabilizer bar to the frame and lower control arm, then loosely install the clamps and retaining bolts.

8. Tighten the bar clamp-to-control arm retaining bolts to 24 ft. lbs. (33 Nm) on 1994-95 models and 124 inch lbs. (14 Nm) on 1996-97 models.

9. Install the frame clamps to the insulators and frames, then tighten the retaining bolts/nuts to 35 ft. lbs. (48 Nm).

10. Remove the jackstands and carefully lower the vehicle.

11. Check and/or adjust the vehicle trim height, as necessary.

Fig. 34 When removing the 4WD stabilizer bar, first loosen the control arm clamp bolts

Fig. 35 Loosen and remove the frame clamp retainers

Upper Control Arm and Bushing

REMOVAL & INSTALLATION

2WD Vehicles

See Figures 36, 37 and 38

➡The following procedure requires the use of a ball joint separator tool such as J-23742 or equivalent.

1. Raise and support the front of the vehicle safely by placing jackstands securely under the lower control arms. Because the vehicle's weight is used to relieve spring tension on the upper control arm, the floor stands must be positioned between the spring seats and the lower control arm ball joints for maximum leverage.

****CAUTION**

With components unbolted, the jackstand is holding the lower control arm in place against the coil spring. Make sure the jackstand is firmly positioned and cannot move, or personal injury could result.

2. Remove the tire and wheel assembly.

3. Remove the brake caliper and support it from the vehicle using a coat hanger or wire. Make sure the brake line is not stretched or damaged and that the caliper's weight is not supported by the line.

4. Remove the cotter pin and retaining nut from the upper ball joint.

5. Position J-23742 or an equivalent ball joint separator tool between upper joint stud and the lower joint/control arm. Use the tool to separate the upper ball joint from the steering knuckle. Pull the steering knuckle free of the ball joint after removal.

➡After separating the steering knuckle from the upper ball joint, be sure to support the steering knuckle/hub assembly to prevent damaging the brake hose.

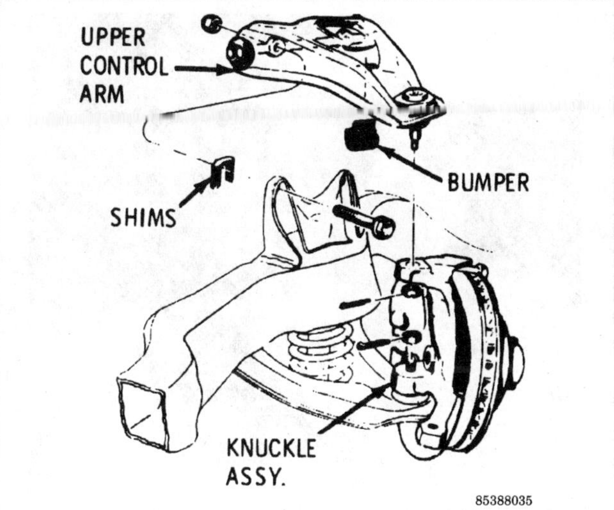

Fig. 36 Upper control arm mounting — 2WD vehicles

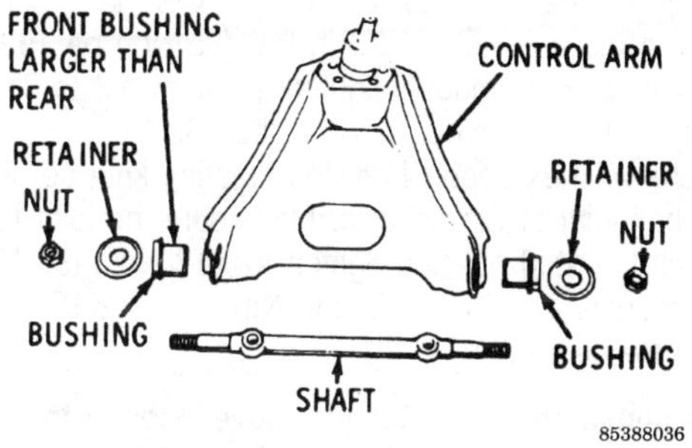

Fig. 37 Exploded view of the upper control arm and bushing components

6. Unfasten the upper control arm-to-frame nuts and bolts, then lift and remove the upper control arm from the vehicle.

➡**Tape the shims together and identify them to assure that they are re-installed in the same place**

7. Clean and inspect the steering knuckle hole. Replace the steering knuckle if any out of roundness is noted.
8. If replacement is necessary, mount the control arm in a vise, then remove the pivot shaft nuts and washers. Use a control arm bushing fixture (C-clamp like tool) along with a slotted washer and a piece of pipe (slightly larger than the bushing) to remove the old bushings.

To install

9. If removed, position the pivot shaft to the control arm and install the bushing using the fixture tool, washer and a length of pipe with the same outer diameter as the bushing.
10. Tighten the tool until the bushing is positioned on the shaft as shown in the illustration. Loosely install the bushing retaining nuts and washers. Tighten the bushing nuts to 85 ft. lbs. (115 Nm).

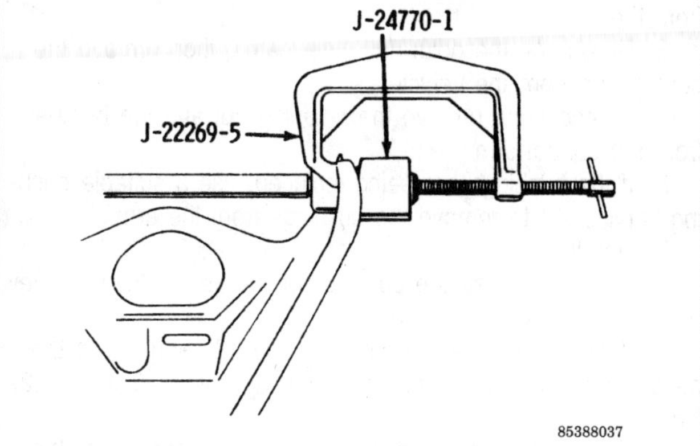

Fig. 38 Upper control arm bushing installation — 2WD vehicles

11. Loosely install the control arm to the frame using the bolts and nuts. Position the shims as noted during removal, then tighten the retainers to 65 ft. lbs. (88 Nm).

➡**On most vehicles, the left upper control arm shaft must have the depression facing inboard.**

12. Remove the support from the steering knuckle, then install the ball joint to the knuckle. Make sure the joint is seated, then install the stud nut. Install a new cotter pin.

➡**When installing the cotter pin, never loosen the castle nut to expose the cotter pin hole.**

13. Reposition and secure the brake caliper.
14. Install the tire and wheel assembly.
15. Remove the jackstands and carefully lower the vehicle.
16. Check and adjust the front end alignment, as necessary.

4WD Vehicles

See Figures 39, 40 and 41

1. Raise and support the front of the vehicle safely using jackstands.
2. Remove the tire and wheel assembly.
3. Remove the cotter pin from the ball joint, then loosen the retaining nut.

➡**After separating the steering knuckle from the upper ball joint, be sure to support the steering knuckle/hub assembly to prevent damaging the brake hose.**

4. Position a suitable ball joint separator tool such as J-36607 or equivalent, then carefully loosen the joint in the steering knuckle. Disengage the tool and the retaining nut, then remove the joint from the knuckle.

➡**The 4WD vehicles covered by this manual do not use shims to adjust the front wheel alignment. Instead, the upper control arm bolts are equipped with cams which are rotated to achieve caster and camber adjustments. In order to preserve adjustment and ease installation, matchmark the cams to the control arm before removal. If the control arm is being replaced, transfer the alignment marks to the new component before installation.**

5. Unfasten the front and rear nuts retaining the control arm retaining bolts to the frame, then remove the outer cams from the bolts.

6. Disengage the bolts and inner cams, then remove the control arm from the vehicle.

7. If necessary, remove the retaining nut and the bumper from the control arm.

8. If the bushings are being replaced, use a suitable bushing service set to remove the bushings from the arm.

To install:

9. If removed, use the bushing service set to drive the new bushings into the control arm.

10. If removed, install the bumper and retaining nut to the control arm. Tighten the bumper retaining nut to 20 ft. lbs. (27 Nm).

11. Position the control arm to the vehicle, then install the retaining bolts (from the inside of the frame brackets facing outward) and the inner cams. The inner cams must be positioned on the bolts before they are inserted through the control arm and frame brackets.

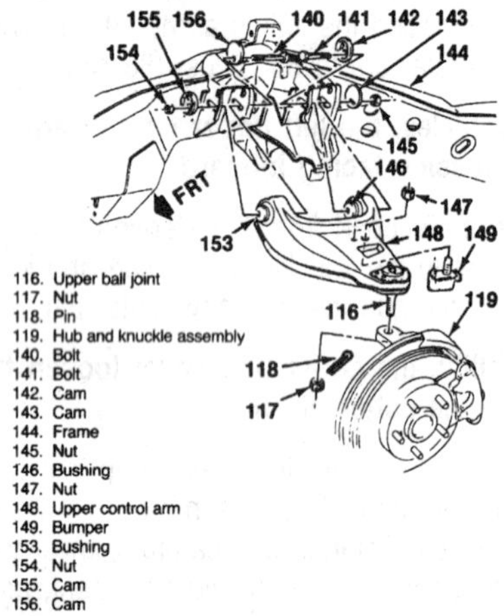

85388038

Fig. 39 Exploded view of the upper control arm mounting — 4WD vehicles

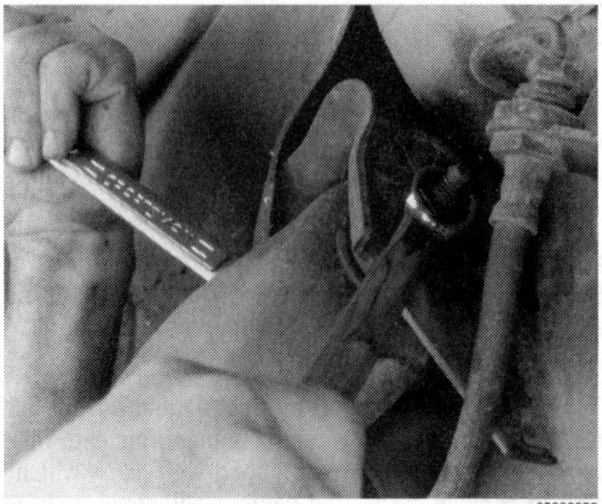

85388039

Fig. 40 Matchmark the cams to the control arm before removal.

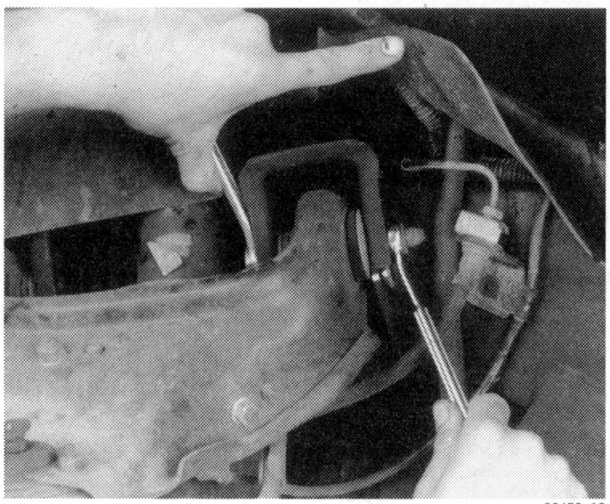

88458p12

Fig. 41 Loosen the end retaining nuts from the upper control arm bolts

12. Position the outer cams over the retaining bolts, then install the nuts to the ends of the bolts at the front and rear of the control arm.

13. Align the cams to the reference marks made earlier, then tighten the end nuts to 70 ft. lbs. (95 Nm) on 1994-95 models. On 1996-97 models tighten the front nut to 85 ft. lbs. (115 Nm) and the rear nut to 72 ft. lbs. (98 Nm).

14. Remove the support from the steering knuckle, then install the ball joint to the knuckle. Make sure the joint is seated, then install the stud nut and tighten to 70 ft. lbs. (95 Nm) on 1994-95 models and 61 ft. lbs. (83 Nm) on 1996-97 models. Install a new cotter pin.

➡When installing the cotter pin, never loosen the castle nut to expose the cotter pin hole, but DO NOT tighten more than an additional $\frac{1}{6}$ turn.

15. Install the tire and wheel assembly.

16. Remove the jackstands and carefully lower the vehicle.

17. Check and adjust the front end alignment, as necessary.

Lower Control Arm and Bushing

REMOVAL & INSTALLATION

2WD Vehicles

➧ See Figure 42

1. Remove the coil spring from the vehicle. For details, please refer to the procedure located earlier in this section.

2. If not done already, remove the tire and wheel assembly.

3. Remove the brake caliper and support it from the vehicle using a coat hanger or wire. Make sure the brake line is not stretched or damaged and that the caliper's weight is not supported by the line.

4. Remove the cotter pin and retaining nut from the upper ball joint.

5. Position J-23742 or an equivalent ball joint separator tool between upper joint stud and the upper joint/control arm. Use

the tool to separate the ball joint from the steering knuckle. Pull the steering knuckle free of the ball joint after removal.

➡After separating the steering knuckle from the upper ball joint, be sure to support the steering knuckle/hub assembly to prevent damaging the brake hose. Also, support the lower control arm and guide it out of the opening in the splash shield.

6. Remove the jam nuts from the back of each lower control arm pivot bolt.
7. Unfasten the pivot bolts (noting the direction in which they are facing), then remove the control arm from the vehicle.
8. If the bushings are beings replaced, use a suitable bushing service set to remove the bushings from the control arm. The front bushing is normally flared and the flare must be driven down flush with the rubber using a blunt chisel before attempting removal.

To install:

9. If the bushings were removed, use the bushing service set to install them to the control arms. If the front bushing is the flared type, use a flaring tool to produce an approximate flare of 45 degrees.
10. Position the control arm to the vehicle.
11. Install the pivot bolts as noted during removal. For most vehicles covered by this manual, that means they should be installed with the heads forward, facing the rear.
12. Install the jam nuts and tighten to 67 ft. lbs. (90 Nm) on both nuts on 1994-95 models. On 1996-97 models tighten the front nut to 85 ft. lbs. (115 Nm) and the rear nut to 72 ft. lbs. (98 Nm).
13. Remove the support from the steering knuckle, then install the ball joint to the knuckle. Make sure the joint is seated, then install the stud nut. Install a new cotter pin.

➡When installing the cotter pin, never loosen the castle nut to expose the cotter pin hole.

14. Reposition and secure the brake caliper.
15. Install the tire and wheel assembly.
16. Remove the jackstands and carefully lower the vehicle.
17. Check and adjust the front end alignment, as necessary.

4WD Vehicles

➧ See Figure 43

1. Raise and support the front of the vehicle safely using jackstands.
2. Remove the tire and wheel assembly.
3. Remove the stabilizer bar. For details, please refer to the procedures earlier in this section. Installation of the stabilizer bar will require use of a torsion bar unloader tool.
4. Remove the shock absorber.
5. Unfasten the lower control arm-to-frame nuts, then withdraw the bolts, noting the direction they were facing for installation purposes. Remove the lower control arm from the truck.
6. If necessary, use a suitable bushing service set to remove the bushings from the lower control arm.

To install:

7. If removed, use the service set to install new bushings to the lower control arm.
8. Position the control arm in the vehicle, installing the front leg of the lower control arm into the crossmember before installing the rear leg into the frame bracket.
9. Insert the control arm retaining bolts in the direction noted during removal. For most vehicles, they should be inserted from the rear of the truck facing forward.
10. Install the lower control arm retaining nuts and tighten them with the suspension at normal trim height to 70 ft. lbs. (95 Nm) for 1994-95 for both nuts. On 1996-97 models tighten both nuts to 81 ft. lbs. (110 Nm)
11. Install the shock absorber.
12. Properly unload the torsion bar, then install the stabilizer bar. Adjust the torsion bar, as necessary. For details, please refer to the procedures located earlier in this section.
13. Install the tire and wheel assembly.
14. Remove the jackstands and carefully lower the vehicle.

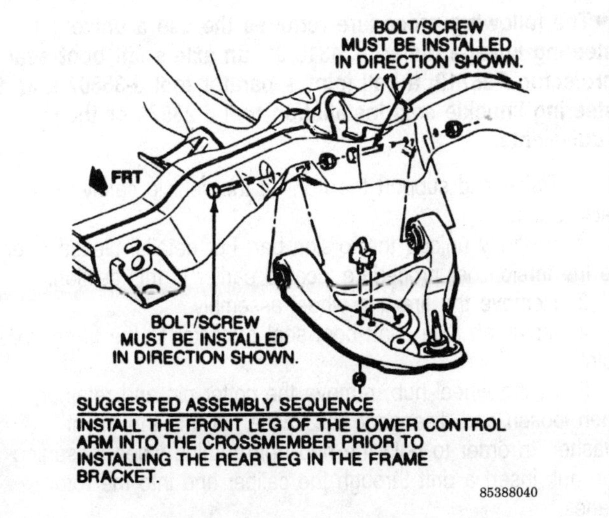

Fig. 42 Lower control arm mounting — 2WD vehicles

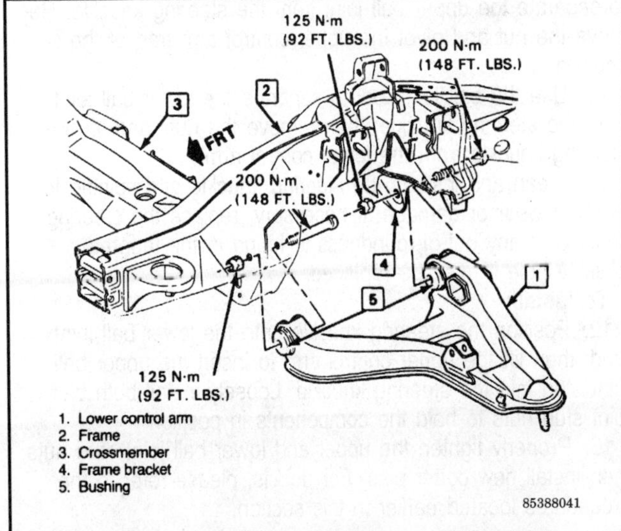

Fig. 43 Lower control arm mounting — 4WD vehicles

Steering Knuckle and Spindle

REMOVAL & INSTALLATION

2WD Vehicles

See Figure 44

1. Raise and support the front of the vehicle frame using jackstands.

When supporting the vehicle on jackstands, DO NOT place the jackstands under the lower control arms as spring tension will be used to help separate the ball joint studs from the knuckle. Place the jackstands under the frame and use a suitable floor jack under the control arm for safety.

2. Remove the tire and wheel assembly.
3. Remove the brake caliper from the steering knuckle and hang it from the vehicle using wire or a coat hanger. Make sure the brake line is not stretched or otherwise damaged.
4. Remove the grease cup, the cotter pin, the castle nut and the hub-and-rotor assembly. For details, please refer to the the brake rotor (disc) procedure located in Section 9 of this manual.
5. Remove the splash shield-to-steering knuckle bolts and separate the shield from the knuckle.
6. At the tie rod end-to-steering knuckle stud, remove the cotter pin and the nut. Using suitable jawed tie rod end puller tools such as J-6627, J-24319-01 or their equivalent to separate the tie rod end from the steering knuckle.
7. Position a floor jack under the spring seat of the lower control arm in order to retain the spring seat. Raise the floor jack until it just contacts the arm.
8. Remove the cotter pins from the upper and lower ball joint studs, then loosen the retaining nuts.
9. Use a ball joint separator such as J-23742 or equivalent to separate the upper ball joint from the steering knuckle. Remove the nut and pivot the upper control arm free of the knuckle.
10. Use the ball joint tool to separate the lower ball joint from the steering knuckle, then remove the nuts and lift the steering knuckle from the lower control arm.
11. Clean and inspect the steering knuckle and spindle for signs of wear or damage; if necessary, replace the steering knuckle. If any out-of-roundness is found in the tapered knuckle hole it must be replaced.

To install:

12. Position the steering knuckle onto the lower ball joint stud, then lift the upper control arm to insert the upper ball joint stud into the steering knuckle. Loosely install both ball joint stud nuts to hold the components in position.
13. Properly tighten the upper and lower ball joint stud nuts, then install new cotter pins. For details, please refer to the procedures located earlier in this section.

When installing a cotter pin, never loosen the castle nut to expose the cotter pin hole.

14. If equipped, position a new steering knuckle gasket.

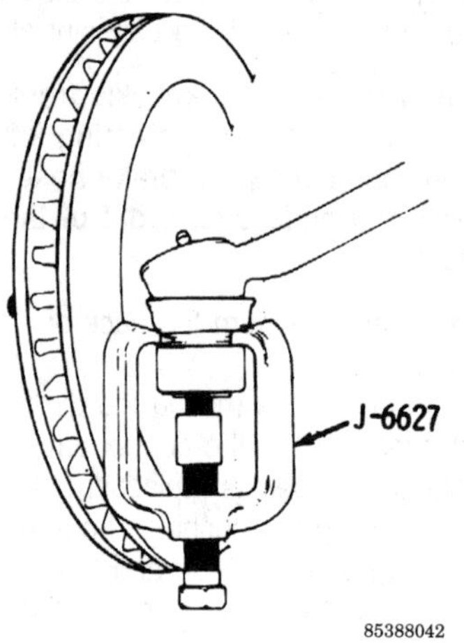

Fig. 44 Use a suitable jawed tie rod end puller to separate the end from the steering knuckle

15. Install the splash shield to the knuckle and secure the retaining bolts.
16. Install the tie rod end to the steering knuckle, then tighten the stud nut to specification and install a new cotter pin.
17. Install the hub and rotor assembly and castle nut. Properly adjust the wheel bearings, then install a new cotter pin followed by the grease cup. For wheel bearing adjustment procedures, please refer to Section 1 of this manual.
18. Remove the support, then reposition and secure the brake caliper.
19. Install the tire and wheel assembly.
20. Remove the jackstands and carefully lower the vehicle.
21. Check and/or adjust the front end alignment, as necessary.

4WD Vehicles

See Figures 45, 46, 47 and 48

The following procedure requires the use a universal steering linkage puller J-24319-01, an axle shaft boot seal protector J-28712, a ball joint separator tool J-36607 and a steering knuckle seal Installation tool J-28574 or their equivalents.

1. Raise and support the front of the vehicle safely using jackstands.
2. Properly unload the torsion bar. For details, please refer to the torsion bar procedure located earlier in this section.
3. Remove the tire and wheel assembly.
4. Install an axle shaft boot seal protector to the tri-pot axle joint.
5. At the wheel hub, remove the cotter pin and retainer, then loosen and disengage the castle nut and the thrust washer. In order to hold the hub from turning when loosening the nut, insert a drift through the caliper and into the rotor vanes.
6. Remove the brake caliper and support it aside using wire or a coat hanger. Make sure the brake line is not stretched or damaged.
7. Remove the brake disc from the wheel hub.

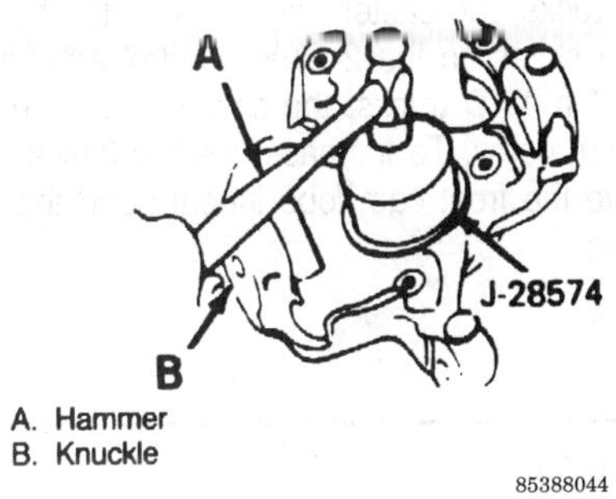

Fig. 45 Installing a new seal on the 4WD steering knuckle

Fig. 46 Remove the cotter pin from the drive axle end nut and retainer

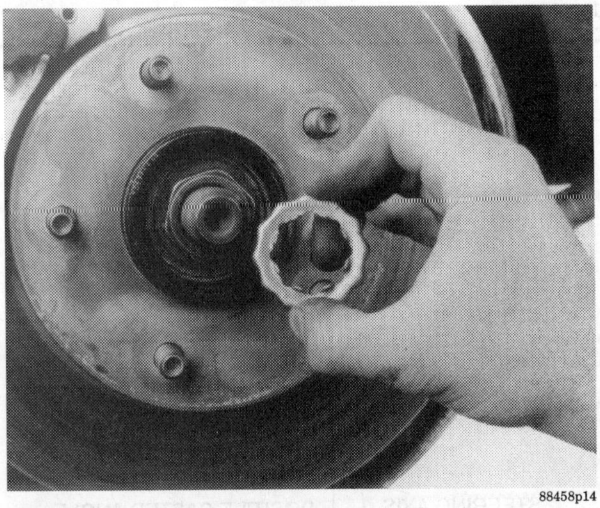

Fig. 47 Remove the retainer for access to the end nut

Fig. 48 Loosen the drive axle nut — here the caliper is installed so a drift could be inserted to keep the disc from spinning

8. Remove the bolts retaining the hub/bearing assembly to the knuckle, then carefully pull the assembly from the splined end of the halfshaft. If available, use J-28733-A, or an equivalent spindle remover to prevent damage to the shaft or hub/bearing assembly.

➡When removed, lay the hub and bearing assembly on the hub bolt (outboard) side in order to prevent damage or contamination of the bearing seal.

9. Remove the splash shield.
10. Remove the cotter pin and castle nut from the tie rod end, then separate the end from the knuckle using a suitable steering linkage puller.
11. Remove the cotter pins from the ball joints, then loosen the stud nuts.
12. Use the ball joint separator tool J-36607 or equivalent to loosen the ball joints in the steering knuckle.
13. Unfasten the ball joint nuts, then separate the ball joints from the knuckle and remove the knuckle from the vehicle.
14. Remove the spacer and the seal from the steering knuckle.
15. Clean and inspect the parts for nicks, scores and/or damage, then replace them as necessary.

To install:

16. Install a new seal into the steering knuckle, using a knuckle seal installation tool such as J-28574 or equivalent.
17. Install the spacer, then position the knuckle and insert the upper and lower ball joints.
18. Install the upper and lower ball joint stud nuts and tighten to specification, then install new cotter pins. For details, please refer to the ball joint procedures located earlier in this section.
19. Align the splash shield to the knuckle, then install the hub and bearing assembly, aligning the threaded holes.
20. Install the retaining bolts and tighten to 77 ft. lbs. (105 Nm).
21. Install the tie rod end of the steering knuckle, then secure using the retaining nut and a new cotter pin.
22. Install the brake disc.
23. Reposition and secure the brake caliper.

24. Install the washer and retaining nut to the end of the halfshaft. Insert a brass drift to keep the rotor and hub from turning, then tighten the shaft nut to 180 ft. lbs. (245 Nm).
25. Install the retainer and a new cotter pin, but DO NOT back off specification in order to insert the cotter pin.
26. Remove the torsion bar unloader tool and the drive axle boot protector.
27. Install the tire and wheel assembly.
28. Remove the jackstands and carefully lower the vehicle.
29. Check and/or adjust the vehicle trim height, as necessary.

Front Wheel Bearings

REMOVAL & INSTALLATION

2WD Vehicles

For wheel bearing removal, packing, installation and adjustment procedures on 2WD vehicles, please refer to Section 1 of this manual.

4WD Vehicles

➡The wheel bearing is installed in the wheel hub assembly and is serviced by replacement only.

Please refer to the appropriate portion of the steering knuckle procedure earlier in this section in order to replace the wheel hub assembly.

Front End Alignment

If the tires are worn unevenly, if the vehicle is not stable on the highway or if the handling seems uneven in spirited driving, wheel alignment should be checked. If an alignment problem is suspected, first check tire inflation and look for other possible causes such as worn suspension and steering components, accident damage or unmatched tires. Repairs may be necessary before the wheels can be properly aligned. Wheel alignment requires sophisticated equipment and can only be performed at a properly equipped shop.

CASTER

➧ See Figure 49

Caster is a measure of the angle between the steering axis and vertical, as viewed from the side of the vehicle when the wheels are in the straight ahead position. Stated another way, it is the tilting of the front steering axis either forward or backward from the vertical. A backward tilt is said to be positive (+) and a forward tilt is said to be negative (-).

Although is it measured using a special instrument, it can usually be seen by observing the location of the upper and lower control arm ball joints. A line drawn through the center of these 2 points represents the steering axis. When looking straight downward from the top of the upper control arm you can see if the ball joints are not aligned, indicating that the caster angle is more or less than 0 degrees. If vehicle has positive caster, the lower ball joint would be located ahead of the upper ball joint center line. If the vehicle has negative caster, the lower ball joint would be located behind the upper joint center line.

On 2WD trucks, the caster may be adjusted by changing placement of shims on the 2 upper control arm pivot shaft-to-frame bolts. On 4WD trucks, the caster is adjusted by turning the adjustment cams. To increase positive caster on a 4WD vehicle, move the front cam lobe inboard and the rear cam lobe outboard.

CAMBER

➧ See Figure 50

Camber is the measure of wheel tilt from the vertical direction, when the wheel is viewed from the rear of the vehicle. Camber is negative when the top of the wheel is inboard and positive when the top is outboard. Always check for bent, damaged or worn suspension components before determining that adjustment is necessary. The amount of tilt is measured in degrees from the vertical and this measurement is called the camber angle.

On 2WD vehicles, camber is adjusted by removing or adding shims at both front and rear pivot shaft-to-frame contact points. To increase camber, subtract shims equally from both locations. On 4WD vehicles, adjustment is once again made using the adjustment cams.

TOE-IN

➧ See Figure 51

Toe is a measurement of how far a wheel is turned in or out from the straight ahead direction. When the front of the wheel is turned in, the toe is positive. When the front of the wheel is turned out, toe is negative. An incorrect toe setting can affect steering feel and cause excessive tire wear.

Stated another way, toe-in is the amount that the front of the wheels are closer together than the backs of the same wheels.

The actual amount of toe-in is normally only a fraction of a degree.

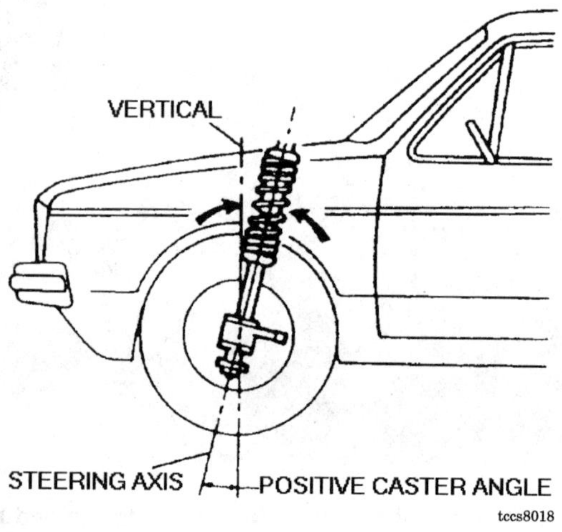

Fig. 49 Caster angle effects straight line stability

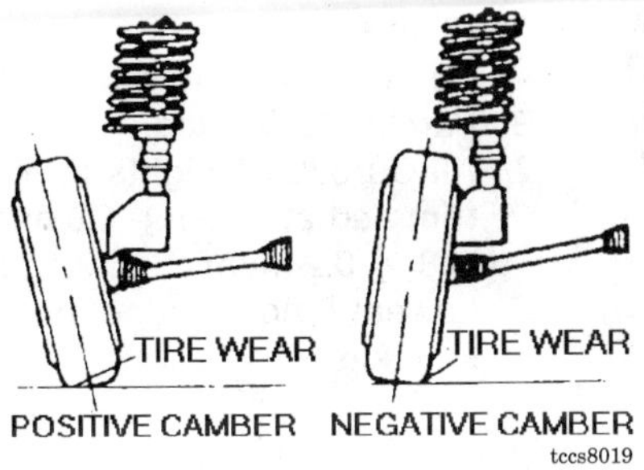

Fig. 50 Camber angle influences tire contact with the road

Toe adjustment is normally performed as the last of the wheel alignment settings (after caster and camber). It is adjusted by turning the tie rod adjustment sleeves in order to obtain the proper specification. After setting, the number of threads inside the adjuster sleeve must be equal, within a tolerance of 3 threads, on either end of the sleeve.

TRIM HEIGHT

See Figures 52, 53 and 54

The trim height "Z" measurement is used as an indicator if the front suspension is properly set-up. The height may be checked following suspension repairs or if damage to the suspension is suspected, such as after hitting a large pot hole. Refer to the illustrations for proper measurements.

On 2WD vehicles, if the measurement is out of specification, check for worn or damaged suspension components. On 4WD vehicles, some adjustment is possible through the torsion bar adjuster. Turning the adjustment bolt one full revolution will increase/decrease "Z" height by 0.2 in. (6.0mm). If a proper adjustment cannot be obtained, check for worn or damaged components. The proper specification for most 4WD models is 4.6-5.0 in. (116-128mm)

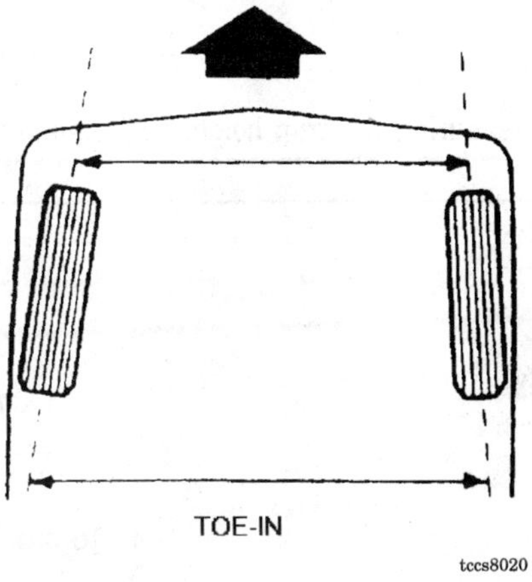

Fig. 51 Toe-in means the distance between the wheels is closer at the front than at the rear of the wheels

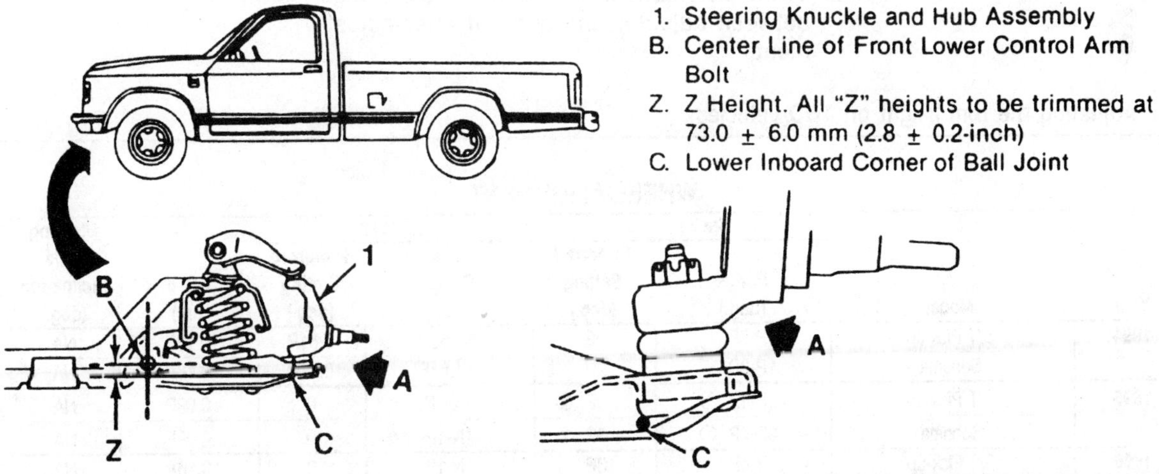

Fig. 52 Measuring the trim height "Z" dimension — 2WD vehicles

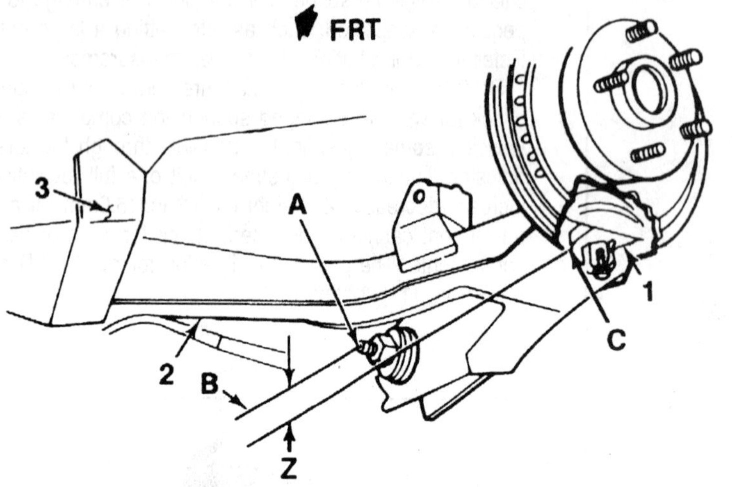

1. Knuckle and Hub Assembly
2. Lower Control Arm
3. Frame

A. Center Line of Pivot Bolt
B. Parallel to Ground
Z. All Curb "Z" Heights to be trimmed at 122.0 ± 6.0 mm (4.8 ± 0.2-inch)
C. Lowest inboard edge of knuckle.

85388056

Fig. 53 Measuring the trim height "Z" dimension — 4WD vehicles

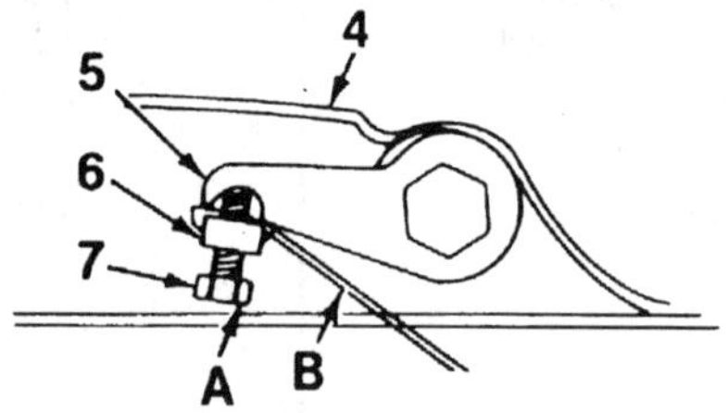

4. Torsion Bar Support
5. Torsion Arm
6. Nut
7. Bolt

A. One revolution of bolt into nut increases front "Z" height by 6.0 mm (0.2-inch).
B. 1 mm (0.04-inch) clearance must be provided between adjuster arm and nut after adjustment.

85388057

Fig. 54 Adjusting the trim height on 4WD vehicles

WHEEL ALIGNMENT

Year	Model	Caster Range (deg.)	Caster Preferred Setting (deg.)	Camber Range (deg.)	Camber Preferred Setting (deg.)	Toe-in (in.)	Steering Axis Inclination (deg.)
1994	S/T Pick-up	1P-3P	2P	0-1.63P	0.81P	0.16P	NA
	Sonoma	1P-3P	2P	0-1.63P	0.81P	0.16P	NA
1995	S/T Pick-up	2P-4P ①	3P ②	1N-1P	0	0.09P	NA
	Sonoma	2P-4P ①	3P ②	1N-1P	0	0.09P	NA
1996	S/T Pick-up	2P-4P	3P	1N-1P	0	0.16P	NA
	Sonoma	2P-4P	3P	1N-1P	0	0.16P	NA
1997	S/T Pick-up	2P-4P ①	3P ②	1N-1P	0	0.09P	NA
	Sonoma	2P-4P ①	3P ②	1N-1P	0	0.09P	NA

NOTE: The Service Parts Identification Label will show all the applicable option codes for the vehicle.

NA - Not Available

① Use 1P-3P for vehicles with the following suspension packages: G51, Z85, ZM6 amd ZR2

② Use 2P for vehicles with the following suspension packages: G51, Z85, ZM6 amd ZR2

88458C01

REAR SUSPENSION

The rear suspension system consists of 3 major components. The double acting shock absorbers, variable rate multi-leaf springs and the solid rear axle assembly. The multi-leaf springs are connected to the frame by a hanger assembly with integral bushings in the front and a shackle assembly with integral bushings in the rear. In response to different road and payload conditions, the shackle assembly allows the leaf spring to "change its length". The rear axle is connected to both the leaf springs and the shock absorbers by various attaching parts.

➡For rear axle service procedures, please refer to Section 7 of this manual.

Leaf Springs

REMOVAL & INSTALLATION

➧ See Figures 55 and 56

➡The following procedure requires the use of two sets of jackstands.

1. Raise and support the rear frame of the vehicle safely using jackstands. Support the rear axle with the second set of jackstands.

➡When supporting the rear of the vehicle, support the axle and the body separately in order to relieve the load on the rear spring.

2. Remove the tire and wheel assembly.
3. Remove the shock absorber.
4. Remove the U-bolt nuts, washers, anchor plate and bolts.
5. Remove the spare tire, if equipped.
6. Remove the shackle-to-frame bolt, washers and nut.
7. Remove the fuel tank, if necessary. For details, please refer to Section 5 of this manual.
8. Remove the front bracket nut, washers and bolt.
9. Carefully remove the spring from the vehicle.
10. If necessary, unfasten the shackle-to-spring nut, washers and bolts, then remove the shackle from the spring.

To install:

11. If removed, install the shackle to the rearward spring eye using the bolt, washers and nut, but do not fully tighten at this time.
12. Position the spring assembly to the vehicle.
13. Install the spring to the front bracket using the retaining bolt, washers and nut, but do not fully tighten at this time.
14. If removed, install the fuel tank.
15. Install the shackle-to-frame bolt, washers and nut, but do not fully tighten at this time. If used, remove the spring support.
16. Install the U-bolts, anchor plate, washers and U-bolt nuts. Tighten the U-bolt nuts using 2 passes of a diagonal sequence. First tighten the nuts to 18 ft. lbs. (25 Nm), then tighten them to 85 ft. lbs. (115 Nm).
17. Position the axle to achieve an approximate gap of 6.46-6.94 in. (164-176mm) between the axle housing tube and the metal surface of the rubber frame bumper bracket. Measure from the housing between the U-bolts to the metal part of the rubber bump stop on the frame.
18. While supporting the axle in this position, tighten the front and rear spring mounting fasteners to 92 ft. lbs. (125 Nm).
19. Install the shock absorber.
20. Remove the jackstands and carefully lower the vehicle.

Shock Absorbers

REMOVAL & INSTALLATION

➧ See Figures 57, 58 and 59

1. Raise and support the rear of the truck safely using jackstands. Support the rear axle securely using a jackstands or a floor jack. The axle must be supported to prevent overextension and damage to the brake lines once the shock is removed.
2. Remove the shock absorber-to-frame retainers at the top of the shock.
3. Remove the shock-to-axle retainers at the bottom of the shock.
4. Remove the shock absorber from the vehicle.

To install:

5. Position the shock in the vehicle and loosely install the upper mounting fasteners to retain it.
6. Align the lower-end of the shock absorber with the axle mounting, then loosely install the retainers.
7. On 1994-95 models, tighten the upper shock absorber retainers to 17 ft. lbs. (23 Nm). Then tighten lower shock absorber fastener to 47 ft. lbs. (64 Nm).
8. On 1996-97 models, tighten the upper shock absorber retainers 22 ft. lbs. (30 Nm). Then tighten the lower shock absorber fastener to 62 ft. lbs. (84 Nm).
9. Remove the jackstands and carefully lower the vehicle.

TESTING

There are 2 possible clues that the shock absorbers are worn and may need replacement. The first is how the vehicle rides and the second is how the shocks appear. The shocks should be checked if the ride of your vehicle has become increasingly bouncy or if oil is visible on the shock, indicating possible fluid leakage.

Visually inspect the shock absorber if trouble or wear is suspected. If the shock absorber is covered with oil and there is evidence of leakage, the shock is defective and should be replaced.

If there is no sign of excessive leakage (a small amount of weeping is normal) but the ride is still suspect, bounce the truck at one corner by pressing down on the rear bumper and releasing. When you have the truck bouncing as much as you can, release the fender or bumper. The truck should stop bouncing after the first rebound. If the bouncing continues past

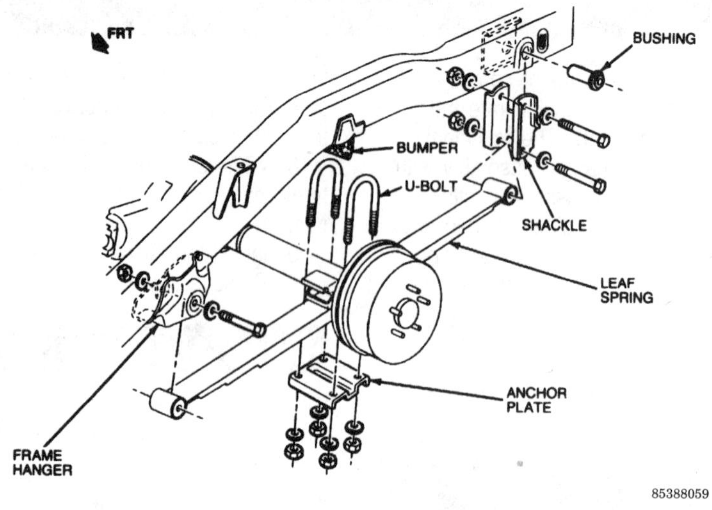

Fig. 55 Rear leaf spring and axle mounting

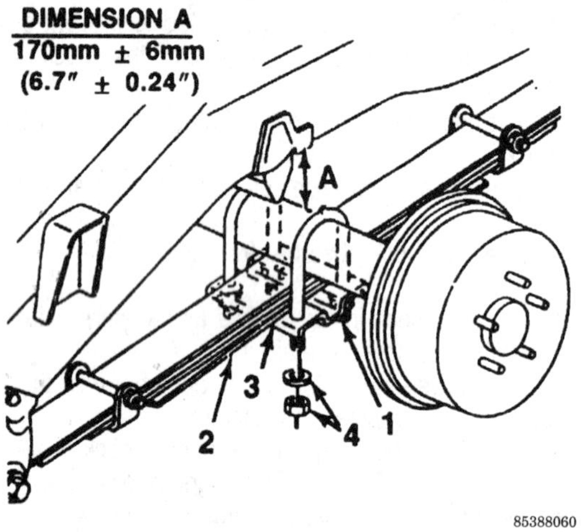

Fig. 56 Leaf spring U-bolts tighten sequence and axle tube-to-bumper bracket dimension

Fig. 58 Unfasten the lower shock retainer

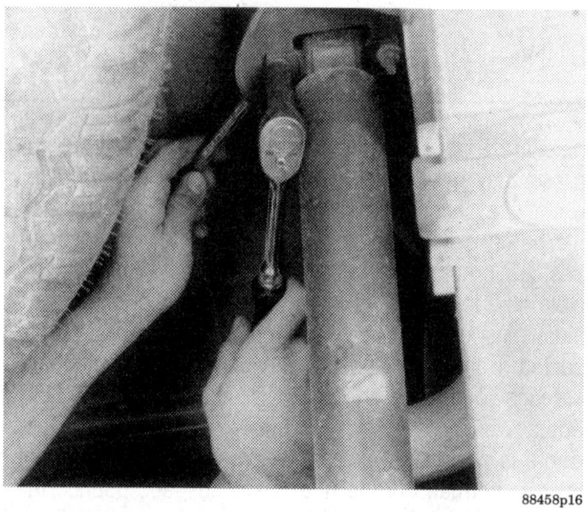

Fig. 57 Loosen the retainers from the upper shock mount — a backup wrench is usually needed

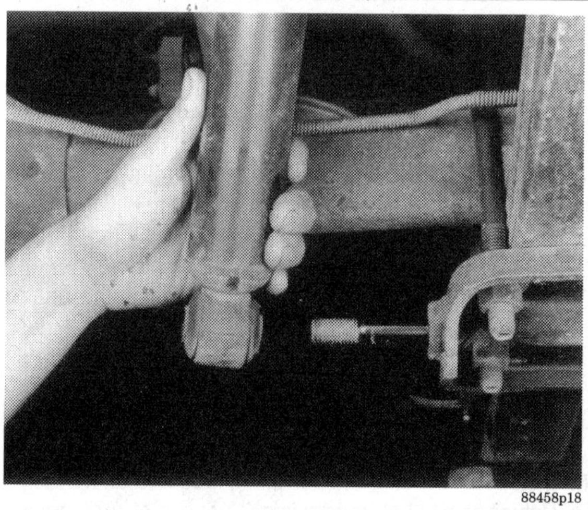

Fig. 59 Loosen and remove the shock from the lower mount

the center point of the bounce more than once, the shock absorbers are worn and should be replaced.

STEERING

The steering box (manual or power) utilizes a recirculating ball system, which transmits force from the worm gear to the sector gear. A relay type steering linkage is used with a pitman arm connected to one end of the relay rod. The relay rod is supported on the other end by an idler arm assembly; the idler arm pivots on a support which is attached to the frame. The relay rod is connected to the steering arms by two adjustable tie rods.

These trucks are equipped with a collapsible steering column which is designed to absorb an impact by collapsing, thereby reducing possible chest injuries during accidents. When making any repairs to the steering column or steering wheel, excessive pressure or force capable of collapsing the column must be avoided. The ignition switch, ignition lock and antitheft system are built into each column.

On the automatic transmission, the ignition key cannot be removed unless the shift lever is in the Park position and the ignition switch is in the Lock position. Placing the key in the Lock position activates a rod within the column which locks the steering wheel and shift lever.

Steering Wheel

REMOVAL & INSTALLATION

See Figures 60, 61, 62, 63, 64, 65, 66 and 67

1. Disconnect the negative battery cable.
2. If equipped, disable the Supplemental Inflatable Restraint System (SIR). Refer to Section 6 of this manual for this procedure.
3. Position the steering wheel so that it is in the horizontal position and the front wheel are straight.
4. If equipped, remove the horn cap from the center of the steering wheel.

If the horn cap or shroud is equipped with an electrical connector it must be disengaged in order to remove the cap/shroud from the steering column.

5. If equipped with an air bag, remove the air bag system inflator module as follows:
   a. Make sure the air bag system is disabled and the negative battery disconnected.
   b. Turn the steering wheel 90 degrees, this will enable you to gain access to the rear shroud holes-to-inflator module.
   c. Insert a prytool and push the leaf spring to release the pin.
   d. Turn the steering wheel 180 degrees to access the remaining shroud holes, then repeat the procedure to release the pin using the prytool.
   e. Tilt the inflator module rearward from the top to access the module electrical wiring, then disengage the wiring from the module and the steering wheel.
   f. Disengage the Connector Position Assurance (CPA) and retainer from the module.
6. Remove the steering wheel-to-steering shaft retainer clip (snapring), then loosen and remove the nut.

Since the steering column is designed to collapse upon impact, NEVER hammer on it!

7. Matchmark the relationship of the steering wheel to the steering shaft. Some models may already be equipped with one or more alignment marks. If not, make your own using a permanent marker.
8. Using a suitable steering wheel puller, such as No. J-1859-03 or equivalent, carefully draw the wheel from the steering column.

To install:

Before installing the steering wheel, be sure that the turn signal switch is in the Neutral position. DO NOT misalign the steering wheel more than 0.8 in. (20mm) from the horizontal centerline.

9. Align the matchmarks and carefully fit the wheel onto the steering shaft splines.
10. Install the retaining nut and tighten to 30 ft. lbs. (40 Nm).
11. If equipped with an air bag, install the inflator module as follows:
    a. Engage the Connector Position Assurance (CPA) and retainer to the module.
    b. Engage the inflator module wiring to the steering wheel and to the module.
    c. Install the inflator module by pressing it into the steering wheel enough to engage and latch all four notched pins in the leaf spring. Make sure the wires are not pinched.
12. If equipped, install the horn pad.
13. Connect the negative battery cable.
14. Enable the air bag system. Refer to Section 6 of this manual for this procedure.

Turn Signal (Combination) Switch

REMOVAL & INSTALLATION

See Figures 68, 69, 70, 71 and 72

When servicing any components on the steering column, should any fasteners require replacement, be sure to use only nuts and bolts of the same size and grade as the original fasteners. Using screws that are too long could prevent the column from collapsing during a collision.

1994 Vehicles

The following procedures require the use of a lockplate compressor tool such as J-23653 or equivalent.

1. Disconnect the negative battery cable.

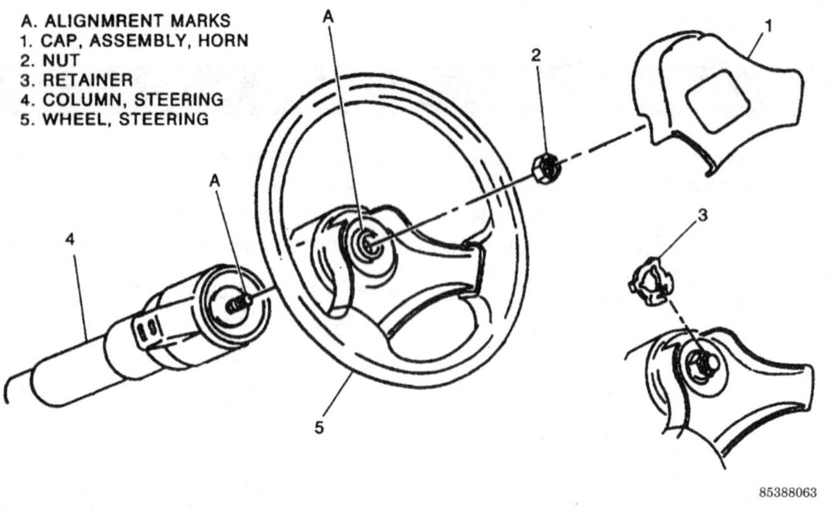

Fig. 60 Exploded view of a steering wheel mounting

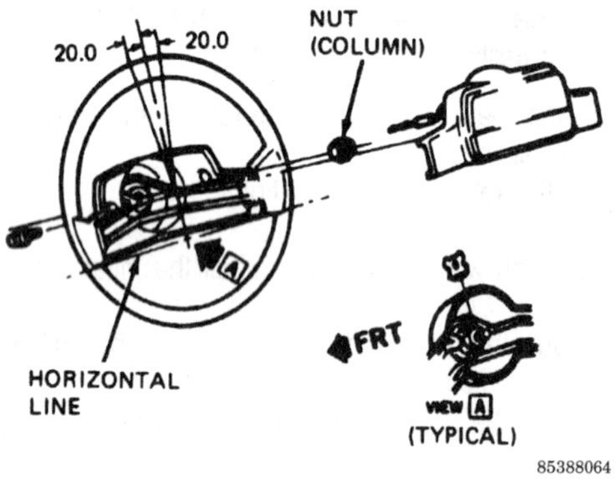

Fig. 61 Steering wheel alignment and installation

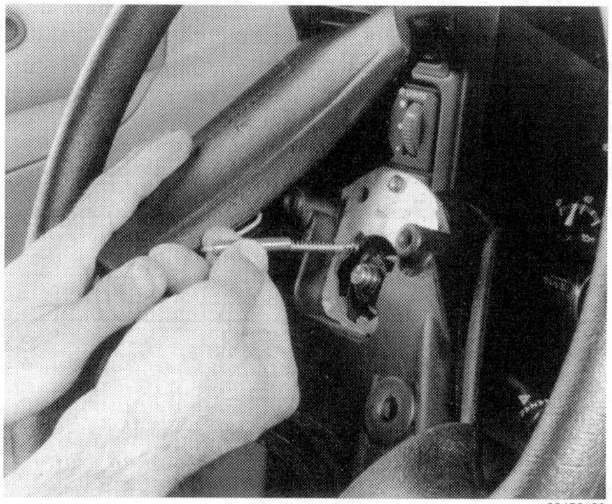

Fig. 63 Disengage the horn wire

Fig. 62 Remove the horn pad

Fig. 64 Loosen and remove the wheel retaining nut

88458p22

Fig. 65 Use a suitable threaded puller to loosen the steering wheel from the shaft

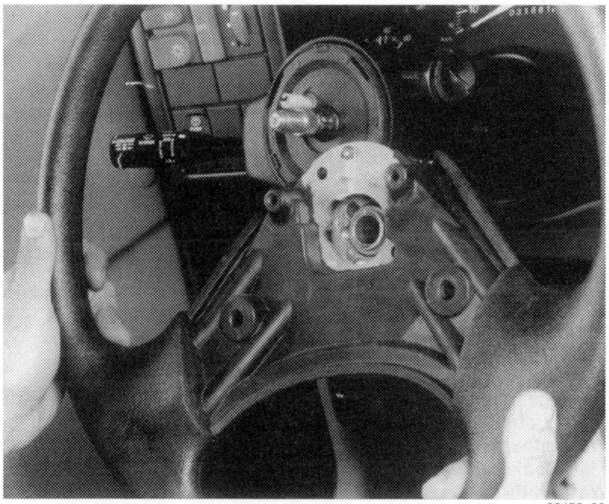

88458p23

Fig. 66 Remove the steering wheel

88458p24

Fig. 67 Matchmark the relationship of the steering wheel to the steering shaft

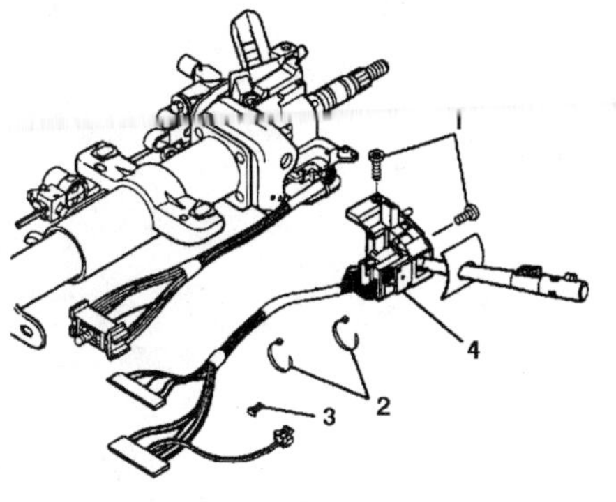

1. Pan hd tapping screw
2. Wire harness strap
3. Axial posn assur connector
4. T/S & multifunc switch asm

88458g11

Fig. 68 Exploded view of the combination switch — 1996 models

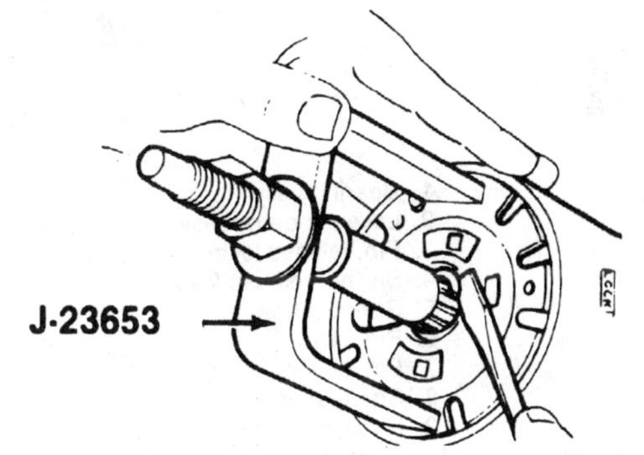

85388072

Fig. 69 Use a suitable lockplate compressor tool when removing the shaft lock

2. Matchmark and remove the steering wheel. Please refer to the procedure earlier in this section for details.

3. Remove the shaft lock cover.

4. Push downward on the shaft lock assembly until the snapring is exposed using the shaft lock compressor tool.

5. Remove the shaft lock retaining snapring, then carefully release the tool and remove the shaft lock from the column.

6. Remove the turn signal cancelling cam assembly.

7. For standard columns, remove the upper bearing spring and thrust washer.

8. For tilt columns, remove the upper bearing spring, inner race seat and inner race.

9. Move the turn signal lever upward to the "Right Turn" position.

10. Remove the access cap and disengage the multi-function lever harness connector, then grasp the lever and pull it from the column.

11. Loosen and remove the hazard knob retaining screw, then remove the screw, button, spring and knob.

12. Remove the screw and the switch actuator arm.

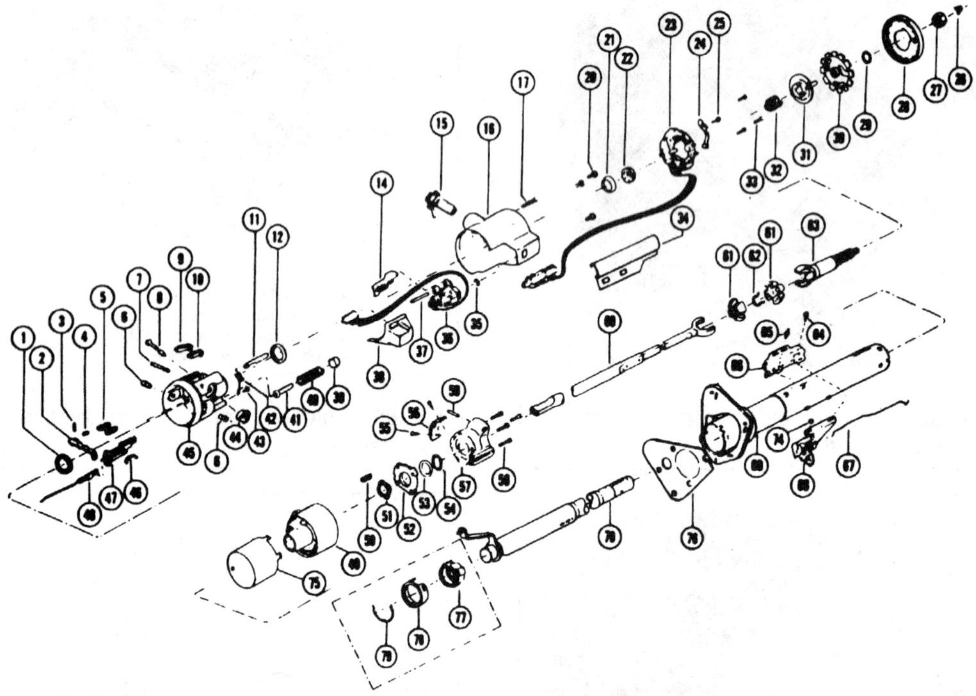

1. Bearing assy
2. Lever, shoe release
3. Pin, release lever
4. Spring, release lever
5. Spring, shoe
6. Pin, pivot
7. Pin, dowel
8. Shaft, drive
9. Shoe, steering wheel lock
10. Shoe, steering wheel lock
11. Bolt, lock
12. Bearing assy
14. Actuator, dimmer switch rod
15. Lock cylinder set, strg column
16. Cover, lock housing
17. Screw, lock retaining
20. Screw, pan head cross recess
21. Race, inner
22. Seat, upper bearing inner race
23. Switch assy, turn signal
24. Arm assy, signal switch
25. Screw, round washer head
26. Retainer
27. Nut, hex jam
28. Cover, shaft lock
29. Ring, retaining
30. Lock, shaft
31. Cam assy, turn signal cancelling
32. Spring, upper bearing
33. Screw, binding head cross recess
34. Protector, wiring
35. Spring, pin preload
36. Switch assy, pivot &
37. Pin, switch actuator pivot
38. Cap, column housing cover end
39. Retainer, spring
40. Spring, wheel tilt
41. Guide, spring
42. Spring, lock bolt
43. Screw, hex washer head
44. Sector, switch actuator
45. Housing, steering column
46. Spring, rack preload
47. Rack, switch actuator
48. Actuator assy, ignition switch
49. Bowl, gearshift lever
50. Spring, shift lever
51. Washer, wave
52. Plate, lock
53. Washer, thrust
54. Ring, shift tube retaining
55. Screw, oval head cross recess
56. Gate, shift lever
57. Support, strg column housing
58. Screw, support
59. Pin, dowel
60. Shaft assy, lower steering
61. Sphere, centering
62. Spring, joint preload
63. Shaft assy, race & upper
64. Screw, washer head
65. Stud, dimmer & ignition switch mounting
66. Switch assy, ignition
67. Rod, dimmer switch
68. Switch assy, dimmer
69. Jacket assy, steering column
70. Tube assy, shift
74. Nut, hexagon
75. Shroud, gearshift bowl
76. Seal, dash
77. Bushing assy, steering shaft
78. Retainer, bearing adapter
79. Clip, lower bearing adapter

85388078

Fig. 70 Exploded view of a common tilt steering column — 1994 models

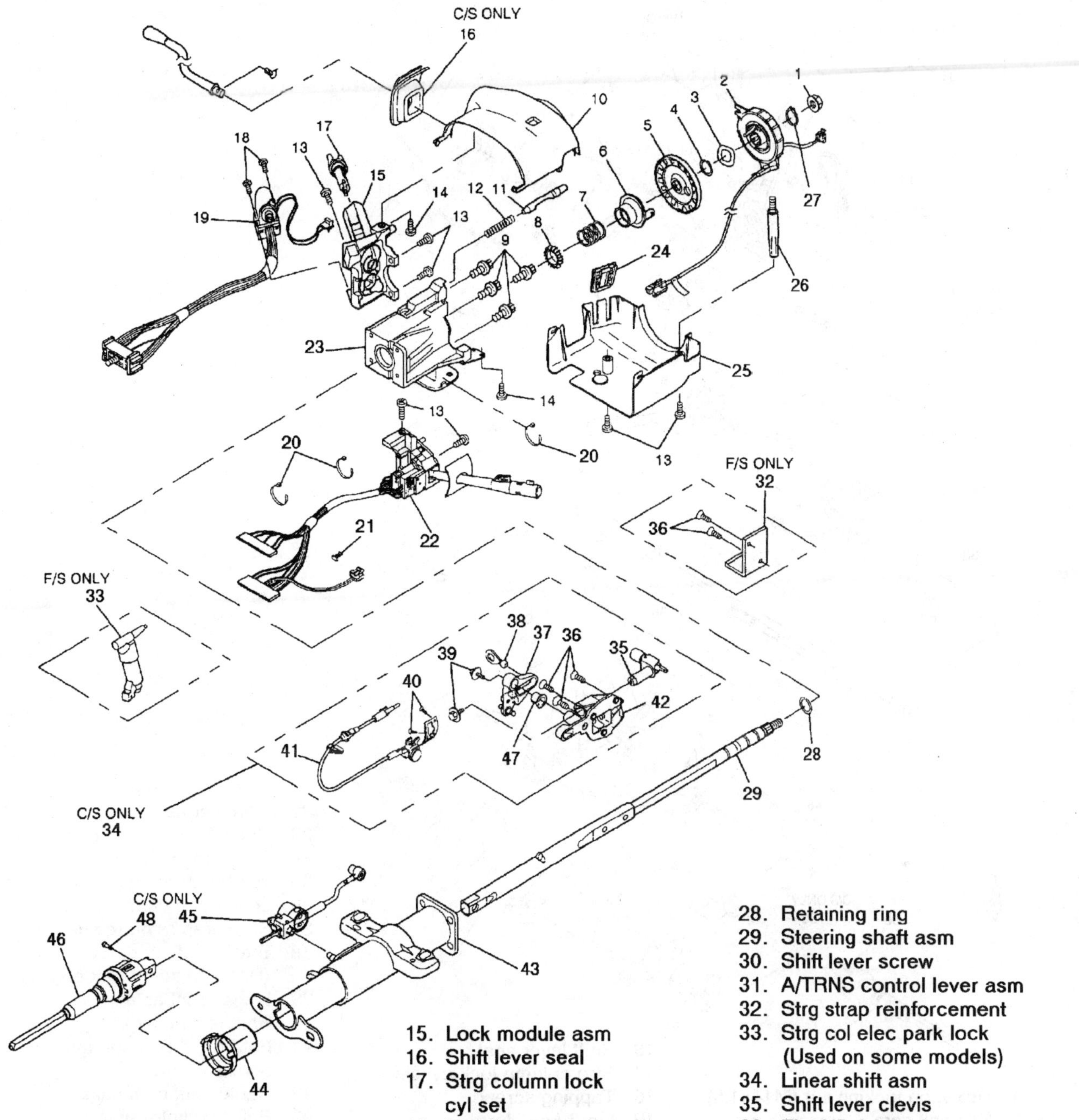

1. Hexagon locking nut (M14x1.5)
2. SIR coil asm
3. Wave washer
4. Retaining ring
5. Shaft lock shield asm
6. T/SIG cancel CAM asm
7. Upper bearing spring
8. Thrust washer
9. Torx head screw
10. Upper shroud
11. Lock bolt asm
12. Lock bolt spring
13. Pan hd tapping screw
14. Torx head screw
15. Lock module asm
16. Shift lever seal
17. Strg column lock cyl set
18. Tapping screw
19. Ign & key alarm switch asm
20. Wire harness strap
21. Axial posn assur connector
22. T/S & multifunc switch asm
23. Strg column housing asm
24. Shroud protector
25. Lower shroud
26. Shroud mounting stud
27. Retaining ring
28. Retaining ring
29. Steering shaft asm
30. Shift lever screw
31. A/TRNS control lever asm
32. Strg strap reinforcement
33. Strg col elec park lock (Used on some models)
34. Linear shift asm
35. Shift lever clevis
36. Flat HD 6-lobed soc tap screw
37. Cable shift cam asm
38. Ball & actuator asm
39. Hex flange head bolt
40. Oval hd 6-lobed soc tap screw
41. Park lock cable asm
42. G/S lever asm support bracket
43. Strg col jacket asm
44. Adapter & bearing asm
45. Electrical (BTSI) actuator
46. CPLG & strg shaft asm
47. CAM bushing
48. Pinch bolt

88458g03

Fig. 71 Exploded view of a common standard steering column — 1995-97 models

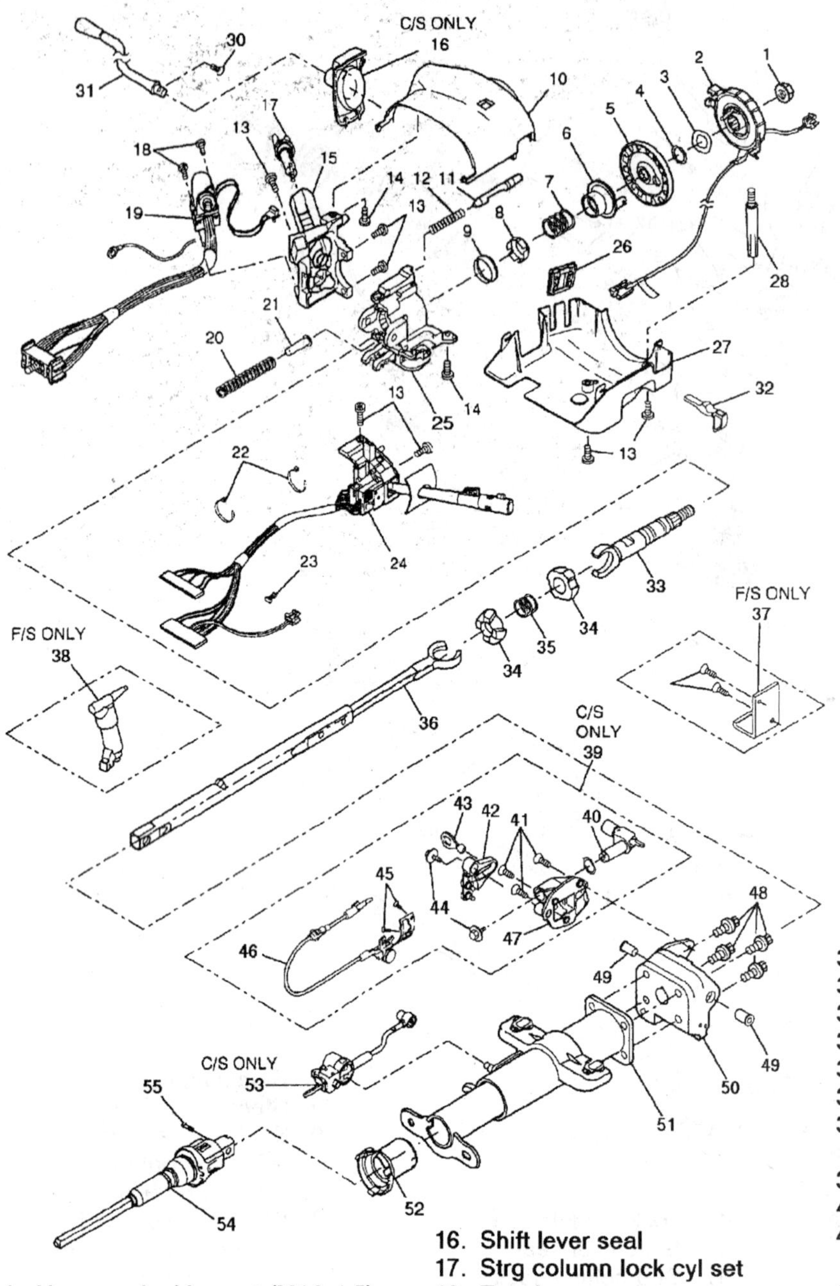

1. Hexagon locking nut (M14x1.5)
2. SIR coil asm
3. Wave washer
4. Retaining ring
5. Shaft lock shield asm
6. T/SIG cancel CAM asm
7. Upper bearing spring
8. Upper bearing inner race seat
9. Inner race
10. Upper shroud
11. Lock bolt asm
12. Lock bolt spring
13. Pan hd tapping screw
14. Torx head screw
15. Lock module asm
16. Shift lever seal
17. Strg column lock cyl set
18. Tapping screw
19. Ign & key alarm switch asm
20. Tilt spring
21. Spring guide
22. Wire harness strap
23. Axial posn assur connector
24. T/S & multifunction switch asm
25. Strg col tilt head asm
26. Shroud protector
27. Lower shroud
28. Shroud mounting stud
29. Retaining ring
30. Shift lever screw
31. A/TRNS control lever asm
32. Tilt lever asm
33. Race & upper shaft asm
34. Centering sphere
35. Joint preload spring
36. Lower strg shaft asm
37. Strg strap reinforcement
38. Strg col elc park lock (Used on some models)
39. Linear shift asm
40. Shift lever clevis
41. Fat hd 6-lobed soc tap screw
42. Cable shift cam asm
43. Ball &actuator asm
44. Hex flange head bolt
45. Oval hd 6-lobed soc tap screw
46. Park lock cable asm
47. G/S lever asm support bracket
48. Torx head screw
49. Pivot pin
50. Strg col support asm
51. Strg col jacket asm
52. Adapter & bearing asm
53. Electrical actuator (BTSI)
54. Cplg & strg shaft asm
55. Pinch bolt

88458g04

Fig. 72 Exploded view of a common tilt steering column — 1995-97 models

13. Remove the turn signal switch retaining screws, then pull the switch forward and allow it to hang from the wires. If the switch is only being removed for access to other components, this may be sufficient.

14. If the switch is being completely removed, disengage the wiring at the base of the column. Attach a length of mechanic's wire to the switch harness connector, then pull the harness through the column, leaving the mechanic's wire in place for installation purposes.

➡On some vehicles access to the connector may be difficult. If necessary, remove the column support bracket assembly and properly support the column, and/or remove the wiring protectors.

15. Remove the switch and wiring harness from the vehicle.

To install:

16. Install the switch and wiring harness to the vehicle. If the switch was completely removed, use the length of mechanic's wire to pull the switch harness through the column, then engage the connector.

➡If the column support bracket or wiring protectors were removed, install them before proceeding.

17. Position the switch in the column and secure using the retaining screws. Tighten the screws to 30 inch lbs. (3.4 Nm).

18. Install the switch actuator arm and retaining screw, then tighten the screw to 20 inch lbs. (2.3 Nm).

19. Install the hazard knob assembly, then install the multi-function lever.

20. Install the thrust washer and upper bearing spring (standard columns) or the inner race, upper bearing race seat and upper bearing spring (tilt columns), as applicable.

21. Lubricate the turn signal cancelling cam using a suitable synthetic grease (usually included in the service kit), then install the cam assembly.

22. Position the shaft lock and a NEW snapring, then use the lock compressor to hold the lock down while you seat the new snapring. Make sure the ring is firmly seated in the groove, then carefully release the tool.

23. Install the shaft lock cover.

24. Align and install the steering wheel.

25. Make sure the ignition is **OFF**, then connect the negative battery cable.

1995-97 Vehicles

1. Disconnect the negative battery cable.

➡Make sure that the turn signal switch is in the OFF (center) position.

2. Disable the Supplemental Inflatable Restraint (SIR) system. For details, please refer to the procedure located in Section 6 of this manual.

3. If equipped, remove the horn cap from the center of the steering wheel.

➡If the horn cap or shroud is equipped with an electrical connector it must be disengaged in order to remove the cap/shroud from the steering column.

4. If equipped with an air bag, remove the air bag system inflator module as follows:

a. Make sure the air bag system is disabled and the negative battery disconnected.

b. Turn the steering wheel 90 degrees, this will enable you to gain access to the rear shroud holes-to-inflator module.

c. Insert a prytool and push the leaf spring to release the pin.

d. Turn the steering wheel 180 degrees to access the remaining shroud holes, then repeat the procedure to release the pin using the prytool.

e. Tilt the inflator module rearward from the top to access the module electrical wiring, then disengage the wiring from the module and the steering wheel.

f. Disengage the Connector Position Assurance (CPA) and retainer from the module.

5. Remove the steering wheel nut.

➡Be sure to note the alignment mark and its relationship to the steering wheel and steering shaft.

6. Using GM tool number J 1859-03, remove the steering wheel. For details, please refer to the procedure earlier in this section.

7. Remove the two pan head tapping screws from the lower steering column cover, then tilt the cover down and slide it back to disengage the locking tabs.

8. Remove the lower steering column cover.

9. Using a Torx® screwdriver, remove the two torx head screws from the upper steering column cover, then remove the cover.

10. Remove the wire harness strap, then remove the two harness straps from the steering column wire harness.

11. Disengage the steering column bulkhead connector from the vehicle wiring harness.

12. Disengage the grey and black connectors of the switch from the steering column bulkhead connector.

13. Remove the two pan head tapping screws.

14. Grasp the lever/multi-function turn signal switch assembly, then remove it by carefully pulling it straight outward.

To install:

15. Install the lever/multi-function turn signal switch assembly, using a small blade screwdriver to compress the electrical contact and move the assembly into position.

➡The electrical contact MUST rest on the cancelling cam assembly.

16. Connect the two pan head tapping screws, then tighten the screws to 53 inch lbs (6 Nm).

17. Engage the grey and black connectors of the switch to the column bulkhead connector.

18. Connect the two wire harness straps to the steering column wire harness, then install the wire harness strap.

19. Install the upper steering column cover, then using a Torx® screwdriver, connect the two torx head screws to the upper column cover, tighten to 12 inch lbs. (1.4 Nm).

20. Install the lower steering column cover, then connect using the two pan head tapping screws, tighten to 53 inch lbs. (6 Nm).

21. Make sure that the lever is in the **OFF** (center) position.

22. Align the steering wheel onto the steering shaft, then install using the marks noted during removal.

23. Install the steering wheel nut, tighten to 30 ft. lbs (40 Nm).
24. If equipped with an air bag, install the inflator module as follows:
   a. Engage the Connector Position Assurance (CPA) and retainer to the module.
   b. Engage the inflator module wiring to the steering wheel and to the module.
   c. Install the inflator module by pressing it into the steering wheel enough to engage and latch all four notched pins in the leaf spring. Make sure the wires are not pinched.
25. If equipped, install the horn pad.
26. Activate the Supplemental Inflatable Restraint (SIR) system. For details, please refer to the procedure located in Section 6.
27. Connect the negative battery cable.

Ignition Switch

REMOVAL & INSTALLATION

1994 Vehicles

For anti-theft reasons, the ignition switch is located on top of the steering column assembly and is completely inaccessible without first lowering the steering column. The switch is actuated by a rod and rack assembly. A gear on the end of the lock cylinder engages the toothed upper end of the actuator rod.

1. Disconnect the negative battery cable.
2. Remove the lower column trim panel, then remove the steering column-to-instrument panel fasteners and carefully lower the column for access to the switch.
3. Place the ignition switch in the **OFF-LOCK** position.
4. Remove the ignition switch-to-steering column retainers, then remove the assembly.

To install:

5. Before installing the ignition switch, place it in the **OFF-LOCK** position, then make sure that the lock cylinder and actuating rod are in the Locked position (1st detent from the top or 1st detent to the right of far left detent travel).

➡Most replacement switches are pinned in the OFF-LOCK position for installation purposes. If so, the pin MUST be removed after installation or damage may occur.

6. Install the activating rod into the ignition switch and assemble the switch onto the steering column. Once the switch is properly positioned, tighten the ignition switch-to-steering column retainers to 35 inch lbs. (4.0 Nm).

⁂CAUTION

When installing the ignition switch, use only the specified screws since over length screws could impair the collapsibility of the column.

7. Raise the column into position and secure, then install any necessary trim plates.
8. Make sure the ignition is **OFF**, then connect the negative battery cable.

1995-97 Vehicles

➧ See Figure 73

1. Remove the column shroud halves.
2. Remove the column-to-dash attaching bolts and slowly lower the steering column, making sure that it is supported.
3. Remove the multifunction switch if necessary.
4. Remove the key alarm switch, if equipped by gently prying the alarm switch retaining clip with a small screwdriver. Rotate the alarm switch ¼ in. (6mm) turn and remove.

⁂WARNING

Extreme care is necessary to prevent damage to the collapsible column.

5. Make sure that the switch is in the **LOCK** position. If the lock cylinder is out, pull the switch rod up to the stop, then go down one detent.
6. Remove the two screws and the switch.

To install:

7. Before installation, make sure the switch is in the **LOCK** position.
8. Install the switch using the original screws. Tighten the screws to 12 inch. lbs. (1.4 Nm).
9. Install the key alarm switch, if equipped . Make sure the retaining clip is parallel to the lock cylinder. Rotate the alarm switch ¼ in. (6mm) turn until locked in place.
10. Install the multifunction switch if removed.

⁂CAUTION

Use of screws that are too long could prevent the column from collapsing on impact.

11. Replace the column. Tighten the nuts to 22 ft. lbs. (29 Nm); the bolts to 20 ft. lbs. (27 Nm).
12. Install the column shroud halves.

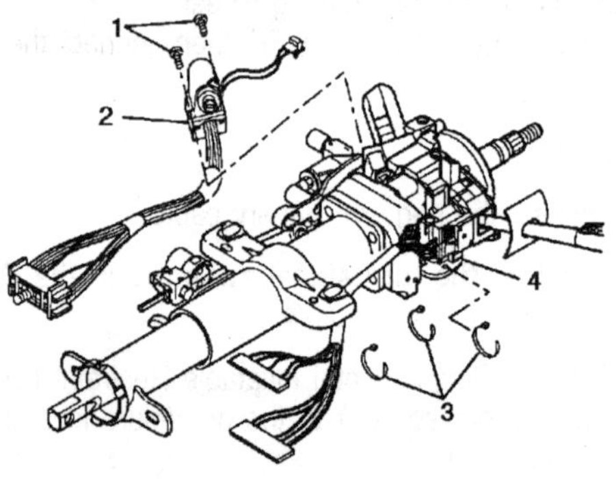

Fig. 73 Exploded view of the ignition and key alarm switch

Lock Cylinder

REMOVAL & INSTALLATION

1994 Vehicles

1. Disconnect the negative battery cable.
2. Matchmark and remove the steering wheel.
3. Remove the turn signal switch from the column and allow it to hang from the wires (leaving them connected). For details, please refer to the procedure located earlier in this section.
4. Remove the buzzer switch assembly.
5. Carefully remove the lock cylinder screw and the lock cylinder. If possible, use a magnetic tipped screwdriver on the screw in order to help prevent the possibility of dropping it.

CAUTION

If the screw is dropped upon removal, it could fall into the steering column, requiring complete disassembly in order to retrieve the screw and prevent damage.

To install:

6. Align and install the lock cylinder set.
7. Push the lock cylinder all the way in, then carefully install the retaining screw. Tighten the screw to 22 inch lbs. (2.5 Nm) on tilt columns or to 40 inch lbs. (4.5 Nm) on standard non-tilt columns.
8. If necessary, install the buzzer switch assembly.
9. Reposition and secure the turn signal switch assembly
10. Align and install the steering wheel.
11. Make sure the ignition is **OFF**, then connect the negative battery cable.

1995-97 Vehicles

See Figures 74, 75 and 76

CAUTION

When performing service around the SIR system components or wiring, the SIR system MUST be disabled. Failure to do so could result in possible air bag deployment, personal injury or unneeded SIR system repairs.

1. Disconnect the negative battery cable and disable the SIR system. Refer to the procedure in Section 6.
2. Remove the upper and lower shroud, air bag module and the steering column.
3. Remove the retaining ring, SIR coil assembly, wave washer.
4. Remove the shaft lock retaining ring using tool J 23653-SIR or its equivalent to push down the shaft lock shield assembly. Discard the ring.
5. Remove the shaft lock shield and turn signal cancel cam assembly.
6. Remove the park lock cable assembly from the lock module assembly.
7. Remove the key alarm switch, if equipped by gently prying the alarm switch retaining clip with a small screwdriver. Rotate the alarm switch 1/4 in. (6mm) turn and remove.

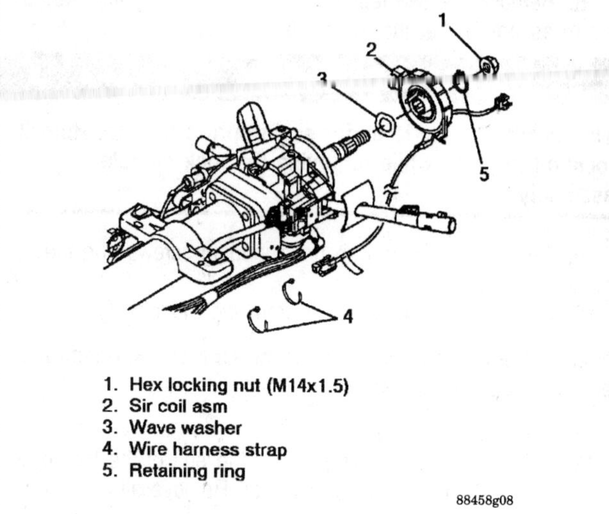

Fig. 74 Exploded view of the SIR coil assembly

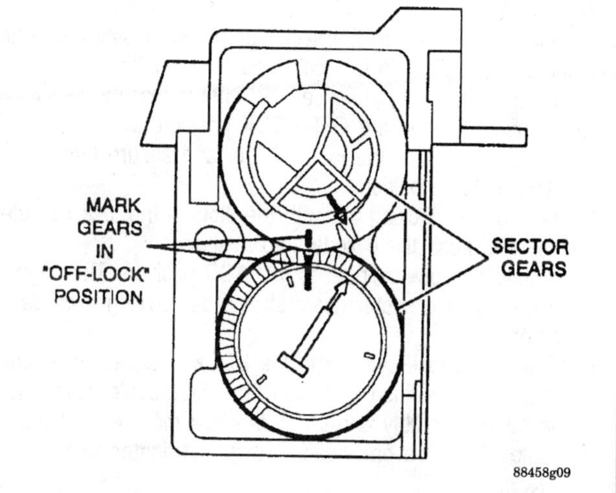

Fig. 75 Exploded view of the sector gear timing position (OFF-LOCK)

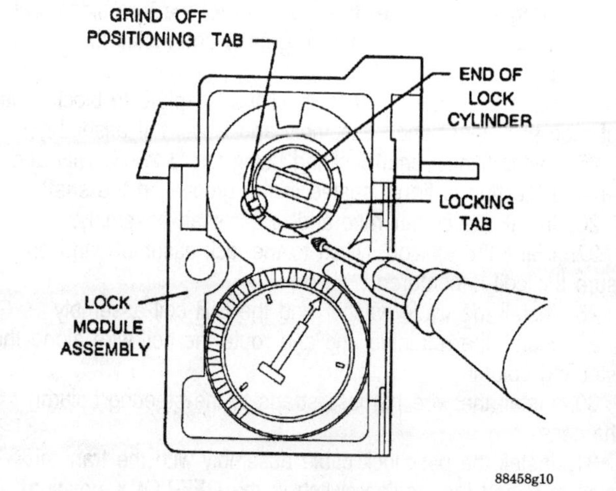

Fig. 76 Remove all burrs from the lock module and cylinder assembly

8. Remove the two tapping screws and the ignition key and alarm assembly. Let the switch hang freely.

CAUTION

The lock assembly is under slight spring tension. Hold the lockbolt in place while removing the lock module assembly.

9. Remove the three pan head tapping screws and the lock module assembly.
10. Remove the backing plate from the module.

➡Mark the two sector gears at the OFF-LOCK position to ensure proper reassembly

11. Remove the sector gears.
12. Remove the positioning tab on the end of the lock cylinder using an 1/8 in. (3mm) burring tool. Remove all burrs from the lock module and cylinder assembly.
13. Push on the locking tab of the lock cylinder from inside the the lock module assembly and remove the lock cylinder.

To install:

14. Align the marks on the sector gears and install the gears and the backing plate to the lock module assembly.
15. Install the lock cylinder set and ensure that the lock module assembly is in the **OFF-LOCK** position.
16. Install the key in the lock cylinder and ensure that it is in the **OFF-LOCK** position.
17. Line up the locking tab with the slots in the lock module assembly and push the cylinder into position.
18. Rotate the lock cylinder to the **ACC** position. The alignment arrows on the sector gears should be pointing towards each other.
19. Rotate the lock cylinder to the **LOCK** position. Push the lockbolt in until it is flush and align the lock module assembly with the head assembly and install the lock module assembly.
20. Install the three pan head screws and tighten to 53 inch. lbs. (6 Nm).
21. Install the ignition and key alarm switch assembly and the fasteners. Tighten the fasteners to 12 inch. lbs. (1 Nm).
22. Install the key alarm switch. Make sure the retaining clip is parallel to the lock cylinder. Rotate the alarm switch 1/4 in. (6mm) turn until locked in place.
23. Lubricate the lower brass surface of the turn signal cancel cam assembly with synthetic grease and install the assembly.
24. Align the inner block tooth of the lockplate to block tooth of race and upper shaft assembly and install the assembly.
25. Install a new shaft lockring using tool J 23653-SIR and ensure the ring is firmly seated in the groove on the shaft.
26. Install the center race and upper shaft assembly.
27. Place the ignition switch to the lock assembly and ensure the coil is centered.
28. Install the wave washer and the SIR coil assembly.
29. Install the retaining ring and route the coil wire along the steering column.
30. Install the wire harness straps to the steering column harness.
31. Install the park lock cable assembly with the transmission in **P** and the ignition switch in the **OFF-LOCK** position.
32. Install the upper and lower covers, lock cylinder set and tilt lever (if equipped).
33. Install the steering column and enable the SIR system. Connect the negative battery cable.

Steering Column

REMOVAL & INSTALLATION

See Figures 77 and 78

1. Disconnect the negative battery cable.
2. Disable the Supplemental Inflatable Restraint (SIR) system. For details, please refer to the procedure located in Section 6 of this manual.
3. Matchmark the relationship of the upper pot joint to the steering shaft, then remove the nut/bolt and separate the joint from the shaft.
4. If equipped with a column mounted shifter, disconnect the transmission control linkage from the column shift tube levers.

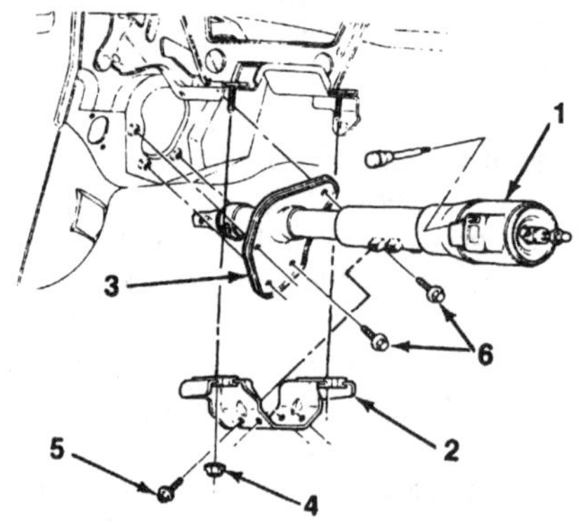

1. Steering column
2. Support bracket
3. Seal
4. Nut
5. Bolt
6. Screws

85388083

Fig. 77 Common steering column mounting

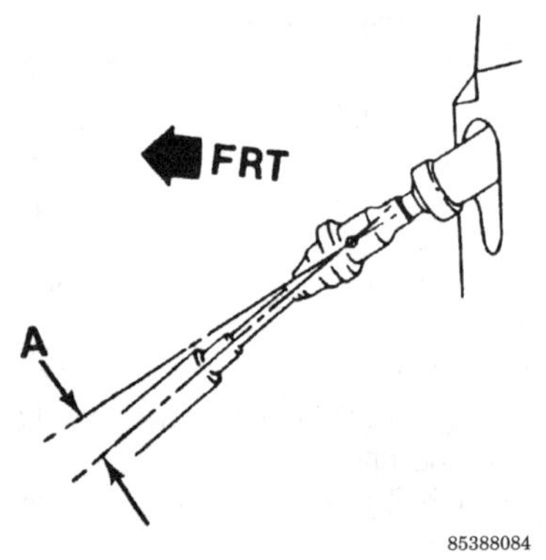

85388084

Fig. 78 The upper pot joint operating angle MUST not exceed 12.5 degrees

5. If equipped, remove the lower steering column trim panel.
6. If applicable, disconnect the shift indicator cable from the shift bowl.
7. If necessary, remove the steering wheel.
8. Remove the bolts from the column floor/toe plate.
9. Remove the column support bracket-to-instrument panel retainers, then carefully lower the column for access to the wiring.
10. Disengage all of the electrical connectors from the steering column assembly.

➡Once the steering column has been removed from the vehicle, be careful not to drop it (especially on it's end), lean on it or damage it in any way; the column is very susceptible to damage.

11. Remove the column from the vehicle. Rotate the column so the shift lever clears the cowl opening.

To install:

12. Position the steering column in the vehicle while carefully guiding the lower end through the cowl.
13. Engage the electrical wiring connectors to the column.
14. Raise the column into position and connect the shift indicator cable to the bowl (if equipped) then loosely install the column bracket-to-instrument panel retainers.
15. Loosely install the column floor/toe plate retainers.
16. Align and connect the pot joint to the steering shaft. Check the pot joint operating angle, it must not exceed 12.5 degrees. Install the nut/bolt and tighten to 45 ft. lbs. (62 Nm).
17. Tighten the column retainers. The floor/toe retainers should be tightened to 120 inch lbs. (13 Nm), the column bracket-to-column bolts (if removed) to 17 ft. lbs. (22 Nm) and the column bracket-to-instrument panel retainers to 18 ft. lbs. (25 Nm).
18. If equipped with a column mounted shifter, connect the transmission control linkage to the column shift tube levers, then check and adjust the shift indicator cable, as necessary.
19. If removed, align and install the steering wheel.
20. If applicable, install the steering column trim panel.
21. Make sure the ignition is **OFF**, then connect the negative battery cable.
22. Enable the Supplemental Inflatable Restraint (SIR) system. For details, please refer to the procedure located in Section 6 of this manual.

Steering Linkage

➧ See Figures 79 and 80

The steering linkage consists of: a forward mounted linkage, crimp or prevailing torque nuts at the inner pivots, castellated nuts at the steering knuckle arm, an idler arm, a steering gear pitman arm, a relay rod and a steering damper (4WD vehicles). Grease fittings are equipped with each joint, for durability. Depending on the application, the relay rod may only be equipped with holes to accept ball studs, or the rod may itself contain ball studs for connection with the pitman/idler arms.

REMOVAL & INSTALLATION

Pitman Arm

➧ See Figure 81

1. Raise and support the front of the vehicle safely using jackstands.
2. If necessary, remove the air snorkel for access to the intermediate shaft.
3. Matchmark the upper and lower intermediate shaft joints, then remove the retainers and remove the intermediate shaft.
4. Disconnect the oil cooler pipes at the crossmember.
5. If equipped, remove the splash shield.
6. Remove the nut from ball stud at the relay rod-to-pitman arm connection.
7. Using a suitable universal steering linkage puller, such as J-24319-01 or equivalent, separate the relay rod from the pitman arm. Pull down on the relay rod and separate the stud.
8. If access to the pitman arm/nut is restricted, remove the 2 lower steering gear bolts (leaving on the top bolt which should be loosened), then pivot the steering gear for pitman arm clearance at the frame crossmember. Support the gear using a block of wood.

➡It may not be possible to pivot the gear for access to the pitman shaft. If necessary, unbolt and remove the gear from the vehicle. For details, please refer to the gear procedures found later in this section.

9. Remove the pitman arm-to-pitman shaft nut, then matchmark the relationship of the arm to the shaft to assure proper alignment during assembly.

➡When separating the pitman arm from the shaft, DO NOT use a hammer or apply heat to the arm.

10. Using a pitman arm remover such as J-6632 or equivalent, separate the pitman arm from the pitman shaft and remove it from the vehicle.

To install:

➡If the pitman arm is being replaced, transfer the alignment mark to the new component.

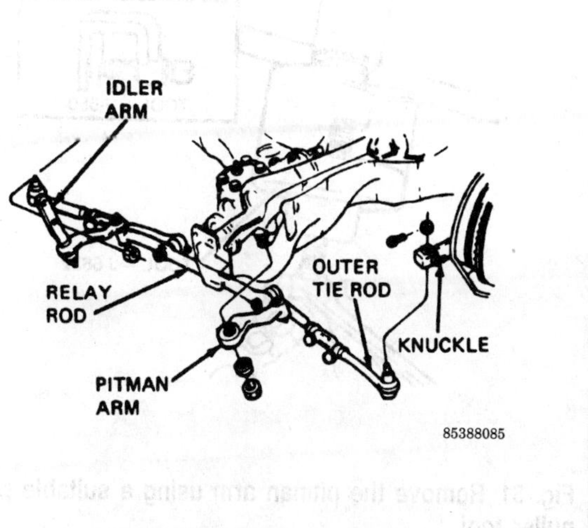

Fig. 79 Common steering linkage components

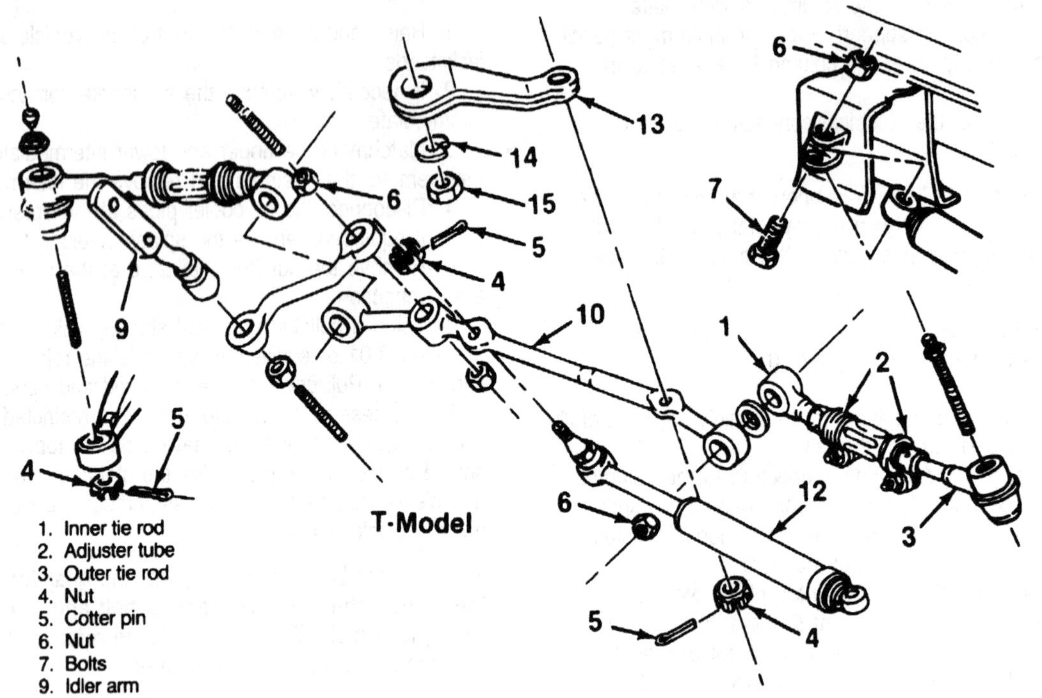

1. Inner tie rod
2. Adjuster tube
3. Outer tie rod
4. Nut
5. Cotter pin
6. Nut
7. Bolts
9. Idler arm
10. Relay rod
12. Steering dampner
13. Pitman arm
14. Washer
15. Nut

85388087

Fig. 80 Common 4WD steering linkage components (with steering damper)

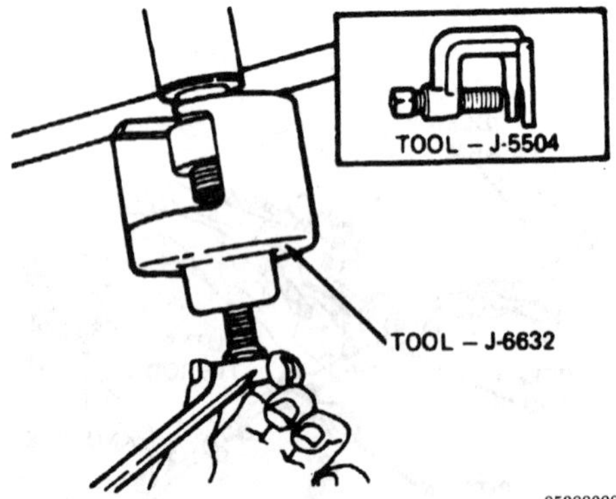

Fig. 81 Remove the pitman arm using a suitable pitman puller tool

11. Install the pitman arm while aligning the arm-to-pitman shaft matchmark. Use a steering linkage installer such as J-29193 (12mm), J-29194 (14mm) or equivalent (as applicable) to properly seat the arm on the shaft, install the correct one onto the shaft and torque it to 40 ft. lbs. (54 Nm) to seat the taper.
12. Remove the installer tool, then install the pitman shaft nut and tighten to 185 ft. lbs. (250 Nm).
13. On vehicles on which the gear was pivoted for access, pivot the gear back into position and install the lower retaining bolts. Tighten all of the retaining bolts to 55 ft. lbs. (75 Nm).
14. Connect the pitman arm to the relay rod (make sure that the seal is on the stud). Use a steering linkage installer such as J-29193 (12mm), J-29194 (14mm) or equivalent (as applicable), install the correct one onto the ball stud and tighten it to 40 ft. lbs. (54 Nm) to seat the taper.
15. After seating, remove the tool, install the lockwasher and nut and tighten to 60 ft. lbs. (82 Nm). If a prevailing torque nut was used (no spring washer) a NEW nut MUST be installed.
16. Install the splash shield, oil cooler pipes, intermediate shaft and air duct, as applicable.

17. Remove the jackstands and carefully lower the vehicle.
18. Check and adjust toe, as necessary.

Idler Arm

See Figure 82

1. Raise and support the front of the vehicle safely using jackstands under the frame so the wheels are free to turn.

Jerking the right wheel assembly back and forth is not an acceptable testing procedure; there is no control on the amount of force being applied to the idler arm. Before suspecting idler arm shimmying complaints, check the wheels for imbalance, runout, force variation and/or road surface irregularities.

2. To inspect for a defective idler arm:
   a. Position the wheels in the straight ahead position.
   b. Position a spring scale near the relay rod end of the idler arm, then exert 25 ft. lbs. (110 Nm) of force upward and then downward. Measure the distance between the upward and downward directions that the idler arm moves. The allowable deflection is 1/8 in. (3.18mm) for each direction for a total difference of 1/4 in. (6.35mm); if the idler arm deflection is beyond the allowable limits, replace it.
3. Remove the idler arm-to-frame bolts/nuts.
4. Remove the nut from the idler arm-to-relay rod ball joint.
5. Use a suitable steering linkage puller such as J-24319-B or equivalent to separate the relay rod from idler arm.
6. Remove the idler arm assembly from the vehicle.

To install:

7. Install the idler arm, then tighten the arm assembly-to-frame bolts to 60 ft. lbs. (82 Nm) on 1994-95 models and 79 ft. lbs. (108 Nm) on 1996-97 models.
8. Connect the relay rod to the idler arm. Use a steering linkage installer such as J-29193 (12mm), J-29194 (14mm) or equivalent (as applicable) to seat the relay rod-to-idler arm ball joint stud. Tighten the tool to 40 ft. lbs. (54 Nm), then remove the tool.
9. Install the idler arm-to-relay rod stud nut and tighten it to 35 ft. lbs. (47 Nm) for 2WD vehicles or 60 ft. lbs. (81 Nm) for 4WD vehicles.
10. Remove the jackstands and carefully lower the vehicle.

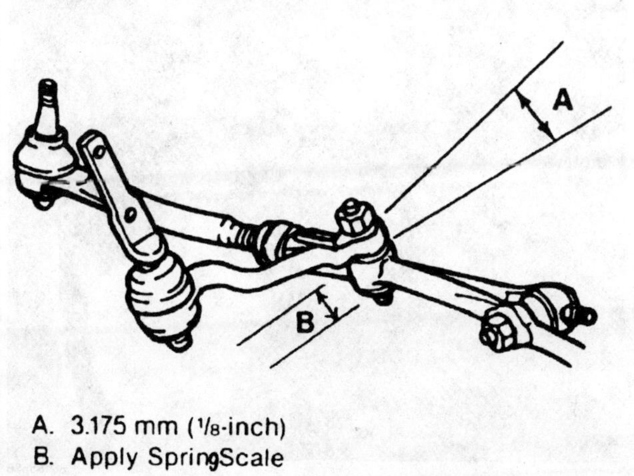

Fig. 82 Checking the idler arm for wear or damage

11. Check and/or adjust the toe-in, as necessary.

Relay Rod (Centerlink)

See Figures 83 and 84

1. Raise and support the vehicle safely using jackstands.
2. Remove the inner tie rod stud nuts, then separate the tie rods from the relay rod using a suitable linkage puller. For details, please refer to the tie rod procedure located later in this section.
3. On vehicles equipped with a steering damper, remove the shock absorber ball stud nut, then separate the shock from the relay rod using a suitable linkage puller, such as J-24319-01 or equivalent.
4. Remove the ball stud nut from the pitman arm-to-relay rod connection, then use a suitable steering linkage puller, such as J-24319-01 or equivalent, to disconnect the pitman rod from the idler arm.
5. Remove the ball stud nut from the idler arm-to-relay rod connection, then use a suitable steering linkage puller, such as

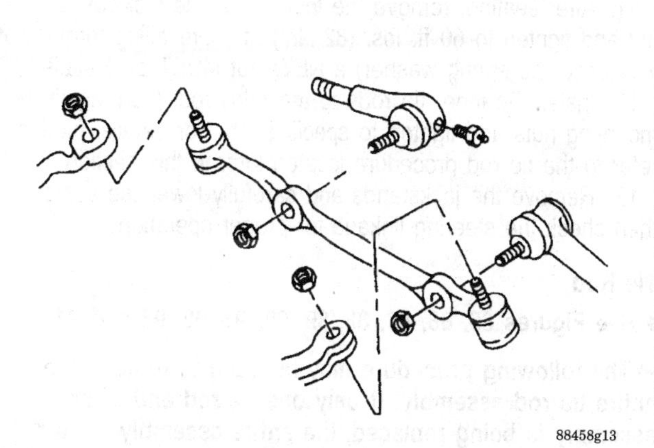

Fig. 83 Exploded view of the relay rod — 2WD model shown

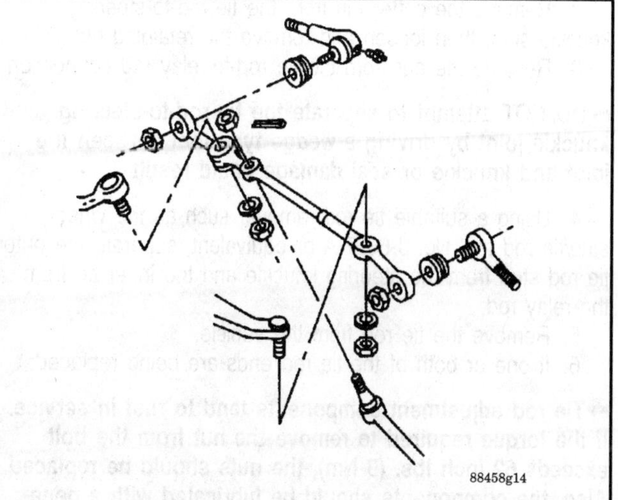

Fig. 84 Exploded view of the relay rod — 4WD model shown

J-24319-01 or equivalent, to disconnect the relay rod from the idler arm.

6. Once the linkage components have been removed from the relay rod, it is free to be removed from the vehicle.

To install:

7. Clean and inspect the threads on the tie rod, the tie rod ends and the ball joints for damage, and replace them (if necessary). Inspect the ball joint seals for excessive wear, and replace them (if necessary).

8. Connect the relay rod to the idler arm. Use a steering linkage installer such as J-29193 (12mm), J-29194 (14mm) or equivalent (as applicable) to seat the relay rod-to-idler arm ball joint stud. Tighten the tool to 40 ft. lbs. (54 Nm), then remove the tool.

9. Install the idler arm-to-relay rod stud nut and tighten it to 35 ft. lbs. (47 Nm) on 2WD models or 60 ft. lbs. (82 Nm) on 4WD models.

10. Connect the pitman arm to the relay rod (make sure that the seal is on the stud). Use a steering linkage installer such as J-29193 (12mm), J-29194 (14mm) or equivalent (as applicable), install the correct one onto the ball stud and tighten it to 40 ft. lbs. (54 Nm) to seat the taper.

11. After seating, remove the tool, install the lockwasher and nut and tighten to 60 ft. lbs. (82 Nm). If a prevailing torque nut was used (no spring washer) a NEW nut MUST be installed.

12. Install the inner tie rods to the relay rod, then install the mounting nuts and tighten to specification. For details, please refer to the tie rod procedure located later in this section.

13. Remove the jackstands and carefully lower the vehicle, then check the steering linkage for proper operation.

Tie Rod

See Figures 85, 86, 87, 88, 89, 90, 91, 92, 93 and 94

The following procedure may be used to remove the entire tie rod assembly. If only one tie rod end of an assembly is being replaced, the entire assembly does not have to be removed from the vehicle. The opposite tie rod end (the end not being replaced) may remain attached to the steering linkage/knuckle, as applicable.

1. Raise and support the front frame of the vehicle safely using jackstands.

2. Remove the cotter pin from the tie rod-to-steering knuckle stud, then loosen and remove the retaining nut.

3. Remove the nut from the tie rod-to-relay rod connection.

DO NOT attempt to separate the tie rod-to-steering knuckle joint by driving a wedge type tool between the joint and knuckle or seal damage could result.

4. Using a suitable tie rod remover such as the wheel stud/tie rod tool No. J-6627-A or equivalent, separate the outer tie rod stud from the steering knuckle and the inner tie from the relay rod.

5. Remove the tie rod from the vehicle.

6. If one or both of the tie rod ends are being replaced:

Tie rod adjustment components tend to rust in service. If the torque required to remove the nut from the bolt exceeds 62 inch lbs. (9 Nm), the nuts should be replaced. Also, the components should be lubricated with a pene-

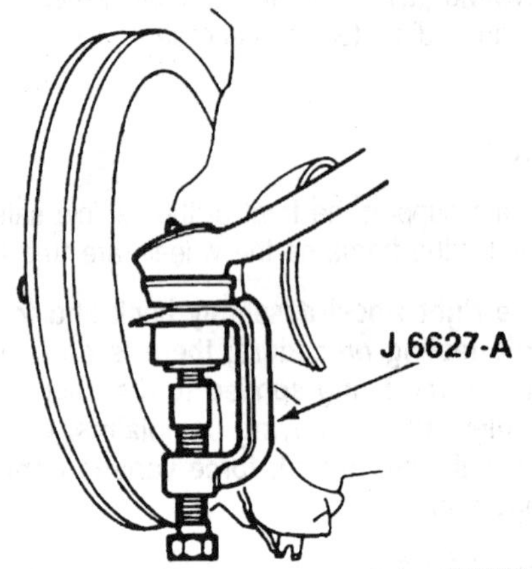

Fig. 85 A proper tools such as the wheel stud remover/tie rod separator tool should be used to free the tie rod ends

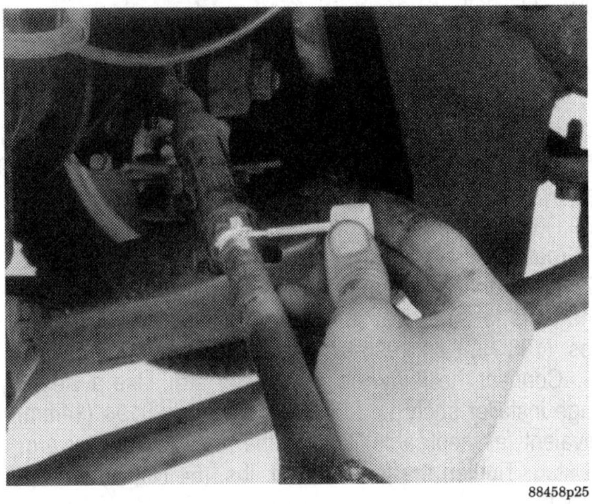

Fig. 86 Matchmark the tie rod before removal, this will aid during installation

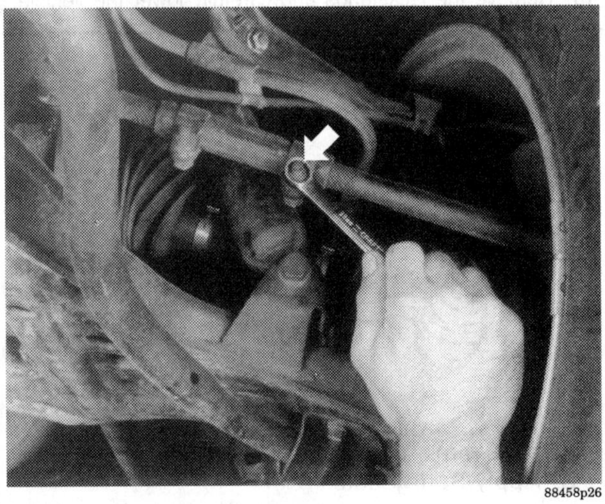

Fig. 87 Loosen the adjuster clamp bolt . . .

88458p27

Fig. 88 . . . then remove the tie rod from the vehicle

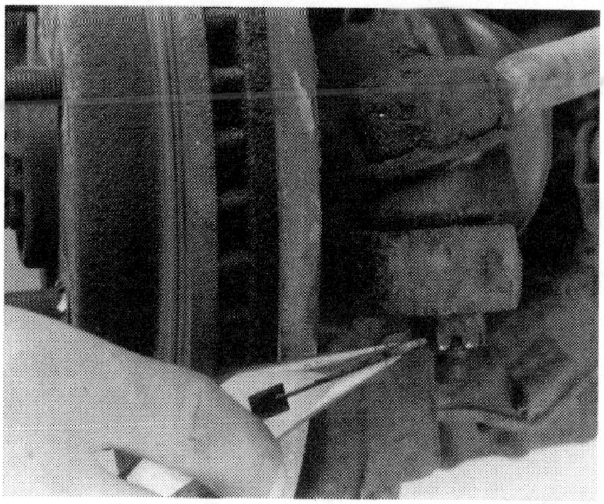

85388092

Fig. 89 When removing a tie rod end, first straighten the ends of the old cotter pin . . .

85388093

Fig. 90 . . . then pull the cotter pin from the ball stud and retaining nut

85388094

Fig. 91 Loosen and remove the stud nut

trating oil, then the clamps should be rotated until the move freely. Pay attention to the clamp positioning before loosening or removing them.

a. Measure the installed length of the tie rod end(s) for installation purposes.

b. Loosen the adjuster tube clamp bolt(s).

c. Unscrew the tie rod end from the adjuster tube; count the number of turns necessary to remove the tie rod end. This can be used to help preserve the toe adjustment during installation.

To install:

7. If one or both of the tie rod ends were removed:

a. Clean, inspect and lubricate the adjuster tube threads.

b. Thread the tie rod end into the adjuster tube using the same number of turns necessary to remove it. Once installed, measure the length of the tie rod end, as done during removal to help assure toe adjustment.

c. Position the clamp bolts between the adjuster tube dimples (located at each end) and in the proper location. Tighten the adjuster tube clamp bolt 14 ft. lbs. (19 Nm).

8. Position the tie rod ends to the steering knuckle and/or the relay rod. Use a steering linkage installer such as J-29193 (12mm), J-29194 (14mm) or equivalent (as applicable), install the correct one onto the ball stud and tighten it to 40 ft. lbs. (54 Nm) to seat the taper(s).

9. Once the ends are properly seated, remove the tool and install the retaining nut(s).

10. Tighten the inner and/or outer tie rod end retaining nuts to 35 ft. lbs. (47 Nm).

11. Install a new cotter pin to the castle nut(s), as applicable.

12. Check and adjust the toe, as necessary.

13. Remove the jackstands and carefully lower the vehicle, then check the steering linkage for proper operation.

Damper Assembly

The damper assembly is used to remove steering wheel vibration and vehicle wander; not all vehicles are equipped

Fig. 92 Use a suitable tool to push the tie rod end free. DO NOT use a wedge-type tool

Fig. 93 Once the ball stud has be unseated, withdraw the tie rod end from the component

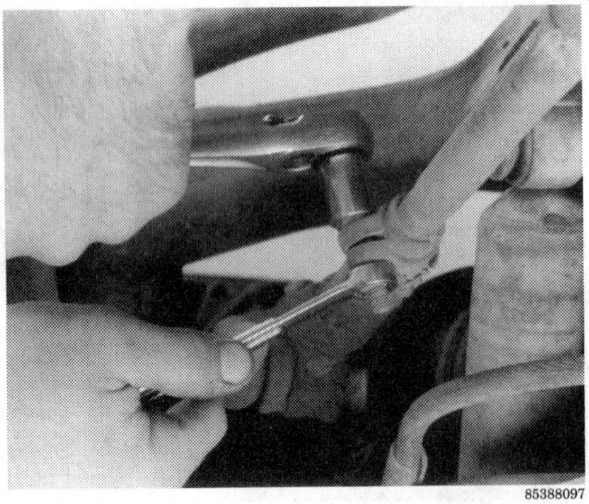

Fig. 94 If replacing a tie rod end (in this case still on the vehicle), loosen the adjuster clamp bolt/nut

with it, though most 4WD vehicles should come with a damper assembly.

1. Raise and support the front frame of the vehicle safely using jackstands.
2. Remove the damper assembly-to-relay rod cotter pin and nut.
3. Use a suitable universal steering linkage puller such as J-24319-01 or equivalent to separate the damper assembly from the relay rod.
4. Remove the cotter pin (if equipped) and the damper assembly-to-frame bracket nut/bolt, then disengage the damper assembly from the vehicle.

To install:

5. Install the damper assembly to the frame bracket, then secure using the retainers. Tighten the bolt/nut to 26 ft. lbs. (35 Nm). If equipped, install a new cotter pin.
6. Position the damper assembly to the relay rod. Use a steering linkage installer such as J-29193 (12mm), J-29194 (14mm) or equivalent (as applicable), install the correct one onto the stud and tighten it to 40 ft. lbs. (54 Nm) to seat the taper.
7. Remove the installation tool, then install retaining nut and tighten to 45 ft. lbs. (62 Nm). Install a new cotter pin.
8. Remove the jackstands and carefully lower the vehicle.

Manual Steering Gear

The recirculating ball type manual steering gear found on most of vehicles covered by this manual is manufactured by Saginaw and is equipped with a mechanical ratio of 24:1.

ADJUSTMENTS

See Figures 95 and 96

Steering gear adjustments are made only as corrections and NOT as periodic adjustments. Before adjusting the gear, check the remainder of the steering linkage and front suspension for wear or damage and repair/replace components, as necessary. Adjustment takes place in 2 major steps. First the worm bearing preload adjustment is made using the adjuster plug, then the overcenter preload is adjusted using the adjuster screw/bolt and jam nut.

➡The following procedure requires the use a steering linkage puller tool such as J-6632 or equivalent, and a 0-50 inch lbs. torque wrench.

1. Disconnect the negative battery cable.
2. Raise and support the front frame of the vehicle safely using jackstands.

➡Before adjustments are made to the steering gear, be sure to check the front end alignment, the shock absorbers, the wheel balance and the tire pressure.

3. Matchmark and separate the pitman arm from the pitman shaft. For details, please refer to the appropriate steps of the pitman arm replacement procedure located earlier in this section. On some vehicles it may be necessary to pivot the gear for access to the pitman arm, if so either temporarily reinstall the gear once the arm is disengaged, or remove the gear

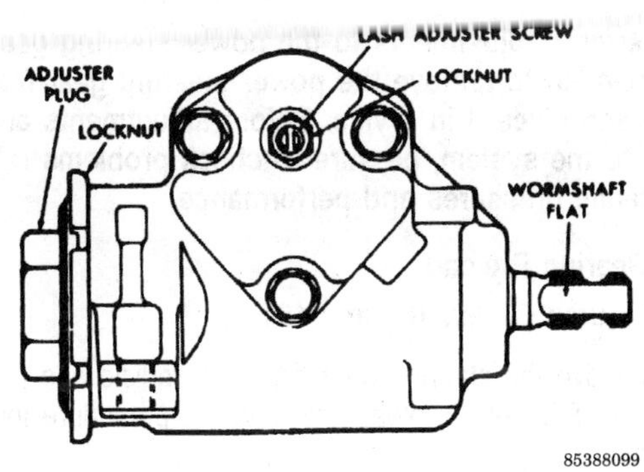

Fig. 95 Manual steering gear adjustment

completely from the vehicle and adjust while measuring preload directly at the gear's input shaft.

4. Loosen the locknut for the steering gear adjuster plug, then back-off the adjuster plug ¼ turn.

5. Remove the horn cap or cover from the steering wheel for access to the shaft nut.

6. Gently, turn the steering wheel (in one direction) to the stop; then, turn it back ½ turn.

➡When the steering linkage is disconnected from the steering gear, DO NOT turn the steering wheel hard against the stops or damage to the ball guides may result.

7. Position a 0-50 inch lbs. (0-6 Nm) torque wrench onto the steering wheel nut, then measure and record the bearing drag. To measure the bearing drag, use the torque wrench to rotate the steering wheel 90°.

8. Have an assistant tighten the adjuster plug slowly as the steering wheel is being turned using the torque wrench. The plug should be tightened to a point where the torque wrench shows a worm bearing preload of 5-8 inch lbs. (0.6-1.0 Nm).

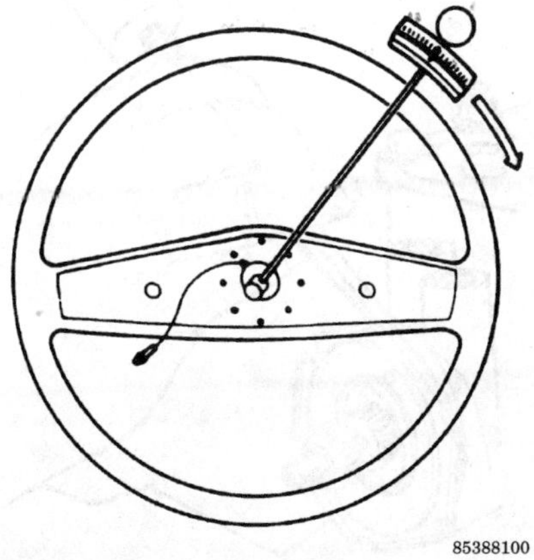

Fig. 96 Use an inch lbs. torque wrench to measure preload (effort necessary to turn the steering wheel/shaft)

After the thrust bearing preload is obtained, tighten the adjuster plug locknut to 85 ft. lbs. (115 Nm).

➡If the steering gear feels lumpy (after adjustment), suspect damage to the bearings, probably due to the improper adjustment or severe impact.

9. After the worm bearing preload is set, adjust the overcenter preload as follows:

a. Loosen the adjuster jam nut.

b. Back off the adjuster screw until it stops, then turn the adjuster screw back inward one full turn.

c. Turn the steering wheel, from one stop all the way to the other stop, counting the number of turns. Turn the steering wheel back exactly ½ way to the center position.

d. Measure and record the torque (preload) necessary to turn the worm shaft (from the steering shaft) with the gear at the center of travel. Use a 0-50 inch lbs. (0-6 Nm) torque wrench to measure preload.

e. Turn the adjuster screw in until the necessary preload torque is 4-10 inch lbs. (0.5-1.2 Nm) more than the first measurement.

f. Hold the adjuster screw from turning and tighten the jam nut to 25 ft. lbs. (34 Nm). Recheck the torque to assure the adjustment did not change while tightening the jam nut.

10. Install the horn cap or cover.

11. Align and install the pitman arm to the shaft, then secure. Refer to the procedure earlier in this section for details.

12. Remove the jackstands and carefully lower the vehicle, then connect the negative battery cable.

REMOVAL & INSTALLATION

See Figure 97

1. Disconnect the negative battery cable.

2. Raise and safely support the front of the vehicle using jackstands under the frame. Turn the wheels so they are facing in the straight ahead position.

3. If equipped, remove the retainers and the shield from the base of the intermediate shaft.

4. Matchmark the intermediate shaft-to-steering gear connection in order to assure proper installation.

5. Remove the intermediate shaft-to-steering gear pinch bolt.

6. Matchmark and remove the pitman arm from the pitman shaft. For details, please refer to the procedure located earlier in this section. It may be easier to save this step for later as access to the pitman arm/shaft may be difficult unless the gear is loosened or removed.

➡When separating the pitman arm from the shaft, DO NOT use a hammer or apply heat to the arm.

7. Unfasten the steering gear-to-frame mounting bolts and washers, then remove the gear from the vehicle.

8. If not done already and, if necessary, remove the pitman shaft from the gear at this time.

To install:

9. If necessary, align and install the pitman shaft to the gear.

10. Position the steering gear to the frame and secure by threading the retaining bolts. On some late model vehicles, if

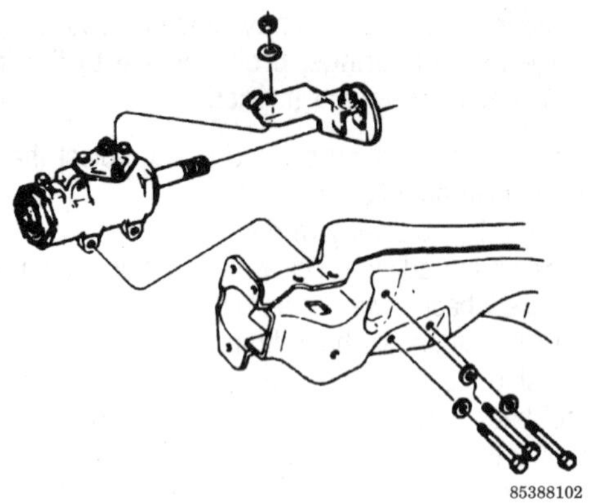

Fig. 97 Common steering gear mounting

not done already, it will be necessary to align and install the pitman arm to the shaft at this time.

11. Install the gear retaining bolts and tighten to 55 ft. lbs. (75 Nm).

➡When installing the steering gear, be sure that the intermediate shaft bottoms on the worm shaft, so that the pinch bolt passes through the undercut on the worm shaft. Check and/or adjust the alignment of the pitman arm-to-pitman shaft.

12. Align and install the intermediate shaft coupling using the pinch bolt. Tighten the bolt to 30 ft. lbs. (41 Nm).
13. If not done already, align and install the pitman arm to the shaft. Refer to the procedure earlier in this section for details.
14. If applicable, install the coupling shield over the intermediate shaft-to-gear coupling.
15. Remove the jackstands and carefully lower the vehicle.
16. Connect the negative battery cable.

Power Steering Gear

The recirculating ball type power steering gear used on these vehicles is basically the same as the manual steering gear, except that it uses a hydraulic assist on the rack piston.

The power steering gear control valve directs the power steering fluid to either side of the rack piston, which rides up and down the worm shaft. The steering rack converts the hydraulic pressure into mechanical force. Should the vehicle loose the hydraulic pressure, it can still be controlled mechanically.

ADJUSTMENTS

Steering gear adjustments are made only as corrections and NOT as periodic adjustments. Before adjusting the gear, check the remainder of the steering linkage and front suspension for wear or damage and repair/replace components, as necessary. Adjustment takes place in 2 major steps. First the worm bearing preload adjustment is made using the adjuster plug, then the overcenter preload is adjusted using the adjuster screw/bolt and jam nut.

➡To perform adjustments to the power steering gear, it is recommended to remove the power steering gear from the vehicle and place it in a vise. Before adjustments are performed to the system, be sure to check problems relating to hydraulic pressures and performance.

Worm Bearing Preload

➧ See Figures 98, 99, 100 and 101

1. Remove the steering gear from the vehicle and position it in a vise. For details, please refer to the procedure found in this section.
2. Using a hammer and a brass punch, drive the adjuster plug locknut counterclockwise and remove it from the end of the steering gear.
3. Use an adjustable spanner wrench such as J-7624 or equivalent, to turn the adjuster plug inward, until it firmly bot-

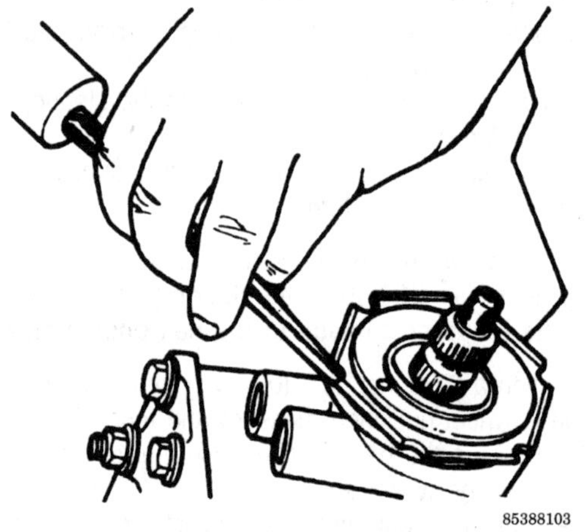

Fig. 98 Remove the adjuster locknut from the gear by driving it counterclockwise

Fig. 99 Matchmark the housing with the adjuster plug hole

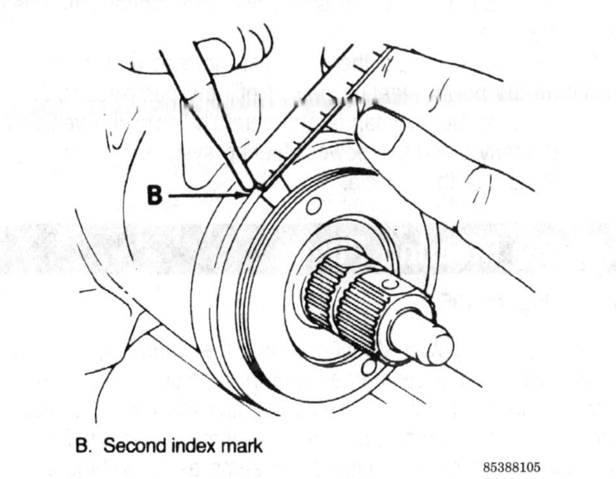

Fig. 100 Measure back (counterclockwise) and scribe a second mark

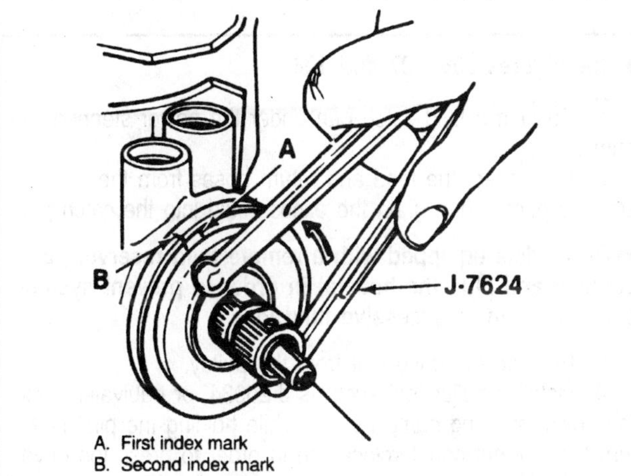

Fig. 101 Use the spanner wrench to align the adjuster plug with the second mark

toms in the housing with a torque of 20 ft. lbs. (27 Nm) on 1994 models and 22 ft. lbs. (30 Nm) on 1995-97 models.

4. Use a scribing tool to place a matchmark (on the housing) next to the one of the spanner wrench holes in the adjuster plug.

5. Using a ruler, measure 1/2 in. (13mm) counterclockwise from the scribed mark (on the housing) and place another mark.

6. Use the spanner to turn the adjuster plug (counterclockwise) until the hole in the adjuster plug aligns with the 2nd scribed mark.

7. While holding the adjuster plug in alignment, install and tighten the adjuster plug locknut.

8. Perform the overcenter preload adjustment.

Overcenter Preload

See Figures 102, 103 and 104

1. Adjust the worm bearing preload. For details, please refer to the procedure earlier in this section.

2. Rotate the stub shaft from stop-to-stop and count the number of turns necessary.

3. Starting from one stop, turn the stub shaft back 1/2 the number of turns (to the center of the gear).

➡With the stub gear centered, the flat on top of the shaft should face upward and be parallel with the side cover; the master spline on the pitman shaft should be in line with the adjuster screw.

4. Loosen the pitman shaft adjuster screw locknut, then turn the adjuster screw counterclockwise until it is fully extended. Turn the screw clockwise one full turn.

5. Place a 0-50 inch lbs. (0-6 Nm) torque wrench vertically on the stub shaft, then rotate it 45° (to each side) and record the highest drag measured near or on the center.

6. Turn the adjuster screw inward until the torque on the stub shaft is 6-10 inch lbs. (0.6-1.2 Nm) greater than the initial reading on 1994 models and 6-15 inch. lbs. (0.7-1.7 Nm) on 1995-97 models.

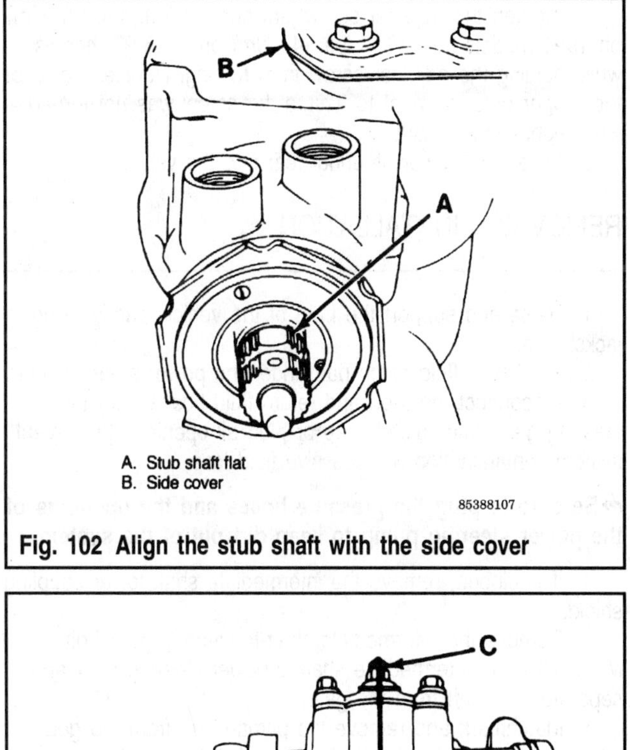

Fig. 102 Align the stub shaft with the side cover

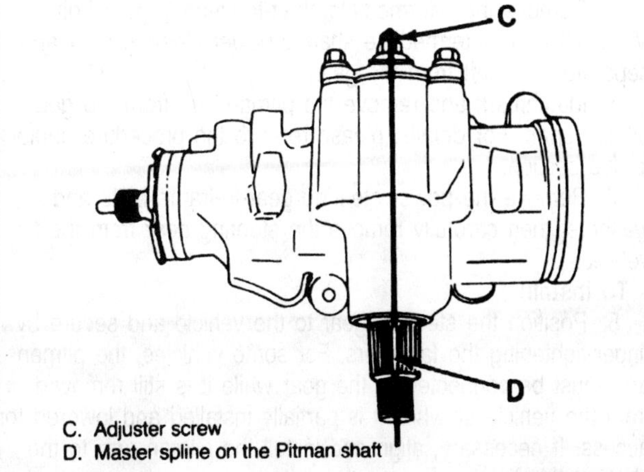

Fig. 103 Align the pitman arm shaft master spline

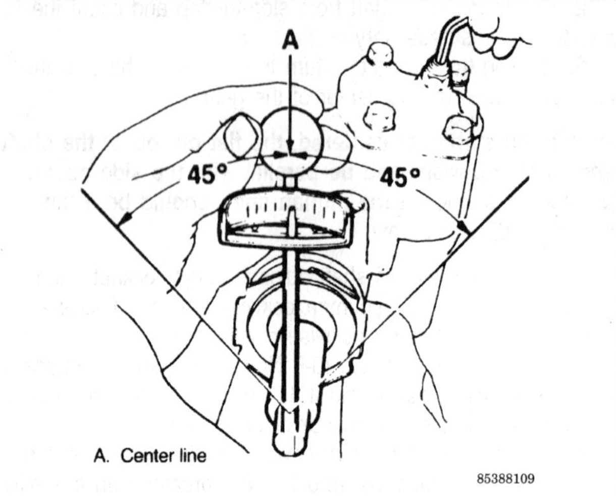

Fig. 104 Use an inch lbs. torque wrench to measure overcenter rotation torque

7. Tighten the adjuster screw jam nut to 20 ft. lbs. (27 Nm) on 1994 models and 36 ft. lbs. (49 Nm) on 1995-97 models while holding the adjuster screw from turning. Double check for the proper measurement to assure the screw was not turned while tightening the nut.
8. Install the power steering gear into the vehicle.

REMOVAL & INSTALLATION

1. Raise and support the front of the vehicle safely using jackstands.
2. Position a fluid catch pan under the power steering gear.
3. Disconnect the feed and return fluid hoses from the steering gear. Immediately cap or plug all openings to prevent system contamination or excessive fluid loss.

➡Be sure to plug the pressure hoses and the openings of the power steering pump to keep dirt out of the system.

4. If equipped, remove the intermediate shaft lower coupling shield.
5. Remove the intermediate shaft-to-steering gear bolt. Matchmark the intermediate shaft-to-power steering gear and separate the shaft from the gear.
6. Matchmark and remove the pitman arm from the gear pitman shaft. For details, please refer to the procedure earlier in this section.
7. Remove the power steering gear-to-frame bolts and washers, then carefully remove the steering gear from the vehicle.

To install:

8. Position the steering gear to the vehicle and secure by finger-tightening the fasteners. For some vehicles, the pitman arm must be connected to the gear while it is still removed from the vehicle or while it is partially installed and lowered for access. If necessary, align and install the pitman arm to the shaft at this time.
9. Tighten the power steering gear-to-frame bolts to 55 ft. lbs. (75 Nm).
10. Align and install the intermediate shaft to the power steering, then secure using the pinch bolt.
11. If equipped, install the shield over the intermediate shaft lower coupling.
12. Remove the caps, then connect the feed and return hoses to the power steering gear. Refill the pump reservoir.
13. Remove the jackstands and carefully lower the vehicle.
14. Properly bleed the power steering system.
15. Road test the vehicle.

Power Steering Pump

➧ See Figure 105

Two types of power steering pumps are commonly found on these vehicles; the submerged and the non-submerged types. The submerged pump has a housing and internal parts which are inside the reservoir and operate submerged in oil. The non-submerged pump functions the same as the submerged pump except the reservoir is separate from the housing and internal parts.

REMOVAL & INSTALLATION

➧ See Figures 106, 107 and 108

1. Position a fluid catch pan under the power steering pump.
2. Disconnect the feed and return hoses from the power steering pump, then drain the excess fluid into the catch pan.

➡On models equipped with a remote fluid reservoir, disconnect and plug the hose(s) in order to prevent system contamination or excessive fluid loss.

3. Remove the drive belt from the pulley.
4. Install a puller tool such as J-25034, or equivalent onto the power steering pump pulley. While holding the pilot bolt, turn the tool nut counterclockwise in order to press the drive pulley from the pump.

➡When installing the puller tool onto the power steering pump pulley, be sure that the pilot bolt bottoms in the pump shaft by turning the head of the pilot bolt.

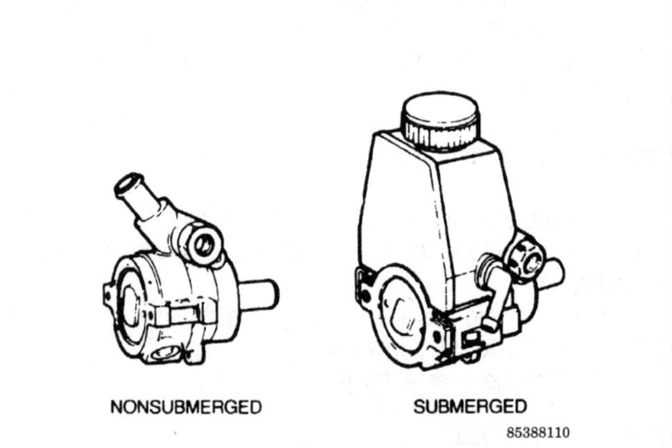

Fig. 105 Two types of power steering pumps are commonly found on these vehicles

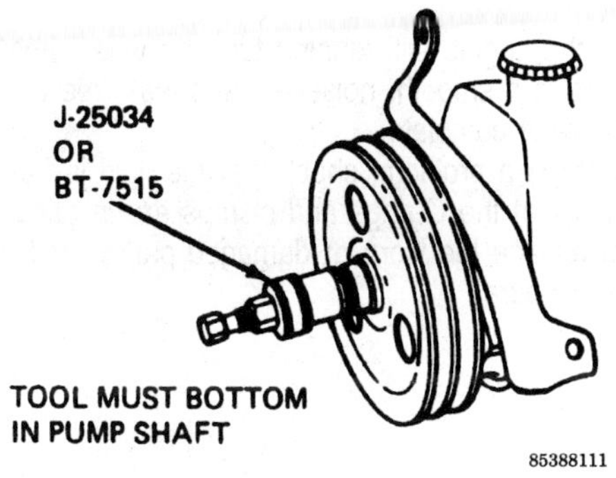

Fig. 106 Installing the pilot bolt

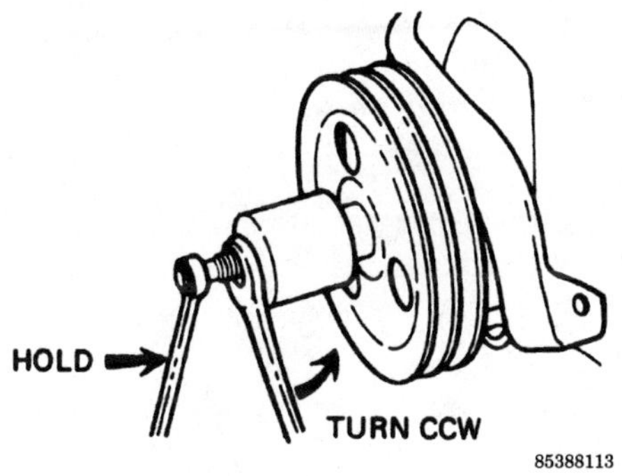

Fig. 107 Removing the power steering pump pulley

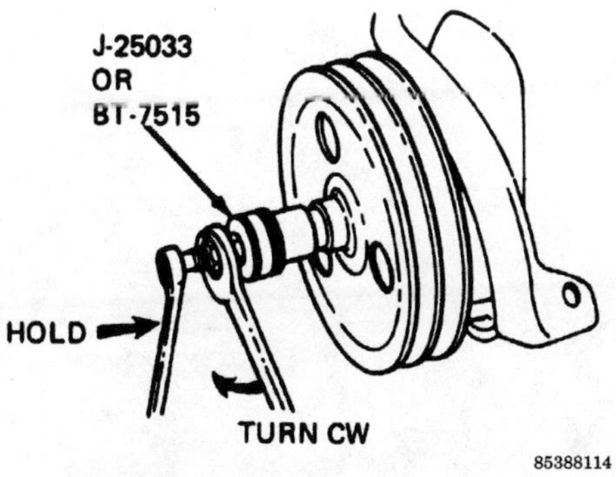

Fig. 108 Installing the power steering pump pulley

5. Remove the power steering pump-to-bracket bolts and, if applicable, the rear brace, then remove the pump from the vehicle.

To install.

6. Position the pump to the vehicle and secure using the retaining bolts to 22 ft. lbs. (30 Nm) on 2.2L engines and 37 ft. lbs. (50 Nm) on 4.3L engines.
7. If equipped, install the rear brace and tighten the retainers to 22 ft. lbs (30 Nm) on 2.2L engines and 31 ft. lbs (41 Nm) on 4.3L engines.
8. Use a pulley installer such as J-25033 or equivalent to press the drive pulley onto the power steering pump. While holding the pilot bolt, turn the tool nut clockwise in order to press the drive pulley onto the pump. Check that the pulley is flush within 0.010 in. (0.25mm) of the shaft end.

➡When positioning the installer tool onto the power steering pump pulley, be sure that the pilot bolt bottoms in the pump shaft by turning the head of the pilot bolt.

9. Properly install the drive belt and, if applicable, adjust the tension.

➡Be sure to secure any hoses which may get in the way or rub other components.

10. Remove the caps, then connect the feed and return hoses to the pump.
11. Properly refill and bleed the power steering system.
12. Test drive the vehicle.

SYSTEM BLEEDING

1994 Models

1. Add fluid to the reservoir until the proper level is reached, then allow the fluid to settle for at least 2 minutes. Start the engine and let it run for a few seconds, then turn it off and check if the level has changed. Repeat this until the level remains constant.
2. Raise and support the front of the vehicle safely using jackstands under the frame to the wheels are free to turn.
3. Start and run the engine, then slowly turn the wheels in both directions (lightly hitting the stops) several times.
4. Stop the engine and check the fluid level. If necessary, add power steering fluid to obtain the level indicated on the reservoir.

➡Maintain the fluid level just above the internal pump casting. Fluid with air in it will have a light tan or milky appearance. This air must be eliminated from the fluid before normal steering action can be obtained.

5. Remove the jackstands and carefully lower the vehicle.
6. Start and run the engine while turning the wheel slowly from stop to stop.
7. Stop the engine and check the fluid level. If necessary, add fluid in order to obtain the proper indicated level.
8. If the fluid is extremely foamy, allow the vehicle to stand for a few minutes, then repeat the procedure through this step.
9. Road test the vehicle to make sure the steering functions normally and is free from noise.
10. Allow the vehicle to stand for 2-3 hours, then recheck the power steering fluid.

1995-97 Models

1. Turn the ignition **OFF**, then turn the wheel to the full left position.
2. Fill the reservoir to the **FULL COLD** level and leave the cap off.
3. Raise the front of the vehicle and support it with jackstands.
4. With the ignition still in the **OFF** position, turn the wheel lock-to-lock at least 20 times (on models with long return lines perform this procedure at least 40 times).
5. Ensure that the fluid level remains at the **FULL COLD** position. and that there is no spilled fluid or air bubbles that could indicate a loose connection or leaking O-ring seal.
6. Turn the ignition **ON** and with the engine idling check the fluid level. If the level is correct install the cap.
7. Return the wheels to the center position and lower the vehicle.
8. With the engine still running turn the wheel from side-to-side. If there is a smooth, noiseless and leak free operation the procedure is complete.
9. If there is a problem, check that the fluid is free of bubbles and that the O-rings and clamps are in good condition. If not replace the worn or damaged part(s) and repeat the bleeding procedure.

TORQUE SPECIFICATIONS

Component	US	Metric
Front Suspension		
Lower Control Arm		
2WD Vehicles		
Front Nut		
1994-95	67 ft. lbs.	90 Nm
1996-97	85 ft. lbs.	115 Nm
Rear Nut		
1994-95	67 ft. lbs.	90 Nm
1996-97	72 ft. lbs.	98 Nm
4WD Vehicles		
Front Nut		
1994-95	70 ft. lbs.	95 Nm
1996-97	81 ft. lbs.	110 Nm
Rear Nut		
1994-95	70 ft. lbs.	95 Nm
1996-97	81 ft. lbs.	110 Nm
Stabilizer Bar-to-frame		
1994-95	30 ft. lbs.	40 Nm
1996-97	26 ft. lbs.	36 Nm
Stabilizer Bar-to-lower Arm		
1994-95	24 ft. lbs.	33 Nm
1996-97	11 ft. lbs.	15 Nm
Steering Knuckle Splash Shield	54 ft. lbs.	73 Nm
Upper Ball Joint		
Nuts	17 ft. lbs.	23 Nm
Stud Nut		
1994-95	70 ft. lbs.	95 Nm
1996-97	79 ft. lbs.	108 Nm
Upper Control Arm		
Nuts		
2WD Vehicles	65 ft. lbs.	88 Nm
4WD Vehicles		
Front nut		
1994-95	70 ft. lbs.	95 Nm
1996-97	85 ft. lbs.	115 Nm
Rear nut		
1994-95	70 ft. lbs.	95 Nm
1996-97	72 ft. lbs.	98 Nm
Shock Absorber		
1994-95		
Upper nuts	54 ft. lbs	73 Nm
Lower nuts	54 ft. lbs	73 Nm
1996-97		
2WD Vehicles		
Upper nuts	106 inch. lbs.	12 Nm
Lower nuts	22 ft. lbs.	30 Nm
4WD Vehicles		
Upper nuts	54 ft. lbs	73 Nm
Lower nuts	54 ft. lbs	73 Nm

88458C03

TORQUE SPECIFICATIONS

Component	US	Metric
Rear Suspension		
Leaf springs		
U-Bolts		
All models		
First pass	18 ft. lbs.	25 Nm
Second pass	85 ft. lbs.	115 Nm
Front bracket/rear shackle Nuts		
1994-95	92 ft. lbs.	125 Nm
1996-97	89 ft. lbs.	122 Nm
Shock Absorbers		
1994-95		
Lower	47 ft. lbs.	64 Nm
Upper	17 ft. lbs	23 Nm
1996-97		
Lower	62 ft. lbs.	84 Nm
Upper	22 ft. lbs	30 Nm
Stabilizer Bar Clamp U-bolt nuts	44 ft. lbs.	60 Nm
Stabilizer Bar-to-link nut		
Lower	50 ft. lbs.	68 Nm
Upper	25 ft. lbs.	35 Nm
Steering Column-to-Floor Plate		
Nuts	22 ft. lbs.	30 Nm
Bolts	120 inch lbs.	13 Nm
Steering Wheel Nut	30 ft. lbs.	40 Nm

88458C04

9

BRAKES

BASIC OPERATING PRINCIPLES

Hydraulic Brake Systems

Hydraulic systems are used to actuate the brakes of all modern automobiles. The system transports the power required to force the frictional surfaces of the braking system together from the pedal to the individual brake units at each wheel. A hydraulic system is used for two reasons.

First, fluid under pressure can be carried to all parts of an automobile by small pipes and flexible hoses without taking up a significant amount of room or posing routing problems.

Second, a great mechanical advantage can be given to the brake pedal end of the system, and the foot pressure required to actuate the brakes can be reduced by making the surface area of the master cylinder pistons smaller than that of any of the pistons in the wheel cylinders or calipers.

The master cylinder consists of a fluid reservoir along with a double cylinder and piston assembly. Double type master cylinders are designed to separate the front and rear braking systems hydraulically in case of a leak. The master cylinder coverts mechanical motion from the pedal into hydraulic pressure within the lines. This pressure is translated back into mechanical motion at the wheels by either the wheel cylinder (drum brakes) or the caliper (disc brakes).

Steel lines carry the brake fluid to a point on the vehicle's frame near each of the vehicle's wheels. The fluid is then carried to the calipers and wheel cylinders by flexible tubes in order to allow for suspension and steering movements.

In drum brake systems, each wheel cylinder contains two pistons, one at either end, which push outward in opposite directions and force the brake shoe into contact with the drum.

In disc brake systems, the cylinders are part of the calipers. At least one cylinder in each caliper is used to force the brake pads against the disc.

All pistons employ some type of seal, usually made of rubber, to minimize fluid leakage. A rubber dust boot seals the outer end of the cylinder against dust and dirt. The boot fits around the outer end of the piston on disc brake calipers, and around the brake actuating rod on wheel cylinders.

The hydraulic system operates as follows: When at rest, the entire system, from the piston(s) in the master cylinder to those in the wheel cylinders or calipers, is full of brake fluid. Upon application of the brake pedal, fluid trapped in front of the master cylinder piston(s) is forced through the lines to the wheel cylinders. Here, it forces the pistons outward, in the case of drum brakes, and inward toward the disc, in the case of disc brakes. The motion of the pistons is opposed by return springs mounted outside the cylinders in drum brakes, and by spring seals, in disc brakes.

Upon release of the brake pedal, a spring located inside the master cylinder immediately returns the master cylinder pistons to the normal position. The pistons contain check valves and the master cylinder has compensating ports drilled in it. These are uncovered as the pistons reach their normal position. The piston check valves allow fluid to flow toward the wheel cylinders or calipers as the pistons withdraw. Then, as the return springs force the brake pads or shoes into the released position, the excess fluid reservoir through the compensating ports. It is during the time the pedal is in the released position that any fluid that has leaked out of the system will be replaced through the compensating ports.

Dual circuit master cylinders employ two pistons, located one behind the other, in the same cylinder. The primary piston is actuated directly by mechanical linkage from the brake pedal through the power booster. The secondary piston is actuated by fluid trapped between the two pistons. If a leak develops in front of the secondary piston, it moves forward until it bottoms against the front of the master cylinder, and the fluid trapped between the pistons will operate the rear brakes. If the rear brakes develop a leak, the primary piston will move forward until direct contact with the secondary piston takes place, and it will force the secondary piston to actuate the front brakes. In either case, the brake pedal moves farther when the brakes are applied, and less braking power is available.

All dual circuit systems use a switch to warn the driver when only half of the brake system is operational. This switch is usually located in a valve body which is mounted on the firewall or the frame below the master cylinder. A hydraulic piston receives pressure from both circuits, each circuit's pressure being applied to one end of the piston. When the pressures are in balance, the piston remains stationary. When one circuit has a leak, however, the greater pressure in that circuit during application of the brakes will push the piston to one side, closing the switch and activating the brake warning light.

In disc brake systems, this valve body also contains a metering valve and, in some cases, a proportioning valve. The metering valve keeps pressure from traveling to the disc brakes on the front wheels until the brake shoes on the rear wheels have contacted the drums, ensuring that the front brakes will never be used alone. The proportioning valve controls the pressure to the rear brakes to lessen the chance of rear wheel lock-up during very hard braking.

Warning lights may be tested by depressing the brake pedal and holding it while opening one of the wheel cylinder bleeder screws. If this does not cause the light to go on, substitute a new lamp, make continuity checks, and, finally, replace the switch as necessary.

The hydraulic system may be checked for leaks by applying pressure to the pedal gradually and steadily. If the pedal sinks very slowly to the floor, the system has a leak. This is not to be confused with a springy or spongy feel due to the compression of air within the lines. If the system leaks, there will be a gradual change in the position of the pedal with a constant pressure.

Check for leaks along all lines and at wheel cylinders. If no external leaks are apparent, the problem is inside the master cylinder.

DISC BRAKES

Instead of the traditional expanding brakes that press outward against a circular drum, disc brake systems utilize a disc (rotor) with brake pads positioned on either side of it. An easily-seen analogy is the hand brake arrangement on a bicycle. The pads squeeze onto the rim of the bike wheel, slowing its motion. Automobile disc brakes use the identical principle but apply the braking effort to a separate disc instead of the wheel.

The disc (rotor) is a casting, usually equipped with cooling fins between the two braking surfaces. This enables air to circulate between the braking surfaces making them less sensitive to heat buildup and more resistant to fade. Dirt and water do not drastically affect braking action since contaminants are thrown off by the centrifugal action of the rotor or scraped off the by the pads. Also, the equal clamping action of the two brake pads tends to ensure uniform, straight line stops. Disc brakes are inherently self-adjusting. There are three general types of disc brake:

1. A fixed caliper.
2. A floating caliper.
3. A sliding caliper.

The fixed caliper design uses two pistons mounted on either side of the rotor (in each side of the caliper). The caliper is mounted rigidly and does not move.

The sliding and floating designs are quite similar. In fact, these two types are often lumped together. In both designs, the pad on the inside of the rotor is moved into contact with the rotor by hydraulic force. The caliper, which is not held in a fixed position, moves slightly, bringing the outside pad into contact with the rotor. There are various methods of attaching floating calipers. Some pivot at the bottom or top, and some slide on mounting bolts. In any event, the end result is the same.

DRUM BRAKES

Drum brakes employ two brake shoes mounted on a stationary backing plate. These shoes are positioned inside a circular drum which rotates with the wheel assembly. The shoes are held in place by springs. This allows them to slide toward the drums (when they are applied) while keeping the linings and drums in alignment. The shoes are actuated by a wheel cylinder which is mounted at the top of the backing plate. When the brakes are applied, hydraulic pressure forces the wheel cylinder's actuating links outward. Since these links bear directly against the top of the brake shoes, the tops of the shoes are then forced against the inner side of the drum. This action forces the bottoms of the two shoes to contact the brake drum by rotating the entire assembly slightly (known as servo action). When pressure within the wheel cylinder is relaxed, return springs pull the shoes back away from the drum.

Most modern drum brakes are designed to self-adjust themselves during application when the vehicle is moving in reverse. This motion causes both shoes to rotate very slightly with the drum, rocking an adjusting lever, thereby causing rotation of the adjusting screw. Some drum brake systems are designed to self-adjust during application whenever the brakes are applied. This on-board adjustment system reduces the need for maintenance adjustments and keeps both the brake function and pedal feel satisfactory.

POWER BOOSTERS

Virtually all modern vehicles use a vacuum assisted power brake system to multiply the braking force and reduce pedal effort. Since vacuum is always available when the engine is operating, the system is simple and efficient. A vacuum diaphragm is located on the front of the master cylinder and assists the driver in applying the brakes, reducing both the effort and travel he must put into moving the brake pedal.

The vacuum diaphragm housing is normally connected to the intake manifold by a vacuum hose. A check valve is placed at the point where the hose enters the diaphragm housing, so that during periods of low manifold vacuum brakes assist will not be lost.

Depressing the brake pedal closes off the vacuum source and allows atmospheric pressure to enter on one side of the diaphragm. This causes the master cylinder pistons to move and apply the brakes. When the brake pedal is released, vacuum is applied to both sides of the diaphragm and springs return the diaphragm and master cylinder pistons to the released position.

If the vacuum supply fails, the brake pedal rod will contact the end of the master cylinder actuator rod and the system will apply the brakes without any power assistance. The driver will notice that much higher pedal effort is needed to stop the car and that the pedal feels harder than usual.

Vacuum Leak Test

1. Operate the engine at idle without touching the brake pedal for at least one minute.
2. Turn off the engine and wait one minute.
3. Test for the presence of assist vacuum by depressing the brake pedal and releasing it several times. If vacuum is present in the system, light application will produce less and less pedal travel. If there is no vacuum, air is leaking into the system.

System Operation Test

1. With the engine **OFF**, pump the brake pedal until the supply vacuum is entirely gone.
2. Put light, steady pressure on the brake pedal.
3. Start the engine and let it idle. If the system is operating correctly, the brake pedal should fall toward the floor if the constant pressure is maintained.

Power brake systems may be tested for hydraulic leaks just as ordinary systems are tested.

⁂WARNING

Clean, high quality brake fluid is essential to the safe and proper operation of the brake system. You should always buy the highest quality brake fluid that is available. If the brake fluid becomes contaminated, drain and flush the system, then refill the master cylinder with new fluid. Never reuse any brake fluid. Any brake fluid that is removed from the system should be discarded.

Adjustments

FRONT DISC BRAKES

Disc brakes are not adjustable. They are, in effect, self adjusting during normal operation. For details on how the disc brakes operate, please refer to the operating principles found earlier in this section.

REAR DRUM BRAKES

See Figure 1

Normal adjustments of the rear drum brakes are automatic and are made during the reverse applications of the brakes. The following procedure should be used ONLY if the linings have been replaced.

1. Raise and support the rear of the vehicle safely using jackstands.
2. Using a punch and a hammer on the rear of the backing plates, knock out the lanced metal areas near the starwheel assemblies on each plate. The metal areas may already have been removed and covered with rubber adjustment plugs, if so remove the plugs by grasping and pulling with a pair of pliers.

➡After knocking out the lanced metal areas from the backing plate, the wheels must be removed and all of the metal pieces discarded, then the wheels should be reinstalled for adjustment.

3. Insert a suitable brake adjustment tool such as J-4735 or equivalent, into the breaking plate slots and engage the lowest possible tooth on the starwheel. Move the end of the brake tool downward to move the starwheel upward and expand the adjusting screw. Repeat this operation until the wheels can JUST be turned by hand. This is a position immediately before the brakes lock.

➡The brake drag should be equal at both wheels.

4. Back off the adjusting screws 24 notches (clicks). By the time you have backed off the adjustment 12 clicks, the brakes should have no drag. If a heavy drag is still present, the parking brake cable is likely in need of adjustment.
5. Make sure both sides of the brakes are properly adjusted. When backing off the brakes on the other side, the adjusting lever must be backed off the same number of turns to prevent side-to-side brake pull.
6. After the brakes are adjusted, install a rubber hole cover into each of the the backing plate slots. To complete the brake adjustment operation, make several stops while backing the truck to fully equalize the adjustment.
7. Road test the vehicle.

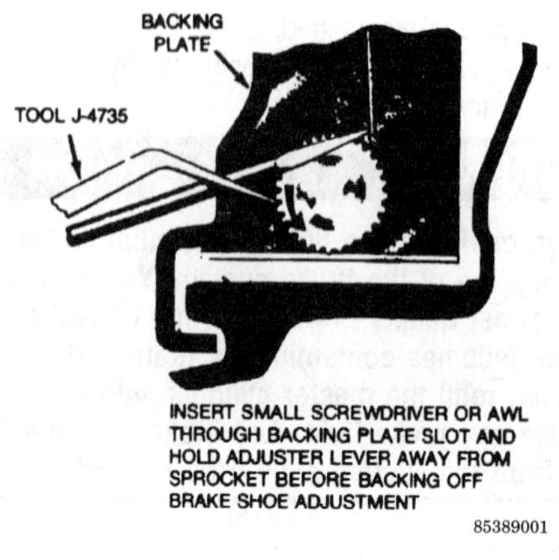

Fig. 1 Drum brake adjustment

BRAKE PEDAL TRAVEL

See Figure 2

The brake pedal travel is the distance the pedal moves toward the floor from the fully released position. On most vehicles covered by this manual it is not adjustable, but checking the distance will give an indication of system condition. Inspection should be made using 100 lbs. (445 N) of pressure on the brake pedal, when the brake system is cold. On power brake equipped vehicles, be sure to pump the brakes at least 5 times to remove vacuum from the booster before making the check.

To check the travel, first measure the distance from the top of the released pedal to the bottom of the steering wheel, then depress the pedal (using 100 lbs. of force) and re-measure the distance. The difference between the 2 measurements (pedal travel) should be approximately 1.7 in. (42mm).

If the pedal travel is excessive, check the pedal and the hydraulic brake system for wear or damage and repair, as necessary.

Brake Light Switch

A brake light switch is mounted to the pedal bracket on all vehicles covered by this manual. The purpose of the switch is to illuminate the brake lights whenever the pedal is depressed,

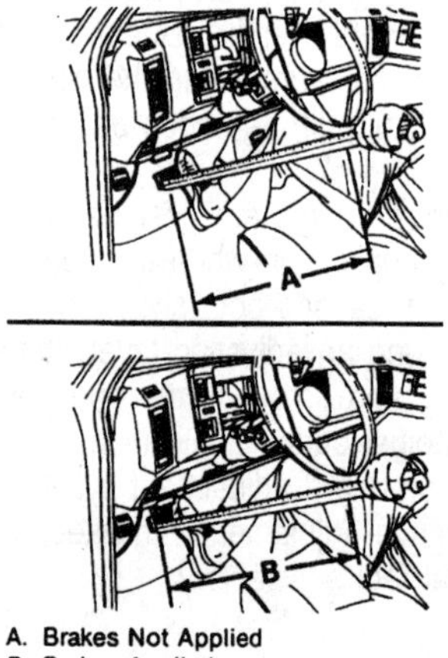

Fig. 2 Checking the brake pedal for excessive travel

therefore proper operation and adjustment is critical to safe vehicle operation. The switch is snapped into position on the pushrod, so no adjustment is necessary or possible.

REMOVAL & INSTALLATION

See Figure 3

1. Disconnect the negative battery cable.
2. Disengage the switch electrical connector.
3. Disengage the retainer from the brake pedal pin, then remove the switch by unsnapping it from the pushrod.

To install:

4. Install the switch by snapping it onto the pushrod, then secure using the retainer on the pedal pin.
5. Engage the switch connector.
6. Connect the negative battery cable and verify proper switch operation.

Brake Pedal

REMOVAL & INSTALLATION

See Figure 4

1. Disconnect the negative battery cable.
2. Remove the lower trim panel, then disengage the electrical connection from the brake light switch.
3. Disengage the retainer from the brake pedal pin, then remove the switch.
4. Disengage the pushrod and remove the bolt.
5. Remove the bushings, spacer and brake pedal.

To install:

6. Insert the spacer and bushings into the pedal, then install the pedal.
7. Install the bolt and nut and tighten to 26 ft. lbs. (35 Nm) on 1994-95 models and 32 ft. lbs (44 Nm) on 1996-97 models.
8. Engage the pushrod and then install the brake light switch.

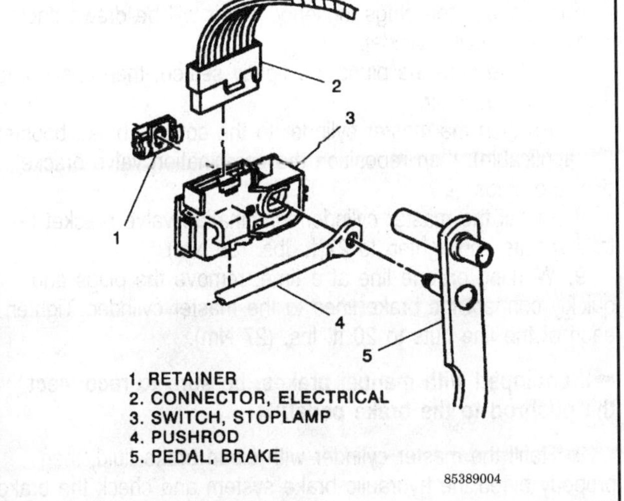

Fig. 3 Brake light switch mounting

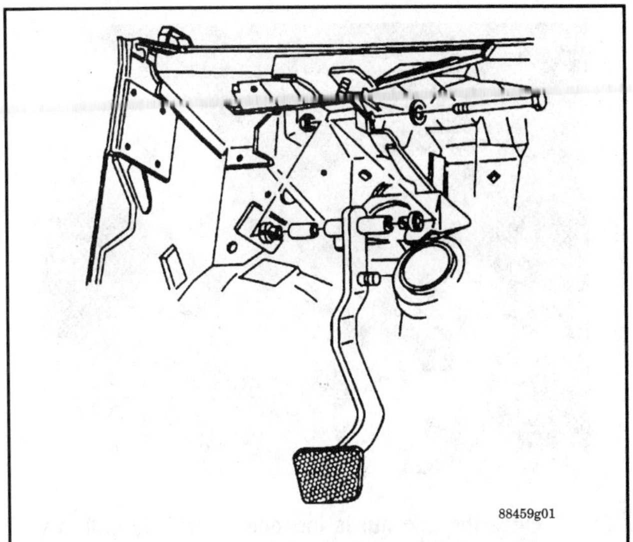

Fig. 4 Exploded view of the brake pedal assembly

9. Engage the brake light switch electrical connection, then install the lower trim panel.
10. Connect the negative battery cable and adjust pedal travel as outlined in this section.

Master Cylinder

REMOVAL & INSTALLATION

See Figures 5, 6, 7, 8, 9 and 10

1. Apply the parking brakes and block the drive wheels.
2. Use a line wrench to loosen and disconnect the hydraulic lines from the master cylinder. Immediately plug the lines to prevent system contamination or excessive fluid loss.
3. If equipped with non-power brakes, disconnect the pushrod from the brake pedal.
4. Remove the master cylinder attachment nuts, then separate the combination valve/bracket from the master cylinder.

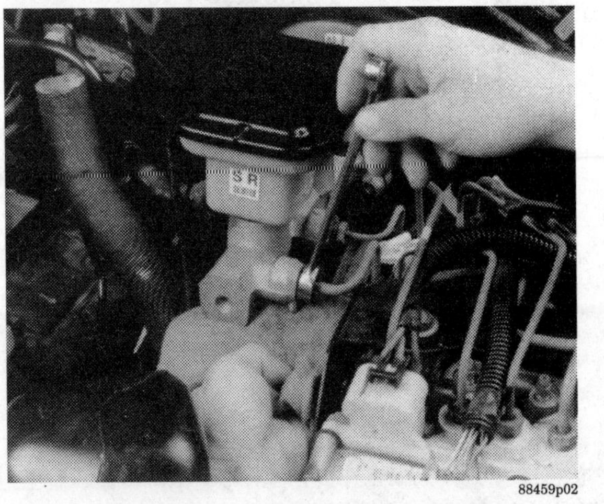

Fig. 5 Place a rag under the line wrench to help minimize spillage when disconnecting the brake lines

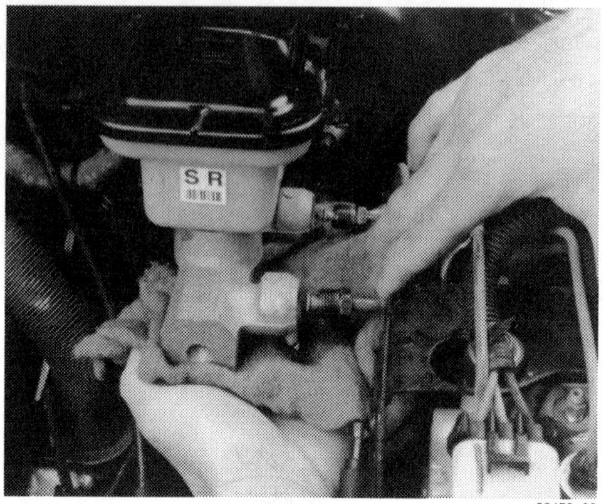

88459p03

Fig. 6 Once the line nut is loosened, carefully pull the fitting away from the master cylinder

88459p04

Fig. 7 Once the lines are disconnected and plugged, loosen and remove the master cylinder retaining nuts

88459p05

Fig. 8 Carefully pull the master cylinder from the mounting studs

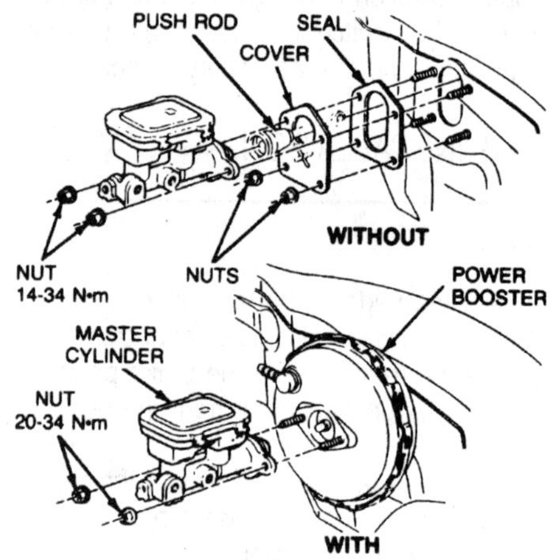

85389005

Fig. 9 Common master cylinder mounting with/without a vacuum booster system

5. Remove the master cylinder and, as equipped, the gasket and/or rubber boot from the vehicle.

To install:

6. In order to ease installation, bench bleed the master cylinder before installation:

a. Plug the master cylinder outlet ports. This can be done using rubber or plastic plugs or, more effectively, using a single length of brake line with appropriately sized flares/flare nuts on each end.

b. Mount the cylinder in a soft-jawed vise with the front end tilted slightly downward.

c. Fill the reservoir with clean brake fluid, then use a tool with a smooth rounded end (such as a wooden dowel or pencil eraser) to stroke the primary piston about 1 in. (25mm) several times. As air is bled from the cylinder, the primary piston will no longer travel the full distance.

d. Reposition the master cylinder in the vise with the front end tilted slightly up, then continue stroking the primary piston to further bleed air.

e. Reposition the master cylinder so it is level, then loosen the plugs one at a time and push the piston into the bore forcing air from the cylinder. DO NOT allow the piston to return with the plugs loosened or air will be drawn back into the master cylinder.

f. Make sure the plugs are tightly sealed, then check and refill the reservoir.

7. Position the master cylinder to the cowl or brake booster (as applicable), then reposition the combination valve bracket over the studs.

8. Install the master cylinder/combination valve bracket retaining nuts and tighten to 27 ft. lbs. (36 Nm).

9. Working on one line at a time, remove the plugs and quickly connect the brake lines to the master cylinder. Tighten each of the line nuts to 20 ft. lbs. (27 Nm).

➡If equipped with manual brakes, be sure to reconnect the pushrod to the brake pedal.

10. Refill the master cylinder with clean brake fluid, then properly bleed the hydraulic brake system and check the brake pedal travel.

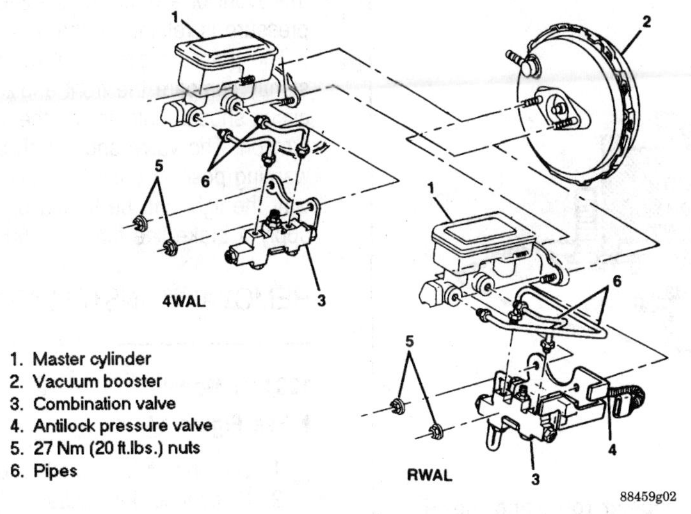

Fig. 10 Exploded view of common master cylinder assembly mountings

11. When all service is finished, remove the blocks from the drive wheels.

Power Brake Booster

The power brake booster is a tandem vacuum suspended unit. Some models may be equipped with a single or dual function vacuum switch which activates a brake warning light should low booster vacuum be present. Under normal operation, vacuum is present on both sides of the diaphragms. When the brakes are applied, atmospheric air is admitted to one side of the diaphragms to provide power assistance.

REMOVAL & INSTALLATION

See Figures 11 and 12

1. Apply the parking brake and block the drive wheels.
2. Remove the master cylinder-to-power brake booster nuts, then reposition the master cylinder and combination valve out of the way; if necessary, support the master cylinder on a wire to prevent damaging the brake lines.

When removing the master cylinder from the power brake booster, it is not necessary to disconnect the hydraulic lines, therefore the brake system should not have to be bled.

3. Disconnect the vacuum hose from the power brake booster.
4. From under the dash, disconnect the pushrod from the brake pedal. On vehicles covered by this manual the retainer and brake switch must be removed.
5. From under the dash, remove the power brake booster-to-cowl retaining nuts.
6. Back under the hood, remove the power brake booster and the gasket from the cowl.

To install:

7. Position the booster to the cowl using a new gasket.

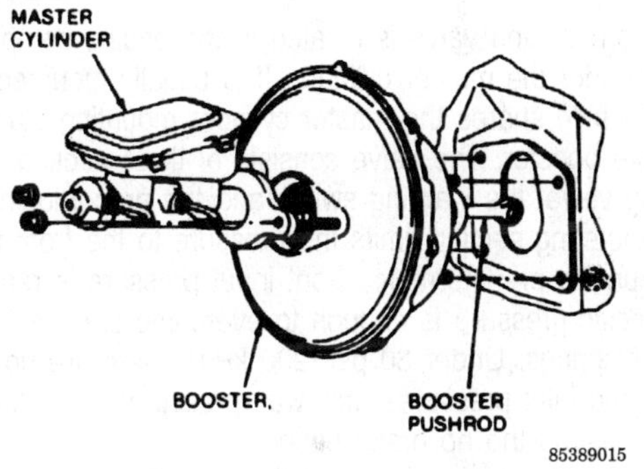

Fig. 11 Common power brake booster attachment

8. Install the booster retaining nuts and tighten to 24 ft. lbs. (32 Nm) for 1994-95 models and 27 ft. lbs. (36 Nm) on 1996-97 models.
9. Connect the pedal pushrod and install the washer or switch and the retainer.
10. Connect the vacuum hose.
11. For all vehicles covered in this manual, gauge the booster rod:
    a. Apply 25 in. Hg (85 kPa) of vacuum using a hand held vacuum pump or apply maximum engine vacuum.
    b. Check the maximum and minimum rod lengths using J-37839 or an equivalent pushrod height gauge.
    c. If the piston is not within limits, install a service adjustable piston rod and adjust it to the correct length.
12. Reposition the master cylinder and combination valve bracket to the booster studs, then secure using the retaining nuts. For details, please refer to the master cylinder procedure located earlier in this section.
13. Start and run the engine, then check for proper booster operation.

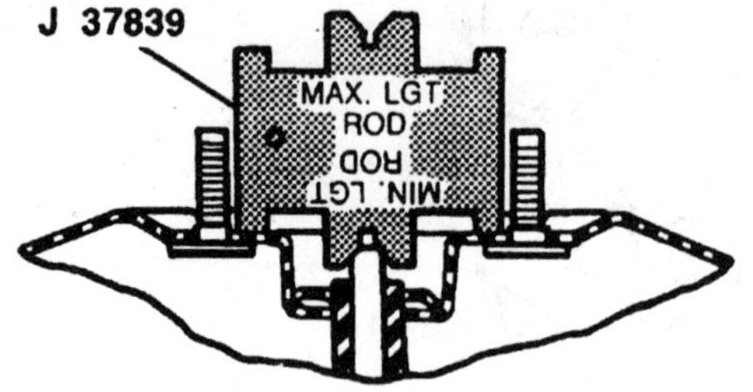

Fig. 12 Checking the piston booster rod using the gauge tool

Combination Valve

See Figure 13

The combination valve is located in the engine compartment, directly under the master cylinder. It is usually mounted to a bracket which shares the master cylinder mounting studs on the brake booster. The valve consists of three sections: the metering valve, the warning switch and the proportioning valve.

The metering section limits the pressure to the front disc brakes until a predetermined front input pressure is reached. The specific pressure is enough to overcome the rear shoe retractor springs. Under 30 psi (200 kPa), there are no restrictions of the inlet pressures; this way pressures are allowed to equalize during the no brake period.

The proportioning section controls the outlet pressure to the rear brakes after a predetermined rear input pressure has been reached; this feature is provided for vehicles with light loads, to help prevent rear wheel lock-up. The by-pass feature of this valve assures full system pressure to the rear brakes in the event of a front brake system malfunction. Also, full front pressure is retained if the rear system malfunctions.

The pressure differential warning switch is designed to constantly compare the front and the rear brake pressures; if one circuit should malfunction, the warning light (on the dash) will turn on. The valve and switch are designed to lock in the warning position once the malfunction has occurred. The only way the light can be turned off is to repair the malfunction and apply a brake line force of 450 psi (3100 kPa).

REMOVAL & INSTALLATION

1994-95 Models

See Figure 14

1. Disconnect the negative battery cable.
2. Disconnect the hydraulic lines from the combination valve one at a time. Immediately plug all openings to prevent system contamination or excessive fluid loss.

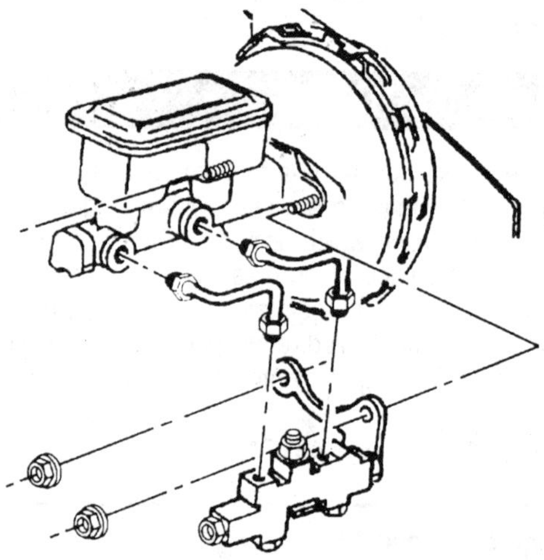

Fig. 14 View of the combination valve mounting (4WAL)

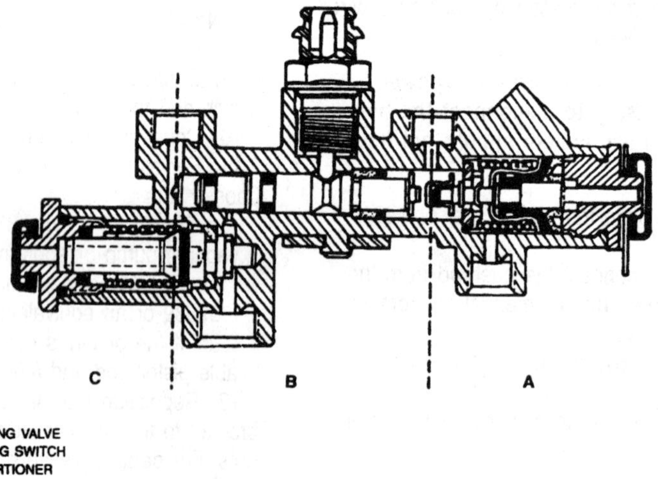

Fig. 13 Cross-sectional view of a combination valve assembly

3. Disengage the electrical connector from the combination valve pressure switch.

4. If equipped with Rear Wheel Anti-Lock (RWAL) brakes, disengage the RWAL pressure valve connector.

5. On most vehicles, remove the master cylinder/combination valve-to-bracket retaining nuts, then remove the valve from the vehicle. On some early model vehicles the combination valve may be removed from the bracket by removing the retaining bolt. If desired, remove the bolt and valve leaving the bracket and master cylinder secured to the booster.

6. If used, remove the RWAL pressure valve.

➡The combination valve is not repairable and must be replaced as a complete assembly.

To install:

7. If applicable, install the RWAL pressure valve.

8. Install the combination valve and bracket assembly, then install and tighten the master cylinder/valve bracket retaining nuts to specification. For details, please refer to the master cylinder procedure located earlier in this section.

9. If used, engage the RWAL pressure valve connector.

10. Engage the pressure switch electrical connector.

11. Remove the caps (one at a time) and connect the brake lines to the combination valve, then tighten the fittings.

12. Check and refill the master cylinder reservoir, then properly bleed the hydraulic brake system.

1996-97 Models

See Figure 15

1. Disconnect the hydraulic lines from the combination valve one at a time. Immediately plug all openings to prevent system contamination or excessive fluid loss.

2. Disengage the electrical connector from the combination valve pressure switch.

3. Unfasten the combination valve retaining nuts and remove the valve.

To install:

4. Install the combination valve and tighten the retaining nuts to 27 ft. lbs. (36 Nm).

5. Engage the electrical connector from the combination valve pressure switch.

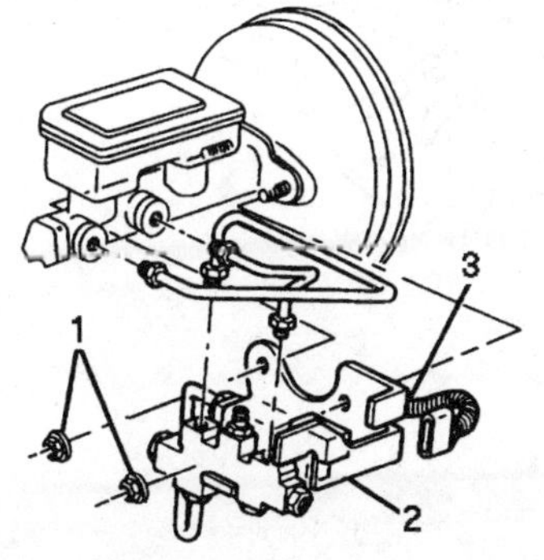

1. Nuts 27 Nm (20 ft.lbs.)
2. Combination valve
3. Antilock pressure valve

88459g04

Fig. 15 View of the combination valve mounting (RWAL)

6. Connect the hydraulic lines to the combination valve and tighten the fittings to 21 ft. lbs. (29 Nm).

Brake Hoses and Pipes

REMOVAL & INSTALLATION

Brake Hose

See Figures 16, 17 and 18

1. Raise the end of the vehicle which contains the hose to be repaired, then support the vehicle safely using jackstands.

2. If necessary, remove the wheel for easier access to the hose.

3. Disconnect the hose from the wheel cylinder or caliper and plug the opening to avoid excessive fluid loss or contamination.

4. Disconnect the hose from the brake line (on 4WD models remove the nut and bolt) and plug the openings to avoid excessive fluid loss or contamination.

To install:

5. Install the brake hose to the brake line and tighten the retainer to 13 ft. lbs. (17 Nm) for rear brakes or 32 ft. lbs. (44 Nm) for front brakes. On 4WD models tighten the nut and bolt to 13 ft. lbs. (17 Nm).

6. If installing a front brake hose, make sure the hose is routed properly, with the loop to the rear of the vehicle.

7. Install the hose to the wheel cylinder or caliper using NEW washers, then tighten the retainer to 36 ft. lbs. (49 Nm).

8. Properly bleed the brake system, then check the connections for leaks.

9. Remove the supports and carefully lower the vehicle.

Brake Line

There are 2 options available when replacing a brake line. The first, and probably most preferable, is to replace the entire line using a line of similar length which is already equipped with machined flared ends. Such lines are usually available from auto parts stores and usually require only a minimum of bending in order to properly fit then to the vehicle. The second option is to bend and flare the entire replacement line (or a repair section of line) using the appropriate tools.

Buying a line with machined flares is usually preferable because of the time and effort saved, not to mention the cost of special tools if they are not readily available. Also, machined flares are usually of a much higher quality than those produced by hand flaring tools or kits.

1. Raise the end of the vehicle which contains the hose to be repaired, then support the vehicle safely using jackstands.

2. Remove the components necessary for access to the brake line which is being replaced.

3. Disconnect the fittings at each end of the line, then plug the openings to prevent excessive fluid loss or contamination.

4. Trace the line from 1 end to the other and disconnect the line from any retaining clips, then remove the line from the vehicle.

To install:

5. Try to obtain a replacement line that is the same length as the line that was removed. If the line is longer, you will have to cut it and flare the end, or if you have decided to

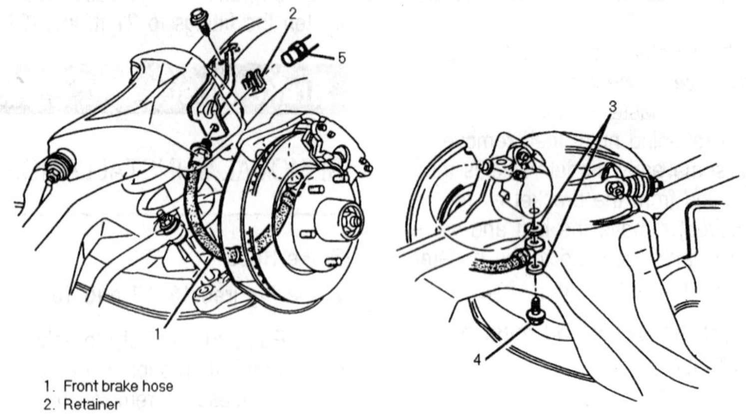

Fig. 16 Common front brake hose routing — 2WD models

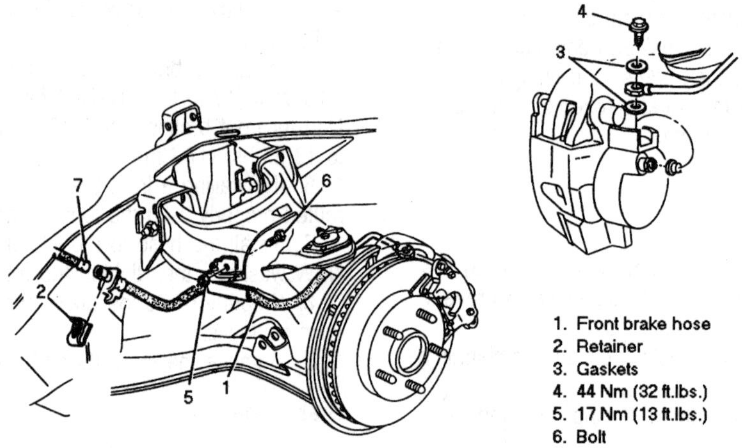

Fig. 17 Common front brake hose routing — 4WD models

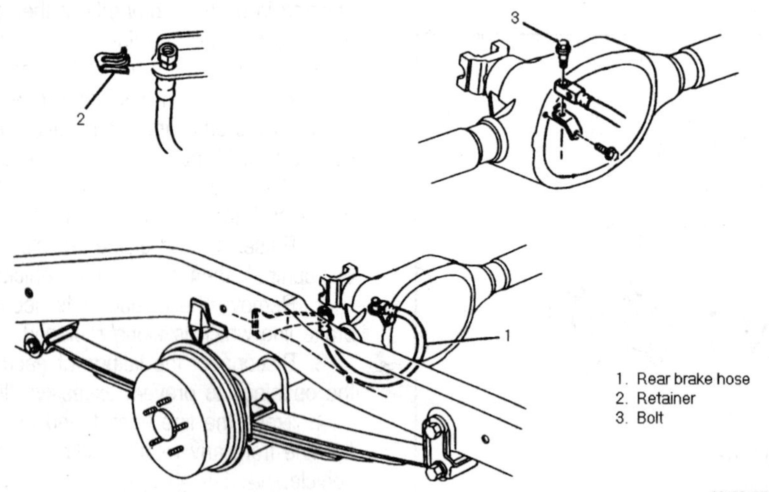

Fig. 18 Common rear brake hose routing

repair a portion of the line, see the procedure on brake line flaring, later in this section.

6. Use a suitable tubing bender to make the necessary bends in the line. Work slowly and carefully; try to make the bends look as close as possible to those on the line being replaced.

➡ When bending the brake line, be careful not to kink or crack the line. If the brake line becomes kinked or cracked, it must be replaced.

7. Before installing the brake line, flush it with brake cleaner to remove any dirt or foreign material.

8. Install the line into the vehicle. Be sure to attach the line to the retaining clips, as necessary. Make sure the replacement brake line does not contact any components that could rub the line and cause a leak.

9. Connect the brake line fittings and tighten to 18 ft. lbs. (24 Nm), except for the rear line-to-hose fitting which should be tightened to 14 ft. lbs. (19 Nm).

10. Properly bleed the brake system and check for leaks.

11. Install any removed components, then remove the supports and carefully lower the vehicle.

BRAKE LINE FLARING

Use only brake line tubing approved for automotive use; never use copper tubing. Whenever possible, try to work with brake lines that are already cut to the length needed. These lines are available at most auto parts stores and have machine made flares, the quality of which is hard to duplicate with most of the available inexpensive flaring kits.

When the brakes are applied, there is a great amount of pressure developed in the hydraulic system. An improperly formed flare can leak with resultant loss of stopping power. If you have never formed a double-flare, take time to familiarize yourself with the flaring kit; practice forming double-flares on scrap tubing until you are satisfied with the results.

The following procedure applies to the SA9193BR flaring kit, but should be similar to commercially available brake-line flaring kits. If these instructions differ in any way from those in your kit, follow the instructions in the kit.

1. Determine the length necessary for the replacement or repair and allow an additional 1/8 in. (3.2mm) for each flare. Select a piece of tubing, then cut the brake line to the necessary length using an appropriate saw. Do not use a tubing cutter.

2. Square the end of the tube with a file and chamfer the edges. Remove burrs from the inside and outside diameters of the cut line using a deburring tool.

3. Install the required fittings onto the line.

4. Install SA9193BR, or an equivalent flaring tool, into a vice and install the handle into the operating cam.

5. Loosen the die clamp screw and rotate the locking plate to expose the die carrier opening.

6. Select the required die set (4.75mm DIN) and install in the carrier with the full side of either half facing clamp screw and counter bore of both halves facing punch turret.

7. Insert the prepared line through the rear of the die and push forward until the line end is flush with the die face.

8. Make sure the rear of both halves of the die rest against the hexagon die stops, then rotate the locking plate to the fully closed position and clamp the die firmly by tightening the clamp screw.

9. Rotate the punch turret until the appropriate size (4.75mm DIN) points towards the open end of the line to be flared.

10. Pull the operating handle against the line resistance in order to create the flare, then return the handle to the original position.

11. Release the clamp screw and rotate the locking plate to the open position.

12. Remove the die set and line, then separate by gently tapping both halves on the bench. Inspect the flare for proper size and shape. Dimension A should be 0.272-0.286 in. (6.92-7.28mm).

13. If necessary, repeat Steps 2-12 for the other end of the line or for the end of the line which is being repaired.

14. Bend the replacement line or section using SA91108NE, or an equivalent line bending tool.

15. If repairing the original line, join the old and new sections using a female union and tighten.

Bleeding the Hydraulic Brake System

The hydraulic brake system must be bled any time one of the lines is disconnected or any time air enters the system. If a point in the system, such as a wheel cylinder or caliper brake line is the only point which was opened, the bleeder screws down stream in the hydraulic system are the only ones which must be bled. If however, the master cylinder fittings are opened, or if the reservoir level drops sufficiently that air is drawn into the system, air must be bled from the entire hydraulic system. If the brake pedal feels spongy upon application, and goes almost to the floor but regains height when pumped, air has entered the system. It must be bled out. If no fittings were recently opened for service, check for leaks that would have allowed the entry of air and repair them before attempting to bleed the system.

As a general rule, once the master cylinder (and the brake pressure modulator valve or combination valve on ABS systems) is bled, the remainder of the hydraulic system should be bled starting at the furthest wheel from the master cylinder and working towards the nearest wheel. Therefore, the correct bleeding sequence is: master cylinder, modulator or combination valve (ABS only), right rear wheel cylinder, left rear, right front caliper and left front. Most master cylinder assemblies on these vehicles are NOT equipped with bleeder valves, therefore air must be bled from the cylinders using the front brake pipe connections.

⁂CAUTION

If the vehicle has rear wheel or 4 wheel anti-lock braking, do not use this procedure without first reading the information on ABS system bleeding found later in this section. Improper service procedures on Anti-Lock Braking Systems (ABS) can cause serious personal injury. Refer to the ABS service procedures.

MANUAL BLEEDING

See Figures 19 and 20

For those of us who are not fortunate enough to have access to a power bleeding, the manual brake bleeding procedure will quite adequately remove air from the hydraulic system. The major difference between the pressure and manual bleeding procedures is that the manual method takes more time and will require help from an assistant. One person must depress the brake pedal, while another opens and closes the bleeder screws.

➡In addition to a length of clear neoprene bleeder hose, bleeder wrenches and a clear bleeder bottle (old glass jar or drink bottle will suffice), bleeding late-model ABS systems may also require the use of one or more relatively inexpensive combination valve pressure bleeding tools (which are used to depress one or more valves in order to allow component/system bleeding). To fully bleed the late model ABS systems, a scan tool should also be used to run the system through functional tests.

88459p06

Fig. 19 Position a bleeder wrench over the wheel cylinder bleeder screw (rear wheels)

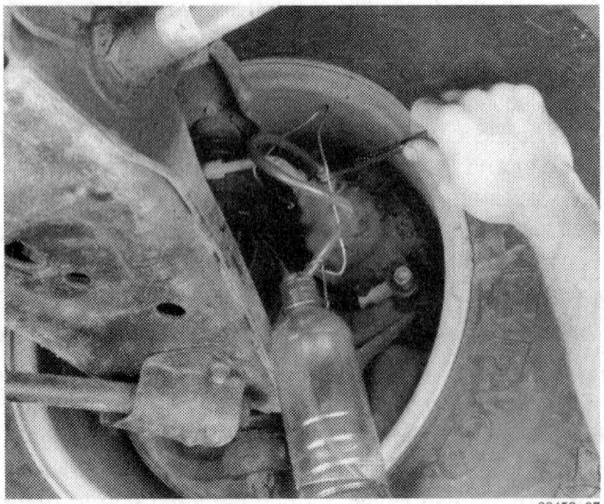
88459p07

Fig. 20 Attach a hose to the screw and submerge the other end in a container of clean brake fluid

1. Clean the top of the master cylinder, remove the cover and fill the reservoirs with clean fluid. To prevent squirting fluid, and possibly damaging painted surfaces, install the cover during the procedure, but be sure to frequently check and top off the reservoirs with fresh fluid.

****WARNING**

Never reuse brake fluid which has been bled from the system.

2. The master cylinder must be bled first if it is suspected to contain air. If the master cylinder was removed and bench bled before installation it must still be bled, but it should take less time and effort. Bleed the master cylinder as follows:
   a. Position a container under the master cylinder to catch the brake fluid.

****WARNING**

Do not allow brake fluid to spill on or come in contact with the vehicle's finish as it will remove the paint. In case of a spill, immediately flush the area with water.

   b. Loosen the front brake line at the master cylinder and allow the fluid to flow from the front port.
   c. Have a friend depress the brake pedal slowly and hold (air and/or fluid should be expelled from the loose fitting). Tighten the line, then release the brake pedal and wait 15 seconds. Loosen the fitting and repeat until all air is removed from the master cylinder bore.
   d. When finished, tighten the line fitting to 20 ft. lbs. (27 Nm).
   e. Repeat the sequence at the master cylinder rear pipe fitting.

➡During the bleeding procedure, make sure your assistant does NOT release the brake pedal while a fitting is loosened or while a bleeder screw is opening. Air will be drawn back into the system.

3. Check and refill the master cylinder reservoir.

➡Remember, if the reservoir is allowed to empty of fluid during the procedure, air will be drawn into the system and bleeding procedure must be restarted at the master cylinder assembly.

4. On late model ABS equipped vehicles, perform the special ABS procedures as described later in this section. On 4 wheel ABS systems the Brake Pressure Modulator Valve (BPMV) must be bled (if it has been replaced or if it is suspected to contain air) and on most Rear Wheel Anti-Lock (RWAL) systems the combination valve must be held open. In both cases, special combination valve depressor tools should be used during bleeding and a scan tool must be used for ABS function tests.
5. If a single line or fitting was the only hydraulic line disconnected, then only the caliper(s) or wheel cylinder(s) affected by that line must be bled. If the master cylinder required

bleeding, then all calipers and wheel cylinders must be bled in the proper sequence:

a. Right rear
b. Left rear
c. Right front
d. Left front

6. Bleed the individual calipers or wheel cylinders as follows:

a. Place a suitable wrench over the bleeder screw and attach a clear plastic hose over the screw end. Be sure the hose is seated snugly on the screw or you may be squirted with brake fluid.

➡Be very careful when bleeding wheel cylinders and brake calipers. The bleeder screws often rust in position and may easily break off if forced. Installing a new bleeder screw will often require removal of the component and may include overhaul or replacement of the wheel cylinder/caliper. To help prevent the possibility of breaking a bleeder screw, spray it with some penetrating oil before attempting to loosen it.

b. Submerge the other end of the tube in a transparent container of clean brake fluid.

c. Loosen the bleed screw, then have a friend apply the brake pedal slowly and hold. Tighten the bleed screw to 62 inch lbs. (7 Nm), release the brake pedal and wait 15 seconds. Repeat the sequence (including the 15 second pause) until all air is expelled from the caliper or cylinder.

d. Tighten the bleed screw to 62 inch lbs. (7 Nm) when finished.

7. Check the pedal for a hard feeling with the engine not running. If the pedal is soft, repeat the bleeding procedure until a firm pedal is obtained.

8. If the brake warning light is on, depress the brake pedal firmly. If there is no air in the system, the light will go out.

9. After bleeding, make sure that a firm pedal is achieved before attempting to move the vehicle.

PRESSURE BLEEDING

➧ See Figures 21 and 22

For the lucky ones with access to a pressure bleeding tool, this procedure may be used to quickly and efficiently remove air from the brake system. This procedure may be used as guide, but be careful to follow the tool manufacturer's directions closely. Any pressure bleeding tool MUST be of the diaphragm-type. A proper pressure bleeder tool will utilize a rubber diaphragm between the air source and brake fluid in order to prevent air, moisture oil and other contaminants from entering the hydraulic system.

1. Prepare a pressure bleeder tool such as J-29567 or equivalent by making sure the pressure tank is at least ⅔ full of fresh, clean brake fluid. In most cases, the bleeder must be bled each time fluid is added. Charge the bleeder tool to 20-25 psi (140-170 kPa).

2. Install a suitable combination valve depressor tool such J-39177 or equivalent, to the combination valve in order to hold the valve open during the bleeding operation.

3. Install the pressure bleeder tool to the master cylinder reservoir.

4. On 4 wheel ABS systems, refer to the ABS bleeding procedures later in this section to bleed the Brake Pressure Modulator Valve (BPMV) of air.

5. Bleed each wheel cylinder or caliper in the proper sequence:

a. Right rear
b. Left rear
c. Right front
d. Left front

6. Connect a hose from the bleeder tank to the adapter at the master cylinder, then open the tank valve.

7. Attach a clear vinyl hose to the brake bleeder screw, then immerse the opposite end into a container partially filled with clean brake fluid.

8. Open the bleeder screw ¾ turn and allow the fluid to flow until no air bubbles are seen in the fluid, then close the bleeder screw and tighten to 62 inch lbs. (7 Nm).

9. Repeat the bleeding process at each wheel.

10. Inspect the brake pedal for sponginess and if necessary, repeat the entire bleeding procedure.

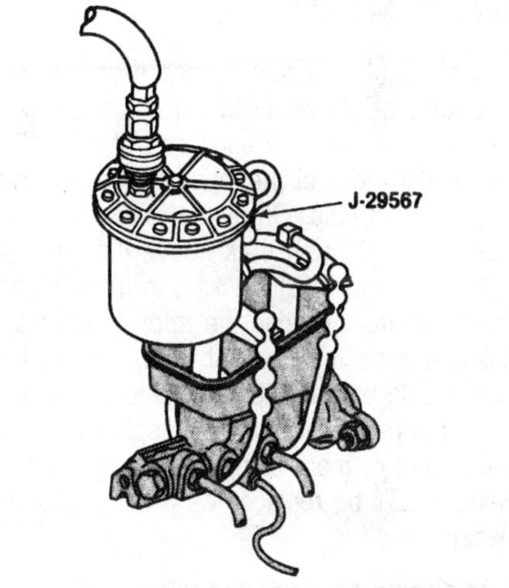

Fig. 21 Pressure bleeding tool

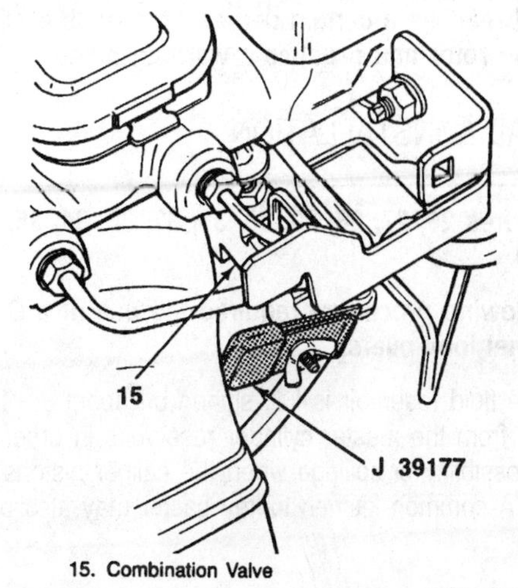

Fig. 22 Depressing the combination valve

11. Remove the depressor tool from the combination valve and the bleeder adapter from the master cylinder.

12. Refill the master cylinder to the proper level with brake fluid.

13. DO NOT attempt to move the vehicle unless a firm brake pedal is obtained.

FRONT DISC BRAKES

⁂CAUTION

Brake pads may contain asbestos, which has been determined to be a cancer causing agent. Never clean the brake surfaces with compressed air! Avoid inhaling any dust from any brake surface! When cleaning brake surfaces, use a commercially available brake cleaning fluid.

Brake Pads

INSPECTION

➧ See Figures 23, 24 and 25

Brake pads should be inspected once a year or at 7,500 miles (12,000 km), whichever occurs first. Check both ends of the outboard pad, looking in at each end of the caliper; then check the lining thickness of the inboard pad, looking down through the inspection hole. On riveted pads, the lining should be more than $^1/_{32}$ in. (0.8mm) thick above the rivet (so that the lining is thicker than the metal backing in most cases) in order to prevent the rivet from scoring the rotor. On bonded brake pads, a minimum lining thickness of $^1/_{32}$ in. (0.8mm) above the backing plate should be used to determine necessary replacement intervals. Keep in mind that any applicable state inspection standards that are more stringent take precedence. All four front pads MUST be replaced as a set if one shows excessive wear.

➡All models should be equipped with a wear indicator that makes a noise when the linings have worn to a degree where replacement is necessary. The spring clip is an integral part of the inboard pad and lining. When the brake pad reaches a certain degree of wear, the clip will contact the rotor and produce a warning noise.

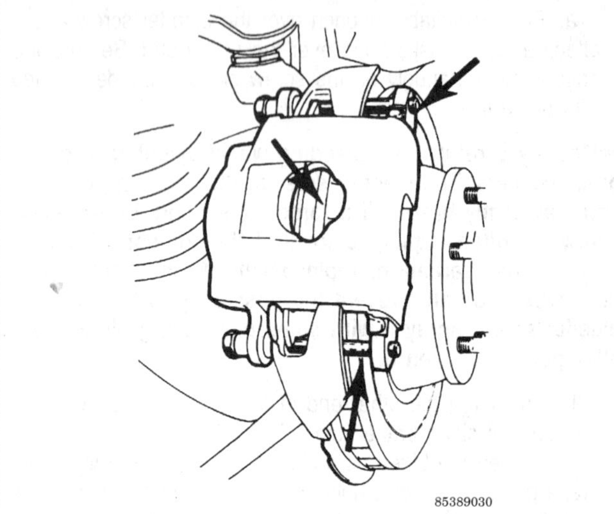

Fig. 23 Disc brake pad inspection

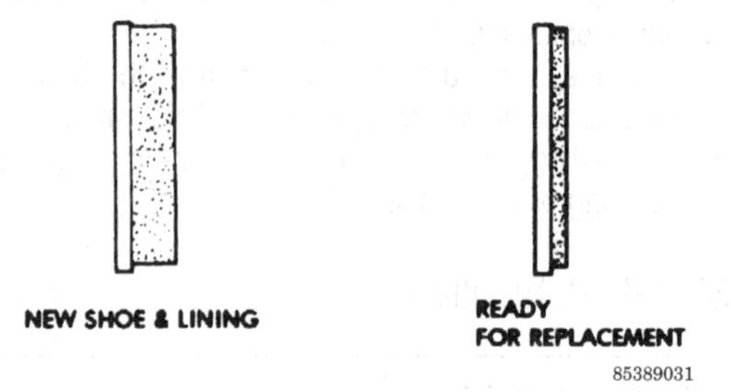

Fig. 24 Relative size differences between a new and worn pad lining

REMOVAL & INSTALLATION

➧ See Figures 26, 27, 28, 29, 30, 31, 32, 33, 34, 35, 36, 37, 38 and 39

➡The following procedure requires the use of a C-clamp and channel lock pliers.

1. If the fluid reservoir is full, siphon off about $^2/_3$ of the brake fluid from the master cylinder reservoirs in order to prevent the possibility of spillage when the caliper pistons are bottomed. A common kitchen turkey baster may also be used to remove brake fluid, but make sure the tool is clean before inserting it in the reservoir.

⁂WARNING

The insertion of thicker replacement pads will push the piston back into its bore and will cause a full master cylinder reservoir to overflow, possibly causing paint damage. In addition to siphoning off fluid, keep the reservoir cover on during pad replacement.

2. Raise and support the front of the vehicle safely using jackstands.

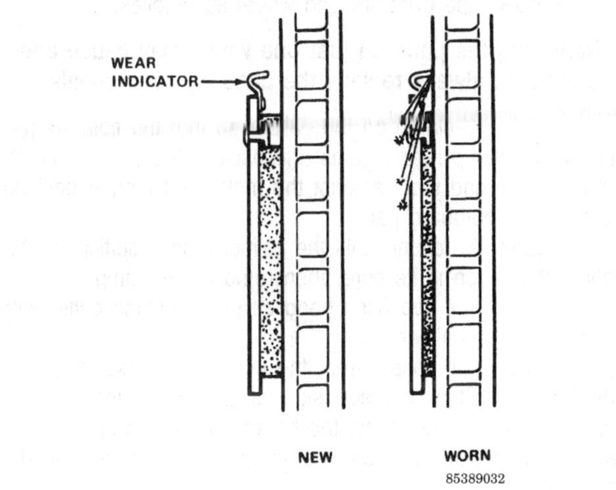

Fig. 25 Front disc brake pads have a built-in wear indicator

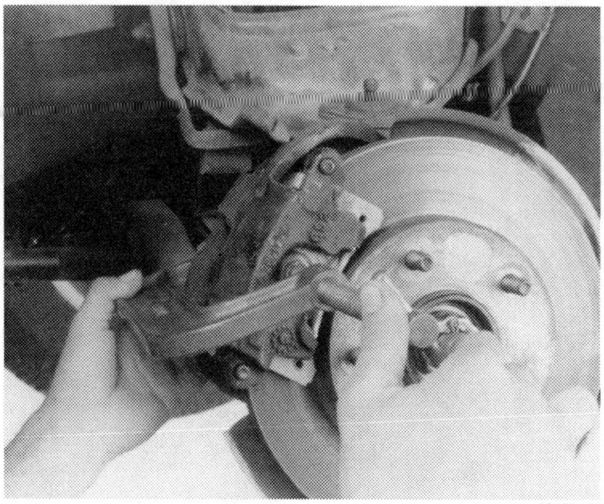

Fig. 28 Use a C-clamp to bottom the piston in the caliper bore

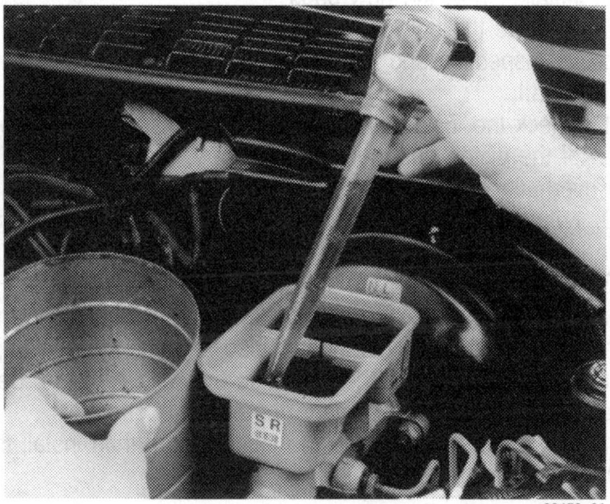

Fig. 26 If the fluid reservoir is full, siphon some fluid from the reservoirs to prevent spillage

Fig. 29 Loosen the caliper mounting bolts/pins

Fig. 27 View of a common disc brake system

Fig. 30 Remove the caliper mounting bolts

88459p12

Fig. 31 After removing the caliper, support the weight of the caliper with mechanics wire or a coat hanger.

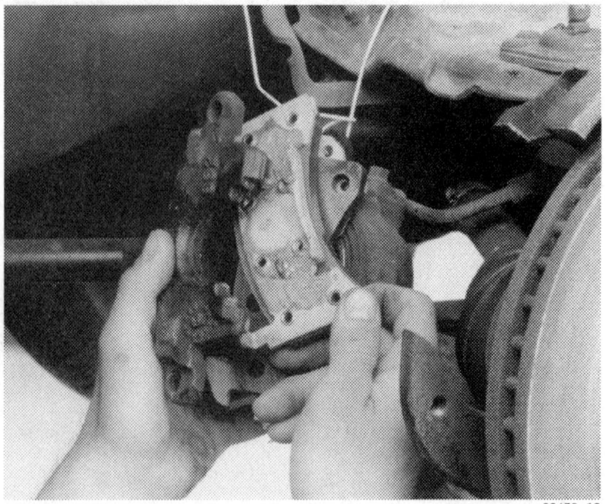

88459p13

Fig. 32 Remove the outboard pad from the caliper

88459p14

Fig. 33 Remove the inboard pad from the caliper piston

3. Remove the front tire and wheel assemblies.

➡Replacing the pads on just one wheel may cause uneven braking; always replace the pads on both wheels.

4. Install a C-clamp on the caliper so that the solid frame side of the clamp rests against the back of the caliper and the driving screw end rests against the metal part (center backing plate) of the outboard pad.

5. Tighten the clamp until the caliper moves sufficiently to bottom the piston in its bore, then remove the clamp.

6. Remove the two Allen head caliper mounting bolts from the back of the caliper.

7. Remove the caliper from the mounting bracket and support from the vehicle's suspension using a coat hanger or length of wire. Do not allow the brake line to support the caliper's weight and be sure the line is not otherwise kinked or damaged.

8. Remove the inboard and outboard pads from the caliper.

9. Remove the inboard pad spring clip from the piston or pad. Remove the spring clip carefully as it must be reused upon installation of the new pads.

10. Remove the bolt ear sleeves and rubber bushings for cleaning, inspection and lubrication.

To install:

11. Check the inside of the caliper for leakage and the condition of the piston dust boot. If necessary, remove the caliper and overhaul or replace it.

12. Lubricate the sleeves and bushings using a suitable silicone lubricant, then install them.

13. Make sure the piston is fully bottomed in the caliper providing clearance for the new brake pads. If the piston is not compressed, install the old inboard pad and use the C-clamp on the pad and back on the caliper to bottom the piston. Be careful not to pinch and damage the piston boot.

14. Install the spring clip to the inboard pad, then install the pad to the caliper.

➡Make sure that the wear sensor is facing in the proper direction. On most vehicles it should face toward the rear of the caliper.

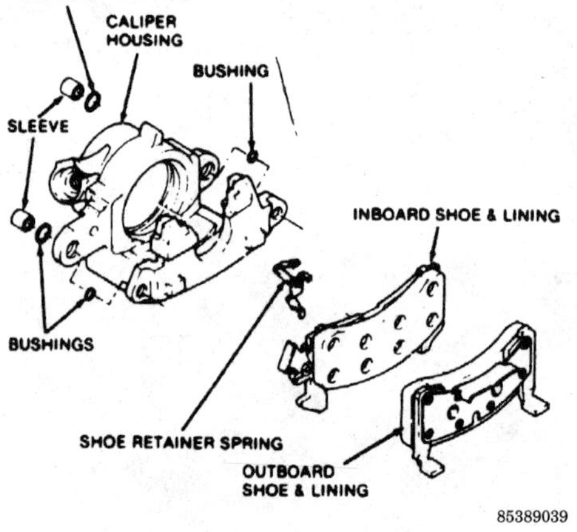

Fig. 34 Exploded view of a common caliper and brake pad assembly

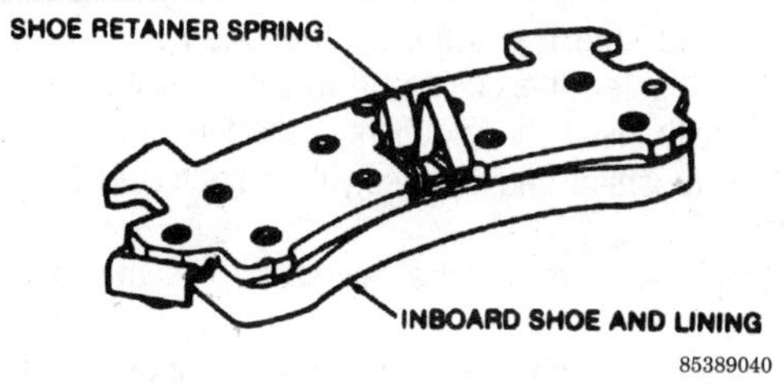

Fig. 35 The spring clip must be properly installed on the inboard pad

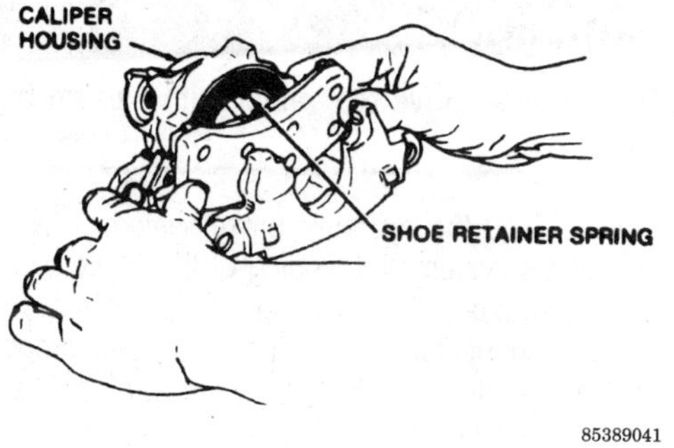

Fig. 36 Install the inboard pad to the caliper by carefully inserting the spring clip in the piston

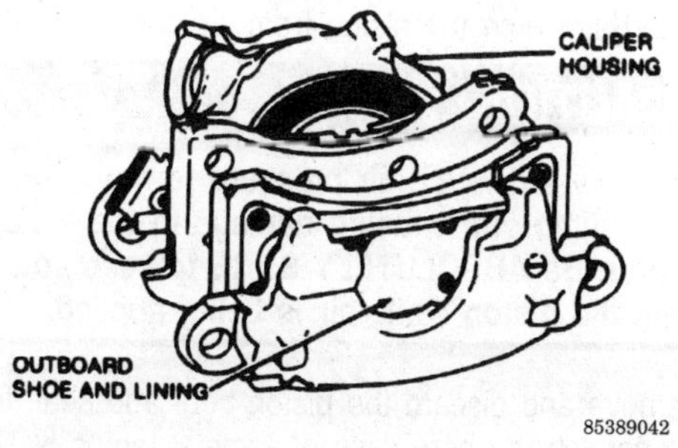

Fig. 37 Position the outboard pad over the caliper ears

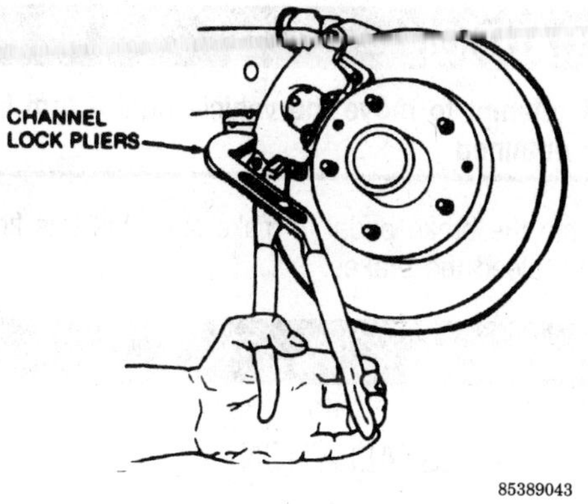

Fig. 38 Compress the brake pad ears using a pair of channel lock pliers

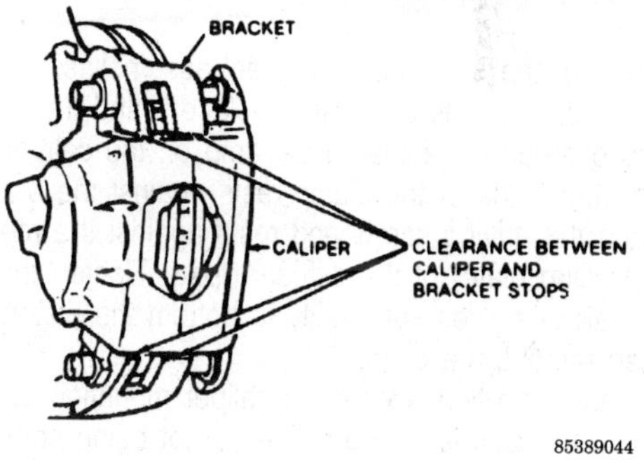

Fig. 39 When the caliper is installed, check for proper caliper-to-knuckle bracket clearance

15. Place the outboard pad in the caliper with its top ears over the caliper ears and the bottom tab engaged in the caliper cutout.

16. Place the caliper over the disc, lining up the hole in the caliper ears with the holes in the mounting bracket. Make sure that the brake hose is not twisted or kinked.

17. Carefully insert the mounting bolts through the bracket and caliper (bushing and sleeves), then tighten to 37 ft. lbs. (50 Nm).

18. Pump the brake pedal a few times to seat the linings against the rotors.

19. Use a pair of channel lock pliers to compress the pad ears so no clearance exists between the pad ears and the caliper.

20. Check the clearance between the caliper and steering knuckle. Clearance at each end of the caliper should be measured individually and the results added together. Clearance should not exceed 0.010-0.024 in. (0.026-0.60mm).

21. Install the wheels, then remove the jackstands and carefully lower the vehicle.

22. Check and refill the master cylinder reservoirs with brake fluid.

CAUTION

DO NOT attempt to move the vehicle until a firm brake pedal is obtained.

23. Pump the brake pedal to make sure that it is firm. If necessary, bleed the brakes.

Brake Caliper

REMOVAL & INSTALLATION

1. If the fluid reservoir is full, siphon off about ⅔ of the brake fluid from the master cylinder reservoirs in order to prevent the possibility of spillage when the caliper pistons are bottomed. A common kitchen turkey baster may also be used to remove brake fluid, but make sure the tool is clean before inserting it in the reservoir.
2. Raise and support the front of the vehicle safely using jackstands.
3. Remove the front tire and wheel assemblies.
4. If the brake pads are being replaced (and the caliper is not being overhauled), install a C-clamp on the caliper so that the solid frame side of the clamp rests against the back of the caliper and the driving screw end rests against the metal part (center backing plate) of the outboard pad. Tighten the clamp until the caliper moves sufficiently to bottom the piston in its bore, then remove the clamp.
5. Remove the two Allen head caliper mounting bolts from the back of the caliper. If the caliper is not being completely remove from the vehicle, remove it from the mounting bracket and support it from the suspension using a coat hanger or length of wire. Do not allow the hose to be stretched, twisted, kinked or otherwise damaged.
6. If the caliper is being completely removed from the vehicle, disconnect the flexible brake hose-to-caliper banjo-bolt, discard the pressure fitting washers (they must be replaced with new ones during assembly), then remove the brake caliper from the vehicle and place it on a work bench.
7. To inspect the caliper assembly, perform the following procedures:
   a. Check the inside of the caliper assembly for pitting or scoring. If heavy scoring or pitting is present, caliper replacement is recommended.
   b. Check the mounting bolts and sleeves for signs of corrosion; if necessary, replace the bolts.

➡If the mounting bolts have signs of corrosion, DO NOT attempt to polish away the corrosion. Instead the bolts must be replaced to assure proper caliper sliding and prevent the possibility of brake drag or locking.

To install:

8. Lubricate and position the caliper bushings and sleeves. Apply Delco® silicone lube or equivalent to lubricate the mounting bolts.
9. With both pads installed to the caliper, place the caliper over the disc, lining up the hole in the caliper ears with the holes in the mounting bracket.
10. If the caliper was completely removed, install the flexible hose to the caliper and secure using the banjo bolt and new washers. Make sure that the brake hose is not twisted or kinked, then tighten the bolt to 32 ft. lbs. (44 Nm).
11. Carefully insert the mounting bolts through the bracket and caliper (bushing and sleeves), then tighten to 37 ft. lbs. (50 Nm).
12. Pump the brake pedal a few times to seat the linings against the rotors.
13. Use a pair of channel lock pliers to compress the pad ears so no clearance exists between the pad ears and the caliper.
14. Check the clearance between the caliper and steering knuckle. Clearance at each end of the caliper should be measured individually and the results added together. Clearance should not exceed 0.010-0.024 in. (0.026-0.60mm).
15. Install the wheels, then remove the jackstands and carefully lower the vehicle.
16. Check and refill the master cylinder reservoirs with brake fluid.

CAUTION

DO NOT attempt to move the vehicle until a firm brake pedal is obtained.

17. Properly bleed the hydraulic brake system. If only a caliper fitting was disconnected, bleeding of the entire system should not be required. Bleed air from the system at the caliper that was disconnected. Check the system for proper operation. If air remains in the system, bleeding at all points in the system may be required.

OVERHAUL

See Figures 40, 41, 42, 43, 44 and 45

1. Remove the brake caliper from the vehicle.
2. Remove the inlet fitting from the brake caliper and drain all brake fluid to help cut down on the inevitable mess.
3. Position the caliper on a work bench and place clean shop towel in the caliper opening. Use a small amount of compressed air, force the piston from it's bore.

CAUTION

DO NOT apply too much air pressure to the bore, for the piston may jump out, causing damage to the piston and/or the operator. Be ABSOLUTELY SURE to keep your fingers away from the piston while air is being applied.

4. Remove and discard the piston boot and seal. Be careful not to scratch the bore. Use of a metal tool is NOT recommended when removing the boot and the seal because of the possibility of scoring and damaging the bore.
5. Inspect the piston and the caliper bore for damage or corrosion. Replace the caliper and/or the piston (if necessary).
6. Remove the bleeder screw and it's rubber cap.

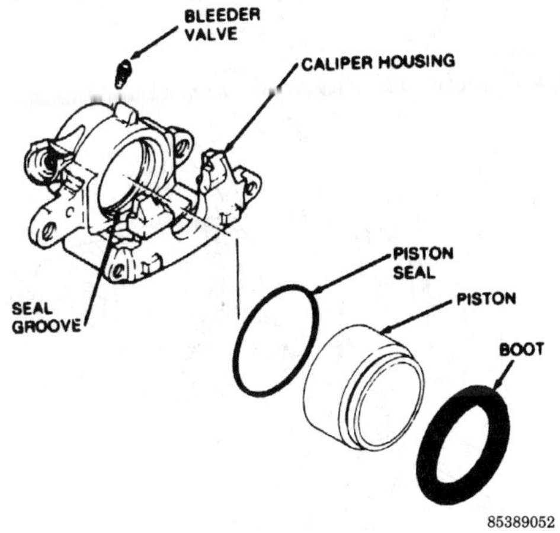

Fig. 40 Exploded view of a common caliper assembly

Fig. 43 Remove the boot from the caliper housing, taking care not to score or damage the bore

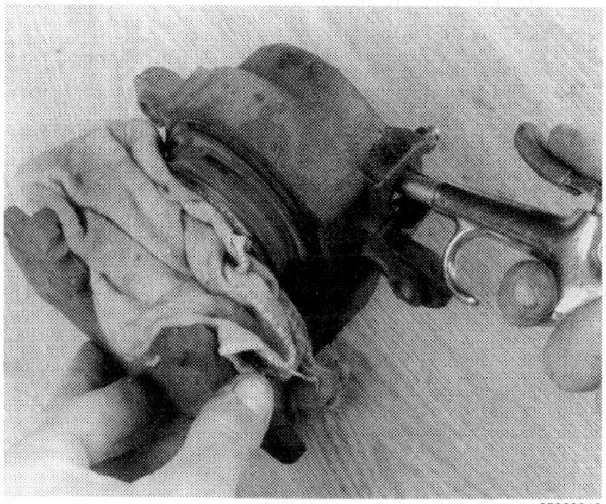

Fig. 41 Apply a small amount of compressed air to push the piston out

Fig. 44 Use extreme caution when removing the piston seal; DO NOT scratch the caliper bore

Fig. 42 Grasp the piston and remove it from the caliper bore

Fig. 45 During assembly use a suitable piston boot driver to properly install the boot to the housing

7. Clean all of the parts with non-mineral based solvent and blow dry with compressed air. All rubber parts should be replaced with those in the brake service kit.

8. Inspect the guide pins for corrosion, replace them (if necessary). When installing the guide pins, coat them with a silicone lubricant.

To assemble:

9. Lubricate the piston, caliper and seal with clean brake fluid.

10. Install the seal into the caliper bore making sure it is not twisted in the caliper bore groove.

11. Install the boot onto the piston, then position the piston into the caliper bore.

12. Bottom the piston into the bore, then secure the boot to the housing using J-26267 or an equivalent piston seal installer tool.

13. Install the bleeder valve and tighten to 62 inch lbs. (7 Nm).

14. Install the caliper to the vehicle and properly bleed the hydraulic brake system.

Brake Disc (Rotor)

INSPECTION

See Figure 46

Check the disc brake rotor for scoring, cracks or other damage. Rotor run-out should be measured while the rotor is installed, while rotor thickness/thickness variation may be checked with the rotor installed or removed. Use a dial gauge to check rotor run-out. Check the rotor thickness to make sure it is greater than minimum thickness and check for thickness variations using a caliper micrometer.

1. Raise and support the front of the vehicle safely using jackstands.

2. Remove the front wheels.

3. Visually inspect the rotor for cracks, excessive scoring or other damage. A light scoring of the surface which does not exceed 0.06 in. (1.5mm) in depth is normal and should not be considered detrimental to brake operation.

➡Before attempting to check rotor run-out on 2WD vehicles, make sure the wheel bearings are properly adjusted. On all vehicles, the bearings must be in good condition and not contain excessive play.

4. Check the disc for excessive run-out using a dial indicator:

a. On 2WD models only, tighten the wheel bearings to eliminate all freeplay.

b. Position and secure a dial indicator so that the button contacts the disc about 1 in. (25.4mm) from the outer edge. Set the dial indicator to zero.

c. Rotate the disc one complete revolution. The lateral run-out reading should not exceed 0.003 in. (0.08mm). If the reading is excessive, recondition or replace the disc.

d. After checking the runout reset the freeplay adjustment on the 2WD models.

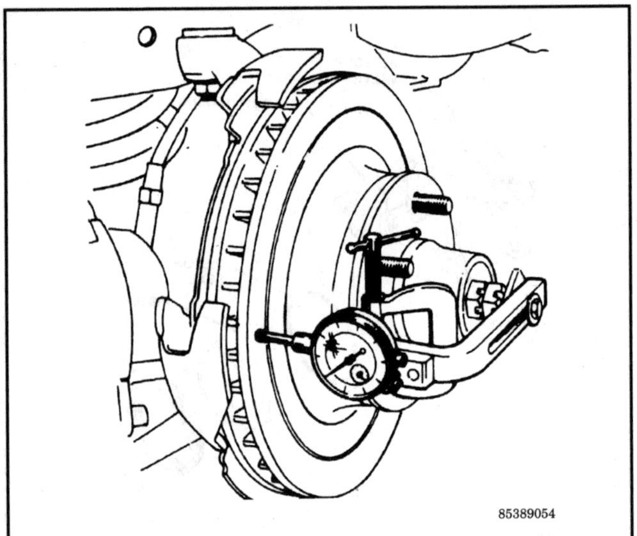

Fig. 46 Check rotor lateral run-out using a dial indicator

5. Check the disc minimum thickness and the disc parallelism (thickness variation):

a. Use a micrometer to check the disc thickness at 4 locations around the disc. Make sure the measuring point is at the same distance from the edge at all locations.

b. The thickness should be greater than the minimum specification (which is normally cast onto the disc) and should not vary more than 0.0005 in. (0.013mm). If the variations are excessive, recondition or replace the disc. A disc which is smaller than the discard dimension MUST be replaced for safety.

REMOVAL & INSTALLATION

2WD Models

1. Raise and support the front of the vehicle safely using jackstands.

2. Remove the tire and wheel assembly.

3. Remove the brake caliper mounting bolts and carefully remove the caliper (along with the brake pads) from the rotor. Do not disconnect the brake line; instead wire the caliper out of the way with the line still connected.

➡Once the rotor is removed from the vehicle the wheel bearings may be cleaned and repacked or the bearings and races may be replaced. For more information, please refer to the wheel bearing procedures in Section 1 of this manual.

4. Carefully pry out the grease cap, then remove the cotter pin, spindle nut, and washer.

5. Remove the hub, being careful not to drop the outer wheel bearings. As the hub is pulled forward, the outer wheel bearings will often fall forward and they may easily be removed at this time.

To install:

6. Carefully install the wheel hub over the spindle.

7. Using your hands, firmly press the outer bearing into the hub.

8. Loosely install the spindle washer and nut, but do not install the cotter pin or dust cap at this time.

9. Install the brake caliper.
10. Install the tire and wheel assembly.
11. Properly adjust the wheel bearings:
   a. Spin the wheel forward by hand and tighten the nut to 12 ft. lbs. (10 Nm) in order to fully seat the bearings and remove any burrs from the threads.
   b. Back off the nut until it is just loose, then finger-tighten the nut.
   c. Loosen the nut 1/4-1/2 turn until either hole in the spindle lines up with a slot in the nut, then install a new cotter pin. This may appear to be too loose, but it is the correct adjustment.
   d. Proper adjustment creates 0.001-0.005 in. (0.025-0.127mm) end-play.
12. Install the dust cap.
13. Install the wheel/hub cover, then remove the supports and carefully lower the vehicle.

4WD Models

See Figure 47

1. Raise and support the front of the truck safely using jackstands under the frame.
2. Remove the tire and wheel assembly.
3. Remove the brake caliper mounting bolts and carefully remove the caliper (along with the brake pads) from the rotor. Do not disconnect the brake line; instead wire the caliper out of the way with the line still connected.
4. If equipped, remove the lockwashers from the hub studs in order to free the rotor.
5. Remove the brake disc (rotor) from the wheel hub.

88459p18

Fig. 47 Removing the rotor from the vehicle

To install:

6. Inspect the disc for nicks, scores and/or damage, then replace if necessary.
7. Install the disc over the wheel hub studs.
8. If used, install the lockwashers over the studs.
9. Install the brake caliper and pads. For details, please refer to the caliper procedure located earlier in this section.
10. Install the tire and wheel assembly.
11. Remove the jackstands and carefully lower the vehicle. DO NOT attempt to move the vehicle unless a firm brake pedal is felt.

REAR DRUM BRAKES

CAUTION

Brake shoes may contain asbestos, which has been determined to be a cancer causing agent. Never clean the brake surfaces with compressed air! Avoid inhaling any dust from any brake surface! When cleaning brake surfaces, use a commercially available brake cleaning fluid.

Brake Drums

REMOVAL & INSTALLATION

See Figures 48 and 49

1. Raise and support the rear of the vehicle safely using jackstands.
2. Remove the rear tire and wheel assemblies.
3. Matchmark the drum to the hub or hub studs for installation purposes.
4. Pull the brake drum from the hub studs. It may by necessary to gently tap the rear edges of the drum using a rubber mallet to start it off the studs.

88459p19

Fig. 48 View of a common brake drum used on the S-series pickups

5. If the drum will not come off past the shoes, it will be necessary to retract the adjusting screw. Remove the access hole cover from the backing plate and turn the adjuster to retract the linings away from the drum.

Fig. 49 Removing the brake drum from the vehicle

To install:

➡The rear wheel bearings are not adjustable, they are serviced by replacement only. If necessary to replace the rear wheel bearings, please refer to the axle shaft, bearing and seal, removal and installation procedures located in Section 7 of this manual.

6. If removed, install a rubber adjustment hole cover before reinstalling the drum.
7. Install the drum in the same position on the hub as removed.
8. Install the rear tire and wheel assemblies.
9. Remove the jackstands and carefully lower the vehicle.

INSPECTION

Clean all grease, brake fluid, and other contaminants from the brake drum using brake cleaner. Visually check the drum for scoring, cracks, or other damage and replace, if necessary.

Check the drum inner diameter using a brake shoe clearance gauge. There are 2 important specifications when discussing rear drum diameters. The refinish diameter is the maximum diameter to which the drum may be machined. This diameter allows room for drum wear after is has been machined and is returned to service. The discard diameter is the point at which the drum becomes unsafe to use and must be discarded. NEVER refinish a drum to the discard diameter. If after refinishing the drum the diameter is within 0.030 in. (0.76mm) of the discard diameter, the drum MUST be replaced.

Brake Shoes

INSPECTION

Remove the drum and inspect the lining thickness of both brake shoes. The rear brake shoes should be replaced if the lining is less than 0.030 in. (0.76mm) thick above the rivet (so that the lining is thicker than the metal shoe backing in most cases) in order to prevent the rivet from scoring the drum. On bonded shoes the same specification should be used and the thickness of the bonded lining should be 0.030 in. (0.76mm) thick above the metal shoe backing plate. As with all brake service, keep in mind that local regulations take precedence over these specifications. Always check with your local authorities to be sure you are in compliance with local laws.

➡Brake shoes should always be replaced in sets.

REMOVAL & INSTALLATION

See Figures 50, 51, 52, 53, 54, 55, 56, 57, 58, 59, 60, 61 and 62

1. Raise and support the rear of the vehicle safely using jackstands.
2. Remove the rear wheels.
3. Matchmark and remove the brake drums.
4. Remove the shoe return springs and disconnect the actuator link (the link may be removed at this time), then remove the shoe guide from the stud at the top of the backing plate.

➡Special brake spring tools are available from the auto supply stores, which will ease the removal and installation of the return springs and the shoe hold-down spring and anchor pin.

5. Remove the shoe hold-down springs and pins.
6. Remove the actuator lever, pivot and return spring.
7. If not done earlier, remove the actuator link.
8. Remove the parking brake strut and strut spring, then remove the parking brake lever from the shoe (it may be easier to wait until the shoe is being removed to separate the lever).
9. Remove the brake shoes, the adjuster screw assembly and the adjuster spring.
10. Clean and inspect all of the brake parts.
11. Check the wheel cylinders for seal condition and leaking.
12. Inspect the axle seal for leakage and replace, if necessary.

To install:

13. Inspect the replacement shoes for nicks or burrs, lightly lubricate the backing plate contact points, the brake cable, the levers and adjusting screws with a white lithium brake grease.
14. Make sure that the right and left hand adjusting screws are not mixed. You can prevent this by working on one side at a time. This will also provide you with a reference for reassembly, just keep in mind that the assembly on one side of the vehicle is the mirror image of the assembly on the other side. The star wheel should be nearest to the secondary shoe when correctly installed.
15. Install the adjusting screw assembly and spring to both shoes, then position the shoes to the backing plate.
16. Install the parking brake lever to the secondary shoe.
17. Install the strut spring to the parking brake strut, then position the strut.
18. Install the actuator lever, lever pivot and the link. Install the lever return spring.
19. Install the shoe hold-down pins and springs.
20. Install the shoe guide over the stud at the top of the backing plate.

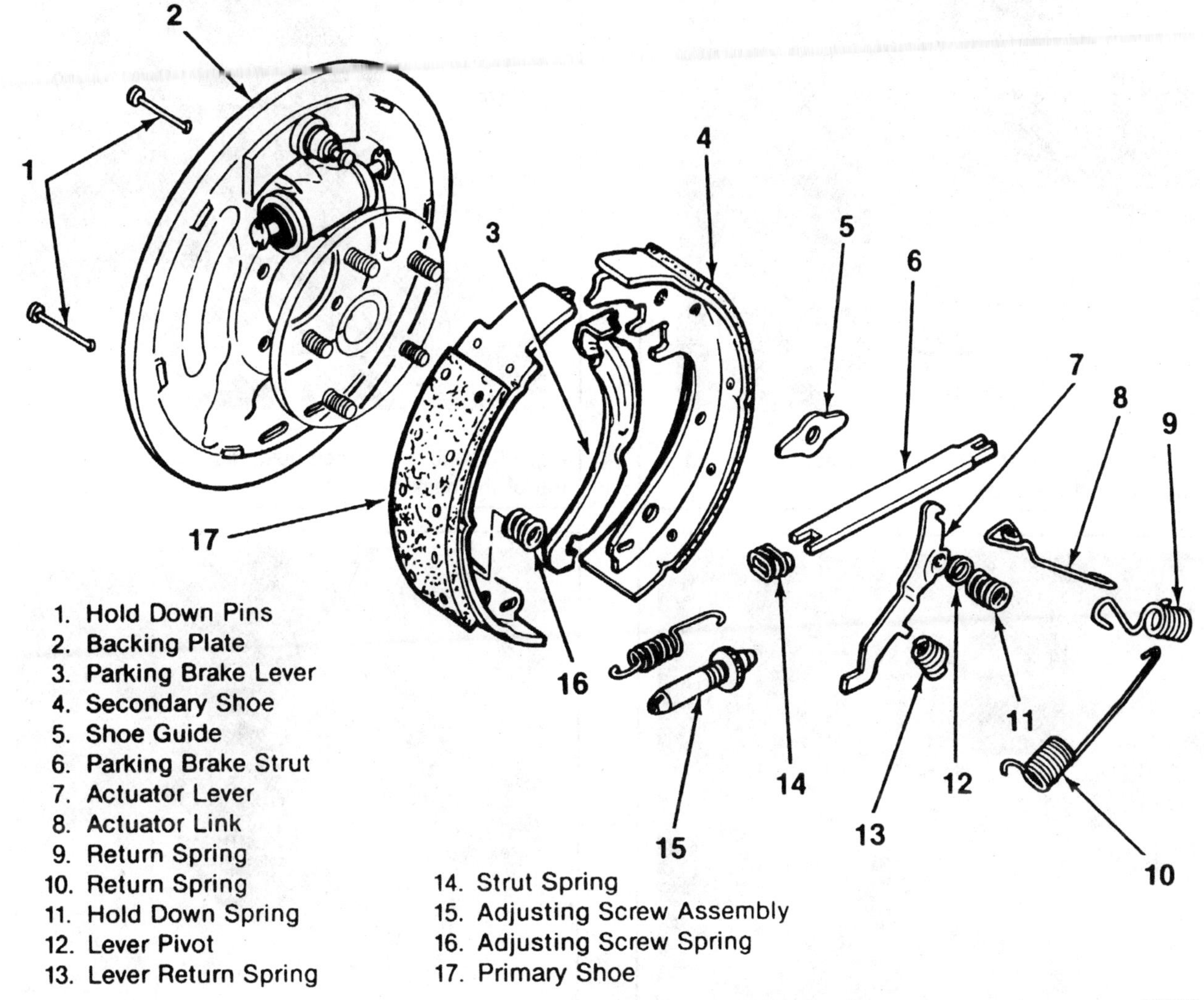

Fig. 50 Exploded view of the drum brake components used on most vehicles covered by this manual

Fig. 51 Use an evaporative spray brake cleaner to remove brake dust from the components

Fig. 52 Use a brake tool to release the return springs

88459p23

Fig. 53 When the first spring is released, pivot it and remove it from the shoe

88459p24

Fig. 54 Remove the second return spring . . . .

88459p25

Fig. 55 . . . then remove the actuator link

88459p26

Fig. 56 Remove the shoe guide from the stud at the top of the backing plate

88459p27

Fig. 57 Use the brake tool to compress the hold-down spring and twist the plate to free the pin

88459p28

Fig. 58 Once the pin and the slot on top of the plate are aligned, separate the hold-down spring and pin

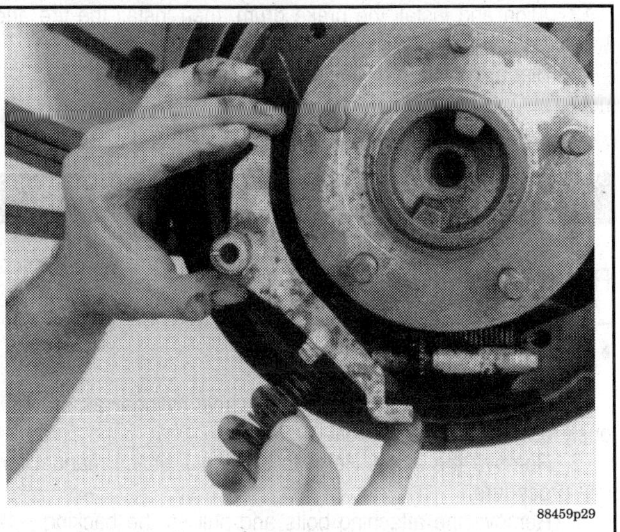

Fig. 59 Remove the actuator lever and return spring

Fig. 60 Remove the parking brake strut and spring

Fig. 61 Remove the shoes from the backing plate

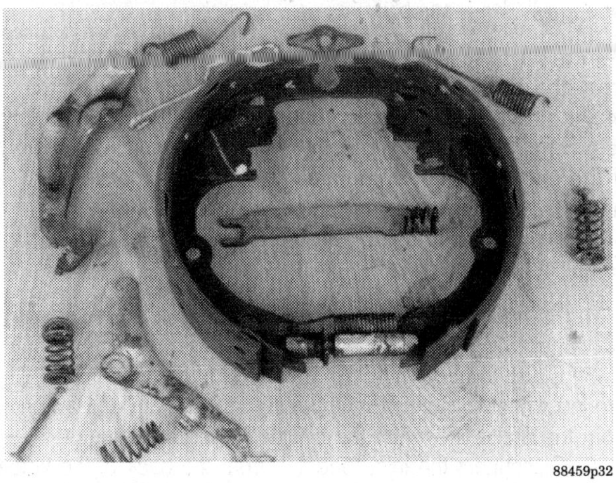

Fig. 62 Exploded view of the drum brake components

21. Install the return springs.
22. Lightly sandpaper the shoes to make sure they are clean, then align and install the drum.
23. Install the rear tire and wheel assemblies.
24. Adjust the brakes as described previously in this section.
25. Remove the jackstands and carefully lower the vehicle, then road test the vehicle.

Wheel Cylinders

REMOVAL & INSTALLATION

See Figure 63

1. Raise and support the rear of the vehicle safely using jackstands.
2. Remove the tire and wheel assembly.

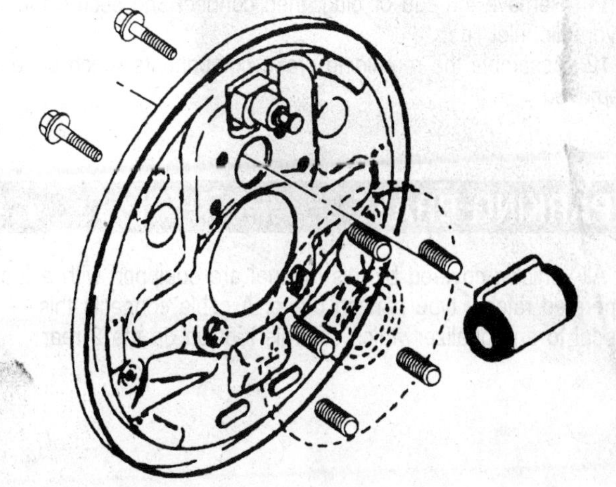

Fig. 63 Exploded view of the wheel cylinder mounting

3. Matchmark and remove the brake drum for access to the wheel cylinder assembly.

➡In most cases, the wheel cylinders may be removed from the backing plate without completely removing the brake shoes and related components, however completely removing the shoes will make the operation MUCH easier. If the shoes are not completely removed, some of the upper springs must be removed in order to allow the shoes to spread and provide the necessary clearance for wheel cylinder removal.

4. Remove the brake shoes or disconnect them sufficiently for wheel cylinder clearance.
5. Clean away all dirt, crud and foreign material from around wheel cylinder. It is important that dirt be kept away from the brake line when the cylinder is disconnected.
6. Disconnect the inlet tube line from the back of the wheel cylinder. Immediately plug or cap the line to prevent system contamination or excessive fluid loss.

➡Wheel cylinders are retained to the rear of the brake backing plate by two types of fasteners. One type uses a round retainer with locking clips while the other simply uses two bolts threaded into the wheel cylinder body.

7. To remove the round retainer type cylinders, insert two awls or pins into the access slots between the wheel cylinder pilot and the retainer locking tabs. Bend both tabs away simultaneously. The wheel cylinder can be removed, as the retainer is released.
8. To remove the bolted wheel cylinders, loosen and remove the bolts from the back side of the backing plate, then remove the wheel cylinder assembly.

To install:

9. For round retainer type wheel cylinders, position the cylinder and hold it in place with a wooden block between the cylinder and the axle flange. Install the new retainer clip, using a 1$^1/_8$ in. 12-point socket and socket extension (to help preserve your fingers). The socket is used to assure that the retainer seats evenly.
10. For bolt type wheel cylinders, position the cylinder, then install the retaining bolts and tighten to 115 inch lbs. (13 Nm).
11. Remove the cap or plug, then connect and secure the hydraulic inlet line.
12. Assemble the remaining brake components which were removed.
13. Align and install the brake drum, then install the tire and wheel assembly.
14. Bleed the wheel cylinder and adjust the brakes (if necessary).
15. Remove the jackstands and carefully lower the vehicle.

Brake Backing Plate

REMOVAL & INSTALLATION

➧ See Figure 64

1. Remove the brake shoes and wheel cylinder as previously outlined in this section.
2. Remove the axles. Refer to Section 7 of the manual for this procedure.
3. Remove the attaching bolts and pull off the backing plate.

To install:

4. Install the axles. Refer to Section 7 of the manual for this procedure.
5. Install the backing plate, then tighten the retaining bolts to 35 ft. lbs. (47 Nm)
6. Install the wheel cylinder and brake shoes as previously outlined in this section.

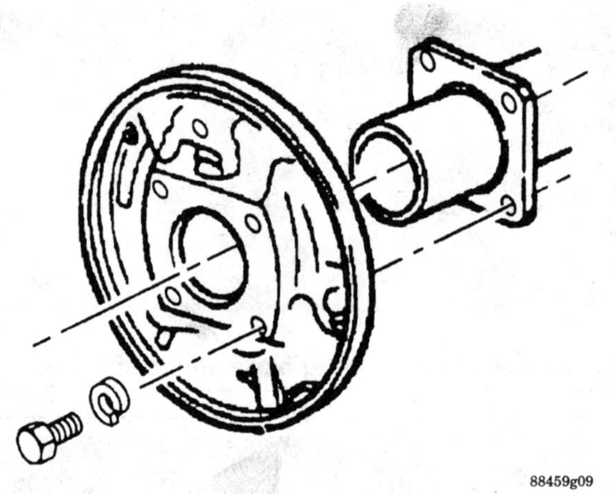

Fig. 64 View of the brake backing plate mounting

PARKING BRAKE

All vehicles covered by this manual are equipped with a foot operated ratchet type parking brake. A cable connects this pedal to an equalizer which controls tension on the 2 rear cables that are attached to the brake shoe levers. Adjustment is made at the equalizer.

Front Cable

REMOVAL & INSTALLATION

See Figure 65

1. Raise and support the front of the vehicle safely using jackstands.

➡The parking brake equalizer threads will often rust in service making adjustment or removal difficult. If necessary, spray a penetrating lubricant on the nut and equalizer threads, then allow time for the lubricant to work.

2. Under the left-center of the vehicle, loosen the nut on the cable equalizer assembly.
3. Separate the front cable from the equalizer.
4. If applicable, remove the front-cable retaining bolts and clips.
5. Bend or squeeze the frame retainer fingers and release the cable from the frame.

➡On some models, it may be necessary to remove the dash trim panels to gain access to the brake pedal.

6. If necessary for access, remove the lower trim panel from the left side of the dash.
7. Release the cowl retainer and grommet, then disconnect the front cable from the parking pedal assembly.
8. Attach a length of wire to the cable, then carefully pull it through the cowl leaving the wire in place for installation purposes. Remove the cable from the vehicle.

To install:

9. Use the wire left in the cowl opening to pull the cable into position.
10. Seat the retainer and grommet to the cowl, making sure the retaining fingers are completely through the hole.
11. Attach the cable to the lever, then if removed for access, install the lower trim panel.
12. Install the cable retainer to the frame, then if applicable, secure any retaining clips.
13. Connect the cable to the equalizer, then properly adjust the parking brake. For details, please refer to the procedure located later in this section.
14. Remove the jackstands and carefully lower the vehicle.

Rear Cables

REMOVAL & INSTALLATION

See Figures 66, 67, 68, 69 and 70

1. Raise and support the rear of the vehicle safely using jackstands.
2. Remove the rear tire and wheel assembly, then matchmark and remove the brake drum.

➡The parking brake equalizer threads will often rust in service making adjustment or removal difficult. If necessary, spray a penetrating lubricant on the nut and equalizer threads, then allow time for the lubricant to work.

3. Under the left-center of the vehicle, loosen the nut on the cable equalizer assembly.
4. Separate the cable from the equalizer.
5. If equipped, release the rear cable retainer from the frame rail.
6. Remove the brake shoes and disconnect the parking brake cable from the shoe lever.
7. Remove the cable retainer from the backing plate by squeezing all of the retainer fingers and pulling the cable/retainer out of the plate. One easy way of accomplishing this is to position a box wrench (which is slightly smaller than the cable retainer) over the retainer to squeeze the fingers, then gently tap the wrench with a hammer to free the cable.
8. If equipped, remove the cable bolt and clip from the frame.
9. Remove the cable from the vehicle.

To install:

10. Position the cable under the vehicle and insert it through the brake backing plate. Seat the retainer on the plate making sure all of the fingers are locked in position. Route the cable

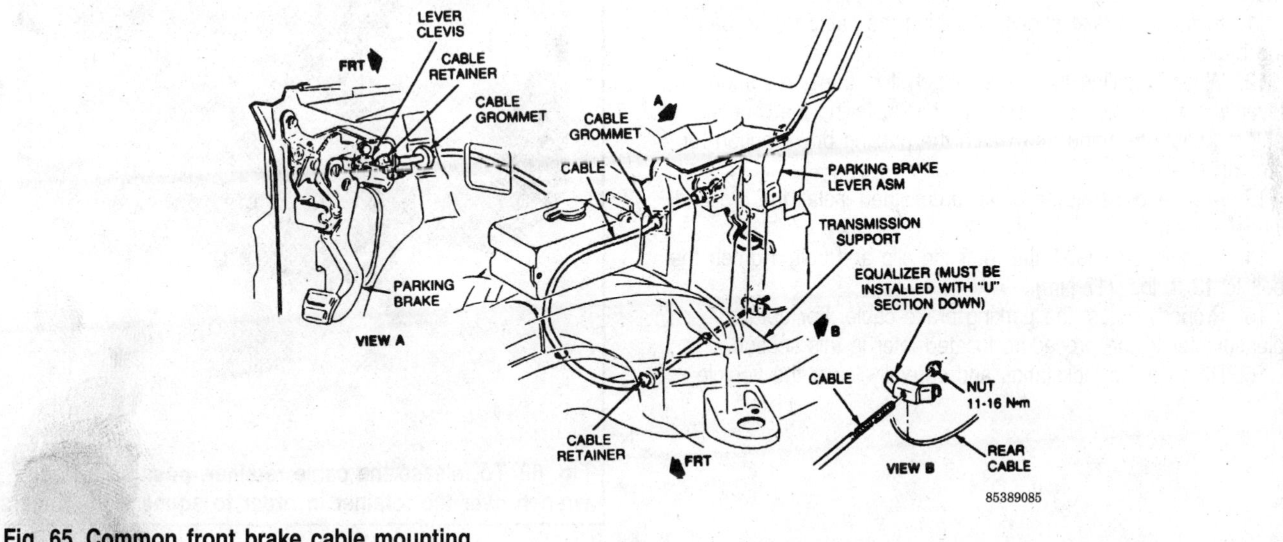

Fig. 65 Common front brake cable mounting

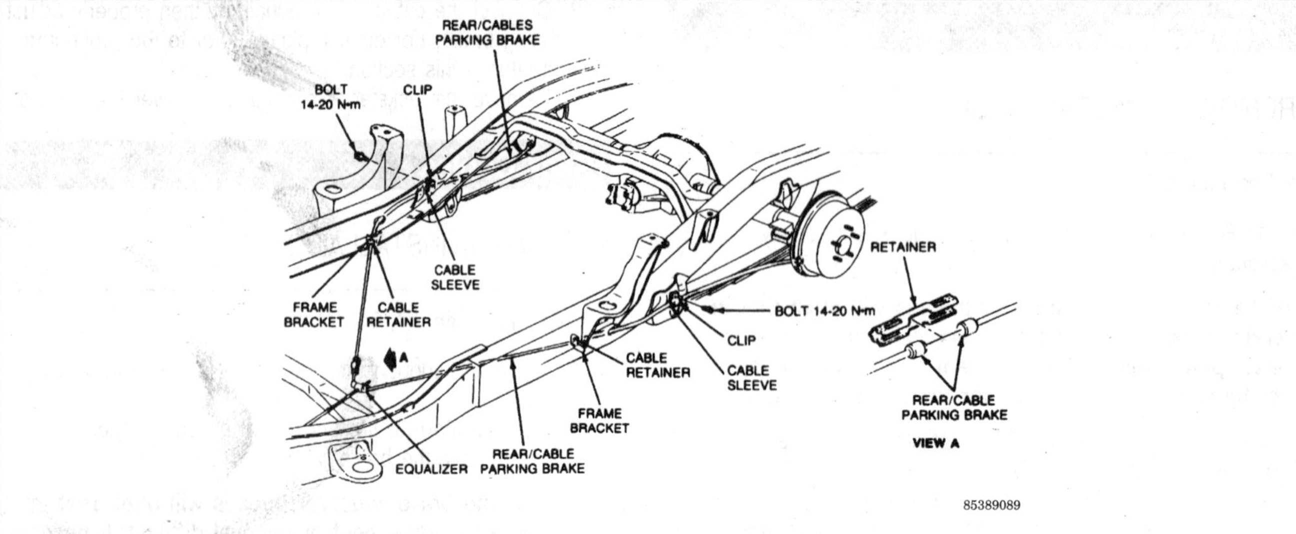

Fig. 66 Common rear parking brake cable mounting

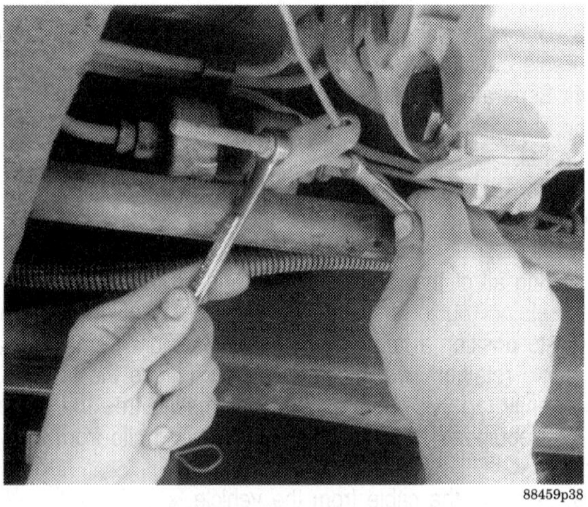

Fig. 67 Hold the adjuster rod from turning while you loosen the nut using a box wrench

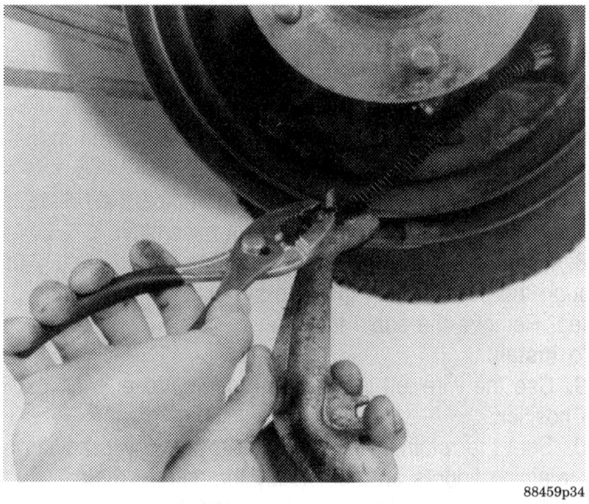

Fig. 68 Use pliers or vise grips when disconnecting the cable from the shoe lever

and, if equipped, secure the frame retainer in the same manner.

11. Install the brake shoes, attaching the cable to the parking brake lever.
12. When installing the cable, attach it to the brake shoe lever and assemble the brakes. Before installing the drums, pull the cable by hand and watch the parking brake action for smooth operation.
13. Align and install the brake drum, then install the tire and wheel assembly.
14. If equipped, install the retaining clip and bolt. Tighten the bolt to 13 ft. lbs. (17 Nm).
15. Properly adjust the parking brake cable. For details, please refer to the procedure located later in this section.
16. Remove the jackstands and carefully lower the vehicle.

Fig. 69 To release the cable retainer, position a box wrench over the retainer in order to squeeze the fingers

Fig. 70 Pull the cable through the backing plate

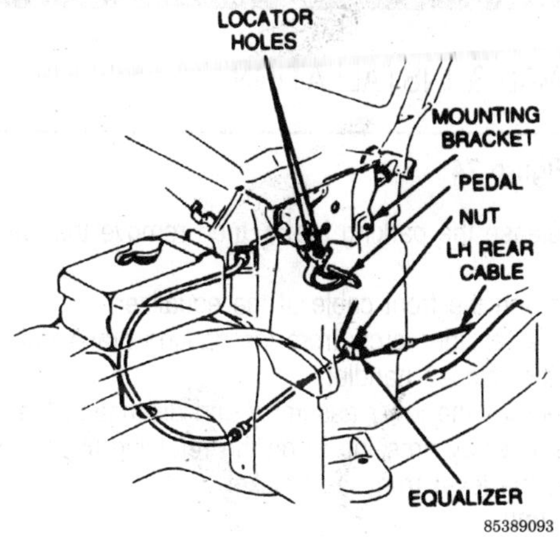

Fig. 71 Parking brake adjustment

ADJUSTMENT

➧ **See Figures 71, 72 and 73**

The parking brake cables must be adjusted any time one of the cables have been disconnected or replaced. Another indication of a need for cable adjustment is if under heavy foot pressure the pedal travel is less than 9 ratchet clicks or more than 13. Remember that the brake shoes must be properly adjusted before attempting to adjust the parking brake cable.

➡Before adjusting the parking brakes, check the condition of the brake shoes and components; replace any necessary parts.

1. Block the front wheels.
2. Raise and support the rear of the vehicle safely using jackstands.

➡The parking brake equalizer threads will often rust in service making adjustment or removal difficult. If necessary, spray a penetrating lubricant on the nut and equalizer threads, then allow time for the lubricant to work.

3. Under the left-center of the vehicle, loosen the nut on the cable equalizer assembly.
4. Set the parking brake pedal to the appropriate number of clicks:
   a. On 2WD models — set the pedal on the 2nd click.
   b. On 4WD models — set the pedal on the 3rd click.
5. Tighten the cable equalizer nut until the rear wheel cannot be turned forward by hand without excessive force.
6. Loosen the equalizer nut until there is just moderate drag when the rear wheels are rotated forward.
7. Release the parking brake and verify that there is no brake drag in either direction.
8. If equipped, tighten the equalizer locknut.
9. Remove the jackstands and carefully lower the vehicle.

Fig. 72 View of the parking cable equalizer assembly

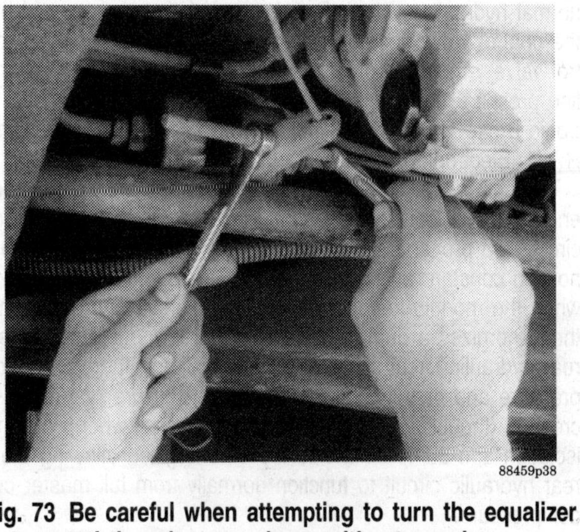

Fig. 73 Be careful when attempting to turn the equalizer nut; rusted threads may release without warning

Parking Brake Pedal

REMOVAL & INSTALLATION

See Figure 74

1. Release the parking brake, then remove the lower trim panel.
2. Loosen the front cable at the equalizer.
3. Unfasten the screw from the parking brake switch, then remove the release handle.
4. Remove the lever assembly and disengage the cable from the lever by pressing in on the retaining fingers and removing the lever from the bracket.

To install:

5. Engage the cable to the lever assembly and install the lever assembly. Tighten the retaining bolts to 18 ft. lbs. (25 Nm).
6. Install the retainer and release handle, then tighten the parking brake switch retaining screw.
7. Install the lower trim panel.

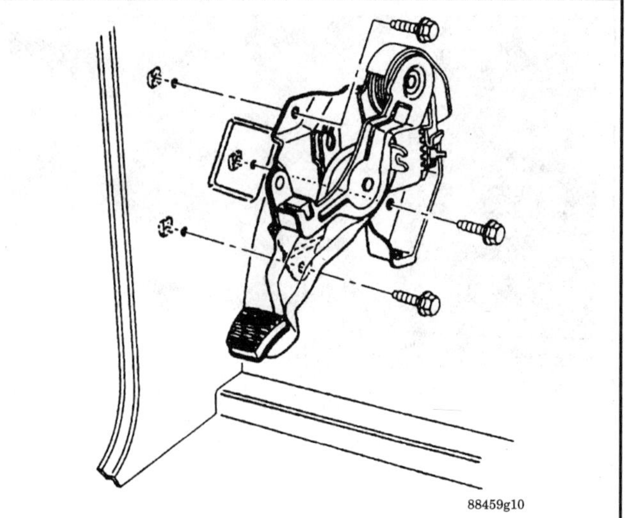

Fig. 74 View of the parking brake pedal mounting

8. Adjust the parking brake. Refer to the procedure outlined in this section.

REAR WHEEL ANTI-LOCK (RWAL) SYSTEM

General Description

See Figures 75 and 76

The RWAL system may be found on most trucks covered by this manual (except on 1994-95 vehicles equipped with the 4 wheel ABS system). The system is particularly useful because of the wide variations of loading the vehicle may experience. Preventing rear wheel lock-up often makes the difference in controlling the vehicle during hard or sudden stops.

Found on both 2WD and 4WD vehicles, the RWAL system is designed to regulate rear hydraulic brake line pressure, preventing rear wheel lock-up during hard braking. On most 4WD vehicles, the system is deactivated when operating in four wheel drive. In this case the braking system acts as a normal hydraulic system. Pressure regulation is managed by the control valve, located under the master cylinder. The control valve is capable of holding, increasing or decreasing brake line pressure based on electrical commands from the Electronic Brake Control Module (EBCM), originally known as the RWAL Electronic Control Unit (ECU).

The control valve holds pressure when the control module energizes the isolation solenoid. This isolates the rear hydraulic circuit and prevents fluid from entering or leaving, therefore holding constant at a given pressure. Pressure is decreased when the module keeps the isolation solenoid energized and then energizes a dump solenoid which allows fluid from the rear hydraulic circuit to enter an accumulator, thereby reducing pressure and preventing wheel lockup. Pressure may be increased (though never over the driver's input) when both the isolation and dump solenoids are de-energized allowing the rear hydraulic circuit to function normally from full master cylinder pressure.

The RWAL ECU/EBCM is a separate and dedicated microcomputer mounted next to the master cylinder; it is not to be confused with the engine management computers also found in these vehicles. The ECU/EBCM receives signals from the speed sensor. The speed sensor sends its signals to the Vehicle Speed Sensor (VSS) buffer (previously known as the Digital Ratio Adapter Controller or DRAC) usually found within the instrument cluster. The buffer translates the sensor signal into a form usable by the computer module. The brake control module reads this signal and commands the control valve to function.

The RWAL system is connected to the brake warning lamp on the instrument cluster. A RWAL self-check and a bulb test are performed every time the ignition switch is turned to **ON**. The brake warning lamp should illuminate for about 2 seconds and then go off. Problems within the RWAL system will be indicated by the brake warning lamp remaining illuminated after this initial test period.

If a fault is detected within the system, the control module will assign a diagnostic fault code and store the code in memory. The code may be read to aid in diagnosis, much in the same way codes are used in the engine emission control systems used by these vehicles.

SYSTEM COMPONENTS

No component of the RWAL system can be disassembled or repaired. Should the control module, control valve containing the isolation/dump valves or the speed sensor fail, each failed component must be replaced as an assembly. If the axle ratio or tire size is changed on the vehicle, the VSS buffer must be replaced with one of the appropriate calibration.

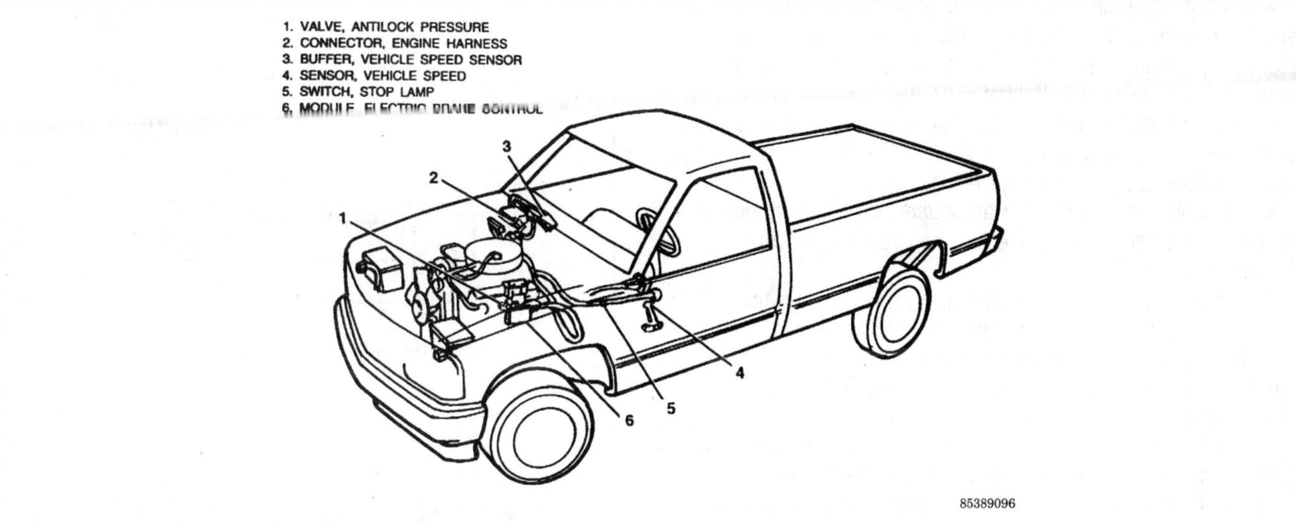

Fig. 75 Component locations for the Rear Wheel Anti-Lock (RWAL) brake system

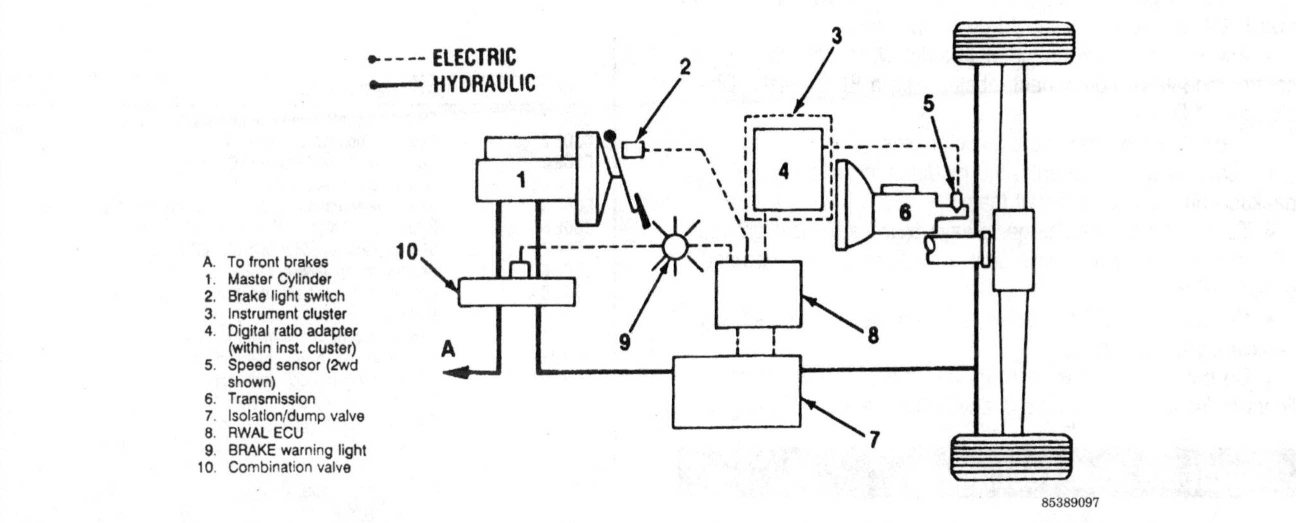

Fig. 76 RWAL brake system schematic

CIRCUIT MAINTENANCE

All electrical connections must be kept clean and tight. Make certain that all connectors are properly seated and all of the sealing rings on weather-proof connectors are in place. The low current and/or voltage found in some circuits require that every connection be the best possible. Special tools are required for servicing the GM Weather-Pack and Metric-Pack connectors. Use terminal remover tool J-28742 or equivalent for Weather-Pack and J-35689-A or equivalent for Metric-Pack connectors.

If removal of a terminal is attempted with a regular pick, there is a good chance the terminal will be bent or deformed. Once damaged, these connectors cannot be straightened.

Use care when probing the connections or replacing terminals; it is possible to short between adjacent terminals, causing component damage. Always use jumper wires between circuit connectors for testing circuits; never probe through weatherproof seals on connectors.

Oxidation or terminal misalignment may be hidden by the connector shell. When diagnosing open or intermittent circuits, wiggling the wire harness at the connector or component may reveal or correct the condition. When the location of the fault is identified, the connector should be separated and the problem connected. Never disconnect a harness connector with the ignition **ON**.

➡When working with the RWAL ECU/EBCM connectors, do not touch the connections or pins with the fingers. Do not allow the connectors or pins to contact brake fluid; internal damage to the RWAL ECU/EBCM may occur.

SYSTEM PRECAUTIONS

- Certain components within the RWAL system are not intended to be serviced or repaired. Only those components with removal & Installation procedures should be serviced. Do not attempt to disassemble or overhaul RWAL system components.

- Do not use rubber hoses or other parts not specifically specified for the RWAL system. When using repair kits, replace all parts included in the kit. Partial or incorrect repair may lead to functional problems.
- Lubricate rubber parts with clean, fresh brake fluid to ease assembly. Do not use lubricated shop air to clean parts; damage to rubber components may result.
- Use only brake fluid from an unopened container. Use of suspect or contaminated brake fluid can reduce system performance and/or durability.
- A clean repair area is essential. Perform repairs after components have been thoroughly cleaned; use only denatured alcohol to clean components. Do not allow components to come into contact with any substance containing mineral oil; this includes used shop rags.
- The RWAL ECU/EBCM is a microprocessor similar to other computer units in the vehicle. Insure that the ignition switch is **OFF** before removing or installing controller harnesses. Avoid static electricity discharge at or near the controller.
- Never disengage any electrical connection with the ignition switch **ON** unless instructed to do so in a test.
- Always wear a grounded wrist strap when servicing any control module or component labeled with a Electrostatic Discharge (ESD) symbol.
- Avoid touching module connector pins.
- Leave new components and modules in the shipping package until ready to install them.
- To avoid static discharge, always touch a vehicle ground after sliding across a vehicle seat or walking across carpeted or vinyl floors.
- Never allow welding cables to lie on, near or across any vehicle electrical wiring.
- Do not allow extension cords for power tools or drop lights to lie on, near or across any vehicle electrical wiring.

Diagnosis and Testing

READING CODES

See Figures 77 and 78

The RWAL (ECU/EBCM) will assign a code to the first fault found in the system. If there is more than 1 fault, only the first recognized code will the stored and transmitted.

Trouble codes may be read either though the use of Tech-1 or equivalent scan tool or by connecting a jumper wire from pin H on the ALDL/DLC to pin A. If the jumper method is used, the fault code will be displayed through the flashing of the BRAKE warning lamp on the dash. The terminals must be connected for about 20 seconds before the display begins. The display will begin with 1 long flash followed by shorter ones — count the long flash as part of the display.

Sometimes the first display sequence will be inaccurate or short; subsequent displays will be accurate.

If using a hand scanner, note if a soft code is stored, only the last recognized code will be retained and displayed on the scanner. Soft fault Codes 2, 3, 4, 6, 7, 8, 9, and 10 can only be read with a scan tool. On some models, Codes 1, 11 and 12 will not read on the scan tool and must be read using the jumper wire method.

Never ground terminal H of the ALDL to terminal A if the BRAKE warning lamp is not lit. Doing so will usually set a false code 9 and illuminate the BRAKE warning lamp. With the brake lamp on, the RWAL system will be disabled.

CLEARING CODES

Stored trouble codes must be cleared with the ignition switch **OFF**. NEVER attempt to clear codes while the ignition switch is in the **ON** position or the computer module will likely be destroyed. Remove the ECM B fuse for at least 5 seconds, then reinstall the fuse.

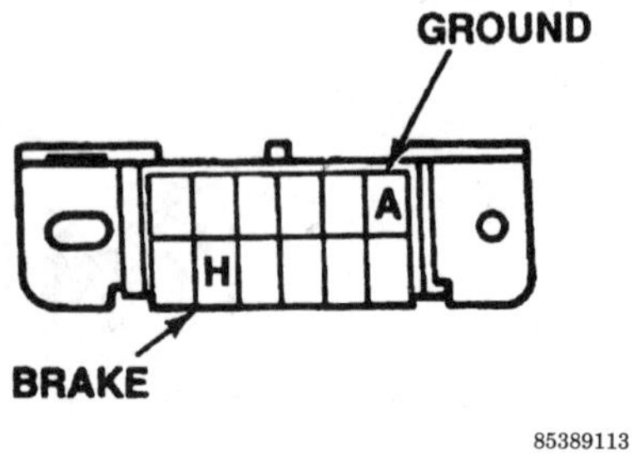

Fig. 77 ALDL/DLC terminal identification for activating trouble code read out

CODE	SYSTEM PROBLEM
CODE 1	Electronic control unit malfunction
CODE 2	Open isolation valve or faulty ECU
CODE 3	Open dump valve or faulty ECU
CODE 4	Grounded antilock valve switch
CODE 5	Excessive actuations of dump valve during an antilock stop
CODE 6	Erratic speed signal
CODE 7	Shorted isolation valve or faulty ECU
CODE 8	Shorted dump valve or faulty ECU
CODE 9	Open circuit to the speed signal
CODE 10	Brake lamp switch circuit
CODE 11	Electronic control unit malfunction
CODE 12	Electronic control unit malfunction
CODE 13	Electronic control unit malfunction
CODE 14	Electronic control unit malfunction
CODE 15	Electronic control unit malfunction

85389114

Fig. 78 RWAL trouble codes

PRELIMINARY DIAGNOSIS

➧ See Figures 79, 80, 81, 82, 83, 84, 85 and 86

Before reading trouble codes, perform the Function Test according to the appropriate charts for your truck. The charts are located in this section. This test will aid in separating RWAL system problems from common problems in the hydraulic brake system. The diagnostic circuit check will direct the reading of trouble codes as necessary.

DO NOT ground the brake trouble code terminal of the ALDL/DLC if the BRAKE lamp is not on indicating a stored trouble code. Attempting to activate trouble code read out with the BRAKE lamp off may set a false Code 9. This will turn the BRAKE lamp ON and disable the anti-lock brake system.

Component Replacement

RWAL ECU/EBCM

➧ See Figure 87

The Electronic Brake Control Module (EBCM), formerly known as the RWAL Electronic Control Unit (ECU), is a non-serviceable unit. It must be replaced when diagnosis indicates it is faulty. Because it is expensive and normally non-returnable, be absolutely sure the module is at fault before replacement.

1. Turn the ignition switch **OFF**. The switch MUST be **OFF** whenever you are connecting/disconnecting power from the module. Failure to do this may destroy the computer.
2. Disengage the wiring harness connector(s) from the computer control module.
3. Grasp the module and remove it by pulling toward the front of the vehicle. If necessary, gently pry the tab at the rear of the module while pulling.

➡Do not touch the electrical connectors or pins; do not allow them to contact brake fluid. If contaminated with brake fluid, clean them with water followed by isopropyl alcohol.

To install:

4. Install the computer module by aligning it and carefully sliding it into the bracket until the tab locks into the hole.
5. Engage the wiring harness connector(s) to the module.
6. Turn the ignition **ON**, then verify proper system operation.

ANTI-LOCK PRESSURE CONTROL VALVE

The Anti-Lock Pressure Valve (APV), formerly known as the isolation/dump or control valve assembly is not serviceable. The entire component must be replaced as an assembly should a malfunction be confirmed.

1. Turn the ignition switch **OFF**. The switch MUST be **OFF** whenever you are connecting/disconnecting power from the module (as will done later in this procedure). Failure to do this may destroy the computer.
2. Disconnect the brake line fittings at the valve, then immediately cap or plug all openings to prevent system contamination or excessive fluid loss. Remember to protect the surrounding paint work from damage by fluid spillage.
3. Disengage the bottom connector from the RWAL ECU/EBCM. At no time should you allow the APV to hang by the wiring.

➡Do not touch the electrical connectors or pins; do not allow them to contact brake fluid. If contaminated with brake fluid, clean them with water followed by isopropyl alcohol.

4. Remove the bolts holding the valve to the bracket.
5. Remove the valve from the vehicle.

To install:

6. Place the valve in position and install the retaining bolts. Tighten the bolts to 21 ft. lbs. (29 Nm).
7. Engage the electrical connector to the RWAL ECU/EBCM.

➡Before engaging the electrical connector, double check to be sure there is no brake fluid on the terminals or the control module may be damaged. If necessary, clean the terminals with water, followed by denatured alcohol.

8. Remove the caps or plugs, then install the brake lines and tighten the fittings to 18 ft. lbs. (24 Nm)
9. Properly bleed the RWAL hydraulic brake system at all 4 wheels.

SPEED SENSOR

➧ See Figure 88

The speed sensor is not serviceable and must replaced if malfunctioning. The sensor is usually located in the left rear of the transmission case on 2WD vehicles and on the transfer case of 4WD vehicles.

The speed sensor may be tested with an ohmmeter; the correct resistance is normally 900-2000 ohms. To remove the speed sensor:

1. Raise and support the vehicle safely using jackstands.
2. Disengage the electrical connector from the speed sensor.
3. If used, remove the sensor retaining bolt.
4. Remove the speed sensor; have a container handy to catch transmission fluid when the sensor is removed.

➡If equipped with the 4L60-E automatic transmission, use J-38417 or an equivalent speed sensor remover/installer tool whenever the sensor is serviced.

5. Recover the O-ring used to seal the sensor; inspect it for damage or deterioration.

To install:

6. When installing, coat the new O-ring with a thin film of transmission fluid.
7. Install the O-ring and speed sensor.
8. If a retaining bolt is used, tighten the bolt to 97 inch lbs. (11 Nm) in automatic transmissions or 107 inch lbs. (12 Nm) for manual transmissions.
9. If the sensor is a screw-in unit tighten it to 32 ft. lbs. (43 Nm).

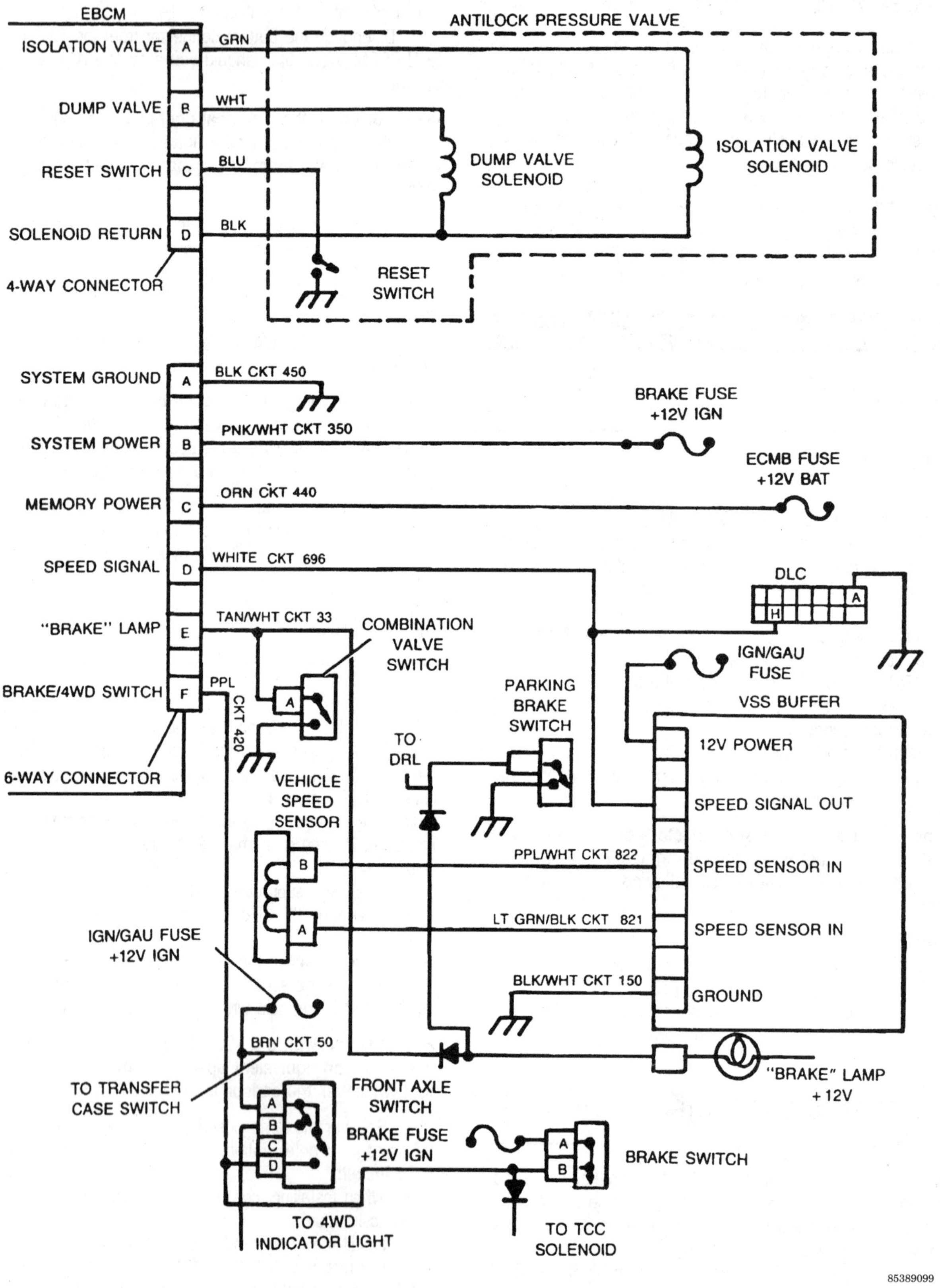

Fig. 79 ABS system wiring diagram

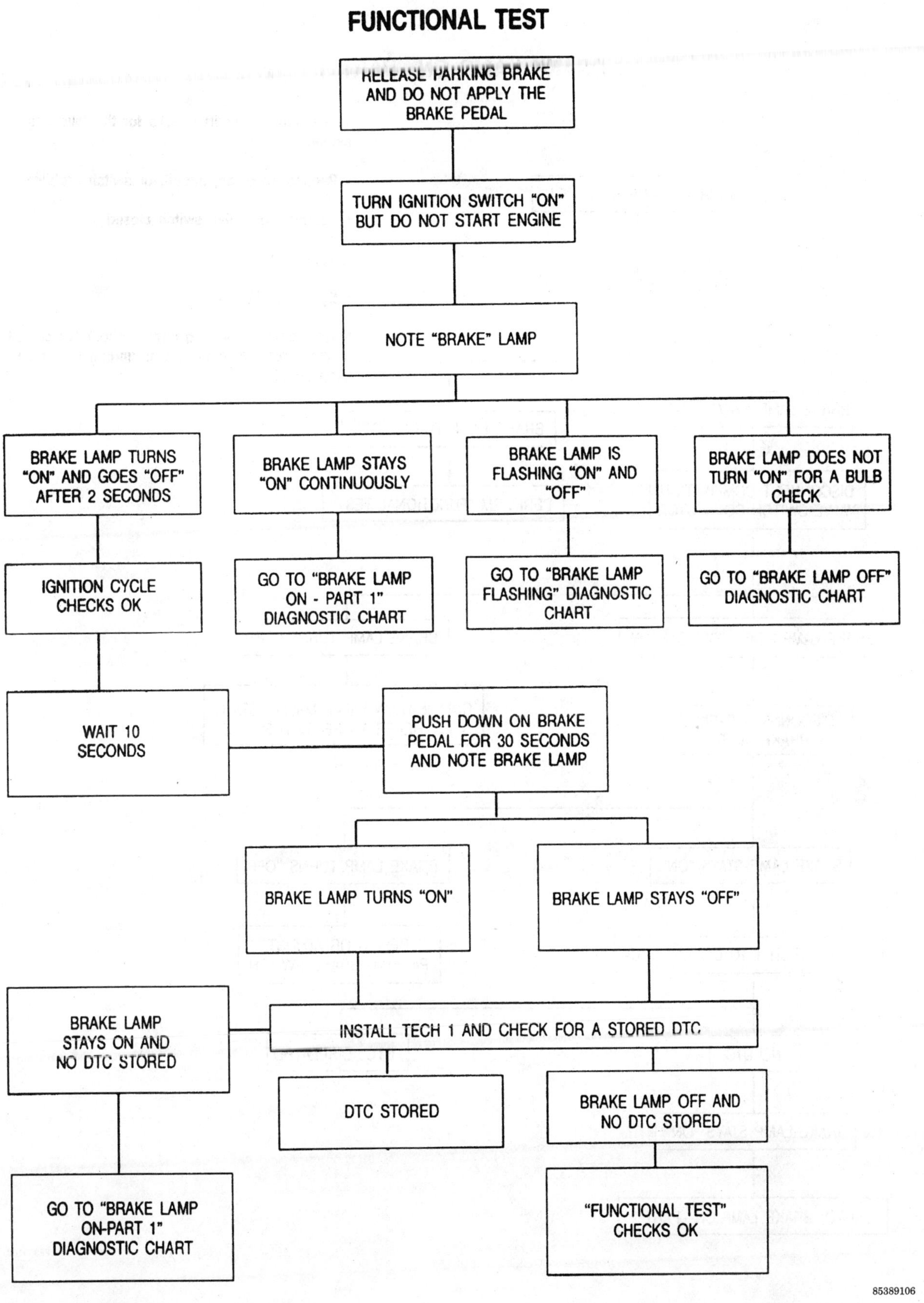

Fig. 80 Functional test

BRAKE LAMP ON—PART 1

This diagnostic chart checks for the following causes:

- Parking brake on, circuit, or switch problem
- Combination valve switch closed
- Stored DTC
- System malfunction

NOTE: When inspecting circuit, check for chafed or cut wires that could be grounding the brake lamp circuit.

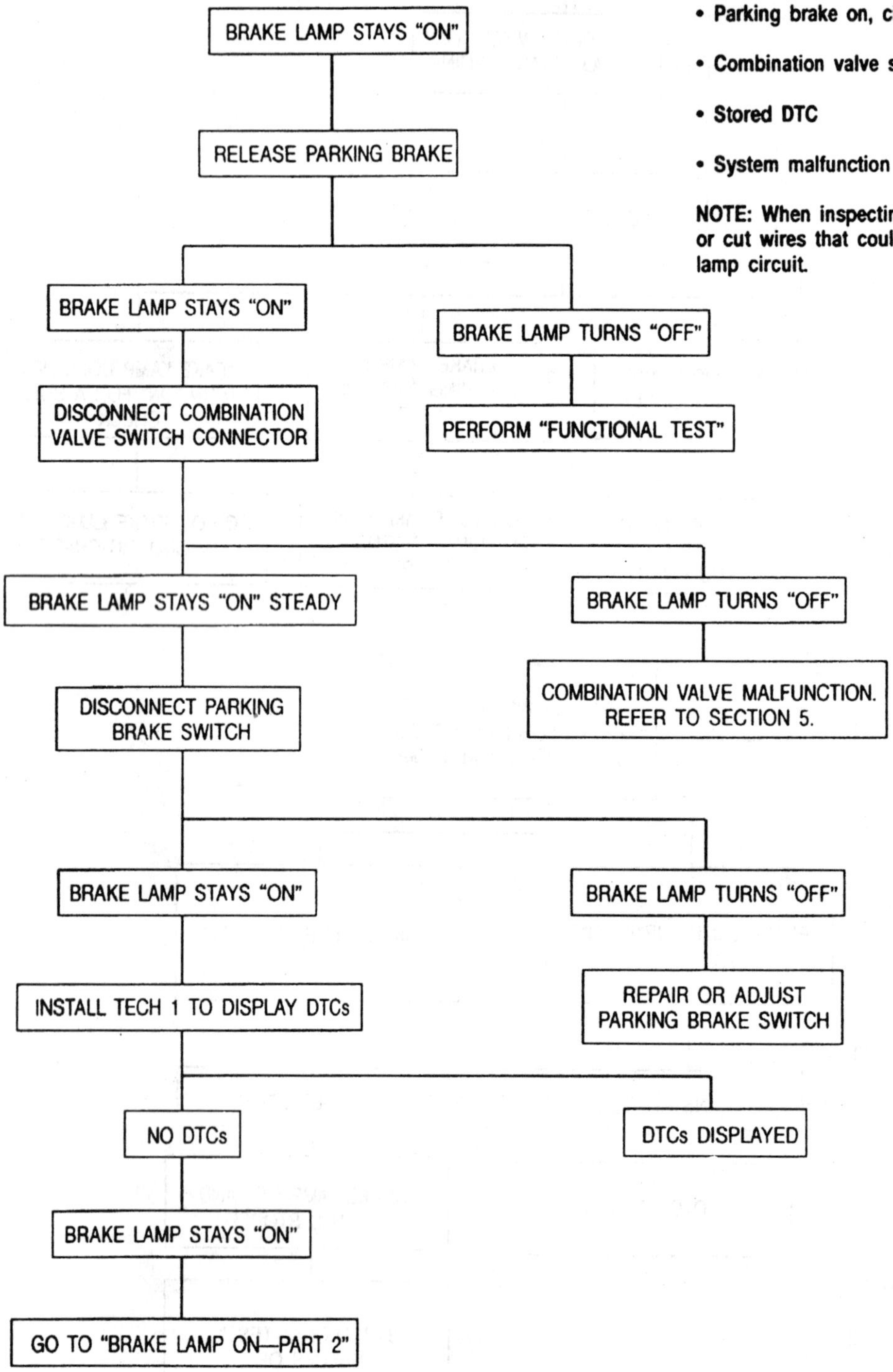

85389107

Fig. 81 Brake lamp on test

BRAKE LAMP ON—PART 2

NOTICE: WHEN MEASUREMENTS ARE REQUESTED IN THIS CHART, USE J 39200 DVM. WHEN A CHECK FOR PROPER CONNECTION IS REQUESTED, REFER TO "INTERMITTENTS AND POOR CONNECTIONS" IN THE DRIVEABILITY, EMISSIONS AND ELECTRICAL DIAGNOSIS MANUAL.

This diagnostic chart checks for the following cause:

- No speed signal voltage to EBCM
- RWAL system or wiring condition
- EBCM malfunction

NOTE: If voltage readings are low or varying, check the battery and charging system or check for intermittent connections.

BRAKE LAMP STAYS ON (FROM BRAKE LAMP ON PART 1)
REMOVE TECH 1
MEASURE VOLTAGE FROM DLC PINS H TO A
0 VOLTS
DISCONNECT EBCM 6-WAY CONNECTOR
MEASURE VOLTAGE FROM EBCM 6-WAY CONNECTOR TERMINAL "D" TO TERMINAL "A"
VOLTAGE STILL MEASURES ZERO
OPEN CIRCUIT OR NO VOLTAGE IN SPEED SIGNAL LINE
CHECK FOR THE FOLLOWING:
- BLOWN VSS CALIBRATOR FUSE
- OPEN WIRING
- OPEN CIRCUIT AT VSS CALIBRATOR CONNECTOR
- FAULTY VSS CALIBRATOR (NO OUTPUT)
- GROUNDED CKT 696
- VEHICLE SPEED SENSOR

8 TO 15 VOLTS
MEASURE VOLTAGE FROM DLC PINS "H" TO "A"
0 VOLTS
CHECK SPEED SIGNAL WIRING FOR OPEN/SHORT CIRCUITS AT—
- DLC
- BULKHEAD CONNECTOR
- VSS CALIBRATOR WIRING OR CONNECTOR

REPAIR FAULT AND RECONNECT
8 TO 15 VOLTS
RECONNECT EBCM 6-WAY CONNECTOR
MEASURE VOLTAGE FROM DLC PINS "H" TO "A"
8 TO 15 VOLTS
REPAIR POOR CONNECTION AT EBCM 6-WAY CONNECTOR
0 VOLTS
REPLACE EBCM

8 TO 15 VOLTS
GO TO "BRAKE LAMP ON-PART 3"

85389108

Fig. 82 Brake lamp on test (con't)

BRAKE LAMP ON—PART 3

NOTICEWHEN MEASUREMENTS ARE REQUESTED IN THIS CHART, USE J 39200 DVM. WHEN A CHECK FOR PROPER CONNECTION IS REQUESTED, REFER TO "INTERMITTENTS AND POOR CONNECTIONS" IN THE DRIVEABILITY, EMISSIONS AND ELECTRICAL DIAGNOSIS MANUAL.

This diagnostic chart checks for the following causes:

- No Power to VSS calibrator
- No battery voltage feed to EBCM
- No Ignition voltage feed to EBCM
- EBCM malfunction

NOTE: The RWAL system is designed to turn the "BRAKE" lamp on if the ignition is on and there is no battery or ignition voltage feed to the EBCM.

NOTE: If voltage readings are low or varying, check battery and charging system or check for intermittent connections.

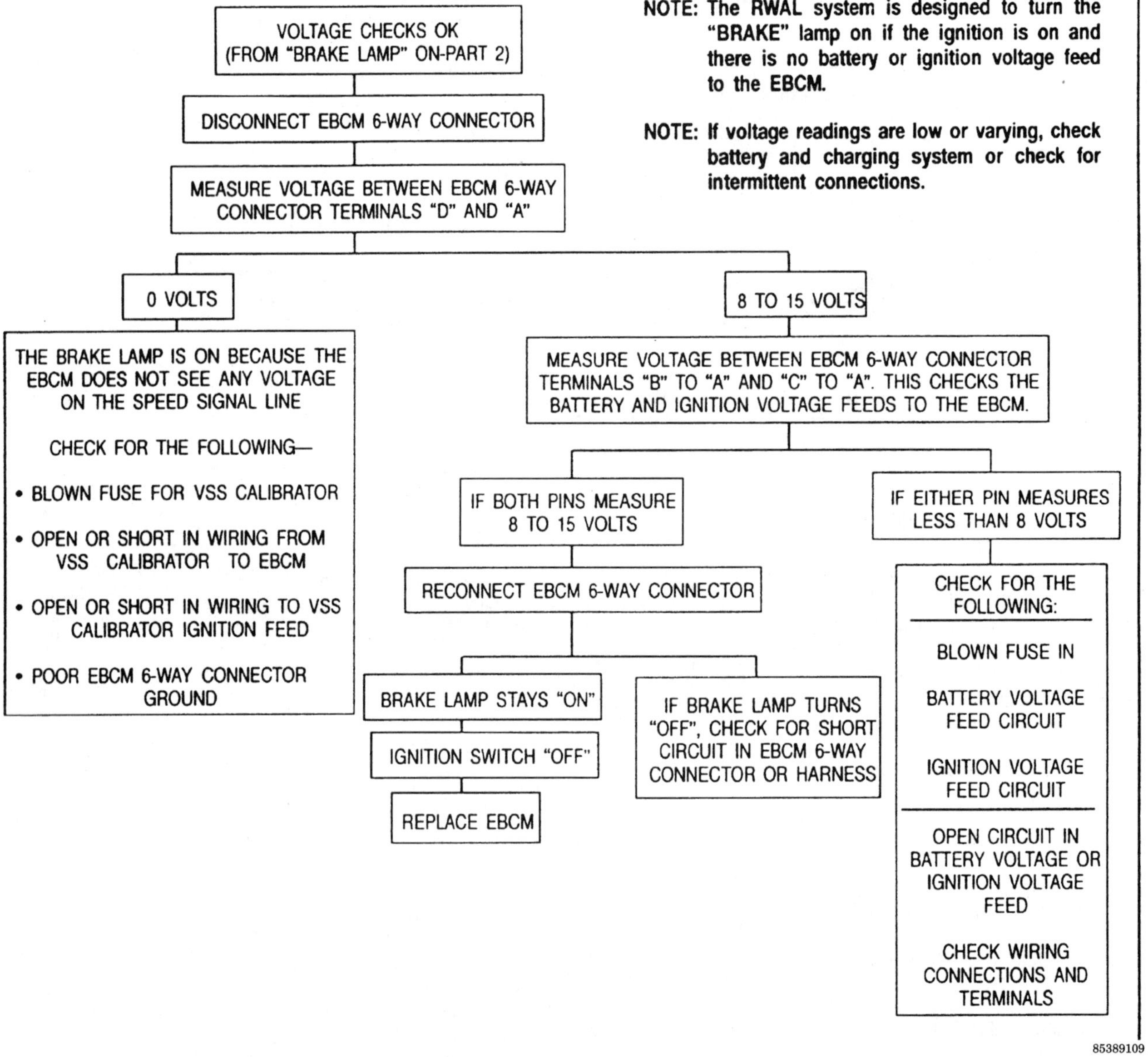

Fig. 83 Brake lamp on test (con't)

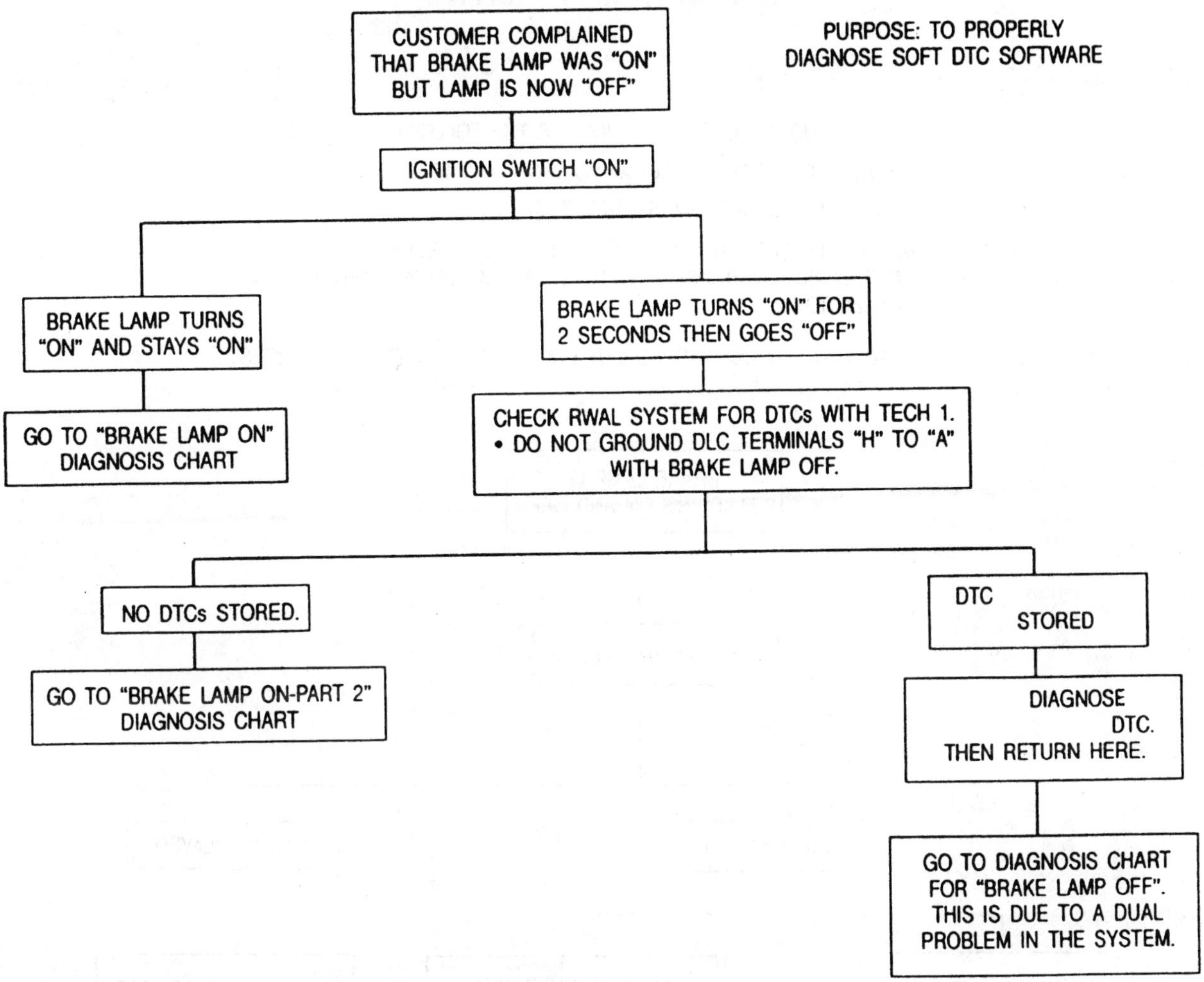

- DO NOT ATTEMPT TO GROUND DLC TERMINALS "H" TO "A" WHEN THE BRAKE LAMP IS OFF. RESULT WILL BE A FALSE DTC 9 STORED.

- SOFT DTCS HAVE BEEN INTRODUCED DUE TO INTERMITTENT CONNECTIONS. IF THE CONDITION GOES AWAY THE DTC WILL BE STORED TO AID IN DIAGNOSTICS. HOWEVER, THE BRAKE LAMP WILL BE TURNED OFF WITH THE NEXT TIME THE IGNITION SWITCH IS TURNED "OFF" AND THE BRAKE LAMP WILL BE TURNED OFF WITH DTC 10 WHEN THE EBCM SEES 12 VOLTS FROM THE BRAKE SWITCH.

85389110

Fig. 84 Brake lamp test

BRAKE LAMP FLASHING

THIS DIAGNOSTIC CHART CHECKS FOR THE FOLLOWING CAUSES:

- INTERMITTENT SPEED SIGNAL VOLTAGE TO THE EBCM
- SYSTEM MALFUNCTION (STORED DTC)

NOTE: IF VOLTAGE READINGS ARE TOO LOW OR VARYING, CHECK BATTERY AND CHARGING SYSTEM OR CHECK FOR INTERMITTENT CONNECTIONS.

NOTE: DTC MAY BE FLASHED OUT UNDER UNUSUAL CIRCUMSTANCES.

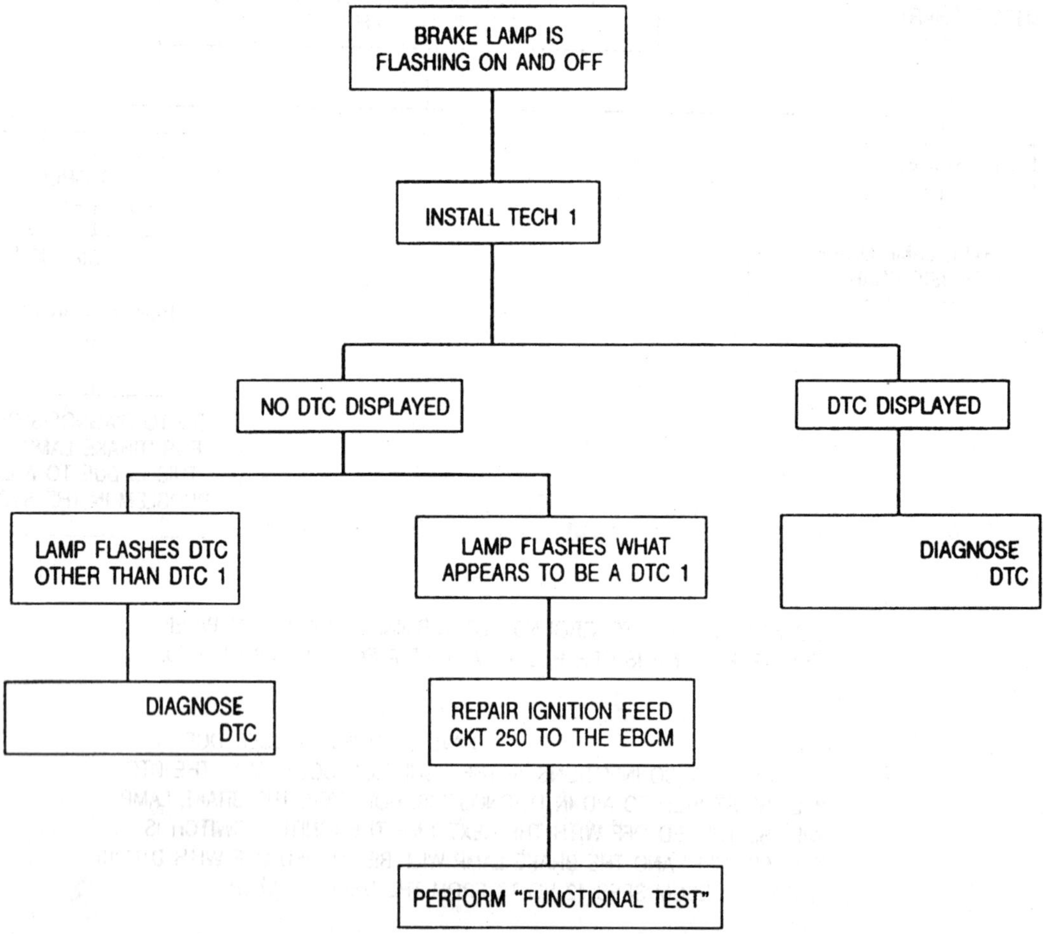

85389111

Fig. 85 Brake lamp flashing test

BRAKE LAMP OFF

The EBCM should perform a BRAKE lamp check when the ignition switch is turned "ON". The EBCM turns the BRAKE lamp on for 2 seconds then turns it off. The Brake lamp going out after 2 seconds indicates that the EBCM ignition cycle checked ok.

NOTE: Operate the parking brake to check the BRAKE lamp circuit. The lamp should come on when the parking brake pedal is applied.

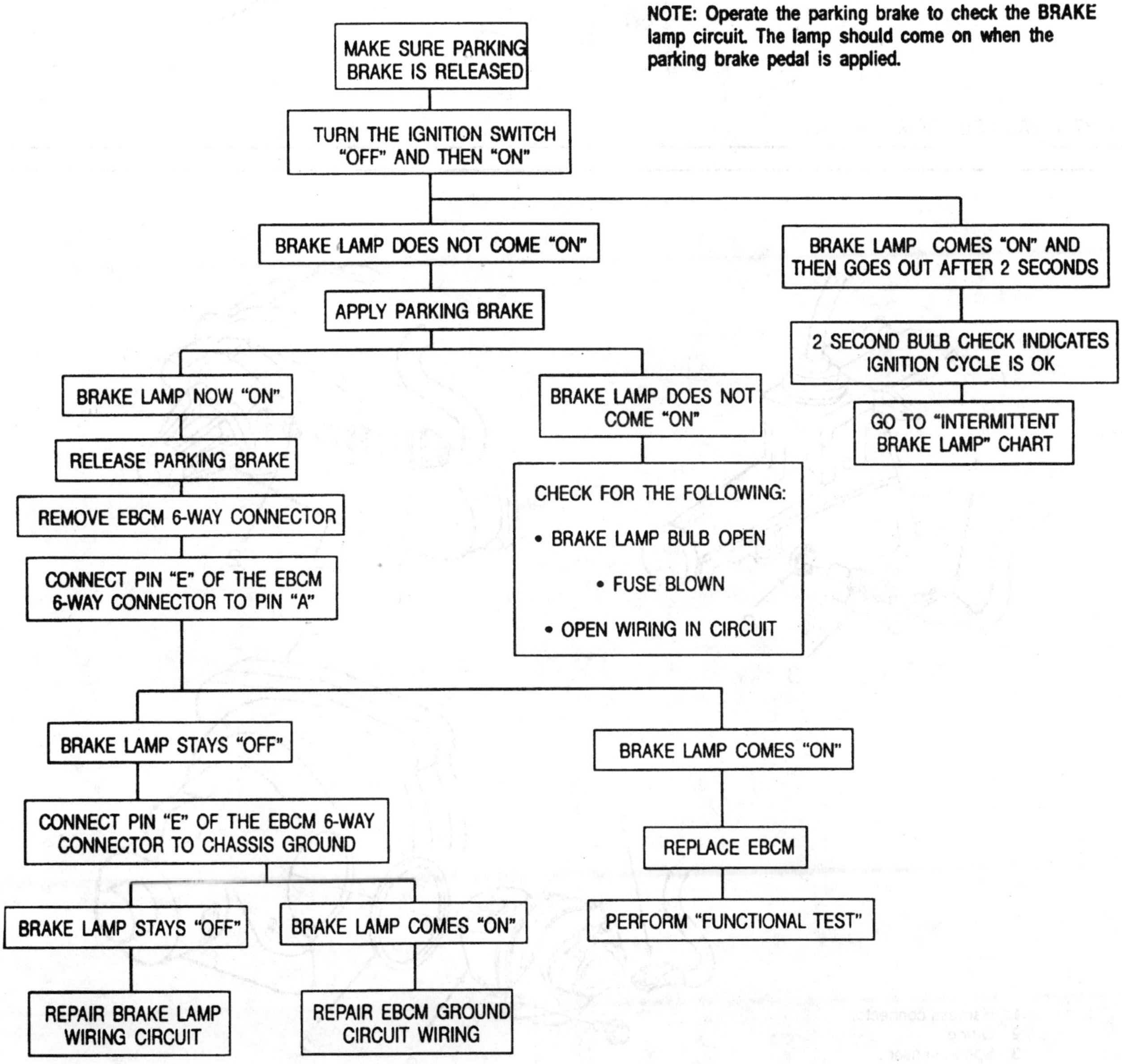

85389112

Fig. 86 Brake lamp off test

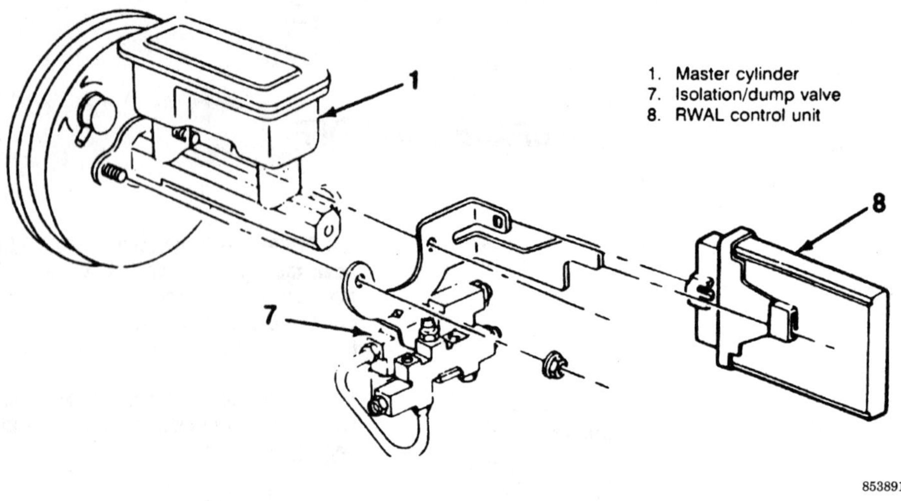

Fig. 87 RWAL ECU/EBCM mounting

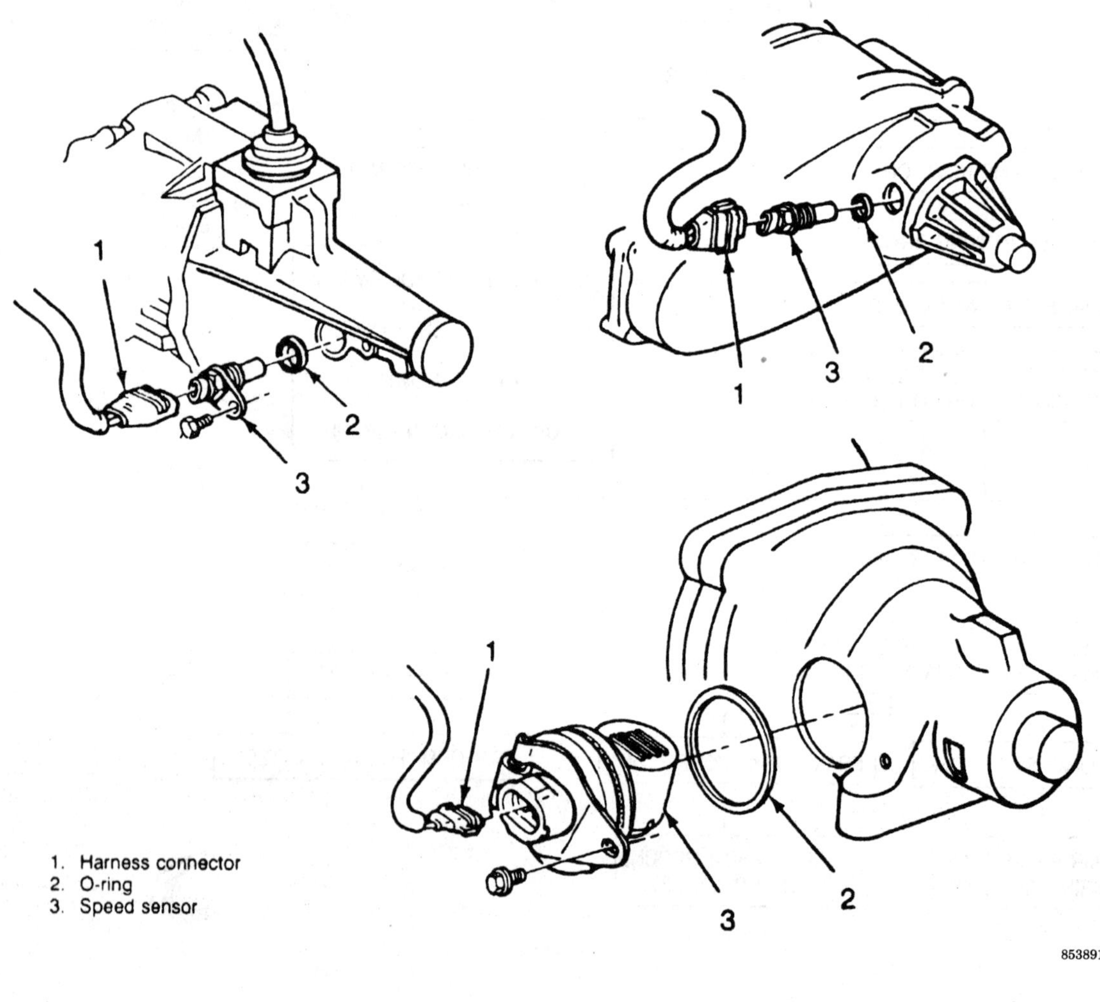

Fig. 88 Common speed sensor mounting locations

10. Engage the wire harness to the sensor.
11. Remove the jackstands and carefully lower the vehicle.

Bleeding the RWAL Brake System

On RWAL a few steps (listed below) should be added to the bleeding sequence in order to ease the procedure and assure all air is removed from the system. If you have access to the additional tools required, you may use these extra steps on all RWAL vehicles to assure proper bleeding.

The use of a power bleeder is recommended, but the system may also be bled manually. If a power bleeder is used, it must be of the diaphragm type and provide isolation of the fluid from air and moisture.

Do not pump the pedal rapidly when bleeding; this can make the circuits very difficult to bleed. Instead, press the brake pedal slowly 1 time and hold it down while bleeding takes place. Tighten the bleeder screw, release the pedal and wait 15 seconds before repeating the sequence. Because of the length of the brake lines and other factors, it may take 10 or more repetitions of the sequence to bleed each line properly. When necessary to bleed all 4 wheels, the correct order is right rear, left rear, right front and left front.

✱✱CAUTION

Do not move the vehicle until a firm brake pedal is achieved. Failure to properly bleed the system may cause impaired braking and the possibility of injury and/or property damage

On all RWAL equipped vehicles, use the bleeding procedure found earlier in this section, with the following additions:

1. Make sure the ignition is in the **OFF** position to prevent setting false trouble codes.
2. After properly bleeding the master cylinder, install J-39177 or an equivalent combination valve depressor tool to the combination valve. This tool is used to hold the internal valve open allowing the entire system to be completely bled.

➡This tool is relatively inexpensive and should be available from various aftermarket companies. Although a homemade tool may suffice, DO NOT attempt to fabricate a homemade tool unless you are CERTAIN it will not damage the valve by over-extension.

3. Recheck the master cylinder fluid level and add, as necessary.
4. Bleed the wheel cylinders as described earlier in this section.
5. Attach the Tech-1 or an equivalent scan tool, then perform 3 RWAL function tests.
6. Re-bleed the rear wheel cylinders.
7. Check for a firm brake pedal, if necessary repeat the entire bleeding procedure.
8. Once you are finished, be sure to remove the combination valve depressor tool.

FOUR WHEEL ANTI-LOCK (4WAL) SYSTEM

General Description

See Figures 89, 90 and 91

There are some slightly different four wheel anti-lock brake systems used on the pick up models. One system utilizes a separate EBCM, like the RWAL and earlier 4WAL systems, while the other system utilizes a Vehicle Control Module (VCM). On the VCM equipped model, the computer control module (which is mounted in the engine compartment) controls both the ABS system and the engine emission control/fuel injection systems.

All versions of the four wheel anti-lock system are designed to reduce brake lock-up during severe brake application. The basic function of each system is similar to the RWAL system described earlier in this manual, the major difference simply being that the 4 wheel system monitors and controls wheel spin/lockup on the front wheels as well as the rear.

Instead of the APV (control valve) used on RWAL systems, the 4WAL systems utilize a Brake Pressure Modulator Valve (BPMV), formerly known as the Electro-Hydraulic Control Unit (EHCU). The EHCU/BPMV is located near the master cylinder and controls the hydraulic pressure within the brake lines.

SYSTEM OPERATION

In a severe brake application, the EHCU/BPMV valve will, depending on the circumstance: allow pressure to increase within the system, maintain (isolate) the pressure within the system, or release existing pressure through the dump valves into the accumulators.

The EHCU/BPMV valve operates by receiving signals from the speed sensors, located at each wheel, and from the brake lamp switch. The speed sensors connect directly to the EHCU/BPMV valve through a multi-pin connector.

The system is connected to the ANTI-LOCK warning lamp on the dashboard. The warning lamp will illuminate for about 2 seconds every time the vehicle is started as a lamp check. The warning lamp will illuminate if the computer detects a problem within the anti-lock system during vehicle operation. If the warning light comes on when the vehicle is started and does not go out, or if the light comes on and remains on during vehicle operation, trouble has been detected by the computer module.

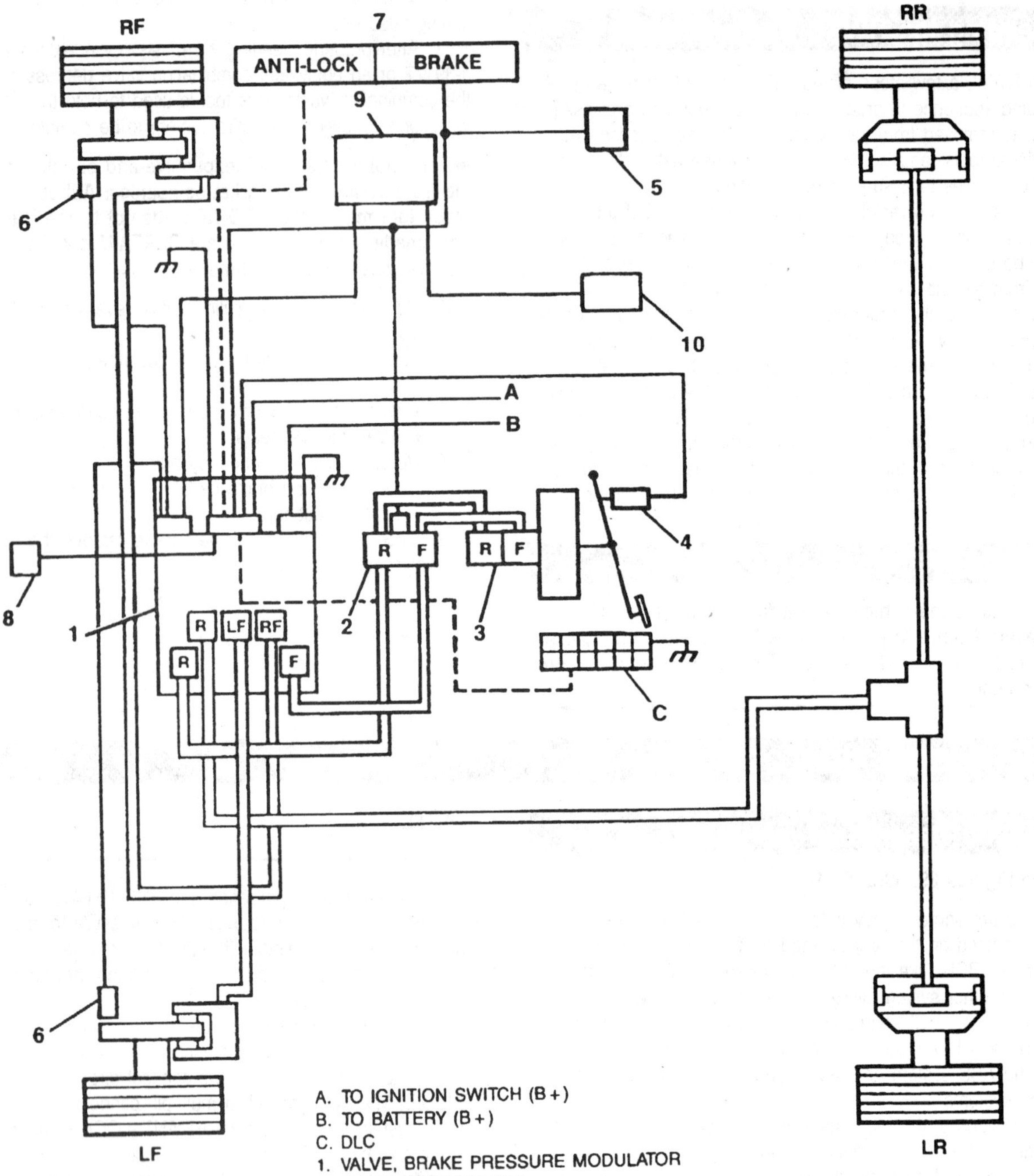

A. TO IGNITION SWITCH (B+)
B. TO BATTERY (B+)
C. DLC
1. VALVE, BRAKE PRESSURE MODULATOR
2. VALVE, COMBINATION
3. CYLINDER, MASTER
4. SWITCH, BRAKE PEDAL
5. SWITCH, PARKING BRAKE
6. SENSOR, WHEEL SPEED
7. LAMPS, WARNING
8. SWITCH, 4WD
9. BUFFER, VSS
10. SENSOR, VEHICLE SPEED (IN TRANSMISSION)

Fig. 89 1994-95 4WAL EBCM system schematic

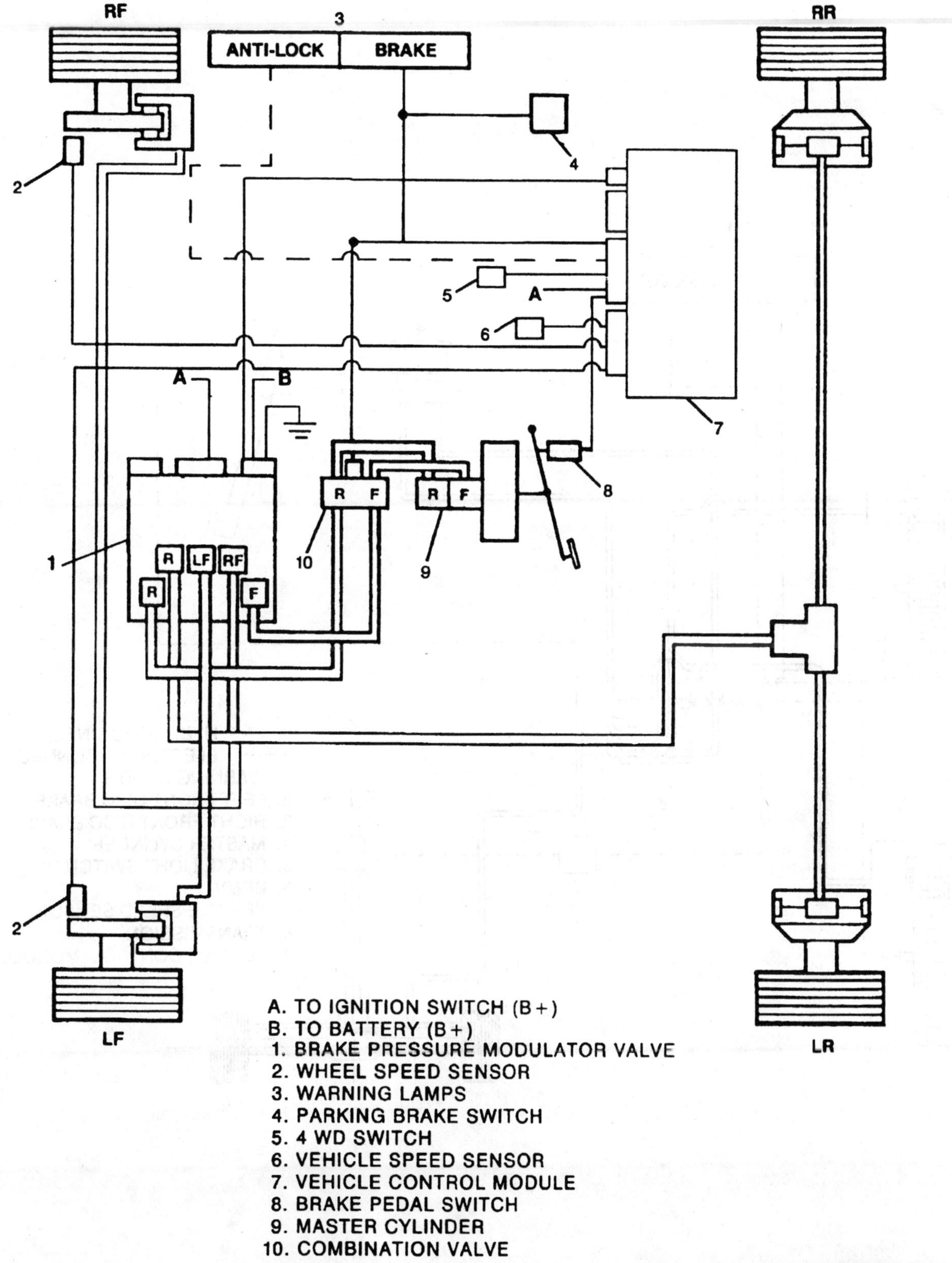

A. TO IGNITION SWITCH (B+)
B. TO BATTERY (B+)
1. BRAKE PRESSURE MODULATOR VALVE
2. WHEEL SPEED SENSOR
3. WARNING LAMPS
4. PARKING BRAKE SWITCH
5. 4 WD SWITCH
6. VEHICLE SPEED SENSOR
7. VEHICLE CONTROL MODULE
8. BRAKE PEDAL SWITCH
9. MASTER CYLINDER
10. COMBINATION VALVE

2905T5014

85389119

Fig. 90 1994-95 4WAL VCM system schematic

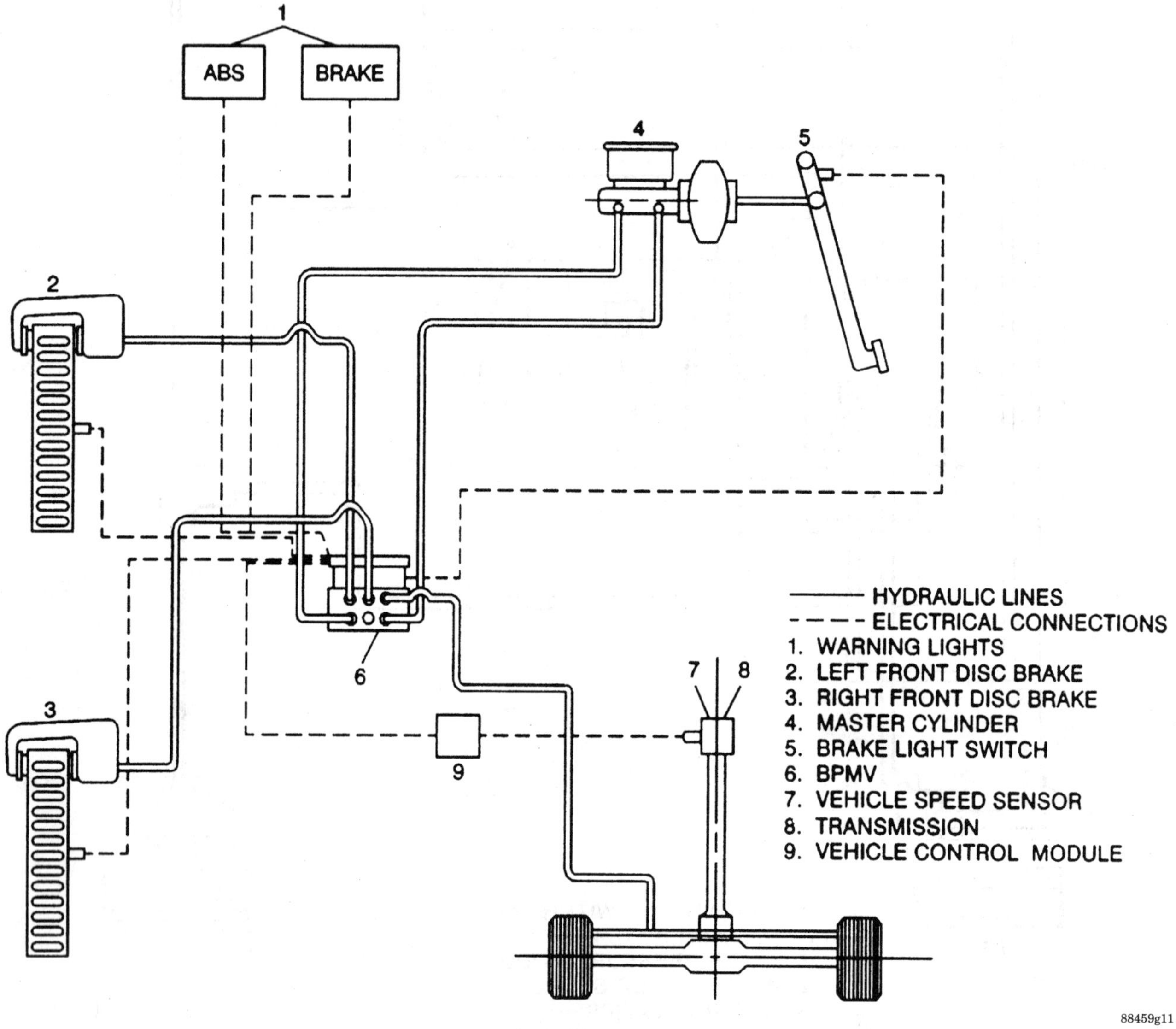

Fig. 91 1996-97 4WAL system schematic

SYSTEM COMPONENTS

EHCU/BPMV Valve

➧ See Figures 92 and 93

The BPMV valve (formerly referred to as the EHCU) is mounted near or under the master cylinder and combination valve assemblies. The valve is not serviceable and must be replaced if malfunctioning. The valve is also the sight for the only additional attention required to properly bleed the 4WAL hydraulic system.

Front Wheel Speed Sensors

➧ See Figure 94

On most 2 and 4WD vehicles covered by this manual, the front wheel speed sensors are permanently mounted to the brake rotor splash shield which must be replaced as an assembly should the sensor fail. On 2WD vehicles, the rotor must be removed for access. On 4WD vehicles, the hub and bearing assembly must be removed.

The front wheel speed sensors operate with the help of sensor tone wheels. The tone wheels are metal rings equipped with teeth on their outer diameter. The AC voltage is produced as the teeth come into and leave alignment with the sensor. The tone wheels are attached to the rotor on 2WD vehicles and the front hub and bearing assembly on 4WD vehicles.

A properly operating speed sensor should have a resistance value of 900-2000 ohms.

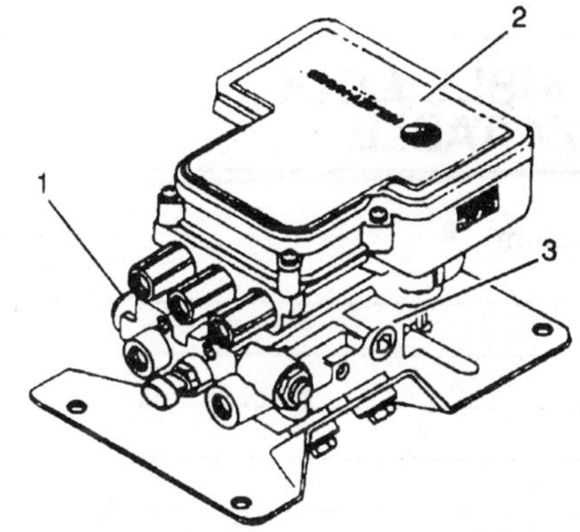

Fig. 92 View of the ECHU and related components

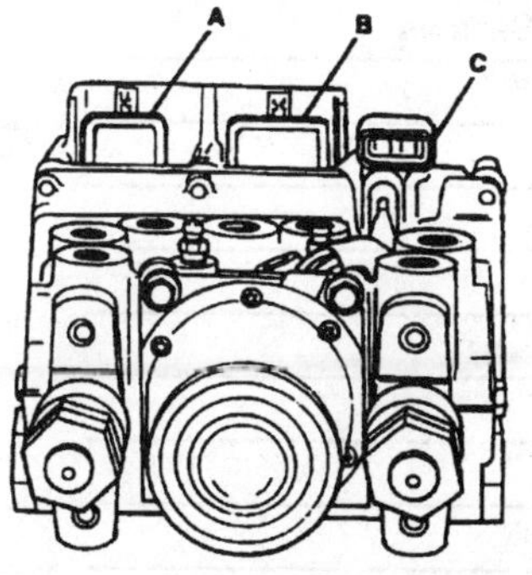

Fig. 93 The 4WAL Brake Pressure Modulator Valve (BPMV)

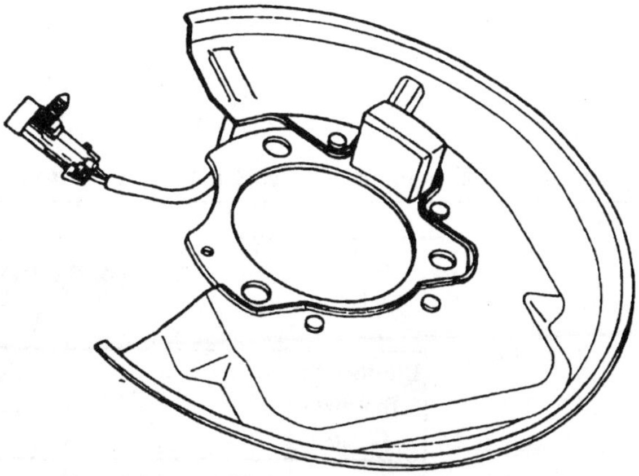

Fig. 94 Common front wheel speed sensor mounting

Diagnosis & Testing

READING CODES

➧ See Figures 95, 96 and 97

Except for on VCM systems, stored trouble codes may be transmitted through the flashing of the ANTI-LOCK dash warning lamp. On these vehicles, the system may be placed in diagnostic mode using a jumper wire, however, the use of the Tech-1 scan tool or its equivalent is highly recommended. On all VCM equipped vehicles, a scan tool must be used to display trouble codes. For all systems, the scan tool will allow performance of the specific system tests called for by the trouble tree for each code.

On vehicles where flash-diagnosis is possible, trouble code read out may be started using a jumper wire to connect Terminal H on the ALDL/DLC (diagnostic connector located under the instrument panel -- refer to self-diagnostics in Section 4 of this manual for more information) to either body ground or to terminal A (internal ground). The terminals must be connected for a few seconds before the code will transmit. Observe the ANTI-LOCK light on the dash and count the flashes in groups: a group of 4 flashes, a pause and a group of 3 flashes indicates Code 43.

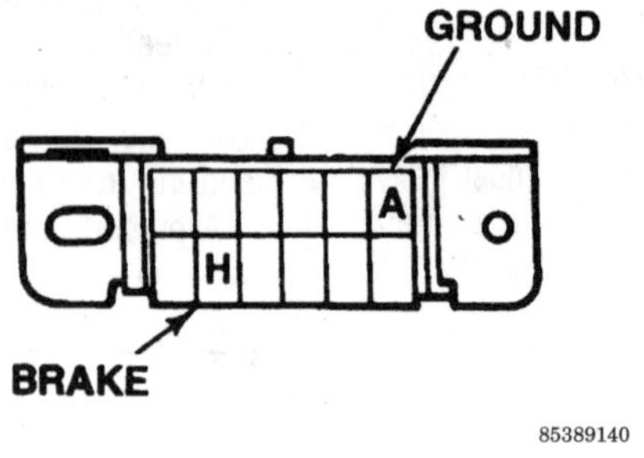

Fig. 95 Non-VCM equipped vehicles may activate trouble code flash diagnosis using the ALDL/DLC

DIAGNOSTIC TROUBLE CODE AND SYMPTOM TABLE

Diagnostic Trouble Code	Description/Symptom
—	Antilock Lamp "ON"
—	Antilock Lamp "OFF"
—	Brake Pedal Pulses
—	Wheel Pull During Hard Braking
21	Right Front Wheel Speed Sensor or Circuit Open
22	Missing Right Front Speed Signal
23	Erratic Right Front Wheel Speed Sensor
25	Left Front Wheel Speed Sensor or Circuit Open
26	Missing Left Front Speed Signal
27	Erratic Left Front Wheel Speed Sensor
29	Simultaneous Drop-Out of Front Wheel Speed Sensors
35	Open or Grounded Rear Speed Signal Circuit
36	Missing Rear Speed Signal
37	Erratic Rear Speed Signal
38	Wheel Speed Error
41-54	Control Valves
65-66	Open or Shorted Pump Motor Relay
67	Open Motor Circuit or Shorted BPMV Output
68	Locked Motor or Shorted Motor Circuit
71-74	Memory Errors
81	Brake Switch Circuit Shorted or Open
86	Shorted Antilock Indicator Lamp
88	Shorted Brake Warning Lamp

85389142

Fig. 96 Diagnostic trouble codes/symptoms — 1994 EBCM 4WAL systems

DIAGNOSTIC TROUBLE CODE AND SYMPTOM TABLE

Diagnostic Trouble Code	Description/Symptom
—	Antilock Lamp "ON"
—	Antilock Lamp "OFF"
—	Brake Pedal Pulses
—	Wheel Pull During Hard Braking
21	Right Front Wheel Speed Sensor or Circuit Open
22	Missing Right Front Speed Signal
23	Erratic Right Front Wheel Speed Sensor
25	Left Front Wheel Speed Sensor or Circuit Open
26	Missing Left Front Speed Signal
27	Erratic Left Front Wheel Speed Sensor
29	Simultaneous Drop Out of Front Wheel Speed Sensors
36	Missing Rear Speed Signal
37	Erratic Rear Speed Signal
38	Wheel Speed Error
41	Right Front Isolation Solenoid or Circuit Open
42	Right Front Pulse-Width Modulated Solenoid or Circuit Open
43	Right Front Isolation Solenoid or Circuit Shorted
44	Right Front Pulse-Width Modulated Solenoid or Circuit Shorted
45	Left Front Isolation Solenoid or Circuit Open
46	Left Front Pulse-Width Modulated Solenoid or Circuit Open
47	Left Front Isolation Solenoid or Circuit Shorted
48	Left-Front Pulse-Width Modulated Solenoid or Circuit Shorted
51	Rear Isolation Solenoid or Circuit Open
52	Rear Pulse-Width Modulated Solenoid or Circuit Open
53	Rear Isolation Solenoid or Circuit Shorted
54	Rear Pulse-Width Modulated Solenoid or Circuit Shorted
64	VCM/4WAL System Voltage Low
65	Pump Motor Relay or Circuit Open
66	Pump Motor Relay or Circuit Shorted
67	Open Motor Circuit or Shorted VCM Output
68	Locked Pump Motor Circuit or shorted Motor Circuit
69	VCM/4WAL System Voltage Low During An Antilock Stop
74	Excessive Isolation Time
75	VCM History Memory Error
81	Brake Switch Shorted or Open
86	Antilock Indicator Lamp Fault

85389143

Fig. 97 Diagnostic trouble codes/symptoms — 1994-97 VCM 4WAL systems

Remember that trouble codes cannot specify the exact cause of the problem, but may only relate which circuit is affected by the problem. Before replacing any component, be sure that it is the cause of the problem, especially when dealing with a control module fault. Control modules are quite expensive and are usually not returnable.

CLEARING CODES

Stored codes may be erased with the hand scanner if available or, on non-VCM equipped vehicles using a jumper wire:

1. If a hand scanner is available, use it to erase the computer module code memory.
2. For VCM equipped vehicles, a code cannot clear on the same ignition cycle it was set. Before attempting to clear the code (using a scan tool as this is the only way to access codes on these vehicles) it may be necessary to cycle the ignition to the **OFF** position for at least 10 seconds, then back to **ON** again to start another cycle.
3. Except for VCM equipped vehicles, codes may be cleared without a scan tool as follows:
   a. Turn the ignition switch **ON** but do not start the engine.
   b. Use a jumper wire to ground ALDL/DLC terminal H to terminal A for 2 seconds.
   c. Remove the jumper wire for 1 second.
   d. Repeat the grounding for 2 more seconds.
   e. When the trouble codes are cleared, the ANTI-LOCK and BRAKE lamps should both illuminate and then extinguish.

PRELIMINARY DIAGNOSIS

Please refer to the charts located in this section. If the chart is used correctly, it will aid in elimination of simple, non-system problems such as blown fuses, failed bulbs or non-ABS related brake failures. The chart will prompt the reading of codes at the proper point in the diagnosis.

➡Some of the diagnostic or repair procedures refer to the performance of a Function Test. This test is performed with the scan tool; it operates all components of the EHCU/BPMV and checks their function. The test cannot be performed without the scan tool.

1994 EBCM Equipped Vehicles

➧ See Figures 98, 99, 100, 101, 102, 103 and 104

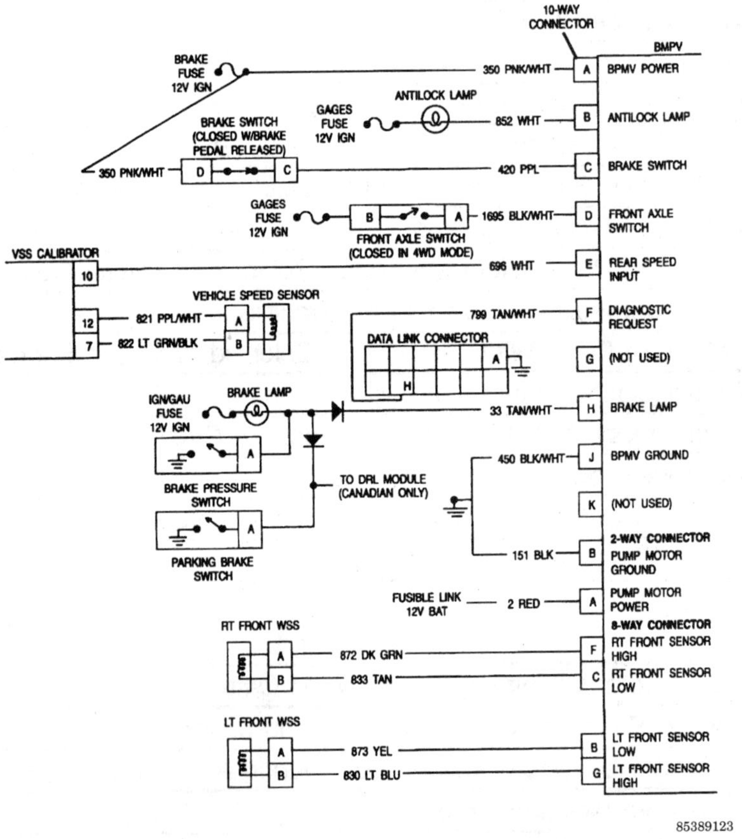

Fig. 98 1994 4WAL EBCM system electrical schematic

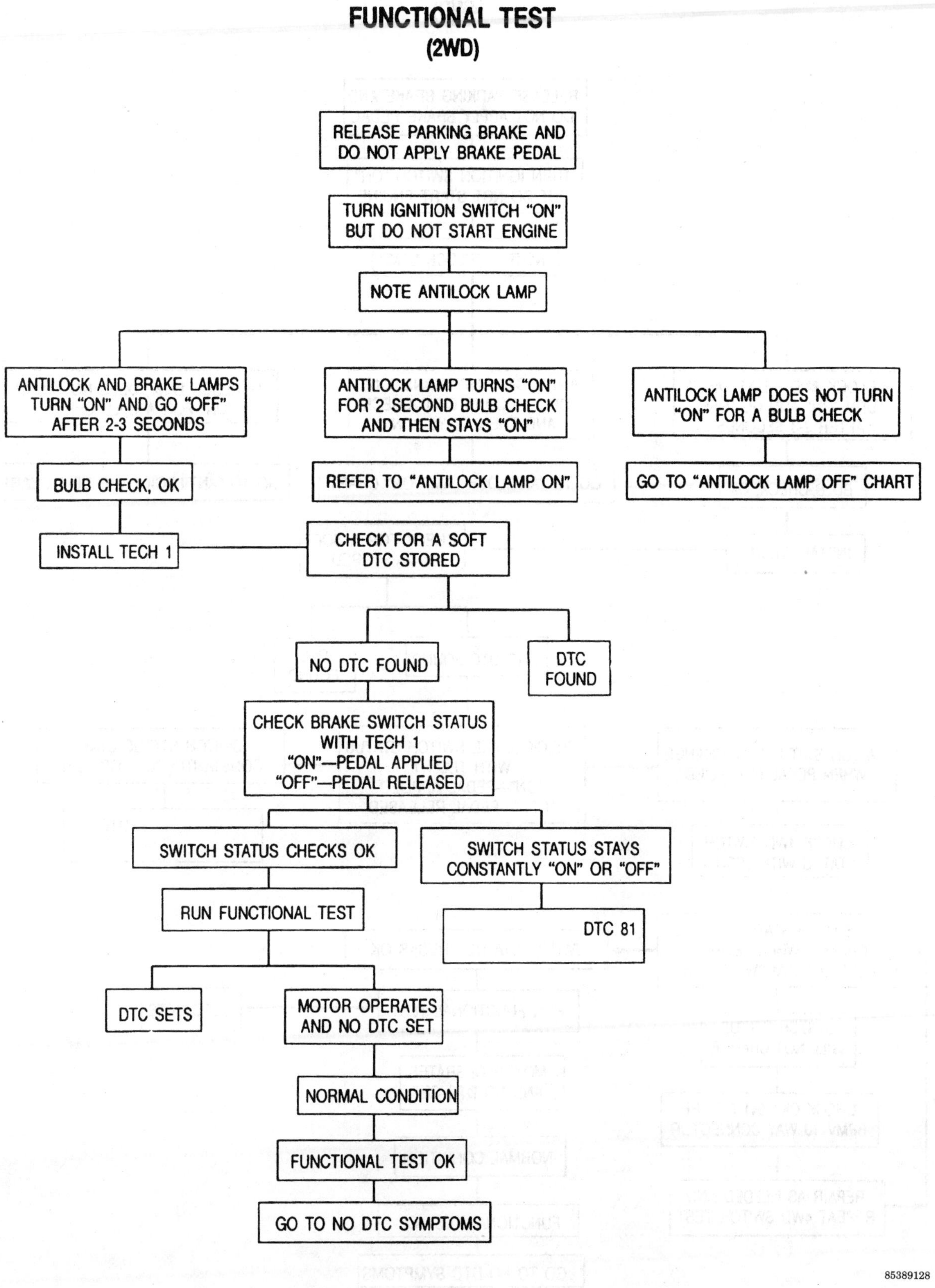

Fig. 99 1994 4WAL EBCM system functional test — 2WD models

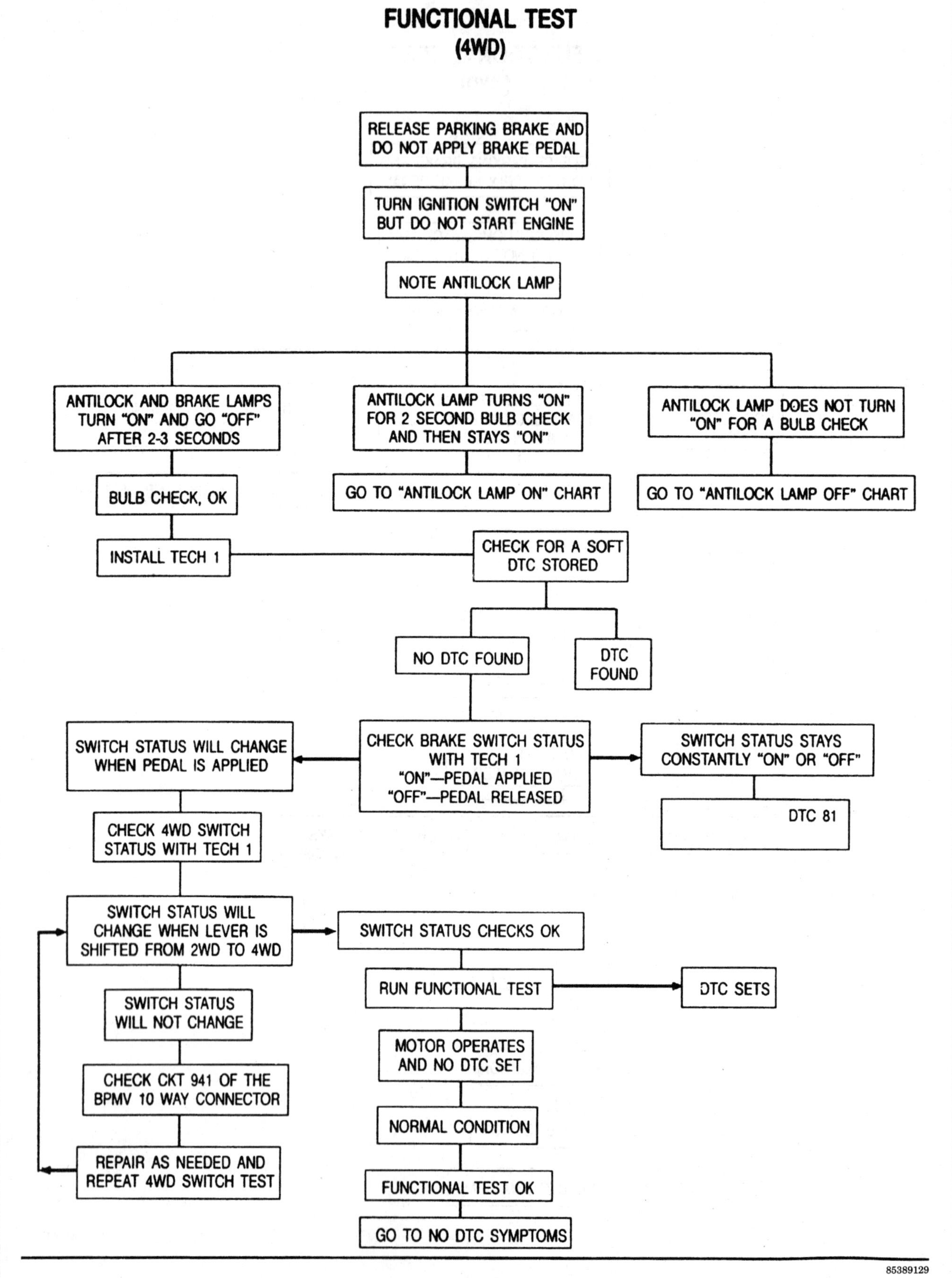

Fig. 100 1994 4WAL EBCM system functional test — 4WD models

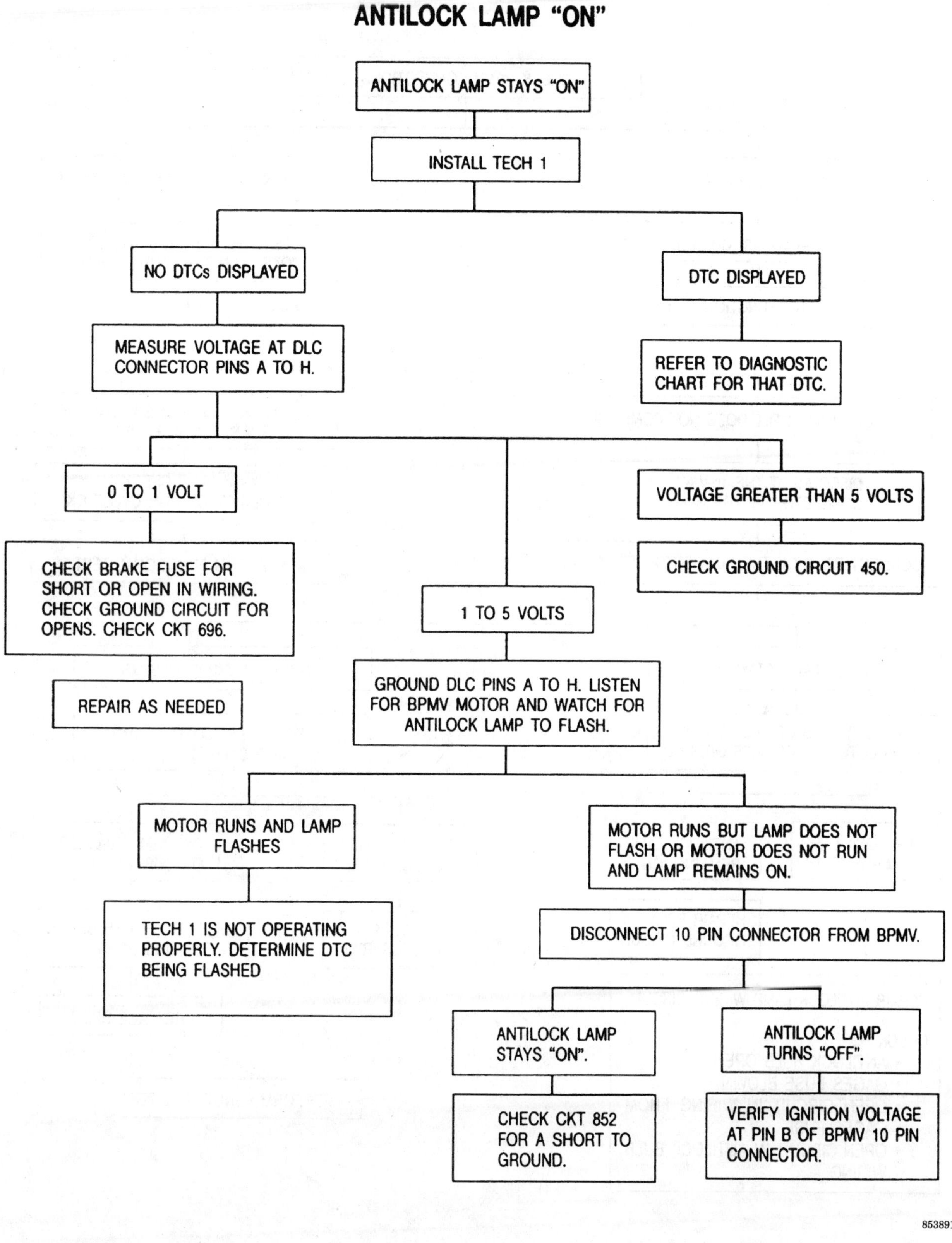

Fig. 101 1994 4WAL EBCM system antilock lamp ON test

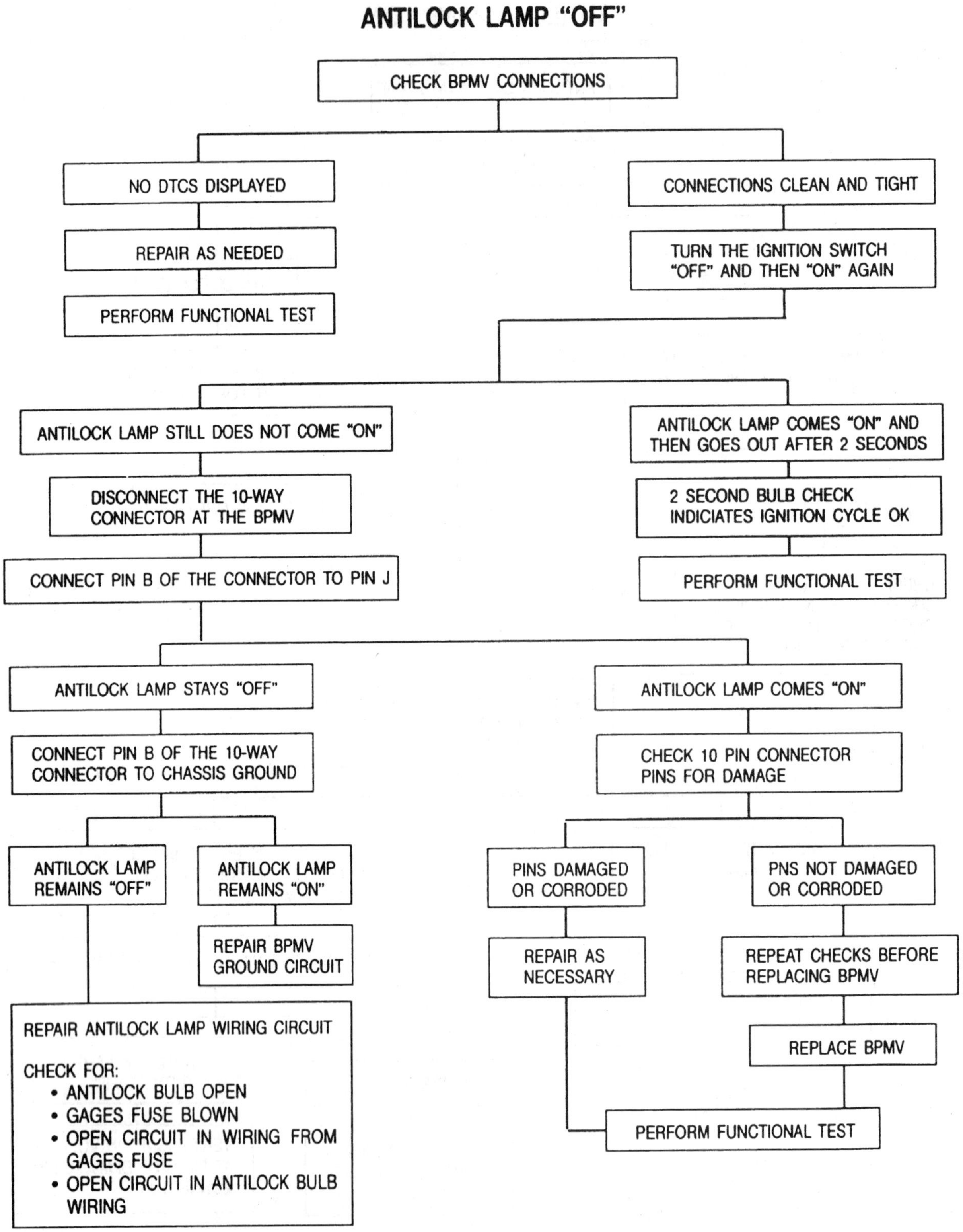

85389131

Fig. 102 1994 4WAL EBCM system antilock lamp OFF test

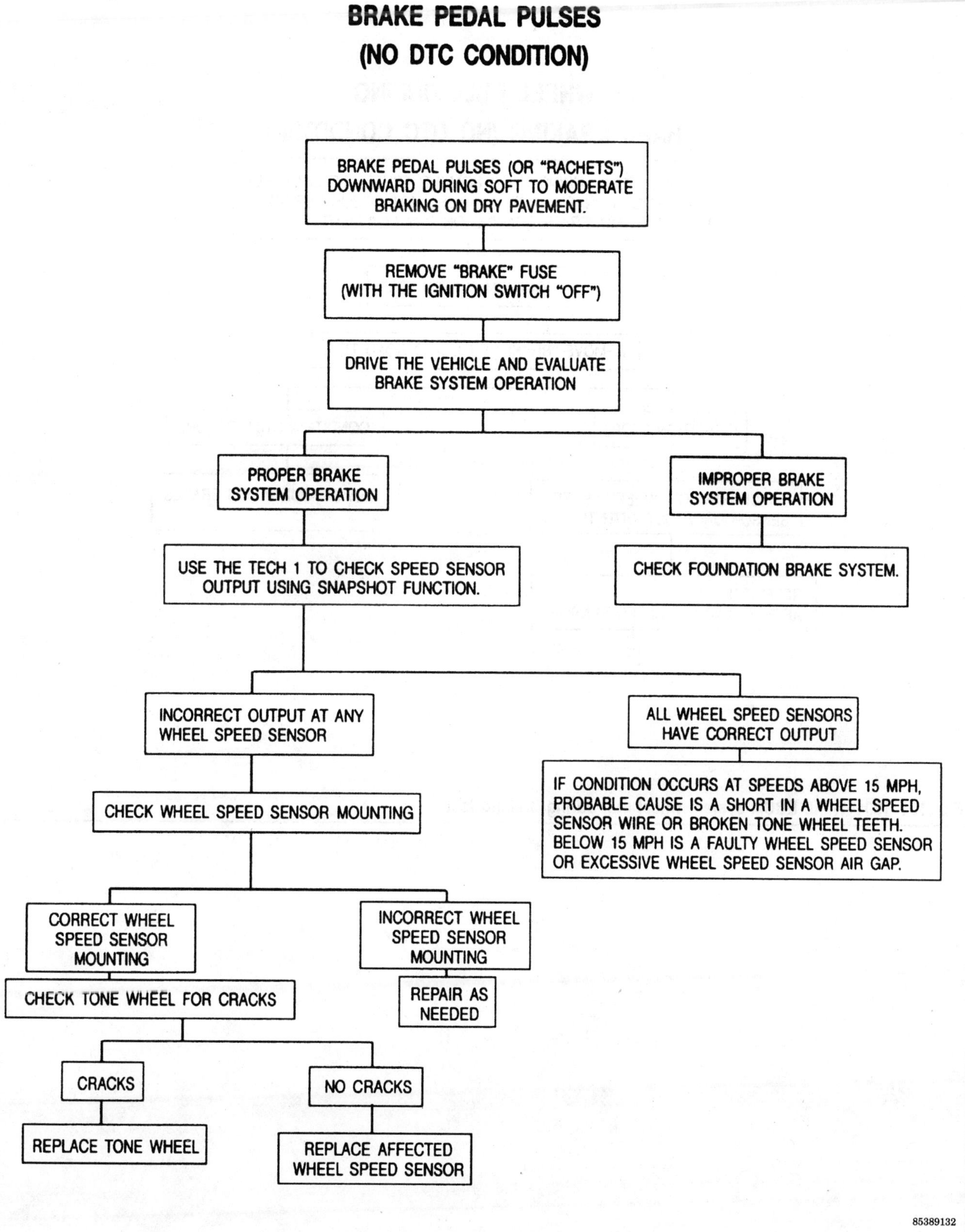

Fig. 103 1994 4WAL EBCM system brake pedal pulse test

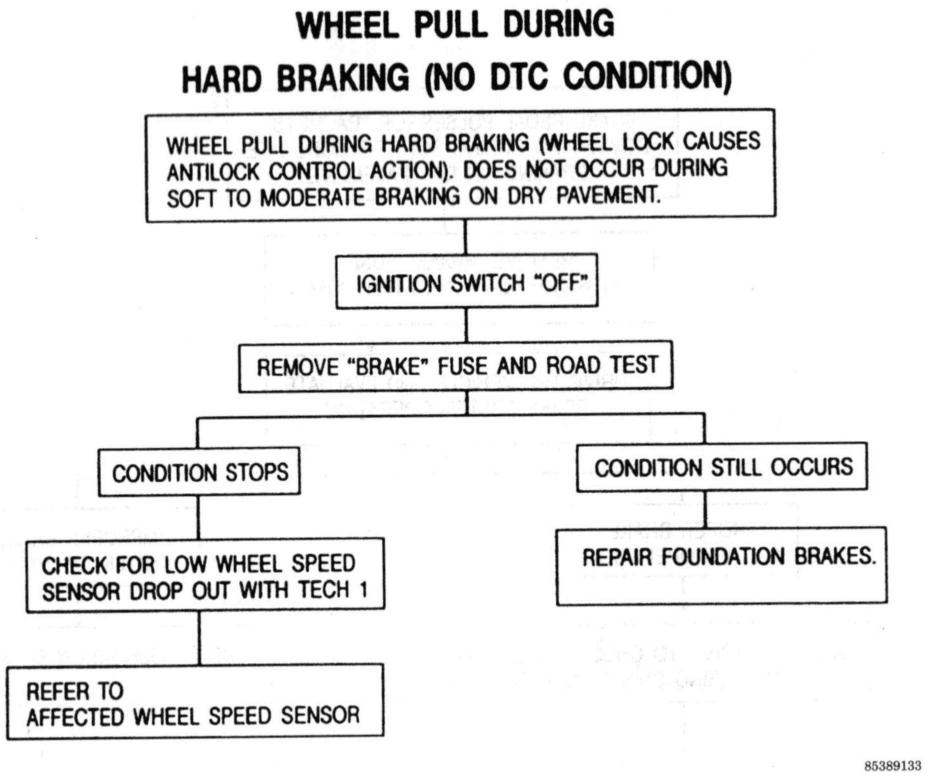

Fig. 104 1994 4WAL EBCM system wheel pull during braking test

1994-97 VCM Equipped Vehicles

See Figures 105, 106, 107, 108, 109, 110, 111, 112, 113, 114 and 115

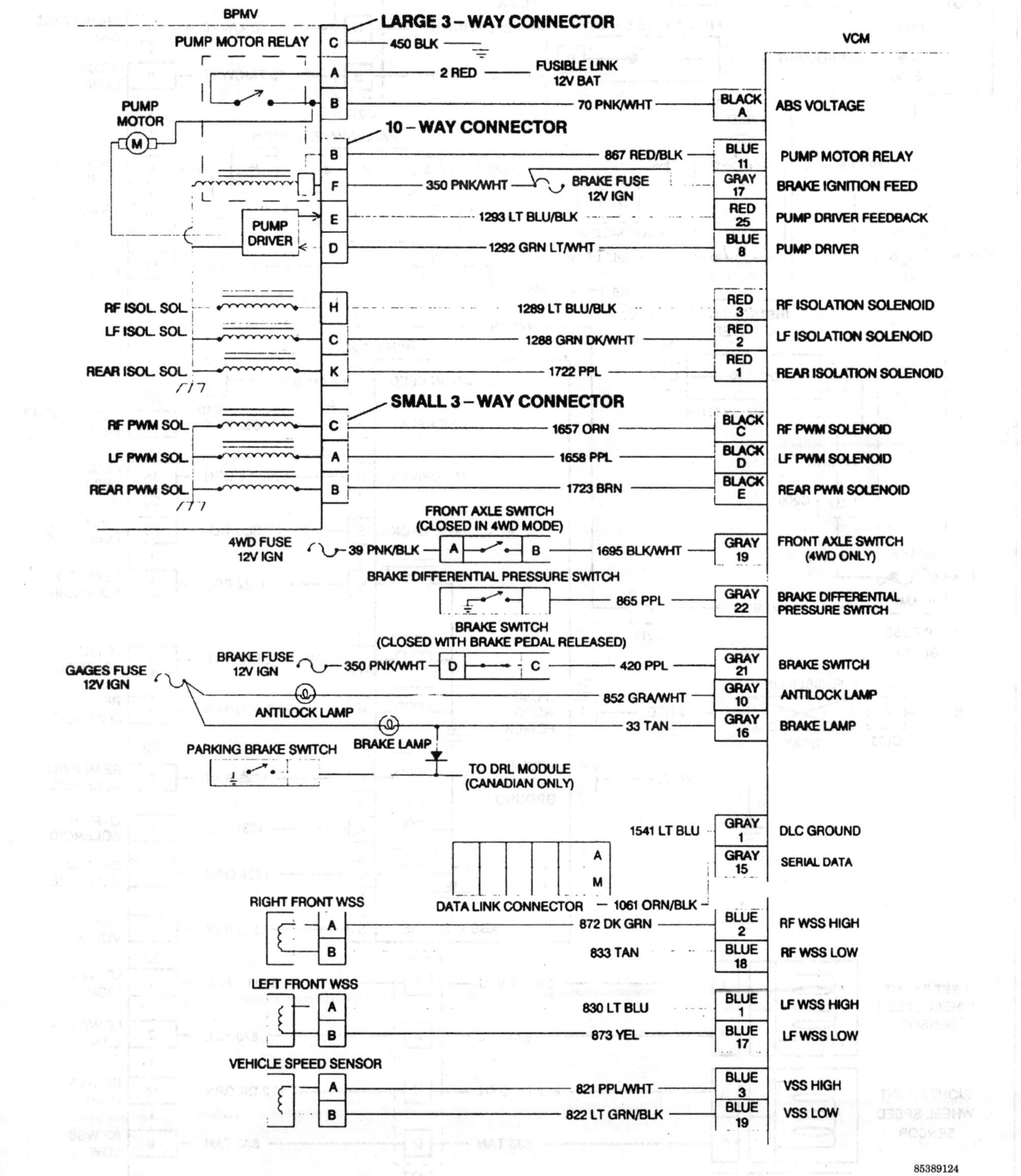

Fig. 105 1994 4WAL VCM system electrical wiring schematic

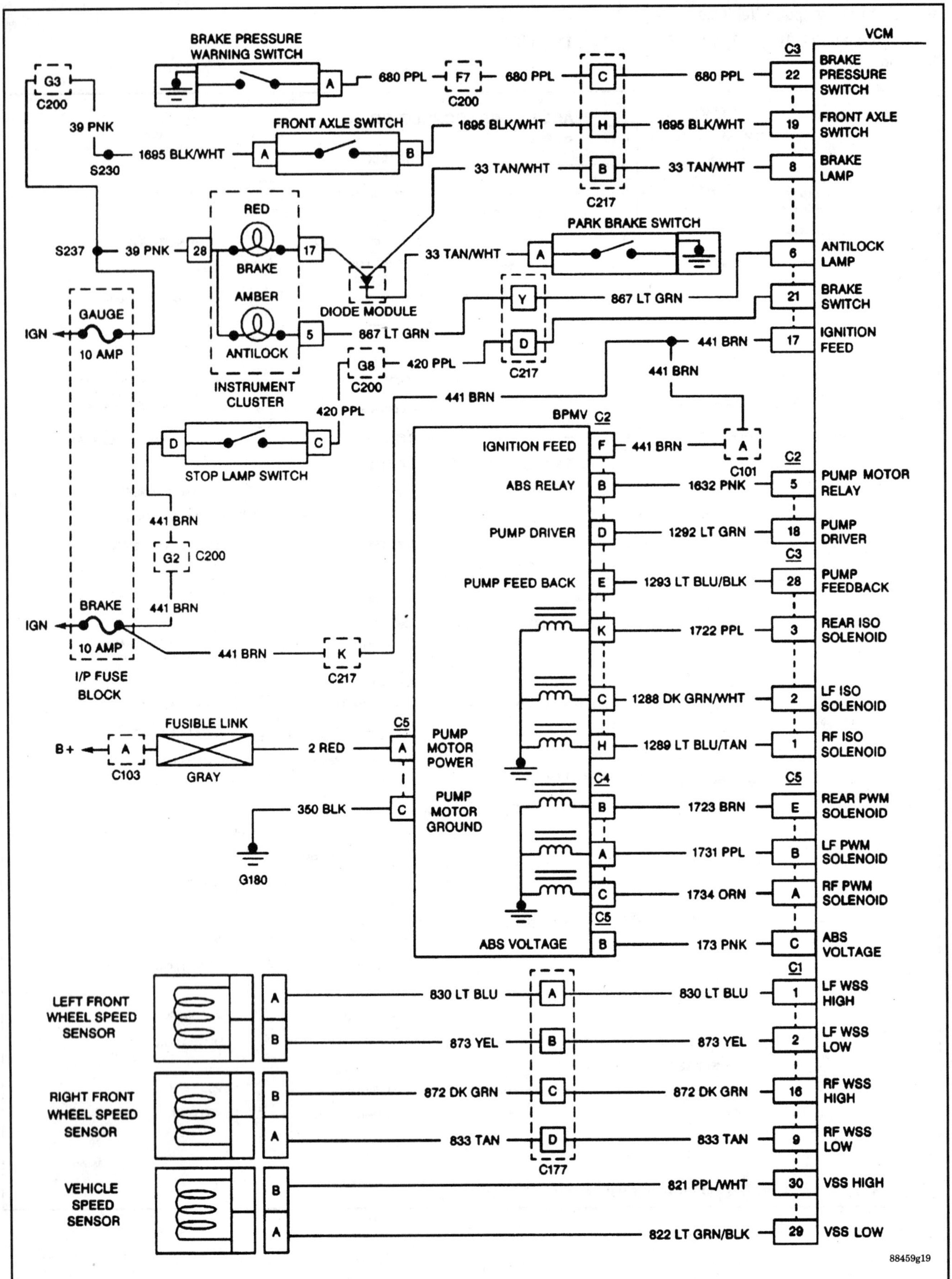

Fig. 106 1995-97 4WAL VCM system electrical wiring schematic

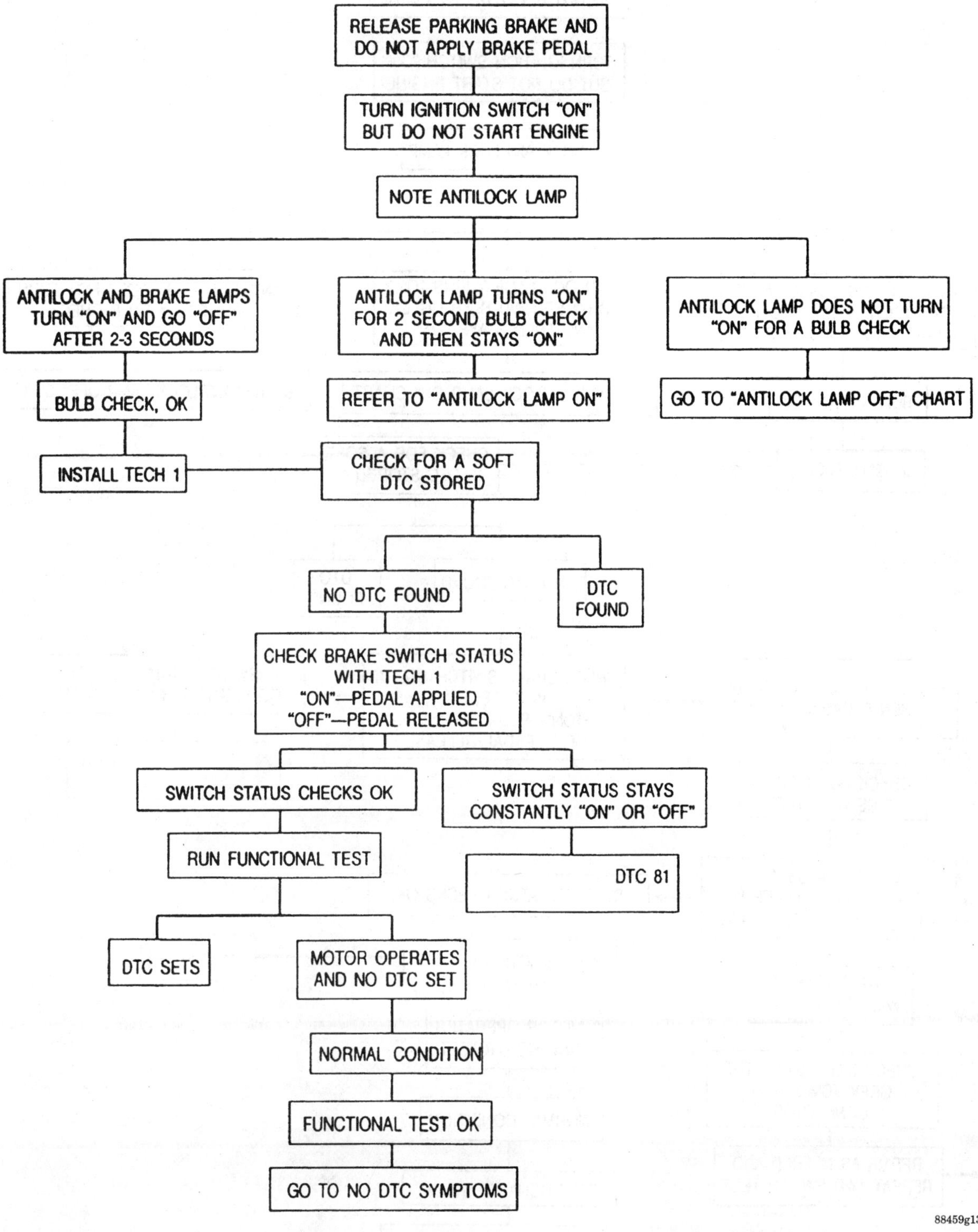

Fig. 107 Functional test — 1994-97 2WD 4WAL VCM models

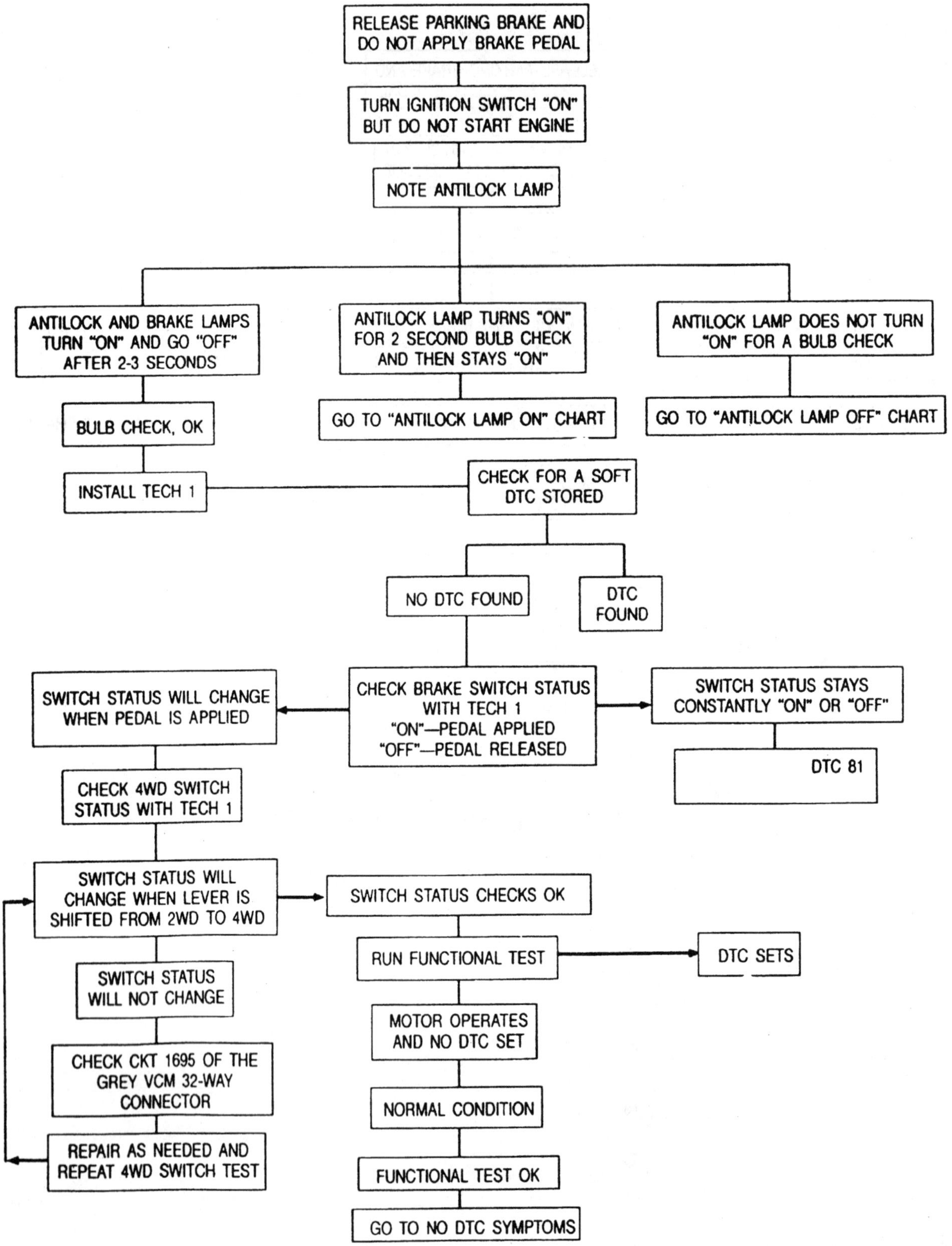

88459g14

Fig. 108 Functional test — 1994-97 4WD 4WAL VCM models

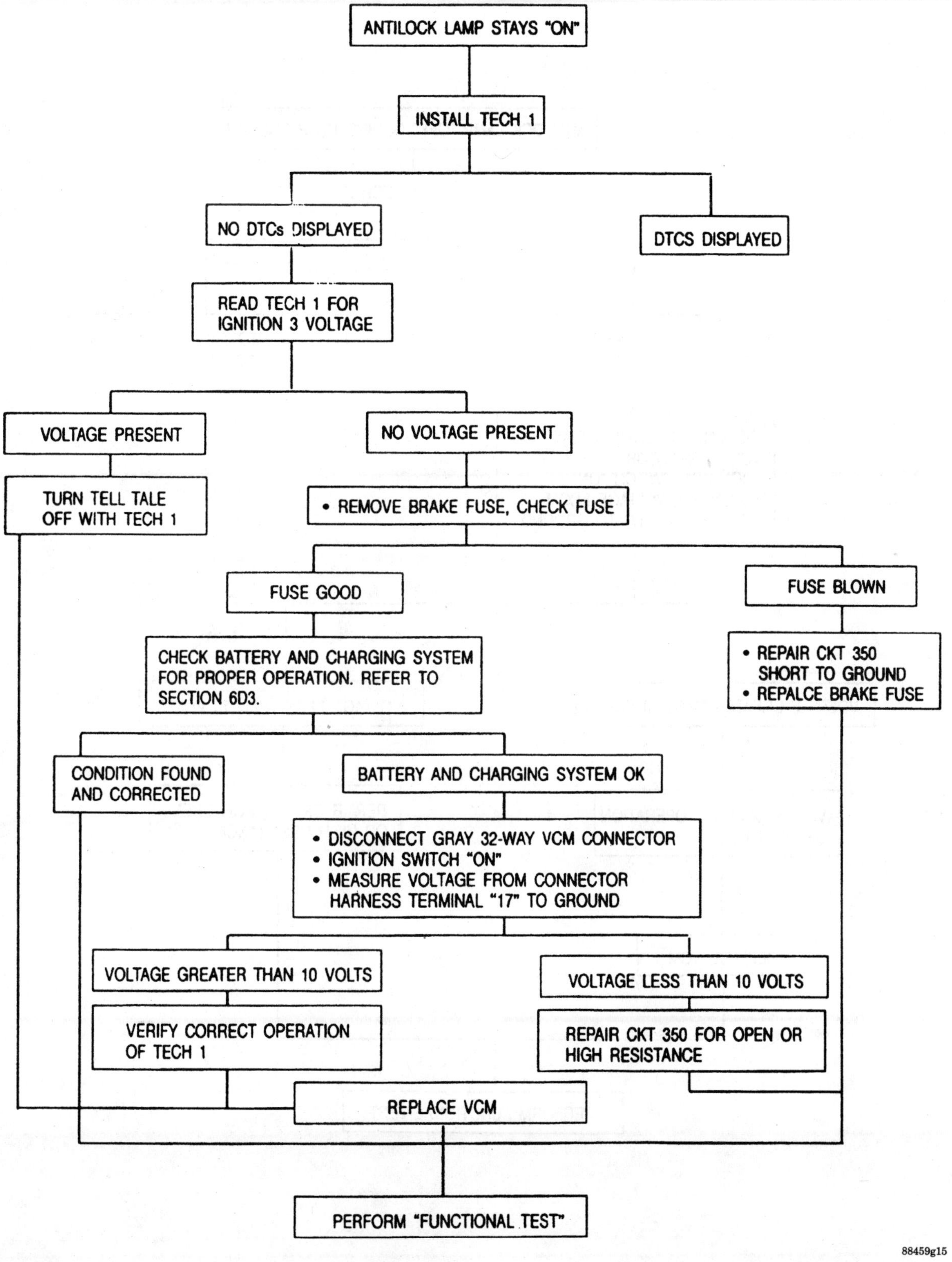

Fig. 109 Antilock lamp ON test — 1994 4WAL VCM models

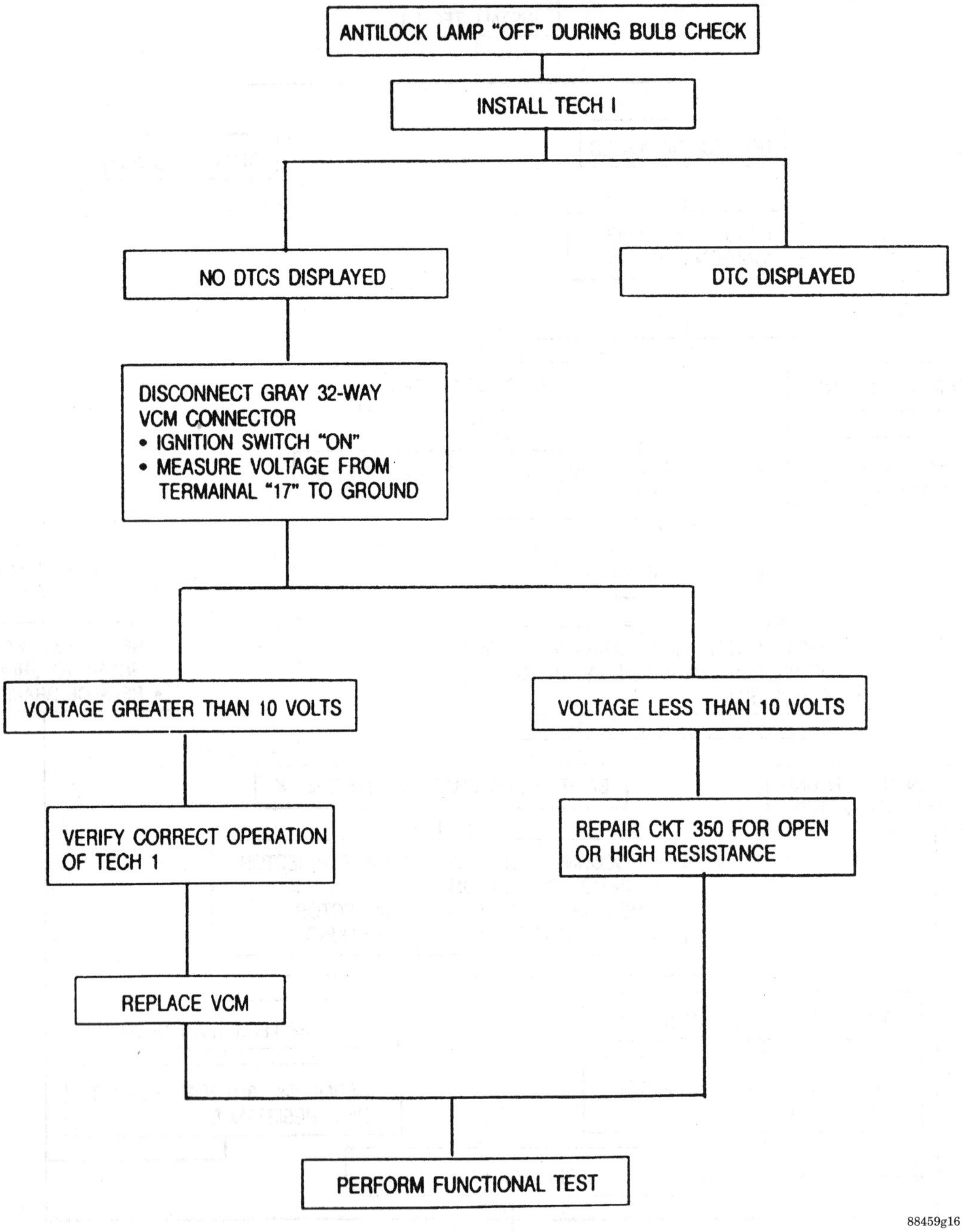

Fig. 110 Antilock lamp OFF test — 1994 4WAL VCM models

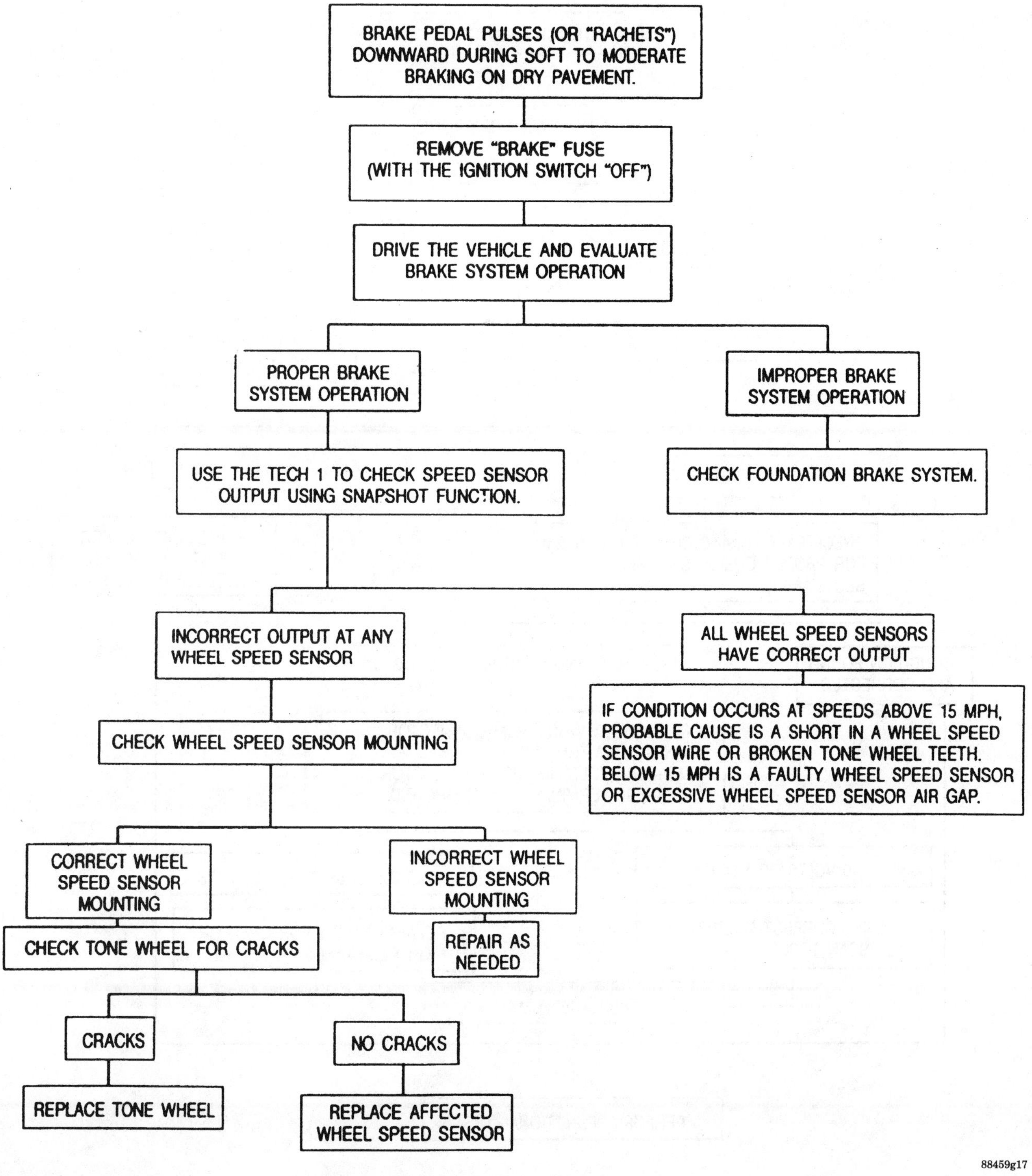

Fig. 111 Brake pedal pulse test (no DTC condition) — 1994 4WAL VCM models

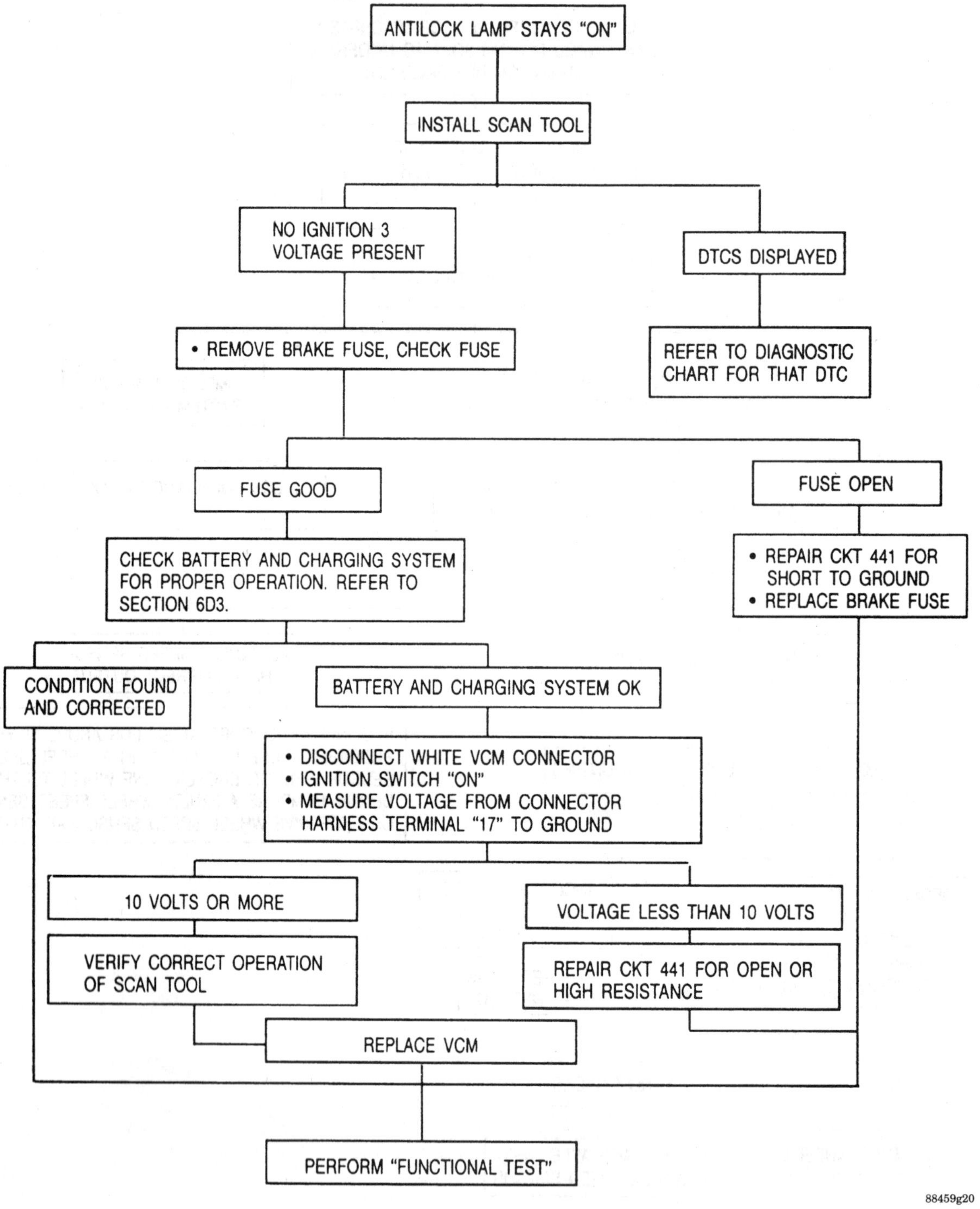

Fig. 112 Antilock lamp ON test — 1995-97 4WAL VCM models

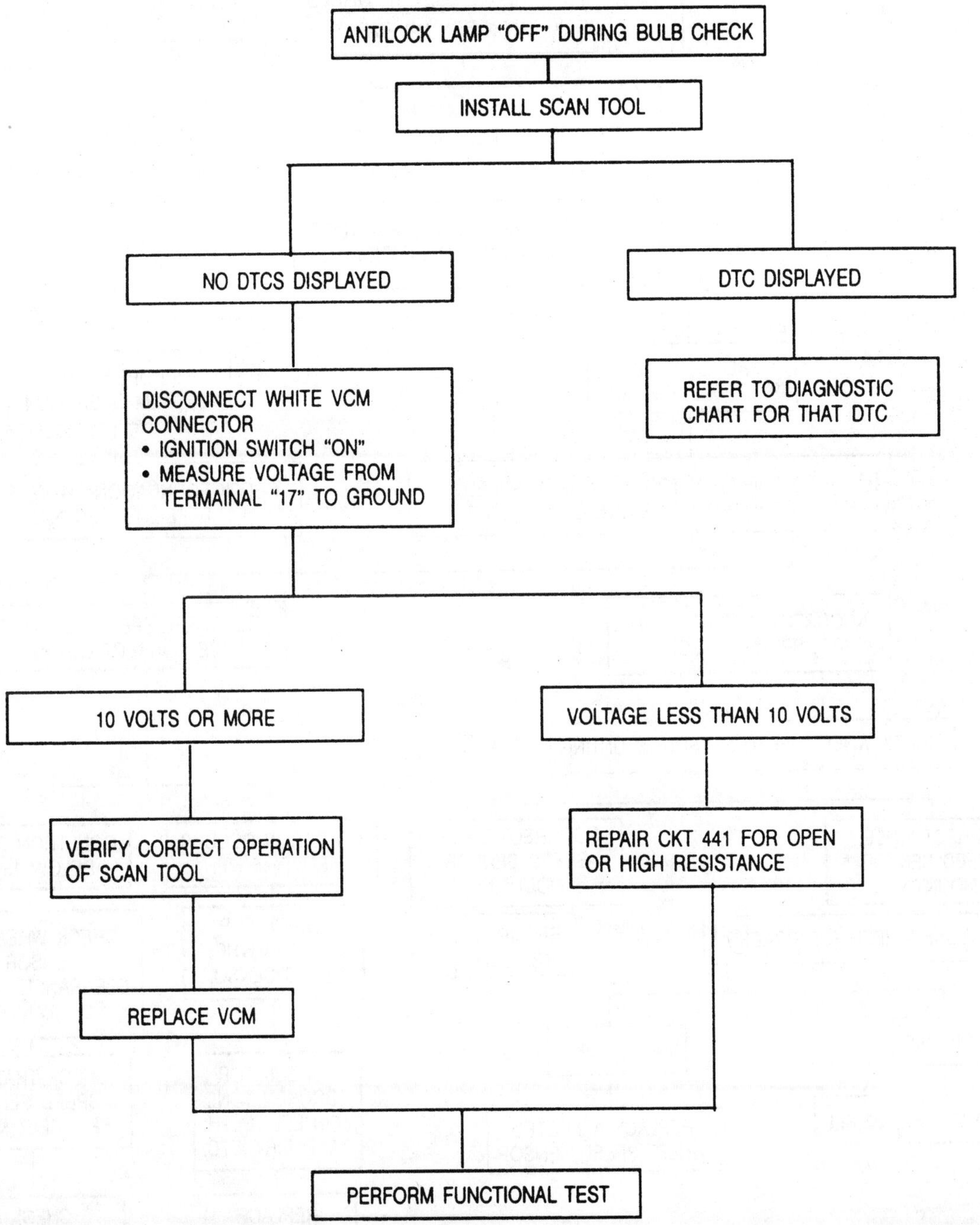

Fig. 113 Antilock lamp OFF test — 1995-97 4WAL VCM models

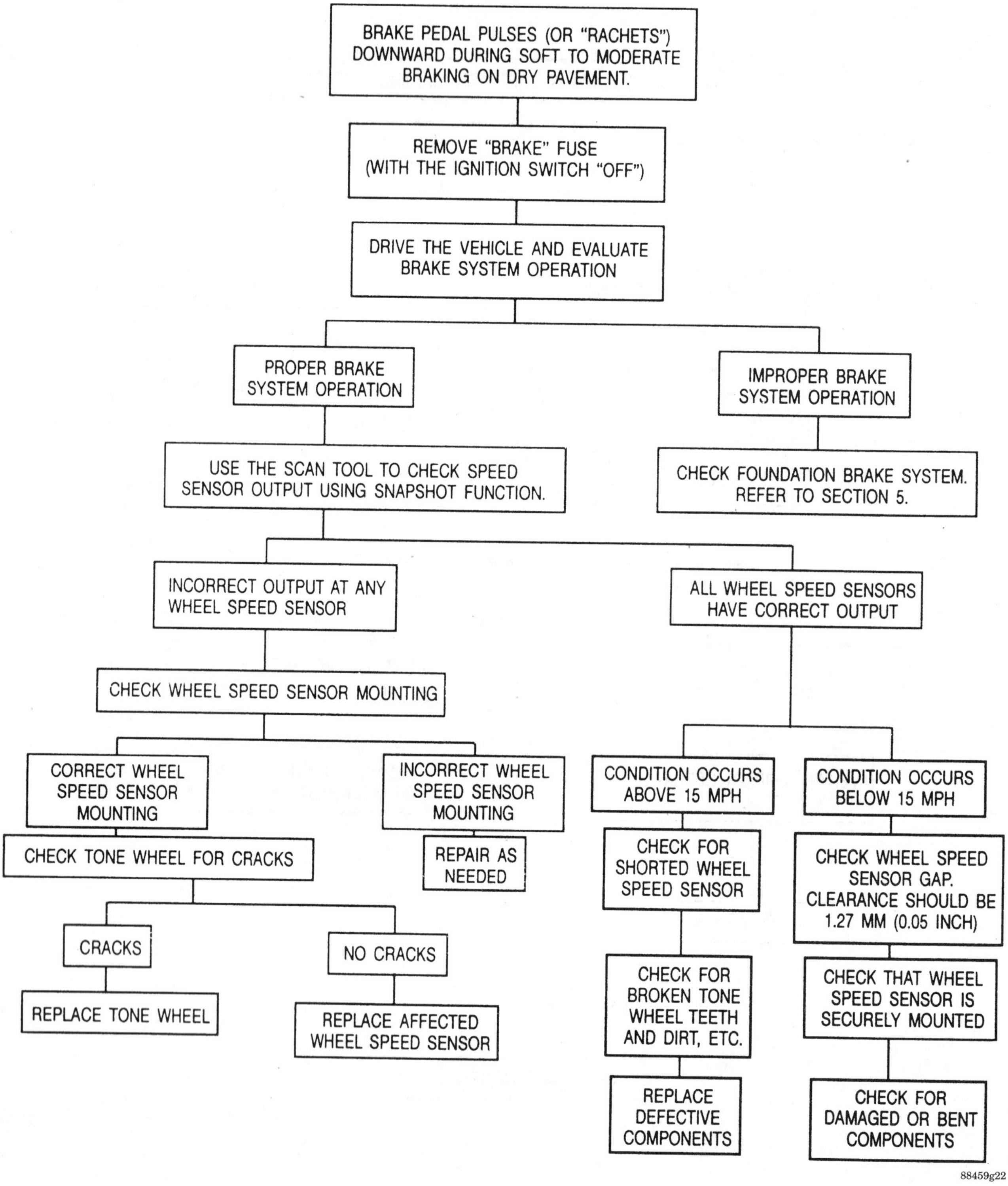

Fig. 114 Brake pedal pulse test (no DTC condition) — 1995-97 4WAL VCM models

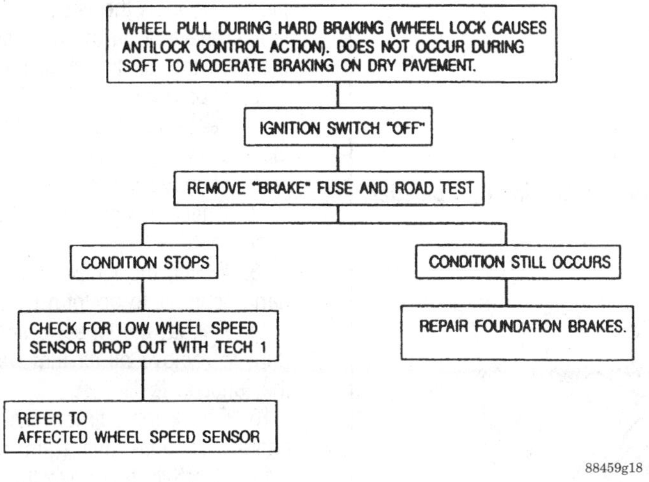

Fig. 115 Wheel pull during hard braking test (no DTC condition) — 1994 4WAL VCM models

Bleeding the Brake System

See Figures 116 and 117

The EHCU/BPMV module is the one component which adds to the complexity of bleeding the 4WAL brake systems. For the most part the system is bled in the same manner as the non-ABS vehicles. Refer to the procedure earlier in this section for details. But because of the EHCU/BPMV's complex internal valving additional steps are necessary if the unit has been replaced or if it is suspected to contain air. These bleeding steps are not necessary if the only connection/fitting(s) opened were downstream of the unit. These steps may or may not be necessary after master cylinder replacement. If in doubt (or without the necessary special tools) thoroughly bleed the system and see if a firm brake pedal can be obtained, if not, the EHCU/BPMV must be bled as well.

As with the RWAL brake system, the use of a power bleeder is recommended, but the system may also be bled manually. If a power bleeder is used, it must be of the diaphragm type and provide isolation of the fluid from air and moisture.

Do not pump the pedal rapidly when bleeding; this can make the circuits very difficult to bleed. Instead, press the brake pedal slowly 1 time and hold it down while bleeding takes place. Tighten the bleeder screw, release the pedal and wait 15 seconds before repeating the sequence. Because of the length of the brake lines and other factors, it may take 10 or more repetitions of the sequence to bleed each line properly. When necessary to bleed all 4 wheels, the correct order is right rear, left rear, right front and left front.

CAUTION

Do not move the vehicle until a firm brake pedal is achieved. Failure to properly bleed the system may cause impaired braking and the possibility of injury and/or property damage

If the EHCU/BPMV requires bleeding, the following procedures may be used to free all trapped air from the component.

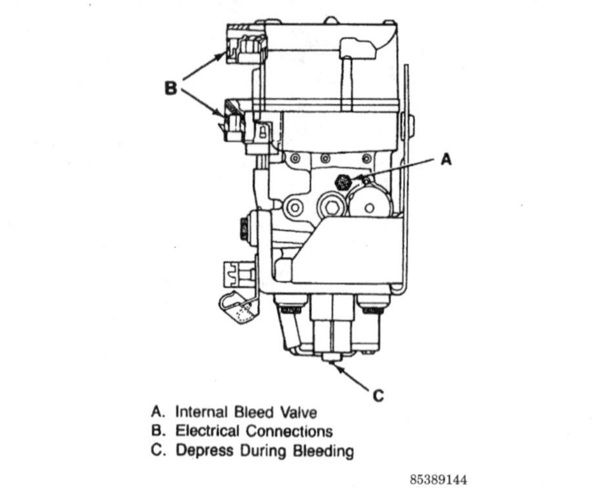

Fig. 116 The EHCU/BPMV valve and the internal bleeder location

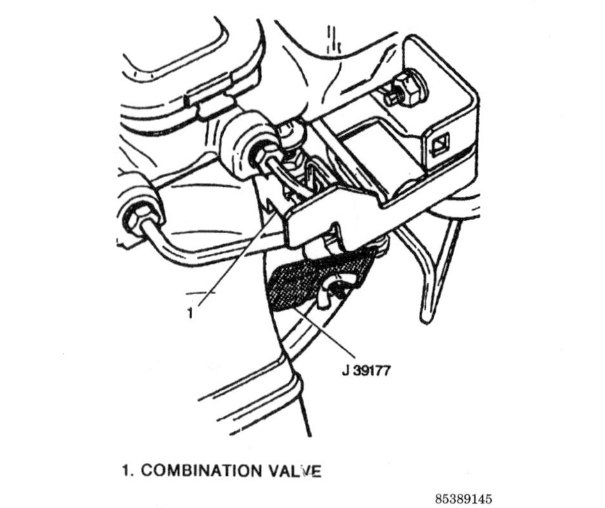

Fig. 117 Depressing the combination valve

The combination valve depressor tools are used to hold the internal passages (combination valve and EHCU/BPMV bleed accumulator bleed stems open allowing the entire system to be completely bled.

➡The combination valve tools are relatively inexpensive and should be available from various aftermarket companies. Although a homemade tool may suffice, DO NOT attempt to fabricate a homemade tool unless you are CERTAIN it will not damage the valve/bleed stem by over-extension.

Finally, remember to always bleed the 4WAL brake system with the ignition **OFF** to prevent setting false trouble codes.

The components used on 1994-97 4WAL systems are usually not equipped with external bleeder screws. Therefore, the unit can only be bled through the downstream bleeder screws (wheel cylinders/calipers). To accomplish this the internal bleeder and the accumulator stems/combination valves must be opened to allow air/fluid to pass through the unit. The Internal Bleed Valves on either side of the unit must be opened ¼-½ turn before bleeding begins. As with most ABS systems found on these trucks, the ignition switch must be **OFF** or false trouble codes may be set.

1. Make sure the ignition is in the **OFF** position to prevent setting false trouble codes.
2. If necessary, properly bleed the master cylinder assembly as directed in the hydraulic brake bleeding procedure found earlier in this section. Check and add additional fluid, as necessary.
3. Open the internal bleed valves ¼-½ turn each.
4. Install one J-39177 or equivalent combination valve depressor tool on the left accumulator bleed stem of the EHCU. Install one tool on the right accumulator bleed stem and install the third tool on the combination valve.
5. Properly bleed the wheel cylinders and calipers. For details, please refer to the hydraulic brake bleeding procedure located earlier in this section.
6. Remove the 3 special tools.
7. Check the master cylinder fluid level, refilling as necessary.
8. Switch the ignition **ON** (engine not running) and use a hand scanner to perform 6 function tests on the system.
9. Repeat the wheel cylinder and caliper bleeding procedure to remove all air that was purged from the BPMV during the function tests.
10. Check for a firm brake pedal. If necessary, repeat the entire procedure until a firm pedal is obtained.
11. Carefully test drive the vehicle at moderate speeds; check for proper pedal feel and brake operation. If any problem is noted in feel or function, repeat the entire bleeding procedure.

Component Replacement

EHCU/BPMV VALVE

➧ See Figures 118 and 119

The EHCU/BPMV valve is not serviceable and must never be disassembled or repaired. If tests indicate the unit is faulty, the entire assembly must be replaced.

1. Tag and disconnect the brake lines from the EHCU/BPMV. Immediately cap or plug all openings to prevent system contamination or excessive fluid loss.
2. Tag and disengage the electrical connectors from the EHCU/BPMV.
3. Remove the retainers holding the EHCU/BPMV upper bracket to the lower bracket and vehicle. Remove the upper bracket and hydraulic unit as an assembly.
4. If necessary, once they are removed from the vehicle, separate the bracket from the EHCU/BPMV.

To install:

5. If removed, assemble the EHCU/BPMV to its bracket. Install the retainers and tighten to 84 inch lbs. (9 Nm). Be careful as overtightening these bolts can cause excessive noise transfer during system operation.
6. Install the assembly into the vehicle, then tighten the retainers 18 ft. lbs. (25 Nm).
7. Engage the electrical connectors as tagged during removal. Make certain each is squarely seated and secure.

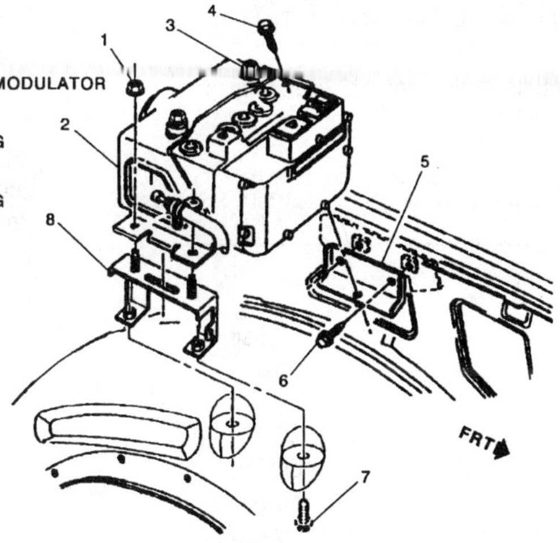

Fig. 118 Brake Pressure Modulator Valve (BPMV) mounting

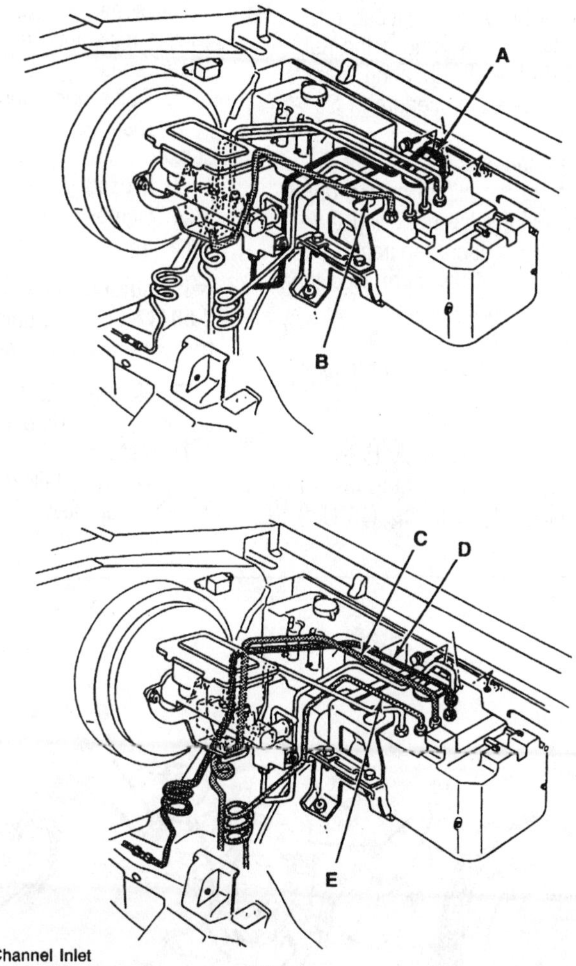

Fig. 119 EHCU/BPMV brake pipe connections — ALWAYS tag the connections to assure proper installation

8. Remove the caps or plugs, then connect the brake lines to their original locations, as tagged during removal. Tighten the fittings to 21 ft. lbs. (29 Nm).

9. Properly bleed the hydraulic brake system, including the EHCU/BPMV valve.

FRONT WHEEL SPEED SENSORS

➧ See Figures 120, 121 and 122

1. Raise and support the front of the vehicle safely using jackstands.
2. Remove the tire and wheel assembly.
3. Remove the brake caliper from the mounting bracket and support aside from the suspension using a coat hanger or wire. Make sure the brake line is not stretched, kinked or otherwise damaged. The line should never support the weight of the caliper.
4. For 2WD vehicles, remove the hub and rotor assembly. For details, please refer to the brake disc procedure found earlier in this section.
5. For 4WD vehicles, remove the brake disc (please refer to the procedure earlier in this section), then remove the hub and bearing assembly. For details on hub and bearing removal, please refer to the steering knuckle procedure in Section 8 of this manual.
6. Disengage the sensor wiring connector.
7. Disconnect the sensor wire from the clip(s) on the upper control arm. On most vehicles this will involve removing the retaining bolt/nut in order to free the clip, then separating the wire from the clip. 4WD vehicles tend to utilize more clips than the 2WD vehicles due to the difference in the front suspension.
8. Remove the splash shield retaining bolts, then remove the shield and sensor assembly.

To install:

9. Mount the sensor and splash shield assembly to the steering knuckle. Install the retaining bolts and tighten them to 19 ft. lbs. (26 Nm) for the outer bolts and 12 ft. lbs. (16 Nm) for the inner bolts.
10. Connect the wiring to the clip(s) on the upper control arm. Check the wiring for correct routing. If removed, install and tighten the clip retaining bolt/nuts, refer to the illustrations for locations and torque specifications. The wiring on some vehicles/components may be marked at the appropriate clip mounting position, look for a paint stripe on the sensor wire.
11. Engage the wiring connector.
12. On 4WD vehicles, install the hub and bearing assembly.
13. Install the brake disc.
14. Remove the support, then reposition and secure brake caliper.
15. Install the tire and wheel assembly, then adjust the wheel bearings on 2WD vehicles.
16. Remove the jackstands and carefully lower the vehicle.

REAR WHEEL SPEED SENSOR

The sensor is usually located in the left rear of the transmission case on 2WD vehicles and on the transfer case of 4WD vehicles.

The speed sensor may be tested with an ohmmeter; the correct resistance is normally 900-2000 ohms. To remove the speed sensor:

1. Raise and support the vehicle safely using jackstands.
2. Disengage the electrical connector from the speed sensor.
3. If used, remove the sensor retaining bolt.
4. Remove the speed sensor; have a container handy to catch transmission fluid when the sensor is removed.

➡If equipped with the 4L60-E automatic transmission, use J-38417 or an equivalent speed sensor remover/installer tool whenever the sensor is serviced.

5. Recover the O-ring used to seal the sensor; inspect it for damage or deterioration.

To install:

6. When installing, coat the new O-ring with a thin film of transmission fluid.
7. Install the O-ring and speed sensor.

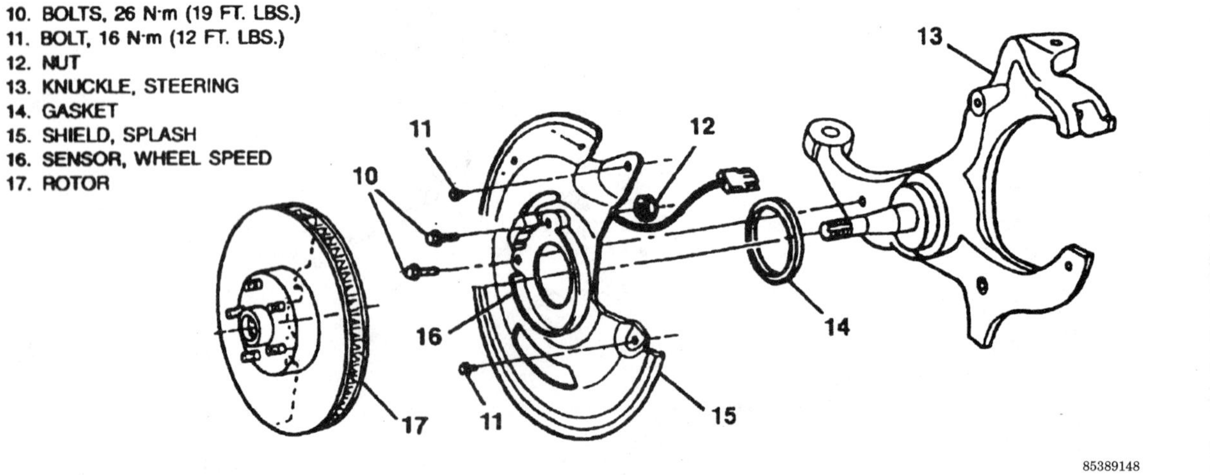

Fig. 120 Front wheel speed sensor/splash shield assembly mounting — 2WD vehicles

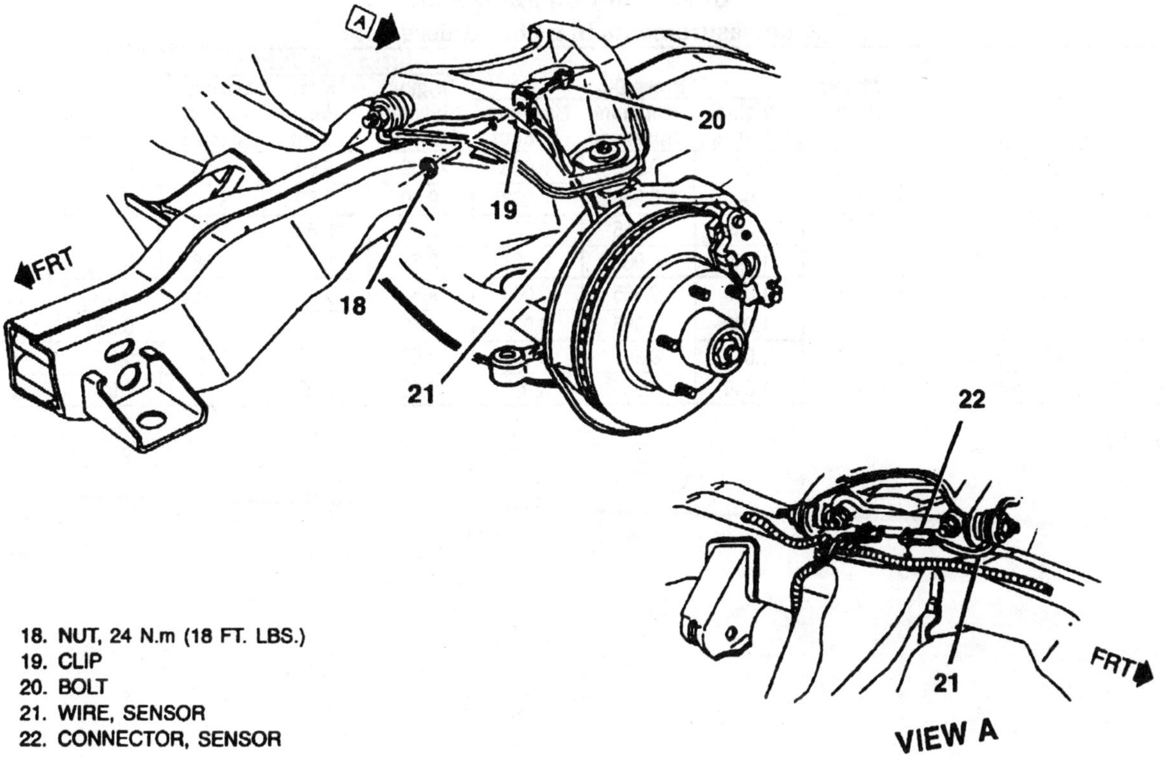

18. NUT, 24 N.m (18 FT. LBS.)
19. CLIP
20. BOLT
21. WIRE, SENSOR
22. CONNECTOR, SENSOR

85389149

Fig. 121 Front wheel speed sensor wire routing — 2WD vehicles

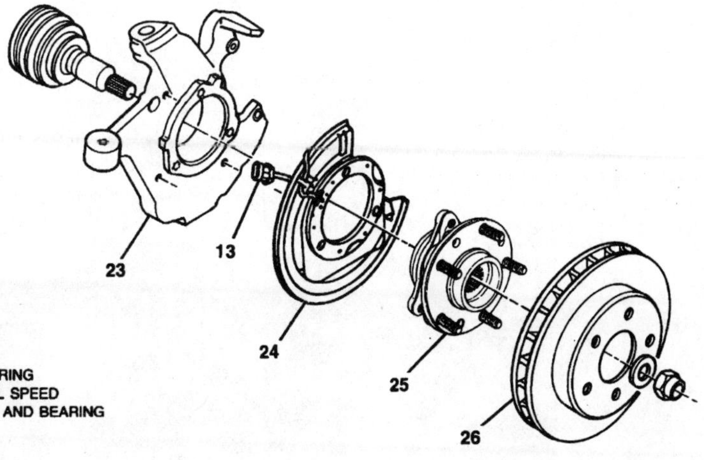

23. KNUCKLE, STEERING
24. SENSOR, WHEEL SPEED
25. ASSEMBLY, HUB AND BEARING
26. ROTOR

85389150

Fig. 122 Front wheel speed sensor/splash shield assembly mounting — 4WD vehicles

8. If a retaining bolt is used, tighten the bolt to 97 inch lbs. (11 Nm) in automatic transmissions or 107 inch lbs. (12 Nm) for manual transmissions.

9. Engage the wire harness to the sensor.

10. Remove the jackstands and carefully lower the vehicle.

BRAKE SPECIFICATIONS

All measurements in inches unless noted

			Brake Disc			Brake Drum Diameter			Minimum Lining Thickness	
Year	Model	Master Cylinder Bore	Original Thickness	Minimum Thickness	Maximum Runout	Original Inside Diameter	Max. Wear Limit	Maximum Machine Diameter	Front	Rear
1994	S/T Pick-up	NA	1.040	0.965	0.003	9.50	9.59	9.56	0.030 ①	0.030 ①
	Sonoma	NA	1.040	0.965	0.003	9.50	9.59	9.56	0.030 ①	0.030 ①
1995	S/T Pick-up	NA	1.040	0.965	0.003	9.50	9.59	9.56	0.030 ①	0.030 ①
	Sonoma	NA	1.040	0.965	0.003	9.50	9.59	9.56	0.030 ①	0.030 ①
1996	S/T Pick-up	NA	1.040	0.965	0.003	9.50	9.59	9.56	0.030 ①	0.030 ①
	Sonoma	NA	1.040	0.965	0.003	9.50	9.59	9.56	0.030 ①	0.030 ①
1997	S/T Pick-up	NA	1.040	0.965	0.003	9.50	9.59	9.56	0.030 ①	0.030 ①
	Sonoma	NA	1.040	0.965	0.003	9.50	9.59	9.56	0.030 ①	0.030 ①

NA - Not Available

88459C01

10

BODY

EXTERIOR

Doors

REMOVAL & INSTALLATION

➧ See Figures 1 and 2

➡The following procedure requires the use of a door hinge spring compressor such as J-36604-A or equivalent.

1. If equipped with power door components, perform the following procedures:
   a. Disconnect the negative battery cable.
   b. Check for access to the wiring by removing the cowl side vent cover. If access is possible, remove the receptacles from the wiring harness, then remove the retainer from the wiring harness grommet. Remove the rubber conduit from the door pillar by pushing it from the vent cover side.
   c. If access is not possible, remove the door trim panel, then disengage the electrical harness connector from the power door lock motor and/or the power window regulator. Remove the harness from the door.
2. If available, apply cloth backed tape to the door and body pillar for protection.

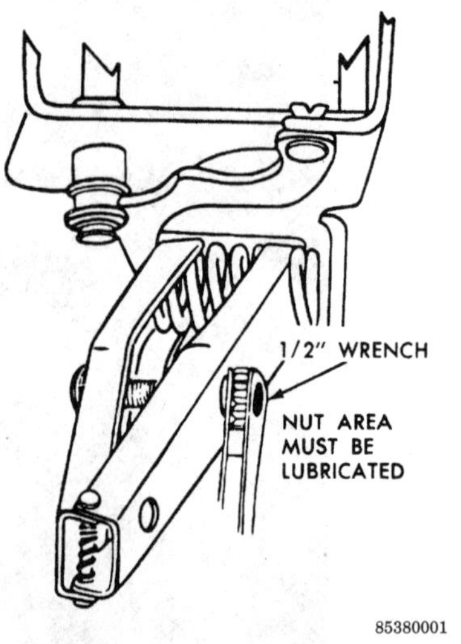

Fig. 1 Exploded view of the door hinge pins

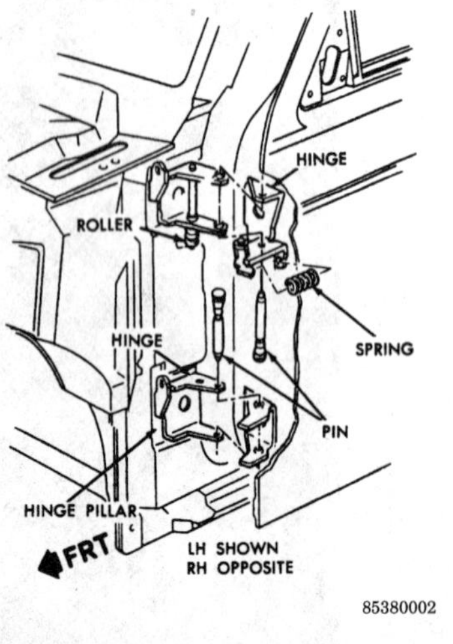

Fig. 2 A spring compressor tool must be used to remove the springs when working on the doors/hinges

CAUTION

Before removing the hinge spring from the door, cover the spring with a towel to prevent the spring from flying and possibly causing personal injury.

3. Using a door hinge spring compressor such as No. J-36604-A or equivalent, compress the door hinge spring and remove it.
4. To remove the door hinge pin clips, spread the clips and move them above the recess on the pin; when the pin is removed, the clip will ride on the pin and fall free of it.
5. Using a soft-head hammer and a pair of locking pliers, remove the lower pin from the door hinge; then, temporarily install a bolt (in the lower pin hole) to hold the door in place until the upper hinge pin is removed.
6. Remove the upper door hinge pin and support the door, then remove the bolt from the lower hinge pin hole and remove the door from the truck.

To install:

7. To install the door, position it on the hinges and insert a bolt through the lower hinge pin hole.
8. Using a new hinge pin clip, install the upper hinge pin.
9. Remove the bolt from the lower hinge pin hole. Using a new hinge pin, install it into the lower hinge pin holes.
10. Compress the door hinge spring and install it into the door hinge using the door hinge spring compressor tool.
11. If equipped with power door components, re-engage the wiring and install the trim panel or pieces, then connect the negative battery cable.

ADJUSTMENTS

Factory installed hinges are welded in place, so no adjustment of the system is necessary or recommended. Service replacement hinges are bolted in position and may be adjusted. If your vehicle is equipped with service replacement hinges, please refer to the door hinge adjustment procedure located later in this section.

Door Hinges

➡The following procedure requires the use of an 1/8 in. (3mm) drill bit, 1/2 in. (13mm) drill bit, a center punch, a cold chisel, a portable body grinder, a putty knife and a scribing tool. Because this procedure requires opening a pinch weld, access to a welder is advisable to properly finish installation.

REMOVAL & INSTALLATION

See Figures 3, 4, 5, 6, 7 and 8

1. Remove the door, and place it on a padded workbench.
2. If necessary, use a putty knife to remove the sealant from the around the edge of the hinge.
3. Outline the position of the hinge(s) on the door and the body pillar using a scribing tool.
4. Center punch the hinge-to-door and the hinge-to-body pillar welds.
5. Drill a pilot hole through each weld using a 1/8 in. (3mm) drill bit. Drill only enough to penetrate the hinge base plate.

When drilling the holes through the hinge welds, DO NOT drill through the door or the body pillar.

6. Using a 1/2 in. (13mm) bit, drill a hole through the hinge base, following the 1/8 in. (3mm) pilot hole. Once again, only drill through the hinge base.

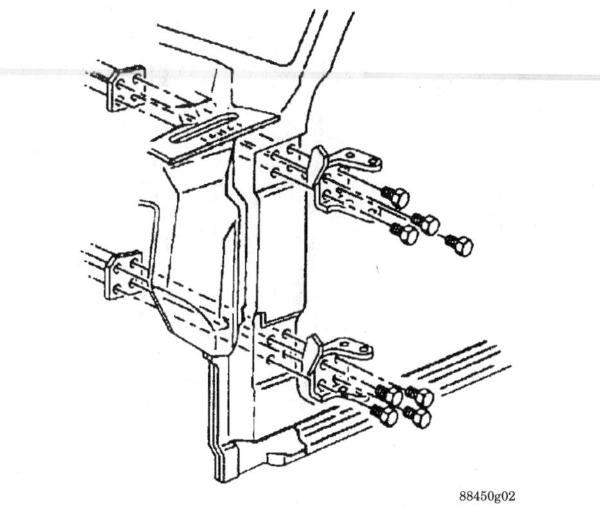

Fig. 5 Body side replacement hinges

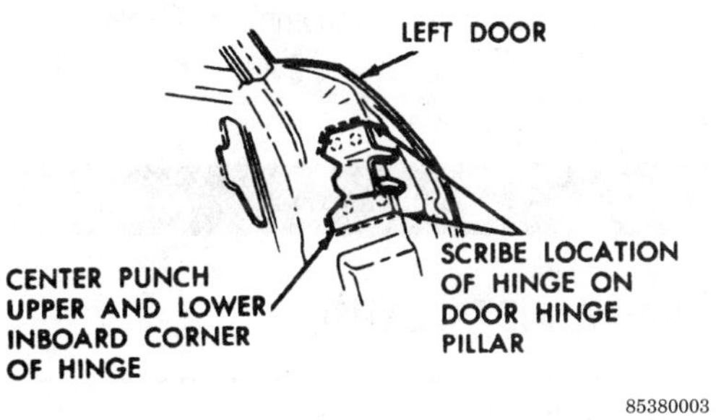

Fig. 3 Marking the door hinges for replacement

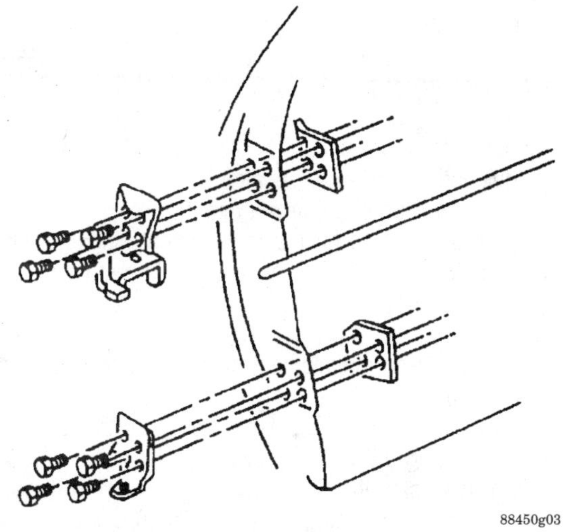

Fig. 6 Door side replacement hinges

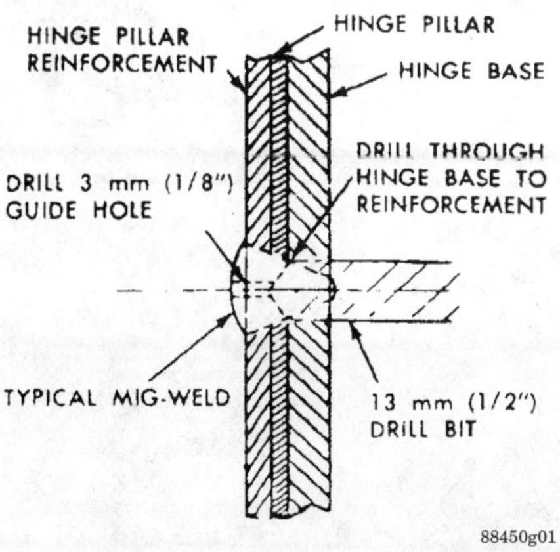

Fig. 4 Use a drill to remove the door hinge welds

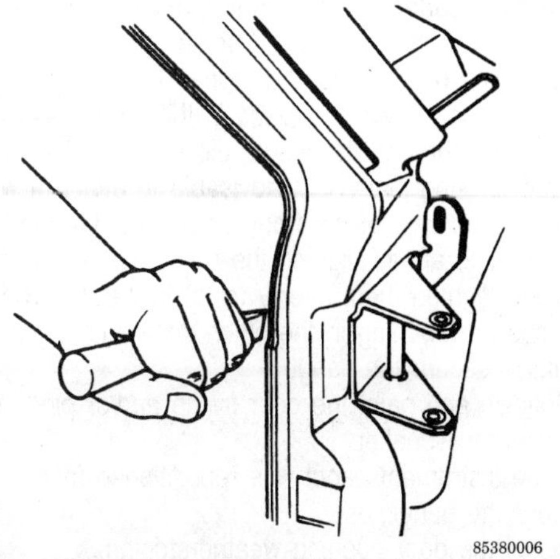

Fig. 7 Using a cold chisel to open the door pillar pinch weld

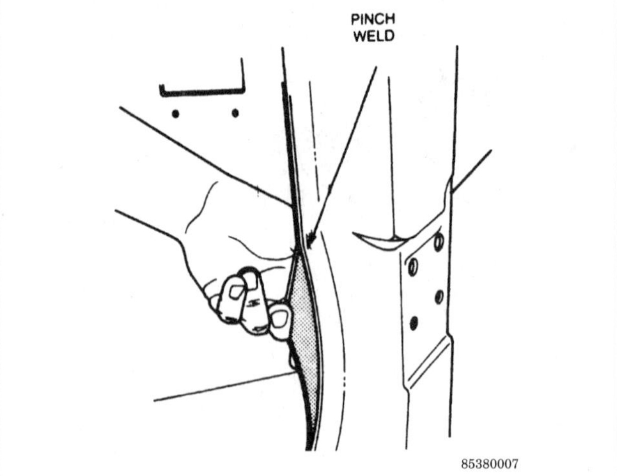

Fig. 8 The door pillar must be opened sufficiently to install the tapped anchor plate

7. Use a cold chisel and a hammer to separate the hinge from the door and/or the body pillar.
8. If replacing the upper door hinge it may be necessary to remove the instrument panel attaching screws, then pull the panel outward and support.
9. Remove the door opening weatherstriping.
10. If equipped, remove the speaker.
11. Remove the trim panel and armrest.
12. Prepare the surface for the replacement hinge(s) using a file or a portable grinder. Clean off any welds remaining on the door or the body pillar.

To install:

13. Align the bolt-on replacement hinge with the scribe lines made during removal.
14. Using the new hinge as a template, mark the location of each bolt hole using the center punch.
15. Drill holes (using the center marks as a guide) through the door and body pillar using a ½ in. (13mm) drill bit.
16. Using a hammer and cold chisel, open the door pillar (body side) pinch weld sufficiently to install the tapped anchor plate.
17. Coat the surface of the hinge that mates to the pillar and door using a medium bodied sealer.
18. Install the hinge bolts and tapped backing plate by aligning the components with the holes in the hinge pillar and door. Place the bolts through the hinge, pillar and/or door and into the tapped backing plate. It is advisable to attach a wire to the instrument panel side of the front lower pillar tapped backing plate in order to aid in aligning the holes. Once the bolts are all threaded, tighten them evenly to 26 ft. lbs. (35 Nm).
19. Close the opening in the pinch weld and, if possible, spot weld to secure the flange.
20. Refinish and paint the door frame and/or pinch weld.
21. Install the speaker
22. If the instrument panel was repositioned for access, pivot and secure the panel.
23. Install the door opening weatherstriping.
24. Install the trim panel and armrest.
25. Install the door and properly adjust the new bolt-on hinges. For details, please refer to the hinge adjustment procedure found later in this section. Check the door-to-frame fit and that the striker properly engages the lock fork bolt.

ADJUSTMENT

➡The ½ in. (13mm) drill hinge holes with the service replacement bolt-on door hinges provide for some adjustment.

1. Loosen the striker and door hinge bolts, then adjust the door up, down, forward, rearward, in or out (as necessary) at the door hinges.
2. Hold the door in position (an assistant is helpful here) and tighten the hinge bolts slightly, then check the for the following specified gaps:
   - Door-to-rocker panel — 0.21-0.27 in. (5-7mm)
   - Door-to-roof panel — 0.21-0.27 in. (5-7mm)
   - Rear of door-to-rear of pillar — 0.16-0.22 in. (4-6mm)
   - Forward edge of door-to-front fender — 0.16-0.22 in. (4-6mm)
   - Door surface flush with other panels to within — 0.03 in. (1mm)
3. Make sure that the striker properly engages the lock fork bolt.
4. When all adjustments are complete, tighten the hinge bolts to 26 ft. lbs. (35 Nm), then tighten the striker bolts securely.

Hood

REMOVAL & INSTALLATION

➧ See Figures 9 and 10

➡To prevent damage to your vehicle an assistant should be used when attempting to remove or install the hood.

1. Raise and support the hood, then place protective covers over the fenders.
2. Remove the right and left cowl vent grille panels.

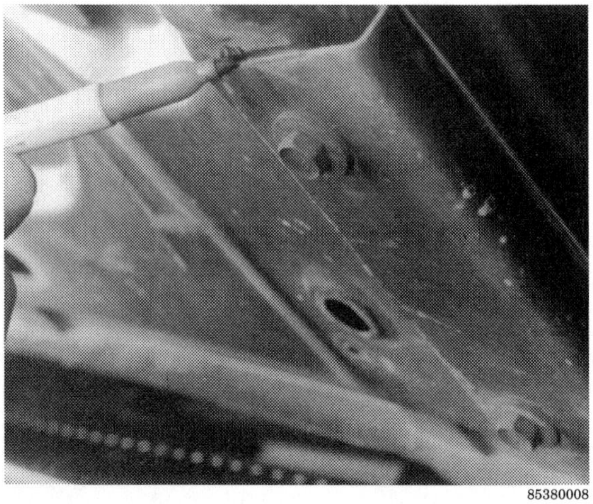

Fig. 9 Matchmark the hood to the hinges in order to simplify installation

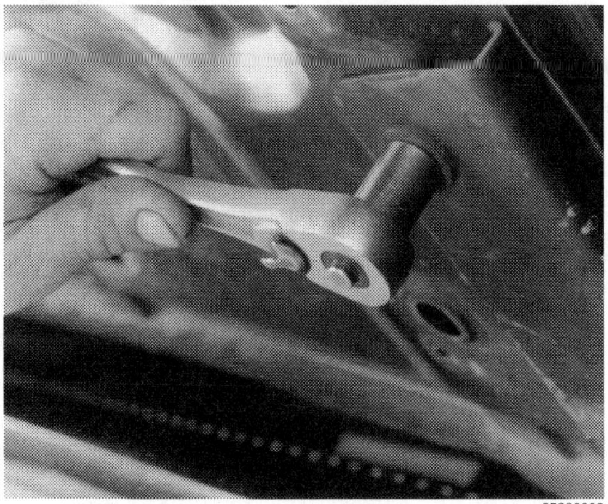

Fig. 10 Hold the hood securely while loosening the mounting bolts

3. If equipped, disengage the underhood lamp wire.
4. Disconnect the windshield washer hoses.
5. Disconnect the vacuum hose from the reservoir
6. Matchmark the alignment of the hood to the hinges using a permanent marker or a scribe tool. This will greatly ease installation and adjustment.
7. Secure the hood (an assistant is needed) and loosen the retaining bolts.
8. Remove the hood from the vehicle.

To install:

9. Install the hood to the vehicle aligning the marks made during removal.
10. Install the hinge bolts and tighten to 18 ft. lbs. (25 Nm).
11. Connect the vacuum hose to the reservoir, then connect the windshield washer hoses.
12. If equipped, connect the wiring to the underhood lamp.
13. Install the right and left cowl vent grilles.
14. Remove the fender covers and gently close the hood to check alignment.
15. If necessary, adjust the hood alignment.

ALIGNMENT

Align the hood so that the gaps between all of the components are equal; it must be flush with the fender and the cowl vent grille. Center the hood in the opening between the fenders, the cowl and the radiator grille. If it is difficult to center the hood or if the hood appears to be out of square, the front end sheet metal may need to be adjusted.

Most of the hood adjustment is achieved through the hinge-bolts, though on some vehicles adjustment may also be obtained through repositioning the striker and/or through the used of bump stops.

Tailgate

REMOVAL & INSTALLATION

See Figure 11

1. Lower the tailgate to the horizontal position.
2. Disengage the cable on the right and left sides from the striker bolts. To accomplish this, pull up on the middle of the cable assembly while raising the gate to a 45 degree angle, but be careful not to pinch the cable between the gate and bed.
3. Remove the tailgate from the vehicle by lifting upward on the left side to separate the left hinge assembly, then disengage the right hinge.

To install:

4. Install the gate to the vehicle by lowering the right hinge assembly into position first, then holding the gate at a 45 degree angle and seating the left hinge assembly.
5. Engage the left and right cables to the striker bolts.
6. Verify proper tailgate latching and operation.

ALIGNMENT

Align the tailgate so the gaps between all of the components are equal; it must be flush with the fenders. Center the tailgate in the opening between the fenders by adjusting the hinges and/or the striker bolts.

Bumpers

REMOVAL & INSTALLATION

Front

See Figures 12, 13 and 14

1. If necessary for better access, raise and support the front of the vehicle safely.
2. If equipped, remove the air dam/deflector retainers and remove the air dam from the vehicle.
3. Remove the grille. For details, please refer to the procedure found later in this section.
4. Remove the brace to bumper nut(s) and bolt(s).
5. Disengage the parking lamp connectors and, if equipped, the fog lamp connectors.
6. Support the bumper (usually a friend is most convenient here), then remove the bumper-to-frame retainers.
7. Carefully lower the bumper from the vehicle
8. Installation is the reverse of the removal. Tighten the retaining bolts and nuts to 30 ft. lbs. (40 Nm).

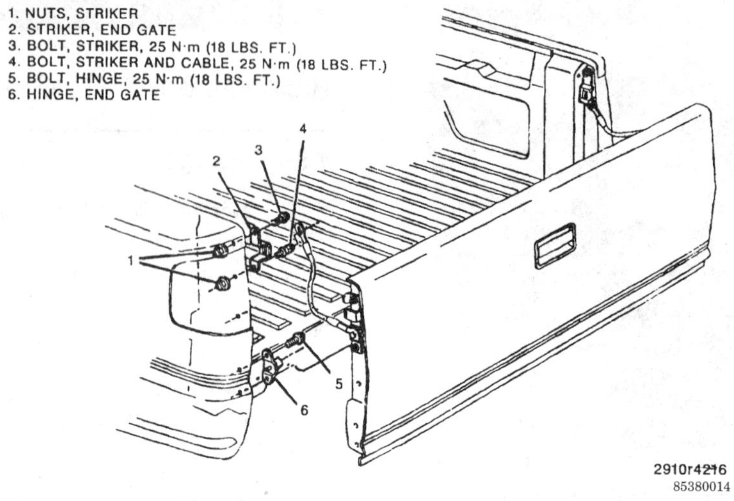

Fig. 11 Tailgate and bed mounted striker components

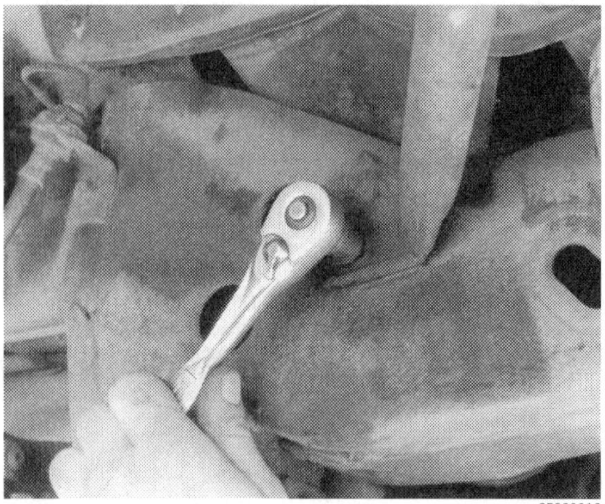

Fig. 12 Most bumpers are reinforced by braces attached further back on the frame

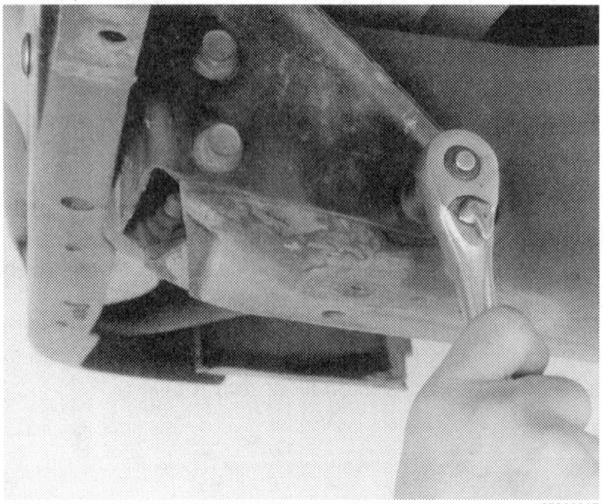

Fig. 13 Loosen and remove the bumper retainers

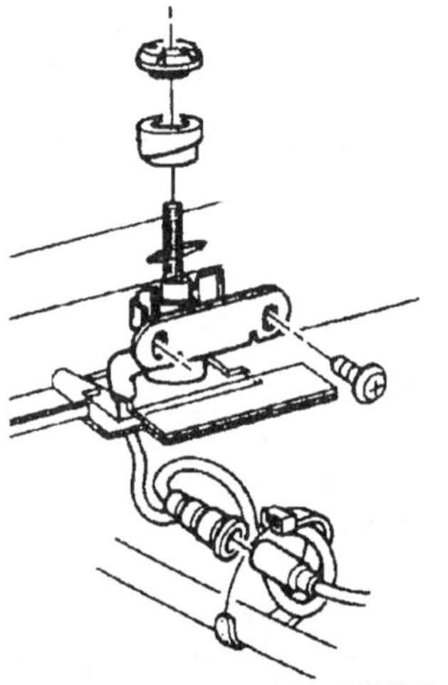

Fig. 14 Exploded view of the bumper assembly

Rear

➧ See Figure 15

1. If necessary, disconnect the license plate lamp harness.

➡Remove the bracket-to-bumper nuts and bolts and lower the bumper from the vehicle with the brackets still installed on frame.

2. On some models one or more additional braces may also secure the rear bumper. If necessary, disconnect the brace from the vehicle or the bumper, as applicable.
3. Carefully lower the bumper from the rear of the truck. If necessary, the bumper brackets may be removed from bumper at this time.
4. Installation is the reverse of the removal. Be sure all brackets and/or braces are properly secured. Most of the brace and bracket retainers should be tightened to 60-70 ft. lbs. (81-95 Nm).

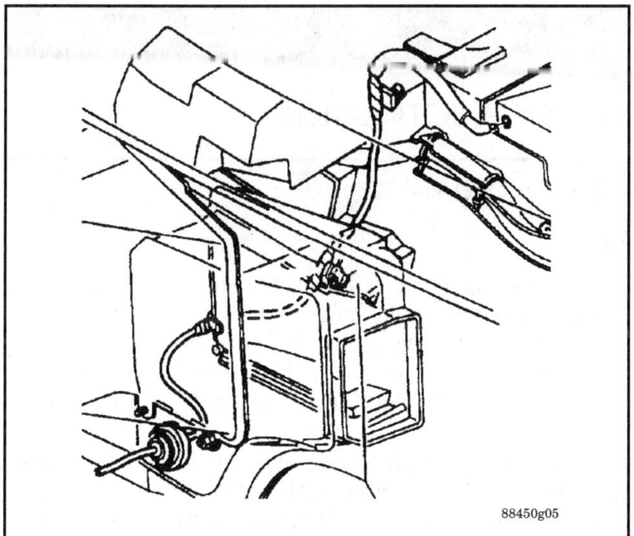

Fig. 15 Exploded view of the rear step bumper

Grille

REMOVAL & INSTALLATION

See Figure 16

1. Loosen and remove the grille-to-fender and grille-to-radiator support retainers.
2. Pull the grille forward sufficiently and disengage any necessary wiring (such as side marker wiring and bulb sockets).
3. Remove the grille from the vehicle.
4. Installation is the reverse of removal. Be careful not to overtighten any of the fasteners as the grille, bezel and fasteners are all easily damaged. Most fasteners should be tightened to no more than 12 inch lbs. (1.4 Nm).

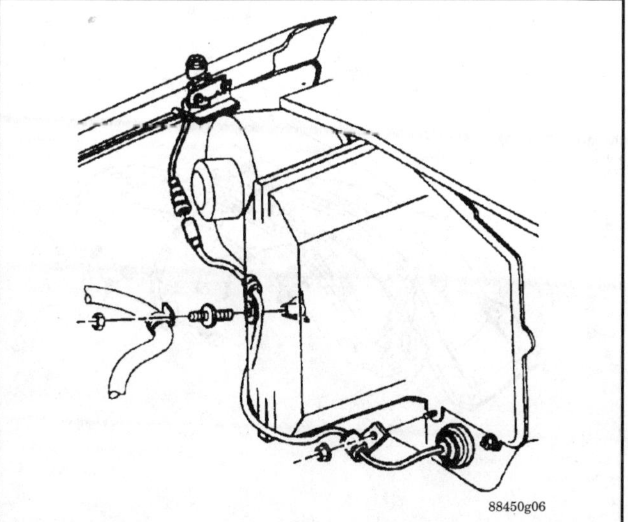

Fig. 16 Exploded view of the grille assembly mounting

Outside Mirrors

See Figure 17

A damaged mirror glass face may be replaced by placing a large piece or multiple strips of tape over the glass then breaking the mirror face. Adhesive back mirror faces should be available for most applications.

When replacing the whole outside mirror assembly, the studs are not accessible from the outside and the door trim panel and water deflector must be removed in order to access the retaining nuts. Once the mirror housing is free it may be removed from the door, but make sure there is no power window option or the wiring harness must first be disengaged.

The water deflector is secured by a strip of adhesive between the deflector and door, as well as waterproof sealing tape. Upon installation, make sure a good seal is achieved to keep water from entering into the body. If necessary, use strip caulking as a sealant between the deflector and door. Tighten the outside mirror retaining nuts to 53 inch lbs. (6 Nm).

Antenna

REMOVAL & INSTALLATION

See Figures 18, 19 and 20

1. Disconnect the negative battery cable.
2. Remove the mast retaining nut, mast and bezel.
3. Disconnect the antenna cable from the receiver cable.
4. Remove the screw and star washer attaching the antenna to the fender.
5. Remove the antenna.

When installing the antenna to the fender make sure the retaining nut is tight. A loose antenna or one that does not make good contact at the fender can cause radio interference.

6. Installation is the reverse of removal.

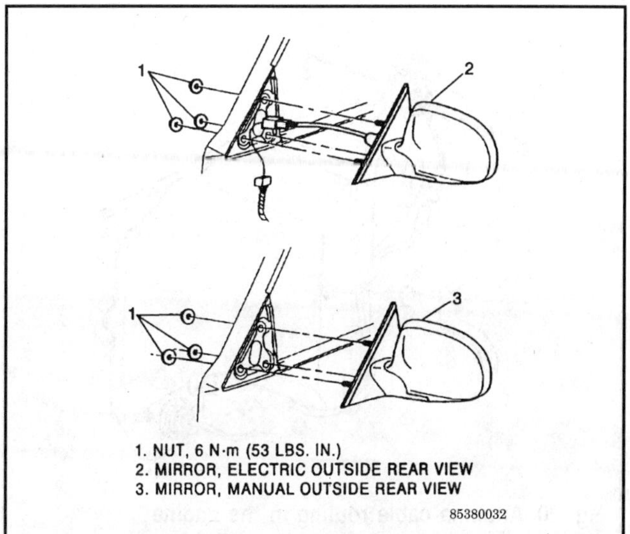

Fig. 17 Outside rearview mirror installation

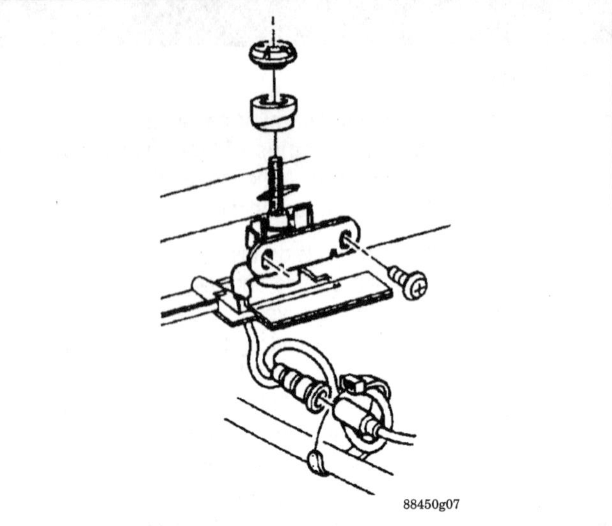

Fig. 18 Radio antenna mounting

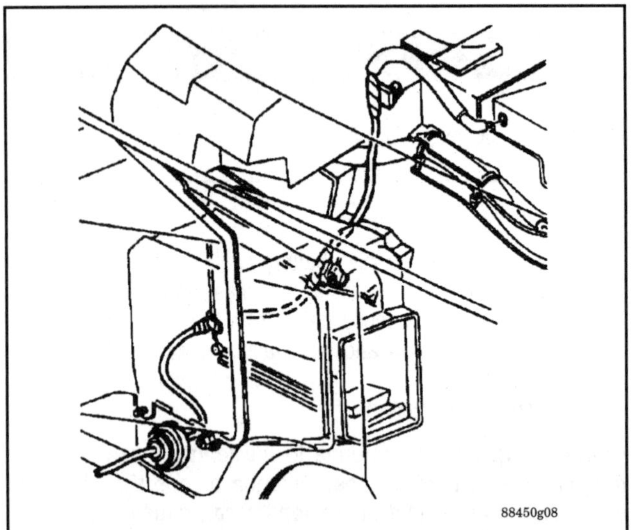

Fig. 19 Antenna cable routing from cowl to radio

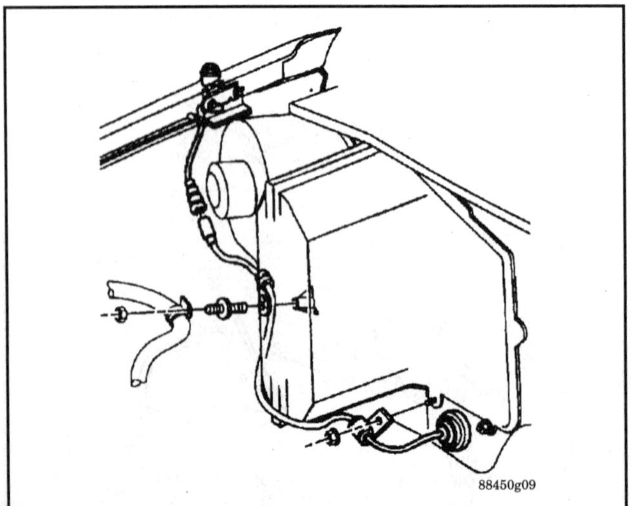

Fig. 20 Antenna cable routing in the engine compartment

Fenders

REMOVAL & INSTALLATION

See Figures 21 and 22

Right

1. Disconnect the negative battery cable.
2. Remove the radiator grille.
3. Remove the bumper end cap must be removed.
4. Matchmark and remove the hood from the vehicle.
5. Remove the battery, battery tray and radiator coolant bottle (if present).
6. Remove the antenna mast and base. For details, please refer to the procedure earlier in this section.
7. Remove the fender retaining bolts. Locations should include all or some of the following, radiator support, reinforcement, wheelhouse panel, door frame and/or door hinge. Keep

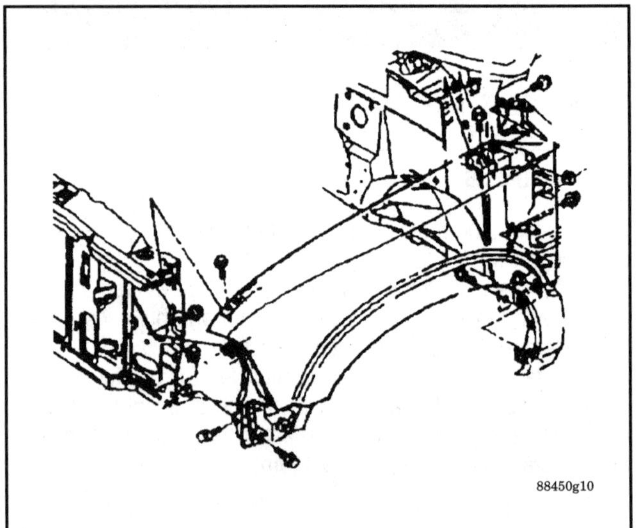

Fig. 21 Fender to radiator support and cowl bolts

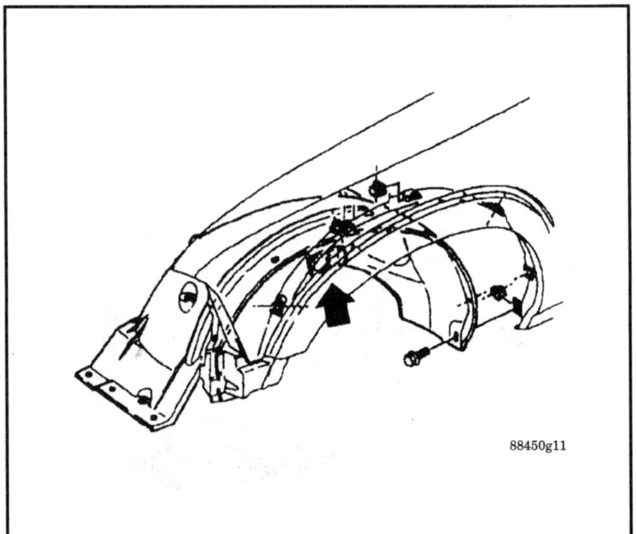

Fig. 22 Fender to radiator support and cowl bolts

track of any shim washers which may come lose after removing fender bolts. The shim washers should be installed in their original locations during assembly.

8. Separate any necessary wiring or vacuum hoses from the fender, then remove it from the vehicle.
9. Installation is the reverse of the removal. Tighten all fender retaining bolts to 21 ft. lbs. (29 Nm).

Left

1. Remove the radiator grille.
2. Remove the bumper end cap.
3. Matchmark and remove the hood from the vehicle.
4. If present on this side, remove the coolant reservoir bottle.
5. Remove the windshield wiper bottle from the fender.
6. Remove the horn from the fender.
7. Remove the hood latch cable.
8. If equipped with 4 wheel ABS, remove the BPMV from the fender. If the assembly cannot be repositioned slightly and supported with the lines attached, the unit must be removed completely from the vehicle. DO NOT kink or damage the brake lines, brake failure and serious personal injury could result.
9. Remove the fender retaining bolts. Locations should include all or some of the following: radiator support, reinforcement, wheelhouse panel, door frame and/or door hinge. Keep track of any shim washers which may come lose after removing fender bolts. The shim washers should be installed in their original locations during assembly.
10. Separate any necessary wiring or vacuum hoses from the fender, then remove it from the vehicle.
11. Installation is the reverse of the removal. Tighten all fender retaining bolts to 21 ft. lbs. (29 Nm).

Cab/Body Mounts

REMOVAL & INSTALLATION

See Figures 23, 24 and 25

Certain procedures covered by this manual (involving the top bellhousing-to-engine bolts) require the cab/body mount bolts to be removed so the body may be raised slightly for access. It is critical that the body NOT be raised any more than necessary for access or twisting and damage could occur. The body must be properly supported at all times.

If a cab/body mount must be removed completely for replacement, ALL mounts on that side of the vehicle MUST be unbolted in order to prevent damage. Again, the body must be suitable supported and multiple points (near each of the mounts) in order to prevent damage.

➡Shims are available in various sized to help level the cab, but the stack should NEVER exceed 0.24 in. (6.0mm).

1. Raise and support the vehicle safely placing jackstands under the body at each of the mounts on that side. Protect the body from the jackstands using wooden blocks. The blocks will help distribute the vehicle's weight on a larger area than the lips of the jackstand. Place at least on jackstand under the frame temporarily for safety.

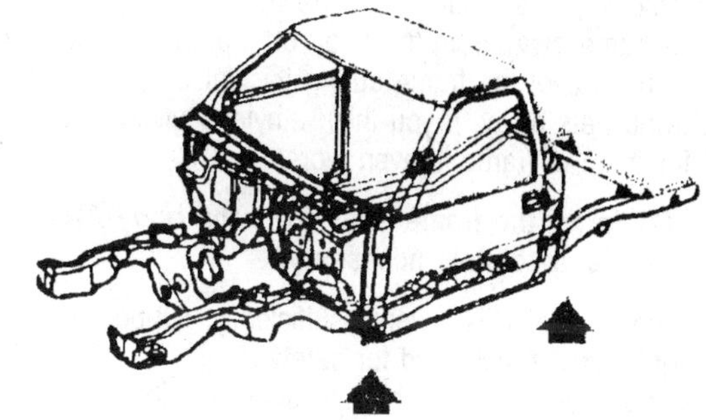

Fig. 24 Cab/body mount locations — regular cab

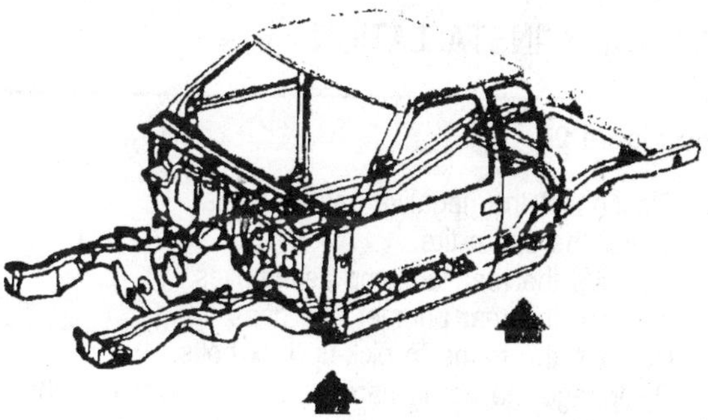

Fig. 25 Cab/body mount locations — extended cab

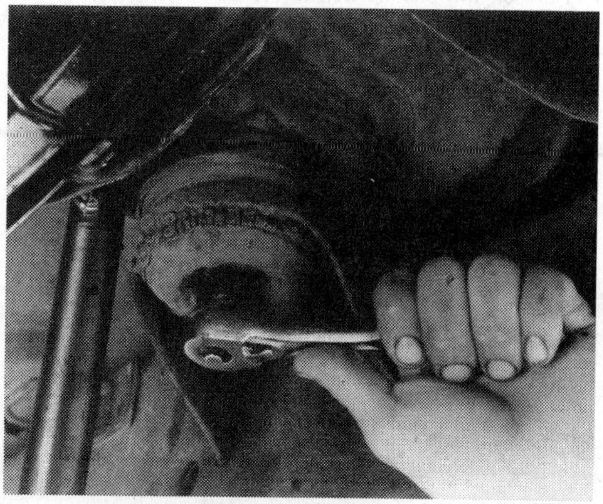

Fig. 23 Some procedures require the left cab/body mounts to be unbolted

2. Loosen and remove the mount bolts on that side of the vehicle. If possible, remove the retainer and lower cushion as well.

3. Remove the jackstand from the FRAME only, then slowly lower the frame away from the body on that side. Make sure you remain clear of the frame during this (also keep small children and pets away, if you think ethylene glycol anti-freeze is bad for them, a frame is even worse).

➡DO NOT lower the frame away from the body ANY MORE than is absolutely necessary.

4. Once the frame is lowered sufficiently, support it at this new height using a jackstand for safety.

5. Remove the upper cushion, spacer and shims, as applicable.

6. Installation is the reverse of removal. Remember, at NO point should you work under the vehicle unless both the body and frame are supported using jackstands. The floor jack IS NOT sufficient to assure safety, even for short periods of time. Tighten the mount bolts to 52-54 ft. lbs. (70-73 Nm).

Pick-Up Box

REMOVAL & INSTALLATION

➧ See Figure 26

1. Disconnect the negative battery cable.
2. Lower the spare tire.
3. Remove the rear tail lamp assemblies.
4. Remove the rear bumper end caps.
5. Remove the frame to pick-up box bolts.
6. Disengage the wiring harness ground wire from the frame.
7. Remove the license plate lamp.
8. Disengage the wiring harness ground wire between the fuel filler neck and the pick-up box.
9. Remove the fuel filler neck to pick-up box screws.
10. Remove the pick-up box from the vehicle.

To install:

11. Position the pick-up box to the vehicle.
12. Install the fuel filler neck to pick-up box retaining screws.

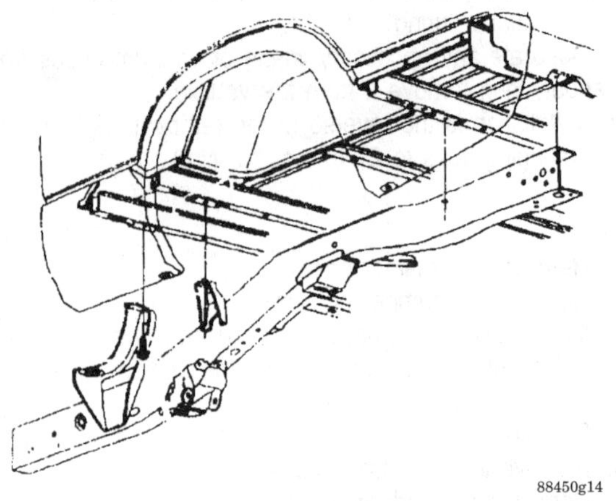

Fig. 26 Pick-up box installation

13. Engage the wiring harness ground wire between the fuel filler neck and the pick-up box.
14. Install the license plate lamp.
15. Engage the wiring harness ground wire from the frame.
16. Install the frame to pick-up box bolts and tighten to 50 ft. lbs. (68 Nm).
17. Install the rear bumper end caps.
18. Install the rear tail lamp assemblies.
19. Raise the spare tire.
20. Connect the negative battery cable.

Spare Tire Carrier

REPLACEMENT

1. Raise and support the vehicle safely using jackstands for access.
2. Lower the spare tire and remove it.
3. Remove the cotter pin and bolts attaching the spare tire hoist to the frame.
4. Remove the spare tire hoist.
5. Installation is the reverse of removal. Tighten bolts to 11 ft. lbs. (15 Nm).

INTERIOR

Instrument Panel and Pad

REMOVAL & INSTALLATION

See Figures 27, 28, 29, 30, 31, 32, 33, 34 and 35

CAUTION

When performing service around the air bag system components or wiring, the air bag system MUST be disabled. Failure to do so could result in possible air bag deployment, personal injury or unneeded air bag system repairs.

1. Disconnect the negative battery cable.
2. Disable the air bag system. Please refer to Supplemental Inflatable Restraint (SIR) System in Section 6.

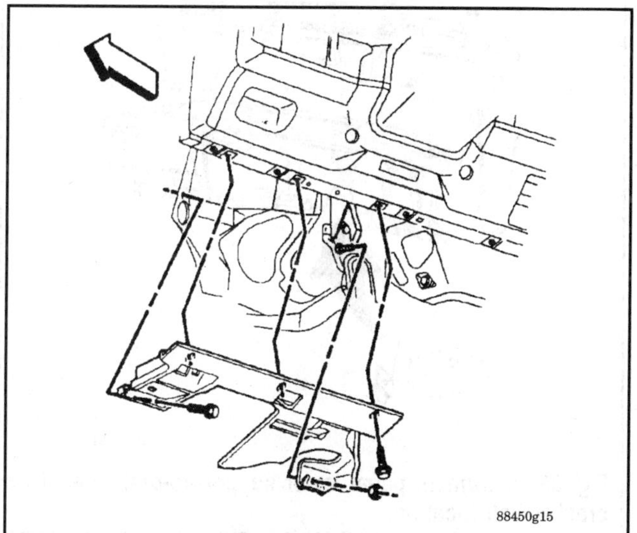

88450g15

Fig. 27 Left instrument panel sound insulator

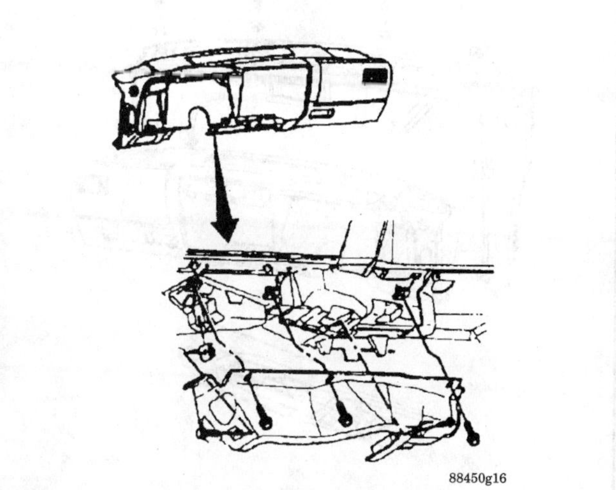

88450g16

Fig. 28 Center instrument panel sound insulator

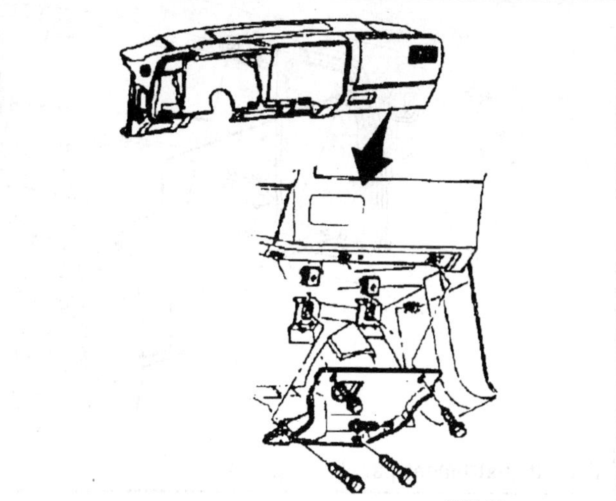

88450g17

Fig. 29 Right instrument panel sound insulator

3. Remove the two screws from the instrument cluster trim plate and remove the cluster trim plate from the instrument panel.
4. Disengage all electrical connectors, as necessary.
5. If equipped with a tilt steering column, move it to the down position.
6. Set the parking brake, block the wheels and place the automatic transmission in low, if equipped.
7. Remove the left instrument panel sound insulator.
8. Unplug the DLC connector.
9. Disengage the RKE/delay module.
10. Remove the center instrument panel sound insulator.
11. Disconnect the parking brake release cable by squeezing the retainers.
12. Disconnect the cable slug from the parking brake mechanism.
13. Remove the right instrument panel sound insulator.
14. Remove the lighter and accessory power outlets, if equipped.
15. Remove the courtesy lamp.
16. Remove the knee bolster from the vehicle.
17. Remove the HVAC control assembly and set aside.
18. Remove the four radio screws, and through the storage compartment, reach behind the radio and unplug the antenna and three electrical connectors.
19. Using a 15 mm wrench, remove the four steering column screws.
20. Remove the following four lower instrument panel support bolts screws across the bottom of the instrument panel.
    a. Remove the left and right instrument panel pivot bolts.
    b. Remove the instrument panel lower support to brake pedal bracket.
    c. Remove the instrument panel lower support bolt.
21. Remove the instrument panel upper support bolts.
22. Remove both speaker grilles.
23. Using a flat bladed tool, remove windshield defrost grilles.
24. Disengage all electrical connectors, as necessary.
25. Remove the instrument panel from the vehicle.

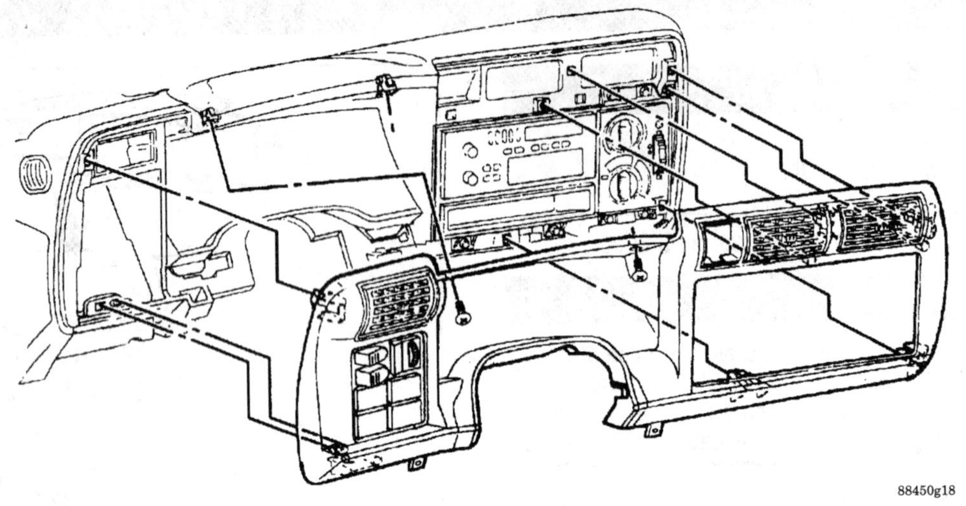

88450g18

Fig. 30 Instrument panel trim panel

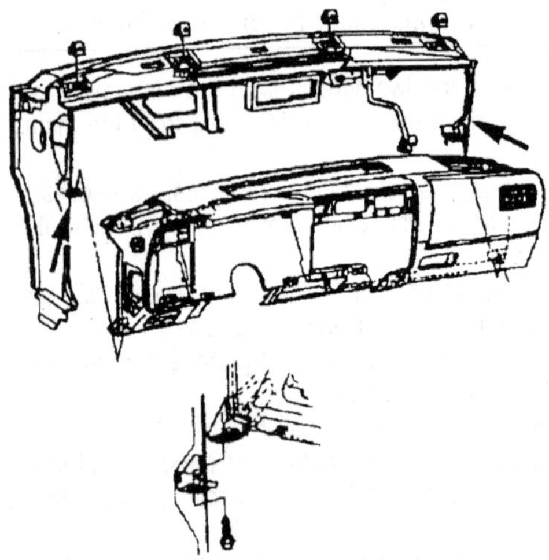

88450g19

Fig. 31 Instrument panel pivot bolt locations

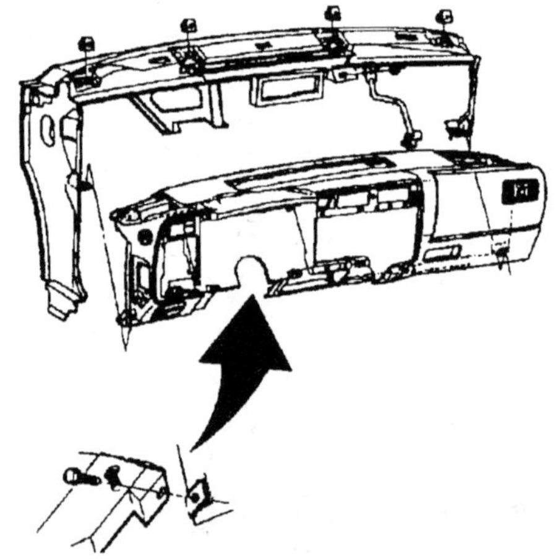

88450g21

Fig. 33 Instrument panel lower support-to-brake pedal bracket bolt location

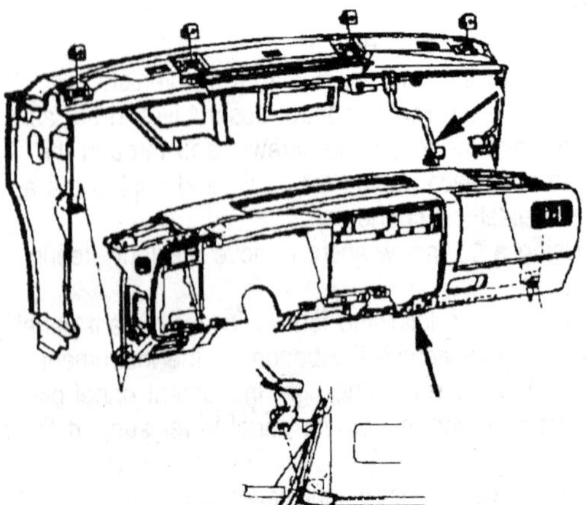

88450g20

Fig. 32 Instrument panel lower support bolts locations

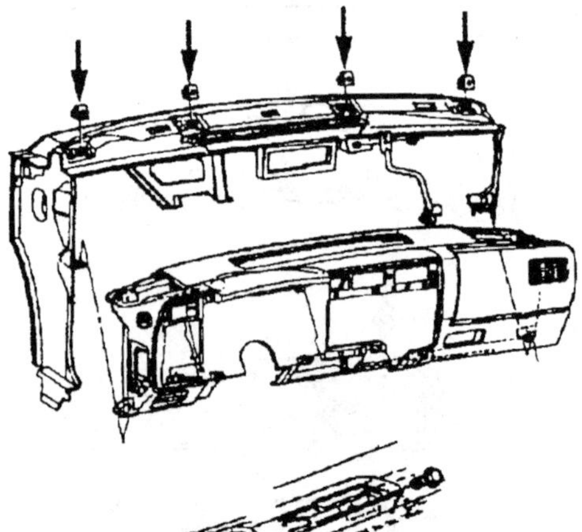

88450g22

Fig. 34 Instrument panel upper support bolts locations

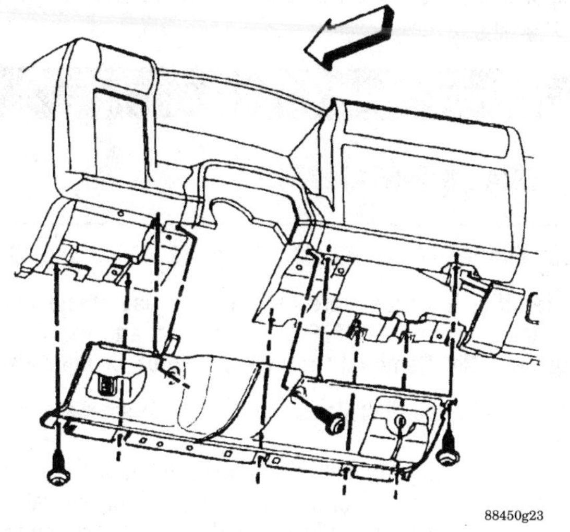

Fig. 35 Knee bolster installation

To install:

26. Position the instrument panel to the vehicle and rest onto the lower pivot studs.
27. Engage all electrical connectors, as necessary.
28. Install the upper instrument panel support screws, but do not tighten.
29. Install the right, center and left lower instrument panel support screws, but do not tighten.
30. Align the instrument panel for the lower screws.
31. Tighten the upper and lower support screws to 66 inch lbs. (7.5 Nm).
32. Install the steering column nuts and tighten to 22 ft. lbs. (30 Nm).
33. Install both speaker grilles.
34. Install the radio and plug the antenna and three electrical connectors.
35. Install the HVAC control assembly and vacuum and electrical connections.
36. Install the instrument cluster trim plate and align with the knee bolster.
37. Instal the knee bolster to the vehicle.
38. Install the courtesy lamp.
39. Install the lighter and accessory power outlets, if equipped.
40. Install the parking brake cable.
41. Install the center instrument panel sound insulator.
42. Install the left instrument panel sound insulator.
43. Engage the RKE/delay module.
44. Plug in the DLC connector.
45. Install the nut to the accelerator stud and tighten to 35 inch lbs. (4 Nm).
46. Install the right instrument panel sound insulator.
47. Enable the air bag system. Please refer to Section 6.
48. Connect the negative battery cable.

Front Console

REMOVAL & INSTALLATION

See Figure 36

1. Remove the transfer case shift lever knob, if equipped.
2. Remove the shift control lever, on manual transmission only.
3. Lift up on the console to release the clips.
4. Unplug the electrical connector, if equipped, and remove the console from the vehicle.
5. Installation is the reverse of removal.

Floor Console

REMOVAL & INSTALLATION

See Figures 37 and 38

1. Remove the cup holder and remove the one console retaining screw.
2. Remove the two screws and the upper console cover.
3. Remove the center nut.
4. Open the storage compartment cover, and remove the storage compartment.
5. Remove the two rear console nuts.
6. Lower the console from the vehicle.
7. Installation is the reverse of removal.

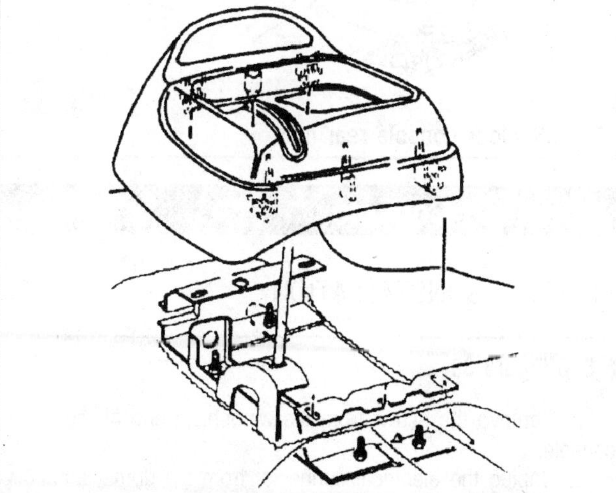

Fig. 36 Front console installation

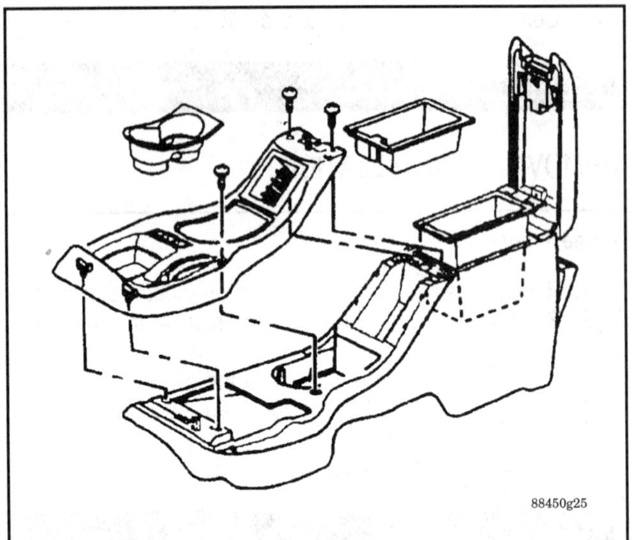

Fig. 37 Floor console installation

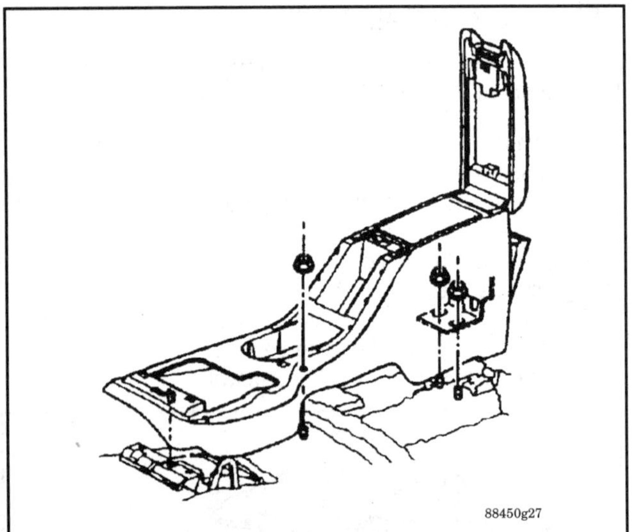

Fig. 38 Floor console rear nuts

Overhead Console

REMOVAL & INSTALLATION

▸ See Figure 39

1. Remove the screw from the windshield end of the console.
2. Unplug the electrical connector from the dome lamp harness.
3. Remove the console by swinging downward and pulling forward to clear the rear mounting tabs.

To install:

4. Insert the rear console mounting tabs into the roof panel.
5. Plug the electrical connector to the dome lamp harness.
6. Install the console by swinging upward and tightening the retaining screw.

Door Trim Panel

REMOVAL & INSTALLATION

▸ See Figures 40, 41, 42, 43, 44, 45, 46, 47, 48 and 49

➡The following procedure requires the use of the Trim Pad Removal tool, J-38778 or equivalent, and the Window Regulator Clip Removal tool No. J-9886-01 or equivalent.

1. Remove the door handle bezel-to-door screws and the bezel.
2. Unless equipped with power windows, use a window regulator clip removal tool such as J-9886-01 or equivalent, to remove the window regulator clip and separate the handle from the door.
3. Carefully pry off the armrest screw cover and remove the armrest-to-door screw and the armrest.
4. If equipped with power windows, remove/disengage the switch mounting panel.
5. Using a suitable trim pad removal tool, remove the nylon fasteners from their seats.
6. Remove the door panel from the vehicle.
7. Installation is the reverse of removal.

Headliner

REMOVAL & INSTALLATION

▸ See Figures 50 and 51

1. Disengage the dome lamp and let it hang down.
2. Remove the coat hooks.
3. Remove the passenger assist handle.
4. Remove the sunshades and retainers.
5. Remove the windshield garnish moldings.
6. Remove the rear side door upper latch cover, if equipped.
7. Pull the body side trim panels loose at the roof line.
8. Grasp the headliner at the front, use a downward motion to disengage the hook and loop fasteners at the rear and slide the headliner forward, past the body side trim panels.

➡New headliners must be pierced to accommodate actual vehicle accessories.

9. Position the headliner to the vehicle.
10. Engage the body side trim panels.
11. Install the windshield garnish moldings.
12. Install the sunshades and retainers.
13. Install the rear side door upper latch cover, if equipped.
14. Install the passenger assist handle.
15. Install the coat hooks.
16. Replace the dome lamp.

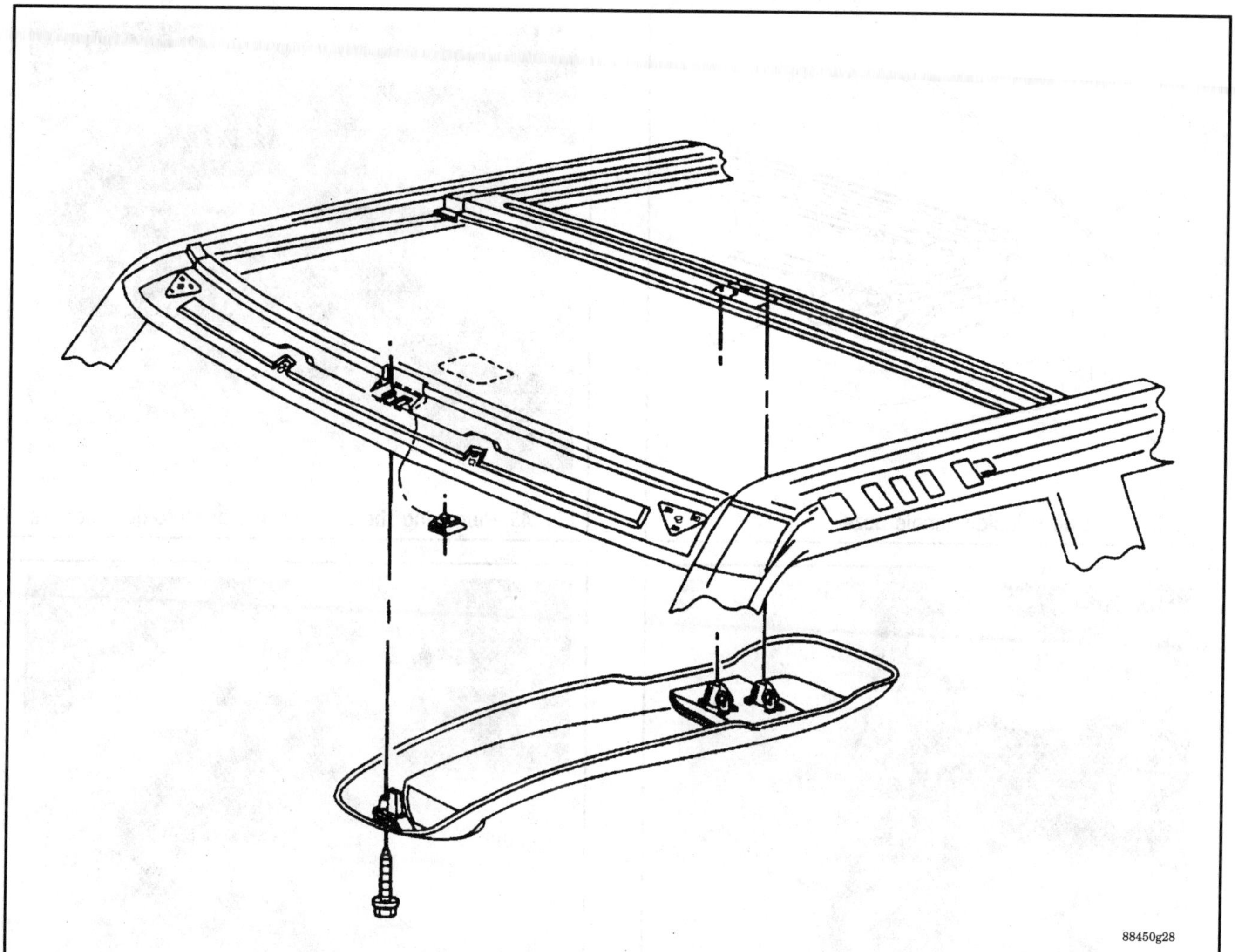

Fig. 39 Overhead console mounting

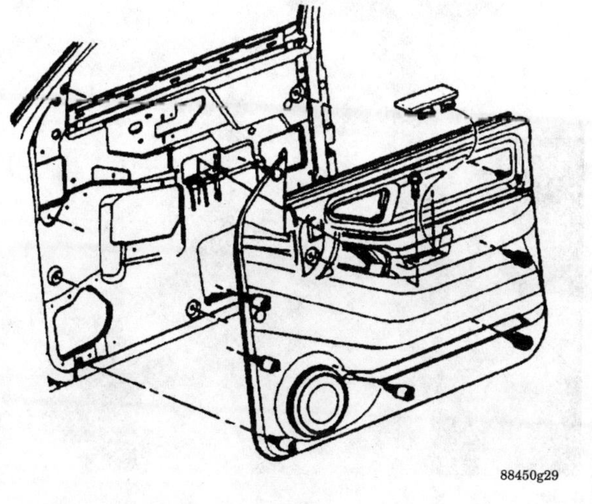

Fig. 40 Front door trim panel

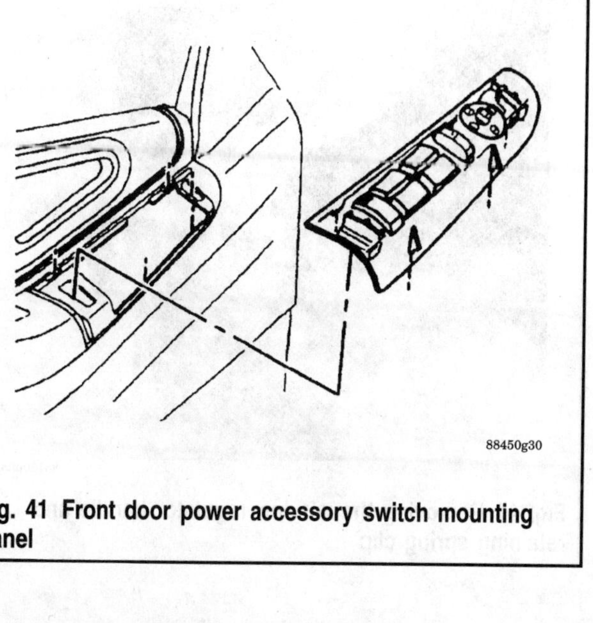

Fig. 41 Front door power accessory switch mounting panel

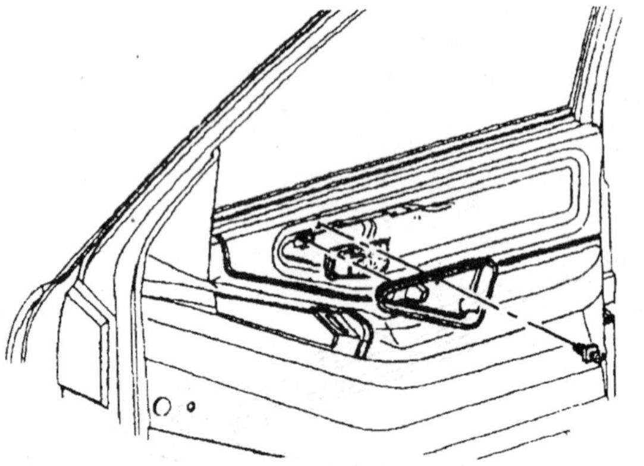

88450g31

Fig. 42 Front door inside handle bezel

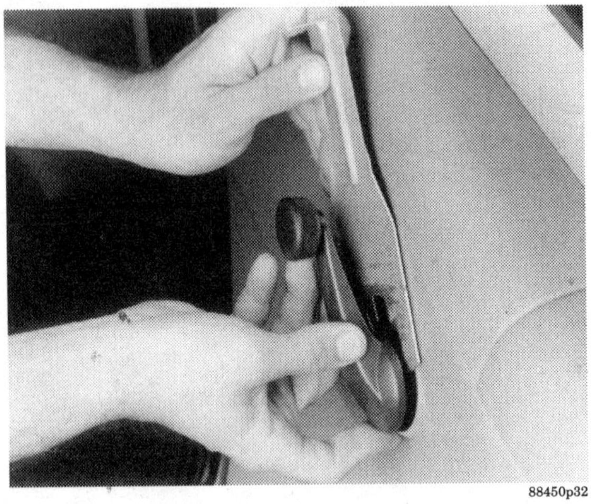

88450p32

Fig. 43 Disengaging the window regulator handle retaining spring clip

88450p33

Fig. 44 Removing the window regulator handle and retaining spring clip

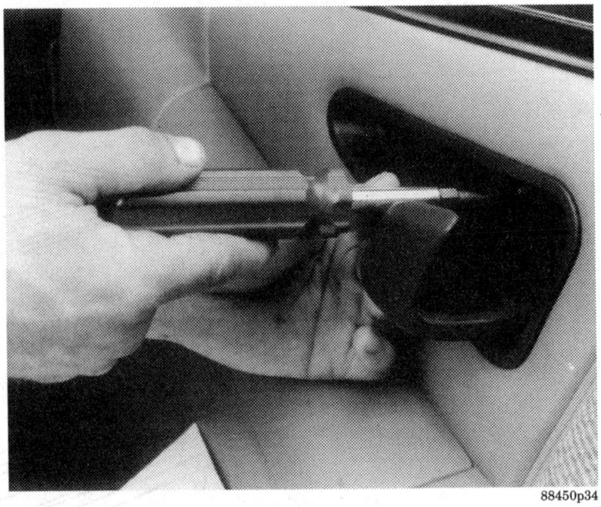

88450p34

Fig. 45 Removing the door handle bezel-to-door screws

88450p35

Fig. 46 Removing the door handle bezel

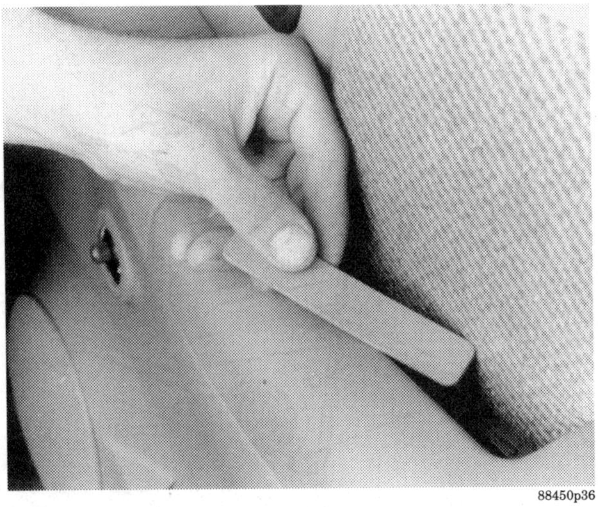

88450p36

Fig. 47 Carefully pry off the armrest screw cover

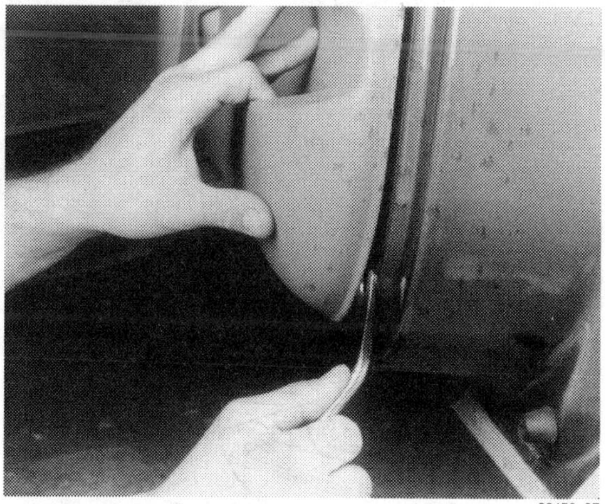

88450p37

Fig. 48 Carefully disengage the trim panel retaining clips

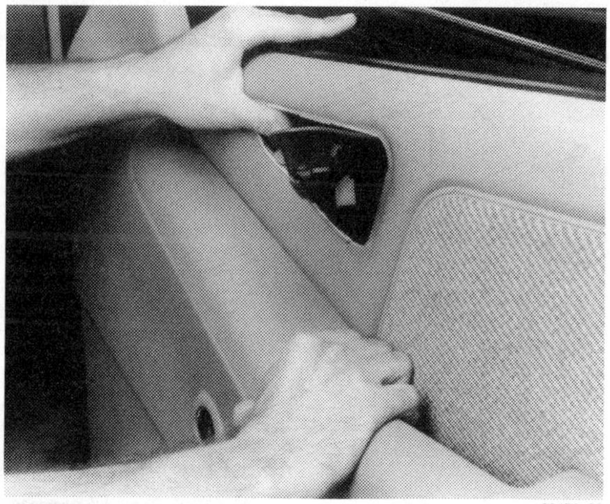

88450p38

Fig. 49 Carefully lift up and disengage the trim panel from the upper door frame

88450g41

Fig. 50 Headliner installation — except extended cab

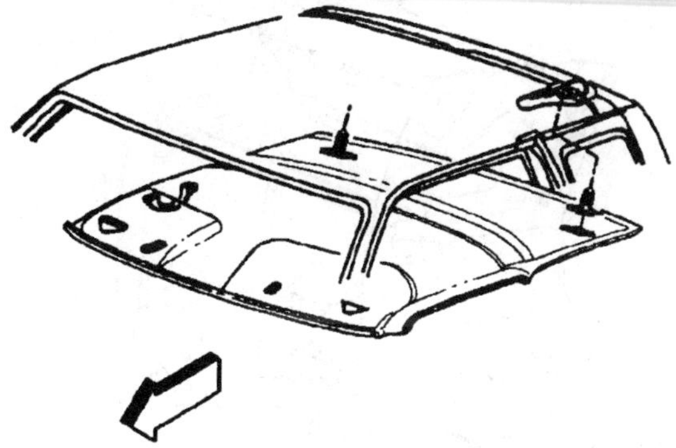

88450g42

Fig. 51 Headliner installation — extended cab

Interior Trim Panels

REMOVAL & INSTALLATION

See Figures 52, 53, 54, 55, 56, 57, 58, 59 and 60

These vehicles use screws and many different types of push-in fasteners to secure interior trim panels. Most of these fasteners can be reused to assemble the trim during various repair procedures. There are times when a push-in fastener cannot be removed without damaging the fastener or the component it is holding. If this is the case, cut or break the fastener and use a new one during installation. Using a suitable fork-type prying tool, pry the fastener from the retaining hole behind the component being removed. When installing, verify the fastener alignment with the retaining hole by hand. Push directly on or over the fastener until it seats.

Many of the attaching screws and pins are hidden by plugs, caps, etc, and if screws aren't present, then the piece is most likely held by clips or the like. Ornamental plugs or caps can

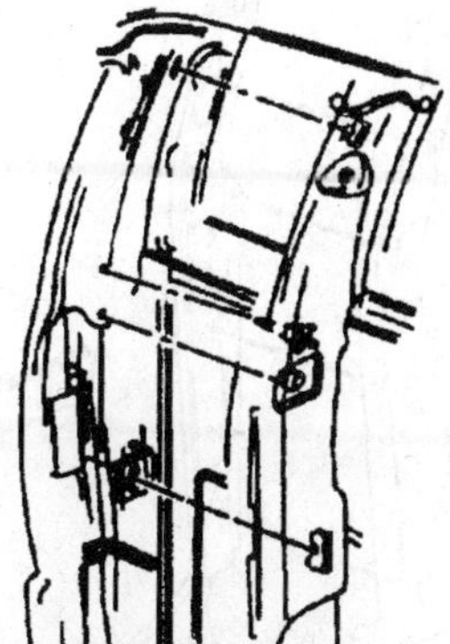

88450g43

Fig. 52 Body side trim panel — standard cab

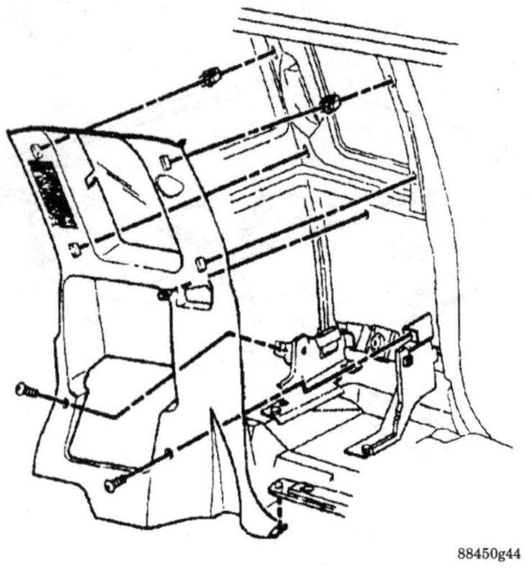

Fig. 53 Body side trim panel — extended cab

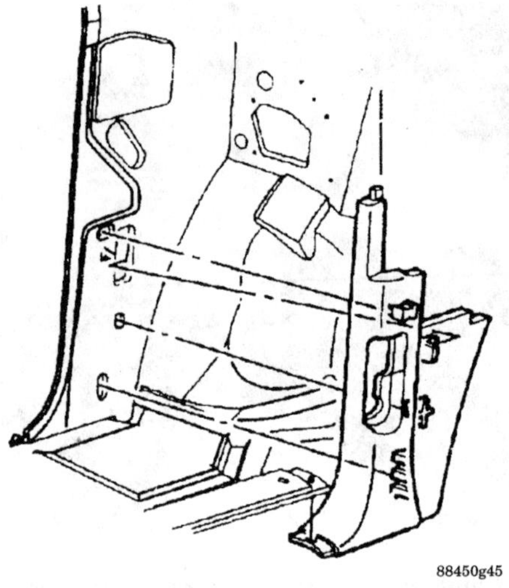

Fig. 54 Left side body hinge pillar trim panel

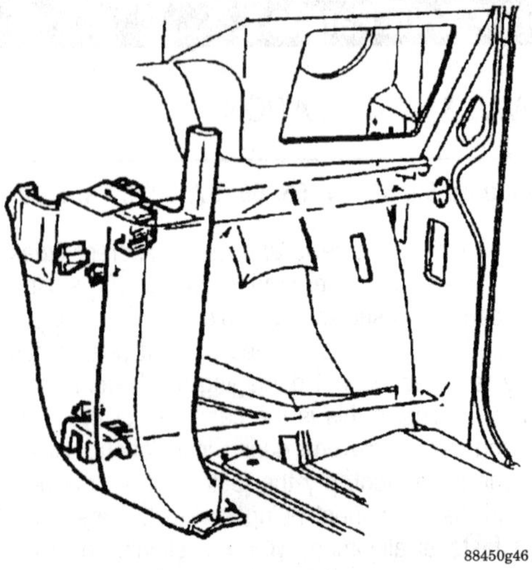

Fig. 55 Right side body hinge pillar trim panel

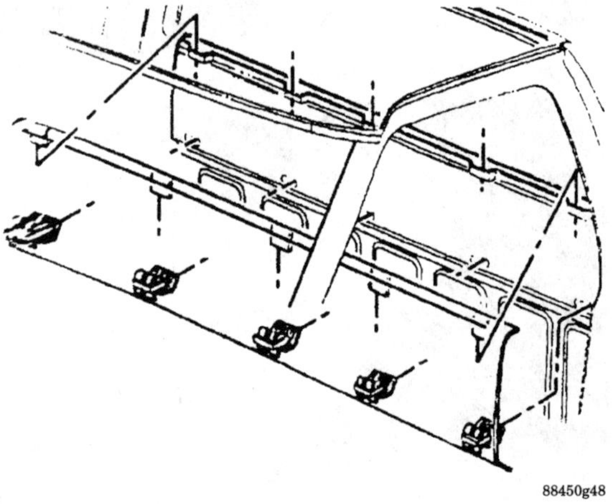

Fig. 57 Rear window garnish molding

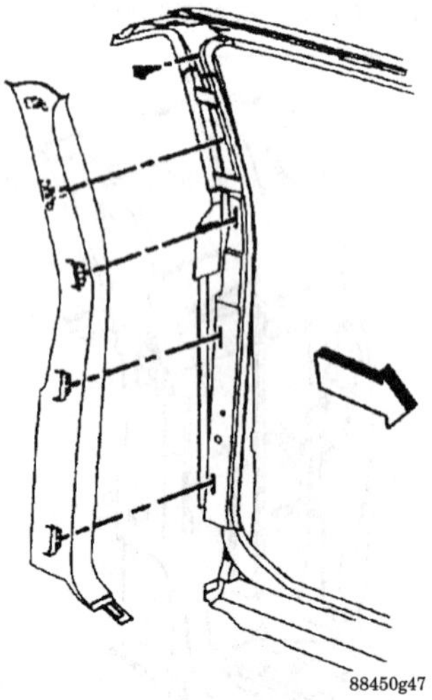

Fig. 56 C-pillar trim panel — extended cab

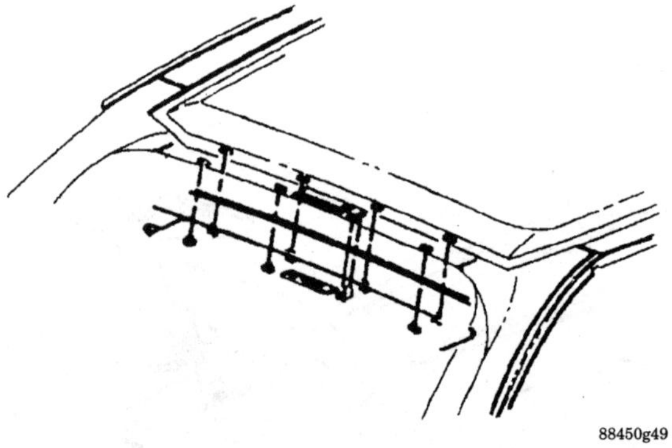

Fig. 58 Roof header garnish molding

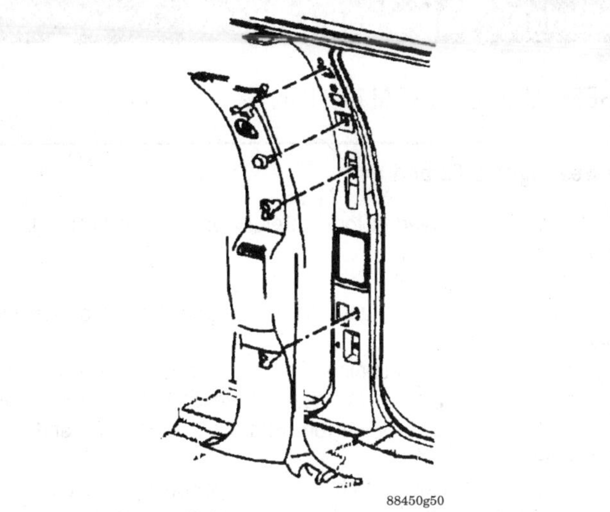

Fig. 59 Front side door lock pillar garnish molding

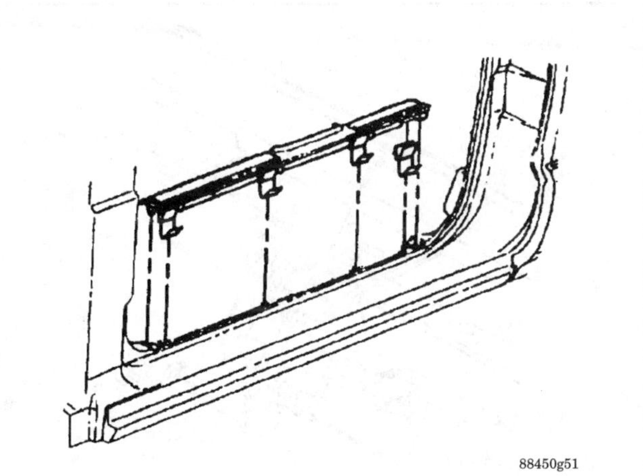

Fig. 60 Sill trim plate

be removed with light prying action. Don't force anything: if the trim piece isn't coming off, it's because you have missed an attaching point somewhere. Most attaching hardware is located around the perimeter or near the center of the piece. Don't forget to reinstall the ornamental plug or cap that hides the screw when the part is put back in place.

Also, some moldings cannot be removed without first removing an adjacent molding. It may seem like more work than necessary, but if you force something that isn't meant to come out before another piece is removed, something is bound to break, and interior moldings are expensive and usually not kept in stock at your local dealership. If seat belts are in the way, be sure to properly tighten the fasteners when reinstalling.

Heater and Air Conditioning Ducts and Outlets

REMOVAL & INSTALLATION

Most outlets are held on by screws, some of which are hidden by other panels i.e. steering column trim panel, glove box door, or other accessory trim panels. If you have removed all visible screws and the outlet will not come out, start removing adjacent panels and look for hidden screws. Inspect the outlet carefully for retaining screws; if none are found, the outlet can most likely be pried out of its opening. Either way, be sure to remove the outlet carefully as it probably has easily-broken tabs on it.

In order to remove any of the system's main duct work, the instrument panel must first be removed. Then remove the retaining screw(s) and remove the duct(s). Be sure to properly seal the duct when it is reinstalled.

Door Locks

REMOVAL & INSTALLATION

Door Lock Assembly

See Figure 61

1. Remove the door trim panel. For details, please refer to the procedure located earlier in this section.
2. If necessary, remove the water deflector.

➡The water deflector is secured by a strip of adhesive between the deflector and door, as well as waterproof sealing tape. Upon installation, make sure a good seal is achieved to keep water from entering into the body. If necessary, use strip caulking as a sealant between the deflector and door.

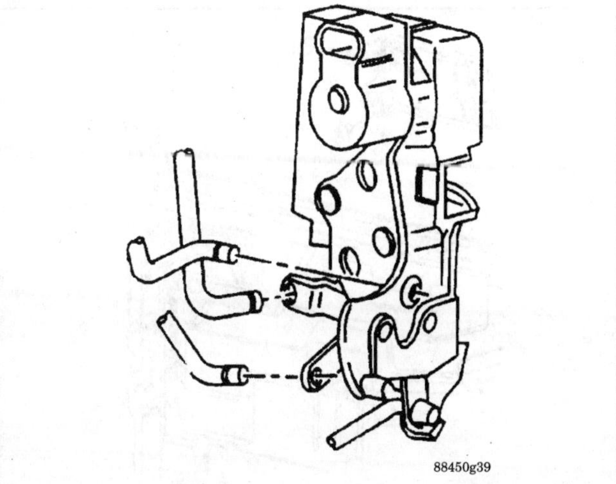

Fig. 61 Front door lock rods and lock actuator assembly

3. Remove the lock rods from the inner door handle housing.
4. Remove the outside handle lock rod from the lock assembly.
5. Remove the lock cylinder rod from the lock cylinder.
6. Remove the lock assembly-to-door retaining screws, then remove the assembly from the door.
7. Unplug the power actuator wiring connector, if equipped.
8. Installation is the reverse of removal. Be sure to check the operation of the lock assembly before installing the door water deflector (if equipped) and trim panel.

Lock Cylinder Assembly

See Figure 62

1. Remove the door trim panel. For details, please refer to the procedure located earlier in this section.
2. Remove the water deflector (if equipped) and roll up the window.

➡The water deflector is secured by a strip of adhesive between the deflector and door, as well as waterproof sealing tape. Upon installation, make sure a good seal is achieved to keep water from entering into the body. If necessary, use strip caulking as a sealant between the deflector and door.

3. Disconnect the outside handle rod from the rod clip.
4. Disconnect the lock cylinder rod from the rod clip.
5. Remove the outside handle mounting bolts.
6. Remove the door lock cylinder from the outside handle housing.
7. Installation is the reverse of removal. Check the operation of the lock cylinder before installing the water deflector (if equipped) and the door trim panel.

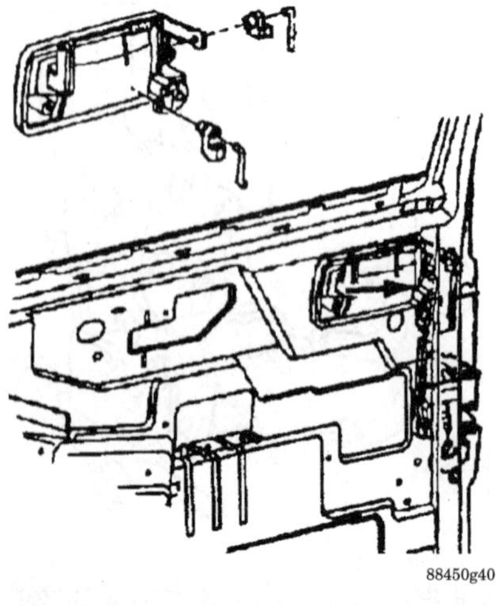

Fig. 62 Front door lock cylinder and outside handle lock rod connections

Endgate Latch and Cable

REMOVAL & INSTALLATION

See Figures 63 and 64

1. Using a flat bladed tool, carefully pry out the latch handle bezel from the top.
2. Open the endgate.
3. Disengage the endgate latch rods from the endgate latch handle as follows:
   a. Separate the retaining clip from the lower latch rod by prying the clip apart at the head of the latch rod:
   b. Slide the lower latch rod from the retaining clip and the handle:
   c. Lift the endgate latch handle to gain access to the upper latch rod retaining clip and separate it from the upper latch rod:
   d. Slide the upper latch rod from the retaining clip.

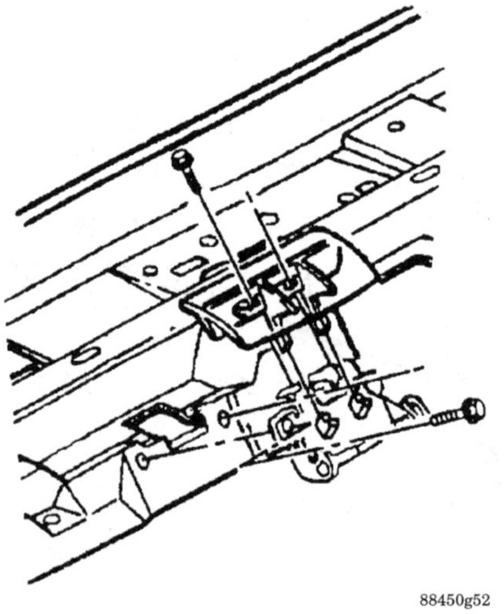

Fig. 63 Endgate handle installation

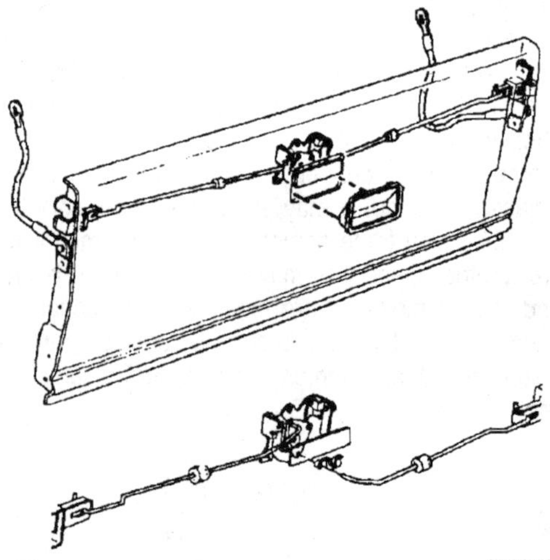

Fig. 64 Endgate handle and latch assembly

4. Disengage the slotted hole at the end of the pick-up box cables from the endgate striker bolts.
5. Remove the bolts that retain the endgate latches to the endgate.
6. Remove the pick-up box endgate latches, cables and latch rods from the endgate.

To install:

7. Position the pick-up box endgate latches, cables and latch rods to the endgate.
8. Install the bolts that retain the endgate latches to the endgate and tighten to 18 ft. lbs. (25 Nm).
9. Engage the slotted hole at the end of the pick-up box cables to the endgate striker bolts.
10. Attach the upper latch rod to the handle and retaining clip.
11. Attach the lower latch rod to the handle and retaining clip.
12. Reposition the latch handle bezel and snap into place.

Door Glass and Regulator

REMOVAL & INSTALLATION

CAUTION

Always wear heavy gloves when handling glass to minimize the risk of injury.

Door Glass

1. Lower the window.
2. Remove the door trim panel. For details, please refer to the procedure located earlier in this section.
3. Remove the water deflector from the door.
4. Remove the front glass run channel retaining screws and and slide the channel from the glass.
5. Remove the glass from the regulator.
   a. Bend the glass sash panel retaining tabs.
   b. Raise the window halfway and push the window forward to remove the window sash from the regulator roller.
   c. Carefully tilt the glass vertically and pull the glass upward to remove the glass sash from the front regulator roller.
6. Remove the glass from the door.

To install:

7. Position the glass to the door.
8. Install the window sash to the regulator.
   a. Rotate the window vertically and slide the window sash downward into the front regulator roller.
   b. Push the glass forward to align to align the rear of the sash with the rear regulator roller.
   c. Bend the retaining tabs back to the original positions.
9. Install the glass run channel and tighten the retaining screws to 18 inch lbs. (2 Nm).
10. Install the water deflector and trim panel.

The water deflector is secured by a strip of adhesive between the deflector and door, as well as waterproof sealing tape. Upon installation, make sure a good seal is achieved to keep water from entering into the body. If necessary, use strip caulking as a sealant between the deflector and door.

Door Glass Regulator

See Figure 65

1. Remove the door trim panel. For details, please refer to the procedure earlier in this section.
2. Remove the water deflector from the door.

The water deflector is secured by a strip of adhesive between the deflector and door, as well as waterproof sealing tape. Upon installation, make sure a good seal is achieved to keep water from entering into the body. If necessary, use strip caulking as a sealant between the deflector and door.

3. Raise the window to the full up position. Using cloth backed tape, securely tape the glass to the door frame.
4. Drill out the regulator-to-door or rivets and separate the regulator lift arm roller from the window sash, then remove the regulator and motor (if applicable) from the door.
5. Installation is the reverse of removal. Use new rivets (when applicable) unless the service kit contains replacement bolts. Be sure to check for proper regulator operation before installing the water deflector and trim panel.

Electric Window Motor

REMOVAL & INSTALLATION

See Figures 65 and 66

1. Remove the door trim panel. For details, please refer to the procedure earlier in this section.
2. Disconnect the negative battery cable.
3. Remove the armrest bracket-to-door screws and the bracket.

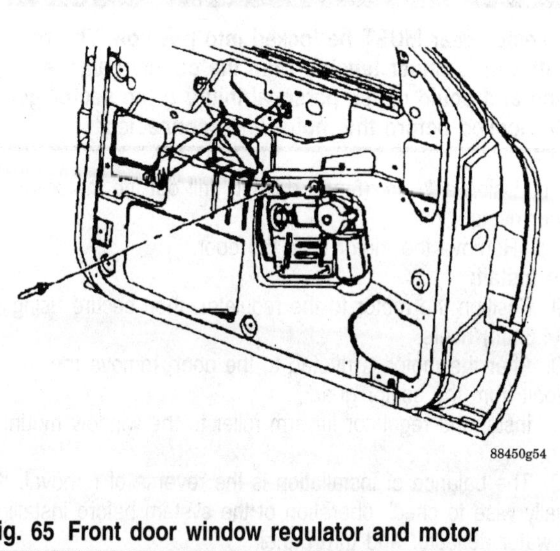

Fig. 65 Front door window regulator and motor

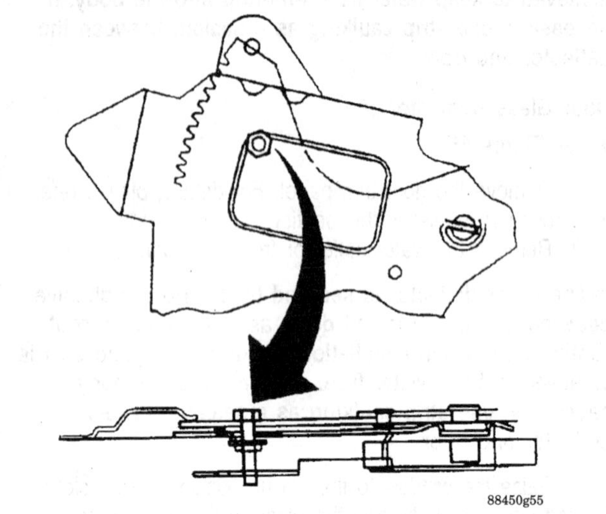

Fig. 66 Installation of the bolt to lock the sector gear

4. Remove the water deflector from the door.

➡**The water deflector is secured by a strip of adhesive between the deflector and door, as well as waterproof sealing tape. Upon installation, make sure a good seal is achieved to keep water from entering into the body. If necessary, use strip caulking as a sealant between the deflector and door.**

5. Raise the window to the full up position. Using cloth backed tape, tape the glass to the door frame.
6. Disengage the electrical wiring connector from the window regulator motor.
7. Separate the regulator lift arm roller from the window sash.
8. To remove the window regulator motor from the door:
   a. Drill a hole through the regulator sector gear and backplate, then install a bolt/nut to lock the sector gear in position.

⁂CAUTION

The sector gear MUST be locked into position. The regulator lift arm is under tension from the counterbalance spring and could cause personal injury if the sector gear is not locked before the motor is disconnected.

   b. Using a $^3/_{16}$ in. (5mm) drill bit, drill out the motor-to-door rivets.
   c. Remove the motor from the door.

To install:

9. Position the motor to the regulator, then secure using $^3/_{16}$ in. (4.8mm) rivets.
10. After the motor is riveted to the door, remove the nut/bolt from the sector gear.
11. Install the regulator lift arm roller to the window mount sash.
12. The balance of installation is the reverse of removal. It is usually wise to check operation of the system before installing the water deflector and trim panel.

Windshield

➧ **See Figures 67, 68 and 69**

➡**Bonded windshields require special tools and special removal procedures to be performed to ensure the windshield will be removed without being broken. For this reason we recommend that you refer all removal and installation to a qualified technician.**

⁂CAUTION

Always wear heavy gloves and safety glasses when handling glass to reduce the risk of injury.

When replacing a cracked windshield, it is important that the cause of the crack be determined and the condition corrected, before new glass is installed. The cause of the crack may be an obstruction or a high spot somewhere around the flange of the opening; cracking may not occur until pressure from the

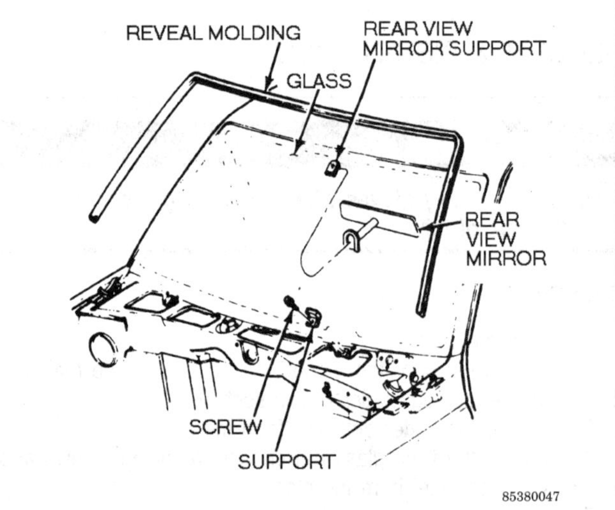

Fig. 67 Common windshield mounting

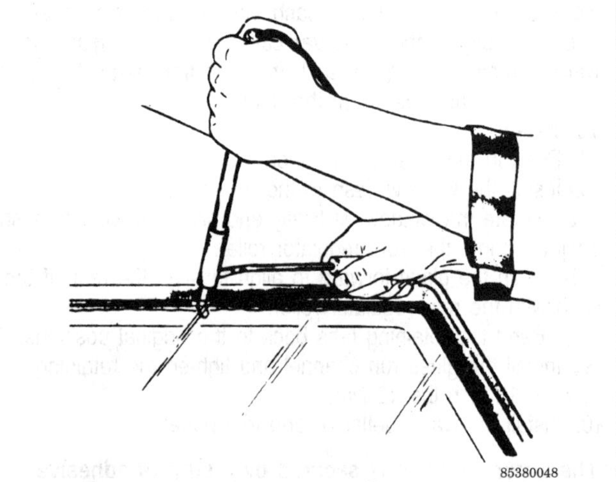

Fig. 68 Using a hot knife or equivalent to remove the windshield

high spot or obstruction becomes particularly high due to winds, extremes of temperature or rough terrain.

When a windshield is broken, the glass may have already fallen or been removed from the weatherstrip. Often, however, it is necessary to remove a cracked or otherwise imperfect windshield that is still intact. In this case, it is a good practice to crisscross the glass with strips of masking tape before removing it; this will help hold the glass together and minimize the risk of injury.

If a crack extends to the edge of the glass, mark the point where the crack meets the weatherstrip (use a piece of chalk to mark the point on the cab, next to the weatherstrip). Later, examine the window flange for a cause of the crack which started at the point marked.

The higher the temperature of the work area, the more pliable the weatherstrip will be. The more pliable the weatherstrip, the more easily the windshield can be removed.

There are two methods of windshield removal, depending on the method of windshield replacement chosen. When using the short method of installation, it is important to cut the glass from the urethane adhesive as close to the glass as possible. This is due to the fact that the urethane adhesive will be used to provide a base for the replacement windshield.

When using the extended method of windshield replacement, all the urethane adhesive must be removed from the pinchweld flange so, the process of cutting the window from the adhesive is less critical.

REMOVAL

➡The following procedure may be used for front and rear glass and requires the use of the Urethane Glass Sealant Remover (hot knife) tool No. J-24709-1 or equivalent, the Glass Sealant Remover Knife tool No. J-24402-A or equivalent.

1. Place a protective covering around the area where the glass will be removed.

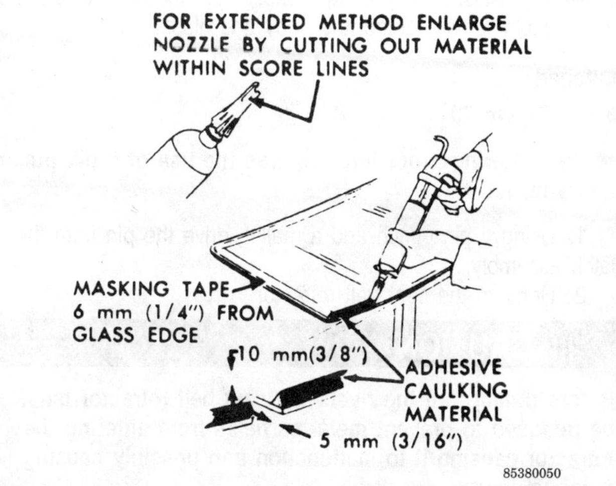

Fig. 69 Applying sealant to the windshield

2. Remove the windshield wiper arms, the cowl vent grille, the windshield supports, the rear view mirror and the interior garnish moldings.

➡If equipped with a radio antenna that is embedded in the windshield, unplug the cable connector from the windshield.

3. Remove the exterior reveal molding and glass supports from the windshield.
4. Using the Urethane Glass Sealant Remover (hot knife) tool No. J-24709-1 or equivalent, and the Glass Sealant Remover Knife tool No. J-24402-A or equivalent, cut the windshield from the urethane adhesive. If the short method of glass replacement is to be used, keep the knife as close to the glass as possible in order to leave a base for the replacement glass.
5. With the help of an assistant, remove the glass.
6. If the original glass is to be reinstalled, place it on a protected bench or a holding fixture. Remove any remaining adhesive with a razor blade or a sharp scraper. Any remaining traces of adhesive material can be removed with denatured alcohol or lacquer thinner.

➡When cleaning the windshield glass, avoid contacting the edge of the plastic laminate material (on the edge of the glass) with a volatile cleaner. Contact may cause discoloration and deterioration of the plastic laminate. DO NOT use a petroleum based solvent such as gasoline or kerosene; the presence of oil will prevent the adhesion of new material.

INSPECTION

Inspection of the windshield opening, the weatherstrip and the glass may reveal the cause of a broken windshield; this can help prevent future breakage. If there is no apparent cause of breakage, the weatherstrip should be removed from the flange and the flange inspected. Look for high weld or solder spots, hardened spot welds sealer, or any other obstruction or irregularity in the flange. Check the weatherstrip for irregularities or obstructions in it.

Check the windshield to be installed to make sure that it does not have chipped edges. Chipped edges can be ground off, restoring a smooth edge to the glass and minimizing concentrations of pressure that cause breakage. Remove no more than necessary, in an effort to maintain the original shape of the glass and the proper clearance between it and the flange of the opening.

INSTALLATION

To replace a urethane adhered windshield, a GM Adhesive Service Kit contains some of the materials needed and should be used to ensure the original integrity of the windshield design. Materials in this kit include:

1. One tube of adhesive material.
2. One dispensing nozzle.
3. Steel music wire.
4. Rubber cleaner.
5. Rubber primer.

6. Pinchweld primer.
7. Blackout primer.
8. Filler strip (for use on windshield installations of vehicles equipped with an embedded windshield antenna).
9. Primer applicators.

Other materials required for windshield installation which are not included in the service kit, are:

10. GM rubber lubricant No. 1051717.
11. Alcohol for cleaning the edge of the glass.
12. Adhesive dispensing gun No. J-24811 or equivalent.
13. A commercial type razor knife.
14. Two rubber support spacers.

Extended Method

1. Clean all metal surrounding the windshield opening with a clean alcohol dampened cloth. Allow the alcohol to air dry.
2. Apply the pinchweld primer found in the service kit to the pinchweld area. Do not let any of the primer touch any of the exposed paint because damage to the finish may occur. Allow thirty minutes for the primer to dry.
3. Follow the steps listed under Short Method for the remainder of the procedure.

Short Method

1. Thoroughly clean the edge of the glass to which the adhesive material will be applied with a clean alcohol dampened cloth. Allow the alcohol to dry.
2. Apply the clear glass primer in the kit to the inner edge of the windshield from the edge of the glass inward 0.03 in. (1mm) from the upper reveal molding, 0.31 in. (8mm) from the bottom of the glass and 0.41 in. (10.5mm) from the left and right sides of the glass. Apply the primer around the entire perimeter of the glass. Allow the primer to cure for thirty minutes.
3. Apply the blackout primer to the glass in the same area as the clear primer. Allow the blackout primer to dry to the touch.
4. Apply a continuous bead of urethane to the primed glass area.
5. Apply spacers to the A-pillar. With the aid of a helper, lift the glass into the opening and align window with the marks.
6. Center the windshield in the opening, push the window upward against the roof.
7. Apply a light hand pressure to the window to wet-out the adhesive and bond the window to the pinchweld frame. Continue to apply pressure until the window is seated against the spacers.
8. Turn the lower support adjuster to maintain windshield position.
9. Spray a mist of water onto the urethane. Water will assist in the curing process.
10. Install the wiper arms.
11. Install the reveal moldings.
12. Install the rear view mirror.
13. Install the cowl vent grille.

➡Leave the door window open to prevent air pressure from dislodging the windshield when the doors are closed. The vehicle should not be driven and should remain at room temperature for six hours to allow the adhesive to cure.

Extended Cab Side Window

REMOVAL & INSTALLATION

Stationary

➡The following procedure requires the use of a urethane glass sealant remover (hot knife) such as No. J-24709-1, and a glass sealant remover knife such as No. J-24402-A, or equivalents.

1. Remove the upper quarter trim molding.
2. Remove the retaining clips.

➡If the glass is cracked, it should be crisscrossed with masking tape to reduce the risk of damage to the vehicle. If a crack extends to the edge of the glass, mark the cab with a piece of chalk at the point where the crack meets the cab; this will aid the inspection later.

3. Working from inside the vehicle, use a urethane glass sealant remover (hot knife) or the glass sealant remover knife to separate the window glass and molding.
4. Remove the molding and the glass from the window frame.
5. Using a scraper or a chisel, remove the adhesive from the pinchweld flange; be sure to remove all of the mounds or loose adhesive.
6. Using alcohol and a clean cloth, clean the pinchweld flange. Allow the alcohol to air dry.
7. Using the pinchweld primer, found in the service kit, apply it to the pinchweld area. DO NOT let any of the primer touch the exposed paint for damage to the finish may occur; allow five minutes for the primer to dry.
8. Apply a smooth continuous bead of adhesive around the molding edge. Be sure that the adhesive contacts the entire edge of the molding and extends to fill the gap between the glass and the primed sheet metal.
9. Using hand pressure, press the glass/molding assembly onto the pinchweld flange. Using retaining clips, secure the glass/molding assembly to the pinchweld.
10. Spray a mist of warm or hot water onto the urethane. Water will assist in the curing process. Dry the area where the reveal molding will contact the body and glass.

Latched

See Figure 70

➡The following procedure requires the use of a pin punch and a mallet.

1. Using a pin punch and a mallet, drive the pin from the latch assembly.
2. Remove the seat belt retractor.

CAUTION

Before drilling out the rivets the seat belt retractor must be removed to prevent metal particles from entering the retractor causing it to malfunction and possibly causing personal injury.

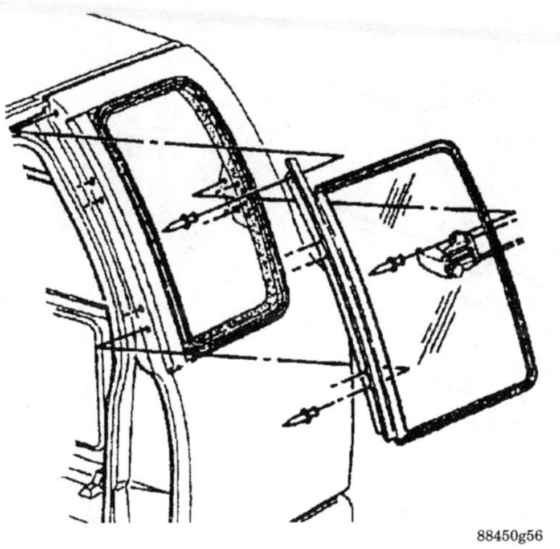

Fig. 70 Exploded view of a common latched side window mounting — extended cab models

3. Open the door for access and drill out the rivets holding the window and remove the glass from the vehicle.
4. Installation is the reverse of removal.

Rear Window Glass

REMOVAL & INSTALLATION

See Figure 71

CAUTION

Always wear heavy gloves and safety glasses when handling glass to reduce the risk of injury. If the glass is cracked but still intact, it should be crisscrossed with masking tape to reduce the risk of damage to the vehicle.

1. Place protective covering around the window removal area.
2. Remove the rear window interior trim moldings.

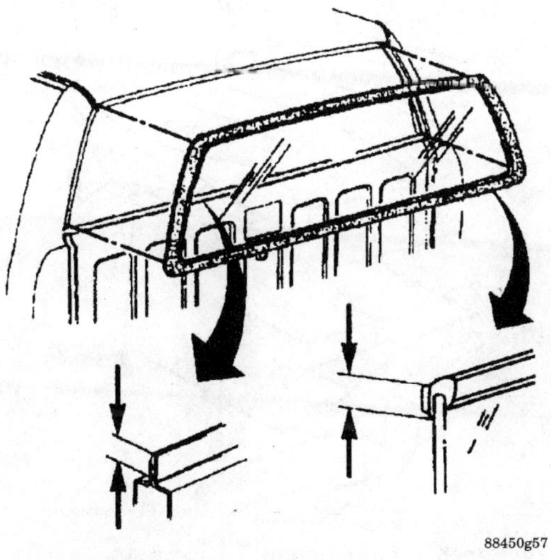

Fig. 71 Rear window installation

3. Cut out the window with the use of the Urethane Glass Sealant Remover (hot knife) tool No. J-24709-1 or equivalent, the Glass Sealant Remover Knife tool No. J-24402-A or equivalent.

To install:

4. Apply glass adhesive as outlined under the windshield installation procedure.
5. With the aid of a helper, align the glass with the body sheet metal, then place the glass in the window frame.
6. Apply a light hand pressure to the window to wet-out the adhesive and bond the window to the frame.
7. Apply a light stream of warm or hot water to the window, but not directly onto the fresh adhesive, and check for leaks.
8. Install the rear window interior trim moldings.

Inside Rear View Mirror

REPLACEMENT

See Figure 72

1. Determine the location of the rear view mirror and using a wax pencil, draw a centerline on the outside of the glass from the roof panel to the windshield base.
2. Draw a line intersecting the centerline approximately 23 1/8 in. (587mm) from the base of the glass. The base of the support will be located at the intersection of these lines.
3. Clean the inside glass within 3 in. (76mm) of the intersecting lines. Using a glass cleaning solution rub the area until completely dry. Reclean with a towel saturated with alcohol.
4. Sand the bonding surface of the rear view mirror support with 320 grit sandpaper. Remove all traces of the factory adhesive if reusing the old support. Wipe the mirror support with alcohol and allow to dry.
5. Apply Loctite® Minute Bond Adhesive 312, or equivalent to the mirror support bonding surfaces.
6. Place the bottom of the support at the premarked line. The rounded edge of the support should face upward.
7. Press the support against the glass for 30-60 seconds with a steady pressure. Allow the adhesive to dry 5 minutes before cleaning.
8. Clean all traces of adhesive and wax from the windshield with alcohol.

Seats

REMOVAL & INSTALLATION

See Figures 73 and 74

Most vehicles covered by this manual are equipped with bench seats. Removal of the bench seat assembly is a relatively simple process. Locate and remove the retainers (usually nuts), then carefully lift the seat and adjuster from the floor pan.

Removal of a bucket seat is also a relatively simple process, once you find the retainers. On some vehicles you will have to remove trim covers which are used to hide the seat adjuster

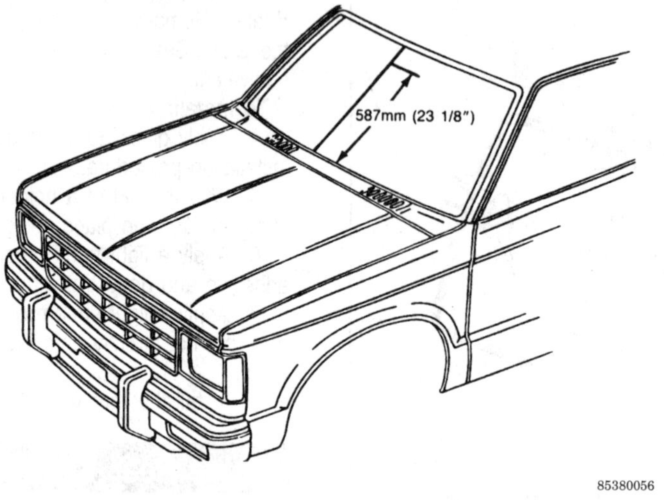

Fig. 72 Locating the mirror support

mounting bolts. Also, power seats will have one or more electrical wiring connectors. Disconnect the negative battery cable then disengage the seat wiring connectors before attempting to remove the seat. Once the nuts are removed and any wiring has been disconnected, lift the bucket seat and adjuster from the vehicle. When installing, all seat adjuster to floor pan nuts are tightened to 33 ft. lbs. (45 Nm).

To remove the jump seat on extended cab models, remove the trim panel and remove the bolts and nuts securing the seat support to the floor. Remove the seat from the vehicle. When installing, tighten the seat support to floor pan nuts and bolts to 35 ft. lbs. (47 Nm).

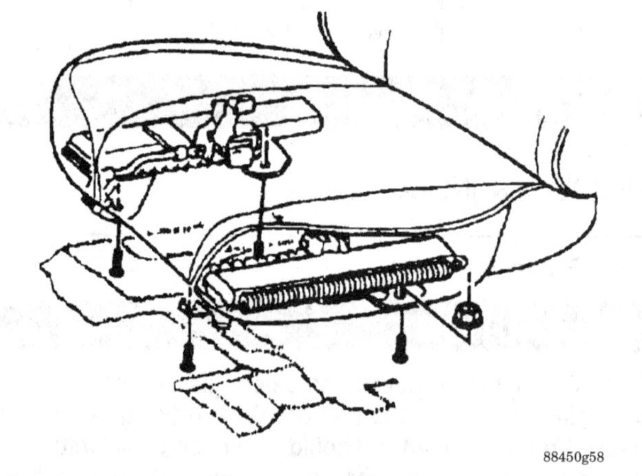

Fig. 73 Bucket seat mounting

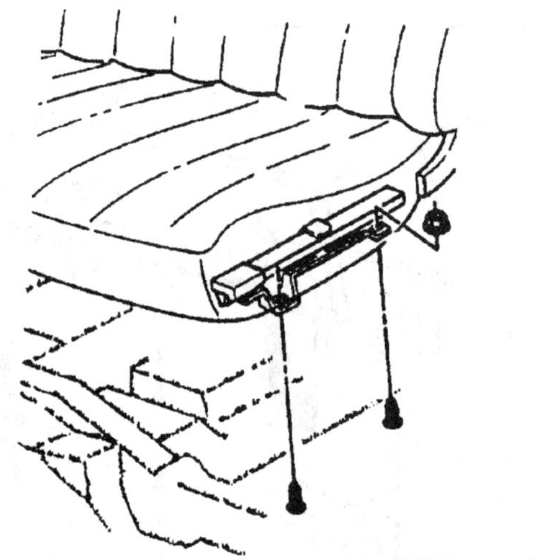

Fig. 74 Bench seat mounting

Seats Belt System

REMOVAL & INSTALLATION

Front Seat Belt

1. Remove the cover from the door pillar anchor plate.
2. Remove the attaching bolt, anchor plate and washer from the door pillar.
3. Remove the bolt cover from the rear of the retractor assembly.
4. Remove the bolt retaining the retractor to the floor panel and remove the retractor.
5. Remove the buckle assembly from the floor panel.
6. Remove the cap which conceals the buckle assembly bolt and remove the bolt.
7. Remove the seat belt warning wire from the driver's side buckle and remove the buckle from the vehicle.
8. Installation is the reverse of removal. Tighten all bolts to 39 ft. lbs. (53 Nm).

Rear Jump Seat Belt (Extended Cab)

With the seat folded in the up position, remove the screws attaching the jump seat trim cover. Remove the through-bolt, then remove the seat belt assembly. During installation, tighten the retaining bolts to 35 ft. lbs. (47 Nm).

TORQUE SPECIFICATIONS

Component	U.S.	Metric
Cab mount bolts	52 ft. lbs.	70 Nm
Endgate bolts		
side hinge	18 ft. lbs.	25 Nm
striker	18 ft. lbs.	25 Nm
to latch	18 ft. lbs.	25 Nm
latch operating handle	18 ft. lbs.	25 Nm
Fender bolts	21 ft. lbs.	29 Nm
Hood hinge nuts	18 ft. lbs.	25 Nm
Front bumper bolts		
brace to frame	30 ft. lbs.	40 Nm
bumper to frame	30 ft. lbs.	40 Nm
bumper to brace	30 ft. lbs.	40 Nm
Rear bumper		
bolts	66 ft. lbs	90 Nm
bracket to frame nuts	66 ft. lbs	90 Nm
Pickup box to frame bolts	50 ft. lbs.	67.5 Nm
Seat mounting bolts		
front	33 ft. lbs.	45 Nm
rear (jump seat)	35 ft. lbs.	47 Nm
Seat belt bolts		
front	39 ft. lbs.	53 Nm
rear	35 ft. lbs.	47 Nm
Steering column bracket nuts	22 ft. lbs	30 Nm

88450C01

GLOSSARY

AIR/FUEL RATIO: The ratio of air-to-gasoline by weight in the fuel mixture drawn into the engine.

AIR INJECTION: One method of reducing harmful exhaust emissions by injecting air into each of the exhaust ports of an engine. The fresh air entering the hot exhaust manifold causes any remaining fuel to be burned before it can exit the tailpipe.

ALTERNATOR: A device used for converting mechanical energy into electrical energy.

AMMETER: An instrument, calibrated in amperes, used to measure the flow of an electrical current in a circuit. Ammeters are always connected in series with the circuit being tested.

AMPERE: The rate of flow of electrical current present when one volt of electrical pressure is applied against one ohm of electrical resistance.

ANALOG COMPUTER: Any microprocessor that uses similar (analogous) electrical signals to make its calculations.

ARMATURE: A laminated, soft iron core wrapped by a wire that converts electrical energy to mechanical energy as in a motor or relay. When rotated in a magnetic field, it changes mechanical energy into electrical energy as in a generator.

ATMOSPHERIC PRESSURE: The pressure on the Earth's surface caused by the weight of the air in the atmosphere. At sea level, this pressure is 14.7 psi at 32°F (101 kPa at 0°C).

ATOMIZATION: The breaking down of a liquid into a fine mist that can be suspended in air.

AXIAL PLAY: Movement parallel to a shaft or bearing bore.

BACKFIRE: The sudden combustion of gases in the intake or exhaust system that results in a loud explosion.

BACKLASH: The clearance or play between two parts, such as meshed gears.

BACKPRESSURE: Restrictions in the exhaust system that slow the exit of exhaust gases from the combustion chamber.

BAKELITE: A heat resistant, plastic insulator material commonly used in printed circuit boards and transistorized components.

BALL BEARING: A bearing made up of hardened inner and outer races between which hardened steel balls roll.

BALLAST RESISTOR: A resistor in the primary ignition circuit that lowers voltage after the engine is started to reduce wear on ignition components.

BEARING: A friction reducing, supportive device usually located between a stationary part and a moving part.

BIMETAL TEMPERATURE SENSOR: Any sensor or switch made of two dissimilar types of metal that bend when heated or cooled due to the different expansion rates of the alloys. These types of sensors usually function as an on/off switch.

BLOWBY: Combustion gases, composed of water vapor and unburned fuel, that leak past the piston rings into the crankcase during normal engine operation. These gases are removed by the PCV system to prevent the buildup of harmful acids in the crankcase.

BRAKE PAD: A brake shoe and lining assembly used with disc brakes.

BRAKE SHOE: The backing for the brake lining. The term is, however, usually applied to the assembly of the brake backing and lining.

BUSHING: A liner, usually removable, for a bearing; an anti-friction liner used in place of a bearing.

CALIPER: A hydraulically activated device in a disc brake system, which is mounted straddling the brake rotor (disc). The caliper contains at least one piston and two brake pads. Hydraulic pressure on the piston(s) forces the pads against the rotor.

CAMSHAFT: A shaft in the engine on which are the lobes (cams) which operate the valves. The camshaft is driven by the crankshaft, via a belt, chain or gears, at one half the crankshaft speed.

CAPACITOR: A device which stores an electrical charge.

CARBON MONOXIDE (CO): A colorless, odorless gas given off as a normal byproduct of combustion. It is poisonous and extremely dangerous in confined areas, building up slowly to toxic levels without warning if adequate ventilation is not available.

CARBURETOR: A device, usually mounted on the intake manifold of an engine, which mixes the air and fuel in the proper proportion to allow even combustion.

CATALYTIC CONVERTER: A device installed in the exhaust system, like a muffler, that converts harmful byproducts of combustion into carbon dioxide and water vapor by means of a heat-producing chemical reaction.

CENTRIFUGAL ADVANCE: A mechanical method of advancing the spark timing by using flyweights in the distributor that react to centrifugal force generated by the distributor shaft rotation.

CHECK VALVE: Any one-way valve installed to permit the flow of air, fuel or vacuum in one direction only.

CHOKE: A device, usually a moveable valve, placed in the intake path of a carburetor to restrict the flow of air.

CIRCUIT: Any unbroken path through which an electrical current can flow. Also used to describe fuel flow in some instances.

CIRCUIT BREAKER: A switch which protects an electrical circuit from overload by opening the circuit when the current flow exceeds a predetermined level. Some circuit breakers must be reset manually, while most reset automatically.

COIL (IGNITION): A transformer in the ignition circuit which steps up the voltage provided to the spark plugs.

COMBINATION MANIFOLD: An assembly which includes both the intake and exhaust manifolds in one casting.

COMBINATION VALVE: A device used in some fuel systems that routes fuel vapors to a charcoal storage canister instead of venting them into the atmosphere. The valve relieves fuel tank pressure and allows fresh air into the tank as the fuel level drops to prevent a vapor lock situation.

COMPRESSION RATIO: The comparison of the total volume of the cylinder and combustion chamber with the piston at BDC and the piston at TDC.

CONDENSER: 1. An electrical device which acts to store an electrical charge, preventing voltage surges. 2. A radiator-like device in the air conditioning system in which refrigerant gas condenses into a liquid, giving off heat.

CONDUCTOR: Any material through which an electrical current can be transmitted easily.

CONTINUITY: Continuous or complete circuit. Can be checked with an ohmmeter.

COUNTERSHAFT: An intermediate shaft which is rotated by a mainshaft and transmits, in turn, that rotation to a working part.

CRANKCASE: The lower part of an engine in which the crankshaft and related parts operate.

CRANKSHAFT: The main driving shaft of an engine which receives reciprocating motion from the pistons and converts it to rotary motion.

CYLINDER: In an engine, the round hole in the engine block in which the piston(s) ride.

CYLINDER BLOCK: The main structural member of an engine in which is found the cylinders, crankshaft and other principal parts.

CYLINDER HEAD: The detachable portion of the engine, usually fastened to the top of the cylinder block and containing all or most of the combustion chambers. On overhead valve engines, it contains the valves and their operating parts. On overhead cam engines, it contains the camshaft as well.

DEAD CENTER: The extreme top or bottom of the piston stroke.

DETONATION: An unwanted explosion of the air/fuel mixture in the combustion chamber caused by excess heat and compression, advanced timing, or an overly lean mixture. Also referred to as "ping".

DIAPHRAGM: A thin, flexible wall separating two cavities, such as in a vacuum advance unit.

DIESELING: A condition in which hot spots in the combustion chamber cause the engine to run on after the key is turned off.

DIFFERENTIAL: A geared assembly which allows the transmission of motion between drive axles, giving one axle the ability to turn faster than the other.

DIODE: An electrical device that will allow current to flow in one direction only.

DISC BRAKE: A hydraulic braking assembly consisting of a brake disc, or rotor, mounted on an axle, and a caliper assembly containing, usually two brake pads which are activated by hydraulic pressure. The pads are forced against the sides of the disc, creating friction which slows the vehicle.

DISTRIBUTOR: A mechanically driven device on an engine which is responsible for electrically firing the spark plug at a predetermined point of the piston stroke.

DOWEL PIN: A pin, inserted in mating holes in two different parts allowing those parts to maintain a fixed relationship.

DRUM BRAKE: A braking system which consists of two brake shoes and one or two wheel cylinders, mounted on a fixed backing plate, and a brake drum, mounted on an axle, which revolves around the assembly.

DWELL: The rate, measured in degrees of shaft rotation, at which an electrical circuit cycles on and off.

ELECTRONIC CONTROL UNIT (ECU): Ignition module, module, amplifier or igniter. See Module for definition.

ELECTRONIC IGNITION: A system in which the timing and firing of the spark plugs is controlled by an electronic control unit, usually called a module. These systems have no points or condenser.

END-PLAY: The measured amount of axial movement in a shaft.

ENGINE: A device that converts heat into mechanical energy.

EXHAUST MANIFOLD: A set of cast passages or pipes which conduct exhaust gases from the engine.

FEELER GAUGE: A blade, usually metal, of precisely predetermined thickness, used to measure the clearance between two parts.

FIRING ORDER: The order in which combustion occurs in the cylinders of an engine. Also the order in which spark is distributed to the plugs by the distributor.

FLOODING: The presence of too much fuel in the intake manifold and combustion chamber which prevents the air/fuel mixture from firing, thereby causing a no-start situation.

FLYWHEEL: A disc shaped part bolted to the rear end of the crankshaft. Around the outer perimeter is affixed the ring gear. The starter drive engages the ring gear, turning the flywheel, which rotates the crankshaft, imparting the initial starting motion to the engine.

FOOT POUND (ft. lbs. or sometimes, ft.lb.): The amount of energy or work needed to raise an item weighing one pound, a distance of one foot.

FUSE: A protective device in a circuit which prevents circuit overload by breaking the circuit when a specific amperage is present. The device is constructed around a strip or wire of a lower amperage rating than the circuit it is designed to protect. When an amperage higher than that stamped on the fuse is present in the circuit, the strip or wire melts, opening the circuit.

GEAR RATIO: The ratio between the number of teeth on meshing gears.

GENERATOR: A device which converts mechanical energy into electrical energy.

HEAT RANGE: The measure of a spark plug's ability to dissipate heat from its firing end. The higher the heat range, the hotter the plug fires.

HUB: The center part of a wheel or gear.

HYDROCARBON (HC): Any chemical compound made up of hydrogen and carbon. A major pollutant formed by the engine as a byproduct of combustion.

HYDROMETER: An instrument used to measure the specific gravity of a solution.

INCH POUND (inch lbs.; sometimes in.lb. or in. lbs.): One twelfth of a foot pound.

INDUCTION: A means of transferring electrical energy in the form of a magnetic field. Principle used in the ignition coil to increase voltage.

INJECTOR: A device which receives metered fuel under relatively low pressure and is activated to inject the fuel into the engine under relatively high pressure at a predetermined time.

INPUT SHAFT: The shaft to which torque is applied, usually carrying the driving gear or gears.

INTAKE MANIFOLD: A casting of passages or pipes used to conduct air or a fuel/air mixture to the cylinders.

JOURNAL: The bearing surface within which a shaft operates.

KEY: A small block usually fitted in a notch between a shaft and a hub to prevent slippage of the two parts.

MANIFOLD: A casting of passages or set of pipes which connect the cylinders to an inlet or outlet source.

MANIFOLD VACUUM: Low pressure in an engine intake manifold formed just below the throttle plates. Manifold vacuum is highest at idle and drops under acceleration.

MASTER CYLINDER: The primary fluid pressurizing device in a hydraulic system. In automotive use, it is found in brake and hydraulic clutch systems and is pedal activated, either directly or, in a power brake system, through the power booster.

MODULE: Electronic control unit, amplifier or igniter of solid state or integrated design which controls the current flow in the ignition primary circuit based on input from the pick-up coil. When the module opens the primary circuit, high secondary voltage is induced in the coil.

NEEDLE BEARING: A bearing which consists of a number (usually a large number) of long, thin rollers.

OHM:(Ω) The unit used to measure the resistance of conductor-to-electrical flow. One ohm is the amount of resistance that limits current flow to one ampere in a circuit with one volt of pressure.

OHMMETER: An instrument used for measuring the resistance, in ohms, in an electrical circuit.

OUTPUT SHAFT: The shaft which transmits torque from a device, such as a transmission.

OVERDRIVE: A gear assembly which produces more shaft revolutions than that transmitted to it.

OVERHEAD CAMSHAFT (OHC): An engine configuration in which the camshaft is mounted on top of the cylinder head and operates the valve either directly or by means of rocker arms.

OVERHEAD VALVE (OHV): An engine configuration in which all of the valves are located in the cylinder head and the camshaft is located in the cylinder block. The camshaft operates the valves via lifters and pushrods.

OXIDES OF NITROGEN (NOx): Chemical compounds of nitrogen produced as a byproduct of combustion. They combine with hydrocarbons to produce smog.

OXYGEN SENSOR: Used with the feedback system to sense the presence of oxygen in the exhaust gas and signal the computer which can reference the voltage signal to an air/fuel ratio.

PINION: The smaller of two meshing gears.

PISTON RING: An open-ended ring which fits into a groove on the outer diameter of the piston. Its chief function is to form a seal between the piston and cylinder wall. Most automotive pistons have three rings: two for compression sealing; one for oil sealing.

PRELOAD: A predetermined load placed on a bearing during assembly or by adjustment.

PRIMARY CIRCUIT: The low voltage side of the ignition system which consists of the ignition switch, ballast resistor or resistance wire, bypass, coil, electronic control unit and pick-up coil as well as the connecting wires and harnesses.

PRESS FIT: The mating of two parts under pressure, due to the inner diameter of one being smaller than the outer diameter of the other, or vice versa; an interference fit.

RACE: The surface on the inner or outer ring of a bearing on which the balls, needles or rollers move.

REGULATOR: A device which maintains the amperage and/or voltage levels of a circuit at predetermined values.

RELAY: A switch which automatically opens and/or closes a circuit.

RESISTANCE: The opposition to the flow of current through a circuit or electrical device, and is measured in ohms. Resistance is equal to the voltage divided by the amperage.

RESISTOR: A device, usually made of wire, which offers a preset amount of resistance in an electrical circuit.

RING GEAR: The name given to a ring-shaped gear attached to a differential case, or affixed to a flywheel or as part of a planetary gear set.

ROLLER BEARING: A bearing made up of hardened inner and outer races between which hardened steel rollers move.

ROTOR: 1. The disc-shaped part of a disc brake assembly, upon which the brake pads bear; also called, brake disc. 2. The device mounted atop the distributor shaft, which passes current to the distributor cap tower contacts.

SECONDARY CIRCUIT: The high voltage side of the ignition system, usually above 20,000 volts. The secondary includes the ignition coil, coil wire, distributor cap and rotor, spark plug wires and spark plugs.

SENDING UNIT: A mechanical, electrical, hydraulic or electromagnetic device which transmits information to a gauge.

SENSOR: Any device designed to measure engine operating conditions or ambient pressures and temperatures. Usually electronic in nature and designed to send a voltage signal to an on-board computer, some sensors may operate as a simple on/off switch or they may provide a variable voltage signal (like a potentiometer) as conditions or measured parameters change.

SHIM: Spacers of precise, predetermined thickness used between parts to establish a proper working relationship.

SLAVE CYLINDER: In automotive use, a device in the hydraulic clutch system which is activated by hydraulic force, disengaging the clutch.

SOLENOID: A coil used to produce a magnetic field, the effect of which is to produce work.

SPARK PLUG: A device screwed into the combustion chamber of a spark ignition engine. The basic construction is a conductive core inside of a ceramic insulator, mounted in an outer conductive base. An electrical charge from the spark plug wire travels along the conductive core and jumps a preset air gap to a grounding point or points at the end of the conductive base. The resultant spark ignites the fuel/air mixture in the combustion chamber.

SPLINES: Ridges machined or cast onto the outer diameter of a shaft or inner diameter of a bore to enable parts to mate without rotation.

TACHOMETER: A device used to measure the rotary speed of an engine, shaft, gear, etc., usually in rotations per minute.

THERMOSTAT: A valve, located in the cooling system of an engine, which is closed when cold and opens gradually in response to engine heating, controlling the temperature of the coolant and rate of coolant flow.

TOP DEAD CENTER (TDC): The point at which the piston reaches the top of its travel on the compression stroke.

TORQUE: The twisting force applied to an object.

TORQUE CONVERTER: A turbine used to transmit power from a driving member to a driven member via hydraulic action, providing changes in drive ratio and torque. In automotive use, it links the driveplate at the rear of the engine to the automatic transmission.

TRANSDUCER: A device used to change a force into an electrical signal.

TRANSISTOR: A semi-conductor component which can be actuated by a small voltage to perform an electrical switching function.

TUNE-UP: A regular maintenance function, usually associated with the replacement and adjustment of parts and components in the electrical and fuel systems of a vehicle for the purpose of attaining optimum performance.

TURBOCHARGER: An exhaust driven pump which compresses intake air and forces it into the combustion chambers at higher than atmospheric pressures. The increased air pressure allows more fuel to be burned and results in increased horsepower being produced.

VACUUM ADVANCE: A device which advances the ignition timing in response to increased engine vacuum.

VACUUM GAUGE: An instrument used to measure the presence of vacuum in a chamber.

VALVE: A device which control the pressure, direction of flow or rate of flow of a liquid or gas.

VALVE CLEARANCE: The measured gap between the end of the valve stem and the rocker arm, cam lobe or follower that activates the valve.

VISCOSITY: The rating of a liquid's internal resistance to flow.

VOLTMETER: An instrument used for measuring electrical force in units called volts. Voltmeters are always connected parallel with the circuit being tested.

WHEEL CYLINDER: Found in the automotive drum brake assembly, it is a device, actuated by hydraulic pressure, which, through internal pistons, pushes the brake shoes outward against the drums.

MASTER INDEX